A COMPANION TO ARISTOPHANES

BLACKWELL COMPANIONS TO THE ANCIENT WORLD

This series provides sophisticated and authoritative overviews of periods of ancient history, genres of classical literature, and the most important themes in ancient culture. Each volume comprises approximately twenty-five and forty concise essays written by individual scholars within their area of specialisation. The essays are written in a clear, provocative, and lively manner, designed for an international audience of scholars, students, and general readers.

ANCIENT HISTORY

A Companion to the Roman Army
Edited by Paul Erdkamp

A Companion to the Roman Republic
Edited by Nathan Rosenstein and Robert Morstein-Marx

A Companion to the Classical Greek World
Edited by Konrad H. Kinzl

A Companion to the Ancient Near East
Edited by Daniel C. Snell

A Companion to the Hellenistic World
Edited by Andrew Erskine

A Companion to Late Antiquity
Edited by Philip Rousseau

A Companion to Ancient History
Edited by Andrew Erskine

A Companion to Archaic Greece
Edited by Kurt A. Raaflaub and Hans van Wees

A Companion to Julius Caesar
Edited by Miriam Griffin

A Companion to Byzantium
Edited by Liz James

A Companion to Ancient Egypt
Edited by Alan B. Lloyd

A Companion to Ancient Macedonia
Edited by Joseph Roisman and Ian Worthington

A Companion to the Punic Wars
Edited by Dexter Hoyos

A Companion to Augustine
Edited by Mark Vessey

A Companion to Marcus Aurelius
Edited by Marcel van Ackeren

A Companion to Ancient Greek Government
Edited by Hans Beck

A Companion to the Neronian Age
Edited by Emma Buckley and Martin T. Dinter

A Companion to Greek Democracy and the Roman Republic
Edited by Dean Hammer

A Companion to Livy
Edited by Bernard Mineo

A Companion to Ancient Thrace
Edited by Julia Valeva, Emil Nankov, and Denver Graninger

A Companion to Roman Italy
Edited by Alison E. Cooley

A Companion to the Etruscans
Edited by Sinclair Bell and Alexandra A. Carpino

A Companion to the Flavian Age of Imperial Rome
Edited by Andrew Zissos

A Companion to Science, Technology, and Medicine in Ancient Greece and Rome
Edited by Georgia L. Irby

A Companion to the City of Rome
Edited by Amanda Claridge and Claire Holleran

A Companion to Greeks Across the Ancient World
Edited by Franco De Angelis

A Companion to Late Ancient Jews and Judaism - Third Century BCE - Seventh Century CE
Edited by Naomi Koltun-Fromm and Gwynn Kessler

A Companion to the Archaeology of Early Greece and the Mediterranean
Edited by Irene S. Lemos and Antonios Kotsonas

A Companion to Assyria
Edited by Eckart Frahm

A Companion to Sparta
Edited by Anton Powell

A Companion to Greco-Roman and Late Antique Egypt
Edited by Katelijn Vandorpe

A Companion to Ancient Agriculture
Edited by David Hollander and Timothy Howe

Literature and Culture

A Companion to Greek and Roman Music
Edited by Tosca Lynch and Eleonora Rocconi

A Companion to Classical Receptions
Edited by Lorna Hardwick and Christopher Stray

A Companion to Greek and Roman Historiography
Edited by John Marincola

A Companion to Catullus
Edited by Marilyn B. Skinner

A Companion to Roman Religion
Edited by Jörg Rüpke

A Companion to Greek Religion
Edited by Daniel Ogden

A Companion to the Classical Tradition
Edited by Craig W. Kallendorf

A Companion to Roman Rhetoric
Edited by William Dominik and Jon Hall

A Companion to Greek Rhetoric
Edited by Ian Worthington

A Companion to Ancient Epic
Edited by John Miles Foley

A Companion to Greek Tragedy
Edited by Justina Gregory

A Companion to Latin Literature
Edited by Stephen Harrison

A Companion to Greek and Roman Political Thought
Edited by Ryan K. Balot

A Companion to Ovid
Edited by Peter E. Knox

A Companion to the Ancient Greek Language
Edited by Egbert Bakker

A Companion to Hellenistic Literature
Edited by Martine Cuypers and James J. Clauss

A Companion to Vergil's *Aeneid* and its Tradition
Edited by Joseph Farrell and Michael C. J. Putnam

A Companion to Horace
Edited by Gregson Davis

A Companion to Families in the Greek and Roman Worlds
Edited by Beryl Rawson

A Companion to Greek Mythology
Edited by Ken Dowden and Niall Livingstone

A Companion to the Latin Language
Edited by James Clackson

A Companion to Tacitus
Edited by Victoria Emma Pagán

A Companion to Women in the Ancient World
Edited by Sharon L. James and Sheila Dillon

A Companion to Sophocles
Edited by Kirk Ormand

A Companion to the Archaeology of the Ancient Near East
Edited by Daniel Potts

A Companion to Roman Love Elegy
Edited by Barbara K. Gold

A Companion to Greek Art
Edited by Tyler Jo Smith and Dimitris Plantzos

A Companion to Persius and Juvenal
Edited by Susanna Braund and Josiah Osgood

A Companion to the Archaeology of the Roman Republic
Edited by Jane DeRose Evans

A Companion to Terence
Edited by Antony Augoustakis and Ariana Traill

A Companion to Roman Architecture
Edited by Roger B. Ulrich and Caroline K. Quenemoen

A Companion to Sport and Spectacle in Greek and Roman Antiquity
Edited by Paul Christesen and Donald G. Kyle

A Companion to Plutarch
Edited by Mark Beck

A Companion to Greek and Roman Sexualities
Edited by Thomas K. Hubbard

A Companion to the Ancient Novel
Edited by Edmund P. Cueva and Shannon N. Byrne

A Companion to Ethnicity in the Ancient Mediterranean
Edited by Jeremy McInerney

A Companion to Ancient Egyptian Art
Edited by Melinda Hartwig

A Companion to the Archaeology of Religion in the Ancient World
Edited by Rubina Raja and Jörg Rüpke

A Companion to Food in the Ancient World
Edited by John Wilkins and Robin Nadeau

A Companion to Ancient Education
Edited by W. Martin Bloomer

A Companion to Ancient Aesthetics
Edited by Pierre Destrée & Penelope Murray

A Companion to Roman Art
Edited by Barbara Borg

A Companion to Greek Literature
Edited by Martin Hose and David Schenker

A Companion to Josephus in his World
Edited by Honora Howell Chapman and Zuleika Rodgers

A Companion to Greek Architecture
Edited by Margaret M. Miles

A Companion to Plautus
Edited by Dorota Dutsch and George Fredric Franko

A Companion to Ancient Near Eastern Languages
Edited by Rebecca Hasselbach-Andee

A Companion to Ancient Greece and Rome on Screen
Edited by Arthur J. Pomeroy

A Companion to Euripedes
Edited by Laura K. McClure

A Companion to Ancient Near Eastern Art
Edited by Ann C. Gunter

A Companion to Ancient Epigram
Edited by Christer Henriksén

A Companion to Late Antique Literature
Edited by Scott McGill and Edward Watts

A Companion to Religion in Late Antiquity
Edited by Josef Lössl and Nicholas Baker-Brian

A Companion to Aristophanes
Edited by Matthew C. Farmer and Jeremy B. Lefkowitz

A COMPANION TO ARISTOPHANES

Edited by

Matthew C. Farmer
Jeremy B. Lefkowitz

WILEY Blackwell

Copyright © 2024 by John Wiley & Sons, Inc. All rights reserved.

Published by John Wiley & Sons, Inc., Hoboken, New Jersey.
Published simultaneously in Canada.

No part of this publication may be reproduced, stored in a retrieval system, or transmitted in any form or by any means, electronic, mechanical, photocopying, recording, scanning, or otherwise, except as permitted under Section 107 or 108 of the 1976 United States Copyright Act, without either the prior written permission of the Publisher, or authorization through payment of the appropriate per-copy fee to the Copyright Clearance Center, Inc., 222 Rosewood Drive, Danvers, MA 01923, (978) 750-8400, fax (978) 750-4470, or on the web at www.copyright.com. Requests to the Publisher for permission should be addressed to the Permissions Department, John Wiley & Sons, Inc., 111 River Street, Hoboken, NJ 07030, (201) 748-6011, fax (201) 748-6008, or online at http://www.wiley.com/go/permission.

Trademarks: Wiley and the Wiley logo are trademarks or registered trademarks of John Wiley & Sons, Inc. and/or its affiliates in the United States and other countries and may not be used without written permission. All other trademarks are the property of their respective owners. John Wiley & Sons, Inc. is not associated with any product or vendor mentioned in this book.

Limit of Liability/Disclaimer of Warranty
While the publisher and author have used their best efforts in preparing this book, they make no representations or warranties with respect to the accuracy or completeness of the contents of this book and specifically disclaim any implied warranties of merchantability or fitness for a particular purpose. No warranty may be created or extended by sales representatives or written sales materials. The advice and strategies contained herein may not be suitable for your situation. You should consult with a professional where appropriate. Further, readers should be aware that websites listed in this work may have changed or disappeared between when this work was written and when it is read. Neither the publisher nor authors shall be liable for any loss of profit or any other commercial damages, including but not limited to special, incidental, consequential, or other damages.

For general information on our other products and services or for technical support, please contact our Customer Care Department within the United States at (800) 762-2974, outside the United States at (317) 572-3993 or fax (317) 572-4002.

Wiley also publishes its books in a variety of electronic formats. Some content that appears in print may not be available in electronic formats. For more information about Wiley products, visit our web site at www.wiley.com.

Library of Congress Cataloging-in-Publication Data
Names: Farmer, Matthew C., editor. | Lefkowitz, Jeremy B., editor.
Title: A companion to Aristophanes / edited by Matthew C. Farmer, Jeremy B. Lefkowitz.
Description: Hoboken, New Jersey : Wiley-Blackwell, 2024. | Series: Blackwell companions to the ancient world | Includes bibliographical references and index.
Identifiers: LCCN 2023050542 (print) | LCCN 2023050543 (ebook) | ISBN 9781119622888 (cloth) | ISBN 9781119622925 (adobe pdf) | ISBN 9781119622956 (epub)
Subjects: LCSH: Aristophanes–Criticism and interpretation. | LCGFT: Essays.
Classification: LCC PA3879 .C557 2024 (print) | LCC PA3879 (ebook) | DDC 882/.01–dc23/eng/20231130
LC record available at https://lccn.loc.gov/2023050542
LC ebook record available at https://lccn.loc.gov/2023050543

Cover Design: Wiley
Cover Image: © Terracotta statuette of an actor, Greek, Attica, late 5th–early 4th century BCE, The Metropolitan Museum of Art Collection API (Public Domain)

Set in 9.5/11.5pt ITC Galliard Std by Straive, Pondicherry, India
Printed and bound by CPI Group (UK) Ltd, Croydon, CR0 4YY
C9781119622888_270224

To our students

Contents

List of Illustrations — xi
Notes on Contributors — xii
Acknowledgments — xvii

Introduction — 1
Matthew C. Farmer and Jeremy B. Lefkowitz

Part I   The World of Aristophanes — 5

1. Aristophanes Among Athenians — 7
   Donald Lateiner and Rosaria Munson

2. The Staging of Old Comedy — 21
   A.C. Duncan

3. Meter and Song — 35
   Anne Mahoney

4. Style, Language, and Obscenity — 46
   Stephen E. Kidd

5. Images of Greek Comedy — 56
   Carl A. Shaw

6. Politics and Aristophanic Comedy — 70
   Edith Hall

Part II   The Comedies of Aristophanes — 89

7. *Acharnians*: Tragedy and Epic — 91
   Stephanie Nelson

8. *Knights*: Political Satire — 107
   Natalia Tsoumpra

9. Clouds: Intellectuals and Philosophy — 127
   Olimpia Imperio

10	*Wasps*: Rhetoric and the Law Nikoletta Kanavou	149
11	Peace: War Elena Fabbro	165
12	Birds: Utopia David Konstan	183
13	*Lysistrata*: Sexuality Kate Gilhuly	196
14	*Women at the Thesmophoria*: Religion and Ritual Helene P. Foley	212
15	*Frogs*: Metaphor and Allegory Anna A. Novokhatko	228
16	*Assemblywomen*: Gender Gwendolyn Compton-Engle	247
17	*Wealth*: Economic Fantasies Ralph M. Rosen	262

Part III The Fragments of Greek Comedy — 279

18	Aristophanes' Lost Plays Christian Orth	281
19	Aristophanes' Predecessors Serena Perrone	292
20	Aristophanes' Contemporaries Sarah N. Miles	304
21	Aristophanes' Successors Anna Uhlig	319

Part IV Aristophanes and His Readers — 337

22	Aristophanes Between Plato and Aristotle Pierre Destrée	339
23	Ancient Scholarship on Aristophanes Andreas Willi	352
24	Aristophanes in Roman Literature Jennifer L. Ferriss-Hill	368
25	Aristophanes and the Second Sophistic Inger N.I. Kuin	381
26	Renaissance and Early Modern Reception of Aristophanes Malika Bastin-Hammou	393

Part V Aristophanes Today — 407

27	Performing Aristophanes Philip Walsh	409
28	Teaching Aristophanes Elizabeth Scharffenberger	423

Index — 438

List of Illustrations

Figure 5.1	Comic actor portraying Perseus onstage before two seated audience members. Attic red-figure chous, Painter of the Perseus Dance, ca. 420, Athens NM BΣ 518.	57
Figure 5.2	Actors portraying (Di)onysus and Phor(mio) from Eupolis' *Taxiarchoi* (ca. 415), Attic polychrome oinochoe, c. 400, Agora P23985. Drawing by Piet de Jong.	58
Figure 5.3	Actor dressed as a fighting cock, Attic red-figure Pelike, ca. 425, Atlanta 2008.4.1. Michael C. Carlos Museum, Emory University.	59
Figure 5.4	(a) Oversized komast riding phallus Pole (Side A), Attic Black-Figure lip cup, unattributed. Florence 3897: Soprintendenza alle Antichità. (b) Oversized satyr riding phallus Pole (Side B), Attic Black-Figure lip cup, unattributed. Florence 3897: Soprintendenza alle Antichità.	60
Figure 5.5	Aulos player with actors dressed as horses and riders, Attic black-figure amphora, ca. 540. Berlin Painter. Inv. F 1697.	61
Figure 5.6	Representation of Aristophanes' *Thesmophoriazusae*, Apulian red-figure bell krater, Schiller painter, ca. 370, Würzburg H5697. Martin von Wagner Museum der Universität Würzburg.	62
Figure 5.7	Dionysus (dressed as Heracles) and Xanthias from Aristophanes' *Frogs* approach Heracles' door, "Berlin Heracles," ca. 375–350, lost (probably destroyed or stolen during World War II), Formerly Berlin Staatliche Museen F3046.	64
Figure 5.8	"New York Goose Vase," Apulian red-figure calyx krater attributed to the Dolon Painter, ca. 400, New York, MMA 24.97.104. Fletcher Fund, 1924.	65
Figure 27.1	Elizabeth Rainey, *Socrates*. Print.	419

Notes on Contributors

Malika Bastin-Hammou is Professor of Greek at the Université Grenoble Alpes (France). She has written widely on Aristophanes and his reception. Her most recent book is *Translating Greek Drama in Early Modern Europe. Theory and Practice* (15th–16th c.) (De Gruyter 2023), co-edited with Giovanna di Martino, Cécile Douduyt, and Lucy Jackson. Her forthcoming book focuses on translations of Aristophanes in early modern France.

Gwendolyn Compton-Engle is Professor of Classics at John Carroll University, where she teaches Latin and Greek language, literature, and culture. She has published articles on costume and performance in Greek comedy, as well as the relationship between comedy and tragedy in the late fifth and early fourth centuries BCE. She is the author of *Costume in the Comedies of Aristophanes* (Cambridge 2015).

Pierre Destrée is a research fellow of the Fondation Nationale de la Recherche Scientifique (Belgium) and a professor at the Université catholique de Louvain, where he teaches ancient philosophy. He is the author of numerous articles and book chapters on ancient ethics, politics, and aesthetics, as well as a French translation and commentary on Aristotle's *Poetics* (Paris, Flammarion 2021). He has co-edited several books, most recently: (with Penelope Murray) *The Blackwell Companion to Ancient Aesthetics*, Wiley-Blackwell, 2015; (with Zina Giannopoulou) *Plato: Symposium – A Critical Guide*, Cambridge University Press, 2017; (with Radcliffe Edmonds) *Plato and the Power of Images*, Brill, 2017; (with F. Trivigno) *Laughter, Humor and Comedy in Ancient Philosophy*, Oxford University Press, 2019; (with D. Munteanu and M. Heath) *The Poetics in Its Aristotelian Context*, Routledge, 2020. He is currently completing a monograph on "Aristotle on Laughter."

A. C. Duncan is Assistant Professor of Classics at the University of North Carolina at Chapel Hill. His research concerns the experience, evaluation, and impact of Greek drama, from its origins in ancient Athens to its reception in our modern, globalized world. In his recent and forthcoming work, he seeks to incorporate non-literary evidence and analytical methods to place the ancient theater within ever-wider cultural and historical contexts. As a director, translator, and occasional performer of Aristophanic comedy, he is particularly concerned with the material, social, and cognitive means through which theater fosters and showcases human creativity.

Elena Fabbro is Professor of Greek Language and Literature at the University of Udine (Italy). She has published numerous studies in the fields of archaic and early lyric poetry (riddles and symposial poetic repertories) and Greek drama, focusing on the comic hero's relationship with divinity, generational conflicts, and the representation of democratic power. She is also interested in classical reception, in particular, Pasolini's re-reading of Greek tragedy and his re-mythologization of the archaic world. She is the author of *Carmina convivalia attica* (Roma Edizioni dell'Ateneo 1995); *Il mito greco nell'opera di Pasolini* (conference proceedings, Udine Forum 2004); and *Aristofane, Le Vespe* (Milano Rizzoli 2012).

Matthew C. Farmer is Associate Professor of Classics at Haverford College. His research focuses on Greek comedy, with a particular emphasis on the study of comic fragments and on the relationships comedy forms with other genres. He is the author of *Tragedy on the Comic Stage* (2017) and *Theopompus: Introduction, Translation, Commentary* (2022).

Jennifer Ferriss-Hill is Professor of Classics at the University of Miami, where she has also held various academic administrative positions. She is the author of three books – *Roman Satire and the Old Comic Tradition* (Cambridge 2015), *Horace's Ars Poetica: Family, Friendship, and the Art of Living* (Princeton 2019), and *Roman Satire* (Brill 2022) – and in addition to her work on Old Comedy, Roman Satire, and Horace, she has also published on Virgil, Varro, and Catullus.

Helene P. Foley is Claire Tow Professor of Classics, Emerita at Barnard College, Columbia University. She is the author of books and articles on Greek epic and drama, on women and gender in antiquity, and on modern performance and adaptation of Greek drama including *Ritual Irony: Poetry and Sacrifice in Euripides*, *The Homeric Hymn to Demeter*, *Female Acts in Greek Tragedy*, *Reimagining Greek Tragedy on the American Stage*, and *Euripides: Hecuba*.

Kate Gilhuly is Professor of Classical Studies at Wellesley College. She is the author of *The Feminine Matrix of Sex and Gender in Classical Athens* (Cambridge 2009), *Erotic Geographies in Ancient Greek Literature and Culture* (Routledge 2017), and co-editor with Nancy Worman of *Place, Space, and Landscape in Ancient Greek Literature and Culture* (Cambridge 2014).

Edith Hall is Professor of Classics at the University of Durham. Her research specialisms are ancient epic and drama, Aristotle, the reception of classical civilization, gender, ethnicity, and class. She has published more than thirty books, including *Adventures with Iphigenia in Tauris* (OUP 2013), winner of an SCS Goodwin Award for Merit, and (with Henry Stead) *A People's History of Classics: Class and Greco-Roman Antiquity in Britain and Ireland 1660–1939* (Routledge 2020). In 2017, she was awarded an honorary doctorate from the University of Athens, and in 2022, she was elected a Fellow of the British Academy.

Olimpia Imperio is Full Professor of Greek Language and Literature at the University of Bari (Italy) and author of books and articles on comic and tragic theater – particularly Aristophanic comedy – and its reception. Her publications include the monographs *Parabasi di Aristofane: Acarnesi, Cavalieri, Vespe, Uccelli* (2004), *Aristofane tra antiche e moderne teorie del comico* (2014), the volume *Fragmenta Comica 10.6: Aristophanes fr. 305–391* for the project KomFrag: Kommentierung der Fragmente der griechischen Komödie (2023), and the translations of Aristophanes' *Frogs* (2017) and *Knights* (2018) sponsored by INDA (Istituto Nazionale del Dramma Antico) for the Greek theatre of Syracuse.

Nikoletta Kanavou is Associate Professor of Ancient Greek Literature at the University of Athens. Her research interests are in fictitious prose narratives, archaic Greek poetry, comedy, literary theory, papyrology, epigraphy, and onomastics. Her work on comedy includes a book on comic personal names as well as articles on the ideology of Aristophanic comedies and the poet's use of myth. One of her current projects explores the comic element in the novel of Achilles Tatius.

Stephen Kidd is Associate Professor of Classics at Brown University, where he specializes in Greek literature of the classical and imperial periods. He is the author of two books – *Nonsense and*

Meaning in Ancient Greek Comedy (Cambridge 2014), which asks why comedy, unlike other genres, gives rise to the perception that some part of it is not meaningful; and *Play and Aesthetics in Ancient Greece* (Cambridge 2019), which explores the ancient Greek concept of play (*paidia*). Now he is writing a book about Lucian of Samosata.

David Konstan is Professor of Classics at New York University. He is the author of books on ancient comedy, the novel, friendship, the emotions of the ancient Greeks, the classical conception of beauty and its influence, forgiveness, and Greek and Roman ideas of love and affection. His most recent book is The Origin of Sin. He is a fellow of the American Academy of Arts and Sciences, an honorary fellow of the Australian Academy of the Humanities, and a past president of the American Philological Association.

Inger N.I. Kuin is Assistant Professor of Classics at the University of Virginia. Her research concerns the intellectual history of ancient Greece and Rome. Her most recent books are *Lucian's Laughing Gods: Religion, Philosophy, and Popular Culture in the Roman East* (University of Michigan Press 2023) and (in Dutch) *Diogenes. Leven en denken van een autonome geest* (Athenaeum – Polak & Van Gennep 2022), and she co-authored a new (also in Dutch) companion to classical literature, *Muze, vertel. De Griekse en Latijnse literatuur van de oudheid* (Amsterdam University Press 2023).

Donald Lateiner, Professor Emeritus of Humanities and Classics at Ohio Wesleyan University, usually researches the historiography of Herodotos (*Historical Method of Herodotos*) and Thoukydides and fifth-century Aegean history, recently misinformation and disinformation in these historians. He also examines ancient narratives, especially Homer (*Sardonic Smile*), Heliodoros' *Aithiopika*, and Apuleius' *Metamorphoses*, topics such as expression of emotions, nonverbal behaviors, particularly affect displays or "leakage" (e.g. blushes, tears), laughter, humiliation and stupefaction, forms of insult, and gendered self-advancement. He once performed one-man scenes from *Lysistrata* for Banned Books Day and appeared as Donald Trump in the 2016 SCS production of The Nerds/Birds.

Jeremy B. Lefkowitz is Associate Professor of Classics at Swarthmore College. He has published a number of studies on Aesop and the ancient fable tradition, and he is the co-editor, with Caterina Mordeglia, of *La favola tra Oriente e Occidente* (forthcoming from SISMEL editrice).

Anne Mahoney is Senior Lecturer in Classical Studies at Tufts University, where she teaches a variety of courses including historical linguistics, Latin, Greek, Sanskrit, and ancient mathematics. She has published articles and reviews on Greek and Indo-European meter, Neo-Latin, drama, and pedagogy, and several textbooks.

Sarah Miles is Associate Professor in the Department of Classics and Ancient History at the University of Durham, UK, where she teaches Greek literature and language. Her research interests and publications focus on Greek comedy, comic fragments, and Greek tragedy; interplay in performance genres from comedy and tragedy to mime and Platonic dialogue; contemporary receptions of Greek myth and Greek epic in popular culture, especially in children's media and animation.

Rosaria Vignolo Munson is the J. Archer and Helen C. Turner Professor of Classics at Swarthmore College. She is the author of *Telling Wonders: Ethnographic and Political Discourse in the Work of Herodotus* (2001); *Black Doves Speak: Herodotus and the Language of Barbarians* (2005); and several articles on Herodotus and Thucydides. She has edited *Oxford Readings in Classical Studies: Herodotus* (2013). Most recently, she has co-edited (with Carolyn Dewald) the "Green and Yellow" commentary on Herodotus Book I for the Cambridge Greek and Latin Classics (2022).

Stephanie Nelson is Professor in the Department of Classical Studies and in the Core Curriculum at Boston University. She teaches widely in Greek and Latin literature and the classical tradition and has written on subjects from Plato and aesthetic theory to translation and literary reception. She is the author of *God and the Land: the Metaphysics of Farming in Hesiod and Vergil* and of *Aristophanes' Tragic Muse: comedy, tragedy and the polis in Classical Athens*. She has also written extensively on Joyce and Homer, including *Time and Identity in Ulysses and the Odyssey*, published by the University Press of Florida in spring 2022.

Anna A. Novokhatko is Associate Professor of Classical Philology at the Aristotle University Thessaloniki. She has published numerous articles on comedy and is the author of a monograph on the embodiment of scholarly discourse on comic stage (De Gruyter 2023). She is a co-editor of, among others, *Measurement and Understanding in Science and Humanities: Interdisciplinary Approaches* (Palgrave Macmillan 2023), *Fragmentation in Ancient Greek Drama* (De Gruyter 2020), *Digitale Altertumswissenschaften: Thesen und Debatten zu Methoden und Anwendungen* (Propylaeum Universitätsbibliothek Heidelberg 2020), *Antikes Heldentum in der Moderne: Konzepte, Praktiken, Medien* (Rombach Verlag 2019), and *Gaze, Vision, and Visuality in Ancient Greek Literature* (De Gruyter 2018). In her recent research, she has concentrated on the interaction of cognitive sciences and classics as well as digital classics.

Christian Orth is Professor in the Seminar für Griechische und Lateinische Philologie at the Albert-Ludwigs-Universität Freiburg. He is a member of the project Kommentierung der Fragmente der griechischen Komödie (KomFrag) and author of several volumes in the series, including *Alkaios – Apollophanes* (2013), *Aristomenes – Metagenes* (2014), *Nikochares – Xenophon* (2015), *Aristophanes: Aiolosikon – Babylonioi (frr. 1-100)* (2017), and *Aristophon – Dromon* (202). With Stylianos Chronopoulos, he edited the volume *Fragmente einer Geschichte der griechischen Komödie – Fragmentary History of Greek Comedy* (Studia Comica 5; Heidelberg 2015).

Serena Perrone is Associate Professor of Classical Philology at the University of Genoa. Her main research interests lie in papyrology and ancient Greek comedy. Her publications include first editions of papyri, particularly fragments held at the University of Genoa, the volume concerning comedy and mime of unknown authorship within the series *Commentaria et Lexica Graeca in Papyris reperta* (CLGP), and the comment on the fragments of the comic poet Crates within the project *Kommentierung der Fragmente der Griechischen Komödie (KomFrag)*.

Ralph M. Rosen is the Vartan Gregorian Professor of the Humanities in the Department of Classical Studies at the University of Pennsylvania. He is the author of numerous articles and books on ancient comedy, satire, and medicine, including *Aristophanes and Politics: New Studies* (Brill 2020l; ed., with Helene P. Foley), *Hip Sublime: Beat Writers and the Classical Tradition* (Ohio State 2018; ed., with Sheila Murnaghan), and *Making Mockery: The Poetics of Ancient Satire* (Oxford U. Press 2007).

Elizabeth Scharffenberger is a senior lecturer in the Department of Classics at Columbia University in New York City. Her research interests include Greek drama and comic literature. Among her publications are papers on dramas by Euripides, Sophocles, and Aristophanes and their modern reception.

Carl A. Shaw is Professor of Greek Language and Literature at New College, the honors college of Florida. His scholarly interests lie broadly in the areas of Greek literature and culture, with a particular focus on drama and archaic performance. His monograph, *Satyric Play: The Evolution of Greek Comedy and Satyr Drama*, was released by Oxford University Press in 2014, and his book on Euripides' *Cyclops* was published by Bloomsbury Press in 2018.

Natalia Tsoumpra is Lecturer in Classical Studies at the Open University. Her research concentrates on Greek comedy and tragedy, but she is also interested in political theory, gender and sexuality, theories of humor, and ancient medicine. She has published various articles on Greek drama and is the editor of *Costume Change in the Comedies of Aristophanes* (*ICS* special issue 2020) and co-editor of *Morbid Laughter: Exploring the Comic Dimensions of Disease in Classical Antiquity* (ICS special issue 2018). From September 2024, she will be a Senior Humboldt Fellow at the Freie Universität Berlin, finishing her book on *The Politics of Power in Aristophanes: Populism, Affect, and Humour*.

Anna Uhlig is Associate Professor of Classics at the University of California, Davis. She is author of *Theatrical Reenactment in Pindar and Aeschylus* (Cambridge University Press 2019) and coeditor (with Richard Hunter) of *Imagining Reperformance in Ancient Culture: Studies in the Traditions of Drama and Lyric* (Cambridge University Press 2017) and (with Lyndsay Coo) of *Aeschylus at Play: Studies in Aeschylean Satyr Drama*, a themed issue of the *Bulletin of the Institute of Classical Studies* (2019).

Philip Walsh is Chair of the Department of Classics at St. Andrew's School (Middletown, DE). He teaches Latin and ancient Greek at all levels, an advanced history seminar on Thucydides and ancient Athens, and sections of English. He is the editor of *The Classical Outlook*, the leading, peer-reviewed publication for teachers of Latin, Greek, and the ancient Mediterranean world. He also edited *Brill's Companion to the Reception of Aristophanes* (Brill 2016). His work has appeared in *Eidolon* and in the *Classical Receptions Journal*.

Andreas Willi holds the Diebold Chair in Comparative Philology at the University of Oxford. His research focuses on the language-literature interface in the ancient world, Ancient Greek sociolinguistics and dialectology, and Greek, Latin, and Indo-European historical-comparative grammar; pertinent book publications include *The Languages of Aristophanes: Linguistic Variation in Classical Attic Greek* (Oxford 2003), *Sikelismos: Sprache, Literatur und Gesellschaft im griechischen Sizilien* (Basel 2008), and *Origins of the Greek Verb* (Cambridge 2018). He is also one of the editors of *Glotta: Zeitschrift für griechische und lateinische Sprache*.

Acknowledgments

We would like to begin by thanking the twenty-nine authors who contributed chapters to this volume. Many of them agreed to join the project just before the outbreak of the pandemic; despite the extraordinary disruptions, delays, and tragedies of these years, our contributors persevered, offered us support and guidance, and cheered one another on throughout the process.

Thanks also to the many dedicated editors, project managers, and other staff at Wiley who steered the project through to completion: Haze Humbert, who solicited the initial proposal for this volume; Todd Green; Ajith Kumar; Andrew Minton; Skyler Van Valkenburgh; Katherine King; Will Croft; Monica Chandrasekar; Pascal Raj Francois; Praveen Kumar Bondili; Sarah Milton; and doubtless many others who supported our work behind the scenes.

Matt would like to thank Haverford College for supporting a sabbatical leave during which much of the work on this volume was completed. He must also express his gratitude to his colleagues Bret Mulligan, Deborah Roberts, Ava Shirazi, and Hannah Silverblank for their generosity, support, expertise, and good cheer throughout the past five years.

Jeremy would especially like to thank the Swarthmore students in his honors seminar on "Aristophanes and the Comic Tradition" who read excerpts from the volume and offered their insights on the needs of students approaching Greek comedy: Kiran McDonald, Kodie Bastian, and Pablo Salvatierra.

Finally, Jeremy and Matt would like to offer their thanks to one another. Looking back over the vicissitudes of the past five years, it's somewhat hard to believe that the project we conceptualized over a lunch at Sang Kee in Philadelphia in August 2018 has in fact become this book. But throughout those years, we've relied on each other for mutual support, camaraderie, and good humor, and I think it is safe to say that neither of us could have done the work without the other.

Introduction

Matthew C. Farmer and Jeremy B. Lefkowitz

A Companion to Aristophanes

It seems that there is now a companion for just about every Greek author and every topic under the sun. Until now, however, Aristophanes had been companionless. To be sure, there have been excellent companions to ancient comedy published in recent years.[1] But this *Companion to Aristophanes* is the first of its kind – a volume dedicated specifically to Aristophanes with updated, sophisticated analyses of the Aristophanic corpus and its place in literary and cultural history. How would Aristophanes have responded to this state of affairs? Would he perhaps have relished being left out of the companion wave, preferring, with Groucho Marx, not to join any club that would have him as a member? Or would he have proudly defended comedy's reputation, claiming that its poets deserve to be taken just as seriously as those working in other genres? We think he probably would have done both.

In recent decades, work on ancient Greek comedy has moved away from an "Aristophanocentric" approach by emphasizing the rich corpus of comic fragments. By offering this volume to Aristophanes, we are by no means seeking to disrupt this trend: as you will see, the fragments of Greek comedy receive extensive attention in the essays that follow, and even in chapters focused on Aristophanes himself, our contributors have consistently drawn on the expansive view of the genre of Greek comedy provided by work on fragmentary authors. Companions, however, are for beginners: whether that means a student reading Greek drama for the first time, a lay reader curious about the state of interpretation and criticism on familiar comedies, or a seasoned classicist or literary critic moving into the subfield of comic studies from some other area of specialization. Almost everyone begins their journey into the world of Greek comedy with the plays of Aristophanes, and for that reason, we believe – whatever Aristophanes himself may have thought of the idea – that his work deserves a companion of its own.

Several goals unite the work of the team of scholars and teachers who have contributed to this volume. Firstly, our purpose has been to make Greek comedy accessible to beginners. Aristophanes' plays are hilarious and compelling, despite the gulf of time that separates our world from his, but they are also offensive, bewildering, frustrating, deliberately contradictory – in need of a guide, or rather, several dozen guides. But secondly, in inviting and selecting authors to serve as guides to our

---

[1] For example, Dobrov 2010, Revermann 2014, Fontaine and Scafuro 2014, Walsh 2016; and see also the individual volumes of the *Bloomsbury Ancient Comedy Companions* series, e.g. Robson 2023.

beginning readers of Aristophanes, we have sought to include a wider range of scholarly voices and perspectives than have sometimes been heard on these subjects.[2] We have asked our authors to open up worlds of possibility for the reader of Aristophanes, to welcome the budding Aristophanist not by cementing old opinions but by gesturing broadly to new horizons. We hope that this volume will equip readers with the tools they need to enter into interpretive conversations and debates about Aristophanes' plays, the lost comedies of his fellow comedians, and the nature of ancient and modern laughter.

The Organization of This Volume

This volume is divided into five sections; collectively, they provide a foundation for reading and interpreting Aristophanes' plays in their literary and historical contexts. Of course, even a volume of this size cannot provide a comprehensive picture of the state of Aristophanic studies, but we hope our contributors' 28 essays offer both a sense of the history of work on Aristophanes and open up new pathways and possibilities for teachers, critics, and readers of the great comedian.

Part I: The World of Aristophanes seeks to establish the historical, political, and literary circumstances in which Aristophanes created his plays. Our opening chapter sets forth the historical situation of Athens in the closing decades of the 5th century BCE and the beginning years of the 4th. The three chapters that follow establish Aristophanes' plays as scripts for performance, with discussions of staging, costumes, actors and choruses, verse and song, and Aristophanes' famously varied language and style. We pair this attempt to reconstruct the Aristophanic stage with a discussion of ancient vase images depicting comedy, a vital source for understanding the plays in performance. This section then closes with an essay that unites the historical and the literary with a focus on Aristophanes' engagement with politics, a topic that has long been central to debates on the interpretation of Greek comedy.

Part II: The Comedies of Aristophanes examines the eleven surviving plays of the Aristophanic corpus. In this section, in many ways the heart of the volume, we set our authors an unusual challenge: to examine one of the extant plays of Aristophanes by pairing it with a particular theme exemplified by that play, and then to explore the ways that theme connects the play to other Aristophanic comedies or the world of Greek comedy as a whole. Each of these chapters can be read as a guide to its play but can also be used as an orientation to particular topics (such as "Gender," "Utopia," or "Religion and Ritual") across Greek comedy. These chapters stand on their own, and we hope they will be widely used by students and teachers approaching individual plays for the first time; but read collectively, they also provide a sweeping overview of what we see as the central interpretive themes of work on Greek comedy in the present and, we hope, the future.

Although Aristophanes is the only comic poet of his period whose plays survive intact, we know of dozens of other authors who competed with him in Athens' dramatic festivals; for many of these authors, we possess substantial bodies of textual fragments and other types of evidence that permit us to broaden our perspective on the literary context in which Aristophanes wrote. In *Part III: The Fragments of Greek Comedy*, our authors provide overviews of this fragmentary evidence while also sketching out a variety of interpretive principles and approaches that can be used to make sense of this challenging material. We survey here both the fragments of Aristophanes' own lost plays – only about a quarter of his literary output survives to the present – and those of his fellow Athenian comic poets, grouping them into broad chronological categories relative to Aristophanes' career. Critical work in recent decades has made it clear that no reader can make complete sense of Aristophanes' plays without the context the fragments of Greek comedy provide.

Part IV: Aristophanes and His Readers showcases historical interpreters, commentators, and translators of Aristophanes' work: ancient Greek philosophers and scholars; Greek and Latin authors

---

[2] See Thonemann 2019 on the traditionally skewed demographics of companions and handbooks, with 7–8 on companions to ancient comedy.

of the Roman Republic and Empire; and Renaissance and Early Modern translators and printers of Aristophanes' plays. Our understanding of Aristophanes' plays has been irrevocably shaped by his reception in the works of these many readers who stand between us and classical Athens, and together these chapters help us understand the creative and interpretive traditions that have developed around his work since antiquity.

Finally, in *Part V: Aristophanes Today* we focus on encounters with Aristophanes in the two settings we most frequently find him today: the stage and the classroom. Both of the chapters in this section speak eloquently to one another: we see the place of performance in the teaching of Aristophanes and the importance of teaching Aristophanes' works as performative texts.

General Resources for Reading Aristophanes

The student of Aristophanes today is well served by resources to support either reading his works in their original Greek or reading them in translation. We offer a few suggestions below to get you started; each of the individual chapters in this volume concludes with a "Guide to Further Reading," which contains much more thorough suggestions.

For the reader of Greek, Wilson's 2007 Oxford Classical Text is the standard edition of Aristophanes' eleven extant plays. Most of the plays are well-served by relatively recent Oxford commentaries; these can be supplemented helpfully by the notes in Sommerstein's Aris and Phillips editions (from which we cite only *Wealth* below) and by the newly appearing volumes of the Michigan Classical Commentaries series. The standard edition of the fragments of Greek comedy, including the fragmentary plays of Aristophanes, is Kassel and Austin's *Poetae Comici Graeci*. The volumes of the project *Kommentierung der Fragmente der Griechischen Komödie* (often known as "KomFrag" and still continuing to appear) provide copious notes and translations on these fragments; the bibliography below cites Orth 2017 as an illustrative example from this extensive series. Olson's *Broken Laughter* provides a thematically arranged selection of fragments with extensive notes.

For the reader of English, there are many translations available. Henderson's Loeb editions are highly readable, hew close to the Greek, and include translations of Aristophanes' fragments. Sommerstein's Aris and Phillips translations are another good starting point, with more substantial notes (particularly for the later plays). Halliwell's Oxford World's Classics translations offer affordable, readable versions in collected printings. In general, we counsel students and teachers to avoid relying on the out-of-copyright translations that can be readily found online, as these tend to bowdlerize Aristophanes' language and to deliberately obscure precisely those features of his plays, such as their lively portrayal of Greek sexual culture, that a modern reader might be most interested in exploring. Instead, see the suggested readings in Chapter 28 ("Teaching Aristophanes") for better, freely available translations. For the fragments of Old Comedy, Storey's Loeb editions are a standard point of entry; Rusten et al.'s *Birth of Comedy* collects and translates many of the most interesting fragments, including fragments of Middle and New Comedy, as well as other textual and visual evidence for Greek comedy.

REFERENCES

Anderson, C.A. and Keith Dix, T. (2020). *A Commentary on Aristophanes' Knights*. Ann Arbor: Michigan Classical Commentaries.

Austin, C. and Olson, S.D. (2004). *Aristophanes Thesmophoriazusae. Edited with Introduction and Commentary*. Oxford: Oxford University Press.

Biles, Z.P. and Olson, S.D. (2015). *Aristophanes Wasps. Edited with Introduction and Commentary*. Oxford: Oxford University Press.

Dobrov, G. (ed.) (2010). *Brill's Companion to the Study of Greek Comedy*. Leiden: Brill.

Dover, K.J. (1968). *Aristophanes Clouds. Edited with Introduction and Commentary*. Oxford: Oxford University Press.

Dover, K.J. (1993). *Aristophanes Frogs. Edited with Introduction and Commentary*. Oxford: Oxford University Press.
Dunbar, N. (1998). *Aristophanes Birds. Edited with Introduction and Commentary*. Oxford: Oxford University Press.
Fontaine, M. and Scafuro, A.C. (ed.) (2014). *The Oxford Handbook of Greek and Roman Comedy*. Oxford: Oxford University Press.
Halliwell, S. (1998). *Aristophanes Birds and Other Plays*. Oxford: Oxford World's Classics.
Halliwell, S. (2015). *Aristophanes Frogs and Other Plays*. Oxford: Oxford World's Classics.
Henderson, J. (1987). *Aristophanes Lysistrata. Edited with Introduction and Commentary*. Oxford: Oxford University Press.
Henderson, J. (1998–2007). *Aristophanes*, vol. 1–5. Cambridge, MA: Loeb Classical Library.
Kassel, R. and Austin, C. (1983–2001). *Poetae Comici Graeci*. Berlin and New York: de Gruyter.
Orth, C. (2017). *Fragmenta Comica 10.3: Aristophanes, Aiolosikon - Babylonioi (frr. 1–100)*. Göttingen: Verlag Antike.
Olson, S.D. (1998). *Aristophanes Peace. Edited with Introduction and Commentary*. Oxford: Oxford University Press.
Olson, S.D. (2002). *Aristophanes Acharnians. Edited with Introduction and Commentary*. Oxford: Oxford University Press.
Olson, S.D. (2007). *Broken Laughter: Select Fragments of Greek Comedy*. Oxford: Oxford University Press.
Olson, S.D. (2021). *Aristophanes' Clouds: A Commentary*. Ann Arbor: Michigan Classical Commentaries.
Revermann, M. (ed.) (2014). *The Cambridge Companion to Greek Comedy*. Cambridge: Cambridge University Press.
Robson, J. (2023). *Aristophanes: Lysistrata*. London: Bloomsbury Ancient Comedy Companions.
Rusten, J.S., Henderson, J., Konstan, D., and Rosen, R.M. (2011). *The Birth of Comedy: Texts, Documents, and Art from Athenian Comic Competitions, 486–280*. Baltimore: Johns Hopkins University Press.
Sommerstein, A.H. (2001). *The Comedies of Aristophanes: Vol. 11: Wealth*. Warminster: Aris and Phillips.
Storey, I. (2011). *Fragments of Old Comedy*, vol. 1–3. Cambridge, MA: Loeb Classical Library.
Thonemann, P. (2019). Gender, subject preferences, and editorial bias in classical studies, 2001–2019. *CUCD Bulletin* 48: 1–24.
Ussher, R.G. (1973). *Aristophanes Ecclesiazusae. Edited with Introduction and Commentary*. Oxford: Oxford University Press.
Walsh, P. (ed.) (2016). *Brill's Companion to the Reception of Aristophanes*. Leiden: Brill.
Wilson, N.G. (2007). *Aristophanis Fabulae*. Oxford: Oxford Classical Texts.

PART I

The World of Aristophanes

CHAPTER 1

Aristophanes Among Athenians

Donald Lateiner and Rosaria Munson

Introduction

When in the 360s BCE the Sicilian tyrant Dionysios Junior asked his Athenian visitor and mentor Plato to describe vividly the people and institutions of Athens, the anti-democratic philosopher allegedly sent him comedies of Aristophanes (*Life of Aristophanes*, Rusten et al., 7.1, p. 274). These critical but ambitious and affectionate portraits of a people could teach him how the Athenians organized (or disorganized) their once unexpectedly successful political life (*politeia*). Attic demes and the Athenian polis selected, arranged, and staged comic productions. Attic "Old Comedy," with mockery of leading politicians – among its other targets, social, intellectual, ethnic, and female – was a civic institution, nearly as old as ostracism – and it perhaps shared the leveling intent (488/7; Sommerstein 2014, p. 292).

Aristophanes lived through his Athenians' best and worst years (450–385 BCE). From the age of twenty-three, he wrote wacky plays with pissed-off, disadvantaged, but plucky little-man heroes (Whitman 1964), preposterous plots, raunchy and lyrical verse, inventively hilarious vocabulary, and outrageous obscenity. We can identify forty titles, although only eleven scripts and hundreds of fragments survive. His dramas furnish us with the only unmangled survivors from Athens' happier days when "Old Comedy" held the stage.[1] Within a vivid portrait of daily life, comic poets participated in public discourse about civic affairs. In this sphere, Aristophanes claimed that he far surpassed his competitors because his ideas benefited the Athenians. As he translates reality into fantasy, his comedies, or rather "trugudies," claim to teach what is right, *to dikaion* (Taplin 1983). The present chapter does not attempt to determine the nature of Aristophanes' overall "political ideology" (an unhelpful and controversial subject; see Rosen and Foley (2020)). It rather examines how the political message of his plays varies over time as it negotiates historical events, public opinion, and Aristophanes' own status in Athenian society, to the extent that we know these external facts from other ancient sources, especially his contemporaries Thucydides, Plato, and Xenophon.

---

[1] See Dover (1972: 210–18); Henderson's annotated Loeb collections (2002, 2007); Rusten et al., Kassel and Austin (*PCG* III.2 1984); Dübner 1842 for the ancient explications (*scholia*). Aristophanes' most successful competitor was Eupolis (*Clouds* 551–9; Eup. F89), who started to write for the comic stage and direct when he was seventeen (429 BCE) and won firsts, for instance, with *Toadies* (*Kolakes*) and *Marikas* (= Hyperbolos the demagogue = *cinaedus*), both in 421.

Aristophanes and the Peloponnesian War

Almost the entirety of Aristophanes' career unfolds against the background of the Peloponnesian War and the internal political antagonisms of post-Periklean Athens, but his last two plays, *Ekklesiazousai* and *Ploutos*, produced after this period are still politically significant. In spite of many, surely strategic, silences, Aristophanes makes his characters and choruses (Ehrenberg 1962) complain about present-day circumstances and criticize in word or by example current policies and the handling of prominent institutions. At least until 411, his consistent message targets ever increasingly demanding Athenian imperialism and his fellow citizens' war appetite: just stop it. It perhaps began with the *Babylonians* (427 BCE), a play that survives only in fragments but appears to have expressed disapproval for, among other things, the Athenians' treatment of the members of their imperial alliance (*Acharn.* 641–42; Panagiotarakou 2009, p. 48–9). And it comes into full flower in the *Acharnians* (425 BCE), which fantasizes a private peace between Dikaiopolis, a local Attic farmer, and the Peloponnesians. Dikaiopolis – "Just City" or "the one who makes the city just" (Strauss 1966, p. 59; contra Bowie 1982, p. 38) – pines for the self-sufficiency of his peaceful country life at the time when the rural population was crammed into the city during the annual Peloponnesian invasions of Attica.[2] He satirizes the causes of the present war and accuses the *Prytaneis* – Councilors in charge of daily business – of wrongdoing for rejecting a god-sponsored settlement (45–54; Henderson 1998, p. 61, n. 10); he ridicules the wasteful Athenian embassies to Persia,[3] the hiring of mercenaries from Thrace, and the pugnacious Athenian general Lamakhos; he sympathizes with the impoverished Megarians and argues that the Spartans are not all in the wrong with regard to this war (61–134, 307–8, 513–19; cf. 646–54). In subsequent years, *Cavalrymen* (424 BCE) features Aristophanes' fellow demes – man from Kydathenaion, the warmongering and divisive demagogue Kleon, out-demagogued by a fast-food sausage seller (cf. Rhodes 2004). *Peace* (421 BCE) looks forward to the imminent end of the war after ten years. Shortly after, the Peace of Nicias was actually concluded, but it would soon become clear that, partly thanks to Alkibiades' machinations, the war had in no way ended. In Aristophanes' play, another sensible, salt-of-the-earth Attic farmer, the vine-grower Trygaios, flies on a feces-chomping, giant, stinking dung beetle to escape from endless assemblies and war to the euphoric and ambrosial divine realm. *Birds* (414 BCE) subtly mocks his countrymen's irrepressible imperialistic overreach and empire. Finally, *Lysistrata* (411 BCE) makes an appeal for Panhellenic concord through the fictional voice of the women from city-states on both sides of the conflict. The fantasies vary; the theme of peace and its benefits endures.

The 420s and 'teens are, however, the time when the most influential leaders (those who claimed to be guardians of the interests of the common people) were radical democrats who also promoted aggressive fighting, expansionism, and control over the tribute-paying subjects. The tribute played an important role in the survival of the Athenian democratic regime by funding payment for public offices, large job-producing infrastructure, and projects for maintaining and replacing the imperial fleet. Aristophanes' stance – at once pro-democratic and anti-war – might therefore have been interpreted as anti-democratic, particularly since he was himself unmistakably a member of the elite and a land owner on the island of Aigina (*Acharn.* 652–4; Figueira 1991, p. 79–93).

The Athenian system had flaws, certainly, which Aristophanes was always ready to amplify for laughs, and his audiences were reasonably self-critical (*Acharn.* 140; Pelling 2000, p. 123–40,

---

[2] Thuc. 2.14–17. Farmer Dikaiopolis' pastoral idea of sustainability (*Acharn.* 29–39) sharply contrasts with Perikles' praise of the *autarkeia* (self-sufficiency) that Athens has achieved thanks to her mastery over the seas, which allows the citizens to enjoy imports from all over the world (Thuc. 2.36.3, 38.2). Panagiotarakou 2009: 72–3.

[3] *Acharn.* 61–134. The Persian king had invaded Greece in 490 and 480 and was defeated by a coalition of Greek states led by Sparta and Athens. During the Peloponnesian War, however, Peloponnesians and Athenians each made overtures to Persia in the hopes of obtaining financial support in their fight against the other side. See esp. Thuc. 4.50 for the year 425.

esp. 133–39; Halliwell 2020, p. 128). In *Cavalrymen* (424 BCE), he makes a scathing attack against the corruption and opportunism of Kleon, self-appointed watchdog and lover of the *demos*. Elected general that very year, when he had "snatched the Pylos focaccia from his colleague Demosthenes" (54–57; cf. 1050–1064), Kleon is almost inseparable from Mr. Demos, the personification of a senescent, spoiled, and gullible dimwit. The impasse is resolved with Mr. Demos' miraculous rejuvenation and final reversal to better counsel (1329–1408). There, the blame for recent follies is cannily attributed to a few unsavory individuals (515). In *Wasps* (422 BCE), the impecunious old men who derive wages and a sense of power from their never-ending jury service are sympathetically portrayed, but the play also exposes a system that makes room for widespread self-dealing: prosecutors bribe defendants, elite defendants are guilty of embezzling public funds, generals profit from campaigns abroad, and politicians with the power of assessing the tribute blackmail the subject allies (*Wasps* 665–930; MacDowell 1995, p. 154–70). In *Birds* (415 BCE), the Athenian protagonists are so annoyed with this whole situation in Athens that they leave to found a new colony and new empire in the sky. All these comedies were successful on the Athenian stage.[4]

At the same time, freedom of political expression (*parrhēsia*) faced some fuzzy limits. The same people could both laugh at a boastful and fraudulent demagogue and trust him with their sons' lives, but one had to steer clear of explicitly dishonoring the polis, the law courts, and the *demos*, as such (see *Acharn.* 631; cf. 503).[5] In the words of the unidentified, cranky but insightful writer now known as the "Old Oligarch,"

> [the Athenian people] forbid abuse in comedy (κωμωιδεῖν) that ridicules the *demos* lest they themselves be disparaged, but they encourage personal attacks, if anyone wishes, knowing full well that the one ridiculed in comedy (ὁ κωμωδούμενος) is not for the most part from the *demos*, but rather a rich, well-born, or powerful man, and just a few poor or ordinary folks are so ridiculed (κωμωδοῦνται); and not even they are, unless they are busy-bodies or try to rise above the *demos*, so that they do not resent it if such people are abused in comedy (κωμωδουμένους). [Ps.-Xen.] 2.18)

Athenian audiences enjoyed seeing influential "names" satirized and attacked. As even Aristophanes' early plays reveal in the years when democracy was still unchallenged, the Athenians harbored a subterranean fear that their institutions were under threat, either by a restricted elite group or by an especially ambitious individual who aimed at tyranny, perhaps even conspiring with the enemy.[6] It was only with the Sicilian Expedition of 415–13, however, that serious doubt would spread among the Athenians about the competence of a sovereign assembly of political equals to pursue domination and expansion abroad. By then, a new generation agitated by the young but ambitious Alkibiades coveted new, post-Periklean expansion for imperial glory. It all started with great fanfare; the general and historian Thucydides, although living now in exile (since 424), described this Generation X's excitement at the prospect of conquering new taxable frontiers as *erós*, irrational passionate attraction (6.24, 31). Similarly, Aristophanes (*Birds* 414) has the King of Birdland use this word to describe the motive of his Athenian visitors/infiltrators. He favors other, more specific terms denoting immoderate desire for drink, sex, food, money, and power.

---

[4] The Athenian judge of selections (*archon* or *archon basileus*) repeatedly included one of Aristophanes' comedies for competitive performance: *Cavalrymen* (424), *Clouds* (423), *Wasps* (422), *Peace* (421). *Babylonians* and *Acharnians* won first prize; *Wasps* and *Birds* came in second. The least political of Aristophanes' comedies, *Clouds*, was also the least successful, coming third in the competition, causing Aristophanes to revise it c. 417 but never produce it in its new, preserved form. Perhaps, as Sommerstein suggests (2014: 298–9; cf. Csapo and Slater 1995: 286–305, for testimonies), the theater audiences were skewed to the wealthier classes, not a representative sample, and held views different from shifting majorities among the mass of less ideological voters (*thetes*) in the assembly.

[5] Notably, *Babylonians* got Aristophanes into some kind of trouble (perhaps an impeachment brought by Kleon) for having defamed the Athenian *demos* at the City Dionysia in the presence of allied delegations and other foreigners. See *Acharn.* 631, 503, 641–42; also 375–84, where Dikaiopolis is partly speaking for Aristophanes. Sommerstein 2004, Henderson 2020; cf. Lateiner 2020 for character silences.

[6] See e.g. *Cav.* 237–8 and, more poignantly, *Wasps* 345, 417, 464, 470, 473–74, 483, 487. MacDowell 1995: 99.

Several decades later (c. 385 BCE), Aristophanes' younger contemporary, the aristocratic snob Plato, staged his comic prose socio-philosophical dialogue *Symposion* (*Drinking Party*) on the day after the tragic poet Agathon's dramatic victory at the Lenaia of 416 BCE. Plato pictures the famous comic verbally competing with Sokrates, on the subject of *erós*—meaning not the lust for adventure and conquest Thucydides speaks about, or Dikaiopolis' longing for "Reconciliation" and peace (*Acharn.* 988–89), but *erós* in the sexual sense. Aristophanes sports a reputation as a heavy drinker (*Symp.* 176b, 185c), and when his turn comes to bloviate wittily, he suffers a toper's hiccups (186b), but eventually amuses his fellow partygoers with a parable of the ancient and divine nature of *erós*. His Zeus solves the pressing divine-community problem of arrogant globular humans, some of them half-women, half-men (189a–193d): heterosexuals will populate earth while same-sex couples will satisfy their lust and get on with more important business.

Plato's myth here trenches on his predecessor Aristophanes' typical territory, an ingenious solution requiring mischief with sex organs and appetites. The Platonic Aristophanes' novel, bright conception is one contribution in a priamel structure leading up to the supreme ironist Sokrates' climactic lengthy recollection of Diotima – another problem-solving high priestess, like Aristophanes' prior Lysistrata. The assembled men of mature years had decided to talk more and drink less, but the young rake Alkibiades crashes the drinking/thinking party. The now presumably fully soused Aristophanes falls asleep over his *kylix*. This is Plato's mild and entirely literary revenge on the far more consequentially distorted caricature of the bumbling sophist Sokrates in the earlier versions of Aristophanes' *Clouds*. At the same time, Alkibiades' comic epilogue gives readers of the *Symposium* a retroactive anticipation of the brilliant but rascally individual who would be appointed as one of the three generals leading the expedition to Sicily in the spring of the following year. When recalled to Athens on charges of impiety, he fled to Sparta and, now a traitor, advised the enemy's strategies (Thuc. 6.61, 88.7–92).

The Failed Peace (420–410 BCE)

Having embarked on a vastly expensive campaign dispatched over 800 miles west to conquer the most powerful city of Sicily, the Syrakusans', the Athenians managed to acquire few allies or financial support. Rather, they encountered determined enemy swords and spears, hunger, and disease. After the desertion of Alkibiades and the death of Lamakhos, the sick and aging Nikias was left in sole command of the expedition, but the Athenians sent a second huge fleet under General Demosthenes. The invasion, however, had lost its surprise advantage, its offense collapsed, and the amphibious force had to turn to defense. After losing control of Syrakuse's harbors, the soldiers and sailors of Athens and their imperial allies straggled away from their misconceived easy target. The demoralized troops were slaughtered even while surrendering. The Syrakousans defended their homeland and annihilated or enslaved the combined Athenian expeditionary forces, first at sea and then on land. More than ten thousand sons, husbands, and cousins perished, a total disaster for the defeated (413 BCE, Thuc. 7.87).

Aristophanes mentions, or even alludes to, no suffering or setback in the overseas Sicilian campaign. *Birds* was produced when the expedition was still in progress but already in difficulty, although the extent to which the public in Athens was aware of the hardships of their troops far distant is unclear. The idea, however, that the plot of the comedy has nothing to do with the expedition the Athenians launched with crazed, irrational enthusiasm in 415 defies belief.[7] But the

---

[7] Hubbard's position (1991: 158–82). He sees the play as a reaction to the double scandal of the mutilation of the Hermai and the profanation of the Eleusinian Mysteries and resulting prosecutions. Like many prominent Athenians, Euelpides and Peisthetairos ("Persuader of companions," members of a *hetaireia*, or aristocratic political group) are escaping legal troubles and sophistically undermine traditional religion and democratic values. In their foundation of Cloudcuckooland (the name recalls one theme of *Clouds*), they replace the Athenian gods with the Birds, ruled by Peisthetairos himself as the "highest of the gods" (1765, *daimonón hypertate*); Hubbard 1991: 158–82.

colonizing enterprise of the two main characters of *Birds* (soon reduced to a single protagonist) is presented not as a military venture, but as their pursuit of a quiet life away from relentless Athenian law courts, lawsuits, and debt – not to mention any profit-seeking encomiastic poet, dishonest prosecutor, inspector, town planner, young man eager to strangle his father, and chresmologue. The colonists cleverly leverage the birds' intermediate position between humans and gods into power to control traffic in animal sacrifice from earthlings, and thus control the outwitted gods themselves. The establishment of a non- or anti-Athens is celebrated as successful, except that the human invader ends up forgetting about democracy and becomes the autocratic ruler of the birds that had welcomed him.[8] Against the real-life backdrop of the Sicilian venture, *Birds* is a spectacular masterwork of elusive irony.[9]

It is of course not surprising that Aristophanes and his characters remain silent, as far as we know, on the Sicilian expedition's disastrous outcome the next year, when the general massacre also claimed the lives of Nikias and Demosthenes, the two ridiculous but somewhat endearing "slaves" of Demos in *Cavalrymen*. In the aftermath of the military catastrophe, 411 BCE, the twentieth long year of the Peloponnesian War, was especially violent and frightening in Athenian domestic politics and because of increasing threats abroad. The Spartan coalition had invaded Attica annually from 431 to 424, but now, while the Athenians were fighting in Sicily, they had established their expeditionary force permanently in a fort in the nearby farming deme of Dekeleia. This had been Alkibiades' strategic advice after he turned traitor (Thuc. 6.91, 7.27); he subsequently helped foment revolts among the subject allies of Athens in Ionia and the islands. There Persia revived her hopes to restore her former dominion. Two satraps prepared to pounce on forces of both Hellenic alliances from their fortified bases on the Turkish littoral.

Alkibiades, now a fugitive from Sparta and eager to return to his city, plays his double game between the satrap of Lydia and an Athens desperate for Persian funds to support her crumbling empire and the war. In Athens, Aristophanes witnesses the vicious run-up to a post-debacle oligarchic revolution – the narrow faction of "the 400" deceitfully promising "the 5,000" – a false hope of a wider hoplite (upper-class), much modified "democracy." Such a government would still have significantly shrunk down from the Athenian *demos* of over 20 000 voters and legislators, but the charade was stillborn. The Athenian fleet, democratic in spirit and leadership, soon would threaten invasion of the oligarch-ruled homeland from Samos, the triremes' current navy dockyard. In the city, the fake news and absurd conspiracy theories of the 420s (Lateiner 2021) have now come true: the democracy will collapse.

Meanwhile, the Dionysiac show goes on. 411 BCE proves a big year for Aristophanes too – his "year of the woman," one might say, with two comedies centered on women, *Lysistrata* and *Thesmophoriazousai*. The first addresses two intertwined political problems. Internally determined demophobes, mostly the upper classes burdened with the expense of the war and loss of their property, confront democrats; internationally, the tribute-paying allies are in rebellion and spoiler Persians triangulate their support between the Lakedaimonians and Athenians. Through his woman commander, the tell-tale named priestess Lysistrata ("Armed Force-Dissolver"),[10] the comic imagines that his people might find an exit from debilitating military siege and warfare-ravaged, olive-tree denuded Attika. In the light of the men's failures, Lysistrata's imagined Hellenic army of

---

[8] Some birds are killed and eaten allegedly because they have rebelled against the "democratic birds" (1583–4). But at the end of the comedy, Pleisthetairos is hailed as a *turannos* (1708) and weds Basileia (sovereignty), the daughter of Zeus (1717–1758). In effect, he has superseded Zeus as "highest of the gods" (see end of preceding note). Hubbard 1991: 171–3.

[9] Henderson disagrees, remarking that *Birds* "lacks a political theme" and that irony "is a technique unparalleled in ancient comedy" (Henderson 2000: 5–6, but see 7).

[10] Note that a near synonym of this name, Lysimache (cf. v. 554) identifies a real Athenian at this time, indeed a historical Priestess of Athena Polias (D.M. Lewis, *BSA* 1955, citing *IG* ii^2 3453; Thonemann 2019). *Lysistrata* is the only comedy titled after an individual woman. See Rusten et al. (2011) who list all comic titles, organized by poet.

females seizes the high ground, literally and moral-metaphorically. The Athenian women capture the fortified Akropolis, the symbolic, spiritual, religious, and financial home of their patron goddess Athena. It was the focus of Athenian life and the polis' Mediterranean display of wealth, power, and beauty. On the day of performance, as today, it towered immediately above the people's seven- or ten-thousand-seat theater (Olson 2012; Rusten 2013; Thonemann 2019). Aristophanes satirizes male testosterone-fueled pretensions to wisdom and enforcement of patriarchal authority. Women held no office and had no vote in the limited democracy, but in this play, by force and logic, the wives under Lysistrata's fragile command compel their surly husbands to listen to them. Not only do they out-argue and outfight their "lords and masters," but they declare a sex strike: no peace, no fuck.

Lysistrata was in all likelihood produced at the Lenaia of 411, which in that year fell later than usual, in early February.[11] By then Peisandros – once an extreme democrat but now turned oligarch – had already traveled to Athens, sent by the Athenian oligarchs from Samos, to lay out the following proposal for the assembly. Athens was desperately short of money needed for the pursuit of the war, and only Persia could provide more funding, but only Alkibiades' assistance could achieve that result, for he exercised considerable influence with satrap Tissaphernes. Therefore, Peisandros advised, the Athenians, in exchange, should grant Alkibiades' requests that he be recalled to Athens and that the city establish a different form of government, one more moderate than this democracy that had exiled the glamorous general in 415. This recommended change of regime presented a tough bargain for the *demos*, but Thucydides reasons that the people, already terrorized (Thuc. 8.65–66), became resigned to the necessity of giving up their power, comforting themselves with the hope that the regime would be temporary. At the same time, Peisandros was secretly rallying support among political friends, the aristocratic-oligarchic members of *hetaireiai* (Thuc. 8.53–54). A considerable number of those most invested in maintaining a sovereign democracy, the lower electoral classes, were away, rowing or repairing the ships of the now Samos-based Athenian fleet. In the city, the profound democratic self-guilt and/or outrage that followed the failure of the Sicilian expedition two years earlier had already manifested itself, when the government was put under the emergency conservatorship of ten elder, upper-class *probouloi* (Thuc. 8.1.3–4; cf. Rusten 2013).

These officials were still at work in 411, since one of them appears in the *Lysistrata* as a bumbling fool, sent up to the Akropolis to bring the uppity women to heel (489–92). Aristophanes' transfer of the veil, a significant "speaking" object, in both *Lysistrata* and *Thesmophoriazousai*, signifies imposed silence and invisibility. The *proboulos* and the equally clunky police attempt these comic repressions of word and hand. They mimic recent (and future) events, silencing the *demos*. Lysistrata rejects any imposition of silence and a silent reign of terror (Thuc. 8.65–6). Likewise, the men of the semi-chorus – elder Athenian citizens and thus retired soldiers, ekklesiasts, and dikasts – are equally pugnacious, dull-witted, and equally poor listeners. As they pine for past glories of Marathon and Salamis, there is little doubt that the Athenians in the audience were aware of the insecurity of democratic traditions on the verge of capsizing. Institutions were about to change. Many who fought or remembered those battles were going to lose citizen rights. Where does Aristophanes, a poet who appreciates popular tastes and wants to win prizes but is also an aristocrat, stand at this point?

Although *Lysistrata* makes unmistakable references to the current instability of Athenian democracy, it treads lightly (see, e.g. *Lys.* 1043–1049). The umbrella covering Aristophanes' rear is a call for peace, one less controversial because of war-weariness and with a stronger Panhellenic message than in *Acharnians*. Women from different city-states, and ones from the opposite bloc, rally to the cause, implying that Persian money should have no role in resolving Greek problems. With Panhellenic unity, there should also come unity within Athens, like that of a skein of well-carded wool in a basket. What/who should be picked out and excluded from the basket? Sheep dung, thorns, and "those who clump and knot themselves together to snag government positions" (*Lys.* 577–78; trans. Henderson), apparently from whatever party or faction – a remarkable attempt

---

[11] Sommerstein (1977) presents the inconclusive evidence for dating *Lysistrata* precisely See, too, Henderson (1987/1991) xv–xxv.

at moral equivalency. One of these spoilers is no doubt Peisandros, who is, however, mentioned as a crooked politician apparently with a reference to his former democratic inclination and not as the oligarchic ringleader he had become (489–92). Who is entitled to be part of the polis? Practically everyone who is a friend of Athens, says Lysistrata, including even metics, foreigners, debtors to the state, and the Athenian colonies. Lysistrata is not, of course, here proposing citizenship for all these categories. Her broad appeal for inclusiveness of disfranchisement by plotting members of the anti-democratic political clubs alludes in the most tactful possible way to threats. This restraint probably reflected the feelings of many in Aristophanes' audience. Whether voluntarily quiet in a mood of justified despondency or with speech suppression imposed by fear of youngish oligarchs, dagger-men (Thuc. 8.69), the men in assembly were intermittently lethargic or considering ill-advised moves.

For all the uneasiness it manages to convey, *Lysistrata* gives no idea of what was about to happen. Just a couple of months after his first trip to Athens, Peisandros returned to the city where the democracy was already being dismantled in the most violent way, with secret assassinations of political opponents (Androkles), repression of speech, and a pervasive atmosphere of fear and mistrust even among friends and neighbors. The sham popular assembly at Kolonos in the spring formalized the change of government. Members of the 400's government, now in power, barged into the *prytaneion* armed with concealed daggers, and accompanied by a posse of young men, they insultingly dissolved the democratic council (Thuc. 8.65–9). In this fraught climate, even the wooly metaphor of the scrubbed fleece for the polis might have been too much, but some political criticism was still permissible at the Lenaia because in February/March, foreigners were unable to sail and attend in stormy wintry weather (*Akh.* 502–6 with scholia to 504).

Thesmophoriazusai, his second comedy of the momentous year 411 BCE, would be different: it would share with *Lysistrata* the motif of the battle of the sexes, but stay mostly clear of domestic or foreign affairs. The few passages where the female Chorus mentions the threat of tyranny (338–39, 1143–4), unconstitutional decrees (361–2), or collusion with the Persians (365–6), although suited to the current political climate, are vague and blended in with laments and imprecation against anyone who acts or conspires against *the women*. More conspicuously, the drama amplifies a theme recurrent in several of Aristophanes' earlier dramas at least since *Acharnians*: the competition of comedy and tragedy in the cultural discourse of the city. It will crash the big time: the Greater Dionysia with Athenians, islanders, and other allies in town. Athenians also saw this production later than usual (in mid-April) because of wartime exigencies and two bubbling political revolutions.[12]

In 411, after the disaster of Syracuse, a significant tranche of the Athenian electorate believed that supersession of the "acknowledged folly" (Alkibiades' sneer at Sparta, Thuc. 6.89.6) was essential for the immediate survival of the Athenian polis and remnants of empire. These Athenians overthrew the democracy with insinuations, intimidations of the organs of government, and murder (Thuc. 8.53–4, 65–6). They would do so again in 404 with backup from Lysander's Peloponnesian armed soldiers (Xen. *Hell.* 2). Many Athenians could argue retrospectively that even early on the *ekklesia* had shown itself dysfunctional in managing all-out war and had forfeited decent opportunities for negotiated peace in 431, 424, and 421. Intellectuals like Thucydides could enjoy and admire the astounding achievements of the democracy without always approving of its decision-making processes.[13]

---

[12] No firm evidence precisely dates *Thesmophoriazousai*, but consensus has settled on the Dionysia of 411. Sommerstein 1977:112–26; Hubbard 1991:186–9. If that is the case, it remains uncertain whether the production occurred before or shortly after the decisive assembly at Kolonos. *Thesm.* 804 and Thuc. 8.42 mention *strategos* Charminos (also 8.30, 73, 76), later dismissed, so these data help date the comedy (Sommerstein 1994:1–4).

[13] We hear that Agathon, Aristophanes' drinking host at Plato's *Symposion*, admired the orator and extremist oligarch Antiphon and his self-defense speech in 411 BCE after the first oligarchical putsch collapsed (Ar. *Eth. Eud.* 1232b4–9). So did Thucydides, exiled by the democracy (4.106, 5.26, 8.68.1–2). Like Euripides, Agathon left Athens for King Archelaos' Makedonian court (ca. 405 BCE, Aristoph. *Frogs* 84–85, Ael. *VH* 2.21), when democratic celebrities might feel nervous, because Peloponnesian forces and Athenian collaborators were battering Athens' perimeter.

Aristophanes and the End of the War

We are not able to divine methodologically the political leanings of playwrights in the same way as we can do so for historians. The former writes fiction that must please his audiences and is more likely to go with the flow. The fact remains, however, that Aristophanes' later plays either *express* oligarchical sympathies or just reveal an increased lack of trust that the democracy could be salvaged—perhaps that was the flow. His silences are even more significant: from 411 to 405 we cannot date any comedy by him, momentous and action-packed as those years were for Athenian military and political fortunes. The rule of the 400 failed to meet any of their goals – obtaining financial support from Persia, the loyalty of the subject allies under newly established oligarchic regimes, and reasonable peace terms with Sparta. They collapsed after a few months, leaving the mostly mysterious moderate oligarchy briefly in charge – the so-called government of 5000. Alkibiades, elected general in Samos, was recalled to Athens after waging a successful campaign on the Hellespont. Mostly under his leadership, the accomplishments of the crews of the Athenian navy led to the restoration of their power – the old, full democracy.

Alkibiades, who had left Athens to pursue the Ionian War, was, however, tripped up when his lieutenant Antiokhos suffered a minor defeat near Notion in 407. He could not regain the trust of his fellow citizens (not again!) and, now persona non grata with Athenians, Spartans, and Persians alike, sought refuge on the Hellespont. The Athenians then elected a new board of generals (inimical to Alkibiades). In a dire emergency, these generals gained a splendid victory against the Peloponnesians at Arginusai (406). But eight of them ended up condemned to death by the democratic assembly for failing to rescue the crews of twenty-five vessels shipwrecked in a storm, about five thousand sailors. Two of the generals escaped a notorious trial; six were executed (Xen. *Hell.* 1.6.12–7.35).

Historically inclined students wonder what Aristophanes the citizen was doing at this time. Tenuous evidence suggests that the loyal democratic tragedian Sophokles, as *proboulos*, voted for establishing the oligarchy of the 400. Of course, we have no way of knowing, except that in 411 many upper-class democrats might have justified that choice in the same way as Sophokles allegedly did: "There was nothing better to do."[14]

Frogs, produced at the Lenaia of 405, shortly after the Arginusai battle and grim aftermath, represents another turning point. As in *Thesmophoriazousai*, one central topic here is theater. *Frogs* features Dionysos traveling to the underworld to retrieve Euripides, who had recently died, leaving the Athenians with a deplorable dearth of good tragedies. Despite being the god of all kinds of drama, Aristophanes' Dionysos is foremost a low-brow comic character, but since he is disguised as Herakles, he also farcically embodies a lofty and heroic (that is to say "tragic") persona. The two choruses, of Frogs and Eleusinian mystic initiates, similarly may symbolize the two genres of poetry (Hubbard 1991:200–3).

But whereas *Thesmophoriazousai* minimized references to public affairs, *Frogs*' literary concerns encompass a political discourse; the theme of the deterioration of drama overlaps with that of the deterioration of the commonwealth. This comedy's didactic intent clearly emerges with the initiates' program, reminiscent of Aristophanes' claims in *Acharnians*, to "utter much that is funny and much that is serious" and "to advise and teach good things for the city" (*Frogs* 389–90, 686–7 cf. above, pp. 1–2). The appeals to unity at home and nostalgia for a better past,[15] and (in a limited way) for peace abroad (1531–1533) make *Frogs* a counterpart of the *Lysistrata*, but the substance of the message is reversed in one important respect. In the earlier comedy, good and harmonious

---

[14] Aristotle *Rhet.* 18.6, 1419 A, lines 25–30, discussed by Jameson (1971):542–3.
[15] In Aristophanes, the desirable past is as flexible as historical vicissitudes are variable and as the reputation of public figures changes. *Lysistrata* celebrates the days of the *Marathonomachoi*, as does *Wasps* 1081 ff. and *Acharnians*. *Frogs* longs for the values of the times of Aiskhylos but also praises Lamakhos (1039, cf. *Thesm.*839–41), once censured as a braggadocious warmonger (*Acharn.*270, 567–625, 1075–1141). While *Eccl.* 356–7 berates Thrasyboulos, *Ploutos* 550 cites him as a paragon of the good leader.

government was said to depend (at least cautiously and allusively) on the exclusion of clubbish individuals who undermined the city's democratic institutions. *Frogs'* conspicuous advice, however, is to stop threatening with prosecution precisely those same now sullied former citizens, that is, the supporters of the oligarchy of the 400. Their past transgressions should now be excused, even "if anyone was tripped up by Phrynichos" (*Frogs* 689).[16] No one should be disenfranchised, the Chorus Leader says, especially when even the slaves who had volunteered to row on the ships at Arginusai have been granted rights equal to those of the honored Plataians – a measure that the Chorus Leader nevertheless applauds.[17] So a fortiori, citizens who have fought for years on the city's side (oligarchs or not), as their fathers did before them, should at least meet with the same generosity at home and allowed to return, if they had been forced into exile.[18] The continuation of the Chorus Leader's speech constitutes an even clearer rebuke to the radical democracy that had been restored in 410. That regime has put in charge new "lowly/bad men" (πονηροῖς, *Frogs* 725; πονηροῖς κἀκ πονερῶν, 731) in place of previous gentlemanly, well-born leaders (καλούς τε κἀγαθούς, 719; εὐγενεῖς καὶ σώφρονας ἄνδρας ὄντας καὶ δικαίους καὶ καλοὺς κἀγαθούς, 727–28), just as Athens has started to use debased silver-plated bronze coins instead of the pure gold ones that it had struck before. The language is here clearly classist and strikingly recalls the distinction between lower-rank citizens (πονηροί) and the elites (χρηστοί) mentioned in the "Old Oligarch" pamphlet.[19]

The crushing defeat at Aigospotamoi after twenty-seven years of war brought Athenian power to an end. The peace terms required the recall of political exiles, many of them oligarchs supported by Sparta. Not, however, Alkibiades: probably at this point most Athenians agreed with the *Frogs'* Aiskhylos and Euripides, who concluded that he should never return (1417–1435). It was perhaps at this historical moment that *Frogs* was produced a second time in order to exploit its message of unity in favor of the new reality.[20] By losing the war, the city also lost her walls, her ships, her autonomy and, in a second, now successful coup, her democracy. During the brutal rule of the tight oligarchical Thirty, who were protected by the Spartan conquerors, the citizen body was split between democratic leaders, common folks, and metics on the one side – some executed by the

---

[16] Perhaps the fact that Phrynikhos had already been assassinated and posthumously tried for treason (Thuc. 8.92.2; Lykourg. 1.112–15) made it easier to scapegoat him for every bad outcome of the 400 and to let bygones be bygones for the others. Cf. Dover 1993:73.

[17] The battle of Arginusai and ensuing crisis are pervasive subtexts in this comedy. The participation of the slaves (and metics) as rowers on the ships (Xen. *Hell.* 1.6.24) and their new freedom with at least partial citizen rights (Hellan. *FGrHist* 323a F 25 = schol. Aristoph. *Frogs* 694) lurk behind the farcical role reversals from master to slave and back again of Dionysus and Xanthias (*Frogs* 494–529, 541–8, 569–64; cf. 33–4, 190–1). The notoriously effeminate Kleisthenes (*Frogs* 57) provides a pun about "embarking" on the ships and "mounting" in a sexual sense (ἐπιβάτευον, 48) and perhaps an obscene joke about fake mourning for the shipwrecked (*Frogs* 422–27; cf. Xen. *Hell.* 1.7.8). In the same context (428–30), the reference to Kallias as "son of Hippobinos" ("Hippocoitus" in Henderson's translation) alludes to both the man's debauchery and impoverished status, suggesting that he was one of the slaves rowing at Arginusai; cf. Nails 2002:72–3. Two politicians named in *Frogs* played important roles in the condemnation of the generals: Arkhedemos (*Frogs* 420–25, 588) was the instigator of the prosecution (Xen. *Hell.* 1.7.2), and the "clever" and "formidable" turncoat ship-captain Theramenes (*Frogs* 541, 967–70) had managed to deflect the blame from himself by scapegoating the generals (Xen. *Hell.* 1.6.35–7.10). Erasinides, compared to long-suffering Oedipus (*Frogs* 1195), was the first to be indicted (Xen. *Hell.*1.7.1–2). Sartori 1974:420–32 provides detailed discussion; Hubbard 1991:208–9.

[18] *Frogs* 687–96. For the disenfranchisement of former supporters of the 400, see Andok. 1.78; [Lys] 20.17–19, 33–36.

[19] [Ps. Xen.] 1.1 and *passim*; see above, p. 3. The positive judgment of the oligarchic sympathizers in *Frogs* is consistent with Thucydides' praise of their leaders (8.27.5, 8.68). Democratic leaders and officials pilloried include a customs man named Thorykion (363), the dead populists Kleon and Hyperbolos (569–70), and the current demagogue Kleophon (678–85, 1504, 1532–1533). Adeimantos, whom Pluto encourages to kill himself in a hurry (*Frogs* 1512), may be targeted as Alkibiades' friend or because of his election to the 406/5 board of generals (Xen. *Hell.* 1.4.21, 1.7.1). Mentioned as broad categories of undesirables are the citizens who foment discord for personal gain, officials who sell out the city in difficult times, betray a fortress or fleet, as members of the 400 did, traffic in duty tariffs or contraband, or persuade others to contribute money to enemies. Furthermore (354–71), the anxious comic condemns those who are not initiated in the Bacchic rites (of comedy) or who antagonize poets (!).

[20] *Frogs* hyp. 1, *Life of Aristophanes* = Kassel and Austin 1984 (*PCG* III.2) pp. 2–3, quoted by MacDowell 1995:298.

regime, others forced to relocate to the Peiraieus or to flee into exile somewhere else – and, on the other side, a privileged class "of 3000" (an entirely theoretical number), who remained in the city and retained nominal citizen rights on the condition of not opposing the junta in power. Aristophanes, like most of the intellectuals we know about from this time (Sokrates, Plato, Thucydides, Xenophon, but with the notable exception of the robbed metic Lysias), must have been part of this second group. This major oligarchic challenge was finally overcome when the democrats forced their re-entry after a series of bloody encounters, and the Spartans, for political interests of their own, gave up control of Athenian internal governance. The democratic constitution was restored and modified to avoid excesses of the past. The assembly declared a general amnesty between the "men of the city" (aside from the top oligarchic leaders) and the victorious but long-brutalized "men of the Peiraieus" (Xen. *Hell.*2.2–4.43; [Aristot.] *Ath. Pol.* 34.2–41).

An admirable legislative program and amnesty, although the wounds of the past proved hard to heal. In 399, a democratic jury convicted Sokrates on charges of corrupting the young and not honoring the city's gods and put him to death. The charges imperfectly disguised the Athenian perception of Sokrates' insistent critique of their now revived but still fragile democracy. According to Sokrates himself, his prosecutors weaponized the false reputation that his intellectual frenemy and fellow-symposiast Aristophanes had created for him many years earlier in the *Clouds* (Plato *Apol.* 18b-19c).

Aristophanes and the Restored Democracy

No poet was brought back from Hades to save Athens and its choruses as Aristophanes' Dionysos had come to hope.[21] No known tragedy or comedy produced after the *Bacchai*'s performance of 405 addresses issues fundamental for city-state politics.[22] Comedy had lost its political sting. This does not mean, however, that we should cease to analyze it politically, since the choice from an "Old Comedy" playwright to be nonpolitical, especially in a moment of crisis, is in itself political, whether he was initially motivated by the scary authoritarian experience of 404/3, or he later learned to adapt to the orthodoxy of PC, new democracy.[23] *Ecclesiazusae*, produced more than ten years after *Frogs*, adapts earlier Aristophanic motifs to the task of addressing more everyday concerns of ordinary folks. Here again (as in *Lysistrata*) the city's women decide to take charge of public affairs. Even in the new fourth-century, basically decent democracy, their complaints still have to do with the divided interests of the *demos* (*Eccl.* 197–8), inconsistent in everything except in its short-term choices of vulgar (πονηροί) politicians who turn out to be one worse than the other (173–85, 193–8, 797–99, 812–29). But desire for peace, so prominent in *Lysistrata* and several other Peloponnesian War comedies, receives no emphasis, even in spite of the fact that Athens was again fighting with Sparta.[24] The disguised women's leader, named Praxagora ("Woman acting in public?"), the *strategos* elected in the assembly, reveals her revolutionary scheme: the establishment of a communist regime that involves the elimination of both private property *and* the family. From now, on all material possessions, women, and children will be held in common (*Eccl.* 596–98).

This imagined scheme may sound like a piece of sophistic theorizing but is a fiction that fantastically intends to solve a real-life economic problem of individual families – the increasing wealth

---

[21] *Frogs* 418–19: ἐγὼ κατῆλθον ἐπὶ ποιητήν. τοῦ χάριν; / ἵν' ἡ πόλις σωθεῖσα τοὺς χοροὺς ἄγῃ.
[22] Whether tragic production and literary quality underwent a decline in the fourth century, the genre still retained its popularity. Didactic values are directed toward the individual spectator rather than to the community of citizens. The comic Timokles F 6 (Kassel and Austin, *PCG* III.2 1984) generalizes comically about tragedy: suffering individuals receive solace when hearing of the tragic suffering of Philoktetes or Niobe; cf. Farmer 2017, Hanink (in Csapo et al., 2014) 194–6.
[23] See Hartwig (in Csapo et al., 2014) 216–20 for other factors behind fourth-century comic developments.
[24] In the so-called Corinthian War (395–87 BCE); Xen. *Hell.* 3.5–5.1.31. *Eccl.* 199–203 only alludes to a prospect of peace soon ruined by the self-serving anger of Thrasyboulos; cf. 356–7.

disparity in fourth-century Athens, including the food insecurity and the shortage of decent warm clothing apparently experienced at this time by a large part of the population (*Eccl.* 408–26, 535–48, 588–94, 605–7, 668; David 1984: 3–11, 19–29; Sommerstein 1984). The welcome result of the reform for Athenian *men* will be the disappearance of debt, thievery, and lawsuits, freedom from work in the fields (the slaves will do that), the promise of free clothing (the women will weave those) and, most especially, communal banquets with plenty to eat and drink for everyone (567, 651–71). This hedonistic solution will assure the salvation (σωτηρία) of the city.²⁵ The other component of Praxagora's scheme, which promises shared and free sex, also seems to please everyone, again especially the men—but only until its logical consequences become clear. The prospect that a son may assault his father because he does not recognize that he is his father is unacceptable (635–36-43). The requirement that young men sleep with old and ugly women before winning the young and beautiful ones is equally repellent. What this looks like is illustrated by the "triumph of the hags" in the name of egalitarianism. By showing what the ultimate democratization of sex comes to, this conclusion may have amused a Trumpianized audience, but the long scene undermines the entire program (*Eccl.* 877–1111; Strauss 1966, p. 277–82; contra, Sommerstein 1984, p. 323).

The more appealing idea of a redistribution of goods has its own disturbing aspects. For one thing, there is always someone who will enjoy public benefits without giving anything back (*Eccl.* 746–876). But that is not the main problem. At the end of the fifth or beginning of the fourth century, the obscure politician Agyrrhios introduced payment for attendance to the assembly and raised it to three obols, in order to encourage broader participation in the affairs of the polis ([Aristot.] *Ath. Pol.* 41.3). But that was not good enough or had somehow become irrelevant for most people. In *Ecclesiazusae,* Agyrrhios is harshly criticized and so is his democratic proposal as a waste of public money (102–9, 183–88, 205–7, 300–10). Who wants to go to assemblies where no laws are ever passed that alleviate real hardships of everyday folks? So, Praxagora's reform introduces an extreme practical democracy (*Eccl.* 411, 631, 945) that will strike a death blow to the useless civic democracy of the past. Courthouses and porticoes will be dining rooms, and the speaker's platform will have the new purpose of storing mixing bowls and water jars or serving as a stage for children's choruses. Ballot boxes will be used for drawing lots to assign citizens to their places for dinner (*Eccl.* 673–86). Her program mostly concerns food. Will constipated Blepyros' gastric affliction (*Eccl.* 320–73) improve with the new alimentary abundance?

Several Aristophanic comedies – *Acharnians, Cavalrymen, Peace, Frogs, Lysistrata* – present a fantastic and impossible solution that would nevertheless be desirable for the audience – *if only* it were possible. In *Ecclesiazusae,* by contrast, a similar happy ending – made especially delightful by the exuberant list of newly obtainable victuals (1168–1178) – does not have the power to communicate anything other than the idea that the Praxagora solution, even if by some miracle it were to become possible, would result in unmitigated disaster. There is, in other words, no solution, imaginary or not, to what ails the democratic city-state. Aristophanes' comic muse has officially given up on democracy per se or any other political remedy. Perhaps for him, as for many of his fellow citizens, an irreversible change for the worse began in 411.

What comedy still can do very well is to create a bond with the audience by simply mocking or deploring the current real-world state of affairs. With *Ploutos,* whose second revised version Aristophanes produced in 388 BCE,²⁶ the embourgeoisement of Old Comedy is almost complete, in that the city of Athens as a political community and public affairs foreign and domestic remain in

---

²⁵ In Athenian political discourse, this term had described "salvation" from war or bad politicians, but here (*Eccl.* 202, 209, 234; cf. David 1984: 23) it refers to the economic crisis.
²⁶ Lines 170–89 provide the *terminus post quem*. They refer to events and leaders of the last years of the Corinthian War. Other topical references date this version at least well after 408, year when this comedy was first produced: to the politician Agyrrhios and the assembly pay he introduced (*Ploutos* 176, 228–31), to the little-known Neokleides (665–6, 716–25, 747), already disparaged (*Eccl.* 254–55, 398–407), and to the amnesty of 403, negotiated by Thrasyboulos (1144, cf. 550). *Ploutos* is Aristophanes' last surviving drama. Only fragments of subsequent comedies remain; *Kokalos* and *Ailosikon.*

the background. The drama mainly focuses on the material circumstances of private households. The ending, desirable this time, once again supersedes the democratic system with all its flaws. Aristophanes has here recycled several themes present in *Ekklesiazousai* (poverty, dearth of food and clothing, self-serving politicians, ineffectual government, and nymphomaniac old women), but he has produced a somewhat less heartless and, we could almost say, consolatory play.

To this end, the comic poet employs two different (and in realistic terms, contradictory) strategies. On the one hand, Poverty, *Penia*, horrifying as she looks (a Fury! *Ploutos* 422) points out that all the tribulations that Khremylos attributes to poverty – starvation, infestation of nasty bugs, rags instead of clothes, busted furniture, etc. – have nothing to do with her, but are gifts from Beggary (Πτωχεία, 535–54). She claims that if she were banished from Greece, all arts and craft, agriculture, and other industry would stop, and consumption goods would become unavailable to all. This argument mirrors Khremylos' earlier speech by which he persuades Ploutos that he is more powerful even than Zeus since he motivates all trades and professions and makes possible sacrifices to the gods, ownership of fine things, success abroad, and assemblies at home (*Ploutos* 507–34; 127–85). The condition of πενία, in other words, is here invested with a measure of dignity. Those like Khremylos, including many Athenians in the audience, are not beggars who lack basic necessities and live off handouts; they contribute to the labor force (David 1984, p. 39). These disadvantaged citizens are also physically more fit and morally better than the rich. By contrast, even honest politicians, when they amass profits in office, become wrongdoers and enemies of the people (557–78).

The second captivating strategy is Aristophanes' creation of two sympathetic leading characters, an imperfect but generous, industrious and frugal man and his plucky slave, both of whom, crucially and understandably, resist Penia's phony exaltation of the working poor (600). Khremylos rejects as unfair the idea that Ploutos should enrich scoundrels while good folks must scrimp and scrape. So, these two proceed in their plan to cure Ploutos' blindness and succeed.[27] While they just celebrate new-found prosperity, the wicked are unhappy, but eventually they will come around. Since Ploutos, now sighted, will only help the good and avoid the wicked, the wicked will all eventually become good (1171–1209). Further, in a sudden, inexplicable plot twist, three remarkably unsavory and not yet reformed individuals – the wealthy Old Woman and her caddish gigolo, and a corrupt priest of Zeus – are welcomed as beneficiaries of Ploutos' new dominance. As the god is installed finally in the temple of Athena on the Akropolis, Athens now features prominently as a unified community. All, good and less good, are restored or elevated to prosperity.[28] This good cheer provides the traditional comic resolution – a chicken in every pot: citizens and slaves, priest and celebrants, young and old share Food, Song, Dance, Sex, and *Ploutos* – Wealth.

GUIDE TO FURTHER READING

For general overviews of Aristophanes' responses to his historical circumstances, see David (1984), Dover (1972), MacDowell (1995), and Pelling (2000). On Aristophanes' relationship to Athenian political structures, see Halliwell (2020), Henderson (2020), Rhodes (2004), Rosen and Foley (2020), Rusten (2013), and Sommerstein (2014). For biographical and programmatic assertions in Aristophanes' plays, see Bowie (1982), Hubbard (1991), Sommerstein (2004), and Whitman (1964).

---

[27] And for jobs that no one wants to do any longer, there are always slaves! (517–8; cf. *Eccl.* 648–52).

[28] *Ploutos* 489–98, 502–4; differently from *Ekklesiazousai* (see above, pp. 10), the terms πονηροί and χρηστοί refer to moral worth, not social class. They are interchangeable with ἄδικοι, δίκαιοι and similar moralizing adjectives; cf. 26–31, 89–98, 217–18, 261–82, 750–950. For prosperity, *Ploutos* 1171–1209. For plot inconsistency, see MacDowell 1995: 344–49.

REFERENCES

Bowie, A.M. (1982). The Parabasis in Aristophanes: prolegomena, *Acharnians*. *The Classical Quarterly* 32: 27–40.
Csapo, E. and Slater, W.S. (1995). *The Context of Ancient Drama*. Ann Arbor: University of Michigan Press.
Csapo, E., Rupprecht Goette, H., Green, J.R., and Wilson, P. (ed.) (2014). *Greek Theater in the Fourth Century BC*. Berlin: de Gruyter.
David, E. (1984). *Aristophanes and Athenian Society of the Early Fourth Century B.C.* Leiden: Brill.
Dover, K.J. (ed.) (1993). *Aristophanes: Frogs*. Oxford: Oxford University Press.
Dover, K. (1972). *Aristophanic Comedy*. Berkeley: University of California Press.
Ehrenberg, V. (1962). *The People of Aristophanes: A Sociology of the Old Attic Comedy*. New York: Shocken Books.
Farmer, M. (2017). *Tragedy on the Comic Stage*. Oxford: Oxford University Press.
Figueira, T.J. (1991). *Athens and Aigina in the Age of Imperial Colonization*. Baltimore and London: John Hopkins University Press.
Halliwell, S. (2020). Politics in the street, some citizen encounters. In: (ed. R.M. Rosen and P.H. Foley), 113–136.
Hanink, J. (2014). Literary evidence for new tragic production: the view from the fourth century. In: (ed. Csapo et al.), 189–206.
Hartwig, A. (2014). The evolution of comedy in the fourth century. In: (ed. Csapo et al.), 207–227.
Henderson, J. (ed.) (1987/1991). *Aristophanes: Lysistrata*. Oxford: Oxford University Press.
Henderson, J. (1998). *Aristophanes, Acharnians, Knights*. Cambridge, MA: Harvard University Press.
Henderson, J. (ed.) (2000). *Aristophanes, Birds, Lysistrata, Women at the Thesmophoria*. Cambridge: Harvard University Press.
Henderson, J. (ed.) (2002). *Aristophanes, Frogs, Assemblywomen, Wealth*. Cambridge: Harvard University Press.
Henderson, J. (2007). *Aristophanes, Fragments*. Cambridge, MA: Harvard University Press.
Henderson, J. (2020). Patterns of avoidance and indirection in Athenian political satire. In: (ed. R.M. Rosen and P.H. Foley), 45–59.
Hubbard, T.K. (1991). *The Mask of Comedy: Aristophanes and the Intertextual Parabasis*. Ithaca and London: Cornell University Press.
Jameson, M.H. (1971). Sophocles and the four hundred. *Historia* 20: 541–568.
Kassel, R. and Austin, C. (1984). *Poetae Comici Graeci (PCG) III.2*. Berlin: de Gruyter.
Lateiner, D. (2020). Silences in aristophanes' drama. In: *Faces of Silence in Ancient Greek Literature* (ed. E. Papadodima), 85–111. Berlin: de Gruyter.
Lateiner, D. (2021). 'Bad news' in Herodotos and Thoukydides: misinformation, disinformation, and propaganda. *JAH* 9 (1): 53–99.
Lewis, D.M. (1955). Who was Lysistrata? *Annual of the British School at Athens* 50: 1–12.
MacDowell, D.M. (1995). *Aristophanes and Athens: An Introduction to the Plays*. Oxford: Oxford University Press.
Nails, D. (2002). *The People of Plato*. Indianapolis: Hackett.
Olson, S.D. (2012). Lysistrata's conspiracy and the politics of 412 BC. In: *No Laughing Matter. Studies in Athenian comedy* (ed. C.W. Marshall and G. Kovacs), 69–81. London and Bristol.
Panagiotarakou, E. (2009), Pursuing Peace with an Iambic Peitho. Dissertation, Concordia University.
Pelling, C. (2000). You cannot be serious: approaching Aristophanes. In: *In Id., Literary Texts and the Greek Historian*, 122–140. London and New York.
Rhodes, P.J. (2004). Aristophanes and the Athenian assembly. In: *Law, Rhetoric and Comedy in Classical Athens* (ed. D. Cairns and R. Knox), 223–237. Swansea: Essays D. M. MacDowell.
Rosen, R.M. and Foley, H. (ed.) (2020). *Aristophanes and Politics: New Studies*. Leiden and Boston: Brill.
Rusten, J. (2013). Political Discourse and the Assembly in four Plays of Aristophanes. In: *Retorica y discurso en el teatro griego* (ed. M.Q. Sagredo and M.C.E. Reguero), 249–260. Madrid.
Rusten, J.S., Henderson, J., Konstan, D., and Rosen, R.M. (2011). *The Birth of Comedy: Texts, Documents, and Art from Athenian Comic Competitions, 486–280*. Baltimore and London: Johns Hopkins University Press.
Sartori, F. (1974). Riflessi di vita politica Ateniese nelle *Rane* di Aristofane. In: *Scritti in onore di Caterina Vassalini* (ed. L. Barbesi), 412–441. Verona.
Sommerstein, A.H. (1977). Aristophanes and the events of 411. *The Journal of Hellenic Studies* 97: 112–126.

Sommerstein, A.H. (1984). Aristophanes and the demon poverty. *The Classical Quarterly* 34 (2): 314–333.
Sommerstein, A.H. (ed.) (1994). *Aristophanes Thesmophoriazusae*. Warminster: Aris & Phillips.
Sommerstein, A.H. (2004). Harassing the satirist: the alleged attempt to prosecute Aristophanes. In: *Free Speech in Classical Antiquity* (ed. I. Sluiter and R.M. Rosen), 145–174. Leiden: Brill.
Sommerstein, A.H. (2014). The politics of Greek comedy. In: *The Cambridge Companion to Greek Comedy* (ed. M. Revermann), 291–305. Cambridge.
Strauss, L. (1966). *Socrates and Aristophanes*. New York: Basic Books.
Taplin, O. (1983). Tragedy and trugedy. *The Classical Quarterly* 33 (2): 331–333.
Thonemann, P. (2019). Lysimache and *Lysistrata*. *Journal of Hellenic Studies* 140: 128–142.
Whitman, C. (1964). *Aristophanes and the Comic Hero*. Cambridge, MA: Harvard Press.

CHAPTER 2

The Staging of Old Comedy

A.C. Duncan

Introduction

This chapter considers how realities of the Athenian theatrical stage shaped Aristophanic Old Comedy. Drawing upon work in the so-called new materialisms – a loose set of allied theoretical approaches which seek to unsettle anthropocentric frameworks and reorient critical attention toward objects and their various connections, "agentic capacities," and "intra-actions" (for these expressions, see Coole 2013; Barad 2007, respectively; more broadly, see Coole and Frost 2010; Grusin 2015) – I make a case for understanding scenic materials such as masks, costumes, properties, and the fixed features of the theater as co-creators of Athenian drama alongside human playwrights and performers. I argue in particular (1) that the creative reuse of available materials inspired and informed Aristophanes' comedy and (2) that the scenic economy such reuse entailed stood in calibrated tension with the novel and extravagant spectacles which have long been taken to characterize the Old Comedic stage.

To situate and support these arguments, I begin by surveying the physical circumstances of the theater of Dionysus as Aristophanes received it in the 420s BCE, suggesting ways his comedies reframed and repurposed aspects of this common performance space. I turn next to several scenes from *Women at the Thesmophoria* which, in addition to offering examples of theatrical objects' agency in theory and practice, present an ancient vocabulary for thinking through ways material circumstances might influence human activity, dramatic performance especially. I conclude by situating Aristophanes' creative reuse of the Athenian stage within the critical and cultural legacy of his work, suggesting that Old Comedy, as a genre extensively and explicitly concerned with the materiality of its presentation, provides a useful case study for theorizing materials' "agency" and "intra-action" in ancient Greek culture more broadly.

Before turning to Aristophanes' stage, it will be helpful to establish the terms and scope of this study given that a culture's conceptualization of dramatic performance reflects and informs production and reception of theater in complex ways. Today, the English verb "stage" and its related forms refer to several distinct albeit associated performance-related practices. The "staging" of a play may refer to the mounting of a full theatrical production or to specific artistic choices therein, including actors' locations and movement (i.e. blocking) as well as the technical design of lighting, costume, and set. By contrast, a "staged reading" is often "staged" only insofar as the script is read aloud in an appropriately theatrical venue, with little attention given to actors' movements, dress, or other scenic technicalities. In wider use, we say both that historical figures or events are "staged" simply by being dramatized and what would otherwise be an empty room is "staged" when it is temporarily outfitted with furniture and decor to assist potential lessees in imagining themselves inhabiting

---

A Companion to Aristophanes, First Edition. Edited by Matthew C. Farmer and Jeremy B. Lefkowitz.
© 2024 John Wiley & Sons, Inc. Published 2024 by John Wiley & Sons, Inc.

the space. Where these varied modern understandings of "staging" most overlap is in their mediation of the abstract and concrete before an audience. For us today, "staging" is not merely the theatrical enactment of a fixed script but the general realization of potential through materials.

Classical Athens had no lexical equivalent and arguably no single concept strictly analogous to modern English "staging." In Aristophanes' time, a small set of terms was commonly used to describe the core components of the theatrical enterprise. Mounting a production was often spoken of as "instructing" (*didaskalein*) performers or "leading a chorus" (*chorāgein*), verbs that respectively referred to the efforts of directors (often, although not always, the playwrights themselves) and financial backers. Both verbs emphasize human agency and dramatic process over theatrical product – a salutary reminder of the interpersonal basis of Greek performance. And yet objects, no less than people, played a defining role in the Greek concept of theater. The crucial importance of materials in defining dramatic performance is particularly evident in vases and sculpture, where masks, costumes, and stage features such as a raised stage or central door regularly leant what Oliver Taplin has called a "scene specificity" that marked these representations as narrowly theatrical as opposed to broadly mythic (see esp. Green and Handley, 1995; Taplin 2007). The importance of materials is also apparent in the technical vocabulary of the theater. This lexicon included, among more precise terms, *skeuē* ("theatrical equipment"; cf. later *diaskeuē*, "revised performance," etc., with Nervegna 2013, pp. 88–99), a word which referred at a minimum to masks and costumes but possibly included stage properties and set pieces as well, and *opsis* ("spectacle"). Although etymologically connected to vision in the broad sense, *opsis* had a narrower meaning in classical-era theatrical contexts, regularly denoting the material aspects of production exclusively. This distinction is made clear in Aristotle's *Poetics* where, shortly before recommending that playwrights avoid errors by visualizing the stage action "before their mind's eye" (*pro ommatōn*, Arist. *Poet.* 1455a23; translations of Greek passages are my own), the philosopher declares *opsis* not to be the proper concern of the literary poet, but rather that of the "properties-maker" (*skeuopoios*, 1450b18–20) or broader "production effort" (*chorēgias*, 1453b7–8). As a technical term of the theater, then, *opsis* had objective, not subjective, meaning: it refers not to vision, per se, but rather to the objects visible on the stage. As such, theatrical *opsis* should be considered a profoundly material concept. Thanks to its (disparaged) prominence in *Poetics*, *opsis* has become a focal point for modern discussion and debate concerning Athenian visual culture (see, most recently, Sifakis 2013; Konstan 2013; Squire 2016; Taplin 2018). *Opsis* is indeed an important concept for the theater, but its theatrical meaning is best understood in the context of the other terms with which Athenians conceptualized their dramatic productions. Evidently, what we call "staging" was for Aristophanes and his contemporaries neither a distinct nor a unified idea. And yet, the realization of potential through the combination of actors and objects, ideas and materials, was as essential for ancient Athenians' idea of the theatrical stage as it is for our own.

However loose its definition, the "stage" of Aristophanes has been a recurrent focus of scholarly interest. Some have approached the comedian's stagecraft by working outward from the texts, investigating his dramatic techniques (Russo 1994; Marshall 2014) and inferring such realia as costumes (Stone 1984; Compton-Engle 2015) and masks (Marshall 1999; Varakis 2010) from the performance script. Others have worked in a complementary direction, drawing upon visual, historical, and epigraphic evidence to sketch an independent yet still culturally embedded image of the Old Comedic stage (see esp. Webster and Green 1978; Taplin 1993; Csapo and Wilson 2020). Many combine these approaches in seeking to situate Aristophanes' stage within broader cultural processes and esthetics. The variety and complementarity of these perspectives suggest that staging should not be viewed merely as an end result but rather as an integral and evolving part of theatrical process.

Discussions of Aristophanic stagecraft often highlight the unique and extravagant elements of the playwright's dramas and justifiably so. The excess, exaggeration, and novelty that characterized the production of fifth-century Athenian Old Comedy, particularly in contrast to the relatively restrained stage of tragedy (cf. Antiphanes fr. 189 K-A), are on full display in Aristophanes' extant works. On the Aristophanic stage elaborate set pieces, large and sometimes quite colorful choruses, motley characters, and supernumeraries all vie for spectators' attention. Old Comedy as a whole seems to have liberally embraced the novel and the spectacular. Still, it must be emphasized that Aristophanes' dramas are no less remarkable for their scenic conservatism, by which I mean, their efficient and ingenious reuse of items readily at hand. To center these less spectacular, but no less significant, items calls for a reappraisal of Aristophanic stagecraft that takes into account the reuse of extant, familiar materials as another essential component of the playwright's ambitious theatrical program.

The creative reuse and recombination of abstract and intangible aspects of Athenian culture, from juridical processes to religious rituals to tragic language and beyond, is a widely recognized and celebrated aspect of Aristophanes' comedy. The same, however, can hardly be said of his repurposing of materials. This is, in part, because such scenic economy runs counter to prevailing notions of what the production of Athenian drama aimed (and sometimes claimed) to be: namely, a propagandistic civic event defined by its conspicuous consumption. Surveying the scattered evidence pertaining to the production of Classical-era Athenian comedy and tragedy, Peter Wilson has written that, at least when it came to costume, "variation and innovation seem to be the keynotes" (Wilson 2000, 86). Novelty would naturally be an important aspect of the broader materialism on display at the Athenian dramatic festivals, venues for wealthy citizens to ostentatiously lavish financial support upon performances and for the city to amass its imperial tribute before the eyes of theatergoers both foreign and domestic. Indeed, the expectation of conspicuous consumption is necessary for making full sense of Aristophanes' several apologies for the apparent frugality of his productions. An animal sacrifice in *Peace*, for example, is described as being moved offstage to "save the producer a sheep" (ll. 1021–1022); in *Frogs*, a shabbily dressed chorus of initiates praises Dionysus for devising a ritual occasion in which they might dress in sandals and rags "for the sake of thrift and a laugh" (ll. 405–410). Such superficial "apologies" are, at a deeper level, clever manipulations of the audience's expectation: by raising the possibility of a more sumptuous spectacle, Aristophanes converts an ostensible production shortfall into a comedic strength, bringing the audience in on the joke. With a wink and a nod, at such moments Aristophanes reminds theatergoers that even the most opulent production budgets are ultimately limited. There is constant incentive for theater-makers to do (and, for Aristophanes, to be recognized as doing) more with less on the stage. Indeed, judicious thrift was a virtue that likely appealed equally to playwrights, producers, and the public. A few years before the start of Aristophanes' theatrical career, the historian Thucydides records the leading Athenian statesman of the time, Pericles, claiming that the pursuit of aesthetic attainment under financial constraint was a core Athenian aspiration: "We love what is beautiful, but with thrift" (Thuc. 2.40). Aristophanes likewise signals that, on his stage, strategic economy may be no less marvelous than scenic extravagance.

Occasional recognitions of his production's thrift notwithstanding, far more often Aristophanes folds scenic economy seamlessly into his plays by reusing items already on the stage. Theater-makers reuse materials for a host of reasons besides efficiency and economy: familiar objects bring unique value to performance, materializing memory in ways that carry the past into the present with a distinctive "aura" (to extend a concept made famous by Walter Benjamin) that resists being reduced to a mere sign in the phenomenally "thick" experience of the theater (see States 1985; Weiss 2023). Aristophanic drama reused materials familiar not only from the theater itself but also from across a wide variety of Athenian social spheres, from the battlefield to the agora to the kitchen to the bedroom. The list of novel items that could be brought onto Aristophanes' absurd stage was limited only by the imagination (the giant dung beetle that serves as an ersatz Pegasus in *Peace* (ll. 1–179) is a particularly memorable example). The materials already familiar to Aristophanes' audience were, by comparison, quite limited. Scholars have tended to practice a "top-down" theorization of Aristophanes' reuse of such known objects, regarding them as the mere medium of the playwright's broader (and more abstract) parodic engagement with Athenian culture. But reused materials of the fifth-century stage may also be considered from the "bottom-up" as possessing agentive capacities of their own (see Duncan 2018) as objects whose accessibility and familiarity exerted a profound influence on the comedian's art and its theatrical reception.

Aristophanes' Creative Reuse of the Athenian Theater

The Athenian theater was a site of recurrent reuse. The three dramatic genres of fifth-century Athens – tragedy, satyr play (competitively subsumed under the rubric of tragedy), and comedy – shared much in common with respect to their material circumstances. All dramatic productions, regardless of genre, were held at the same annual competitive Dionysian religious festivals, in the same performance area (*theatron*, "theater," literally "seeing place"), and with financial backing from the same small pool of wealthy aristocrats known as *chorēgoi* (sg. *chorēgos*, "producer"; see Wilson 2000). Recent scholarship concerning the smaller deme theaters of Attica, as well as other major venues abroad, has reinvigorated important debates over the reproduction of Aristophanic drama (see esp. Paga 2010; Hunter 2017; Wiles 2017; Bosher 2012, 2021). It remains safe to say that, however, during Aristophanes' career the theater of Dionysus on the south slope of the Athenian Acropolis was not only the most important dramatic venue in Greece but also the intended site for the premier of most of Aristophanes' extant plays. Indeed, Aristophanes occasionally references the theater space or festival context in his scripts (e.g. "in this very location last year," *Thesm.* 1060; "we are alone at the Lenaia," *Ach.* 504, etc.), underscoring the recurrent spatial and festival contexts of his productions. For theatergoers, of course, the effects of the space on performance were ever-present. One may easily take for granted the semi-annual reuse of this illustrious performance space, but the theater of Dionysus's cultural resonances allowed Aristophanes to engage with his audience's collective and spatial memory in ways impossible for a rotating venue (on the importance of theatrical space within an urban landscape, see Carlson 1993; Rehm 2002).

Beyond its specific spatial and cultural importance, the form of the theater of Dionysus, too, offered Aristophanes many opportunities for creative reuse. Theatergoers sat in a zone commonly referred to today by its Latin title, the *cavea:* a concave, sloped seating area which evolved from recessed hillsides into the massive marble structures that would become a hallmark of Hellenistic-era cities. One such monumental fourth-century structure superseded the theater used during Aristophanes' lifetime, frustrating modern attempts to reconstruct the precise parameters of his fifth-century stage. What historical and archeological evidence remains suggests a modest, therefore selective, fifth-century audience of between 4000 and 7000 spectators seated, at least in part, on wooden bleachers (*ikria*, cf. Ar. *Thesm.* 395). If Eric Csapo (2007) is right in suggesting these stands were reassembled for each festival, their reconstruction materially anticipated and literally supported the social "reassembly" of their audiences.

Drama relies upon its theatergoers no less than the theater itself. The demographics of Aristophanes' audience are poorly evidenced, but most scholars follow Roselli (2011) in taking an inclusive and pluralistic approach to fifth-century spectatorship that allows for stratification along such lines as social class or even, as Martin Revermann (2006a) has framed the issue, theatrical "competency." No two theatrical audiences are ever truly identical, but from year to year Aristophanes relied upon a significant quorum of theatrical "regulars" to establish certain continuities and connections between productions past and present. Aristophanes' blandishing praise of his audience as "shrewd" (*dexios*, cf. *Eq.* 228; *Nub.* 521) and "wise" (*sophos*, cf. *Eq.* 1210; *Nub.* 575; *Ran.* 700; etc.), his frequent reference to past performances, and ultimately the success he found in competition all attest to Aristophanes' close familiarity with his audience's cultural knowledge and comedic preferences. That is to say, the audience, itself, could be "reused."

Aristophanes also depended upon the simple *presence* of his theatergoers no less than their expertise or complex predilections. Ancient Greek drama was staged in open-air, sun-lit theaters, giving theatergoers the intersubjective experience of being seen while seeing. Although the integral presence of the audience can be felt across all genres of Attic drama (see Duncan 2023), Old Comedy is distinctive for its overtly meta-theatrical references to theatergoers who are addressed individually (cf. the priest of Dionysus at *Ran.* 297) and *en masse*. Direct audience address highlights and further involves spectators in their role as subjects of the theatrical experience; it also converts them, however partially or briefly, into proper objects of the comedy themselves. In directly addressing his audience, Aristophanes makes comedic "material" out of theatergoers themselves.

Although the modern concept of a proverbial, imaginary "fourth wall" separating actors and audience is not particularly applicable to Attic Old Comedy, certain distinctions were made and maintained between Aristophanes' "stage" and his "stands." Spatially separating the two was a circular area of level ground known as the *orchēstra* (literally, "dancing place"), the most archaic zone of the Greek theater that remained its performative kernel and visual center. The irregular and often rectilinear seating arrangements common to fifth-century theaters lacked the graceful arc of Hellenistic-era theaters (on the experience of such early spaces, see Wiles 2017), but the essential circularity of the orchestra was culturally significant and practically spacious. In Aristophanes' time, the orchestra routinely hosted dithyrambic performances (known as "circular choruses"), dramatic dances featuring 50 men (or boys) energetically moving together. For the more modestly sized choruses of drama (24 *choreuts*, "dancers," for comedy, and as few as 12 for tragedy and satyr play), the *orchēstra* provided space for dancers to move even while dressed in the large and ungainly costumes of Old Comedy's spectacular "animal" (or, as in *Clouds*, otherwise trans-human) choruses (on these choruses, see Sifakis 1971; Rothwell 2006). Furthermore, as in tragedy, the large *orchēstra* allowed Aristophanes or his director to place performers and set pieces in meaningful arrangements. Although physical interactions between the chorus and characters are not absent from tragedy, particularly where hostages or suppliants are concerned, Aristophanes' plays are nevertheless remarkable for the dynamism of this engagement. Aristophanic characters frequently rouse, inspect, threaten, hide among, and otherwise engage with the chorus, taking advantage of the dancers' distribution across the *orchēstra* and their proximity to important spectators in the front rows. Inheriting an *orchēstra* whose size, shape, and performative conventions were well established, Aristophanes nevertheless had artistic room to reimagine this archaic space for his own purposes.

The *orchēstra* was accessed by two *eisodoi* ("entrances," sometimes also called *parodoi*) stretching to the left and right of the seating area, long pathways along which arriving performers became only gradually visible to the audience. Tragedy leveraged the pomp and circumstance of these *eisodoi* to cultivate a sense of anticipation or grandeur, often narrating an important entrance over several verses. Although the *eisodoi* were poorly suited for the sudden and surprising entrances of the comedic stage, Aristophanes nevertheless found creative ways to extract humor from the pathways' gradual disclosure of performers. For example, in *Clouds* the playwright has a character gratuitously specify that the highly anticipated arrival of the spectacular chorus is taking place "by the *eisodos*" (*Nub.* 326; cf. *Av.* 296 and fr. 388 K-A). In *Frogs*, Aristophanes inverts the ornate entrance descriptions of tragic entrances when describing the bogey Empousa, who is described as serially changing not only her location but also her form (ll. 285–305). The historical details of Empousa's remarkable staging are controversial and obscure, but the long *eisodoi* may at least have facilitated her many humorously frightening (dis)appearances and transformations.

A single *eisodos* is sufficient for most entrances and exits. The presence of two pathways, often used by tragedy to enrich the imagined topography of a broader scene (see Lowe 2006, p. 63), in Aristophanes' hands notably supported the temporally overlapping arrival and departure of characters (cf. *Ach.* 954–959; *Nub.* 1254–1259; *Av.* 948–959; 990–1021, etc.). Indeed, despite their literal meaning as "entrances," *eisodoi* were about going as much as coming for actors and audience members alike. Theatergoers themselves may have used these wide paths as a convenient exit after performance, a practical and spatial overlap that would have blurred distinctions between fictive plot and real life. When, for example, Aristophanes' characters invite others to accompany them to a celebratory after-party (cf. *Ach.* 1231–1234; *Peace* 1341–1359), it is as if theatergoers themselves are asked to follow in the characters' footsteps. In a clever and spatially efficient move, Aristophanes conflates his protagonist's success with the competitive victory of his own comedies. As a result, spectators were to exit the theater by way of the *eisodos* and thereby "follow" the actor characters to a promised (real) party, they might be seen as literally voting with their feet, throwing in their lot with Aristophanes' production as the comedy most deserving to win.

Last but not least among the permanent features of the theater was the stage building, situated between the *eisodoi* and across the *orchēstra* from the audience. The building comprised a raised platform backed by a walled, single-story structure known as a *skēnē* (the origin, via Latin *scaenae frons*, of the English word "scene"). In contrast to the *orchēstra* and *eisodoi*, whose essential form changed little during the Classical period, the *skēnē* underwent a series of practical improvements near the middle of the fifth century. Evidence is scanty but nevertheless suggests that each of these permanent changes was initially introduced for the sake of tragic competition. As early as Aeschylus' *Oresteia* trilogy in 458 BCE, for example, the *skēnē* could not only support an actor on the roof but represent interior scenes as well, likely by means of a wheeled platform known to Aristophanes as the *ekkyklēma* (cf. *Ach.* 408–409; *Thesm.* 96). Further developments followed. Aristotle credits the tragedian Sophocles, who first entered competition around the time of the *Oresteia*, with introducing pictorial backdrops, "scene painting" (*skēnographia*) to the Athenian theater (Arist. *Poet.* 1449a18). By the 430s, the stage building also boasted a permanent crane, which Aristophanes calls the *mēchanē* or "device" (cf. *Pax* 174), that placed actors in aerial positions for divine epiphanies or the transcendent (and often transgressive) acts of certain mortals (Mastronarde 1990). It is striking that all of these durable architectural features, even if they were introduced for the sake of tragedy, were employed only occasionally within that genre. The cultural cachet that allowed tragedy to commission such improvements also privileged the genre to eschew their reuse when inconvenient. Aristophanes and his fellow Old Comedians, by contrast, seem to have adapted these structural improvements eagerly and extensively without demanding any permanent changes to the theater's architectural form of their own. In Aristophanes' hands, the decorated *skēnē* was often more than a static backdrop, representing homes (*Wasps*), citadels (*Lysistrata*), and schools (*Clouds*) dynamically under siege or attack. The *ekkyklēma* revealed tableaux with numerous objects and characters – notably, as discussed further below, of playwrights at work (*Acharnians, Women at the Thesmophoria*). The *mēchanē* supported religious iconoclasts (*Clouds*) and mock-heroic expeditions (*Peace*), while the *skēnē* roof (*Wasps, Clouds*) and door (*passim*) enabled sudden and surprising entrances impossible to stage from the long *eisodoi*. Aristophanes' characters routinely call attention to these special effects with demonstratives and technical terms and meta-theatrical references that not only provide our surest historical evidence of these improvements but also demonstrate the comedian's unabashedly creative reuse of the old tricks of the stage. The generic origins and associations of these fifth-century improvements give their reuse tragic overtones that could be quite salient (cf. esp. *Ach.* 408–409, *Thesm.* 96). Even so, the parodic resonances of such aspects of the stage building were not necessarily the sole or even the overriding consideration for their adoption among Aristophanes' many adaptations of the permanent theater.

The fixed features of the theater of Dionysus had profound effects on the stagecraft of Aristophanes and his contemporaries, but it was through portable items such as properties and costumes that individual playwrights could most distinguish themselves in competition. Such items were likely of particular concern for the financial backers, *choregoi*, who were responsible for the often substantial outlay required to produce these numerous, often bespoke, materials. When it came to tragic costume, Rosie Wyles (2011, pp. 23–24) has suggested that certain expensive or hard-to-fabricate items, such as a leather cuirass, might well have been directly sourced from non-theatrical contexts. Aristophanes may have been particularly open to such appropriations, particularly where inexpensive and available, yet distinctive and memorable, items might be humorously substituted for others, as when a basket of coal or wineskin stands in for a child hostage (*Acharnians, Thesmophoriazusae*), or when household items stand in for witnesses in a court case (*Wasps*). Expensive items, too, might find reuse, as when a general's feathered helmet is borrowed to serve container for (mimed) vomit, its crest serving as an emetic (*Ach.* 585–6; on Aristophanes' use of metaphor, see Anna Novokhatko's chapter in this volume).

The Greek theatrical body, itself, was extensively mediated by materials. All performers, with the notable exceptions of scantily clad satyr chorus and the aulos player, were dressed in materials from head to foot which instantly and clearly signaled the main genres on the dramatic stage. The comedic body of Aristophanes' day was typified by grotesque padding, including an outsized paunch and, in the case of male characters, dangling phallus. These items were complemented by a mask that displayed similarly "distorted" and "ugly" features (cf. Arist. *Poet.* 1449a), including gaping and irregular mouths, pronounced wrinkles, and, for adult men, baldness or receding hairlines (on the costumes of Aristophanes' actors, see Anne Duncan's chapter in this volume). The practicalities, politics, and esthetics of Old Comedic costume have been much discussed (see esp. Foley 2000), particularly in contrast to those of tragedy, which came much closer to the norms and ideals as elsewhere expressed in contemporary Athenian culture (see Halliwell 1993).

The stereotypical and recurrent features of comedic costume, although not yet codified in Aristophanes' time into a fixed set of stock characters, may nevertheless have encouraged reuse within the genre. The differences between comedic and tragic costume prevented their casual reuse across genres, but the aesthetic contrast could provide a powerful visual means of marking cross-generic engagement in comedy. A fictionalized visit to the home of the real tragic playwright, Euripides, in *Acharnians*, several scenes from *Women at the Thesmophoria Festival* as well as certain pieces of visual evidence, most famously as the so-called Choregoi vase (see Taplin 1993), all suggest that Classical-era audiences were fascinated by the aesthetic gulf between Athens' two chief dramatic genres. One today can only speculate about the historical particulars of any given fifth-century production, but in light of the material economies practiced by theater-makers across time and culture, one might hazard certain intriguing possibilities for Aristophanes' stage. C. W. Marshall (1999, p. 194), for instance, has suggested that Aristophanes might have reused an aged Papposilenus mask from satyr play to represent the aged and notoriously satyr-like features of Socrates in *Clouds*. If such direct cross-generic reuse of theatrical materials did in fact occur, it would have had more than merely formal significance for Athenian audiences. Such material appropriation would show Aristophanes having the upper hand over his fellow dramatists, not only through imitation but through direct possession and physical control of the very stuff out of which their theater was made. *Pace* Aristotle, costume could be very much the concern of the playwright. The idea, if not the reality, of comedy laying claim to the materials from tragedy is a special case of Aristophanic reuse considered further in the section "Material Agency and Affordances in *Women at the Thesmophoria Festival*."

To summarize this survey of the Athenian theater as Aristophanes received it, the late-fifth-century stage was a site not only of recurrent but also of inventive reuse. Theater-makers reused scenic materials not only for the sake of efficiency but also for the unique effects familiar items have on the production and reception of drama. David Wiles (2017, p. 64) has suggested that, by the late-fifth century, the increasingly permanent and prestigious nature of Attic theater exerted a limiting effect on "artistic innovation." Wiles' observation, while true enough on its own terms, may nevertheless be reframed from a materialist perspective. Although Aristophanes made few permanent or prestigious innovations to the theater himself, he constantly *renovated* his stage, drawing upon the theater's established material and cultural traditions in pursuit of comedic novelty that underscored his own critical and creative powers as a playwright. By marking his ability to give second-hand materials a second life on stage, Aristophanes signals a dialectic between his individual genius as a bricoleur-dramatist, on the one hand, and, on the other, the distributed agency of theatrical materials (on the concept of bricolage, see Lévi-Strauss 1966, pp. 17–22; on distributed material agency, see Barad 2007). Indeed, Aristophanes explores such dialectical dynamics between playwrights and materials in several of his plays, dramatizing a Greek cultural awareness of the unique and formative powers of materials on artistic creation.

Material Agency and Affordances in *Women at the Thesmophoria Festival*

Women at the Thesmophoria Festival, which premiered in 411 BCE, is profoundly concerned with the generative power of materials in theatrical composition. Complexly echoing Aristophanes' earlier efforts in *Acharnians*, first produced over a dozen years earlier at the Lenaia festival of 425 BCE, *Women at the Thesmophoria Festival* once again dramatizes a visit to the home of tragic poet actively engaged in the composition (on the mimetic complexities of the play's engagement with *Acharnians*, see Farmer 2017, pp. 155–194). Euripides, the tragedian whose reliance on ragged costume was already thoroughly satirized in *Acharnians*, is promoted from a memorable cameo into one of two major roles in *Women at the Thesmophoria Festival*. In this play, Euripides and his unnamed "Inlaw" (whom some modern editions, following ancient precedent, call Mnesilochus) join forces to subvert a plot against the playwright's life, ostensibly on account of his tragedies' misogynistic portrayal of women. A complexly meta-theatrical work in which important issues of gender, religion, and performance loom equally large, *Women at the Thesmophoria Festival*'s critique of Euripidean stagecraft has received perhaps the lion's share of scholarly attention (on the play and its scholarly reception, see Helene Foley's contribution to this volume). The play's meta-theatrical interests are hardly limited to tragedy, however. *Women at the Thesmophoria Festival* is also reflexive and self-interpretative as a comedy in its own right, one that reveals how the creative reuse of objects spans not only time and genre but also an entire play, wringing fresh humor and renewed spectacle out of familiar objects already on the stage.

Women at the Thesmophoria Festival begins with Euripides and his Inlaw arriving at the home of the upstart tragic poet, Agathon. A rising star of the Athenian social and theatrical scenes in the 410s, Agathon was as remarkable for his youthful effeminacy as his precocious success in tragic competition (cf. Pl. *Symp.*). The playwright's transgressions of established Athenian norms of gender and genre are jointly mocked by Inlaw. Euripides, for his part, hopes that his fresh-faced fellow tragedian will agree to infiltrate the Thesmophoria and forestall the plot being hatched against Euripides's life. When Agathon politely declines this proposal, Euripides pivots to seeking material assistance from Agathon in order to give the boorish Inlaw a gender-bending makeover. This leads Euripides to raid Agathon's closet and personal items in ways familiar from the parallel scene in *Acharnians* which likewise meditates on the reflexive relationship between a playwright's material identity and his dramatic output. The theoretical and practical engagement with the performance materials at Agathon's home is more substantial than that which occurs in *Acharnians*, however, as the scene articulates a theory of materially enabled composition that sets the stage for several parodic improvisations to follow.

Euripides and Inlaw first observe Agathon as he is rolled out on the *ekkyklēma* (l. 96, see section "Aristophanes' Creative Reuse of the Athenian Theater"), wearing several items of women's clothing and rehearsing a choral song that the coarse Inlaw, for one, finds ludicrously effete. Many direct parallels between the scenes at the homes of Euripides and Agathon make the differences all the more striking. Unlike Dicaeopolis in *Acharnians*, who instantly infers a causal connection between Euripides's ragged clothes and his ragged characters (repeatedly declaring "no wonder," *ouk etos, Ach.* 411 and 413), Inlaw is at first unable to interpret the significance of the Agathon's appearance. He is confused by the "mishmash" (*taraxis, Thesm.* 137) of materials on Agathon's person, items Inlaw regards as either stereotypically masculine (viz., lyres, ll. 137–138; oil flask, l. 139; sword, l. 140) or feminine (saffron-colored gown, l. 138; hairnet, l. 139; and mirror, l. 140). Such gendered objects are powerful (and, in this case, humorously discordant) cultural symbols whose semiotic incongruity leads Inlaw to deride Agathon as a sexual deviant (see esp. Zeitlin 1996; Duncan 2000; Duncan 2006; Stehle 2002). Responding to Inlaw's crude perplexity, Agathon provides a materialist account of dramatic composition which, in its detail and theoretical richness, far surpasses Dicaeopolis' intuitive connection between clothes and characters. Agathon explains:

> ἐγὼ δὲ τὴν ἐσθῆθ' ἅμα γνώμῃ φορῶ.
> χρὴ γὰρ ποιητὴν ἄνδρα πρὸς τὰ δράματα
> ἃ δεῖ ποιεῖν πρὸς ταῦτα τοὺς τρόπους ἔχειν.
> αὐτίκα γυναικεῖ' ἢν ποιῇ τις δράματα,
> μετουσίαν δεῖ τῶν τρόπων τὸ σῶμ' ἔχειν.
>
> I change my clothing along with my thinking.
> For it is necessary for the man who is a poet to have the same
> personal habits as the dramas he must compose.
> For example, if someone composes plays featuring women,
> it is necessary to participate bodily in their personal habits.
>
> (ll. 148–152)

Without suggesting causal directionality (the Greek preposition *hama*, 148, conveys simply coincidence, see LSJ s.v. ἅμα), Agathon links abstract thought with concrete clothes, the material component of those personal habits (*tropous*, l. 150) associated with his body (*to sōm'*, l. 152). After another scurrilous interjection from Inlaw, the tragedian continues his explanation:

> If some man composes manly dramas, this (sc. "manliness")
> is already present in his person. That which we do not possess,
> imitation (*mimēsis*) chases down in turn.
>
> ἀνδρεῖα δ' ἢν ποιῇ τις, ἐν τῷ σώματι
> ἔνεσθ' ὑπάρχον τοῦθ'. ἃ δ' οὐ κεκτήμεθα,
> μίμησις ἤδη ταῦτα συνθηρεύεται.
>
> (ll. 154–156)

Given its combined concern with gender, performance, and *mimēsis* (this is the earliest instance of the noun being used to refer to artistic representation; for further discussion, see Halliwell (2002, p.15 n. 33)), it is unsurprising that these few lines have attracted much scholarly interest. The influential connections Plato and Aristotle would later develop between *mimēsis* and abstract form (see Porter 2010), however, should not obscure the essential materiality of Agathon's description, which emphasizes embodiment (cf. *en tōi sōmati*, 154), immanence (*enesth'*, l. 155) and physicality (the verbs *kektēmetha*, l. 155, and *synthēreuetai*, l. 156, along with their neuter direct objects). For Agathon, at any rate, dramatic *mimēsis* both follows from (cf. *hēdē*, l. 156) and gathers together materials.

Mimēsis has been a primary target of scholarly criticism in these verses, but arguably the most important word in Agathon's explication for understanding Aristophanes' own approach to the stage is the rather unassuming participle, *hyparchon* (l. 155). The verb *hyparchein*, which in Modern Greek has come to express existential being, was in ancient Greek used, among other things, to express temporal priority, "to be in existence, to be ready" (LSJ s.v. ὑπάρχειν I.B.2) or logical subsistence (III.A.3). In surviving texts from Classical-era Athens, the verb frequently appears, as here, in neuter participial form, particularly in the set phrase *ta hyparchonta*. *Ta hyperchonta* could refer to "existing circumstances" generally, but it is often deployed with an eye toward utility, so that the expression may often best be rendered, "present advantages" or "means" (IV.A.1–2). For Aristophanes and his audience, *hyparchei* was the proper term for referring to material conditions salient to the undertaking of some action.

As such, *ta hyperchonta* shares strong affinities with the ecological materialism of James J. Gibson's (1979) concept of "affordances," the established and potential interactions of objects within an environment as perceived by some subject. A chair, for example, although definitionally a discrete piece of furniture used for sitting, may have various further affordances depending on context. As circumstances demand, a chair may "become" a stool for reaching a high cabinet, a door jam to block an intruder, a projectile to throw at an adversary, etc. An item's affordances are determined jointly by its inherent material properties (e.g. size, shape, weight, composition, etc.) and by what Gibson labels the item's ecological circumstances: its perceived connections and combinations with other objects. According to Gibson and subsequent generations of materialist-minded scholars, objects are never absolute but exist in constant and dynamic relation with each other as well as perceiving subjects. In our bustling world, let alone the kaleidoscopically evolving Old Comedic stage, an object's affordances often defy prediction. As already explored in the section "Aristophanes' Creative Reuse of the Athenian Theater," Aristophanes' ingenious repurposing of established theatrical objects showcased the latent affordances of these items, involving theater-goers in playfully imaginative and shifting subjectivities. Aristophanes' characters lead others by example to take an improvisational approach to the stage. In Agathon's case, the playwright's corporeal manliness (a suggestive gesture might accompany the demonstrative *touth'*) automatically supports the composition of "manly" poetry, but objects that, properly speaking, are external to the playwright's body are no less generative. Learning at the tragedian's side the ecological basis of dramatic composition, Inlaw leaves Agathon's home armed not only with women's clothing and cosmetics but also with a sensitivity to the material affordances enabling performance.

The significance of Agathon's programmatic words becomes clearer as *hyparchein* recurs on several occasions in *Women at the Thesmophoria Festival*. Inlaw, who is ultimately discovered and held captive by the women, is compelled to improvise several dramatic fictions of his own in order to escape. Combining established Euripidean plots with the present advantages of materials at hand, Inlaw puts into practice Agathon's theory of ecological composition, reusing and recombining familiar ideas and objects. These parodic scenes not only satirize peculiarities of Euripides' use of the stage and its materials but also offer insight into the pliable ways Aristophanes and his audiences reimagined materials' roles in performance.

After an initial failed attempt to escape the women which involved material-led improvisation that parodied a hostage scene from Euripides' *Telephus*, Inlaw is left alone with his thoughts, wondering aloud what new "device" (*mēchanē*, l. 765), "way" (*peira*, l. 766), or "idea" (*epinoia*, l. 766) might lead to salvation. His thoughts shift from the abstract to the concrete when Inlaw decides "some messenger" (*tin' angelon*, l. 768) must first be sent to Euripides, leading Inlaw to suddenly recall a way (*poron*, l. 769) out of his bind. He adapts a peculiar scene from Euripides's lost *Palamedes* in which Oeax, the eponymous hero's brother, writes on oar blades that he scatters out to sea like so many messages in bottles. But Inlaw's plot comes up against a material constraint. He has no oars:

ἀλλ' οὐ πάρεισιν αἱ πλάται.
πόθεν οὖν γένοιντ' ἄν μοι πλάται πόθεν; πόθεν
τί δ' ἄν, εἰ ταδὶ τἀγάλματ' ἀντὶ τῶν πλατῶν
γράφων διαρρίπτοιμι; βέλτιον πολύ.
ξύλον γέ τοι καὶ ταῦτα, κἀκεῖν' ἦν ξύλον.

But the oars aren't here!
Now, where might I get some oars? Where? Where?
Ah, what if I could write on these votive offerings here,
and toss them out? That's much better!
These, too, are wooden, you know, and those were wooden.

(ll. 771–775)

Oeax's improvised use of oars as writing tablets in Euripides' *Palamedes* – a resourcefulness that seems to have fallen below tragedy's generally solemn approach to materials – may have attracted Aristophanes' parody. At any rate, the comedian extends the chain of material-led improvisation: Oeax, lacking wooden tablets, resorts to wooden oars; Inlaw, lacking wooden oars, resorts to wooden offerings. Wood offers Gibsonian affordances (e.g. inscription, manipulation, flotation, projection, etc.) that scaffold Inlaw's comparison and shape his plot. The semantics of the Greek word for "offerings," *agalmata*, are wide, making it unclear whether the votives in the Thesmophorion were sculptural or were already, themselves, flat writing tablets, inscribed with prayers. Their form is quite literally immaterial to Inlaw, who calls attention to the objects' at-hand accessibility (cf. the proximal deictic, *tadi*, l. 773) and their material composition, capping both ends of his closing verse with the word "wooden" (*xulon*, l. 775).

Aristophanes' parody wrings much humor from the economic and religious meanings of these wooden objects. Timber was a familiar commodity for Aristophanes' audience as both building material and fuel (see Olson 1991) which, as today, might be repeatedly salvaged or reclaimed for different purposes. The reuse of wood may have been especially on Athenian minds in 411 BCE, when the city was rebuilding its navy after a major defeat while under extreme economic duress (cf. Thuc. 8.1). Although his situation is ludicrous, Inlaw may not have been the only in the theater at that time tasked with improvising wooden oars from objects at hand. And yet, as religious offerings, the *agalmata* Inlaw appropriates were properly exempt from such economical circulation, having become, in Alan Sommerstein's (1994 *ad* 773) words, "like all other dedications. . . the property of the god(s) of the sanctuary." Mutilating and hurling the goddesses' possessions from the holy precinct, Inlaw compounds his sacrilege at the same time that Aristophanes advances the plot while delightfully appalling his audience through the ingenious reuse of items already on stage as part of the *mise-en-scène* of the sanctuary.

When the oar plot bears no fruit, Inlaw turns to another Euripidean contrivance adapted from the tragedian's *Helen*, first produced at the Dionysia festival of the previous year. For this improvisation,

Inlaw does not need to scan his surroundings for suitable materials. In the same breath that he mentions the play, Inlaw observes how his own material circumstances support its restaging:

ἐγᾦδα· τὴν καινὴν Ἑλένην μιμήσομαι.
πάντως ὑπάρχει μοι γυναικεία στολή.

I know – I'll portray his new *Helen*!
After all, I already have a woman's outfit.

(ll. 850–851)

Marking the present advantages of his borrowed clothes with the verb *hyparchei*, Inlaw verbally and sartorially recalls Agathon's programmatic exposition of materially enabled dramatic composition (l. 155). The situation also recalls that of Menelaus in *Helen* (1079–1080), who, as Donna Zuckerberg (2016, p. 64) has noted, makes much of the "convenience" of his rags for the deception Helen poses – a moment Craig Jendza (2020) has labeled "paracomic." Within and across Athenian dramatic genre, then, creative reuse of materials seems to be a driving force in the theater. Scenic materials' agency is subtle but powerful: the effeminacy of Inlaw's garments and their association with Agathon have led even this uncouth character to play the role, not merely of a woman but also of a tragic playwright composing a new scene.

Hyparchein occurs for its third and final time in *Women at Thesmophoria* during the play's final Euripidean parody. Inlaw, now securely fastened to a post and under the watchful guard of a Scythian archer, despairs his rescue until he sees Euripides signaling from the wings:

ἁνὴρ ἔοικεν οὐ προδώσειν, ἀλλά μοι
σημεῖον ὑπεδήλωσε Περσεὺς ἐκδραμών,
ὅτι δεῖ με γίγνεσθ' Ἀνδρομέδαν· πάντως δέ μοι
τὰ δέσμ' ὑπάρχει.

It appears the man will not betray me, but has
covertly signaled to me that he's going to play Perseus,
and that I must become Andromeda — after all, I already
have the chains!

(Ar. *Thesm.* 1010–1014)

Here, although the idea for the parody is not his own, Inlaw nevertheless immediately recognizes the appropriateness of his material circumstances to the part he is asked to play. Inlaw's use of the words *pantōs, moi, and hyparchei* – a near verbatim repetition of his earlier expression (851) – links this scenic improvisation to that of the *Helen* parody. A spatial imitation of *Andromeda*, too, may be at play. In a passage mentioned above (section "Aristophanes' Creative Reuse of the Athenian Theater") to highlight Aristophanes' self-conscious reuse of the theatrical space, a character recalls how a similar scene was enacted "last year, in this same place" (l. 1060). It may be, further, that "this same place" refers not merely to the theater as a whole but the specific location on stage, creating a historically stereoscopic visual experience. In sum, the reuse of scenic objects and space in the parodies of Euripidean drama in *Women at the Thesmophoria Festival* reveals materials to be not only a medium of satiric engagement but also a driving creative force for performance in general. "After all," to borrow Inlaw's phrase, the present advantages of Athens' materially and culturally rich theater afforded Aristophanes staging opportunities which no new set piece, however spectacular or sumptuous, could hope to match.

Conclusion

Aristophanic drama dramatizes ways that, for all its ostentatious opulence and novelty, fifth-century Athenian theater remained an economical institution. Through practical and creative reuse of physical aspects of its stage, theater-makers leveraged materials' unique powers (their object histories, affordances, and beyond) in performance. Calling theatrically self-conscious attention to various cases of scenic economy that demonstrate his creative and critical powers as a playwright, Aristophanes celebrates materials' ability to not simply realize but also inspire and shape dramatic performance. Aristophanes' frequent manipulations of familiar and readily available materials complemented the exaggeration and excess widely hailed as the hallmarks of Old Comedy. Although creative reuse pervades Aristophanes' stagecraft, his parodies of tragic costume in plays like *Acharnians* (see esp. ll. 383–495), *Frogs* (38–47, 460–674), and especially *Women at the Thesmophoria Festival* provide a particularly meta-theatrical and evocative framework for exploring material reuse. In the scenes studied above, Agathon theorizes and Inlaw enacts ways material-led improvisation and creativity might inform theatrical production more broadly. Engagement with tragic costume in all of these plays underscores the distributed nature of Athenian theater and the various intra-actions of scenic objects. As the ancient Greek terms nearest in meaning to English "staging" (viz., *didaskalein, choragein, skeuē*, and *opsis*) suggest (see section "Introduction"), Athenian drama was an intensely collaborative production involving not only poets, performers, and producers but costumes, properties, and the fixed features of the theater as well. As scholars including James I. Porter (2010), Melissa Mueller (2016), Mario Telò (2016), and Amy Lather (2021) have begun to explore, materials exerted a profound influence not simply on ancient drama (which necessarily depended upon actors and objects as a medium of communication) but on broader Greek cultural esthetics as well. Reusing and theorizing the scenic objects in memorable ways, Aristophanes' stage offers convenient examples of and, valuable insight into, the wider workings of materials in the ancient world.

GUIDE TO FURTHER READING

Much has been written about Aristophanes' stage, but such a practically and theoretically rich subject leaves much to uncover. Seminal work by twentieth-century classicists, including Bieber (1961), Webster and Green (1978), and others, laid a theatrical- and art-historical foundation for the study of Old Comedy that remains solid today. More recent work, including Wilson (2000), (2007), and Csapo et al. (2014), draws further upon disparate documentary sources to refine our knowledge of the stage. Pickard-Cambridge (1968), although now dated in certain respects, remains an efficient and accurate overview of the Athenian dramatic festivals and includes a well-illustrated section on comedic costume. Csapo and Slater's (1995) sourcebook makes scattered ancient evidence accessible in a single English edition.

On Aristophanes' use of the stage in particular, Russo (1994) and McLeish (1980) provide thorough, although sometimes speculative accounts of the surviving plays. Dearden (1976) works outward from the features and conventions of the theater. In addition to a concise overview of Aristophanes' theatrical conditions, Dover (1972) discusses key staging issues with authority. Marshall (2014) highlights essential formal features of Aristophanic comedy and their function in performance. On Aristophanic costume, Stone (1984) presents an exhaustive and textually informed assessment; Varakis (2010) and Compton-Engle (2015) take a more thematic approach. On the semiotics of the tragic costume with which Aristophanes was so often engaged, see Wyles (2011). There remains no book-length study of properties in Old Comedy, but the theatrical commentaries of Ewans (2011, 2012) helpfully list all necessary properties and discuss their deployment in a handful of comedies. Revermann (2006b) inspects Aristophanic drama through a theoretically informed performance lens, offering many important local and general observations.

The New Materialisms resist easy summary, but Coole and Frost (2010) and Grusin (2015) present useful and influential surveys. Gibson (1979) remains an oft-cited touchstone for ecological interactions between materials and man, incorporated in the scholarly discourse on Athenian drama for decades (Rehm 2002), even before Barad (2007) and Bennett (2010) brought such ideas as "intra-action" and "vibrant materialisms" to the scholarly fore. New Materialist approaches to the tragic stage are well underway, including Mueller (2016) and Telò and Mueller (2018). These and certain vanguard studies of Aristophanes, including Telò (2016), may be bellwethers for further materially informed studies of Old Comedy to come.

REFERENCES

Barad, K. (2007). *Meeting the Universe Halfway: Quantum Physics and the Entanglement of Matter and Meaning.* Duke University Press.
Bennett, J. (2010). *Vibrant Matter: A Political Ecology of Things.* Duke University Press.
Bieber, M. (1961). *The History of the Greek and Roman Theater.* Princeton: Princeton University Press.
Bosher, K. (ed.) (2012). *Theater outside Athens: Drama in Greek Sicily and South Italy.* Cambridge University Press.
Bosher, K. (2021). *Greek Theater in Ancient Sicily* (ed. E. Hall and C. Marconi). Cambridge University Press.
Carlson, M. (1993). *Places of Performance: The Semiotics of Theater Architecture.* Cornell University Press.
Compton-Engle, G. (2015). *Costume in the Comedies of Aristophanes.* Cambridge University Press.
Coole, D. (2013). Agentic capacities and capacious historical materialism: thinking with new materialisms in the political sciences. *Millennium: Journal of International Studies* 41 (3): 451–469.
Coole, D. and Frost, S. (ed.) (2010). *New Materialisms: Ontology, Agency, and Politics.* Duke University Press.
Csapo, E. (2007). The men who built the theatres: Theatropolai, Theatronai, and Arkhitektones. In: *The Greek Theatre and Festivals: Documentary Studies* (ed. P. Wilson), 87–115. Oxford University Press.
Csapo, E. and Slater, W.J. (1995). *The Context of Ancient Drama.* University of Michigan Press.
Csapo, E. and Wilson, P. (2020). *A Social and Economic History of the Theatre to 300 BC.* Cambridge University Press.
Csapo, E., Goette, H.R., and Green, J.R. (ed.) (2014). *Greek Theatre in the Fourth Century B.C.* Berlin, De Gruyter.
Dearden, C.W. (1976). *The Stage of Aristophanes.* Athlone Press.
Dover, K.J. (1972). *Aristophanic Comedy.* University of California Press.
Duncan, A. (2000). Agathon, essentialism, and gender subversion in Aristophanes' Thesmophoriazusae. *European Studies Journal* 17/18(2/1): 25.
Duncan, A. (2006). *Performance and Identity in the Classical World.* Cambridge University Press.
Duncan, A.C. (2018). The familiar mask. In: *The Materialities of Greek Tragedy: Objects and Affect in Aeschylus, Sopcholes, and Euripides* (ed. M. Telò and M. Mueller), 79–95. Bloomsbury.
Duncan, A.C. (2023). Seeing together: joint attention in attic tragedy. In: *Minds on Stage: Greek Tragedy and Cognition* (ed. F. Budelmann and I. Sluiter), 173–195. Oxford University Press.
Ewans, M. (2011). *Aristophanes: Lysistrata; The Women's Festival; and Frogs.* University of Oklahoma Press.
Ewans, M. (2012). *Aristophanes: Acharnians; Knights; and Peace.* University of Oklahoma Press.
Farmer, M.C. (2017). *Tragedy on the Comic Stage.* Oxford University Press.
Foley, H.P. (2000). The comic body in Greek art and drama. In: *Not the Classical Ideal: Athens and the Construction of the Other in Greek Art* (ed. B. Cohen), 275–311.
Gibson, J.J. (1979). *The Ecological Approach to Visual Perception.* Houghton-Mifflin.
Green, J.R. and Handley, E.W. (1995). *Images of the Greek Theatre.* British Museum Press.
Grusin, R. (2015). *The Nonhuman Turn.* University of Minnesota Press.
Halliwell, S. (1993). The function and aesthetics of the Greek tragic mask. In: *Intertextualität in der griechisch-römischen Komödie*, 195–211. M&P Verlag für Wissenschaft und Forschung.
Halliwell, F.S. (2002). *The Aesthetics of Mimesis: Ancient Texts and Modern Problems.* Princeton University Press.
Hunter, R. (2017). Comedy and reperformance. In: *Imagining Reperformance in Ancient Culture: Studies in the Traditions of Drama and Lyric* (ed. R. Hunter and A. Uhlig), 209–231. Cambridge University Press.
Jendza, C. (2020). *Paracomedy: Appropriations of Greek Comedy in Tragedy.* Oxford University Press.
Konstan, D. (2013). Propping up Greek tragedy: the right use of opsis. In: *Performance in Greek and Roman Theatre*, (ed. G. Harrison and V. Liapis), 63–76. Brill.
Lather, A. (2021). *Materiality and Aesthetics in Archaic and Classical Greek Poetry.* Edinburgh University Press.
Lévi-Strauss, C. (1966). *The Savage Mind.* Chicago: University of Chicago Press.
Lowe, N. (2006). Aristophanic spacecraft. In: *Playing Around Aristophanes: Essays in Honour of Alan Sommerstein* (ed. L. Kozak and J. Rich), 48–64. Warminster: Aris & Phillips.
Marshall, C.W. (1999). Some fifth-century masking conventions. *Greece & Rome* 46 (2): 188–202.

Marshall, C.W. (2014). Dramatic technique and Athenian comedy. In: *Cambridge Companion to Greek Comedy*. Cambridge University Press.

Mastronarde, D. (1990). Actors on high: the skene roof, the crane, and the gods in attic drama. *Classical Antiquity* 9 (2): 247–294.

McLeish, K. (1980). *The Theatre of Aristophanes*. Thames & Hudson.

Mueller, M. (2016). *Objects as Actors: Props and the Poetics of Performance in Greek Tragedy*. University of Chicago Press.

Nervegna, S. (2013). *Menander in Antiquity: The Contexts of Reception*. Cambridge University Press.

Olson, S.D. (1991). Firewood and charcoal in classical Athens. *Hesperia* 60 (3): 411–420.

Paga, J. (2010). Deme theaters in Attica and the Trittys system. *Hesperia* 79 (3): 351–384.

Pickard-Cambridge, A., Gould, J., and Lewis, D.M. (1968). *The Dramatic Festivals at Athens*. Oxford: Clarendon Press.

Porter, J.I. (2010). *The Origins of Aesthetic Thought in Ancient Greece: Matter, Sensation, and Experience*. Cambridge University Press.

Rehm, R. (2002). *The Play of Space: Spatial Transformation in Greek Tragedy*. Princeton University Press.

Revermann, M. (2006a). *Comic Business: Theatricality, Dramatic Technique, and Performance Contexts of Aristophanic Comedy*. Oxford University Press.

Revermann, M. (2006b). The competence of theatre audiences in fifth- and fourth-century Athens. *Journal of Hellenic Studies* 126: 99–124.

Roselli, D.K. (2011). *Theater of the People: Spectators and Society in Ancient Athens*. University of Texas Press.

Rothwell, K.S. (2006). *Nature, Culture, and the Origins of Greek Comedy: A Study of Animal Choruses*. Cambridge University Press.

Russo, C.F. (1994). *Aristophanes: An Author for the Stage* K. Wren, Trans., 2nd ed. Routledge.

Sifakis, G.M. (1971). *Parabasis and Animal Choruses: A Contribution to the History of Attic Comedy*. University of London: Athlone Press.

Sifakis, G.M. (2013). The misunderstanding of opsis in Aristotle's poetics. In: *Performance in Greek and Roman Theatre*, (ed. G. Harrison and V. Liapis), 45–62. Brill.

Sommerstein, A.H. (1994). *Aristophanes: Thesmophoriazusae*. Aris & Phillips.

Squire, M. (ed.) (2016). *Sight and the Ancient Senses*. Routledge.

States, B.O. (1985). *Great Reckonings in Little Rooms: On the Phenomenology of Theater*. University of California Press.

Stehle, E.M. (2002). The body and its representations in Aristophanes' Thesmophoriazousai::where does the costume end? *American Journal of Philology* 123 (3): 369–406.

Stone, L.M. (1984). *Costume in Aristophanic Poetry*. Ayer Company.

Taplin, O. (1993). *Comic Angels and Other Approaches to Greek Drama through Vase-Paintings*. Clarendon Press.

Taplin, O. (2007). *Pots and Plays: Interactions between Tragedy and Greek Vase-Painting of the Fourth Century B.C.* The J. Paul Getty Museum.

Taplin, O. (2018). Aristotle's poetics and skênikoi agônes. In: *Eris Vs. Aemulatio: Valuing Competition in Classical Antiquity*, 141–151. Brill.

Telò, M. (2016). *Aristophanes and the Cloak of Comedy: Affect, Aesthetics, and the Canon*. University of Chicago Press.

Telò, M. and Mueller, M. (ed.) (2018). *The Materialities of Greek Tragedy: Objects and Affect in Aeschylus, Sophocles, and Euripides*. Bloomsbury Academic.

Varakis, A. (2010). Body and mask in Aristophanic performance. *Bulletin of the Institute of Classical Studies* 53 (17–38).

Webster, T.B.L. and Green, J.R. (ed.) (1978). *Monuments Illustrating Old and Middle Comedy*, 3rd ed. Institute of Classical Studies.

Weiss, N. (2023). *Seeing Theater: The Phenomenology of Classical Greek Drama*. University of California Press.

Wiles, D. (2017). The environment of theatre: experiencing place in the ancient world. In: *A cultural history of theatre in antiwquity* (ed. M. Revermann), 63–81. Bloomsbury.

Wilson, P. (2000). *The Athenian Institution of the Khoregia: The Chorus, the City, and the Stage*. Cambridge University Press.

Wyles, R. (2011). *Costume in Greek Tragedy*. Bristol Classical Press.

Zeitlin, F. (1996). Travesties of gender and genre in Aristophanes' Thesmophoriazusae. In: *Playing the Other: Gender and Society in Classical Greek Literature*, 375–416. University of Chicago Press.

Zuckerberg, D. (2016). The clothes make the man: Aristophanes and the ragged hero in Euripides' Helen. *Classical Philology* 111 (2): 201–223.

CHAPTER 3

Meter and Song

Anne Mahoney

Introduction

For us, Greek drama is primarily a set of texts. We have only a few dozen fragments of musical notation (available in West 1992, 2001), of which none at all are from comedy and only a couple are from fifth-century tragedy. No choreography survives, nor do costumes, masks, or props, though we do have pictures of performances on many vases. Thus, it can be easy to forget that a fifth-century performance, whether of tragedy or of comedy, was a musical spectacle, more like *The Magic Flute* or *Oklahoma!* than like *A Midsummer Night's Dream*. The music was an integral part of the show. To get any sense at all of what that music may have been like, we may study the meters of the songs. In this chapter, I will review the basic meters Aristophanes uses, spoken and sung, and how song fits into the plays. The text is cited from Wilson (2007), with some adjustments to colometry for clarity. Metrical notation and terminology follow West (1982).

First of all, Aristophanes uses different meters for different parts of a play. Certain meters are appropriate for spoken dialog, while songs, sung by the chorus, the actors, or both, use lyric meters similar to those of the choral poets (like Pindar and Stesichorus) and the tragedians. Meter thus supports the structure of the play and helps make it audible. A play normally begins with speech, either a monolog (as in *Acharnians, Clouds, Assemblywomen*) or, more often, a dialog (as in *Knights, Wasps, Peace, Birds, Lysistrata, Women at the Thesmophoria, Frogs, Wealth*). After a while, the chorus enters, normally singing; one or more of the actors may sing with them (as, for example, in *Birds*, where the Hoopoe sings a showy lyric to summon the chorus, 209–262). Thereafter, sung passages and spoken ones alternate. Eight of the 11 extant plays have a parabasis, in which the chorus addresses the audience directly, normally speaking for the poet. The exceptions are *Assemblywomen, Wealth*, and *Lysistrata*. The parabasis typically consists of a song in strophe and antistrophe, with a speech after each stanza. After the parabasis, the second part of the play may be fairly episodic, with new, often unnamed characters entering, interacting with the main characters, and disappearing – *Birds* is a good example. These episodes are punctuated by choral songs, often simpler metrically than those of the first half of the play. The play may end with spoken lines (*Knights, Peace*), with a song (*Acharnians, Wasps, Birds, Lysistrata, Assemblywomen*), or with a passage in anapests (*Clouds, Women at the Thesmophoria*) as tragedy normally does. *Frogs*, after some dialog in spoken anapests, ends with a tag from the chorus in epic meter.

Meter is useful for more than just structure, though. It can be helpful in establishing the text. An iambic trimeter, for example, has to have at least 12 syllables; if it has only 11, something is wrong and the text needs to be emended. We see this at *Peace* 402, for example, κλέπται γὰρ νῦν εἰσὶ μᾶλλον ἢ πρὸ τοῦ, where although the line makes sense, there is clearly a syllable missing (and editors supply

---

A Companion to Aristophanes, First Edition. Edited by Matthew C. Farmer and Jeremy B. Lefkowitz.
© 2024 John Wiley & Sons, Inc. Published 2024 by John Wiley & Sons, Inc.

something like γε to fill in). Similarly, strophe and antistrophe must respond metrically, and when they do not, at least one is wrong.

Greek meters, like the rest of the Greek language, are descended from Proto-Indo-European, though there has been considerable development within Greek. Of the four major metrical families, aeolic is closest to its Indo-European antecedents: aeolic forms allow variation at the start of the line, in the aeolic base, but not at the end, and they do not permit either resolution of a long element (putting two short syllables into a single position) or contraction of a biceps element (putting a long syllable in the place of two shorts). Dactylic meter is most familiar from epic, though the epic line probably developed from something closer to the dactylo-epitrite forms used in choral lyric. This family allows contraction but not resolution. The iambic and trochaic family gives us most of the meters of spoken dialog; it allows resolution but not contraction. Finally, the anapestic family allows both resolution and contraction. In aeolic and iambo-trochaic meters, there can be anceps elements, a metrical position where either a long syllable or a short syllable is permitted. It is useful to distinguish between the elements, which are the positions in the underlying metrical pattern, and the actual syllables a poet uses to realize a metrical pattern: there can be anceps elements in the pattern, but there are no anceps syllables in a poem, as each syllable in its context is either long or short.

Aside from the texts themselves, we can learn about Greek verse from Alexandrian and Byzantine metrical theorists, some of whose work is summarized in the extant scholia to the plays. These scholars analyzed Greek verse into metra, small units (typically three or four syllables) that can be repeated. This works nicely for the epic line, which is why we call it the "dactylic hexameter," and for the principal line of dramatic dialog, called the "iambic trimeter," but it does not produce satisfactory analyses of more complicated forms, like the songs of drama. In fact, the dactyl (–⏑⏑), the iambus (x–⏑), the trochee (–⏑x), and the other feet they identify do not actually exist independently. Originally, all these metrical forms are made from cola (from κῶλον, "limb"), somewhat longer units, typically 8–10 syllables, characteristic of each family. This was rediscovered in the early nineteenth century by August Böckh, as he was editing Pindar, and confirmed by comparative evidence from Sanskrit and elsewhere in Indo-European.

In what follows, we will consider first the dialog meters and then the lyrics.

Dialog Meters

The spoken dialog is generally in iambic trimeters, as in all Greek plays. There are also dialog passages in trochaic tetrameters catalectic (for example, *Ach.* 305–334), iambic tetrameters catalectic (as at *Kn.* 333–381), and anapests (such as *Cl.* 314–456). All of those except the iambic trimeter can also be used for the spoken parts of the parabasis (the parabasis speech and the epirrheme and antepirrheme). The schema of the iambic trimeter is basically the same as for tragedy: x–⏑–x–⏑–x–⏑–, with colon break, and thus normally word end, after the fifth or seventh element. All long elements except the last can be resolved (that is, realized with two short syllables), just as in tragedy, but the third and seventh elements, always short in tragedy, can also be treated as resolvable ancipitia. Resolution is much more common than in tragedy, in fact so common that one of the simplest ways to mark paratragedy is to have a series of unresolved trimeters. Here is an example of typical trimeters, the opening lines of *Clouds*, with resolutions in bold:

ὦ **Ζεῦ βασι**λεῦ τὸ χρῆμα τῶν νυκτῶν ὅσον·	⏑–⏑⏑⏑–⏑⏑–⏕–⏑ ‖B	
ἀ**πέραν**τον. οὐ**δέποθ**' ἡμέρα γενήσεται;	⏑⏑⏑–⏑⏑–⏑–⏑–⏑–	
καὶ μὴν **πάλ**αι γ' ἀλεκτρυ**όνος** ἤκουσ' ἐγώ·	–––⏑––⏑⏑⏑–⏑– ‖H	
οἱ δ' οἰκέται ῥέγκουσιν. ἀλλ' οὐκ ἂν πρὸ τοῦ.	–⏑–⏑–⏑⏑–⏑–⏑ ‖H	
ἀ**πόλ**οιο **δῆτ**', ὦ **πόλ**εμε, πολλῶν οὕνεκα,	⏑⏑––⏑⏑––⏑–⏑ ‖B,H	5
ὅτ' οὐ**δὲ κολάσ**' ἔξεστί μοι τοὺς οἰκέτας.	⏑–⏑⏑⏑–––⏑–⏑–	

(Strepsiades: Dear Lord Zeus, what a night. It never ends. Won't it ever be day? Though long ago I did hear a rooster. The slaves are snoring. But they wouldn't have back in the day. Drop dead, War, when because of all your nonsense I can't even punish my slaves.)

Note resolved long elements in lines 3, 5, and 6, resolved ancipitia in lines 2 and 5 (twice each), and a resolved short element in line 1. The metrical pattern of line 1 would not be possible in tragedy, though lines 3 and 6 would be. In tragedy, an anceps position may be resolved to accommodate a proper name like Ἀντιγόνη or Ἀγαμέμνων, but usually only the actual long elements are resolved. It is not common to have two resolutions in a single line in tragedy, as lines 2 and 5 here, and it would be quite unusual to have seven resolved elements in six lines in tragic dialog, but this is fairly ordinary in comedy.

Aristophanes uses trochaic tetrameters catalectic more often than the tragedians do; every play except *Wealth* has a passage in this meter. The schema is —⏑—x—⏑—x|—⏑—x—⏑—, always with word end after the eighth element, which is the colon boundary. This is the same schema as for tragedy but, just as for the iambic trimeter, the ancipitia can be resolved, and resolution is more frequent than in tragedy. A passage in this meter often ends with a pnigos, which is a group of trochaic dimeters ending with a catalectic dimeter, normally in a single long period which may also be a single syntactic unit. The pnigos is not restricted to trochees: a passage in anapests may also end with a pnigos, in anapestic dimeters ending in catalexis. Perhaps the most famous pnigos or quasi-pnigos in Aristophanes is at the close of *Ecclesiazusae*, where the chorus describes the imminent party in a dactylic pnigos: a long run of dactyls including a compound word of some 70 syllables.

Tragedy does not use the iambic tetrameter catalectic, but Aristophanes occasionally does. The schema is x—⏑—x—⏑—|x—⏑—⏑—— with colon break always after the eighth element. As in the other iambo-trochaic dialog meters, both the long elements and the ancipitia can be resolved. An example comes from the *Agon* of *Knights*, 411–414:

ἔγωγε, νὴ τοὺς κονδύλους, οὓς πολλὰ δὴ 'πὶ πολλοῖς

ἠνεσχόμην ἐκ παιδίου, μαχαιρίδων τε πληγάς,

ὑπερβαλεῖσθαί σ' οἴομαι τούτοισιν, ἢ μάτην γ' ἂν

ἀπομαγ**δα**λιὰς σιτούμενος τοσοῦτος ἐκτραφεὶς ἤ.

(Sausage-Seller: I swear by every knuckle sandwich – and I've had a lot of them since I was a boy – and every knife-stroke, I will get beyond you in all this, or else I've been raised on table-scraps for nothing.)

The only resolutions in these lines are in the first and third elements of the last line. Note that each line falls into two parts, with word break after the eighth element. Other passages in iambic tetrameters catalectic occur in *Clouds*, in the *agon* between father and son after Pheidippides has taken a course at the Phrontisterion (1351 ff); in *Peace* as a final exhortation to the farmers hauling Peace from the cave (508–511); in *Lysistrata* as a transition into the *agon*, which is conducted in anapestic tetrameters (467 ff); and in both *Assemblywomen* (285 ff) and *Wealth* (253 ff) at the entrance of the chorus.

Extended dialogs in spoken anapests are also different from tragedy. In tragedy, spoken anapests come in short passages, often between a song and the following iambic trimeters (for example, *Antigone* 376–383), or perhaps at the entry of a new character (as *Antigone* 526–530), and they are usually organized in dimeters. There are also passages in which anapests alternate with stanzas in different meters (as in the parodos of *Antigone*, 100 ff), sometimes with the chorus using lyric meters and an actor using anapests (as in *Agamemnon* 1448 ff, between Clytemnestra and the chorus) and sometimes the other way around (*Antigone* 817 ff, in which Antigone sings, mainly in aeolic meters, and the chorus sings anapests). Aristophanes uses those structures as well but also has non-lyric dialog in anapests, often extending to dozens of lines. Here, the line is a catalectic tetrameter, whose schema is basically ⏑⏑–⏑⏑–|⏑⏑–⏑⏑–, but because the longs can be resolved and the shorts can be contracted, the effective schema is ⏒⏔⏒⏔⏒⏔⏒⏔⏒⏔⏒⏔. While this seems chaotic, in practice, anapests are easy to scan by ear. The passage may end in a pnigos. For example, the discussion between Socrates and Strepsiades, eventually joined by the chorus leader, after the entrance of the chorus of *Clouds*, 314–456, involves 63 separate turns. Strepsiades closes the passage with a pnigos from 439 to 456. No anapestic passage in tragedy is anywhere close to this length. As in tragedy, Aristophanes may also use anapests at points of transition between song and speech, though he does so much less often than the tragedians. An example is *Acharnians* 1143–1149.

Although the syntax of comic dialog is generally relatively straightforward, Aristophanes does use hyperbaton as any other Greek poet does, and, as is typical for verse in all the older Indo-European languages, the parts of a phrase in hyperbaton will be at verse boundaries: syntax and meter work together. An example occurs at *Peace* 840:

ἀπὸ δείπνου τινὲς

τῶν πλουσίων οὗτοι βαδίζουσ' ἀστέρων

ἰπνοὺς ἔχοντες, ἐν δὲ τοῖς ἰπνοῖσι πῦρ.

(Trygaeus: They're some of the rich stars coming home from dinner carrying lanterns, and there's fire in the lanterns.)

Here, the verb and the subject pronoun separate the two parts of the genitive phrase, which occur at start and end of the verse. The tendency to put distracted phrases at colon boundaries is called Watkins' rule; it is easily seen in Greek epic but occurs in nearly all Greek poetry, and Latin and Sanskrit as well, see Watkins (1995, 40–41) and Mahoney (2014).

Eight of the 11 extant plays have a parabasis, in which the chorus addresses the audience directly, normally speaking for the poet. The exceptions are *Assemblywomen*, *Wealth*, and *Lysistrata*. The typical form of the parabasis is an *envoi*, an opening speech (which is strictly what "parabasis" refers to, though the term is normally applied to the entire episode), and a song in strophe and antistrophe with a speech after each part; these two speeches are the epirrheme, or epirrheme and antepirrheme, and the unit consisting of the song and the epirrheme is sometimes called the epirrhematic syzygy. The *envoi* is a line or two in which the chorus dismisses the characters, saying something like "good-bye and good luck." In a couple of plays (*Acharnians, Knights, Peace, Birds*), the chorus adds "we're about to do the anapests," another general term for the parabasis even when the speeches are not actually in anapestic meter. The parabasis speech and epirrheme are always in catalectic tetrameters of one sort or another. In most of the plays, the parabasis speech is anapestic. In *Clouds*, though, this speech is in eupolidean meter, a sort of catalectic variant of the choriambic dimeter, which Aristophanes uses only here; its schema is o o ⏑ x –⏑⏑– | o o ⏑ x –⏑⏑–, with mandatory word break between the cola. Here, the symbols o o represent the aeolic base, two elements that can have two long syllables or one long and one short in either order, but not two short. The epirrheme and antepirrheme are trochaic tetrameters catalectic, except in *Peace* where the parabasis has a song but no epirrhematic speeches. *Thesmophoriazusae*, on the other hand, does not have a parabasis ode, just an anapestic speech and a trochaic one. *Frogs* (674–737) has an epirrhematic syzygy without an opening speech, though there is an anapestic passage in the parodos (354 ff) which is similar to the parabasis speeches of other plays; the spoken parts of the parabasis are trochaic tetrameters catalectic as in the other plays. In the parabasis, the chorus leader, and perhaps the whole chorus, may break character and speak for the poet, either about the competition they are currently engaged in or the poet's prior career, or current affairs in Athens. The chorus of *Birds* is a striking exception as its parabasis is entirely in character, giving a bird's-eye view of the history of the world from creation to the present.

Lysistrata does not have a parabasis presumably because the chorus is divided into warring factions, male versus female, for most of the play. Moreover, the parabasis normally gives advice to the city, and as the *agon* between Lysistrata and the Proboulos has done exactly that, there is no need for an additional exhortation from the chorus. That *Wealth* and *Assemblywomen* do not have them suggests that the form of comedy was changing by the start of the fourth century and the parabasis had fallen out of fashion. In *Wealth*, moreover, the chorus is much less integrated into the plot and even sings unrelated songs not composed by Aristophanes. Henderson suggests, in his introduction to the play (v. 5, p. 416), that this might have been the first play to use choral songs not composed by the playwright (though the notation χοροῦ, for a song not in the text, does also appear at *Assemblywomen* 730, 877).

Oracles are given in dactylic hexameter, as they would be in tragedy or even in prose. One example is the scene in *Knights*, 997–1110, where half a dozen oracles are concocted and parodied. Epic, too, may be parodied, as at the end of *Peace* (1270–1293), and these passages are also in dactylic hexameter.

There are even occasional bits of prose, normally quoting or parodying ritual language. The herald in the opening scene of *Acharnians*, calling the assembly to order, speaks prose, as does the leader of the festival in *Thesmophoriazusae*; this is the longest prose passage in Aristophanes, 295–311.

The chorus itself is, as in tragedy, a collective group who act together. They may support the main character, as in *Wasps*, or they may be somewhat hostile, as in *Clouds*. In *Frogs*, the main chorus, of initiates in the underworld, is somewhat apart from the action, observing the contest between Aeschylus and Euripides but not appearing to favor either side. In *Lysistrata*, as noted above, the chorus spends the first half of the play divided into warring factions. While the choruses of tragedy are usually human, or anthropomorphic divinities like the Furies or the Oceanids (in *Prometheus*), in comedy they may be animals, like the Birds, or more abstract divine figures, like the Clouds. The Birds are all of different species, named as they enter (267 ff). Other poets used even less humanized choruses: for example, Athenaeus tells us that in *The Letter Play*, Callias's chorus consists of the 24 letters of the Greek alphabet (Ath. 453c). The chorus in tragedy may be made up of slaves, as in *Medea*, or low-ranking soldiers, as in *Ajax*. In the extant plays of Aristophanes, the human choruses are citizens, though usually not aristocratic (except for *Knights*). Any Athenian man in the audience can identify with the jurors of *Wasps* or the farmers of *Peace*, and if he does not see himself in the *Assemblywomen* or the *Women Celebrating Thesmophoria*, his wife will.

Songs and Lyric Meters

Although the songs in the surviving plays of Aristophanes are generally not as complicated as the great kommos of *Libation Bearers* or the "Ode to Man" in *Antigone*, they are inventive and metrically well crafted. The personalities of the choruses sometimes include signature metrical motifs, like the Acharnians' cretics or the Birds' twittering. Actors may sing, in dialog with the chorus or occasionally in solo song; almost all the major characters have at least a brief sung passage.

The songs are in lyric meters, using all the usual metrical families: aeolic, iambo-trochaic, dactylic, and anapestic. Dochmiacs are generally paratragic and not especially common. Ionic meter occurs rarely, and there is no song that is primarily ionic. Lyrics are almost always strophic, just as in tragedy, and sometimes the same stanza is repeated several times, especially for the detached sarcastic songs in the second half of a play. Astrophic lyrics include the Hoopoe's song in *Birds*, Agathon's in *Thesmophoriazusae*, and Dicaeopolis's celebration in *Acharnians*.

In tragedy, lyrics use a conventionalized Doric dialect, which mostly means original long α is used instead of the η that results from a characteristic Attic (and Ionic) sound shift, so a word like Attic ἀρχή may appear in its common-Greek form ἀρχά. Other Doric features, like ποτί for πρός, are uncommon. Aristophanes, on the other hand, uses the same Attic in the songs as in the spoken dialog. When a Doric dialect appears in the plays, it is in the speech of a non-Athenian character, like the Spartans in *Lysistrata*, and it is a specific regional variety rather than the generic, conventional choral form.

As a concrete example of Aristophanes' metrical practice, we will take *Peace*. Here is a metrical overview. The play opens with dialog in iambic trimeters between two of Trygaeus's slaves, who are preparing food for the beetle and explaining to the audience how crazy their master seems to be. Trygaeus, on beetle back, is first heard at 62, and by 82 he is visible. From 82 to 101, the dialog is in anapests, returning to trimeters at 102 as Trygaeus explains his plan. At 114, his daughters enter, singing in dactylic meter; there are four tetrameter lines followed by one hexameter, and Trygaeus replies in hexameters. Most of this passage parodies Euripides: the beetle motif comes from *Bellerophon* and the daughters' lament from *Aeolus*. Iambic trimeters resume at 124. After the children leave, Trygaeus addresses the audience at 149 and then goes into anapestic dimeters at 154 as he exhorts the beetle. At 173, he abruptly returns to iambic trimeters, calling out to the stagehand managing the *mechane*. The scene shifts to Zeus's front door, through which Hermes enters at 180. After Hermes explains what has happened to Peace, and War appears with his mortar for grinding the Greek cities, Trygaeus summons the chorus, moving to trochaic tetrameters in mid-sentence at 299. Dialog between Trygaeus and the chorus continues in tetrameters, ending with a pnigos from Trygaeus at 339.

The first song is at 346–360, with an antistrophe at 385–399 and a second antistrophe at 582–600. Between the strophe and the first antistrophe is a brief dialog in iambic trimeters. In the strophe, the chorus asks Trygaeus what to do now and looks ahead to the peaceful time to come. In the first antistrophe, they turn to Hermes, pleading with him not to tell Zeus what they're doing. The second antistrophe is part of the joyful reaction to the emergence of Peace, as the chorus welcomes her. In both tragedy and comedy, it is not uncommon to have some dialog between strophe and antistrophe, but it is rather rare for a strophe to be repeated later in the play. Here, the three occurrences of the same tune (and, presumably, the same choreography) frame the actual rescue of Peace. The lyric itself is cretic.

After the first antistrophe, Trygaeus has the clever idea of telling Hermes the Sun and Moon are conspiring against the Olympians, which (somehow) convinces Hermes to help out. Dialog continues in iambic trimeters until 426, when Trygaeus switches to trochaic tetrameters to encourage the chorus, and they respond in the same meter. Hermes then prays in iambic trimeters (with a ritual exclamation *extra metrum*), and this meter continues until 459 when the chorus begins pulling on the ropes. They sing a sort of work song, mostly in anapests, at 463–472 ~ 490–499. Before each stanza are some exclamations which could be taken as part of the song, as Olson and Wilson do, or *extra metrum*, with Parker and Henderson. Since the last lines (εἶα ἔτι μάλα, 462, εἶα, νὴ Δία, 480) don't quite respond, it seems better to treat them as separate from the lyric. Between the stanzas and after this song, dialog continues in iambic trimeters until 508, when Trygaeus and Hermes call on the farmers in iambic tetrameters. At 512–519, the chorus makes one last good pull on the ropes and Peace emerges; here they sing in lyric iambics.

From 520, dialog returns to iambic trimeters. Trygaeus greets Peace, and he and Hermes laugh at the reaction of the armament makers they (claim to) see in the audience. At 553, we have trochaic tetrameters, ending with a pnigos from 571 to 581, followed by the second antistrophe of the framing song.

After the song, dialog returns to trochaic tetrameters. Hermes gives a comic account of the start of the war, explaining how both sides are to blame for driving Peace away. Trygaeus closes the trochaic passage with a pnigos at 651, and from 657, iambic trimeters resume as Peace asks Trygaeus, through Hermes, how things are going on earth. Eventually, Trygaeus prepares to return home, with Peace and her attendants, and Hermes points him in the right direction; the beetle will be staying behind. With the exit of the other characters, the chorus is alone and the parabasis begins at 729; the parabasis speech is in anapestic tetrameter. (Line 733, however, is trochaic, for no obvious reason; presumably, it is a quotation, but its source has not been identified.) The parabasis song, 775–795 ~ 796–818, is mainly in dactylo-epitrite, with a brief aeolic passage (in aristophaneans). There is no epirrheme in this parabasis.

The parabasis speech begins with praise of Aristophanes as an innovative poet and also one not afraid to challenge the greatest monsters in society. From 745, the speech abruptly switches to the first person: now the chorus leader speaks as Aristophanes and boasts of his successes. In the pnigos, 765–774, the chorus leader predicts that when Aristophanes succeeds, it will become cool to be bald: our poet, only about 30 years old, was already losing his hair. The parabasis song satirizes other dramatists. Strophe and antistrophe open with a passage adapted from the *Oresteia* of Stesichorus (fr. 210–212 Campbell), calling on the Muses to reject war and sing of peace, an invocation that fits nicely into the context of the play. But at 781, the chorus tells the muses to ignore Carcinus if he calls on them, since he and his sons are inferior poets and dancers. In the antistrophe, the victims are the tragic poets Morsimus and Melanthius. Instead of supporting them, the Muses should play with our poet and his chorus.

The second part of the play, in which Trygaeus celebrates his wedding to Opora ("Harvest" or Henderson's (1998) felicitous "Cornucopia"), is almost all in iambic trimeters. Trygaeus returns to his home at 819 and asks his slaves to take his new bride inside, after a bit of banter about the fluttering souls of recently deceased poets. At 856–867, the chorus and Trygaeus sing a brief lyric, starting in aeolic and ending in iambics, celebrating Trygaeus's exploit. The antistrophe is at 909–921. Between strophe and antistrophe is some sexual play with Peace's other attendant, Theoria ("Holiday" or "Festival"), whom Trygaeus offers to the public officials. Trygaeus then turns his attention to preparing for his wedding, beginning with a suitable sacrifice. Although the obvious offering to Peace would be bloodless, he and his slave settle on a sheep, and there is some clever word play around the difference between Ionic οἴ and Attic οἰί. As the slaves go off to fetch a sheep, the chorus sings another song, 939–955, mainly in iambics, first celebrating Trygaeus's divinely sanctioned success, then satirizing the aulos player Chaeris. The antistrophe comes at 1023–1038, when the sheep is taken inside to be dealt with.

Trygaeus then prepares the sheep for sacrifice, sprinkling water so it will nod its head in assent, and putting a bit of barley on the altar. This is also an excuse for tossing some barley or other small snacks to the audience. Trygaeus then prays to Peace, in anapests, 974–1015, assisted by his slave. He then asks the slave to sacrifice the sheep, and the slave observes that blood must not be shed on the altar of Peace, so Trygaeus tells him to take the animal inside – adding, meta-theatrically, that then the choragus can keep his sheep. At this point, the chorus sings the antistrophe matching the prior strophe, praising Trygaeus.

As Trygaeus prepares the wedding feast, Hierocles interrupts him. In *Peace*, as also in *Acharnians* and *Birds*, the second half of the play, after the parabasis, has a series of characters we have not seen before who come to the main character and ask to share in his good fortune. The main character may or may not be sympathetic: Dicaeopolis in *Acharnians* is happy to pour out a bit of his private peace for the wedding party but gives the sycophant short shrift; Peisetaerus in *Birds* gives the young father-beater wings and sensible advice, but the oracle-monger and sycophant get nothing. Similarly here, Trygaeus has no interest in the oracles offered by Hierocles and no sympathy for the arms merchants' economic difficulties. Hierocles demands to know what god Trygaeus is sacrificing to, and when he hears it is Peace, he produces oracles claiming that it is not now time to make peace. The oracles are of course in hexameters, and Trygaeus replies in the same meter, so the dialog from 1062 to 1114 is an epic-oracular pastiche. At 1115, Trygaeus breaks off, turns to the audience, and invites them (in iambic trimeter) to join in the meal, dismissing Hierocles.

As he slinks away, the chorus begins a second parabasis. The ode, 1127–1139 ~ 1159–1171, is mainly in cretics, celebrating the pleasures of peace, the strophe describing a winter's afternoon near the fire, and the antistrophe the ripe fruits of summer. The epirrhematic speeches are in trochaic tetrameters catalectic. While in the main parabasis the chorus leader spoke for Aristophanes, here he speaks for himself and in character, as a citizen benefiting from the return of Peace.

After this, a sickle-maker enters. Trygaeus greets him cordially and invites him into the feast. He is followed by several arms dealers, who are angry: peace hurts their business. Trygaeus offers to buy some of their stock, at ridiculous prices; they are insulted and depart. The son of Lamachus and the son of Cleonymus come out from the wedding party, apparently to practice the songs they will be performing later. Lamachus's son quotes from the epic cycle, in epic verse of course, and Trygaeus replies in the same meter, insisting that these warlike songs are out of place today. Cleonymus's boy sings Archilochus fragment 5, "I ditched my shield and saved myself," no more peaceable than the previous boy's, and, of course, an excuse to twit Cleonymus. The fragment is in elegiac couplets, though the boy only gets through the first one before Trygaeus cuts him off.

Trygaeus himself then sings a lyric in iambics inviting everyone to eat, 1305–1312, and the chorus replies with the antistrophe, 1313–1317, as Trygaeus goes inside to put on his wedding clothes. He emerges and prays for prosperity, in anapests. Finally, the wedding song that closes the play, 1329–1359, is aeolic.

The parabasis song from *Peace* (775–795 ~ 796–818) is a good example of Aristophanes' lyric technique. Here, each colon is printed on a separate line, and cola belonging to the same period are indented. (In dactylo-epitrite, the link elements between D, e, and E cola may be treated as part of the previous colon or the following one; I have followed the matching word ends.)

strophe:

Μοῦσα, σὺ μὲν πολέμους	— ‿‿ —	775
ἀπωσαμένη μετ' ἐμοῦ	⌣ ‿‿ —	
τοῦ φίλου χόρευσον,	— — ‿ —	
κλείουσα θεῶν τε γάμους	— — ‿‿ —	
ἀνδρῶν τε δαῖτας	— ‿ — —	
καὶ θαλίας μακάρων·	— ‿‿ — ‿ —	
σοὶ γὰρ τάδ' ἐξ ἀρχῆς μέλει.	⌣ — ‿ — — ⌣ |H	780
ἢν δέ σε Καρκίνος ἐλθὼν	— ‿‿ — ‿‿ —	
ἀντιβολῇ μετὰ τῶν παίδων χορεῦσαι,	— ‿ — ‿ — — — —	
μήθ' ὑπάκουε μήτ' ἔλ-	— ‿ — —	785
θῃς συνέριθος αὐτοῖς	— ‿ — —	
ἀλλὰ νόμιζε πάντας	— ‿ — ⌣ |B	
ὄρτυγας οἰκογενεῖς, γυλιαύχενας ὀρχηστὰς	— ‿ — ‿ ‿‿ ‿ — —	
νανοφυεῖς, σφυράδων ἀποκνίσματα, μηχανοδίφας.	— ‿ — ‿‿ ‿ ‿‿ — |H	790
καὶ γὰρ ἔφασχ' ὁ πατὴρ ὃ παρ' ἐλπίδας	— ‿‿ — ‿‿ —	
εἶχε τὸ δρᾶμα γαλῆν	— ‿‿ —	795
τῆς ἑσπέρας ἀπάγξαι.	— — ‿ — ||	

antistrophe:

τοιάδε χρὴ Χαρίτων	D	
δαμώματα καλλικόμων	⌣ D	
τὸν σοφὸν ποιητὴν	ith (= E^)	
ὑμνεῖν, ὅταν ἠρινὰ μὲν	⁻ D	
φωνῇ χελιδὼν	⁻e⁻	800
ἡδομένη κελαδῇ,	D	
χορὸν δὲ μὴ 'χῃ Μόρσιμος	ᵛ E |H	
μηδὲ Μελάνθιος, οὗ δὴ	D ⁻	

πικροτάτην ὄπα γηρύσαντος ἤκουσ᾽,	D ⁻e⁻	805
ἡνίκα τῶν τραγῳδῶν	arist ∫	
τὸν χορὸν εἶχον ἀδελ-	arist ∫	
φός τε καὶ αὐτός, ἄμφω	arist |B	
Γοργόνες ὀψοφάγοι, βατιδοσκόποι Ἅρπυιαι,	5 da^	810
γραοσόβαι μιαροί, τραγομάσχαλοι ἰχθυολῦμαι·	6 da|H	
ὧν καταχρεμψαμένη μέγα καὶ πλατὺ,	6 da	815
Μοῦσα θεά, μετ᾽ ἐμοῦ	D	
ξύμπαιζε τὴν ἑορτήν.	⁻ith	

(Muse, put war aside and dance with me, your friend, singing the fame of the gods' weddings, men's banquets, and the celebrations of the Blessed, for these have been your concern from the beginning of time. And if Carcinus comes along and asks you to dance with his sons, don't listen, don't go work for them, but know they are all house-bred quail, neckless dwarfy dancers, little balls of goat dung, invention-hunters. For their father, who unexpectedly had an actual play in hand, tells us that Old Mouser strangled it last night.

It is these public songs of the fair-haired Graces that the skillful poet must sing, when the swallow sings of springtime, delighting in her voice, and Morsimus has no chorus, nor Melanthius either. I heard him singing in that sharp, shrill voice of his when he and his brother had a chorus for the tragedies; they are both epicurean Gorgons, Harpies greedy for skate, pestilent old-lady-rejecters, fish-gobblers with the armpits of a goat. Spurn them, spit on them, Divine Muse, and come play festival with me.)

The colometry is uncontroversial because Aristophanes has made the structure quite clear. That is, we can easily recognize the periods, which are all marked with hiatus or with brevis-in-longo, and the cola are familiar types, almost all divided at word end rather than overlapping or dovetailed.

The first period ends with hiatus in the strophe, at line 781. It is dactylo-epitrite, closing with an ithyphallic, which is also the catalectic variant of the E colon. The second is marked by brevis-in-longo, also in the strophe, line 787; that is, the final syllable of this line is short but the metrical pattern has a long element. It starts out as more dactylo-epitrite but ends with a run of three aristophaneans, an aeolic colon. The third period, purely dactylic, is marked by hiatus in the antistrophe, line 814. The fourth is also dactylic until a final ithyphallic, echoing the end of the first period and tying the stanza together.

A scholion tells us that the opening of each stanza is taken from Stesichorus, though it does not quote the earlier poet's precise words. The dactylo-epitrite meter is typical for Stesichorus, Pindar, and Bacchylides, but Aristophanes does not use it very often; as Parker observes, he "uses dactylo-epitrite rarely, but to interesting effect" (1997, 89). *Knights* has a pure dactylo-epitrite song at 1264–1273 ~ 1290–1299, but otherwise Aristophanes tends to mix it with other meters, as in this song. Because it is associated with high-art poets of the past, it is the appropriate meter for the Pindaric poet of *Birds*, and for the high-flown chorus of *Clouds*. Here, the allusion to Stesichorus, in both words and meter, "suggests an alliance between the grand old poet, the skilled poet-comedian, . . . and the Muse who inspires both against the bogus, would-be-grand poets of the present day" (Parker 1997, 8–9). Metrical allusion or emulation can sometimes extend to metrical parody, most obviously in *Frogs* where Aeschylus and Euripides satirize each other's metrical quirks (1264–1363); on metrical terminology in this passage, see Mahoney (2007).

After the opening adapted from Stesichorus, each stanza refers to contemporary tragic poets, Carcinus and sons in the strophe and Morsimus and Melanthius in the antistrophe. Carcinus had won at the City Dionysia in 446, but in this song he seems to be having trouble writing another play; Olson (1998) *ad loc.* suggests "Karkinos is allegedly so lacking in talent that even he is surprised when he produces something." Perhaps he has not had a significant play since the victory 20-odd years earlier. Is this the first recorded appearance of the schoolchild's standard excuse, "the dog ate my homework"? His sons are dancers who appear at the end of *Wasps* (1501–1537). Morsimus is great-nephew of Aeschylus, but Aristophanes treats him as a rather poor poet in passing insults in *Knights* (401) and *Frogs* (151). Melanthius comes in for abuse in *Birds* (151) apparently for a skin condition; Aristophanes does not mention his poetry elsewhere. The chorus asks the Muse to play with them, not with these tragic poets, not only because the other poets are not as good but also because they write tragedy, and now that Peace has been restored to earth, comedy is more appropriate.

The second period moves from dactylo-epitrite to aeolic. Dale (1948, 182) points out that "it is quite usual for the dactylo-epitrites of drama to disintegrate, as it were, at some point in the stanza into separate dactylic and iambic or trochaic cola, often reassembling into orthodox compounds in a subsequent period." Here, the ithyphallics in the first and last periods are iambic, related to E, and the aristophaneans of the second period are aeolic but, as Dale notes, "treated as if they were orthodox hemiepe" (183). The colon is —⏑⏑—⏑—, which is something like a dragged D, or like D⁻ with one short left out. As both aeolic forms and dactylo-epitrite mix single-short and double-short cola, the effect is not jarring.

In the dactylic third period, the bombastic insulting compounds are prominent because the word ends all match: strophe and antistrophe have the same rhythm. Moreover, in each stanza, the compounds at the ends of the cola rhyme, ending in -ας in the strophe and in -αι in the antistrophe. Obviously, nouns of the same declension in the same case will end the same way, but Aristophanes seems to have taken care to place the ones with matching endings in matching positions; there are other words in each stanza with different endings, so the arrangement seems not to be accidental. Both cola end in two long elements. The second is an ordinary hexameter with the final long element contracted as it always is in epic, but the first colon has an odd number of elements. It ends in —⏕—, which is a dactyl with its long element contracted followed by one more long element, in other words by a dactyl missing its second element entirely.

The final period starts with a pure dactylic colon, echoing the third period, then a hemiepes, as if returning briefly to dactylo-epitrite, and then ends with an ithyphallic, echoing the one earlier in the stanza. The song has moved from short cola, set off by word breaks, to longer dactylic runs, and this final period moves back to the shorter cola, making a metrical ring.

Conclusion

Aristophanes' comedies have the same sort of structure as contemporary tragedies, with songs sung by a chorus, actors, or both; spoken dialog mostly in iambo-trochaic meters; and anapestic passages at points of transition. He uses such "transitional anapests" less often than the tragic poets and uses a larger set of dialog meters. The songs are generally metrically straightforward, possibly also musically uncomplicated (though we have no way of knowing this), to let the humorous words come through clearly.

GUIDE TO FURTHER READING

Parker (1997) is the standard reference on Aristophanes' practice, particularly in the lyrics. Her introduction is a useful orientation to classical Greek metrical practice, not limited to Aristophanes himself, and she continues with analysis of every sung passage in the 11 plays. See also Gasparov (1996) for a historically oriented overview of quantitative meters. West (1982) is the main handbook on Greek meter in English. West (1992) explains what is known about ancient Greek music, with transcriptions of the extant fragments. A good example of how metrical analysis can bring out additional details in a drama is Scott (1984).

REFERENCES

Dale, A.M. (1948). *The Lyric Metres of Greek Drama*. Cambridge: Cambridge University Press.

Gasparov, M. L. (1996). *A History of European Versification*, trans. G. S. Smith and M. Tarlinskaja, ed. G. S. Smith with L. Holford-Strevens. Oxford. [Original publication Очерк истории европейского стиха, Moscow, 1989]

Henderson, J. (1998). *Aristophanes: Clouds, Wasps, Peace*. Loeb Classical Library 488, Cambridge.

Mahoney, A. (2007). The feet of Greek and Sanskrit verse. In: *Greek and Latin From an Indo-European Perspective. (Proceedings of the Cambridge Philological Society supplementary volume 32.)* (ed. C. George, M. McCullagh, B. Nielsen, et al.). Cambridge: Cambridge University Press.

Mahoney, A. (2014). "Colometry in Vergil's hexameters: structure, style, and sense," New England Classical Journal 41 (4) (2014), 320–331.

Olson, S.D. (1998). *Aristophanes: Peace*. Oxford: Oxford University Press.

Parker, L.P.E. (1997). *The Songs of Aristophanes*. Oxford: Oxford University Press.

Scott, W.C. (1984). *Musical Design in Aeschylean Theater*. Hanover: University Press of New England.

Watkins, C. (1995). *How to Kill a Dragon: Aspects of Indo-European Poetics*. Oxford: Oxford University Press.

West, M.L. (1982). *Greek Metre*. Oxford: Oxford University Press.

West, M.L. (1992). *Ancient Greek Music*. Oxford: Oxford University Press.

West, M.L. (2001). *Documents of Ancient Greek Music*. Oxford: Oxford University Press.

Wilson, N.G. (ed.) (2007). *Aristophanis Fabulae*. Oxford: Clarendon Press.

CHAPTER 4

Style, Language, and Obscenity

Stephen E. Kidd

Introduction

Aristophanes is probably the luckiest comedian ever. In a landscape of weighty classics – epic with its desperate struggles for *kleos*, tragedy with its *oimoi*'s and *aiai*'s, history with its bleak analyses, and philosophical dialogue with its probing questions – Aristophanes stands out as the lone voice of classical Greek literature talking about the more immediate parts of our lives: what goes on in the kitchen, the bedroom, and the outhouse. And he does this in no uncertain terms: we find in Aristophanes a lexical rainbow of particulars from cheese-graters, ladles, and lentil soup, to fellating, foreskin, and doggie-style, to shitting, diarrhea, and unsightly garment stains – not to mention long lists of obscenities that we could never learn if only the other genres survived. For whatever reason, all these particulars seem to have some relationship to that other phenomenon Aristophanes practically monopolizes in this period – laughter. And this is what makes him so incredibly lucky: he has become, through the sheer act of surviving, not just a comedian of the classical period, but The Comedian.

It is sometimes easy to forget this fact when discussing Aristophanes' style. Even though there were dozens of other comedians writing about the same things that Aristophanes was writing about, and hundreds of comedies rapid-firing the same sorts of jokes, all of these comedies have been lost but for a handful of fragments. If we were writing about the style of some fifth-century tragedian – say, Euripides – our first step would be to compare him to those other two surviving tragedians (Aeschylus and Sophocles) and ask: what makes Euripides' style unique? With Aristophanes, by contrast, what tends to happen is that his writing style gets compared not to his closest rivals – for example, Cratinus and Eupolis – but to non-comic authors like Euripides or later romantic comedians like Menander, who was writing a different genre of comedy altogether. The outcome of such stylistic comparisons is that Aristophanes often appears to be not just refreshing but revolutionary, since his "style" amounts to the stuff of Old Comedy itself – jokes, mockery, obscenities, and the earthy vocabularies of bodily pleasures.

As I will suggest in this chapter, however, a study of Aristophanic style needs to distinguish, first and foremost, Aristophanes from the Old Comedy that he represents. If *langue* is the traditional term for the sum total of what's spoken in a language, and *parole* is the language used by one particular speaker, we might think of an Old Comic *langue* within which there is an Aristophanic *parole*. It is the latter – what is specific to Aristophanes – that we are searching for when searching for an author's "style." What happens instead – again, because Aristophanes is the sole survivor – is that stylistic analyses tend to light upon the Old Comic *langue* itself. But is it possible to discern an Aristophanic *parole* within the Old Comic *langue* and not treat the two as identical? I begin with a couple of excellent treatments of Aristophanes' style – one written by the modern critic Michael

A Companion to Aristophanes, First Edition. Edited by Matthew C. Farmer and Jeremy B. Lefkowitz.
© 2024 John Wiley & Sons, Inc. Published 2024 by John Wiley & Sons, Inc.

Silk, the other written by an ancient authority, Plutarch. Both stylistic studies are enriching, but it often seems that the style being described pertains as much to Old Comedy as it does to Aristophanes. I then offer three close readings of three pairs of passages, comparing and contrasting Aristophanes' treatment of a theme with a treatment by one of his rivals. The point here is not to claim something that is definitively "Aristophanic" – a tall order considering the utter lack of complete, non-Aristophanic comedies for contrast – but, rather, to imagine how we would treat Aristophanes' style if he were not the lone survivor of this distinctive brand of comedy.

Aristophanes' Style: A Modern and Ancient View

One of the best modern discussions of Aristophanes' style is found in Michael Silk's *Aristophanes and the Definition of Comedy*. Ranging across centuries of different authors, including several modern ones, Silk manages to capture not just the ebullient spirit but also core essentials of Aristophanes' verbal brilliance. After discussing the notion of "mobility" – the way an author shifts lexical registers, tone, and technique in their writing – and noticing how Aristophanes indulges in such mobility with remarkable frequency, Silk proceeds to organize his stylistic observations into three broad categories. Aristophanes' style can be recognized by (1) its physicality, (2) its tendency toward accumulations, and (3) its discontinuity.[1]

With "physicality," Silk has in mind examples like the following: in *Acharnians*, Dikaiopolis considers the various "treaties" (*spondai*) on offer from Sparta. *Spondai* in Greek can mean either "treaty" or "libations" (since pouring libations were traditionally part of the treaty-making ceremony), but Aristophanes, instead of resting on that abstract notion of "treaty" – as we would find in other genres – takes the word in a physical, gustatory direction: Dikaiopolis actually tastes these treaties/libations (186–92). When he tries the "five-year" sample, he says, "Yuck!... it smells of pitch and fixing ships." When he tries the "10-year" sample, he says, "These samples smell of embassies to cities..." To the 30-year sample, he exclaims, "Dionysia! These smell of ambrosia and nectar, and not having to get three days worth of provisions; they are saying in my mouth: go wherever you want!" "Treaties," in short, are not left as abstractions but converted into something physical and sensuous. We could include many other examples here: for "treaties" alone, Aristophanes, the following year in *Knights*, brings out physical "treaties" on stage, now two women that are the objects of the lead character, Demos', desire. When he sees them, Demos says (1390–1), "My! How gorgeous they are! Am I allowed to thirty-yearify them?" Here, we are not tasting a "30-year" treaty but being asked to imagine it as a physical sex act. There is more to "physicality," though, than making abstract concepts into concrete and sensuous objects: Silk also includes Aristophanes' rich lexicon of specifics ("an all purpose container: A dish for dirt, a prosecutions pot, a lamp... a tray" *Ach.* 936–9), as well as that "most aggressively physical feature of Aristophanic poetry," obscenity ("Grab my cock, hand it round! Girls get it up!", *Ach.* 1216–17).[2]

The second category on Silk's list is "accumulations." Aristophanes tends to pile up words in a lexical heap, rather than parcel out each word image over larger syntactical units. These accumulations occur not only at the level of the sentence – where we regularly find lists like "garlic, spring cucumbers, pomegranate, apple" (*Peace* 1001) or, from *Clouds* (1012–15): "glistening chest, fresh complexion, big shoulders, little tongue, big butt, short cock" – but also at the level of the word, where we find accumulative compounds like *tribolektrapel'* or *gliskhrantilogexepitriptou* (Clouds 1003–4), the longest being the 79-syllable compound describing a celebratory meal, found at the end of *Assembly Women* (136). What is the purpose of such accumulations? Silk describes it well: whether at the level of the sentence or the word, the effect is one of "relish" and a "gusto [that] is palpable, irrespective of the satirical or non-satirical function of the new composite" (135).

---

[1] Silk (2000) 121–5 for physicality, 126–135 for accumulations, and 136–59 for discontinuity.
[2] I am using Silk's translations here to avoid confusion and will continue to do so while discussing Silk's examples.

Silk's third category is "discontinuity." If Aristophanes starts a sentence with one idea or in one register, it is very unlikely that he will end the sentence with that idea or register. Instead, he "switches" (137). For example, if a sentence begins with standard language, he will switch to an absurd coinage; if it begins politely he'll switch to something indecent ("sighing, yawning, stretching, *farting*") (*Ach.* 30); if it begins with everyday language, he'll switch to paratragic language ("I know one thing I saw that *did entrance my heart*", *Ach.* 5). As Silk puts it, often "the principle is of a sudden switch *from* a norm *to* something incompatible with it—and then a switch back again" (138). Verbal disjunctions bring cognitive surprises to the audience, and such disjunctions are ubiquitous in Aristophanes, from "devoted to my country and my toes" to "to country-folk you meant oats and salvation" to – as was seen above – "smelling of pitch and naval preparations" (146–7). We can think of all of these verbal phenomena under the heading of the "discontinuous."

There is much to appreciate in Silk's treatment of Aristophanes' style via these three categories: physicality, accumulations, and discontinuity. But it is hard not to wonder: should we imagine that the other comedians were doing something different? Was their poetry in fact not physical, accumulative, and discontinuous? Silk himself notes in regard to physicality (121) that it is a "predisposition of all comedy" (and we might add here Bakhtin's more general notion of that celebratory spirit opposed to all that is "high, spiritual, ideal, abstract").[3] The same might be said of the category of the "discontinuous": switching registers or concepts mid-sentence – whether it be with an obscenity, a coinage, or simply a verbal surprise – is a phenomenon that humor theorists have long studied under the rubric of "incongruity." If, as incongruity theorists maintain, all jokes function via some clash of two disparate ideas – whether the clash arises from a word that does not fit the context, an obscenity that does not fit the polite tone, a tragic bombast that does not fit the lowly situation being described, or some other incompatibility – how would Aristophanes' rivals have been able, as comedians, to make audience's laugh at all, if only Aristophanes wrote such discontinuous zingers?

Aristophanes' style in Silk thus starts to look a lot like the style of Old Comedy. But such blurring is a phenomenon not just found in modern writers. Plutarch, writing in the late first-/early second-century CE, compares Aristophanes with the late fourth-/early third-century BCE comedian Menander. Far more popular than Aristophanes in Plutarch's day, Menander was part of the school curriculum, wielding a cultural capital similar to that of Shakespeare today. Plutarch (or his speaker) is clearly not a fan of Aristophanes, so we are a good distance away from Silk's positive assessment:

> You find coarseness, vulgarity and low-class talk in Aristophanes' language, but never in Menander's. The uneducated average joe is captivated by Aristophanes' style, but the educated person hates it: I mean things like antitheseis, similar endings, and puns... Aristophanes uses these stylistic features often, without good timing, and in a way that makes us cringe.[4]

Plutarch proceeds to list a number of examples of these puns, antitheseis, and homoioteleuta, which we might arrange according to Plutarch's categories, even though most instances partake in more than one. For the puns, there are, for example, "I will arrive at Gela via gelastics" and the military commander Lamachus' lament toward the end of *Acharnians*: "this plume-moth has eaten up my plumes." For the homoioteleuta, examples include "this guy is blowing either north-east or litigious-beast" and "he doused the bankers, because they weren't bankers but wankers." For the antitheseis, we find Dikaiopolis and Lamachus' interchange toward the end of *Acharnians*: "Lam. Bring here the gorgon-faced shield circle." "Dik. And for me the cheese-faced cake circle!" Although it is impossible to translate puns and other such verbal antics, it is enough to notice that

---

[3] Silk (2000) 121: "the predisposition of all comedy toward the material, toward the 'specific embodiment'..."; Bakhtin (1984) 19: "The essential principle of grotesque realism is degradation, that is, the lowering of all that is high, spiritual, ideal, abstract." Cf. Silk (2000b) 300.
[4] Plutarch *Comparison of Aristophanes and Menander*, 853b. My translation.

Plutarch – whatever we make of his judgment of Aristophanes – is acute in his observation of stylistic features. His list of Aristophanic puns, antitheseis, and homoioteleuta can be extended for many more pages, since, formally speaking, such "nauseating nonsense" is the stuff of Aristophanic poetry.

Plutarch may censure Aristophanes for "jokes that are bitter and harsh, containing a vicious, painful fierceness" (854c) and feel disgust at his relentless torrent of puns and wordplay, but, in this case, context is everything. All of these stylistic observations are made not simply about Aristophanes in a vacuum, as it were, but Aristophanes as a contrast to the smooth and polished Menander, who was writing a very different brand of romantic comedy roughly a century later. How would Plutarch's observations on Aristophanes' style read if they were set, not against that later romantic comedian but against the comedians of Aristophanes' day? Should we imagine that Aristophanes' contemporary rivals generally avoided puns and other cheap verbal fireworks? Did they, unlike Aristophanes, avoid "bitter and harsh" jokes? Or does Plutarch's comparison of Aristophanes and Menander ultimately boil down to a general stylistic comparison between Old Comedy and New Comedy – which is to say, Plutarch isn't identifying anything particularly "Aristophanic" at all? If we turn to some examples from Aristophanes' rivals, this stylistic picture becomes clearer still.

"Aristophanic" Style in the Other Comedians

To begin with Plutarch's puns, antitheseis, and homoioteleuta, Plutarch offered the ongoing responsion game between Dikaiopolis and Lamachus: "Lam. Bring here the gorgon-faced shield circle. Dik. And for me the cheese-faced cake circle!" It is easy to think of such style as Aristophanic if we compare it to the stichomythia of Euripides or Menander, but far less so when we compare it to a snippet of dialog from Aristophanes' comic rivals, for example, Eupolis. In Eupolis' *Dyers* fr. 84 we find the following interchange: Speaker A claims "The treatment I am receiving is unholy, *by the goddesses (Numphas)!*" to which Speaker B responds "Long deserved, *by the cabbages (krambas)!*" Plutarch would be groaning as much at Eupolis as Aristophanes.[5] What about puns like Aristophanes' "I will arrive at Gela via gelastics" and "this plume-moth has eaten up my plumes"? Standard fare, it seems: Archippus repeatedly puns on fish names in his comedy *Fish* (fr. 16): Speaker A asks: "What are you saying? That there are soothsayers in the sea?" to which Speaker B responds: "Sturgeons (*galeoi*), the best of all soothsayers", punning on *Galeotai*, the soothsayers of Sicily. Cratinus meanwhile gives us the cringeworthy pun on "Syria" (the region) and "syria" (the name of a garment) in *Seriphioi* (fr. 222): Speaker A says, "From there you will travel high up on the breezes to Syria" to which speaker B says, "A useless garment when the north wind blows." Demetrius in his comedy *Sicily* puns on the word for "bread" (*artos*), while Pherecrates puns on the word *kitharos* "flatfish" and *kithara* "lyre": everyone was indulging in puns, it seems, and there are numerous examples.

So much for Plutarch's summary of Aristophanic style, what about Silk's notions of Aristophanes' physicality – that is, his preference for concrete, physical language? Here too, he seems to have kept good company: there is Alcaeus' *Palaestra* fr. 22: "if I tell anything more than a baby mouse," and Crates I's *Lamia* fr. 21 "words sliced thick Thessalian style,"[6] and Cratinus' fr. 314 "having the face of a leathered prawn," and Eupolis' *Cities* fr. 220 description of the politician Syrakosios as one of those "little dogs" barking "on the walls." We could also add the glutton from Hermippus' *Fates* fr. 46 who can "gulp down down the whole of the Peloponnese" and Metagenes' rivers of "sausages and minced meat" (*Thuriopersians* fr. 6) and Pherecrates' "garland of nettles" (*Deserters* fr. 29), and Plato's "men with hairy butts" (*Adonis* fr. 3) – not to mention his observation that pigs, once

---

[5] For antitheseis, compare Ameipsias fr. 9, Cratinus fr. 248, fr. 270, fr. 326, Eup. fr. 116, fr. 157, fr. 270, fr. 331, Hermippus fr. 3, fr. 28.

[6] Crates I fr. 21. For these fragments, I am using Storey's easily accessible translations throughout to reduce confusion.

eaten, leave nothing behind but the "tail, the mud, and the squeal" (*Festivals* fr. 27). Theopompus meanwhile tells us in *Aphrodite* fr. 5 that Philonides' mother had sex with a donkey – and that Philonides was the offspring.

Theopompus' fragment leads us to the related question of obscenity. Is there anything particularly Aristophanic about dropping f-bombs as a matter of poetry? The fragments offer a resounding "hell no!": Ameipsias fr. 23, Eupolis fr. 359, and Pherecrates all say "go to hell!" (*es korakas*). Callias I fr. 14 meanwhile gives us "white ass!" (*leukoproktos*), Cephisodorus fr. 3 says, "I'll be fucked" (*laikasomai*) as well as "wide anused" (*lakkoprokt-*); Crates I fr.20 allows "farted" (*eperdeto*), while Cratinus fr. 3 and 339 revels in "anus" (*proktos*), fr. 27 "leaping and farting," fr. 42 "cow patties and sheep dung," fr. 53 "I found Cercyon taking a crap at dawn and throttled him," and fr. 299 "cock" (*peos*). Eupolis fr. 64 describes Autolycus as "well-drilled" (*eutresios*), fr. 92 gives a special word for "anus" (*batalus*), while fr. 104 tells of "fucked young men," fr. 176 and 240 "shit," and fr. 247 "cunt." Hermippus says, "whore-for-all" (*pasiporne*), Pherecrates fr. 159 says "sluts" (*laikastrias*), and fr. 253 "screwed" (*lekoumesth-*), and Plato fr. 3 says "hairy-anused" and fr. 43, 125, and 188 all contain "fuck" words with fr. 202 on being a fucked politician. Strattis fr. 54 offers "shit" (*kheso*), and there are many more.

So much for physicality and obscenity. What about Silk's category of accumulations? Aristophanes, as we saw earlier, regularly indulges in word piles such as "garlic, spring cucumbers, pomegranate, apple" or "glistening chest, fresh complexion, big shoulders, little tongue, big butt, short cock." But so does, it seems, everyone else: in Callias I fr. 26, we find "soup, fire, turnips, radishes, tree-ripened olives, flat-cakes"; in Cratinus fr. 105, there are "lilies, roses, white lilies, larkspur, violets and bergomot mint..."; in Eupolis *Goats* fr. 13, the goats sing that they "feed off every sort of tree: fir tree, prickly oak, and strawberry tree..." (cf. Eupolis 218, 317, 338). In Metagenes fr. 18, there are "radish, wheat roll, porridge, nuts, soup, pasta," in Nicophon *Hand-to-Mouth* fr. 10 "sardine sellers, charcoal sellers, fig sellers, leather sellers, etc." (cf. 1 and 6), in Pherecrates fr. *Slave-Trainer* fr. 50 there is "sliced eel, squid, lambchop, a slice of sausage, a boiled pigs foot" (cf. 106, 158, 201), and in Philyllius *Cities* fr. 13 a "coal-seller, sieve maker, gardener, barber" (cf. Philyllius 12). The same can be said for the verbal accumulations at the level of the word, such as Aristophanes' *tribolektrapel'* or *gliskhrantilogexepitriptou* (*Clouds* 1004). In Cratinus alone, there is *arguropisteras* (fr. 239), *Androkolonokles* (fr. 281), *euripidaristophanizon* (fr. 342), and *Choeriloekphantides* (fr. 502; cf. Storey 375–6 for Eupolis' compounds). So a tendency toward accumulation does not seem to be particularly Aristophanic either.

Finally, there is discontinuity, which, as we noticed above, resembles the incongruity that many humor theorists consider to be a staple of jokes and comedy in general. In Aristophanes, there were examples like *Wasps* 1118: "who's never picked up an oar, a spear, a *blister* for his country?" (152), or *Peace* 240–1: "Lord of terror, lord of shields, lord of what runs down your legs?" (154). But compare Cratinus fr. 345: "some story has come upon us – an ignorant, *pig-pennish* one" or the paratragedy of Philonides fr. 7, which riffs on Sophocles' (fr. 811) "As for the oaths of women, I write them in water" with something more scandalous: "As for the oaths of adulterers, I write them in ashes" (since singeing of pubic hair was one of the punishments for adulterers). Aristophanes takes us to the heights of discontinuity at *Peace* 174 when Trygaeus breaks the fourth wall and calls to the crane operator ("Crane operator! Pay attention!"), but so does Strattis – not once but twice (*Atalantus* fr. 4, *Phoenician Women* fr. 46).

If all Old Comic poetry indulged in Plutarch's puns, antitheseis, and homoioteleuta, and all Old Comic poetry reveled in Silk's physicality, accumulations, and discontinuity, how do we winnow out something that we might call "Aristophanes' style"?[7] The impulse is to pair up passages of Aristophanes with those of his rivals and see whether Aristophanes is somehow being *more* physical, *more* accumulative, or *more* discontinuous. But this is to describe style in a rather one-dimensional way, as if it could be simply a matter of quantity (Aristophanes is *more* discontinous) or quality

---

[7] Though not quite "style," Silk (2000b) identifies a fixation on tragedy as particularly Aristophanic; Farmer (2017) 19–24 studies early philotragic contemporaries that cannot be easily dismissed as Aristophanic copycats.

(Aristophanes is *better* at being discontinuous). But, as we will see, often the stylistic differences are not a matter of "more" or "better" to be measured on some scale that can only be moved leftward or rightward. Nor should we expect things to work this way: if we consider our appreciations of different comedies and comedians today, we enjoy different comedians for different reasons, and no one would wish to keep only the "best" one, whatever that could mean. Instead, as we will see, Aristophanes and the other comedians simply approach their topics from different angles, applying the various colors of comedy's poetic palette in their own unique ways.

Some Close Readings

Placing a passage of Aristophanes beside a comic fragment and exploring stylistic differences will necessarily exclude a great deal of context. The issue of priority, for example – is one comedian alluding to or riffing on the other, and which comedy came first? – will be set aside. Instead, we will simply think of each passage as two poets trying to work out a particular theme or problem in poetry. Each fragment, of course, works within an over-arching comedy – spoken, for example, by particular characters with particular agenda – but here we will simply treat them as comedic samples, avoiding broader issues of interpretation or reconstruction. Finally, one of the most obvious differences that would strike us immediately if we were listening to these passages in ancient Greek is the meter and rhythm of the poetry. Since we are working in translation, it is best to set that aside as well. Nevertheless, even with all of this removed from our object of inquiry, we still have more than enough to sink our teeth into.

Let us begin with metaphors. In the following example – already paired in the scholia – Aristophanes and Cratinus are describing poetry as a flow of water, but each develops the metaphor in different ways. Here is how Aristophanes does it in *Knights* (526)

>....flowing once on a great deal of praise,
>> he was flowing through the simple plains, and sweeping away from their locations carrying off oak trees and plane trees and his enemies by the roots.

Here's how Cratinus does it in *Wine-Flask* (fr. 198 = schol. to *Knights* 526a):

> Lord Apollo – the flow of words!
> Fountains are splashing: there are twelve springs in his mouth,
> An Ilissus in his throat. What could I say further?
> For if someone will not plug his mouth,
> He will flood everything here with his poems.

Both poets begin the image with the common word for "flow" (*rheo*), and Aristophanes in fact uses the verb twice in that first sentence (*rheusas, errei*) – whether weakly or not, I will leave it to the reader to decide. For Aristophanes, "flow" moves in the direction of a "flood": across the "simple" fields – an esthetic term punningly applied. What is he/the flood sweeping away? Here is where Aristophanes really shines by taking the metaphor's vehicle as far as possible from the tenor like a Homeric simile: we are now talking about the types of trees that this flood is sweeping away (oak trees, plane trees, and so forth), and just as quickly as we have been rubberbanded to those distant images, he pulls us back to the literal: what he is really sweeping away (by the roots) are the "enemies." But like any great image the swept trees cannot fully resolve: who are the oaks supposed to represent? Who the plane trees?

Cratinus does not do this. He clings more tightly to his image (perhaps unexpectedly since Aristophanes' flood is describing the poetry of Cratinus), yet is able to build on it with increasing layers upward, rather than expanding haphazardly outward. Now we are not dealing with the muddy floods of uprooted trees but spring water, implicitly pure: the fountains are "splashing" (like Aristophanes' esthetic "simple," Cratinus' spring water carries its own poetic weight). Unlike Aristophanes, he develops the image with inward precision (how many springs? a dozen; which river? the Ilissus) rather than outward additions (what is the flood destroying?). But where Cratinus really excels is the development of the last two lines: we have not budged from the spring analogy (if we were to follow Aristophanic range, perhaps it would have developed outward with unresolvable water jugs that citizens are bringing to the spring) but have entered a contrafactual. We are now being told not what the spring/mouth is actually doing (as in Aristophanes' river) but what would happen in some other situation: if someone tried to "plug" this fountain/poet, "it will flood everything," as if the force of the water could only be felt by the imagined attempt to restrain it. Then comes the surprise word to draw the fountain-poet image back together: he will flood everything "with poems."

The inclination is to put the two passages side by side and say one is "better" – like Euripides and Aeschylus weighing words in the *Frogs* – as if we could mark off Aristophanes for using *rheo* twice in one sentence, or mark off Cratinus for not taking the vehicle far enough away from the tenor to achieve a more brilliant comic absurdity. But in fact, both excel in their own way, and we can appreciate the differences in each. Aristophanes comes across in the comparison as the greater risk-taker, pulling the metaphor to its limits; Cratinus is the more artful. For Aristophanes, the poet himself *is* the flood, while for Cratinus it is what proceeds from his mouth, that is, his poetry. Just as two comedians today, we would not wish to lose one, even if we had a slight preference for a certain comic flavor. One poet takes us horizontally to the ruthlessly flowing poet river; the other takes us vertically to a fountain gurgling from a poet's mouth. There is more than one way to develop a comic metaphor.

What about jokes? One joke repeated by the comedians over and over again regards an incident that occurred in 408 BCE during the first performance of Euripides' *Orestes*. The lead actor playing Orestes, Hegelochus, fumbled the crucial, solemn line meant to announce Orestes' restored sanity: "After the stormy waves, I once again see calm (*galén'*)," he was supposed to say. Instead, Hegelochus said: "After the stormy waves, I once again see a weasel (*galên*)." Little could Hegelochus have known that the botched syllable would insure his immortality (unlike his more flawless thespian contemporaries). While alive, however, he was regularly reminded of this low point in his professional life. Here is how Aristophanes detonates the joke in *Frogs*. After suffering some (imagined) terror, Xanthias wishes to assure Dionysus that there is no longer anything to be scared about and so deploys the contemporary reference to make the joke (303–4):

> All is well,
> and it's possible for us to say, like Hegelochus:
> "After the stormy waves, I once again see a weasel."
> The witch is gone.

His contemporary Sannyrion makes the same joke in the *Danae*. Zeus is trying to figure out how to get into the chamber where Danae is being held, but he makes this mental pitstop along the way:

> What should I turn into in order to fit into this hole?
> Let's see... I know! I might become a weasel.
> Hegelochus, though, would reveal me—
> the tragedian—and cry out in a loud voice.
> After the stormy waves, I once again see again a weasel.

Aristophanes aims for the quicker setup and punchline. Xanthias and Dionysus have been wringing laughs out of the audience for a number of lines – Dionysus is so terrified that his eyes are closed, and Xanthias is describing all the (nonexistent) terrors Dionysus cannot see – and so Aristophanes wants to milk a few more laughs out of Dionysus' fright with an unexpected incongruity. What is most remarkable here is the simplicity of Aristophanes' side flick of the wrist, the flank attack when we're not expecting it: he does not need to add anything to the joke other than simply quote the line. That is enough to jolt us suddenly from the immediate dramatic context and produce the desired guffaw.

Sannyrion's version meanwhile seems the more baggy of the two: "the tragedian" (*ho tragikos*) of line four seems practically like an unnecessary gloss for "Hegelochus." As Aristophanes shows, all that is needed to spark the joke is the actor's name, yet Sannyrion continues with the plodding: "the tragedian. . ." and takes three lines to do what Aristophanes does in two. But to read it as a failure in this way, I think, would be to mistake what Sannyrion is doing. This joke about Hegelochus has been repeated both on and off the stage since that fateful performance of *Orestes*. Everyone in the audience knows what's coming – probably as soon as the word "weasel" first appears at the end of the line. So what Sannyrion seems to be doing is delaying the punchline on purpose, deferring the expected joke's detonation with "the tragedian. . ." The irritating dilation is its own delight. As with the metaphors, here too we would be missing too much by limiting our analysis to which joke is better. There are so many ways to make a joke, and each comedian finds his own momentary angle.

What about obscenity? One common use of obscenity among the comedians has to do with contemporary politicians. Unlike the great leaders of the past who were characterized by their hard work, bravery, and honest dealings, today's politicians are characterized primarily by their penchant for getting "fucked."[8] Here is how Aristophanes explores this obscenity in *Knights*: the demogogue Cleon and his new political rival, the sausage seller, are arguing over their respective achievements. When Cleon claims to have put an end to the men who allow themselves to "get fucked" (*binoumenous*), the sausage seller retorts (878–80):

> Isn't it clever of you to keep anal watch (*prōktotērein*), and put a stop to those men who allow themselves to get fucked (*tous binoumenous*). There's no way that it wasn't out of envy that you stopped them – so that they not become politicians.

Compare those lines of Aristophanes to a similar fragment from his rival Eupolis where, again, politicians are being described as men who take the "fucked" role (fr. 104):

> King Miltiades and Pericles, please do not allow these fucked young men – who drag the generalship around their ankles – to hold office any longer.

Here too we find this certain breed of new politician – not the great ones from days of yore like Miltiades (brought back to life to set things straight in this play). This new breed lacks the old-time courage and virtue, and instead is characterized by their repeatedly being "fucked" and, presumably, enjoying that position.

Both Aristophanes and Eupolis are dancing around the same theme of sexual preferences and using obscenities in that dance. How might we compare Aristophanes' and Eupolis' use of obscenities here? Aristophanes follows the explosion of his obscenity with a series of negatives, the things which did not happen – "there is *no way* that Cleon was *not* envious," "so that they *not* become politicians" – as if to lend emphasis to the one thing that everyone can agree did happen as a matter of course – these politicians getting fucked. Interestingly, the final surprise joke trigger – "so that they not become *politicians*" – is not formulated according to the usual laws of joke potency, where the verbal surprise ought to come last. Instead, Aristophanes ends the line with one of the blandest and most innocuous words in Greek ("become"). The obscenity itself, meanwhile, gets tucked away in the middle of the verse.

What about the Eupolis fragment? Here, we find the obscenity "fucked" at a more prominent position at the end of the second line. "Stop allowing those young men, who allow themselves to be *fucked*." Aristophanes' obscenity is characterized by nonchalance, but this one is more emphatic, as if Eupolis were not simply loosening the audience with an everyday obscenity (much as we might say "fuck/fucking" today with friends), but forcing it to work for laughs as if the obscenity itself functioned as the joke's trigger. Unlike Aristophanes, who follows his obscenity with a string of negatives, Eupolis turns to a metaphor: these young men drag around their ankles "the generalship." Like the "fucked" of the second line, the "generalship" of the third line is saved for last,

---

[8] Although this may appear homophobic to modern readers, the ancient phobia is surprisingly different (though no less hateful). For the classic introduction, see Dover (1989).

detonating the surprise of the joke. Rather than preferring a more nonchalant version of obscenity like Aristophanes, Eupolis wishes to harness the force of obscenity with a more typical joke frame.

We could extend these stylistic comparisons with many more examples, but it is worth remembering that, due to the necessity of selection, such comparisons can be nothing more than an exercise. What Aristophanes does in one passage is not what he necessarily does in another passage, so nothing of the above ought to be taken as representative of Aristophanes as a whole (or any other comedian). At the same time, such close readings are the stuff of stylistic analysis: when we read the comparisons in the late-antique scholar Platonios that "Aristophanes has forged a style balanced between [Cratinus and Eupolis], since he is not too bitter, like Cratinus, nor <too> charming, like Eupolis, but possesses both the power of Cratinus against wrongdoers and the pervasive charm of Eupolis,"[9] we are at such an abstract level of description that Aristophanes' style seems to slip through our fingers altogether. Modern critics do much better: for example, Zimmermann (2000: 278) who describes a rival's comic song as lacking "the spirit, humour, and malignancy that we find in comparable passages in Aristophanes" and suggests that "perhaps [Aristophanes] really *was* the best" (2000: 279).[10] Even with such descriptions, though, there is a noticeable gravitational pull toward those *Frogs*-ian scales of "better." But, as we have seen, "who is better?" often obscures more of style than it captures.

It is also worth remembering that, if we continued in our close readings, weaving together a genuinely "Aristophanic" style against the background of Old Comedy, something else would happen long before that style could fully emerge. We would encounter a fundamental problem. A handful of fragments can only get us so far, and, no matter how much we conjecture and contextualize, too many crucial contrasts have been lost. As Chremylus puts it in *Wealth*: "our cloak has quite a few holes in it" (715).

Conclusion

This leads us to the final point about Aristophanes' style. I have been suggesting that when considering Aristophanes, we ought to think of an Aristophanic *parole* that works within an Old Comic *langue*. That is, we should be observing not *that* Aristophanes makes jokes, but how he makes jokes differently; not *that* he uses obscenities but how he uses obscenities in a characteristically "Aristophanic" way. But this is only a half-truth. The reality is that when students are first delighted by their experience reading Aristophanes – the freshness, the vividness, the fact that no one else in classical Greek literature seems to be doing what he is doing, the Aristophanes that Silk presents so well – Aristophanes' status as the lone exemplar seems to be an irreducible part of that joyful experience. As strange as it is to say, his singular nature seems to be somehow part of his style. Not historically, of course, but what we all experience as his style today is deeply related to the fact that he is the only one in an otherwise fairly serious canon who is able to make us feel those exhilarating Old Comic feelings. Once we are drawn in by *that* Aristophanes, we of course wish to dig deeper, put him in his context, and discover what makes Aristophanes "Aristophanic" as opposed to his Old Comic rivals. But this "Aristophanes," unlike the first, can never be more than a partial reconstruction, even a mirage.

We might think, then, of two versions of "Aristophanes' style" – the one experienced by the first-time reader (where the style essentially is the Old Comic *langue*) and the one reconstructed by the Aristophanic scholar (where the style is the Aristophanic *parole*). Neither "Aristophanes" should be

---

[9] Platonius *On the Different Sorts of Styles* (Storey i.4 = Koster II). Cf. Anonymous *On Comedy* (Storey i.7 = Koster V): "Now Aristophanes was more technically adept than his contemporaries in creating comedy, and being recognized as such shone forth among them all." The translations are Storey's.

[10] Cf. Storey's concession "Aristophanes may have done it better" (377), and Silk (2000) 313 for Dover and Norwood's assessments.

privileged over the other. While the scholar's Aristophanes may be the more historically accurate, the first-time reader's Aristophanes – the Aristophanes who makes us laugh at 2500-year-old jokes and regales us with other stylistic delights – is never really escaped. It is the Aristophanes we all know – and will always know – best.

GUIDE TO FURTHER READING

For accessible studies published in English on Aristophanes' style, Silk (2000: 98–159) manages to convey so much of Aristophanes' ebullience without directly tackling issues of jokes and humor; Robson (2009: 52–78) and Hall and Swallow (2020) focus on humor, which is in many ways inextricable from a comedian's style; Zimmerman (2014: 135–41) covers many aspects in a short space; still valuable are older treatments like Stanford (1958: xxxiii–xliii) and Starkie (1909: xxxviii–lxii), who offers handy lists of puns and such. For comparisons of Aristophanes' style and language to that of contemporary comedians, see Zimmermann (2000), Silk (2000b), Storey (2003: 366–77), and Olson (2017: 24–27). For language – a topic which includes host of issues beyond that covered by "style" – see Willi (2002: 111–68) and (2010: 471–510) on the language of old comedy more broadly; Colvin (1999) on dialects. For obscenity, Henderson (1991 [1975]) is the classic study (cf. Robson 2009: 115–33); see Halliwell (2008: 215–63) and Rosen (2015) for old comedy's obscenities (*aischrologia*) in its festival context.

REFERENCES

Bakhtin, M. (1984). *Rabelais and His World*. H. Iswolsky, trans. Bloomington: University of Indiana Press.
Colvin, S. (1999). *Dialect in Aristophanes and the Politics of Language in Ancient Greek Literature*. Oxford: Oxford University Press.
Dover, K.J. (1989). *Greek Homosexuality*. Cambridge, MA: Harvard University Press.
Farmer, M. (2017). *Tragedy on the Comic Stage*. Oxford: Oxford University Press.
Hall, E. and Swallow, P. (ed.) (2020). *Aristophanic Humour: Theory and Practice*. London: Bloomsbury.
Halliwell, S. (2008). *Greek Laughter*. Cambridge: Cambridge University Press.
Henderson, J. (1991[1975]). *The Maculate Muse: Obscene Language in Attic Comedy*. Oxford: Oxford University Press.
Olson, S.D. (ed.) (2017). *Fragmenta comica: Kommentierung der Fragmente der griechischen Komödie. 8, 1, Eupolis, Testimonia and Aiges-Demoi (frr. 1-146): introduction, translation, commentary*. Heidelberg: Verl. Antike.
Robson, J. (2009). *Aristophanes: An Introduction*. London: Duckworth.
Rosen, R. (2015). Aischroloy in old comedy and the question of 'Ritual Obscenity'. In: *Carnaval et comédie* (ed. M. Bastin-Hammou and C. Orfanos), 19–33. Besançon: Pr. Universitaires de Franche-Comté.
Silk, M. (2000). *Aristophanes and the Definition of Comedy*. Oxford: Oxford University Press.
Silk, M. (2000b). Aristophanes versus the rest: comic poetry in Old Comedy. In: *The Rivals of Aristophanes: Studies in Athenian Old Comedy* (ed. D. Harvey and J. Wilkins), 299–315. London: Duckworth.
Stanford, W.B. (1958). *Aristophanes: The Frogs*. London: Bristol Classical Press.
Starkie, W.J.M. (1909). *The Acharnians of Aristophanes*. London: Macmillan and Co.
Storey, I.C. (2003). *Eupolis, Poet of Old Comedy*. Oxford, New York: Oxford University Press.
Willi, A. (2002). Languages on Stage: Aristophanic language, cultural history, and Athenian identity. In: *The Language of Greek Comedy* (ed. A. Willi), 111–168. Oxford: Oxford University Press (check).
Willi, A. (2010). The language of old comedy. In: *Brill's Companion to the Study of Greek Comedy* (ed. G.W. Dobrov), 471–510. Leiden: Brill.
Zimmermann, B. (2000). Lyric in the fragments of old comedy. In: *The rivals of Aristophanes: studies in Athenian Old Comedy* (ed. D. Harvey, J.M. Wilkins, K.J. Dover, and M. Tristram), 273–284. Swansea: Classical Press of Wales.
Zimmermann, B. (2014). Aristophanes. In: *The Oxford Handbook of Greek and Roman Comedy* (ed. in A. Scafuro and M. Fontaine), 132–159. Oxford: Oxford University Press.

CHAPTER 5

Images of Greek Comedy

Carl A. Shaw

Introduction

Modern audiences can best access Ancient Greek comedy through textual remains, but ancient audiences, including visual artists, thought of comedy above all as performance, not as text. Extant visual evidence, with its numerous images of Greek comedy, can thus vastly expand our understanding of the original theatrical experience. Ancient vases, in particular, enhance elements alluded to in comic texts and illuminate details that are omitted from scripts, such as the nature of costumes, masks, props, scenery, and stage action, as well as more abstract concepts like the role (or lack of role) of dramatic illusion. There are, however, a number of challenges when analyzing ancient images of Greek comedy, and any study of comic visual representations, particularly in relation to Aristophanes, is destined to disappoint with its multitude of unavoidable caveats. In this chapter, we will consider some of the connections between Greek visual evidence, ancient performance, and extant texts, as well as some of the limitations of this sort of comparative analysis. In the end, we will see that although conclusions are almost always uncertain and are often varied and various, visual materials (including those from disparate times and places) offer an extensive range of possibilities for reflecting on and understanding Aristophanes' comic texts as performative experience.

Contemporaneous Athenian Evidence

It is frustrating, and perhaps more than a little surprising, that of the vast number of extant Greek vases depicting ancient comic performance, no visual evidence from Aristophanes' lifetime definitively illustrates his comedies. This absence of evidence may be due in part to chance, but it is also probably due to particular artistic conventions of the time. During the first half-century or so of comedy's performance, Attic visual artists appear to have been interested above all in representing choruses, but just as Aristophanes' career began in 427, they shifted their attention to actors, which are more challenging to identify than choruses. In addition, as Taplin (1993, 79–80) observes, few Athenian visual artists embraced either the theatricality or the grotesqueness of Old Comedy. So even if artists were inclined to depict Aristophanic performance, they did not necessarily present it in the mode we associate with images of ancient Greek comedy (most of which is constructed from a multitude of South Italian evidence), with distorted costumes and masks.

Despite these challenges, there are some rather interesting pieces of evidence that illuminate Aristophanic comic performance and, more generally, comic conventions of the time. For example, a fascinating Attic red-figure chous (Figure 5.1) from around the start of Aristophanes' career

---

A Companion to Aristophanes, First Edition. Edited by Matthew C. Farmer and Jeremy B. Lefkowitz.
© 2024 John Wiley & Sons, Inc. Published 2024 by John Wiley & Sons, Inc.

Figure 5.1 Comic actor portraying Perseus onstage before two seated audience members. Attic red-figure chous, Painter of the Perseus Dance, ca. 420, Athens NM BΣ 518. Source: With permission from Konstantinos Kontos, National Archaeological Museum, Athens.

depicts a comic, costumed Perseus onstage, standing before the *skênê*, holding a sickle and *kibisis* (Perseus' signature magical sack). The vase is not of the highest artistic quality and does not add a great deal to our understanding of any particular play of Aristophanes, but it is exceptional for its overt theatricality, showing the stage and members of the audience, and even more so for its detailed depiction of Perseus' costume. While we typically think of comic costumes as bulging with padded stomach, breasts, and buttocks, Perseus is portrayed here less exaggeratedly. The artist has incorporated some unmistakably comic elements: an oversized, coiled phallus; an outward-facing stance (which was reserved for slaves and comic figures); a not-quite comically distorted but decidedly not-tragic mask; and lines drawn on ankles and wrists to indicate a comic body suit (*somation*). On the other hand, his figure is well proportioned in a way that is not common to ancient representations of comedy. It is impossible to know whether this is an accurate portrayal of the production's costume and mask, but it does suggest a broader range of costume types than we typically associate with Aristophanic comic actors. This vase makes it seem quite possible that Athenian comic characters, including those in Aristophanes' comedies, were not always costumed as grotesquely as comic actors on South Italian vases of the following century.

A roughly drawn oinochoe (Figure 5.2) found in a well in the Athenian Agora provides another noteworthy piece of contemporary visual evidence, and as the only Attic vase that definitively illustrates a known Athenian comedy, it is especially valuable to modern scholars. Two figures on the vase, one labeled ("Di)onysus" and the other labeled "Phor(mio)," represent the main characters from Eupolis' *Taxiarchoi*, which was performed in Athens during Aristophanes' lifetime, around 415. In the play, which is very fragmentary, the god Dionysus decides to join the military as a means of escaping someone or something; the Athenian general Phormio (an actual contemporary historical figure known for his severe and disciplined nature) trains the god in a range of military fundamentals. The plot juxtaposes the excessively hedonistic figure of Dionysus with the

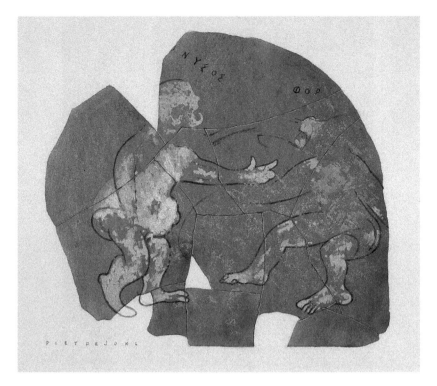

Figure 5.2 Actors portraying (Di)onysus and Phor(mio) from Eupolis' *Taxiarchoi* (ca. 415), Attic polychrome oinochoe, c. 400, Agora P23985. Drawing by Piet de Jong. Source: With permission from Piet de Jong, American School of Classical Studies at Athens: Agora Excavations.

harsh, militaristic Phormio, and much of the humor lies in Dionysus' unwillingness and inability to adapt to military life. The scene on the vase, while hastily painted, clearly shows Dionysus with a padded comic costume and a distorted comic mask. Phormio too wears a comically proportioned *somation*, which suggests that, in Athens, heroic comic figures during the time of Aristophanes acted both with and – like Perseus above – without excessively distorted, padded costumes.

While neither of the previous vases illustrates a comedy by Aristophanes, they both provide insight into staging conventions of the age. Two more Attic vases, both of which illustrate the same comic performance, offer what is likely the most famous visual representation of a comedy from Aristophanes' lifetime, and have in fact repeatedly been connected to Aristophanes' own plays. The first (formerly Malibu 82.AE.83) well-known Attic red-figure calyx krater (ca. 425) shows a double-aulos player between two costumed fighting cocks; the second (Figure 5.3) shows a dancer in comic bird costume. Scholars once linked the image of fighting roosters and an aulos player to the chorus of Aristophanes' *Birds*, but since roosters are not among the avian figures named in the play, the connection has been dismissed. A more plausible link can be made to the *agon* of Aristophanes' *Clouds*, since, according to an ancient scholar's comment (Σ N. 889c), Greater and Lesser Arguments were portrayed onstage as fighting cocks. The main difficulty with this argument is the depiction of only one bird in Figure 5.3. The remarkable similarity of costume on both vases suggests that they almost certainly illustrate the same performance, but an artist wishing to represent the *Clouds' agon* would presumably have included both roosters to convey the confrontational nature of the scene. Ultimately, it is impossible to know whether or not the fighting roosters on these vases represent an Aristophanic performance. Nevertheless, the inclusion of an aulos player on both vases (Figure 5.3, on the reverse), the clear signs of costuming, and the humorously oversized *phalloi* clearly suggest a comic performance. These vases are, then, even if not illustrations of an Aristophanic comedy, invaluable for the window they offer into the elaborate style of costuming that was available to Aristophanes as he staged plays with avian choruses and characters.

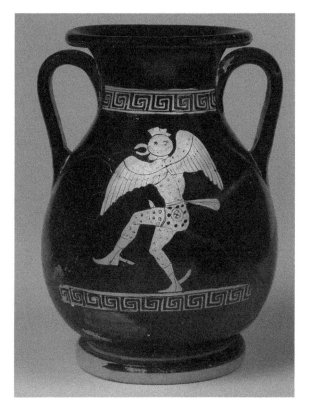

Figure 5.3 Actor dressed as a fighting cock, Attic red-figure Pelike, ca. 425, Atlanta 2008.4.1. Michael C. Carlos Museum, Emory University. Source: Bruce M. White, 2008.

Pre- and Proto-comic Performances in Athens

While the surviving visual evidence from Aristophanes' lifetime is somewhat discouraging, these Attic vases help us imagine certain elements of Aristophanic performance. As we will see in this section, earlier Athenian evidence can also be informative, since a wide range of artistic modes influenced fifth-century comedy. Aristophanes' allusive and parodic style fostered a close engagement with a number of earlier texts, including comic, tragic, epic, and lyric works; but popular civic-religious performances also influenced him, and earlier vases can provide insight into Aristophanes' world of non-text-based inspiration. To fully appreciate and understand Aristophanic comedy, we will look at illustrations of Attic performance, especially humorous performance, that predates Aristophanes' own plays: phallic processions, padded komasts, dithyrambic performances, and choral "riders."

Komasts are the earliest comic performers found on Attic vases. Likely imported from Corinth, they are typically depicted with a large padded stomach, breasts, buttocks, and (occasionally) a phallus. These costumes in many ways resemble the costumes of Athenian actors from fifth- and fourth-century comedy, but depictions of komasts decrease in popularity nearly a century before comedy's official introduction to the City Dionysia, making a direct connection unlikely. Although Athenian comic poets may not have integrated these older komastic performers directly into their plays, their costume probably continued to be used in various performative contexts, thereby shaping the development of comedy.

One of the most fascinating examples of a komastic vase comes from a mid-sixth-century Athenian cup (Figure 5.4a) that depicts an oversized komast riding on a phallus pole carried in procession by six men. The padded komast of this vase relates generally to the costumes of Athenian comedy, and the phallus procession represented here, which was a major part of the festival in

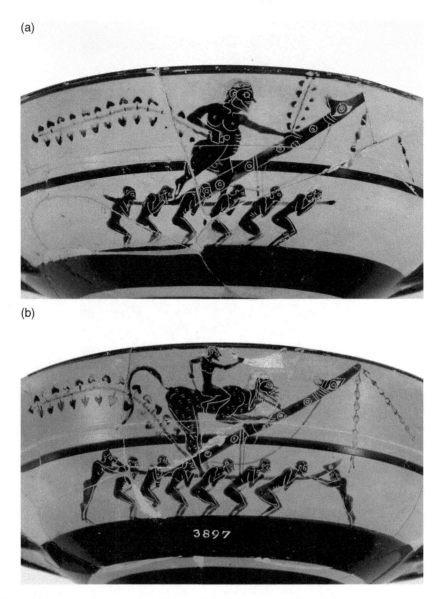

Figure 5.4 (a) Oversized komast riding phallus Pole (Side A), Attic Black-Figure lip cup, unattributed. Florence 3897: Soprintendenza alle Antichità. (b) Oversized satyr riding phallus Pole (Side B), Attic Black-Figure lip cup, unattributed. Florence 3897: Soprintendenza alle Antichità. Source: Stephan Eckard.

honor of Dionysus (note Dionysus' ivy in front of and behind the komast float), relates specifically to the *phallophoria* in Aristophanes' *Acharnians* 241–279. While many details of the phallus-carrying scene are specific to the play (particularly Dicaeopolis' personally negotiated peace treaty), other details seem related to the civic-religious festival. Dicaeopolis starts this section by stating/singing "O Lord Dionysos, may my performance of this procession and this sacrifice be pleasing to you," and twice he tells his slaves to keep the phallus straight, details that no doubt are connected to the phallophoria. All Greek and translations of Aristophanes come from Henderson's Loeb. Similarly, he says that he "will bring up the rear and sing the Phallic Hymn," which starts out "Phales, friend of Bacchus, revel mate, nocturnal rambler, fornicator pederast." Presumably, this song parodies an actual processional song, and the repeated calls for the carriers to keep the phallus erect can be related to the precarious shouldering of the phallus on the vase.

Figure 5.5 Aulos player with actors dressed as horses and riders, Attic black-figure amphora, ca. 540. Berlin Painter. Inv. F 1697. Source: Johannes Laurentius / Art Resource, NY / Antikensammlung, Staatliche Museen, Berlin, Germany.

Early Athenian vases also point to the influence that dithyramb and humorous "rider choruses" had on comedy. Many vases show choruses of men dressed as or riding on animals, including dolphins, horses, ostriches, bulls, and birds. Csapo (1986) and Rusten (2006) have persuasively argued that these animal rider choruses depict dithyrambic performance, and that they connect to Old Comedy's use of animal choruses. An Attic black-figure amphora from around 540, dubbed the Berlin Knights (Figure 5.5), offers what is likely both a humorous rider chorus and an important dithyrambic precursor to Athenian Comedy. On the left, there is a formally dressed aulos player escorting a chorus of three men outfitted as horses; they, in turn, carry three other men wearing helmets. The scene is probably dithyrambic, but its humorous costuming and movement also warrant calling it a "pre-comic" performance: the masks and tails, as well as the ridiculous action of acting like a horse while another man rides on top, are undoubtedly comical. Once again, this vase provides a glimpse into some of the options for the costuming of comic choruses and may help us understand how poets of Old Comedy like Aristophanes staged comedies with animals and animal choruses.

West Greek Comic Vases

While early Attic vases can help illuminate certain elements of Aristophanic comedy, later vases are able to reveal the influence Aristophanes' plays had on Greek visual artists and, possibly, what Aristophanic comedies themselves looked like. There are, though, a number of dangers in using later evidence to reflect back on Aristophanes' plays. Not only must we remember that these vases were painted chronologically and geographically distant from Aristophanes' original productions, but it is also important to remember that, despite certain general conventions, individual artists always had the freedom to make individual choices. While many vases may accurately display a particular comic scene, they are not photographs of performance, and there were innumerable opportunities for variation. Some details may be altered, missed, forgotten, or added. Some scenes may be combined. Some characters may be represented with no discernible markers of costume, while others may be illustrated hyper-realistically, with clear indicators of masks and stage garments. Nevertheless, comic vases produced in Southern Italy (formerly known as the so-called phlyax) are probably the best visual representations of Athenian comedy, including that of Aristophanes.

In previous generations of scholarship, fourth-century comic vases discovered in "Magna Graecia" (i.e. Southern Italy) were connected to native Italic performances, known as phlyax plays, rather than to Athenian fifth-century comedy. The term "phlyax" itself is a misnomer based on Athenaeus' discussion of Italic comic performance but, terminology aside, the date and location of these vases posed serious problems to the notion that they depicted Athenian comedy of the previous century. In the 1980s and 1990s, however, Eric Csapo and Oliver Taplin independently demonstrated that these South Italian wares portray Athenian fifth-century comic productions. Sometime in the second half of the fifth century, it seems, Athenian visual artists moved to Greek colonies in Southern Italy, where they set up shops to make and sell vases to local Greek and non-Greek audiences. From around 400 to 360, as they painted a vast number of comic images in these new artistic centers, they developed a unique character that differed from their Athenian predecessors. As Taplin (1993, 32) observes, "They openly flaunt their theatricality, and they delight in the indecorousness and everyday clutter of comedy."

The most important of these vases (and the one at the heart of Csapo's and Taplin's work) is the so-called Würzburg krater, an Apulian red-figure bell krater (Figure 5.6), that depicts the climactic scene of Aristophanes' *Thesmophoriazusae*. The play's action is precipitated by Euripides' fear that women at the religious Thesmophoria festival are plotting to kill him for his depraved depictions of women on the tragic stage. He decides, therefore, to have an impostor infiltrate the secret rites and convince them of his innocence. With Euripides' fellow tragedian Agathon unwilling to take on this role, he compels his in-law to shave, dress as a woman, and secretly enter the Thesmophorion. The women, though, are alerted to the presence of a spy, and a number of farcical scenes ensue, all of which parody episodes from Euripides' own tragedies. The first, a comic recreation of a scene from Euripides' *Telephus*, is the subject of the Würzburg krater. In the original tragic production, the titular character is recognized as a Greek enemy, and to protect himself, he grabs Agamemnon's child and holds it hostage at an altar, with a knife to its throat. In the *Thesmophoriazusae*, when the

Figure 5.6 Representation of Aristophanes' *Thesmophoriazusae*, Apulian red-figure bell krater, Schiller painter, ca. 370, Würzburg H5697. Martin von Wagner Museum der Universität Würzburg. Source: With permission from C. Kiefer.

women determine that the in-law is male, he re-enacts Telephus' actions by grabbing a baby and running to the altar with a sword. As soon as the women threaten to start a fire beneath him, he unwraps the baby from its swaddling and discovers that it is not a child but a wineskin. A clever and humorous dialog follows, until finally the in-law threatens to cut the "baby's" throat, which upsets the bibulous women.

Although Aristophanes' original play was staged in 411 in Athens, and the Würzburg krater was fabricated approximately 40 years later in Southern Italy, a handful of distinct details make it clear that the two works of art were related:

a) the pseudo-sacrifice takes place at an altar.
b) the in-law's phallus is hidden by a long chiton (*krokotos*, 252–256).
c) the in-law wears a headband (257–260 and 941).
d) the in-law holds a wineskin wearing booties (734).
e) the baby's mother rushes to the altar with a basin to collect the "blood" (i.e. the wine).
f) the in-law wears a beardless mask with marks of stubble from the shaving scene (221–232).
g) the mirror from the previous shaving scene hangs above and between the actors (233).

As Csapo and Taplin have shown, it is very unlikely that any sort of Italian farce served as an intermediary between Aristophanes' *Thesmophoriazusae* and the Würzburg krater. Instead, the artist appears to make a genuine effort to inform viewers that they are looking at a representation of Aristophanes' play. As Csapo (2010: 115) notes, even the mirror, which was almost certainly not onstage during the *Telephus* parody, "impart[s] essential background to the visual narrative," and "is added as a clue to the interpretation of a scene to which it does not strictly belong."

Austin and Olson (2004, lxxvi–lxxvii) note a handful of divergences between the vase and the text, such as a lack of brushwood piled around the altar on the vase, but we must remember that ancient visualizations are almost never exact representations of a text or a photographic reproduction of performance. Artists may not even have had access to a text and, more importantly, they were compelled to make choices on how best to convey a particular moment in a particular performance of a play within the limited scope that a vase allowed. As Csapo (2014) explains, "many (on the whole minor) discrepancies between the painter's image and the actor's performance may arise paradoxically, out of the painter's very desire to provoke recognition of the specific performance from whose details he deviates."

Aristophanes' *Frogs*, Before and After 405 BCE

While many extraordinary vases shed light on Greek comedy, the remainder of this chapter will focus on Aristophanes' *Frogs*, since earlier Attic and later Italic visual remains reveal some of the opportunities to relate ancient images to Aristophanes' comedies – even when there is no direct connection. The plot of the *Frogs* follows Dionysus and his slave Xanthias on their journey to the underworld. They set off to find the recently deceased tragedian Euripides and bring him back to Athens because, much to the god's dismay, there are no more skilled tragic poets alive in the city. At the start of the production, Dionysus, wearing a lion skin and bearing a club, approaches Heracles' house to inquire about the best route to Hades. The hero humorously offers a number of ways for Dionysus to kill himself, but ultimately the god hops aboard Charon's boat to access the land of the dead. When he arrives, however, his Heracles costume is too convincing, and he is threatened with punishment for the crimes his half-brother had previously committed. Dionysus makes a couple of rapid costume changes with his slave Xanthias, which ultimately leads to both characters being whipped repeatedly; but when Dionysus is recognized as the god of the theater, he is asked to judge a poetic competition between Euripides and Aeschylus. Hades holds a seat of honor for the best tragedian, and although Aeschylus has long held the title, Euripides is trying to usurp the throne. As the play nears its end, Dionysus fumbles for a resolution and ultimately contradicts his earlier desire to bring back Euripides. He dubs Aeschylus the best tragedian in the underworld and returns with him to Athens, leaving Sophocles to temporarily hold the tragedian's seat in Hades.

While no contemporaneous visual representation of Aristophanes' *Frogs* is extant, an Italic vase from around 375–350 appears to preserve an illustration of the play (Figure 5.7). The vase, which was either lost or destroyed during the Second World War, presents the production's opening scene, in which Dionysus and his slave approach Heracles' door. Dionysus holds the hero's club and lion skin, while Xanthias, carried by a donkey, holds the god's ridiculously oversized baggage on a pole over his shoulder. As Dionysus himself makes clear at the start of the play, the point of Aristophanes' scene is to parodically (and ironically) critique the ubiquity of comic baggage scenes, in which slaves use scatological double entendres to complain about the heavy burdens they carry. The vase's artistry, like the depiction of Aristophanes' *Thesmophoriazusae* above, is not particularly skillful, and although the vase clearly corresponds to the play in a number of details, there are certain discrepancies with the text. In particular, Dionysus simply wears a body stocking and *somation* on the vase (note the lines around the ankles in particular), while the text mentions tragic boots and a krokotos. The artist appears to have painted a comic Heracles rather than a comic Dionysus-cum-Heracles, presumably to ensure the correct identification of the character and the play, which would be incredibly difficult to interpret if not painted skillfully (and perhaps even if it were painted skillfully).

The visual discrepancy between play and vase is just one of the problems faced when using South Italian reproductions to understand Athenian comedy. Not only are we separated from the original theatrical experience by the artist's particular choices but also by the director's choices, since the *Frogs*' reproduction was staged a decade or more after Aristophanes' death. Nevertheless, a closer look at the Berlin Heracles may help us make reasonable suppositions about comic staging conventions that were imported from Athenian and Aristophanic comedy. The illustration of the body stocking, the masks, the shape of the faces, the hair and beards, as well as the props and scenery are all invaluable. One of the most fascinating issues that comes to light here is whether or not animals were regularly used onstage. At first glance, Xanthias appears to ride an actual donkey, but as Csapo (2010, 59) points out, the line running up the animal's front right leg likely represents the seam of a costume. If this is true, then the production, and presumably Aristophanes' own play, employed an amusing pantomime horse, with two actors synchronizing their movements as they carried Xanthias across the stage.

Figure 5.7 Dionysus (dressed as Heracles) and Xanthias from Aristophanes' *Frogs* approach Heracles' door, "Berlin Heracles," ca. 375–350, lost (probably destroyed or stolen during World War II), Formerly Berlin Staatliche Museen F3046. Source: Photo from M. Bieber, *Die Denmäler zum Theaterwesen im Altertum* (Berlin 1920), Tafel 80.

As with the costume of Dionysus-Heracles, the artist has simplified the representation in order to make it more recognizable to audiences, but he also includes clues to the viewer about the artifice. If this interpretation is correct and animals were portrayed by costumed actors, this vase informs our understanding not only about the *Frogs* but also about many other Athenian plays.

We can also gather, or at least speculate on, certain other details about the *Frogs* by examining comic vases that do not depict the play directly. For example, one of the most famous Italian vases is the "New York Goose Vase" (Figure 5.8), an Apulian red-figure calyx krater attributed to the Dolon Painter (ca. 400). Numerous features of the illustration suggest a comic performance. On the right, the artist has clearly painted a raised stage, which holds a dead goose, a basket with two kids inside, and an actor in the mask and costume of an old woman. At the center of the scene, an actor wearing an old-man mask and a comic body stocking with exaggerated body parts (buttocks, phallus, stomach, and breasts) stands on his tiptoes with hands raised above his head. To the left, there is a younger character, wearing similar comic costuming and holding a stick.[1] The inscriptions on the vase make clear that the elderly woman has handed over the old man, most likely a slave, for torture.

There is much to appreciate about this vase, from its discernible representation of comic costuming to the helpful plot contextualization offered by the inscriptions. The most relevant piece of information for discussion of the *Frogs*, though, is the elderly slave's quote: "He has bound up my hands." While the image's lack of rope troubled some earlier scholars,[2] Csapo is surely right to

Figure 5.8 "New York Goose Vase," Apulian red-figure calyx krater attributed to the Dolon Painter, ca. 400, New York, MMA 24.97.104. Fletcher Fund, 1924. Source: The Metropolitan Museum of Art / Dolon Painter / Public Domain.

---

[1] Other details include the mask at the top of the painting and the youth without any stage artifice standing above at the far left labeled "tragóidos." [An Apulian red-figure bell krater (McDaniel Painter, ca. 370, Boston MFA 69.951) confirms the comic performance.]
[2] E.g. Beazley (1952).

suggest that the vase depicts "a splendid example of illusionistic comic acting."[3] In the performance, the slave was not actually bound up with a rope and hit with a cane but rather *acted* as if the young man had tied his hands together and lifted him into the air until his feet barely touched the ground. Once on his tiptoes, as if hoisted up by a rope, the actor would simulate being hit by the guard's staff, jumping, writhing, and crying out in feigned pain. And while we cannot know for certain that this vase represents an Attic comedy (rather than an Italic comedy in the Doric Dialect), the words uttered by each character, with the exception of the Scythian guard who speaks Circassian, are in the Attic dialect, despite its Italic provenance.[4] This is helpful, then, as we imagine Attic performances, including those of Aristophanes, since it gives a sense of how poets, actors, and audiences expected imagination and dramatic illusion to work. Not all props were physically present, and their absence would encourage virtuosic acting that was probably much funnier than if every item found in the text were actually used onstage.

The simulation of abuse found on the New York Goose Vase may help illuminate the whipping scene in Aristophanes' *Frogs*. After Dionysus and Xanthias, each wearing the Heracles costume in turn, are mistaken for the hero, Aeacus decides to torture them. He hopes to figure out who is immortal and who is a slave, since a god should not feel the pain of a beating. Xanthias says, "whichever of us you catch yelping first, or caring at all that he's getting flogged, him you can consider no god." Xanthias and Dionysus are forced to strip, and both wince and exclaim when lashed, but quickly cover up their pain with quips and silly justifications. Whether a real whip, a fake whip, or (more likely, I think) no physical prop was used at all, the whole scene likely operated like the beating represented on the New York Goose vase, with a good deal of illusionistic comic acting. Aeacus presumably mimed whipping Xanthias and Dionysus, while they in turn each offered hilarious physical reactions to the simulated flogging. While modern audiences may find this sort of lack of props surprising, Greek theater had different conventions, and Aristophanes' audiences had different expectations, particularly regarding realism and theatrical illusion.

Using fourth-century Italic vases in this way, we see that even visual evidence not directly connected to Aristophanes can help explain Aristophanic performance. The same is true of pre-comic vases. In fact, the Athenian cup examined above (Figure 5.4a,b) may help us better understand the rowing scene in Aristophanes' *Frogs*, in which Dionysus boards Charon's boat and crosses the lake to the underworld. As noted earlier, the procession of the phallus represented on the vase was one of the most important religious features of the Dionysiac festival. Tradition suggests that the parade memorialized events surrounding the incorporation of Eleutherae into the region of Attica. The citizens of Eleutherae celebrated their new political relationship with Athens by offering a statue of Dionysus to the city, but the Athenians turned down the offer and were punished by the god. As the scholiast to Aristophanes' *Acharnians* 243 reports, Dionysus cursed the Athenians with "a disease of the genitals" (likely ithyphallicism and an inability to satisfy their sexual desire) and "the sole cure was for them to hold the god in all reverence. Therefore, in obedience to these pronouncements, the Athenians privately and publicly constructed *phalloi*, and with these they paid homage to the god, making them a memorial to their own suffering" (trans. Csapo and Slater, 1995, p. 111).

Participants at the *phallophoria* carried a wide range of bronze and wooden phalloi from outside the city toward Dionysus' temple near the Athenian Acropolis, and as the vase shows, some of these phalloi were quite large and included oversized phallus riders. The komast and satyr on this vase, I think, help illuminate Dionysus' action in the rowing scene. As soon as he and Xanthias arrive at the lake that Heracles has described to them, they see Charon approaching in a boat. After negotiating details regarding Xanthias (who must run around the lake because he is a slave), Charon addresses the god:

---

[3] Csapo (2010: 111).

[4] The words uttered by each character are not in iambic meter but rather seem to suggest that the artist is conveying the context without actually accessing the text. Csapo (2010, 112): "These details seem to indicate that the artist is not trying to write verse, but remembering the gist of a dialogue, not getting the foreign dialect quite right, and writing the sounds down in a way that comes naturally only to a Tarentine."

Χα. κάθιζ' ἐπὶ κώπην. εἴ τις ἔτι πλεῖ, σπευδέτω.
οὗτος, τί ποιεῖς;
   Δι. ὅ τι ποιῶ; τί δ' ἄλλο γ' ἢ
ἵζω 'πὶ κώπην, οὗπερ ἐκέλευές με σύ;
Χα. οὔκουν καθεδεῖ δῆτ' ἐνθαδί, γάστρων;

Charon: (to Dionysus) Sit to the oar. If anyone else is sailing, hurry it up.
Hey you there, what do you think you're doing?
Dionysus: Who me? Just sitting on the oar, right where you told me.
Charon: No, sit over here, fatso.

Charon's command to sit down is difficult to translate because the preposition ἐπὶ with the accusative case can mean "to" but also "onto." The joke here is that Charon intends the former, but Dionysus interprets the latter, leading Dionysus to sit upon the oar rather than at the oar, a fitting action for the doltish god.

The phallophoria represented on the Attic cup in 4a and 4b helps provide a different interpretation of Dionysus' action here. The god sits not "upon" the oar or "to" the oar but rather "onto" the oar, as if being penetrated by it anally. In the first image, the komast stands upright in a manner that suggests he is the rider of the phallus, but the satyr is bent over in a manner that, as Burkert (1983: 69, n. 51) points out, suggests he is enabling anal penetration by the phallus. This sort of stage action would be justified for a number of reasons. First, phalloi and phallic jokes were abundant in Old Comedy, and comic poets rarely seem to have missed an opportunity to refer either straightforwardly or obliquely to the male genitalia. Second, the comic representation of Dionysus often highlighted his less noble qualities, such as cowardice, drunkenness, and the inability to control his passions, which included a desire to be the passive partner in a homosexual encounter.

The penetration of the satyr in the phallophoria may even relate to Dionysus' own penetration in other religious contexts. There is an anecdote about Dionysus wishing to descend to the Underworld that is quite similar to Aristophanes' *Frogs*. Although much later, Clement of Alexandria (*Protrepticus* 2.34.3) writes that Dionysus, not knowing how to get to Hades, paid his way by being the passive sexual partner. In the tale, which is also related by Pausanias (2.37.5–6), Dionysus wishes to visit Hades but cannot find an entrance. Prosymnos offers to give him directions, but only if he can have anal sex with the god when he comes back from Hades. Once Dionysus returns, he finds that Prosymnos has died, but the god aims to repay the negotiated cost regardless, so he carves a phallus out of fig wood and, out of his own desire, penetrates himself anally. The phalloi in Greek cities, Clement says, serve a public and religious purpose, much like those paraded at the Athenian *phallophoria*.

Dionysus' payment of sex is clearly similar to the scene in the *Frogs*, where it appears Dionysus either desires to be penetrated as part of his trip to the Underworld or believes that Charon is ordering the god to sodomize himself on an oar before crossing the lake. Unfortunately, the age and origin of the Prosymnos story are uncertain, but the tale, taken alongside the satyr on the Attic phallophoria vase, suggests at least a notional connection between the rowing scene in the *Frogs* and the anal penetration of Dionysus (and Dionysus' companions, the satyrs). In both stories, the god is sodomized beside a lake that he crosses to descend to the underworld, and even if the Prosymnos story was not known to Aristophanes, it seems entirely possible that Dionysus in the *Frogs* is at the very least taking part in his own phallophoria. Like the satyr on the vase, Dionysus is "being ridden" by the phallus. If this interpretation of the Frogs is correct, we have here a rather simplistic one-off sodomy joke based on a complex religious ritual (the phallophoria) and, perhaps, a deeper myth about Dionysus' descent to the underworld. Aristophanes appears to intertwine Dionysiac religion and public spectacle into a quick physical joke, and without the Attic cup in 4a and 4b, we would not be able to appreciate the stage action in this scene.

While the oar joke and rowing scene probably took place onstage with a boat and oars, the New York Goose Vase and the oinochoe representing Eupolis' *Taxiarchoi* (Figure 5.2 above) force us to consider still another option. As we have seen, not all props were physically present, and a good deal of stage action required the use of the audience's imagination. The oinochoe, in fact, may represent a Dionysiac rowing scene very similar to *Frogs*, and if the vase accurately portrays the action, it all occurred without a boat or oars. In one of the extant fragments of Eupolis' comedy, a character says "hey you at the bow, will you stop splashing us?" If this is Dionysus speaking to Phormio as the general is training him how to row, then perhaps the vase depicts this scene, since Phormio appears to be in a crouched position with his arms extended in a rowing position. The vase, though, is rather sloppily sketched, and with such a fragmentary play, it is impossible to be sure what scene the artist depicts. If the attribution is correct, though, and a boat was not used onstage, perhaps the entire rowing scene in *Frogs* was also mimed. This would have made for a spectacular scene, requiring astonishing and amusing physical feats on the part of actors. Dionysus would not have actually sat in a skiff and rowed across stage; he would have squatted down and mimicked rowing. Nor would he have sat upon the oar in the manner discussed above. Once again, we would not have thought that the scene was potentially mimed without the existence of vases that show the importance of audience imagination.

Conclusion

As this final discussion of the *Frogs* reveals, our study of vases does not offer much in the way of concrete details. The few Athenian vases contemporary with Aristophanes, as well as images found on earlier Attic and later South Italian vases, provide no snapshot of Aristophanes' comedies. We can extrapolate and speculate a good deal, but we cannot know the accuracy of our speculations. Ultimately, we gain more questions than answers, but many enlightening possibilities emerge as we approach these vases imaginatively. We cannot guarantee that Aaecus imitated whipping Dionysus and Xanthias. Nor can we be sure that Dionysus made a sexually suggestive allusion to the phallophoria and Dionysiac religion. But when dealing with something as important as reconstructing and understanding original performances, creativity and possibility are more valuable than limiting ourselves to entirely known quantities. Even though Aristophanes was clearly obsessed with words and texts, performance is at the heart of his comedy, and visual evidence, whether earlier or later, Attic or Italic, provides a window (blurry though it is) onto Aristophanic comedy that texts alone cannot reveal.

GUIDE TO FURTHER READING

Taplin 1993 remains the standard point of entry for the study of vase images related to Greek comedy. The earlier collections of Trendall (1959) and Webster (1978), including their collaborative work (Trendall and Webster 1971), were foundational and are still very useful. Csapo and Slater 1995, as well as Rusten et al. 2011, collect vase images alongside other testimonia for the history of ancient comedy; Storey (2011: 425–451) provides a helpful catalog of relevant vases, though without illustrations. The many publications of J.R. Green are vital to our current understanding of this material; Green 2012 is just one example. Piqueux 2022 focuses on the body of the performer in images of Greek comedy and includes a wealth of high-quality images.

REFERENCES

Austin, C. and Olson, S.D. (2004). *Aristophanes Thesmophoriazusae*. Oxford.
Beazley, J.D. (1952). The New York 'Phlyax-vase. *AJA* 56: 193–195.
Burkert, W. (1983). *Homo Necans: The Anthropology of Ancient Greek Sacrificial Ritual and Myth*. Transl. Peter Bing. Berkeley and Los Angeles: University of California Press.
Csapo, E. (1986). A note on the Würzburg bell-crater H5697 ("Telephus Travestitus"). *Phoenix* 40: 379–392.
Csapo, E. (2010). *Actors and Icons of the Ancient Theater*. Oxford, Malden: Wiley.

Csapo, E. (2014). The iconography of comedy. In: *The Cambridge Companion to Greek Comedy* (ed. M. Revermann), 95–127. Cambridge, New York: Cambridge University Press.

Csapo, E. and Slater, W.J. (1995). *The Context of Ancient Drama*. Ann Arbor: The University of Michigan Press.

Green, J.R. (2012). Comic vases in South Italy: continuity and innovation in the development of a figurative language. In: *Theater outside Athens* (ed. K. Bosher), 289–342. Cambridge.

Piqueux, A. (2022). *The Comic Body in Ancient Greek Theatre and Art, 440–320 BCE*. Oxford.

Rusten, J.S. (2006). Who 'invented' comedy? The ancient candidates for the origins of comedy and the visual evidence. *AJP* 127: 37–66.

Rusten, J.S., Henderson, J., Konstan, D., and Rosen, R.M. (2011). The birth of comedy: texts. In: *Documents, and Art from Athenian Comic Competitions*, 486–280. Baltimore: The John Hopkins University Press.

Storey, I. (2011). *Fragments of Old Comedy*, vol. 3. Cambridge, MA: Harvard Univ. Press.

Taplin, O. (1993). *Comic Angels: And Other Approaches to Greek Drama through Vase-Painting*. Oxford.

Trendall, A.D. (1959). Phlyax vases. *BICS Suppl.* 8: London.

Trendall, A.D. and Webster, T.B.L. (1971). *Illustration of Greek Drama*. London: Phaidon.

Webster, T.B.L. (1978). Monuments illustrating old and middle comedy. *BICS Suppl.* 39: London.

CHAPTER 6

Politics and Aristophanic Comedy

Edith Hall

Critics and Complexities

Athenian Old Comedy guaranteed its authors a right to interrogate their contemporaries. As the "Old Oligarch" wrote (2.18), any individual's identity and conduct could be satirized, for the benefit of the people. Only the *dēmos* itself was protected from comic attack because only a constitution where the *dēmos* held the power made "accountability comedy" possible. This guarantee was rooted in comedy's status as a democratic organ enabled by the Cleisthenic revolution and funded by public authorization. It suited a genre associated with the emergence of democracies, not only at Athens but in Sicily and Megara, where it was said that comedy was introduced simultaneously with democracy (Arist. *Poet.* 1448a).

In 486 BCE, comedy was integrated into the programme of the drama competitions of the Athenian state.[1] This was decades later than tragedy. The man responsible for introducing the tragic competitions had probably been Peisistratos, the last successful tyrant of Athens. He courted the favor of his citizens and advertised the glory of their city to the wider Greek world by bankrolling spectacular entertainments at festivals.

But comedy, introduced after the Athenian democratic revolution and the repulse of Darius, was different. It did not glamorize mythical heroes in ways pleasing to a tyrant: it insulted rulers and well-known citizens. It mocked anybody who "put their head about the parapet" in public. It addressed corruption, private life, and personal habits. It subjected powerful individuals and groups to trial by vituperation which makes modern equivalents—*Saturday Night Live*, *Spitting Image*—look anodyne. The intensity of the abuse individuals suffered in comedy ensured that only robust, popular, and clever statesmen survived to be re-elected. Dover saw that Aristophanes never criticized the state's constitutional structure (Dover 1972: 33). Yet, of "all the men whom we know from historical sources to have achieved political prominence at Athens during the period 445–385, there is not one who is not attacked and ridiculed in the extant plays of Aristophanes or in the extant citations from the numerous lost plays of the period."[2] In Aristophanes alone, the *kōmōidoumenoi* number is at least three hundred (Storey 1998).

The *ad hominem* abuse may have been connected with a mythical structure underlying comic plots—the relationship between Dionysus and Hephaestus, and their eternal drunken procession, replayed by Athenian citizens at the Anthesteria. These two gods return in noisy triumph to Olympus after outcast Hephaestus, the most banausic Olympian, has by his intellect and humor

---

[1] *Suda* χ 318, Chionides; see Rusten (2011) 100.
[2] Dover (1972) 34.

A Companion to Aristophanes, First Edition. Edited by Matthew C. Farmer and Jeremy B. Lefkowitz.
© 2024 John Wiley & Sons, Inc. Published 2024 by John Wiley & Sons, Inc.

outwitted Ares and Hera, who have insulted him (see Hall 2018a). Old Comedy's political dimension also fits the ostensibly historical origin of comedies recorded in late sources:[3] farmers who had suffered harm traversed the streets by night near the houses of their persecutors, shouting aloud their sufferings. These farmers later did this again in the theatre, where they needed to preserve their anonymity through fear of reprisals and covered themselves with wine-lees. The aim of this public declaration of wrongs was to stop the guilty Athenians from further wrongdoing by publicly shaming them.

No comedy survives for the six decades between 486 and Aristophanes' earliest extant play, *Acharnians*. The question of Aristophanes' politics has been repeatedly asked but has received staggeringly diverse answers.[4] Cavalier theatre managers used him to protest against the Puritan closure of their venues. Fielding thought he championed freedom of speech and used him to question censorship. Wieland felt that Aristophanes had anticipated his own critique of the demagogic excesses of the French revolution. Shelley reconfigured Aristophanes as a democratic revolutionary, while the early Victorian impresario J.R. Planché thought he opposed enfranchising the poor and uneducated. Nietzsche saw Aristophanes as a spokesperson for oligarchic sympathizers and Laurence Housman as an advocate of women's suffrage.[5]

Murray thought he was a pacifist (1933; see also Dickinson 1957), while Hugill (1936, 1937) considered federal Panhellenism was his guiding ideal. Gomme saw, beneath Aristophanic personae, correspondences with specific politicians and partisan viewpoints which require precise unpicking (1938); this approach has been revived by Sidwell, who argues that Aristophanes, Cratinus, and Eupolis engaged in a perpetual contest that "was not merely aesthetic, but fundamentally political" (Sidwell 2009: 302). Yet scholars writing about politics in Aristophanes have generally neglected its aesthetics and *vice versa*. In a much-cited discussion, de Ste. Croix assumed that "literary" humor and reliable historical evidence in Aristophanes could be surgically detached (1972: 232–4). Nichols, while emphasizing Aristophanes' literary innovations and "radical imagination," unquestioningly assumes that they serve his "profound conservatism," moral, social, and political (1998: vii). Ussher controversially ignored the political dimension of Aristophanes in his 1979 survey, merely concluding that Aristophanes was not a "pacifist, pamphleteer, or propagandist," nor a "spokesman for any 'cause' (not even peace) of for any philosophy or party" (1979: 41). In 1987, Heath notoriously claimed that Old Comedy "had no designs on the political life from which it departed." Comic fantasy transforms political reality; it "did not and was not intended to have a reciprocal effect on political reality" (1987: 42).

More recently, Spielvogel, noting the prominence of themes of production in Aristophanes, reads his politics through an economic lens (2001, 2003). Reinders thinks that Aristophanes' politics are revealed in his evolving presentation of the relationship between the *dēmos* and the poet (2001). Hutchinson views the hierarchical power relations in each comic household as illuminating each comedy's political meaning (2011). Villacèque emphasizes the parabasis, arguing that through it poets trained audiences in the practice of deliberation, mirroring the deliberative processes in the Assembly (2013: 85–103). But Mhire and Frost present Aristophanes, rather, as a pioneer of political theory (2014: 1–2): "it is hard to name a single political theme of foundational significance that is not in some way discussed in his eleven extant plays."

Croiset, who alleged that Aristophanes spent his boyhood in the countryside "among the peasants of Attica," admiring his father Philippos' activities as a "hardworking small landowner" (1909 [1906]: 9), identified Aristophanes as the peasants' advocate. Yet it is as plausible to argue that the people most honored in Aristophanic comedy are oarsmen (Hall 2022). Dozens of jokes,

---

[3] Conveniently edited by Koster (1975) as Proleg. IV 1–11, XVI 1.14 ff., XVIIIa 1–19, XXIa 25–56, XXXIII 2.1–12. See Hall (2018a) 375–6.

[4] For a shrewd historical commentary on political meanings imposed on Aristophanes by scholars, see Reinders (2001) 6–10.

[5] Nietzsche (1922), comments made in a lecture in 1874/5; all other sources specified and discussed in Hall (2007a) and Hall (2007b). See now Swallow (2023), 42–62, 63–89, 130, 214–227.

hardly ever negative about the navy, require knowledge of rowing. They are largely in plays written for the Lenaea festival. In all the fifth-century plays we know were performed at the Lenaea (*Acharnians, Knights, Wasps, Frogs*), there is an extended rowing sequence. At this festival, metics, some of whom worked on the ships,[6] could play key roles including *chorēgos* (IG II³ 4 41). Such sequences would have pleased the audience majority that Aristophanes needed on his side. The professional rowers will have been at home during the midwinter Lenaea, outside the sailing season. But in the plays written for the Dionysia (*Clouds, Peace, Birds*), there is no extended rowing sequence. *Lysistrata*, unlike the other 411 play, *Thesmophoriazusae*, features rowing, which suggests it premiered at the Lenaea (Hall 2022).

Aristophanes' conflicted reception history implies that the texts have been used to reflect critics' politics rather than those of Aristophanes in his own time and space. His primary goal was to win the competition at the particular festival of Dionysus where the comedy premiered. Although the judges were randomly selected in order to forestall corruption, they could not ignore the opinion of the audience, expressed in applause or disapproval.[7] But the Athenian citizenship was impetuous in decision-making, reactive to events as they unfolded, and swift to turn on leaders it had previously idolized. Pleasing enough of these volatile and rivalrous people sufficiently to secure more applause than two other comic playwrights would have been a challenge even if the spectators all had similar backgrounds. But they did not.

Audiences reflected the diversity of social classes holding Athenian citizenship. They were divided into four "official" financial categories of men who could produce 500, 300, and 200 measures of produce a year (Pentakosiomedimnoi, Knights, and Zeugitai, respectively) and the majority, the thetes, who had to sell their labour. Within these categories, however, political views varied: some rich men favored the democracy, and some poor men disliked it. Aristocratic hereditary landowners may have despised rich man whose money came from industry, like Cleon.

A further political factor was deme identity. The Cleisthenic constitution had divided the Attic demes into three types: urban, inland, or coastal; the peasants of the inland demes were regarded as more conservative, pro-Spartan, and anti-war than those of the inner city and Piraeus. But deme identity was further complicated by the tribes: Cleisthenes had placed each deme in one of ten tribes that contained all three types of deme. This matters to the politics of comedy because the festival organization attributed greater importance to the tribes in comedy than in tragedy. The *chorēgoi* who sponsored tragedy were allocated by the magistrate, who selected them from among the richest citizens. This was originally the case with the comedies, but the responsibility for providing *chorēgoi* was transferred to the tribes (Arist. *Ath. Pol.* 56). The importance of tribal identity to comedy was greater than we are in a position to understand. In *Acharnians*, for example, the chorus and Lamachus share a tribe, Oeneis, to which the poor farmer Dercetes, who arrives at the end of the play, also belongs.[8]

Evaluating the political trajectory of each Aristophanic comedy therefore requires embracing its specificity. Festival culture itself and the memories of collective participation were instrumental in creating a sense of unity, shared history, and identity among all sectors of the citizen and metic population of Attica at the Lenaea, and all the Athenians' allied city-states at the Dionysia. But such issues relate to the realist plane of Aristophanes' works, overlooking one of its most distinctive dimensions—the supernatural. This was inseparable from its democratic agenda. The surreal or supernatural elements are central to Old Comedy's use of what Ruffell calls its "art of the impossible," through which it can "interrogate Athenian politics, culture, and society"; the genre uses "the naïve, implausible, impractical, utopian and downright silly," which "can certainly change our perception of the real world" (2011: 429). But this definition, through necessary, is insufficient. Ruffell's art of the impossible needs a class component; the impossible is achieved now by lower-class men.

---

[6] IG III 1032 vol. vii l. 226.
[7] See the testimonia translated in Rusten (2011) 112–14.
[8] See Hall (forthcoming) ch. 3.

Aristophanes invests several non-elite comic heroes with supernatural powers. They are relatively humble mortals, but, in the innovative presentation of these "ordinary men in the street" as "superheroes," they are also aesthetic projections of the freedoms and rights of the citizen spectator in the democratic city-state. Their supernatural powers offer opportunities for the instigation of laughter through subversion of the authority of gods and powerful humans (Hall 2020a).

The plays are set in the "here-and-and-now" of classical Athens, with recognizable topography, buildings, and civic personnel, as well as topical jokes and colloquial language. But a surreal dimension is grafted onto this realist base, incorporating theriomorphic hybrids, journeys to the (in reality) unseen gods or the Underworld, and the ability to move vast distances in a split second without apparent scene change. The citizen-class heroes possess paranormal, supernatural powers in other literature confined to revered heroes and divinities. But the actual gods impersonated in the plays are ineffectual and usually outwitted by their human antagonist. The supernatural powers of Aristophanes' déclassé heroes are as much a political as an aesthetic or epistemological phenomenon (Hall 2020a).

The Plays in their Specific Contexts

At the Dionysia of 426, Aristophanes' script for *Babylonians*, about which we know little for certain, may have infuriated Cleon, the pro-war and radically democratic politician whose star rose after Pericles' death. Speaking in the persona of Dikaiopolis in *Acharnians*, Aristophanes says that "because of my comedy last year," Cleon denounced him in the Council, telling lies (*Ach.* 277–82). Later, Dikaiopolis says (502–6),

> Cleon shall not badmouth me now
> on the ground that I slander the city-state in the presence of *xenoi*.
> We are by ourselves and the festival is the Lenaea.
> The *xenoi* are not yet present; for neither the tributes
> nor the allies from the city-states are arriving.

Although perhaps implying it, he takes care *not* to say explicitly that Cleon had actually prosecuted him for slandering the city. Yet, combined with unreliable scholia, and unnuanced responses to the picture of Cleon in *Knights* and *Wasps* (see below), these two passages have produced a consensus that Cleon had formally indicted Aristophanes for slandering Athens, especially its treatment of its subject allies. Consequently, *Babylonians* has been speculatively reconstructed as a heartfelt protest against the oppression of rebellious allies.[9] Cleon may have disliked the portrait Aristophanes painted of him. But his sole formal action against Aristophanes may have been to claim that, since he had Aeginetan connections, his enrolment in the Cydathenaean deme and thus registration as an Athenian citizen were suspect (see *Vita Aristoph.* 19).

Far more solid evidence is constituted by Aristophanes' characterization of the Lenaea festival as a venue where dramatists could wash Athens' dirty linen because only Athenian residents were present. Saxonhouse has compellingly argued that one sense in which Aristophanes is political is that his plays consistently ask how political membership and agency can be constituted (2014). The conceptual distinction between Greek and barbarian, suitable for identity formation at the Dionysia where the audience was Panhellenic, was prominent in *Babylonians* (fr. 81b). In *Acharnians*, however, the scrutinized identity belongs to an Attic inhabitant. Whitehorne has argued that *Acharnians* "presents a melange of definitions of Athenian identity, an album of one young man's snapshots of what it meant to be a citizen of Athens in 425 BC" (2005: 34). But Dikaiopolis' experience was not confined to citizens: the identity at stake is that of Attic *resident*.

---

[9] See, e.g., Starkey (2013).

What this audience had in common was neither citizenship nor first language. It was physically dwelling in Attica, the rural areas of which were ravaged by the Spartans. These inhabitants had to eat; they were all affected by market conditions and by their geographical proximity to the city-states of Megara and Boeotia. Residents of smallholdings outside the walls at a distance from the harbours or the city centre, which could be supplied by sea, were the most vulnerable. The viewpoint of citizen is, however, privileged over that of either metics or slaves: Aristophanes is also careful, as in all his Lenaea plays, to court the applause of the Piraeus oarsmen (161–163, 544–57, 673–82). But his specific project is to ask the occupiers of Attic space what the true definition of a *xenos* might be to a rustic peasant household, and the answer is anyone—including fellow Athenians—who did not act in smallholders' interests. This included preventing trade with the neighboring state of Megara under the economic sanctions imposed by the Megarian Decree of 432 BCE (*Ach.* 530–7).

Aristophanes dramatizes interactions with foreigners, both *barbaroi* and *xenoi*. Dicaeopolis of Cholleidai (near Hymettus) talks to (supposed) Persians, Thracians, and sympathetically portrayed Megarians and Boeotians.[10] He interacts with figures from the demes of Eleusis, Acharnai, Phlya, and Phyle. He is a complex avatar of the ordinary Athenian's identity at the height of the Athenian Empire: he can cut a deal with the mysterious divinity Amphitheus, thus behaving like an epic hero, an Achilles or Odysseus who can talk directly to gods and expect special treatment from them. He can drink a treaty that smells of divine nectar and ambrosia, and liberates him from all laws of nature and nation. Amphitheus can travel instantaneously to negotiate unilaterally on behalf of this single peasant with the Spartan Foreign Office. Dicaeopolis' own special powers are confirmed after the *parodos*, when he is found to have travelled instantaneously himself, to his farm in the deme of Cholleidae, miles south-east of the city at the southern end of Mt. Hymettus. Here, he inaugurates his private Dionysiac festival and truce with Sparta (247–252). He travels instantaneously, again, to Euripides' house (393–395). Although it is unclear whether Euripides lives in central Athens, in his ancestral estate on Salamis or in his parental deme of Phlya, north of Hymettus, all these alternatives mean travelling for hours from Dicaeopolis' farmstead.

No doubt encouraged by laughs his references to Cleon had won in *Acharnians*, for the Lenaea the following year Aristophanes created a complex fantasy on the theme of Cleon set in the urban epicentre. The hero of *Knights*, the market-place sausage seller who becomes a respected statesmen and is renamed "Agorakritos," "Pick of the agora," hails, like both Cleon and Aristophanes, from the quintessentially inner-city deme of Cydathenaeum, which included the agora.

Knights was enjoyed by its original audience, for it was awarded first prize. Our appreciation of the "real" Cleon has been obscured by the uncritical reproduction of his contemporary caricature as a screaming warmonger, not only in *Knights* but also in *Wasps* (422 BCE), *Peace* (421 BCE, produced the spring after Cleon's death), and especially Thucydides (see Hall 2019). But by reassessing accounts of Cleon, and by reading *Knights* from the perspective of one of his many supporters, we can see—and hear—a different, more likable leader.[11] The comic version of Athenian democracy staged in *Knights*, a response to the new political climate of Athens after the plague and Pericles' demise, can be understood as the most radical in ancient literature (Hall 2018b).

Knights contains neither gods nor instantaneous travel. But both *parabaseis*, delivered by the chorus of upper-class knights, contain fantasies of paranormal occurrences, talking steeds and warships, respectively. In the first, the chorus-men recall when their beloved warhorses sat on the benches to row the warships and spoke Greek (like Achilles' horses in the *Iliad* (19.404–417)), calling out to one another (600–603); in the second, the chorus remember when the Athenian war-triremes discussed how to foil Hyperbolus' plan to take a fleet to Carthage (1300–1315). This perhaps recalls the sentient ships of the Phaeacians, who need no man to steer them, in the *Odyssey* (8.557–8). In Aristophanes' *Holkades, Merchant-Ships*, produced at the following year's Lenaea, everyday Athenian citizens may have listened to other seagoing vessels speak. But in *Knights*, the real

---

[10] Colvin (1999: 303–4) thinks that Aristophanic representations of dialects and languages other than Attic Greek is merely realistic, rather than promoting a sense of Athenian superiority.
[11] Hall (2018b). My argument here is similar to that made in a very short but brilliant essay by Morley (1997).

supernatural work is done by the most low-class Aristophanic citizen hero, and the one with the most vertiginous rise in Athenian society, the sausage seller, who promises to uphold the rights of oarsmen. He is invited by Demos to join him as special counsellor and fellow diner in the Prytaneum.

The sausage seller performs a feat reminiscent of the miraculous rejuvenation of the aged hero Iolaus in Euripides' *Heraclidae*, who prays to Hebe and Zeus to be made young again to avenge himself on Eurystheus (849–866). In *Knights*, the proletarian superhero announces, "I have purified Demos by boiling him down and made him beautiful instead of ugly" (1321). Demos now looks exactly as he did in the days of Aristides and Miltiades (1325–6.). He can respond with enthusiasm when a female personification of a Thirty Years' Peace Treaty is presented to him (1388–1395). The sausage seller, it turns out, possesses the same power to produce truces with Sparta as the god Amphitheus in *Acharnians*.

In Strepsiades, Aristophanes chose a less appealing protagonist. He is a venal Athenian from the countryside, married into the urban aristocracy, and solely concerned with his private financial position. *Clouds* addresses Athenian advanced education and, besides *Thesmophoriazusae*, is the least overtly political of Aristophanes' plays: the institution it examines is not the public, civic Assembly or Council but Socrates' private *phrontisterion*. Although Socrates seems to have been loyal to Cleon and to have had a distinguished career as a hoplite, which may have affected Aristophanes' choice of target and some aspects of the philosopher's characterization,[12] it is not the dominant strand in the caricature. But this means that Lombardini is likely to be incorrect in suggesting that Aristophanes' critique of Socrates is motivated by "a concern over the antidemocratic implications" of Socrates' "purported scientific and philosophical activities" (2014). The chorus is not a particular category of citizens like the bellicose residents of Acharnai, or the Knights, or the dicasts of *Wasps*, but a peculiar entity personifying a combination of weather divinity and a concept in natural science. The play is unusual for many reasons, not least that the supernatural agent, the cloud chorus, as instrument of divine justice, prevails over the mortal protagonist. But it is understandable why the first version of *Clouds* took third place at the Dionysia of 423. Visitors from other city-states may have cared little about Socrates and his hyper-educated colleagues; the peasant farmers and sailors who formed the bulk of the audience may not have found hilarity in the minutiae of rhetoric, physics, and loan-processing by more prosperous citizens.

Besides the personifications of the Right and Wrong Arguments, who do not interact with humans, the only significant supernatural feature of *Clouds* is the chorus. But Strepsiades enjoys a special relationship with them. His response on hearing them approach, accompanied by thunderclaps, reveals the comic effects Aristophanes could produce by combining demotic heroes with supernatural epiphanies (293–295). By the end, however, Strepsiades can summon the Cloud-goddesses and hold a sombre moral dialogue with them (1452–1466).

In *Wasps* of 422 BCE, Aristophanes scrutinized the legal system, in which men prominent in public life laid charges against one another as they jostled for political supremacy. The most popular politician remained Cleon, known for using the courts to neutralize opposition. His supporters dominated the juries. Aristophanes' hero Philocleon, "Cleon-Lover," is addicted to jury service. The chorus consists of similar men, presented as wasps, swarming about the city and stinging statesmen. But they are older, more decrepit, and poorer than Philocleon: Aristophanes emphasizes that if deprived of jury service, for which they are paid, their families may go hungry (291–311).[13]

The play stages a trial, which, for all its absurdism, represents our best source for democratic Athenian law-court procedure. The system, whatever its drawbacks, was revolutionary. The democracy had replaced adjudication by expert individuals or panels with citizen juries. Volunteers had to be over 30 years of age and full citizens. The jury voted immediately after the speeches. There was neither judge's summation nor sequestered deliberation. The principle was that each individual juror exercised independent judgement; by using large juries, the opinion of the people was measured by a form of hive mind.

---

[12] See Edith Hall (2024).
[13] Well brought out by Olson (1996).

The trial in *Wasps* differs because it takes place in Philocleon's house. His son, who hates Cleon and wants to cure his father of jury mania, confines him at home but organizes a domestic court so he can continue adjudicating. Philocleon does not even know who the litigants are, but says he has already decided on his verdict—a joke referring to the apparent fondness for decisions in favor of the plaintiff. The household dog, Labes, is accused of stealing a Sicilian cheese by a dog from Cydathenaeum. The dogs are recognizable as the generals Laches and Cleon. The trial represents the rivalry between them after Laches' naval operations in Sicily. Philocleon says that the cheese he smells on Labes' breath is evidence of guilt. His son begs him not to reach a verdict before hearing the other side (919–20). But the prosecuting dog incites Philocleon against Labes. Since Labes is incapable of defending himself, the younger man speaks on his behalf. But his father resolves to vote for conviction.

Many scholars have thought that Aristophanes was inexorably opposed to Cleon and to the conduct in civic debate and legal process of his large lower-class faction. Konstan has argued that the play fundamentally advocates an aristocratic viewpoint, the preferability of moneyed leisure to democratic participation (Konstan 1985). But Cleon remained a man of high repute. The most revealing element of this trial is not Philocleon's undeniable lack of objectivity. It is the overwhelming weakness of the defence speech for the dog Labes which Bdelycleon delivers. No evidence is used to disprove that he stole the cheese; Bdelycleon admits that he did. No case is made that there were mitigating circumstances and that, in the interests of equity, Labes should therefore not be punished. Instead, Bdelycleon generalizes about Labes' good character and competence as a servant, uses his children to elicit pity, and appeals to the class identity of the jury. He implies that Labes is, like most of them, not a member of the elite. This somehow makes the theft acceptable (950–9).

Bdelycleon actually tricks his father into acquitting Labes by swapping the voting pots. But despite Philocleon's precipitate decision, prejudice in favor of the Cleon-dog, and failure to concentrate on details, he reaches the correct conclusion. Moreover, as Harriott saw, there is "no serious criticism of the procedures of courts…although forensic rhetorical clichés and appeals for pity are ridiculed" (1986: 149).

The weakness of Bdelycleon's arguments must have been obvious to Aristophanes' audience, many of whom supported Cleon. By the late 420s, Athenian citizens had been trained for decades to analyze argumentation and assess the legitimacy of evidence, not only through jury service but through participation in magistracies, committees, boards, the Assembly, and the Council. If Aristophanes intended to imply that the jurors of classical Athens were incompetent, then he would have done so. But *Wasps* shows that Athenian, jury-trained audiences were more than capable of spotting a weak legal argument when they saw it.

The supernatural elements in *Wasps* include the hybrid insect–humans of the chorus. The dog trial requires one of the actors costumed as a dog to deliver speeches (907–931). But most revealing is Philocleon's self-identification with Zeus. After describing the pleasures of jury service and the sovereignty it has bestowed on ordinary Athenians like him, he compares his power to that of Zeus (620–7). When he and the other men of his class create the din or *thorubos* associated with law courts, people liken the sound to Zeus's thunder; he uses the metaphor of discharging the lightning, traditionally Zeus's prerogative, to demonstrate the power he wields over "rich and august men" (622–627).

The relationship between the internal content of the comedy to its external "frame" of the drama competition is closer in *Peace* than in any other Aristophanic play. The hero of *Peace*, Trygaeus, is a vine-growing peasant from Athmonon (190–1), an extra-mural inland deme far north-east of the city centre. Trygaeus is the most Panhellenic of Aristophanes' heroes, leading a chorus from numerous Greek states in the retrieval of Peace. He enacts in the realm of comic fiction the present in which his audience found themselves.[14]

The previous summer the Athenians were defeated in the brutal battle of Amphipolis. But Cleon and Brasidas, the generals on either side, had died as a result, leaving the way open for negotiations

---

[14] Argued in greater detail in Hall (2006) ch. 11.

(Thuc. 5.16.1). By the time of the Dionysia, the terms of a treaty had been agreed. Two aspects of this diplomatic procedure are central to *Peace*. First, the treaty was ratified, according to Thucydides, "immediately after the City Dionysia" (5.20.1), which probably means that the Athenian assembly met on the day after the festival ended to elect the delegation which would go to Sparta, where the truce was ratified a few days later (Thuc. 5.18–19). *Peace* was therefore performed just days before peace was inaugurated in reality, and in front of an audience from numerous Greek cities interested in the collective truce. Second, the first clause of the treaty was itself concerned with festivals:

> With regard to the sanctuaries held in common, everyone who so wishes shall be able, according to the customs of his country, to sacrifice in them and visit them and consult oracles in them and attend the festivals in them (*theōrein*) in safety (Thuc. 5.18.1).

The mute character *Theōria*, whom Trygaeus bestows upon the Athenians, is thus simultaneously a reference to the increased right to enjoy attending festivals to be assured by the imminent treaty, and one of the play's exceptional number of cases of "audience participation."[15]

The importance of ensuring that nothing derailed the imminent treaty explains why the homology *Peace* creates between comic plot and civic context is extreme. Trygaeus' mission is to create in his fantastic world a group identity that can, with superficial light-heartedness, accommodate not only all Athenians but all Greeks present at the Dionysia. This group sensibility relies on the implication that all opponents of the treaty are not only party poopers but pursuing self-interested agendas. This play molds political opinion and identities on both pan-Athenian and Panhellenic levels.

The hero of *Peace* is invested with more superpowers than any other figure in Old Comedy, and more than most mythical heroes. Trygaeus, whose name suggests that he is a quasi-daemonic agent or representative of the Dionysiac spirit of comedy (Hall 2006: 328–335), can imitate the heroes Perseus and Bellerophon by acquiring a giant dung beetle and riding it to heaven. There he converses with Hermes. He witnesses the personification of War toss foodstuffs representing Greek states into a mortar and give orders to his slave, the personification of Tumult familiar from the *Iliad* (5.593, 18.535). Trygaeus summons a congress of Panhellenic farmers who arrive instantaneously (292–300). Alongside Hermes, he supervises their riotous hauling of the personification of Peace from the cave (459–519). He can even receive communications from the statue because Hermes translates for him her whispered messages (670–705). He can marry the personification of Harvest, Opōra, and outrageously break the fourth wall when he hands over her companion Theōria to the Councillors sitting in the front row (715, 871–909). He can return to the earth within the space of a chorus even without his dung beetle, which has been sequestered for the use of Zeus (728–819). He can see the flitting souls of deceased poets as he descends (829–832).

We have seen in *Knights* how reading Aristophanes' politics through the prism of Thucydides' prejudiced retrospective account can distort interpretation, and the same is true of *Birds*. The conventional reading is that Cloud-cuckoo-land is Athens or Sicily or both: some believe that the play reflects Aristophanes' dislike for Athenians' litigiousness; "Cloud-cuckoo-land is Athens with feathers, and Peisetairos re-creates the hustle and bustle he claimed he was trying to escape" (Mahoney 2007: 271). But the pervasive "political" reading, first popularized by Johann Wilhelm Süvern (1835), perceives a satire on Athens' fantasy of extending her empire to Sicily. This fantasy's denouement in 413 BCE is narrated tragically in Thucydides VII (Süvern 1835). Such an approach inevitably means introducing Alcibiades and the Hermocopid scandal into the discussion (Vickers 1995).

A few excellent studies have assessed the depiction in *Birds* of tyranny as a political constitution, including the contention of Saxonhouse and Meyer that the comedy provided a model for Plato's *Republic* (Saxonhouse 1978; Meyer 2014). Henderson has suggested that Peisetairos possesses practical and political gifts which unite the community (1997: 141–4); Aristophanes, on this

---

[15] Slater (2002), ch. 6, especially 130–1.

account, was prepared to think, at least in fiction, about the possibility that a tyranny could be beneficial. Ambler takes a less extreme approach. He agrees that, despite Peisetairos' hubris and self-aggrandisement, Aristophanes does not appear to condemn him. Ambler infers that Aristophanes believes that while a gullible populace wanting an empire must also embrace a Peisetairos, the price would be accepting that their tyrannical ruler would milk the system for personal advantage (Ambler 2012). But what none of these readings accommodates is the play's multiple references to the north, the Black Sea and Thrace as arenas for Athenian political life.[16]

When *Birds* was performed at the City Dionysia in Athens in 414 BCE, much of the Athenians' attention was fixed on the north, where their relationships had been jeopardized by the shocking loss of Amphipolis. The Thracian cities in the old Athenian *phoros*, tribute-paying district,[17] wanted independence. Many spectators of *Birds* will have had experience of military operations in Thrace, which had historically loomed much larger in their heads than Sicily. From 415 to 413, the Athenians maintained naval operations round the northern Aegean. The denseness of allusions to Thrace in *Birds* undermines the oft-repeated claim that the comedy is an ironic critique of the imperial ambitions underlying the Sicilian expedition (Hall 2020b).

"Thrace" was a vast territory with which the Athenian ruling class had always held intimate links and where they possessed personal fiefdoms and estates. In Thrace that they found refuge and accumulated fortunes when they were in political trouble at home.[18] These Athenians were a familiar enough phenomenon that their compatriots had a nickname for them, *Thraikophoitai* or "Thrace-frequenters"; tellingly, the author who introduces us to this term is Aristophanes, in his lost *Gerytades* (fr. 156b.9).

Birds satirizes the murky doings of individual opportunistic Athenians in the Thracian hinterland of their empire. Peisetairos unambiguously establishes himself as the tyrant of a new town-cum-aerial-toll station and goes partly native. He makes a more vertiginous ascent in terms of status even than the sausage seller by wresting the very power over the universe from Zeus. This spectacular denouement follows a plot conducted in the supernatural realm from near the outset. Peisetairos and Euelpides can visit a mythical king, Tereus, who has been transformed into a bird, talk to him, and other birds, and eat a magic root which turns them partially into birds themselves. Peisetairos supervises the building of an aerial city and converses with Iris, Poseidon and the Triballian god, the Titan Prometheus, and Heracles.

Peisetairos' ascent of the cosmic status ladder reveals an enthralling characterization as a comic citizen hero, even if a sinister one, with superpowers. He wants to leave Athenian *polupragmosunē* (44); the "quiet" life he desires is one in which he is unaccountable to democratic constraints. Peisetairos becomes increasingly autocratic. He pressurizes Zeus by threatening him with a replay of the gigantomachy (1248–1252) and consolidates his power by marrying Basileia, the divine principle of Sovereignty; along with her Peisetairos acquires access to his father-in-law Zeus's powers, in particular, his thunder.[19]

Public play-acting of intimacy with divinity was a longstanding tradition among tyrants; Peisistratos was said to have been equipped by his allies with a tall woman costumed as Athena, besides whom he entered Athens (Hdt. 1.60). There is a mythical counterpart in Sisyphus' brother Salmoneus. After becoming king of Elis, Salmoneus demanded that his subjects call him Zeus. He drove his chariot through the city dragging bronze kettles to simulate thunder and throwing torches to simulate lightning.[20] Peisetairos is, hilariously, arrogating to himself not only the sovereignty of the universe but the rights of the upper classes of history and myth to outrageous, hubristic misbehavior.

---

[16] An exception is constituted by some insightful comments on Thracian references in *Birds* in Tsakmakis (1997: 40–2).
[17] On which see Edson (1947).
[18] Isaac (1986); Lavelle (1992); Sears (2013) 3.
[19] If in this context winning Basileia from Zeus can function, as it does in Bacchylides fr. 41 (in Campbell *Greek Lyric* vol. IV), as a metaphor for winning immortality, then Peisetairos is shattering the biggest human ontological constraint of them all.
[20] Pseudo-Apollodorus, *Bibliotheca* 1. 9. 7; Hyginus, *Fabulae* 60, 61; Strabo 8.356.

No Aristophanic comedy except *Peace* is more closely tied to its specific historical occasion than *Lysistrata*. The appeal of the sex-strike motif has historically occluded Lysistrata's other strategy, the occupation of the Acropolis by the older women to protect the silver in Athena's treasury from being used to finance the war (175–79, 240–45, 421–23, 487–93). Thonemann has stressed the immediacy of this and other contemporary references such as the figure of the Proboulos (a magistracy only created in late 413 BCE) and criticism of the demagogue-turned-oligarch Peisander (2020: 489–92). The Athenians at the beginning of the war had established a financial reserve of 1,000 silver talents, to be stored on the Acropolis and never spent, along with one hundred ships; they even made any proposal to spend the money (unless there was a clear and present danger of a direct naval attack) punishable by death (Thuc. 2.24.1–2). But in the crisis following the Sicilian disaster, in the summer of 412, Chios seceded from Athens, and the dazed Athenians subsequently voted to access the reserve (Thuc. 8.15.1; Schol. *Lys.* 174=*FGrH* 328 F138). Lysistrata's campaign to improve the financial management of Athens must be a response to this decision.

Furthermore, Lysistrata seems herself to be modeled on a historical individual, the priestess of Athena in 411, whose name was Lysimache (Lewis 1955). According to Pliny, Lysimache held office for 64 years (*Natural History* 34.76). Lysistrata means "the woman who disbands the army," and Lysimache means, "the woman who puts a stop to the fighting." It seems improbable that the original audience of *Lysistrata* would not have connected their most important priestess's name with that of Aristophanes' heroine. Lysistrata herself seems to refer to the priestess when she is addressing the Proboulos: she says that she and her female comrades will be successful in their aims and be known among the Greeks as Lysimaches, "the women who put a stop to the fighting" (551–4). Ten years earlier, in *Peace*, Trygaeus had prayed to the goddess Eirene "to resolve our fights and quarrels, so that we can name you Lysimache, the woman who pus a stop to the fighting" (991–2). Lysistrata's comrade Myrrhine may also be named after the first priestess of Athena Nike (appointed by 424/3 BCE), Myrrhine, daughter of Kallimachos (Lougovaya-Ast 2006; Thonemann (2020: 133–4).

We do not know whether Lysimache had complained on behalf of the women of Athens about the devastating recent fatalities. Henderson argues that mass bereavement might have prompted "real female discontent, even rebelliousness" (Henderson (1987: 128). But Hugill was overstating his case for consistency over time in Aristophanes' political position on the empire when he argued that it was "sincere" (1937: 190), and that the government-textile allegory in *Lysistrata* (572–86) is the most explicit expression of it: there is no basis for Hugill's inference that "Lysistrata's plan is the negation of imperialism, and the restoration of confederation" (1936: 99).

The supernatural in *Lysistrata* plays a diminished role compared with the plays featuring male citizen protagonists. Unnaturally, swift movement between cities does seem possible, and Lysistrata herself, though apparently an Athenian housewife, shares features not only with Lysimache but with Athena (Hall 2010). She can also summon a personification of Reconciliation (1114). But the comedy does not significantly confound the laws of nature. Still less does *Thesmophoriazusae*, which, despite its inventive burlesques of Euripidean tragedy, contains not one miraculous, paranormal, or supernatural element; no divinities, talking animals, instantaneous travel, unreal locations, or magical powers. The overt central problem to be solved is not a matter of civic interest (war, demagogues, law courts, treatment of the navy, colonization, whether to retrieve Alcibiades, how to address poverty) but a fictitious plot by non-citizens (women) against a poet who composes fictions. The protagonist is Euripides' boorish Inlaw, who is doing a private favor to a kinsman.

Yet this comedy premiered in 411 BCE, almost certainly at the City Dionysia three months after *Lysistrata* at the Lenaea. The atmosphere in democratic Athens was tense. The Athenians had agreed to negotiations with both the Persian satrap Tissaphernes and the exiled Alcibiades, hoping to get Persian help against Sparta. Peisander (within two months to act as one of the leaders of the oligarchic coup) had persuaded even his opponents to let him use an unprecedented bargaining chip with Tissaphernes. This was the possibility that the Athenians might switch to what he ambiguously called "a more moderate form of government, and put the offices into fewer hands, and so gain the king's confidence, and forthwith restore Alcibiades, who is the only man living that can bring this about" (Thuc. 8.53.3). The *dēmos* took the mention of oligarchy badly but allowed

Peisander to use the bargaining chip, assuming that they could change the constitution back later (8.54.1). Peisander "also went the round of all the clubs already existing in the city for help in lawsuits and elections, and urged them to draw together and to unite their efforts for the overthrow of the democracy; and after taking all other measures required by the circumstances, so that no time might be lost, set off with his ten companions on his voyage to Tissaphernes" (Thuc. 8.54.4). He may already have left Athens by the time of the Dionysia. But it is unknown how far Aristophanes' audience believed or feared that the democracy would be destroyed and replaced by a government of only 400 councillors and 5,000 voting citizens.

There is no reason to suppose that *Thesmophoriazusae* criticizes democracy by ridiculing the procedures of the male Assembly meetings on the Pnyx (Harriott 1986: 154). Perhaps its apolitical nature indicates that it is a complete evasion. The targets are "safe" (women and a barbarian). The extent of the obscenity, unparalleled in Aristophanes (de Wit-Tak 1968), could deliberately mask the absence of political clout.

A very few passages could be interpreted as explicit warnings that an oligarchic coup was imminent, and this is how Karamanou reads it (2013). Critylla opens the "assembly" episode with a parody of the prayer that opened the male citizens' Assembly, including the lines calling for destruction on anyone "who plots any evil to the *dēmos* of the women, or negotiates with Euripides or the Medes in order to inflict harm on the women, or wants to rule as a tyrant or to restore the tyrant" (335–9). The chorus also sing, "It is appropriate for me to call here to our dance Pallas, lover of the dance, the virgin unwed maiden, who rules our city... Appear, as is proper, you hater of tyrants!" (1137–45). These two passages represent slim pickings, however, as they recycle formulaic imprecations integral to civic discourse since the Cleisthenic revolution. Dover thinks that the conspirators themselves would have echoed 1143–5, "arguing that they were not really overthrowing *nomos* and that what they envisaged was not 'tyranny'" (1972: 172).

Similarly, when trying to prove female superiority, the women use names as evidence: "Charminos is weaker than Nausimache ['Naval Battle', a name for a woman or a ship].... As for Aristomache ['Excellent Battle'], that one at Marathon, and Stratonice ['Army Victory'], it has been a long time since any of you has even attempted to compete with either one of them" (804–7). But the reference to the defeat of Charminus at the naval battle of Syme the year before merely expresses nostalgia for the good old days of Athenian victories during the Persian Wars.

A remote possibility is that the prolonged ridicule of the Scythian archer is related to the association of the archers with the oligarchic faction. Aristarchus, soon to be general under the Four Hundred, was the most ardent opponent of the democracy and the oligarch keenest to overthrow it (Thuc. 8.90, 92; Xen. *Hell.* 2.3.46). After the oligarchs were deposed, his final act of treachery was to escape to the Athenian garrison at Oenoe on the Boeotian frontier, and betray it the Boeotians. Thucydides tells that he took with him on this dangerous mission, when his survival was at stake, "some of the most barbaric of the archers" (8.98).

Finally, the ending has the women capitulate to Euripides with unexplained speed, just possibly reflecting allegorically the Assembly's agreement to negotiate with Tissaphernes and Alcibiades. Euripides became associated with antidemocratic ideas (see *Frogs* 952–3, 967; Redfield 1962: 117–19). At the end of the play the chorus even assists Euripides and the kinsman, by giving false directions to the archer (1218–24, as in *Iphigenia in Tauris* 1294–301), indicating that it is for Euripides to deal with the barbarian threat (1171). But if there is such a political allegory, it is veiled indeed.

Events moved fast between the production of *Thesmophoriazusae* in 411 and *Frogs* at the 405 Lenaea. After the oligarchic revolution, the Athenian fleet, based at Samos, repudiated the change of government, and under Alcibiades' leadership succeeded in having the democracy reinstated; by a series of naval victories they recovered parts of their empire. But the Persians supported the Spartan fleet under Lysander, the brilliant general appointed navarch for Aegean operations in 407. In 406, the allied Spartan and Persian ships defeated the Athenians at Notium. The Athenian radical democrats opposed to Alcibiades removed his command and he retired to the Thracian Chersonese.

The Athenians hastily put a new fleet together, partly manned with slaves and metics, and in 406 won a surprise victory (repeatedly mentioned in *Frogs*) at the Battle of Arginusae, near Lesbos.

The victory must partly have been the result of Lysander's replacement by a less able Spartan admiral. Celebrations were ruined by the unnecessary deaths of many shipwrecked sailors of 25 ships and the trials and summary executions of six of the eight admirals for negligence. By the Lenaea festival the following winter, many Athenians, exhausted internally from both the bitter reprisals against the admirals and the oligarchic faction of 411 and secret sabotage by mutinous gangs of aristocratic youths, must have realized that their city was in parlous danger, especially since Lysander returned to effective naval command after Arginusae.

It would be good to know how Aristophanes himself stayed apparently unharmed either by the oligarchs or the leaders of the consequent democratic backlash (Dover 1972: 172). But *Frogs* is the work of a playwright keen, as ever, to please the majority of his audience, seeking consensus across political divides. There are problems understanding of the specificity of the play to the winter of 405, since its parabasis met with such approval that there was a repeat performance, with some changes to the text, at an unspecified time.[21] But the political agenda remains clear, and it is absorbed from the Eleusinian Mysteries, the most inclusive Athenian festival. Initiation, which held out the promise of a blessed afterlife, was open to all who could speak Greek, free and slave alike (Evans 2002). The dramatic action concludes, like the experience of the Mysteries, with torches and communion with the dead, as Aeschylus is escorted back to Athens by the chorus of mustai.

Aristophanes makes political use of the Eleusinian festival's social inclusivity. He calls for an Athens which embraces a wider citizenry than hitherto. On the one hand, he advocates the recall of Alcibiades, felt by many to be indispensable to the defence of Athens against Lysander, and the reinstatement of prominent citizens who had fallen foul of the democracy, but he also approves the recent emancipation (and almost certainly naturalization as citizens) of a significant number of slaves. They had been freed in recognition of their contribution as rowers at Arginusae.[22] The scale of the crisis and acute shortage of manpower had made even this desperate expedient acceptable (Hunt 2001). There is little reason to suppose that the new citizens enfranchised by Arginusae were not present in the audience at the première of *Frogs*: several lines seem designed to cultivate their applause (33–4, 190–2, 693–9). Arginusae also almost certainly inspired the creation of the clever and resilient Xanthias, whose significant role, as a slave, is unprecedented. The newly enfranchised are likely to be gratified by the prospect of a slave with superpowers and the ability better to endure being flogged than a god.

The katabasis plot of *Frogs* is inherently supernatural; Aristophanes also used it in *Gerytades*, in which a delegation of poets descended to the Underworld. Great heroes had been able to visit the Underworld in myth and archaic literature – Odysseus, Heracles, Theseus – but in *Frogs* Aristophanes offers us a katabasis performed by an Olympian divinity, Dionysus, attended by a brave, resourceful, and human slave. After leaving Heracles' house, and before Xanthias' role ends when he decides to enter the Underworld proper and stay there, both god and slave encounter further figures whom the laws of nature would prevent any member of Aristophanes' audience from seeing in reality; the monster Empousa, a talking corpse, Charon, frogs singing in Greek, Aeacus, and the (presumably human but deceased) maid.

Assemblywomen is political in a more abstract and theoretical way than Aristophanes' fifth-century works. Interpretations have centered on its treatment of poverty in Athens after the loss of her empire (Zumbrunnen 2006), and on its disputed relationship with contemporary discussions by philosophers of communism and female civic participation, notably Socrates' views as articulated in Plato's *Republic* 15 years later.[23] Yet the concept of the civic festival can show that the play is politically analytical in a different way. A component of festivals was the processional journey, with its own bends, inclines, bridges, landmarks, and traditional places where the participants paused at shrines to perform a hymn or sacrifice. A psychologically familiar route was taken by the opening procession of the Panathenaea in high summer; the participants, who included metics, gathered at

---

[21] This is reported in the hypothesis; see Rosen (2015).
[22] See Hall (2006: 200).
[23] See Ellis (2011) and the extensive bibliography that was already available to Adam (1926: 345).

the Dipylon gate in the north of the city and moved down the Panathenaic way via the agora to the Acropolis and thence the Parthenon.

In *Assemblywomen*, an important scene relies on the audience's shared knowledge, as Athenian residents, of the Panathenaic procession. After the women have inaugurated the new regime, Chremes responds to Praxagora's edict ordering everyone to take their private possessions to the agora and donate them to the state (711–14). He lines up the contents of his larder as if they were members of the *polis* assembling for the Panathenaic procession (730–45). His sieve is to take the place of the basket-bearer (*kanēphoros*), the young woman who led the procession. She is to be followed by a blackened cooking pot (representing the chair-bearer), a jug (the pitcher-bearer), and other "participants" including honey-combs, branches which may suggest the older men who took part, a tripod, oil flasks and the "crowd" who brought up the rear, represented by smaller items of culinary equipment. The Panathenaea marked the Athenians' New Year, and Chremes' domestic Panathenaic procession marks another fresh start, since it "inaugurates the new age" (Bowie 1993: 262). The plan for the new age was conceived, says Praxagora, at the Skira festival (17–18, 59), a women-only celebration of Demeter and Kore held the previous month. But in the world of the play the new era delivers female political power and socioeconomic communism, characterized by the joint ownership of possessions including kitchen equipment.

In understanding the community function of festivals, sociologists, and anthropologists today employ a model proposed by Durkheim in *The Elementary Forms of Religious Life* (1912). Durkheim argued that everyday life, governed by the need to work and perform domestic chores in order to fulfil physical needs, weakens individual people's commitment to shared beliefs and social bonds. It develops a sense of secular individualism that is "centrifugal"—it pulls each person away from the society's communal centre and toward their separate and self-interested place on its periphery (Etzioni 2000). Societies are threatened by these centrifugal and individualistic pressures. The threat creates a need for activities which look toward the centre of the community and reinforce commitments to mutual values, beliefs, and practices. Rituals offer a mechanism for the symbolic recreation of society, in which its members share charged experiences.

These had been eloquently summarized in 403 BCE when the city was enduring the reign of terror under the so-called Thirty Tyrants at the end of the Peloponnesian War. The exiled democrats won a victory, after which their spokesman Cleocritus addressed the defeated aristocrats in a speech which shows how the shared experience of festivals was fundamental to citizens' sense of group identity (Xen. *Hell.* 2.4.20):

> Fellow citizens, why are you keeping us out of Athens? Why do you seek our deaths? For we have never done you any harm. We have taken part alongside you in the most hallowed rituals and sacrifices, and in the finest festivals. We have been your co-dancers in choruses and co-students, as well as your co-soldiers.

Aristophanes exposes the tension between Cleocritus' centripetal ideal and cynical centrifugal impulses in the same episode of *Assemblywomen* as Chremes' Panathenaic marshalling of his chattels in the public cause. Another citizen enters and declares that it would be the height of folly to contribute his possessions, the fruit of his sweat and thrift, to the public store (746–9).[24] After an extended debate, the second man secretly decides to evolve some scheme by which he can keep his own things and yet take a share of the common feast (872–7). And in this comedy, where women (who had not in reality benefitted from Cleisthenes' extension of sovereign power to their menfolk) are the primary agents, and where the selfishness and un-democratic instincts of individuals supply much humor, there is scarcely any element of the supernatural at all (Hall 2014).

There is a conspicuous absence of political satire in the last of Aristophanes' extant plays, and in some ways it anticipates the more domestically focussed plots of New Comedy. But in one sense *Wealth* is profoundly political: it gives its most important role to Cario, an outstandingly intelligent

---

[24] The man is not named in the manuscript, but should almost certainly be identified with Chremes, the friend of Blepyrus who reports what happened at the momentous meeting of the Assembly when the women took power.

slave. Dover innovatively insisted on the centrality of Cario's role, asking whether it reflected real-world socioeconomic shifts in early fourth-century Athens (1972: 205, 207). Sommerstein also acknowledges Cario's prominence (2001: 24, 27, 160) and has stressed the collaboration between Aristophanic citizens and their slaves in terms of effecting ambitious solutions to problems (2009). But others who have discussed Cario tend to assume a morally censorious tone (Olson 1989: 194–6).

Yet, if we read the role of the undoubtedly self-interested Cario from the perspective of a spectator wishing to laugh, he emerges as the most significant—because by far the funniest—character (Hall 2020c). Hesk and Lowe have urged us to retune our critical antennae when interpreting ancient comedy, including its politics, to reinstate the primacy of laughter generation.[25] Of the bids for laughter discernible in *Wealth*—jokes, puns, punchlines in sequences of dialogue, and physical stunts—Cario is given the overwhelming majority.

The Cario actor also needs to change costume and mask and transform himself into Poverty, who looks like an Erinys from a tragedy (423). In the debate with Chremylus, Poverty delivers an economic analysis, which, as Bowie argues, needs to be taken seriously; it explains why hard labour, and therefore slavery, remain unavoidable.[26] The same actor who uses mirth to undermine the logic of slavery by showing his cleverness and psychological leadership ironically also plays the role of a tragic goddess who articulates, with precision logic, the necessity of slavery.

Most revealingly of all, however, is that the strongest superpowers here belong not to a citizen but to an able slave. Chremylus, a poor citizen, does consort with Ploutos and hold a debate with Poverty. But his slave Cario reports seeing the divinities Asclepius, Iason and Panacea in the Asclepeion (696–709); he also reports the fantasy utopian Phaeacia-like state in which the household finds itself after Ploutos is cured; the flour bins, wine jars, treasure chests, oil tank, perfume bottles, and fig store are overflowing, wooden wares have turned into fine metals, and the slaves can play games all day (802–822). The happy return to prosperity is clinched when the god Hermes begs Cario to let him join this human household; the gods are now poor, having lost Wealth to mankind (1099–1170). Aristophanes' response to the decline in living standards in the Athenian democracy is to create his most exaggerated plot in terms of ordinary humans, citizens and slaves, exchanging situations with gods altogether; the humor in the scenes from the moment when Ploutos recovers his sight is almost entirely produced by Cario, gleefully acting out repercussions of the new utopia.

Citizen Supermen

Aristophanes never criticizes democracy nor its institutions—the Council, Assembly, and law courts. He seems to have retreated from the political when democracy was in imminent danger, is averse to extreme positions of any kind, and attuned to mainstream opinion; he positions his comedy as the authoritative mouthpiece of the community's central, traditional, collective value system, and seeks consensus, rather than subverting authority from a viewpoint characterized as oppositional, radical, or marginal. He is always mindful of large constituencies in audiences such as farmers and sailors, and of the different makeups of the audiences at the Dionysia and Lenaea. But he mercilessly lambasts and holds to account individuals who put themselves forward as leaders and influencers. He also invests some of his democratic heroes with superpowers.

The three plays with female choruses, however, form a distinct category in terms of the supernatural as well as gender issues. The women comedies do not take us to heaven, down into the Underworld, or to join communities of fauna. The premise of *Assemblywomen* may have seemed almost as improbable, to ancient male audiences, as talking birds or farmers flying on dung beetles,

---

[25] Hesk (2000, 2007); Lowe (2007); Hall (2020a, b, c); see also Swallow and Hall (2020).
[26] Bowie (1993) 284-9; see also McGlew (1997).

but it contains no more supernatural elements than *Thesmophoriazusae*. *Lysistrata* resembles the plays with male citizen protagonists only slightly more.

Women competent enough to take over the Acropolis or the Assembly may well have been seen as *preter*natural–going *beyond* what was deemed natural for people of their sex – but they were not supernatural. During the civil war in 427 BCE, there was a street battle in Corfu's main town. Thucydides describes how women on the democratic side joined in the fighting "with great daring, hurling down tiles from the roof-tops and standing up to the din with a courage that went further than what was natural (*para phusin*) to their sex" (3.74). But the women of Aristophanes, except Lysistrata, come nowhere near commandeering the powers of gods or mythical heroes. In my view, this is because Aristophanes did not regard the women of classical Athens as participating in the thrilling project of citizen self-refashioning as agents of sovereignty in the democratic city. This was a prerogative of the men. Women could not assume the superpowers which were within the imaginative grasp of their fathers, sons, and husbands. They might even be within the imaginative grasp of male slaves like Xanthias or Cario, who could fantasize, because of events like those after Arginusae, that they might be citizens themselves one day. Aristophanic comedy made superheroes out of its citizens, its *politai*. This was its most daring achievement.

The hero with superpowers of democratic comedy was a ludic emanation of the political consciousness shared by the mass of poor, male-free citizens of Athens. They had acquired sovereign power with the democratic revolutions, and their worldview and attitude to authority had been revolutionized as a result, opening up, for the playwrights of the new comic genre which the democracy had grafted onto its festivals, a rich seam of hilarity. Freedom to run their own city brought the freedom not only to imagine the impossible, but to fantasize collectively about acquiring powers to reject established authorities hilariously and to over-ride the laws of nature absurdly, to discharge Zeus' thunderbolts as jurymen. The supernatural powers of the heroes in Athenian comedy disappeared, to be replaced by Menandrean ethical naturalism and heroes with no superpowers at all, at the precise moment when the democracy was etiolated after the Macedonian conquest (Hall 2020a).

GUIDE TO FURTHER READING

Useful treatments of Aristophanes and Athenian politics include Croiset 1909 (1906), de Ste. Croix (1972), Gomme (1938), Heath (1987), Hall (2020a, 2022), Nichols (1998), Reinders (2001), Sidwell (2009), Spielvogel (2003), Villacèque (2013), and Whitehorne (2005). On the aesthetics and language of Aristophanic political comedy, see Colvin (1999), Hall (2019), forthcoming, Ruffell (2011), de Wit-Tak (1968), Hesk (2007), Hutchinson (2011), Slater (2002), and Storey (1998). On Aristophanes portrayal of demagogues and tyrants see Ambler (2012), Meyer (2014), Hall (2018b), Konstan (1985), Morley (1997), and Olson (1996). On Aristophanes in relation to Greek (particularly Platonic) political theory, see the essays in Mhire and Frost (2014), as well as Adams (1926), Ellis (2011), and Saxonhouse (1978). On the intersection of Athenian religion and politics, see Bowie (1993), Etzioni (2000), and Evans (2002). On Aristophanes' portrayal of non-Greeks, see Hall (2006, 2020b) and Karamanou (2013). On the Athenian institution of slavery as reflected in comedy, see Hall (2020c), Hunt (2001), and Sommerstein (2009).

REFERENCES

Adam, J. (ed.) (1926). *The Republic of Plato*. Cambridge: Cambridge University Press.
Ambler, W. (2012). Tyranny in Aristophanes's "Birds". *The Review of Politics* 74: 185–206.
Bowie, A. (1993). *Aristophanes: Myth, Ritual, Comedy*. Cambridge: CUP.
Colvin, S. (1999). *Dialect in Aristophanes and the Politics of Language in Ancient Greek Literature*. Oxford: OUP.
Croiset, M. (1909 [1906]). *Aristophanes and the Political Parties at Athens*. London: Macmillan and co., English translation by James Loeb of *Aristophane et le partis à Athènes*. Paris.

de Ste. Croix, G. (1972). *The Origins of the Peloponnesian War*. London: Duckworth.
de Wit-Tak, T. (1968). The Function of Obscenity in Aristophanes' "Thesmophoriazusae" and "Ecclesiazusae". *Mnemosyne* 21: 357–365.
Dickinson, P. (1957 *trans*). *Aristophanes against war: The Acharnians, The Peace, Lysistrata*. London: Oxford University Press.
Dover, K. (1972). *Aristophanic Comedy*. London: B.T. Batsford Ltd.
Edson, C. (1947). Notes on the Thracian Phoros. *Classical Philology* 42: 88–105.
Ellis, H. (2011). The Ecclesiazusae and the Republic. *International Journal of the Humanities* 9: 177–186.
Etzioni, A. (2000). Toward a theory of public ritual. *Sociological Theory* 18: 44–59.
Evans, N.A. (2002). Sanctuaries, sacrifices, and the eleusinian mysteries. *Numen* 49: 227–254.
Frost, B.-P. (2014). *Introduction* (ed. Mhire and Frost), 1–9. Albany, NY: SUNY University of Press.
Gomme, A.W. (1938). Aristophanes and politics. *Classical Review* 52: 97–109.
Hall, E. (2006). *The Theatrical Cast of Athens*. Oxford: OUP.
Hall, E. (2007a). *Aristophanic Laughter Down the Centuries* (ed. Hall and Wrigley), 1–29. Oxford: Legenda.
Hall, E. (2007b). The English-speaking Aristophanes. In: *Aristophanes in Performance* (ed. E. Hall and A. Wrigley), 66–92. Oxford: Legenda.
Hall, E. (2010). The many faces of Lysistrata. In: *Looking at Lysistrata* (ed. D. Studdard), 29–36. London: Duckworth.
Hall, E. (2014). Comedy & Athenian festival culture. In: *Cambridge Companion to Greek Comedy* (ed. M. Revermann). CUP.
Hall, E. (2018a). Hephaestus the hobbling humorist: the club-footed God in the history of early Greek comedy. *Illinois Classical Studies* 43: 366–387.
Hall, E. (2018b). The boys from Cydathenaeum: Aristophanes versus Cleon again. In: *How to Do Things with History (Festschrift for Paul Cartledge)* (ed. D. Allen, P. Christensen, and P. Millett), 339–363. OUP.
Hall, E. (2019). Competitive vocal performance in Aristophanes' knights. In: *Poet and Orator* (ed. A. Markantonatos and E. Volonaki), 71–82. de Gruyter.
Hall, E. (2020a). *The Hilarious Politics of the Supernatural in Aristophanic Comedy* (ed. Swallow and Hall), 89–99. London: Bloomsbury.
Hall, E. (2020b). Aristophanes' *Birds* as Satire on Athenian opportunists in Thrace. In: *Aristophanes and Politics* (ed. R.M. Rosen and H.P. Foley), 187–213. Leiden and Boston: Brill.
Hall, E. (2020c). In Praise of Cario, the Nonpareil Comic Slave of Aristophanes' *Wealth*. In: *Ancient Greek Comedy (Essays in Honour of Angus M. Bowie)* (ed. A. Fries and D. Kanellakis), 219–237. Berlin: de Gruyter.
Hall, E. (2022). Rowing and democratic memory: Salamis in Aristophanic comedy. In: *Salamis and Democracy* (ed. N.C. Kyriazis and E.M.L. Economou). Cham: Springer.
Hall, E. (2024). Relatively Funny: Re-Reading the *Phrontistērion* in Aristophanes' *Clouds*. In: *Portrayals of 'Intellectuals' in the Ancient World* (ed. T. Fögen). Berlin: de Gruyter.
Hall, E. (forthcoming). *Aristophanes' Citizen Superheroes*.
Harriott, R. (1986). *Aristophanes: Poet and Dramatist*. London and Sydney: Croom Helm.
Heath, M. (1987). *Political Comedy in Aristophanes*. Göttingen: Vandenhoeck & Ruprecht.
Henderson, J. (1987). Older women in Attic Old Comedy. *TAPhA* 117: 105–129.
Henderson, J. (1997). Mass versus elite and the comic heroism of Peisetairos. In: *The City as Comedy: Society and Representation in Athenian Drama* (ed. G. Dobrov), 135–148. Chapel Hill, NC: University of North Carolina Press.
Hesk, J. (2000). Intratext and Irony in Aristophanes. In: *Intratextuality* (ed. A. Sharrock and H. Morales), 227–262. Oxford: OUP.
Hesk, J. (2007). Combative capping in Aristophanic comedy. *Cambridge Classical Journal* 53: 124–160.
Hugill, W.M. (1936). *Panhellenism in Aristophanes*. Chicago: Chicago University Press.
Hugill, W.M. (1937). The last appeal of Aristophanes. In: *Manitoba Essays: Written in Commemoration of the Sixtieth Anniversary of the University of Manitoba by Members of the Teaching Staffs* (ed. R.C. Lodge), 190–219. Toronto: Macmillan Co. of Canada.
Hunt, P. (2001). The Slaves and the Generals of Arginusae. *AJP* 122: 359–380.
Hutchinson, G.O. (2011). House politics and city politics in Aristophanes. *CQ* 61: 48–70.

Isaac, B.H. (1986). *The Greek Settlements in Thrace Until the Macedonian Conquest.* Leiden: Brill.

Karamanou, I. (2013). As threatening as the Persians: Euripides in Aristophanes' *Thesmophoriazusae.* In: *Bulletin of the Institute of Classical Studies. Supplement No. 124, Marathon—2,500 Years,* 155–164. Oxford University Press.

Konstan, D. (1985). The Politics of Aristophanes' *Wasps. TAPA* 115: 27–46.

Koster, W.J. (ed.) (1975). *Scholia in Aristophanem 1.1A.* Groningen: Bouma.

Lavelle, B.M. (1992). The Pisistratids and the Mines of Thrace. *GRBS* 33: 5–23.

Lewis, D.M. (1955). Notes on Attic inscriptions (II): XIII. Who was Lysistrata? *ABSA* 50: 1–12.

Lombardini, J. (2014). *Seeing Democracy in the Clouds* (ed. Mhire and Frost), 13–27. Albany, NY: SUNY University of Press.

Lougovaya-Ast, J. (2006). Myrrhine, the first priestess of Athena Nike. *Phoenix* 60: 211–225.

Lowe, N.J. (2007). *Comedy.* Cambridge: CUP.

Mahoney, A. (2007). Key Terms in *Birds. Classical World* 100: 267–278.

McGlew, J. (1997). After Irony: Aristophanes' *Wealth* and Its Modern Interpreters. *American Journal of Philology* 118: 35–53.

Meyer, M. (2014). *Peisetairos of Aristophanes' Birds and the Erotic Tyrant of Republic IX* (ed. Mhire and Frost), 275–303. Albany, NY: SUNY University of Press.

Mhire, Jeremy, J., and Frost, B.-P. (ed.) (2014). *The Political Theory of Aristophanes.* Albany, NY: SUNY University of Press.

Morley, N. (1997). Cleon the misunderstood? *Omnibus* 35: 4–6.

Murray, G. (1933). *Aristophanes: A Study.* Oxford.

Nichols, P. (1998). *Aristophanes' Novel Forms: The Political Role of Drama.* London: Minerva Press.

Nietzsche, F. (1922). Geschichte der griechischen Literatur. In: *Gesammelte Schriften,* vol. V (ed. R. Oehler and F. Würzbach). Munich: Beck.

Olson, S.D. (1996). Politics and Poetry in Aristophanes' *Wasps. Transactions of the American Philological Association* 126: 129–150.

Redfield, J. (1962). Comedy, Tragedy, and Politics in Aristophanes' "Frogs". *Chicago Review* 15: 107–121.

Reinders, P. (2001). *Demos Pyknites: Untersuchung zur Darstellung des Demos in der alten Komödie.* Stuttgart and Weimar: J.B. Metzler.

Rosen, R.M. (2015). Reconsidering the Reperformance of Aristophanes' *Frogs. Trends in Classics* 7: 237–256.

Ruffell, I.A. (2011). *Politics and Anti-realism in Athenian old comedy: the art of the impossible.* Oxford: Oxford University Press.

Rusten, J. (ed.) (2011). *The Birth of Comedy.* Baltimore, MD: Johns Hopkins U.P.

Saxonhouse, A. (1978). Comedy in Callipolis: Animal Imagery in the *Republic. American Political Science Review* 72: 888–901.

Saxonhouse, A. (2014). *Boundaries: The Comic Poet Confronts the "Who" of Political Action* (ed. Mhire and Frost), 89–108. Albany, NY: SUNY University of Press.

Sears, M.A. (2013). *Athens, Thrace, and the Shaping of Athenian Leadership.* Cambridge & New York: Cambridge University Press.

Sidwell, K. (2009). *Aristophanes the Democrat.* In: *The Politics of Satirical Comedy during the Peloponnesian War.* Cambridge: CUP.

Slater, N. (2002). *Spectator politics: metatheatre and performance in Aristophanes.* Philadelphia, Pa.: University of Pennsylvania Press.

Sommerstein, A. (2001, ed. and trans.). *Aristophanes' Wealth.* Warminster: Aris & Phillips.

Sommerstein, A. (2009). Slave and citizen in Aristophanic comedy. In: *Talking About Laughter: And other Studies in Greek Comedy,* 137–154. Oxford: OUP.

Spielvogel, J. (2001). *Wirtschaft und Geld bei Aristophanes.* Frankfurt: Marthe Clauss.

Spielvogel, J. (2003). Die politische Position des athenischen Komödiendichters Aristophanes. *Historia: Zeitschrift für Alte Geschichte* 52: 3–22.

Starkey, J. (2013). Soldiers and sailors in Aristophanes' *Babylonians. CQ* 63: 501–510.

Storey, I. (1998). Poets, Politicians and Perverts: Personal Humour in Aristophanes. *Classics Ireland* 5: 85–134.

Süvern, J.W. (1835). *Essay on "The Birds" of Aristophanes,* trans. W. R. Hamilton. London: John Murray.

Swallow, P. (2023). *Aristophanes in Britain.* Oxford: OUP.

Swallow, P. and Hall, E. (ed.) (2020). *Aristophanic Humour*. London: Bloomsbury.
Ussher, R.G. (1979). *Aristophanes [Greece & Rome New Surveys in the Classics 13]*. Oxford: OUP.
Vickers, M. (1995). Alcibiades at Sparta: Aristophanes' *Birds*. *Classical Quarterly* 45: 339–354.
Villacèque, N. (2013). *Spectateurs de paroles! Délibération démocratique et Théâtre à Athènes à l'époque classique*. Rennes: Press Universitaires de Rennes.
Whitehorne, J. (2005). O City of Kranaos! Athenian Identity in Aristophanes' "Acharnians". *Greece & Rome* 52: 34–44.
Zumbrunnen, J. (2006). Fantasy, Irony, and Economic Justice in Aristophanes' *Assemblywomen* and *Wealth*. *TheAmerican Political Science Review* 100: 319–333.
Τσακμάκης, Α. (1997). Κατασκευάζοντας το θεατή των Ορνίθων Τσακμάκης. In: *Όρνιθες* (ed. M. Christopoulos and A. Tsakmakis), 335–332. Athens: Οψεις και Αναγνώσεις μιας Αριστοφανικής Κωμωδίας.
Thonemann, P. (2020). Lysimache and « Lysistrata ». *The Journal of Hellenic Studies* 140: 128–142. https://doi.org/10.1017/S0075426920000063.
Olson, S.D. (1989). Cario and the new world of Aristophanes' Plutus. *TAPA* CXIX: 193–199.

PART II

The Comedies of Aristophanes

CHAPTER 7

Acharnians: Tragedy and Epic

Stephanie Nelson

Aristophanes, Literature, and Politics

The *Acharnians* is the earliest Aristophanes play to survive. Before winning first prize in 425 at the Athenian drama festival, the Lenaia, with this play (and at the tender age of around 25), Aristophanes had presented the *Banqueters* in 427 and the *Babylonians* in 426, winning second and probably first prize with them, but these plays exist only in fragments. All three plays were produced not by Aristophanes himself but by Callistratus, which was not in itself unusual but notable enough to merit Aristophanes' comic explanations in the parabasis of *Knights* (507–547), the first play he produced in his own name, and then again in those of *Wasps* (1018–1035) and *Clouds* (527–534).[1]

The *Acharnians* displays a fascination with other forms of literature, and particularly tragedy, that was to persist throughout Aristophanes' long career as one of Athens' foremost comic poets. Immediately, however, two qualifications need to be made. In the first place, since composing poetry was not, in Classical Athens, thought of as a "job" in our sense, "career" is not really the appropriate term here. And more importantly, as should become clear, our term "literature," like our term "art," fails to capture how vibrantly poetry, in all its many forms, permeated Athenian life. As it permeated Athens, it also permeated the works of Aristophanes. Many years after the *Acharnians*, in the *Frogs* of 405, Aristophanes' primary topic was to be tragedy and its relation to the city. In fact, of the 11 surviving plays, two are about tragedy (*Women at the Thesmophoria*, *Frogs*), two make tragedy central (*Acharnians*, *Wasps*) (Wright 2013: 205–225; Farmer 2017: 117–154) and all contain continual, ongoing references to tragedy, as well as to both epic and lyric verse. The *Acharnians*, a play largely about the need to end the ongoing Peloponnesian War, opens with its protagonist lamenting having to see a play by the tragic poet Theognis, rather than one by Aeschylus (10–12). It is a concern that continues not only throughout the play but also throughout Aristophanes' life.

Aristophanes' continual reference to what are, in our terms, various literary genres, displays, however, far more than merely an esthetic sensibility. Classical Greece was in many ways created as a culture through poetry, and fifth-century Athens very much continued the tradition. To be "Greek" (or rather, "Hellenic") in the classical world meant to speak the language of Homer; the Homeric poems were the basis of any education, and nearly all great public festivals included

---

[1] Aristophanes would later have Callistratus produce both *Birds* (414) and *Lysistrata* (411), while *Frogs* (405) would be produced by Philonides.

recitations of Homer.[2] Similarly, to be Athenian was to participate in the great Athenian festivals, particularly the City (or "Greater") Dionysia, where poetry was performed. Literature and the political were completely intertwined. Even before the Athenian democracy was established, the great civic festival, the Panatheneia, included recitations of Homer alongside athletic contests and (every 4 years) the great ritual procession enshrined on the Parthenon frieze. Similarly, the City Dionysia included not only the competitions for tragedy, comedy, and dithyramb but also the most political of ceremonies, such as the actual physical presentation of the tribute paid by Athens' "allies" to the city they were in fact subject to, or the parade of young men whose fathers had been killed in war, who had been raised at the expense of the city, and who, at the age of 18, were welcomed into full citizenship with the bestowal of armor by the city (Rehm 1994: 16–18; Goldhill 1990; Griffin 1998; Carter 2000; Rhodes 2003).

In such an atmosphere, "literature" (in our terms) could hardly fail to be political – but also, and correspondingly, what it means to be "political" (that is, related to the *polis* or Greek city-state) takes on a coloring rather different from, say, that of the United States in the twenty-first century. The contests in dithyramb at the City Dionysia provide an excellent example. The dithyramb was a choral ode to a god, here sung by 50 voices. Singers had, by law, to be full Athenian citizens, and each of the ten "tribes" into which Athens was divided contributed a chorus for both the mens' and the boys' competitions. The contests, as a result, not only reinforced the community of the tribe but also reinforced Athenian democracy as such, since this division (in accordance with which Athenians also governed themselves in the Assembly and were called into military service) was the one established by Cleisthenes when the Athenian democracy was first formed in 507 (Wilson 2000: 75–81; Ieranò 2013: 368–386; Farmer 2017: 196).

Not only the singers of dithyramb but also the chorus members in Athenian drama had, by law, to be Athenian citizens. Given three tragedies competing against each other, each with a chorus of 12 or 15 members, and five comedies also competing against each other, each with a chorus of 24, each festival would bring between 156 and 165 Athenian chorus members onto the stage, along with the 1000 dithyramb singers. The experience was also intense. Chorus members (all male) rehearsed for months before the festival and were excused from military service to do so, and this during the lengthiest and most destructive war in Athenian history (Wiles 2000: 131, 135; McLeish 1980: 32–34). As Revermann has pointed out, this means that a great number of members of the audience would have themselves participated in, and presumably become invested, in the poetic performances (Revermann 2006). The lavish festival, funded by the *polis*, was thus performed before an audience that had a stake in the literary competition in more ways than one.

Aristophanes' comedies continually assume an interest in and familiarity with epic, drama, and lyric poetry, and since he frequently won with them, the assumption seems to have been justified. Moreover, the plays were, pretty much by definition, designed for a popular audience. For ordinary Athenians then, drama and lyric, alongside epic as nearly a given, must have been simply an element of their common world. Nor is this surprising. For one thing, just as the "literary" in Athens was intertwined with the religious, the religious was not distinct from the political, as the Parthenon (which held not only the great 38-ft gold and ivory statue of Athena Parthenos but also the treasury of Athens' Delian League), the public festivals that celebrated Dionysus, and the name "Athens" itself all indicate. Similarly, Athenians, like all Greeks, regularly consulted oracles, and oracles were delivered in verse, as quoted both by Herodotus and, extensively, in a parodied version, by Aristophanes. Not only Aristophanes' *Knights*, which makes oracles a main weapon in the political contest between Cleon and his comic challenger, but also *Peace* (1051–1126) and *Birds* (859–891) include "oracle-mongers" as an ordinary feature of politics, and references to oracles run

---

[2] See Revermann in Bakola et al. 101: "Greek literary history can, in fact, plausibly be seen as a long series of responses to epic in the form of the Homeric poems: lyric poetry, tragedy, historiography and the novel (let alone the epic poetry of Apollonius, Tryphiodorus or Nonnus) all cannot but interact with Homeric epic as a critical part of their artistic and ideological self-definition."

throughout the plays (as *Wasps* 158–162, 799–804, *Lysistrata* 765–780, *Wealth* 32–55, and throughout). In *Birds*, in fact, a city cannot even be founded (at least in the view of the poet) without a poet to provide the requisite verse for the occasion (*Birds* 904–957).

Aristophanes, Euripides, and the *Telephus*

In this atmosphere, Aristophanes' interest in "literature" inevitably spoke as well to what it meant to be an Athenian. From what we know of the *Banqueters*, Aristophanes' lost first play, the difference between the Buggered and the Virtuous Boy included a preference for new-fangled and morally dubious rhetoric and song, in contrast to the good old-fashioned values expressed by Homer and Aeschylus. The same contrast would appear 4 years later, when the young man Pheidippides, corrupted by the relativism of the Sophists (here in the person of Socrates), actually comes to prefer Euripides to Aeschylus and the even more traditional lyric poet, Simonides (1353–1376). In *Women at the Thesmophoria*, a play in which Euripides becomes a main character, Euripides' tendency to corrupt the Athenian character appears again, though now in the upside-down form of depictions that are only too realistic. And the contrast appears again in *Frogs*, many years later and in very different circumstances, when, needing a poet to save the city from its all too imminent destruction (as Athens was on the brink of losing the Peloponnesian War), Dionysus himself descends to Hades to bring back Euripides, only to be persuaded that in fact it is Aeschylus that Athens truly needs.

It is also, however, important to remember that Aristophanes is not necessarily interested in tragedy for its own sake; he is composing comic plays, not a pre-Aristotelian *Poetics* (Platter 1993: 42–62; Wright 2013: 11–12, although see also Wright 2012: esp. 2–5). Literature consequently enters his plays as an element of particular comedies, each designed to explore a particular topic. This is nowhere more true than in the *Acharnians*, where Aristophanes makes a single tragedy, Euripides' now lost *Telephus*, thematic throughout, but uses the tragedy to explore the comedy's more basic theme, which is peace and war (MacDowell 1995: 46–79; Ruffell 2011: 172–179). The plot of the play is in equal parts simple and brilliant. The hero, Dikaiopolis (whose name means "just-city"), opens the play frustrated in the Assembly by the high and mighty officials and ambassadors who profit off the war. In a masterful version of the "great idea" that often supplies Aristophanes' motif (establishing a bird city in *Birds*; a sex strike to end the war in *Lysistrata*), Dikaiopolis decides to buy a peace just for himself and his family, aided by the fact that the Greek word, *sponde*, means both "wine" (poured as a libation at the signing of a truce) and a peace treaty. Opposed in his plans by a chorus from the particularly aggressive deme of Acharnae (hence the play's title, *The Acharnians*), Dikaiopolis, who has now identified himself with Aristophanes, decides that his best defense lies in becoming the Euripidean character Telephus and parodying that tragedy. After a visit to Euripides and a detailed parody of his play Dikaiopolis triumphs. Even more specifically, he triumphs over the (actual) Athenian general Lamachus (whose name, as it happens, means "very-warlike"), who takes the role played by Achilles in the Euripides play and who is brought in by the Acharnians to support their cause.

In the second half of the play, however, there is a strange change (Silk 2000: 293–296). After a parabasis in which Aristophanes again speaks in his own voice, though now, as was conventional, through the chorus, we find that Dikaiopolis has not returned to the farm he longed for in the opening of the play, but rather set up his own private marketplace. Here, as he foretold (623–625), he trades with Athens' enemies, a Megarian and Theban. He also picks and chooses which Athenians he will let share his peace – not including the Chorus in the number. As the play ends the *Telephus* returns, but now with Lamachus, who has been wounded fighting off a raid, in the role of Telephus, and Dikaiopolis as one of the ones, feasted at the public expense, that he complained about so bitterly in the play's opening scene.

There is another major complication as well. While Aristophanes makes Euripidean tragedy central to his play, he also uses it in contradictory ways, both structuring *Acharnians* around the *Telephus* and also maintaining his usual condemnation of Euripides as a corrupting force. Moreover, a coinage by Cratinus, one of Aristophanes' rival comedians, makes it clear that his "Aeschylus vs. Euripides" motif is more complex than it seems, since the coinage, "euripidaristophanizing," links Aristophanes not to Aeschylus but to Euripides (Scholium at Plato, *Apology* 19c; O'Sullivan 2006: 163–169). Aristophanes, it seems, not only ridicules Euripides' new, relativistic, anti-heroic point of view but also shares it (Nelson 2016: 69–73; Farmer 2017: 157–158, 188–194). The self-contradiction, of course, is his privilege as a comedian. It also, however, proves to be central not only to Aristophanes' play but also to his critique of what it means to be an Athenian.

The fact that Euripides produced the *Telephus* in 438, 14 years before *Acharnians,* seems to indicate how great an impact Athenian drama could have (Henderson 2020: 40–41). The impact of this particular play appears again in Aristophanes' returning to it, 14 years after *Acharnians*, in his *Women at the Thesmophoria*. It also appears in an Italian vase, dated around 370, which pictures the *Telephus* parody from that play, implying that references to drama had a significant and ongoing commercial, and even exportable, appeal (Csapo 1986; Rusten 2011: 435; Farmer 2017: 155–194). Passing references and parodies to earlier plays, both comedies and tragedies, made by both Aristophanes and his fellow comedians, imply much the same, that some significant part of the audience of perhaps 15,000 paid attention and remembered earlier plays (Pickard-Cambridge 1968: 263). After all, there is no reason to put in a joke, particularly when one is trying to win a comedy contest, if no one is going to get it.

Even further, the significance of *Telephus* in the *Acharnians* points, in its own way, to the theme of the *Banqueters, Clouds,* and *Frogs* – that the poetry the city attends to also shapes the sort of city it is (and see *Republic* 376e–402d). In *Acharnians*, however (although Aristophanes can never resist sprinkling in a number of other comic targets), the focus is more narrow than usual. The primary issue is peace and war. As the first of a series of plays positioned against the ongoing Peloponnesian War (*Peace, Lysistrata,* and with scattered references throughout the corpus), *Acharnians* pits Dikaiopolis and his private peace against Lamachus in a contest, essentially, over who is the "true citizen" (*polites chrestos* 595; Prauscello 2013: 324). It also pits him against a very particular kind of Athenian, as exemplified by the chorus. As Thucydides reports (2.20), when the Spartan king, Archidamus, first invaded Attica at the opening of the war he chose Acharnae to devastate. His rationale was that these notoriously tough and belligerent farmers, now cooped up within the city walls, from which they could see their homes being destroyed, would be most easily provoked to leave the protection of the walls and give battle. And while the Spartans failed to achieve the infantry battle they wished for, they certainly succeeded in provoking the Acharnians into an undying opposition to Sparta (Thucydides 2.21), which is where the *Telephus* comes in.

As we will see below, Euripides' *Telephus* appears largely to have been about who is an "us" and who is a "them," and, in pursuing this theme, to have been about what values are most important to an individual and a community. The play also asked these questions specifically in the context of peace and war. In the traditional story, which Euripides developed, Telephus, the king of Mysia (in Asia Minor, near the Troad) is the son of Heracles by Auge, who was banished from Greek Tegea by her father, king Aleos (Collard et al. 1995: 15–52). Telephus is thus, in fact, not barbarian (which, to the Greeks, meant simply someone who was not Greek) but Greek. When the Greek forces invade Mysia on their way to attack Troy, Telephus leads the resisting army and is wounded in the battle by Achilles. Having learned from Apollo that only the one who caused the wound can cure it, Telephus disguises himself as a poor beggar and infiltrates the Greek camp in search of Achilles. When he is discovered, perhaps after a defense of the Greeks' enemies, he seizes Agamemnon's young son, Orestes, as a hostage, and threatens to sacrifice him unless he is healed. The Greeks, who have heard an oracle that they cannot take Troy without his leadership, agree, although Achilles protests that he knows nothing about medicine. Telephus is then healed when Odysseus realizes that the healer is not Achilles but the spear which wounded Telephus, whose filings are able to cure him. Although Telephus refuses to join the Greek expedition, on the grounds that his wife is Priam's daughter, he agrees to lead the Greeks to Troy, the guidance that is fated to grant them success.

The remains of Euripides' play leave a number of questions unclear, in particular, the relation of the hostage scene to Telephus' "great speech," evidently in defense of the Greeks' enemies, as well as the question of precisely how Telephus' identity, first as king of Mysia and then as in fact Greek, was discovered (Collard et al. 1995: 18–20; Farmer 2017: 168–172). The fragments, however, make it clear that the play focused on the issue of disguise and true identity and, in particular, Telephus' status as Greek rather than Mysian (as fragments 719 and 727c). Moreover, the plot of the play seems to make it clear that it was not Telephus' arguments that ended the Greeks' hostility toward him but rather the discovery of his true identity as a Greek. Reason, in other words, gives way to the question of us versus them.

Themes in *Acharnians*: Us versus Them

As we have seen, Aristophanes puts the *Telephus* to contradictory uses in *Acharnians*, both to ridicule Euripides as undermining true Athenian values and also to furnish the framework of his play. The contradiction reflects a central question, or perhaps contradiction, in the *Acharnians* itself, one that also centers around the issue of us versus them, though in a more complex way than in the plot of the *Telephus*. In terms of the *Telephus* plot Dikaiopolis emerges, like Telephus, as neither beggar nor alien, but as the true Athenian. In terms of Aristophanes' usual ridicule of Euripides' non-heroic heroes, however, Dikiopolis, in his Euripidean disguise, seems a negative character, one who, having swallowed down shifty Euripidean rhetoric, prepares to deceive the Chorus (415–417, 440–458, 484). The contradiction reflects a long-standing critical debate about whether Dikaiopolis is a purely positive figure in the play, such as Trugaios in *Peace* or Lysistrata in *Lysistrata*, or an ambiguous, altered, or negative hero, like Peisetairos in *Birds*, Dionysus in *Frogs*, or Strepsiades in *Clouds*. Those who argue for the first position point to the close identification of Dikaiopolis with Aristophanes that we will examine below. In this light, Dikaiopolis' final triumph in the Festival of the Pitchers and consequent public feasting foreshadows his creator's victory (and post-celebration dinner, as 1150–1161) in the comic festival. In contrast, those who have a negative view of Dikaiopolis point out how, in the second half of the play, he seems to separate himself both from the "true Athenian values" he represented earlier and from most of the Athenians he meets (as also perhaps implied at 1150–1161) (Dover 1972: 87–88; Parker 1991; MacDowell 1995: 75–77; Olson 2002: xliii–xlv).

Rather than defending either position, I wish to explore the idea that Dikaiopolis is presented, deliberately, as ambivalent – and that it is this ambivalence that Aristophanes points to in his use of the *Telephus*. As we will see below, the ambivalence that Aristophanes brings out through the *Telephus*, and through his references to the role of literature generally in Athens, reflects both an ambivalence in Dikaiopolis and tensions within Athens itself. As we will see, these tensions exist between Homeric and democratic values, between public and private values, and within Athenian identity generally. The first topic we will consider, however, is the one most directly related to both Dikaiopolis' ambiguity and Aristophanes' use of the *Telephus*. This is the basic question of us versus them.

A great deal of the *Acharnians* centers around what seems to have been a central question of the *Telephus*, what it means to be one of "us." This is also precisely the issue that renders Dikaiopolis ambivalent, and it is explored by Aristophanes through theater. The opening of *Acharnians* deliberately prepares the audience to identify with Dikaiopolis, as he sits waiting for the Assembly to open, thinking about the playwrights and musicians he prefers (*Achar.* 9–15), just as the audience has just been sitting, waiting for the play to begin. His adoption of the ragged Telephus costume achieves the same goal. In contrast to the parade of "phonies" that occupy the first scene, the self-serving ambassadors, the actually Athenian retinue of the King's Eye, and the Odomanti who seem to be no such thing, Dikaiopolis' costume enables him to reveal himself, as Telephus did, as not a beggar at all, but as actually a "true citizen" (595) – and so accordingly as natively one of "us."

The first half of *Acharnians* thus leads to a triumph for its hero: he wins over the Chorus, is restored to peace and the countryside and family he longed for, and is acknowledged as the true Athenian citizen, while Lamachus, the "Very-warlike," plays the role that Dikaiopolis has cast off, of the rejected outcast, and even scapegoat (Bowie [1993] 27–35). The triumph of the hero in the Festival of the Pitchers at the play's end repeats this success, ratifying the triumph of the values of peace over those of war. At the same time, however, the second half of the *Acharnians* has complicated the issue and done so specifically in terms of a theatrical "us" and "them," as Dikaiopolis repeatedly refuses to share his private peace and its benefits, most tellingly with the Chorus (*Achar.* 1008–1017, 1037–1046). Dikaiopolis' rejection of Decertes, a small farmer destroyed by the war, seems designed to remind the audience of the difference between the countryman Dikaiopolis yearning for his farm (32–36), the figure they initially identified with, and the now prosperous merchant trading with Athens' enemies.

Aristophanes, however, goes a good deal further than this in using the present involvement of the audience to address the question of "us" versus "them." In one of the most striking moments in the play Dikaiopolis, beginning his self-defense before the chorus, and speaking as Aristophanes himself, specifically appeals to the Athenian audience as "us":

> For this time Cleon will not slander me, saying that
> with strangers (*xenoi*) present I speak badly of the city.
> For we are by ourselves [literally "we are ourselves"] and the contest is the Lenaia
> and no strangers are here yet; neither tribute nor troops
> have arrived from the allied cities [as at the Greater Dionysia],
> But this time we are by ourselves, completely winnowed,
> for I figure the resident aliens as the bran of the town.
>
> (502–508)[3]

Both the current appeal and the reference to Aristophanes' struggle with Cleon are completely theatrical, as that struggle originated and was carried on in Aristophanes' plays (as *Acharn.* 377–382, 660–664, *Wasps* 1029–1042, *Peace* 751–761, *Clouds* 549–550) – as the audience would have seen.

And yet, while Dikaiopolis' identification of himself with Aristophanes seems to clinch his identity as one of "us," his response to acquiring his Telephus costume adds a different dimension:

> "O Zeus, thou seer through all and under" –
> Euripides, since you've granted this favor,
> give me those things too that accompany the rags,
> the felt cap for the head, the Mysian one,
> "For today I must seem to be a beggar
> and be the very thing I am, but seem not so";
> the audience should know me, who I am,
> but the chorus should stand there like fools
> so that for them, with my phraselets, I might give them the finger
>
> (440–444)

Dikaiopolis' deliberate separation of himself from the Chorus, opening with first the paratragic play with disguises that reveal more than they hide, and moving then to an apparent quote from the *Telephus* (Olson 2002: 189) has a rather different feel than the Chorus' coming, and expected, references to "our producer" and "this poet" (628, 649) in the parabasis. Aristophanes may use the *Telephus* to encourage the audience to see his hero as one of us, but, on the other hand, we are currently watching a comedy, not a tragedy.

Dikaiopolis' declared plan of tricking the Chorus is all the more significant as his winning them over, as in many Aristophanes' comedies, is a key move in the success of his plan. His separation is then further underlined, again metapoetically, when the Chorus complains of the producer Antimachus cheating them out of their due post-production feast – soon after pointing out Dikaiopolis' disinclination to share the feast he is busily preparing (1037–1046, 1150–1161). Moreover, as Dikaiopolis, in character, celebrates first his own private Rural Dionysia, usually celebrated in December, and then the February Festival of the Pitchers (the only festival in which,

---

[3] Aristophanes' text is taken from the Oxford Classical Text, edited by Nigel G. Wilson (2007); translations are my own.

traditionally, Athenians drank alone), he skips over the festival that Athens is currently collectively engaged in, the Lenaia (Bowie 1993: 35–39). It seems to be not only his private peace that he is inclined not to share.

There is a good reason, even beyond the connection to culture that we saw above, that Aristophanes might use the Athenian experience of poetry to explore the question of an "us" and a "them." Dithyramb was not only explicitly organized by democratic tribes, that is, around specifically Athenian groupings of who is "us," but was also by its nature collective. Comedy also readily divides the "us" who appreciate the joke from the "them" who may well be its butt.[4] Tragedy, in a rather different way, can do the same. As I have argued elsewhere, the effect of Greek tragedy was an intensity of effect that Gorgias likened to trickery (*apate*) (DK 82.B23 = Plutarch, *Moralia* 348c) and that Plato feared as able to sway the firmest of souls (*Republic* 492a5-c10, 605d2 and see *Ion* 535b1-536b10; Nelson 2016: 171–173; Farmer 2017: 180–181). This intensity also serves to bring the audience together – one reason that the Dionysia was so appropriate as a political venue. Even the setting reinforced the collectivity. When the ambassadors from the tributary states presented their tribute to the Athenians assembled in the theater, they looked up past the ten generals seated in the front row, and up past the dignitaries around them, and then up past the audience of ordinary Athenians, to the Parthenon and the 30-foot bronze statue of Athena Promachos, with its drawn spear glinting in the sunlight. In fact, while the City Dionysia, unlike the Lenaia, was not simply "us," the presence of foreigners could simply reinforce the collective feeling created by the setting, as with Aristophanes' joke in *Peace* (45–49) on the "Ionian fellow" making guesses about the plot.

The collective spirit appealed to by poetry was, moreover, reinforced in Athens by the striking resemblance between the theater and the paramount institution of Athenian democracy, familiar (at least presumably) to all citizens, the Assembly, with its 6000-person quorum. *Acharnians*, moreover, employs exactly this resemblance in its first scene, by implicitly using the theater audience as a stand-in for the citizens attending Dikaiopolis' Assembly. The resemblance is noted in sources as disparate as Cleon's speech in Thucydides (3.38), Plato (*Republic* 492b-c), and even implicitly in the *Oedipus Tyrannos*, as Oedipus' first address to the Theban priest, elders, and citizens before him, is performed by an actor facing the priest of Dionysus, the assembled officials, and the citizens of Athens. In both venues, the Athenians sit collectively and judge speeches. And in both, in one of the few places where Cleon and Aristophanes seem to have agreed, they are liable to be tricked (Slater 2002: 42–67).

Dikaiopolis' appeal to his audience as "ourselves alone at the Lenaia" makes the association of the theater with Athens as a unified community explicit. By going even further, and explicitly identifying Dikaiopolis with himself, in opposition to his enemy Cleon, Aristophanes also makes it personal on a whole other level. While Athenian comedy often uses the parabasis to break the fourth wall of the drama, with the chorus explicitly identifying themselves as the chorus, and defending "our poet" (literally, or at least etymologically, "our maker") this level of identification is extreme. It is also at a curious disconnect with the *Acharnians*' parabasis, where Aristophanes, who suddenly identifies himself with Aegina rather than Athens (652–654), insists that peace is not desirable at any price, and claims that his importance lies in stopping the Athenians from being deceived by flattering speeches (633–645) (Bowie 1982; Biles 2011: 78–80; Sidwell 2012: 37). And there is another curious element in Dikaiopolis' identifying himself as Aristophanes – as Aristophanes makes explicit in his following plays, at the time of *Acharnians* Aristophanes was deliberately not linking himself to the production of the play. The theme of "us" versus "them," it seems, is rather more complex than the *Telephus* (at least on a superficial view) would suggest.

---

[4] Prauscello (2013: 322): "The comic author tends to create an 'ideology of exclusiveness' for his implied audience: '[t]he poet addresses the spectators as if they belonged to his friends' group'" quoting Zanetto (2001: 74); and see Halliwell (1991).

Themes in *Acharnians*: Epic Values and Democracy

We will look again at Aristophanes' relation to the production of *Acharnians* when we consider the theme of identity at the end of this piece. First, though, I want to turn to two other sets of contradictions or tensions in Athenian culture explored through the *Telephus*. The first is the tension between Homeric and democratic values, and the second is the tension between the public and the private.

Aristophanes' use of the *Telephus* in *Acharnians* points not only to his specific take on peace and war but also addresses a curious aspect of Athenian culture. Beginning with its opening contrast of Aeschylus and Theognis, the *Acharnians* sets comedy against tragedy. In so doing, it also sets itself against the world of Homeric epic, which was the setting for Greek tragedy. Just as the grounding of Greek culture generally was in Homer, Aeschylus is said to have declared that all his dramas were slices from the great feast of Homer (Athenaeus 8347e and see *Frogs* 1040–1042), while Plato refers to Homer as the first and greatest of the tragedians (*Republic* 595c1). It is also Euripides' undermining of this ethos that Aristophanes particularly ridicules throughout his plays. The ragged, unheroic heroes mocked at *Acharnians* 410–80 appear again in the joke on Euripides' Bellerophon in *Peace* (135–148), in Agathon's effeminacy in *Women at the Thesmophoria* (95–167 and see 173–174) and culminates in *Frogs* with the contrast between Aeschylus' Homeric "noble six-footers ... breathing spears and lances and white-crested helms and casques and greaves and seven-oxhide spirits" and Euripides' duty shirkers, lowlifes, and rogues (*Frogs* 1013–1017).

But at the same time that Aristophanes is ridiculing Euripides for degrading the great Homeric values, he is conducting a rather intensive parody of his own. Throughout his portrait of Lamachus, who enters addressed as "O Lamachus, hero!" (575), Aristophanes stresses his Homeric panoply, his cloak, shield with its Gorgon device, and helmet with its lofty crest, all of which are made thematic first in Dikaiopolis' debased uses for the heroic instruments of war (581–592, and see the same theme in *Peace* 1210–1264) and then in the great final contest which pits helmet plumes against roast fowls, spears against sausages, and bucklers against flat cakes (1095–1142).[5] Although it is sadly lost to us, Lamachus' costume, whose splendor clearly set off Dikaiopolis' borrowed rags, must have been hugely funny in itself, and all the more so as it adorned Lamachus, who, being notoriously poor, seems to have been given this role primarily because of his name (Plutarch, *Nicias* 15.1, *Alcibiades* 21; Olson 2002: 149–150). The parody thus appropriately culminates with Dikaiopolis triumphing over Lamachus, limping and supported, returned from a skirmish, rather unheroically wounded by a vine-prop, and calling for a doctor. As we have seen, the surprise is that Lamachus, with all his outdated Homeric heroism, seems now to have become the sympathetic Telephus figure.

As we have seen, Aristophanes' use of the *Telephus* points to a distinctive feature of comedy: its ability, in contrast to tragedy, and in some cases rising even to a generic imperative, to be self-contradictory. Rather than being merely license (although it can be that too), comedy's self-contradiction is often the source of the humor, as in the protest in *Wealth*: "you won't persuade us, even if you persuade us" (600) or Groucho Marx's classic "I would never belong to a club that would have me for a member." In this regard, as I have argued elsewhere, comedy reveled in playing against tragedy's intense emotional response, and against its related resistance to breaking the fourth wall (Nelson 2016: 171–176). Since the *Telephus* itself is lost we cannot know what emotional response it might have been designed to create. Whatever that was, however, it could hardly be as divided against itself as *Acharnians*, and not least in its view of martial valor.

Just as Dikaiopolis appears to switch roles in the course of the *Acharnians*, so does Lamachus. Initially, Lamachus, the bombastic militarist growing rich off the public coffers, is contrasted to

---

[5] Revermannin in Bakola et al. (2013: 120): "In *Acharnians* the juxtaposition, embodied by the pair of contrasting central characters, between the doomed grandeur of epic and comedy's celebration of survival and the good life culminates in the play's showdown, the arming scene and its aftermath (1071–1234). Staged as a *tableau* of parallel actions (and parallel ways of living) the scene's conceptual core, the lavish description of the hero getting ready for battle, is profoundly Homeric."

Dikaiopolis and his like who suffer the actual fighting (595–617). At the end of the play, however, Dikaiopolis, the underdog, the poor but honest representative of the demos, is feasting at the public expense (1085–1093) while Lamachus suffers the ills of war. One can argue, and critics certainly have, that this is only right, as it is a war of Lamachus' own making – and Aristophanes certainly' continues to assert the advantages of peace over war. Nonetheless, we may need to reconsider the play's insistence that the heroic values of the past are absurd when compared to the values of the demos day to day.

The point goes to the heart of Athenian identity – or even more, to the self-contradiction that lies at the heart of Athenian identity. The complexity appears most clearly in the fact that Lamachus is not only a representative of militarism but also a Homeric representative of militarism, an association that appears again at the end of *Peace* when the boy singing Homeric martial poetry turns out to be Lamachus' son (1292). In *Acharnians*, moreover, Lamachus' role contains virtually no obscenities, which is very unusual for a major character in an Aristophanes play, but suits his Homeric origins. In short, Lamachus is an Iliadic hero, a role that inevitably resonated in a culture whose focus on competition and whose ethos, *aien aristeuein* (*Iliad* 6.208): "always be best," were grounded in Homer.

But Athens, of course, was also a democracy. Lamachus may have been a *strategos* or "general," and so among the few elected officials in a system where most appointments were made by lot (593 and see 599, 606), but even there Athens took seriously the subordination of its officials to the people. Nor were the Athenians under any illusions about the "rule of the *demos*," praised by Pericles as allowing the poor as well as the rich to serve the state (Thucydides 2.37). The "rule of the *demos*" is also the "rule of the many" and since in Athens, as everywhere, the many are poor and the few are rich, democracy meant also the dominance of the poor, for example, the sailors who manned Athens' warships for a wage, against the rich hoplites, whose expensive armor (*hopla*), unless they were war-orphans, was paid for by themselves. Thus, when Dikaiopolis, formerly disguised in the rags he has begged from Euripides, reveals himself to be not a beggar at all but rather an honest citizen, the distinction might not be as apparent to everyone as Dikaiopolis intends.

The distinction also reflects an ambivalence in the Athenian relation to war itself, a self-contradiction that appears, for example, at the end of *Peace*, where the martial poetry sung by Lamachus' son is set against the son of Cleonymus singing Archilochus' spoof on martial valor (1265–1304; Telò 2010 in Bakola et al. 2013: 129–154). Trugaios, like Dikaiopolis, rejects Lamachan militarism – but then equally rejects Cleonymus' alleged cowardice, just as Aristophanes ridicules both war-mongering and those who are not fit and ready to fight, ridiculing Euripides' unheroic heroes or Cleonymus' throwing away of his shield as often as he mocks those who promote the war.

In short, the contradiction between Aristophanes ridiculing Euripides for not maintaining the glory of the Homeric hero, and then basing his own play on exactly the degraded hero that Euripides championed, only reflects an internal contradiction within Athens itself. Classical Athens was among the most militaristic and aggressive of societies, and yet prided itself, at least as Pericles reports, on its appreciation of leisure (*schole*, the origin of our word "school") and the finer things that leisure gives rise to. Pericles thus celebrates an Athenian cultivation that is open to all and yet expects Athens to be remembered forever as the state that "ruled over more Greeks than any other Greek state" (Thucydides 2.64; Samons 2004: 54–57). And above all, while Athens exemplified every bit as much as Sparta the ethos of always excelling, it did so within a culture that explicitly elevated the low and common over the well-born and aristocratic.

Themes in *Acharnians*: The Public and the Private

Aristophanes, then, incorporates tragedy into its opposite genre, comedy, at least in part to point out the self-contradictions inherent in Athenian society. Nor, while this may serve as a critique, is it necessarily a criticism. As Alcibiades says in Sparta (Thucydides 6.89) or as Socrates seems continually to have pointed out (as *Gorgias* 515a–522e, *Republic* 488a–489d), pure democracy, the idea that anyone can govern, whether they are competent or not, is an agreed-upon madness. Nonetheless, Aristophanes seems to have been able to both point out the absurdity and be fervently a part of the *polis*. The "great idea" of the *Acharnians*, the procuring of a private peace, is like a Volkswagen Bug sporting a sign: nuclear-free zone; it is an absurdity (though a very, very attractive absurdity) presented as a logical solution. Similarly with the individual and the community. When Dikaiopolis/Aristophanes tells 15,000 spectators that it is just us here alone at the Lenaia it is a joke – and yet he means it. That may be contradictory, but it is no less true for that.

The *Telephus* asked its audience to judge between peace and war in a number of ways, not least of which was in deciding what one ultimately values most. In what seems to have been the centerpiece of the play, a speech we know largely from the *Acharnians'* parody, the audience is asked how they can condemn an enemy's behavior when it is precisely what they would have done themselves. As Dikaiopolis puts it, had the Spartans denounced one of the allies' puppy dogs Athens would have retaliated: "and suppose we then that Telephus would not?" (541–551). The challenge not only problematizes the question of us and them, it does so in a very specific way, by raising the question of what one considers "one's own" and so necessary to fight for, and by contrasting private and public motivation. Thus, in Dikaiopolis' version, the Peloponnesian War actually began with Pericles retaliating for prostitutes stolen from his mistress, Aspasia (526–540), just as Pericles was regularly said to have had war declared against Samos to support Aspasia's original home, Miletus (Plutarch, *Pericles* 25).

The issue is also central to the *Telephus*. In a reprise of the dilemma posed by the need to sacrifice his daughter, Iphigenia, in order to set out for Troy (as dramatized in Aeschylus' *Oresteia*), Agamemnon in the *Telephus*, must choose between his hostility to a war enemy and his attachment to his young son, who is being held hostage. Telephus too must choose between his allegiance to his wife's family and joining the expedition of his newfound countrymen. Even the underlying paradox of the play, the idea that only that which caused the wound can heal it, raises questions of what is one's own and what is owed to others. It is notable, for example, that in the parallel scene in *Acharnians*, when Dikaiopolis refuses to give Decertes a curative drop of peace, he declares, "I'm not the public doctor" (1030–1032 and see 1222–1223).

The importance of the question of one's ultimate values appears in the fact that it is the *Telephus'* sacrifice scene that seems to have made the greatest impression, parodied in both *Acharnians* and *Women at the Thesmophoria*, and from *Women at the Thesmophoria* on the Italian vase mentioned above. The theme of what one values is also the focus of the parodies. Just as Agamemnon had to choose what mattered most to him when faced with the threatened sacrifice of his son, the Acharnians face the dreadful possibility of losing "the most dear of those dear to you" (325), a basket of charcoal (325–357) (charcoal being what the district was known for), while Mica in *Women at the Thesmophoria* faces the danger of losing her child, which is in fact a wineskin (women in comedy being notoriously bibulous) (*WT* 688–764). In the *Acharnians*, moreover, it is the reminder of what matters most, the private (taking deme affairs as "private" to the Acharnians, as opposed to the concerns of Attica as a whole), that compels the Chorus to listen to the argument of the "other." Thus, the play singles out the argument that what "they" have done is in fact only just what "we" would have done in the same circumstances – and what that is is to protect our own.

The human contradiction that Aristophanes seems to be honing in on is the idea that it is precisely what is private that we all have in common. As Achilles says in Book Nine of the *Iliad*, as he steps out of the great contest between Trojan and Greek, the Atreidae are not the only men who love their wives (9.340–41). This is also how Dikaiopolis establishes his rapport with the audience at the opening of *Acharnians* – yearning for his own home, his own things and his own deme, where one was not always being urged to "buy" "buy" "buy" from others (32–36). It is also how Dikaiopolis first experiences the joys of his newfound (or rather, newly purchased) peace, returned to his own deme, celebrating not the common City Dionysia but his own local Rural Dionysia, with his own wife, daughter, and servant. Dikaiopolis' ambivalence also begins to emerge in this regard, since, after what was no doubt his first ever purchase of wine (peace), his private market comes to seem more and more public. As Dikaiopolis heads off to celebrate his victory with the priest of Dionysus (who is in fact sitting in the front row of the theater) it is again the public world he enters.

We also note that, while it is completely positive in a comic hero to replace family with more nubile companions (as Trugaios does in *Peace*), Dikaiopolis' final festive procession is in marked contrast to his Rural Dionysia, as his wife and daughter have now disappeared.

It has been argued that in a play such as the *Birds*, or even the *Assemblywomen*, Aristophanes' humor derives from showing how the attempt to reform only recreates the original problem (McLeish 1980: 69–74). *Acharnians* also can be seen as showing us Dikaiopolis quite rightly valuing the goods of the private over those of the public and then losing both in the process. In any case, he certainly ends the play more like the ambassadors he despised at the play's opening than like Decertes, the farmer he refused to help. He also seems as far as ever from the rural home he once longed for. This is not to say that Aristophanes means to undermine his picture of the value of peace and the private realm, which he certainly does not. Rather, what seems to emerge is the mutual dependence of the public and private, however antithetical and contradictory their values. Like Dikaiopolis, we value the public because it enables us to protect the private, and in the course of so protecting it we endanger it. One does not need to go to war to see the point – paying taxes does it just as well.

This tension between the public and private is also directly related to the role of "literature" in Athenian life. Art in Athens, like architecture, was overwhelmingly public. Paintings appeared not inside private houses but on the public stoas, and statuary adorned not private gardens but public sites such as the Agora or Acropolis. As we have seen, theater and dithyramb contests were publicly funded political events, and this would have been as true of the smaller deme festivals as it was of the larger and more elaborate Lenaia and City Dionysia. Only personal ornaments such as jewelry, and decorated vases, primarily intended for private use, were specifically private – and even here the prizes of olive oil at the Panathenaic games had their own very specific style of vase to contain them. The exception, the sympotic songs composed and sung for private parties, may in fact also prove the rule, as these were associated with aristocratic clubs or *hetaireiai* regarded by the demos with deep suspicion. When Dionysus in the *Frogs* reads Euripides' *Andromeda* by himself on shipboard rather than seeing it at the festival, there is, from a fifth-century point of view, something distinctly wrong.[6]

But while Athenian literature, as Athenian art generally, may have been essentially public, it was also profoundly concerned with the private. The essentially public nature of Greek drama, for example, is vividly illustrated by the convention that the acting space was "outside" or public space, while "inside" or private space was confined to the space behind the *skene*, which could be revealed, largely in tableau, only with the *ekekkluma*. And yet Greek drama is very much about the private, and, from Aeschylus' *Oresteia* on, about the conflict between public and private. Women, of course, were designated to the private and inside realm – and yet they appear prominently in drama (Foley 1982, 2001). While the themes are in no way strange to us, the effect of following a story such as that of Antigone or Medea not in the privacy of one's home, but at an immensely political public and male-dominated festival, can only have brought out the inherent tension of literature itself, which exists in some ways as a means of collectively experiencing what is most individual and private.

Themes in *Acharnians*: Identity

The final theme that Aristophanes' *Acharnians* takes over from the *Telephus* is identity. As the summary of Euripides' plot makes clear, the play hinged on the "real" identity of Telephus and used the basic motif of disguise to bring this out. Had there been any doubt about this, *Acharnians* clobbers us with the idea, as Dikaiopolis and Euripides go, seriatim, through the costumes of Oeneus,

---

[6] Ford (2003); Henderson (2020: 39): "I will suggest that until very late in Aristophanes' fifth-century career, most spectators still knew, and comic poets expected them to know tragedy only through performance, however familiar the spectators may have been with written texts of other kinds of poetry."

Phoenix, Philoctetes, and Bellerophon before lighting on that of Telephus, with Thyestes and Ino then thrown in for good measure (418–434). On an even more meta-level Aristophanes ensures that we "recognize" Euripides by going through all the jokes that will become standard in Aristophanic comedy: Euripides is a sophist, self-centered, amoral, a wool-gatherer; he panders to lowlifes; his heroes are degraded, and his mother peddles vegetables (385–478).

The disguise theme, moreover, is one that Aristophanes has already carefully established. The *Acharnians'* initial scene with the ambassadors opens the question of who is a true citizen. It also ties that question to disguise by focusing on the costume and pseudo-Persian babbling of the King's Eye (94–97), revealing his companions to be the Athenians Cleisthenes and Strato (115–122), and questioning the identity of the Odomanti (155–158). Dikaiopolis' elaborate play with the need "be the very thing I am, but seem not so" (441) and his final triumphant throwing off his ragged costume to reveal himself as a true citizen, calls attention as well to the many costumes that continue to run throughout the play: Lamachus' war gear, the Megarian's "piggies," the "packing-up" of the informer, Nicarchus (926–958), Decertes' white outfit (1024 – whatever the joke), and the groomsman, bridesmaids, etc. (1048–1067) (Olson 2002: lxv–lxviii, 222–223). As is a given in Aristophanes, particularly in his penchant for cross-dressing, who you are seems very closely tied to how you dress, a point Dikaiopolis makes in noting that when Euripides dresses like a particular character, that is the character he then creates (420–429, and see *WT* 149–172; Wright 2012: 123–124; Farmer 2017: 158–162; Bobrick in Dobrov 1997: 177–197; Muecke (1982a,b); Slater 2002: 155).

The question of disguise, of course, particularly as Aristophanes ties it to theatrical costume, introduces a meta-theatrical element that Aristophanes hammers home in identifying himself with Dikaiopolis. This also, however, complicates the issue. As we saw before, although Athenian comedy often identifies the comic hero with the playwright, and regularly uses the parabasis to let the Chorus speak directly for him or to have him speak in his own first-person voice, Aristophanes' identification with Dikaiopolis is on a whole new level (McLeish 1980: 56–58; Olson 2002: xlv–xlviii; Wright 2012: 10–16). But as we also noted, in the *Acharnians* the identifications in the parabasis and with comic hero seem to be at odds, while, on yet another meta-level, Callistratus, not Aristophanes, produced the play (Hubbard 1991: 41–59). Just as Dikaiopolis both is and is not Aristophanes, Aristophanes, it seems, both is and is not the "our producer/director" or "poet" or "this poet" of the parabasis (628, 633, 649, 654), who is somehow associated with Aegina (652–654) but also, in the first person, defies Cleon to attack him (660–664).[7] It is all very confusing. But then, that is comedy for you.

The confusion, or perhaps better, the point that we are all many people, also extends to the question of why Aristophanes is using the *Telephus* in the first place. Aristophanes makes the parallel between the *Telephus* and the situation of Athens, which must choose between peace with Sparta and Pericles' aggressive pro-war policy, as explicit as it could possibly be. Thus as Dikaiopolis dresses up as Telephus in disguise to argue against Athenian aggression, he "secretly" reveals that he is Aristophanes and is actually speaking about Athens. As such he introduces his appeal to the audience as "ourselves alone at the Lenaia" with the lines:

> Do not bear me ill will, you men of the audience
> if, being a beggar, I mean to speak among the Athenians
> about the city while making a trugedy,
> since trugedy too knows what is right.
> I will speak out (*ego de lexo*) shocking things, but ones right and just.
> For this time Cleon will not slander me ...
>
> (497–502)

---

[7] See Parker (1991) and Sidwell (2012) for additional complications as to Dikaiopolis' identity; Sommerstein (1980: 189) for no known connections between either Aristophanes or Callistratus and Aegina, but Olson (2002: 241–2) for possibilities.

Aristophanes' use of "trugedy" here, his coinage for comedy in its relation to tragedy, and his declaration that trugedy *also* knows what is right point directly to the relation of comedy and tragedy (Taplin 1983; Foley 1988; Wright 2012: 17–19). What is rather surprising is that while both may know what is right, usually, but apparently not here, they express that knowledge quite differently.

The basic point of the *Acharnians* is quite simple: war is bad and peace is good. That Aristophanes has chosen to make this point by parodying a tragedy, however, adds an additional, and very peculiar, level of discourse. As Euripides' later plays such as the *Hecuba* or *Trojan Women* make clear, he, like Aristophanes, could use his plays to try and make his audience see the uglier side of Athenian aggression. As a tragedian, however, working in a genre all but invariably grounded in heroic myth, Euripides (like Telephus) had no choice but to make his argument in disguise. Aristophanes, in contrast, had no such need, since Athenian comedy was explicitly political and expected to focus on contemporary debates. Why then use tragedy?

The question brings us back to the issue of identity and the reason we choose to use disguises. On the surface, we disguise ourselves for the same reason that makes Euripides cloak his criticisms of the Peloponnesian War in epic garb, or that makes Telephus dress as a beggar, so that we can gain something not available to us in our own person. When Dikaiopolis describes this as his motive in begging tragic rags from Euripides, however, the case begins to look rather more complicated:

> And what I suffered myself at Cleon's hands
> I myself know, on account of last year's comedy.
> Having dragged me into the Council chamber
> he kept slandering me and talking me down with lies
> and torrenting and washing down on me, so that
> I nearly perished, dirty-dealing-fullified.
> So that now, first of all, before I speak, give me leave
> to costume myself out as wretchedly as possible.
>
> (378–384)

The layering is funny in itself, as Dikaiopolis reveals that not only will he be Dikaiopolis pretending to be a poor beggar, he will also be Aristophanes pretending to be Dikaiopolis pretending to be a poor beggar (Fisher 1993). As the layers become more and more extreme, however, they also beg the question raised above in regard to Aristophanes' use of tragedy. Unlike Telephus with the Greeks, the Acharnians know perfectly well who Dikaiopolis is, so the costume seems of little use. Similarly, the audience knows perfectly well that the comedy is making a political point, and they know that Aristophanes is writing Dikaiopolis' lines for him. Dikaiopolis' disguise is hardly going to prevent Cleon from realizing that Aristophanes is behind the attack. So what is its purpose?

I would suggest that the layers upon layers of disguise may be a hint (along with the quite serious political point Aristophanes is making) that we adopt disguises not just as a means to an end but because we like disguises. Dikaiopolis dressing up as Telephus is in this way not so different from Euripides' costuming his heroes, Lamachus dressing as a warrior, or the bridesmaid dressing to suit her role. We dress up both as who we are not and also as who we are, perhaps because in the end we do not see that much difference between the two.

The underlying idea seems to be, as we saw earlier, that deep down we are all many people. As a result, being "us" is not simply a given condition – one has to keep working at it. And as this is true for each of us individually, it is true in spades for us as a collective. Dikaiopolis begins the *Acharnians* completely identifying with the community that is his deme and ends it with a completely different set of values, those of his private marketplace.[8] Similarly, I would argue, the Athenian audience begins the play collectively seeing Dikaiopolis as "us" and Lamachus as "them" only to have their sympathies reversed. Even while we vicariously enjoy Dikaiopolis' victory, Lamachus seems to be expressing what we all have to undergo. The joke seems to be how easily the switch occurs. We may

---

[8] Adding another twist, Dikaiopolis' apparently rural deme, Cholleidae (406) was in fact in the city, as Olson (2002: 78, 180); Sidwell (2012: 40).

believe we are a community because we all believe x. In fact, *Acharnians* may be suggesting, we all decide to believe x (at least for now) because we need to be a community.

Given this reading of what community means it is not difficult to see how it might be exemplified in theater. As Plato described:

> when the many are seated all together in a throng, in Assemblies or the Courts or theaters or army-camps or some other common gathering of a multitude, and with a great tumult censure some of the things that are said or done and praise others, doing either in excess, and calling out and clapping hands, and at that both the rocks and the area all around echoing makes a redoubling of the tumult of censure and praise, in such a case how do you suppose a young man's heart is moved, as they say?
> (*Republic* 492b3–c4)

The feeling of experiencing laughter, or delight, or pity, or fear collectively is powerful – even while each individual in the end can experience it only for him or herself (Prauscello 2013: 322–326). But even more deeply, Aristophanes seems to suggest, literature, and theater in particular may best express us as a community because it is make-believe. At least for comedy, it seems that we are what we believe ourselves to be, and that is a faculty that we exercise, above all, through literature.

In this light, Aristophanes' *Acharnians* may also have one more comment to make on the nature of our being an us and its relation to drama. Dikaiopolis rather notably moves in the play from being merely a pawn, as it were, of the high and mighty who push him and his fellows about, to directing the action himself (McLeish 1980: 68–70). Thus, as the play begins, he is at the mercy of the Prytaneis, the Herald who silences him, the Ambassador who interprets the words of the King's Eye, and even the Odomanti, who steal his garlic. In contrast, at the end of the play, and in an elaborate staging, Dikaiopolis orders others to bring out for him, one by one, all the benefits of his peace. It is almost as if the hero has managed somehow to become the author / director of his own play, rather than merely one of the grunts that get moved around by others. It is an attractive position, but as Aristophanes seems to have shown, one that elicits rather less sympathy from the audience.

Aristophanes has thus used the inherently paradoxical idea of a private peace to bring out, in all its comic glory, the themes also present in the *Telephus* – the importance and even irrational importance of community, the inevitable human identification of insiders and outsiders, and the paradox that as human beings we tend to be most ourselves when we are in disguise. In this regard as well comedy's use of literature generally, and of tragedy in particular, is crucial. Literature provides a way for each of us to explore our private emotions as individuals – and yet it does so for all of us. This occurs nowhere more vividly than in a performance of tragedy, where the emotion of a collective audience can reinforce each individual experience. And then comedy comes along to remind us that it was all purely our own invention, and yet no less real for all that.

GUIDE TO FURTHER READING

Among the numerous accounts of Aristophanes' relation to tragedy, see Taplin (1996), Silk (2000), Dobrov (2001), Rosen (2006), and Farmer (2017), and for *Acharnians* in particular Foley (1988) and Platter (2007). For Aristophanes' relation to other forms of literature, see Rosen (1988), Hall (2006), Harvey and Wilkins (2000), Zanetto (2001), Platter (2007), Biles (2011), Wright (2012), and Bakola et al. (2013). Dover (1972), Bowie (1993), MacDowell (1995), and Slater (2002) are all excellent overall studies of Aristophanes with particular chapters on *Acharnians*.

REFERENCES

Bakola, E., Prauscello, L., and Mario Telò, M. (ed.) (2013). *Greek Comedy and the Discourse of Genres*. Cambridge University Press.

Biles, Z.P. (2011). *Aristophanes and the Poetics of Competition*. Cambridge University Press.

Bowie, A.M. (1982). The parabasis in Aristophanes: prolegomena, Acharnians. *Classical Quarterly* 32: 27–40.
Bowie, A.M. (1993). *Aristophanes: Myth, Ritual, and Comedy*. Cambridge: Cambridge University Press.
Carter, D.M. (2000). Civic ideology and the problem of difference: the politics of Aeschylean tragedy, once again. *Journal of Hellenic Studies* 120: 34–56.
Collard, C., Cropp, M.J., and Lee, K.H. (1995). *Euripides: Selected Fragmentary Plays*, vol. 1. Warminster: Aris & Phillips.
Csapo, E. (1986). A note on the Wurtzburg bell-crater H5697 ("Telephus Travestitus"). *Phoenix* 40: 379–392.
Dobrov, G.W. (ed.) (1997). *The City as Comedy: Society and Representation in Athenian Drama*. Chapel Hill, NC: University of North Carolina Press.
Dobrov, G.W. (2001). *Figures of Play: Greek Drama and Metafictional Poetics*. Oxford and New York: Oxford University Press.
Dover, K.J. (1972). *Aristophanic Comedy*. Berkeley: University of California Press.
Farmer, M.C. (2017). *Tragedy on the Comic Stage*. Oxford: Oxford University Press.
Fisher, N.R.E. (1993). Multiple personalities and Dionysiac festivals: Dicaeopolis in Aristophanes' Acharnians. *Greece and Rome* 40: 31–47.
Foley, H.P. (1982). The 'female intruder' reconsidered: women in Aristophanes' Lysistrata and Ecclesiazusae. *Classical Philology* 77: 1–21.
Foley, H.P. (1988). Tragedy and politics in Aristophanes' Acharnians. *Journal of Hellenic Studies* 108: 33–47.
Foley, H.P. (2001). *Female Acts in Greek Tragedy*. Princeton: Princeton University Press.
Ford, A. (2003). From letters to literature: reading the 'song culture' of classical Greece. In: *Written Texts and the Rise of Literate Culture in Ancient Greece* (ed. H. Yunis). Cambridge.
Goldhill, S. (1990). The great Dionysia and civic ideology. In: *Nothing to Do with Dionysos? Athenian Drama in its Social Context* (ed. J.J. Winkler and F.I. Zeitlin), 97–129. Princeton University Press.
Griffin, J. (1998). The social function of attic tragedy. *Classical Quarterly* 48: 39–61.
Hall, E. (2006). *The Theatrical Cast of Athens: Interactions between Ancient Greek Drama and Society*. Oxford and New York: Oxford University Press.
Halliwell, S. (1991). The uses of laughter in Greek culture. *Classical Quarterly* 41: 279–296.
Harvey, D. and Wilkins, J. (ed.) (2000). *The Rivals of Aristophanes: Studies in Athenian Old Comedy*. London: Duckworth/Classical Press.
Henderson, J. (2020). Old comic citation of tragedy as such. In: *Fragmentation in Ancient Greek Drama* (ed. A. Lamari, F. Montanari, and A. Novokhatko), 39–48. Berlin: de Gruyter.
Hubbard, T.K. (1991). *The Mask of Comedy: Aristophanes and the Intertextual Parabasis*. Ithaca: Cornell University Press.
Ieranò, G. (2013). 'One who is fought over by all the tribes': the dithyrambic poet and the city of Athens. In: *Dithyramb in Context* (ed. B. Kowalzig and P. Wilson), 368–386. Oxford.
MacDowell, D.M. (1995). *Aristophanes and Athens: An Introduction to the Plays*. Oxford.
McLeish, K. (1980). *The Theatre of Aristophanes*. New York: Taplinger Publishing Company.
Muecke, F. (1982a). A portrait of the artist as a young woman. *Classical Quarterly* 32: 41–55.
Muecke, F. (1982b). 'I know you—by your rags': costume and disguise in fifth-century drama. *Antichthon* 16: 17–34.
Nelson, S.A. (2016). *Aristophanes and his Tragic Muse: Comedy, Tragedy and the Polis in 5th Century Athens*. Leiden: Brill.
O'Sullivan, N. (2006). Aristophanes' first critic: Cratinus fr. 342 KA. In: *Greek Drama III: Essays in Honor of Kevin Lee* (ed. J. Davidson, F. Muecke, and P. Wilson), 163–169. London: Duckworth.
Olson, S.D. (2002). (Ed. and Comm.), *Aristophanes: Acharnians*. Oxford.
Parker, L.P.E. (1991). Eupolis or Dicaeopolis? *Journal of Hellenic Studies* 111: 203–208.
Pickard-Cambridge, A.W. (1968). *The Dramatic Festivals of Athens*, 2nd ed. rev. (ed. J. Gould and D.M. Lewis). London: Oxford University Press.
Platter, C.L. (1993). The uninvited guest: Aristophanes in Bakhtin's «History of laughter». *Arethusa* 26: 201–216.
Platter, C. (2007). *Aristophanes and the Carnival of Genres*. Baltimore: The Johns Hopkins University Press.
Prauscello, L. (2013). Comedy and comic discourse in Plato's Laws. In: *Greek Comedy and the Discourse of Genres* (ed. E. Bakola, L. Prauscello, and M. Telò), 319–342. Cambridge.

Rehm, R. (1994). *Greek Tragic Theatre*. London and New York: Routledge.
Revermann, M. (2006). The competence of theatre audiences in fifth- and fourth-century Athens. *Journal of Hellenic Studies* 126: 99–124.
Rhodes, P.J. (2003). Nothing to do with democracy: Athenian drama and the polis. *Journal of Hellenic Studies* 123: 104–119.
Rosen, R.M. (1988). *Old Comedy and the Iambographic Tradition*. Atlanta: Scholars Press.
Rosen, R.M. (2006). Aristophanes, old comedy, and Greek tragedy. In: *The Blackwell Companion to Tragedy* (ed. R. Bushnell), 251–268. Oxford.
Ruffell, I. (2011). *Politics and Anti-Realism in Athenian Old Comedy: The Art of the Impossible*. Oxford.
Rusten, J.S. (ed.) (2011). *The Birth of Comedy: Texts, Documents, and Art from Athenian Comic Competitions, 486–280*. Baltimore: Johns Hopkins University Press.
Samons, L.J. (2004). *What's Wrong with Democracy: From Athenian Practice to American Worship*. Berkeley: University of California Press.
Sidwell, K. (2012). Aristophanes' Acharnians and Eupolis again: Metacomedy in action. In: *No Laughing Matter: Studies in Athenian Comedy* (ed. C.W. Marshall and G. Kovacs), 35–54. London: Bristol Classical Press.
Silk, M.S. (2000). *Aristophanes and the Definition of Comedy*. Oxford.
Slater, N.W. (2002). *Spectator Politics: Metatheatre and Performance in Aristophanes*. Philadelphia: University of Pennsylvania Press.
Sommerstein, A.H. (1980). (Ed., Trans. And Comm.), *Aristophanes: Acharnians*. Warminster: Aris & Phillips.
Taplin, O. (1983). Tragedy and Trugedy. *Classical Quarterly* 33: 331–333.
Taplin, O. (1996). Comedy and the tragic. In: *Tragedy and the Tragic: Greek Theatre and beyond* (ed. M.S. Silk), 188–202. Oxford.
Telò, M. (2010). Embodying the tragic father(s): autobiography and intertexuality in Aristophanes. *Classical Antiquity* 29: 278–326.
Wiles, D. (2000). *Greek Theater Performance: An Introduction*. Cambridge.
Wilson, P. (2000). *The Athenian Institution of the Khoregia: The Chorus, the City and the Stage*. Cambridge.
Wilson, N.G. (2007). *Aristophanis Fabulae I*. Oxford.
Wright, M. (2012). *The Comedian as Critic: Greek Old Comedy and Poetics*. London: Bristol Classical Press.
Wright, M. (2013). Comedy versus tragedy in Wasps. In: *Greek Comedy and the Discourse of Genres* (ed. E. Bakola, L. Prauscello, and M. Telò), 205–225. Cambridge.
Zanetto, G. (2001). Iambic patterns in Aristophanic comedy. In: *Iambic Ideas: Essays on a Poetic Tradition from Archaic Greece to the Late Roman Empire* (ed. A. Cavarzere, A. Aloni, and A. Barchiesi), 65–76. Lanham, MD: Rowman & Littlefield.

CHAPTER 8

Knights: Political Satire

Natalia Tsoumpra

Introduction*

One year after receiving first prize for his *Acharnians*, produced under the name of Callistratus at the comic festival of the Lenaia in 425 BCE, Aristophanes returns to the festival with the *Knights*, this time producing the play himself. The *Knights* has been commonly viewed as a personal and political indictment of the popular leader Cleon, who dominated the political scene both as a politician and as a general after Pericles' death in 429 until his own death in 422 BCE. However, in many ways, the play is more of a critique of the *dēmos* and its questionable attitude toward participation in the democratic politics of the time. The plot is based on an extended allegory that mixes the private with the public in the favorite manner of Aristophanes: the city of Athens is represented by a private household, and the *dēmos* of Athens is embodied in the character of Demos, a decrepit old man and the owner of the "house" of Athens. Demos has acquired a new steward, a tanner from Paphlagonia, who stands for Cleon. The vile Paphlagon has managed to gain the full trust of Demos by feeding him flattery and lies while hoarding all the wealth and power for himself. There are two other slaves in the household (perhaps identified with the generals Demosthenes and Nicias)[1] who wish to serve Demos and share in the power but are kept at a distance by Paphlagon. In an attempt to bring Paphlagon down, they steal his oracles, where they discover that he is the last in a long succession of vendor–politicians, each worse than the previous one, and that he is destined to be overthrown by an even viler figure, a Sausage seller. Seizing the moment, the two slaves immediately recruit a random sausage seller on his way to the market and convince him that he has all the right qualifications to fight against Paphlagon-Cleon and win his position. The Sausage seller, who is also supported by the chorus of the aristocratic Knights, outdoes Paphlagon in a series of contests before the Chorus and the slaves, before the Council, and before Demos, using all of Paphlagon's tricks: shouting down the opponent, abusive and violent discourse, foul language, flattery, and lies. He is eventually chosen by Demos as his new steward, henceforth becoming his wise advisor Agorakritos, while Paphlagon is banished to the edges of the marketplace. At the end of the play, Agorakritos magically boils and rejuvenates Demos, restoring him to his former glory of the days of Marathon and Salamis. Guided by Agorakritos, Demos now renounces all his former behavior, vows not to repeat his past mistakes, and gets his sexual rewards in the form of a young well-endowed boy, and two girls, who represent peace treaties.

What is the picture that emerges about the contemporary Athenian political landscape? There are various political players who are embedded in complicated power relationships: Paphlagon/Cleon,

---

* I wish to thank the editors of the volume for their valuable help and comments.
[1] Henderson (1998) denies the identification, while Sommerstein (1981) accepts it.

who employs shady political tactics and has a very public, if unofficial role in steering and manipulating the *dēmos*; the mysterious figure of the Sausage seller, a low-born and vile man, who outdoes Paphlagon in baseness, but in the end seemingly emerges as the new benevolent patron of the *dēmos*; Demos, who as the *dēmos* of Athens occupies a deliberately passive role in political debates within the context of the participatory Athenian democracy, but in the end also seemingly changes his ways under new patronage; and the chorus of the Knights, members of Athens' second-highest socio-economic class, whose curious partnership with the Sausage seller goes against obvious class affiliations. Studies on the play have attempted to shed light on the political/ideological stance it puts forward: some focus on the rhetorical strategies of Paphlagon/Cleon and the Sausage seller, and their connection with the ideological agendas of different factions on the post-Periclean political scene (Woodhead 1960; Edmunds 1987; Lind 1990; Atkinson 1992; Lafargue 2013; Burns 2014); others comment on the state of the contemporary political debate, such as the abusive talk (Worman 2008), the political implications of the use of culinary imagery (Wilkins 1997, 2000), or the intersection between political and erotic discourse (Wohl 2002); and others ponder on the implications of the Sausage seller's victory and Demos' transformation for the political vision of the play: does Aristophanes champion a new era of partnership between politicians and the *dēmos* (McGlew 1996, p. 357, 2002, pp. 106–107) and celebrate lower-class intelligence in battling elites (Zumbrunnen 2004, pp. 671–672, 2012, pp. 85–98) while championing a Cleon-type politician (Hall 2018, 2019) and absolving the *dēmos* from all blame (Henderson 1990), or should the joy of the hyper-democratic ending be viewed ironically? (Reckford 1987; Bennett and Tyrell 1990; Bowie 1993; Tsoumpra 2018). Drawing occasionally on some of these studies, I shall provide a commentary on the competition between Paphlagon and the Sausage seller, focusing on the reimagining of the standard comic slanders against politicians as reasons for praise in the *Knights*, and on the play's criticism of the *dēmos*. I shall then turn to a more extended discussion of the tropes of political satire in Aristophanic comedy, and occasionally other contemporary literature, before concluding with some thoughts about the political role of aggressive/offensive humor.

Paphlagon/Cleon Versus the Sausage Seller/Agorakritos

Even though there is no doubt that Paphlagon was intended to represent Cleon, he is never tied to him by name. In fact, Cleon is only mentioned by name in line 976, in a choral passage that is not directly related to Paphlagon. This was probably deliberate. There was a long-standing dispute between Aristophanes and Cleon that simmered for a number of years, and Cleon had supposedly initiated legal action against the poet (Atkinson 1992, pp. 56–61; Storey 1998; Hesk 2000, pp. 263–264; Sommerstein 2004; Rosen 1988, 2007 considers the conflict a mere dramatic fiction), the repetition of which Aristophanes would have been keen to avoid. Two of Aristophanes' plays before the *Knights* (*Babylonians*, Dionysia 426, and the aforementioned *Acharnians* in 425), and one after (*Wasps*, Lenaia 422) contain extended and not-so-veiled attacks on Cleon. Only fragments survive from the *Babylonians*, but based on information from the parabasis in the *Acharnians* and the ancient scholia on *Acharnians* 378, we can infer that the subject matter was a satire of the administration of Athens by Cleon. The chorus of Babylonians, working as slaves in a mill (fr. 71), may have represented the allied city-states (Norwood 1930 and Storey 2005 argue against this view; see Starkey 2013 for the view that the chorus served in the Athenian navy). The *Acharnians* provides a sequel to the dispute between Aristophanes and Cleon: we find out that the production of the *Babylonians* earned Aristophanes (or the producer Callistratus) a prosecution from Cleon (*Ach.* 377–382), but this did not stop Aristophanes from abusing Cleon again (659–664) and announcing the renewal of his attack in the following year's play (299–302). The ongoing invective supposedly led to renewed attempts by Cleon to silence Aristophanes (*Vesp.* 1284–1291), but Aristophanes takes up again in the *Wasps* Cleon's caricature as the corrupt patron and false protector of the jurors, and as a malevolent watchdog in a domestic trial scene (*Vesp.* 902–930), despite his tongue-in-cheek promise not to "make mincemeat out of Cleon again" (*Vesp.* 62–30).

Even after his death, Cleon still earns continued abuse in Aristophanes' comedies (*Pax* 47–48, 269–270, 313–315, 648–656, 752–760; *Ra.* 569).

The *Knights* is the most systematic denunciation of Cleon and his policies, and one that Aristophanes was most proud of: in the re-worked version of the *Clouds* that has come down to us, the poet reflects on his sustained attack of Cleon in the *Knights*, boasts about his courage to take Cleon down at the height of his power (549–550), and claims to have started a new trend of comedy that other playwrights copied and followed (549–559). Both Paphlagon and the Sausage seller embody the standard political charges made against prominent political individuals in Aristophanic comedy, namely, that they are corrupt, that they are of foreign descent and have low social origins, and that they are effeminate and/or passive homosexuals (Storey 1998; Robson 2009, p. 167). These accusations are articulated in the *Knights* in a much more clear, consistent, and self-aware manner than in any other of Aristophanes' plays. However, in the "bizarro" world of the play, the slanders become commendations, and the traits of unworthiness highly sought-after qualities. The play almost advocates a homeopathic therapy, curing an evil with another evil through a *similia similibus* formula (Faraone 1991, pp. 5–10): if Paphlagon is vile, the politician to take him down has to be, if not equally vile, then viler, since politics is no longer a job for decent people. The *Knights* depicts a parody of succession myths (Bowie 1993, pp. 58–66; Henderson 2018), such as Hesiod's account in the *Theogony* of the sequence Uranus–Cronus – Zeus, which culminates in Zeus' victory and the creation of a stable cosmos under his tutelage. While, however, in the *Theogony* there is a progressive shift in the creation of the cosmos from primitive to civilized forces, the sequence of politicians in the *Knights* is of increasing awfulness (128–143). The narrative of decline resembles that of Hesiod's Myth of the Races and corrupt dystopias in other comic plays that collapse myth and contemporary politics (Ruffell 2000, pp. 491–492).

We are not allowed to forget what a sordid business politics is, as the two contestants engage in a competition of corruption, ignorance, and duplicity that is expressed through a number of metaphors, such as alimentary, hunting, wrestling, cooking, and sexual. The "entry requirements" are spelled out clearly even before the competition begins. The Sausage seller relates a story about how as a boy he would steal meat from the butchers, hide it up his crotch, and swear that he was innocent (417–424). His scandalous behavior prompted a politician to predict that he would have a great future in politics (425–426), since, as the slave Demosthenes points out, he stole, lied about stealing perjuring himself, and "had someone's meat up his ass" (427–428). In short, he displayed thievishness, corruption, deception, and clear signs of passive homosexuality (Sommerstein 1981, p. 166; Henderson 1991, pp. 68, 129). In an earlier passage, the slave Demosthenes adds ignorance, bad education (193), repellant voice, and low origins (218) to the list of the traits of a successful politician.

Let us trace how both of the two contestants fulfill the criteria of their candidacy.

Corruption: In Whose Interest Does the Leader Lead?

Paphlagon excels in bribery, embezzlement, thievishness, aggressive persecution of political adversaries, and back-stabbing, all in the interest of his personal gain and to the detriment of the *dēmos*. He is a vile blackmailer, constantly in pursuit of bribes and illegal gains. The Chorus jokes that the only tune he can master with his lyre is the *dōrodokisti* (996), a pun on the Dorian mode of music and bribe-taking (*dōrodokein*). Paphlagon openly admits that he steals (296), and he is constantly accused of a rapacious and voracious appetite (137, 203, 204, 248), often exercised in the prytaneum (280–281, 709). Although he pretends to make provision for Demos' meals, he consumes most of the food himself, as the Sausage seller points out:

> Sure, you feed him, just like the nannies: badly! You chew some food and feed him a morsel, after you have bolted down three times as much yourself.[2] (716–718)

---

[2] All translations are quoted from Henderson (1998), slightly modified.

Instead of acting as the "guardian dog" of Demos, Paphlagon chews down his food:

> "Mark well, son of Erectheus, the dog Cerberus,
> Trafficker in bodies,
> Who wags his tail at you when you are dining and watches,
> And when you happen to gape in another direction,
> Eats up your entree,
> And at night steals into your kitchen all unseen and doglike
> Licks clean the plates and the islands."
>
> (1030–1034)

Food imagery is pervasive in the play, and food consumption becomes an extended metaphor for Paphlagon's political corruption and rapaciousness (Whitman 1964, pp. 92–93; Littlefield 1968; Marr 1996; Wilkins 2000, pp. 187–192). In the final competition, both Paphlagon and the Sausage seller bring out various goodies for Demos (1166–1191), but it turns out that Paphlagon has kept the best cheesecake for himself, giving Demos only a tiny piece (1218–1220). The Sausage seller helpfully explains that this has been Paphlagon's practice all along: embezzling public funds and leaving only little money for distribution within the state (1221–1223).

That food stands for money, resources, or strategic plans, and its aggressive consumption for Paphlagon's thieving and surreptitious political practices, is obvious in other passages too:

> Why, just the other day I whipped up a Spartan cake at Pylos, and by some very dirty trick he outmaneuvered me, snatched the cake, and served it up himself - the one I'd whipped up!
>
> (54–57).

The slave Demosthenes insinuates here that Paphlagon/Cleon stole his idea about capturing the island of Sphacteria from the Spartans by attacking it from Pylos and passing it off as his own (Sommerstein 1981, p. 147).[3] Cleon took the credit for the plan and became a hero. The victorious plan is represented by a cake, and by extension, the snatching-up of the cake symbolizes the intellectual property theft and deception. The same idea is repeated in lines 1166–1167, where Paphlagon offers Demos a cake made from grain imported from Pylos.

Paphlagon gobbles up (258, *katesthieis*) public funds and squeezes magistrates at their audit, as if they were figs, to check who is ripe (260, *pepon*) to "give up the juice," that is, offer a bribe to Paphlagon so that they pass off audit unchallenged. The same charges are reiterated in lines 824–827, where Paphlagon is accused of gulping down (826, *katabrochthizei*) the "stalks" (824, *kaulous*) of the audits and scooping up public money like bread in soup (827, *mustilatai*). Paphlagon licks (103, *leiksas*) the sauce off confiscated cakes (103, *epipasta dēmioprata*), another metaphor for Paphlagon's theft of the confiscated property of condemned criminals, and his profit-making to the detriment of the state. It is not incidental that the imagery of predatory beasts and animals feeding themselves is often applied to Paphlagon (197 eagle, 1037 lion, 1052 hawk, and 403 an insect sucking from "bribery" flower), and that he is likened to animals renowned for their greediness (375–381 pig, 956 seagull) or aggression (at 496 he is expected to fight like a cockerel) (Bowie 1993, p. 62; Wilkins 1997, p. 260; Sommerstein 2009, pp. 163–167; Tsoumpra 2014, pp. 113–114).

Food metaphors are important for emphasizing the voracious and monstrous character of Paphlagon, but they also feature as an important element of the rivalry between Paphlagon and the Sausage seller, as their competition is often presented in terms deriving from the preparation, cooking, and eating of food (Wilkins 1993, 1997, 2000, pp. 179–201; Tsoumpra 2014, pp. 98–150). The political business is no different from the cooking business, as the slave Demosthenes claims (213–216): it involves mixing and stirring, and feeding the people flattery and lies instead of food.[4] The Sausage seller has an advantage over Paphlagon, since he is a meat vendor, someone who slaughters and butchers a sacrificial animal and prepares its meat for consumption. He tops

---

[3] Thucydides also downplays Cleon's role in the capture of Pylos and presents Cleon's claims that he could end the siege easily within 20 days as a self-aggrandizing and empty posture (4.27–8).

[4] Cf. the pun on *dēmos* (δῆμος) = people and *dēmos* (δημός) = fat in l.954.

Paphlagon's threats of incessant devouring with his capacity to gobble up, at one go, the paunch of a cow and the tripe of a pig together with their broth (356–358). But, unlike Paphlagon, he is not only a food consumer but also a food provider, and will finally emerge as a sacrificial cook, treating Demos himself as a piece of meat (Reckford 1987, pp. 113–120; Wilkins 1993, 2000; Tsoumpra 2014, pp. 138–146). Throughout the competition, the Sausage seller counters Paphlagon's offers to Demos with offers of meat (1178–1179 pork bellies and broth, 1184 intestines) and appropriates Paphlagon's thieving tactics by snatching the hare that Paphlagon was about to offer to Demos (1192–1201). His hamper is empty because he has given everything to the *dēmos* (1215–1216), thus proving his loyalty.

Low Origins

Paphlagon's profession displays his non-aristocratic background: he is a tanner, which is viewed as a lowly, crude activity. He does not come from an important ruling family, nor does he own any land: he is simply a seller. This profile may serve the comic critique and not correspond entirely to reality (Henderson 1990, pp. 279–284): according to a scholion on *Knights* l. 44, Cleon's father owned a tannery staffed by slaves, and the inscription IG ii2 2318.35 informs us that he was wealthy enough to be a *chorēgos* for the dithyramb competition of 459 BCE at the city Dionysia.

The Sausage seller as a butcher is the lowest of the low. He exercises his profession at the city gates, a most disreputable location, as it is frequented by sex workers and sellers of dogs' and asses' meat (Sommerstein 1981, p. 208). His education is limited to poor knowledge of reading and writing (188–189), and he was raised on disputes in the marketplace, hence his name Agorakritos (1257–1258).

Just as the Sausage seller menaces Paphlagon with a butcher's techniques, most of Paphlagon's threats against the Sausage seller draw on practices from the tanning profession (e.g. 369 "I will stretch your hide on the tanning-bench"). The implication is that both characters are associated with the noisy, brash, lower-class character of the Athenian marketplace, and that, therefore, the political discourse, the verbal mode, and the rhetorical style they employ fit those of a lowly, aggressive market worker.

Paphlagon's name implies that he is not only a low-class trader but also of foreign birth. The Paphlagonians in ancient tradition form part of groups of people on the Euxine coast, whose characteristics mark them as separate from the Greek world (Bowie 1993, pp. 59–61). In the comic poet Hermippus (fr. 66 20–1 K-A), Paphlagonians are associated with acorns, one of men's earliest foods, which were abandoned once men got out of their primitive condition. Paphlagon's name, therefore, not only indicates a slave from the primitive area of Paphlagonia but also combines a pun about Cleon's manner of public speaking (*paphlazō* = splutter), which was loud and aggressive (Bowie 1993, p. 62; Storey 1998, p. 91). The "spluttering" may also ridicule Cleon's barbarized Greek. There is no evidence in the text that Paphlagon speaks "barbarous" Greek on stage, and it is true that Paphlagon's foreign origin is not foregrounded in the play (MacDowell 1993, p. 359), but the allegation of foreign ancestry cannot be disassociated from the slur of servile origin, as non-Greek ethnic origins were associated mostly with slaves. As will be shown later, evidence from other plays suggests that misuse of the Greek language due to foreign identity was a common jibe, (Sommerstein 1996a, pp. 214–215; Colvin 2000, 288–289). Other instances of foreigners' speech in Aristophanic comedy show that linguistic proficiency was correlated to intellectual and cultural properties (Willi 2002, pp. 111–150). Therefore, the "Paphlagonian/foreign descent" slander operates on three levels: as a foreigner, Paphlagon/Cleon does not/should not belong to the citizen body, and, most importantly, should not hold a position of power; he is linguistically and culturally inferior and barbaric; and, lastly, paired with the fact that Paphlagon is also a slave, his primitive origin betrays a low social background, someone of non-aristocratic blood, who is not fit to become a member of the ruling class.[5]

---

[5] That all politicians are represented as slaves in the play is important: this is the only dystopian scenario in Aristophanic comedy, albeit in the form of allegory, where slaves have the upper hand. This was never part of the poetic imagination, even as a fantasy scenario, unlike gynecocracy.

Effeminacy/Passive Homosexuality

Another stereotypical comic attack hurled at both Paphlagon and the Sausage seller is that of effeminacy and passive homosexuality. A hint that Paphlagon is dangerously prone to effeminate behavior is provided by his intemperate and uncontrollable consumption, mentioned above. Indulging the appetites of the belly and lacking self-control means stooping to the level of slaves and women, and is, therefore, highly condemned in ancient tradition (Hes. *Op.* 374–375, Th. 593–599, Archil. 124b, Hippon. 118.1–3, 128, Pl. *Ti.* 73a6, Xen. *Mem.* 1.6.10). Since women were regarded as lacking in control, men who exhibit immoderation do not observe their proper gender role and are vulnerable to accusations of softness, effeminacy, and sexual passivity (Carson 1990, p. 135; Worman 2008, pp. 72–83; Ormand 2009, pp. 16–17). In particular, bodily excesses (such as intemperate talking and eating, or engaging in excessive sexual activity) tend to be labeled as feminine traits in the ancient world, and open apertures make one suspect (Worman 2008, p. 72). Both Paphlagon's apertures, mouth and anus, are constantly open. His mouth does double duty: it ingests food and expels words at the same time. Before he even enters the stage, Paphlagon is described as notorious for his loud, raucous voice (137) and the first line the Sausage seller addresses to him denounces this very feature (274; cf. 302 and 311–312). When he is beaten by the chorus, Paphlagon appeals to his ability of shouting and bawling (255–256) and threatens to run his enemies down with his loud cries (275). The slave Demosthenes is worried that Paphlagon's ability to "bawl a bawling" (487) will win over the Council to his side. His ear-splitting volubility is his trademark as the guardian dog of Demos (1017–1023). He is truly the politician of the "open mouth" (Worman 2008, pp. 62–92).

More worryingly, Paphlagon's mouth is identified with his anus, which is also constantly agape, so much so that the Sausage seller threatens to stuff it like a sausage skin (364). Paphlagon's hands are among the Aetolians and his mind in Clopidae,[6] but his arse is in Chaonians (78), that is, agape (with a pun on *chaos* = gaping void). When the slave Demosthenes urges the Sausage seller to examine Paphlagon's tongue, making a reference to the butchers' practice of examining pigs before the sacrifice and checking if they showed signs of tapeworm, what gapes wide is his anus and not his mouth. It is, therefore, signs of sexual passivity, and not of any sickness, the inspectors should be attentive to. Crucially, Paphlagon is envious of other "buggers" (877, 879, *kinoumenous*), whom he persecuted (878, *prōktotērein*, literally "hunted their asses down"), because they had high chances of becoming politicians.

Yet it is the Sausage seller that is the *par excellence* "open anus" politician (Worman 2008, pp. 62–92). His trick of hiding meat in his buttocks as a boy has already been mentioned above, but there is an even clearer sign of the Sausage seller's engagement in passive homosexual practices: he did not sell just sausages in the marketplace but also himself, as he announces in no uncertain terms (1242); he was a male prostitute (Henderson 1991, p. 152). Even though prostitution was not legally prohibited, men who engaged in prostitution lost key citizenship rights, among them the right to speak in the assembly (Ormand 2009, p. 76). It was also ethically problematized, since the male prostitute was supposed to willingly take the part of the penetrated partner in sex, a role which was only to be assumed by a woman. Therefore, a man who was found out to have engaged in prostitution was publicly disgraced and could face disenfranchisement.[7] Yet in the debased politics of the play male prostitution becomes an advantage.

The Sausage seller is expected to continue his practices in the Prytaneum (167, with *laikaseis*, "you will suck cocks" as a surprise substitute for "dine"). His anus and its functions become a recurrent point of reference during the competition: he threatens to cover Paphlagon with excrement (295), while Paphlagon threatens to drag him by his ass (365); heartened by the fart of a "bugger" which he interprets as a good omen (638–639), he knocks aside the barrier of the council chamber by waggling his rump and shouts out "gaping widely" (640–642); his arsehole knows well

---

[6] Both puns on *aiteō* = to demand and *klōps* = thief.
[7] As Aeschines' speech *Against Timarchos* clearly demonstrates.

how to expand and contract (720); and he offers himself up to Demos to be dragged by the balls to Cerameicus (772). The Sausage seller systematically makes himself available as the lubricious, penetrable type (Robson 2018).

Even though effeminate and sexually submissive behavior is ascribed to both contestants, paradoxically, at the same time, they pose as rival lovers of Demos. In a parodic *paraklausithuron* scene, whereupon an excluded lover sings love songs from the street to his beloved within the house, Paphlagon and the Sausage seller knock on Demos' door and profess their love to him (732, *philō, erastēs,* 733 *anterastēs*). Thus, the relationship between Demos and the politicians is described in terms of a pederastic relationship, where the politicians occupy the position of the active *erastēs,* while Demos is reduced to that of the passive *eromenos* (737 "you are like the boys who have lovers"), albeit an unconventional one, since he is "a grumpy, hard-of hearing old man" (42–43) – a most unappetizing picture. The play parodies the funeral speech of Pericles (Thuc. 2.43.1) who urges the Athenians to become lovers of their city. In the *Knights*, the eroticized metaphorical discourse is literalized: pederastic courtship and prostitution become the debased models of politics (Wohl 2002, pp. 73–123; Scholtz 2004; Yates 2005). Offered "whorish pleasures" (Wohl 2002, p. 96) by its politicians, the *dēmos* also turns into a whore,[8] who gives himself to unworthy lovers (738–740).

Demos/the *dēmos*

Demos occupies a peculiar position in the *Knights*: at times apathetic, at times naïve and susceptible to flattery, and at times manipulative, striving for his personal gain. Even though he is all powerful, as he occupies the position of the master in the household/city (40, *despotēs*), the politicians/slaves do business on his behalf and he may employ and dismiss them as he pleases, for the largest part of the play he does not exercise any agency. He only appears on stage when the play is already halfway (728), completely ignorant of the current household situation, and sits through the competition as a passive observer, happily receiving the flattery and bribery of the two politicians. While Paphlagon and the Sausage seller prove to be masters of deceit and manipulation, as they strive to cap each other's efforts to control or hold sway over Demos, Demos himself is unable to establish a coherent line of thought and action, and make decisions based on discernible logic and worthy values. This is demonstrated in particular in the scene with the recitation of the oracles. Demos enjoys listening to oracles about his future (61) and is childishly delighted by the one that predicts that he will become "an eagle in the clouds" (1012–1013). However, when the two rivals recite their oracles, Demos professes *aporia* every time and relies on Paphlagon and the Sausage seller for interpretation (1021, 1041, 1059). This is highly problematic, as the meaning of the oracles is never stable but open to arbitrary interpretations, misinterpretations, and counter-interpretations. The referent of the oracle is constantly negotiated and manipulated by the rival so that a final interpretation becomes impossible (Ruffell 2011, pp. 69–70). Even when Demos ventures a guess, he stands corrected by the Sausage seller (1069–1070) and is easily convinced by the ridiculously tenuous associations on which he bases his interpretation (1073–1077, the dog in the oracle stands for a trireme because they are both fast-moving, and the fox stands for soldiers because they both eat grapes). He truly assumes the position of the *pais-erōmenos*, who is educated by his wise *erastēs* (1098–1099).

In the end, what matters for Demos is who best serves his appetite: he is not to be disturbed when dining (59–60), and, just like the members of the Council, who are won over by the Sausage seller's report about the cheap price of sardines and the free offer of coriander and onions (642–682), he makes his final decision based on who is better "for him and his belly" (1207–1208). There is a twist in the play, right before the final competition, when Demos answers the Chorus' accusations that he is easily flattered and deceived by every orator (111–120): Demos claims that he is being intentionally stupid; his apathetic stance is feigned and deliberate, as he enjoys "fattening up" politicians like sacrificial victims and striking them down when they are full up and do not serve him any more (1121–1130, note again the alimentary metaphor here). Demos seems to place

---

[8] The word 'whore' reflects the pejorative stereotypes that accompanied a *pornos* (male sex worker).

an emphasis on the demotic judicial power over the assembly: the politicians are raised in the assembly (1137) but are forced to disgorge the goods that they have stolen in the courts (1148–1150), using the wicker funnel that hid judges' votes as a "probe." The dominance of the political leaders in the assembly is reversed and remedied by the control of the *dēmos* of the judicial function (Cammack 2022). The courts are where the *dēmos* shows its supremacy; in the assembly, Demos hands over his power to the politicians, passively listening and gaping at them (755, 1203). However, it is still the case that Demos' political practices trap him – trap the *dēmos* – in a vicious cycle of corruption and deception, from which he cannot break free. Demos thinks his political practices are clever but they only perpetuate the dysfunction of the political system. For a proper resolution, more drastic measures are needed, hence the boiling and magical metamorphosis of Demos by his new advisor, Agorakritos.

The magic boiling performed by Agorakritos has been often compared to the story of Pelias in the Medea myth (Wilkins 2000, p. 198; Bowie 1993, pp. 54 and 76). It almost holds the place of a comic *deus ex machina* resolution: Agorakritos, as a newly emerged divinity, restores order in the household and the city. Demos who used to be senile, disoriented, and apathetic now appears on stage as younger (Olson 1990; against Edmunds 1987, p. 256) and wiser: he expresses feelings of shame and regret about his earlier behavior (1349, 1355) and seems to adopt a more active participation in the political scene and to regain his power of decision-making (1356–1383). The messages are conflicting: on the one hand, Demos' new decisions appear to pursue the rights of the *thētes* over the higher classes (Hall 2018), in ensuring that the rowers are paid promptly and stopping hoplites getting their names transferred from less desirable lists onto others (1366–1371). On the other hand, his rejuvenation signals a return to traditional values and the days of Marathon and Salamis (Carey 2013, pp. 141–142): he is hailed as a king and a monarch (1330, 1333), and he is dressed in the style of an Athenian elite (1331–1332), imitative of eastern luxury (Worman 2008, p. 108, n. 155; Kallet 2003, pp. 138–139), who smells of libations instead of voting pebbles (1332); he professes that young men should be banned from the agora and seems to have abandoned his earlier confidence in his power of conviction in the court (1358–1362). Most significantly, he is still prompted and guided by Agorakritos in his decisions, who pats him on the back and reassures him that his past behavior was not his fault (1356–1357), and finally presents him with the customary Aristophanic end-of-play rewards: sex and food.

It has been argued that comic criticism of the *dēmos'* exercise of power was always directed at bad leaders rather than the *dēmos* itself (Henderson 1990, p. 288ff., 1998, p. 271ff., 2003, p. 159ff), "that the demos is unhappy and frustrated because it has chosen bad leaders; that it has done so because those leaders have deceived, flattered and bullied the demos; and that the demos has forgotten that they, not the leaders, are sovereign" (Henderson 1993, p. 308). The ending of the *Knights* seems, at first glance, to support this view. Some read it as a renewal of democracy, the restoration and establishment of Demos' power over demagogues (Ehrenberg 1951, p. 47; Littlefield 1968, pp. 21–22; Ford 1965, pp. 108–109; Dover 1972, p. 98; Brock 1986, p. 23; Henderson 1993, p. 313; Macdowell 1995, p. 106) but a more nuanced perspective is perhaps advisable (Hesk 2000, p. 257; Zumbrunnen 2012, pp. 94–95; Tsoumpra 2018). The *Knights* is the closest an Aristophanic play gets to challenging, or at least problematizing, the sovereignty of the *dēmos*: the reassurance of Demos by Agorakritos that he is not to blame for his behavior rings artificial and ironic, especially because the play has made absolutely clear that Demos is, in fact, responsible. Eager deception is as great an indictment of the *dēmos* as a comment on bad politicians. If Demos in the *Knights* represents the image of popular sovereignty, this image is far from ideal.

Political Satire in Aristophanic Comedy

As mentioned above, the obvious political nature of *Knights* is not an isolated phenomenon in Aristophanes' production: it is perhaps the most representative example of a sustained attack on a politician, but it belongs in a series of Aristophanic plays that combined an attack on Cleon and denunciation of his tactics and policies with criticism of the *dēmos*. These plays (*Babylonians, Acharnians, Knights, Wasps*) marked a change from the way political comedy was done previously: political themes were not conveyed straightforwardly but mostly through mythical plots and characters (Henderson 2013). For instance, in Cratinus' *Dionysalexander*, Dionysus impersonates Alexander-Paris and abducts Helen an act that leads to a series of burlesque episodes, but the final sentence of the hypothesis reveals the hidden political undertones of the play: "Pericles is very skilfully ridiculed for having brought the war on the Athenians" (P. Oxy. 663). By contrast, Aristophanic comedy engages with political/public issues in a systematic, thematic way, making them the backbone of the plot (e.g. demagoguery and corrupt political practices in *Knights*, the war and its impact in *Acharnians*, the supposed corruption of the courts in *Wasps*), and it inaugurates the so-called genre of "demagogue" comedies (Sommerstein 2000) by developing straightforward, topical modes of attack against Cleon and the other "new politicians" who came into ascendancy after Pericles' death in 429 BCE (Henderson 2003). Aristophanic comedy targets often, but not exclusively, men who competed for the political favor of the public in the assembly and the courts, as well as men who were involved in politics in other capacities (e.g. generals, *probouloi*, members of embassies). What can be seen as a common thread in Aristophanic political satire is the advancement of a narrative of decline in contemporary politics, and a nostalgia for the good old times of the Athens of the Persian Wars. The imaginary, ideal world that the Aristophanic satire contemplates is fashioned from past rather than future visions and is something that can be felt rather than reasoned. As such, the Aristophanic political interventions aim rather at impression formation and leaving an affective footprint rather than education or imparting of political knowledge.

I am now going to trace these themes surrounding the narrative of decline (bribery/low origins/passive homosexuality) in other comic plays and explore the intersections that emerge between class, sexuality, and politics.

Bribery/Embezzlement

In the *Knights*, bribery and embezzlement constitute the main tenets of Paphlagon/Cleon's corruption. Even though the two are distinct – bribery referring to giving and receiving money and non-monetary gifts to attain a political favor, thus affecting public policies, going against state interests, and perverting justice, while embezzlement refers to the theft of public funds – the two are often coupled (e.g. *Eq.* 802 *harpazēs kai dōrodokēs*) and, as court cases show, it was common that charges of both bribery and embezzlement were brought against a man in the same trial (Lys. 21; 27; 28). Old Comedy – as well as other literary sources – gives the impression that both the giving and taking of bribes were habitually practised by most politicians and permeated every aspect of everyday Greek life. Cleon and Laches, who served as a general in Sicily from 427 to 425 BCE, are both satirized for their bribery-taking in *Wasps*, in the burlesque domestic trial of the dogs. The prosecutor, the dog Kyon of Cydathenaeum that stands for Cleon, brings a legal case against the dog Labes, that is the general Laches (a pun with *labein*, "to take," indicating a thievish attitude), for the theft of a piece of Sicilian cheese. The main point of the prosecution is not the embezzlement itself but the fact that Laches enjoyed the money he made out of his generalship in Sicily on his own, giving no share to Cleon (907–930).[9] Once again Cleon is portrayed as prosecuting men who were *hupeuthunoi*, that is, were undergoing examination of their actions about handling public money, in the hope of making money out of them by blackmail. A similar point is made by Bdelycleon in the *agon* (648–724), that politicians make large personal profits from the Athenian empire by shady methods (bribery by allied cities and blackmail are mentioned in lines 669–671, and a long list of bribe items in lines 675–677) at the expense of the poor jurors.

---

[9] On the ideological background and political dimension of the dogs' trial, see Olson (1996, pp. 138–142), Rosenbloom (2002, pp. 294–300), and Biles and Olson (2015, pp. lii–lvi).

The accusations of bribery and theft against popular leaders like Cleon cannot be separated from the "low origins invective" (on which see below). Politicians who were not members of old wealthy families but came into money later in life through trade garnered much more suspicion of corruption and thievishness because, on the one hand, public positions of responsibility did not "naturally" belong to them, and on the other hand, they might have been thought to have accrued their wealth dishonestly. Political orators in the fourth century BCE were at pains to show that they were men of substance, while at the same time exhibiting the right amount of modesty and self-control, and serving the state through liturgies (Ober 1989, pp. 230–240). A politician who possessed personal wealth was perceived as freed from the need to take money from those who wanted to betray the interests of the *dēmos* (Ober 1989, pp. 238–240).

Of course, the accusation of bribery was not just leveled against popular leaders but was thought to be a widespread practice. Even the god Hermes in *Peace* has to be bribed with a golden cup to be persuaded to pull Peace out of a cave (423–425). A form of bribery routine satirized in Old Comedy could be described as "weaponised incompetence," that is, public officers dawdling over public business in order to draw as much pay as possible (Harvey 1985; Apostolakis 2021, p. 47). In Aristophanes' *Acharnians*, Athenian ambassadors draw out their sojourn in the court of the Persian king in order to take advantage of the daily pay they receive for their service (64–93).[10] The ambassadors reap the benefits of their position while pretending they are breaking ground in their negotiations with the Persian King (102–103), who is clearly not going to send any money (104, 113–114). Another embassy sent to the court of Sitalces in Thrace employs the same methods to draw hefty pay, all the while making false promises of imminent aid (134–137). Fragments from other comic poets show that bribery was commonly satirized (Cratinus mentions goddesses of bribes in fr. 70 and 401 K-A; two ambassadors to the Persian King receive golden vessels as bribes in Plato's fr. 127). Similar invective is used by elite public speakers against political opponents in fourth-century deliberative oratory: Demosthenes accuses Aeschines of acting as a fake ambassador of Athens in Macedonia, a hireling of Philip and Alexander (18.52 *misthōton*), and of wasting time at the expense of Athens while taking gifts and payments as bribes from the Macedonians (19.8 *dōra kai misthous*). The willingness to be bribed stems from a desire to become rich, which, Demosthenes argues, is to be much more expected from an individual who comes from an impoverished humble background, such as his opponent Aeschines. Here again, as in comedy, there is no sympathy for poverty in political leadership: "if poor, then bribable" (Ober 1989, p. 237).

The Class/Origins Problem

As we have seen, the Sausage seller in the *Knights* accuses Demos of choosing base leaders, not among those who are of aristocratic birth, wealth, and good education, as well as morally upstanding citizens (738 *kalous te kagathous*)[11] but "lamp-sellers and cobblers and shoe-makers and tanners" (740). This is a recurring theme of political satire in Aristophanic comedy. Paphlagon/Cleon, the tanner, in the *Knights* stands for a whole class of "new politicians" (Connor 1971, p. 155), young men who came from non-aristocratic backgrounds, had commercial occupations and businesses, and launched a new kind of democracy by appealing to the citizenry at large.[12] The hostility of Aristophanes against Cleon and this new class of politicians – and indeed the hostility of most elite ancient sources against Cleon (such as Thucydides 3.36–8, Plut. *Per.* 33, *Nic.* 2–3) – has been attributed to the disdain against the nouveau riche men on the rise and has been used as evidence of a shift in the social class of leadership at Athens after Pericles. For the first time in Athens' history, men whose family had no illustrious forebears or aristocratic connections, and who had made their fortune from commerce and manufacturing – rather than land and agriculture – became leaders of

---

[10] Cf. Lys.30.2, where Nicomachos took six years to write up Solon's laws, a task that was supposed to take four months.
[11] For the alignment of class with physical and moral characteristics, see Dover (1974, pp. 41–45).
[12] *pace* Mann (2007) who denies that non-aristocratic politicians first appeared after Pericles' death.

the people. However, there are counter-indications to a reading of certain politicians, such as Cleon, as lower class (Hershkowitz 2018, pp. 209–210), and it has been suggested that the comic profiles of politicians as sellers were largely fictional and offered as political critique (Henderson 1990, pp. 279–284).[13] In the *Knights*, apart from Cleon, two more shopkeeper statesmen are alluded to: Eucrates of Melite, who was said to be a dealer in bran and hemp and Lysicles, a sheep leader (Sommerstein 1981, pp. 150–151). We know very little about the heritage of Eukrates or Lysikles, but both names do appear in aristocratic circles in the fifth century (Hershkowitz 2018, p. 210).[14]

After Cleon's death, the main target of comic playwrights becomes Hyperbolus, who figured prominently in plays by Eupolis (*Marikas*), Hermippus (*Bread-sellers*), and Plato (*Hyperbolus*), from 421 to 418 (Sommerstein 1996b, p. 333, 2014). In Aristophanes, Hyperbolus is ridiculed for his lamp-selling business (*Eq.* 739; *Pax* 690; cf. Cratinus fr. 209 K-A), while, another prominent individual, Cleigenes, who served as a council secretary in 410/9 and may be the ruthless litigator mentioned in Lysias 25.25 (Henderson 1998, pp. 122–123), is "the vilest bath-keeper" (*Ra.* 710). Cleophon, the most influential popular politician after 410 BCE, is labeled as a "lyre-maker" (see scholia at Ar. *Ra.* 681; [Arist.] *Ath. Pol.* 28).

It should be noted that, apart from the case of Cleon, whose loudness, shamelessness, greediness, and rapaciousness are criticized extensively, no proposed policies or political actions of those individuals are mentioned as grounds for their satire: their banausic occupations and low origins are reasons enough for their ridicule. Moreover, the identification of those politicians by their occupation may imply another form of assault: while citizens were normally identified by a first name and a patronymic and/or a demotic, occupation was used as an identifying trait for slaves, and became part of their name (Hansen 1991, p. 39). Therefore, by using a politician's occupation as an identification tag, the comic poets implicitly also labeled them as slaves (Lape 2013, p. 80). Judicial invective in fourth-century oratory shows that accusing one's opponent of servile origins was quite common (Aeschin. 2.78, 180, 3.171–172; Dem. 18.129–131, 22.61; Donelan 2021, p. 27).

To the slave/tradesperson comic slander, allegations of foreign descent were frequently added with the aim of undermining and discrediting the individuals against whom they were leveled (Heath 1990; Storey 1998; Colvin 2000, pp. 288–291; Lape 2013, pp. 78–81; Tsoumpra 2020a, p. 86). An ancient scholion on *Clouds* 552 reports that the comic poet Hermippus portrayed the mother of Hyperbolus as a foreigner. Eupolis, Hermippus, and Plato mock Hyperbolus as a Persian, a Lydian and a runaway slave. A fragment from Plato's *Hyperbolus* (fr. 183 K-A) mocks the homonymous politician for being unable to speak proper attic Greek: his Greek is "barbarized," not in the sense that it is the "broken" Greek of a foreigner but a sociolect of substandard Attic, a low urban variety of Attic (Colvin 2000, pp. 289–290). The implications are again those of someone who comes from a low social background, and is not fit to be a member of the ruling class.

Similarly, in *Frogs*, Cleophon's speech is likened to a "double-talking" Thracian swallow (*Ra.* 674–682), implying that he is of a Thracian origin and that his language is unintelligible as the chirping of a swallow (with a double jibe at the politician's dishonesty). An ancient scholion on this line in *Frogs* tells us that the comic poet Plato in his *Cleophon* portrayed the politician's mother speaking "barbarian" Greek to him (fr. 61 K-A *barbarizousan*) and notes that she was called "Thrassa." Cleophon is deemed by the chorus in *Thesmophoriazusae* to be "worse than Salabaccho" (805), a courtesan. The accusation here is double-edged: by being associated with a foreign courtesan, Cleophon is not only mocked for his foreign descent but also for being a *kinaidos*[15] – all comic stereotypes happily combined.

Other less prominent public figures are ridiculed in Aristophanic comedy for being of non-Greek origin (non-Athenian origin, interestingly, was never singled out for mockery). Even though it is

---
[13] The only evidence for the association of Cleon with the tanning business outside Aristophanes is a comic adespoton 297 K-A.
[14] The "tradesperson" label as critique was not applied only to politicians: it was a recurrent joke for the tragedian Euripides too. Aristophanes routinely refers to Euripides' man as a greengrocer, which is supposed to be a jibe at his low-class origin (*Eq.* 18–19; *Ach.* 475–478; *Th.* 387). In reality, Euripides may have had noble origins (Ruck 1975).
[15] On which see below.

not always clear whether the accusations had a standing in reality (for instance, Cleophon's father was an Athenian, and, if Cleophon was born before Pericles' citizenship law of 451/0, he was lawfully an Athenian citizen), foreign origin was risible because it implies much more than linguistic difference: it carries connotations of inferiority in intelligence, education, and culture, and is associated with slavery.[16]

It must be clear by now that all the different elements of the invective against popular leaders, bad education, low social background, foreign origin, and slavery form part of one coherent narrative. The value system of political leadership in the Aristophanic comedy can be clearly seen in the famous coinage analogy of the parabasis in *Frogs* (718–737), where the *dēmos* is denounced for preferring the "new, base copper coins" to the "old, gold and silver" ones. The sentiment is very similar to the aforementioned passage in the *Knights* (736–740), but the associations are spelled out here in greater detail: the old coins stand for noble (727 *eugeneis*), just, well-born and outstanding citizens (728 *dikaious kai kalous te kagathous*), who receive a physical training in wrestling schools and an education in the arts (729), whereas the new, vile metal indicates foreigners (730 *ksenois*), slaves (*purriais*),[17] of low origins and morals and with bad ancestors (731 *ponērois ka'k ponērōn*). The play's view that the *dēmos* chooses the latter over the former leaders sounds off a very similar line to that of the Old Oligarch, namely that the *dēmos* chooses leaders who are base and stupid because the *dēmos* themselves are base and stupid (1.1 and 1.5). Even though the etiology of the bad choice of leadership is not clearly articulated in the Aristophanic play as it is in the Old Oligarch, it can be easily surmised.[18]

Where Have All the Real Men Gone?

Aristophanic comedy often displays (and rejoices in) the reversal of gender and sexual norms within the ancient Greek community: women exercise power over men more or less permanently (*Lysistrata*, *Ecclesiazusae*), female characters appropriate male speech and behavior (Lysistrata, Praxagora), male characters are routinely ridiculed and emasculated, and the use of drag emphasizes the artificiality of gender construction. However, Aristophanic comedy is an unapologetically phallocentric genre which contains the tensions it creates and ends up confirming and upholding gender stereotypes: aggressive and excessive masculinity is celebrated and rewarded, while effeminacy and passive homosexuality are ridiculed. As Henderson (1991, pp. 208–209) has argued, in comedy, homosexuality "is made to represent and exemplify corruption, decadence, shamelessness, wickedness, or 'perversion.'" It is perhaps not unexpected that accusations of effeminacy and passive homosexuality become *topoi* of political invective in Aristophanes. This must have been part of the political arsenal that public speakers employed in debates in the assembly and the court, using it as a weapon against their opponents – or perhaps both the rhetorical and the comic invective drew from the same value system of classical Athens, which upheld notions of masculinity that required a man to be the active, penetrating partner in sex (Halperin 1990; Walters 1997). The adult male who performed the role of the passive partner was characterized by deviancy and excessive appetites and was known as a *kinaidos*, a term that suggested not simply sexual passivity but also "an effeminate style and an inability to control one's appetites to the point of engaging in degrading sexual activity" (Glazebrook 2013). Evidence shows that accusations of deviant sexuality were common in attacks on a political opponent's character (Glazebrook 2013; Sapsford 2022). For instance, in the fourth-century speech *Against Timarchos* Aeschines labels his opponent Demosthenes as a *kinaidos* in the courtroom in order to besmirch his masculinity and his moral upstanding (1.181, 2.88); his clothing and lifestyle

---

[16] See Hall (2002, pp. 111–117) for a discussion of the term *barbaros*.
[17] Red hair indicates a foreigner and/or a slave.
[18] Henderson (1990, p. 310) insists that "Comedy uses the language of democracy to attack the leaders whom the demos chose" and that the inherent rightness of the demos to rule is never questioned or problematized. I beg to disagree. Consider also that the *dēmos* are often portrayed as "wide-arsed" just like their politicians (*Ach.* 104, 604, 635; *Eq.* 755, 1203; *Nu.* 1083–1084): base people choose base leaders.

show *anandria* (unmanliness) and *kinaidia* (1.131, 2.99). Sexuality, morality, and politics are tightly bound up together: if a politician cannot control his sexual appetites, how can he be trusted to show restraint in political office or in the management of funds?

Allegations of sexual deviancy are common in Aristophanes' extant comedies. In *Knights*, as we have seen, the political opponents either accuse one another of or boast about their willingness to be anally penetrated. But such sexual invective occurs outside the context of a political debate too: prominent individuals are described as being of a doubtful sex, of a feminine appearance (cross-dressing, long hair, smooth bodies) and sexually promiscuous; 24 characters are singled out as being pathics (Henderson 1991, pp. 213–215), in terms that reflect the individual's willingness to be sexually penetrated (*katapugōn*, "total bugger," *euruprōktos*, "wide-arsed"; *chaunoprōktos*, "with gaping arse"). In *Frogs*, the chorus proclaims that the politician Cleisthenes "is plucking his arsehole and tearing his cheeks" (422–424), while another politician, Callias, the son of "Hippocoitus" (Henderson's 1998 translation), is "dressed with a lionskin made of cunt" (430). Cleisthenes, in particular, is routinely made fun of for looking like a woman: in *Acharnians*, he is ridiculed as a beardless effeminate, who shaves his ass (118–122); in *Thesmophoriazusae*, he is an ally of the women because he is kindred in appearance and lifestyle (574–576) and is "crazy about women's ways" (576, *gunaikomanō*); in *Lysistrata*, he is imagined to scheme with the women (621). But Aristophanes takes the invective one step further: not only are certain politicians ridiculed because of their effeminacy, but it is repeatedly claimed that *all* politicians are effeminate and that buggery is a surefire way into politics (Henderson 1991, p. 209). Political leaders are those who "suck cocks" and are "bottoms" (*Ach.* 79). In *Ecclesiazusae*, Praxagora claims that the men "who have been pounded the most" are the best speakers (112–113) and cites the example of a certain Agyrrhius whose career exploded when he engaged in passive sex (102–103); men in assemblies look like women (*Ec.* 167–168); prosecutors, tragedians, and public speakers are all "wide-arsed" (*Nu.* 1088–1094). The joke probably reflects popular ideas about homosexuality at the time, as it is not just limited to Aristophanic comedy but found in other comic poets too: the comic playwright Plato makes a similar joke (fr. 202.5 "you've been screwed; therefore you will become a politician") and Eupolis complains that Athens is governed by "young boys who are being screwed" (fr. 100). Aristophanes, as a character in Plato's *Symposium*, is hung up on his assertion that the boys who are in pederastic relationships go on to become eminent in politics (192a1–b2).

The willing subjection to anal intercourse is not just an *insignium* of public speakers but of any prominent individual in the public realm: performing certain sexual acts is a means of progressing in higher circles. The tragic poet Agathon is the most popular target for his promiscuous passive homosexuality: in *Thesmophoriazusae*, he is chosen by Euripides to infiltrate the women's assembly because he looks like a woman (191–192), and his feminine appearance and obvious lack of any "masculine" cues is ridiculed by Euripides' In-law, who is the carrier of aggressive masculinity in the scene and threatens to mount Agathon (157–158). Agathon is someone that everyone has shagged (35), but this seems to be a necessary rite of passage, in order to be accepted in the poetic circle, as Euripides claims that he was like Agathon when he started out (172–173).

The invective against prominent public figures in Aristophanes for being "sissies" and "buggers" is complemented by the overly aggressive masculinity that the male comic heroes exhibit. This can be observed during the course of many plays, but it is especially typical of the "happy ending": as we have seen at the end of the *Knights*, Demos regains his sexual potency and is allowed to satisfy his sexual urges with a young boy and the young girls representing the peace treaties. A similar situation occurs in the *Acharnians*, where the male hero Dikaiopolis strikes his private peace treaty with Sparta and at the end of the play enjoys the sexual attention of two young girls as his prize. In the *Birds*, Peisetairos consolidates his leadership in the new bird society by harassing the wife of the former leader, Tereus, threatening the goddess Iris with sexual abuse, and finally stealing Zeus' trusted "stewardess" Basileia. The end of the play celebrates their union as Peisetairos is hailed "the highest of divinities" (1765). Similarly, the victory of the hero in *Peace* is marked out in sexual terms, as he becomes the bridegroom of Peace (859–862, 1316–1359) and gives Theoria as a plaything to the councilors to enjoy (868–917): the aggressive sexual act functions as a collective male fantasy which symbolizes the return to normality and peace (Robson 2015; Tsoumpra 2020a, p. 93).

The comic trope "there are no real men anymore" forms the backbone of the plot for the "women on top" comedies of Aristophanes. In both *Lysistrata* and *Ecclesiazusae*, the idea that women will now conduct politics stems from the fact that men have failed so badly in their roles that the gender role inversion might be the only solution to the political crisis. In both plays, the political decline is marked by the effeminization of men (Foley 1982; Bowie 1993): in *Lysistrata*, the magistrate loses the debate with Lysistrata and is forcefully dressed like a woman and ordered to start sewing because political decisions about the war are now the business of women (536–538). The male chorus complains about their emasculation by the women and are eager to prove that they are "real men" (662–663; Tsoumpra 2020b, pp. 376–377). Even though the women suffer because of their sex strike, it is the men who give in to their urges first – a blatant reversal of the gender stereotypes that view the women as the ones with the unbridled, uncontrolled sexuality. The reinstatement of men in the control of the state is signaled by the reclaiming of their dominant sexual role, as they are dividing up the body of Reconciliation on stage (1164–1187). In *Ecclesiazusae*, men are suspiciously keen to stay indoors and abstain from political participation in the assembly (462–464), thus behaving like women. Blepyrus, who runs out of the house in his wife's clothes in order to relieve himself but unable to "reproduce," emblematizes the feminization and disempowerment of men in the play (Leitao 2012, p. 147; Tsoumpra 2020b, pp. 388–392).

The satire of politicians and men involved in the running of the state as passive homosexuals in comedy is one side of the coin: aggressive masculinity and macho discourse is the other side. It is worth noting that this type of sexualized discourse persists in western contemporary politics, even though expectations about the performance of gender roles are supposed to have changed and the negative effects of toxic masculinity have been brought to the forefront of public discourse and popular culture. In recent times, there has been a revival of a coarse, vulgar, sexualized discourse ("Stammtisch" discourse; Mudde and Kaltwasser 2014, p. 64) in politics, characteristic of male leaders, who highlight their virility with every opportunity and engage in "locker room" talk. One can think here of Silvio Berlusconi in Italy, who fervently cultivated the image of the playboy politician,[19] and Donald Trump's many examples of macho public discourse,[20] addressed both to opponents and to the general public.

Aggressive/Offensive Humor in Aristophanes' Political Comedies

Satire and invective have been recognized as the trademarks of comedy ever since antiquity. Plato, in his discussion about whether tragedy and comedy should be allowed in his ideal city, makes the following observations about the nature of comedy:

> And no bad men either, so it would seem: those who are cowardly and who do the opposite of what we were talking about just now, abusing and ridiculing each other, and using foul language (*aischrologountas*) whether drunk, or even sober, or also the other wrongs that such people perpetrate against both themselves and others in word and deed.[21]

(Pl. *Resp.* 395e7)

---

[19] Berlusconi has been variously accused of frequenting minors, sleeping with an escort girl, and holding debauched parties at his Sardinian villa. He was charged in 2011 and initially convicted of paying for sex with an underage prostitute and abusing his office to cover it up; he was acquitted on appeal in 2015. He is notorious for using misogynistic language. In an interview with the Chi magazine, he denied the accusations that he had paid for sex claiming "For those who love to conquer, the joy and the most beautiful satisfaction is in the conquest. If you have to pay, what joy is there?" https://www.theguardian.com/world/2009/jun/24/silvio-berlusconi-scandal-magazine-interview.

[20] In a 2005 recording obtained by The Washington Post before the presidential election, Donald Trump, making a cameo appearance on the set of Days of Our Lives, talks about women in vulgar terms. Some of the quotes read: "You know, I'm automatically attracted to beautiful – I just start kissing them. It's like a magnet. Just kiss. I don't even wait. And when you're a star, they let you do it. [. . .] Grab them by the pussy. You can do anything." https://www.nytimes.com/2016/10/08/us/donald-trump-tape-transcript.html.

[21] Transl. Emlyn-Jones and Preddy (2013).

Comedy is not a suitable form of mimesis for guardians because it involves abuse, ridicule and using foul language. In his *Laws* (935d), Plato also notes "comedy's zeal to mock individuals" (*geloia eis tous anthrōpous legein*). Similarly, Aristotle recognized the important place of personal abuse in comedy, claiming that its origins are found in the iambographic tradition and that comedy arose from the tradition of poets who first made poems of abuse (*Poet.* 1488b27). Horace also assigns the origins of satire to fifth-century Attic comedy (*Sat.* 1.4.1–5):

> Eupolis, Cratinus, and Aristophanes and all the other poets of Old Comedy would point out with great freedom anyone who deserved to be put down as a bad person or a thief, an adulterer, a cutthroat, or in some other way notorious.[22]

Personal abuse seems to have been well established as comedy's business in antiquity. The connections between the iambic tradition and comedy, as well as possible reasons for the selection of the satirical targets (Halliwell 1984; Sommerstein 1996b; Henderson 2013) have been explored by various scholars in recent years (Rosen 1988, 2007; Degani 1993; Henderson 1991, pp. 17–23, 243–244; O' Higgins 2003). It has been suggested that Aristophanic comedy enjoyed a special license for mockery and obscenity, that it exemplified "institutionalized shamelessness" and marked a carnivalesque break from reality (Halliwell 1991, 2002, 2004). According to this view, the humor of Aristophanic comedy offered an opportunity for a pleasurable and shameless breach of social norms, and physical and mental release with no fear of consequences, since engaging in or laughing with verbal and sexual aggression, and exchange of vulgar insults and obscenities were not acceptable in public. However, the audience of Aristophanic comedy was much more desensitized to "shameless" behavior than this view allows. The provocative and offensive humor of Aristophanic comedy (such as verbal and sexual violence) did not necessarily signal a deviation from an acceptable standard but enlisted and replicated existing social norms. We have seen that many of the themes of the comic invective are not limited to comedy but crop up also in historiography (e.g. the violence and shamelessness of Cleon feature in both Thucydides and Plutarch) and are central in forensic and deliberative speeches (such as the low origins, bribery and *kinaidos* slanders). Thus, they form part of a wider discourse to which the theater audience was not simply exposed: it actively contributed to their formation and circulation. By presenting verbal and sexual aggression as humorous and amusing, Aristophanic comedy does not suspend or overturn the cultural norms: it further normalizes them. In this respect, the satire and invective of Aristophanic comedy can be compared to the use of verbal violence in contemporary political discourse: the heated and aggressive language that politicians use, and the ridicule, insults, and put downs that they direct against one another, as well as external targets, in political debates often aim to engender a humorous effect, which then neutralizes the aggression of the rhetoric. The tendentious jokes are often phrased as acts of subversion, as defiance against political correctness. Donald Trump offers a wide range of examples of such discourse. For instance, one of his presidential campaign quotes against his Democratic rival Hillary Clinton read: "If Hillary can't satisfy her husband, what makes her think she can satisfy America?."[23] In another instance, while speaking at a rally in North Carolina about the next president's power to appoint supreme court justices, he implied that gun owners should shoot Hillary Clinton to protect the Second Amendment:

> "If she gets to pick her judges, nothing you can do, folks. Although the second amendment people, maybe there is, I don't know. But I'll tell you what, that will be a horrible day."[24]

---

[22] Transl. Henderson (2013).
[23] Source: https://www.theguardian.com/us-news/2016/may/10/donald-trump-quotes-fictional-presidential-victory-speech.
[24] Source: https://www.theguardian.com/us-news/2016/aug/09/trump-gun-owners-clinton-judges-second-amendment.

Both remarks are phrased as humorous utterances, attempting to create bonds of solidarity between the in-group that is in on the joke and at the same time disparage and humiliate the political opponent. They create an ideological space, where harmful stereotypes about women's "designated" sexual role are strategically perpetuated (the first quote), imbued with nostalgia for a time when white male culture was dominant and women were kept sexually and politically subordinate, while physical violence is plainly endorsed as a reasonable act of defense (the second quote). This rhetoric, situated in between political critique and public entertainment, shows how the logic of humor might impinge upon other spheres and ways of thought and create its own ideology. The aggression and offensiveness of the Aristophanic political satire might function in a similar way: not as transgressive or subversive, but as reflecting and upholding contemporary social, political, and ethical standards while offering the comfort that it is "just a joke."

GUIDE TO FURTHER READING

For attempted reconstructions of Aristophanes' conflict with Cleon, see Welsh (1978), Storey (1995), Sommerstein (2004), and Lafargue (2013, pp. 21–26). Rosen (1988, 2007) considers the conflict a mere dramatic fiction. For more parallels between the comic invective and the judicial/deliberative invective in the fourth century BCE, see Heath (1997) and the Papaioannou et al. (2017) co-edited volume.

The corpus of scholarly criticism devoted to the political significance of Aristophanic Comedy is extensive: for the view that comedy echoed the vox populi, representing the feelings and views of the *dēmos*, and reminding them that they have the ultimate authority over the state, see Henderson (1990, 1993, 2003); Konstan (1995) argues that comedy offered a sort of ideological retreat and safety valve for popular discontent; Ober (1998) that it provided education to the masses on their role; and Rosenbloom (2002) that it subjected democratic audiences to right-wing harangue. Ruffell's monograph (2011) is a great resource for the ways in which humor and impossibility are central to the political and ideological interventions of Old Comedy. She examines how the anti-realism of comic metatheatricality makes various political points through audience address, the construction of model audiences, and their interaction with the fictional content. The recent volume by Rosen and Foley (2020) offers the latest reprise of the "Aristophanes and Politics" subject: a collection of essays on the ways in which Aristophanes is a thoroughly political poet.

REFERENCES

Apostolakis, K. (2021). Comic invective and public speech in fourth-century Athens. In: *Comic Invective in Ancient Greek and Roman Oratory* (ed. S. Papaioannou and A. Serafim), 43–64. Leiden, Boston (MA): Brill.

Atkinson, J.E. (1992). Curbing the comedians: Cleon versus Aristophanes and Syracosius' decree. *Classical Quarterly* 42: 56–64.

Bennett, L.J. and Tyrell, W.M.B. (1990). Making sense of Aristophanes' Knights. *Arethusa* 23: 235–254.

Biles, Z.P. and Olson, S.D. (2015). *Aristophanes Wasps*. Oxford: Oxford University Press.

Bowie, A.M. (1993). *Aristophanes: Myth, Ritual and Comedy*. Cambridge: Cambridge University Press.

Brock, R.W. (1986). The double plot in Aristophanes' Knights. *Greek, Roman, and Byzantine Studies* 27: 15–27.

Burns, T.W. (2014). Anger in Thucydides and Aristophanes: the case of Cleon. In: *The Political Theory of Aristophanes: Explorations in Poetic Wisdom* (ed. J.M. Mhire and B.-P. Frost), 229–258. Albany, NY: SUNY Press.

Cammack, D. (2022). The popular courts in Athenian democracy. *The Journal of Politics* 84: 4. Available at https://ssrn.com/abstract=3587081.

Carey, C. (2013). Marathon and the Construction of the Comic Past. *Bulletin of the Institute of Classical Studies* (Supplement 124): 123–142.

Carson, A. (1990). Putting her in her place: woman, dirt, and desire. In: *Before Sexuality: The Construction of Erotic Experience in the Ancient Greek World* (ed. F.I. Zeitlin, J.J. Winkler, and D.M. Halperin), 135–170. Princeton, NJ: Princeton University Press.

Colvin, S. (2000). The language of non-Athenians in old comedy. In: *The Rivals of Aristophanes: Studies in Athenian Old Comedy* (ed. F.D. Harvey, J. Wilkins, and K.J. Dover), 285–298. London: Duckworth.
Connor, W.R. (1971). *The New Politicians of Fifth-Century Athens*. Princeton, NJ: Princeton University Press.
Degani, E. (1993). Aristofane e la Tradizione dell'Invettiva Personale in Grecia. In: *Aristophane* (ed. I.M. Bremmer and E.W. Handley), 1–49. Vandoeuvres/Genève: Fondation Hardt.
Donelan, J. (2021). Comedy and insults in the Athenian law-courts. In: *Comic Invective in Ancient Greek and Roman Oratory* (ed. S. Papaioannou and A. Serafim), 25–42. Leiden, Boston (MA): Brill.
Dover, K.J. (1972). *Aristophanic Comedy*. Berkeley and Los Angeles: University of California Press.
Dover, K.J. (1974). *Greek Popular Morality in the Time of Plato and Aristotle*. Oxford: Blackwell.
Edmunds, L. (1987). The Aristophanic Cleon's 'disturbance' of Athens. *American Journal of Philology* 108: 233–263.
Ehrenberg, V. (1951). *The People of Aristophanes: A Sociology of Old Attic Comedy*. Oxford: Blackwell.
Emlyn-Jones, C. and Preddy, W. (2013). *Plato Republic, Books 1–5*. Cambridge, MA and London: Harvard University Press [Loeb Classical Library].
Faraone, C.A. (1991). The agonistic context of early Greek binding spells. In: *Magika Hiera: Ancient Greek Magic and Religion* (ed. C.A. Faraone and D. Obbink), 3–32. Oxford, New York: Oxford University Press.
Foley, H.P. (1982). The "female intruder" reconsidered: women in Aristophanes' *Lysistrata* and *Ecclesiazusae*. *Classical Philology* 77: 1–21.
Ford, G.B. (1965). The Knights as a source of Aristophanes' attitude toward the demagogues and the demos. *Athenaeum n.s.* 43: 106–110.
Glazebrook, A. (2013). Sexual rhetoric. In: *A Companion to Greek and Roman Sexualities* (ed. T.K. Hubbard), 431–445. Oxford and Malden, MA: Wiley Blackwell.
Hall, J.M. (2002). *Hellenicity: Between Ethnicity and Culture*. Chicago: University of Chicago Press.
Hall, E.M. (2018). The boys from Cydathenaeum: Aristophanes versus Cleon again. In: *How to Do Things with History: New Approaches to Ancient Greece* (ed. D. Allen, P. Christesen, and P. Millett), 339–364. Oxford, New York: Oxford University Press.
Hall, E. (2019). Competitive vocal performance in Aristophanes' « Knights ». In: *Poet and Orator: A Symbiotic Relationship in Democratic Athens* (ed. A. Markantonatos and E. Volonaki), 71–82. Berlin, Boston (MA): De Gruyter.
Halliwell, F.S. (1984). Aristophanic satire. *Yearbook of English Studies* 14: 6–20.
Halliwell, F.S. (1991). Comic satire and freedom of speech in classical Athens. *Journal of Hellenic Studies* 111: 48–70.
Halliwell, F.S. (2002). Aristophanic sex: the erotics of shamelessness. In: *The Sleep of Reason: Erotic Experience and Sexual Ethics in Ancient Greece and Rome* (ed. M.C. Nussbaum and J. Sihvola), 120–142. Chicago: Chicago University Press.
Halliwell, F.S. (2004). Aischrology, shame, and comedy. In: *Free Speech in Classical Antiquity* (ed. I. Sluiter and R.M. Rosen), 116–144. Leiden, Boston (MA): Brill.
Halperin, D.M. (1990). *One Hundred Years of Homosexuality and Other Essays on Greek Love*. New York: Routledge.
Hansen, M.J. (1991). *The Athenian Democracy in the Age of Demosthenes: Structure, Principles and Ideology*, trans. J. A. Crook. [Original publication Det athenske demokrati i 4. århundrede f. Kr. Copenhagen, 1978.]. Oxford: Oxford University Press.
Harvey, F.D. (1985). Dona ferentes: some aspects of bribery in Greek politics. *History of Political Thought* 6 (1/2): 76–117.
Heath, M. (1990). Aristophanes and his rivals. *Greece & Rome* 37 (2): 143–158.
Heath, M. (1997). Aristophanes and the discourse of politics. In: *Society and Representation in Athenian Drama* (ed. G. Dobrov), 230–249. Chapel Hill and London: University of North Carolina Press.
Henderson, J. (1990). The demos and comic competition. In: *Nothing to Do with Dionysus? Athenian Drama in its Social Context* (ed. J.J. Winkler and F. Zeitlin), 271–313. Princeton, NJ: Princeton University Press.
Henderson, J. (1991). *The Maculate Muse: Obscene Language in Attic Comedy*. New Haven and London: Yale University Press.
Henderson, J. (1993). Comic hero versus political elite. In: *Tragedy, Comedy and the Polis* (ed. A.H. Sommerstein), 307–319. Bari: Levante Editori.
Henderson, J. (1998). *Aristophanes, Acharnians and Knights*. Cambridge, MA: Harvard University Press [Loeb Classical Library].

Henderson, J. (2003). Demos, demagogue, tyrant in attic old comedy. In: *Popular Tyranny: Sovereignty and Its Discontents in Ancient Greece* (ed. K.A. Morgan), 155–180. Austin: University of Texas Press.

Henderson, J. (2013). A brief history of Athenian political comedy (c. 440–c. 300). *Transactions of the American Philological Association* 143: 249–262.

Henderson, J. (2018). Hesiod and comedy. In: *The Oxford Handbook of Hesiod* (ed. A.C. Loney and S. Scully), 295–310. Oxford: Oxford University Press.

Hershkowitz, A. (2018). *Rise of the Demagogues: Political Leadership in Imperial Athens After the Reforms of Ephialtes*, PhD thesis. Rutgers, the State University of New Jersey.

Hesk, J. (2000). *Deception and Democracy in Classical Athens*. Cambridge University Press.

Kallet, L. (2003). Demos tyrannos: wealth, power, and economic patronage. In: *Popular Tyranny: Sovereignty and Its Discontents in Ancient Greece* (ed. K.A. Morgan), 117–153. University of Texas Press.

Konstan, D. (1995). *Greek Comedy and Ideology*. Oxford: Oxford University Press.

Lafargue, P. (2013). *Cléon: Le Guerrier d'Athéna*. Paris: Ausonius Press.

Lape, S. (2013). Slavery, drama and the alchemy of identity in Aristophanes. In: *Slaves and Slavery in Ancient Greek Comic Drama* (ed. B. Akrigg and R. Tordoff), 76–90. Cambridge: Cambridge University Press.

Leitao, D.D. (2012). *The Pregnant Male as Myth and Metaphor in Classical Greek Literature*. Cambridge: Cambridge University Press.

Lind, H. (1990). *Der Gerber Kleon in den "Rittern" des Aristophanes: Studien zur Demagogenkomödie*, Frankfurt am Main. Peter Lang.

Littlefield, D.J. (1968). Metaphor and myth: the unity of Aristophanes' *Knights*. *Studies in Philology* 65: 1–22.

Macdowell, D.M. (1993). Foreign birth and Athenian citizenship in Aristophanes. In: *Tragedy, Comedy and the Polis* (ed. F.S. Halliwell, A.H. Sommerstein, J. Henderson, and B. Zimmermann), 359–371. Bari: Levante Editori.

Macdowell, D.M. (1995). *Aristophanes and Athens*. Oxford: Oxford University Press.

Mann, C. (2007). *Die Demagogen und das Volk. Zur politischen Kommunikation im Athen des 5. Jahrhunderts v. Chr. (Klio Beihefte, Neue Folge, 13.)*. Berlin: Academie Verlag.

Marr, J. (1996). History as lunch: Aristophanes, *Knights* 810–19. *Classical Quarterly* 46 (2): 561–564.

McGlew, J. (1996). Everybody wants to make a speech: Cleon and Aristophanes on politics and fantasy. *Arethusa* 29: 339–361.

McGlew, J. (2002). *Citizens on Stage: Comedy and Political Culture in the Athenian Democracy*. Ann Arbor, MI: University of Michigan Press.

Mudde, C. and Kaltwasser, C.R. (2014). *Populism: A Very Short Introduction*. Oxford: Oxford University Press.

Norwood, G. (1930). The Babylonians of Aristophanes. *Classical Philology* 25 (1): 1–10.

O' Higgins, L. (2003). *Women and Humor in Classical Greece*. Cambridge: Cambridge University Press.

Ober, J. (1989). *Mass and Elite in Democratic Athens: Rhetoric, Ideology, and the Power of the People*. Princeton, NJ: Princeton University Press.

Ober, J. (1998). *Political Dissent in Democratic Athens: Intellectual Critics of Popular Rule*. Princeton, NJ: Princeton University Press.

Olson, S.D. (1990). The new demos of Aristophanes' *Knights*. *Eranos* 88: 60–63.

Olson, S.D. (1996). Politics and poetry in Aristophanes' *Wasps*. *Transactions of the American Philological Association* 126: 129–150.

Ormand, K. (2009). *Controlling Desires: Sexuality in Ancient Greece and Rome*. Westport, CT: Praeger.

Papaioannou, S., Serafim, A., and da Vela, B. (ed.) (2017). *The Theatre of Justice: Aspects of Performance in Greco-Roman Oratory and Rhetoric*. Leiden, Boston (MA): Brill.

Reckford, K.J. (1987). *Aristophanes' Old-and-New Comedy*, Six Essays in Perspective, vol. 1. Chapel Hill: University of North Carolina Press.

Robson, J. (2009). *Aristophanes: An Introduction*. London: Duckworth.

Robson, J. (2015). Fantastic sex: fantasies of sexual assault in Aristophanes. In: *Sex in Antiquity: Exploring Gender and Sexuality in the Ancient World* (ed. M. Masterson, N.S. Rabinowitz, and J. Robson), 315–331. London: Routledge.

Robson, J. (2018). Whoring, gaping and hiding meat: the humour of male-on-male sexual insults in Aristophanes' *Knights*. *Archimède* 5: 24–34.

Rosen, R.M. (1988). *Old Comedy and the Iambographic Tradition*. Atlanta: Scholars Press.

Rosen, R.M. (2007). *Making Mockery: The Poetics of Ancient Satire*. Oxford: Oxford University Press.
Rosen, R.M. and Foley, H.P. (ed.) (2020). *Aristophanes and Politics. New Studies*. Leiden and Boston: Brill.
Rosenbloom, D. (2002). From Ponēros to Pharmakos: theater, social drama, and revolution in Athens, 428–404 BCE. *Classical Antiquity* 21: 283–346.
Ruck, C. (1975). Euripides' mother: vegetables and the phallos in Aristophanes. *Arion* 2 (1): 13–57.
Ruffell, I.A. (2000). The world turned upside down: utopia and utopianism in the fragments of old comedy. In: *The Rivals of Aristophanes: Studies in Athenian Old Comedy* (ed. F.D. Harvey, J. Wilkins, and K.J. Dover), 473–506. London: Duckworth and the Classical Press of Wales.
Ruffell, I.A. (2011). *Politics and Anti-Realism in Athenian Old Comedy: The Art of the Impossible*. Oxford: Oxford University Press.
Sapsford, T. (2022). *Performing the Kinaidos: Unmanly Men in Ancient Mediterranean Cultures*. Oxford: Oxford University Press.
Scholtz, A. (2004). Friends, lovers, flatterers: demophilic courtship in Aristophanes' *Knights*. *Transactions of the American Philological Association* 134: 263–293.
Sommerstein, A.H. (1981). *Aristophanes Knights*. Warminster: Aris & Phillips.
Sommerstein, A.H. (1996a). *Aristophanes Frogs*. Warminster: Aris & Phillips.
Sommerstein, A.H. (1996b). How to avoid being a Komodoumenos. *The Classical Quarterly* 46 (2): 327–356.
Sommerstein, A.H. (2000). Platon, Eupolis, and the 'demagogue comedy'. In: *The Rivals of Aristophanes: Studies in Athenian Old Comedy* (ed. F.D. Harvey, J. Wilkins, and K.J. Dover), 437–451. London: Duckworth.
Sommerstein, A.H. (2004). Harassing the satirist: the alleged attempts to prosecute Aristophanes. In: *Free Speech in Classical Antiquity* (ed. R.M. Rosen and I. Sluiter), 145–174. Leiden: Brill.
Sommerstein, A.H. (2009). Monsters, ogres, and demons in old comedy. In: *Talking About Laughter and Other Studies in Greek Comedy* (ed. A.H. Sommerstein), 155–175. Oxford: Oxford University Press.
Sommerstein, A.H. (2014). The politics of Greek comedy. In: *The Cambridge Companion to Greek Comedy* (ed. M. Revermann), 291–305. Cambridge: Cambridge University Press.
Starkey, J. (2013). Soldiers and sailors in Aristophanes' *Babylonians*. *The Classical Quarterly* 63 (2): 501–510.
Storey, I.C. (1995). Wasps 1284-91 and the portrait of Kleon in Wasps. *Scholia* 4: 3–23.
Storey, I.C. (1998). Poets, politicians and perverts: personal humour in Aristophanes. *Classics Ireland* 5: 85–134.
Storey, I.C. (2005). But comedy has satyrs too. In: *Satyr Drama* (ed. G.W.M. Harrison), 201–218. Swansey: Classical Press of Wales.
Tsoumpra, N. (2014). *Comic Leadership and Power Dynamics in Aristophanes*, DPhil thesis. Oxford: Oxford University Press.
Tsoumpra, N. (2018). The politics of hopelessness: Thucydides and Aristophanes' *Knights*. In: *Hope in Ancient Literature, History and Art* (ed. G. Kazantzidis and D. Spatharas), 111–129. Berlin: De Gruyter.
Tsoumpra, N. (2020a). Identities. In: *A Cultural History of Comedy: Antiquity*, vol. 1 (ed. M. Ewans), 79–96. London: Bloomsbury.
Tsoumpra, N. (2020b). "Undressing and cross-dressing: costume, ritual, and female empowerment in Aristophanes," in N. Tsoumpra (ed.), Costume Change in the Comedies of Aristophanes. Special Issue of Illinois Classical Studies 45.2, 368–98. Champaign-Urbana: University of Illinois Press.
Walters, J. (1997). Invading the Roman body: manliness and impenetrability in Roman thought. In: *Roman Sexualities* (ed. J.P. Hallet and M.B. Skinner), 29–43. Princeton, NJ: Princeton University Press.
Welsh, V. (1978). *The Development of the Relationship Between Aristophanes and Cleon to 424 B. C.* London: King's College.
Whitman, C.H. (1964). *Aristophanes and the Comic Hero*. Cambridge: Harvard University Press.
Wilkins, J. (1993). The regulation of meat in Aristophanes' *Knights*. In: *Tria Lustra (Liverpool Classical Papers 3)* (ed. H. Jocelyn), 119–126. Liverpool Classical Monthly.
Wilkins, J. (1997). Comic cuisine: food and eating in the comic polis. In: *The City as Comedy: Society and Representation in Athenian Drama* (ed. G.W. Dobrov), 250–268. Chapel Hill and London: University of North Carolina Press.
Wilkins, J. (2000). *The Boastful Chef: The Discourse of Food in Ancient Greek Comedy*. Oxford: Oxford University Press.
Willi, A. (2002). Languages on stage: Aristophanic language, cultural history, and Athenian identity. In: *The Language of Greek Comedy* (ed. A. Willi), 111–150. Oxford; New York: Oxford University Press.

Wohl, V. (2002). *Love Among the Ruins: The Erotics of Democracy in Classical Athens*. Princeton, NJ: Princeton University Press.
Woodhead, A.G. (1960). Thucydides' portrait of Cleon. *Mnemosyne* 13: 289–317.
Worman, N. (2008). *Abusive Mouths in Classical Athens*. Cambridge: Cambridge University Press.
Yates, V. (2005). Anterastai: competition in eros and politics in classical Athens. *Arethusa* 38 (1): 33–47.
Zumbrunnen, J. (2004). Elite domination and the clever citizen: Aristophanes' *Acharnians* and *Knights*. *Political Theory* 32: 656–677.
Zumbrunnen, J. (2012). *Aristophanic Comedy and the Challenge of Democratic Citizenship*. Rochester, NY: University of Rochester Press.

CHAPTER 9

Clouds: Intellectuals and Philosophy

Olimpia Imperio

Introduction

Clouds was performed at the Dionysia of 423 BCE, where it placed third after Cratinus' *Damianus* and Amipsia's *Connus* (cf. especially Ar. *Nu. Arg.* V Wilson). The text we possess is a *diaskeuē*, that is, a version revised by the playwright in later years.[1] The nature and extent of this revision are highly controversial.[2] Nonetheless, as documented for us by ancient scholarship (cf. especially Ar. *Nu. Arg.* VI Wilson), we can be certain that the revisions concerned to a substantial extent at least three parts of the play:

(1) the recited section of the parabasis, which, rewritten in "eupolidean" verse, recalls two post-423 events, namely the death of Cleon and the performance of the *Marikas* of Eupolis (cf. vv. 518–562 and, for the novelty of the meter, Σ [vet] Ar. *Nu.* 520), as well as the defeat of the original version of Clouds itself in 423;
(2) the epirrhematic agon between the Better Argument and the Worse Argument (vv. 889–1104), in which obvious signs of structural and content disorganization are generally recognized (see below);
(3) the final scene (vv. 1476–1511), with the burning of the *Phrontisterion*, which is explicitly referred to in a scholium *vetus* in v. 543.

From ancient evidence (in addition to the *hypothesis* VI Wilson, cf. the scholium *vetus* at v. 553), we also know that such a remake was never brought to the stage, and we can reasonably assume that it was probably not even completed by the playwright. There are numerous inconsistencies of scenic character and content, as well as conspicuous traces of incompleteness and compositional layering recognizable in the transmitted text, which compel us to assume that the unfortunate patchwork effect produced by the revision convinced Aristophanes to give up the idea of bringing the revised play to the stage.[3]

---

[1] Probably no later than 417 BCE, presumably the year of the ostracism of Hyperbolus, the demagogue who, as is clear from vv. 551 to 559, taken from the parabasis of the so-called *Second Clouds*, will have been up to that time the victim of the fury of Aristophanes' rival playwrights.
[2] The extensive critical debate, already reconstructed in detail by Dover (1968, lxxxv–cviii), is retraced more recently by Torchio (2021, 12–25).
[3] MacDowell (1995), 134–136, 144–149 and Sommerstein (1997) = 2009; however, the possibility of subsequent "reperformances" of the *Second Clouds* has been revived by Marshall (2012).

A Companion to Aristophanes, First Edition. Edited by Matthew C. Farmer and Jeremy B. Lefkowitz.
© 2024 John Wiley & Sons, Inc. Published 2024 by John Wiley & Sons, Inc.

The precise reason for the play's cold reception at the Dionysia in 423 escapes us. Apart from the claims of Aristophanes himself, who, both in the parabasis of the *Wasps* (vv. 1044–1050) and in that of the so-called *Second Clouds* (i.e. the second version of the *Clouds*, or *Clouds* II vv. 520–526), attributes the failure of the play to the inability of the audience to understand its merits (Sonnino 2005; Platter 2007, 84–107), the specific reasons for this failure remain unknown, and hypotheses on the subject have been remarkably diverse:

(1) the play's lack of verve (Bücheler 1861, 682 = 1915, 315), due to its use of culturally sophisticated themes, which, although highly topical in the narrow circle of intellectuals, were of little appeal to a general public more intrigued by political satire (Gelzer 1960, 149; Carey 2000, 431);
(2) the superior artistic quality of the two other winning competitors' dramas (Biles 2011, 154);
(3) the lack of originality of the plot, which would have reiterated the motifs of upbringing and generational clash already experienced in the *Banqueters* of 427 BCE (Römer 1896, 247);
(4) or, conversely, its bold experimentalism (Hose 1995, 46f.; Sommerstein 2001, 250); the spectators' irritation at the tendentious characterization of Socrates as an ungodly sophist corrupting the young (Kaibel 1895, 977), an ungenerous misrepresentation that might have been accentuated by an original ending in which Strepsiades triumphed over Socrates with the same cavillous and deceptive arguments that the old man had learned to free himself from creditors (Howald 1922, 38–42);
or, on the contrary, because of Aristophanes' ill-concealed sympathy for the philosopher and the Sophists, revealed by Strepsiades' miserable succumbing before the final triumph of Pheidippides, in comparison with which the burning of the *Phrontisterion* introduced in the revised version would thus represent a moralizing corrective (Kunst 1919, 23–25; Murray 1933, 87f., 104f.; Schmid and Stählin 1946, 264–267; Whitman 1964, 135–137; De Carli 1971, 24f.; MacDowell 1995, 144–149; Biles 2011, 210);
(5) nor, conversely, has the possibility of a connection between the failure of the first *Clouds* and the content of its ending been ruled out, with the sudden turnabout of the chorus (on which see below) and (presumably) the absence of the hero's final triumph already in the play's first draft (Hubbard 1991, 106, 112; Sommerstein 1997, 278f. = 2009, 185f.; Revermann 2006, 230).

Performed at a particularly dramatic moment during the first phase of the Peloponnesian War, in the thick of the ensuing moral and political crisis in Athens, *Clouds* focuses on the conflict between tradition and modernity, between fidelity to the values of the democratic *polis* and the new sophistic-Socratic culture that those values strongly challenged. This conflict, expressed in the comic plot on the dual familial/generational and cultural/philosophical levels, with its important ethical, political, and sociological implications, sheds invaluable light on the peculiar status of intellectuals and philosophers in Athens during the 420s. This chapter will explore the figure of the intellectual in Athenian society, against the backdrop of the so-called Greek enlightenment of the classical age, together with the problem of the historicity of the character of Socrates sketched in the *Clouds*. After a brief summary of the plot, we will turn to the idea of the fraudulence of arguments from science, rhetoric, sophistry, and philosophy, and, in general, the polarity between practical life and intellectual activity.

The Plot of *Clouds*

During a sleepless night, an elderly farmer named Strepsiades, burdened with debts from his son's foolish and costly obsession with horses, devises a criminal plan: he will convince his son Pheidippides to attend the Socratic *Phrontisterion* ("thinking place"), where he will learn the "Worse Argument," capable of winning even unjust causes. Having mastered the intricacies of this infamous "Worse Argument," the old man and his son will thus be able to escape the completely legitimate claims of their creditors. Pheidippides' disdainful refusal to go to school, however, forces Strepsiades to become a schoolboy himself and to enter into a cultural universe that is totally foreign to him. Crude, obtuse, and forgetful as he is, Strepsiades will in fact prove to be entirely incapable of grasping the subtle precepts taught by a rather impatient Socrates, who will eventually expel the old man. In the second part of the play, at the suggestion of the chorus of Clouds, aerial and multiform tutelary deities of the Socratics, Strepsiades finally persuades his son to study with the intellectuals in the *Phrontisterion* under Socrates, and to learn the "Worse Argument," promoter of modern Sophistic education, which will triumph over the "Better Argument," champion of traditional education. From this full immersion in the life of the *Phrontisterion* Pheidippides re-emerges profoundly "socratized," with all of the cunning dialectical skills required to free his father from his creditors for good. But the son's education (*paideia*) will prove all too successful, and before long the consequences will backfire on the father himself: during an argument that breaks out at the dinner table over differences of taste and poetics, Pheidippides will beat up Strepsiades and, availing himself of the captious sophisms learned from the "Worse Argument," he will defend the lawfulness of disrespectful and even violent behavior of children toward their parents. Bitterly repentant, and with the support of the god Hermes, at the end of the play Strepsiades takes revenge on the Socratics, who urged him to repudiate the gods, by setting fire to the *Phrontisterion*.

Socrates and the Intellectuals: Science, Rhetoric, Sophistry, and Philosophy

The comic mask of the philosopher brought to the stage in Attic comedy reproduces an intellectual type that turns out to be substantially imported from Ionia: it had been the Ionian Anaxagoras of Clazomene, friend and teacher of Pericles, who had proposed to the Athenians the first model of the wise man who, as is already apparent only from the conspicuous anecdotal evidence reported by Diogenes Laërtius (II 6–15 = 59 A 1 D.-K.; cf. 59 A 21 D.-K.), appears to ordinary people as a strange being because of his austere attitude toward life and his fellow man, his serene disinterest in the turmoil of politics, his almost exclusive interest in the study of nature, and his indifference to the judgment of the crowd. And it is precisely that extravagant abstractness of behavior and that austere personality, contemptuous and detached from mundane, everyday things that make the Aristophanic Socrates the "priest" of those sciences of which the Clouds, in the play named after them, are tutelary deities (cf., e.g., the attitude of σεμνοπροσωπεῖν, the "putting on airs," attributed by Strepsiades to Socrates in *Nu.* 363 and see Imperio 1998a, 227f., regarding Call.Com. fr. 15 K.-A.).

In the *Clouds*, Socrates appears on stage perched in a basket suspended in midair and immediately declares, "I move through the air and scan the sun (ἀεροβατῶ καὶ περιφρονῶ τὸν ἥλιον)" (v. 225: a statement that will be mockingly echoed by Strepsiades in v. 1503) when he climbs onto the roof of the *Phrontisterion* to set it on fire, in the play's finale, and, implicitly likening the nature of his own thought to the air, he gives the reason for his unusual vantage point: "I would never have exactly discovered celestial phenomena if I had not suspended my mind and mingled thought, which is subtle, with the air, which is similar to it. If I had remained on the ground, observing from below the things that are above, I would never have discovered anything; for the earth draws to itself powerfully the mood of thought, just as it does to the watercress (vv. 227–234)" (on this last simile and its philosophical matrices, generally and too generically traced to the thought of Diogenes of Apollonia on the authority of Hermann Diels, see Fazzo 2013, 107–112). To investigate *ta meteora*, Socrates thus becomes himself *meteoros*: a term that does not simply allude to a generic sublimity of mind but encompasses a range of referents that includes the studies of astronomy, the practice of which, repeatedly evoked as one of the thinker's primary activities (cf. vv. 95–97, 171f. 191–194, 201), establishes a direct connection between the teaching imparted by the Socrates of the *Clouds* and the physical-naturalistic doctrines of Anaxagoras, and of his disciple Diogenes of Apollonia (in particular, regarding the aerial and subtle nature of thought, theorized in vv. 227–234, cf. 64 A 19–20 D.-K and the Hippocratic treatise *On Airs, Waters and Places*, 8; but the role of this eclectic and unassuming philosopher in the "meteorological" theories of the Aristophanean Socrates has been appropriately downplayed by, among others, Turato 1973, 47–49), and is the prerequisite for those accusations of impiety and atheism that in the course of the play strike, directly or indirectly, at Socrates as a representative intellectual figure of all the learned *alazones* (frauds or braggarts) who populate the plays (on the history of the terms μετέωρος, μετεωρολογία and related, see Capelle 1912, 414–448; and particularly on the negative connotations that these two terms, and related acquire in relation to Anaxagorean speculation and the sophists' interest in this sphere of inquiry, 428–441).

The theoretical foundation of this atheism is clearly recognizable in the study of *ta meteora*, that is, astronomy and meteorology.[4] Ultimately, in the figure of Socrates as he appears to be sketched by Aristophanes in the *Clouds* (but also in fragments from other comedies of the *archaia*), what we have already identified as the two "souls" of intellectualism portrayed by the play are exemplified and merged in the most accomplished manner, namely, that ambiguous and contradictory suspension between a purely aerial and theoretical dimension and an all too earthly and concrete reality toward which the intellectual is hopelessly drawn. This is a dialectic which had perhaps already proved its dramatic vitality in the figures of those intellectuals who were to form the chorus of Cratinus' *Panoptai/All-Seers* (performed probably between 435 and 432 BCE), in which for the first time, to our knowledge, the elements of the comic satire of intellectuals were fixed in an ingenious and lasting way in Attic comedy. In this comedy, the sophists were presented in the guise of monstrous beings, endowed with two heads and (like the mythical monster Argos, from whom their mask was perhaps inspired) countless eyes (fr. 161 K.-A.). And if it is permissible to assume that the innumerable eyes gave substance to the insatiable cognitive curiosity and that impiety by which, precisely because they were *Panoptai*, "all-seeing," they probably believed themselves to be similar to Zeus or some other deity, it is equally plausible to imagine that the two heads represented the stage reification of this disagreement between heaven and earth, theory and praxis, from which precisely comedy springs.

The *Phrontisterion* is thus the school in which the "thinkers," that is, Socrates' colleagues and disciples, defined precisely by Strepsiades, in v. 101, "small-minded thinkers" (μεριμνοφροντισταί); and from φροντισταί was composed the chorus of the *Connus*, the other anti-Socratic comedy (named after a person known in tradition as Socrates' music teacher) with which Amipsias competed in the same contest as the *Clouds* by placing second; that moreover the historical Socrates was nicknamed, perhaps jokingly, φροντιστής is documented by Xen. *Smp.* 6, 6; and in Pl. *Apol.* 18b Socrates himself, recalling the old popular rumors about him, culminating first in Aristophanes' play, then in the trial of 399 BCE (the Testimonia on Socrates' trial, condemnation and death are now collected in P36-P42 Laks-Most), in which he states that people branded him as τὰ μετέωρα φροντιστής. In fact, the *Phrontisterion* is primarily a school of meteorology, understood as the science of *meteora*: that in the enclosure of his school Socrates spends his time investigating the paths and revolutions of the moon is explained to Strepsiades as early as the prolog (vv. 171–175) by the Disciple who, in v. 181, will open the door of the *Phrontisterion* for him; and Socrates himself declares when he enters the scene (v. 225) that he devotes himself to scrutinizing the sun with scientific suavity. Collectively, this is enough for Strepsiades to establish with mischievousness that meteorology = atheism, an equation that Socrates forcefully reiterates in vv. 247–249.

---

[4] This is moreover, confirmed by the insulting epithet ἀλιτήριος, "cursed," with which, in a comic couplet perhaps attributable to the *Flatterers* of Eupolis (fr. 157.2f. K.-A. = fr. *157b Olson), a character is apostrophized (equally doubtfully identifiable with that Protagoras who, included in the play among the figures of "illustrious" flatterers of the wealthy Callia, is qualified as ὁ Τήιος in another trimeter of the lost play: fr. 157.1 K.-A.= fr. 157a Olson), precisely insofar as he "shoots lies around heavenly things (ἀλαζονεύεται ... περὶ τῶν μετεώρων), while eating the things that come from the earth." A similar statement is made in an untitled fragment of Aristophanes in which the speaking character stigmatizes the canonical dyscrasia between the mental aptitude for abstraction and the inescapable need to satisfy the material needs of practical life, experienced by an unidentified philosopher or intellectual (Socrates or Protagoras, for Bergk 1841, 1190; Kock 1880, 557), "who ponders invisible things, but eats the produce of the earth (ὃς τἀφανῆ μεριμνᾷ/τὰ δὲ χαμᾶθεν ἐσθίει)" (fr. 691 K.-A.).

The Socratic teaching of scientific atheism (vv. 314–411) that opens the first episode (vv. 314–509) stands in continuity with the previous initiation scene (on which see below), constituting its coherent development: it is a matter of persuading Strepsiades to accept the Clouds as the only deities and to induce him to permanently sever his relationship with traditional religion. On the one hand, therefore, a rationalistic explanation of atmospheric phenomena must be provided by appealing, according to an analogical procedure, to everyday experience, in order to clear the mind – particularly that of the neoadept – of false superstitions and archaic and outmoded beliefs (cf. vv. 364–411); on the other hand, there is a need to replace old with new idols: the "ethereal Vortex," the Air, the Aether, Chaos, the Tongue, and the Clouds, precisely, to which are transferred the most visible signs of Zeus' power, such as thunder and lightning (cf. vv. 365, 423f.). The nexus of meteorology = atheism, with the denial of Zeus' existence, is thus the common thread linking the first lesson given by Socrates to Strepsiades to the lesson Strepsiades will give to Pheidippides when, after the parabasis, he tries to persuade him to attend the *Phrontisterion* instead (vv. 814–831), and to the ending of the play, when Strepsiades will trace the *hybris* of Socrates and his disciples toward the gods precisely to their speculations about the moon (vv. 1506–1509). The connection made by the play between the influence exerted by the new ideas on the traditional way of life and the accusation of impiety is, moreover, also made explicit in the rebuke that, in a fragment perhaps taken from the *Autolycus* of Eupolis (on its problematic attribution, to Eupolis or Aristophanes, see Olson 2017, 213), an unknown character to his interlocutor: "you, miserable (ὦ μοχθηρός), spend your unholy existence (ἀσεβῆ βίον) devoted to exceedingly new ideas (ἐπὶ καινοτέρας ἰδέας)" (fr. *60.1 K.-A.). And the charge of impiety (*asebeia*) must have already been made by Cratinus, in the *All-seeing* (fr. 167 K.-A.; cf. Σ Clem.Al. *Protr.* 24.2 [I, p. 304.28 St.]) to the ἄθεος Hippon (38 A 4, 6, 8, 9; B 2, 3 D.-K.) as the author of the revolutionary theory of the oven-shaped sky (38 A 2 D.-K.): a theory evoked by Strepsiades in the prolog, when he explains to the reluctant Pheidippides that the "wise souls" of the Socratic *Phrontisterion* teach that "the sky is an oven (πνιγεύς)" and that "we are the coals (ἄνθρακες)" (vv. 94–97), and perhaps also in the play's finale (vv. 1504f.), where Socrates and one of his Disciples realize that shortly thereafter they will end up one burned (κατακαυθήσομαι), the other suffocated (ἀποπνιγήσομαι): see Picot (2013).

Anaxagoras, who had theorized the extreme subtlety of air (59 A 92 D.-K.) and of mind, the subtlest of all things (59 B 12 D.-K.), is a primary source of the meteorological material of the *Clouds*. Anaxagorean parody is present in the notion of λεπτόν and λεπτολογεῖν in vv. 230, 320 and 741 (with Strepsiades' mocking reprise in the play's finale, in v. 1496, where, armed with his torch, he declares his intention to "engage in a subtle dialogue (διαλεπτολογοῦμαι)" with the rafters of the *Phrontisterion*). By the time of the *Clouds*, Anaxagoras had been dead for years, far from Athens, but Aristophanes could not have been unaware of his revolutionary cosmology, which, like Socrates, had so influenced Euripides (see Schorn 2004, 197–201, 220–243). By likening the sun, moon, and stars in general to "fiery stones," Anaxagoras had stripped the heavens of their sacredness, provoking popular hostility toward the "new science," toward the "tortuous deceptions of the meteorologists" (Eur. fr. inc. fab. 913.4f. Kn.): as evidenced, on the one hand, by the trial for impiety brought against him shortly before the outbreak of the Peloponnesian War, which was aimed at striking down Pericles by projecting on him a suspicion of atheism (the Testimonia on Anaxagoras' trial are now collected in ANAXAG. P23-P26 Laks-Most), and on the other by the fact that all apologetic literature would later be committed to clearing Socrates of the charge of anaxagoreanism. To the point that it can be concluded that in Athens, for popular feeling as well as for the educated classes, anaxagoreanism, meteorology, and atheism were synonymous: this is confirmed by the later Plato, who in the *Laws* (e.g., in *Lg.* 886d) stigmatizes the persuasive ideas and speeches of the "modern savants," whose followers have convinced themselves that those supernatural realities, such as the sun, moon, stars, and earth, on which the first proof of the existence of the gods is based, are nothing but earth and stones; this certainty undermined the spontaneous and confident faith of the fathers, on which instead the indoctrinated children look with contempt.

At the door of the *Phrontisterion*, on which the uncouth Strepsiades knocks violently, thus causing the Disciple to "abort" the thought he was "conceiving" (vv. 133–137), there appears a group of disciples whose appearance leaves Strepsiades dumbfounded: to him they look like strange "beasts" (θηρία), emaciated like the Spartans deported from Pylos, and with their eyes fixed on the ground, precisely like animals. The Disciple explains to him that they investigate things underground, not in search of onions, as the rough peasant is automatically led to believe, but to peer into the darkness at the bottom of Tartarus (vv. 184–192). At the same time, being bent downward, they turn their bottoms toward the sky, with which they learn astronomy. But in the philosophical tradition, having one's eyes turned downward is also a sign of inward reflection (see the comic characterization of Platonists and Pythagoreans in fourth-century comedy: Imperio 2019; Zimmermann 2023). And for that matter, inward reflection, the basis of that celebrated Delphic precept of γνῶθι σεαυτόν ("know thyself") that played so much part in Socratic thought and dialog (for a survey of passages, see Reale 2000, 45–69), permeates the characterization of the Socrates of the *Clouds* on several occasions (beginning with the explicit allusion contained in v. 842, in which to Pheidippides who asks what advantage he will gain from attending the *Phrontisterion*, Strepsiades replies that he will be able to know himself, and understand how ignorant and uncouth he is: γνώσει δὲ σεαυτόν, ὡς ἀμαθὴς εἶ καὶ παχύς: a circumstance that would seem to be confirmed by the obvious references to Aristophanic comedy scattered particularly throughout the Platonic *Phaedrus* (see now especially Moore 2015). Conversely, astronomy "forces the soul to look upward and distracts it from things down here" (Pl. *R.* 529a). Now, it does not appear that the Socrates outlined by the philosophical tradition was in favor of this kind of research (Pl. *R.* 529a–530b; Xen. *Mem.* IV 7.5); on the contrary, judging from the *Apology* (18b), Socrates decisively rejected this rumor, which carried in the common mind a dangerous stigma of quackery and atheism: and as such this practice was considered typically sophistic (cf., e.g., Gorgias, *Encomium of Helen*, 82 B 11, 13 D.-K.; Eur. fr. 913 Kn.; Hippocrates, *Ancient Medicine* 1; Plu. *Life of Nicias* 23. Hippias of Elis gave lectures on this matter: cf. Pl. *Prot.* 315c, *Hipp.Ma.* 285cd). There are, however, traces of an Anaxagorean phase in Socrates: in a famous passage in the *Phaedo* (97b–98b) Socrates recalls that in his youth he had adhered to the theories of Anaxagoras, who, in his astronomical speculations, had advocated the unheard-of theory that the sun was a mass of glowing metal, roughly the size of the Peloponnese (Diog. Laert. II 8; cf. 59 A 19, 20 D.-K.) and had been tried for impiety and forced into exile from Athens for "speeches teaching about the heavens" (λόγους περὶ τῶν μεταρσίων διδάσκοντας, Plu. Per. 32.1, with MacDowell 1978, 200f.).[5]

But, at the entrance to the *Phrontisterion*, an increasingly bewildered and incredulous Strepsiades is also shown the thinkers' working tools (vv. 200–217). These objects are unidentifiable to us, which on the stage, however, allowed for an association with astronomy and geometry (Bromberg 2012), which is in fact identified with geography (he is in fact shown a map of the entire earth: a scene recalled by Plato in the *Theaetetus* (172a–177a), until, in v. 218, Socrates appears, hovering in the air inside a ταρρός (v. 226), generally identified with a basket (a kind of astronomical observatory), suspended from a support referred to as a κρεμάθρα, a tool whose nature cannot be specified, but which provided a movable foothold that allowed the basket to swing and thus the actor not only to descend from above but also to perform midair evolutions (cf. ἀεροβατῶ, of v. 225): an expedient Aristophanes also makes use of for the *ex machina* appearance of Euripides in the *Acharnians* and Agathon in the *Thesmophoriazusae*. With the help of some of his disciples (cf. vv. 257 and 259), Socrates invites Strepsiades to lie on the sacred bunk and take a garland (vv. 255f.), and then to sprinkle him with παιπάλη, that is, with the finest flour (v. 262): crowning the initiatory ritual of purification preliminary to the meeting with the Clouds of that neophyte who only two verses earlier had declared his intention to become, under Socrates' guidance, precisely παιπάλη, the finest flour, that is, metaphorically, a refined and shrewd speaker.

The comic characterization of Socrates as a proponent of new and foreign deities also, evidently, incorporates the esoteric dimension, steeped especially in Orphic and Pythagorean reminiscences (Morrison 1958, 199–209; Bowie 1998, 61–65; Marianetti 1992, 63–73; Willi 2003, 113–116; Morosi 2018), within which the *Phrontisterion* is cast, a dimension that does not seem, moreover,

---

[5] On Socrates' "conversion" from the physical sciences to dialogical technique, which, described in the *Phaedrus* passage, would seem to be retraced in the plot of the *Clouds*, see Cerri (2012, 155–161).

to have been foreign to the real life of the Socratic circle (cf., e.g., *Theaet.* 155e, *Smp.* 120c–d, 209e, Clem. Al. *Strom.* I 21, and see Adkins 1970; Riedweg 1987; Janko 1997). After all, from the very first moment when, upon entering the *Phrontisterion*, Strepsiades had attempted to approach the ideas of the Socratics, the Disciple had explained to him, in language steeped in the stylistics proper to religious language, that the activities of the school are "mysteries (μυστήρια, v. 143)," to which for an "outsider" "it is not permissible" (οὐ θέμις) access (v. 140) except after a proper initiation rite. Already peculiar to religious language is the formula οὐ θέμις (Harrison 1962), employed to express the prohibition against divulging the contents of mystery rites to the uninitiated (cf., e.g., Ar. *Th.* 1150s; Pl. *Grg.* 497c and vd. *h.Cer.* 478f. with Richardson 1974, 304–309); significant in this sense, in the initiatory rite enacted in vv. 250–274, are also the references to the proem of Parmenides' poem (Iribarren 2013). On the parody of mystery language in Strepsiades' initiation scene, see in detail Marianetti (1993).

In the initiation scene, after inviting the elderly neophyte to gather in religious silence and listen to prayer (εὐφημεῖν χρὴ τὸν πρεσβύτην καὶ τῆς εὐχῆς ἐπακούειν) (v. 263), Socrates moves on to invoke the "Immense Air," the "Splendid Ether," and the Clouds, σεμναί θεαί "venerable goddesses," and βροντησικέραυνοι, "thunderbolting" (v. 265). For his oaths and prayers, therefore, the philosopher will not invoke the traditional gods, who are now "out-of-date currency" (vv. 247f.), but rather the Breath (Ἀναπνοή), Chaos, and Aere (v. 627), and as the only deities he will recognize precisely Aere, Aether, and Clouds (cf. vv. 252f., 264f.) or the triad formed by Chaos, Clouds and Tongue (cf. vv. 423f.): just as "newly minted" are the deities (Aether, Whirlwind of Tongue, Intellect, and Nostrils) invoked by Euripides in the *Frogs* (vv. 892f.), who already in the *Thesmophorazusae*, swore by the Αἰθήρ (v. 272). In perfect consistency with such premises, Socrates goes so far as to assert that Zeus does not exist (v. 367) and that it is the "ethereal vortex" (v. 380) that produces and governs weather phenomena, and Strepsiades concludes, just as consistently, that it is not Zeus, but the Vortex (Δῖνος) that rules in his stead (vv. 380, 828): a statement that, as the scholia attest (Σ vet *Nu.* 380a–b), was common knowledge among the φυσικοί, who by the term δῖνος, "vortex" (in the naturalistic–scientific sense more often attested in the feminine, δίνη) meant to explain the movement of the sky, and in particular its circular and whirling turning. The theory of περιδίνησις (the circular and whirling motion of the sky) played a particularly prominent role in the cosmology of Empedocles (cf. 32 A 67 D.-K., with EMP. D 116–117 Laks-Most) and atomists such as Democritus (68 A 67, B 167 D.-K.; cf. ATOM. D 82 Laks-Most) and Leucippus (67 A 24 D.-K.; cf. ATOM. R 86 Laks-Most), but its evocation in the *Clouds*, according to the ancient commentators, would have had as its specific philosophical referent the thought of Anaxagoras, who attributed the separation of the primordial elements of the cosmos and their re-aggregation to form matter to a process of περιχώρησις ("turning over") imparted by the Nous, the "Intellect" (59 A 71 D.-K.; cf. 59 B 9, 12, 13 D.-K. and see Ferguson 1971, 1972–1973, 1978–1979; Perilli 1996, especially 79–85; Willi 2003, 103–105). This theory will be forcefully reiterated, in the exodus of the play,[6] in vv. 1470–1474, by a Pheidippides who has by now perfectly assimilated to the most extreme consequences the dictates of Socratic thought: to him Strepsiades tries in vain to make him understand that Δῖνος, one of the new Socratic deities in whom he had been induced to believe, is in fact nothing but a δῖνος, that is, an urn: and a jar was to be placed at the entrance of the *Phrontisterion* as a material symbol of the cosmic whirlpool, replacing the herm placed to guard the house of every ordinary Athenian (cf. Σ vet 1473a–b), to be perhaps thrown to the ground by Strepsiades after v. 1474, as a sign of dissent against the ungodly Socratic doctrines (for this hypothesis, see Revermann 2006, 234f.).

The initiate Strepsiades is thus allowed to see the Clouds, invoked by Socrates (vv. 263–274) as deities and presented to him as a σμῆνος θεῶν, a "swarm of goddesses" (v. 297), and, immediately after the antistrophe of the parodos song that punctuates their appearance and entrance into the orchestra, again described by Socrates to the new adept as μεγάλαι θεαί (v. 316; cf. v. 365). Strepsiades

---

[6] A theory which, moreover, will earn Socrates the epithet ὁ Μήλιος (v. 830), with clear reference to the atheism of Diagoras, the poet from Melos often mentioned in the catalogs of atheists handed down in ancient sources, who was tried for impiety in 415/14 BCE for criticizing the Eleusinian Mysteries, and consequently expelled from Athens (on the figure of Diagoras of Melos, see now Winiarczyk 2016), and who in Aristophanes reappears in *Av.* 1073, and perhaps in *Ra.* 320, in a passage that is difficult to decipher (Sommerstein 1999, 129).

offers irreverent comments: to him they first appear similar to mortal women, then to flakes of wool, and then not even to women anymore, because "these here are provided with noses!" (v. 344). The Clouds' noses have been repeatedly speculated upon (Brown 1983), but the easiest assumption is that they allude to the manly member, in the comic costume emphasized in the grotesque leather phallus. Whatever the point of the joke, which evidently escapes us, the dominant feature of Socrates' description of them is their chameleon-like mutability ("they become what they want…"), which also allows them to reveal the φύσις of others (v. 352). More precisely, immediately after the song sung in the parodos by the chorus of clouds, in which powerful reminiscences of Empedocles' cosmology have been recognized (Saetta Cottone 2013), Socrates explains to Strepsiades that these are celestial clouds, great gods for the idle men (ἀνδράσιν ἀργοῖς), who "provide the opinions, dialectic, intelligence, and the art of telling extraordinary things, of resorting to periphrases, of making turns of phrase, of striking with verbal assaults and knocking down with retorts" (vv. 315–318). And a little later Socrates further specifies the nature of these deities, who "nurture a great many intellectuals (*sophistas*) : diviners from Turii (Θουριομάντεις), experts in the medical arts (ἰατροτέχνας), slackers with rings that serve as seals and with manicured nails and long hair (σφραγιδονυχαργοκομήτας), twisted musicians of cyclic choruses (κυκλίων χορῶν ἀσματοκάμπτας), aerial hucksters (ἄνδρας με τεωροφένακας) braggarts (οὐδὲν δρῶντας) do-nothings (ἀργούς), devoted only to celebrating them over and over again in their compositions" (vv. 331–333).

In these words of Socrates, we allow ourselves to recognize some specific categories of σοφισταί, of intellectuals precisely:

(1) soothsayers (called "of Thurii" after the name of the Panhellenic colony of Magna Graecia whose foundation, promoted by Pericles between 446 and 443 BCE, was led as founder by the well-known soothsayer Lampon: cf. D.S. XII 10.3–4; Plu. *Per.* 15; Σ vet Ar. *Av.* 521);
(2) physiologist-naturalist physicians; and
(3) musicians of the "new dithyramb" (renowned for the daring experimentalism that connoted the music of their circular choruses), and perhaps also that of the "modern" poets (among whom the prime suspect is obviously Euripides).

All of these categories are characterized substantially as ἀλαζόνες, "impostors," insofar as they share a generic propensity for ἀργία (cf. vv. 316, 332, 334), they all move in the smoky realm of sophistic rhetoric (cf. vv. 316–318). As such, they are expert manipulators of the *logos*, dealing with disciplines that have to do with a purely "aerial" dimension and are evidently removed from the sphere of normal life. These prerogatives are implicitly evoked in v. 333, by the epithet μετεωροφένακες (cf. the compounds μετεωροσοφιστής); in v. 360, in reference to the sophist Prodicus, and μετεωρολέσχας, "chatterers with their heads in the air"; and in a fragment dubiously attributed to the *First Clouds*, about philosophers, "because they ponder celestial phenomena" (fr. *401 K.-A., with Torchio 2021, 54f., and evoked by Plato in *R.* VI 489c). In the course of this play (cf., e.g., vv. 102–104, 449, 1492), they are attributed, in particular, to the Sophists and the scholars of the *Phrontisterion* but, more generally, are found referred, by Aristophanes and other playwrights, to the entire class of "modern" intellectuals (Zimmermann 1993; Imperio 1998b).

And yet access to the privileged, initiatory, and mystery sphere of intellectuals entails great hardships. The disciples of the *Phrontisterion* must prove their καρτερία, that is, that physical and spiritual fortitude without which true wisdom cannot be drawn: anyone who wishes to attend the school must have memory and aptitude for reflection but also the ability to endure hardship and discomfort and to resist hunger and thirst; not to suffer too much from the cold; to be able to control and master the urges of sex: "O man who desires great wisdom from us, you will be blessed among the Athenians and Hellenes: If you are endowed with memory and capacity for reflection, and perseverance finds a place in your soul; if you do not grow weary of standing or walking; if you do not suffer too much from the cold and have no eagerness to eat, but keep away from wine and gymnasiums and all other dissension, and, as befits an intelligent man, consider this to be the supreme good: to win in action, in decisions and in contentions of the tongue" (vv. 412–419). In presenting his son with the *Phrontisterion* "of wise spirits" (ψυχῶν σοφῶν, v. 94) and their activities

(vv. 95–99), Strepsiades qualifies them, among other things, as "persons of regard (καλοί τε κἀγαθοί, v. 101)": an appellation that Pheidippides immediately reverses into the opposite "wretches (πονηροί)": two evaluations which, as will be seen later, will take on socio-political implications. These are "waifs" (as ἀλαζόνες will later be qualified by Strepsiades himself in the play's finale, in v. 1492) of cadaverous complexion who walk around barefoot (τοὺς ἀλαζόνας/τοὺς ὠχριῶντας, τοὺς ἀνυποδήτους λέγεις) among them are that "wretched" (κακοδαίμων) "Socrates and Chaerephon" (vv. 102–104).

Not a mere comic gimmick, but a character trait historically documented by Plato (cf., e.g., *Smp.* 174a, 219e–220b) and Xenophon (cf., e.g., *Mem.* 1.2.1, 1.5.6, 1.6.2), Socrates' *karteria* was probably also to be the object of derision in Amipsia's anti-Socratic comedy (which competed with the original *Clouds*), the *Connus*: in fr. *9 K.-A., in addition to being explicitly apostrophized as καρτερικός (v. 2), the philosopher is described as a source of trouble for shoemakers (v. 3) and, according to the testimony of Diogenes Laërtius (II 28), must have presented himself on stage as a "starving man, wearing a humble, worn-out cloak" (on this fragment, see Orth 2013, 233–243). Paradigmatic manifestations of Socratic *karteria* are thus, for the two playwrights, *anypodesia*, that is, the habit of walking barefoot even in harsh weather conditions (which Aristophanes also ascribes to the Socratics in v. 363 of the *Clouds*), the extraordinary ability to endure hunger (to which Aristophanes repeatedly refers in the *Clouds*, in vv. 175–179, 416–417, and 441, and in the *Birds*, in v. 1282) and the use of the humble cloak designated as τρίβων, a distinctive sign of poverty (cf., e.g., Ar. *V.* 33, 116, 1131, *Ec.* 850, *Pl.* 714, 842–846, 882; Eup. frr. 280.3 and 298.6 K.-A., Lys. 32.16) and frequently associated, especially in comedy, with the unkempt look of philosophers, which Aristophanes attributes to Socrates in v. 870 of the *Clouds* (where Pheidippides goes so far as to insultingly identify the philosopher with his own tattered cloak!). Not coincidentally, it is at Socrates' invitation that in v. 497 Strepsiades, before being admitted inside the *Phrontisterion*, strips himself of his ἱμάτιον, which he later never retrieves: as is evident from the exchange of jokes with his son Pheidippides in vv. 856f., and as Strepsiades himself reiterates in v. 1498.

Socratic frugality becomes, in the warping lens of comedy, also failure to take care of personal hygiene (ἀλουσία): in vv. 836–838 of the *Clouds*, Strepsiades presents to his son the disciples of the *Phrontisterion* as intelligent men (ἄνδρας δεξιούς), with plenty of brains (νοῦς ἔχοντας), who, to save money, never go to the barber to get a haircut, use ointments, nor have any of them ever go to the public baths to wash, with obvious, derisive reference, to the philosopher's lack of attendance, documented by the Platonic *Symposium* (174a), at the public baths; and in the same terms the chorus of Aristophanes' *Birds* speaks of Socrates, in vv. 1553–1564.[7] It is clear that here, as in the Clouds – where the *Phrontisterion* is presented by the Disciple as the abode of "wise spirits (ψυχῶν σοφῶν, v. 94)" who, all curved, peer over Erebus to Tartarus (v. 192), and whose access is later described by Strepsiades as a veritable catabasis in an underground quarry (vv. 506–508), which will make the unfortunate man resemble Chaerephon, that is, a corpse (vv. 503f.) – Aristophanes plays on the semantic ambiguity of the term ψυχή, which from Homer onwards habitually designated the souls of the dead, ghosts, but which precisely in Socratic language will come to indicate a man's mind, that part separate from the body that was to be cared for and cultivated much more than the body itself (cf., e.g., Pl. *Ap.* 29d–30b, *La.* 186a, *Prt.* 313a), with the intention of mocking the pale and emaciated appearance of the Socratics, who resemble, precisely, ghosts with cadaverous faces – more precisely, yellowish, as they are described by Pheidippides to his father in v. 103 (with which the invitation to enter and not to linger outside the *Phrontisterion*, addressed to them by the Disciple, in vv. 198f., with the argument that it is not good for them to stay too long in the open air).

This somewhat greenish pallor was depicted most likely on the masks of Socrates and his disciples, and later, beginning in v. 1171, on that of Pheidippides himself; already in v. 718 Strepsiades declares that he has lost his complexion, and, in v. 1112, he predicts that his son, in order to

---

[7] As a "psychagogical" practice, this is fully reflected in the *psychagogia* described by Plato in the *Phaedrus* (261a–271a), the brief *nekyia* that takes place in the swamp of the Schadefeet is described (cf. Sommerstein 1987, 300; Dunbar 1995, 711f.; Moore 2015).

become a perfect σοφιστής, would become ὠχρόν, "yellow in the face," and κακοδαίμονα, "unhappy"; in v. 1017, then, a χροιὰν ὠχράν, "yellowish skin," is promised to Pheidippides as a result of his teaching. This skin color was, in the traditional mentality, connected with an idea of softness and lack of manliness, and was attributed, in particular, to women, intellectuals, foreigners, in short, to all those who were not participants in the ethical-athletic system of traditional society: the tanned complexion is in fact characteristic of those who live in the open air, under the sun, the only life that the knights, coming from the wealthier classes and notoriously conservative and hostile to innovations and scruffiness of the intellectuals, and, of course, an admirer of theirs such as Pheidippides, can agree to live (cf. vv. 119f.). The dark complexion is thus the sociologically discriminating trait between those who participate in the traditional model of gymnastic-athletic *paideia* and those who remain excluded from it because, evidently, they adhere to a model of life other than the one accepted as dominant, that is, they practice a humble, banausic craft.

To Socrates' wish that he would be as good and diligent a student as Chaerephon (*Nu.* 500–503), Strepsiades replies fearfully, "poor me: I shall look half-dead (ἡμιθνής)!" (v. 504): similarly, in a fragment of Aristophon's *Plato*, the speaking character, perhaps the philosopher himself, vouches that he can make one of his own students emaciated and skeletal (like a corpse, the interlocutor comments) in only three days (fr. 8 K.-A.; and on Plato's character in fourth-century comedy, see Farmer 2017; Imperio 2019). Precisely, as a paradigm of the contrite and emaciated intellectual, Chaerephon of Sphettus, a friend and disciple of Socrates (Pl. *Ap.* 21a, *Chrm.* 153b), was also a favorite target of the playwrights: already in the first version of the *Clouds* (or *Clouds* I) he was likened to an ephemeral nocturnal butterfly (fr. 393 K.-A.), and in the *Birds* he is apostrophized as νυκτερίς, and thus compared to a bat (vv. 1296, 1564). Again in the *Seasons* Aristophanes describes him as a "son of the night" (fr. 584 K.-A.); and in a fragment of the *Cities* (fr. 253 K.-A.) Eupolis calls him πύξινος, "made of boxwood," because of his yellowish complexion (also mocked in Ar. *V.* 1412–1414). His connection with Socrates, moreover, evidently gave rise to the attack made on him by Cratinus in the *Damianus*, where he was mocked for being "dirty and poor" (αὐχμηρὸν καὶ πένητα: fr. 215 K.-A.); and it is likely that even with the insulting epithets affixed to him by Aristophanes in the *Telmessians* (where he apostrophizes him as a "sycophant": fr. 552 K.-A.), and in another lost play entitled *Dramas or Niobe* (where she describes him as a κλέπτης: fr. 295 K.-A.), and by Eupolis in the *Adulators* (where she mentions him explicitly as one of the *kolakes*, the flatterers of the rich Callias: fr. 180 K.-A.), his membership in an alleged Sophistic-Socratic entourage was targeted (see Imperio 1998b, 110; Tylawsky 2002, 37–41; Revermann 2006, 190 with n. 20 and 226 with n. 107). It should be noted, however, that although repeatedly mentioned throughout the *Clouds* since the prolog (in vv. 104, 144–147, 156; and, outside the prolog, in vv. 503 and 1465), and with a prominent role in the *Phrontisterion*'s teaching staff, Chaerephon never appears on the scene as *dramatis persona*.[8]

However, the *phrontistai* do not only study *ta meteora*, but are also concerned with the natural sciences, particularly zoology: when the door to the *Phrontisterion* opens in the prolog, the Disciple explains to Strepsiades that Socrates and Chaerephon are intent on measuring the length of a flea's leap (vv. 144–152) and on analyzing the mechanics of the sound emitted by the intestines of mosquitoes (vv. 156–164). Here, then, in the scene beginning in v. 144, we find the first arrangement of the comic motif of the futility and insubstantiality of the research of intellectuals and philosophers, destined to remain typical in the history of comedy. It should be said at once that λεπτότης (meagerness or subtlety) is established as one of the chief features of the dialectical skill of the sophist-Socratics of the *Clouds*: it has already been evoked in Strepsiades' comments on the Disciple's account of these two "typical" lectures given by the Master in the *Phrontisterion* ("O lord Zeus, what subtlety of thought [τῆς λεπτότητος τῶν φρενῶν)!", v. 153); and it is metaphorically

---

[8] Hence, the fortunate theory that in the early *Clouds* Chaerephon had a dramaturgical vitality of his own, or, alternatively, that Aristophanes intended to give this character a larger role in the later revision that remained incomplete: cf. fr. 393 K.-A. and see especially Dover (1968, xcv–xcvii), Russo (1994, 102–104, 106f.), and Torchio (2021, 22–23, 43–46).

related to the airy and elusive dimension of their thought. Initially, old Strepsiades, forgetful and tardy as he is, takes issue with the fact that he cannot grasp their speeches "sharp as splinters" (vv. 129f.). Implicitly evoked in the course of the geometry lesson given by the Master, who scatters *thin* ashes on the table, on which it would be rather necessary to distribute food, (v. 177), "thinness" will immediately be felt by Strepsiades as a condition of his own ψυχή, which, as soon as he heard the voice of the *Clouds*, "took flight" (v. 320). In v. 358, Socrates will be hailed by the chorus as a "priest of the subtlest nonsense (λεπτοτάτων λήρων ἱερεῦ); and in v. 741 Socrates himself will exhort Strepsiades to give free rein to his subtle thinking (τὴν φροντίδα λεπτήν) in order to be able to distinguish and ponder everything correctly; and the puny chest (στῆθος λεπτόν), along with yellowish complexion, narrow shoulders, long tongue and small buttocks, will be pointed out by the Stronger Argument as one of the negative effects produced in the bodies of those who follow" the fashions of the people of today" (v. 1018).

In a long untitled fragment of Epicrates (fr. 10 K.-A.) we witness emblematic evidence of the debt incurred by later playwrights to Aristophanes' comic characterization of the philosopher. In this fragment, a botany session is presided over, under Plato's supervision, by his two disciples Speusippus and Menedemus, in the Academy; each of the participants attempts to offer precise classifications of different plant species, and in particular, but ultimately inconclusively, into the definition of the nature of the gourd. This session, described by an outside hearer, is blatantly modeled on that Socratic lecture on zoology; but the comic point of both scenes is the mockery of the absurd, futile, inconclusive naturalistic pursuits in which the two philosophers and their pupils engaged: the speaker of the Epicrates fragment goes on to recount that, in the face of the sterile futility of such a debate, an unidentified physician from Sicily farted in mockery, accusing the Platonic pupils of raving (v. 29), without, however, eliciting any reaction from those or their Master, who, after witnessing the debate, unperturbed and not at all upset (vv. 32f.), patiently had the students resume their investigation, guiding and helping them to complete the classification (vv. 35–37). It is interesting to note how philosopher and disciples are marked by an imperturbability that allows them to be unaffected by derision or provocation from the outside world: in a word, by that *semnotes*, that is, by a characterization that, together with *atopia*, that is, strangeness of attitudes and speech, unites them with their direct Socratic ancestors in *Clouds*. Like those ancestors (cf. *Nu.* 175–180; cf. also vv. 133–137), they also stand still in silence and keep their foreheads down, intent as they are on meditating at length on the question that has been posed, and, still with their eyes downcast, they continue their search (vv. 20–24).

Even before he admits him into the *Phrontisterion*, the Disciple explains to Strepsiades that Socrates devotes himself to studying the paths of the moon by looking up with his mouth open, resulting in being struck by the droppings of a gecko (vv. 169–174), and then describes his intent on devising a fraudulent trick that will ensure dinner for the *phrontistai* (vv. 175–179): the comic depiction of pauperism (cf. also vv. 420–422), of *karteria* and indifference to the needs of the body, typical of philosophers and thinkers, devoted to abstract speculation and as such indifferent and distracted with respect to material needs and everyday life, is combined with the comic motif of greed and the propensity for theft and deception (cf. vv. 801–814, 876) and culminates in the immediately following evocation of the figure of Thales of Miletus, the "father" of Greek philosophy. Both the one and the other gag are destined to have great fortune in the anecdotal flourishing around the characterization, not only comic, of the intellectual. Indeed, the well-known anecdote about Thales recalled in Plato's *Theaetetus* (174a–b) is generally evoked in this regard (on the fortune on this anecdote see P12 n. 1 Laks-Most), in which the comic potential inherent in the figure of the intellectual, understood as a pure theorist, can easily be discerned: a story was told of Thales who, while studying the stars and having his eyes turned to the heavens, fell into a well, and a fine and witty Thracian servant girl mocked him, telling him that he took great pains to know the things of the heavens but did not notice what was before him. Comedy arises here, evidently, from that irreconcilable conflict between the abstractness of pure theory investigated by the philosopher and the "common sense" of the common man. This anecdote, which seems to find a precise mirroring in the story (told by the Disciple to Strepsiades in *Nu.* 169–174) of the gecko pissing on a Socrates intent on looking up with his mouth open to peer at the motions of the moon, stigmatizes the image of the disinterested, distracted wise man totally absorbed in his meditation, and has an emblematic counterpart in another anecdote about Thales, related by Aristotle in the *Politics* (1.11, 1259a10–18): "Because he was poor and the futility of philosophy was held against him, they say that, having foreseen on the basis of certain astronomical calculations of his own an abundant olive harvest, still in the middle of winter, and having a small sum at his disposal, he seized all the olive presses in the area of Miletus and Chios, for a derisory sum, when they were still in little demand; but when the time of harvest came, since many were looking for the presses all together and urgently, he rented them at the price he had imposed: in this way he amassed great wealth and proved that it is indeed easy for philosophers to get rich if they want to, but that this is not really what they are concerned about." Another image of the wise man reverberates in the episode: no longer just the pure theoretician, the thinker devoted primarily to abstract speculation, but also the one who knows how to astutely put his knowledge to use in practical life, drawing personal gain and advantage from it – an image evidently different from, and in some ways opposed to, the other, both images inherently bearing negative valences and at the same time fruitful in humorous and satirical insights. And it is precisely in the groove of this ambiguous polarity that the characterization of intellectuals in Greek comedy moves (Zimmermann 1993; Imperio 1998b).

Socrates is figured as the hierophant, shaman, supreme officiant of the worship of the goddesses Clouds, but the Clouds themselves, evoked by him in the parodos, apostrophize him as ἱερεύς, priest (v. 359): priest, however, of "subtlest subtlety": and of the subtle word and their worshippers, the μετεωροσοφισταί, the Clouds self-represent themselves as tutelary deities. And here the goddess-clouds explicitly state that they lend their ear, if invoked (ὑπακουσαίμεν, v. 360), solely to Prodicus, for his doctrine (σοφία) and intelligence (γνώμη), and to Socrates for his disdainful strutting in the streets, his ability to walk barefoot (*anypodesia*) and endure many evils, and his solemn air (*semnotes*): a description that coincides with that of the philosocratic writers (cf. Pl. *Phdr.* 117b, 229a; Xen. *Mem.* 1.6.1–3; Pl. *Ap.* 30 and 31a). And it is precisely the comic compound *meteorosophistes* that enshrines the synthesis of the two dimensions of intellectual activity that Aristophanes intends to stigmatize by condensing it in the figure of a Socrates presented as a thinker expert at once in physics, in the manner of the Milesians, Anaxagoras, and his disciple Archelaus (implicitly evoked in the course of the play: see Betegh 2013, 87–106), and in heresy, in the manner of Prodicus, Protagoras, and the other sophists.

This then explains the place assigned to Prodicus among the μετεωροσοφισταί praised in *Nu.* 361, a sophist particularly renowned for his onomatological, semantic, and synonymic investigations, conducted on the basis of those eminently Protagorean categories of ὀρθοέπεια and ὀνομάτων ὀρθότης (on which see below). Prodicus is repeatedly evoked in various passages of Aristophanes' comedies, and in the parabasis of *Birds*, the sophist from Ceos is also called upon as a scholar of τὰ μετέωρα (cf. Ar. *Av.* 690–692, and cf. Imperio 2004, 344–350 with further bibliography). It is also explained that the sophist is apostrophized as a wordsmith (ἀδολέσχης) in Aristophanes' *Fryers* (fr. 506 K.-A.): the same accusation leveled by Strepsiades at Socrates and his disciples in the finale of the *Clouds*.[9] Alongside the meteorology-atheism nexus, another significant pairing is thus established: that between μετεωρολογία and ἀδολεσχία, which, explicitly formalized by Plato in relation to Anaxagorean speculation (cf. *Cra.* 401b, *Phdr.* 270a), then seems to be grafted into the fabric of the articulate polemic that the philosopher conducts against sophistry (cf. *R.* 488e, 489a).

Once Strepsiades has vowed to repudiate the traditional deities and believe only in the new "trinity" (vv. 425f.), the chorus promises him that he will have fame high to the heavens (vv. 460f.), the fame that will befall Thales after his death, as we read in the epitaph reported by Diogenes Laertius (I 39 = *Anth. Pal.* VII 84): a far more ambitious prospect, therefore, than that to which Strepsiades aspires, who is instead interested only in escaping his creditors; and Socrates, after declaring that he

---

[9] See vv. 1480, 1485. It is precisely on the pithy wordsmith Socrates that the contempt of the *persona loquens* of an anepigraphic fragment of Eupolis [μισῶ ... τὸν πτωχὸν ἀδολέσχην, fr. 386.1–2], probably as part of a similar Socratic-sophistic polemic of which traces also remain in fr. 388 (see Olson 2014, 138; and on the epithet ἀδολέσχης, 133f.).

wants to preliminarily test his character and memory and impart some notion of astronomy, and after promising him that he will end up looking like Chaerephon, retires with his new pupil to the *Phrontisterion*, not without first making him leave his cloak at the entrance (vv. 478–509).

Thus begins the parabasis (vv. 510–626), whose strophic part (vv. 563ff.) features highly traditional content. The two odes, in fact, with the sole exception of Aether, mentioned in the strophe, contain canonical invocations to some of the main Olympian deities: Zeus, Poseidon, and Helios (as well as precisely Aether), in the strophe; Apollo, Artemis, Athena, and Dionysus in the antistrophe, which commemorates some of the main Panhellenic festivals (those of Delos for Apollo, of Ephesus for his sister Artemis, the Panathenae for Athena, and the Delphic festivals for Dionysus, a grand tour of Panhellenic celebrations, here retraced perhaps also as a tribute to the audience gathered in Athens for the Great Dionysia). Prominent in the strophe, as mentioned above, is the presence of Aether, the only Sophistic deity we have seen invoked in v. 265 by Socrates (and who, as will be discussed below, is also invoked by the Aristophanic Euripides of *Thesmophoriazusae* 171 and *Frogs* 892), but who occupies a prominent place in late archaic thought: as a divine figure, alongside other entities such as Chaos or Eros, he appears among the primal forces in the Orphic cosmologies (1 B 12 D.-K.; cf. COSM. T 18 Laks-Most), in the *Genealogies of* Acusilaus (9 B 1 D.-K.; cf. COSM. T 21–22 Laks-Most) and in Ferecides of Syrus (7 A 9 D.-K.), and then returns in the tragedies of Aeschylus (cf., e.g., *Prom.* 88, fr. 70 R., where Aether is assimilated to Zeus), certainly not with polemical intentions against traditional deities; and as a natural element Αἰθήρ, the Aether, sometimes identified with Ἀήρ, the Aere, constitutes one of the four cosmological elements of pre-Platonic science. And it will be seen later how even in the two epirrhemata of the parabasis the traditional superstitious mentality re-emerges, whereby atmospheric phenomena, from thunder to lightning to rain to eclipses, are perceived as omens to be heeded at critical moments in the life of the city, such as assemblies, battles, and elections: emblematic is the reference to the atmospheric disturbances that must have accompanied Cleon's election as strategus for the year 424/23 BCE, described in the epirrhema (vv. 581–586) as an inauspicious omen overlooked by the Athenians. The same vein goes the complaints of the moon and, through it, of the gods, defrauded of the sacrifices and festivals provided for in the religious calendar, of which the Clouds make themselves spokesmen in the antepirrhema (vv. 615–619). The warning expressed by the chorus in the only epirrhema of the second parabasis (vv. 1115–1130) will then turn out to be of a similar significance: the judges of the theatrical agon are shown both the benefits of a judgment formulated "according to justice" and respect for the divine Clouds, and the punishments they will suffer if they incline in the opposite direction (see below).

After the parabasis Socrates comes out of the *Phrontisterion* exasperated, invoking a new trinity (Chaos, Breath, and Aere), in which, compared to the triad by which Strepsiades had previously sworn, Chaos alone finds himself reconfirmed: the philosopher's teachings, which one imagines in the meantime continued retrospectively, clash against the coarseness of his rustic disciple. This is the section of the play in which most markedly Socrates assumes the "sophistic" appearance of a master of rhetoric. The scene that opens in v. 627, in which the teaching continues publicly, is the earliest preserved evidence of the comic theme of the "paradoxical lesson," which, in vv. 636–692, deals with meters (of recited poetry – trimeters and tetrameters), rhythms (of sung poetry – dactyls and enoplians), and grammar (particularly the masculine and feminine gender of words, which, according to tradition, Protagoras was the first to study, dividing nominal genders into masculine, feminine and neuter: cf. Pl. *Phdr.* 266df = A 26 D.-K.; Arist. *Rhet.* 1407b7–8 = A 27 D.-K.). Central, in this scene, is the role of the bug-infested crib (vv. 634, 699, 709–715, 725), on which Strepsiades is forced first to follow the lesson (v. 633) and then to "give birth" to some thoughts (vv. 694f.): a reprise of the initiatory scene, in which Strepsiades is invited to lie down on the sacred cot (v. 254), but also an allusion to the Pythagorean principle, shared moreover by both Orphism and other currents of archaic thought (cf. vv. 319, 331), of detachment from the ground as a prerequisite for deeper concentration. Further on, Strepsiades wraps himself in lambskin blankets (vv. 729f.) to concentrate and meditate; however, bereft as he is of speculative skills, he emerges from it intent on handling the leather phallus applied to his comic actor's costume (v. 734) and is therefore urged by Socrates to cover himself again (vv. 735, 740), to "break up the subtle thought into small parts" and to "fathom" and "analyze carefully" (vv. 740–742), and invited, when confronted with a possible *aporia* in any of his "thoughts," to leave that one momentarily aside, and then resume "shaking it in the mind" and "weighing it up" (vv. 743–745). In the cultic sphere, the neophyte or priest covers his face to isolate himself from the world around him and draw in the divine; in the savory Aristophanic deformation, Strepsiades hides under the hairy blanket to masturbate!

Strepsiades also seems to take up his Master's solicitations, however, as he declares that he has succeeded in grasping a swindling idea (v. 747): having a Thessalian sorceress pull down the moon, so that at the end of the month creditors cannot claim interest on the money lent (vv. 749–756). Socrates is pleased with the idea but subjects him to another test of intelligence: he wants to see if he can come up with "a clever stunt (τι δεξιόν)" to wipe out a lawsuit for five talents that might eventually be brought against him (vv. 757–763). Strepsiades thinks of the further magical practice of catoptromancy to catch the moon (vv. 764–773), and at that point, growing more and more admiring, Socrates asks him what he would do if he had the knowledge that he would lose in a trial for lack of witnesses, but Strepsiades finds no other answer than to think of suicide by hanging: once he is dead, no one can sue him (vv. 775–783). It is this unsuccessful response, as well as the evidence of his forgetfulness, that makes Socrates impatient and causes the chorus to advise him to send a son, if he has one, with a younger and more receptive mind in his place (vv. 785–803). The son, reluctant but compelled by his father (vv. 814–888), thus finds himself witnessing the contest between the two discourses (vv. 889–1114). These are two strange personifications that certainly exhibit human likenesses (see vv. 908, 1033, 1103 with Σ vet. 1033a–b),[10] which may have been inspired by the dialogical–philosophical tradition of Epicharmic origin (and in particular by the title of Epicharmus' drama Λόγος καὶ Λογίνα, *Male and Female Logos*), and which reveal from the outset, in the violent exchange of insults in vv. 889–933, their respective natures and peculiarities. The Discourse Best, which programmatically declares that it will destroy the opponent (vv. 892, 899), is an advocate of the just and believes in Dike (vv. 900, 904) and is mocked by the Worse Argument as *archaios*, "old-fashioned" (v. 915; cf. vv. 984f.), demented and out of tune (v. 908), and brought back to the days of Kronos (v. 929), as well as mocked for his unkempt appearance and dry, wrinkled skin (v. 910). The Worse Argument in turn is repeatedly accused by the Better Argument of being insolent (θρασύς, vv. 890, 915), and furthermore a καταπύγων ... κἀναίσχυντος, a bugger and shameless (v. 909), a buffoon (βωμολόχος, v. 910), and parricidal (πατραλοίας, v. 911). The Worse Argument's peculiarities are the ability to invent new thoughts (γνώμας καινὰς ἐξευρίσκειν, v. 896), maybe to defeat his opponent – as he programmatically declares – by inversion (ἀναστρέφειν) and rebuttal (ἀντιλέγειν); of proving that Justice does not exist (vv. 902–905), of corrupting the youth (v. 928), and of training them only in talk (λαλιὰν μόνον ἀσκῆσαι, v. 931). They are brought back to order by the Chorus, which puts an end to μάχη and λοιδορία, that is, the canonical exchange of insults that preludes the agonal confrontation; once they establish the order of the two speeches, the debate turns to the comparison between the old and the new education. It is easy to observe that the choice of this theme disregards the expectations explicitly announced since the prolog by both Strepsiades and the Disciple of the *Phrontisterion* as well as by Socrates himself. Among the various inconsistencies and contradictions that characterize this agon (Dover lvii–lxvi; MacDowell 1995, 139–143), this is one of the most conspicuous, especially in view of two additional critical issues. First, the arguments of the Better Argument coincide perfectly with the educational ideal of Socrates as described to us by the set of Platonic dialogs: although the Socrates of the play does not speak on the subject because he strategically exits the stage at the moment when the agon is about to begin (vv. 886f.), the Clouds, his goddesses and advocates, nevertheless openly encourage the Better Argument in a partisan manner when he is about to deliver his "tirade" (vv. 959f.) and cheer him with vibrant enthusiasm when he has concluded it (vv. 1024–1033). Second,

---

[10] Despite the information reported by the much-debated Σ vet 889c, according to which "the Speeches are presented on the scene in intertwined cages in the act of fighting like birds" (which could, however, refer to the dramaturgical setup of the original version of the agon: for a summary of the *status quaestionis* see Revermann 2006, 212–219.

the arguments of the Worse Argument turn out to be decidedly stronger and more pertinent than those of its antagonist: the Better Argument, which is the "just" one on the ethical level, but "weaker" on the dialectical level, is defeated by the Worse Argument, which, conversely, is the "unjust" one on the ethical level, but "stronger" on the dialectical level.

At the beginning of the agon, the Worse Argument explains that he is so called because he first conceived of the idea of opposing arguments against laws and justice, choosing weak arguments to then win (vv. 1038–1043). So the discourse that is victorious at the test of dialectical confrontation is called "weaker" and the losing discourse "stronger." In its premise, Weaker Speech also emphasizes the substantial affinity between ἀντιλέγειν, that is, the practice of antilogy, of opposing arguments contrary to the laws and norms of justice (v. 1040), which is the prerogative and slogan of the royal sophists, and ἐλέγχειν (v. 1043), that is, the practice of refutation, which is the prerogative and slogan of the real Socrates; and, although, in refuting the stronger Argument, the weaker Argument turns out to be the winner, in the final judgment of the Clouds, and thus, by implication, of Socrates, it will instead be he who turns out to be refuted by the facts.

The Better Argument begins to speak; he illustrates the ἀρχαία παίδευσις, the "ancient education" (v. 961), inspired by sound principles such as justice and σωφροσύνη, "prudence" (v. 962), the basic features of which are reminiscent of the ideal model that ancient sources envisaged for the austere Spartan education (cf. Xen. *Lac. Resp.* 3.5): the nakedness of the children, who had to march in line in the street without a cloak, even in snow (v. 965); the obligation of silence (v. 963); the mnemonic learning of a traditional rhythmic-musical heritage, based on choral music and adherence to ancient melodies (vv. 967f.); corporal punishment inflicted on the unruly (v. 972); athletic and gymnastic education (vv. 1002, 1009–1023); respect for elders (vv. 993f., 998f.); disdain for the public square and baths (v. 991); worship of the Marathonomachoi ("Marathon veterans," v. 986) and courage (v. 992); love of rural life (vv. 1006–1008); condemnation of autoeroticism (v. 966), casual sexual practices (vv. 996f.); and passive homosexuality (καταπυγοσύνη, vv. 1022f.).

The insinuation that behind such lifestyle practices (the letting one's hair grow, the custom of toughening one's person with labors and privations) lay an admiration of Socrates for Spartan customs is made explicit in the herald's pronounced praise of Peisetaerus, founder of the city of the Birds: "once, before you founded this city, all men were crazy about Sparta (ἐλακωνομάνουν): there was the fashion of long hair (ἐκόμων), they fasted (ἐπείνων), they went around dirty (ἐρρύπων), they behaved Socratically (ἐσωκράτουν) they carried sticks (ἐσκυταλιοφόρουν)" (*Av.* 1280–1283a). It finds significant parallels as well in the philosopher's repeated criticisms of the Athenian democratic regime as recorded by Plato and Xenophon, and in the appreciation expressed by him and his friends and pupils from the aristocratic area toward the governments of Sparta and Crete as examples of *eunomy* (cf., e.g., Pl. *Cri.* 52e; and see Dunbar 1995, 636).

It is clear, then, that *karteria*, *anypodesia*, and dressing up in a humble, threadbare cloak in the *Clouds* do not simply function as part of the elaboration of the comic typology of the self-sufficient and ascetic savant – following a procedure frequently enacted by later period comedy and Lucian's satire – but are taken up as a metaphor for a stern and contemplative ideal of life, which treated the body and its needs with detached and sometimes provocative superiority: attitudes that "committed" fifth-century comedy must have felt to be alien (if not antagonistic) to the values of the democratic *polis*, and therefore potentially dangerous.

The image of a "sophist" Socrates teaching dialectic for a fee should also be interpreted in this perspective (cf. vv. 98–99, 244–246, 467–473, 1146–1147 and vd. Tell 2009): an image that must have been exploited for comic purposes already by Cratinus in the *Trophonius*, where the dialectical art is explicitly linked to banking in the figure of the "banker who coins speeches" (ἀργυροκοπιστὴρ λόγων, fr. 239 K.-A.). One of the historical knots of the Socratic question is linked to this image, as is well known, since the apologetic literature denies that Socrates ever made a profession of rhetoric for hire, and that in the *Clouds* dialectic and heresy are configured in explicitly Protagorean terms. Emblematic, in this sense, is Socrates' recourse to the Protagorean categories of ὀρθοέπεια and ὀρθότης ὀνομάτων (cf. Pl. *Cra.* 391b–c = 80 A 24 D.-K., *Phdr.* 267c = 80 A 26 D.-K. (with D 22b Laks-Most), *Prt.* 339a = 80 A 25 D.-K.), which, as noted above, occupied a central place in the linguistic disquisitions on poetry and prose conducted by the Sophists in the fifth century and were the privileged object of Prodicus' onomatological investigations (cf. Pl. *Cra*. 383a–b, 391b–c, 430d, *Chrm*. 163b–d, *Euthd*. 277e, *La*. 197d, *Men*. 75e, *Prt*. 337c, 340a, 341b; Arist. *Rh*. 3.5, 1407b6–8, *Top*. 2.6, 112b22), and which in the *Frogs* will be configured as a foundational element of the Euripidean poetic *lexis* (cf. vv. 1119–1197). In fact, Socrates suggests to Strepsiades, as he searches for a bold idea that can finally free him from debt, that he "distinguish and examine the facts little by little *correctly*" (κατὰ μικρὸν περιφρόνει τὰ πράγματα ὀρθῶς διαιρῶν καὶ σκοπῶν, v. 742). And in the rhetoric lesson given to Strepsiades (vv. 627–699) Socrates conspicuously assumes the role of the "Protagorean" sophist, when he states that he wants to teach his elderly pupil the ability to distinguish *correctly* (cf. the meaning of the adverb ὀρθῶς in v. 659 and v. 679) between nominal genders. And it is precisely this "Protagorean" Socrates that Hyperides will have in mind when, in the oration *Against Autocles*, he states that Socrates was punished *for his speeches* (ἐπὶ λόγοις, XI, fr. 55 Jensen): an accusation that – at least according to the wording preserved in the spurious oration *Against Andocides*, written on the occasion of the trial for the desecration of the Mysteries and the mutilation of the Hermes – is similar to that which had been brought against Diagoras: Andocides, the author of the oration asserts (Lys. 6.17) – was even more ungodly (ἀσεβέστερος) than Melian Diagoras, who had caused outrage (ἠσέβει) *by speeches* to the cults and festivals of others (i.e., of the Athenians), in that he committed impiety *by deeds* against the sacred rites of his own city.

The Worse Argument proceeds to refute point by point the arguments of the Better Argument, resorting as much to well-known mythical *exempla* as to objectifiable experience in everyday life. Why condemn the hot baths, which even the valiant Heracles used for refreshment from his labors (vv. 1045–1052)? Why condemn the public square, in which even Homer made Nestor and all the other σοφοί, the "wise men," speak (vv. 1055–1059)? Why extol the chastity that brought trouble to so many characters of myth, and renounce all the pleasures of life (vv. 1060–1082)? Why condemn homosexuality, which is so widespread even among spectators (vv. 1085–1104)? The arguments of the Worse Argument are tight and stringent, and the Better Argument itself acknowledges its defeat: it leaves its cloak and exits the stage; this defeat is then sealed by the chorus' ominous warning to Strepsiades in vv. 1113f. This leads to another suspension of the stage action, with the brief second parabasis (vv. 1115–1130), in which, in line with the strophic part of the first parabasis, the chorus of Clouds formulates terrifying warnings to humans who will not observe their worship (Totaro 2000, 63–77).

Since before the parodos, the Clouds had been presented by Socrates as spirits (δαίμονες) (v. 253a), "venerable" (v. 265) and "honored" (v. 269), goddesses of the intellectuals (cf. also vv. 291f., 316–318, 329, 365, 423f.); a role they themselves confirmed by appearing on stage as deities intent on granting the philosopher's requests (vv. 359–363; cf. vv. 804–806). Now, the second parabasis falls at a decisive moment precisely in defining the character and dramatic role of the chorus. At the conclusion of the agon of the two *Logoi*, they decree the success of the Worse Argument and induce the old Strepsiades to entrust the Socratic *Phrontisterion* with the Sophistic education of his son Pheidippides (vv. 1105–1112). In dismissing the exiting actors, the chorus expresses a personal comment on Strepsiades' decision to have Pheidippides educated that takes the form of a sinister omen: Strepsiades will come to regret his decision (vv. 1113f.). It is a judgment that stigmatizes the mistake made by the elderly parent, deluded by the prospect of being able to solve his debt problem, thanks to his son's rhetorical skill, and that hazily foretells the *nemesis* that will befall him. Yet, until before the agon, it was the Clouds themselves who had continually urged him, first to launch himself personally into the intellectual experience of the *Phrontisterion*, with the prospect of supreme happiness (vv. 412–419, 427–436, 459–475, 510–517), and then, in light of his inability, to study, to have his own son educated (vv. 794–796). The ominous foreboding formulated by the chorus in vv. 1113f. recalls the similar foreboding formulated by Pheidippides before he enters the *Phrontisterion*, in v. 865, only to find its more explicit sequel in the song of vv. 1303–1320, and foreshadows an orientation of the chorus that, after the second parabasis, will become increasingly explicit. First and foremost, the song of vv. 1303–1320, at the conclusion of the confrontation between Strepsiades and the creditors, will reiterate the conviction that the old man will soon outgrow his enthusiasm for wanting to make Pheidippides an unscrupulous rhetorician.

In the course of the violent conflict between father and son, then, the Clouds will not hesitate to stigmatize Pheidippides' attitude as impudent and shameless (vv. 1348f.), and to blame his father's conduct (vv. 1454f.). Finally, in vv. 1458–1461, they will make clear to an exasperated Strepsiades the purpose of their actions. From tutelary deities of the sophists and inspirers of fraudulent thoughts, the Clouds now reveal themselves to be the guardians of traditional religious values, founded primarily on respect for the gods and a strict concept of justice (at the end of the play, the chorus urges Strepsiades to beat up the Socratics, especially for their offensive doctrines toward the deities of the polis). In the light of this epilog, the demand for victory contained in the epirrheme of the second parabasis acquires greater meaning and dramatic depth, since it is formulated precisely on the basis of those two fundamental principles: the judges will accrue benefits in return for favoring Aristophanes' play according to justice (vv. 1115f.), or punishments for their disrespect for the deity of the Clouds (vv. 1121f.). And those two principles acquire relevance precisely because they are affirmed at the dramatic moment in which the next "turn" of the chorus is foreshadowed: Pheidippides' off-stage education prepares for the final comic catastrophe. Indeed, it should be noted that during the performance of the second parabasis Socrates accomplishes with Pheidippides what he had failed to do with Strepsiades in the extrascenic time covered by the first parabasis (vv. 510–626), namely, a fruitful sophistic education, which is also manifested by a visible change in the physical appearance of Pheidippides, who, now pale, quarrelsome and resentful, has taken on a "typically Attic" look (vv. 1171–1176). And it has been seen that values such as justice and respect for the divinity of the Clouds also guide the chorus' criticism of the spectators in the epirrheme of the first parabasis (vv. 575–594): here, the goddesses are said to be indignant because, despite the benefits rendered to the city, they are neglected in their sacrifices and libations; nor are they heeded when, through atmospheric signals (rain, lightning, thunder), they discourage the Athenians from making bad decisions (as was the case with the unfortunate election of Cleon to the strategy in 424/23 BCE). The same aversion to the greedy demagogue, for whom condemnation to the pillory is desired, is an unmistakable indication of the high sense of justice that inspires the work of the Clouds (Segal 1969): a sign of the ambiguous characterization of this Aristophanic chorus, which even before the "turn" of vv. 1458–1461 exhibits traits antithetical to the dictates of sophistry.

When the stage action resumes, Pheidippides returns home (vv. 1131–1213), and Strepsiades, confident in the fact that Pheidippides has successfully learned the Worse Argument, sings a hymn to Ἀπαιόλη (v. 1150), that is, Fraud, "queen of the Universe" just as earlier, in v. 814, cursing at his reluctant son, he had invoked the Ὀμίχλη, the Mist, the deified vapor of which the Clouds are composed (cf. v. 330). He then launches into a reckless and unscrupulous self-defense against the two Creditors (vv. 1214–1320), after having adequately practiced the dialectic of Pheidippides. He will emerge victorious from this performance, so much so that he is referred to as "the sophist" by the Chorus (v. 1309), in that choral ode in which he foretells the catastrophe about to befall Strepsiades and utters the first words of condemnation of his actions.

In v. 1321, Strepsiades comes running out of his house, pursued by his son who is beating him, and addresses him as a parricide, a scoundrel, and a corrupter (vv. 1327, 1330), and then tells the Chorus about the genesis of the conflict with him: this is the famous symposium scene in which father and son quarrel over their different musical tastes (the son refuses to perform a song by Simonides on the lyre and to recite a passage from Aeschylus, to which he prefers an embarrassing *rhesis* from Euripides' *Aeolus* (vv. 1353–1372). Hence the brawl: father and son come to blows, and the generational clash is consummated; this consummation takes place on the dialectical plane in a second agon. Pheidippides is addressed by the chorus as "expert at shaking and forcing new words" (v. 1397) and invited to find some avenue of persuasion that might make him appear as an advocate of right things (v. 1398). He turns out victorious, starting with the assumption that "it is sweet to occupy oneself with new and intelligent things and to be able to despise the constituted laws (νόμων καθεστώτων)." He then claims familiarity with the "{subtle speech and thought}" we have come to know (γνώμαις δὲ λεπταῖς καὶ λόγοις), boasting that he will prove that "it is right to punish one's father" (vv. 1399–1405). In the end, he goes so far as to declare that he would just as legitimately beat his mother (vv. 1443–1450).

After beginning to engage in an afterthought announced in the address to the elders of the audience (vv. 1437–1439), Strepsiades lashes out at the Clouds, who are responsible for leading him down the road to perdition, but the Clouds retort that he is the cause of his own strident woes: they drive to ruin the man in love with dishonest deeds so that he may learn to fear the gods (vv. 1454–1461), only to repent, declare that his is a just punishment (v. 1462), and finally meditate revenge: the burning of the *Phrontisterion* and the attack on Socrates' disciples (vv. 1476–1511), guilty of scrutinizing the poses of the Moon (v. 1507) but especially of offending the gods (vv. 1506, 1509).

We are deprived of the traditional final song of jubilation by the chorus: without taking leave of the audience, to whom it addresses no exhortation to applaud, nor any peroration of victory, the chorus asks only to leave the stage. The play closes with the teaching derived from the expression pathei mathos, that is, the tragic principle of knowledge through suffering (v. 1509): Strepsiades now "knows because he has seen" (εἰδώς) that, in a foolish attempt to evade his debts by resorting to the foolish Socratic-sophistic tricks he has committed the ἁμαρτία, the "mistake," of outraging the gods, and for this act of his *hybris*, which has aroused the ill will of the gods (φθόνος τῶν θεῶν), he is hopelessly doomed to defeat: he will eventually admit his errors and be punished, thus coming to recognize, through personal suffering, the impiety of the Socratics and the unquestionable power of the traditional deities. The typically tragic theme of πάθει μάθος, evoked by the Chorus Leader in vv. 1458–1461, in the context of the sudden turnabout of the chorus, famously constituted a foundational motif of Aeschylean theodicy, experienced especially in the *Oresteia* and theorized particularly in *Ag.* 160–183 and 360–398 (see Newiger 1957, 67f.; 1961, 427f. = 1996, 114f.; Rau 1967, 173–175; Zimmermann 2006; 2010, 104–106).

Conclusion

In the course of the play, in fact, the chorus of the multiform and chameleon-like Clouds seems to demonstrate toward the Socratics an extremely fickle and changeable behavior, which has not failed to attract the attention of modern exegetes: in the first part of the play, and at least until the beginning of the contest between the *Logoi*, the Clouds loom as tutelary deities of the *Phrontisterion* (vv. 252f., 264–274) and, with the promise of a happy outcome to his dastardly plans, encourage Strepsiades first to submit himself in person to Socratic teaching (vv. 412–415, 427–436, 450–475, 510–517) and then to have his son Pheidippides instructed in the *Phrontisterion* (vv. 793–796). After the agon, however, their attitude of increasingly marked distancing from the Socratics and the shady plots of Strepsiades begins to take hold (cf. vv. 1113f., 1303–1320), until the final "turning point" of vv. 1451f., 1458–1461, where the chorus reveals its true nature as a guarantor of traditional ethical–religious values, by virtue of which it will support to the end the repentant Strepsiades' plan of revenge against the inhabitants of the *Phrontisterion*, guilty of outraging the shifting deities.[11]

The bleak ending of this play, with traits more tragic than comic, has posed thorny exegetical problems. The most conspicuous anomaly is found on the structural level: instead of a choral ode sealing with the usual joyous κῶμος the triumph of the comic hero, it closes rather hastily with a very brief anapestic intervention by the Chorus Leader (vv. 1510f.), which would seem to be inadequately prepared (Gelzer 1970, col. 1446) and divorced from the preceding context (although in fact a parallel is found at least in the close of the *Thesmophorazusae* (vv. 1227–1231; and the same irrelevance is often imputed to the entire concluding scene of the *Knights*). Far from concluding with a happy ending, with the protagonist's victory crowned by some form of celebration, the *Clouds* present a rather somber, catastrophic ending, with the burning of the Socratic *Phrontisterion* as an extreme and fierce act of revenge (though not necessarily gratuitous, and indeed endorsed by a deity,

---

[11] On the ambiguous characterization of the Clouds' chorus and its controversial change of attitude in the last part of the play (accidental according to some, the result of the inconsistencies produced by the unfinished revision; according to others, instead, deliberate, and cleverly prepared throughout the entire drama), see especially Dover (1968), xxiiis, lxixs, with *Addenda*, pp. 269f., Segal (1969), Köhnken (1980), Scodel (1987, 334f.), Hubbard (1991, 106–111), Marianetti (1992, 76–107), Bowie (1993, 124–130), Katsouris (1997, 51–75), and Saetta Cottone (2011, 315–318).

Hermes: cf. vv. 1478–1485; and perhaps dictated by an intimate desire for justice: cf. vv. 1485–1492, 1488, 1498, 1504f.), perpetrated, among other things, by a comic hero characterized by strong traits of negativity: crude, dull-witted and petty as he is, he ultimately proves to be the loser and therefore vents his frustration with a gesture of blind violence, and is therefore characterized as an "anti-hero" utterly incapable of earning the solidarity of the audience.

On the dramaturgical level, the most conspicuous problems are represented by the manner in which the fire was carried out and by the singular recitative regime of the finale, which from v. 1493 onward would seem to involve more than three or four speaking actors, not normally permitted in classical theater. It is impossible to determine what exactly took place on the scene and especially whether, as has sometimes been speculated, along with the *Phrontisterion* they also burned Socrates and his followers: an outcome that, in addition to being fraught with consequences for the controversial seriousness of Aristophanes' attack on Socrates, would make this ending almost the only case in surviving classical dramatic production of a violent scene acted out before the eyes of the spectators, in contrast to fifth-century BCE theatrical practice, notoriously reluctant to depict violent episodes, whether on the comic or tragic stage (for a detailed survey of the critical debate on this subject, see Di Bari 2013, 311–320, *ad* Ar. *Nu.* 1504f.).

This is the paradox whereby this character, who has exerted on the entire spiritual tradition of the West an influence of immense magnitude, was put into comedy in the same year and in the same Dionysian comic contest by Aristophanes in the *Clouds* and by Amipsias in the *Connus*; and then, a quarter of a century later, he was tried and sentenced to death by "democratic" Athens on the very basis of the charges brought against him by the playwrights. These charges were that by his teaching he corrupted the young and that he did not recognize the gods worshipped by the city, but rather new and different gods; and that he propagated doctrines that undermined the foundations of traditional religion, family, and state. But it will be worth reflecting on the singular circumstance that, although on the one hand, the character of Socrates presents – obviously amplified, deformed, and degraded – physical and personal aspects of the Socrates described by a distinctly apologetic and celebratory tradition such as that represented by the Socratic works of Xenophon and especially Plato (who, moreover, it is precisely from the comic characterization that he takes the starting point to elaborate the polemical rehabilitation of Socrates in the *Apology*), on the other hand, the analysis of the play shows that Aristophanes, freeing himself from all instances of strict historical veracity, intends to make Socrates the embodiment of the new sage as he appeared to the distrustful mentality of the common Athenian. To do so, Aristophanes does not hesitate to attribute to him those cosmological and naturalistic interests that in the *Apology* he denies ever having practiced; those unscrupulous rhetorical–dialectical techniques peculiar to sophistry that allow the Worse Argument to take over from the Best; and that formalized and paid teaching, which he considered a commodification, and therefore a devaluation of knowledge, a prejudice that permanently came to stigmatize intellectual activity in the ancient world as well as in the modern world.

GUIDE TO FURTHER READING

If, for the text of the *Clouds*, the canonical critical edition is now Wilson's comprehensive Oxford edition (Wilson 2007), the most recent annotated critical editions of the *Clouds* remain to date those of Dover (1968), Sommerstein (1982), and Guidorizzi (1996). For a detailed treatment of the many issues related to the text, dramaturgy, and remaking of the *Clouds*, see Revermann (2006, 179–235), but also important are the contributions of Nussbaum (1980), Fisher (1984), Henderson (1993), and Rosen (1997). For the Aristophanic characterization of intellectuals, see Zimmermann (1993), and, more specifically, for sophistry in ancient Attic comedy, after De Carli (1971), see O'Regan (1992) and Carey (2000, 419–436). A useful *excursus* concerning the characterization of Socrates in the *Clouds* and in modern comic production has been traced by Brown (2004, 2007). For the characterization of the character of Socrates in the two different versions of the play, see Gelzer (1956) and Montuori (1966), and for the problem of the historicity of the character of Socrates in the *Clouds* see Turato (1973). Finally, for the personifications of the chorus and the two *Logoi of* the *Clouds*, one must see Newiger (1957, 50–71, 134–155).

REFERENCES

Adkins, A.W.H. (1970). Clouds, mysteries, Socrates and Plato. *Antichthon* IV: 13–24.
Bergk, Th. (1841). Aristophanis Fragmenta. In: *Fragmenta Comicorum Graecorum collegit et disposuit A.Meineke*, (I–V.1–2), vol. II 1, 894–1224. Berlin: Reimer.
Betegh, G. (2013). Socrate et Archélaos dans les « Nuées »: philosophie naturelle et éthique. In: *Comédie et philosophie: Socrate et les « Présocratiques » dans les « Nuées » d'Aristophane* (ed. A. Laks, R. Saetta Cottone, and M. Trédé-Boulmer), 87–106. Paris: Pr. de l'École Normale Supérieure.
Biles, Z.P. (2011). *Aristophanes and the Poetics of Competition*. Cambridge; New York: Cambridge University Press.
Bowie, A.M. (1993). *Aristophanes: Myth, Ritual, and Comedy*. Cambridge: Cambridge University Press.
Bowie, E.L. (1998). Le portrait de Socrate dans les « Nuées » d'Aristophane. In: *Le rire des anciens: actes du colloque international (Université de Rouen, École normale supérieure, 11-13 janvier 1995)* (ed. M. Trédé, P. Hoffmann, and C. Auvray-Assayas), 53–66. Paris: Pr. de l'École Normale Supérieure.
Bromberg, J.A. (2012). Academic disciplines in Aristophanes' « Clouds » (200-3). *Classical Quarterly* 62 (1): 81-91.
Brown, C. (1983). Noses at Aristophanes, Clouds 344 ? *Quaderni Urbinati di Cultura Classica* 14: 87–90.
Brown, P. (2004). Socrates in comedy. In: *Socrates: 2400 Years Since His Death: (399 B.C. – 2001 A.D.): International Symposium Proceedings, Athens-Delphi 13–21 July, 2001* (ed. V. Karasmanis), 525–535. European Cultural Centre of Delphi: Athens.
Brown, P.G. (2007). The comic Socrates. In: *Socrates From Antiquity to the Enlightment* (ed. M.B. Trapp), 1–16. Aldershot: Ashgate.
Bücheler, F. (1861). *Über Aristophanes' Wolken*. Jahrbücher fur Classische Philologie LXXXIII: 657–689 = Kleine Schriften I. Leipzig; Berlin 1915: Teubner: 288–323.
Carey, C. (2000). Old comedy and the sophists. In: *The Rivals of Aristophanes: Studies in Athenian Old Comedy* (ed. D. Harvey, J.M. Wilkins, K.J. Dover, and M. Tristram), 419–436. Swansea: Classical Pr. of Wales.
De Carli, E. (1971). *Aristofane e la sofistica*. Firenze: La Nuova Italia.
Di Bari, M.F. (2013). *Scene finali di Aristofane: « Cavalieri », « Nuvole », « Tesmoforiazuse »*. Lecce: Pensa Multimedia.
Dover, K.J. (ed.) (1968). *Clouds*. Oxford: Clarendon Press.
Dunbar, N.V. (ed.) (1995). *Birds*. New York: Oxford University Press.
Farmer, M.C. (2017). Playing the philosopher: Plato in fourth-century comedy. *American Journal of Philology* 138 (1): 1–41. https://doi.org/10.1353/ajp.2017.0000.
Fazzo, S. (2013). Le cresson de « Socrate » dans les « Nuées »: note en marge d'une relecture de Diogène d'Apollonie. In: *Comédie et philosophie: Socrate et les « Présocratiques » dans les « Nuées » d'Aristophane* (ed. A. Laks, R. Saetta Cottone, and T.-B. Monique), 107–112. Paris: Pr. de l'École Normale Supérieure.
Ferguson, J. (1971). Δῖνος. *Phronesis* XVI: 97–115.
Ferguson, J. (1973). Δῖνος on the stage. *The Classical Journal* LXVIII: 377–380.
Ferguson, J. (1979). Δῖνος in Aristophanes and Euripides. *The Classical Journal* LXXIV: 356–359.
Fisher, R.K. (1984). *Aristophanes Clouds, purpose and technique*. Amsterdam: Hakkert.
Gelzer, T. (1956). Aristophanes und sein Sokrates. *Museum Helveticum* XIII: 65–93. https://doi.org/10.5169/seals-14000.
Gelzer, T. (1960). *Der epirrhematische Agon bei Aristophanes*. München: Beck.
Gelzer, T. (1970). Aristophanes der Komiker. In: *Paulys Realencyclopädie der classischen Altertumswissenschaft. Supplementband, XII Nachtr.*, 1392–1569.
Guidorizzi, G. and Dario, D.C. (ed.) (1996). *Le Nuvole*. Roma: Fondazione Lorenzo Valla.
Harrison, J.E. (1962). *Epilegomena to the study of Greek religion.: Themis. A study of the social origins of Greek religion*. New York: New York Univ. Books.
Henderson, J. (1993). Problems in Greek literary history: the case of Aristophanes' Clouds. In: *Nomodeiktes: Greek Studies in Honor of Martin Ostwald* (ed. R.M. Rosen and J. Farrell), 591–601). Ann Arbor (Mich.):. University of Michigan Press.
Hose, M. (1995). Der Aristophanische Held. In: *Griechisch-römische Komödie und Tragödie* (ed. B. Zimmermann), 27–50. Stuttgart: M und P, Verl. für Wissenschaft und Forschung.
Howald, E. (1922). Ἀέναοι Νεφέλαι. *Sokrates* X: 23–42.
Hubbard, T.K. (1991). *The Mask of Comedy: Aristophanes and the Intertextual Parabasis*. Ithaca, NY: Cornell University Press.

Imperio, O. (1998a). Callia. In: *Tessere: frammenti della commedia greca: studi e commenti* (ed. A.M. Belardinelli), 195–254. Adriatica Ed: Bari.

Imperio, O. (1998b). La figura dell'intellettuale nella commedia greca. In: *Tessere: frammenti della commedia greca: studi e commenti* (ed. A.M. Belardinelli), 43–130. Bari: Adriatica Ed.

Imperio, O. (ed.) (2004). *Parabasi di Aristofane: « Acarnesi », « Cavalieri », « Vespe », « Uccelli »*. Bari: Adriatica Ed.

Imperio, O. (2019). Plato (2) (comic treatment of). In: *The Encyclopedia of Greek Comedy* (ed. A.H. Sommerstein), 723. Hoboken: Wiley.

Iribarren, L. (2013). Sophistique contre cosmologie: à propos d'une allusion à Parménide dans les « Nuées ». In: *Comédie et philosophie: Socrate et les « Présocratiques » dans les « Nuées » d'Aristophane* (ed. A. Laks, R. Saetta Cottone, and M. Trédé-Boulmer), 133–149. Paris: Pr. de l'École Normale Supérieure.

Janko, R. (1997). The physicist as hierophant: Aristophanes, Socrates and the authorship of the Derveni Papyrus. *Zeitschrift für Papyrologie und Epigraphik* 118: 61–94.

Kaibel, G. (1895). Aristophanes [12]. In: *Paulys Realencyclopädie der classischen Altertumswissenschaft*. II 1, 971–994.

Katsouris, A.G. (1997). Reversals in Aristophanes' clouds and in tragedy. Δωδώνη 26: 51–92.

Kock, T. (1880). *Comicorum Atticorum Fragmenta*, vol. I. Leipzig: Teubner.

Köhnken, A. (1980). Der Wolken-Chor des Aristophanes. *Hermes* CVIII: 154–169.

Kunst, K. (1919). *Studien zur griechisch-römischen Komödie mit besonderer Berücksichtigung der Schlusz-Szenen und ihrer Motive*. Wien; Leipzig: Gerold's Sohn.

MacDowell, D.M. (1978). *The Law in Classical Athens*. Ithaca, NY: Cornell University Press.

MacDowell, D.M. (1995). *Aristophanes and Athens: An Introduction to the Plays*. Oxford; New York: Oxford University Press.

Marianetti, M.C. (1992). *Religion and Politics in Aristophanes' Clouds*. Hildesheim: Olms-Weidmann.

Marianetti, M.C. (1993). Socratic mystery-parody and the issue of asebeia in Aristophanes' Clouds. *Symbolae Osloenses* 68: 5–31. https://doi.org/10.1080/00397679308590865.

Marshall, H.R. (2012). « Clouds », Eupolis and reperformance. In: *No Laughing Matter: Studies in Athenian Comedy* (ed. C.W. Marshall and G.A. Kovacs), 55–68. London: Bristol Classical Press.

Montuori, M. (1966). Socrate tra Nuvole prime e Nuvole seconde. *Atti della Accademia di Scienze morali e politiche della Società nazionale di Scienze, Lettere ed Arti di Napoli* LXXVII: 56.

Moore, C.R. (2015). Socrates and self-knowledge in Aristophanes' « Clouds ». *Classical Quarterly* N. S. 65 (2): 534–551. https://doi.org/10.1017/S0009838815000257.

Morosi, F. (2018). Inside out, upside down. Creating the Φροντιστήριον in Aristophanes' Clouds. *Antiquorum Philosophia* 12: 119–138. https://doi.org/10.19272/201830201008.

Murray, G. (1933). Aristophanes. A Study. Oxford: Oxford Clarendo Press.

Morrison, J.S. (1958). The origins of Plato's philosopher-statesman. *Classical Quarterly* LII: 198–218.

Newiger, H.-J. (1957). *Metapher und Allegorie: Studien zu Aristophanes*. München: Beck.

Newiger, H.-J. (1961). Elektra in Aristophanes' Wolken. *Hermes* LXXXIX: 422–430.

Nussbaum, M.C. (1980). Aristophanes and Socrates on learning practical wisdom. *YCIS* XXVI: 43–97.

Olson, S.D. (ed.) (2014). *Fragmenta comica: Kommentierung der Fragmente der griechischen Komödie. 8, 3, Eupolis frr. 326-497: translation and commentary*. Heidelberg: Verl. Antike.

Olson, S.D. (ed.) (2017). *Fragmenta comica : Kommentierung der Fragmente der griechischen Komödie. 8, 1, Eupolis, Testimonia and Aiges-Demoi (frr. 1-146) : introduction, translation, commentary*. Heidelberg: Verl. Antike.

O'Regan, D.E. (1992). *Rhetoric, Comedy, and the Violence of Language in Aristophanes' Clouds*. Oxford: Oxford University Press.

Orth, C. (ed.) (2013). *Fragmenta comica : Kommentierung der Fragmente der griechischen Komödie. 9, 1,: Alkaios-Apollophanes : Einleitung, Übersetzung, Kommentar*. Mainz: Verl. Antike.

Perilli, L. (1996). *La teoria del vortice nel pensiero antico: dalle origini a Lucrezio*. Ospedaletto (Pisa): Pacini.

Picot, J.-C. (2013). L' image du πνιγεύς dans les « Nuées »: un Empédocle au charbon. In: *Comédie et philosophie: Socrate et les « Présocratiques » dans les « Nuées » d'Aristophane* (ed. A. Laks, R. Saetta Cottone, and M. Trédé-Boulmer), 113–129. Paris: Pr. de l'École Normale Supérieure.

Platter, C.L. (2007). *Aristophanes and the Carnival of Genres*. Baltimore, MD: Johns Hopkins University Press.

Rau, P. (1967). *Paratragodia: Untersuchung einer komischen Form des Aristophanes*. München: Beck.

Reale, G. (2000). *Zu einer neuen Interpretation Platons: eine Auslegung der Metaphysik der grossen Dialoge im Lichte der « ungeschriebenen Lehren »*. Paderborn: Schöningh.

Revermann, M. (2006). *Comic Business: Theatricality, Dramatic Technique, and Performance Contexts of Aristophanic Comedy.* Oxford; New York: Oxford University Press.
Richardson, N.J. (ed.) (1974). *The Homeric Hymn to Demeter.* Oxford: Oxford University Press.
Riedweg, C. (1987). *Mysterienterminologie bei Platon, Philon und Klemens von Alexandrien.* Berlin: De Gruyter.
Römer, A. (1896). Zur Kritik und Exegese der Wolken des Aristophanes. *Sitzungberichte der Akademie der Wissenschaften* 221–256.
Rosen, R.M. (1997). Performance and textuality in Aristophanes' Clouds. *The Yale Journal of Criticism* 10 (2): 397–421.
Russo, C.F. (1994). *Aristophanes, An Author for the Stage.* New York; London: Routledge.
Saetta Cottone, R. (2011). Nuvole e demoni: Empedocle e Socrate nelle « Nuvole » di Aristofane. In: *La storia sulla scena: quello che gli storici antichi non hanno raccontato* (ed. A. Beltrametti), 315–335. Roma: Carocci.
Saetta Cottone, R. (2013). Aristophane et le théâtre du soleil: le dieu d'Empédocle dans le chœur des « Nuées ». In: *Comédie et philosophie: Socrate et les « Présocratiques » dans les « Nuées » d'Aristophane* (ed. A. Laks, R. Saetta Cottone, and M. Trédé-Boulmer), 61–85. Paris: Pr. de l'École Normale Supérieure.
Schmid, W. and Stählin, O. (1946). *Handbuch der Altertumswissenschaft, VII,1,4: Geschichte der griechischen Literatur, I: Die klassische Periode.* München: Biederstein Verl.
Schorn, S. (2004). *Satyros aus Kallatis. Sammlung der Fragmente mit Kommentar.* Basel: Schwabe Verl.
Scodel, R. (1987). The ode and antode in the parabasis of clouds. *Classical Philology* 82: 334–335.
Segal, C. (1969). Aristophanes' cloud-chorus. *Arethusa* II: 143–161.
Sommerstein, A.H. (ed.) (1982). *The Comedies of Aristophanes, III: Clouds.* Warminster: Aris and Phillips.
Sommerstein, A.H. (ed.) (1987). *The Comedies of Aristophanes, VI: Birds.* Warminster: Aris and Phillips.
Sommerstein, A.H. (1997). The silence of Strepsiades and the agon of the first clouds. In: *Aristophane: la langue, la scène, la cité: actes du colloque de Toulouse 17-19 mars 1994* (ed. P. Thiercy and M. Menu), 269–282. Bari: Levante Ed.
Sommerstein, A.H. (1999). The anatomy of euphemism in Aristophanic comedy. In: *Studi sull'eufemismo* (ed. M. Caroli, F. De Martino, and A.H. Sommerstein), 181–217. Bari: Levante Ed.
Sommerstein, A.H. (ed.) (2001). *The Comedies of Aristophanes. 11: Wealth.* Warminster: Aris and Phillips.
Sonnino, M. (2005). Aristofane e il concorso lenaico del 422: la parabasi delle « Vespe » e il contenuto delle « Nuvole Prime ». *Seminari Romani di Cultura Greca* 8 (2): 205–232.
Torchio, M.C. (2021). *Aristophanes: Fr. 392-486.* Fragmenta Comica 10.7, Göttingen.
Totaro, P. (2000). *Le seconde parabasi di Aristofane.* Stuttgart: Metzler.
Turato, F. (1973). *Il problema storico delle Nuvole di Aristofane.* Padova: Antenore.
Tylawsky, E.I. (2002). *Saturio's Inheritance: The Greek Ancestry of the Roman Comic Parasite.* Bern; Frankfurt am Main: Lang.
Whitman, C.H. (1964). *Aristophanes and the Comic Hero.* Cambridge: Harvard University Press.
Willi, A. (2003). *The Languages of Aristophanes: Aspects of Linguistic Variation in Classical Attic Greek.* Oxford; New York: Oxford University Press.
Wilson, N.G. (ed.) (2007). *Aristophanis Fabulae.* Oxford: Clarendon Press.
Winiarczyk, M. (2016). *Diagoras of Melos: A Contribution to the History of Ancient Atheism.* Berlin: De Gruyter.
Zimmermann, B. (1993). Aristophanes und die Intellektuellen. In: *Sept exposés suivis de discussions: Vandœuvres-Genève, 19-24 août 1991* (ed. J.M. Bremer and E.W. Handley), 255–286. Vandœuvres-Genève: Fondation Hardt.
Zimmermann, B. (2006). « Pathei mathos »: strutture tragiche nelle « Nuvole » di Aristofane. In: *Κωμῳδοτρα γῳδία: intersezioni del tragico e del comico nel teatro del V secolo a.C* (ed. E. Medda, M.S. Mirto, and M.P. Pattoni), 327–335. Pisa, Ed. della Normale.
Zimmermann, B. (2023). Pythagoristen. Philosophenspott in der griechischen Komödie. In: *Von der Antike begeistert! Philologie, Philosophie, Religion und Politik durch drei Jahrtausende. Festschrift für Christoph Riedweg* (ed. C. Semenzato and L. Hartmann), 39–58. Basel: Schwabe Verl.

CHAPTER 10

Wasps: Rhetoric and the Law

Nikoletta Kanavou

Introduction

In classical Athens, rhetoric was a mainstay in the education of male citizens; rhetorical training, combined with an understanding of legal matters, was a prerequisite for careers in the public sphere. In particular, rhetoric was the most important weapon for forming and directing opinions in the democratic Assembly and the popular courts: the people's perception of what was "right" or "just" could be manipulated with the use of rhetorical tricks. It is the Athenians' gullibility in the face of persuasive, but dishonest rhetoric, and the people's fascination with courtrooms that fall victim to Aristophanes' satire in *Wasps*.

The play was performed at the Lenaia festival in 422 BCE and won second place in the poetic competition. At the time of the play, Athens and Sparta, at war against each other since 431 BCE, rekindled their old conflict around the city of Amphipolis in Thrace (cf. *Wasps* 288 and Thucydides 4.102–8); the demagogue politician Cleon, who fought there in 422 BCE, is targeted in *Wasps*, though mostly for his dubious politics – including his corrupt handling of the justice system – and not his military action. Cleon was the main satirical target of *Knights* (424 BCE). Much like *Clouds* (423 BCE), *Wasps* draws additional humor from the theme of the troubled relationship between a father and a son; but unlike in the earlier play, in *Wasps* it is the father, not the son, who causes trouble, and it is the son who attempts to redeem the situation and chastise his father. The father, Philocleon, is a juror locked in a corrupt system, who suffers from an extreme passion for law courts, a personal affliction that (as often in Aristophanes) reflects broader social problems: Athenian proneness to litigation, the abuse of the Athenian justice system by both politicians and the people for their own advantage, and the use of dishonest rhetoric, mainly by politicians, to sway public opinion toward things that are neither just nor truly beneficial to the people. The son, Bdelycleon, recognizes the reality of the situation and tries to divert his father toward an apolitical, carefree mode of living. As in *Clouds* (though with reversal of the function of father and son), the efforts of the "castigator" (son, Bdelycleon) to restrict the behavior of the "villain" (his father, Philocleon) lead to questionable results.

In its satire of the people's relationship with its politicians and of a familial conflict, *Wasps* thus seems to combine themes previously used in *Clouds* and *Knights* (see Lutz 2014, p. 41).[1] The plot's central idea of curing a character from a basic flaw further echoes Cratinus' *Pityne* "Wine-flask"; Aristophanes' jury-obsessed Philocleon mirrors Cratinus' alcoholic poet-hero (Biles and Olson 2015, pp. xxix–xxxii; cf. Farmer 2017, pp. 139–145). But *Wasps* is unusual in employing such a well-defined pair of antagonists

---

[1] On similarities between *Wasps* and *Knights*, see Mirhady 2009, pp. 372 ff.

(Philocleon and Bdelycleon, also juxtaposed in their names) to bear the play's central conflict; in other plays, this function is diffused among several characters (Konstan 1995, p. 17).

The Chorus, from which – as frequently in Aristophanes – the play is named, consists of old men, Philocleon's colleagues from the *hēliaia*. Some receive personal names which give them a fleeting individuality (230–234). Members of the Chorus are conceived by poetic imagination as wasps (a "swarm" of wasps, 425) and presumably wore wasp costumes, complete with *kentron* "sting" (406–407; 1071–1073). This *kentron* is a sign of their aggressiveness and a metaphor for the bite of the jurors' judgment in the Athenian law courts; there are repeated references to their anger, *orgē*, a sentiment which is also comically attributed to the poet in the *parabasis* (1030; it is there directed against the demagogue politicians, particularly Cleon).

As frequently in Aristophanes, the play opens with the appearance of two slaves; these carry the typical slave names Xanthias and Sosias. They have been ordered by Bdelycleon to guard his father, Philocleon, and make sure he does not leave home to pursue his detrimental addiction to jury service. The very lively Prologue (1–229) mainly consists of dialogue (involving the two slaves, but also the two protagonists, father and son, when they enter the scene after 135), but it further includes a lengthy exposé of Philocleon's affliction by the slave Xanthias (83–135) and culminates in the old man's desperate escape attempts. One such attempt means passing through the chimney (143–151). Another attempt results in a memorable comic scene (169–196), in which Philocleon hides beneath a donkey and introduces himself, like another Odysseus, as Outis "Noone" (183–189; this false introduction may be paralleled with the vague fake identity assumed by the Inlaw at *Thesmophoriazusae* 620 to escape the women). Philocleon seeks to emulate the cunning of Odysseus, but unlike Odysseus, who deceives the Cyclops and escapes (*Odyssey* 9.364–414), the old man gets caught. The appearance of the Chorus in the *parodos* (230–290) introduces Philocleon's partners-in-crime, his fellow jurors, old and poor Athenian citizens accompanied by their young children (a rather unrealistic – and hence perhaps ridiculous – detail given the men's advanced age; cf. MacDowell 1971, p. 10). In a song of his own (317–333), Philocleon laments his forced stay at home and his inability to follow the other jurymen to the *hēliaia*. In the Episode that follows (334–525), he makes a further escape attempt, provoking the reaction of Bdelycleon, and, in turn, the Chorus' aggressive response, until all three parties agree to solve their dispute via rhetoric. In the *agōn* (526–724), Philocleon and Bdelycleon provide a rhetorical defense of their pro-Cleonian and anti-Cleonian positions, respectively, and Bdelycleon's view prevails. A concluding song follows (725–759), and then another episode, in which Bdelycleon, to console his father for his retirement from jury service, proceeds to install a private law court in his home (760–862, followed by prayer and song, 863–890). A comic trial involving two dogs named Cyon and Labes takes place at this court, resulting in the latter's acquittal (891–1008; this is probably a satire of a real conflict between Cleon and the general Laches, on which see below). In the *parabasis* (1009–1121), the Chorus voices praise for the poet's courageous satire of demagogue politicians, especially Cleon. In the Episode that follows (1122–1264), Bdelycleon undertakes to introduce his father to a better way of life: he makes him exchange his juror's *tribōn* for more luxurious garments and prepares him to attend a dinner party by rehearsing appropriate conversation topics and songs. A second *parabasis* (1265–1291) returns briefly to the topic of the poet's conflict with Cleon. The play's final Episode (1292–1449) is an account of Philocleon's new behavior, which has gotten out of control. Despite Bdelycleon's best efforts and Philocleon's proclaimed artistic side (cf. his earlier characterization by the Chorus as a *philo͞dos* "lover of song," 270), the old man fails as a symposiast, as his crude nature prevails: he causes fights and finally snatches a flute girl. Several individuals come to complain to Bdelycleon about his father's behavior: Myrtia, the bread seller, accuses Bdelycleon of beating her and stealing (1388–1414); a man accuses him of beating (1415–1441). The danger of new trials (with Philocleon in the place of the accused) comically returns, only to be met with the old man's indifference; absorbed in a newly discovered hedonism, he has no further interest in litigation. This situation is reflected in a song (1450–1473). In the *exodos* (1474–1537), Philocleon engages in a manic dance and calls the sons of Carcinus, a dancer and tragic dramatist (the sons were also dancers), to compete with him; *Wasps* ends on a note of wild hilarity.[2]

---

[2] For a useful schema of the play's action, see Biles and Olson (2015, p. xl).

The sections that follow take a deeper look at the play's plot by exploring in detail the role of rhetoric and the law, as two main sources of satirical humor in this comedy, in various aspects of the action. The first section treats reflections in *Wasps* on the Athenian justice system and its relationship with the city's politics as a building block of the *Wasps*' comedy. Then, in the second section, the focus moves to the role of rhetoric in holding together a comic plot that may appear fragmented due to the seemingly different interests of its first and second parts (comedy of jury service vs. dinner parties). After that, in the third section, the relationship between Bdelycleon and Philocleon, which is largely marked by their rhetorical juxtaposition, is scrutinized in its legal aspects and comic function. The fourth section, on the satire of Cleon, is dedicated to one of the play's main comic targets, a real politician who is mocked for misusing both law and rhetoric. A final section briefly ponders the poet's self-image in the play and his relationship with his audience.

Politics and the Athenian Justice System

Jury-obsessed Philocleon and the Chorus of elderly and desperate jurymen carry Aristophanes' satire of the perceived malfunctions of the Athenian justice system. The state of this system at the poet's time, on which the humor of *Wasps* draws, may be roughly described as follows. Because of the financial difficulties caused by the Peloponnesian war, many Athenians sought to secure a salary as members of the *hēliaia*, the body of Athenian citizens that took on the role of jurors and tried legal cases in the name of the people. The body of jurors numbered about 6000 individuals (cf. *Wasps* 661–662) over the age of 30, who were selected each year, and provided the pool from which the juries of individual cases were formed; the size of these juries varied but may have been as large as several hundred jurors, which reflects the direct involvement of the people in the allocation of justice in democratic Athens. There was no limit to the number of times someone could serve as juror; Philocleon (and his fellow jurymen that formed the Chorus) could well have been active in that post for years. The *hēliastai*, as these jurors were called, received a daily remuneration of two obols, which was increased by Cleon to three obols (that is, if Sch. Ar. *V.* 88a and 300b are to be relied on). In a poignant comic scene of *Wasps*, Chorus members enter with their children, who lament the deprivations which they suffer (291–315). One child wonders how his family will secure their daily bread, if his father is not appointed as juror (303–308). Although Philocleon has an apparent lack of financial need and deliberately ignores his son's reminders that he can have a good life without working (which increases the absurdity of his obsession with jury duty, cf. 341, 503–506), he gives voice to the poor Athenian of his time in one instance, when he emphasizes the joy which his three obols bring to his household and their effect on his quality of life (605–615). In reality, the body of Athenian jurors seems to have been of a rather mixed socio-economic background (see Gagarin 2020, pp. 44–46); clearly, jury duty at the *hēliaia* emerged as a welcome job opportunity for many (cf. Kapparis 2019, p. 47), but perhaps especially for the poor and the lazy (cf. Isocrates 7.54) and for men of advanced age who were less likely to find other sorts of employment (MacDowell 1978, pp. 34–25; Ober 1989, pp. 142–144).

Wasps suggests that jury duty became associated with corruption at least partly because of the jurors' proneness to accept bribes – a real problem which the practice of allocating jurors to different courts by lot, the threat of criminal suits (cf. Demosthenes 46.26) and the swearing of the judicial oath (on which see Gagarin 2020, pp. 105–107) seemed unable to prevent completely, although Aristophanes' comedy surely exaggerated the situation (Gagarin 2020, p. 173). As Xanthias implies in his description of Philocleon's obsession (83–135), individuals under trial (*hypeuthynoi*) seek to improve their situation by offering bribes (102). In fulfilling their duties, jurors also expect favors and gifts from the defendants in exchange for lenience, a practice which may equal *adikia* "injustice" (as pointed out by Bdelycleon, 589). Lawyers are as corrupt as the jurors and indeed make more money than the latter (686–695). Furthermore, the dependence of the *hēliastai* on state-approved salaries and their greed gave leeway to demagogue politicians to manipulate them and exercise control of the judicial system (see also "The Cleon satire").

A further fault associated with the allocation of justice in Athens, which particularly lends itself to parody, is the subjection of juries to emotional blackmail. It was apparently true that the outcome of trials often relied more on emotional appeals and stunts (sometimes involving the appearance of begging children) and less on examination of the evidence (*Wasps* 560–587, 952–978; similar criticism is found in Plato, *Apology* 34c–35b).[3] The emotional blackmail attempted by the appearance of the defendants' children is turned into hilarious parody at the trial of the dogs, when puppies of the accused dog are called to appear in court (976–978). Aristophanes' jurors, however, do not seem to empathize much with the defendants. The jurymen of the Chorus can be unreasonably harsh (403–407, 578–587), even though they do not quite share Philocleon's obsession with law courts; this harshness is a side effect of their lack of accountability (*anupeuthynoi*, 587) and perhaps reflects the mentality of the demagogues who influence the jurors. In his function as juror, Philocleon also appears unjustly harsh and corrupt (106–109, 277–280, 389–390, 603–604, 1200–1201), although his eagerness to convict whatever the case may be is probably a comic exaggeration, and so is the constant bias which he and his co-jurors display (Gagarin 2020, pp. 106, 111). Philocleon's and the jurors' hard stance against the accused indeed inspires numerous comic retorts (159–160, 193–195, 223–227, 276–289, 321–322, 389–390, 999–1002).

In the *agōn*, Philocleon's bragging about the jurors' sense of "power" alerts us to a further malfunction of the system. He claims that his power as juror is not inferior to that of Zeus, and that he is addressed like Zeus (620–621). The comparison of this funny old man to the most powerful of the gods is of course meant to raise laughs, but it also suggests a tendency to abuse juristic power in real Athenian courts, a tendency memorably exemplified in the jurors' proposed (terrible) treatment of a daughter due to inherit her father's property (*epiklēros*, 583–589; see also below). In addition to this, the juror's job is highly addictive, as proven by Bdelycleon's failed attempts to divert his father from it – perhaps an exaggerated reflection of the Athenians' proneness to litigation but also of some jurors' inability to adhere to good sense and measure in the exercise of their duties. A juror who lacks self-control is by default incapable of being just (on a psychological level) or of serving justice (on a social level); the virtues of justice (*dikaiosynē*) and temperance (*sōphrosynē*) go hand-in-hand, and if one is lacking, the other suffers too (Kanavou 2016).[4] This whole situation is described as a *nosos* "malady" (651), a description that corresponds to the early designation of Philocleon's passion for law courts as a "strange disease" (71). The cure proposed by Bdelycleon is *apragmosynē*, that is, abstinence from public life and its negative qualities and concentration on private matters (North 1966, pp. 97–99; Rademaker 2005, pp. 230–233; Carter 1986 esp. 81–87). *Apragmosynē* is identified with *sōphrosynē* in Plato (Kanavou 2016, p. 184; Lanni 2016, pp. 114–115), an implication also present in the exhortation of the *Wasps*' Chorus to Philocleon to change his ways, not be *aphrōn* "foolish" and adopt his son's advice (729–730, 747–749). Philocleon comically fails to benefit from it, as he replaces one sort of folly with another (jury obsession with wild partying).

The ills of the justice system are not an isolated target in *Wasps*. The broader cadre of Athenian democratic life, of which popular law courts form an important part, comes under fire. Citizens that gather at the Pnyx, the place of the Athenian popular Assembly, are imagined as sheep, that is, as feckless beings, easily manipulated by the top demagogue Cleon, who in comic imagination assumes the appearance of a disgusting animal, a merge between a greedy whale and a fat she-swine (31–40; Bowie 1990, pp. 31–32 on the sexual overtones of this joke). The Chorus alludes to "flatterers" of the people, men in power who pretend to defend the people's interests while only caring for their own (419). In the *Wasps*' satire, there is a clear link between broader Athenian politics and the justice system. Philocleon and his fellow jurors have become subservient to the interests of these demagogues, who mock the people and flatter the jurors in order to be able to manipulate the courts to get the trial outcomes they want in a seemingly democratic fashion (515–520, 590–600).

---

[3] On the use of such practices at law courts, see Lanni 2006, pp. 41–64 and Gagarin 2020, p. 91; on the use of character evidence, Adamidis 2017.

[4] On the treatment of *sōphrosynē* in Aristophanes see Rademaker 2005, pp. 223–233; North 1966, pp. 66, 96–97.

Opponents and doubters of demagogue politics are unjustly labeled as anti-democratic. Athenian popular courts, seen as a bulwark of democracy, host the trials of individuals unfairly accused as "conspirators" against democracy (486–507); this is the charge bestowed on Bdelycleon by the Chorus on account of his anti-demagogue and anti-Cleonian sentiment[5] a charge which Bdelycleon artfully evades by claiming that concern for his father's well-being, not politics, is his motive for removing him from the law courts (503–507). City officials can be corrupt and may steal from public funds, and the same goes for army officers (556–557; the trial of Labes [=general Laches], sued by Cyon [=Cleon] also demonstrates this). Bdelycleon alludes to the connection between corrupt politics and corrupt justice quite explicitly. Demagogue politicians not only embezzle public money but also have the power to threaten and blackmail the city's allies and make considerable profit while keeping the jurors happy with only a fraction of what they themselves earn (666–685; cf. the critique of Athenian imperialism at 707–711 and *Knights* 839–840). Cleon's role as a "protector" of justice in *Wasps* shows nothing but disrespect for justice. This implies a moral attitude that may be compared to the sophistic discourse of Platonic dialogs that interprets *dikaiosynē* and *pleonexia* as the justice of the stronger or the more powerful (*Gorgias* 483a–d, *Republic* 343a–344c; see also Thucydides 5.105.2, and especially Cleon's position in the Mytilene debate, 3.36–48).

One might question whether the *dēmos* really was as vulnerable to the demagogues' bogus politics as comically suggested in *Wasps*. The Athenian *dēmos* was a large body of citizens with decisive power in the Assembly and the courts (Demosthenes 57.56 on the power of juries; see also Lanni 2006, p. 131). It is implied, however, that it is their lack of moral integrity that makes them weak (Kanavou 2016, p. 188). Because of their narrow focus on self-interest and lack of prudence, the Athenians prove unable to select wise advisors and fall prey to incompetent, selfish leaders (such as Cleon), who show no interest in the good of the *dēmos* and in the ideal of justice. Concern for self-interest is, of course, not always a bad thing[6] but it becomes bad when it leads to greed, selfishness, or dishonesty, and comes to threaten the public good. Greed is emphasized in *Wasps* as an abominable quality of the city's democratic leadership (655–724; Balot 2001, p. 197), and the "Old Oligarch" criticizes the self-interest of the *dēmos* (Balot 2001, p. 186 ff. Marr and Rhodes 2008, pp. 17–18 and *passim*). The corruption of everyday people also manifests itself in behaviors such as stealing, of which both Philocleon and the Chorus members are guilty. The Chorus boast of committing theft (235–239, 354–355), while they react with comic indignation at the idea of themselves falling victims to theft and fraud (758–759, 1098–1101; but cf. Konstan 1995, pp. 19–21 for the idea that this behavior is not indicative of bad moral character, but of an "anterior social order" which accepted the impulse of getting what one could get).

The satire of poor morals is not limited to law courts and politics but moves to the private sphere with Philocleon's partying at the end of the play and his repeated attacks on innocent citizens. New legal situations of private nature result from his trespasses: injured parties appear with witnesses and threaten to prosecute the old man (1388–1414; 1415–1441; cf. *Clouds* 493, where Strepsiades says that when someone hits him, he looks for witnesses and then goes to court).[7] The charge brought against Philocleon is one of *hybris* (1417–1418), a term which in legal language covers serious injuries done to the person (the relevant law is cited in Demosthenes 21.47). The bread seller Myrtia further intends to appeal to the *agoranomoi* for loss of property (1406–1408); the *agoranomoi* were magistrates, 10 in number, who were responsible for maintaining order at the market (Lanni 2016, pp. 63–64; MacDowell 1978, p. 157; on the scenes of Philocleon's encounter with injured parties, see Halliwell 2020, pp. 124–128). Aristophanes' depiction of Philocleon's extremely deviant behavior is a comic subversion of moral norms. Cf. Aristotle's words: "Justice is a virtue which assigns to each man his due in conformity with the law; injustice claims what belongs to others, in opposition to the law" (*Rhetoric* 1366b9–11); "Now the term 'unjust' is held to apply both

---

[5] cf. 417, 463–465, and MacDowell 1995, p. 160 on tyranny as a common accusation at that time.
[6] See Mirhady 2009, p. 374, on self-interest as a democratic value, against interest in the good of the *polis* as an aristocratic concern.
[7] See Thür 2005 on the role of witnesses in Athenian courts.

to the man who breaks the law and the man who takes more than his due, the unfair man.... 'The just' therefore means that which is lawful and that which is equal or fair, and 'the unjust' means that which is illegal and that which is unequal or unfair" (*Nicomachean Ethics* 1129a32–4).[8]

In addition to ideological issues associated with jury service and the attribution of justice, *Wasps* alludes to systemical and procedural details and uses a wealth of relevant terms (on legal terms found in *Wasps* and other plays, see Willi 2003, pp. 72–79; Buis 2014, pp. 322–325; the present survey does not propose to be exhaustive). Apart from the familiar term *dikē* "lawsuit," which occurs several times, there is the comic diminutive *dikidion* ("little case," 511), the also frequent *dikastēs* "judge," "juror"/*sundikastēs* "fellow juryman," *dikastērion* "court of justice" (and comic diminutive *dikastēridion*, 803), the phrase *dikazein dikas* ("to judge lawsuits," 414), and the term *graphē* "public suit," that is, in the interest of the state (842, 894, 907; on the much-discussed distinction between *dikē* and *graphē*, see, e.g. Osborne 1985, pp. 40–44). There was no "judge" in the modern sense of the word; cases were judged directly by the jurors, under the supervision of magistrates, at the popular courts, various of which are mentioned: the New Court (120), the Court at Lycus (819), and the Courts of the Archon, the Eleven and the Odeion (1108–1109).[9] We further encounter numerous terms of technical legal language. In his rant about the jurors' supposed omnipotence, Philocleon alludes to the processes of *euthyna* (public examination of official conduct, 571) and *dokimasia* (judicial process to establish a right, 578), both of which offer opportunities to the jurors to abuse their power. Philocleon also mentions a father's *diathēkē* "testament" regarding the fate of an *epiklēros* "heiress" (583–589), which the jurors are prepared to ignore and give the bride to the highest bidder (on the emerging suit, see Phillips 2013, pp. 235, 252–253, 257, 269). Philocleon further takes a jibe at a potential accused who "comes into court" (verb *eiserchomai*, 579). We also hear of the decree, by virtue of which the Assembly orders guilty perpetrators to be put on trial (590–591); this process is called *eisangelia* "state prosecution" (Hypereides 3.7–8 and further Sommerstein 1983, p. 193). A wronged individual would issue to the perpetrator a "summons before a court"; relevant technical terms (verbs *kaleō* "call a case" 851 and *eisagō* "bring to trial" 826) are used in the episode of the dogs' trial, which is fashioned as a public indictment (*graphē*), and in the context of the lawsuits that threaten Philocleon at the end of the play (forms of the verbs *kaleō* [1441] and *[pros]kaleomai* "summon into court" [1334, 1335, 1406, and 1417–1418; cf. *prosklēsis* "judicial summons" 1041; *klētēr* "witness to summons" 1408, 1416]). There is also vocabulary related to punishment (*timēma* "penalty" 897; cf. verb *timaō* "assess a penalty" 106, 847; *epibolē* "fine" 769) and acquittal (*afiēmi* 922; cf. *apoluō* 571 and *apofeugō* 579). There are references to various further roles and functions relevant to judicial praxis, for example, *synēgoros* ("advocate" 482, and *synēgorikon* "fee of the public advocate" 691), *kēryx* ("herald" 752), *martyres* ("witnesses" 782, etc., and *martyria* "testimony" 1041), *thesmothetēs* (archon in charge of legal matters, 775), *polemarchos* ("polemarch," one of the archons, 1042), *antōmosia* ("affidavit" 1041), and *xenia* (an indictment against someone suspected of citizenship fraud, 718).

Finally, there are many allusions to elements of the courtroom space and tools of real trials; many of these allusions feature in a parodic manner in the account of the creation of Philocleon's private court, in which some proper courtroom tools are comically substituted with everyday objects. Terms of the real courtroom space include *dryphaktos* (the bar of law courts, 830, cf. 386 and 552), *kigklis* (latticed entry gates, 124, 775), *klepsydra* (water clock used in court to measure duration of speeches, 857–858, replaced by a thunder mug at the dogs' trial), *ksylon* (jury bench, 90), *kion* (pillar outside the law court, on which notices are posted, 105), and *sanides* (boards with notices of trials 349, 848). Some terms pertain specifically to the casting of jury votes, which were secret: *psēphos* ("pebble" used for voting, 94, etc.; an alternative voting token was *choirinē* "mussel shell" 333, 349), *kadiskoi* ("voting urns," in which the jurors dropped their voting tokens; these were two

---

[8] The fifth book of this work is dedicated to the nature of justice, on whose importance in classical thought see further Nussbaum 2001 *passim*; Havelock 1969; cf. Rawls 1999 for a modern philosophical perspective.
[9] On these courts, see MacDowell (1971, pp. 273–275).

in number, one for conviction and one for acquittal [853–854, cf. 321–322], and are replaced by ladles at the dogs' trial, 853–854), *kēmos* (top of the voting urn, 99, 754, 1339), *lithos* (stone on which the jurors count votes, 332–333), and *pinakion timētikon* ("penalty tablet" 167).

Aristophanes' use of such a significant amount of legal terminology implies that his audience was familiar with judicial terms and procedures (Willi 2003, pp. 78–79). Indeed, most Athenians were involved in one or another sort of legal business, were at least occasionally active as jurors, especially if they lived near the city, and presented (both prosecuted and defended) their own cases in court, although some would have hired a *synēgoros* and/or a *logographos* "speech writer" (a *synēgoros* could also be publicly appointed, e.g. *Wasps* 691–694). Thus, most (if not all) of the juristic terms used in *Wasps* would have been part of everyday Athenian discourse and express notions and situations known and experienced by the poet's general audience. At the same time, a number of details in Aristophanes' comic depiction of judicial issues have invited discussion as to their relationship with real-life procedures. For example, at the dogs' trial the comic *timēma* "penalty" (897), a fig-wood collar, is put forward during the indictment, before the jurors' vote, which seems not to have been the normal process (Adamidis 2017, pp. 80–81). At the same mock trial, Bdelycleon's cross-examination of the canine defendant (963–966) may reflect real-life courtroom practice, despite doubts regarding the use of this method in real Athenian courts (Todd 1990, p. 29). The appearance of a female litigant (Myrtia) subverts reality, since women in real Athens were represented in law by a male relative (*kyrios*); Myrtia's legal language (1406–1408) sounds more comic in view of her gender. If the inevitable comic distortions are filtered out, however, *Wasps* is seen by scholars as useful source of knowledge on Athenian legal practices, in addition to the surviving forensic speeches and inscriptional evidence (cf. Buis 2014, p. 322). This play is frequently cited by scholars of Athenian law.

Wasps is also informative about Athenian politics, despite its comic distortion of reality. The grimly funny picture painted by Aristophanes of the judicial system, the *dēmos*, and the politicians is of course a comic exaggeration. MacDowell (1995, pp. 177–178) rightly claimed, however, that the satire of courts is "food for thought." The political character of *Wasps* is hard to ignore and has fruitfully (even if not entirely conclusively) been analyzed before. *Wasps* emphasizes endorsement of Cleon, expressed in Philocleon's name and role, as a disastrous choice, but it also cheats its audience of any expectations that an anti-Cleonian stance or the option of *apragmosynē* will lead to an improvement of the protagonists' lives. So, does Aristophanes take a political side? On the one hand, his hero Bdelycleon is comically suspected of conspiring against the rule of the people, which is represented by the demagogue (*Wasps* 344–345, 417, 470, 473–477). On the other hand, Cleon explicitly aligns himself with the poor Athenians (the *rhyppapai*, 909) and Philocleon identifies himself with the people (the *koinon*, 917). The comedy thus presents a conflict between two different positions, which may be read as "democratic" and "aristocratic" (Konstan 1985, pp. 39–40) or "radical democratic" and "conservative democratic" (the former in each pair is represented by Cleon; Olson 1996, esp. pp. 145–149; see also Biles and Olson 2015, p. lx), or one may prefer to avoid such labels altogether (Mirhady 2009, pp. 375–377, 380 reviews the Konstan-Olson debate and concludes that the poet's stance is hard to discern, and Lutz 2014, pp. 5–6, n. 9 is rather ambivalent). But there is no doubt that the Philocleon–Bdelycleon conflict (solidified in their names, on which see below) mirrors the faults and absurdities of Athenian justice and related politics. While the play's satire treats Cleon's group as no true democrats, and Bdelycleon's proposed alternative stance as failed, the plot's outcome suggests that it is neither the pro-Cleon nor the anti-Cleonian feeling that endangers democracy but the lack of *sōphrosynē* on both sides; in order to be viable, democracy needs to be a *sōphrōn* state of affairs, where justice reigns (Kanavou 2016, p. 189; cf. Harris 2005, pp. 18–19). It is important to note that democracy as a principle is not criticized, and the sovereignty of the *dēmos* is not subverted: despite their anticipation of the *agōn*'s outcome as decisive for their fate (518, 535, 540–547), the jurymen of the Chorus do not follow Philocleon in his new way of life, and they do not take any part in the hero's grotesque final act and will continue to function as jurors (1120–1121; cf. Olson 1996, pp. 130–131). But perhaps comedy's jokes about tyranny (mainly the hilarious conception of Bdelycleon as a "tyrant") draw inspiration from a real fear of it.[10] Indeed, a few years later, in 411 BCE, democracy would briefly yield its place to oligarchy – possibly the outcome of (among other factors) the lack of wisdom that had brought to power the new demagogue politicians and the lack of justice that corruption has brought with it (Kanavou 2016, p. 189).

While the Athenians' relationship with the law is a main source of humor in *Wasps*, it also gives fodder to satire in other Aristophanic comedies (Buis 2014, pp. 326–333). Parallels for the *Wasps*' satire of jury duty and Athenian litigiousness are found in *Knights* (797–800) and *Peace* 348–349 (poor regard for jurymen), 533–534. The Athenians are accused of *philodikia* in *Peace* 505 (cf. *Wasps* 800–804), while the heroes of *Birds* decide to leave Athens in order to escape from their fellow citizens' litigiousness among other things (39–48). In *Clouds* (207–208), Strepsiades cannot believe that a spot on the map is Athens because he can see no jurors convening. Aristophanes was not the only comic poet to draw satirical inspiration from the judicial system. Among the relevant fragmentary evidence (collected by Buis 2014, pp. 333–334), the title of a lost comedy by the fifth-century BCE poet Thugenides, *Dikastai* "Jurors," is closely analogous to Aristophanes' *Wasps*; its sole surviving, one-line fragment (1 K-A) refers to *antidikia* "litigation." On Athenian litigiousness (also frowned upon by the "Old Oligarch," 3.2), see further Christ (1998). Legal matters, particularly regarding family law, are also strongly present in the comedies of Menander.

The Unity of the Plot and the Power of Rhetoric

In terms of structure, the play is divided into two distinct parts (e.g. Konstan 1995, p. 16). In the first part, up until the *parabasis*, the plot centers on Bdelycleon's attempts to talk his father out of his juridical passion; in the second part, after Philocleon's conversion is achieved, the son tries to instill in his father a more pleasurable and carefree way of life.

A number of scholars have argued convincingly in favor of the unity of the plot, despite the apparent discrepancy between its first part, the depiction of Philocleon's passion for jury duty, and the second, which shows the old man's new life and is dominated by wild party scenes. An indicator of the unity of the plot is the poet's foreshadowing and allusion techniques that link earlier with later scenes (for example, lines 341 and 736–740 foreshadow the pleasures that await Philocleon once he quits jury duty). There is also an analogy between the two types of places frequented by Philocleon before and after his conversion, respectively, the law courts and the symposium: the function of both relies on social form which is disrespected by Philocleon (MacDowell 1971, p. 7, n. 1; MacDowell 1995, p. 178 ["it is the character of Philokleon that unifies the play"]; Konstan 1985, pp. 42–44; Olson 1996, p. 143). Both as a juror and as a dinner-party guest, the hero displays nasty behavior toward the people he comes in contact with (what Strauss 1966, p. 134 termed as "malice," which he called "a necessary ingredient of the Aristophanic comedy"). Philocleon's behavior may also be taken to reflect a lack of the virtue of moderation and of respect for true justice, a lack which defines his character from beginning to end and thus suggests itself as a further strong unifying thread between the play's first part and its final scenes; the absence of moderation first takes the form of an obsession with law courts and then re-emerges in Philocleon's excessive partying (Kanavou 2016, pp. 186–187).

If the unity of the plot is to be sought in the flawed morals of its central character, the transition from the first to the second part of the play lies in the effect of rhetoric. Indeed, this transition depends on Bdelycleon's success in changing the heart of his father and the Chorus, a success which is, above all, a comic celebration of the power of words. Having defied his son's attempt to keep him at home by force or by the allure of *euōchia* (341), Philocleon, a victim of

---

[10] On this "very real fear of tyranny and oligarchy," also attested by Thucydides, see Ostwald 1986, p. 224.

the demagogues' misleading oratory, will perhaps be persuaded by the sort of rhetoric that is deemed honest and right by the terms of the play (so Bdelycleon hopes, 512–514). The old man's fellow jurymen and members of the Chorus also declare that their mood can only change if they hear persuasive talk (646–647). Ironically, even though Bdelycleon wishes to direct his father to *apragmosynē*, rhetoric – the basic tool of politicians – cannot be avoided and must be used as a means to an end (cf. Konstan 1995, pp. 23–25). That is to say, Philocleon's and the Chorus' conversion depends on rhetoric, and verbal arguments will be enlisted to demonstrate the failures of contemporary politics and dispel Philocleon's illusion that Cleon is a well-meaning protector (cf. 596–598; this role was indeed assumed by Athenian political orators, see Ober 1989, pp. 316–317), and that jury service is a worthwhile activity. Similarly, Philocleon will use rhetoric to support his position and as a weapon to extricate himself from the pressure of his son. His case rests on the power of the jurors, the respect paid to them by important men, and the financial bonus of jury duty; these are all substantial considerations for the common people, with whom Philocleon identifies (593).

The views aired by father and son in the *agōn* (526–724) are assessed by the Chorus of wasp-jurors. They are a challenging audience. Their comic appearance as aggressive insects underlines their harsh and immoral nature and further establishes a sad contrast with the glorious past which the old men assert; the alleged connection of their wasp nature with the courage they showed in the Persian Wars (1071–1101) only increases the comic effect, as does the very claim that they fought the Persians (at the time of Aristophanes there would have been very few survivors of these wars, aged older than 80 years, and surely rare to find among serving members of the *hēliaia* in the early 420s; hence, this claim is perhaps a little more extravagant than MacDowell 1971, p. 10 allowed, and it seems to have been a comic *topos*, cf. *Knights* 781, 785). Their association with the distant past (also expressed in their taste for the early tragic poet Phrynichus, 269) further serves to suggest these old jurors as rooted in a bygone world, with little contact with contemporary reality (cf. their claim that they had no interest in acting as rhetors or sycophants, like men of the present time often do, 1094–1097). They initially side with Philocleon (cf. the Chorus' exhortation to him at 526–528, 531–534, and their enthusiastic reaction to Philocleon's contributions to the *agōn*). Bdelycleon, as a representative of the younger generation, undertakes the task to inform their knowledge and cure them of their misconceptions.

Given the importance of jury duty for the poorer members of the citizen body and the democratic significance of popular courts, it is no surprise that in the eyes of the Chorus, Bdelycleon is initially a *misopolis* ("hater of the city" 411), a *misodēmos* ("hater of the people" 473), and a lover of tyranny (474, 463–470). But this impression is reversed after Bdelycleon's rhetorical defense of his anti-Cleonian and anti-jury-duty position. He argues that his father and fellow jurymen are being exploited by corrupt, self-serving politicians, who turn them into pawns; the jurors' function is a sham, and they are badly paid for it, compared to the earnings of the demagogues (see previous section). Both Philocleon and the Chorus, who – for the purposes of comedy – appear to be more clueless about the truths exposed by Bdelycleon than real-life jurors might have been, are shaken. In the *agōn* (especially after 696), Philocleon's political convictions falter. The Chorus now praises Bdelycleon's advice, which Philocleon should follow (728–732, 747–749); the old jurymen are eventually convinced that Bdelycleon "loves the people more than anyone else in his generation" (888–890). The Chorus' description of Philocleon's completely new behavior (1292 ff.) signposts the latter's full conversion to a new way of life. As noted already, the Chorus does not follow the hero's new lifestyle; this highlights the exaggeration involved in Philocleon's conversion and serves as a reminder of their different social and financial circumstances. Unlike Philocleon, the members of the Chorus are poor old men, who are entirely dependent on jury pay (*Wasps*, 300–316, 463, 703) and seem indeed to hail from the lower social class (Ostwald 1986, p. 235; for Konstan 1985, pp. 35–36, 45–46, the Philocleon–Bdelycleon–Chorus triptych reflects Athenian class conflict). However, in the play's first part, the characterization of Philocleon and the Chorus shares common elements, and the hero and his fellow jurymen are united in their faith in Cleon and jury service, while Bdelycleon's arguments later convince both his father and the Chorus. This (at least partial) "collapse of class distinctions" (Konstan 1985, p. 45, 1995, p. 27) is very much the product of endorsement of a common ideology, which is driven by rhetoric-first that of the demagogues, then Bdelycleon's rhetoric.

There is no doubt that *Wasps* reflects Athenian democratic discourse and the "culture of persuasion" that holds central place in the Athenian democracy (McGlew 2004). In the life of real Athenian courts, the important role of speeches and speechmakers is a manifestation of the close relationship between rhetoric and the law (Carey 2015; Wohl 2010), which persists to the present day. But at the same time, rhetoric is comically treated by Aristophanes not as a true servant of law and justice, but as suspicious throughout; this concerns not just the demagogues' rhetoric but also Bdelycleon's (cf. the mock name Demologocleon "populist Cleon" which Bdelycleon initially earns, 342). For all its importance for the plot's progress, in the end rhetoric only provides an illusory winner. Bdelycleon's view prevails, but it is not a view that leads to a good outcome. This is not surprising as (1) we are in a comic world, (2) rhetoric's relationship with truth and righteousness is inherently ambivalent, as sophistic activity in classical Athens amply demonstrates; the question of "good" and "bad," "right" and "wrong" is never clearly settled. In *Clouds,* we find arguments in favor of the new sophistic education (1060–1082), of which rhetoric is an important part; but it only proved detrimental to the fates of the play's heroes.[11]

The Father–Son Conflict

The ambivalent outcome of rhetoric described above may further be interpreted as a manifestation of the inherent difficulty in the relationship between father and son (and by extension, between Bdelycleon and the Chorus). While *Clouds* also portrayed a difficult father–son relationship, the *Wasps*' conflict of generations (expressed poignantly at 1067–1070, 1133–1134) inverts stereotypes by assigning to the son feelings and mentality that are normally the property of the father and vice versa (cf. Philocleon's outrageous hope for financial independence after his son dies, 1352–1359; see further Whitman's analysis [Whitman 1964, pp. 143–166]). That we are dealing here with comic inversion is implied by the usual status of father–son relationships in real Athens. From a legal point of view, father and adult son were both independent and equal, and the latter had no right to impose his will on the former; still, in a regular household, the father could have been expected to patronize the son, but not the opposite (cf. Kapparis 2019, p. 133 n. 15). While it was the father's right to punish his son if he deviated from accepted behavior (*Clouds* 1434), it was not expected of sons to control the behavior of fathers, like Bdelycleon does in *Wasps*. In *Clouds,* it is the father who, as expected, takes charge of the son's "education" (1380); in *Wasps,* it is the opposite (736, 1004).

This inversion of roles is at least partly explained by Philocleon's advanced age, as a result of which Bdelycleon is in charge of his father's *oikos* (cf. 612–614; note that he is also the master of the slaves, who once answered to his father [67–68, 142, 442]). As a result, the son further sees himself as responsible for the father's welfare and behavior and by extension of the *oikos* as a whole. This situation was not unusual in real Athens (see Kapparis 2019, pp. 85–86; MacDowell 1978, pp. 91–92). Similarly, immature parental behavior that bothers children was not unheard of: Isaeus 6.18–24 concerns a father's passion for a *hetaera*, which causes trouble to his son (their names, Euctemon and Philoctemon, respectively, contain the same second component and are uncannily reminiscent of the names of the *Wasps*' heroes); this conflict is solved with a compromise (Kapparis 2019, p. 133 n. 15). Another example is the passion of the orator Hypereides for the *hetaera* Myrrhine, which made him expel his son from the parental home (at least according to Athenaeus XIII 590c–d, who cites Idomeneus of Lampsacus as his source). But comedy naturally exaggerates the potential of this scenario. Toward the end of the play (1352–1359), Philocleon's drunken promises to the slave girl whom he has abducted is a hilarious reversal of a situation a

---

[11] See O'Regan 1992 for an analysis of the "dark" side of rhetorical practice.

young man might find himself in. A comic sexual competition between father and son ensues, which almost culminates in violence, when Philocleon threatens to punch Bdelycleon if he takes the slave girl away (1379–1387).

Contrary to the view of young men in *Clouds* as immature and dangerously impressionable (the fashionable view), the young man of *Wasps*, Bdelycleon, appears at first well balanced and prudent, and he is seemingly guided by good intentions (to help his father improve his quality of life). But the seemingly wise son is presented to act wrongly on all counts. He orders a slave to beat his father and the old men of the Chorus (456–459) – a reversal of the accepted practice of a father beating a son when necessary for the purposes of *paideia* (Strauss 1993, p. 82) and a reproachable act, even if the son does not carry out the beating himself (Pheidippides and Hetton/Adikos Logos in *Clouds*, 904–906, 911, 1321–1325, are presented as father beaters, and Pheidippides even composes a new law to allow children to beat their fathers, 1405; in real Athens, father beaters were liable to serious legal punishments, see Kapparis 2019, p. 122; MacDowell 1978, p. 92). What is more, Philocleon's obsession with law courts is reminiscent of Pheidippides' with horses. Strepsiades struggled to divert Pheidippides' interest from expensive horses to sophistry and rhetoric and came to regret it (*Clouds* 1406–1407). The results of Bdelycleon's efforts are also highly dubious. The alternative lifestyle that he proposes, which is that of the Athenian bourgeoisie, is also ridiculed, to the point that it seems hardly a better option than jury service (the Chorus' praise of Bdelycleon's filial devotion and successful conversion of his father to a better way of life sounds ironic, 1462–1473). In fact, Bdelycleon must have struck spectators as not an altogether positive force from the moment that he appeared on scene. Allusions to his appearance (he sports a long beard and a mustache, 466; 473–477) are hardly meant as compliments (long hair was associated with wealth and the class of cavalrymen, but also with ostentation – a frequent fault of sophistic rhetoric – and the Spartans, the city's great enemy in war and politics). His character is criticized (the slave Xanthias sees him as annoyingly arrogant and haughty, 134–135).

Strauss (1993, pp. 161–163) rightly noted that "*Wasps* refuses to give either generation the last word." The rhetorical *agōn* between the younger and the older generation produces no winner. The conflict is comically resolved when it becomes apparent that both father and son are flawed characters – much like Strepsiades and Pheidippides in *Clouds* – and each of them promotes a lifestyle that lends itself to satire. Thus, the satire of courts gives its place to the satire of high society life and pretentious behavior at dinner parties that attract some prominent Athenians (including the orator Antiphon [1301–1302], who was associated with the *apragmōn* way of life envisaged by Bdelycleon for his father; Lanni 2016, pp. 114–115). Allusions to *dikas*, the feared outcome of Philocleon's unruly behavior, persist, but the old man no longer cares (cf. his insolent responses to his victims' complaints, e.g. 1392–1395); his conversion is not reexamined. In the end, the father–son contrast serves first and foremost the interests of comedy. Indeed, the obscene and hedonist nature of Philocleon's new life has a salient Dionysian element (see Biles and Olson 2015, pp. xxxiv–xxxviii). Philocleon, the main focus of the play, is a wildly comic character, whose stage presence, consisting of not only his spoken lines but also his bodily movement and antiques – which contradict his old age – must have greatly amused the play's audience.

The Cleon Satire

Like in other Aristophanic comedies, several fellow citizens of the poet fall victims to personal satire in *Wasps* (note, for example, early in the play, the extended mockery of Cleonymus the *rhipsaspis* [15–27] and of Cleon's supporter Theorus, which includes a joke at the expense of Alcibiades [42–51]). But despite the programmatic statement that Cleon will not come under extended attack in *Wasps* (62–63), as he did in *Knights*, the politician, who was also targeted in *Babylonians* (426 BCE) and *Acharnians* (425 BCE), is the most attacked individual in the play. The most influential of demagogue politicians, Cleon acquired more leverage after participating (with the general

Demosthenes) in the capture of Spartan soldiers on the island of Sphacteria in 425 BCE and was elected general the following year. After the capture of Amphipolis by the Spartans in 424 BCE, he was not re-elected, but he went on to fight at Amphipolis against the Spartan commander Brasidas in 422 BCE (which is where they both met their deaths; Thucydides 5.10). A central figure in the war effort, he was also very much involved in everyday Athenian politics and the justice system, which Aristophanes satirizes here. Cleon's prominence as a satirical target in *Wasps* is reflected in the names of the play's two main heroes, Philocleon and Bdelycleon, which are purposeful comic formations (Kanavou 2011, pp. 80–83): Philocleon "loves Cleon" because he supports the *hēliastai* (he is a *philēliastēs* "lover of the *hēliaia*" 88); Bdelycleon hates the man because he sees him as responsible for his father's unhealthy obsession with trials. Philocleon indeed appeals to Cleon for help in escaping his son's guard (197), and the Chorus call him "our protector" (242) – which he is only in a very twisted sense, as Bdelycleon's arguments show (cf. some of the Chorus' own statements, e.g. 242–244, with Harris 2013, pp. 316–317; note also Paphlagon's [= Cleon's] call for the jurors' protection in *Knights*, 255–257).

The satire of Cleon in *Wasps* includes his presentation as a disgusting whale (31–40, with a reference to the much-ridiculed tanning business ran by his family), the mock-name Demologocleon "populist Cleon" (342, bestowed upon Bdelycleon), and his inclusion in the guest list of the parties to be attended by Philocleon (1220); the list also comprises other victims of Aristophanes' satire, such as Theorus. Cleon is implicitly mocked as a *xenos* "foreigner" (1221), an allusion to the character of the Paphlagonian slave in *Knights*, a thinly veiled satire of the politician. He is further imagined as singing the song of Harmodius (1224–1226), which reflects the demagogue politicians' populist use of antityrannical sentiment; the song is paraphrased to lead from the praise of the tyrannicide to the mockery of the demagogue as a "scoundrel" and a "thief" (1227).

The high point of Cleon's satire in *Wasps* is an extraordinarily comic scene, in which the dog Cyon from the deme Cydathenaion (Cleon's own deme) takes another dog called Labes from the deme Aixone to trial on account of consuming some Sicilian cheese (891–1008); the trial takes place at Philocleon's newly founded private court, a mock version of a real courtroom built with comic substitutes for real objects and procedures (including courtroom rhetoric), and has attracted much scholarly interest for its metatheatricality (Farmer 2017, p. 134). The connection between "Cyon" and Cleon is reinforced by the canine theme, which is persistent in Aristophanes' mockery of Cleon, both in *Wasps* and in other comedies (Kanavou 2011, pp. 89–90). In *Wasps* 1031–1032, he is imagined as having "saw-like teeth," a feature of dogs (cf. *Knights* 1017 and *Peace* 754), and he is associated with a prostitute called Cynna (cf. *Peace* 755); in *Knights*, he ironically presents himself as the "watchdog" of the Athenian people, in comic comparison to the dog Cerberus who guards the gates of Hades (1017–1024; 1030). The name of the other dog, Labes "Snatcher" (from *labein*), is a comic distortion of the name Laches, of a man from the deme Aixone, who served as a general in Sicily a couple of years earlier (Thucydides 3.115; Harris 2013, p. 315). The dog trial is a substitute (an even more comic version) of the envisaged comic trial of Laches, which would have been judged by Philocleon and the jurymen of the Chorus, should the former not have been forcefully kept at home by his son (240–244; Cleon had asked the jurymen to show exceptional harshness). Although the historical circumstances of the comic trial are dubious, they must reflect a real enmity (if not real litigation) between Cleon and Laches. In particular, the comic indictment of the dog Labes may imply that Cleon accused Laches of embezzling funds from the Sicilian campaign. Lawsuits known as *euthynai* (examination of public officials) seem to have been a favorite activity of the demagogues (Ostwald 1986, pp. 211–212). Aristophanes appears to mock Cleon's dissatisfaction not with the act of usurpation itself but with Laches' unwillingenss to share his booty (the Sicilian cheese!) with him (hence the comic name "Labes"). Significantly, Bdelycleon's defense of Labes (as *synēgoros*) implies that, while both are corrupt, Cleon is a worse character than Laches (968–972; Cleon notably exercised a pro-war policy, while Laches was associated with the brief truce of 424 BCE and, later, the peace treaty known as "Nicias' peace"). Philocleon's intention to convict the dog Labes, even after hearing Bdelycleon's defense of the dog and after the anti-Cleonian discourse of the *agōn*, betrays the tight grip still held on him by the ideological position represented by the demagogue. In the end, Philocleon is cheated by his son into letting Labes walk free – Cleon is defeated by accident, but he is defeated nevertheless.

Satire of Cleon's litigious side abounds in *Knights*, where it is suggested that he prosecutes officials for financial and political gain and that he manipulates jurors (the relevant passages are collected in Harris 2013, p. 316). His misuse of the law courts is mainly attested in comedy, but it is also implied in Thucydides (Ostwald 1986, pp. 204, 211, 220–221; Harris 2013, p. 334). Comic satire of Cleon further targets his use of rhetoric as a means of controlling people; he seems indeed to have been a master of persuasion (Ober 1989, p. 93; O'Sullivan 1992, pp. 115–124; *Wasps* 36 is a jibe at the sound of his voice). However, Aristophanes' depiction of Cleon's corrupt nature and involvement with the law courts and jury duty must entail a degree of comic exaggeration (MacDowell 1971, pp. 1–4). He is certainly not the only politician to be mocked for using less than fair tactics in the courts. Hyperbolus, another prominent demagogue and a target of Aristophanes' satire in several comedies, is accused of deceiving the jurors in *Wasps* (1007).

The Poet and His Audience

Wasps is a comedy, in which the poet's "voice" resonates particularly strongly, and the poet appears to reflect quite openly on his relationship with his audience. As early as the prolog, and after an opening that includes a sequence of *onomasti* jokes, the slave Xanthias introduces the play as a "clever" piece of work, though not cleverer than its audience (64–65). The poet's satire of his fellow citizens indeed goes hand-in-hand with flattery, and allusions to the Athenians' capability of good judgment occur elsewhere (see, in particular, *Knights* 1119–1120, with Ostwald 1986, pp. 226–227); the poet does not forget that these are the judges of his plays. *Wasps*' "cleverness" consists in that it will not repeat familiar brainless modes of entertainment (such as Megarian slapstick, 66), but it will make use of an original funny plot. The *parabasis* of *Wasps* further attributes to the poet exceptional courage, manifested in his fearless satire of Cleon (1030–1042, cf. 1284–1291) and "new ideas" (1044); while comedy enjoyed a considerable freedom of speech, satire of a powerful demagogue like Cleon seems to have entailed a degree of risk (cf. *Acharnians* 645, 377–382 [implying that Cleon took legal action on account of the *Babylonians*], and see, e.g. Henderson 2020, pp. 46–49; Sommerstein 1983, pp. 233–234). The poet's judgment and intellect are further presented as beneficial to his viewers (he received similar praise by the Chorus of *Knights*: "He acted discreetly, and didn't leap mindlessly in and spout rubbish," 545).

The concept of the comic poet as an educator has been much discussed (Bertelli 2013, pp. 99–125, with bibliography), but the poet's role certainly had limits. There is a comic reference to these limits in *Wasps* 650–651, when Bdelycleon states that to cure "an old illness of the city" a strong intellect is needed – stronger than the comic poet's. Indeed, a comic comparison of the poet's function may be recognized in Bdelycleon as the young, long-haired revolutionary who fails to change his father (or the world). There is no doubt that the performance of Aristophanic comedy was first and foremost entertainment and not persuasive rhetoric or political advice. It is clear that *Wasps* examines the irrationalities of Athenian life, as do other plays (cf. Nelson 2014, pp. 109–136), but it is hard to identify a "serious" message amid comic jokes and contradictions. The issues raised in the *agōn* are not met with suggestions of any concrete solutions - for example, could the jurors of the Chorus not demand a pay rise to correct the supposed injustice in the division of the city's income? The only outcome of the debate is one individual's decision to remove himself from these issues, first by privatizing jury duty (in the form of the mock trial of the dogs, cf. 799–804) and then by entirely giving up jury life. Bdelycleon's and Philocleon's private court is reminiscent of Dicaeopolis' private peace that excludes most others; the Chorus only expresses envy that Philocleon has such a good adviser (731–732). The seriousness of the issues addressed would, of course, have hit the audience (see further Wright 2012, pp. 18–20; Sommerstein 2005, pp. 197–201 listed concrete changes in Athenian public life [suggesting an "alternative democracy"], which Aristophanes might have wished for). But despite being introduced as a political and artistic innovator in the *parabasis*, the poet cannot expect to influence the life of his audience in a way other than helping them to interpret everyday reality with a sense of humor.[12]

As noted at the beginning of this chapter, *Wasps* came second in the poetic competition (followed by Leucon and his *Ambassadors* in the third place; Hyp. I). It is virtually certain that the play that won first prize, *Proagon*, which was brought upon the stage in the name of Philonides, was also by Aristophanes (MacDowell 1971, p. 20; Biles and Olson 2015, p. xxviii). This play was perhaps a satire of the official presentation (*proagōn*) of the dramas (with their poets, choruses, and actors) that were to compete at the Great Dionysia, and it apparently had Euripides as a main subject (KA iii.2: 253) – a satirical target that also featured in *Acharnians*, and of whom *Wasps* purportedly does not deign to make use (54–66), instead turning its focus to a more original and intellectually demanding topic (this promise is not wholly kept: Euripides may not appear as a character like he did in *Acharnians*, but satire of Euripidean themes is far from absent; see further Farmer 2017, pp. 117–153 on Philocleon as a character "obsessed with tragedy," who speaks in tragic lines and adopts tragic behavior). *Clouds*, which won third place the previous year, had fared even worse than *Wasps*; the Chorus of *Wasps* complains about this (1017, 1043–1050). While both *Clouds* and *Wasps* are clearly intelligent and provocative dramas, and it is possible that the poet would have rejoiced in their victory, we cannot infer with any certainty that Aristophanes regarded any of his plays as "favorites"; what certainly seems to be the case is that he turned his disappointments, in both politics and theater, into further comedy.

GUIDE TO FURTHER READING

Commentaries on *Wasps* include MacDowell (1971), Sommerstein (1983), Lutz (2014), Biles and Olson (2015), and Rothwell's student commentary (2019). On law and the justice system in ancient Athens, see Harrison (1968-1971), MacDowell (1978), Todd (1993), Lanni (2006, 2016), and Phillips (2013). On comic representations of legal matters, see the relevant chapters in Cairns and Knox (2004) and Harris et al. (2010). For Aristophanes' politics (a tangled issue), see further Sidwell (2009), Sommerstein (2005, 2013), and now Rosen and Foley (2020).

REFERENCES

Adamidis, V. (2017). *Character Evidence in the Courts of Classical Athens. Rhetoric, Relevance and the Rule of Law*. London/New York: Routledge.

Balot, R.K. (2001). *Greed and Injustice in Classical Athens*. Princeton, NJ: Princeton University Press.

Bertelli, L. (2013). Democracy and dissent: the case of comedy. In: *The Greek Polis and the Invention of Democracy: A Politico-Cultural Transformation and Its Interpretations* (ed. J.P. Arnason, K.A. Raaflaub, and P. Wagner), 99–125. Malden, MA/Oxford/Chichester: Wiley-Blackwell.

Biles, Z.P. and Olson, S.D. (2015). *Aristophanes. Wasps*. Oxford and New York: Oxford University Press.

Bowie, E. (1990). *Marginalia Obsceniora:* some problems in Aristophanes' *Wasps*. In: *Owls to Athens: Essays on Classical Subjects Presented to Sir Kenneth Dover* (ed. E.M. Craik), 31–38. Oxford: Oxford University Press.

Buis, E. (2014). Law and Greek comedy. In: *The Oxford Handbook of Greek and Roman Comedy* (ed. M. Fontaine and A.C. Scafuro), 321–339. Oxford: Oxford University Press.

Cairns, D.L. and Knox, R.A. (ed.) (2004). *Law, Rhetoric and Comedy in Classical Athens. Essays in Honour of Douglas M. MacDowell*. Swansea: Classical Press of Wales.

Carey, C. (2015). Law, speech-writers, and rhetorical context. In: *The Oxford Handbook of Ancient Greek Law* (online edn) (ed. E.M. Harris and M. Canevaro). Oxford Academic https://doi.org/10.1093/oxfordhb/9780199599257.013.8.

---

[12] For the relationship between poet and audience in *Wasps*, see further Biles and Olson (2015, pp. xxviii–xxix, xxxiii, xliv, 379, 392–393).

Carter, L.B. (1986). *The Quiet Athenian*. Oxford: Clarendon Press.
Christ, M.R. (1998). *The Litigious Athenian*. Baltimore: The Johns Hopkins University Press.
Farmer, M.C. (2017). *Tragedy on the Comic Stage*. Oxford: Oxford University Press.
Gagarin, M. (2020). *Democratic Law in Classical Athens*. Austin: University of Texas Press.
Halliwell, S. (2020). Politics in the street: some citizen encounters in Aristophanes. In: *Aristophanes and Politics: New Studies* (ed. R.M. Rosen and H.P. Foley), 113–136. Leiden, Boston (MA): Brill.
Harris, E.M. (2005). Was all criticism of Athenian democracy necessarily anti-democratic? In: *Democrazia e antidemocrazia nel mondo greco (Atti del Convegno Internazionale di Studi Chieti, 9–11 April 2003)* (ed. U. Bultrighini), 11–23. Alessandria: Edizioni dell'Orso.
Harris, E.M. (2013). *The Rule of Law in Action in Democratic Athens*. New York: Oxford University Press.
Harris, E.M., Leão, D.m.F., and Rhodes, P.J. (ed.) (2010). *Law and Drama in Ancient Greece*. Bristol: Bloomsbury.
Harrison, A.W.R. (1968–1971). *The Law of Athens*, The Family and Property, Procedure, vol. 1, 2. Oxford: Clarendon Press.
Havelock, E.A. (1969). "Dikaiosynē": an essay in Greek intellectual history (in tribute to George Grube, the distinguished author of "Plato's thought"). *Phoenix* 23: 49–70.
Henderson, J. (2020). Patterns of avoidance and indirection in Athenian political satire. In: *Aristophanes and Politics* (ed. R.M. Rosen and H.P. Foley), 45–59. Leiden: Brill.
Kanavou, N. (2011). *Aristophanes' Comedy of Names: A Study of Speaking Names in Aristophanes*. Berlin/New York: De Gruyter.
Kanavou, N. (2016). Sōphrosynē and justice in Aristophanes' *Wasps*. *Greece & Rome* 63: 175–191.
Kapparis, K.A. (2019). *Athenian Law and Society*. London/New York: Routledge.
Konstan, D. (1985). The politics of Aristophanes' *Wasps*. *Transactions of the American Philological Association* 115: 27–46.
Konstan, D. (1995). *Greek Comedy and Ideology*. Oxford/New York: Oxford University Press.
Lanni, A. (2006). *Law and Justice in the Courts of Classical Athens*. New York: Cambridge University Press.
Lanni, A. (2016). *Law and Order in Ancient Athens*. Cambridge: Cambridge University Press.
Lutz, L. (2014). *Aristophanes Wespen*. Berlin/New York: De Gruyter.
MacDowell, D.M. (1971). *Aristophanes: Wasps*. Oxford: Clarendon Press.
MacDowell, D.M. (1978). *The Law in Classical Athens*. London: Thames and Hudson.
MacDowell, D.M. (1995). *Aristophanes and Athens: An Introduction to the Plays*. Oxford: Oxford University Press.
Marr, J.L. and Rhodes, P.J. (ed.) (2008). *The "Old Oligarch": The Constitution of the Athenians Attributed to Xenophon*. Oxford: Aris & Phillips.
McGlew, J.F. (2004). "Speak on my behalf": persuasion and purification in Aristophanes' *Wasps*. *Arethusa* 37: 11–36.
Mirhady, D. (2009). Is the Wasps' anger democratic? In: *The Play of Texts and Fragments (Essays in Honour of Martin Cropp). (Mnemosyne Suppl. 314)* (ed. J.R.C. Cousland and J.R. Hume), 371–387. Leiden/Boston: Brill.
Nelson, S. (2014). Aristophanes and the polis. In: *The Political Theory of Aristophanes: Explorations in Poetic Wisdom* (ed. J.J. Mhire and B.-P. Frost), 109–136. Albany, NY: SUNY Press.
North, H. (1966). *Sōphrosynē: Self-Knowledge and Self-Restraint in Greek Literature*. Ithaca, NY: Cornell University Press.
Nussbaum, M.C. (2001). *The Fragility of Goodness: Luck and Ethics in Greek Tragedy and Philosophy*. Cambridge, New York: Cambridge University Press.
Ober, J. (1989). *Mass and Elite in Democratic Athens. Rhetoric, Ideology, and the Power of the People*. Princeton, NJ: Princeton University Press.
Olson, D. (1996). Politics and poetry in Aristophanes' *Wasps*. *Transactions of the American Philological Association* 126: 129–150.
O'Regan, D.E. (1992). *Rhetoric, Comedy and the Violence of Language in Aristophanes' Clouds*. Oxford: Oxford University Press.
Osborne, R. (1985). Law in action in classical Athens. *Journal of Hellenic Studies* 105: 40–58.
Ostwald, M. (1986). *From Popular Sovereignty to the Sovereignty of Law: Law, Society, and Politics in Fifth-Century Athens*. Berkeley/Los Angeles: University of California Press.
O'Sullivan, N. (1992). *Alcidamas, Aristophanes and the Beginnings of Greek Stylistic Theory. (Hermes Einzelschriften 60)*. Stuttgart: Franz Steiner Verlag.

Phillips, D.D. (2013). *The Law of Ancient Athens. Law and Society in the Ancient World.* Ann Arbor, MI: University of Michigan Press.
Rademaker, A. (2005). *Sōphrosynē and the Rhetoric of Self-Restraint: Polysemy and Persuasive Use of an Ancient Greek Value Term.* Leiden: Brill.
Rawls, J. (1999). *A Theory of Justice.* Cambridge MA: Harvard University Press [Revised ed.].
Rosen, R.M. and Foley, H.P. (ed.) (2020). *Aristophanes and Politics: New Studies.* Leiden/Boston: Brill.
Rothwell, K.S. Jr. (2019). *Aristophanes' Wasps.* Oxford: Oxford University Press.
Sidwell, K. (2009). *Aristophanes the Democrat: The Politics of Satirical Comedy during the Peloponnesian War.* Cambridge/New York: Cambridge University Press.
Sommerstein, A.H. (1983). *Aristophanes' Wasps.* Warminster: Aris & Phillips.
Sommerstein, A.H. (2005). An alternative democracy and an alternative to democracy in Aristophanic comedy. In: *Democrazia e antidemocrazia nel mondo greco (Atti del Convegno Internazionale di Studi Chieti, 9–11 April 2003)* (ed. U. Bultrighini), 195–207. Alessandria: Edizioni dell'Orso.
Sommerstein, A.H. (2013). The politics of Greek comedy. In: *The Cambridge Companion to Greek Comedy* (ed. M. Revermann), 291–305. Cambridge, Cambridge University Press.
Strauss, L. (1966). *Socrates and Aristophanes.* Chicago: University of Chicago Press.
Strauss, B.S. (1993). *Fathers and Sons in Athens: Ideology and Society in the Era of the Peloponnesian War.* Princeton, NJ: Princeton University Press.
Thür, G. (2005). The role of the witness in Athenian law. In: *The Cambridge Companion to Ancient Greek Law* (ed. M. Gagarin and D. Cohen), 146–169. Cambridge: Cambridge University Press.
Todd, S. (1990). The purpose of evidence in Athenian courts. In: *Nomos: Essays in Athenian Law, Politics and Society* (ed. P. Cartledge, P. Millett, and S. Todd), 19–38. Cambridge: Cambridge University Press.
Todd, S. (1993). *The Shape of Athenian Law.* Oxford: Clarendon Press.
Whitman, C.H. (1964). *Aristophanes and the Comic Hero.* Cambridge, MA: Harvard University Press.
Willi, A. (2003). *The Languages of Aristophanes: Aspects of Linguistic Variation in Classical Attic Greek.* Oxford: Oxford University Press.
Wohl, V.J. (2010). *Law's Cosmos: Juridical Discourse in Athenian Forensic Oratory.* Cambridge, New York: Cambridge University Press.
Wright, M. (2012). *The Comedian as Critic: Greek Old Comedy and Poetics.* London: Bristol Classical Press.

CHAPTER 11

Peace: War

Elena Fabbro

Introduction

An elderly Attic farmer, who bears the significant name Trygaios (190) (derived from tryghē, "vintage," and trygan "to harvest fruit," providing the occasion for wordplay in vv. 913 and 1339–1340; cf. Kanavou (2011a) 98–100), is so exasperated by the long-drawn-out war that he hatches a plan to ascend to the heavens to ask Zeus for an explanation. His means of transport is a dung beetle from Mount Etna, clearly a parody of Pegasus (76–77 cf. Eur. fr. 306 Kn.; 154–156 cf. fr. 307 Kn.), the winged horse that carried Bellerophon, the hero of Euripides' homonymous tragedy, as he attempted his impious ascent to the heavens to question the gods concerning their rule over men. Resisting the pleas of his servants and his two young daughters, who the servants bring in to strengthen their entreaties, Trygaios makes the audacious ascent on his own and quickly reaches his destination (for details of the scene in terms of acting, see Slater (2002) 116–119). But Hermes, acting as a sort of doorman, informs him that neither Zeus nor the other gods are there, having withdrawn to the farthest part of the heavens from men (198–199, 207–209) in disgust at the behavior of the Greeks, who provoked the conflict and obtusely insist on continuing it. In their stead, as concrete proof that war has been the winning cause up to this point, the field is occupied by the very personification of war, Polemos and his henchman Kydoimos ("Turmoil"), as we learn from an agitated dialog between the two, commentated by Trygaios (234–288) (Kloss (2001) 164–166).

Polemos has buried Peace in a deep cave and is preparing to "make a pulp of" the cities of Greece in a monstrous mortar. But the plan is foiled because he lacks a pestle, given that both the Athenian and Spartan ones are broken: the pestles are metaphors of the leaders of the pro-war faction, the demagogue Cleōn and the general Brasidas who died in the same battle.

At this point, Trygaios calls on all Greeks to disinter Peace (292–294, 296–299), and his appeal is answered by the chorus of Panhellēnes who, although Trygaios urges restraint, cannot contain their boisterous exultance, nor the irrepressible desire to dance.

But Hermes intervenes to announce that Zeus has condemned to death anyone who seeks to retrieve Peace. After a long bout of verbal fencing alternating supplication with *bōmolochos* ("buffoon")-style quips, like Trygaios offering to reveal the Moon and Sun's presumed plot against the gods (406–413), Hermes is persuaded to hide the disinterment (anodos) of Peace from Zeus, and in fact becomes a fundamental collaborator in the plan. Despite sabotage attempts by Boiotians, Argives, Spartans, Megarians, and even Athenians who are not as cooperative as they should be, Peace is pulled out of the deep cave in which Polemos had hidden her and reappears with two companions from her retinue, Theōria and Opōra "symbolic representations of the significance of panhellenic festivals and of nature's harvest respectively, both of Dionysian relevance and to be enjoyed only at a time of peace" (Kanavou (2011a) 100, see Newiger (1957) 108–111; Whitman

---

A Companion to Aristophanes, First Edition. Edited by Matthew C. Farmer and Jeremy B. Lefkowitz.
© 2024 John Wiley & Sons, Inc. Published 2024 by John Wiley & Sons, Inc.

(1964) 111; Smith (2011) 79–81). After initial celebrations, Hermes, at the chorus' request, recaps the causes of the outbreak of war and mediates a reciprocal exchange of information between men and Peace, and bids them to return to the countryside. He then sends Trygaios on his way, indicating a route that, unlike his outbound trip, is completely trouble-free, along with Peace, Theōria, and Opōra; Hermes also bestows the latter on Trygaios as his bride.

The first parabasis (729–817) occupies the virtual time of the return trip, after which Trygaios, following the instructions he has been given, delivers Theōria – who, on the basis of her speaking name, is responsible for sacred embassies and communications on the organization of city festivals – to the prytaneis of the Boulē (887–891), as well as carrying out the sacrifice of a sheep to Peace. Through the chorus (751–760), the poet restates – with an almost verbatim reprise of *V*. 1029–1037 – his strong ethical–political commitment in favor of the Athenians and their allies in combatting Cleōn-the-monster, and he boasts of having liberated comedy from the vulgar amusement produced by his rivals (739–747; cf. *V.* 64–66; Hubbard (1991) 144–153).

Wedged between the two parabases is the episode of Hierocles, a *chrēsmologos* ("oracle monger") who, after labeling peace as inopportune in magniloquent terms, tries to partake of the sacrificial banquet but is chased off (1043–1126). The second parabasis (1127–1190) represents the celebration of the Attic farmers' return to their fields, where they can once again enjoy the pleasures of a simple, serene life, as opposed to the corruption and oppression of the city during wartime (Totaro (1999) 113–114). At this point, Trygaios' wedding feast begins offstage (1191–1196).

Successively, while waiting for the banquet table to be set for Trygaios and Opōra's wedding, an arms dealer, speaking for himself and for his colleagues, a weapon maker and a lance-maker, laments the collapse of their market due to peace; Trygaios lampoons them at length (1210–1264). Trygaios also pre-emptively censures the songs to be sung at the wedding feast, banning any mention of the warrior tradition or of Homeric epic (1270–1297). As the bride appears, the play ends with the canonical hymenaios hymn (1332–1356).

Peace was staged at the City Dionysia in 421, before a potentially panhellenic audience, and came in second after Eupolis' *Kolakes* ("*Flatterers*"); the third prize went to Leucon for his *Phratores* ("*Clansmen*"); see *Argumentum* A3.47–50. The previous summer, the simultaneous deaths on the front at Thrace beneath the walls of Amphipolis of the Spartan Brasidas and the Athenian Cleōn – the main advocates for drawing out the war, albeit for very different reasons, according to Thucydides (5, 16, 1) – had laid the grounds for the peace of Nicias, named for the Athenian general who had led the negotiations. Based on that agreement, stipulated a few days after the City Dionysia, the two cities and their respective allies committed to a 50-year peace (Thuc. 5, 18, 3–4; 20. 1) which, through the principle of restitution or compensation, effectively re-established the territorial *status quo* that had preceded the outbreak of war in 431. The clear relationship between the subject of the play and the contemporary political situation weighs on the judgment of critics, who had long considered *Peace* a *pièce d'occasion*, "a minor comedy" (Russo (1994), 134) constructed around a series of episodes with no specific structural progress, and without the tension usually conveyed by the *epirrhematic agon*, especially in the second part (see Whitman (1964) 103–104; Solomos and Feldheim (1974) 141; Cassio (1985) 35–39), redeemed only by the brilliant opening scene with the dung beetle (von Wilamowitz-Moellendorff (1935) 304 n. 3). The absence of an antagonist in the *agon* seems to respond to the absence of any real rhetorical opposition to the protagonist's plan (Gelzer (1960) 245), which appears to be fairly well developed, albeit not in words, by the chorus (McGlew (2001) 76–77). As far as scene construction is concerned, the play does not offer narration of offstage events, and attention seems to be focused exclusively on the theater as a point of contact between actors, chorus, and audience (Cassio (1985) 37–39; Russo (1994) 49).

Men and Gods

The incipit of *Peace* reprises the dramaturgical schema previously used for The *Knights* and The *Wasps*, opening on two slaves – like-minded, aside from a bit of jokey bickering – commiserating over the troubles caused by the anomaly of the comical situation. In *Knights*, the troubles were extreme, as a new servant had been set up in Demo's house and had quickly become tyrannical and overpowering; in *Wasps*, the slaves' anxiety is caused by an elderly master who is addicted to serving on juries at trials and whose son has ordered them to keep him from exercising his desired function.

As in *Wasps* (for a comparative analysis see Moulton (1981) 84; Slater (2002), 116), in *Peace*, the characters' factions and motivations are not immediately revealed, leaving room for apparently unrelated comic relief: in *Wasps*, an interpretation of dreams that proves to be loaded and tendentious with regard to the demagogical regime; and in *Peace*, the regressive and infantile pleasure of excrementitious language, referring to the enormous, insatiable beetle whose demands require the servants to keep up a frenetic pace of preparing and providing adequate quantities of its food (on this theme and on the important role of olfactory imagery in *Peace*, and the connection between war and excrement, see Hubbard (1991)141–144; Bowie (1993) 135–137 and Tordoff (2011)).

On other occasions, Aristophanes explicitly disassociates himself from this type of humor, especially in the incipit of *Frogs* (1–18); here, he gives himself over to it with a delayed effect, intended to arouse the spectators' curiosity. Before the scatological material is effectively worked into the comic action, there is room for a malicious insult of the memory of the hated Cleōn, now relegated to Hades (47–48, 647–650), but here compared to the beetle and reviled as a coprophagist (48), in a clear link between the sphere of warfare and excrement.

The beetle is the instrument Trygaios uses to carry out a plan that one of the slaves calls mad, in fact quite singularly mad (54, *cholē* 66, connected with the melancholy surfeit of bile that seems to affect Euripides' Bellerophon, see Riedweg 1990, 49–50): to investigate and verify Zeus' supreme authority with regard to the war, which in 421 has been going on for a decade. Trygaios views the war as an enormous disaster for all of Greece and takes on the risky flight as a panhellenic mission "in defence of all Greeks" (59, 63, 93, 105–106, 108, 150 [with metatheatrical reference to the spectators], 266, 292, 995–998; see Cassio 1985, 56). Thus, Trygaios or the chorus (292, 301–302) frequently try to overcome Hermes' hostility (204, 408, 421, 436) by appealing to a collective salvation. Of course, once the divinity has been won over, the suspicion that certain cities have little propensity for peace will come up sporadically during the play, as the basis of gags between Hermes and Trygaios with reference to the lack of zeal in disinterring Peace shown by the chorus, which is made up of Boeotians (466), Argives (475, 493), Spartans (478–480), Megarians (481, 500) and Athenians (503), in the presence of General Lamachos (473), which may be a metatheatrical suggestion, according to Olson (1998) 175. The shift implies an unshakable conditioned reflex that materializes, for example, when the chorus or Trygaios himself justifies the Athenian retaliation that followed the first Peloponnesian invasion of Attica (Thuc. 2. 23), perpetrated, according to Hermes, against "totally innocent men" (627): in fact, the god's line of argumentation is not even dented by their interruptions (628–631). Nelson (2016) (225–228) suggests that the panhellenic identity of the chorus is constructed solely as a means to contrast the gods and loses its bearings as soon as Hermes begins to support humanity's plan.

The father of the gods is thus blamed for the situation, both according to the slave's gossip (58), and also, redoubling an already strong stage effect, in an apostrophe by Trygaios himself from inside the house (62–63): this accusation is particularly heretical because it insinuates that Zeus "uproots all the cities before he knows what he's done." Similarly, in Euripides' *Herakles* (347), Amphitryon tries to explain Zeus' disregard for his lineage and family line by offering the dual hypothesis that the god is lacking in justness or intelligence. Trygaios' disgruntlement is further underscored by his intention, should Zeus remain unresponsive to his request, to formally accuse him of medism (107–108), that is, of colluding with the Persian army, a remark that clearly echoes the dynamics of the political struggle in Athens at the time (Olson (1998) 89).

Trygaios is insolent to Zeus (*loidoreitai* 57) in the same way that Dikaiopolis, in the *Acharnians* (38), proposed attacking (*loidorein*) the political adversaries of peace, or anyone who diverted attention from that sole topic worthy of attention, either in bad faith or out of simple-mindedness.

The ethical–political obsession that is one of Trygaios' characteristics ("all day long he looks up at the heavens with his mouth open" 56–57) is the basis upon which his madness is diagnosed (54–55), but while Dikaiopolis operates within the sphere of institutions delegated to resolve problems via political means – but in reality putting those institutions to a final test, and taking their place when they fail it – Trygaios contends with a much broader field, going toe to toe with a god perceived as hostile (Sicking (1967) 119, (1998) 80–81); his madness lies in challenging the gods (as a *theomachos*) and is the same madness that Teiresias attributes to Pentheus in Euripides' *Bacchae* (325). Trygaios' antagonism toward Zeus, summoned up in the first verses (58–59, 62–63; see Sicking (1967) 119), is exemplified along the same lines as that of Prometheus: they share the belief that he is responsible for humanity's evil and the condition of isolation that said disposition brings to bear (on the Promethean paradigm in the design of the character and the development of the comic action, see Morosi's accurate analysis (2013) based on cues from Albini (1971) 24 and Hubbard (1991) 142). As in the *Acharnians*, the protagonist's isolation from the universal condition is resoundingly reversed when the autonomous initiative, the "Great Idea," meets with success and general consensus, proving a posteriori to be the true wisdom, while true madness lies in conformism (on the centrality of creative capacities in defining the role of the protagonist in *archaia* comedy see Given (2009) building on Arrowsmith (1973), Sommerstein (1980) 11–13, Storey and Allan (2014) 174–175, and Grilli's *distinguo* (2022) 95–103).

Through Aristophanes' prodigious inventiveness, the conceptual theme – in this case, the "impious" abolition of the distance between man and god – is literalized: Trygaios undertakes an ascent to the heavens to achieve concrete and direct contact with the divinity. Among the initiatives of Aristophanes' protagonists, this one certainly stands out owing to its brilliant, adventurous nature, although, in my opinion, it is not so different from those of other comedies as to be viewed as the seed of a new literary genre, the romance (as Moulton suggests (1981) 101–106).

An initial attempt has failed, with Trygaios tumbling from a ladder he had had built, but he perseveres doggedly and hits on an efficacious plan to procure the winged beetle. We can glimpse an intertextual relationship with *Bellerophon*, of which just over a hundred verses remain (frr. 285–312 Kn.) along with the remnants of two *argumenta* (iii a–b Kannicht), which must have marked one of the most profoundly important points of heroic unease and solitude ever explored in the world of tragedy (for details on the centrality of the parody, see Rau (1967) 89–97), Dobrov (2001 (89–104), and Mastromarco (2012). This tragedy is also the source of fr. 286 Kn., the most vehement text against traditional religion and theodicy that Greek culture has passed down to us; based on the immoral order of the world in which wrongdoers are "happier than pious men" (fr. 286. 8–9 Kn.), it deduces that "there are no gods in heaven" (fr. 286. 2–3 Kn.) – differing from the common belief labeled as "antiquated discourse" (*palaios logos*) – or that "if the gods do anything senseless (*phaulon*), they are not gods" (fr. 286b. 7 Kn.).

The happiness of wrongdoers is reiterated in Sophocles' *Philoctetes* (446–452) and, transcribed into the comedic register, it forms the social framework that is successfully revolutionized in *Plutus*. In reference to the Aristophanean context, it is important to note that even in the fragment of *Bellerophon*, all the negativity of the world is already concentrated on the political side, denouncing the tyranny that strips men of their possessions and their lives, and the fate of small, pious cities devastated by a superior military power (fr. 286. 5–11 Kn.).

It is evident that precisely and solely the development of an intertextual, paratragic discourse makes comic impiety allowable, conserving, in my view, a meaningful ideological system, that is, a firm conviction regarding the unacceptability of reality. The substitution of a dung beetle for a quintessentially "noble" winged (*gennaios pteros* 76) steed plays on a mythical-literary redetermination that recalls an Aesopian fable (*Fab.* 3 Perry; *Vita Aesopi* 135–139; cf. V. 1446–1449, *Lys.* 694–695, see Schirru (2009) 99–103). In that story, the beetle itself takes a polemical stance toward Zeus and his sacred bird, the eagle (Hall (2013), 294–296; Zogg (2014) 70–84; Mann (2017) on the collision between comic and tragic genres associated with the two animals), but in the play, Trygaios bursts out with an irresistible economistic rationalization when the lack of dignity compared to the model is decried by his daughter, who had advised him to appear before Zeus like an authentically tragic hero astride Pegasus (135–136), and, the veil of parodic mediation having been dropped, warns him at the same time of the risk of becoming fodder for tragic plotlines (Slater (2002) 117–118). The father's response: "But my dear girl, I'd have needed double rations. As it is, whatever food I eat, I can use again to feed this creature" (137–139) seems a mere quip, but in reality it underscores, with a sort of synaptic link, that war above all leads families to experience poverty and hunger (see Xantou (2010) 310), introducing the difficulties that Trygaios mentions in vv. 119–121: "I'm fed up with you when you keep asking me for bread and calling me 'daddy' and there absolutely isn't even a drop of money in the house at all" (see Sommerstein (1985) 140). A similar conflict with children is attributed to the impoverished, elderly judges who constitute the chorus of *Wasps* (248–257, 291–314).

Parody is also commonly found in the remodulation of spaces and movements accompanying the journey from the human world to the divine one (see Mastromarco (2012) 112–117; Morosi (2021) 205–207), which here Trygaios and the beetle comically undertake with great difficulty: due to the beetle's coprophagistic habits, the ascent is contrasted by its opposite trajectory – a backslide in every sense, not least of which stylistically (on the organization of stage movements, see Russo (1994) 137–139). The riskiness of this heroic undertaking (*tolmēma neon* 94) is trivialized, as Trygaios defends himself against it with a grotesque appeal, addressed to the audience but also to Athenians as a whole, to avoid any bodily evacuations for three days – a command that seems on the verge of being flouted several times during the course of his brief journey, provoking funerial outcries and threats of retaliation from the protagonist (164–172). Trygaios' apostrophe addressed to the stagehand during his "flight" ("if you don't take care, I'll be giving the beetle a meal!" 174–176) confirms a metatheatrical significance, the subject of a detailed study by Slater (2002) 117–118; but see also Mastromarco (2012) 115–116).

Upon arrival, Trygaios immediately recognizes "the house of Zeus" (178) (on the lack of spatial references to represent the new scenario, see Morosi (2021) 207). He is greeted, or rather challenged by Hermes with a hostility (182–184) similar to that with which Aeacus, the doorkeeper of Hades, in *Frogs* 465–466 apostrophizes Dionysus disguised as Heracles, but there the harangue refers to Heracles' prior misdeeds in Hades, while in *Peace*, the transgression of which the visitor is accused is simply being mortal (on the general use of knocking on the door as a signal for the passage from one plane of reality to another, see Brown (2008)). But the dialog takes an unexpected turn, as Trygaios assumes the dominant role, refusing to tell Hermes his name and replacing it with the same insult that the god has aimed at him (*miarotatos*), making it a banner of cockiness (183–188): a repetitive comic gag, but also an expression of awareness and faith in his purpose.

When Hermes formulates the specific question regarding the reason for his visit, it is clear that his role, here seen above all as the god of commercial transactions (cf. *Ach.* 742–743, 816; Bowie (1993, 138–142) but also as a mediator on the vertical axis between gods and men (Auger (1997), is not to stand in for Zeus in a discussion on the fundamental problems of humanity. Trygaios declares that he has come "to bring you this meat" (192): he limits himself to dismissing the residual hostility by making recourse to common corruption, in a burlesque variation on sacrificial homage and more generally the *do- ut-des* that governs Greek religion (cf. also 378–379, 385–389, 390–399, 417–423; Olson (1998) 106; Pulleyn (1997) 16–18). And one cannot fail to mordantly note how the divine interlocutor immediately changes his tune.

But the expected confrontation that is the real motive for the journey is thwarted, because Zeus and the other gods have abandoned their headquarters: only Hermes has stayed behind, and solely to serve the needs of their "relocation." This news brings about a radical shift on the comic plane. First and foremost, the scenario of the presumed theomachy falls apart. In fact, it seems that between Trygaios and Zeus there is no difference of opinion concerning the war, because the reason the gods have withdrawn to somewhere else, as high up as possible (207), is, precisely, their anger (204) at the Greeks' obstinacy in refusing reciprocal peace proposals: whichever of the two sides accidentally found itself in a position of superiority persisted in exploiting it to the extreme (211–219). The protagonist's error in judgment is, however, redressed, unlike in the tragic model, by his reactivity to the new situation (Dobrov (2001) 100): Trygaios in fact readily acknowledges the reliability of Hermes' account, explicitly assuming collective responsibility (220).

But the agreement on this point between god and man is still far from producing the salvific renewal of peace for which the protagonist set out on his journey: while not responsible for, and in fact averse to the war, Zeus himself does not have the power to stop it, but only to punish men, not by quashing their vices but by giving them over to their vices. The disappearance of the Olympians, which recalls that of Aidōs and Nemesis in Hesiod's *Erga* (197–200), orients the comic action to the specific message that if men are responsible for war, then it is men who must – quite literally, given that she proves to be a statue – make peace (Nelson (2016) 220, 223).

In a process typical of Aristophanean language, with a shift from the abstract to the concrete, a value-based choice is made through concrete, physical deeds, so the gods have installed (katōikisan) "where they used to live" (205) Polemos, who is by no means a member of their community, but rather, with a metaphor translated into a theatrical character, the personification of war (Newiger (1957) 112–120), and of the Greek poleis' desire for destructive and self-destructive power (Paduano 2002, 43).

The cruel culinary preparations carried out by Polemos, the horrid kōmastēs ("fellow roisterer") in *Ach.* 977–985, here accompanied by his attendant Kydoimos, are part of the arrangements for a perverse feast – according to Moulton (1981) 85–92, a preview by antiphrasis of the one that will be celebrated in honor of peace – which are suddenly hampered by the unavailability of the "pestles" Cleōn and Brasidas. No connoisseur of Aristophanes would be surprised at the gleeful cynicism with which the death of the two military men is instrumentalized, nor at the lack of qualms about placing them on the same level.

At this point, at the moment when the action takes an unexpected turn, Trygaios convokes – or rather evokes, as if by magic – the chorus, and the orchestra is filled with Greek men (292), who are then called on by social and geographical category, with particular attention to those most damaged by the war ("peasants and merchants and carpenters and craftsmen and immigrants and foreigner and islanders, come hither all ye people, as quickly as you can, bringing shovels and crowbars and ropes," 296–299).

The paradox by which the same risk-filled space reachable only through a heroic undertaking now becomes accessible to the multitude of the chorus is the stage corollary of a shift of tasks and responsibilities. The transformation seems in perfect symmetry with what happened in the *Acharnians*: there, the failure of civic existence experienced by Dikaiopolis through his participation in the assembly led to the idiosyncratic choice of a separate peace; here, the unrealizability of an individual dialog with the divine interlocutor gives rise to a unified community all working toward the same objective.

The solidarity between the chorus and the protagonist arises surprisingly, after Trygaios has been accused of madness by his own household; with regard to the chorus, he seems to have an intellectual superiority comparable to the influence Lysistrata brings to bear on other women, first overcoming their reluctance to participate in the sexual strike, and then quashing their attempts to defect. Similarly, Trygaios successfully contains the chorus' premature and boisterous expressions of joy, which risk drawing Polemos' attention (309–345), and also manages to channel their wild vitality into an effective, coordinated effort (299, 361).

But just as the work is beginning, another encounter with the divine, or another glitch, occurs. The action seems to get underway only to retreat back on itself, because the allocution with which Hermes, returning to the scene, accosts the protagonist is once again *miare* (362), the *Stichwort* on which the earlier comical wordplay had lingered. But Hermes' explicit obligation to report (380–381) is quickly dealt with when the request is converted into a bribe and the symbolic gesture of offering the god a libation bowl is promptly translated into a venal enticement to which the god is not immune (424–425).

In this case, Hermes, as in Aeschylus' *Prometheus*, assumes the official function of mouthpiece for Zeus' threats and prohibitions, a schema that is repeated in the finale of *Plutus* when Hermes arrives at Chremylus' house (1112–1116), and is also in part comparable to the magniloquent injunction issued by Iris, sent as a mediator for the gods in *Av.* 1230–1233, 1238–1242, although the end result common to all of these situations is that the intervention has no effect.

Zeus' prohibition against disinterring Peace is not easy to explain; certainly, Zeus has not become a supporter of war or is he an alter-ego of Polemos – as Olson suggests (1998, 148), reprising a misinterpretation that had already circulated in antiquity, as evidenced by *schol.* 236c **V** (42 Holwerda). Rather than a confirmation of divine punitive intent (62–63) manifested in the convergence of the representation of Polemos and Cleōn, who is dead but not yet innocuous (319–320; see Slater (2002) 281 n. 24), what seems to be at work here is a dramaturgical function that ensures the comic hero's undertaking will have the context of obstacles and tensions necessary to lend it the nature of event, unavoidably countering or at least differentiated from the principle of reality. Disobedience to Zeus is the realization of the unprecedented venture (*tolmēna neon* 94) that in the previous scene had allowed Trygaios an unimaginable, albeit temporary, control over divine space.

The repetition of Hermes' aggression might lead us to suspect that it is destined to peter out as it had before, but this time the god's venality goes much further. When Trygaios reminds him of the earlier offer (378–379), Hermes counters with his obligation to report everything to Zeus, leading to an upping of the offer to excessive levels. First, the generic promise of "sacrifices and great processions" (396–399), which brings to mind the mediation role and honors proffered in Aeschylus' *Eumenides*, in that case a negotiation between Athena and the divine Erinyes (*Eum.* 867–921). Then, in an apparently hyperbolic addendum that in fact reveals the real issue at stake, Trygaios offers to dedicate to Hermes the entire religious calendar, including Panathēnaia, Dipolia, and Adōnia (416–422). But what convinces the god in the end is not a future scenario, but Trygaios' concrete, physical, immediate gesture (prōton, 423) of offering him a golden bowl; it is for this that Hermes reserves, in *aprosdoketon*, his "compassion" (*eleēmōn*, 425).

At this point, Trygaios, addressing the chorus, pronounces the phrase that concludes what we might call the supernatural dispute and marks the definitive shift of the peace question into the human sphere: "Now then, men, it's over to you" (*hymeteron enteuthen ergon*, 426).

The very human nature of the undertaking is not diminished by the fact that Hermes assumes the role of consultant or even director of the exhumation effort (428–516) and perhaps also of divine protector of thieves (401–402; *Eq.* 297, see Whitman (1964) 115), and later takes on the didactic function of recounting the reasons for Peace's disappearance from the Greek world (603–648). Hermes does these things because he is "the most friendly to men and the most generous" of gods (*philanthrōpotate kai megalodōrotate*, 392–394), "the most benign" (*eunoustate*, 602), from a strictly human point of view, although once this part of the action is concluded, he remains in the heavens, after bidding Trygaios adieu with fervent solidarity (718–719).

The divine world, which through self-exile had emphasized its absence and the impotence of Zeus' threats against those who worked for peace, is now revealed to be effectual only via Hermes as an aid to the protagonist as he prepares to resolve the impasse in another conflict, now on the strictly human front (Cassio (1985) 54–56; Olson (1998) XXXIX–XLII; Jay-Robert (2002) 16–19; Given (2009) 110 and 114–117). In *Plutus*, where Zeus is rightly blamed as the cause of human unhappiness, after Plutus' recovery has put the world to rights, Hermes passes effortlessly to the human side, transforming himself into an overeager petitioner for a new occupation.

In *Peace*, the conflict is more limited in scope and milder than in *Birds* or *Plutus*, in which Zeus is divested of his power: here, there is no doubt that Zeus will return to his realm, if he has not done so already, as would seem to be suggested by the paratragic hint, again from *Bellerophon*, on the fate of the beetle which "yoked to the car of Zeus, bears lighting" (722 = fr. 312 K.-A.).

Upon emerging from the cave, Peace is enigmatic and mute: her obstinate silence, interpreted as a sign of animosity toward men, now identified with the spectators (657–659), is mediated by the words of Hermes himself, who serves as interpreter (661–667, 670, 679; see Auger (1997) 162–165). The other two divine figures, who accompany Peace, Opōra, and Theōria (523), are also mute (*kōpha prosōpa*): like the Spondai ("Peace terms") in *Eq.* 1389–1391, Diallagē ("Truce") in *Lys.* 1114–1188, and Basileia in *Birds*, they are represented onstage as real women, considered beneficial for the pleasant fragrances they emanate (523–538), and objects of vitalistic sexual interest as well (868–908, see Stafford (2000) 34–35; Sulprizio (2013). Peace, on the other hand, whose divine status is emphasized repeatedly (315, 520, 560, 657), was likely represented onstage as a statue, perhaps on a grand scale, a theatrical expedient that was the object of parodies by Eupolis (fr. 62 K.-A.) and Plato (fr. 86 K.-A.), according to *Schol. Plato Apology* 19 c (421 Greene). She has a central function in the rest of the play, because after her descent to earth, with the establishment of her cult (hidrysis) and her permanent placement on the *ekkyklēma* at the central door (Dover (1972) 135), she remains the guarantor of the peace between gods and men, between the space of the gods and the space of mortals (Morosi (2021) 215). We know of no other cases in which the personification of peace could appear on stage, except perhaps the dubious case of Aesch. 451n *TGrF*, and it is very difficult to establish whether the cult of Peace was already present in Athens at the time (Stafford (2000) 173–177; Smith (2011) 77–79); for a discussion on the mythical and religious dimension of *Peace*, see Olson (1998) xxxv–xxxviii and Parker (1996) 229–230.

Cooperation between a mortal and an isolated, philanthropic god is thus the real turning point of the play: the liberation of Peace, which guarantees peace on earth, is made possible solely by the temporary mediation of a conflict between men and gods, which paradoxically arises from a shared disgust with regard to war, and represents the autonomy that human action achieves or is forced to achieve.

Politicians and Farmers, or, War Versus Peace

Peace is marked by another contradiction: despite the insertion into a fantastical space, there is no other Aristophanes play that is closer to reality, to the point that it celebrates a sort of conciliation with it (McGlew (2001) 88). The peace that is so impossible in *Acharnians*, so incompatible with the Ecclēsia (26–27, 39), was, in the 421 City Dionysia, a certainty about to be formalized. The historical framework – which in any case does not constitute a limitation on the poet's creative imagination (Moulton (1981) 82–83) – not only makes the depiction of a united panhellenic community plausible but also brings harmony and a conciliatory element to the ongoing relationship between author and audience, as declared in the parabasis (Paduano (2002) 18–22). In the framework of *Acharnians*, however, the poet's intellectual and social mission was entirely polemical, and consisted of presenting the "right things," exposing the truth – even through reproach – to the public, which he presumed would greatly benefit from it (655). The commitment to defending justice and heroism that the dramaturg illustrated particularly in the struggle against the demagogue Cleōn is proposed again in the parabases of *Knights*, *Wasps*, and *Peace* (Hubbard (1991) 146–150), but in the latter is limited to an animated self-elegy, with none of the accusations of betrayal or ingratitude on the part of the audience found in *Clouds* (cf. *V.* 1044–1045; *Nu.* 533).

But while the climate is oriented toward harmony and unanimous volition, the carrying out of the great community effort takes on a dramatic structure precisely because it is thrown into confusion by a series of upsets, dissatisfactions, and contestations that testify to and unforgivingly point a finger at particularism (496, 499). The alternation between praise and blame for the undisciplined contingent led by Trygaios is the subject of an interesting comparison by McGlew (2001) 84–87 with Agamemnon's role in the Homeric review of troops (*epipolēsis*) during the crisis of the Greek coalition in *Iliad* 4. But Homer's poem deals with a unity that risks being torn apart, while here we have one in the process of formation despite numerous difficulties, and the development of a new leadership that is not only individual but also class-based.

This is the paradoxical outcome of the process by which the rose of communities seems to inexorably drop its petals one by one: first Thebes, the indomitable enemy of Athens (466); then not just Athens, but the Athenian faction of the war, embodied by the antagonist of *Acharnians*, Lamachos (473); then Argos, the neutrality of which with regard to the other factions is labeled as ambiguous and opportunistic (491–493); then Sparta, divided over the defense of the Pylos prisoners (479–480); then Megara, exasperated by the consequences of the Athenian embargo (481–482). The significance of this diaspora lies in the implicit caveat that unanimously wishing for the end of the horrors and hardships of war is not enough to actually *have* peace; there must also be an open inclination toward concord and integration in order for the panhellenism prematurely vaunted by Trygaios (93) to become a reality. All of these defections and obstacles to cohesion lend the chorus a changeable identity, which is one of the play's thorniest problems (for different approaches to this, see Sifakis (1971) 29–32; Dover (1972) 137–139; Hubbard (1991) 241–242; Sommerstein (1985) xviii–xix; Cassio (1985) 75–77; Zumbrunnen (2012) 35–36, and above all McGlew (2001)).

While when it first enters the scene, the chorus in fact represents not only all Greeks (292, 302) but also all of the categories and professions that Trygaios calls upon with an appeal to the audience itself (244, 263, 276, 286), in the end, those who are "craving for peace" (497–498) are clearly identified based on profession and class, and not nationality: they are the farmers alone (508). This is presented as a given and accepted by Hermes as such (511), but it is principally an axiological assertion, most loftily expressed in the invocation of a "day long yearned for by peasants and honest men" (556), a clear hendiadys that overlaps the two categories. The dramaturgical innovation of the new identity taken on by the chorus, which must not have corresponded to a visual re-identification in the staging, seems consonant with the idea that peace requires a re-definition of the political body, or, even more radically, of the citizens of all the cities in conflict (McGlew (2001) 82).

In fact, there is an affinity between peace and agriculture in terms of semantic and symbolic fields, which is evidenced in an invocation to Eirene in *Geōrgoi* (fr. 111 K.-A.) and in *Peace Second* (on which see Kassel–Austin (1984) 170–173; Olson (1998) xlviii–li) in fr. 305 K-A, a dialog where Geōrgia, the personification of agriculture, declares herself "trusty nurse, housekeeper, fellow-worker, guardian, daughter and sister of Peace, friend of all mankind" (Stafford (2000) 187–188).

Thus, it is clear that Hermes intends to explain Peace's long absence to the farmers, in particular, in a speech that outlines a brief political–moral history of the conflict (605–648; see Cassio (1985) 87–95), with a didactic function that makes it comparable to a parabasis epirrhemes (see Cassio (1985), 84–85; Gelzer (1960) 104, 152–153). Before extending his address to all the Athenians in the audience (619, 607, 641, 647, cf. 642), the god calls on them (*ō sophōtatoi geōrgoi, ō sophōtatoi geōrgoi* 603) – as the ideological counterpart to those responsible for the war, whose horizon is strictly limited to the sphere of human motivations (Zumbrunnen (2012), 24–25) – and sets up the entire situation as a phenomenology of political praxis. In fact, to give Peace a proper reception, there must be a reckoning, a conscious memory of the transgressions and errors of the recent past. Here, the orientation is the same as in *Acharnians* and was confirmed by Aristophanes on other occasions as well – that is, one of absolute condemnation of the speciousness and mystification that constitute the very fabric of the political system and especially of the omnipresent private interests that epitomize the abuse of power.

And as in *Acharnians* (523–539), the underlying cause of the war is laid at the door of the figure most representative of the system itself, Pericles, whose megalomania is also highlighted in *Ach.* 530 by the ironic epithet "olympian" and the Megarian embargo. In particular, the specious pretext – that is, the reciprocal kidnapping of women by Megarians and Athenians (524–529) – suggests a parody of the political use of the traditional myth of the origins of hostilities between Europe and Asia, discussed in the Herodotean proem (1. 1–5, 2) (Pelling (2000) 151–154; Olson (2002) LIII; Kanavou (2011b) 385–387). In Hermes' speech, that conflict, which Thucydides considered the most massive ever produced (1. 1.2), was nothing but a gigantic diversionary maneuver by Pericles aimed at evading a showdown in the polis regarding his power, which had begun to show the first threatening cracks in the lawsuit brought against his friend Pheidias for embezzling (605; Filoch. *FGrH* 328 F 21 *ap.* Schol. *ad* 605 (95–96 Holwerda); Ephor. *FGrH* 70 F 196; see Cassio (1985) 87–88). Pericles, fearing that he would be dragged into it and aware of the natural aggressivity of Athenians (606–607), was said to have devastated the city with the Megarian decree. This then triggered an equally oversized chain reaction, which transcended individual volition in a fatal, sinister automatism described through the burning of a vineyard and the destruction of wine jars (612–613), a sort of "a collapse of Dionysiac" (Olson (1998) 198).

The story – implausible, as the interlocutors themselves as good as acknowledge (615–617) – epitomizes the essential irrationality of war, which Trygaios does not fail to stigmatize with paradoxical irony, responding to a successive objection from the oracle monger Hierocles, and instead asserting a policy of friendly dealings as the objective: "But what *should* we have done? Never stopped waging war? Or cast lots for which of us should be made to howl the louder, when we had the chance to make peace and rule Greece together?" (1080–1082).

After brief comments by Trygaios and the chorus, Hermes' account of the prelude to war shifts to the enemy camp: the allied cities, fearing an increase in the tribute they would have to pay for war expenses, tried to bribe the profit-greedy Laconians (622), who then sparked the war, which proved lethal to the guiltless Spartan peasants (625–627), probably the Perioeci considered with particular empathy from an Attic-centric perspective (so suggests Cassio (1985) 98–99).

The guiding purpose of every move on the international chessboard in a game of actions and reactions continues to be the private interests of the ruling classes – of Sparta and the allied cities – who are presumed to be implicitly accustomed to the language of bribery and corruption. The distinction is called for in relation to the brachylogical language of the text; Aristophanes intends something quite different when he uses the term "city" to indicate the populace, the free society of the Greek world liberated from the brutality and misery of war and equated, via anthropomorphism, to friendly relations between private individuals: "look now and see how all the states have been reconciled, how they're talking to one another and laughing in gladness" (538–540). Although in his chronicle Hermes underscores how the distortions of the Athenian political system stirred up the rebellion of the allied cities, another critical political question remains in the shadows – that of the legitimacy of Athenian dominion over its allies/subjects (Cassio (1985) 105–118; McGlew (2001) 80 n. 12).

And then the pendulum of Hermes' discourse swings again to Athens and to the successive phase of war, with the forced urbanization of Attic farmers following the Peloponnesian invasions: in the same way, the gullible masses, vulnerable to deceit (633) find themselves "sold out" (pōloumenos, 633), subjected to a perverse strategic use of the economic factor. On the one hand, the demagogues instrumentalized the farmers' penury to coerce them (632–635) – a phenomenon previously described in *V.* 703–705 – and on the other, persecuted the richest of the allies to squeeze them as well (*Eq.* 326–327; *V.* 288–289; Ps. Xen. *Ath. resp.* 1, 16), finding them easy prey, and in fact they responded to these extortionary tactics with groveling bribes (639–647): a *modus operandi* ascribed, as in *Knights*, to Cleōn, here demonized even though dead (647–648).

Much later, in the second parabasis (1127–1190), where the chorus consists mainly of Athenian farmers, a new burning question involves another abuse of power perpetrated on farmers by the dominant class, in this case the taxiarchs, who are in charge of enlistment rolls and are accused of executing their function arbitrarily (cf. *Eq.* 1369–1371): "they do intolerable things: they enter some of our names on the lists and erase others, higgledy-piggledy, two or three times" (1179–1181). The manipulation traps the victims in their unsophisticated ingenuousness, to the point that some of them, unexpectedly finding their names on the enlistment roll, appeal to one of the basic guarantees of the democratic order, the formal audit (*euthynai*) of officials at the end of their terms (1182–1187). But the institutional deferment of such proceedings reduces this prospect to an ineffectual threat, and the sensation of generalized injustice prevails (1188).

The primary victims of this state of things, the peasants, are also the only social group capable of remedying the situation, exhuming, along with peace, the world that preceded the disruption, colored by political idealizations and nostalgia (566–579; cf. *Ach.* 201–202, *Eq.* 805–807, frr. 109, 111 and 112 K.-A. of the *Geōrgoi* likely staged in 424; see Hanson (1995) 216; Smith (2011) 78–79; Saïd (2000), 195–200; Ceccarelli (2020), the utopian and abstract traits of which were perhaps overemphasized by Sicking (1967) 123–124, (1998) 83–84).

The restoration is based on a process of strict consequentiality, clearly conveyed in the urgency with which Trygaios, no more than 30 verses after the appearance of Peace, asks Hermes to send the peasants home (550). The invitation to pick up their tools and go back to their work in the fields is immediately translated into a proclamation (551–555) which initially has the allure of the official decree "Hear ye, o people!" (*akouete leōi* 551; cf. *Ach.* 1000, *Av.* 448).

The real execution on the part of the chorus will coincide with the comic finale and the hierogamy with Opōra (1320), in which the call to return to the fields (1329–1331) addressed to the bride replaces her ritual entrance into the house.

If, as Dikaiopolis asserts (*Ach.* 596), in wartime every citizen becomes a soldier (*stratōnidēs*), then the end of war would mean a return to usual activities, as was hoped for in *Eq.* 805 "if he (Demos), ever goes off to the country again and lives in peace (*eirēnaios*)": on ideological links between urban and agrarian spheres, see Compton Engle (1999). But in *Peace*, this transition is tinged with incredibly fervid pathos in the reciprocal reunion of man and the environment, in a sort of personal, almost carnal dialog with nature, of an intensity not seen even at the apex of bucolic poetry, as compared by Moulton (1981), 93–101: for example, in vv. 557–559 "I wish to greet my vines, and it is my eager desire, after a long, long time, to re-salute the fig trees that I planted as a young man," a recurrent symbolic association with peacetime (575–576, 596–597, 634, 1323–1324; cf. *Ach.* 995–996, *Av.* 588–590). The idyl is also reproduced in the parabasis with references to the song of the cicada, the quintessence of summertime, and to ripe fruit which, almost by sympathetic transmission, becomes plump like the body of a man finally delivered from the hunger he suffered during the war (1159–1171).

The symbolization of pleasure through the imagination of agricultural products, re-semanticized in terms drawn from erotic poetry, like pothos (yearning) and its derivatives (556, 579, 583, 587), leads to the boldest construction, the *hieros gamos* of Trygaios and Opōra. This is sanctioned in the official terms of the marriage bargain (706–707; cf. Men. *Perik.* 1013–1014, *Dysk.* 842–843, *Sam.* 726–727) by Hermes, substituting for the father or *kyrios* of the bride, with a solemn promise addressed to Peace by Trygaios in the name of the community to never let her go again (705). But the bureaucratic regularity, sanctioned by the actual and above all symbolic location of the event (en tois agrois / *tautēi xunoikōn*), is overcome by the mythopoetic language, which introduces a paradoxical coherence capable of reifying the symbol conveyed by the signifier, specifically of the names of the bride and groom: "produce grapes for yourself" (708) is the unexpected closing in place of a ritual formula like "to plow legitimate children" (*gnēsiōn / paidōn ep'arotōi*), testified to in the cited passages from Menander, which is in turn an agricultural metaphor (Olson (1998) 212).

But the symbolic dimension does not expunge the personal relationship, unlike in another Aristophanean hierogamy, the wedding of the protagonist of *Birds* to Basileia, the female personage Prometheus mentions in his counsel. She embodies the power of Zeus with her variegated spectrum of abilities and is fully identified with that power, in addition to receiving the only ritual title in praise of femininity (*kallistē korē* 1537).

Here, however, Trygaios' reception and courting of his bride bely a passionate impulse ("Come here, darling, and give us a kiss" 709), barely dimmed by a preoccupation with his own sexual efficacy "after such a long interval" (710), which sketches out the generative idea of *Lysistrata*, that is, that war is so incompatible with love and sex that it leads to dishabituation. But upon returning to earth, the chorus notes that Trygaios will benefit from a magical rejuvenation, more like that of Demos in the *Knights* than Philocleōn's paradoxical tendency in the *Wasps*: "you will be enviable, an old man turned young once again, anointed with perfume" (860–862), encouraging his salacious vitality (863). The metaphorical projection of complete happiness – including sexual satisfaction – brought about by peace in a synesthetic fusion that touches on all the senses (see also *Ach*. 198, 263–265, 277–278; Edmunds (1980) 6, 20; Ruffell (2017) 49–53) culminates, as in *Birds*, with the choral hymenea of the *exodos* clinched by ritual allusions to the sex act (1351–1352), which include the verb *trygaō* (1339–1340), dually referring to agricultural work and the protagonist's name (Taplin (1983) 333; Hall (2006) 329; Kanavou (2011a) 99).

Another object of desire is Theōria, but this is a question of sexuality in general and not within a relationship, an expression of the collective (and self-reflexive) ritual dimension it exemplifies (Sulprizio (2013) 57–59; Voelke (2014) 144–150): given its public dimension – the term also refers to official missions within the sphere of panhellenic agones – her return to the Boulē, the council representing the citizenry to which she once belonged (713–717), is accompanied by metaphorical language related to feasts, sacrifices, and sports competitions, events that delegations attended (Cassio (1985) 122–126), culminating in a series of *double entendres* set in motion by erotic sports metaphors (894–904; see Campagner (1998) and García Romero (1995) 67–76). Probably delivering her to the prytanis sitting in the *proedria*, a defined area, front and center in the audience, Trygaios metatheatrically unites the dramatic space with that of the real Athens (Slater (2002) 127–128).

The Social Divide

We have seen how Trygaios' mad and heroic individualism, oriented toward ensuring the collective well-being of the Greeks, and not just his own (as in *Acharnians*), evolves into a collective effort for the same purpose (see, in particular, Newiger (1975) 184, (1980), 227; Thiercy (1986), 207–215; McGlew (2001), 93–95). The course of his undertaking is akin to that of *Lysistrata*, although in *Peace* it is produced in abrupt and surprising terms, compared with the linearity of the later play, where the conception of the sexual strike is individual, but its realization must necessarily be collective in order to be effective.

The action in *Peace* also presents us with a further distinction between collective and universal, as compared with *Lysistrata*, where the agreement reached between Athenians and Spartans structurally entails harmony both in the political sphere, between the two cities, and in the private sphere with the return of familial happiness from which no one is excluded.

In the second part of *Peace*, the chorus having vanished into the dramatic background, the scene focuses once again on the house and on dealing with the success that has been gained. The mechanism by which Trygaios exercises his power is based on inclusion or exclusion from the well-being that he has symbolically attained, represented here by participation in the feast for his wedding to

Opōra (1040–1312). Once again, the focal point is the liminal threshold of the door (942, 1023), through which various supplicants may or may not pass based on a criterion he has established: their position in favor of or against the war. This sets off a series of scenes that have often been wrongly interpreted as episodic or extemporaneous moments of respite in the comic action; on the contrary, they serve two fundamental purposes. The first, an ideological aim, is to establish the thesis that by marginalizing social groups who hold incongruous – or worse, contrary – values and interests to those of the community, society does not create division, but true unity; however, it should be noted that incongruousness and opposition are always argued out, so this is not a ritualistic "scapegoating" mechanism. The second function, which is wholly dramaturgical, is to fully focus on a strategy of dialectic dynamics between the self and the other, which is a common theme in Aristophanes' plays. The protagonist's attainment of well-being entails not only privileged access to the most basic pleasures, food, and sex (see most recently Grilli (2022) 239–243) but also an understanding of his power in terms of aggressive impulses that associate pleasure with violence perpetrated against others. This is often physical, sometimes gratuitous violence that does not serve any purpose, as in the case of Philocleōn in the *Wasps* (1322–1323) who, leaving the banquet, hits everyone he comes across (Riess (2012), 291–295). But in other cases it is a violence carried out through the mechanism of exclusion of the other – the antagonist or an entire community – from the exclusive enjoyment of benefits acquired.

The extreme case is in *Acharnians* where the protagonist excludes *all* of his fellow citizens from the achieved peace, including the chorus which had shifted from an initial opposition to a position of supportive, but necessarily *not* participatory, admiration (see Morosi (2021) 69–71). Conversely, the dramaturgical mechanism in *Plutus* focuses on the public prosecutor, the sycophant, the only person excluded from the well-being brought about by the healing of Plutus' blindness: the singularity is significant because it contradicts the principle that since men are only dishonest to make themselves wealthy, if wealth is given to the honest, then everyone will be honest and consequently rich (494–497). This position is not without a pinch of sinister grandeur on his part, an impenitent unwillingness to give up his perverse political activism (850–958).

But *Birds* is the play that is, at least from the quantitative point of view, by far the most enmeshed in this spatial semantics. As critics and scholars have shown, the part dedicated to the seekers who aspire to enter the new city has a length and a dramaturgical function not found in any other surviving comedies. It follows a rapid, two-track sequence through a dual series of refusals: the first concerns intrusions into the sacrificial celebration of the birth of the new city, and the second a request for the wings necessary to effectively become one of its citizens (903–1057 and 1337–1469).

Of the initial seekers, only the first, an encomiastic poet who boasts of having celebrated the newborn Cloud-Cuckoo-Land "from way back," has his requests for a coat and a cloak reluctantly met, simply to be rid of him (931–932, 940). An oracle monger on the founding of the new city, the scientist/city planner Meton, an inspector dispatched to check on the correctness of the city's colonial procedures, and finally a decree-seller peddling legislation to govern international relations are all sent packing. The second series of seekers – a parricide, the dithyrambographer Cynesias and a sycophant – also meet with unremitting refusal. In general terms, what is rejected is a linear attempt by old society (Athenian or generically human) to impose its model on the new city; the bittersweet treatment reserved for the poet is owing to the irrelevance attributed to his social function.

There are two scenes in *Peace* that establish the exclusion of two categories that had been favored by the state of war: arms dealers, and oracle mongers, who had increased their prestige, thanks to the proliferation of responses attested to by Thucydides 2. 8. 2. One of them, going by the speaking name Hierocles, turns up at the ritual sacrifice carried out to establish the cult of a divinity (*hidrysis*) with Trygaios officiating in honor of Peace, now installed (923) on stage (Cassio (1985) 126–128; Slater (2002) 125–126). A servant mistakes him for a mere scrounger who has come "drawn by the aroma of sacrifice" (1050; cf. *Av.* 983). But Trygaios has a clearer picture of the situation, suspecting that the intruder wants to object to the peace (1049), and his diffidence is immediately confirmed by the man's vehement harangue revealing a point of view incompatible with what the return of Peace has generated. Rather than panhellenic solidarity, Hierocles maintains an obtusely partisan position, addressing the Athenians and accusing them of having made an imprudent deal with an untrustworthy enemy, the Spartans, who he compares, without naming them, to monkeys (1065), and more explicitly to deceitful foxes (1067–1068), a high-handed cliché that also recurs in *Ach.* 308

and *Lys.* 629 (cf. Hdt. 9. 54.1; Thuc. 5. 105. 3–4; Eur. *Andr.* 445–452; *Suppl.* 187). This argument that peace was "premature" must have been infuriating for those who had experienced the war as interminable suffering periodically marked by failed attempts to end it, as Hermes suggested (211–219). Moreover, the unnatural formulation he uses ("for this is not yet pleasing to the blessed gods, / to cease from warfare, 'til a wolf shall wed a sheep'," 1075–1076) has the air of a mocking postponement ad infinitum, a reflection not of a temporal determination but of an *adynaton*; in fact, Trygaios reveals it as such in his snappish retort ("And how, curse you, could a wolf ever wed a sheep?", 1076a), and only digs the hole deeper with two successive recombinations of proverbial sayings of the same rhetorical type, also based on animal symbolism (1083 and 1086). Hierocles also reiterates the "too soon" topos by confusingly applying the Greek "hasty bitch" proverb to a goldfinch (1078; cf. Aes. 223 Perry; Arch. fr. 196a 39–40). Rather than a textual error (on which see Borthwick (1968), and Olson (1998) 276), this incongruence should be ascribed to an aggressive and mocking treatment of the character, as indicated in *Schol. ad* 1077 (157 Holwerda).

The impression is that the recourse to the theme of premature timing is an antiquated pretext, familiar to oppositionists of every era and for any measure they deem impossible or inopportune to contest based on content. But the consideration of timing is more malicious in relation to the professional figure of the oracle monger, whose attribute is precisely to know in advance what has not yet happened. In fact, whenever something happens of which the seer was not previously aware, his competence and social function are called into question, and the monopoly attributed to him on important questions that interest the entire community is threatened. Here, Aristophanes is using a brilliant defensive strategy that consists of switching the roles, maintaining that the fault is not that of the prophet, but of reality itself: that is, it is not that his foreknowledge is delayed, but rather that the unexpected event is incongruously early in relation to a necessity identified as what "is pleasing to the blessed gods" (1075) – an assertive and authoritative logical short circuit.

This is the only possible response to the obvious accusation of *post-eventum* prophesying, as Trygaios does not fail to note (1085). Similarly, in *Birds* (964–965) Pisthetaerus asks the oracle peddler why he had not foretold the founding of the city before (964–965) and is told that a god had impeded him from doing so.

It is precisely Hierocles' uselessness, which reduces his self-importance to nothing more than a scam (1087), that leads to his expulsion. Trygaios initially expresses his disdain by pretending not to see him as he busies himself with preparations for the sacrifice (1051, cf. the analogous expedient used for the opposite purpose of including Heracles in *Av.* 1579 ss.); in the end, the formal rejection of his attempt to meddle in the sacrificial ritual (1058, 1060) comes as a pastiche of Homeric expressions (1090–1094), twisted from oracular response into contextual invective against the interlocutor (1094; see Zogg (2014) 135–144). In response to the mention of the famous Sibylla (1095), in a parodic, triple-coded discourse (comedy, epic, oracles) facilitated by the continuity of the meter, Trygaios offers, as a far more authoritative oracular source, another Homeric citation: the words with which Nestor sought to stimulate the reconciliation between Agamemnon and Achilles: "No clan, no right to justice, no hearth does that man have who lusts after the horrors of intestine war" (1097–1098 = *Il.* IX 63–64). In terms of literary connotations, we can note that the model and the citation together generate an ideological stretch regarding a situation that is not completely congruous in either case; in fact, defining the Peloponnesian war a "civil war" (*polemou* [. . .] *epidēmiou*) is just as inappropriate as defining the division that arose within the Greek coalition at the walls of Troy as such (see Ruffell (2011) 329; differently interpreted by Olson (1998) 279). But, just as Nestor plays every card to restore the disrupted order, so Aristophanes implicitly, but no less intensely, testifies to panhellenic brotherhood (Paduano (2002) 34).

After the exclusion of a useless individual, a climax points toward that of a harmful entity, namely the arms merchants who profited from the state of war. Earlier, in the initial phase of the liberation of Peace, after the ritual libation, Trygaios had denounced such economic motives, and was seconded by a deprecatory formula from the chorus (447–449). In that situation, he was referring to another category of public enemy: soldiers eager to advance their careers (444) to attain the status of stratēgoi (450). Subverting the values and codes of war (1229, 1264), through the success of Trygaios' undertaking Aristophanes reintroduces one of his favorite polemics, identifying profit as the decisive driver of social action: consider, for example, the question asked by the proboulos in an admixture of malice and diversionary ingenuousness in *Lys.* 489: "so we're at war on account of the money?"

The attack on the arms dealers, clarifying the dialectic between politics and economics interests, completes Hermes' analysis of the causes of the war, tracing – in Marxist terms – the superstructure back to the structure; in other words, these men are dangerous especially because they are the true fathers of war, and not just its privileged sons.

In vv. 545 ff., Hermes and Trygaios were complicit in imagining the helmet-maker tearing his hear out over the nose dive his market takes, damage exacerbated by the mockery of makers of agricultural tools, like hoes and scythes. The scenario they imagine becomes an onstage reality after the second parabasis, when the protagonist in first person (and most likely the poet along with him) takes charge of the derision. After the chorus enthusiastically celebrates the benefits of peace in the second parabasis, Trygaios re-enters the scene and gives the servant orders concerning the preparation of the banquet. On the heels of a scythe merchant and an amphorae seller who have been invited to Trygaios' wedding (1198-1207), a group consisting of an arms dealer, a helmet-maker and a lance-maker ruined by the return of Peace begins to complain (1210-1264), in perfect antithesis with the atmosphere of festive anticipation. Without batting an eyelid, Trygaios suggests he might be a potential customer: with the definitive end of the state of war, everything has changed, and their goods must be sold off at a deep discount, or be assigned a re-semanticized use based on a strictly economic evaluation (on the parody of objects as a metonymic signal of the end of the old order see Camerotto (2007) 131-138). Haggling, he suggests that some helmet crests (*lophoi* 1214, 1222) – which, from the moment of Lamachos' entrance in *Acharnians*, were a pompous symbol of military prestige that Trygaios interprets here as an illness (*lophāis* 1211) – might serve to dust off the table (1218). In another instance of war being collocated within the scatological sphere, a cuirass, given its greatly reduced market value, proves perfect for a certain bodily function (1228-1238); the military trumpet can, with certain alterations or additions, become either a cottabus target or a scale weight (1240-1249); the helmets are excellent "for measuring out laxative" (1254), or, with the addition of two handles, as wine cups (1258-1259); and lances are devalued to the point of becoming "stakes, at a drachma for a hundred" (1263; on grapevines as a paradigm symbolizing subversion and wartime destruction in *Acharnians* and *Peace*, see Camerotto (2007) 136-137; Xantou (2010) 303).

But Trygaios' apparent willingness to bargain is only an intermediate level of his attack: when the interlocutors seem ready to accept ridiculously low offers for lack of anything better – and are thus forced to reveal the extent of their financial woes – their customer backs out, in an about face that is in itself mocking but is intensified by even more ridiculous pretenses: the helmets are "rubbish" with their "hair falling out" (1222-1223) and the cuirass "chafes" (v. 1239).

Once the recycling proposals have been exposed and foiled by their proponent himself, the only path left to take is head-on hostility toward the war merchants, who are chased off by the head of the household (1221, 1239, and 1253). Whether their elimination can be understood as a realistic or historically practicable option is a different question; however, there is no reason to see this scene as an attempt on the author's part to soften or avoid a controversial subject by limiting himself to targeting a few unfortunate characters, given the same treatment here as is reserved in other plays for sycophants or snitches, who similarly encapsulate a negative model of citizen activity, as McGlew interprets it (2001) 91-92. The example is rather unfortunate, because sycophants are targeted not as individuals deviating from the democratic civic standard, but as cogs in the wheels of justice who exercise a function that is in itself legitimate and in fact institutional (cf. *Pl.* 906-925). Nonetheless, they are blamed for being damaging to the community (cf. *Ach.* 515-519, 908-958), and their distortional effects are constantly the object of comic aggression and hostility (on the social dynamics these outsiders created, see Christ (1998), 59-71).

The same diptych schema is repeated in the clash between the sons of two targets of ridicule, General Lamachos and Cleonymos – the latter notorious for having abandoned his shield in battle, or more likely for his failure to report for conscription (cf. 446, 673, and *Ach.* 88, *Eq.* 1372, *Nu.* 353, 400, *V.* 19-23, 592, *Av.* 290, 1473-1481; Storey (1989) 255-260) – over the songs they intend to perform during the wedding banquet (1268-1301): the former intends to sing – as explicitly indicated (1267, 1270, 1273-1274, 1276, 1279, 1282-1283, 1287, 1289) – blaring battle-themed hexameters adapted from the *Epigones* (fr. 1 Bernabé, Davies) and the *Iliad* (see Zogg (2014) 144-163 on the interaction between text and model) and is mocked by Trygaios, who identifies the singer's warmongering father as the cause of his predilection. Trygaios makes every effort to shift the singing toward another sphere of heroic rituality, the banquet (1280–1281), which interacts with the theme of war (see Telò (2013) 144–149). But the boy's compromise proves unsatisfactory (1286–1287 ~ *Epigones* fr. dub. 7 Bernabé; fr. adesp. 2 Davies), and he is quickly rebuffed with the reprise of a play-on-words based on the polysemy of *thorēsso* (1286), which in *Ach.* 1134–1135 for Lamachos referred to "arming oneself for battle," and for Dikaiopolis "getting drunk at a symposium": not only the objects but the words themselves, polarize the dynamics of the semiotic codes of war and peace.

The other boy, following the thread of the citation, responds with the first couplet of Archilochus' celebrated elegy on the loss of a shield (1298–1299 = fr. 5, 1–2 W.) and is promptly panned by Trygaios who completes the boy's responding hemistich, an adaptation of fr. 5, 3 (auton d'exesaōsa), with another passage from Alcaeus (fr. 6, 13–14 V. kai mē kataischynōmen [/eslois tokēas gas ypa ke[imenois): Second Boy: "But I saved my life" (psychēn d'exesōsa) – Trygaios: "And put your parents to shame" (katēischynas ge tokēas 1301). But the reuse of the poetic device proves to be tendentious: by cutting out the negation "mē" from the Alcaeus passage, and thus undermining the epic-style alcaic incitement to be valorous and demonstrate worthiness of one's ancestors (cf. Hom. *Il.* 6, 209; Ar. *Av.* 1451–1452), Trygaios takes the opportunity to once again stigmatize the cowardice of Cleonymos (Zogg (2014) 64). The barbed quip does not seem to be triggered so much by comic aggression as by the need to underscore that love of peace is a virtue, and not a screen to hide a lack of courage or civic-mindedness. In the end, Lamachos' son is unyielding and thus warrants an unceremonious dismissal (1294), while Cleonymos' son, albeit bearing the mark of familial infamy, is allowed to enter the banquet (1302), as is the chorus (1305–1306, 1312) which seems to share Trygaios' appreciative delight in the bride (1338–1341, 1346, 1353–1354). After the *hymenaios*, the chorus sings itself offstage with final good wishes to enjoy the pleasures of the wedding feast (1365–1367), inclusively engaging – like Trygaios (1357–1359) – the entire collective group of spectators/fellow citizens (cf. *Ec.* 1141–1148). The return of peace, which had called upon all citizens to focus on a common interest, is now translated onstage into a collective enjoyment of its benefits.

GUIDE TO FURTHER READING

For annotated editions, see Sommerstein (1985) and Olson (1998); also, good interpretative suggestions in Paduano (2002).

The principal interpretative study on *Peace* is Cassio (1985), who analyzed numerous questions of composition technique, outlining peculiarities in the choice and organization of the dramatic materials. A few more recent lines of exegesis have focused in particular on the intensely metatheatrical aspect of the play (Slater (2002) 115–131; Hall (2006) 333–338) and the elaborate, not only tragic, intertextuality of the plot as a sort of "comic prism" (Hall (2006) 341) through which some of the most important poetic traditions of the time are refracted (see Zogg 2014). More recent critical debate has focused attention on the intensely meta-literary quality of *Peace*, highlighting its paratragic references and a pervasive interplay with epic-lyric, oracular, and folk tale traditions (Hall (2006) 341–349; Dobrov (2001) 89–104; Telò (2010) 308–317; Telò (2013)).

The intertextual relationship with Euripides' *Bellerophon* is examined from various perspectives in numerous studies: in addition to Rau (1967) 89–97; Olson (1998) XXXII–XXXIV, and Dobrov (2001) 89–103; see Telò (2010) 308–317, Mastromarco (2012), and Zogg (2014) 94–130, who also focus on the "stage-scenic" and "metrical-musical" memory triggered by the parody; see also Bierl's (2007, 2009) anthropological approach to the shamanic nature matrix of Trygaios' flight, and reservations regarding said approach expressed by Grilli (2022) 28–32.

In focusing on the protagonist's function, a few critics have interpreted the hero Trygaios as an identification or allegory of concrete historical figures: for Hall (2006, 326–328) he is the "shadow" of Nicias or of other comic rivals, for Sidwell (2009, 205–215), that of Cratinus and Eupolis, in a complex hypothetical network of intertextual relationships with comedies of rivals (metacomedy). On the opposite side of a consolidated line of exegesis, Sicking (1967, 123–124; 1998, 82) focused on the "Great Idea" and its fantastical concretization within the framework of universal happiness as the structural pattern of *Peace*, a pattern to which nearly all of the surviving plays by Aristophanes adhere. Moulton (1981, 82–83) advises prudent consideration of historical contextualization: "it is unwise to infer that the progress of the negotiations had a limiting effect on Aristophanes' imagination." On the opposite side of another consolidated line of exegesis which interprets *Peace* in the light of a widespread feeling of hopefulness and a non-contentious climate, Chronopoulos (2021) underscores the dystonia of values and economic interests linked to a long phase of passage between peace and war, which this "social drama" problematizes on stage.

For pathological impairment or "madness" as a visible sign of the comic hero's ethical–political obsession (54–55, 65, *V.* 71, 80, 87, *Av.* 31, 426) which forces him to face the world and overcome its problems to his own advantage, faithful to the sole value of self-affirmation, see Dover (1972, 31–41), Paduano (1974, 361–362) and Grilli (2022, 146–149).

For a parallel between Trygaios' wedding and the *hieros gamos* of Dionysus enacted in the Anthesteria, see Bowie (1993, 146–150); for assonances with other ritual structures, Edmunds (1980, 20–21) and Thiercy (1986, 307–310). For the intertextual and inter-genre aspect of the poetry-competition scene between the sons of the symbols of poetry of war and peace (1265–1304), in detail, see Kloss (2001, 86–89), Zogg (2014, 144–163), and Telò (2013).

The continuous "symbiosis of the higher and lower mimetic" that characterizes the ambivalent relationship between tragedy and comedy is emphasized right from the protagonist's name, which embodies both fertility and self-reflexive qualities and echoes with the term "trygōidia," formed by analogy with the word "tragedy," with which Aristophanes defines his play; see also *Ach.* 496–500 and 886, and, on comic poets as trygōidoi *V.* 650, 1537 (Hubbard (1991) 140–141; Dobrov (2001) 50–53; Hall (2006) 328–335; Wright (2012) 11–21); on his apparent *paronomasia*, see Taplin (1983). The clear implication is that comedy is one of the Dionysiac elements *intrinsically* associated with peace. Reconstruction of the staging of *Peace* is an open question for Aristophanes scholars due to the numerous setting changes called for by the text, which seem to be explainable as "diegetic" changes; see Morosi (2021) 207.

REFERENCES

Albini, U. (1971). La *Pace* di Aristofane una commedia minore? *Parola del Passato* 26: 14–25.
Arrowsmith, W. (1973). Aristophanes' *Birds*: the Fantasy Politics of Eros. *Arion* 1: 119–167.
Auger, D. (1997). Dieux médiateurs dans la comédie d'Aristophane. *Uranie* 7: 153–171.
Bierl, A. (2007). Le "chamanisme" et la comédie ancienne. Recours générique à un atavisme et guérison (avec une application à l'exemple de la *Paix* d'Aristophane). *Methodos* (online) 7 http://journals.openedition.org/methodos/625> [reprinted in Jaeder, Müller (2009)]: 13–55.
Bierl, A. (2009), 'Schamanismus' und die Alte Komödie: Generischer Rückgriff auf einen Atavismus und Heilung (mit einer Anwendung am Beispiel von Aristophanes' *Frieden*). In: *Religion: Lehre und Praxis. Akten der Kolloquiums Basel, 22 Oktober 2004* (ed. B. Jeder and P. Müller), Archaiognosia Suppl. 8, 1–30. Athens: University of Athens.
Borthwick, E.K. (1968). Beetle, bell, goldfinch, and weasel in Aristophanes' *Peace. Classical Review* 18: 134–139.
Bowie, A.M. (1993). *Aristophanes: Myth, Ritual and Comedy*. Cambridge: Cambridge University Press.
Brown, P. (2008). Scenes at the Door in Aristophanic Comedy. In: *Performance, Iconography, Reception. Studies in Honour of Oliver Taplin* (ed. M. Revermann and P. Wilson), 349–373. Oxford: Oxford University Press.
Camerotto, A. (2007). Guerra e pace. Poteri della parodia. In: *Diafonie. esercizi sul comico* (ed. A. Camerotto), 129–154. Padua: SARGON.
Campagner, R. (1998). Una *Boule* a luci rosse (Aristofane, *Pax* 894–904). *Quaderni Urbinati di Cultura Classica* 58: 33–40.
Cassio, A.C. (1985). *Commedia e partecipazione. La* Pace *di Aristofane*. Naples: Liguori.
Ceccarelli, S. (2020). Un paesaggio ameno contro la guerra. Aristofane e l'idealizzazione della campagna attica. In: *Experiencing the Landscape in Antiquity*, vol. BARS3015 (ed. A. Cristilli, A. Gonfloni, and F. Stock), 261–266. Oxford: Bar Publishing.
Christ, M.R. (1998). *The Litigious Athenian*. Baltimore/London: Johns Hopkins University Press.
Chronopoulos, S. (2021). The difficult passage from war to peace: liminality, transition, and tension in Aristophanes' *Peace* 8. *Histos Suppl.* 12: 63–85.
Compton Engle, G. (1999). From Country to City: the Persona of Dicaeopolis in Aristophanes' *Acharnians. The Classical Journal* 94 (4): 359–373.
Dobrov, G.W. (2001). *Figures of Play: Greek Drama and Metafictional Poetics*. Oxford: Oxford University Press.
Dover, K.J. (1972). *Aristophanic Comedy*. Berkeley/Los Angeles: University of California Press.
Edmunds, L. (1980). Aristophanes' *Acharnians*. In: *Aristophanes: Essays in Interpretation*. Yale Classical Studies 26. (ed. J. Henderson), 1–41. Cambridge: Cambridge University Press.

García Romero, F. (1995). *Ἔρως Ἀθλητής*: les métaphores érotico-sportives dans les comédies d'Aristophane. *Nikephoros* 8: 57–76.
Gelzer, T. (1960). *Die Epirrhematische Agon bei Aristophanes: Untersuchungen zur Struktur der attischen alten Komödie*, Munich: Beck.
Given, J. (2009). When Gods Don't Appear: Divine Absence and Human Agency in Aristophanes. *Classical World* 102: 107–127.
Grilli, A. (2022). *Aristofane e i volti dell'eroe. Per una grammatica dell'eroismo comico* Pisa: ETS.
Hall, E. (2006). *The Theatrical Cast of Athens, Interactions between Ancient Greek Drama and Society.* Oxford.
Hall, E. (2013). The Aesopic in Aristophanes. In: *Greek Comedy and the Discourse of Genres* (ed. E. Bakola, L. Prauscello, and M. Telò), 277–297. Cambridge: Cambridge University Press.
Hanson, V.D. (1995). *The Other Greeks: The Family Farm and Agrarian Roots of Western Civilization.* New York: Free Press.
Hubbard, T.K. (1991). *The Mask of Comedy. Aristophanes and Intertextual Parabasis.* Ithaca/London: Cornell UP.
Jay-Robert, G. (2002). Fonction des dieux chez Aristophane. Exemple de Zeus, d'Hermès et de Dionysos. *Revue des Études Anciennes* 104 (1–2): 11–24.
Kanavou, N. (2011a). *Aristophanes' Comedy of Names: A Study of Speaking Names in Aristophanes.* Berlin and New York: de Gruyter.
Kanavou, N. (2011b). Political myth in Aristophanes: another form of comic satire? *Greek, Roman, and Byzantine Studies* 51: 382–400.
Kassel, R. and Austin, C. (ed.) (1984). *Poetae comci graeci, III 2.* Berolini/Novi Eboraci: de Gruyter.
Kloss, G. (2001). *Erscheinungsformen komischen Sprechens bei Aristophanes.* Berlin and New York: de Gruyter.
Mann, K. (2017). The rejected eagle in Aristophanes' *Peace*. *Mnemosyne* 70: 299–307.
Mastromarco, G. (2012). Dal Bellerofonte di Euripide alla *Pace* di Aristofane. In: *Textos fragmentarios del teatro griego antiguo: problemas, estudios y nuevas perspectivas* (ed. A. Melero, M. Labiano, and M. Pellegrino), 93–118. Lecce: Pensa Multimedia.
McGlew, J. F. (2001). Identity and ideology: the farmer chorus of Aristophanes' *Peace*. *Syllecta Classica* 12: 74–97.
Morosi, F. (2013). Prometeo comico. Un paradigma trascurato nella *Pace* di Aristofane. *Dioniso* 3: 61–96.
Morosi, F. (2021). *Lo spazio della commedia. Identità, potere e drammaturgia in Aristofane.* Rome: Edizioni di Storia e Letteratura.
Moulton, C. (1981). *Aristophanic Poetry*. Göttingen: Vandenhoeck & Ruprecht.
Nelson, S. (2016). *Aristophanes and his Tragic Muse. Comedy, Tragedy and the Polis in 5th Century Athens.* Leiden/Boston: Brill.
Newiger, H.-J. (1957). *Metapher und Allegorie. Studien zu Aristophanes.* München: Beck.
Newiger, H.-J. (1975). Krieg and Frieden in der Komödie des Aristophanes. In: *ΔΩPHMA: Hans Diller zum 70. Geburtstag. Dauer und Überleben des antiken Geistes* (ed. A.D. Skiadas), 175–194. Athens: Hellenic Society for Humanistic Studies.
Newiger, H.-J. (1980). War and peace in the comedies of Aristophanes. In: *Aristophanes: Essays in Interpretation.* Yale Classical Studies 26. (ed. J. Henderson), 219–237. Cambridge: Cambridge University Press.
Olson, S.D. (ed.) (1998). *Aristophanes.* Peace, *edited with introduction and commentary*. Oxford: Oxford University Press.
Olson, S.D. (ed.) (2002). *Aristophanes.* Acharnians, *edited with introduction and commentary*. Oxford: Oxford University Press.
Paduano, G. (1974). Su alcune costanti dell'eroe comico in Aristofane. *Bollettino del centro internazionale di studi di architettura Andrea Palladio* 16: 345–369.
Paduano, G. (ed.) (2002). *Aristofane.* La Pace Milan: Rizzoli.
Parker, R. (1996). *Athenian Religion. A History.* Oxford: Oxford University Press.
Pelling, C.B.R. (2000). *Literary Texts and the Greek Historian.* London: Routledge.
Pulleyn, S.J. (1997). *Prayer in Greek Religion.* Oxford, New York: Oxford University Press.
Rau, P. (1967). *Paratragodia: Untersuchungen einer komischen Form des Aristophanes.* München: Beck.
Riedweg, C. (1990). The 'Atheistic' fragment from Euripides' *Bellerophontes* (286 N²). *Illinois Classical Studies* 15: 39–53.
Riess, W. (2012). *Performing Interpersonal Violence. Court, Curse, and Comedy in Fourth-Century BCE Athens.* Berlin/Boston: de Gruyter.
Ruffell, I.A. (2011). *Politics and Anti-realism in Athenian Old Comedy: the Art of the Impossible.* Oxford, New York: Oxford University Press.

Ruffell, I. (2017). (What's so funny 'bout) peace, love and understanding? Imagining peace in Greek comedy. In: *Peace and Reconciliation in the Classical World* (ed. E.P. Moloney and M. Stuart Williams), 44–65. London: Routledge.

Russo, C.F. (1994). *Aristophanes an author for the stage* [trans. K. Wren]. London and New York: Routledge [original publication Aristofane autore di teatro. Florence 1962.].

Saïd, S. (2000). La campagne d'Aristophane. In: *Où courir? Organisation et symbolique de l'espace dans la comédie antique. Colloque international (20–21–22 janvier 2000, Crata), Pallas*, vol. 54 (ed. C. Cusset, J.-C. Carrière, M.-H. Garelli-François, and C. Orfanos), 191–206.

Schirru, S. (2009). *La favola in Aristofane*. Berlin: Verlag Antike.

Sicking, C.M.J. (1967). Aristophanes Laetus? In: *ΚΩΜΩΙΔΟΤΡΑΓΗΜΑΤΑ: Studia Aristophanea Viri Aristophanei W.J.W. Koster in honorem* (ed. R.E.H.W. Boerma), 115–124. Amsterdam: Hakkert [reprinted in Sicking (1998), 77–84].

Sicking, C.M.J. (1998). *Distant Companions. Selected Papers*. Leiden, Boston and Köln: Brill.

Sidwell, K.C. (2009). *Aristophanes the Democrat: The Politics of Satirical Comedy During the Peloponnesian War*. Cambridge, New York: Cambridge University Press.

Sifakis, G.M. (1971). *Parabasis and Animal Choruses. A Contribution to the History of Attic Comedy*. London: Athlone Press.

Slater, N.W. (2002). *Spectator Politics. Metatheatre and Performance in Aristophanes*. Philadelphia: University of Pennsylvania Press.

Smith, A.C. (2011). *Polis and Personification in Classical Athenian Art*. Leiden/Boston: Brill.

Solomos, A. and Feldheim, M. (ed.) (1974). *The living Aristophanes*. Ann Arbor (Mich.): University of Michigan Press.

Sommerstein, A.H. (ed.) (1980). *The Comedies of Aristophanes*. Acharnians, vol. 1. Warminster: Aris and Phillips.

Sommerstein, A.H. (ed.) (1985). *The Comedies of Aristophanes*. Peace, vol. 5. Warminster: Aris and Phillips.

Stafford, E. (2000). *Worshipping Virtues: Personification and the Divine in Ancient Greece*. London/Swansea: The Classical Press of Wales.

Storey, I.C. (1989). "The blameless shield" of Cleonymos. *Rheinishes Museum für Philologie* 132: 247–261.

Storey, I.C. and Allan, A. (2014). *A Guide to Ancient Greek Drama* [2005]. Malden MA/Oxford/Chichester: Blackwell Publishing.

Sulprizio, C. (2013). You can't go home again. War, women and domesticity in Aristophanes' *Peace*. *Ramus* 42: 44–63.

Taplin, O. (1983). Tragedy and Thrugedy. *Classical Quarterly* 33: 331–333.

Telò, M. (2010). Embodying the tragic father(s): autobiography and intertextuality in Aristophanes. *Classical Antiquity* 29: 278–326.

Telò, M. (2013). Epic, nostos and generic genealogy in Aristophanes' Peace. In: *Greek Comedy and the Discourse of Genres* (ed. E. Bakola, L. Prauscello, and M. Telò), 129–152. Cambridge: Cambridge University Press.

Thiercy, P. (1986). *Aristophane, fiction et dramaturgie*. Paris: Les Belles Lettres.

Tordoff, R.L.S. (2011). Excrement, sacrifice, commensality: the osphresiology of Aristophanes' *Peace*. *Arethusa* 44: 167–198.

Totaro, P. (1999). *Le seconde parabasi di Aristofane*. Stuttgart/Weimar: Metzler.

Voelke, P. (2014). Entre communauté civique et communauté hellénique: Theôria l'hetaïre dans la *Paix* d'Aristophane. *Quaderni Urbinati di Cultura Classica* 106: 135–152.

Whitman, C.H. (1964). *Aristophanes and the Comic Hero*. Cambridge (MA): Harvard University Press.

von Wilamowitz-Moellendorff, U. (1935). Über die *Wespen* des Aristophanes. In: *Kleine Schriften. I. Klassische griechische Poesie* (ed. P. Maas), 284–346. Berlin: Weidmann [original publication *Sitzungsberichte der Kgl. Preussischen Akademie der Wissenschaften*. Berlin 1911. 460–491; 504–535].

Wright, M. (2012). *The Comedian as Critic: Greek Old Comedy and Poetics. Greek Old Comedy and Poetics*. London: Bristol University Press.

Xantou, M.G. (2010). Contextualizing Dikaiopolis persona. Urban life, rural, space, and rural perceptions of urbanity in Aristophanes' *Acharnians*. *Hellenika* 60 (2): 297–314.

Zogg, F. (2014). *Lust am Lesen. Literarische Anspielungen im* Frieden *des Aristophanes*. München: Beck.

Zumbrunnen, J. (2012). *Aristophanic Comedy and the Challenge of Democratic Citizenship*. Rochester: University Rochester Press.

CHAPTER 12

Birds: Utopia

David Konstan

Introduction

"A utopia is a society that has abolished the difference between public and private life" (Wenglinsky 2020).

"l'utopiste rêve en effet d'une coïncidence parfaite entre individu et collectivité—d'où le contrôle exercé sur la famille, susceptible de saper la solidarité communautaire, et sur la culture livresque, ferment d'individualisme" (Jouanno 2008: 19).

In Aristophanes' *Birds*, two Athenians, Peisetaerus (the name means "He Who Persuades his Companion") and his sidekick, Euelpides ("Of Good Hopes"), seek a place to settle down where they can avoid litigation (38–48) and evade their debts (114–16). To this end, they consult Tereus, formerly a human being but transformed into a hoopoe, since, as a bird, he has seen much of the world. They travel alone, unencumbered by wives, children, or other relatives. What kind of life do they imagine for themselves? Well, Euelpides hopes for friends who will invite him to a wedding feast but expect nothing from him if they should find themselves in trouble (128–34). Peisetaerus, in turn, wishes that his friends will reproach him if he does not fondle their handsome young sons (136–42). So, free food, free sex, without the bother of having a family of one's own. It is a recurring dream in connection with a certain kind of utopia, which reconciles private desires with public order by promising their fulfillment at no cost. After the pair discount several possible locations, Tereus suggests that they consider the realm of the birds themselves. He points out that birds do not carry wallets since there is no money, and they dine on seeds and mint, which Euelpides compares to wedding cakes. Amid such primitive simplicity, there is no room for deceit or competition. At this point, Peisetaerus suddenly announces a bold idea, by which, he says, the birds will achieve power (162–63). This is an odd development. No sooner does Peisetaerus hear of what might appear to be an ideal community in which to escape liabilities and lawsuits, than he proposes to transform it, by making the birds lords of the universe. We shall follow this development, in a moment, but we may first pause to situate the plot of *Birds* in the tradition of utopian literature. For the society that the two Athenians encounter, and the one they propose to realize in its stead, manifest aspects, sometimes regarded as polar opposites, of the utopian tradition.

A Companion to Aristophanes, First Edition. Edited by Matthew C. Farmer and Jeremy B. Lefkowitz.
© 2024 John Wiley & Sons, Inc. Published 2024 by John Wiley & Sons, Inc.

Utopia and Dystopia

Utopias are commonly regarded as ideal societies. Thus, the *Merriam-Webster Dictionary* gives as the first definition, "a place of ideal perfection especially in laws, government, and social conditions," though it adds (2) "an impractical scheme for social improvement" and (3) "an imaginary and indefinitely remote place."[1] So too, the *New Oxford American Dictionary* (2005) gives as the definition, an "imagined place or state of things in which everything is perfect," and the online http://Dictionary.com offers "an ideal place or state" and "any visionary system of political or social perfection." Perfection is the abiding characteristic, but of course we are immediately moved to ask: perfect in what respect? What constitutes perfection?

Answers will differ, according to place and circumstances. Utopias are projections, imagined as remedying perceived flaws in one's own society. In Aristophanes' *Birds*, as we have seen, one such fault is the inveterate litigiousness of Athenians, which the two heroes of the comedy seek to escape. Others may fantasize about a world of earthly delights. Not everyone may agree on what is most desirable, and some may stand to gain more than others from any given arrangement. The paradise of bachelors may have as its foundation a Tartarus of maids, to borrow from the title of Herman Melville's mordant short story. But whereas such inequalities may be sustained by brute force, utopias are stable because they rest on universal consent. Everyone – or very nearly everyone – is content in the ideal community. Utopias are harmonious, because no one wishes to change the social order. There is no tension between individual desire and the integrity of the collective, no space carved out for a strictly personal life, which may have its own ends and purposes. In Thomas More's *Utopia*, which gave the world the word, "Every house has a front door to the street and a backdoor to the garden. The double doors, which open easily with a push of the hand and close again automatically, let anyone come in – so there is nothing private anywhere" (More 1989; 46). There is no need for privacy where there is universal concord, no reason why one's most intimate thoughts, if not necessarily one's most intimate acts, must be concealed. Just because all its citizens are presumed to be perfectly happy with the way things are, the most consistent quality of utopias is, as Martin Wenglinsky observes in the headnote to this chapter, the abolition of the distinction between public and private.

This very feature invites a comparison with utopia's ostensible opposite, the dystopia.[2] Doubtless the most famous example of such an oppressive regime is George Orwell's *Nineteen Eighty-Four*, in which the character who represents the totalitarian state asserts: "If you want a picture of the future, imagine a boot stamping on a human face — forever." This horrific image suggests anything but social concord, as though resistance was permanently built into the social structure and needed always to be crushed by greater power. But the fuller context of the quotation reveals another sense:

> There will be no curiosity, no enjoyment of the process of life. All competing pleasures will be destroyed. But always — do not forget this, Winston — always there will be the intoxication of power, constantly increasing and constantly growing subtler. Always, at every moment, there will be the thrill of victory, the sensation of trampling on an enemy who is helpless. If you want a picture of the future, imagine a boot stamping on a human face — forever.

Winston, the would-be rebel against the dominant order, whose love for his girlfriend is subversive precisely because it is personal and hence a "competing pleasure," will himself, in the end, share in "the thrill of victory." For he will be overcome by joy as he watches the armies of his own state, represented on a screen by abstract arrows, advance victoriously against the enemy. Winston need no longer hide from the cameras that are installed in every home, to spy on one's most private acts. To be sure, his betrayal of his beloved and submission to the state are achieved by a brutal process of brainwashing. But that is only because the systematic indoctrination by the state has somehow failed to be complete in Winston's case. Winston represents the imagined reader's revulsion at the tyrannical and one-dimensional regime, which is not annulled, like Winston's, at the end of the

---

[1] https://www.merriam-webster.com/dictionary/utopia; accessed 15 August 2020.
[2] On the relation between utopias and dystopias in modern and classical literature, see Konstan 2021.

novel. Within the state, however, concord reigns. This is why Wenglinksy can say that his definition "does away with the need to distinguish between utopias and dystopias."

In Aldous Huxley's *Brave New World*, which is again marked by a hierarchical class structure, all citizens are conditioned to accept their role by means of biological and psychological engineering, supplemented by the euphoria-inducing drug, soma. Here too, there are a few misfits who insist on "the right to be unhappy" and serve to afford the novel its dramatic tension and to represent the implied reader's rejection of the conformity that characterizes the system. Ayn Rand's novel, *Anthem*, imagines a world in which the first-person singular pronoun has been excised from the language, and people can express themselves only in the plural, "we." The discovery of the word "I" enables the rebellious couple – as usual, there are nonconformists, who are motivated at least in part by sex – to express their love for each other as individuals. The breakdown of the ideal society is signaled by the eruption of private desires, the "competing pleasures" that undermine its perfect concord.[3]

But surely we can imagine societies in which individuals are free to pursue their own happiness and fulfill their private desires without jeopardizing the solidarity of the whole. Where technology or some other development has put an end to the scarcity of goods, all can, as Marxists have envisioned, satisfy their personal needs and desires without diminishing the well-being of the rest.[4] In such a world, there would be no need for a state, with its mechanisms of enforcement, both military and ideological, nor for the regimentation of its citizens and invasion of their private lives. Describing communities of this sort poses, to be sure, a challenge to the writer of fiction: it is hard to create enough sense of drama to sustain interest in an entire novel or play. To ring a change on the famous opening line of Leo Tolstoy's *Anna Karenina*, "Happy societies are all alike; every unhappy society is unhappy in its own way." One might, of course, introduce purely idiosyncratic dissenters, like the narrator in Dostoyevsky's *Notes from Underground*, who simply refuses to go along. Won't there always be such naysayers, whatever the delights on offer? Perhaps. As we shall see, Aristophanes provides an amusing example. If there is no opposition at all, however, then individual desires will coincide with the collective interest, and once more, the distinction between private and public will collapse.

In a recent collection of short stories called *A People's Future of the United States* (Anders 2019), the majority, as is increasingly common these days, depict some kind of disaster scenario, whether ecological (including epidemics) or social, in which machines go berserk or race or gender conflicts are hugely amplified. One, for example, is introduced with the alarming heading, "RACIST ROBOTS RECALLED BY MANUFACTURER."[5] These are not precisely dystopias: they do not pretend to limn an ideal or harmonious society, even one that rests on coercion. There is one story, however, that views the future more benignly; it is by Hugh Howey, and titled, rather mysteriously, "No Algorithms in the World" (Anders 2019: 264–73). It begins:

> "Look at these damn commies." I glance up from my holo to see what Dad's cussing about this time. It could be anything from a concrete building with bland architecture to a queue of people outside an ice-cream shop. The older he gets, the wider the commie circle of ire and bile .... Today it appears to be the Muslim couple crossing the street in front of our car, her with a hijab and him with his ghutra.

This might seem like the lead-in to a typical doomsday setup, with the world on the verge of all-out ethnic warfare, but in fact it is a decoy. The story continues:

> "Not all Muslims are communists," I say, even though it's pointless. Qatar, Kuwait, and the UAE were among the first to give universal basic income a go, and so for Dad, the Middle East is patient zero in what he calls "a plague of joblessness." It's been twelve years here in the States, and most Americans have come around to accept the new system, especially once the checks started arriving on schedule . . . .

---

[3] In science fiction, cloning is sometimes imagined as resulting in a homogeneity of minds. One such fantasy is the so-called Borg, that is, "cybernetic organisms linked in a hive mind called 'the Collective'" (*Wikipedia*, s.v.), as represented in the television series *Star Trek*.
[4] On Marxism and utopia, see Ollman 2005.
[5] Charles Yu, "Good News Bad News," in Anders 2019: 307–20; quotation from p. 307.

And yet a solid 30-plus percent of the population is like my dad, cashing their checks and complaining about the world unfolding around them and vehemently opposed. Mostly, Dad gets annoyed by how other people spend their free time. Not working hard enough, he says (p. 264).

The narrator has a secret, however, that he has been struggling to reveal to his father. He has decided to give up his well-paying job, which he regards as pointless, and his pregnant wife will be leaving hers as well. He explains: "We don't need the money. We're working just to work, and neither of us looks forward to going in." To which his father replies: "That's why it's called work, son. You aren't supposed to like it." The narrator tries to comfort the recalcitrant old man: "We're going to stay in Houston, at least for a while. So you and Mom can be around the baby. But we want to travel, to spend our time learning together and teaching her what we can. Spending every moment we can together" (p. 272).

The father's resistance to the new world looming before him is based on values and a sense of self that have been the bedrock of our modern culture: work and responsibility as the condition for leisure, the fundamental complementarity of what the Romans called *otium* and *negotium*. Without work, the son's life is rootless and indeterminate. True, there is the family, reduced to a nucleus of three, but it is no longer a node of privacy within the nexus of the wider economy, a locus of domesticity as opposed to the public world of labor and the marketplace (see Richter 2015).

Cloud-Cuckoo-Land

In Aristophanes' *Birds*, as we have noted, Peisetaerus seek a community that will satisfy their pleasures and allow them to shirk their obligations to the state, but then, seemingly out of the blue, Peisetairus comes up with a revolutionary scheme to transform the very world he found into an avian empire. Peisetaerus's plan will succeed, but before we examine its implications, we may consider what it is about the birds' society in its original condition that might have seemed attractive to the two companions. We know some things about it. Tereus, for example, has a servant or henchman (a *therapôn*), who answers the door to Tereus' house when the Athenians first arrive. As he explains, he was formerly Tereus' slave and wished to be metamorphosed along with him (he calls himself a "slave bird," ὄρνις δοῦλος, 70), so that he could continue to serve him as attendant and servant (ἀκόλουθον, διάκονον). Euelpides is surprised that birds should require servants, but the slave bird explains that it is because Tereus was formerly a human being, and so has special needs, for example, for certain kinds of fish, which he can fetch for him (75–76). Regular birds evidently have no concern for such luxuries. We know too that, at least from a human perspective, birds are wholly unambitious and flit around aimlessly, with no sense of place (165–70). Indeed, the first step in Peisetaerus' revolutionary plan is to mark out boundaries, by which the indeterminate sky or "pole" (Greek *polos*) through which the birds fly may be converted into a fixed city or *polis* (179–84). When, later in the play, the birds are set to the task of building a wall around the heavens, so as to lay claim to the territory of the firmament and thereby block transit between human beings on earth and the gods on high, they accomplish this feat with incredible speed. Peisetaerus himself is amazed at their efficiency (1164–1167), so much so that he regards the report of their achievement as "seeming truly like lies" (1167). Their secret is a combination of specialized abilities – herons carry hods, geese use their feet as shovels, woodpeckers carve the gates – with immense numbers (thirty thousand cranes, ten thousand storks), and total collaboration with no further incentive than the job at hand. As Peisetaerus exclaims, "Why would anyone hire wage-laborers anymore?" (1152). To be sure, the birds are now working in the context of the new civic regime, in which Peisetaerus gives the orders. But their collective solidarity is a sign of the absence of competing individual desires. They seem to operate as a unit, as though, despite the variety of their species, they are all clones of one another, constituting a hive-like entity such as bees or ants, or, if you prefer, a Borg. When, in the fantasy of Aristophanes, such an integrated community is given direction and purpose by a human mind, it is invincible.

Do the birds have families? This is more difficult to answer. Of course, Aristophanes was aware that many kinds of birds form couples, brood over their eggs in nests, and care for their chicks until they are self-sufficient. In the comedy, however, there is no sign of domesticity, save for a scene toward the end, when a young man with a reputation for beating his father arrives, hoping to join the society of the birds, since he is passionate, as he says, for their customs or *nomoi* (1345).[6] In the topsy-turvy bird world, it turns out that, as Peisetaerus concedes, it is considered a manly thing (ἀνδρεῖόν, 1349) for a nestling to strike its father, although in Greece it was the very worst of offenses.[7] Earlier, the chorus of birds had invited the audience to join their way of life, "for all the things that are ruled out as shameful according to the law (*nomos*) where you are, are the very things that are virtuous among us birds" (755–56) – and the example they offer is father-beating. (They add that slaves, foreigners, and sympathizers of the disenfranchised are welcome as well.) This certainly appears to be a thoroughgoing inversion of Greek mores and calls into question whether anything like a normal family structure exists. Peisetaerus immediately adds, however, that there is also an ancient custom, inscribed in the tablets of the storks,[8] that stipulates that when a father has reared his young so that they may fly from the nest, they are then responsible for his support. Such an obligation was traditional at Athens,[9] and the father-beater naturally protests that his trip to the realm of the birds was useless. Peisetaerus gives him the old-fashioned advice that he had received when he was young: "Don't beat your father. . .! Let your father live, but since you're so warlike, fly off to Thrace and make war there" (1364, 1368–1369) observing too that the young man can support himself on a soldier's wages.

We cannot, of course, expect complete consistency in a comedy by Aristophanes. There is, moreover, a characteristic structure to his more utopian concoctions, in which a new order is established in the first part of the play and then put to the test in the latter part, in what are sometimes called exemplificatory scenes: *Birds* stands out as having the greatest number of these among the surviving comedies (see Henderson 2000:2). In any case, the birds' society has already been radically altered by Peisetaerus, who is now fully in command, and there is no reason to equate it with the utopian vision that initially attracted him and Euelpides. We remember too that Peisetaerus had just a little earlier concluded that there was no need, among the birds, for hired labor, such as he now recommends to the violent young fellow. But of course, no one in the audience would have supposed that there really was such legislation among the birds. It is an on-the-spot invention of Peisetaerus, designed to insure that the communal polity of the birds, which originally had no need of laws and regulations, does not turn out to be hospitable to human perversity. Instead of an absence of rules or anomy, to which the birds were by nature adapted, Aristophanes subtly shifts the image of his utopia to one characterized by good rules or what we may call "eunomy" (Thomas More first toyed with the name "Eutopia" for his ideal society).[10]

Left to themselves, animals, have often been regarded as following nature rather than submitting to prescribed laws.[11] This is why animals have readily served as models of a harmonious

---

[6] Cf. the reference to the *arkhaioi thesmoi*, "ancient sanctions" (331) among the birds, by which human beings were admitted into their realm.

[7] Compare the behavior of Pheidippides in Aristophanes' *Clouds*, when he has fallen under the spell of Socrates' sophistry:
 Pheidippides: Consider cocks and other animals—
 they avenge themselves against their fathers.
 And yet how are we different from them,
 except they don't propose decrees?
 Strepsiades: Well then,
 since you want to be like cocks in all you do,
 why not sleep on a perch and feed on shit?
 (1427–32), trans. Johnston 2017.

[8] The storks laws are on *kurbeis* (1354), triangular tablets on which some ancient legislation was inscribed at Athens, as opposed to the *stelai* on which modern laws were normally published.

[9] The obligation was a matter of law; see Harrison 1968:77.

[10] For the different ways in which utopias may be constructed, whether by the absence of conventional norms (anomy), or their inversion (antinomy), or by imposing good norms (eunomy), or, finally, by pushing all norms to their limits (megalonomy), see Konstan 1995:29–44.

[11] A current in classical philosophy held that, since non-human animals are incapable of entering into contracts, justice cannot govern our relations with them and hence it is legitimate to subject them to our uses and kill them for the sake of food, irrespective of whether they are dangerous. On the Epicurean view of animal minds, see Verde 2020.

community, without the need for compulsion. Lacking individuality, they conform instinctively to the requirements of the collective; they have no individual identity that separates them from the group. An ancient example is the comedy *Thêria* or "Wild Animals," by Aristophanes' older contemporary, Crates, of which, unfortunately, only a few fragments survive. One of these runs as follows:

> (A) Then absolutely no one will get a slave man or woman,
> but an old man will have to be his own servant?
> (B) No! I'll make everything able to walk.
> (A) But what good is that to them? (B) Each of the utensils
> will come to you by itself, when you call it. "Appear
>   beside me, table!
> set yourself! Grain-sack, knead the dough!
> ladle, pour! Where is the wine cup? Go and wash yourself!
> up here, bread-dough! The pot should spit out those beets!
> Come here, fish." "But I'm done only on one side yet."
> "Then turn yourself over, and baste yourself – with a
>   little salt."[12]

The concept of a world without slaves depends on notion that objects are animated and thus eliminate the need for work. Aristotle conceivably had this (or a similar) passage in mind when he wrote:

> if it were possible that every utensil accomplished its task when summoned or on its own initiative, and, like the objects made by Daedalus, as they say, or the tripods of Hephaestus, which the poet says, "on their own enter the divine assembly" [Homer, *Iliad* 18.376], and if shuttles could weave and plectrums pluck the lyre this way, then builders would have no need of workers or masters of slaves" (*Politics* 1253^{b}33-38).

The difference is that, in Crates dramatization, material objects (including dead fish) are endowed with speech and at least a limited intelligence, and so can stand in for perfect slaves, since they apparently have no will but to obey the commands they are given or that they intuit. We cannot be sure of the identity of the speakers in the dialogue, but if they were animals (or if one of them was), then it is they who imagine, quite exceptionally in ancient Greek literature, a strictly classless society.[13] A similar conceit is at work in Jonathan Swift's representation, in *Gulliver's Travels*, of the Land of Houyhnhnms, those super-rational horses who have no emotion and live in perfect harmony, a bit like Mr. Spock in the *Startrek* series (or later, the robotic character Data). In George Orwell's *Animal Farm*, the several domesticated animals rebel against the human farmer and establish a society based on equality and freedom, even if, in the end, the pigs fashion themselves as a new ruling class, under the dictatorial authority of their leader, Napoleon, now in league with human farmers. Something analogous takes place in the avian utopia dreamt up by Aristophanes, as we shall see. But the initial impulse to Orwell's satire on Soviet Communism was to see in animals a figure of the selfless solidarity that Marx imagined as emerging from the socialized labor of the proletariat.

The city that Peisetaerus creates for the birds, while different from their pre-civilized condition, is attractive in its own right, and, seduced by the idea of acquiring wings and hence the ability to fly, humans, like the would-be father-beater, flock to the new polity.[14] It is these visits that constitute the exemplificatory scenes mentioned above. Some are promptly sent packing, like the geometer Meton, who proposes to measure the sky off into individual plots of land (995–96). For all that the birds' city is now bounded by a wall, it will not be internally sectioned off into privately owned tracts. When Meton inquires whether there is civil strife *(stasis)* in the newly founded city, Peisetaerus replies, Not at all, since "they have decided of one accord to beat up all charlatans" (1014–1016;

---

[12] Translated by Jeffrey Rusten (in Rusten 2011 : 139).
[13] See Konstan 2012 for a somewhat different take on the play.
[14] On the possibly ambivalent representation of wings as prostheses, see Gerolemou 2020.

the word ἀλαζών here may also mean braggarts or pretenders). Peisetaerus takes Meton himself to be a prime instance of the type, and sure enough he is driven from the city with blows. Nevertheless, there is something alarming about a unanimity that results in the pummeling and expulsion of anyone who threatens the strict cohesion of the group. The same treatment is meted out to an inspector or commissioner, who arrives to oversee the city's affairs.

There are internal dissensions in the new city as well, to which we will come in a moment. But first, we may remark on the most profound change that the birds experience, the one that lies at the heart of Peisetaerus plan. With a sublime instinct for psychological manipulation, Peisetaerus persuades the birds that they had been lords of the universe before the gods had ruled, and indeed before the Earth itself existed. He thus instills in them a passion to recover the power that was usurped by the Olympian deities. Peisetaerus begins, with feigned sympathy: "I'm so sorry for you, who once were kings" (466–67), to which the leader of the bird chorus replies: "Us, kings? Of what?" Peisetaerus, now on a roll, continues: "You were kings of all that is, of me, first, and of this one here, and of Zeus himself. You were born more anciently and earlier than Cronus and the Titans, and even the Earth" (468–70). The chorus leader is stunned: "Earlier than the Earth?" "Yes, by Apollo," replies Peisetaerus, rather insouciantly swearing by one of the gods that he means to replace. "This, by Zeus," exclaims the chorus leader, "I never heard." Peisetaerus tells him that he is ignorant, lacks curiosity (not always regarded as a bad thing in antiquity), and never set foot on Aesop's fables, where he would have learned that

> the lark was the first bird of all to be born, earlier than the earth, and then his father died of disease, but because there was no earth, he was laid out for burial for five days, till the lark, in a quandary for lack of means, finally buried her father in her head (471–75).

Peisetaerus' strategy is brilliant. He arouses in the birds a desire for sovereignty over the universe by representing it as something they once possessed but have since lost, even if the image of their primitive empire is palpably absurd (the chorus leader was right to ask, "kings of what?," given that the earth itself did not yet exist). Till now, they were self-sufficient, without memory and hence without ambition: this was indeed the secret of their idealized existence. Once they are made to believe that they have fallen from a higher estate, they become passionate to recover it – in this respect, not different from the Athenians, possessed by a restless will to power. The birds must win it all back.

To this end, they place an embargo on the transmission of sacrificial smoke to the gods, which they can do since they have now gained control of the intervening space, and succeed in starving them into submission. Under the suzerainty of the birds, human life too will improve, since they will eliminate agricultural pests, predict weather so that merchants may sail safely, reveal the sites of buried treasure, and subtract from their own years to extend the lives of mortals. As Peisetaerus concludes, "if they believe that you are god, that you are life, that you are earth, that you are Cronus, that you are Poseidon, they will obtain all these good things" (586–87). The future that the birds offer is in effect a return to the golden age, the pre-Jovian epoch of spontaneous bounty, the ever-fresh dream of Eden. It was a vision enshrined in Hesiod's myth of the five ages in the *Works and Days*, and in various versions of Orphic and related cosmogonies.[15] Peisetaerus' reference to Cronus, the father of Zeus whose reign was imagined as benevolent, evokes that primeval age of

---

[15] The details of the Orphic cosmogony are obscure, and it is not clear how far back in time to place its origins, since the evidence is largely late. There seems, however, to have existed at some point a sequence of six divine kings, namely Phanes, Night, Uranos, Cronus, Zeus, and Dionysus, and this was possibly known to Plato; at all events, some such account seems to lie behind Socrates remark toward the very end of the *Philebus*, "But in the sixth generation," says Orpheus, "cease the order of the song" ('ἕκτῃ δ' ἐν γενεᾷ', φησὶν Ὀρφεύς, 'καταπαύσατε κόσμον ἀοιδῆς', 66C8–10). There are hints too that Dionysus was sometimes identified with Phanes, in which case his reign at the end of the succession of generations will represent not simply a new and latest world order but in some sense a return of the primal deity. Cf. Bossi 2010.

plenty. But the restoration of the primordial regime takes the form in *Birds* of the realization of an imperial ambition, even if their victory proves benign for their new subjects.[16]

The conceit that a primitive society, uncorrupted by wealth and private interests, may overrun its more sophisticated neighbors was not unfamiliar to the Greeks – their image of the Scythian tribes is one example – and has remained a potent image to this day (think of the "Dune" novels). But a model for the birds' will to power was closer to hand in the year 414 BCE, when the comedy was produced. The Athenians, together with their allies, had recently launched a great armada, with a view to bringing the island of Sicily under their sway and thus severing Sparta and the Peloponnesus from their overseas confederates. Thucydides provides a vivid description of the hopes and passions that the fleet inspired, which, he avows, was the greatest military undertaking in Greek history (6.31). The grand project of the birds, by which they rule the entire cosmos, might have appeared to Aristophanes' audience as an augmented image of their own expansionist drive.

In the finale of *Birds*, the gods surrender and Peisetaerus marries Basileia, "Queen" or "Princess," formerly the consort of Zeus, whose place he has taken. As king, the birds too are subject to Peisetaerus' authority. Indeed, he is described as tyrant (*turannos*, 1708), which strictly speaking signifies a person or group that has usurped power but at the same time suggests the coercive rule of an autocrat. Most surprisingly, Peisetaerus appears on stage roasting the flesh of some birds who are said to have rebelled against the popular party (1583–1585, cf. 1688). What was their offense? We do not know. In the end, Aristophanes plants the bare hint that this utopia too must resort to force in order to ensure complete concord among the populace.

Comic Utopias

Among the surviving comedies of Aristophanes, two others evoke utopian societies. Both were composed late in his life, after the turn of the fourth century. The earlier is *Ecclesiazusae* or *Assemblywomen*, produced around 392; the other is *Ploutos* or *Wealth*, produced posthumously by Aristophanes' son in 388. Like *Birds*, *Assemblywomen* begins with an expression of discontent with the situation in Athens, this time focusing not on the courts and financial impositions but rather on the more general civic malaise caused by the mismanagement of the city's affairs as a whole. Nor is it just a pair of disgruntled citizens who seek an alternative, but rather the women of Athens as a whole, and their complaint is that the men who govern are dishonest and above all changeable and inconsistent. Women, on the contrary, stick to the traditional ways, tried and true. They are also economical in managing the household, and care deeply for their children, and so will not frivolously engage in wars. Inspired by their leader, Praxagora, the women agree, not to form their own society, but rather to pack the Assembly and propose a bill to transfer political power entirely to them. And so it transpires. But as soon as they are granted full control, they install a radical regime, in which all property is pooled, whether land or money or even domestic goods. There will no longer be a distinction between rich and poor, but all will live off the common store, dining in public mess halls. But that is not all. In addition, Praxagora decrees that men may sleep with any woman they desire, and women can produce children with whatever man they wish (614–15). But Praxagora's husband objects, handsome young men (or rich ones, 611–13), and pretty girls will have a monopoly on sex and the old and decrepit will have to do without. To this, Praxagora replies that, according to the new rules, the ugliest will have first dibs, and only when they have been satisfied may one proceed to the more good-looking ones. A further result is that fathers will not know which children are theirs, nor children their fathers. This is Plato's Republic, but with a vengeance, since the abolition of private property and the family will extend not only to the ruling class but to all citizens (slaves are not included in Praxagora's dispensation, and their labor will sustain the

---

[16] We may compare Plato's account of the ideal society of Atlantis, which nevertheless harbored world-conquering ambitions; see *Timaeus* 24E–25A, and the incomplete *Critias*.

system, 652). As Praxagora puts it, "I will make the city a single household" (673–74). No more complete collapse of the distinction between public and private can be imagined.

Of course, there will be dissenters, whose resistance is exhibited in a pair of exemplificatory scenes. One man decides to hold off contributing his goods to the central depot even as he takes advantage of the free meal service. Then, a young man seeks a tryst with his young lover, but much to his chagrin, three old women appeal to the new law and oblige him to take them on first (the details are set out in the chapter, in this volume, devoted to *Assemblywomen*). There follows a universal invitation to join the collective banquet, and with this festive moment the comedy concludes.

Unlike *Birds*, in *Assemblywomen* Athens harbors within itself the agents of its transformation, in that part of the citizen population that had hitherto been disenfranchised and so had no special stake in the dominant order, whether political (men only could vote) or domestic, since each household was headed by a male guardian or *kurios* who alone had legal standing. Women are, in this respect, analogous to animals: the distinctions that mark the patriarchal order are foreign to them, and when given a chance, they do away with them entirely. By satisfying all the basic needs of citizens, including sexual, the new community can hope to eliminate internal strife and promote the solidarity of its members. There will be no theft, Praxagora proclaims, because all will be provided for. Still, individual preferences will remain, and the boy and girl who are so enamored of one another might well prefer a less equitable sexual regime. Had Aristophanes been disposed to introduce a romantic theme, of the sort that was the mainstay of New Comedy, where *erós* took center stage, he might have intimated a desire on the part of the young couple to flee this new regime, thereby highlighting its oppressive nature in the manner of *Brave New World*. That was not Aristophanes' mode, however, and in any case, in classical Athens no young maiden of citizen status would have been as forward and immodest as the girl in *Assemblywomen*. Of course, there is now a new social order, and things have changed, but there is reason to believe that an Athenian audience would have perceived the girl as a budding hetaera or courtesan. Still, the world the women make shows signs of fissures, not unlike the finale of *Birds*, though in a different register.

The communism of *Assemblywomen* rests on the supposition that slaves can produce a sufficient surplus to provide for the needs and even the luxuries of the free citizens. Xenophon, in a brief essay called the *Poroi* or, as it is sometimes translated, the *Ways and Means*, proposed that all Athenians might receive an economic subsidy from the profits of the silver mines at Laurion, which were manned by as many as 20 000 public slaves. Whether the redistribution of this and other slave-based revenues from farming and manufacturing could enable the transition from property-based individualism to a communal way of life may be doubted. In any case, Aristophanes' last play, *Wealth*, constructs a utopia rather on the premise of limitless affluence that is magically conjured up, thanks to the beneficence of the god of wealth himself. The plot, which is discussed in greater detail in another chapter in this volume, is straightforward enough. The protagonist, Chremylus, seeks a solution to the pervasive corruption of Athenian society, in which the evil prosper and the few who are decent and honest dwell in miserable poverty. He consults the oracle of Apollo at Delphi, which instructs him to follow the first person he sees as he leaves the precinct. This turns out to be a decrepit old sightless man, who, as it happens, is Ploutos himself, blinded by Zeus because, he says, Zeus resented human beings (ἀνθρώποις φθονῶν, 87), and because Ploutos visited only those who were just, wise, and well behaved. Chremylus comes up with the bold plan of restoring Ploutos' sight, which will not only allow him to distinguish again between the righteous and the wrongdoers, and so reward only the deserving, but also to regain his original power and replace Zeus as the ruling deity. With this, he will bring limitless bounty to the world – after all, he is wealth personified – and poverty will be driven out once and for all.

There is a certain inconsistency in the way Aristophanes represents the economic problem in Athens. On the one hand, Chremylus sees it as the unfair distribution of wealth, with the result that only the corrupt are rich (though they are taken to be very numerous). Once Ploutos recovers his sight, this injustice will be remedied, since he is, by his own account, a morally responsible deity, unlike Zeus. On the other hand, Ploutos' blindness is also a symbol of his defeat at Zeus' hands, and once he can see again, he regains his former station. With this, there is not just a fairer distribution of existing resources but a limitless profusion of everything. This is the kind of utopia the birds promised, where all will prosper equally. In the first scenario, wherein the condition of decent and crooked citizens is simply inverted, one can see why some, who had flourished in the old order, might have grounds for complaint in the new regime. But if everyone will be affluent, why would anyone protest? In the exemplificatory scenes, we see why. First, a just citizen arrives on the scene, whose fortunes have taken a sudden turn for the better. Immediately thereafter there enters a sycophant, which is to say, a citizen who takes it upon himself to denounce and bring to trial evildoers, as he perceives them. This kind of officious busybody was a natural butt for satire, and from his first words one might conclude that, as a malicious snitch, he has simply got his comeuppance under the new dispensation, where the tables have been turned and the wicked have lost their advantage. "Haven't I suffered something criminal? I have lost my entire home thanks to this god. He'll go blind again, if there's any justice" (856–59). The just man and Chremylus' slave, Cario, deduce at once that he is wicked and deserves his misery. But in fact, the sycophant defends his profession as necessary to the city. When the just citizen says, "But wouldn't you want to live in leisure, enjoying peace and quiet?" the sycophant responds, "But you're describing a sheep's life, where there'll be no occupation in life." The just man continues: "Won't you change your mind?" To which the sycophant answers, "Not if you should give me Wealth himself and all the silphium in Cyrene" – an expression equivalent to "all the tea in China" (921–25). The idle life, where no one works and everything is freely available, appalls the sycophant. We may recall the father in the story by Hugh Howey, who "gets annoyed by how other people spend their free time. Not working hard enough." The sycophant is stripped and humiliated, and sent packing.

Next comes an old woman, who has a particular grievance: a poor but handsome young man who had cozied up to her for her gifts, has abandoned her now that he, like everyone else, is in the money. Even where material needs are provided for, love may be lacking, or unequally bestowed. When the young gigolo himself appears, he insults the old lady cruelly. Later, after Hermes has capitulated and a priest, who is now starving because no one offers sacrificial dinners any more (people only worship when they are in need), is appeased, the old woman turns up again, just a few verses from the end. To her worried query, Chremylus replies: "It will all work out. The young man will come to you this evening" (1200–1201). Out of earshot, Chremylus cracks one more nasty joke at her expense (ridicule of the sexuality of old women was a staple of ancient humor), but this new world, like that of *Assemblywomen*, will guarantee (we are not told how) that no one's erotic needs will go unmet.

The utopian fantasy of *Ploutos* has been interpreted as a protest against the class divisions that emerged in the wake of Athens' defeat in the Peloponnesian War, and it is certainly possible that such a social agenda is implicit in the comedy. In a radical democracy like Athens, where an ideal of political equality co-existed with real differences in wealth within the citizen class, a dream of universal prosperity might have some appeal, however impractical. In the movie, *Elysium*, the super-rich have created an alternative environment on a space station that circles the earth and have a monopoly on all amenities, including advanced medical care, while the masses below struggle to survive on a barely habitable planet.[17] In the end, rebels from earth succeed in reprogramming the computer on Elysium so that it now recognizes all human beings as citizens, with the result that its facilities become available to all. Evidently, there was always more than enough to go around; the solution is comparable to the resuscitation of Wealth in Aristophanes' play, except that a technological fantasy substitutes for the role of the god (Nephelokokkygia, or "Cloud-Cuckoo-Land," as the avian city in *Birds* is dubbed, bears some analogy to Elysium).

---

[17] The movie opened in 2013, produced and directed by Neill Blomkamp, and starring, among others, Matt Damon and Jodie Foster.

Conclusion

Another film of the same stripe, *In Time*, imagines a world where the upper class has a monopoly not on money as such but on years of life, which are calculated on a clock genetically built into each person's forearm. Those who are poor in the new currency die within a year of their 25th birthday, whereas those who have banked extra time can live on forever, remaining physically unchanged (one can give one's own time to others, as the birds promise to do in Aristophanes' play).[18] Here too, action heroes (including a renegade from the privileged Time Zone of New Greenwich) break into the vault where time capsules are stored and distribute years to those in need. Once more, it seems that existing resources are sufficient to go around, and it is only the greed and arrogance of the upper class, rather than scarcity, that is responsible for the early deaths and poverty of the masses. The fault in the system is simply hoarding. The limitless abundance promised by technology today could only be imagined, in antiquity, as a result of magically self-propelled objects that take the place of slaves (as in Crates' *Theria*) or else as the return of a mythical age of plenty.

Poverty and misrule are not the only afflictions that inspire fantasies of a better world. War too, and especially civil war or dissension, may give rise to imagined reigns of peace and harmony. In Aristophanes' *Eirene* or *Peace*, produced in 421 just before the first phase of the Peloponnesian War was halted by the truce sponsored by Nicias, an Athenian citizen concocts a scheme for rescuing the goddess Peace, who is being held captive by War. His plan is to overfeed a dung beetle till it is large enough to carry him to Olympus, where, with the help of Greeks drawn from all over, he will liberate Peace. This achieved, he brings back to earth two other deities, Harvest (whom he will marry) and Festival, who will preside over a restored and idealized world of rustic merriment. Arms makers and their like have no place here and are obliged to turn their swords into plowshares or some comparable piece of domestic equipment. Francisco Barrenechea has made a strong case regarding Eirene not merely as an ad hoc personification in the play but as a goddess with a cult of her own. As he notes, Peace received some form of worship in classical Greece, though the evidence for Aristophanes' own time is not conclusive (Barrenechea makes a similar case for Ploutos as a genuine deity; see Barrenechea 2018).

The revival of a reign of peace has affinities with the archetype of the return of a displaced deity that generates the utopias of *Birds* and *Wealth*. The same motif was available to the Roman poet Tibullus, when he imagined a new era of peace that, as many hoped, the triumph of Octavian over his rivals and his rise to sole ruler over the empire would inaugurate. The tenth elegy of the first book of Tibullus's elegies begins:

> Who was he, who first forged the fearful sword?
> How iron-willed and truly made of iron he was!
> Then slaughter was created, war was born to men.
> Then a quicker road was opened to dread death.
> But perhaps it's not the wretch's fault we turn to evil
> what he gave us to use on savage beasts?
> That's the curse of rich gold: there were no wars
> when the beech-wood cup stood beside men's plates.
> There were no fortresses or fences, and the flock's leader
> sought sleep securely among the diverse sheep.
> I might have lived then, Valgius, and not known
> sad arms, or heard the trumpet with beating heart.
> Now I'm dragged to war, and perhaps some enemy
> already carries the spear that will pierce my side
>
> (1–14, trans. Kline 2001, slightly modified).

The early days of mankind were a time of simple wants, easily satisfied. Although this image of rural ease is not the exuberant abundance of a lush paradise, all were content and there were no barriers between plots of land. Sadly, this epoch gave way to one of war and danger, specifically, of course,

---

[18] Opened in 2011, directed and produced by Andrew Niccol and starring Amanda Seyfried and Justin Timberlake.

the great conflict between Octavian and Marc Antony, with the support of Cleopatra, but perceived more generally as a long era of bellicosity and greed. But Tibullus ends his poem on a hopeful note:

> Meanwhile let Peace tend the fields. Bright Peace first
> bowed the oxen for plowing under the curved yoke.
> Peace nurtured the vines and laid up the juice of the grape
> so the son's wine might pour from the father's jar.
> Hoe and plowshare gleam by Peace, but rust seizes
> the grim weapons of the cruel soldier in darkness.
> ...
>
> Then come, kindly Peace, hold the wheat-ear in your hand,
> and let your radiant breast pour out fruits before us (45–50, 67–68).

Editors and translators vary over whether and where to capitalize Pax: some do so throughout, others only in the penultimate verse, when Peace is addressed directly, and still others not at all. Pax received official recognition and a cult in the time of Augustus, who dedicated the famous *Ara Pacis* to her as well as a temple in the newly created *Forum Pacis*. She is called the foster mother or nurse of Ceres, with whom she shares some conspicuous traits, in Ovid's *Fasti* (1.697–704). It is unclear whether Tibullus imagined the goddess Pax (capital P) reigning in the earliest stage of human history. If he did, as I am inclined to believe, then he adapted the scenario that Aristophanes portrayed in his *Birds* and *Wealth* (and in modified form in the *Peace*), by which an ideal life is associated with the return to power of a displaced deity. In any case, Tibullus was invoking the three-tiered conception of human history as beginning in a golden age, which then gave way to an epoch of conflict and toil, but with a promise of a future redemption. One convention identified the prior world with the reign of Cronus (the Latin Saturn), whose overthrow by Zeus (or Jupiter) ushered in an age of penury and violence. The third, utopian phase was the return to peace and plenty, under the aegis of a new deity or one restored to power, as intimated in the Orphic cosmologies and by Aristophanes in several of his utopian comedies – and perhaps by Tibullus as well.[19]

The ideal of a return to the land has persisted up to our own time, sometimes envisaged and even put into practice as local communes, more rarely conceived of on a global scale, usually supported by ecologically benign technologies. In the ancient world, where products of the earth constituted a larger proportion of overall wealth than they do today, and where a majority of people still worked the land, such a vision was nearer to everyday experience. But a farmer's life is a hard one, and also competitive. As Hesiod puts it, in his praise of the good kind of *eris* or contention:

> She stirs up even the shiftless to toil; for a man grows eager to work when he considers his neighbor, a rich man who hastens to plough and plant and put his house in good order; and neighbor vies with his neighbor as he hurries after wealth. This Strife is wholesome for men. And potter is angry with potter, and craftsman with craftsman, and beggar is jealous of beggar, and minstrel of minstrel (*Works and Days* 20–26, trans. Evelyn-White 1914).

Menander's *Dyscolus* or *Grouch* gives a more sober picture of what it is like to eke a living out of Attica's meager soil. A working farmer's idea of the good life may be less that conjured up by an upper-class poet like Tibullus (who was of the rank of *eques* or knight in Rome), and more a vision of an end to toil as such, stripped of its romantic or ethical penumbra. Let slaves do the work, as in *Assemblywomen*: then there will be no need for private property. Or let the birds take care of it, or let wealth be there for the taking, as though everyone had the touch of Midas. Extend the vision of plenty to include as much sex as one may desire, and with whomever, and gone is the need and very concept of privacy. With all one could wish at everyone's fingertips, social harmony is guaranteed, and there is no place for conflict between the private and the public realms. Only spoilsports will

---

[19] In Tibullus 1.7, for example, it is Messalla's genius or personal tutelary deity that occupies this role. The most famous Roman example of the pattern is Virgil's fourth *Eclogue*, which proclaims, *redeunt Saturnia regna* (Saturn's reign returns, v. 5).

complain. If they continue to abide in a perfect world, it may be because each utopia reflects in a distorted way the values that it seeks to supersede. Even in Cloud-Cuckoo-Land, there will be objectors to the new regime, who may find themselves in the roasting pan – and not at all disposed, like the fish in Crates' utopia, to flip themselves over happily when they are done on one side.

GUIDE TO FURTHER READING

For Aristophanes' *Birds* in English, see Henderson (2000); for commentary on the Greek text, see Dunbar (1998). On utopia as a theme in Greek and later literature, see Jouanno (2008), Konstan (1995, 2012, 2021), Ollman (2005), and Wenglinsky (2020). More's *Utopia* can be approached through the edition of Logan and Adams (1989).

REFERENCES

Anders, C.J. (ed.) (2019). *A People's Future of the United States*. New York.
Barrenechea, F. (2018). *Comedy and Religion in Classical Athens: Narratives of Religious Experiences in Aristophanes' Wealth*. Cambridge.
Bossi, B. (2010). A riddle at the end of the *Philebus*: why should we stop at the sixth generation? (*Phil*.66 c 8-10 = OF 25 B. = 14 K.). In: *Orfeo y el Orfismo: Nuevas Perspectivas* (ed. A. Bernabé, F. Casadesús, and M.A. Santamaría), 372–386. Alicante. Available at: http://www.cervantesvirtual.com/obra/orfeo-y-el-orfismo-nuevas-perspectivas--0.
Dunbar, N. (1998). *Aristophanes Birds*. Oxford: Edited with Introduction and Commentary.
Evelyn-White, H.G., trans. (1914). *Hesiod*. Cambridge, MA: Loeb Classical Library.
Gerolemou, M. (2020). Why can't I have wings? Aristophanes' *Birds*. In: *Classical Literature and Posthumanism* (ed. G.M. Chesi and F. Spiegel), 175–182. London.
Harrison, A.R.W. (1968). *The Law of Athens*, vol. 1. Oxford.
Henderson, J. (ed. and trans)(2000). *Aristophanes Birds, Lysistrata, Women at the Thesmophoria*. Cambridge MA: Loeb Classical Library.
Johnston, I. (2017). ΆΡΙΣΤΟΦΑΝΟΥΣ Νεφέλαι *ARISTOPHANES' Clouds*. Oxford: Ohio.
Jouanno, C. (2008). L'utopie, état de la question. *Kentron: Revue Pluridisciplinaire du Monde Antique* 24: 13–22.
Kline, A.S. (2001), Tibullus and Sulpicia (55 BC–19 BC) – The Poems. Accessible at https://www.poetryintranslation.com/PITBR/Latin/Tibullus.php#anchor_Toc532635316 (accessed 4 July 2021).
Konstan, D. (1995). *Greek Comedy and Ideology*. Oxford.
Konstan, D. (2012). A world without slaves: Crates' *Thêria*. In: *No Laughing Matter: New Studies in Athenian Comedy* (ed. C.W. Marshall and G. Kovacs), 13–18. London.
Konstan, D. (2021). Post-Utopia: The Long View. *Humanities* 10: 65. https://doi.org/10.3390/h10020065 (accessed 4 July 2021).
More, T. (1989). Utopia. Ed. G.M. Logan and R.M. Adams. Cambridge: Cambridge University Press.
Ollman, B. (2005). The utopian vision of the future (then and now): a Marxist critique. *Monthly Review* 57: 78–102.
Richter, A.G. (2015). *At Home in Nineteenth-Century America: A Documentary History*. New York.
Rusten, J. (ed.) (2011). *The Birth of Comedy: Texts, Documents, and Art from Athenian Comic Competitions*, 486–280. Baltimore.
Verde, F. (2020). Momenti di riflessione sull'animalità nel Kepos: Epicuro, Lucrezio, Ermarco e Polistrato. In: *La voce e il logos: Filosofie dell'animalità nella storia delle idee* (ed. S. Gensini), 53–78. Pisa.
Wenglinsky, M. (2020). Utopias. In: *Wenglinsky Review*. July 26. Available online: https://www.wenglinskyreview.com/wenglinskyreview-a-journal-of-culture-politics/2020/7/26/utopias (accessed 15 November 2020).

CHAPTER 13

Lysistrata: Sexuality

Kate Gilhuly

Introduction

Aristophanes' *Lysistrata* is the most famous of Greek comedies and is frequently performed and adapted, with contemporary audiences drawn to its depiction of sexually actualized women-in-charge and its anti-war message. Recent adaptations include Spike Lee's provocative film *Chiraq*, set on the South side of Chicago, in which a character called Lysistrata tries to end gang violence through a sex strike, posing serious questions about sexual and racial attitudes, and on the lighter side, *Lysistrata Jones*, a Broadway musical comedy depicting cheerleaders of a college basketball team who refuse to have sex with their boyfriends until the team wins a game. These very different takes on the ancient comedy attest to the enduring appeal of the premise. If we consider the play in the context of fifth-century Athens, with attention to the constraints of ancient comedy and Athenian attitudes toward sexuality, however, *Lysistrata* becomes more notable for the way the image of the sexually empowered woman and the anti-war theme has a very specific meaning in that context. Both of these themes are nuanced, complicated, and interrelated. We find that ancient Greek sexuality was distinctly *different* from our own, and appreciation of this difference in turn enriches our understanding of the play.

A brief encapsulation of the plot will lay the groundwork for the discussion that follows: the play begins when Lysistrata has called together a meeting of the women of Greece to propose a plan for how they can stop the Peloponnesian war. At first local women arrive, Athenians, their neighbors and allies in the war, and then the women from abroad arrive, representatives of Athens' enemies: a Spartan woman, a Boeotian, and a Corinthian woman. Lysistrata presents her scheme to the women, first getting them all to agree that they are tired of the war. She proposes that they refrain from sex with their husbands until they quit fighting. The women balk, until Lysistrata gets the Spartan Lampito to agree to her plan, and then the others follow. Next in a ridiculous ritual procedure, the women swear an oath and sacrifice a wineskin to seal the deal, promising that they will seduce their husbands, but stop short of having sex with them. The young women return home ready to enact their plan, while the older women seize the Acropolis. Having learned of the takeover, a magistrate comes to investigate. The women easily overwhelm him, dressing him as a woman and then as a corpse. Eventually, all the women, young and old, gather on the Acropolis. Here, their willpower starts to wane, and Lysistrata has trouble keeping them there and has to resort to fabricating an oracle. At this point, Kinesias enters, hard up for his wife, Myrrhine, and under Lysistrata's direction, Myrrhine teases her husband and then leaves him in the lurch. Finally, the Spartans and the Athenians yield to the women, sending ambassadors to negotiate a peace treaty, which Lysistrata oversees in the presence of a desirable naked woman named Diallage. The comedy resolves in a feast and a festive mood, with the Spartans and Athenians taking turns singing and dancing.

Lysistrata was performed in 411, most likely at the Lenaia, a festival in honor of the god Dionysus, a domestic celebration with no foreigners or allies present. Ancient drama was state sponsored, and theatergoing was an integral aspect of citizenship. At the time of performance, the Athenians were still fighting a war against the Spartans and their allies, primarily Corinth and Boeotia. While the Athenians had suffered a major setback with their infamously misguided expedition to Sicily in 413, they had recently forced a naval retreat of Peloponnesian ships into a Corinthian harbor and had appointed an extraordinary body, the *Probouloi* to handle war-time finances. The Spartans were garrisoned at Deceleia, which meant that trade routes crucial to food supplies were cut off, and Athens' allies were on the verge of revolt. It is hard to square this political context, being in the middle of fighting a war, with the common interpretation that *Lysistrata* is a pro-Spartan peace play. Thus, rather than trying to impart a narrow political agenda to Aristophanes, it seems likely that his goal was to win the dramatic contest (see Hall 2014; Rosen 2018). All of Athenian drama was presented as part of a competition, and in one comedy, Aristophanes even appears onstage articulating his desire to win (*Clouds* 547–574). Consequently, it seems the poet's aim was to appeal to the broadest range of his audience members; in the case of *Lysistrata*, this means communicating a message that appealed to all Athenians, as much to the war-weary as to the bellicose.

Ancient Greece and the History of Sexuality

It has only been in the relatively recent past that scholars have considered sexuality a legitimate area of study and to discuss and translate frankly the sexuality depicted in ancient literature. Prior to this, the "dirty" parts of ancient Greek literature were translated into Latin, and in the Latin lexicon the definition would be provided in French, rendering ancient sexuality something that only polyglots could access. In 1975, Jeffrey Henderson published the *Maculate Muse*, the first full-length study to directly address obscenity and sexuality in Greek Comedy. Since then, sexuality has become a legitimate object of scholarly attention and the current standard is to speak frankly about what the Greek text is actually communicating, a practice followed in this article.

Ancient Greece has played a pivotal role in the history of sexuality, because Michel Foucault used the Greek culture of pederasty to make the argument that sexuality is not, as was previously thought, natural, but rather culturally determined, and therefore changing over time (Foucault 1990). Foucault's work appeared just after Sir Kenneth Dover published his groundbreaking study, *Greek Homosexuality*, which anchored Foucault's claims in learned philological readings and a broad consideration of vase painting (Dover 1980). Pederasty refers to the erotic pursuit of late adolescent boys by older men. Dover argued and Foucault broadcast the notion that the distinctive feature of Greek pederasty was that the love of someone of the same sex did not determine one's sexual identity.

In contemporary Western culture, the gender of the object of desire defines one's sexuality as homosexual or heterosexual; in ancient Greece, however, as Dover and Foucault argued, men who loved boys were often married with families, and this love did not define their identity in any particular way. As long as the man wanted to penetrate the object of his desire, his masculinity went unquestioned. For a man, to desire penetration would liken him to a woman and affect his identity. For example, in *Lysistrata* (621), Aristophanes depicts the chorus of old men fearing that the Spartans are gathering at Kleisthenes' house, inciting the women as they take over the Acropolis. Kleisthenes, a politician, was a frequent butt of comic ridicule because he was clean shaven, or unable to grow a manly beard and thus was characterized as effeminate. The Athenians imagine the Spartans gathering at his house, because they thought that Spartans were especially fond of anal sex with grown men (Henderson 1987). The association of Kleisthenes' effeminacy with a willingness to be penetrated aligns with Dover and Foucault's model. This paradigm was further elaborated by David Halperin, who describes the Athenian conception of "sex as phallic action" promoting an image of masculine civic identity as self-controlled, dominant, and insertive (Halperin (1990), 101–102). Foucault's influence is also evident in the watershed edited volume *Before Sexuality* in which Classicists engaged with the insight that sexuality, as "the most intimate feature of an individual, that dimension of the personality which it takes longest to fathom, and which, when finally known, reveals the truth about much of the rest" is a modern construction, in a range of essays that brilliantly opened up avenues of inquiry for Classicists about the various different ways the Greeks organized themselves around erotic experience (Halperin et al. 1990).

In his study of homosexuality in early Christianity, John Boswell articulated a different stance from the constructionist position of Dover, Foucault, and Halperin, arguing for a trans-historical category of the homosexual, claiming that, "if the categories 'homosexual/heterosexual' and 'gay/ straight' are the inventions of particular societies rather than real aspects of the human psyche, there is no gay history" (Boswell (1982) 93, see also Boswell 1994). Later, James Davidson argued forcefully that the conceptualization of homosexual love as a zero-sum competition is "obnoxious myth-making," that oversexualizes the Greeks, misses the larger context of Greek erotics, and suggests that interpreting homosexual love based on a heterosexual model is driven by homophobia (see Davidson 2001, quote from 49). The impasse created by these two positions, referred to, respectively, as constructionists and positivists, has recently been circumvented by Queer theorists, who find affinity in nonnormative identities in the past, while respecting their historical specificity (Dinshaw 1999). This body of work tends to emphasize the multiplicity of subject positions and opens up an expansive field for seeing sexual identity in the past. While these criticisms and modifications to early efforts to study the history of sexuality have been important interventions, some of the early insights about the distinctiveness of ancient Greek sexuality, both the fact that pederasty was culturally sanctioned and that sexual identity was not necessarily determined by the object of one's desire, are generally accepted, and it is clear that Foucault's thinking about sexuality in ancient Greece has been extremely productive for both his critics and his followers.

With pederasty at the heart of this discussion, male sexuality has been crucial to the history of sexuality. While there has been an efflorescence of interest in gender over the last 50 years, and women's lives in the ancient world, the construction of sexualities involving women, heterosexuality and lesbianism, has not been central to the discussion of the history of sexuality. But sexualities exist in a constellation, and if we follow Foucault in his claim that sexuality is historically contingent, then all forms of sexuality should be expected to change over time, including heterosexuality. *Lysistrata* provides invaluable insight into what is distinctive about Athenian attitudes to sexuality, especially women's roles in heterosexual relationships. It also is concerned with sex as commodity, pederasty, and the role of place in defining sexual cultures as well. We can use a consideration of the play to illuminate attitudes toward these aspects of sexuality in classical Athens, remembering that these erotic depictions are substantially shaped by the generic concerns of ancient comedy.

It is crucial to keep in mind that we really do not have access to ancient sexual practices, rather the traces of ancient sexuality are all found in representations, whether textual or graphic. It is therefore important to be thoughtful about how representations work. Here again Foucault's insights are extremely useful, in particular, his theory of discourse: he identifies discourse as the medium through which power and knowledge are transmitted. Discourse is conceived of as an open field in which a multiplicity of elements can circulate and be used for various strategies. They are made up of "tactical elements or blocks operating in the field of force relations; there can exist different and even contradictory discourses within the same strategy; they can, on the contrary, circulate without changing their form from one strategy to another, opposing strategy" (Foucault (1990) 101–102). Silences or discretions function not as the limit of discourse, but alongside them and within them. Expanding on this notion, Eve Sedgwick has emphasized that we do not encounter a discursive regime as a coherent totality, but we allow for incoherence, irrationality, and understand that we are catching glimpses of a system in process (Sedgwick (1990) 44–48). I think this provides a useful model for conceptualizing how we encounter sexuality in *Lysistrata*. It is as though we are dealing with a marketplace of different ways of talking about sexuality, with various discourses being deployed for different strategies. Thus, we can think of Halperin's notion of sex as phallic power as one ancient discourse about ancient sexuality, and Davidson's notion of pederasty as being contextualized through the language of gift exchange and self-control as other discursive elements. In what follows, rather than trying to illuminate a single coherent system of ancient sexuality that lurks behind Aristophanes' humor, we will examine the range of strategies Aristophanes uses to articulate different facets of ancient sexuality in the service of his comedy, embracing contradictions, ruptures, and incoherence. In a sense this aligns with a tenet of Queer theory, that sexuality is heterogeneous (Dinshaw 2012 1–39). A key advantage of this approach is that it is capacious and allows us to include various approaches to ancient sexuality and take advantage of a range of the many important insights that have been advanced in the last 50 years about ancient Greek sexuality and the way it takes shape in Aristophanes' *Lysistrata*.

Greek Comedy, Constraints, and Incitements

Athenian comedy provides a unique vantage from which to investigate sexuality, because it is a genre fundamentally concerned with phallic potency and civic reproduction. The comedies were performed as part of a ritual to honor Dionysos. They were preceded by a phallic procession (Cole 1993; Csapo 1997; Hedreen 2004). The name comedy derives from *komos*-singers, with a *komos* being a drunken ritual carousing. Early depictions on vases depict dancers wearing costumes that exaggerate the front and behind, sometimes with a phallus, and they are generally grotesque. Aristotle theorizes that the origins of comedy and tragedy lie in the festivals of Dionysos, associating comedy with the phallic songs still customary in his own day. Comedy is the representation of baser men, he says, characterized by the ridiculous (*Poetics* 1449a 32–37). As such, comedy embraces the material world, assumes a middling to low economic and social perspective, revels in bodily functions, and speaks bluntly about sexuality. For the Athenians, sexuality, including the ridicule of sexual behavior, was intrinsic to public life (Florence 2013).

Consequently, contemporary audiences can find the plays extremely explicit or even offensive. In fifth-century Athens, there were strictures about what was appropriate to say on the comic stage about citizens and their family members, but these constraints are very different from our own (Halliwell 1991). It seems it was forbidden in Athenian comedy to mock a citizen calling him a father-beater, a mother-beater, or to say that a warrior is the kind who would throw away his shield, but it was perfectly fine to represent politicians, the cultural elite, and one's audience as senselessly buggered (*The Clouds* 1086–1104), to use animal metaphors to talk about female genitalia (*Acharnians* 719–835), or to introduce a character as he empties his bowels in the middle of the street (*Assemblywomen* 311–325).

Lysistrata was the first of the trio of so-called "women plays," followed by *Women at the Thesmophoria*, and *Assemblywomen*, plays that focus on collective groups of Athenian women, in their domestic, civic, and ritual roles. When these plays were originally performed, it was not appropriate to speak publicly about an Athenian woman identifying her by her name (Schaps 1977; Sommerstein 1980), and unmarried daughters were not portrayed on the comic stage (Henderson 1975). A woman could be referred to as someone's daughter, or wife, but to call her by her own name was to bring shame on her. The ideal of keeping women out of public discourse was most famously expressed in Pericles' Funeral Oration as represented by Thucydides in the *History of the Peloponnesian War*. Addressing the wives of the war dead, he says, "It is a great glory is to be least mentioned by men, whether in terms of praise or blame" (Thuc. 2.45.2). In Attic oratory, we notice that only those women are named whose reputation is being besmirched, and it would seem that the same practice held true on the comic stage. Aristophanes is thus writing about Athenian wives in a context that was much more constrained than it was for men. Indeed, it was a comic practice to ridicule well-known male public figures. Cleon and Euripides were frequent targets of Aristophanes, as were his poetic rivals, even Dionysos, the god of theatre is not spared Aristophanes' ridicule. The send-up of Socrates in the *Clouds* (423 BCE) was so effective that Plato has Socrates address the portrayal in his *Apology*, set almost 25 years later. This kind of treatment, however, would have been unthinkable for a woman. As we move through a discussion of the play, we will see how this conventional silence about Athenian women in comedy shapes Aristophanes' discursive strategy.

The opening scene contains some essential comic tropes about women and comic approaches to sexuality that are consistent throughout old comedy. First, comedy represents women as lushes. In the very first line, Lysistrata laments that if she had invited the women to drink wine, she would have no problem motivating them to get together. Second, women on the comic stage are sex crazy. The first woman to interact with Lysistrata is Kalonike, who asks about the matter Lysistrata wants to discuss, inquiring if it is big and hard. Lysistrata answers yes, and as a result Kalonike cannot understand where everyone is (21–24).

Sexuality and Place

A bit later, the foreign women arrive. In this scene, we get our first glimpse of the comic penchant for linking the culture of sexuality to place. First Lampito is objectified in a very particular way:

Sweetheart, how beautiful you are!
You have such great color, and your body
is full to bursting! You could strangle a bull.

(79–81)

Lysistrata sizes Lampito up remarking on her beauty, healthy color, and the vigor of her body. Her assessment takes a strange turn when she comments, "You could throttle a bull (81)." Unlike Athenians, Spartan women were encouraged to exercise, and Aristophanes is using this cultural distinction for humorous purposes. Lampito responds in a comic Spartan accent that she exercises by kicking her butt, alluding to a famous Spartan dance. Kalonike notices her formidable breasts, and Lampito ends this objectifying survey by saying, "You are feeling me up like a sacrificial animal (84)." The Boeotian woman is noted for her beautiful plain and neatly plucked "pennyroyal," the flora of her homeland standing in for her pubic hair. The depilation of the pubic area was figured in comedy as an essential element of femininity, clearly a practice that provoked fascination in men. Indeed, the very masculine kinsman in *Thesmophoriazousai*, having been convinced to pose as a woman and infiltrate the women at ritual puts on women's clothes, hides his own genitals, and then improbably has to singe his pubic area to pass as female. Finally, Lysistrata asks about the Corinthian woman, and Myrrhine describes her as "fine in front and behind (93)," perhaps alluding to Corinth's two harbors, but certainly sexually objectifying her. It is worth emphasizing that these three women are singled out from the others who have gathered and that they represent the city-states of Athens' antagonists in the Peloponnesian Wars.

Intriguingly, the eroticization of women by women that we encounter in this passage is rarely remarked upon, but it does find a counterpart in the Spartan poet Alcman's "Maiden Song," which seems to lurk behind some of the humor in the oath-swearing passage (Gilhuly 2018, see also Bierl 2011). Both the Corinthian and Boeotian women are also represented through the trope of woman as land, which is pervasive throughout Greek literature. The figuration of woman as a fertile field, ready to be furrowed, has been analyzed thoroughly through a psychoanalytic lens by Page Dubois (1988). The representation of Lampito is somewhat more complicated. Like the other two women, she stands for the distinctive culture of Sparta in her fitness, but her remark that she feels she is being treated like a sacrificial animal belongs to the register of ritual and renders the other remarks about her physique less explicitly sexual than the description of the other two women. There are numerous allusions to women's ritual practice throughout the play, as will be discussed below, and I suggest that it is an important aspect of Aristophanes' strategy for depicting the sexuality of married Athenian women on stage.

In these characterizations of the women from abroad, we see that different locations are thought to be the home of very distinctive sexual cultures. The association of place with sexuality as well as other characteristics is a favorite trope of comedy, and in Aristophanes' surviving texts we find a range of neologisms that situate different proclivities all around the map. To act like an Egyptian meant to be a prostitute, like a Cretan meant to lie, like someone from Lesbos meant to do shameful (sexual) things. The verb to act like a Corinthian means to be a courtesan, encapsulating the Athenian image of Corinth as a travel hub with a hospitality industry that capitalized on people passing through. The verb *lakonizein*, to act like a Spartan meant to eat the humble diet of the Spartan military, to ascribe to Sparta's conservative political ideology as well as to prefer anal sex. Henderson says that Spartan men had a penchant for sex with other adult men, thus diverging somewhat from the Athenian practice of pederasty that considered younger males on the verge of manhood as one of many appropriate objects of desire (Henderson (1987) 152). These local erotic associations with Sparta are crucial to understanding the action of the play as it unfolds (Gilhuly 2018).

The Prostitute and The Priestess

As mentioned above, there were constraints on talking about Athenian wives in public; however, two types of women were excluded from this rule. It was permitted to mention prostitutes and priestesses by their names in public: prostitutes because they were not afforded as much respect as married women; and priestesses because they were afforded more. Aristophanes avails himself of the discourses that surround the *hetaira* or courtesan, and women involved in ritual, in order to construct a representation of Athenian wives as sexual agents taking on a leadership role in public. Indeed, we can read the plot of the play, and much of its humor as being shaped by the superimposition of these two roles onto the depiction of the wives as they use their sexuality and ritual authority to get the men to stop fighting the war.

The clearest interaction in the play that suggests we are meant to think of sex traffic as we watch the sex strike unfold occurs after the women have roused their husbands and have joined the older women who first took over the acropolis, dousing the fire-bearing chorus of old men with water. Myrrhine's husband Kinesias approaches the acropolis, where all the women are now gathered. He is gripped by an urgent desire to be with his wife. Lysistrata is watching guard and when he asks if he can see Myrrhine, Lysistrata says, "What will you give me?" (861), speaking as though she is a madame negotiating the terms for sex with a client. Much of the women's language in the play is erotic and takes place in the public domain. In their oath, the women describe seductive clothing, slippers, and the makeup they will wear to seduce their husbands, and the sex positions they will refrain from, such as legs in the air, and the lioness-on-the-cheesegrater. We do not know exactly what the cheesegrater in this position refers to, although Leaina, translated here as Lioness, was the name of a famous Athenian courtesan, and presumably this position involves crouching on all fours. Seductive clothing, makeup, and a knowledge of sex positions would be known as well to wives as any other women; however, talking about these things in public was strictly the domain of the prostitute. "For a wife to be represented trading in her sexuality meant for the fifth-century audience of comedy, that she is no longer for all intents and purposes, a wife. In the representational mind of the audience, she becomes another kind of woman altogether (Stroup (2004) 41)." Making an effort to be sexually attractive and talk of sex positions is the purview of courtesans. Indeed, Athenaios, a Greek antiquarian preserves in his *Deipnosophistai* numerous mostly comic depictions of courtesans manipulating their appearance to be more seductive (e.g., Athenaios 568a–d), and there are a scattering of references to ancient sex manuals allegedly written by prostitutes from which genre, incidentally, our word pornography derives.

Since 1955, when David M. Lewis pointed out the similarity of Lysistrata's name to Lysimache, the priestess of Athena Polias at the time the play was performed, scholars have assumed that Aristophanes meant Lysistrata to be associated with this prestigious priestess (Lewis 1955; Foley 1982; Henderson 1987; Faraone 2006; Thonemann 2020). Lysistrata means "loosener of armies," and Lysimache means "loosener" of battles. To emphasize the association between the two, Aristophanes has Lysistrata remark that if the women's sex strike is successful and the men of Greece stop fighting one another, "I think then we will be called Lysimaches among the Greeks!" (554), suggesting that Lysimache was known to oppose the war with the Peloponnesians. According to Jeffrey Henderson, "Lysimache would thus be one of only two examples of a respectable woman being publicly named by a free man not related to her" (Henderson (1987) xxxix). Lewis also suggested that Myrrhine should be associated with the priestess of Athena Nike, based on an epitaph that identifies someone named Myrrhine as being the first to hold the post. Myrrhine was, however, a very common name, that also has sexual implications: Myrrhine means myrtle and was slang for female genitalia. Recalling that it would have been derogatory to identify a woman by her first name, we note that the name Lysistrata merely suggests the idea of Lysimache and that Myrrhine cannot be linked to any specific individual, and so no Athenian woman would be insulted. But Lampito was the exact same name as the mother of Agis, the King of Sparta who was besieging Deceleia and directing the Spartan military efforts against the Athenians. Aristophanes may have been intentionally insulting the Spartans by putting a character on stage named after the king's mother.

It may seem counterintuitive that depictions of women as priestesses have anything to do with sexuality, projecting our own beliefs about the relationship between the sacred and the sexual onto the ancient Greek context. Thus, one scholar suggests that Myrrhine could not be associated with the priestess of Athena Nike because her name is very common and her role in the play is so explicitly erotic (Henderson (1987) xli). When Lysistrata sends Myrrhine out to tease the aroused Kinesias, he is ready to go, and she further inflames him, as she keeps running off to get a mattress, pillow, blanket, and perfume. The scene represents a rare glimpse, if even a comic one, of young married heterosexual love, with the husband and wife almost equally desirous of one another, and Myrrhine's devotion to her young baby in the mix. It is important to remember that certain ritual roles were performed by just the type of woman Myrrhine represents, a regular Athenian-born woman. In fact, some sacred positions, like the Priestess of Athena Nike, were assigned by lot, others like the Priestess of Athena Polias were long term and may have been reserved for the women of elite families and associated with behavior requirements. There were indeed some ritual offices that had an explicitly erotic dimension, like the role of the Basilinna in the Spring time festival called the Anthesteria. The role of this woman was to take part in a sacred ritual marriage to Dionysos, which some scholars believe portrayed the sexual consummation as part of the rite (see Robertson 1993).

Another ritual that seemed to showcase at least one aspect of feminine sexuality was the Adonia, a festival celebrated in honor of Adonis, the beautiful young love of Aphrodite who met an untimely death when he was gored by a boar. In fact, one scholiast notes that an alternate title for Lysistrata was *Adoniazousai,* or women celebrating the Adonia. While many scholars have dismissed this note, recently Laurialan Reitzammer has explored the many subtle allusions to this rite that are found in this play, including references to boars, myrrh, Aphrodite, Adonis gardens, and lamentation (Reitzammer 2008). This rite is linked to the myth about Aphrodite's love for a younger man, Adonis, and involved forcing young shoots on rooftop gardens. The Adonia was a private festival that seems to oppose civic values, since it enacts a kind of failed fertility, or as Marcel Detienne suggested, the festival engaged with notions of improper farming, seduction, and the failure of reproduction. As Reitzhammer has argued, the allusions to this ritual reveal that Aphrodite, and the untamed, irresistible feminine sexuality that she represents are just as central to the themes of *Lysistrata* as the restrained, virginal civic-minded mentality of Athena. Indeed, Nicole Loraux sees the competition between these two goddesses and the spaces they are associated with, the acropolis and the bedroom, as the conflict that lies at the heart of the comedy (Loraux 1993).

While most scholars writing on this play over the last three decades acknowledge the influence of the image of both the prostitute and the priestess on the characterization of the wives in the play, there has been some pushback. Laura McClure argues that the notion that the sex-striking wives are modeled on the figure of the *hetaira* has eclipsed the importance of their depiction as married women, "The young wives must be viewed primarily as free citizen wives rather than as hetaeras, given the domestic setting of the sex strike and the close connection of female sexuality with reproduction (McClure (2015) 55)." Nicholas Smith has recently argued against the connection between the women in the play with priestesses, claiming that Aristophanes "does nothing to reinforce the association (Smith (2017) 39)."

What these readings confuse is the realm of discourse with realia. McClure is right to note that the women in the play *are* wives, and that is an essential element of the play. She bases part of her argument on a discussion of clothing and makeup, arguing that what the women say they will wear to seduce their husbands, saffron gowns, perfume, slippers, rouge, and transparent dresses (42–48) are represented elsewhere as the standard adornment of the Athenian housewife, as though courtesans wore some other type of apparel distinct from alluring women's clothing. In Athens, courtesans were not necessarily visibly distinct from other women. In practice, one significant anxiety about the courtesan in Athenian law courts is that she might pass as a wife. In fact, the ps. Demosthenes "Speech Against Neaira" alleges that a woman who was once a courtesan has posed as a citizen's wife for 20 years (Patterson (1994) 207). That speech also mentions that a go-between could charge a man extra for arranging sex with a married woman ([Dem.] 59.41), thus blurring the distinction between courtesan and wife even further. The one factor that does seem to separate a wife from a courtesan is space (Davidson (1998) 78). As Sarah Stroup notes "the public display of female sexuality is incompatible with the social category of 'wife' in Attic drama (Stroup (2004) 40)."

Smith is also correct to note that Aristophanes never says the women are priestesses. But he depicts Lysistrata leading the women in an oath that is secured by a ritual that mingles sacrifice and libation. As Helene Foley notes, Lysistrata deploys the power, authority, and strategies that derive from a woman's role in cult, including the weaving of a cloak and the redirecting of resources toward peaceful ends (Foley (1982) 8–9). The figure of the *hetaira* and the priestess operate in this play on the level of discourse, and the confluence of these roles allows Aristophanes to present what would have been a fantastic notion to his audience, that women could lead the *polis* by means of their sexuality. Thus, Aristophanes evokes the discourse of the *hetaira* when he depicts women negotiating with sex in public, and he calls upon the discourse of the priestess or woman at ritual to give the women authority to address Athenian political interests (e.g., 639–47). The prostitute and the priestess evoke notions of economics and morality that would not be elicited by the image of the wife alone. The prostitute evinces the suggestion of short-term sexual gratification, as well as marketplace transactions and the commodification of sex, while the priestess mediates between the city and the cosmic order, thus introducing a longer term framework and conferring a ritual logic to the plot, one that we will explore further when we come to our analysis of the Diallage scene below.

Temporality and Sexuality

Recently, work by Queer theorists has illuminated the extent to which representations of sexuality, whether they are reproductive or not, are bound up with notions of time. If the temporal arc of normative sexuality involves growing up, getting married, and having children, there is concomitantly always a path that does not follow this teleological temporality. As Carolyn Dinshaw notes, there is a temporal dimension to queerness, which represents "forms of desirous, embodied being that are out of sync with the ordinarily linear measurements of everyday life. . ." (Dinshaw (2012)4). As Valerie Rohy describes it, "queer time is nonlinear, antifamilial, non-reproductive, antihistorical, nonnormative and anachronistic, while straight time is normative, linear, teleological, genealogical, and developmental" (Rohy (2017) 250).

The insight that sexuality and gender influence the way that temporality is experienced is useful for understanding the role of the Adonia in *Lysistrata*, as well as the notion that contradictory models of temporality coexist in a single culture. There is a poignant misunderstanding involving a clash of temporalities when the magistrate complains about the women's behavior as the men are voting to make their doomed expedition to Sicily:

I remember once in the assembly – Demostratus, curse him, was saying, "Sail to Sicily," and his wife, dancing on the roof, she cried, "Alas for Adonis!" Then Demostratus went on to say, "We should enlist some hoplites from Zacynthus," and the woman on the roof – she was a little tipsy, she was saying, "Beat your breast for Adonis!" But he was aggressive, hateful to the gods, loony ox. That's the sort of licentious behavior you get from women. (390–398)

While the drunken woman celebrating the Adonia strikes the magistrate as inappropriately indulgent, the call and response between Demostratus and his wife demonstrates the very divergent spheres or even temporal dimensions that men and women inhabited in Classical Athens. While the men are carrying on the business of the city, women are celebrating a ritual that involves day drinking. The experience of time in ritual has long been contrasted to the temporality of conducting business, with the repetition of religious rites imparting a cyclical structure to time, while secular activities tend to be thought of as happening in a temporal structure that is linear and teleological. Even in the Proboulos' telling, with hindsight the Athenians came to regret the decision to go to Sicily. Far from being an irrational interruption, the woman's lament for the loss of the beautiful young man seems to be prescient, since the Athenians lost so many of their men on the ill-considered imperial expedition to Sicily. The lament of the woman performing ritual collapses the time between the decision and its consequences. Through this brief interlude, Aristophanes conveys the sense that temporality was gendered; furthermore, this feminine erotic ritual, representing the love of Aphrodite for the lost youth, is brought into conversation with the masculine domain of politics. Through the alignment of male politics and feminine ritual, the decision to go to Sicily is thus associated with the same anti-civic values that the Adonia enacts, that is, a failure of fertility.

Consuming Women: Sex and Food

Superimposing the feminine figure representing sexuality over the one who is most closely associated with sacrifice allows for enormous comic play along the axis of sex and food.

In this play, when the men come to an agreement over Reconciliation's body, Lysistrata offers, "We women will host a dinner for you in the Acropolis. We'll use the food we brought here in our baskets." (1182–4) The word for baskets, *kistai* denotes round wicker baskets that are often used in festive processions, but also there is a pun on the word *kusthos*, which signifies female genitals (Henderson (1987) 206). The remainder of the play depicts these festivities, but one may wonder how it is that a picnic resolves the tension created by a sex strike. In the logic of the play, where sex and sacrifice have been so consistently intertwined, one can seamlessly be substituted for the other, and a communal dinner is a satisfying resolution to the pent-up sexual tension created by the women's refusal to satisfy their husbands in bed.

James Davidson's book *Courtesans and Fishcakes: The Consuming Passions of Classical Athens* explores discourses of desire and appetite, demonstrating how the pursuit of pleasure was condoned as long as it was within reason. He analyzes the discourse surrounding the consumption of fish, wine, and sex, showing that control over appetite was a central concern of Athenian masculinity. He suggests that because the consumption of sea foods was not regulated by ritual, as meat was, Athenians expressed their enthusiasm for eating fish in an almost erotic way. "Fish mania was comparable to a mania for sex and women…and sea foods came to be described in Greek literature, and above all in Greek comedy, as sexual objects (Shaw (2014) 2)." Courtesans were frequently called anchovies; Apollodoros, whom Athenaeus cites as writing a treatise on Athenian courtesans speaks of sisters called anchovies because "they were pale, lean, and had big eyes." Another slang for courtesan was eel: Aristophanes may be playing on this association (*Lyisistrata* 702) when a member of the women's chorus talks about not being able to invite her friend (*hetaira*) to a festival, who then turns out to be an eel, in a joke about import taxes. The word for cuttlefish, Sepia, was a common name for a courtesan, and in the fragments of the comic poet Antiphanes, courtesans were assimilated to cray-fish, sprats, sting-rays, and red mullets as well (Shaw (2014) 20). The comic association of courtesans with fish, delicacies that can be consumed outside of a civic or ritual framework, characterizes sex with *hetairai* as a harmless indulgence. This analogy bears the imprint of the fact that the cultural discourse of Athens was an overwhelmingly masculine sphere, and feminine sexual identity or agency, or even the bare acknowledgment of the humanity of women, was not always a matter of concern. Masculine sexual behavior is what is at stake in the representation of feminine sexuality and what we see is a way of structuring it through the depiction of women as comestibles.

Sexualized women are not only associated with seafood. In fact, we find there is a spectrum of animal analogies for women, which bear different meanings. Related to the link between sex and sacrifice is the persistent association of women with animals in this play, in Greek comedy, and pervasively in Greek literature. "There is a network of imagery and metaphor which associates women in their role in sex and marriage with animals, especially the taming, the yoking, and breaking in of animals, and with agriculture," (Gould (1980) 53). In *Lysistrata*, for example, the sow is a metaphor for women's anger (683), it represents their pubic hair (824) and is used as a slang term for their genitals (1001). Similarly in the *Acharnians*, a starving Megarian disguises his daughters as piglets, punning on the same sexual slang, and trades them for garlic and salt (*Ach.* 719–835). Pandora, the "the mother of the race of women" as Hesiod describes her, is exceedingly lovely on the outside, bedecked and bejeweled with the gifts of the gods, a deceitful exterior that hides the mind of a bitch within (*Works and Days* 78–87, See also *Theogony* 573–597). Semonides' *Catalog of Women* imagines ten types of women, seven of which are animals, the pig, fox, dog, donkey, ferret, and mare. The one good wife is a bee. Beyond just characterizing women as closer to nature and somehow subhuman through this persistent metaphorical association with the animal world, when it relates to sacrifice, this trope reflects an objectifying representational strategy that casts the sexualized woman as something to be consumed, or when the animal is a predator, she is something that is capable of consuming a man, as in the case of Pandora as a bitch, or the representation of Medea as a lioness (Eur. *Med.* 1342).

Reconciliation

In *Lysistrata*, the conflation of sex and sacrifice culminates at the end of the play in the scene when Lysistrata introduces Diallage, whose name is often translated as Reconciliation. The word *diallage* means exchange or change, to take one thing for another, as in to change from enmity to friendship, and can also indicate a surrogate, or substitute, when one thing stands for another. In a way, we can look at Diallage as a ritual surrogate, embodying many of the various ways we have seen feminine sexuality represented in this play.

When she comes on stage, the Spartan and Athenians are mesmerized by the woman's sexual attractiveness. Greek comedy often ends with a scene like this that features a beautiful naked woman. Aristophanes' earliest preserved play, The *Acharnians*, is about an Athenian citizen who brings about a private peace treaty with the Spartans to end the Peloponnesian War. It ends with Dikaiopolis drinking and dancing with a girl on either arm. In *Thesmophoriazousai*, Euripides is on the verge of being killed by the women of Athens, who are angry at him for depicting them in an insulting way in his tragedies. He convinces his kinsman to infiltrate their celebration of the Thesmophoria, a fertility rite in honor of Demeter. The kinsman is discovered, and held captive by a Scythian archer. After failing at various strategies that involve parodies of his tragic plays, Euripides finally hits upon a solution appropriate to comedy, and is able to convince the archer to release his kinsman by seducing him with a dancing girl and a flute player (Zeitlin (1996) 398). In *Peace,* the comic hero Trygaeus, after flying to Olympus on a dung beetle, frees Peace and brings about an end to the Peloponnesian war. He is rewarded with a wedding to a woman named Harvest, who along with another woman called Festival, both mute nude attendants of Peace, are said to have been raised in a brothel (849). In all of these three plays, the introduction of the mute nude female, designed to appeal to the male heterosexual gaze, signifies a resolution of the play's tension into a state of fertility, abundance, and social stability. Scholars are unsure whether these roles were played by actual courtesans, or men dressed up as naked women (Vaio 1973: 379; Stone 1981: 147–50;

Zweig 1992: 78–81 and 85; Henderson 2002: 195–6). Whether she was a woman, or a woman played by a man, Diallage can be seen as a prostitute and serves as an appropriate anchor for the discourse of the prostitution that has circulated in this play. As Laura McClure notes, Diallage's representation as a prostitute is even more emphatic than elsewhere in Aristophanes' comedies, and Lysistrata's character is affected by this depiction: "As if being pimped out by a madame, (Diallage) stands naked before the Spartan and Athenian representatives, who, swollen with desire... cannot possibly resist her, nor peace."

The Spartans and the Athenians negotiate for different parts of Diallage's body:

Spartan Ambassador: We must demand this promontory here return to us.
Lysistrata: Which one?
Spartan Ambassador: This one in back. We are asking for it for a long time. We can almost feel it.
Athenian Ambassador: By Poseidon, you'll never get it.
Lysistrata: Give it to them, good man!
Athenian Ambassador: What do we get then?

Lysistrata: You'll ask for other land in return for this.
Athenian Ambassador: Let's see now. I know. First of all, hand over to us Echinos here, the Malian gulf that runs behind it, also the two Megarian legs.
Spartan Ambassador: My dear Ambassador, you are net getting it all.
Lysistrata: You will give it. Don't quibble over legs.
Athenian Ambassador: I want to strip and plow naked!
Spartan Ambassador: Me first! I want to spread the manure.

(1162–1174)

The men divide up Diallage' using body parts to represent contested territory in the Peloponnesian war: The Spartans claim Pylos, (1162), and in return the Athenians ask for Echinos, the Malian gulf, and Megarian legs (1169–71). Thus, Diallage is represented as land in the same way that the Boeotian woman was when she was described as a beautiful plain with her pennyroyal neat and clean-plucked. In comedy, peace and fertility go together, perhaps revealing comedy's origins in agrarian rites. In general, Aristophanes associates peace with natural abundance, replete with food, wine, and sex. Heterosexuality is central to this depiction, and *Lysistrata* makes heterosexual marriage the centerpiece of its focus. Matthew Dillon has argued that unlike Aristophanes' other peace plays, (*Acharnians* and *Peace*, with fragmentary plays as well including *Farmers*), *Lysistrata* has notably little agrarian imagery, suggesting that this reflects the Spartan investment of Deceleia in 413 BCE, which Thucydides tells us (7.27–8) effectively stopped all agricultural activity in Attica (the territory including and surrounding Athens). Dillon suggests that the characterization of women in this play carries the entire burden of the agrarian themes that we see in other comedies, and so we are confronted with a pronounced and repeated assimilation of woman to land. Furthermore, as a consequence of the thematic emphasis on the role of women in the play, Aristophanes was inspired to depict women in a more expansive and realistic way, depicting the real-life effects of war on the women who give birth to warriors, and bury the dead as well (Dillon 1987).

At the same time that Diallage represents the topography of Greece, it is clear that the men are dividing the body of Diallage, just as a sacrificial animal would be divided and shared out. Unlike fish, which can be consumed without invoking the significance of ritual, there are civic and religious implications in this depiction. We can think of Diallage then as representing the animal sexuality of women in general, but more specifically she reprises the scene in which Lampito entered, embodying those same qualities specifically attached to the women who represent Athenian enemies: she is represented as a sacrificial victim, a sexual object, and land.

The image of Diallage's body as a map of Greece, which the Athenian and Spartan delegates parce out, provides Aristophanes with a further opportunity to explore the link between place and sexuality. Thus, when the Athenians and Spartans want to come to terms to end the sex strike, the Athenians suggest that they call for Lysistrata, and the Spartans offer that they should appeal to

Lysistratos too, the masculine version of the name, again emphasizing their predilection for sex with men. Further, as the two sides lay claim to various parts of Diallage's body, the Athenians desire the parts that align with the frontside: the legs and the parts in between, while the Spartans are interested in the backside. The Athenian ambassador exclaims, "I want to strip and plow naked," and the Spartan ambassador replies, "Me first! I want to spread the manure!" (1173–74). This agricultural metaphor aligns with the trope of woman as land. However, the significance goes deeper: the Athenian interests are associated with heterosexual reproduction, linked with abundance and peace in comedy, while the Spartans are not only devoted to pederasty but also desire anal sex with a woman.

In this way, Aristophanes' *Lysistrata* poses an interesting question for the scholarly view about pederasty and its relationship to gender in ancient Greece. If, as discussed above, the Greek sexual system is notably different from ours insofar as a person's sexual identity was determined not by the gender of the person they had sex with but rather by the role one played, why is it that Spartan sexual culture is mocked in *Lysistrata* as harboring a desire to have sex with women as they would with boys? It seems that in the constellation of sexuality in this play, the gender of the partner, together with the type of sex act, does in fact make a difference to the identity of the insertive partner. Here, we have perhaps located an inconsistency in Athenian sexual discourse, whereby sex with boys can be thought of as on analogy to sex with women, but the reverse is not true. By exploiting this dissonance, Aristophanes distinguishes Spartan sexual culture from Athenian and excludes them from those aspects of heterosexuality that are so central to the genre of comedy: fertility and reproduction of the civic order.

Civic and Sexual Reproduction on the Comic Stage

Depictions of sexuality are dependent on the context in which they are found, and thus we must imagine that they are shaped by genre as well as intended audience. So, for instance, while Athenian pederasty was always the subject of much anxiety, it receives its most favorable treatments in texts set in elite milieux and written for members of the upper class. "The cultural image of pederasty is always elitist" (Hubbard 1998). Comedy did not share the same elite identification but rather served as an arm of "the rule of the demos" (Henderson 1990, 313), and so its take on pederasty diverges from what we might encounter in the writings of Plato or Xenophon. Thus, in *The Clouds*, Stronger Logic extols the virtues of a traditional education in gymnastics and music by conjuring an idealized Athenian pederastic fantasy: rows of strong, tan young boys with well-developed glutes and small penises, obedient, modest, and orderly (961–1023). When Weaker Logic speaks on behalf of the new education, he defends adultery by claiming that it may not be so bad to be one of the *euruproktoi*, or wide-assed – the result of the punishment owed by an adulterer to the cuckolded husband, to be penetrated in the anus by a radish (1068–1083). Weaker Logic then coaxes Stronger Logic to agree that most of the Athenian cultural elite in the audience are wide-assed, and Stronger Logic runs off to join them (1086–1104). As Hubbard notes, this interaction attests to the notion that the men who desire young boys are those who themselves were courted when they were young. That is, the penetrators were once the penetrated. Comedy does not uphold the logical inconsistency of a culture that valorizes pederasty and at the same time strictly defines the masculine sexual role as insertive.

Comedy celebrates peace, fertility, abundance, maintenance of the status quo, and reproduction of the civic order. Endorsing these values, comedy tends to be somewhat more critical of pederasty, and, as we see in the text of *Lysistrata*, other types of non-reproductive sex as well. In *Lysistrata*, the fact that the Spartans desire non-reproductive sex with Diallage positions them on the outside of the bounty conferred by the normative heterosexual erotic resolution of comedy. Thus, while on the surface *Lysistrata* is a play about ending the war with Sparta and her allies and establishing a Panhellenic peace, the subtext is hostile to Sparta, demeaning Lampito by calling her by her name and resolving the sex strike with no promise of a future for Sparta. In this sense, we can see that *Lysistrata* is a peace play, with an undercurrent of hostility toward the Spartans and their allies.

Feminine Sexuality: Subject and Object

Insofar as the Diallage scene recapitulates the entrance of Lampito and her associates with the shared themes of sexual objectification, sacrifice, and topography, the relationship between these two scenes raises an interesting aspect of the depiction of feminine sexuality in ancient Greek literature. Lysistrata and Lampito both act as leaders in the oath scene, as the women take on the role of ritual practitioners. But when Lampito is first greeted and sized up by the other women, she complains that they treat her like a sacrificial animal. Lampito is characterized as both ritual actor and victim, or to put it another way, as both subject and object. We can dismiss this offhand comment until the theme is echoed in the division of Diallage's body into parts like a sacrificial victim. In this scene, the ritual motif reappears but Diallage, or the surrogate is clearly represented only as victim. This division of the self into a higher and lower element, and the projection of the lower aspect onto a surrogate which is then violated conforms with what Maurice Bloch has identified as a core ritual process (Bloch 1992, 1–7). Through this projection, Diallage can be read as a stand-in for Athens' enemies.

Significantly, this instability between subject and object finds a parallel in other representations of feminine sexuality in Greek literature and is distilled in the depiction of the prostitute. The prostitute was a woman who engaged as a subject with men in making exchanges and yet at the same time was herself the object being trafficked (Gilhuly 2007). In a trenchant analysis of the discourse of prostitution in ancient Greece, Leslie Kurke addresses the opposition between the *hetaira* (courtesan) and *porne* (streetwalker). She notes that the name *hetaira* is the feminization of *hetairos* or male companion – a term for the male associates who would celebrate symposia or drinking parties together. This derivation tantalizingly suggests a parity between the two roles. Indeed, the *hetaira* too was associated with the symposium, elite culture, and gift exchange. The name *porne,* on the other hand, derives from the Greek verb *pernemi,* meaning to sell, often in the context of slave traffic, and these prostitutes were associated with the marketplace, where they provided sex for pay to whoever wanted their services. As Kurke notes, on the level of discourse, the opposition between the *hetaira* and the *porne* operates within an ideological framework that opposes elite to egalitarian culture, and the discourse of prostitution, with its various terms and their attendant associations was well-suited to represent this distinction. At the symposium, the courtesan occupies ambiguous territory: she serves as a mirror to the symposiasts, but in her sexual role she is other. This instability finds expression in slippage between the language and associations surrounding the two terms: occasionally in the same text a woman would be introduced in the idiom of the *hetaira* and then refashioned in the language of the *porne*. As Kurke notes, "the trafficking of the agora infiltrates the symposium, as the celebrants struggle desperately to distinguish themselves from the women they have introduced, now become bearers of difference" (Kurke (1999) 219). Jess Miner (2003) has analyzed this slippage at work in the ps. Demosthenes speech Against Neaira, noting that Apollodoros seems to depict Neaira as a wife who once was a courtesan, but then as he comes to the climax of his speech he derogatorily uses a verb related to *porne,* asking the jurors "will you leave a woman who has blatantly prostituted herself throughout the whole of Greece unpunished for insulting the city so shamefully. . .?" (ps. Dem 59.107). The *hetaira* refashioned as *porne* is always vulnerable to seeing her status as quasi-coequal symposiast reconfigured as sex object.

Victoria Wohl identifies a similar dynamic regarding the portrayal of feminine subjectivity in Greek tragedy. She argues that in its near-obsessive dramatization of the exchange of women, tragedy imagines the possibility of a female subject, a potential which is always foreclosed: "the female subject is always shown to be invalid, subjected, dangerous or impossible" (Wohl (1998) xxi). Nonetheless, she argues that the ambiguous status of woman as both object of the exchange and subject allows for the confirmation of male hegemony at the same time that it is potentially subversive, "calling attention to its own exclusions and violences, and laying open to critique the society and subjectivities founded upon it"(Wohl (1998) xxi). Wohl acknowledges that this female subject is always a male fantasy, which is also the case with the women depicted in *Lysistrata*. It is interesting that there seems to be a persistent pattern in depictions of women, especially those that relate to sexuality, that they occur in a discursive or ideological framework that allows for the temporary projection of female subjectivity which then ultimately resolves into objectification and silence.

Clearly, Wohl outlines a similar mechanism to what we see in *Lysistrata*. By the end of the play, all the empowered women who were able to pull off Lysistrata's scheme, controlling all Greek men with their sexuality to achieve their desired political ends, have returned to their roles as anonymous wives. The only women to remain in the public eye are Lysistrata and Diallage, who we can align either with the priestess and her sacrificial victim, or a madame and a common prostitute. The depiction of the wives as *hetairai* has now been refigured in the depiction of Diallage as *porne*. The vacillation between subject and object that we have traced unifies Aristophanes' use of the discourse of the prostitute and the priestess in this play. *Lysistrata* thus describes the mechanism that allows the male fantasy of female sexual subjectivity and its foreclosure as one that aligns with the logic of sacrifice.

Conclusion

If we are to understand Lysistrata as a male projection, what has the temporary exploration of female sexual subjects allowed Aristophanes to examine? At the end of the play, as the women recede, the men come to the fore. When they are ready to negotiate, Lysistrata instructs Diallage to lead the men together, advising her, if the Spartans do not offer a hand, take them by the "tail," an animal metaphor, slang for penis (1119). And in fact, it is the men who capitulate to the women's demands, unable to withstand their own desire for sex. The play concludes with drinking and merriment, an alternation of Athenian and Spartan dances. The men are shown to be just as animal, subject to their sexual desire, and fond of drinking with neighboring Greeks as the women were (Gilhuly 2009; Bowie 1993).

In the process of imagining a world of empowered sexualized women in charge, Aristophanes' *Lysistrata* engages with a range of discourses. While all these tactics for speaking about sexuality – the discourse of the prostitute and the priestess, as well as the *hetaira* and the *porne*, the comic spin on pederasty, the implication of time and space in sexual culture, the notion of sex as commodity, and the assimilation of sex to ritual – do not add up to a coherent totality, they do serve the overarching purpose of the play, to bring a robust consideration of the feminine into the public domain. In this way, Aristophanes prompts the audience to think about the consequences of war from a broader perspective, considering the impact on widows, lonely unmarried women, young couples missing out on the pleasures of marriage, and older couples yearning for the comfort and care of their partner. The play evokes images of the effects of war in the marketplace, on the arable fields, and in the temple. Ultimately, Aristophanes' imaginative play with the idea of women on top has asked the Athenian theatergoers to imagine a fuller version of themselves and to consider the impact of their political decisions in that context.

GUIDE TO FURTHER READING

For sex (and gender) in *Lysistrata*, see Faraone (2006), Foley (1982) Gilhuly (2009) McClure (2015), Reitzammer (2008), and Stroup (2004). For sexuality and place in Aristophanes *Lysistrata*, see Gilhuly (2018). For sexuality and ritual in Greek culture, see Goff (2004); for the discourse of the *hetaira*, see Kurke (1999) and Davidson (1998). For the history of sexuality, see Boswell (1982), Davidson (2001), Dover (1980), Foucault (1990), Halperin (1990); Halperin et al. (1990), and for an overview Ormand (2013).

REFERENCES

Bierl, A. (2011). Alcman at the End of Aristophanes' *Lysistrata*: Ritual Interchorality. In: *Archaic and Classical Choral Song: Performance, Politics and Dissemination* (ed. L. Athanassaki and E. Bowie), 415–436. Berlin, Boston: de Gruyter.

Bloch, M. (1992). *Prey into Hunter: the Politics of Religious Experience*. Cambridge, New York: Cambridge University Press.

Boswell, J. (1982). IV Towards the Long View Revolutions, Universals, Categories. *Salmagundi* 58: 89–113.
Boswell, J. (1994). *Same-sex Unions in Premodern Europe*. New York: Villard Books.
Bowie, A.M. (1993). *Aristophanes: Myth, Ritual, and Comedy*. Cambridge: Cambridge University Press.
Cole, S.G. (1993). Procession and celebration at the Dionysia. In: *Theater and Society in the Classical World* (ed. R. Scodel), 25–38. Ann Arbor: University of Michigan Press.
Csapo, E. (1997). Riding the Phallus for Dionysus: Iconology, Ritual, and Gender-Role De/Construction. *Phoenix* 51: 253–295.
Davidson, J.N. (1998). *Courtesans and Fishcakes: the Consuming Passions of Classical Athens*. Hammersmith, London: HarperCollins.
Davidson, J. (2001). Dover, Foucault and Greek Homosexuality: Penetration and the Truth of Sex. *Past and Present* 170: 3–51.
Dillon, M. (1987). The Lysistrata as a Post-Deceleian Peace Play. *TAPA* 117: 97–104.
Dinshaw, C. (1999). *Getting Medieval: Sexualities and Communities, Pre- and Postmodern*. Durham, NC: Duke University Press.
Dinshaw, C. (2012). *How Soon is Now?: Medieval Texts, Amateur Readers, and the Queerness of Time*. Durham, NC: Duke University Press.
Dover, K.J. (1980). *Greek Homosexuality*. New York: Bloomsbury Academic.
DuBois, P. (1988). *Sowing the Body: Psychoanalysis and Ancient Representations of Women*. Chicago: The University of Chicago Press.
Faraone, C.A. (2006). Priestess and courtesan: the ambivalence of female leadership in Aristophanes' Lysistrata. In: *Prostitutes and Courtesans in the Ancient World* (ed. C. Faraone and L. McClure), 205–223. Madison: University of Wisconsin Press.
Florence, M. (2013). *The Body Politic Sexuality in Greek and Roman Comedy and Mime* (ed. Hubbard 2013), 366–380.
Foley, H.P. (1982). The "Female Intruder" reconsidered: women in Aristophanes' *Lysistrata* and *Ecclesiazusae*. *CP* 77 (1): 1–21.
Foucault, M. (1990). *The History of Sexuality*. New York: Pantheon Books.
Gilhuly, K. (2007). Bronze for gold: subjectivity in Lucian's "Dialogues of the Courtesans". *AJP* 128 (1): 59–94.
Gilhuly, K. (2009). *The Feminine Matrix of Sex and Gender in Classical Athens*. New York: Cambridge.
Gilhuly, K. (2018). *Erotic Geographies in Ancient Greek Literature and Culture*. Abingdon: Routledge.
Goff, B. (2004). *Citizen Bacchae: Women's Ritual Practice in Ancient Greece*. Berkeley: University of California Press.
Gould, J. (1980). Law, custom and myth: aspects of the social position of women in classical Athens. *JHS* 100: 38–59.
Hall, E. (2014). Comedy and Athenian Festival Culture. In: *The Cambridge Companion to Greek Comedy* (ed. M. Revermann), 306–321. Cambridge.
Halliwell, S. (1991). Comic Satire and Freedom of Speech in Classical Athens. *JHS* 111: 48–70.
Halperin, D.M. (1990). *One Hundred Years of Homosexuality: And Other Essays on Greek Love*. New York: Routledge.
Halperin, D.M., Winkler, J.J., and Zeitlin, F.I. (ed.) (1990). *Before Sexuality: the Construction of Erotic Experience in the Ancient Greek World*. Princeton.
Hedreen, G. (2004). The Return of Hephaistos, Dionysiac Processional Ritual and the Creation of a Visual Narrative. *JHS* 124: 38–64.
Henderson, J. (1975). *The Maculate Muse: Obscene Language in Attic Comedy*. New Haven: Yale University Press.
Henderson, J. (1987). *Aristophanes: Lysistrata*. Oxford.
Henderson, J. (1990). The Demos and the Comic Competition. In: *Nothing to Do with Dionysos?: Athenian Drama in Its Social Context* (ed. J.J. Winkler and F. Zeitlin), 271–313. Princeton.
Henderson, J. (2002). Strumpets on Stage: the Early Comic Hetaera. *Dioniso* 1: 78–87.
Hubbard, T.K. (1998). Popular Perceptions of Elite Homosexuality in Classical Athens. *Arion* 6 (1): 48–78.
Hubbard, T.K. (ed.) (2013). *A Companion to Greek and Roman Sexualities*. Hoboken: John Wiley & Sons Inc.
Kurke, L. (1999). *Coins, Bodies, Games, and Gold: the Politics of Meaning in Archaic Greece*. Princeton.
Lewis, D.M. (1955). Notes on Attic Inscriptions (II) XXIII: Who Was Lysistrata? *ABSA* 50: 1–12.

Loraux, N. (1993). *The Children of Athena: Athenian Ideas about Citizenship and the Division Between the Sexes.* New Jersey: Princeton.

McClure, L. (2015) Courtesans Reconsidered: Women in Aristophanes' Lysistrata, EuGeSta 5.54-84.

Miner, J. (2003). Courtesan, Concubine, Whore: Apollodorus' Deliberate Use of Terms for Prostitutes. *AJP* 124 (1): 19–37.

Ormand, K. (2013). *Foucault's History of Sexuality and the Discipline of Classics* (ed. Hubbard), 54–68.

Patterson, C. (1994). The case against neaira and the public ideology of the athenian family. In: *Athenian Identity and Civic Ideology* (ed. A. Scafuro and A. Boegehold), 199–216. Baltimore: Johns Hopkins University.

Reitzammer, L. (2008). Aristophanes' Adoniazousai. *CA* 27 (2): 282–333.

Robertson, N. (1993). Athens' Festival of the New Wine. *HSCP* 95: 197–250.

Rohy, V. (2017). Exchanging Hours: A Dialogue on Time. *GLQ: A Journal of Lesbian and Gay Studies* 23 (2): 247–268.

Rosen, R.M. (2018). Sparta and Spartans in Old Comedy. In: *The Greek Superpower: Sparta in the Self-definitions of Athenians* (ed. Cartledge and Powell), 139–156. Swansea.

Schaps, D. (1977). The Woman Least Mentioned. *CQ* 27 (2): 323–330.

Sedgwick, E. (1990). *Epistemology of the Closet.* Berkeley: University of California Press.

Shaw, C.A. (2014). 'Genitalia of the Sea': seafood and sexuality in Greek comedy. *Mnemosyne* 67 (4): 554–576.

Smith, N. (2017). Aristophanes "Lysistrata" and the Two Acropolis Priestesses. *The International Journal of Literary Humanities* 35–40.

Sommerstein, A.H. (1980). The Naming of Women in Greek and Roman Comedy. *Quaderni di Storia* 6 (11): 393–418.

Stone, L. (1981). *Costume in Aristophanic Comedy.* New York: Arno Press.

Stroup, S.C. (2004). Designing Women: Aristophanes' "Lysistrata" and the "Hetairization" of the Greek Wife. *Arethusa* 37 (1): 37–73.

Thonemann, P. (2020). Lysimache and Lysistrata. *JHS* 140: 128–142.

Vaio, J. (1973). The Manipulation of Theme and Action in Aristophanes' *Lysistrata. GRBS* 14: 369–380.

Wohl, V. (1998). *Intimate Commerce: Exchange, Gender, and Subjectivity in Greek Tragedy.* Austin: University of Texas Press.

Zeitlin, F. (1996). *Playing the Other: Gender and Society in Classical Greek Literature.* Chicago: University of Chicago Press.

Zweig, B. (1992). The mute, nude female characters in Aristophanes' plays. In: *Pornography and Representation in Greece and Rome* (ed. A. Richlin), 73–89. Oxford.

CHAPTER 14

Women at the Thesmophoria: Religion and Ritual

Helene P. Foley

Introduction

In Aristophanes' *Women at the Thesmophoria* of 411–410 BCE, the tragic poet Euripides attempts to infiltrate the festival of the Thesmophoria, an ancient rite exclusive to women performed all over Greece, but for three days in numerous locations throughout Attica in the month Pyanopsion (September–October). The women plan to condemn Euripides for plays featuring adulterous heroines and other inappropriate female behavior foreign to tragedy (but not comedy) such as excessive wine drinking, petty domestic theft, and introducing suppositious children; heroines such as Euripides' Phaedra, who falls in love with her stepson Hippolytus, have purportedly introduced suspicion into the households of Attica, so that husbands attempt to interfere with their wives' domestic world. Euripides initially plans to persuade the beautiful androgynous young tragic poet Agathon to take on the role of his defender at the festival, but he is forced to settle on transforming and disguising his hairy hypermasculine Relative (sometimes named Mnesilochus in later texts) as a woman to do the job. The Relative enters the festival and offers a speech in Euripides' defense that compounds the original offense by enumerating all the outrageous illegitimate female behavior that Euripides' plays did not reveal. He unsurprisingly fails to persuade the women, who plan to attack him. He is then exposed as male after the effeminate Cleisthenes arrives to reveal Euripides' plot to the women. The Relative seeks to escape punishment by borrowing from four plays by Euripides; after the first two, Euripides arrives in disguise to help; each attempt at rescue fails. Euripides finally reconciles with the women, promising not to denigrate them in his future plays if they allow the Relative to escape, but threatening to reveal their secrets if they renege. The women agree and allow Euripides to invent a successful new stratagem to trick the Scythian bowman guarding the Relative. Euripides and the Relative escape, as the chorus of women assists by confusing the pursuing Scythian and then moves toward a return home.

To the degree that we can reconstruct the highly secret rite of the Thesmophoria, the festival involved married citizen women worshipping the goddess of grain Demeter Thesmophoros ("bringer of laws" or the gifts of civilization) and her daughter, queen of the underworld, Kore or Persephone. On the first day of the festival, the Anodos or "way up," the women left their homes and assembled, perhaps moving up the hill (1045) toward the Pnyx below the acropolis to set up tents. On the second day, the Nesteia or fasting day, the occasion for Aristophanes' play, the women slept on mats made from antaphrodisiac plants and mourned with Demeter, grieving over the loss of her daughter to the underworld. Public business ceased (78–80) and prisoners were released. The third day, Kalligeneia ("beautiful birth"), entailed celebrating a return to fertility and birth in

A Companion to Aristophanes, First Edition. Edited by Matthew C. Farmer and Jeremy B. Lefkowitz.
© 2024 John Wiley & Sons, Inc. Published 2024 by John Wiley & Sons, Inc.

the natural and human worlds accompanying Persephone's emergence into the world above. According to a scholion on Lucian' *Dialogues of the Courtesans* 2.1, at some point during the festival women exchanged obscene jests and insults during a nighttime ritual that may have derived from the jokes or gestures performed for the grieving Demeter by mythical female figures called Iambe or Baubo. A group of women called Bailers, who had refrained from sexuality before the rite, retrieved from deep *megara* or pits the rotting remains of sacrificed piglets mixed with cakes in the shape of snakes (who were said to guard the pits) and male genitalia and pine branches. In popular slang, female genitalia were called piglets; pigs are particularly prolific animals. This sacred compost could be mixed with the seed corn to promote the growth of grain. This ritual was said to have originated during the rape of Kore by Hades, when the pigs of the swineherd Eubouleus were swallowed along with her into underworld. (For recent discussions of the ritual, see especially Lowe (1998), Dillon (2002) 110–20, and Parker (2005) 270–83. For discussions more focused on the ritual within the play, see Versnel (1992), Bowie (1993), Habash (1997), Tzanetou (2002), and Bierl (2009)). Male citizens approved and financed this festival, and women known to be adulterous were in fact excluded from participating in it. There may be an indirect reference in the play to myths/stories in which male intruders to the rite were threatened by female sacrificers, since the Relative, once exposed as an infiltrator, is threatened while seated at an altar with serious punishments by the women (Detienne (1989), Bowie (1993) 212, Dillon (2002), Tzanetou (2002) 329, Parker (2005), and Osborne (1993) on female sacrifice).

Aristophanes' play does not reveal the august secrets of the Thesmophoria. Although the play may refer to an actual ritual pursuit when the women search for the presence of another male intruder in their sacred space and mentions torches, sacrificial bowls, altars, and fasting, the women's opening assembly to condemn Euripides comically adapts a meeting of the male political assembly on the Pnyx; references to the myth of Demeter and Persephone so central to the women's religious experience are indirect at best. The occasion of the Thesmophoria serves to frame the play, but once the assembly is over and the Relative is imprisoned, the audience is regularly reminded of the rite primarily through choral prayers and hymns sung and danced for a range of gods. In this respect, the play differs in significant ways from other treatments of ritual and religious festivals in Aristophanes, including in Aristophanes' two other extant "women plays," *Lysistrata*, probably performed earlier in the same year at the Lenaia festival, and the *Women at the Assembly* (ca. 391–90bce). In these two plays, however, the main female characters play far more central roles in a civic context that includes references to ritual at various points.

Unlike these two plays, *Women at the Thesmophoria* focusses on male experience, and in particular on male experience in characterizing and performing women, above all in dramatic contexts, where all female roles were in fact played by male actors. Performing and transforming excerpts from tragic plots involving confinement, rescue, and escape (a *mēchanē sōterias*, Euripides' *Helen* 1034; *mēchanē*, *Women at the Thesmophoria* 87 and 1132) in a comic context that undermines them also brings the relation between tragedy and comedy continually into focus. This chapter will begin by considering the two topics central to the action, men playing women and the dialogue between tragedy and comedy, and then turn to a more extended consideration of the unusual role of religion and ritual in the play in comparison to a limited selection of other Aristophanes' plays.

Men Playing Women

Women at the Thesmophoria opens with Euripides and his Relative approaching the house of Agathon. Following an introduction by his servant, Agathon is rolled in on a theatrical platform (the *ekkyklēma*) dressed in female garb and accompanied by costumes and props to compose/ rehearse a Trojan female chorus that sings in honor of Demeter and Persephone and other deities (101–29). He alternates between the role of leader and chorus. This song, honoring gods relevant to the occasion of the Thesmophoria, seems to have been performed (unlike the chorus' later hymns to the gods) in a provocative manner suggestive of the so-called new music, since he produces erotic thrills in the Relative (130–33) (Muecke (1982) 46–48). Agathon explains that when composing/rehearsing female parts he needs to suit his clothing and his habits to his thoughts in order to acquire the proper inspiration (146–52). Yet both his beautiful white (untanned) and beardless mask, costume, which lacks both phallus and breasts, his props, which include a lyre, a breastband, a mirror, an oil flask, a hairnet and a sword, and his modulated voice suggest an androgynous nature (Taaffe (1993) 81, 124–25, Compton-Engle (2015) 98–101). As he asserts somewhat contradictorily: "it is necessary to create works similar to one's nature" (167). He clearly can pass as a woman (Zeitlin (1996b) 383), which is why he claims that entering the Thesmophoria himself is too risky.

After Agathon's refusal to help Euripides infiltrate the festival, the Relative is, much to his horror, shaved, depilated with a torch in his lower parts – a phallic gesture to his backside that makes him fear becoming a sacrificial pig (*delphakion*, 237, perhaps suggestive of female genitalia) – and dressed in female garb. Gazing at himself in the mirror, he shows the first signs of entering his role, which he then begins to enact as he enters the festival, speaking in a higher-pitched voice, asking the goddesses for suitable matches for his daughter Pussy and good sense for his son Dicky, and swearing mostly by the proper deities (Taaffe (1993) 86). Although his outrageous speech in defense of Euripides alienates the women, they fail to recognize him as a male and do not deny female sexual improprieties in principle. So far, the Relative is successfully playing at being a woman, while revealing his male identity in his slips into masculine obscenity (McClure (1999) 213). The threat of exposure then requires him to adopt a female role in an increasingly humiliating fashion. He must squat to urinate like a woman and gives himself away by confusing male and female urinals. He desperately tries to hide and in principle deny the existence of his dangling comic phallus, a revealing sign of his masculinity, by pushing it back and forth away from observers. (This discussion owes much to Stehle (2002); see also Taaffe (1993).)

After drawing on some devices from the male tragic roles of Euripides' Telephus and Palamedes (discussed below) to fashion an escape fails, the Relative then turns to the female roles of the innocent Helen and the virginal Andromeda. As Helen, he conflates the heroine's suffering with his own and literally throws himself on the mercy of his male rescuer Menelaus/Euripides. His central desire now becomes a safe return as male to wife and family. But as Andromeda, bound to a plank and still in the female costume he wished to escape, he is even threatened with becoming a sexual object and with feminizing male penetration from the rear (1105–22). Here, he not only plays a female role but virtually becomes a suffering heroine, as he mingles Andromeda's sorrows with his own line by line and uses a mix of male and female pronouns (1015–55). In Euripides' plays, male transgressors are often punished by sharing painful female experiences. In *Hippolytus*, Hippolytus fulfills Phaedra's final wish by experiencing something equivalent to her suffering (*Hippolytus* 728–31; Zeitlin (1996a) 391; see also Stehle (2002), Foley (1992, 2001)). The Relative is similarly forced to experience a comic version of female entrapment and pain before he is released. These last two tragic escape plots implicitly exonerate Euripides from the misogyny of which he is accused by creating virtuous women and set the stage, if not explicitly, for a reconciliation between Euripides and the women and for the actual rescue of the Relative.

Critics have been divided on how to evaluate the play's representation of men playing women as well as male actors performing the play's "real" women (Duncan (2006)). As Froma Zeitlin ((1985) 69) has argued, in tragedy: "Functionally women are never an end in themselves, and nothing changes for them once they have lived out their drama on stage. Rather, they play the roles of catalysts, agents, instruments, blockers, spoiler, destroyers, and sometimes helpers or saviors for masculine characters. When elaborately represented, they may serve as antimodels as well as hidden models for that masculine self." This principle partly holds true for *Women at the Thesmophoria* and provides a tragic coloring to the action. The male invaders of this play do not get away with their intrusion into a legitimate female ritual space. All except the Scythian bowman undergo some form of feminization (Tzanetou (2002) 330). Only in the case of Euripides in the final scene does a male playing a female succeed in carrying out a planned stratagem. In this play, performing a woman at first consists of donning a series of props – female clothing not a gendered body (Ferris (1989) 20–28). Men put gender on and off like a costume (Stehle (2002) 377); their female disguises fail (Taaffe (1993) 78; Compton-Engle (2015) 98 and 101); they experience a comic version of tragic suffering and humiliation to their sense of male identity. Euripides and the Relative are forced to play his own tragic characters (Zeitlin (1996b) 382), reconcile with the women, and flee in female dress, escaping rather than triumphing, as does the typical male comic hero in Aristophanes, whose great ideas succeed and eventuate in feasting, erect phalluses, and sexual fulfillment with women (Stehle (2002) 370; see more on Aristophanic heroes below).

Yet the play also confirms and expands on typical masculine and especially comic clichés about women and delights in perpetrating them. The women are angry because Euripides has disrupted their lives by revealing sexual and other domestic misbehavior that they admit to doing. Earlier old comedies based on myth or representing women who are courtesans, old women, or market women had established a range of comic expectations for women, if less extensively for wives (Henderson (2000)). In the Telephean hostage scene (see below), they confirm their reputation as heavy drinkers. The women also fail to imitate men successfully. In conducting their assembly, the women even want to deny a key democratic privilege, *parrhēsia*, or free speech to the Relative (540–41) (Slater (2002) 169). They ineptly fail to recognize the Relative as male. In the scene where Critylla guards the Relative, she reveals herself to be a very literal and unsophisticated viewer of tragedy. Nevertheless, Euripides' offending plays, which probably began in the 430 s, hardly represent a tragic tradition and his supposed mistreatment of women comes across as limited in comparison to the Relative's new revelations and in many respects alien to his extant tragedy (Hubbard (1991) 185, Bobrick (1991) 191, Bowie (1993) 227, Austin and Olson (2004) lv–lvi). Even his would-be adulteresses like Phaedra, cited by the first female speaker, resist and fail to accomplish their illicit desires.

The self-defense of womanhood offered by the women in the Parabasis (785–845) even asserts women as the superior sex. If women are such a bad thing, they ask, why do men desire and guard them so carefully? Women's names, such as Nausimache (Naval Battle, 804), offer a more positive civic image of their nature than ordinary male names (although the name Salabaccho (805) that they mention belongs to a well-known courtesan). When they pilfer, it is minor household goods, not, like men, public funds. Indeed, women preserve domestic goods (the loom-beam, weaving rod (*kanōn*), work baskets, and parasol (*skiadeion*)), whereas men have lost their rod (*kanōn*) and spear and thrown away their shields (*skiadeion*), both images of masculinity (819–29). Motherhood, they argue, should be publicly recognized. Women who bear good sons should be honored, and mothers of bad sons should not be allowed to lend money for interest (a pun on *tokos*, meaning birth and interest, 843). The contradictory argument of the parabasis makes an arguably absurd case for women (see, most extensively, Bierl (2009) 190–91), especially in comparison to the one made by the women in *Lysistrata*, where they establish their status as citizens by reference to their role in civic ritual (see below).

As mentioned above, once the women have turned over the Relative as hostage to the polis, they return to performing song and dance in honor of the gods as they would no doubt have done at the Thesmophoria, and move toward a return home and a normal family life. They put aside gender conflict and have the last word in the play. I shall argue below that these concluding choral performances re-establish the women in an authoritative ritual role that serves the polis more effectively.

Paratragedy

Aristophanes' first known engagement with Euripidean paratragedy began in his *Acharnians* of 425 BCE. In this play, the hero Dicaeopolis borrows from Euripides a disguise, a hostage device, and a speech (or speeches) from perhaps his most wretched, lame, and beggarly hero, Telephus. He uses this tragic role to create what he calls a *trugōidia* (499), or tragic-comic performance that will allow him to borrow the prestige and authority of serious theatre (*tragōidia*) in order to defend making a separate peace with Athens' enemy in the Peloponnesian Wars, Sparta. The borrowing and refashioning of Euripides' play works. Dicaeopolis persuades his opposition and celebrates his private peace. In Aristophanes' later play, *Peace*, the comic hero Trygaeus similarly and successfully borrows the mythical flight to heaven of Euripides' hero Bellerophon on the winged horse Pegasus to make a heroic journey on the back of a dung beetle in order to bring Peace back to Greece.

His hero succeeds where Euripides' failed. In both cases, Aristophanes refashions tragedy to serve his own comic agenda. Aristophanes' rival comic poet Cratinus (307K, 342 K-A) called this process Euripidaristophanizing (*euripidaristophanizein*). Aristophanes may mock Euripides' propensity for his wretched heroes in *Acharnians* and other plays, but in another comic fragment he himself is represented as admitting to imitating self-consciously while making less pedestrian (*agoraios*) Euripides' terse style (488K-A, 471K).

In all four cases, comic refashioning of Euripides' tragedies in *Women at the Thesmophoria* distorts and undercuts his tragic plots and fails to win the Relative's release from imprisonment. After Euripides finally reconciles with the women, he develops a plan that combines tragedy (it adapts a Euripidean plot) and comedy to win the Relative's release. Critics have generally interpreted this sequence of events as a contest between comedy and tragedy in which comedy successfully undermines tragedy and emerges as victor in an intergeneric contest or even punishes tragedy for transgressing into comic territory (Zeitlin (1996b) 380, Bowie (1993) 219–220, Gibert (2000) 227, Tzanetou (2002) 339). This is in a narrow sense not wrong. Yet, as becomes increasingly clear, successfully performing tragedy on a comic stage is in principle impossible, due to the generic need to maintain dramatic illusion (Farmer (2017) 168), and the attempt simply invites comedy to demonstrate this while enhancing its own virtuosity. Hence, I will argue for a more complex interpretation of the intergeneric dialogue here. In this respect, I am sympathetic to Matthew's Farmer's argument (2017) that tragedy and comedy here share a self-conscious response to earlier dramatic tradition (what he calls an engagement with "secondariness" in relation to earlier tradition and a mutual generic dependence), but I want to put more emphasis on how comedy's experimental game with tragedy works. Comedy, not tragedy, is in control here, and to the degree possible it is important to understand how paratragedy serves its own agenda.

In the play's first engagement with an Euripidean tragedy, *Women at the Thesmophoria* borrows from both *Telephus* and Aristophanes' refashioning of it in *Acharnians*. Here, the emerging dialogue between tragedy and comedy serves new and complex ends. Even before he "defends" Euripides in the assembly, the Relative shows hints of Telephean lameness in his opening dialogue with Euripides (22–24) (Moulton (1981) 113). Like Mysian Telephus, he then makes in disguise an outrageous speech that dares to offer unwelcome truths before his enemies and fails to persuade his audience. In so far as we can tell, his speech is unrelated to what appears to have been an arguably serious argument in Euripides' original, where Telephus probably either claimed that the Mysians appropriately resisted an unprovoked attack by the Greeks or defended Troy. The hero even seems to have won the sympathy of the play's one female, Clytemnestra, for his cause; she very likely allowed him to hold her child Orestes hostage at an altar. In Euripides, the hostage device apparently won Telephus another hearing and an eventual cure for his lameness from Achilles. In *Women at the Thesmophoria*'s version of the hostage device, the Relative snatches a baby (now a girl), seats himself on an altar, and threatens to murder the child if he is not released. The notoriety of this comic scene seems to be confirmed by an Apulian bell krater (ca. 370bce, Martin von Wagner Museum der Universität Würzburg H 5697) displaying a version of it. The device fails to persuade the women, whose plans to surround the altar with flames are cut short as the Relative strips and then cuts the throat of the "child," who turns out to be a wine sack with booties. The women, eager to share the wine, are diverted by the rush to find a bowl to catch as much of the sacrificial "blood" as they can; calling on the two goddesses of the Thesmophoria, the women promise godless deeds in exchange for the action of the Relative (718–23). Here, comedy performs at an altar a "perverted" sacrifice that Euripides' tragedy consistently avoided in favor of alternative outcomes. A knowledgeable audience member would have been able to appreciate the clever (and misogynist) outrage comedy (with the help of its bibulous woman) had performed (in a fashion differently from *Acharnians*) on Euripides' original.

The Relative's next inept and cryptic effort to escape involves borrowing a device from Euripides' *Palamedes* of 415 BCE. In this play Oiax, the brother of the mythical inventor of writing Palamedes, apparently inscribed a message on oar blades and floated them out to sea into order to inform his father of his brother's unjust condemnation to death by the Greeks and request (with eventual success) revenge for it. In this case, the Relative, confined to the altar, notices some dedicatory tablets and writes a barely legible message on them. The device, isolated from a more complex play that probably included a far more relevant Telephean-style defense speech by its hero (Austin and Olson (2004) lix; for liberties taken with the original, see Rau (1967), Pucci (1961), and Scodel (1980)), may have seemed, as the Relative complains, a bit cold (*psuchros*, 848) and far-fetched even in the original, but it would be hard to blame Euripides for the failure of an escape plot that apparently did not exist in the original. If anything, the Relative inappropriately/impiously refunctions a religious dedication with his crude writing on it, probably followed by his awkward attempt to throw the tablets into an imaginary sea (Slater (2002) 170). The oar blades presumably made no physical appearance on Euripides' stage and offered a long-term solution at best. The Relative makes the device comic from the start. Euripides fails to respond to this botched effort.

As many others have noted, in the first two borrowings from Euripides' tragedy the Relative adopts male roles irrelevant either to escaping or defending Euripides for his supposed crimes against women. Now, dressed in the right costume for the role (and the Thesmophoria), the Relative turns more adeptly to recent escape dramas by Euripides with virtuous heroines. The first play, Euripides' *Helen*, performed the previous year (412 BCE), exonerates Greek mythology's most notorious heroine. In this version, the Trojan War was fought for Helen's image; Helen herself was abducted like the virginal Persephone to the Hades-like world of Egypt to await rescue by her husband Menelaus after the war. The play staged a recognition scene for the couple that deliberately recalled the romantic reunion of the faithful Penelope and Odysseus in the *Odyssey*. (In *Women at the Thesmophoria*, the first speaker Mika chastised Euripides for never staging Penelopes, 547–48.)

The Relative begins to perform Helen's role; Euripides soon arrives costumed in sailor's rags as Menelaus to rescue his damsel in distress. The plan fails for several reasons. First, the literal-minded Critylla, who is guarding the Relative, reads the performance as reality. She is not wrong. Like Critylla, the audience sees the visibly male and aged comic Relative in female dress absurdly staging a romantic reunion with the aged Euripides/Menelaus dressed in sailor's rags in a context not resembling fictional Egypt. Then, just as Critylla realizes an escape plan is also afoot, a magistrate (Prytanis) and a Scythian archer to guard the prisoner arrive to put an end to possible escape. Tragedy's need to maintain dramatic (in this case hardly tragic) illusion certainly gives comedy a theatrical advantage here. Yet it is important to emphasize that the audience never sees tragedy actually performed in this play, but always a comic revision of Euripides' originals.

For those who recalled *Helen*'s recent performance, the scene shows off comedy's clever refashioning of Euripides' original. In Euripides' play, the virtuous Helen carries out her reformed role to the hilt; she is the author of the couple's escape plot herself and will become a deity after her death. Euripides' Menelaus, who experiences near comic mockery for arriving on stage in rags, has to be dragged into a romantic reunion with his faithful wife. Yet he now plays, despite his untragic rags, the dominant romantic role in Aristophanes' restaging. In a stylistic tour-de-force elegantly outlined by Nieddu (2004), Aristophanes' scene fast-forwards the first half of Euripides' play while performing (probably in mock "tragic" performance style) extensive quotations from the original, and even absurdly finds a new role for Critylla as Theonoe, the Egyptian king Theoclymenus' sister, as blocking figure, rather than pious facilitator, as in the original. The tragic diction and style are largely consistently Euripidean. Yet in Aristophanes' new unEuripidean version Helen becomes a passive object of rescue who frantically turns in the excited tragic dochmiac meter for help and a kiss to Menelaus (Bobrick (1991) 184, Austin and Olson (2004) lx, lxv). Euripides' heroically scheming Helen disfigures her beauty by marring her cheeks in a false lament for her dead husband; the Relative as Helen instead draws attention to his crudely shaved cheeks (903) and then sexualizes the marital embrace with a pun ("To your wife's arms" (*es chēras*, 912), becomes "to your wife's hearth/genitals," *eschēras*, if this is the correct text). The new version eliminates the explanation for Helen's innocence: her image went to Troy while she was wafted to Egypt. Did Aristophanes aim to have the Relative and the Poet himself correct Euripides' novel, assertive, and guiltless heroine, by turning her into a virginal and helpless Andromeda, the subject of the next paratragic escape and rescue attempt? The Relative's untragic asides makes the performance hard to categorize. Unpacking the generic dialogues implicit in this complex and sophisticated scene is not easy, but Aristophanes rewriting and restaging of the original plays the dominant role.

The deserted Ethiopian princess Andromeda opens Euripides' play *Andromeda* (412bce) bound to a rock and waiting to be devoured by a sea monster. She is eventually married to the hero Perseus, who fails in love with and rescues her on his return from killing the Gorgon Medusa. Euripides' novel romance left a long-lasting impression on later Antiquity (Gibert (2000) 76–78), beginning with Aristophanes' own Dionysus in *Frogs* (52–54) who, struck with desire while reading Euripides' *Andromeda*, journeys to Hades to bring back the dead poet. Andromeda sings a monody which is repeated by the voice of Echo from a cave (*Andromeda*, frag. 114K). As a chorus of contemporary maidens arrives to console her, she asks Echo to cease so that she can mourn with her friends (*Andromeda*, frag. 118K). The Relative, now bound to a board while still dressed in female garb and guarded by the Scythian policeman, takes a cue from Euripides, who probably dashes by dressed as Perseus. This time the Relative immerses himself in the role, mingling his own wretched situation with that of Andromeda, and reaching out to a chorus of women (ō *gunaikes*, 1036), who are perhaps meant to be the chorus women at the Thesmophoria, to share his lament. This paratragic moment is interrupted by the appearance of Echo, who claims that she collaborated with Euripides in last year's play (1060–61). In contrast to many critics, I think (see also Gilula (1996), Slater (2002) 175–76, Farmer (2017) 184 with note) that Echo is not played by the actor playing Euripides/Perseus, but by a virtuoso actor dressed as an *old* woman (her age perhaps suggesting being a bit-out-of date; then she is addressed later as a man, 1037), who comically undercuts the Andromeda lament and forces the Relative to break role due to her frustrating repetitions. (Among other issues, if Euripides as Echo turns to a comic performance that undercuts his own tragic plot, the scene becomes mystifying from a generic perspective. He would also be choosing to play a female role and a comedian before the final scene, where the gender change makes explicit sense.) Andromeda's original attempt to silence Echo in Euripides no doubt set up this comic reinterpretation. The Scythian then enters and his bastard Greek is immediately echoed by Echo; invisible to him, she leads him on a frantic comic chase to catch her. Euripides' novel musical innovation has become a purely comic device.

Euripides then enters, probably flying on the stage machine as Perseus (though other scholars think he only runs on (see Farmer (2017) 181, n. 74)), but his attempt to stage falling in love with and unbinding the Relative is interpreted literally by the Scythian as a desire to penetrate a man from behind. Euripides, frustrated by this response to his novelties (*kaina*, 1130), decides to turn to a device (*mēchanē*, 1132) suitable to a barbarian mind (1129). From a thematic point of view, the virginal and innocent Andromeda implicitly sets the stage for Euripides' reconciliation with the chorus of women. (The Relative's turn in his lament to addressing chorus women both in and outside the play may offer an implicit appeal for reconciliation.) Euripides' promise not to slander women has already been accomplished twice over with *Helen* and *Andromeda*. Aristophanes' comic undercutting of *Andromeda* displays a novel virtuosity, while paying an indirect tribute to the Euripides' theatrical brilliance. As has often been pointed out, paratragedy fails with inferior target texts (Rose 1979; see also Hutcheon 1985). Moreover, as in this case, barbarian viewers are hardly critics to be taken seriously.

The majority of critics have interpreted the final scene of the play, in which Euripides disguises himself as an old woman and distracts the Scythian from guarding the Relative by offering him a quick lay with a female dancer, Fawn, as a final defeat of tragedy by comedy, or at the very least an ironic victory for Euripides. From this perspective, Euripides' own plots have failed, and he is forced to play a woman himself and borrow from comedy to rescue the Relative. (For some reservations, see Moulton (1981) 141–43). Or, as Zeitlin suggests, Aristophanes finally gives Euripides a chance to use comedy's own mimetic tricks ((1996b) 386). However, as Edith Hall 1989 points out (see also Bobrick (1991), Wright (2005) 51–52), the device used in this scene – creating escapes for Greek characters by tricking a gullible barbarian – had already appeared in recent Euripidean tragedy (*Iphigenia Among the Taurians, Helen*). Escape plots were also typical of comedy in a different form; here tragedy and comedy visibly draw from a similar repertoire and converge to serve the play's final reconciliation (Zeitlin (1996b) 398–99, Farmer (2017) 217). Euripides' mastery in staging the scene hardly undercuts his notoriously intergeneric theatrical talent. The performance is immediately appreciated by the women, who voluntarily misdirect the barbarian's search for Euripides/Artemisia (a queen of Halicarnassus who performed brilliantly on the Persian side in the Greek naval battle against Xerxes). The chorus of *Iphigeneia Among the Taurians* had previously misdirected the play's barbarian king Thoas (Hall (1989) 50, n.71), and Euripides manages for the first time to make theatrical illusion work for the Scythian (Bobrick (1997) 192–93) even though he is not staging a "tragedy."

In the last quarter of the fifth century BCE, Aristophanes regularly turned to novel paratragic responses to Euripides, while Euripides himself more frequently deployed what could be described as comic theatrical devices, including the very use in *Helen* of ragged heroes mocked by Aristophanes in *Acharnians* and *Women at the Thesmophoria*. On the basis of those plays available to us, *Women at the Thesmophoria* no longer "needed" to borrow a tragic role from Euripides to win authority for his Telephean hero Dicaeopolis as in *Acharnians;* this particular shared role/device/plot now belongs more to Aristophanes in *Women at the Thesmophoria* than to Euripides and is attributed explicitly to neither poet in the text (see Slater (2002) and Farmer (2017) 162–63 for further discussion). Aristophanes' later *Frogs* does question and mock aspects of Euripides' dramaturgy in a broad range of ways (see below). By contrast, *Women at the Thesmophoria* appropriates outrageous slander of female behavior attributed to Euripides and the violation of tragic conventions/scenes based on ritual (the hostage scene and perhaps the abuse of religious dedications at an altar) for comedy, which already owned them. It deploys *Helen* to celebrate its games with theatrical illusion – very likely a novel comic gesture – and reconfigures both *Helen* and *Andromeda* to display comic virtuosity through its intertextual dialogue with and abuse of tragedy. I would argue that the focus throughout these paratragic scenes remains more on comic brilliance, what Zeitlin calls "opportunistic displays of Aristophanic skill" ((1996b) 388), than tragic failure.

Aristophanes, always openly in competition with other comic poets (Csapo (2000)), found in tragedy a chance to expand the range and sophistication of comedy due to cultural familiarity with it without intimidating his audience, as he claims to have done in his treatment of Socrates and "philosophy" in the second parabasis of *Clouds*. The conventions of tragedy could only permit indirect replies to comedy, although the ragged Menelaus of *Helen* may be one pointed example (Foley (2008)). By the time of *Frogs* Aristophanes even claims to count on his sophisticated audience's book knowledge of tragedy (1109–18). As Lowe (2000) (267) put it: "While it is hard to demonstrate that tragedy ever needed comedy, comedy is constantly defining itself in relation to tragedy, a genre that is rapidly evolving and rewriting its own poetics." The *Frogs* chorus of Eleusinian initiates suggests that comedy even owns the combination of the serious (*spoudaia*) and the humorous (*geloia*) (390–94), and comedy here implicitly takes its place along with Aeschylus in preserving the city's future dramatic choruses. In *Women at the Thesmophoria*, Aristophanes builds an entire play on Euripides' tragedies to show off the capacities of comedy's self-conscious and wide-ranging theatrical *mimēsis* (imitation). (On the broader implications of mimesis in the play, see especially Zeitlin (1996b), who thinks that the play asks questions about genre, imitation, and representation through gender (375–77s), and Farmer (2017) 157.)

Festival and Choral Performance

Many Aristophanes' plays besides *Women at the Thesmophoria* do refer, sometimes in some detail, directly to rituals and festal performances practiced in classical Athens. To give one example, in Aristophanes' *Acharnians*, Dicaeopolis stages a private version of a ritual performed in Attic demes during the Rural Dionysia in order to celebrate his private peace. A phallus is carried in honor of Dionysus, his daughter serves as basket bearer, and his wife watches from the roof, as the hero calls for holy silence and then sings a phallic song. In the last scene of *Acharnians*, Dicaeopolis has won a drinking context at the Choes, or feast of the Pitchers, a part of the public ritual of the Anthesteria. This festival, among other things, celebrated the new wine and performed rites in honor of the god Dionysus. Each man drank from his own cup at separate tables. At a trumpet signal, the person who drank his mixed wine up fastest received a wineskin. Dicaeopolis is invited to an official version of this festival and is promised a prize from the King Archon. He returns home inebriated with neat wine from his pitcher accompanied by two slave girls caressing his erect phallus. Both festal scenes emphasize the hero's successful return to the country and then to civic life. Yet he has excluded others from what was normally a communal procession at his Rural Dionysia along with his later household festivities and has managed to join a communal cultural ritual of the Choes while maintaining his separate peace. In the final lines of the play, Dicaeopolis asks the chorus to sing an Olympic victory song, the *tēnella kallinikos*, in his honor (1224–37). The chorus agrees and follows him, as he takes up his wineskin with no promise of sharing it. Dicaeopolis' name means "just city." But the exclusion of most of his fellow citizens from his private peace leaves the audience with unanswered questions.

Two early plays that closely followed *Acharnians* deployed a similar concluding festal pattern. In *Peace*, the hero Trygaeus flies to heaven to find out how to rescue Peace from her entombment in a cave below the earth. With the help of the god Hermes, Trygaeus invites those on earth, even foreigners, to share in rescuing Peace and establishing her cult (292–300). The plot resembles in some respects the rescue of Persephone from Hades. Like Kore/Persephone, Peace will restore fruitful regularity to the seasons (571–81) (Bowie (1993) 145–46). Hermes, the god who brings souls up from and down to Hades, inaugurates the rites to raise Peace, and with the help of Greeks both eager and reluctant, Peace (a statue) is raised. Weapons are turned into farming tools. Peace's handmaiden Theoria (Festival) is given to be shared to the assembly or Boule. A rejuvenated, semi-divinized Trygaeus celebrates a holy marriage rite with the fragrant Opora (Harvest). The concluding festival (*heortēn*, 817) also includes details suggestive of the Anthesteria, among them the celebration of new wine (916) and athletic (also sexual) competitions (Bowie (1993) 145–50). Although a few interlopers like oracle dealers and arms dealers are excluded from the celebration, the final feast even includes festivity at home for the women (966–71).

In *Birds*, two Athenians leave Athens to escape social and political difficulties. The hero Peisetaerus founds a new kingdom of the birds between earth and Olympus, Cloud-Cuckoo-Land (*Nephelococcugia*). Those on earth will now worship the birds, represented on stage by the chorus, but the gods on Olympus are excluded from human sacrifices and disenfranchised. Peisetaerus marries Zeus' female symbol of authority, Basileia, and acquires his thunderbolts. The new kingdom accepts but also excludes many immigrants eager for wings and liberation. In the final marriage ritual and festivity that closes the play, the hero offers hints of authoritarian behavior, including roasting "traitor" birds to be consumed at the feast (1583–84). As in *Acharnians*, the festivities affirm the hero's success, but, as critics agree, leave unresolved questions about the newly created utopia. (On ritual, religion and festival in *Birds*, see Straus 2018.)

These three early plays have established a similar narrative and festal pattern for similar male comic heroes. Against this background, I shall begin by considering the more indirect relation to a festal setting staged in *Women at the Thesmophoria*. As noted above, the play concludes not with the triumphant festal celebration for male protagonists that closed the three earlier plays but a return to ordinary home life. Once the barely individualized female characters have played their roles speaking in the assembly and guarding the Relative, all the women at least symbolically merge with the dancing and hymning chorus. The chorus moves abruptly at the end of the second day of the Thesmophoria toward home and the establishment of normality, apparently bypassing the third day (Kalligeneia) and further festivities altogether (Austin and Olson (2004) lxvi and Bierl (2009) 272–73). The other two plays that put women in charge more actively discussed below, *Lysistrata* and *Women at the Assembly*, do conclude with triumphant heterosexual festal celebration, however. *Women at the Thesmophoria*'s comic denigration of women is in principle also at odds with this important and respected female civic rite. Second, the emphasis on male transvestism and escape attempts distract from a possible focus on female ritual experience. Nevertheless, once the play's choral performance shifts from staging and serving the condemnation of Euripides at an assembly, it moves gradually away from concern over male intruders to the Thesmophoria to performing hymns and dances in honor of Olympian and other deities. The odes (as can often happen in comedy) become more loosely connected with the action and then engage with the divine world. The content and the performance of these songs restore dramatically a traditional civic and maternal role for Athenian women that is claimed in a more tongue in cheek fashion in the Parabasis. By addressing a broad range of deities, the chorus affirms a religious role in the polis no longer mixed with humorous imitations of the male assembly, as in the Parodos.

Critylla, appropriately for the Thesmophoria, opens the second day of the festival with an invocation to Demeter, Persephone, Plutus, and Kalligeneia (298–300). The chorus' final ode returns to invoking the two goddesses. Yet elsewhere direct references to the central myth celebrated in the Thesmophoria are minimal, including in the choral songs. Euripides' attempt to rescue his Relative has been viewed as parallel to Demeter's search for and effort to win back her lost daughter. In the *Andromeda* scene, the Relative becomes like Kore a maiden in need of rescue (Zeitlin (1996b) 181-94). During the hostage scene adapted from *Telephus*, the girl baby is indirectly described with the term *korē*, but this reference mainly serves to make a pun (Moulton (1981) 125). Mika is asked who took away her *korē* (*exekorēse*, 760) – her virginity/child. In the final scene, Euripides' disguise as an old woman accompanied by a young woman has been interpreted as reflecting the reunification of the grieving mother Demeter and her lost daughter, despite the fact that the "daughter" figure is a dancing girl who lures a supposedly Hades-like Scythian to remunerated sex. Moreover, the girl, Euripides, and the Relative split up as they exit (Stehle (2002) 399).

The play's early choruses frame the speeches concerning Euripides' condemnation. The Parodos (opening song) combines hymns in honor of the Olympians, who might have been celebrated in the Thesmophoria as well, with the inauguration of a male political assembly (Haldane 1965). In reality, the Thesmophoria was organized by female leaders or *Archousai,* but we know nothing of what was involved; close parallels with this comic assembly scene seem unlikely. This opening does establish the women as worshippers of civic deities, yet it simultaneously characterizes them as imitating male institutions with the behavior of typical comic women. The choral odes that comment on each of the speeches about Euripides continue to reflect an assembly format typical of debate scenes in Aristophanes until the Relative is unmasked as male and Cleisthenes departs to turn him over to male authorities.

The ode at 663–85 represents an important transition in the choral performance. On the one hand, the women perform a search around the orchestra for additional male intruders. They gird themselves up in male fashion, take up their torches, strip off their mantles, and are imagined to run through rows of tents set up for the festival (655–62). As noted earlier, a ritual pursuit (perhaps for Kore) may have played a role in the Thesmophoria, although search scenes are also common in comedy. Here, the women humorously search for a man before a male theatrical audience. They probably surround the Relative confined to the central altar in a potentially threatening fashion (Bierl (2009) 100). Yet this ode opens a way beyond the women's earlier focus on revenge by putting considerable emphasis on rejecting impiety to the gods, on the importance of maintaining belief in them (in contrast to Euripides' supposed denial of their existence), and on expressing reverence for divinity. Second, the circular performance of this dance is likely to have been typical in female festivals and rituals, whereas the chorus' earlier odes in the assembly may have imitated male processions and formations.

Circular dance is also central to the next ode (953–1000), which follows the Parabasis and the *Helen* paratragedy. At this point, the Relative has been removed from supervision by the women; the chorus turns away from the original plot and focuses exclusively on festal dance. The women detail their evolving dance movements, a feature typical of ritual performance (Bierl (2009) 83). Their song describes an opening turn to performance customary to their holy rites (*orgia semna,* 948) for the two goddesses during sacred seasons. After a quick joke about a starving artist named Pauson, whose hunger imitates their own ritual fasting, the women turn to honoring the race of the Olympians in an ecstatic dance. They now reject speaking abusively of men. (The touch of *aischrologia* offers more sympathy than insult to Pauson.) They honor both the virgin goddess Artemis and, for the first time, the goddess of marriage Hera along with rural deities, and then finally turn ecstatically (but still in control, in contrast to comic mockery of women's propensity for ecstatic and foreign dance) to Dionysus, god of the theatrical festivals. The argument of some scholars such as Versnel (1992, 251–54) and Bierl (2009) that the women here move from a symbolic virginity toward maternity seems in my view fairly speculative, however. The growing emphasis on the women's larger civic religious role is consolidated in their final ode (1136–89), where they begin by calling on the virginal Athena guardian of city, who hates tyrants, to bring peace and then summon the two Thesmophoroi to come with torches and join their rites that are forbidden for men to see. The audience is appropriately not included in these further sacred rites. Instead, Euripides appears to negotiate his treaty with the women, and they allow and even help him to rescue the Relative.

Since the Nesteia included the release of prisoners, this conclusion is apt (Bierl (2009) 133). The women close the play announcing a return to their own homes and request recompense from the two goddesses for their performance (1227–30). Although Aristophanes' other play entitled *Women at the Thesmophoria* included a nurse Kalligeneia as a character and was probably set on the third day of the festival, this play avoids any direct sharing of rites and myths focused on the two goddesses. Instead, the overall emphasis is first on return to performance segregated by gender and then to traditional familial roles. No more will be said of female misbehavior. As Habash ((1997) 37–39) stresses, the original Thesmophoric setting is re-established with an added coloring, and with the appeal to Dionysus, the song includes the City Dionysia itself. Overall, the sequence of the choral performance seems to offer an implicit reply to the play's comic calumny supported by a turn in the last two paratragedies of *Helen* and *Andromeda* to staging virtuous women. It performatively separates female ritual performance for the gods from the comedy's representation of outrageous female behavior.

In *Lysistrata*, by contrast to *Women at the Thesmophoria*, women across Greece devise and successfully implement a sex strike for peace. The men in this play become the object of critique by proving both inadequate to resolve public issues on their own and even more vulnerable to sexual desire than the women. They have not only failed to make peace but have wasted the women's "taxes" (589–90, 651, sons) and deprived younger women of reproducing children. The play, probably performed at the Lenaia festival in 411 before *Women at the Thesmophoria* at the later City Dionysia, may have been the first old comedy that puts women in charge (Henderson 2000). The women's authority here derives implicitly from traditional female domestic and public roles, which includes their ability to martial ritual to serve their plans. The women's international plot may have evolved from festal contexts. Some of the women met their contemporaries from Boeotia at a feast of the goddess Hekate (700). The audience could arguably link Lysistrata's name to that of the contemporary Priestess of Athena Polias, Lysimache, since both names mean disbander of armies (Lysimache is also named at *Peace* 992); her associate Myrrhine shares a name with the in reality much older priestess of Athena Nike; and the women's Spartan ally Lampito shares a name with the mother of King Agis the II of Sparta (see further Foley (1982) 8). Lysistrata shows none of the comic vices attributed to women in *Women at the Thesmophoria*. Represented as a public figure whose husband is never named, the Athena-like Lysistrata shows extraordinary self-control, eloquently overpowers male rhetoric, and demonstrates extensive strategy and persistence. Even the young and seductive Myrrhine proves able to manipulate her husband, Cinesias, who arrives with her male child and sporting an erection; she tempts, then abandons him when he proves unsympathetic to the peace plan.

The sex strike occurs simultaneously in homes, where wives refuse to have sex with their husbands, and on the sealed acropolis where older women have staged a takeover of the Treasury on the pretext of sacrificing there. Rites normally performed by women for Athena on the Acropolis justify their presence there, even though they have shut the men out from their stored money for war. The chorus of women in their Parabasis claim authority to act in the city's interest due to their religious education. "At seven I served as an Arrēphoria (one of two girls seven to eleven chosen to help weave and carry Athena's robe), then at ten I was an *aletris* (grinder) for Artemis and shed my saffron robe as a bear at the Brauronia; as a beautiful girl I carried the Basket wearing a necklace of dried figs" (640/1–644/5–67). When Lysistrata proposes to the skeptical Proboulos (magistrate) to weave a cloak (*chlaina*, 586) to unite citizens, the enormous robe (*peplos*) woven every four years by chosen girls and women for the goddess Athena could easily have come to mind (Bowie (1993) 185). The women also use their control of ritual as a weapon. Drawing on their skills in cloth making and preparing dead bodies for the grave, they feminize the Proboulos by dressing him as a corpse (599–607). Lysistrata then wittily promises a third day offering at his grave (608–10). By contrast, the chorus of men, who frequently make misogynist remarks, attempts to violate the acropolis by burning it and threatening Athena's sacred olive as well as penetrating it with phallic sticks. In response, the women throw a "nuptial bath" of water over the chorus of old men to put out their fires and make them grow (374–81) (see Faraone 1997).

Although the outraged men compare the women to Amazons, the women, despite vulnerability to female comic vices, prove able to carry out their mission. The opening scene refers to the female propensity for ecstatic religious rites, and the Proboulos mentions how their disruptive female rites for Adonis at the Adonia interrupted deliberations at the assembly (387–98). They are typically reluctant to give up sex, and predictably cement their oaths over a large bowl of wine. Later several of the women make a failed attempt to escape back from the Acropolis to their bedrooms. Yet Lysistrata finally deploys female sexuality to seal a Peace treaty over the body of Reconciliation for the universally erect men. The chorus of older women reclothes and domesticates the hostile chorus men. In the final scene, the women close the doors of the acropolis, share their boxes (*kistai*, 1184, suggesting sexual organs as well as sacred objects) with the men, host them, and return home as married couples. The chorus promises support both for sons and for daughters in their ritual role as basket bearers (1188–94). While the increasingly wine-filled men show a propensity to squabble at the play's conclusion, the women's reconciliation on the acropolis serves to re-establish it as space for religious celebration. As in *Peace*, this festal celebration includes both sexes but is now orchestrated by women. This play celebrates "woman in her legitimate role as ritual performer in the interests of the polis" (Foley (1982) 11, with further bibliography. On these aspects of *Lysistrata*, see also Vaio (1975), Hansen (1976), Henderson (1996) and (Faraone 1997)).

The third extant play with an active female protagonist once again offers a more complicated representation of women in control than *Women at the Thesmophoria*. Yet when the heroine of *Women at the Assembly* Praxagora succeeds in her plan to have the women take over the polis in disguise as men because men have so mishandled running it, references to ritual are much less specific. The women do hatch their plan at the Skira (18), another ritual for Demeter, and Praxagora defends female ethical superiority by referring to their ability to keep religious secrets at the Thesmophoria (443). By turning the polis into a domestic world governed by the women through their skills at making meals and clothing, the closing celebration is even more all inclusive than *Lysistrata* and resembles both a civic and domestic festival. When Chremes brings out domestic pots and pans to donate them to the new communist utopia that Praxagora created, he martials them as if they were participants in the Panathenaia, the largest Attic festival in honor of Athena (730–45) (Bowie (1993) 262). The revised festival marks, like the Panathenaia, the beginning of a new regime/year and gives a certain legitimacy to the heroine's plan even if Chremes' companion is not ready to make the gesture himself. Despite the mixed gender final celebration of the play, women remain permanently in charge. The plot feminizes the men by depriving them of their civic, military, and agricultural roles. Praxagora's novel plan for sexual reproduction – older people must be served sexually before younger ones – is performed in a scene where a young man is entrapped by three libidinous old crones and cannot reach his attractive girlfriend. The off-stage festal conclusion, though shared by all throughout a city that has turned into a heterosexual banqueting space, seems less celebratory in the light of the previous scene in contrast to that of *Peace* or *Lysistrata*, although it does not reinstitute female comic misbehavior across the board (Foley (1982), Saïd (1987)).

Thomas Hubbard (1991) argued that *Women at the Thesmophoria* responds directly to and revises *Lysistrata* performed earlier in the same year. Why then does *Women at the Thesmophoria*, performed at the larger and more international City Dionysia, create no positive (rather than punitive) agenda for an active and effective female protagonist? *Lysistrata* and *Women at the Assembly* exploit women's active roles in public ritual and in the household (or a household become state). The secret world of the Thesmophoria apparently generates fears about female behavior already traditional in myths about the rite. The later *Frogs* returns to the issue of exploring the relation between drama, ritual, and the implications of performing gender issues more systematically. Examining its elaborate structure more closely can at least give a fuller perspective on these questions.

The second chorus of *Frogs* (405 BCE), which presides over the contest between Aeschylus and Euripides in the underworld for the chair of tragedy, consists of Initiates in the Eleusinian Mysteries. They arrive on stage imitating a version of the journey to Eleusis that precedes the enactment of the Mysteries. Before the procession, the *prorrhēsis* or proclamation announced to prospective initiates that those tainted with blood guilt and those unable to speak Greek were excluded from the Mysteries. Initiates, wearing old clothes and having purified both themselves and a piglet (later sacrificed at some unknown point) by going "to the sea" at Phaleron, moved toward Eleusis chanting the name Iacchus (a version of Dionysus) during the procession. *Aischrologia* took place on the journey at a bridge over the Cephisus river. All night dances occurred on arrival (*pannychides*, 371; 446–47); many torches were carried (for these details, see Parker (2005) 347–351). The *Frogs*' chorus of initiates at least initially appears to include both men and women (Sommerstein (1996) 184 and Dover (1993) 65–68). The play concludes with the choral accompaniment and celebration of the tragedian Aeschylus as he departs as victor in the contest toward the world above (1500–33), where he will continue to ensure and revitalize dramatic performances that keep the city's dramatic festivals alive.

As in *Women at the Thesmophoria*, this chorus does not take us beyond the opening procession of the Mysteries to reveal secrets of the Eleusinian ritual. Instead, it goes on to observe first the initiatory experiences of Dionysus (in disguise as the mythical proto-initiate Heracles) and his slave Xanthias before their reception by Persephone and Plouton/Hades and then the tragic contest. Its Parodos (316–430) celebrates the blessed life of initiates dancing, throwing off the cares of age, and singing in sacred meadows of Persephone in the underworld; the chorus calls on Iacchus, on Athena as Savior (377–80), and processes toward Demeter as goddess of the Mysteries (385–87). The song concludes with brief *aischrologia*. In this song, "mystic identity is interwoven with Athenian civic consciousness" (Lada-Richards (1999) 100; see also Bowie (1993) 244). The chorus' mocking *prorrhēsis* (351–71) excludes from its rites those with unclean thoughts and those who betray or divide the city in various ways. But it also rejects those who have not seen and danced in the secret rites of the noble Muses and the Bacchic mysteries of bull-devouring Cratinus' (the now deceased older rival of Aristophanes) language (355–57). Those who nibble away at the fees of poets because they were satirized in the (theatrical) rites of Dionysus are also unwelcome (367–68). As noted earlier, the chorus also aims to share both humorous and serious things (389–90) during Demeter's upcoming festival. Starting with this parodos, this chorus gradually establishes itself as eager and by-and-large initially non-partisan observers of the contest who also define themselves as knowledgeable and sophisticated viewers of and initiates in the rites of drama.

Aristophanes seems to be claiming these adapted Eleusinian rites for his own genre, which by the conclusion becomes defined implicitly as perhaps even more encompassing than tragedy. Aeschylus (however old-fashioned) remains important to the goal of preserving dramatic choral performances for Athens, but he emerges as victor through a contest defined by comedy. A native of Eleusis, he opens the contest by swearing by Demeter and hopes to be worthy of her mysteries (886–87); his silent veiled characters (911–13) also suit this tradition. The contest offers a far wider range of pointed literary satire of tragedy than *Women at the Thesmophoria* or earlier plays. It sets out for tragedy civic goals (advice to save the city) and new ethical and aesthetic standards concerning style, prologues, range of subject matter, range and identity of speakers, language, music, and meter. Through Aeschylus, Aristophanes now objects morally to Euripides' articulate women and his concern with domestic affairs (*oikeia pragmata*, 959, 974–79) as well as to his expanded group of shameless women, who have even provoked suicides in respectable female citizens (1043–44, 1054–55, 1078). In the course of the tragic *agōn* (contest), genre boundaries dissolve and comedy emerges enriched (Lada-Richards (1999) 323). Even before Dionysus asks Euripides and Aeschylus for their advice concerning the city, Aristophanes' parabasis (718–37) has upstaged the tragic poets with more direct and comprehensible advice for which he may have been given the honor of a second performance of the play. It advises the city to restore political rights to those raised in wrestling schools, choruses, and *mousikē* (729, theatrical and song culture). In this play, then, Aristophanes for the first time uses adapted ritual and festival along with paratragedy as a context in which to redefine and even police theater/comedy and its role in the city. As Taplin argues ((1996) 198),

Aristophanes offers "a kind of bid for comedy to stand on a civic pedestal beside that of tragedy." In *Women at the Thesmophoria* paratragedy serves comedy's agenda in a more diffuse fashion, often strongly articulated through gender; ritual performance by the chorus of women eventually separates itself off from the engagement between tragedy and comedy to restore the cultural status quo, in contrast to *Frogs*' fuller integration of the two aimed at defining theater's role in the city.

Aristophanes' comic plots, themselves enacted at Athens' inclusive Dionysiac festivals, typically aim to recreate through rituals/festivals a sacred and secular community that resists divisions created by war or civic disunity (see further Hall (2014)). Those comedies (*Peace, Lysistrata, Frogs, Women at the Assembly*, and *Wealth*, a play I have not been able to include here) that unify the city, the citizens, the genders, or even the entire Panhellenic world through a shared festal conclusion give a more celebratory and expansive role to ritual than those that that retain social hierarchy (*Birds*), exclude fellow citizens (*Acharnians*), or reach a détente between genders that achieves a ritual normality not shared by all (*Women at the Thesmophoria*). *Frogs* embraces a broader Athenian citizenship and reconciles dramatic genres and *Peace* (815–18) even includes the theater audience in its celebration. In *Women at the Thesmophoria*, Euripides and the Relative merely escape a series of transgressions by both genders into each other's space. It may be significant that the women do not perform the final day of their annual rite.

GUIDE TO FURTHER READING

The most path-breaking and influential interpretative essay on *Women at the Thesmophoria* is F.I. Zeitlin (1996b) (originally 1981), "Travesties of Gender and Genre in Aristophanes' *Thesmophoriazusae*." Other valuable literary studies are Moulton (1981), Muecke (1982), Hall (1989), Taaffe (1993), Slater (2002), Henderson (1996), and Farmer (2017). For literary studies more focused on ritual in the play, see Bowie (1993), Habash (1997), and Tzanetou (2002). Bierl (2009) examines the play's chorus in its larger context. On costume, see Compton-Engle (2015). For commentaries, see Sommerstein (1994) and Austin and Olson (2004). Parker (2005) is the most up-to-date source on Attic rituals. For those interested in looking at relations between myth, ritual, and the gods in old comedy more generally, Bowie (2000, 2010), Given (2009), Straus (2011), Scullion (2013), Hall (2014), Revermann (2014), and Barrenechea (2018) on *Wealth* can fill out a broader picture not undertaken in this essay.

REFERENCES

Austin, C. and Olson, S.D. (2004). *Aristophanes Thesmophoriazusae*. Oxford: Oxford University Press.
Barrenechea, F. (2018). *Comedy and Religion in Classical Athens: Narratives of Religious Experiences in Aristophanes' Wealth*. Cambridge: Cambridge University Press.
Bierl, A. (2009). *Ritual and Performativity: The Chorus of Old Comedy*. Cambridge, MA and London: Harvard University Press.
Bobrick, E. (1991). Iphigeneia revisited: *Thesmophoriazusae* 1160–1225. *Arethusa* 24: 67–76.
Bobrick, E. (1997). The tyranny of roles: playacting and privilege in Aristophanes' *Thesmophoriazusae*. In: *The City as Comedy* (ed. G. Dobrov), 177–197. Chapel Hill and London: University of North Carolina Press.
Bowie, A.M. (1993). *Aristophanes. Myth, Ritual and Comedy*. Cambridge: Cambridge University Press.
Bowie, A.M. (2000). Myth and ritual in the rivals of Aristophanes. In: *The Rivals of Aristophanes* (ed. D. Harvey and J. Wilkins), 317–340. Swansea: Classical Press of Wales.
Bowie, A.M. (2010). Myth and ritual in comedy. In: *Brill Companion to Aristophanes* (ed. G.W. Dobrov), 143–176. Leiden and Boston: Brill.
Compton-Engle, G. (2015). *Costume in the Comedies of Aristophanes*. Cambridge: Cambridge University Press.
Csapo, E. (2000). From Aristophanes to Menander? Genre transformations in Greek comedy. In: *Matrices of Genre: Author, Canons, and Society* (ed. M. Depew and D. Obbink), 115–133. Cambridge, MA: Harvard University Press.
Detienne, M. (1989). The violence of wellborn ladies: women in the Thesmophoria. In: *The Cuisine of Sacrifice Among the Greeks* (ed. M. Detienne and J.-P. Vernant), 129–147. Chicago: Chicago University Press.

Dillon, M. (2002). *Girls and Women in Classical Greek Religion*. New York: Routledge.
Dover, K. (1993). *Aristophanes Frogs*. Oxford: Oxford University Press.
Duncan, A. (2006). *Performance and Identity in the Classical World*. Cambridge: Cambridge University Press.
Faraone, C. (1997). Salvation and female heroes in the parodos of Aristophanes' *Lysistrata*. *Journal of Hellenic Studies* 117: 38–59.
Farmer, M.C. (2017). *Tragedy on the Comic Stage*. Oxford: Oxford University Press.
Ferris, L. (1989). *Acting Women: Images of Women in Theatre*. New York: MacMillan.
Foley, H.P. (1982). The 'female intruder' reconsidered: women in Aristophanes' *Lysistrata and Ecclesiazusae*. *Classical Philology* 19: 1–21.
Foley, H.P. (1992). Anodos dramas, Euripides' *Alcestis* and *Helen*. In: *Innovations of Antiquity* (ed. R. Hexter and D. Selden), 133–160. Routledge.
Foley, H.P. (2001). *Female Acts in Greek Tragedy (=Martin Classical Lectures 1995)*. Princeton: Princeton University Press.
Foley, H.P. (2008). Generic boundaries in late fifth-century Athens. In: *Performance, Reception, Iconography* (ed. M. Revermann and P. Wilson), 15–36. Oxford: Oxford University Press.
Gibert, J. (2000). Falling in love with Euripides (*Andromeda*). *Illinois Classical Studies* 24–25: 75–92.
Gilula, D. (1996). A singularly gifted actor (Ar. *Th*. 1056–1096). *Quaderni di Storia* 44: 159–164.
Given, J. (2009). When Gods don't appear: divine absence and human agency in aristophanes. *Classical World* 102: 107–127.
Habash, M. (1997). The odd Thesmophoria of Aristophanes' *Thesmophoriazusae*. *Greek, Roman and Byzantine Studies* 38: 19–40.
Haldane, J.A. (1965). A scene in the *Thesmophoriazusae* (295–371). *Philologus* 109: 39–46.
Hall, E.M. (1989). The archer scene in Aristophanes' *Thesmophoriazusae*. *Philologus* 133: 38–54.
Hall, E.M. (2014). Comedy and Athenian festival culture. In: *The Cambridge Companion to Greek Comedy* (ed. M. Revermann), 306–321. Cambridge: Cambridge University Press.
Hansen, H. (1976). Aristophanes' *Thesmophoriazusae*: theme, structure and production. *Philologus* 120: 165–185.
Henderson, J. (1996). *Three Plays by Aristophanes: Staging Women*. London: Routledge.
Henderson, J. (2000). Pherekrates and the women of old comedy. In: *The Rivals of Aristophanes: Studies in Athenian Old Comedy* (ed. D. Harvey and J. Wilkins), 135–150. Swansea: Classical Press of Wales.
Hubbard, T.K. (1991). *The Mask of Comedy: Aristophanes and the Intertextual Parabasis*. Ithaca: Cornell University Press.
Hutcheon, L. (1985). *A Theory of Parody*. New York and London: University of Illinois Press.
Lada-Richards, I. (1999). *Initiating Dionysus: Ritual and Theater in Aristophanes Frogs*. Oxford: Oxford University Press.
Lowe, N.J. (1998). Thesmophoria and Haloa: Myth, Physics and Mysteries. In: *The Sacred and the Feminine in Ancient Greece* (ed. S. Blundell and M. Willliamson), 149–173. London and New York: Routledge.
Lowe, N.J. (2000). Comic plots and the invention of fiction. In: *The Rivals of Aristophanes: Studies in Athenian Old Comedy* (ed. D. Harvey and J. Wilkins), 259–272. Swansea: Classical Press of Wales.
McClure, L. (1999). *Spoken Like a Woman: Speech and Gender in Athenian Drama*. Princeton: Princeton University Press.
Moulton, C. (1981). *Aristophanic Poetry*. Göttingen: Vandenhoeck und Ruprecht.
Muecke, F. (1982). A portrait of an artist as a young woman. *Classical Quarterly* 32: 41–55.
Nieddu, G.F. (2004). A poet at work: the parody of *Helen* in the *Thesmophoriazusae*. *Greek, Roman and Byzantine Studies* 44: 331–360.
Osborne, R. (1993). Women and sacrifice in classical Greece. *Classical Quarterly* 43: 392–405.
Parker, R. (2005). *Polytheism and Society at Athens*. Oxford: Oxford University Press.
Pucci, P. (1961). *Aristofane ed Euripides: recherche metriche e stilistiche*. Rome: Accademia nazionale dei Lincei.
Rau, P. (1967). *Paratragoedia: Untersuchung einer komischen Form des Aristophanes. Zetemata* 45. Munich.
Revermann, M., ed. (2014), Divinity and Religious Practice. In: *The Cambridge Companion to Greek Comedy* (ed. M. Revermann), 275–90. Cambridge: Cambridge University Press.
Rose, M. (1979). *Parody/Metafiction*. London: Croom Helm.
Saïd, S. (1987). Travestis et travestissements dans les comédies d'Aristophane. *Cahiers du GITA* 3: 217–248.
Scodel, R. (1980). *The Trojan Trilogy of Euripides*. Göttingen: Vandenhoeck und Ruprecht.
Scullion, S. (2013). Religion and the Gods in Greek Comedy. In: *The Oxford Handbook of Greek and Roman Comedy* (ed. M. Fontaine and A.C. Scafuro), 340–358. Oxford: Oxford University Press.

Slater, N.W. (2002). *Spectator Politics: Metatheatre and Performance in Aristophanes*. Philadelphia: Pennsylvania State University Press.
Sommerstein, A.H. (ed.) (1994). *Thesmophoriazusae*, vol. 8. Warminster: Aris and Phillips.
Sommerstein, A.H. (ed.) (1996). *Frogs*. Warminster: Aris and Phillips.
Stehle, E. (2002). The body and its representations in Aristophanes' *Thesmophoriazusae*. *American Journal of Philology* 123: 369–406.
Straus, M. (2011). Aristophanes' *Clouds* in its ritual setting. *Leeds International Classical Studies* 10 (1): 1–28.
Straus, M. (2018). Ritual aspects of Aristophanes' *Birds*. *Acta Classica LXI* 125–157.
Taaffe, L. (1993). *Aristophanes and Women*. London: Routledge.
Taplin, O. (1996). Comedy and the tragic. In: *Tragedy and the Tragic* (ed. M.S. Silk), 188–120. Oxford: Oxford University Press.
Tzanetou, A. (2002). Something to do with Demeter: ritual and performance in Aristophanes' *Women at the Thesmophoria*. *American Journal of Philology* 123: 329–367.
Vaio, J. (1975). The manipulations of theme and action in Aristophanes' *Lysistrata*. *Greek, Roman and Byzantine Studies* 14: 369–380.
Versnel, H. (1992). The festival for the Bona Dea and the Greek Thesmophoria. *Greece & Rome* 39: 31–55.
Wright, M. (2005). *Euripides' Escape Tragedies: A Study of Helen, Andromeda and Iphigeneia Among the Taurians*. Oxford: Oxford University Press.
Zeitlin, F.I. (1985). Playing the other: theater, theatricality and the feminine in Greek drama. *Representations* 11: 63–94. reprinted in (1990), *Nothing to Do with Dionysus*, eds. J. Winkler and F. Zeitlin. Princeton: 63–96 and in Zeitlin's *Playing The Other*.
Zeitlin, F.I. (1996a). The power of Aphrodite: Eros and the boundaries of the self in Euripides' *Hippolytus*. In: *Playing the Other: Gender and Society in Classical Greek Literature*, 219–284. Chicago and London: University of Chicago Press.
Zeitlin, F.I. (1996b). Travesties of gender and genre in Aristophanes' *Thesmophoriazusae*. In: *Playing the Other: Gender and Society in Classical Greek Literature*, 375–416. Chicago and London: University of Chicago Press.

CHAPTER 15

Frogs: Metaphor and Allegory

Anna A. Novokhatko

θάνατον γὰρ εἰσέθηκε, βαρύτατον κακόν
Ar. *Ra*. 1394

Introduction

Aristophanes' *Frogs* (Βάτραχοι) performed in Athens at the Lenaea of 405 BCE won the first prize and was performed a second time the following year.[1]

A summary of the plot is as follows: As Athens is doing badly politically and culturally, Dionysus travels to the underworld with his slave Xanthias to bring an important poet who has already died back to this world. After a discussion with Heracles about the best way to get there, they arrive at Charon, who, however, only accepts Dionysus in his boat, while Xanthias must walk. During the crossing, the god feels disturbed by the croaking of frogs.

Once in the underworld, Dionysus disguises himself as Heracles. He changes clothes several times with his slave and thus also confuses Hades' servant Aiakos. His attempt to identify the god through a torture test also fails. A conversation between Xanthias and Aiakos reveals that Aeschylus held the place of honor at Hades' side. After Euripides' entry into the underworld, however, he gained great popularity there and proved to be a serious rival. Dionysus pits the two against each other, but without stating the reason. The two poets now take turns praising their own works and censuring those of the other. Since no result can be determined, they throw their verses into a scale at the behest of the god and declaim them. The scales always tip in Aeschylus' favor. His proposed solutions to political and military problems also find more favor. Dionysus declares Aeschylus the winner. Hades allows the playwright to return to earth and at the same time asks Dionysus to inform the current rulers and high officials of Athens that they may soon enter the realm of the dead.

The *Frogs* occupies a distinctly special and peculiar place in relation to Athenian politics, social life, and the history of poetics and literary criticism. Much work on *Frogs* over the last decades has focused on the unification of three dimensions of the play, the political, the ritual, and the poetic.[2] The transformation of Dionysus' character which bridges two halves of the comedy has been

---

[1] Sommerstein (1993, pp. 461–466) suggests the Lenaea of 404 BCE.
[2] Konstan (1987, 1995, pp. 61–74).

analyzed from various viewpoints.[3] In what follows, I will discuss the comedy and identify these main themes and approach them through an analysis of metaphor. I will suggest that conceptual metaphors and allegories for death are essential to the structure and setting of *Frogs*. The concepts of *katabasis* and Eleusinian mysteries are crucial in this regard. In addition, I will point out some allegorical figures and allegorical scenes in the comedy and show how cognitive approaches can shed new light on these issues.

Studies on Metaphor: Some Preliminary Assumptions

Metaphor enables a principal reimagining and reinterpretation of language and reality.[4] Following discussions of the subject that have come to be known as cognitive/conceptual metaphor theory, metaphors are viewed as being created by transferring the entities and structure of very skeletal images of concrete bodily experiences to more abstract entities.[5] Metaphorical expressions reflect conceptual associations in the speaker's mind that are formed on the basis of conceptual associations that are also based on particular physical experiences of the world. The concrete concepts that arise from people's interactions with their environment form the basis for associations with more abstract concepts and thus contribute to understanding these concepts.

The postulates of conceptual metaphor theory are clearly important for any analysis of comedy, as seen, for example, in the bodily experiences implied by the image schemata.[6] Bodily experiences are indispensable to theatrical performance and to the language of comedy. Comedy absorbs and reflects various linguistic registers, frequently simulating spoken everyday language.[7] Metaphor is par excellence a matter of everyday speech and thought, mapping and blending domains of experience and cognition. It is also one of the greatest weapons for talking about ideas and experiences that are difficult to articulate using more literal language.[8]

In this chapter, I will suggest that metaphors play a crucial role in the structure, the setting and plot of Aristophanes' *Frogs*. Six postulates of the cognitive theory of metaphor are of particular importance for our analysis of *Frogs*: (1) metaphors are all-pervasive, found in every area of human thought and expression; (2) metaphors are whole systematic sets of corresponding elements between two domains of experience, not merely the comparisons of two isolated entities; (3) metaphors use more concrete domains to understand more abstract domains; (4) metaphors occur primarily in thought; (5) conceptual metaphors arise from embodied experience; and (6) the metaphorical structures arising from our shared experience of embodiment are "predominantly universal."[9]

An essential contribution is made by the recent interest in multimodal metaphors, non-verbal manifestations of conceptual image schemas, and the way they can be visually instantiated or physically performed. Metaphors draw on combinations of visuals, gestures, sound, and music. The investigations of non-verbal metaphors found in visual art, theater, dance, and music are also promising for any analysis of Aristophanic comedy. Conceptual metaphor makes it possible to

---

[3] For a solid bibliographical overview, see Tsoumpra (2020, p. 199, f. 2).
[4] There is neither a single cognitive (or conceptual) theory of metaphor nor agreement on what exactly the cognitive theory of metaphor might be. For a very good overview of the interface between the history of metaphor studies and cognitive studies, see Lancaster (2021, pp. 236–249).
[5] The bibliography on cognitive approaches to metaphor is vast, starting with Reddy's exploration of the "conduit metaphor" (Reddy 1979), Ortony's juxtaposition of metaphorical language and metaphorical thought (Ortony 1979), and the seminal (Lakoff and Johnson 1980). See Eubanks (2017) in detail.
[6] On the performative elements of Greek theater analyzed from a cognitive perspective, see Meineck (2018).
[7] Willi (2002, pp. 13–14, 18). On registers, technical languages, sociolects, and (comic) idiolects in Aristophanes, see Willi (2003).
[8] Gibbs (2017, p. 223). On conceptual metaphor and blending, see Dancygier (2017).
[9] Kövecses (2017, pp. 13–19) and Lancaster (2021, pp. 243–244).

coherently describe different moments and profiles of an action according to the same underlying scheme. In addition to importing and maintaining a set terminology, the presence of a conceptual metaphor promotes the retrieval of terms based on limiting the number of pathways available.

Metaphors function within tradition, which means the authors are not necessarily aware of the metaphors at play. The interplay between the unconscious layers and the creative imagination of the author remains crucial to understanding the function of conceptual metaphor in literary texts. New terms might be supported by the metaphorical framework provided by a tradition: even a word that occurs only once in the comedy might be considered significant due to the systematic conceptual metaphors that structure the play as a whole.

Metaphors are thus useful devices employed by the comic poet in performance on stage on a number of different levels. They should not, however, be considered self-explanatory simply because they come from shared areas of experience. They might simultaneously be challenging, perplexing, and strange, just as they might address or evoke "real" bodily experiences. The tensions integral to metaphorical language are in fact central to its comicality. Different people construe the same metaphors against a background of different experiences, and embodied experience varies over time or place and from person to person. The manner in which embodiment constrains the use and understanding of metaphors varies.[10] Here, Aristophanes' *Frogs* will be analyzed through the prism of a specific conceptual metaphor that runs through the text, serving as an axis for the comedy.

The theme of death has been previously considered as a structural paradigm for the consolidation of multifaceted variety of topics in *Frogs*.[11] While metaphor was previously seen as a product of creative poetic will, the theory of conceptual metaphor allows us to connect the conceptual or urmetaphors for DEATH at play with everyday discourses, and to interpret them as fundamental to the human concept of mind, in both the Aristophanic and modern senses. Examining conceptual metaphors for DEATH as a central theme and motif of the comedy and looking at them holistically contributes to the creation of a model for the transmission of information and the understanding of internal dialogue within the play, as well as highlighting the similarities and differences between ancient and modern conceptualizations of DEATH. The final part of this chapter discusses certain cognitive approaches to allegory and analyses the function of allegory in the *Frogs* connecting it to conceptual metaphors for DEATH.

Conceptual Metaphors for DEATH

Discussing general metaphorical ways people conceive birth, life, and death, Lakoff and Turner argue that although the human imagination enables the creation and comprehension of even bizarre connections, there are relatively few basic metaphors for life and death that are a part of human culture.[12] In all cultures, human beings move from the concrete – accessed through the senses and experienced as embodied human beings interacting with our physical and social environment – to the abstract. The evolution of human cognition has enabled us to develop models of mind from which emerge from the most basic forms of interaction with the natural and social environment. DEATH itself is connected to various fundamental concepts of mind such as fear (DEATH IS AN ADVERSARY, DEATH IS DARKNESS), love (DEATH IS LOSS), and framing of space and time (DEATH IS DEPARTURE, DEATH IS JOURNEY), and such like. Through the use of these mechanisms of thought, metaphor serves as a main mediator of the conceptual link between various concrete concepts related to DEATH taken from the natural environment and DEATH as a more abstract concept.[13]

---

[10] Littlemore (2019, pp. 105–122).
[11] Reckford (1987) and Bassi (2016, pp. 144–185).
[12] Lakoff and Turner (1989, pp. 1–56).
[13] Cairns (2018/2019, p. 19).

DEATH *Metaphors and the Setting: Katabasis*

As has been emphasized by Charle Forceville, interpreting something as a metaphor requires deciding three parameters: which are its two parts, which is its target and its source, and which features are to be mapped from source to target.[14] Already in Homer DEATH is associated with a range of ideas and images: DEATH is a departure, journey, night, darkness, sleep, winter, these being common to various cultures and epochs.[15] Aristophanes' approach is quite different. He subverts any natural understandings of death, staging situations that clash with common understandings. The mocking of death creates space for serious reflection.

The theme of visiting the underworld and returning alive was taken up, changed, and transmitted in ancient tradition. The journey was usually a descent (*katabasis*) to a dark and gloomy place where oblivion and punishment reigned, but the visitor could also travel east or west to the realm of fabulous creatures.[16] Aristophanes' *Frogs* is constructed around a narrative of a journey to the underworld (DEATH IS DEPARTURE, DEATH IS JOURNEY).

The god Dionysus accompanied by his slave Xanthias goes to Hades to lead the recently deceased Euripides from the realm of the dead back to Athens.[17] In his cross-cultural analysis of mysterious cults, Mircea Eliade painted the descent into Hades as signifying an "initiatory death," an experience which can establish a new way of being. Dionysus, in particular, was characterized by his death and rebirth, part of an eternal cycle of life.[18]

The initial impulse is thus provided by the emphasis on DEATH: Dionysus being closely linked with death rituals and Euripides' death. After a contest in Hades between Euripides and Aeschylus, who has already been long dead, Dionysus decides to bring not Euripides but Aeschylus back to the world of the living.

The underworld to which Dionysus journeys is described in detail, this being probably the most comprehensive extant description of the underworld in Greek literature (Ar. *Ra.* 137–164).[19] It consists of a big bottomless lake at the outset (ἐπὶ λίμνην μεγάλην ἥξεις πάνυ ἄβυσσον, 137–138), then thousands of serpents and other beasts who look horrific (ὄφεις καὶ θηρί' ὄψει μυρία δεινότατα, 143–144), this is followed by a vast sea of mud and eternal dung (βόρβορον πολὺν καὶ σκῶρ ἀείνων, 145–146) where sinners lie, and then, all around, the music of pipes will be heard (αὐλῶν τίς σε περίεισιν πνοή, 154), and the Mystic initiates who live very close by the road, at Pluto's palace doors (οὗτοι γὰρ ἐγγύτατα παρ' αὐτὴν τὴν ὁδὸν ἐπὶ ταῖσι τοῦ Πλούτωνος οἰκοῦσιν θύραις, 162–163), will appear in beautiful light (ὄψει τε φῶς κάλλιστον, 155), as will myrtle groves (μυρρινῶνας), and happy companies of men and women (θιάσους εὐδαίμονας ἀνδρῶν γυναικῶν), and there will be much clapping of hands (κρότον χειρῶν πολύν, 156–157). All the recipient's sensorimotor senses – sight, hearing, taste, touch and smell – are engaged to experience this transition to DEATH in Heracles' enactive narration.[20] The vocabulary consists of physical, environmental, and spatial

---

[14] Forceville (2016, p. 244), see also Forceville (1996, p. 108).
[15] On the metaphors for DEATH in Homer, see Zanker (2019, pp. 82–86, 97–98). On metaphorical conceptions of death in world literature, see Lakoff and Turner (1989, pp. 1–56); on the paradigmatic analysis of death in John Milton see Turner (1987, pp. 78–104). On different approaches to the reality of dying and dead bodies in different societies, see Rehm (2017, pp. 133–134).
[16] On pagan and early Christian representations of the journey to Hades, see Ekroth and Nilsson (2018).
[17] This scenario is based on the legend of Dionysus' search for his mother Semele whom he then brought to Olympus, with the theme of death and immortality rooted in the myth. See Whitman (1964, pp. 233–234).
[18] Eliade (1972, p. 27).
[19] Stavru (2021, p. 161). On the ritual enactment of catabatic myths and the descent in the fifth-century BCE poetry, see Franklin (2017, pp. 169–177). The mission to the underworld was mentioned in other comedies such as Aristophanes' *Gerytades* (fr. 156 PCG), Eupolis' *Demoi* (fr. 99.56-7, 64–65 PCG), Pherecrates' *Krapataloi* (frr. 86 and 100 PCG) and *Metallēs* (fr. 113 PCG), Strattis incert. fr. 64 PCG, Ameipsias incert. fr. 22 PCG. On fifth-century drama with the theme of the descent to Hades, see Sommerstein (1996, pp. 9–10), Lada-Richards (1999, pp. 119–120), and Maggi (2020, pp. 311–312, f. 734). On the journey to the underworld in the *Frogs*, see Higgins (1977), Hooker (1980), and Edmunds Radcliffe (2004, pp. 111–158).
[20] On Heracles' experience of Hades in the ancient literary and iconographic tradition, see Verbanck-Piérard (2018).

elements, creating a three-dimensional description of the underworld, actively embodying smells and sounds. An indicator of DEATH, the water barrier known from mythical tradition, such as the Acherusian Lake or the river Acheron or the lake Lerna/Alkyonia or some other, separates the two realms and serves as an indication of the transition (εὐθὺς γὰρ ἐπὶ λίμνην μεγάλην ἥξεις, 137).[21]

Charon, the ferryman of the dead, is mentioned in a number of earlier sources but appears on stage for the first time in the *Frogs* in extant Greek literature. Heracles begins by describing the old sailor (ἀνὴρ γέρων ναύτης, 139–140) who would take Dionysus and Xanthias over on the other side of the lake. Once Heracles has prepared the scene, it is performed (180–209).[22] Charon stands in his boat, speaks like a real ferryman, and teaches Dionysus how to row. The god Dionysus is supposed to stretch out his hands (οὔκουν προβαλεῖ τὼ χεῖρε κἀκτενεῖς, 201), set his feet against the stretcher (ἀντιβὰς, 202), strike the oar into the water (ἐμβάλῃς, 206), and row (ἐλαύνειν, 203, 205). This detailed bodily, sensorimotorial description of the terrifying transition from life to death provides an additional effect, as physical movement contrasts with and reduces the terror associated with the moment of death.[23]

The two-obol fare, which was also the entrance fee to the theater, is a metatheatrical inflation of the legendary one obol given to Charon (δύ' ὀβολὼ μισθὸν λαβών, 140).[24] The joke presumes some kind of a death of theater: since the deaths of Euripides and Sophocles, the price of a theater ticket is equated with the price of entry into the realm of the dead.[25]

The "real" Athens is at that moment depicted as impotent and miserable and so Dionysus sets out on his quest to bring back a tragic playwright with physical generative power: "If you looked for a fertile poet (γόνιμον δὲ ποιητὴν), who would utter forth a noble phrase, you could not find anybody," declares Dionysus (96–97). Fertile poets are dead, while the barren and the dead are alive, the passage belonging to a cluster of DEATH IS LIFE incongruity, which will be discussed further below.

The comic here is in Aristophanes' subverting the separation of the worlds of life and death, and representing Hades as vital and "real."[26] Dionysus asks his half-brother to refer to the underworld, as though the underworld were an attractive holiday resort. He asks him to describe the harbors (λιμένας), bakeries (ἀρτοπώλια), brothels (πορνεῖ'), places to rest (ἀναπαύλας), right turnings (ἐκτροπάς), springs (κρήνας), roads (ὁδούς), cities (πόλεις), accommodation (διαίτας), and the hostesses who have the fewest bedbugs (πανδοκευτρίας, ὅπου κόρεις ὀλίγιστοι, 112–115).

Further, continuing his touristic itinerary, he asks after the fastest route to Hades (117–118). The fast route is by hanging, via rope and bench (ἀπὸ κάλω καὶ θρανίου, κρεμάσαντι σαυτόν, 121–122). Dionysus answers this by engaging in a somatic level of emotion: he dislikes it, as he finds it somewhat stifling (πνιγηρὰν, 122). The second route is via hemlock (κώνειον); a well-beaten shortcut (ἀτραπὸς ξύντομος τετριμμένη) is by way of mortar (ἡ διὰ θυείας, 123–124). Dionysus dislikes this too, his answer containing physiological details on bodily temperature: this way of suicide is cold and wintry (ψυχρὰν γε καὶ δυσχείμερον, 125); it freezes one's shins straight out (εὐθὺς γὰρ ἀποπήγνυσι τἀντικνήμια, 126). A third route comes by throwing hurling oneself from a tower, at a pace and directly downhill (ταχεῖαν καὶ κατάντη, 127). Creep down to Kerameikos (καθέρπυσόν νυν εἰς Κεραμεικόν, 129), climb to the top of the tall tower (ἀναβὰς ἐπὶ τὸν πύργον τὸν ὑψηλόν, 130), watch

---

[21] On archaic and classical sources on the water of Acheron, see Sourvinou-Inwood (1995, pp. 307–316) and Sommerstein (1996, p. 168).
[22] On the fifth-century BCE representations of Charon, see Sourvinou-Inwood (1995, pp. 303–361) and Sommerstein (1996, p. 172).
[23] Sourvinou-Inwood (1995, pp. 316–317).
[24] Whitman (1964, p. 235).
[25] Moorton (1989).
[26] For an implicit mockery of Euripides' literary taste, while depicting the infernal world as a place where all the imaginable comforts of home are provided and the personal possessions of the inhabitants take center stage, see Bassi (2016, p. 168). The longing of Dionysus for Euripides is a pretext to represent the realm of death as a materialistic paradise full of food and the objects stolen previously by Heracles.

the start of the torch-race (ἀφιεμένην τὴν λαμπάδ' ἐντεῦθεν θεῶ, 131), and then when the spectators say "they're off!" – fall down from the tower (τόθ' εἶναι καὶ σὺ σαυτόν. . . κάτω, 133). Dionysus would perish this way, squashing his two brain rissoles into smithereens (ἀπολέσαιμ' ἂν ἐγκεφάλου θρίω δύο, 134). Dionysus thus provides a thoroughly enactive account of "dying," recalls various bodily reactions, and changes in the organism and the environment depending on the chosen mode of death (121–134).[27] Comicality and nausea are blended here, much as in many contemporary horror films, with the range of emotions, the fear and trembling before DEATH, distorted and derided through a focus on systems of bodily regulation.[28]

Two important dimensions of the play, the political and the ritual, both end in the salvation of Athens. Here, I intend to argue that they are the omnipresent conceptual metaphors for DEATH that merge these two strands. For it is the attempt to resurrect the past that presupposes precisely the death of that past.[29] Thus, the play contains a plenty of dead bodies and is full of jokes about death.[30] One example is the short scene with an embodiment of DEATH, the *ekphora* (procession to the tomb) with its anonymous corpse (170–178). Look, here is a corpse they are carrying to the grave (τιν' ἐκφέρουσι τουτονὶ νεκρόν, 170), says Dionysus. The corpse (τεθνηκότα, 171) refuses to take Dionysus' luggage to Hades except for the exorbitant payment of two drachmas (δύο δραχμὰς μισθὸν τελεῖς; 173). Dionysus offers him nine obols, and the indignant corpse refuses: "May I resurrect if I take them!" (ἀναβιῴην νυν πάλιν, 177), rather than the "may I die!" which would be the normal refusal for the living.[31] Dead bodies appear in burlesque intertextual associations: Aeschylus in the agon throws a verse with "corpses" and death onto the scale of critical judgment, thus weighing down the balance. His verse "chariot upon chariot, and corpse on corpse" (ἐφ' ἅρματος γὰρ ἅρμα καὶ νεκρῷ νεκρός, 1403) from the lost tragedy *Glaukos of Potniae* emerges as the winner.[32] In both passages, the corpses are emphatically material and have physical weight. The first corpse that is carried does not want to take on any further weight itself and refuses to take on the baggage of Dionysus. The embodiment of the second multilayered metaphor of weighing verses lies in the physical weight of the mass itself being weighed: the significant verses "weigh" more, and the most "weigh" the verses that contain corpses. The absurdity, then, lies at the heart of both scenes: the physical weight that belongs to the world of the living is the central component and measure of death.

The connection of the topic of death with the historical and political goings-on has been commented upon: Aristophanes seems especially to allude to the battle near Arginusae where corpses were tossed in the sea. The victory at Arginusae led to one of the worst disasters experienced by the Athenians during the Peloponnesian War. Due to incompetent leadership, excessive sailor fatigue, and a sudden storm, the commanders on the ground failed to rescue the crews of the 25 Athenian ships that had been damaged during the battle. Thousands of wounded suffering men clung to the wrecks of their ships and died. When the Athenians received the news, they were horrified. They deposed the eight generals who had been in command during the battle. Two of the leaders went into exile, and the six who returned to Athens were tried, convicted, and eventually executed.[33] Corpses and especially unburied corpses as reminders of Athenian shame and at the same time embodied symbols of DEATH, had a special symbolic function in the Athenian reality of the time.

Political crisis and the urgent call for redemption of Athens are linked to the ritual dimension of DEATH metaphors in the play. The Eleusinian Mysteries were initiations held every year for the cult of Demeter and Persephone. They are a well-known Panhellenic symbol of the life of the Athenian polis, for the ritual performance of the Mysteries was a way for the city to define its territory, and

---

[27] Sommerstein (1996, pp. 166–168).
[28] On the interplay of physiological changes and conceptual model of emotion, see Cairns (2016).
[29] Karen Bassi calls death "the driving metaphor of the comedy," see Bassi (2016, p. 172).
[30] See Reckford (1987, pp. 405–408).
[31] Dover (1993, pp. 211–212). On metatheatrical joking with "carrying things" (σκεύη φέρειν in v. 15, σκευάρι' εἰς Ἅιδου φέρειν in v. 172) and on Pluto giving Aeschylus at the end of the play instruments of suicide to carry back to the living, see Bassi (2016, p. 168).
[32] Sommerstein (1996, p. 283).
[33] Worthington (1989), Sommerstein (1996, pp. 2–3), and Allan (2012).

the boundaries of the community and its influence.³⁴ Aristophanes used a pattern of initiations to frame his plot: the Mysteries represented the myth of the abduction of Persephone by Hades, in a cycle with three phases: the descent and loss, the search, and the ascent (ἄνοδος) of Persephone and the reunion with her mother.³⁵ Although the chorus of *mystai* entering the scene is not explicitly referred to Eleusinian initiates, there is no doubt that Aristophanes and his audience were well aware of the primary reference. The appearance of the chorus is marked by sensorimotor vocabulary: first the sound of pipes is heard (οὐ κατήκουσας; . . .αὐλῶν πνοῆς, 312–313), and then later the mystic steam of the torches is breathed upon (δᾴδων γέ με αὔρα τις εἰσέπνευσε μυστικωτάτη, 313–314). Iacchus is celebrated and invited to escort the choral dancers (Ἴακχε φιλοχορευτά, συμπρόπεμπέ με, 412), and the god Dionysus agrees to play and dance with good friends (ἐγὼ δ' ἀεί πως φιλακόλουθός εἰμι καὶ μετ' αὐτῆς παίζων χορεύειν βούλομαι, 414–415). He emerges here rather as an Eleusinian pilgrim might from the darkness following the passage through DEATH into the torchlight.³⁶ The barriers between the living and the dead are blended. In the spring of 405, real-world Athens was full of discord and factions, largely deprived of its power over the other Greek states and unable to organize the celebration of the Mysteries. The chorus of initiates is thus placed in the underworld, the realm of death. In other words, metaphors for DEATH bring together, consolidate, and merge the ritual and the political aspects of the play. What is impossible in the city of Athens is staged in the living underworld.

Yet the chorus continues to highlight the distinction between the realms of upper and the underworlds. For the chorus is dancing in flowering meadows (326–336, 344–352, 447–453), but is wearing cheap poor sandals (τὸ σανδαλίσκον) and rags (τὸ ῥάκος, 405–406).³⁷ The identity of this chorus is connected through the conceptual metaphors for DEATH with the salvation of Athens, which is itself dependent on the continuation of traditional Athenian festivals and rituals. The decline of the chorus symbolizes a *danse macabre* of theater: it signifies the end of the traditional rituals and thus of the political, cultural, socio-economic, and religious life of Athens. The procession with which the play concludes serves as "a reverse funeral rite": the joyful move that accompanies the tragic playwright back to the upper world, where he is once again initiated into a renewal of the joyful play.³⁸

DEATH remains the main background until the end of the text: the comedy ends with Pluto issuing an invitation to a number of Athenian politicians to come to him quickly and not waste any more time (ταχέως ἥκειν ὡς ἐμὲ δευρὶ καὶ μὴ μέλλειν, 1508–1509). The instruments of suicide mentioned at the beginning of the play (121–134) appear again, thus forming a ring composition. The god of death prescribes the necessary medicine "this, this and this" (τουτὶ, τουτουσὶ, τόδε, 1504–1505, 1507) to the politicians, in all probability pointing to the material objects referred to by Heracles at the beginning of the play, so that their descent to the underworld occur as quickly as possible.

By equating the world of the dead with the "real" Athenian world, Aristophanes undermines the usual distinctions between the living/strong/powerful and the dead/weak/powerless, the familiar and the alien, life and death. Everything is mixed up, and one no longer knows who is alive and who is dead. The conceptual metaphors for DEATH challenge the boundaries, in which LIFE IS DEATH and DEATH IS LIFE.³⁹ Euripides' much-quoted paradox blending life and death, "one of the most poignant motifs of the play," is referred to twice in the *Frogs*.⁴⁰ On the first occasion,

---

[34] Burkert (1983, pp. 248–297, 1987). See also Bowie (1993, pp. 228–230) with bibliography.
[35] On Aristophanes' use of the parallel pattern of the Dionysus' myth about his descent to Hades to bring to the Olympus his mother Semele, see above.
[36] On Aristophanes' Dionysus gaining a new identity in the infernal world as well as on the metatheatrical identification of Dionysus with the genre of comedy itself, see, e.g. Segal (1961), Epstein (1985), Reckford (1987, pp. 403–439), Moorton (1989), Padilla (1992), Lada-Richards (1999), Habash (2002), Biles (2011, pp. 219–233), and Tsoumpra (2020).
[37] On archaic epic association of flowery meadows with the concept of death, see Brockliss (2019, pp. 191–218).
[38] Reckford (1987, p. 432).
[39] Edmunds Radcliffe (2004, p. 125): "Perhaps Aristophanes is suggesting that despite the separation of the realms of the living and the dead, Athens is not far from death, a grim reminder of Athens' precarious war situation in 405 BCE."
[40] Whitman (1964, p. 257).

Aeschylus blames Euripides for undermining social values and displaying women who declared that "to live is not to live" (φασκούσας οὐ ζῆν τὸ ζῆν, 1082). On the second Dionysus, having chosen that Aeschylus be taken back with him to the living, mocks Euripides. "Who knows whether to live is indeed to be dead (τίς δ' οἶδεν εἰ τὸ ζῆν μέν ἐστι κατθανεῖν), and to breathe is to dine, and to sleep is a sheepskin?" replies Dionysus providing a response to Euripides' fury (1477–1478) in pseudo-Euripidean verses. Euripides' tragedy *Polyidus* is in all probability the source in both cases of the quote. The plot of this tragedy may have been built around the seer Polyidus who restored to life the boy Glaucus, the speaker of the verses being perhaps Pasiphae, mother of Glaucus (fr. 638 TrGF)[41]:

τίς δ' οἶδεν εἰ τὸ ζῆν μέν ἐστι κατθανεῖν,
τὸ κατθανεῖν δὲ ζῆν κάτω νομίζεται;
Who knows whether to live is to be dead, and to be dead means to live below?

"Living below" (ζῆν κάτω) corresponds to "the upper dead" (ἐν τοῖς ἄνω νεκροῖσι, 420), by which the chorus of initiates refers to the living. Living and dying, the upper and the below, are deliberately and repeatedly blended in conceptual metaphors for DEATH.

The double chorus of the play is involved in the game as well. The much-discussed ambiguity and uncertainty of the first frog chorus are interwoven with the metaphors for DEATH.[42] The short-bodied tailless amphibian frog is a symbol of transition in and of itself, since it moves easily between land and water, and serves as a mystical guide between the worlds of life and death. The lake of the singing frogs is also a limen of the land of the dead, a boundary zone separating life from death. The frogs participate in Dionysus' rite of passage singing a hymn to Dionysus and thus associating him with the limen of death on the evening of the Choes and the beginning of the Chytroi devoted to the dead, this being particular to the Dionysiac cult (211–219).[43] The frog chorus functions in opposition to the chorus of initiates, the two choruses signifying the old and modern art of comedy.[44] The frogs are thus reminiscent of the old theriomorphic choruses belonging to the past, staged by the ancient playwrights such as Magnes and Callias.[45] The invisibility of the frogs has been taken by various scholars as a metaphor for the dying of the old comedy, while the Eleusinian initiates dressed in rags (v. 405–410) serve as a metaphor for the financial hardship now besetting dramatic production. Due to the dynamic of the comic, Aristophanes provides a further constituent of the conceptual metaphors for DEATH: he merges two separate choruses into a single choral concept that is seen as the decline of comedy from the old no longer visible days of animal choruses to the present misery and poverty of choreuts, the decline of the theater festival in toto.

Conceptual metaphors for DEATH that shape the setting and plot of the comedy are able to capture and combine two dimensions of the play, the political and the ritual. Through discussion of historical reality in terms of the death ritual and through visualizing a ritualized death and descent to Hades as a contribution to political discourse, Aristophanes makes use of fundamental conceptual metaphors that embody the abstract notion of the end of an era.

DEATH in the *Frogs* functions as a CONTAINER for the thoughts and feelings of the author and the spectator, as well as for props on stage. In what follows I will argue that the third dimension of the play – the theory of poetics and literary criticism – belongs to this CONTAINER and is interwoven into the fabric alongside political and ritual elements.

---

[41] Cf. also Eur. *Phrixos* fr. 833 TrGF, Pl. *Grg.* 492e. See Sommerstein (1996, pp. 253–254, 293).
[42] Allison (1983), Campbell (1984), and Kanellakis (2020, pp. 182–184).
[43] Moorton (1989, pp. 310–312, 315–316). On a musical agon between the frogs and the Dionysus and Dionysus' victory in the final pnigos (263–267), see D'Angour (2020).
[44] Hubbard (1991, pp. 201–202, f. 123). On the symbolic significance of the "frogs" for traditional old comedy, see also Reckford (1987, pp. 408–413).
[45] On the comedies *Batrachoi* by Magnes and by Callias, see Allison (1983, pp. 12–13).

DEATH *Metaphors and Tragedy*

Aristophanes' *Frogs* is the only theatrical play which is regularly considered as a critical text in its own right. It serves as a landmark in the history of poetics and literary criticism.[46] At the very beginning of the play the god of Athenian theater Dionysus, who is a passionate lover of tragedy, claims to be suddenly struck with a longing (ἐξαίφνης πόθος τὴν καρδίαν ἐπάταξε πῶς οἴει σφόδρα, 53–54, πόθος Εὐριπίδου, 66) for the recently deceased tragic playwright after having read his tragedy *Andromeda* on the ship (ἐπὶ τῆς νεὼς ἀναγιγνώσκοντί μοι τὴν Ἀνδρομέδαν πρὸς ἐμαυτόν, 52–53). Now he wills to get him back (ἐλθεῖν ἐπ' ἐκεῖνον, 69) from the realm of the dead. For competent tragic, poets are no longer to be found (οἱ μὲν γὰρ οὐκέτ' εἰσίν), and those who can be found are useless (οἱ δ' ὄντες κακοί, 72). This provokes Heracles' implicit equation of Dionysus' longing with necrofilia (καὶ ταῦτα τοῦ τεθνηκότος; 67).

The passion for Euripides is further developed in the second half of *Frogs*, which explores the nature of tragedy. But it is not only Dionysus who was a lover of tragedy. Aristophanes is exceptional not only for his metapoetic discourse, which was common to many comic playwrights, but for his interest in tragedy per se, and for his setting out a set of criteria for the critical evaluation of tragedy.[47]

Conceptual metaphors for DEATH connect Aristophanes' analysis of tragedy to the first part of his comedy, to the political and the ritual aspects of comedy discussed above. Tragedy as drama is itself centered and focused on the spectacle of death.[48] Apart from the panorama of DEATH in tragedy, the continuous expectation of illness, fury, blindness, and such like, DEATH is fundamental to the destruction staged in tragedy, and to the prayers of lamentation that follow. The mythological idea of DEATH in tragedy is depicted through a departure from the world of living into the underworld (DEATH IS DEPARTURE). Thus, the messenger in Euripides' *Hippolytus* (428 BCE) introduces the description of Hippolytus' death by stating that human optical faculties are hardly sufficient to perceive it: εἰσορῶσι δὲ κρεῖσσον θέαμα δεργμάτων ἐφαίνετο "the spectacle for the those who were seeing was more powerful than their eyes," Eur. *Hipp.* 1216–1217). In her analysis of tragedy, Olga Freidenberg (1890–1855) claimed that almost every tragedy is a "drama of bodies," initially not receiving burial but – following a long chain of complex events – eventually buried. This was the only way that conceptual thinking could make sense of the staged myths, myths which figuratively depicted the hero's death at the moment of transition from life to the underworld.[49] Tragedy occupies the spectator with a kind of death that is stretched over the course of the action: the suffering passion (πάθη) that is transmitted to the spectator in the form of affects, according to Aristotle, is the constitutive element of tragedy (Arist. *Poet.* 19, 1456a37–b4). Unlike comedy, tragedians did not bring corpses to act on stage (compare Aeschylus' ghost of Darius (εἴδωλον Δαρείου) or the ghost of Clytaemnestra (Κλυταιμνήστρας εἴδωλον) or Euripides' ghost of Polydorus (Πολυδώρου εἴδωλον), who are emphatically illusory characters). But tragedians stage those who are destined to die. The narrative of death as well as its expectation are indispensable in the spectacle of tragedy.

Frogs is not the only comedy where Aristophanes focuses on tragedy, but no other comedy has so many references to DEATH in its discussion of tragedy as *Frogs*. Here, Aristophanes works intensively with conceptual metaphors for DEATH and their connection to the genre of tragedy: the competition of the poets is placed in the realm of the dead. Hades as a spatial indicator underlines the DEATH IS DEPARTURE metaphor, tragedy comically being placed in the underworld as a "dying" performance medium up there in Athens in its "real" social presence. This medium is located now

---

[46] Halliwell (2011, p. 93). On the *status quaestionis* as well as the problematic issues involved in approaching Aristophanes as a literary critic, see Halliwell (2011, pp. 93–154) with bibliography.

[47] Cf. Halliwell (2011, p. 95): "The evidence suggests that his paratragic obsession with Euripides, in particular, was not paralleled by any of his predecessors or rivals, though things may have been changing by the time a younger comic poet like Strattis came on scene towards the end of the fifth century."

[48] See Freidenberg (1997, p. 202).

[49] Freidenberg (1997, pp. 189–271).

in the past and being anatomized on a scale in a contest between words and things.[50] The DEATH metaphors are used in a mise-en-abîme-technique (a play within a play), for Aristophanes "kills" tragedy himself, placing it in the literal setting of the underworld but at the same time adding that it was no longer worth watching, and it costs the same price to go to the theater as to enter to the realm of death. The reading and the scrupulous "forensic pathologist" textualization of the tragedy through fragmenting, quoting, segmenting, disjointing, and paraphrasing as a substitute for the performance in the original evokes the imagery of DEATH.[51]

In the agon, in which two dead tragic playwrights are to compete for the art of tragedy, metaphors for DEATH are a fundamental constituent of the setting.[52] Aeschylus memorably cries foul because his own poetry had not died with him (ἡ ποίησις οὐχὶ συντέθνηκέ μοι, 868), while Euripides' poetry died with its author (τούτῳ δὲ συντέθνηκεν, 869). The further emphatically dead object is Euripides himself (τεθνηκότος 67, τεθνηκότα 1476). The third comparable dead object is a comically personified "bowl from last year" (τὸ τρύβλιον τὸ περυσινὸν τέθνηκε, 985–986), Dionysus mocking Euripides' diction.[53] The extraordinary use of the verb "to die" applied to an everyday kitchen utensil increases the paratragic effect. This embodiment of DEATH, in other words, a physical and sensorimotor regulation of the abstract DEATH, equates *ad absurdum* a bowl, a poet and his poetry, and perhaps anticipates Dionysus' choice of Aeschylus to return to the world of the living.

DEATH is accorded further poetological connotations in the famous scene of weighing individual verses on a scale (1364–1413).[54] In a dual allusion to the Homeric *kerostasia*, the weighing of human fates (*Il.* 8, 69–74 and *Il.* 22, 209–213) and Aeschylus' lost tragedy *Psychostasia*, the weighing of souls in order to see which are doomed to die, Aeschylus proposes that Dionysus weigh out his verses against those of Euripides (1365–1367).[55] Here, on the second attempt, Euripides' verse on Persuasion, who has "no other temple than a word" (οὐκ ἔστι Πειθοῦς ἱερὸν ἄλλο πλὴν λόγος, 1391), proves no match for Aeschylus' "For alone of the gods Death loves no gifts" (μόνος θεῶν γὰρ Θάνατος οὐ δώρων ἐρᾷ. 1392) from his lost *Niobe*.[56] Persuasion stands for rhetoric, Death stands for tragedy: tragedy is heavier. In epic poetry, the sinking down of the heavier pan of the scale denotes DEATH. In *Frogs*, the heavy DEATH-pan signifies victory, and Aeschylus' release from Hades back into the world of the living. As Dionysus explains, Aeschylus' pan dips lower because "death" is much heavier (θάνατον γὰρ εἰσέθηκε, βαρύτατον κακόν, 1394) than the lightweight language of "persuasion" (πειθὼ δὲ κοῦφόν ἐστι, 1396). In the final trial, Aeschylus puts "death" once again on the scale, as has been already mentioned above, and his massive DEATH verse "chariot on chariot, corpse on corpse" (ἐφ' ἅρματος γὰρ ἅρμα καὶ νεκρῷ νεκρός, 1403) emerges victorious.[57]

The body-based metaphors for DEATH belong to a CONTAINER in which the political, ritual, and poetic/poetological dimensions of *Frogs* intermingle and condense. This CONTAINER blends both parts of the play and allows the burlesque journey of Dionysus to the underworld to be seen as a unity with the sophisticated critique of tragedy. The language, characters, plot, and setting of the comedy can be read in terms of DEATH. Multifaceted metaphors for DEATH enable the macabre

---

[50] Bassi (2016, p. 156). See the sparkling study on Aristophanes' *Frogs* in Karen Bassi's book (pp. 144–185). This convincingly emphasizes the increasing importance of the written text at the end of the fifth century BCE, and the gradual replacement of theatrical performance by the text of tragedy, which were intended for reading. However, the tragic playwrights and the re-performances of Attic tragedy in the fourth century BCE and later render the death metaphor for the whole process somewhat exaggerated.
[51] Bassi (2016, p. 161).
[52] Hanink and Uhlig (2017, pp. 59–69).
[53] Bassi (2016, p. 167). On Aristophanes' and more generally Greek "continuous battle between the tendency to personify and the opposite tendency to schematize" (p. 10), see Webster (1954).
[54] Verrall (1908) and Dover (1993, pp. 365–369).
[55] Vermeule (1979, p. 76).
[56] On the real tragic playwright Aeschylus' imagery of weighing, see Rehm (2017).
[57] Whitman (1964, p. 243). On Aeschylus' balance between living beings and corpses, see Rehm (2017).

laughter on stage around this fundamental and complex abstract concept of mind because they emerge directly and naturally from the embodied imaginative human understanding.

In the last part which follows allegories in *Frogs* will be considered and the ways in which they arise from bodily experience and interact with metaphors for DEATH.

Allegory in the *Frogs*

The cognitive turn in the humanities has triggered a great deal of research on allegory in recent decades, parallel to metaphor studies. Allegory characterizes a fundamental aspect of human language use, and as a mode of interpreting and understanding is cognitive by nature. What renders allegory close to metaphor is its fundamental principle of "duality": a phenomenological simultaneous appearance of two things in the same image, in the same space, and at the same time. In allegory, one thing is said or shown and another is meant.[58] Its cognitive effect is attributed to the visual aspects of other speaking and to its capacity to awaken the listener's imagination and create vivid images in the mind's eye. This, in turn – as in the case of the DEATH metaphors discussed above – is particularly important for Aristophanic comedy with all the essential elements of Greek drama such as music, poetry, innovative narrative plot, and visual art par excellence. The means and the nature of the visual and verbal interaction, the costumes, the props, the gestures, the facial expressions, the positions, and the actions are all significant for the interpretation of the allegory. Both the allegorical experience and that of metaphor arise from ordinary bodily actions of the physical world in everyday life.[59]

The dynamic function of allegory may lie most fundamentally in its mobilization of the intersecting energies of interpellation and interpretation.[60] Visual allegories deploy these energies with force because, as objects designed for particular environments and as images that represent abstract ideas in embodied form, they operate in the physical world of the senses.

What is crucially different in allegory in comparison to metaphor is that the allegorical is not reconstructed as a meaning identical to the initial meaning, but as a second, additional, at times hidden, meaning about major issues in human experience related to politics, religion, love, and death.[61] In the case of metaphor, there is a fusion and blend of meanings (such DEATH IS DEPARTURE); in the case of allegory, there is more of a leap in meaning (such as the allegory of scale).[62]

In the following, I will outline and discuss some of the most important allegories in Aristophanes' *Frogs*, their interaction with metaphors as well as their role and function in the structure and plot of the play.

Allegorical Characters and Allegorical Scenes

In contrast to a number of other Aristophanic comedies, it has been argued that the *Frogs* include neither allegorical characters nor allegorical debates.[63] In comparison to the *Knights* with its allegorical character Demos, and to the *Clouds* with Just and Unjust Arguments, to *Peace* with its mute Eirene, Opora, and Theoria as well as with its speaking Polemos and Kydoimos, and finally to the paradigmatic *Wealth* with allegorical protagonists Penia and Ploutos, the *Frogs* does not include characters with clearly allegorical characteristics.

However, following Paul De Man's sense in which allegory is understood as the omnipresent incompatible coexistence of two different levels of reading, certain characters in the play can be read

---

[58] Machosky (2013, p. 1).
[59] Gibbs and Okonski (2022).
[60] Baskins and Rosenthal (2007, pp. 1–4).
[61] Gibbs and Okonski (2022, p. 213).
[62] Kurz (2004, pp. 35–36); see also Ritchie (2017, pp. 98–100).
[63] Waites (1912, pp. 29–33), Lever (1953, p. 221), and Newiger (2000) (= 1957).

allegorically. The complexity of the interpretation can "only appear in the juxtaposition of two readings in which the first forgets and the second acknowledges the linguistic structure that makes it come into being."[64] For example, Dionysus represents the community of Athens, which is at first disjointed but gradually acquires a civic cohesion through a rite of passage in search of its own salvation, and the salvation of its country. Dionysus' variety of clothes (lion skin (λεοντῆν, 46) and club (ῥόπαλον, 47) as mythic-heroic symbols vs. saffron-colored robe (ἐπὶ κροκωτῷ, 46) and boots of tragedy (κόθορνος, 47) as theatrical symbols) and his shift of costumes first with Heracles and then with Xanthias (498–629) conveys an air of uncertainty, on both political and social levels. Dionysus' development within the play, and the gradual construction of his identity as the god of theater, constitutes an allegory for the salvation of both the polis, and theater itself.[65]

Aeschylus and Euripides also serve as allegories. They embody metonymies of the AUTHOR for the type of TEXT the author composes, the play characters of tragic playwrights being identified as the authors' own work.[66] These two metonymies represent allegorically different periods in the history of Athenian politics and Athenian theater. Aeschylus notably stands for firm faith and public solidarity in the days after Marathon, the time when tragedy was flowering. Euripides represents divisive forces, the new education, contemporary decay, the rhetorical, and sophist movements.[67]

Further, the allegorical scenes, or rather a number of important allegorical dimensions that run throughout the scenes, create a symbolic reinforcement of the events surrounding conceptual metaphors for DEATH discussed above.

The Allegory of Death

The monstrous encounter between the shock-producing Empousa (285–305) and Xanthias at the outset of the journey to Hades – the earliest literary reference to this ghostly inhabitant of the underworld – can, to cite but one example, be read as an allegory of fear and trembling in the face of Death itself (DEATH IS AN ADVERSARY).[68] Xanthias hears a noise (καὶ μὴν αἰσθάνομαι ψόφου τινός, 285), Dionysus and Xanthias both glance behind (ὄπισθεν, 286) and in front (ἐν τῷ πρόσθε, 287), and then Xanthias claims to see an enormous beast (καὶ μὴν ὁρῶ νὴ τὸν Δία θηρίον μέγα, 288). Dionysus cannot see anything and asks him to describe the monster. It is horrifying (δεινόν, 289), says Xanthias, it can take different forms (παντοδαπὸν γοῦν γίγνεται, 289), that of a cow (τοτὲ μέν γε βοῦς, 290), a mule (νυνὶ δ' ὀρεύς, 290), a beautiful woman (τοτὲ δ' αὖ γυνὴ ὡραιοτάτη τις, 290–291), or a dog (ἀλλ' ἤδη κύων, 292). At this point, Dionysus is certain that Xanthias can see Empousa (Ἔμπουσα τοίνυν ἐστί, 293). Xanthias goes on to describe the monster's whole face blazing with fire (πυρὶ γοῦν λάμπεται ἅπαν τὸ πρόσωπον, 293–294). She has one leg made of bronze (σκέλος χαλκοῦν, 294) and the other of cow dung (βολίτινον, 295). After this terrifying description, both Dionysus and Xanthias try to escape from the creature (296–297). We are dying (ἀπολούμεθ', 298), exclaims Xanthias.

Like DEATH, the monstrous figure of Empousa dissolves the identity of the living individual, corresponding to Vernant's "second face" of death which "embodies the unsayable, the unbearable."[70] Aristophanes' choice of Empousa has Eleusinian echoes, for there the initiates see

---

[64] De Man (1979, p. 51).
[65] Segal (1961), Epstein (1985), Given (2009, pp. 108–109, 115).
[66] On the use of the metonymy AUTHOR for TEXT in Greek and Latin literature, see Zanker (2016, pp. 148–163).
[67] Vaio (1985), Woodbury (1988), Dover (1993, pp. 10–37), Schmidt (1998), and Bassi (2016, pp. 144–185).
[68] On the encounter with Empousa, see Brown (1991), Patera (2015, pp. 249–290), Aguirre (2018, pp. 268–270), and Maggi (2020, pp. 325–326). On the metaphor DEATH IS AN ADVERSARY in Homer, see Zanker (2019, pp. 83–85).
[69] Cf. Dionysus' echo in "dying" some lines further: "Which of the gods shall I blame of being dead?" (τίν' αἰτιάσομαι θεῶν μ' ἀπολλύναι; 310).
[70] Vernant (1996, p. 55) and Brockliss (2019, p. 219).

a fearsome female figure emerge from the darkness.[71] The real or imaginary encounter with Empousa, associated with the dark Hecate and with the underworld, evokes in Aristophanes' description of enactive mechanisms that provoke a range of emotions such as fright, shudder, revulsion, fear, horror, and lead to empathy when a reader or viewer encounters the image of a human body. Among the conceptual metaphor DEATH IS AN ADVERSARY Aristophanes employs a personified allegory of DEATH. The emotional and aesthetic horror caused by death is depicted in the associated imagery, the monstrous changing shapes and sounds, a face blazing with fire, and its different legs with their "real" biological or material clues. The physiological and material details contribute to an emotionally engaging image and reveal that allegory has its roots within ordinary bodily experience. Empousa functions in the comedy as an allegory of the encounter with death, and as a visual symbol of DEATH, serving to emphasize the fear and trembling of the unseeable and unknowable.

The Allegory of Political Deception

If the monster serves as a literally physiological allegory, there are further allegories rooted in everyday human experience. It is, for example, a political allegory which interacts with the DEATH metaphors in the comic scene of Xanthias exchanging places with his master Dionysus in front of Pluto's palace (494–673). The chorus leader emphasizes this allegory in the parabasis: it is shameful to change from slaves into masters (καὶ γὰρ αἰσχρόν ἐστι... εἶναι κἀντὶ δούλων δεσπότας, 693–694).[72] In 410 BCE, many of the oligarchs, people who had fought naval battles for Athens, were alienated from Athenian citizenship as a punishment for the coup in 411 BCE. In the second half of 406 BCE, the Athenians freed the slaves who had fought in the battle of Arginusae and gave them citizenship, but condemned the victorious generals to death. If slaves can be citizens, the chorus leader in *Frogs* says, why should the former oligarchs not be pardoned, and allowed to contribute to the country through instruction and advice (697–699). Dionysus and Xanthias change costumes several times and act out on stage the process of slaves becoming masters while masters become slaves. The scene has allegorical traits as it has a hidden meaning of disguise, façade, and deception with gloomy social and political connotations. However, these traits remain in the context of the ubiquitous patterns of bodily action in the real-world experience and imagination.

The Allegory of Comedy

Conventional metaphors can reflect larger allegorical themes and serve as metonymic references to broad allegorical complexes. Extended metaphors can emerge into allegories, and there are common cognitive processes based on concrete empirical evidence needed to interpret extended metaphors and allegories.[73] Thus, the two choruses discussed above in terms of DEATH metaphors can be read as an allegory for the decline of comedy.[74] The fifth-century BCE history of comedy at Athens is embodied in the performance: the first chorus of the frogs represents the old theriomorphic choruses. Their short appearance as well as their invisibility stands in this case for the disappearance of the old comedy, while the second chorus of the initiates dressed in rags emphasizes the crisis and fall of comic production. Aristophanes here presents the whole double-chorus setting as an allegory for the falling state of contemporary comedy, a self-referential development of both the theatrical institution and the literary genre.

---

[71] Aguirre (2018, p. 269).
[72] Sommerstein (1996, p. 217).
[73] Gibbs and Okonski (2022, pp. 216–217).
[74] Dover (1993, pp. 55–69).

The Allegory of Tragedy

The small ληκύθιον scene in Aeschylus' and Euripides' contest in Hades (1198–1247) provides a further allegorical interpretation. Aeschylus destroys Euripides' prologs "from a little bottle of oil" (ἀπὸ ληκυθίου, 1200–1201), by adding "he lost his little bottle of oil" (ληκύθιον ἀπώλεσεν, 1198–1248).[75] These white-ground *lekythoi* were used in funerary rites.[76] Here, the allegorical dimensions of the whole scene should be outlined. Aeschylus criticizes redundancy, metrical inconsistency, and lack of stylistic quality in Euripides' prologs. A possible fertility metaphor associates the "little bottle of oil" with the phallus, the tragic playwright's creativity being impotent. The loss of ληκύθιον as an oil flask that Greek athletes took to the gymnasium, the wrestling school, or bath reduces heroic diction through the familiarity of an everyday object.

Tragedy is notably embodied and personified in *Frogs*. The relationship between materiality and metaphor is of particular importance here. Euripides in the agon points out the shortcomings of Aeschylus' tragic art and highlights the merits of his own. He uses the personification of poetry to emphasize his achievements in the advancement of art in his narrative. When he took tragedy over from Aeschylus (ὡς παρέλαβον τὴν τέχνην παρὰ σοῦ, 939), claims Euripides, it was swollen (οἰδοῦσαν) with bombast and ponderous phrases (ὑπὸ κομπασμάτων καὶ ῥημάτων ἐπαχθῶν, 940). The gender constituent is important here, as being a male speaker Euripides narrates his manipulation of a female object. He first slimmed her down (ἴσχνανα μὲν πρώτιστον αὐτὴν) and removed the heaviness (τὸ βάρος ἀφεῖλον, 941) with a course of versicles (ἐπυλλίοις), walking exercises (περιπάτοις), and little white beets (τευτλίοισι λευκοῖς, 942) giving her a chatter potion (χυλὸν διδοὺς στωμυλμάτων), which he pressed out of books (ἀπὸ βιβλίων ἀπηθῶν, 943). After this slimming cure, he fed her again on a diet of monodies (ἀνέτρεφον μονῳδίαις), adding some Cephisophon (Κηφισοφῶντα μειγνύς, 944). The embodied art of tragedy is an object of physiological and physical manipulation. Following the Euripidean narrative, it had been sick and had now been healed through his intervention. Language having texture, weight, volume, and taste perceived materiality in terms of its form, meter, and arrangement. Metaphors bridge the tactile medical work through the creation of a text and render the process of embodiment a useful category to describe the experience of writing a tragedy. However, the scene as a whole depicts a "loosing" Euripidean tragedy and reflects a larger allegorical theme of the decline of tragedy.

The Allegory of Justice in Hades

The weighing of verses on a scale (1364–1413) can also be read as allegory. The scales depict the primary metaphor CHOOSING IS WEIGHING which draws on another metaphor, IMPORTANCE IS BIG/HEAVY.[77] In the agon, Aeschylus speaks second with the advantage of the heavier last word, but the end result is predicted, since Aeschylus always wins over his rival's verses. The whole episode is a parody of the judicial process, for the scale is a traditional symbol of justice personified (the ancient Egyptian goddess Ma'at and later Isis or the Greek deities Themis and Dike are often depicted with a scale, typically suspended from one hand, measuring the strength of the proponents and opponents of a cause).[78] The scales represent the weighing of evidence, and the scales lack a foundation in order to signify that evidence should stand on its own and thus constitute an allegory of justice. The scales in Hades (DEATH IS JUSTICE) embody an abstract idea, placing it on the physical stage and bringing it "before the eyes." Again, a recurring pattern of everyday experience stands for a larger allegorical theme.

---

[75] On this extensively discussed scene on a variety of opinions about what *lekythion* could symbolize, see Sommerstein (1996, pp. 263–268) and Collins (2004, pp. 30–43). See further Navarre (1933), Henderson (1972), Bain (1985), Sider (1992), Gerö and Johnsson (2002), and Sansone (2016).
[76] Oakley (2004).
[77] Bocharova (2016, p. 55).
[78] Vermeule (1979, p. 76) and Leone (2017). Cf. also Δίκας τάλαντον in Bacchyl. 4, 11–13 and 17, 25–26 Snell-Maehler.

Allegory is revealed here as a communicative strategy, a discursive mode, based on the duality of analog operations, especially in relation to action through personification, space through topification, and time through narrative.[79] Aristophanes is cognitively and consciously aware of the benefits of allegory as a facilitator of conceptual understanding. The dreadful monster Empousa (=fear of death), the artful interdependence of the two choruses (=the decline of comedy), the playful scenes with change of costumes (=political instability) or the loss of the oil flask (=the decline of tragedy), and the reference to fateful scales (=justice) – all these show Aristophanes' pride in his allegories and the awareness of doing something special with them. Aristophanic strategies demonstrate to us the universality of metaphors and allegories based on bodily and everyday experiences: the current political crisis interwoven with the theatrical crisis at the end of the fifth century BCE at Athens is illustrated by a multitude of metaphors and allegories that build on certain popular models of communication determined by context, culture, and environment.

Conclusion

There is an implicit social arrangement in Aristophanes' use of metaphor and allegory in comedy, namely an agreement about the social world in which the recipients find themselves, as the background for the humor.[80] We cannot judge the degree of "absurdity" in Aristophanes' *Frogs* because we do not know what the criteria of "absurdity" actually were in the minds of fifth-century BCE Athenian spectators. However, it is significant that comic laughter bridges the political, ritual, and poetological dimensions of the play. Conceptual DEATH metaphors play a similar bridging role. The comic effect results from the incongruity of different worlds or different patterns of thought, the incongruity of humor and death serving as a central tension that gives life to the play.[81] In a triumph of eclecticism, the clash of multiple "mental spaces," triggered by the embodiment of political, social, and poetological discourses in the comic performance, has produced new patterns of interpretation in clashing of fundamental archaic concept of death and the comic realities on stage beyond those that would result from the comparison and juxtaposition of these worlds that we consider incompatible.[82]

The ridiculousness in *Frogs* is superimposed on the three principal dimensions of the play, the political, the religious/ritual, and the poetical. Metaphors trigger, as we have seen, the embodiment of abstract concepts and map from a more concrete source domain (an arrogant rotting corpse on his way to the grave) to a more abstract target domain (the cultural memory of the naval battle of Arginusae). Euripides' medical treatment of the sick body of Aeschylus' personified tragedy (a more concrete source domain) dramatizes the experience. The recipient laughs and reflects on the development of the medium and genre of classical tragedy (a more abstract target domain).

However, what is different about DEATH compared to various everyday actions is that it is never actually experienced. One can experience LOVE, HATE, COMFORT, REVENGE, and such like, even (giving) BIRTH, and through this experience conceive them. DEATH itself, although it is certainly one of our most fundamental concepts in life and thought, cannot actually be physically experienced, and Aristophanes, who nevertheless embodies this experience on stage, again deliberately and intentionally creates an absurdity. The enactivist approach to death is crucial in Aristophanes' comedy: DEATH is presented through a series of conceptual metaphors and allegories, and is perceived as an earthy, somatic, and sensorimotor interaction with the environment, forming the background for more complex, politically and socially motivated and culturally clear-cut metaphors. They represent different varieties of figurative conceptualizations.[83] Some recipients have never personally

---

[79] Harris and Tolmie (2011, p. 109). See also Kurz (1979, pp. 16–17).
[80] Critchley (2002, pp. 3–4).
[81] On the detailed treatment and criticism of incongruity theories, see Latta (1999, pp. 99–234).
[82] On the function of blending metaphors in comics (in the current sense of the term), see Fludernik (2015).
[83] For various examples of primary metaphors underlying the use of complex metaphors, see Dancygier (2017, pp. 37–39).

experienced anything of the realm of Aristophanes' conceptual DEATH metaphors, but their cultural background 'is saturated' with examples to draw on.[84]

We repeatedly discover the extensive presence of DEATH metaphors and allegories at all levels of linguistic and cognitive description, linking mind to body, body to culture, language to culture, and language to brain. Both metaphor and allegory function as cognitive and not linguistic or stylistic mechanisms. Cognitive approaches to metaphor and allegory offer novel perspectives even to such a paradigmatic text as Aristophanes' *Frogs*. The conceptual metaphors and allegories for DEATH unite different registers and different parameters of the *Frogs* in blending the real with the metaphorical. These exist in the structure, the setting, and the plot. DEATH is directly rooted in basic bodily experience diachronically and cross-culturally. There is a very earthly, self-absorbed attitude toward death – wrote Johan Huizinga in bodily terms in 1919 about late Middle Ages – it is not about mourning the loss of loved ones, but about regretting one's own approaching death, which can only be felt as misfortune and horror.[85] There is no critical separation between everyday human events and abstract symbolic, metaphorical, and allegorical meanings. These meanings arise from the way they are experienced in bodily experience and daily routine. Athenian reality, the imaginative power of Aristophanes, social institutions such as the ritual festivals or the theater, and the cultural memory of the spectators are blended into a whole through the conceptual metaphors and allegories for DEATH in *Frogs*.

GUIDE TO FURTHER READING

Griffith (2013) and Marshall (2020) offer valuable introductions to the comedy. For commentaries, see Dover (1993) and Sommerstein (1996). For the setting of the comedy and the interplay of the political, the poetic and the ritual, cf. Konstan (1987), Hubbard (1991, pp. 157–219), Konstan (1995, pp. 61–74); see also Schmidt (1998). For studies more focused on ritual in the play, see Segal (1961), Bowie (1993), Lada-Richards (1999), Habash (2002), and Edmunds Radcliffe (2004). For political context in the *Frogs*, see Allan (2012) and Worthington (1989); for literary criticism, see Hunter (2009, pp. 10–52) and Halliwell (2011, pp. 93–154). For those interested in looking at cognitive metaphor theory and its application to ancient texts, see Cairns (2016), Horn and Breytenbach (2016), Zanker (2019), and Novokhatko (2021). For allegory, see an inspiring survey by Silk (2021).

REFERENCES

Aguirre, M. (2018). Dread in the dark? From modern fiction to classical antiquity. In: *Landscapes of Dread in Classical Antiquity. Negative Emotion in Natural and Constructed Spaces* (ed. D. Felton), 259–276. Abingdon: Routledge.

Allan, A. (2012). Turning remorse to good effect? Arginusae, Theramenes and Aristophanes' *Frogs*. In: *No Laughing Matter: Studies in Athenian Comedy* (ed. C.W. Marshall and G. Kovacs), 101–114. Bloomsbury Academic.

Allison, R.H. (1983). Amphibian ambiguities: Aristophanes and his *Frogs*. *Greece & Rome* 30 (1): 8–20.

Bain, D. (1985). Ληκύθιον ἀπώλεςεν: some reservations. *The Classical Quarterly* 35 (1): 31–37.

Baskins, C. and Rosenthal, L. (2007). Introduction. In: *Early Modern Visual Allegory: Embodying Meaning* (ed. C. Baskins and L. Rosenthal), 1–10. London and New York: Routledge.

Bassi, K. (2016). *Traces of the Past: Classics Between History and Archaeology*. Michigan Press.

Biles, Z.P. (2011). *Aristophanes and the Poetics of Competition*. Cambridge: Cambridge University Press.

Bocharova, J. (2016). Personification allegory and embodied cognition. In: *Personification: Embodying Meaning and Emotion* (ed. W.S. Melion and B. Ramakers), 41–69. Leiden-Boston: Brill.

---

[84] Ritchie (2017, p. 104).
[85] See Johan Huizinga's discussion of death in the Middle Ages from 1919. Huizinga (1996, pp. 170–171).

Bowie, A.M. (1993). *Aristophanes: Myth, Ritual and Comedy*. Cambridge: Cambridge University Press.
Brockliss, W. (2019). *Homeric Imagery and the Natural Environment*. Cambridge, MA: CHS.
Brown, C. (1991). Empousa, Dionysus and the mysteries: Aristophanes, frogs 285ff. *The Classical Quarterly* 41 (1): 41–50.
Burkert, W. (1983). *Homo Necans: The Anthropology of Ancient Greek Sacrificial Ritual and Myth*. Transl. by P. Bing. Berkeley, Los Angeles and London: University of California Press.
Burkert, W. (1987). *Ancient Mystery Cults*. Cambridge, MA and London: Harvard University Press.
Cairns, D. (2016). *Mind, Body, and Metaphor in Ancient Greek Concepts of Emotion*. L'Atelier du Centre de recherches historiques [En ligne], 16. http://journals.openedition.org/acrh/7416.
Cairns, D. (2018/2019). ΘΥΜΟΣ in Homer: philological, oral-poetic, and cognitive approaches. *Quaestiones Oralitatis* 4: 13–30.
Campbell, D. (1984). The frogs in the *Frogs*. *The Journal of Hellenic Studies* 104: 163–165.
Collins, D. (2004). *Master of the Game: Competition and Performance in Greek Poetry*. Washington, DC: CHS.
Critchley, S. (2002). *On Humour*. London and New York: Routledge.
Dancygier, B. (2017). Figurativeness, conceptual metaphor and blending. In: *The Routledge Handbook of Metaphor and Language* (ed. E. Semino and Z. Demjén), 28–41. London and New York: Routledge.
D'Angour, A. (2020). The musical frogs in *Frogs*. In: *Ancient Greek Comedy: Genre – Texts – Reception* (ed. A. Fries and D. Kanellakis), 187–197. Berlin, Boston: De Gruyter.
De Man, P. (1979). *Allegories of Reading: Figural Language in Rousseau, Nietzsche, Rilke, and Proust*. New Haven, CT: Yale University Press.
Dover, K. (1993). *Aristophanes' Frogs*, ed. with an introd. and comm. Oxford: Clarendon Press.
Edmunds Radcliffe, G. III (2004). *Myths of the Underworld Journey: Plato, Aristophanes, and the 'Orphic' Gold Tablets*. Cambridge: Cambridge University Press.
Ekroth, G. and Nilsson, I. (ed.) (2018). *Round Trip to Hades in the Eastern Mediterranean Tradition: Visits to the Underworld from Antiquity to Byzantium*. Leiden-Boston: Brill.
Eliade, M. (1972). *Zalmoxis, the Vanishing God: Comparative Studies in the Religions and Folklore of Dacia and Eastern Europe*. Chicago, IL: University of Chicago Press.
Epstein, P. (1985). Dionysus' journey of self-discovery in the *Frogs* of Aristophanes. *Dionysus* 9: 19–35.
Eubanks, P. (2017). Epilogue: metaphors for language and communication. In: *The Routledge Handbook of Metaphor and Language* (ed. E. Semino and Z. Demjén), 517–528. London and New York: Routledge.
Fludernik, M. (2015). Blending in cartoons: the production of comedy. In: *The Oxford Handbook of Cognitive Literary Studies* (ed. L. Zunshine), 155–175. Oxford: Oxford University Press.
Forceville, C.J. (1996). *Pictorial Metaphor in Advertising*. London and New York: Routledge.
Forceville, C.J. (2016). Pictorial and multimodal metaphor. In: *Handbuch Sprache im multimodalen Kontext* (ed. N.-M. Klug and H. Stöckl), 241–260. Berlin, Boston: De Gruyter.
Franklin, J.C. (2017). 'Skatabasis'. The rise and fall of Kinesias. In: *Poeti in agone: competizioni poetiche e musicali nella Grecia antica* (ed. A. Gostoli, A. Fongoli, and F. Biondi), 163–221. Turnhout: Brepols.
Freidenberg, O. (1997). *Image and Concept: Mythopoetic Roots of Literature*. Ed. and annot. by N. Braginskaia and K. Moss. Transl. by K. Moss. London and New York: Routledge.
Gerö, E.C. and Johnsson, H.R. (2002). A comment on the Lekythion-scene in Aristophanes' *Frogs*. *Eranos* 100: 38–50.
Gibbs, R.W. Jr. (2017). *Metaphor Wars: Conceptual Metaphors in Human Life*. Cambridge University Press.
Gibbs, R.W. Jr. and Okonski, L. (2022). Allegory and bodily imagination. In: *Allegory Studies: Contemporary Perspectives* (ed. V. Brljak), 213–234. New York and London: Routledge.
Given, J. (2009). When gods don't appear: divine absence and human agency in Aristophanes. *The Classical World* 102 (2): 107–127.
Griffith, M. (2013). *Aristophanes' Frogs*. New York: Oxford University Press.
Habash, M. (2002). Dionysos' roles in Aristophanes' "Frogs". *Mnemosyne* 55 (1): 1–17.
Halliwell, S. (2011). *Between Ecstasy and Truth. Interpretations of Greek Poetics from Homer to Longinus*. Oxford: Oxford University Press.
Hanink, J. and Uhlig, A. (2017). Aeschylus and his afterlife in the classical period: "my poetry did not die with me". In: *The Reception of Aeschylus' Plays through Shifting Models and Frontiers* (ed. S.E. Constantinidis), 51–79. Brill.
Harris, R.A. and Tolmie, S. (2011). Cognitive allegory: an introduction. *Metaphor and Symbol* 26: 109–120.
Henderson, J. (1972). The Lekythos and *Frogs* 1200-1248. *Harvard Studies in Classical Philology* 76: 133–143.

Higgins, W. (1977). A passage to Hades: the *Frogs* of Aristophanes. *Ramus* 6 (1): 60–81.
Hooker, J.T. (1980). The composition of the "Frogs". *Hermes* 108: 169–182.
Horn, F. and Breytenbach, C. (ed.) (2016). *Spatial Metaphors. Ancient Texts and Transformations.* Berlin: Edition Topoi.
Hubbard, T.K. (1991). *The Mask of Comedy: Aristophanes and the Intertextual Parabasis.* Ithaca and London: Cornell University Press.
Huizinga, J. (1996). *The Autumn of the Middle Ages*, transl. by R. J. Payton and U. Mammitzsch. The University of Chicago Press.
Hunter, R. (2009). *Critical Moments in Classical Literature. Studies in the Ancient View of Literature and Its Uses.* Cambridge: CUP.
Kanellakis, D. (2020). *Aristophanes and the Poetics of Surprise.* Berlin, Boston: De Gruyter.
Konstan, D. (1987). Poésie, politique, poétique, et rituel dans les *Grenouilles* d'Aristophane. *Métis* 1: 291–308.
Konstan, D. (1995). *Greek Comedy and Ideology.* New York – Oxford: Oxford University Press.
Kövecses, Z. (2017). Conceptual metaphor theory. In: *The Routledge Handbook of Metaphor and Language* (ed. E. Semino and Z. Demjén), 13–27. London: Routledge.
Kurz, G. (1979). Zu einer Hermeneutik der literarischen Allegorie. In: *Formen und Funktionen der Allegorie* (ed. W. Haug), 12–24. Stuttgart: Metzler.
Kurz, G. (2004). *Metapher, Allegorie, Symbol.* Göttingen: Vandenhoeck & Ruprecht.
Lada-Richards, I. (1999). *Initiating Dionysus: Ritual and Theatre in Aristophanes' "Frogs".* Oxford: Clarendon Press.
Lakoff, G. and Johnson, M. (1980). *Metaphors We Live by.* Chicago, IL: University of Chicago Press.
Lakoff, G. and Turner, M. (1989). *More than Cool Reason. A Field Guide to Poetic Metaphor.* Chicago, IL and London: University of Chicago Press.
Lancaster, M.D. (2021). Metaphor research and the Hebrew Bible. *Currents in Biblical Research* 19 (3): 235–285.
Latta, R.L. (1999). *The Basic Humor Process. A Cognitive-Shift Theory and the Case Against Incongruity.* Berlin – New York: Mouton De Gruyter.
Leone, M. (2017). Weight problems: an enquiry into scales and justice. *Insights: Journal of the Institute of Advanced Study, University of Durham* 10 (12): 1–20.
Lever, K. (1953). Poetic metaphor and dramatic allegory in Aristophanes. *Classical World* 46: 220–223.
Littlemore, J. (2019). *Metaphors in the Mind: Sources of Variation in Embodied Metaphor.* Cambridge: Cambridge University Press.
Machosky, B. (2013). *Structures of Appearing: Allegory and the Work of Literature.* New York: Fordham University Press.
Maggi, L. (2020). *La critica dei culti nel teatro del V secolo. Aristofane interprete di Euripide.* Baden-Baden: Academia.
Marshall, C.W. (2020). *Aristophanes' Frogs.* London-New York: Bloomsbury.
Meineck, P. (2018). *Theatrocracy. Greek Drama, Cognition, and the Imperative for Theatre.* London and New York: Routledge.
Moorton, R.F. Jr. (1989). Rites of passage in Aristophanes' "Frogs". *The Classical Journal* 84 (4): 308–324.
Navarre, O. (1933). Ληκύθιον ἀπώλεσεν. *REA* 35: 278–280.
Newiger, H.-J. (2000). *Metapher und Allegorie: Studien zu Aristophanes, 2. unveränderte Auflage.* Stuttgart-Weimar: Metzler (= 1957, Beck, München).
Novokhatko, A. (2021). Contemporary metaphor studies and classical texts. *Mnemosyne* 74 (4): 682–703.
Oakley, J.H. (2004). *Picturing Death in Classical Athens: The Evidence of the White Lekythoi.* Cambridge: Cambridge University Press.
Ortony, A. (1979). Metaphor: a multidimensional problem. In: *Metaphor and Thought* (ed. A. Ortony), 1–16. Cambridge: Cambridge University Press.
Padilla, M. (1992). The Heraclean Dionysus: theatrical and social renewal in Aristophanes' *Frogs. Arethusa* 25: 359–384.
Patera, M. (2015). *Figures grecques de l'épouvante de l'antiquité au present. Peurs enfantines et adultes.* Leiden: Brill.
Reckford, K.J. (1987). *Aristophanes' Old-and-New Comedy. Six Essays in Perspective.* Chapel Hill and London: University of North Carolina Press.

Reddy, M.J. (1979). The conduit metaphor – a case of frame conflict in our language about language. In: *Metaphor and Thought* (ed. A. Ortony), 284–324. Cambridge: Cambridge University Press.

Rehm, R. (2017). Aeschylus in the balance: weighing corpses and the problem of translation. In: *The Reception of Aeschylus' Plays Through Shifting Models and Frontiers* (ed. S.E. Constantinidis), 131–146. Brill.

Ritchie, L.D. (2017). *Metaphorical Stories in Discourse*. Cambridge: Cambridge University Press.

Sansone, D. (2016). Whatever happened to Euripides' *Lekythion* (*Frogs* 1198-1247)? In: *Wisdom and Folly in Euripides* (ed. P. Kyriakou and A. Rengakos), 319–333. Berlin-Boston: de Gruyter.

Schmidt, J.-U. (1998). Die Einheit der *Frösche* des Aristophanes: demokratische Erziehung und 'moderne' Dichtung in der Kritik. *Würzburger Jahrbücher für die Altertumswissenschaft* 22: 73–100.

Segal, C. (1961). The character and cults of Dionysus and the unity of the *Frogs*. *HSCP* 65: 207–242.

Sider, D. (1992). Ληκύθιον ἀπώλεσεν: Aristophanes' limp phallic joke? *Mnemosyne* 45 (3): 359–364.

Silk, M. (2021). Invoking the other. Allegory in theory, from Demetrius to de Man. In: *Allegory Studies: Contemporary Perspectives* (ed. V. Brljak), 41–65. New York: Routledge.

Sommerstein, A.H. (1993). Kleophon and the restaging of *Frogs*. In: *Tragedy, Comedy, and the Polis* (ed. A. Sommerstein, S. Halliwell, J. Henderson, and B. Zimmermann), 461–476. Bari: Levante Editori.

Sommerstein, A.H. (1996). *Aristophanes, Frogs*, ed. with transl. and notes. Class. Texts. Oxford: Aris & Phillips.

Sourvinou-Inwood, C. (1995). *'Reading' Greek Death: To the End of the Classical Period*. Oxford: Clarendon Press.

Stavru, A. (2021). Pythagoreische Seelenreisen bei Aristophanes: Katabasis als transformativer Wissenserwerb. In: *Seelenreise und Katabasis: Einblicke ins Jenseits in antiker philosophischer Literatur* (ed. I. Männlein-Robert), 139–176. Berlin – Boston: De Gruyter.

Tsoumpra, N. (2020). The shifting gender identity of Dionysus in Aristophanes' *Frogs*. In: *Ancient Greek Comedy: Genre – Texts – Reception* (ed. A. Fries and D. Kanellakis), 199–216. Berlin, Boston: De Gruyter.

Turner, M. (1987). *Death Is the Mother of Beauty: Mind, Metaphor, Criticism*. University of Chicago Press.

Vaio, J. (1985). On the thematic structure of Aristophanes' *Frogs*. In: *Hypatia. Essays in Classics, Comparative Literature, and Philosophy Presented to Hazel E. Barnes on her Seventieth Birthday* (ed. W.M. Calder III, U.K. Goldsmith, and P.B. Kenevan), 91–102. Boulder, CO: University of Colorado Press.

Verbanck-Piérard, A. (2018). Round trip to Hades: Herakles' advice and directions. In: *Round Trip to Hades in the Eastern Mediterranean Tradition: Visits to the Underworld from Antiquity to Byzantium* (ed. G. Ekroth and I. Nilsson), 163–193. Leiden-Boston: Brill.

Vermeule, E. (1979). *Aspects of Death in Early Greek Art and Poetry*. Berkeley, Los Angeles, London: University of California Press.

Vernant, J.-P. (1996). Death with two faces. In: *Reading the Odyssey, Selected Interpretative Essays* (ed. S.L. Schein) transl. by J. Lloyd, 55–61. Princeton, NJ.

Verrall, A.W. (1908). The verse-weighing scene in the *Frogs* of Aristophanes. *The Classical Review* 22 (6): 172–175.

Waites, M.C. (1912). Some features of the allegorical debate in Greek literature. *Harvard Studies in Classical Philology* 23: 1–46.

Webster, T.B.L. (1954). Personification as a mode of Greek thought. *Journal of the Warburg and Courtauld Institutes* 17 (1/2): 10–21.

Whitman, C.H. (1964). *Aristophanes and the Comic Hero*. Cambridge, MA: Harvard University Press.

Willi, A. (2002). The language of Greek comedy: introduction and bibliographical sketch. In: *The Language of Greek Comedy* (ed. A. Willi), 1–32. Oxford: Oxford University Press.

Willi, A. (2003). *The languages of Aristophanes: aspects of linguistic variation in classical Attic Greek*. Oxford.

Woodbury, L. (1988). The Poetry of tongue and of *phren* in the Frogs. In: *Language and the Tragic Hero: Essays on Greek Tragedy in Honor of Gordon M. Kirkwood* (ed. P. Pucci), 175–185. Atlanta: Scholars Press.

Worthington, I. (1989). Aristophanes' 'Frogs' and Arginusae. *Hermes* 117 (3): 359–363.

Zanker, A.T. (2016). *Greek and Latin Expressions of Meaning. The Classical Origins of a Modern Metaphor*. München: Beck.

Zanker, A.T. (2019). *Metaphor in Homer: Time, Speech, and Thought*. Cambridge; New York: Cambridge University Press.

CHAPTER 16

Assemblywomen: Gender

Gwendolyn Compton-Engle

Introduction

The very title of this play signals an interest in both gender and the workings of Athenian democracy. Although usually translated as a noun, *Assemblywomen*, the Greek title is the participle *Ekklesiazousai* ("participating in the Assembly") in the feminine plural, hence "Women Participating in the Assembly." Like its title, the play infuses the functioning of democracy with the politics of sex and gender. In so doing, it revisits some of the features of *Lysistrata* and *Women at the Thesmophoria*, extending the gender reversals of the "women" plays of 411 into its own milieu, the postwar era of the late 390s. *Assemblywomen* engages with similar questions of gender construction as did *Women at the Thesmophoria* but inverts the action: then a man had dressed as female to infiltrate an all-female religious gathering, but now women take on male disguise to enter the male political assembly. The preoccupation of *Women at the Thesmophoria* with incongruous costumes and theatrical performance recurs here, but *Assemblywomen* applies these metatheatrical techniques to the city's civic institutions and its household dynamics. The protagonist Praxagora, a woman rallying her female compatriots to take action for the good of the polis, embodies some of the same leadership as Lysistrata did, but her actions extend much further into the structures of the polis, placing her in a position of official political power – at least until she disappears from the play completely. Her plan blends comic and philosophical utopias to enact an all-encompassing reordering of Athenian society that inverts its fundamental norms and promises a communal prosperity. Through its female-led revolution, the play also raises the perennial questions of Old Comedy: Who will save the city? What is the relationship between self-interest and the public good, or between the individual household and the larger community? Is there a way that we can have it all, in a life of ease and pleasure? Despite signs of fourth-century evolution in comedy, including the disappearance of the chorus from the text of the play's second half, *Assemblywomen* shows Aristophanes as engaged as ever with contemporary Athens.

The overall structure of *Assemblywomen* follows a pattern typical of Aristophanes' plays: a protagonist conceives and enacts a big idea against some opposition, and the remainder of the play showcases some consequences. The play falls into three main movements: preparation for the Assembly takeover, presentation of Praxagora's full plan, and demonstration of some consequences. In the first sequence, the women practice for their political coup. Praxagora gathers a group of women who have brought items of male costume in order to impersonate men and attend the Assembly. These women also form the chorus of the play. After some practice, they depart for the Assembly in their male guises. The second major segment of the play introduces the male perspective and sets Praxagora in dialogue with male skeptics of her plan. Praxagora's husband appears in his wife's clothing as he seeks relief from intestinal blockages. His neighbor Chremes reports the news that the Assembly has handed over control to the women of the city. Praxagora and her posse return, and after feigning ignorance of the events of the Assembly, she unveils a radical plan that involves dissolution of individual households, sharing of communal property, free meals, and new rules about who has sex with whom. Finally, in the play's third portion, two episodes showcase some results of this radical plan: first, a rule-following citizen and a scofflaw dispute whether it is best to comply with the new rules or to game the system; second, a young woman and a group of old hags compete for the sexual favors of a young man. The play concludes with an encompassing invitation to a feast.

Praxagora and the Chorus

The opening scene of *Assemblywomen* introduces central themes that will recur in varied form throughout the play. First of all, the women's cross-gender disguise and preparation for the role they will play in the Assembly demonstrate the construction of gender through costume, movement, and speech. The female-to-male cross-dressing brings a particular new focus on the performance of masculinity. The scene also highlights the theatrical quality of politics, as the assembly and the theater become conflated (Zeitlin 1999, 167–172; Slater 2002, 212–214). It establishes Praxagora as a skilled manipulator of audiences, both political and theatrical (Rothwell 1990; McClure 1999, 236–246; Slater 2002, 207–234; Moodie 2012). And while details of the political program that Praxagora will implement are reserved for a later scene, the costuming of this first section introduces the key principle of inversion, while the group actions of the women introduce a central dialectic between the collective good and individual self-interest.

The apparel worn and carried by the women in the first part of *Assemblywomen* employs the typically gendered signifiers of the comic stage to present a version of cross-dressing, female-to-male, that has not yet been seen on the comic stage. Normally, the male comic actor, in order to play a female character such as Praxagora, wears a white mask and an ankle-length *chiton* (tunic) on top of his padded bodysuit. This white mask and long robe, as well as sometimes a longer female cloak (*himation*) are the two most clearly distinguishing signifiers of the female on the comic stage. In contrast, an actor playing a male character would typically wear a darker, usually bearded mask, and would wear a very short tunic, often with an additional short *himation* (Stone 1981, 22–31, 155–97; Compton-Engle 2015, 17, 60–61). The female characters of *Assemblywomen* have altered both their costume bodies and their clothing to pass as male. They have brought fake beards (24–5, 68–72, 99–101, 118–27) and have allowed themselves to grow body hair (60–61, 65–67). They also claim to have tanned their faces (62–4, 126–7), although the degree to which they have visibly achieved this is uncertain, since later reports from the Assembly indicate that these "men" were unusually pale (385–7, 427–28). The women at the start of *Assemblywomen* still wear typical female garments but have brought their husbands' cloaks, walking sticks, and shoes, which they explicitly indicate they have stolen from the men (26, 40, 275). Throughout the initial scene, their long female chitons are still visible to the audience, until Praxagora gives them instructions at 268 to gird them up, presumably to a typical male-shortened length. The women depart at 285 fully "in costume" as men. The initial presentation of these characters as female, followed by the addition of a male layer of costume, helps the audience to see the outward signs of maleness being donned.

The cross-dressing of the women in *Assemblywomen* presents the inverse of the male-to-female transvestism in *Women at the Thesmophoria*, where Euripides' Relative removes his beard and body hair and takes on women's clothing as part of his female disguise (*Thesm.* 213–79). Since the groundbreaking work of Froma Zeitlin, the performance of gender in Greek drama has been viewed through the lens of "playing the other," with special attention to male-to-female cross-dressing in *Women at the Thesmophoria* and Euripides' *Bacchae* (Zeitlin 1996, 341–74, 375–416). Zeitlin elucidates how *Women at the Thesmophoria*, by disguising the Relative as female and making him act out roles from Euripidean tragedy, explores the implications for male actors, especially those performing tragedy, who embody female characters and perform femininity (Zeitlin 1996, 375–416;

Foley in this volume). But the opening of *Assemblywomen*, by having a male actor play a woman who is in turn playing a male role, turns the spotlight back on masculinity, focusing its attention not so much on men representing the female other as on men playing *themselves*. The interposed female layer creates space for a recognition that not only is there an "artifice of femininity," as stressed by scholars such as Zeitlin and Taaffe, but that masculinity as well is a set of signs performed for an audience.

The women's attempt to perform masculinity in the opening of *Assemblywomen* extends beyond costume to movement and speech (Taaffe 1993, 115–22; McClure 1999, 240–43; Slater 2002, 211–12). In lines 149–50, Praxagora instructs them, "Come on, see to it that you speak like a man (*andristi*) and well (*kalōs*), leaning your body on your staff." This exhortation to talk like a man has its counterpart in the cross-dressing scene in *Women at the Thesmophoria*, where Euripides urges the cross-dressed Relative to speak in a feminine way (267–68; see McClure 1999, 226–35). In *Assemblywomen*, the gendered nature of speech is further emphasized when the women in their rehearsal repeatedly use expressions that are marked as female and then corrected, such as swearing by the two goddesses at 155, addressing the imaginary assembly as "women" (*gynaikes*) at 165, and swearing by Aphrodite at 189 (see McClure 1999, 205–15; Willi 2003, 157–97; Sommerstein 2009, 15–42 on features of female speech in Aristophanes). Praxagora's final instructions to the women stress their comportment and speech, as she tells them to lean on their walking sticks, sing, and imitate the manner of rustics (276–79); when they return, they keep up their act by clomping around noisily in their shoes (483).

One final piece of costume emphasizes that these female characters are not only playing "men" but playing "men-at-Assembly," that is, citizen male participants in democracy. Right after the women attach their false beards, as they begin to rehearse their lines for the Assembly, each speaker in turn puts on a garland as she is about to speak. The text calls attention repeatedly to this garland, which was worn by real speakers at the Assembly (122, 131, 133, 148, 163, 170–71; cf. *Birds* 463, *Thesm.* 380). Thus, the assumption of masculinity, signified by the beards, is followed immediately by the assumption of political speech, signified by the garland. In contrast with *Women at the Thesmophoria*, the primary referent for the role-playing is not tragic performance but the enactment of democracy itself.

In keeping with this political role-playing, the performance venue is simultaneously the Theater of Dionysus and the imagined Assembly of the citizen body on the Pnyx. Niall Slater notes, for example, that when the members of the chorus enter, they sit with their backs to the audience, making the theatrical audience part of the imagined Assembly space (Slater 2002, 212). The spectators of this performance are simultaneously the theatrical audience and the *demos* as a political body. This overlap between spectators and citizens is further emphasized later, when the chorus exhorts Praxagora to bring a new solution to the citizen body (*politen. . .demon*, 574–75), a wise discovery that the *polis* needs (577), and she prefaces her *political* agenda with a reference to the *theatrical* audience (583–85): "Indeed I believe I'll teach them good things; but the spectators (*tous theatas*), will they be willing to hear something new and not dwell too much in their old ways? This is what I fear most." The conflation of spectators and political *demos*, theater and Assembly, harks back to the opening of *Acharnians*, in which the setting is imagined to be the Pnyx, and an Assembly is enacted, complete with a herald, opening rituals, formulaic expressions, and ambassadors, right there in the theater (see Rhodes 2004 for a review of the Athenian Assembly in Aristophanes; McClure 1999, 15–19 on the dialectical relationship of theater with other civic institutions). In both plays, the theatrical audience is encouraged to think of itself also as a political body, but in *Assemblywomen*, the disguises and rehearsing put further emphasis on the performative element of political participation. As Zeitlin indicates, Aristophanes highlights the "theatricalization of civic experience" by showing the degree to which all aspects of civic life are performances (Zeitlin 1999, 167–68).

The opening scene also establishes a focus on female leadership and the collective action of women, recalling and surpassing the political action taken by women in *Lysistrata*. Like Lysistrata before her, Praxagora has formed a plan for the salvation of the city (396–7; *Lys.* 30, 41, 525) and has called together a group of women to set that plan in motion. In both plays, the action begins with the solo female protagonist on stage awaiting the other women who have not shown up yet (1–29; *Lys.* 1–4). Praxagora's opening address to the lamp, especially lines 7–14 emphasizing the sexual positions and depilation that the lamp has witnessed, hints at a sexualized plot akin to *Lysistrata* (an expectation that is deferred until the play's penultimate scene). Following the precedent of Lysistrata, Praxagora rallies and coordinates her group of female conspirators by emphasizing aspects of their social role as stewards of the household (211–12; *Lys.* 493–95) and as mothers of soldiers (233–35; *Lys.* 523–26, 588–90, 648–51), as well as deploying the comic stereotypes that women are very fond of wine (14–15, 132–46, 227; *Lys.* 194–239) and natural deceivers (236–38; cf. Sommerstein 1998, 160 for many parallels).

Praxagora herself, in her male garb, takes on a publicly active role that was impossible for a woman in classical Athens, and even more radical than that of her predecessor Lysistrata. Scholars generally agree that Lysistrata's character is to some extent modeled after the priestess of Athena, Lysimache, an affiliation that gives some "cover" to her prominent role by aligning her with a position in the city that was acceptable for women (Lewis 1955; Henderson 1987; reconsidered by Reverman 2006, 236–43). Christopher Faraone has supplemented this reading by demonstrating that Lysistrata exhibits traits of two somewhat contradictory personas: the traditional religious piety concordant with that priestess role and the savvy manipulation of men's desire that is characteristic of a madam running a brothel (Faraone 2006). These, Faraone suggests, were the only two models of female leadership available to women on the comic stage when *Lysistrata* was produced.

Yet two decades later in *Assemblywomen*, Praxagora does much more. We have already seen her directing the show that the women will perform in the Assembly. Her claim that she will instruct her audience (*didaxo*, lines 215 and 583) echoes claims made by the comic poet himself in other plays (*Ach.* 626ff., esp. 658; *Frogs* 1007–10). Her training of the women, that is, the chorus and actors, for their Assembly role puts her in the mode of a comic producer/director (*didaskalos*) like Peisetaerus in *Birds*, who trains the chorus of birds and furnishes characters with pieces of costume (Slater 2002, 138; Compton-Engle 2015, 129–43). (Further similarities between Peisetaerus and Praxagora will emerge as *Assemblywomen* continues.) Indeed, the only other characters in extant Greek drama to direct a rehearsal scene are the playwright Euripides in *Women at the Thesmophoria* and the god of theater himself, Dionysus in the *Bacchae*.

Not limited to metatheatrical directorship, Praxagora will hold public office and direct public policy. Her name, meaning "one who acts in the public meeting-place" (124) designates her as a political actor of wide-ranging scope, as opposed to the single-issue focus denoted by Lysistrata's name ("dissolver of armies"). The women say that if Praxagora's plan to give authority to women is approved, they will elect her as general (*strategos*, 246–7). Sure enough, when the chorus members return from the Assembly, they call her their *strategos* (491, 500), and Blepyrus affirms this appellation at 727; later she is called *strategis* (835, 870), the female version of the word "general."

Furthermore, Praxagora displays the verbal dexterity necessary for effective action in the Athenian public sphere (Rothwell 1990). Her use of language in the opening scene shows her to be an astute rhetorician capable of persuading various audiences – the immediate audience of women around her, the imagined Assembly audience, and the theatrical audience. She does not make the same gendered linguistic slip-ups that the other women do (Taaffe 1993, 120; McClure 1999, 243). As the women practice their speeches for the Assembly, Praxagora starts dispensing political advice like a seasoned orator. Beginning at line 170 and continuing through 240, she establishes her own concern for the best interest of the city, criticizes the city's leadership and its policies, blames the *demos* for its self-interest, and proposes that the women be put in charge. When the other women express their amazement at her speaking ability, she claims that she acquired it from listening to orators while living in exile on the Pnyx (243–44).

Praxagora's persuasive skill, like that of Peisetaerus (but not Lysistrata), bears some hallmarks of sophistic rhetoric (Rothwell 1990, 83–91, Hubbard 1997, 37). She is described as *sophos* ("wise"), *dexios* ("clever"), *deinos* ("awesome/clever"), and *xynetos* ("shrewd"). The chorus at 571–82 urges her to employ her "shrewd intelligence and philosophical mind" as she prepares to unveil her plan. Although these qualities are remarkable in a female character, Athenians did not regard rhetorical skill as an unambiguous good, even in male speakers. A suspicion of verbal chicanery runs through

Greek literature, and comedy often associates rhetorical prowess with an effete elite (e.g., *Knights* 421–25, *Clouds* 1088–94). Rothwell attributes Praxagora's persuasive success to the infusion of politics with the dynamic of *eros*, and, in particular, the *erastes/eromenos* (homoerotic lover/ beloved) dyad that comedy often caricatures as underlying the training of elite politicians (Rothwell 1990, 77–81). Praxagora invokes passive homoeroticism right after she completes her own rhetorical set piece. When asked how women could possibly offer public speeches, she responds, "They say that whoever of the young men are screwed the most are the most clever at speaking- and we (women) have that advantage by chance already" (113–14). The implication is that political discourse is already debased in a way conducive to female participation (Saïd 1996, 287–88). Just a few lines earlier, she mentions Agyrrius, a politician who (she says) "used to be a woman" and stole another man's beard, but is now doing big things in the city (102–4). This reference to Agyrrius and his supposedly feigned masculinity points to a precedent for the women's cross-dressed political speech. Although Rothwell presents a fairly positive portrayal of Praxagora's use of persuasion, Laura McClure interprets her speech in a much more sinister light as "undermining the normative social order" through seductive rhetoric associated with pathics and demagogues (McClure 1999, 238, 244–46). While Praxagora persuades skillfully, her success may be colored by these associations with sophistry and with speakers of questionable masculinity.

At the same time, there is also some indication that the playwright is going to extra lengths to establish rapport between Praxagora and the *theatrical* audience. Erin Moodie's recent study of "pretense disruption" has observed that the female characters of *Assemblywomen*, especially Praxagora, engage in frequent linguistic strategies to win the sympathy of the audience (Moodie 2012). Different from standard rhetorical devices, these features of comic speech that break the dramatic pretense, such as second-person addresses directly to the audience, are usually employed by lower-status characters like slaves and parasites (Moodie 2012, 263–65; Moore 1998). While these features are rare in *Lysistrata* and *Women at the Thesmophoria*, Praxagora uses direct audience appeal frequently, inserting it into her opening speech at line 22 and continuing through the second-person addresses in her speech to the audience/imagined Assembly beginning at line 173. This usage is parallel with that of male protagonists who dispense political advice, such as the sausage seller of *Knights,* and may help make her unusual role as a prominent woman more palatable to the audience.

Establishing some rapport with the audience is especially necessary because Praxagora's proposal to hand over the city to the women – not to mention the content of the radical program itself, which has not yet been revealed – is so potentially threatening that it needs to be disarmed in whatever way possible, so that the audience does not immediately reject it. The women's seizure of power to save the polis is represented in this play as simultaneously well-intentioned and threatening. Rule by women evokes mythic examples of gynecocracy such as the Amazons, the archetypal opponents of Greek civilization; or the Lemnian women, who killed all the men on their island (Saïd 1996, 289–90; Zeitlin 1999). Yet at this point in *Assemblywomen*, Aristophanes opts not to emphasize these mythic gynecocracies. More proximate to contemporary Athens is the threat of oligarchy and political conspiracy, and the play does hint in that direction (Sheppard 2016; Tordoff 2017). When Praxagora first mentions the other women (line 23), she calls them *hetairai*, a word whose basic meaning is "comrade" or "companion," but can be understood in multiple ways. In its feminine form, the word normally refers to courtesans, a connotation that might again promise a play full of sexual shenanigans as in *Lysistrata*. Yet the masculine form can also be used as companions in a political conspiracy, and the related abstract noun *hetaireia* refers to a conspiratorial group with political (usually anti-democratic) goals (cf. Lysias 12.4; Sommerstein 1998, 139). Praxagora refers twice to deliberations the women made at the religious festival of Skira (18, 59), recalling the female conspiracy hatched at a religious gathering in the *Women at the Thesmophoria*. Tordoff notes that *Lysistrata* and *Women at the Thesmophoria* were staged under the specter of oligarchy in 411 and suggests that *Assemblywomen* "deliberately and provocatively recalls his earlier plays plotted around the theme of female conspiracy, both written at a time when Athens did in fact succumb to an oligarchic revolution" (Tordoff 2017, 165). On the other hand, Praxagora reassures her audience that women are the most conservative of all (214–28). She appropriates the jargon of contemporary political discourse, with its emphasis on restoring ancestral constitutions and reconstructing a shared civic past, when she claims that women preserve the *archaios nomos* ("ancient law/custom") by engaging in all their traditional activities (Sheppard 2016; Tordoff 2017).

Despite the unsettling association with conspiratorial groups, it is precisely the leadership of collective action taken for the benefit of the whole polis that distinguishes both Praxagora and Lysistrata from other, more self-interested comic protagonists. Comparison with *Acharnians* shows a contrasting pursuit of private interest. That play begins with Dicaeopolis alone, awaiting the start of the Assembly. Disgusted by the failure of his fellow citizens to act, he soon gives up on civic endeavors, instead proceeding only in his own private interest, creating his own individual peace with Sparta, and relishing the benefits of peace that he alone enjoys. *Assemblywomen*, like *Acharnians*, also opens with a protagonist anticipating the start of an Assembly, but unlike Dicaeopolis, Praxagora is soon joined by the group of women who are already her allies. The fact that the chorus appears so early in the play (they begin to appear at line 30), without their normal entrance song and without a need to be persuaded to the protagonist's cause themselves, establishes them immediately as her supporters and aligns Praxagora with a collective from the start. Praxagora explicitly states that her goal is to accomplish something good for the polis (108), and she castigates the *demos* for taking public money but acting only in their own private interest (205–208). The combination of the civic-mindedness of Praxagora and the group action that she initiates places their agenda on the side of the common good, in what will become a major theme of the play, the tension between individual self-interest and public welfare.

By line 285, when the chorus puts the final pieces of its male disguise in place and tromps off to the Assembly, all the play's themes have been introduced. Through their disguises, women have assumed the tangible and behavioral signs of male prerogative, and Praxagora has directed them in a rehearsal for the role of male citizen participants in democracy. This introductory section of the play offers a mixture of reassurances and unsettling aspects in its presentation of Praxagora's initiative. The inversion of gender norms and the specter of conspiracy raised by the women's plotting are mitigated by the remarkable persuasive powers of Praxagora and by her emphasis on the public good against individual self-interest.

The New City

The departure of the throng of women, including (unusually) the chorus, leaves the theater completely empty for the entrance of a lone man, Praxagora's husband Blepyrus. The next portion of the play shows the events of that morning's Assembly through the eyes of three male characters – Blepyrus, his unnamed neighbor, and Chremes, who reports on the Assembly action – and begins to address more directly the impact of female power on men. The largely sympathetic portrayal of Praxagora that was created in the opening scene gets put to the test as she confronts a man, her own husband, who stands to lose from the women's action. When Praxagora engages in direct conversation with the men, she reveals a far more radical plan than anything the play had yet indicated, including the complete dissolution of the boundary between oikos (household) and polis (city-state).

The physical appearance of Blepyrus immediately reprises the theme of costume, gender, and power. In multiple ways, this scene insists that the counterpart to a powerful woman is an emasculated man. Unable to find his own clothes, Blepyrus is forced to wear his wife's robe and her Persian slippers as he leaves the house to unload his bowels (311–326). As a male dressed in incongruous female garb, he presents an obvious visual inverse of Praxagora's opening appearance. His neighbor appears soon in the same predicament (327). Blepyrus has no idea where his cloak is, but the neighbor knows that his own wife has taken his cloak and shoes. That the clothes are something that the women have *taken* from their husbands underscores the detriment to men when their wives take power (Compton-Engle 2005). Power, like the pieces of costume, operates here on a zero-sum logic: only one gender can have it at a time.

The feminization of Blepyrus extends beyond his dress, to impact his body. In his difficulty passing a bowel movement, he calls on the goddess of childbirth, Eileithyia, for assistance (369). As he hears about the women's regime, he fears that he and the other men will experience sexual coercion (465–71), as though suddenly aware of the relationship between rape and power. Blepyrus exemplifies in comic form the association of bodily suffering with the feminine, as Zeitlin has articulated for tragedy: "[a]t those moments when the male finds himself in a condition of weakness, he too becomes acutely aware that he has a body – and then perceives himself, at the limits of pain, to be most like a woman" (Zeitlin 1996, 350). Blepyrus even presents his disempowerment as metaphorical death. When Praxagora returns, he accuses her of stripping him and leaving him laid out as a corpse, all but wreathing him and adding a funerary jar, a *lekythos* (536–38; see Slater 1989 on the oil jar as symbol of death, Compton-Engle 2005 on cloak-stealing and death). Meanwhile, the women's return to the stage includes reminders of their appropriation of male power: they repeatedly call Praxagora *strategos* (491, 500), and she praises them for becoming the "most manly" (*andreiotatoi*, 519) in the Assembly.

The transvestism of Blepyrus is consistent with the presentation throughout Greek drama of cross-dressed male characters, who experience humiliation, loss of control, and metaphorical death correlated with their female garb (Zeitlin 1996, 375–416; Saïd 1987, 234; Taaffe 1993, 113; Compton-Engle 2015, 94–102). The magistrate of *Lysistrata* is involuntarily dressed first as a woman and then as a corpse by the women (599–61). The Relative in *Women at the Thesmophoria* wears the same type of female saffron gown (*krokotos*) as does Blepyrus at line 332 (*Thesm*. 253, 941, 945, 1043, 1220), and the Relative is stripped by the female chorus (*Thesm*. 636–40), as Blepyrus claims has happened to him via the theft of the cloak from his sleeping body. Blepyrus also resembles a recent tragic figure, Pentheus of Euripides' *Bacchae*, who exits his palace dressed in female clothing and soon thereafter experiences gruesome death at the hands of women. Like Pentheus, Blepyrus faces a throng of women who have abandoned the private sphere of the household and transgressed into the public realm. His cross-dressed state matches the cross-spatial displacement that has left individual men trapped in the oikos while the female collective takes control of the polis. From the male perspective presented by Blepyrus, this is all looking very bad.

The grievances and fears expressed by Blepyrus set up a challenging rhetorical situation for Praxagora, by putting her face-to-face with a member of her own household whose interests are so clearly threatened by the women's usurpation of power. Her first strategy is to deceive him, pretending that she knows nothing about the events of the Assembly (553–59). In this calculated deception of her husband, she follows the precedent of tragic heroines like Clytemnestra professing concern for Agamemnon's safety, or Medea feigning reconciliation with Jason (McClure 1999, 27). The rhetorical challenge only grows larger when Praxagora begins to outline her political plan, which will necessitate a drastic restructuring of almost the entire Athenian society. Before Praxagora embarks on the exposition of her plan, the chorus frames her speech with reference to her intelligence (571–73, "concentrated intelligence and philosophical mind") and to the city's need for a new discovery. Both the chorus and Praxagora herself directly appeal to the desires of the audience (simultaneously theatrical and political), gauging whether they are ready to hear something new (583–85).

Praxagora's plan involves the complete recalibration of the interests of the oikos and the polis, as well as the tension between individual self-interest and the common good. The plan's main components are centered around the key word *koinos*, "common." Everyone will share everything in common, rather than having inequities of wealth and property. Land, money, food, clothing, sexual partners, parents, and children – all will be held in common. The physical space of the city will be transformed into one household, with walls knocked down between individual houses (673–4). The public buildings and equipment used as mechanisms for democracy – the law courts, stoas, speaker's platform, jury allotment machines – all will be repurposed for dining and entertainment (676–86). There is a brief acknowledgment that some work must be done, but not by citizen males: slaves will continue to farm the land (651) and women will continue to weave clothing (653–54). (Ober 1998, 151 on further exclusion of slaves in this imagined society.) Otherwise, all of the social problems that plague Athens (assault, theft, informing, litigiousness, debt) will disappear or be easily managed. In sum, "everyone will have everything" (605), the free male's only concern will be going glistening to dinner (651–2), and food, wine, and sex will all be supplied in abundance (690–716).

Despite her claim to novelty, Praxagora's agenda draws on utopian strains from the literary tradition and also from ongoing discussions in political philosophy. Some of the promised outcomes of Praxagora's plan echo the traditional comic fantasies of unlimited food, wine, sex, and prosperity, a return to a Hesiodic Golden Age where life is easy and responsibilities are vanishingly few. (On comic representations of the Golden Age, see Baldry 1953; Heberlein 1980.) Yet instead of the traditionally rural fantasies of a return to pre-civilized, spontaneous natural abundance, as presented in extant plays such as *Peace* and *Acharnians*, or lost plays such as Cratinus' *Wealths* or Crates' *Beasts*, Praxagora offers a political program centered around the question of how to arrange the rules of urban life to bring maximum prosperity to its citizens. In contemplating a new social order, this venture bears some similarity with *Birds*, whose alternate universe is created by the protagonists' flight from Athens and then a virtual re-creation of their polis in the sky. But Praxagora's utopia is much more closely connected to the existing polis than is the Cloud-Cuckoo-Land of *Birds*, since her program is located in Athens itself and created by the Athenians' own Assembly, albeit an Assembly hijacked by female interlopers.

Explorations of alternative *nomoi* (customs, norms, laws) had been circulating among Greek intellectuals throughout the fifth century, as evidenced in Herodotus' fascination with the social customs of other peoples, frequently involving the reversal of Greek sexual norms (Saïd 1996, 282–83, 307; Dawson 1992, 18–21). Another historical factor, the founding of new colonies by Greek city-states, provided an impetus for both physical planning and social planning, the influence of which can be felt in *Birds* (Dawson 1992, 21–26). Property equalization, a key idea in *Assemblywomen*, was proposed for new colonies by Phaleas of Chalcedon in the late fifth century (Ar. *Pol.* 2.7; Dawson 1992, 29–31; Hubbard 1997, 37). Furthermore, the prominence of Sparta at the end of the Peloponnesian War and in the postwar decades surrounding the production of *Assemblywomen* led to a flurry of interest in the Spartan constitution, which included social elements like communal dining (*syssitia*, 715).

Several of the ideas in Praxagora's plan, such as the proposed elimination of private property and the abolition of the individual household, would eventually appear as features of the life of the guardian class in Plato's *Republic* (416d–417b, 449c–450c, 457c–466a), which was likely composed in the 370s. Most scholars now reject the view that Aristophanes accessed some kind of advance draft of the *Republic* and incorporated those ideas in parodic form into *Assemblywomen* (see Tordoff 2007 for a good overview). There is no evidence for this, and Ober rightly questions the comic benefit of doing so: "It was one thing for a comedian to poke fun at a philosophical public figure like Socrates, quite another to expect to get laughs out of parodying a (putative) privately circulated advance draft of an abstruse work of moral and political philosophy" (Ober 1998, 154). On the other hand, scholars are still continuing to assess whether Plato was directly influenced by the ideas advanced by Praxagora in this play. Sommerstein argues affirmatively, cataloging the similarities between the two programs and pointing out that Plato expresses particular concern that these ideas will be taken as ridiculous (*Rep.* 452a–d), perhaps an acknowledgment of their comic origin (Sommerstein 1998, 12–17). Robert Tordoff, building on arguments of Andrea Nightingale about Plato's relationship with comedy, argues that Book Five of the *Republic* "shows marked Platonic anxiety about the sort of intellectualising comedy" that *Assemblywomen* presents (Tordoff 2007, 261; Nightingale 1995, 172–92).

However seriously Plato might have taken its ideas, *Assemblywomen* is not a treatise in political theory, but a production of comic theater. A comedy, even an intellectual one, does not labor under the expectation that it will produce a consistent theoretical framework for social planning. Inconsistency, multiplicity, and flights of fancy are hallmarks of the genre (see Ruffell 2006 on the multi-stranded nature of comic discourse). In a study of utopianism in *Birds*, David Konstan has demonstrated that several different types of utopian thought are interwoven throughout that play in ways sometimes inconsistent and paradoxical (Konstan 1997). He identifies these utopian modes as anomia (freedom from laws), antinomia (the reversal of existing norms), eunomia (having the most just laws), and megalonomia (an exaggerated inflation of existing norms), each coming to the fore in different aspects or moments of *Birds*. Applying Konstan's categorization helps us to see that *Assemblywomen* draws most strongly on the antinomian strand of utopianism, particularly in its inversion of sexual roles. In *Assemblywomen*, the reversal in gender roles, an antinomian element straight out of the most mind-blowing of topsy-turvy alternate worlds, works alongside the political concept of equalization and the economic proposition of commonality of possessions, the "common livelihood" (*koinon. . .bioton*, 594) so heavily emphasized by Praxagora. Suzanne Saïd argues that these two dynamics are connected, that is, that the transposition of power from men to women is inherently intertwined with the communistic agenda: "[W]omen becoming powerful is a way of saying that the power has changed, that politics as such exist no more, and that economics has invaded everything" (Saïd 1996, 298).

The prologue has prepared for both the antinomian and the communitarian elements in Praxagora's plan, and both are reinforced in the brief exchange between Blepyrus and Chremes that precedes Praxagora's return. The cross-dressing of Praxagora and Blepyrus, a clearly antinomian element, is reiterated in political terms when Chremes confirms to Blepyrus that all the responsibilities of male citizens will be removed from them and transferred to the women (458–60). Meanwhile, the collective action of the women, set against the initial solitariness of Blepyrus, prepares for the emphasis on the communal (*to koinon*). Furthermore, Chremes' summary of the arguments made in the Assembly includes the idea that women already share clothing, gold, silver, and drinking cups with each other (446–51). The play's unusual emphasis on clothing helps to bridge these two dynamics, since not only do the cloaks stolen by the women represent the gender role reversal, but Praxagora also promises a communal provision of clothing (668–71).

The combination of the antinomian with the communitarian can help to explain how *Assemblywomen* presents the relationship between the private realm of the oikos and the public realm of the polis. As a central and contested polarity in Greek life (Vernant 1983, 127–75), often connected with gender roles in Greek drama, the oikos–polis dialectic deserves more extensive examination here. A starting point for understanding this dynamic in drama was outlined by Michael Shaw, who in a 1975 article identified a pattern in which female characters in drama intrude on the male domain, stepping out of the oikos into the world of the polis in response to male failure to act on its behalf. On the surface, this would seem to describe exactly the action of *Lysistrata* and *Assemblywomen*, where the women leave their houses to take political action because the city's male leaders have failed in their role to protect the oikos. But in an important article, Helene Foley argues that this straightforward schematic of "male:polis::female:oikos" is too simplistic for Greek drama, which instead displays a "complex symbolic reciprocity" between these two realms (Foley 1982, 4). For example, Athenian women do regularly perform public religious roles on behalf of the polis (see Foley in this volume), and male characters navigate the interests of both oikos and polis in plays like *Acharnians* or *Wasps* that precede the introduction of prominent female characters into comedy (Crane 1997; Papathanasopoulou 2020).

In both *Lysistrata* and *Assemblywomen*, the female protagonists claim that they will save the state by applying the values and structures of the domestic world to the public realm. Lysistrata's extended analogy of woolworking to the management of the state (*Lys.* 567–86) is the most obvious example of this. In *Lysistrata*, although "the distinction between acropolis and home collapses" on a metaphorical level, the boundaries are not really violated; the play concludes with everyone restored to their proper roles (Foley 1982, 7). *Assemblywomen*, with its combination of permanent role reversal and communal living, presses things further. The communal aspect of Praxagora's plan extends *Lysistrata's* analogy of household to state into a more literal demolition of boundaries: the household is not *like* the state, the household *is* the state. Praxagora intends to make the whole city into one single enormous oikos, literally knocking down walls to create one common dwelling (673–4). But at the same time as she elevates the household so that it subsumes the city, she also overturns other traditional interests of the oikos, such as patrilineal succession or inheritance (Foley 1982, 5). In the antinomian spirit that permeates *Assemblywomen*, the primacy of the household as a political unit also brings with it the abandonment of democratic political structures like the court system, symbolized in the repurposing of the jury allotment machines, the stoas, and the speaker's platform. The center of civic life will now be, in essence, a dining room.

Blepyrus is fully converted by this vision and is now eager to follow his wife and be called "the husband of the general" (727), in yet another inversion of norms. This complete capitulation to his wife's leadership should raise some eyebrows. His departing wish to follow her and be seen (*apoblepomai*, 726) in this subordinate role finds its closest parallel in Pentheus' deranged wish to be taken through the middle of Thebes in his feminized Bacchic garb (*Bacch.* 961).

New Sexual Norms in Praxagora's Athens

In the final section of *Assemblywomen*, two scenes test out the consequences of shared property and reversal of sexual norms, respectively. The first of these two scenes (730–876) explores the potential problem of compliance with the new regime's requirement to surrender private possessions. The neighbor of Blepyrus dutifully has his possessions carried out of his house so that he can bring them to the agora and turn them over to the public supply, in accordance with the new rules. He addresses these objects in affectionate, anthropomorphic terms and sets them up in a mock religious procession likely modeled after the Panathenaic procession (730–45). An unnamed skeptical interlocutor calls him foolish, arguing that no reasonable person would relinquish his possessions; even the gods take rather than give; no one else is going to comply; and the laws keep getting changed all the time anyway. Why not wait? Then, a heraldess proclaims that amazing piles of food, wine, and clothing are ready, presumably in the agora. The economic utopia seems to be coming to fruition. The selfish man decides he is going to dinner anyway, without turning in his property. The audience never learns whether or not he gets away with this plan. In either case, this scene is hardly a scathing indictment of communal living. This imagined consequence of Praxagora's plan only raises the problem of what to do with the holdouts, whose actions are presented as selfish, unfair, and in contravention of the communal spirit, but not catastrophic (Ruffell 2006, 93–98). If this is the worst consequence that Aristophanes can imagine resulting from the abolition of private property, then communism doesn't look so bad–or at least it doesn't have much comic potential.

But while the public sharing of formerly private goods receives relatively mild comic treatment, the upending of sexual norms creates more drastic outcomes, exacerbated by generational conflict. In an extended and riotous sequence (877–1111), four women compete for the sexual favor of a young man. This scene uses multiple forms of speech (songs, spells, obscenity, and legalisms), as well as the play's third example of ridiculously incongruous costume, to reverse and confuse categories of gender and age. First, an old woman and a young woman (a *kore*, really an adolescent girl) contest the right to have sex with the young man, and then two even older and uglier women each assert their claim. The seeds for this encounter are planted at 611–629, when Praxagora explains to Blepyrus how sexual relations will work in a society with communally shared sexual partners: anyone desiring to have sex with a young and attractive partner must first sleep with an older and uglier one. Thus, a typically comic generational opposition pitting the young against the old is added onto the gender polarity of male and female, so when the new sexual rule is put into practice, two inversions happen simultaneously. Furthermore, Praxagora's earlier statement that she intends to put a stop to all the prostitutes (718–20) leaves the remaining women acting as de facto *hetairai* (courtesans), as they all solicit sex from the young man. The communal sharing of women thus obliterates the firewall between the statuses of prostitute and citizen that Athenian society sought so hard to maintain (Halliwell 2002, 127–133).

The appearance of the *kore* in this scene is significant in the development of comic roles for women. As the first unmarried young woman in extant Greek comedy to speak independently, she shatters existing Athenian norms simply by speaking in public. (The daughters who speak in *Acharnians* and *Peace* appear with their fathers.) The role of this *kore* extends one step further *Lysistrata's* radical move of presenting citizen wives on the comic stage and blurring the lines between wife and *hetaira* (Stroup 2004; see Henderson 2000 on the precedents for comic *hetaira* roles in non-extant plays). Although it is possible that the *kore* of *Assemblywomen* speaks only from a window (she is described as peeping out at 924, and the young man asks her to come down at 961), nevertheless, she is doing exactly what the whole system of secluding unmarried women was meant to avoid: she is planning a sexual rendezvous with a young man when her mother is not home (911–14). The girl prefigures the important role for the nubile *kore* character in the future development of comedy; likewise, the interaction of a young male and young female love interest, blocked by the old woman, also anticipates the pairs of thwarted young lovers who will come to dominate comedy in later eras.

Furthermore, the erotic lyrics that the young pair sing to each other (952–75) exhibit reversals of gender and generic expectation. This song is an early example of a *paraclausithyron*, a type of song sung by a drunken male reveler at the closed door of a lover, imploring her to open the door. In this example, however, the girl initiates the song, speaking of her own desire, and uses language appropriate to the male (Olson 1988; Sommerstein 1998, 221–22; Halliwell 2002, 133 suggests the influence of subliterary mime). Recently, Natalia Tsoumpra has suggested that the girl's words echo an *agoge* spell (a kind of love charm common in Greek magical texts), intended to lead the man to her, but here again the normal gender roles are reversed, with the female applying the spell, in contrast with surviving real-life examples of these spells that are overwhelmingly cast by men (Tsoumpra 2019, 541–43).

The girl's appearance in opposition to the first older woman also breaks what has heretofore been a solidarity of women in *Assemblywomen*. Until this point, the female characters have been acting with no apparent divisions among them. Compare this to *Lysistrata*, which divides women into two groups by age from the start and sends them off with age-specific tasks as part of its bipartite plot (the wives enact the sex strike while the older women seize the treasury). But rather than working in parallel toward the same goal, as the two groups of women in *Lysistrata* do, this old woman and young woman are in direct competition. Here, too, song plays a role. The old woman beckons the Muses to help her find a tune (882–83), and she even directly calls on the theatrical piper to start playing (890–92), but instead of a lovely song, it turns into a raucous, rivalrous, and obscene antiphony. As soon as the girl appears, the two women begin to hurl insults at each other, both in dialogue and in alternating lyric stanzas (893–935). The young woman praises her own youthful body and suggests that the old woman should be death's girlfriend; the old woman retaliates by casting a horrible curse on the girl (906–10; Tsoumpra 2019, 535–41). So much for the female collective.

In this scene, the persuasion of Praxagora has been replaced not only by the language of erotic lyric and love magic but also by the language of legal claims; for these old women also brandish legal documents. At 944–5, the first old woman claims that it is right (*dikaion*) for her to have sex with the young man according to the law (*kata ton nomon*). At 1012, she produces a physical copy of a *psephisma*, a decree, which she proceeds to read aloud to demonstrate that the man must comply (see Fletcher 2012 on the distinction between law and decree). The second old woman then claims that the first one is acting against the law (1049–51). Throughout the scene, references to the law and legal remedies continue to proliferate (1022, 1041, 1056, 1064–65, 1077, 1090). In addition to the sexual mores that have been overturned by these new laws, legal agency has been inverted, so that no man has legal authority (i.e., is *kyrios*) over contracts worth more than a bushel (1024–5), a restriction previously applied to Athenian women. McClure argues that the women's use of legalisms "reflects the profound disturbance of normative gender roles brought about by the new government" (McClure 1999, 255).

Of equal importance is the incongruous costume that marks the old women's appearance and links them to the play's earlier costume inversions. When the first old woman emerges, alone on the stage at the start of the scene, she wears a *krokotos* (879), the same ultra-feminine garment that Blepyrus had worn in his first appearance. This parallel with Blepyrus would be reinforced if, as is likely, the old woman exits from the same central door as he had (Sommerstein 1998, 28–30 on the staging). (She could even be played by the same actor.) This time the incongruity created by the *krokotos* is not one of gender but of age (Taaffe 1993, 126). Attention to the masks of all three old women (but not the *kore*) highlights their artificiality and links the three women with death (Compton-Engle 2015, 44–45). The first old woman mentions at her entrance that she has plastered her face with white lead (878), a reversal of the tanning process that the women in the play's opening scene had used to de-feminize their appearance. She is trying very hard to be feminine, but the effect of her mask points to death instead. A reference to the white lead of her mask is repeated at 928, and again for the third old woman at 1072. This white paint is then analogized to the white-ground technique with which funeral jars (*lekythoi*) were decorated (Slater 1989). When she demands a kiss, the young man insults her by saying that her boyfriend paints *lekythoi* (996); he later suggests she should prepare herself for a funeral, including the placing of *lekythoi* (1030–33). As he is being dragged off by the third old woman, he says that she should be placed on his tomb in place of a *lekythos*. Thus, the funerary jar that Blepyrus had imagined in his exaggerated description of his own metaphorical death (538) comes back to haunt the stage in the faces of the old women, culminating in the young man's "death."

There is no doubt that the multiple inversions and norm violations in this scene create chaos (a "ludicrously disordered demimonde," in the words of Halliwell 2002, 131) but the age differentiation that is introduced at this point in the play also complicates any effort to determine how the original audience might have reacted to the scene. Sommerstein and Henderson both suggest that the young man's cries of protest are ridiculously out of proportion to what he actually suffers (one might compare the hyperbolic self-pity expressed so often by New Comedy's young men in love) and that the older men who seem to be the target audience of Old Comedy might relish seeing the young man discomfited (Sommerstein 1984; Henderson 1987, 118–19; Slater 2002, 226–30). Some Schadenfreude at the young man's fate would be more likely if the young man in this scene is the very same unnamed person who had declared his intention to flout the rules about communal property in the previous scene (a possibility mentioned in Slater 2002, 222–23). Halliwell sees this scene as no more outrageous than the treatment of sex elsewhere in Old Comedy, which he argues "offers, with scarce exceptions, a grotesquely paradoxical erotics within which the disadvantages of 'ugliness' are transformed into the supremacy of shamelessness" (Hailliwell 2002, 125). Yet other scholars observe that the coupling of sexuality and death in the presentation of the old women creates an image of sterility that contrasts with the Greek marital ideal (Saïd 1996, 310–313; Zeitlin 1999, 187; Tsoumpra 2019). In this way, *Assemblywomen* moves in the opposite direction from *Lysistrata*, which begins with war-imposed sterility but ends with a celebration of fecund marital union. In this interpretation, the specter of the old women, with their resemblance to monstrous mythical figures like the Erinyes and Empousa (1056), can only cast a negative light on Praxagora's whole endeavor. As *Assemblywomen* draws to a close, the progressively older age of each of the women and the foot-in-the-grave imagery associated with them also contrasts with the rejuvenation that old male Aristophanic protagonists usually receive at the end of a play.

But this play is not over. In one last reversal, *Assemblywomen* does in fact offer a final scene of celebration reminiscent of a typically festive Aristophanic ending. This finale reassures its predominantly male audience, by transferring the role of protagonist from Praxagora to Blepyrus and replacing the outrageousness of the previous scene with pleasures that await him. Immediately after the young man's departing lament, a maid appears to announce blessings upon the *demos*, the land, her mistress, all the women who stand near, all the neighbors and demesmen – and herself (1112–14). There is a city-wide party to which even the audience is invited (1140–43). Blepyrus, when he emerges, wants to ensure that the invitation is extended to all ages: "don't leave anyone out, but generously call old man, young man, and child" (1145–46). The collective is back, and this time it includes men. Blepyrus himself receives the usual perks afforded a male protagonist at the end of a play: some young women to accompany him to the feast (1138, 1152), arranged for him by his wife, no less.

And what did happen to Praxagora, after all? While she is presumably the mistress listed among the blessed at line 1113, she herself is not present for this final scene, as the maid's *report* of her orders at 1137 makes clear. In fact, Praxagora spoke her last words approximately 400 lines ago (at 724). After converting both the Assembly and her own husband to her will in the first two sections of the play, she has retreated into the background. The contrast with the end of *Birds* is notable. Peisetaerus, having used his own sophistry to persuade the birds to make him king over a utopian world of his design, ends his play holding supreme power over the universe, gods and humans included; the play culminates in his marriage to Basileia ("Reign"). Praxagora, who likewise used skilled persuasion and metatheatrical directorship to enact her utopian plan, had seemed to be on her way to becoming a scaled-down Peisetaerus, with a position as *strategos/strategis* that, while less grandiose than the limitless power of Peisetaerus, nevertheless is commensurately bold for her station as a woman. Yet she cannot be shown partaking in the festivities. As Naomi Scott has recently demonstrated, female protagonists in Aristophanes are not featured enjoying food like male protagonists routinely consume (Scott 2017). Like *Lysistrata*, then, this play ends with a restoration of gender norms. In *Lysistrata*, the male power structure ultimately remains intact, and the division of Reconciliation's "territory" orchestrated by Lysistrata makes clear the continued sexual subjugation of women for men's pleasure. In *Assemblywomen*, the women remain technically still in power in the city, and in that sense this play extends female agency further than *Lysistrata* did. Nevertheless, the play ends by depicting a male character, a substitute protagonist, reaping the rewards. In the final scene, the chorus' direct address to the judges for their support (1155–62) suggests one motivation: audience appeal. One thing this highly imaginative playwright could not conceive, or dare to stage, is a successful woman enjoying herself.

GUIDE TO FURTHER READING

The edition of Sommerstein (1998) with its introduction, translation, and commentary is an indispensable starting point; the commentary of Ussher (1973) remains helpful, especially for those who know Greek. For the historical and political milieu, Ober (1998) is foundational and can be supplemented with Sheppard (2016) and Tordoff (2017). Rothwell (1990) and McClure (1999) treat rhetoric and female speech in this play. Hubbard (1997) and Zeitlin (1999) assess its utopian ideas, while Tordoff (2007) provides a good entry point to the relationship with Plato's *Republic*. Ruffell (2006) re-assesses the longstanding dispute over whether Praxagora's program should be seen in a serious or ironic light. Aspects of theater and staging are the focus of Slater (2002); costume, gender, and transvestism are treated in Zeitlin (1996) and Compton-Engle (2015). Taaffe (1993) offers a reading of all three plays that focus on women. For the development of female roles in comedy, see Henderson (1987 and 2000) as well as Taaffe (1993) 23–47 on the plays prior to *Lysistrata*. Foley (1982) and Saïd (1996) examine the relationship of women to the Athenian *polis*; for matters of sex and gender at the play's end, Halliwell (2002) and Tsoumpra (2019) offer complementary perspectives.

REFERENCES

Baldry, H.C. (1953). The idler's paradise in Attic comedy. *G&R* 22: 49–60.
Compton-Engle, G. (2005). Stolen cloaks in Aristophanes' *Ecclesiazusae*. *TAPA* 135: 163–176.
Compton-Engle, G. (2015). *Costume in the Comedies of Aristophanes*. Cambridge: Cambridge University Press.
Crane, G. (1997). Oikos and agora: mapping the polis in Aristophanes' *Wasps*. In: *The City as Comedy: Society and Representation in Athenian Drama* (ed. G.W. Dobrov), 198–229. Chapel Hill: University of North Carolina Press.
Dawson, D. (1992). *Cities of the Gods: Communist Utopias in Greek Thought*. New York and Oxford: Oxford University Press.
Faraone, C.A. (2006). Priestess and courtesan: the ambivalence of female leadership in Aristophanes' *Lysistrata*. In: *Prostitutes and Courtesans in the Ancient World* (ed. C.A. Faraone and L. McClure), 207–223. Madison: University of Wisconsin Press.
Fletcher, J. (2012). The women's decree: law and its other in *Ecclesiazusae*. In: *No Laughing Matter: Studies in Athenian Comedy* (ed. C.W. Marshall and G.A. Kovacs), 127–140. London: Bristol Classical Press.
Foley, H.P. (1982). The 'female intruder' reconsidered: women in Aristophanes' *Lysistrata* and *Ecclesiazusae*. *CP* 77: 1–21.

Halliwell, F.S. (2002). Aristophanic sex: the erotics of shamelessness. In: *The Sleep of Reason: Erotic Experience and Sexual Ethics in Ancient Greece and Rome* (ed. M.C. Nussbaum and J. Sihvola), 120–142. Chicago: University of Chicago Press.

Heberlein, F. (1980). *Pluthygieia. Zur Gegenwart bei Aristophanes*. Frankfurt: Haag und Herchen.

Henderson, J. (1987). Older women in Attic Old Comedy. *TAPA* 117: 105–129.

Henderson, J. (2000). Pherekrates and the women of Old Comedy. In: *The Rivals of Aristophanes: Studies in Athenian Old Comedy* (ed. D. Harvey and J. Wilkins), 135–150. Swansea: Classical Press of Wales.

Hubbard, T.K. (1997). Utopianism and the sophistic city in Aristophanes. In: *The City as Comedy: Society and Representation in Athenian Drama* (ed. G.W. Dobrov), 23–50. Chapel Hill: University of North Carolina Press.

Konstan, D. (1997). The Greek polis and its negations: versions of utopia in Aristophanes' *Birds*. In: *The City as Comedy: Society and Representation in Athenian Drama* (ed. G.W. Dobrov), 3–22. Chapel Hill: University of North Carolina Press.

Lewis, D.M. (1955). Notes on Attic inscriptions (II), XXIII: who was Lysistrata? *ABSA* 1: 1–13.

McClure, L. (1999). *Spoken Like a Woman: Speech and Gender in Athenian Drama*. Princeton: Princeton University Press.

Moodie, E.K. (2012). Aristophanes, the *Assemblywomen* and the audience: the politics of rapport. *CJ* 107 (3): 257–281.

Moore, T. (1998). *The Theater of Plautus: Playing to the Audience*. Austin: University of Texas Press.

Nightingale, A.W. (1995). *Genres in Dialogue: Plato and the Construct of Philosophy*. Cambridge: Cambridge University Press.

Ober, J. (1998). *Political Dissent in Democratic Athens: Intellectual Critics of Popular Rule*. Princeton: Princeton University Press.

Olson, S.D. (1988). The 'love duet' in Aristophanes' *Ecclesiazusae*. *CQ* 38: 328–330.

Papathanasopoulou, N. (2020). Strong household, strong city: space and politics in Aristophanes' *Acharnians*. In: *Aristophanes and Politics: New Studies* (ed. R.M. Rosen and H.P. Foley), 163–186. Leiden: Brill.

Revermann, M. (2006). *Comic Business: Theatricality, Dramatic Technique, and Performance Contexts of Aristophanic Comedy*. Oxford.

Rhodes, P.J. (2004). Aristophanes and the Athenian Assembly. In: *Law, Rhetoric, and Comedy in Classical Athens: Essays in Honour of Douglas M. MacDowell* (ed. D.L. Cairns and R.A. Knox), 223–237. Swansea: Classical Press of Wales.

Rothwell, K.S. (1990). *Politics and Persuasion in Aristophanes' Ecclesiazusae*. Leiden: Brill.

Ruffell, I.A. (2006). A little ironic, don't you think? Utopian criticism and the problem of Aristophanes' late plays. In: *Playing Around Aristophanes: Essays in Celebration of the Completion of the Edition of the Comedies of Aristophanes by Alan Sommerstein* (ed. L. Kozak and J. Rich), 65–104. Oxford.

Saïd, S. (1987). Travestis et travestissements dans les comédies d'Aristophane. *Cahiers du GITA* 3: 217–248.

Saïd, S. (1996). The *Assemblywomen*: women, economy, and politics. In: *Oxford Readings in Aristophanes* (ed. E. Segal), 282–313. [Original publication "*L'Assemblée des Femmes*: les femmes, l'économie et la politique," in J. Bonnamour and H. Delavault (eds.), *Aristophane, les femmes et la cité*, 33–69. Fontenay-aux-Roses, 1979.] Oxford: Oxford University Press.

Scott, N. (2017). Women and the language of food in the plays of Aristophanes. *Mnemosyne* 70 (4): 666–675.

Shaw, M. (1975). The female intruder: women in fifth-century drama. *CP* 70 (4): 255–266.

Sheppard, A. (2016). Aristophanes' *Ecclesiazusae* and the remaking of the ΠΑΤΡΙΟΣ ΠΟΛΙΤΕΙΑ. *CQ* 66 (2): 463–483.

Slater, N.W. (1989). *Lekythoi* in Aristophanes' *Ecclesiazusae*. *Lexis* 3: 43–51.

Slater, N.W. (2002). *Spectator Politics: Metatheatre and Performance in Aristophanes*. Philadelphia.

Sommerstein, A.H. (1984). Aristophanes and the demon poverty. *CQ* 34: 314–333.

Sommerstein, A.H. (ed. and trans.) (1998). *Aristophanes: Ecclesiazusae*. In: *The Comedies of Aristophanes: vol. 10*. Warminster: Aris & Phillips.

Sommerstein, A.H. (2009). *Talking About Laughter: And Other Studies in Greek Comedy*. Oxford.

Stone, L.M. (1981). *Costume in Aristophanic Comedy*. New York: Arno Press.

Stroup, S.C. (2004). Designing women: *Lysistrata* and the 'hetairization' of the Greek wife. *Arethusa* 37 (1): 37–73.

Taaffe, L.K. (1993). *Aristophanes and Women*. London: Routledge.

Tordoff, R. (2007). Aristophanes' *Assembly Women* and Plato, *Republic* Book 5. In: *Debating the Athenian Cultural Revolution: Art, Literature, Philosophy, and Politics 430–380 BC* (ed. R. Osborne), 242–263. Cambridge: Cambridge University Press.

Tordoff, R. (2017). Memory and the rhetoric of Σωτηρία in Aristophanes' *Assembly Women*. In: *Clio and Thalia: Attic Comedy and Historiography (Histos Suppl. 6)* (ed. E. Baragwanath and E. Foster), 153–210. Newcastle: Histos.

Tsoumpra, N. (2019). Sex can kill: gender inversion and the politics of subversion in Aristophanes' *Ecclesiazusae*. *CQ* 69 (2): 528–544.

Ussher, R.G. (ed.) (1973). *Aristophanes: Eccleziazusae*. Oxford.

Vernant, J.-P. (1983). *Myth and Thought Among the Greeks*. London: Routledge & Kegan Paul.

Willi, A. (2003). *The Languages of Aristophanes: Aspects of Linguistic Variation in Classical Attic Greek*. Cambridge.

Zeitlin, F.I. (1996). *Playing the Other: Gender and Society in Classical Greek Literature*. Chicago: University of Chicago Press. [Ch. 8 original publication in *Representations* 11 (1985) 63-94. Ch. 9 original publication in H. P. Foley (ed.), *Reflections of Women in Antiquity*. London, 1981].

Zeitlin, F.I. (1999). Aristophanes: the performance of utopia in the *Ecclesiazousae*. In: *Performance Culture and Athenian Democracy* (ed. S.D. Goldhill and R.G. Osborne), 167–197. Cambridge: Cambridge University Press.

CHAPTER 17

Wealth: Economic Fantasies

Ralph M. Rosen

Introduction: Aristophanes' "Latest" Play

Sometime in the sixth century BCE the Greek poet Hipponax, who composed short satirical poems in a comic meter known in antiquity as "limping iambics," complained in a surviving four-line fragment (fr. 36W = 44 Dg) that the god Wealth (*Ploutos*) had never come to *his* house to make him rich. It might have been nice, the poet muses, to hear Wealth say "Hipponax, I'm giving you thirty minas of silver and lots of other things as well!" (2–3). Why did Wealth skip out on Hipponax, leaving him poor and miserable but others rich? Hipponax answers his own question by irreverently suggesting that the god Wealth must be "totally blind" (*liēn tuphlos*, 1), a conceit that occurs here for the first time in Greek literature, and which comes to form the premise of Aristophanes' last surviving play, *Wealth* (*Ploutos*). From the simple and common observation that people become rich or poor for no predictable or consistent reason – whether they are good or bad, diligent or lazy – the idea of a blind god of wealth was full of dramatic possibilities in the hands of Aristophanes, who spun it out into a rich fantasy of comic desire and characteristically untethered, scattershot social commentary.

We know from one of the Hypotheses (III) attached to the manuscripts that *Wealth* was produced in 388 BCE, but little more information is provided. The date of production makes it the latest of the surviving plays, and likely one of the last of his career.[1] In many ways, this fact has been a liability in modern assessments of the play since the consciousness of its "lateness" colors so many aspects of critical discussion in a highly prejudicial manner. In terms of its structure, there are some obvious ways in which *Wealth* differs from the fifth-century plays, notably the apparently diminished role of the chorus and lyric passages in general and an *agōn* that does not quite follow the pattern of earlier examples in more familiar Aristophanic plays.[2] It has been difficult for many to resist the temptation to attribute such differences to the play's lateness, imagining, for example, that as Aristophanes aged his creative powers began to flag, or that evolving tastes of an audience, now in a "new century" (from our periodizing perspective) must have put new pressures on the

---

[1] Aristophanes wrote two plays after the *Wealth* of 388, probably produced by his son Araros (see Hypothesis IV of *Wealth* = Henderson 2007, pp. 112–113, testim. ii.) – *Cocalus* (produced in 387) and *Aeolosicon* (not securely datable, but likely shortly after 387).
[2] On the play's formal structure, see Sommerstein (2001, pp. 23–25).

A Companion to Aristophanes, First Edition. Edited by Matthew C. Farmer and Jeremy B. Lefkowitz.
© 2024 John Wiley & Sons, Inc. Published 2024 by John Wiley & Sons, Inc.

poets. A long critical tradition has deemed the play less funny, "poor," belonging "entirely to Middle Comedy," lacking "*brio*" (Norwood 1931, p. 272), showing evidence of Aristophanes' "decline in agility, in sparkle of wit, in theatrical inventiveness" (Sommerstein 1984, p. 314).[3]

While recent scholars have begun to take a more positive and appreciative view of the play (e.g. Hall 2020), its biographical and chronological "lateness" have trailed its reception and obscured its many points of literary interest and comic delight. In this chapter, then, we will try to approach *Wealth* with an awareness, at least, of our own aesthetic prejudices, especially the common assumption that it is somehow "inferior" to Aristophanes' earlier plays. We leave it to individual readers to answer for themselves the many subjective questions that have been traditionally invoked to diminish the play – whether, for example, the play is funny enough, whether its characters are as "vivid" and convincing as the more celebrated figures of earlier plays, whether its moral outlook is too direct and simplistic, or whether the episodes cohere or the plot suffers for not having an active chorus.

After orienting ourselves with a description of the play's plot and dramatic structure, we will focus for the rest of this chapter on notable scenes and some broad themes of *Wealth*, particularly with an eye on how we should analyze and interpret them in the context of a comedy. The themes I refer to would be for the most part transparent to the audience and explicitly flagged by the characters, and when abstracted from the plot raise fundamental questions about human society that would resonate in any historical era. One could even say the play touches on some of the deepest questions of economic and political philosophy – moral questions about wealth that even venture here into theodicy. Why, for example, do the gods always seem to sanction economic inequities? Why are good people allowed to be poor and bad rich? Is poverty a positive or negative force in a justly organized human society? Is Aristophanes taking any kind of stance on Athenian slavery through the important enslaved character Cario? These, and many others, are real and important questions that might well occur in some form to anyone watching *Wealth* as the plot unfolds. But does Aristophanes seem to be doing anything specific or intentional with them? If the questions are philosophical, is the play actually attempting to *answer* any of them? Our discussion of the various substantive issues raised in *Wealth* will intersect, as we shall see, with a set of meta-questions about the very nature of Aristophanic comedy – how, for example, the comic dynamics of the play mediated an audience's reception of the parts that appear to be serious, and how, in the end, both a contemporary Athenian audience and later audiences and readers of any era are encouraged by the text to understand the play.

Literary Background and Plot

The production of *Wealth* in 388 BCE was not the first time Aristophanes had explored the comic potential of the god Wealth. Isolated fragments and comments in the scholia indicate that Aristophanes had produced an earlier play with the title *Wealth* in 408 BCE, but they offer no basis for determining whether the two plays were entirely different, or if the later play was simply a revision of the earlier one.[4] Earlier in the fifth century, possibly around 429 BCE (see Storey 2011, p. 347), Cratinus had produced a play called *Wealth-gods* (*Ploutoi*, the plural form of Ploutos,

---

[3] It is curious that even Sommerstein (2001, p. 23) concedes that "if we possessed only a synopsis of *Wealth* it would probably have been impossible to show convincingly that it was written towards the end of Aristophanes' career," his point being that in terms of basic plot structure, at least, *Wealth* is similar to the earlier plays and shows no particular signs of "decline." For further comments on *Wealth* as a "late play," see Flashar (1967, pp. 154–156) (Engl. tr. = 1996, pp. 314–315) who identifies "irony" as the main hallmark of Aristophanes' late style on display in *Wealth*.
[4] Eight small fragments have come down to us from the earlier *Wealth*, but these offer little information about its content. MacDowell (1995, pp. 324–325) argued for the second *Wealth* as a revision of the first, but see, contra, Sommerstein (2001, pp. 28–33), who makes a case that the later *Wealth* was an entirely new play. See also Pellegrino (2015, p. 266).

identified in the play as a chorus of Titans, an older generation of gods who could bring wealth to mortals; cf. Cratinus fr. 171.11–12 K-A), which, while its plot was different from Aristophanes' *Wealth*, seems to have shared its premise that too many Athenians had been getting rich unjustly.[5] Another of Aristophanes' contemporaries, Archippus, also wrote a play called *Wealth*, produced probably around the same time as Aristophanes' play (Storey 2012, p. 3). The handful of extant fragments tell us little about its plot, but a few (frr. 37–40 K-A) do suggest that it featured a character (or characters) who, like Chremylus in Aristophanes' *Wealth*, complained about human and divine badness, and became unexpectedly rich (Miccolis 2017, p. 224).[6] In the early decades of the fifth century, the Sicilian comic poet Epicharmus also wrote a play called *Hope, or Wealth* (frr. 31–37 K-A; see Olson 2007, pp. 55–58). Again, our scanty fragments tell us little about its details, but the title suggests that its plot involved allegorizing wealth in some fashion (Hertel 1969, pp. 33–34). It is clear, then, that Aristophanes was working with a theme – wealth and the inequities of its distribution – already with a long tradition in earlier Greek comedy, even if some of the particulars of his version would have been regarded as innovative.

It is important to keep this earlier tradition of Greek "wealth-comedies" in mind when thinking about Aristophanes' portrayal of Athenian socioeconomic dynamics in his own *Wealth*, especially if we are tempted to assume, as many have been, that his play was intended to reflect, and perhaps even indict, specific conditions at Athens at the time of its production. Certainly, we cannot entirely rule out that possibility, but we also cannot rule out the possibility that a similar social critique did not also drive the various "wealth-comedies" from the fifth century when economic conditions were different from those of early fourth-century Athens. To put this another way: is there anything so idiosyncratic about the plot of Aristophanes' *Wealth* that could not have worked for Epicharmus' or Cratinus' wealth-plays, for example, or even for Aristophanes' first *Wealth* of 408? Or does any comic plot containing an allegorized Wealth god (blind or not) come already pre-packaged with a general critique of economic disparities that would resonate with virtually any audience at any period? We will have further occasion below to address the question of the play's ideological underpinnings, and indeed broader meta-questions as well about the very nature of "comic meaning" in a play such as *Wealth*.

Before we enter such interpretive terrain, it will be useful to lay out the details of the play's plot and note some of the issues that arise along the way. *Wealth* opens with one of Aristophanes' most fully developed and dramatically central enslaved characters (more on whom below), Cario, who explains the background to the opening scene but registers with the audience his perplexity. His master, Chremylus, in a comic paradox ("doing the opposite of what he ought to do," 14) is shown following a blind man who is soon revealed to be the god Wealth himself. Chremylus explains his frustration that despite his "god-fearing and just" life, he remained "unsuccessful and poor" (28–29), while plenty of obviously bad people became rich (30–31). He decides, therefore, to ask Apollo at Delphi whether he should urge his only son to abandon a life of goodness and become instead a thoroughgoing scoundrel and criminal. The god cryptically told Chremylus to follow the first person he ran into leaving the temple and to take him home with him. That person, as we find out in the opening scene, turned out to be the blind god Wealth. Wealth explains (89–93) that Zeus had blinded him out of resentment for humans and wanted to prevent Wealth from enriching only good and honorable people.

This initial setup allows the plot to unfold in typical Aristophanic fashion – a problem is presented (Wealth is blind, so the bad are as likely to get rich as the good), a solution is proposed and implemented (Chremylus schemes to restore Wealth's sight so he will thenceforth visit only good people), and the consequences are played out in subsequent episodes. The actual scene in which Wealth regains his sight at the temple of Asclepius takes place off-stage (see further below) but is

---

[5] See further Bakola (2010, pp. 122–141), Storey (2011, pp. 346–361), Bianchi (2017, pp. 126–130).

[6] Scholars have speculated about whether Archippus' *Wealth* influenced Aristophanes, or vice versa (as Kaibel 1899, p. 55), but we can say little more in the absence of a secure dating of Archippus' play. For details, see Miccolis (2017, pp. 224–225).

recounted in memorable detail by Cario at 654–747.[7] A series of episodes builds up to this scene after Chremylus takes the blind Wealth home. Cario first tells Chremylus' friends (Chremylus refers to them as his "fellow farmers," *suggeōrgoi*, 223) about his (literal) acquisition of Wealth and the plan to restore his sight, and promises them all their own share of the wealth they deserve. Chremylus's friend Blepsidemus, suspicious at first that Chremylus has become rich unscrupulously, eventually celebrates the plan as well. An important scene follows (415–626) in which the allegorized character Poverty enters and engages in what amounts to an *agōn* with Chremylus over the question of whether society can even function without poverty looming in the background as a motivating force for work and ultimate prosperity. This scene has been understandably central to the question of whether Aristophanes is trying to offer something resembling a coherent economic critique of *Wealth* and whether we can glean from it any meaningful information about the contemporary Athenian economy.[8] Whatever the philosophical merits of Poverty's argument, she *must*, of course, lose this debate, since she is a negative, unwelcome force in human life that has no role to play in a comic world of abundance and mirth.

After Cario recounts to Chremylus' wife how Wealth's sight was restored at the temple of Asclepius (641–770), Chremylus and Wealth return to the house in triumph, with Wealth proclaiming grandiloquently that he can now "show to all humankind that I never willingly gave myself to bad people (*ponēroi*)" (780–781). The remaining episodes imagine, through a series of encounters between Wealth and a succession of characters, the effect that unlimited wealth exclusively for the "good" might have on Athenian society. In this section, too, we face the temptation to affirm a distinct moral position in the play, but there seems nothing especially controversial about a world in which all honest citizens can become wealthy. In fact, as is typical with Aristophanic scenes of this sort where characters are brought on the stage in succession to enact the possible consequences of an abstract idea ("wealth for all good people"), Aristophanes shows far more interest in the comic potential of such interactions than in ideological or even logical consistency. Here, for example, a "just" (or "honest/virtuous" – *dikaios*) man is first to arrive to show his gratitude to Wealth for his enrichment (828–31). He describes himself (825) as "a man who was once miserable, but is now fortunate," and explains that he had exhausted his modest resources helping friends in need, but that they never reciprocated when he needed *them*. On the surface, the "just man" is exactly the kind of character we would expect to embody in a world in which Wealth has become able to distinguish the good from the bad. But in the end Cario quietly ridicules even this supposedly honorable figure as something of a clueless chump, leaving the impression that this "just man" may not be such an appealing paradigm of virtue after all. Cario's banter at the expense of the "just" is the main dramatic focus of this short scene, not a rumination about the man's goodness.

Next comes an informer, emblematic of a "bad" man (described at 862 as a "bad coin") who complains to Wealth about his recent impoverishment. The informer, predictably, declares he is a good and beneficial citizen, describing himself as a "patriot" (*philopolis*, 900) who works "for the good" (*euergetein*, 912) of the city. This detail may hint that if the world really were set up such that wealth only was apportioned to good people, there would always remain the question of how to define goodness or badness. But informers are consistently presented in Aristophanes as irremediably bad people preying on fellow citizens for their own gain, so it hardly seems likely that Aristophanes introduces him here to point out that some people might well suffer unfairly in a new world in which wealth only comes to the good. The scene exposes the Informer as unarguably "bad" in the eyes Wealth, despite his protestations to the contrary, and the audience would be expected to agree that his claims to goodness were all unambiguously false.

The scene that follows has sometimes puzzled modern readers because it also seems to make a muddle of the plot's moral logic. Here, an old woman comes to Chremylus to complain that her young lover has stopped paying her favors. As she explains (775–779), the lover was a good sort,

---

[7] At 649–650 Cario even notes the thoroughness of the account he is about to give: "I will relate everything from top to bottom [lit.: from the feet to the head]."
[8] See, e.g. Konstan and Dillon (1981), Sommerstein (1984), Olson (1989, 1993), and McGlew (1997).

but earlier he had been poor. Now that he has become rich under the new order, however, he no longer needs to ask the old woman for money to buy clothes or food for himself and his family. In fact, she complains, he now wants to cut off all ties with her completely (1023–1024), breaking a promise he made to never leave her (1032). Once again the entire scene is interspersed with banter and sarcasm from Chremylus and the lover, as the old woman herself recognizes (973: "you're mocking me!"). She claims that her lover's behavior shows he was never a very good person to begin with so he should not be rewarded with riches; but since he has now been so rewarded, he should be forced to keep up their former relationship so she can continue to reap the benefits. The lover himself is portrayed here as something of a comic rogue by Chremylus, although Chremylus also admires him in his own roguish way: "The guy was no idiot—he certainly knew how to eat up the savings of a lusty old woman!" (1024). Chremylus half-heartedly points out that the lover should keep up his end of the bargain and not abandon her, but despite this high-minded pretense, he makes the point crudely and for obvious comic effect: "...well, since you saw fit to drink the wine, you just have to drink down the dregs as well!" (1084–1085). There is no real resolution to the moral conundrum – the young lover goes inside the house to dedicate some garlands to Wealth, with the old woman trailing behind him and still hopeful of his attentions, while Chremylus leaves the audience with another comic image: "King Zeus! how tightly that little old lady was sticking to the boy—like a barnacle!" (1095–1096).

Two final episodes run with the gag that humans, once rich, will no longer need to sacrifice to the gods or support their priests. In the first, Cario banters with the god Hermes, who brings threats of punishment from Zeus for cutting off sacrifices to the gods. Cario stands up to him and in a comic theodicy charges the gods with harming humans despite all the various offerings they receive from them (1123). That altercation is quickly defused when Hermes accepts to work as kitchen servant in Cario's household. A priest next appears with the same complaint, namely that he is now hungry because no one needs him to perform sacrifices any more. He offers to give up on Zeus and stay with Chremylus, but any tension this might cause is resolved when Chremlyus points out that Zeus is equivalent to Wealth anyway (1190), so they can now proceed to install him as a guard over the inner chamber of the goddess Athena, which is to say, the Athenian treasury on the Acropolis.

This is not, however, the absolute final image we are left with, for in 1197, Aristophanes brings back the old woman for the sake of one more joke at her expense – a pun that once again mocks her aged physical appearance. When she reappears on the scene, she still wants to know when she will get what she came for from the young man. Chremylus promises her that the young man "will come to you tonight," but this is likely delivered to sound patronizing and unconvincing, and we soon see why she is really brought back. After she agrees to put two pots of offerings on her head for the projected installation of Zeus/Wealth on the Acropolis, Chremylus closes the play by addressing the audience for the sole purpose of showcasing the pun: "Hey, look how these pots are doing the opposite of other pots! || For in other pots a 'wrinkled skin' sits on the top; || but here the pots are on top of a wrinkled skin!" (1204–1206).

The play ends, then, with the audience presumably laughing at a bit of wordplay that belittles the old woman and her claims to a kind of justice. Any of the serious questions raised by the play's fantasy of universal wealth for all (good) people remain in the end irrelevant and even distracting from the entertaining inconsistencies and illogicalities that the absurd premise entails. Neither the old woman nor her young lover are portrayed as especially admirable characters – each exploits the other for their own selfish reasons, and having the lover suddenly become rich offers no particular moral clarity. If anything it merely exposes the disingenuousness of their earlier relationship when the lover was poor. Wealth is here *supposed* to enrich only the "just," but it is difficult to imagine even an Athenian rushing to defend the lover's character.[9] This scene, of course, is relatively quick and

---

[9] Dover's comment on this (1972, p. 204): "He does not sound to us like a Just man, but perhaps to the Athenians his ingratitude to a randy old woman raises no moral issue at all." The fact that the lover's behavior is held up as questionable in the play itself, however, does suggest that his precipitous abandonment of a settled agreement with the old woman was, as we might say, "not okay" in the eyes of the audience.

minor in the course of the plot, but its placement toward the end, and then its gratuitous reprise in the final lines, speaks to the particular comic tone and style that pervades the entire play. Unlike several other more celebrated Aristophanic plays, *Wealth* does not engage even in a very convincing *pretense* of moralizing its central dilemma; its flirtation with anything resembling seriousness dissipates almost as quickly as it appears, as we shall explore more fully in the following section.

Set Pieces and Notable Scenes

Agōn between Poverty and Chremylus (415–609)

As with most other Aristophanic, *Wealth* also features a discrete scene that functions as an *agōn* – a more or less formalized contest between two characters who argue for opposing positions on a specific topic. The *agōn* of *Wealth* is more integrated into the flow of the plot than others and not marked by the structural and metrical features that typify more formal *agōnes*.[10] Nevertheless, this major scene (415–609) functions unmistakably as an *agōn*. A new character, Poverty (allegorized as an old woman) is introduced to argue against Chremylus' plan to restore sight to Wealth. At 467 Poverty herself constructs the scene as a formal debate: "Well then, on this matter I'm willing to make my case to both of you [*Chremylus' friend Blepsidemus is also on stage*] right here on the spot." The structure is forensic, with each side allowed to present a case and penalties agreed upon for the loser. At 487–488, the chorus leader formalizes the opening of the contest in a manner that calls to mind similar exhortations in more expansive *agōnes*, such as we find, for example, in *Clouds* or *Frogs*: "but now you have to say something clever which will defeat her, countering her position in your speeches, and don't expose any weakness." The two opposing positions are stated clearly and formally in the ensuing lines: Chremylus declares that, as a result of Wealth's blindness, too many bad people become rich and too many good people remain poor and hungry; Poverty counters that redistributing wealth equally to all good people will be a social disaster, because no one will want to do any of the work that needs to be done since with all their material needs taken care of, they will have no need to do so.

It would be easy to turn a topic like this into a serious debate about economic policy, social structures, or even human desires and the pursuit of pleasure. Some Aristophanic *agōnes* indeed do present what appear to be tenable if debatable positions (e.g. modes of education in the *agōn* of *Clouds*, or the aesthetic positions ascribed to Euripides and Aeschylus in *Frogs*), even if they invariably dissolve into some kind of comic absurdity or silliness. Here, the case is never allowed to get very serious, because the premise of the entire enterprise is so absurd that it can never be removed from the realm of fantasy. At least in the case of *Assemblywoman* (see Chapter 15), another play that imagines a radical redistribution of wealth (and to which *Wealth* is often compared),[11] its fantasy of shared community property is not actually unthinkable in the real world – no gods or allegorical characters, in other words, are necessary. In *Wealth*, Poverty is the one character who attempts something resembling an argument and views herself as engaged in an actual debate (note at 523, e.g. she explicitly questions Chremylus' "argument," *logos*). The philosophical question of whether a society in which everyone (the *agōn* is not consistent on whether it would be only the "just") is automatically wealthy would end up paralyzed by its own indolence is never taken up by Chremylus, who is predictably unwilling to entertain the idea that poverty could ever be a desirable condition for anyone.

At 550–554, Poverty tries to counter Chremylus bleak portrayal (535–547) of a life lived in poverty by accusing him of conflating the life of a poor man (*penēs*) with that of a beggar (*ptōkhos*).

---

[10] For a brief overview of the Aristophanic *agōn*, see Storey and Allan (2005, pp. 183–184). More detail in Marshall (2014, pp. 133–138), Gelzer (1960).

[11] See Sommerstein (1984, 2001, pp. 20–22).

Beggars, she explains, have nothing; but poor men work hard and are thrifty – *that* is the what she means by poverty, not the caricature of poverty she accuses Chremylus of offering. When Chremylus responds with a sarcastic joke, Poverty's objection is emblematic of perhaps *the* central tension of Aristophanic comedy (if not, indeed, all comedy that thrives on parody, satire, and mockery): "You're trying to mock (*skōptein*) and joke (*kōmōidein*), and have no care for being serious (*spoudazein*)" (557).[12] Twice during the *agōn* Chremylus all but agrees with Poverty's arguments, coming close to taking her seriously, but he is unwilling to make any concessions that might complicate the hedonistic goal of restoring Wealth's sight. After Poverty notes (567–570), for example, that impoverished politicians are honest but rich ones corrupt, Chremlyus has to admit she is right, but dismisses her with insults nevertheless:

> Well, you're not lying about anything there, though you're still a total witch!
> But do not go crowing about that—you'll weep nonetheless for trying
>   to persuade us on this point, that poverty is better than wealth. (571–573)

After more banter from Chremylus at the expense of Poverty and her arguments, Chremylus has had enough and sends Poverty off stage with an envoi that once again goes far to sum up the Aristophanic comedic agenda: 598–600

> Now scram, and no more grumbling from you, not a word!
> You won't persuade me, even if you...do persuade me!

As Poverty leaves the stage, reciting a tragic line from Euripides' *Telephus* (601) and warning that Chremylus will one day send for her to return (608), Chremylus affirms the simple calculus of the comic world that Aristophanes has placed him in: "It's better for me to be rich, and for you to go straight to hell!" (611–612). These are all fast-paced scenes, fleeting and funny in their self-contradictions, and presumably accompanied by plenty of stage business, but they help us as distant readers to calibrate the play's tone as unwaveringly comic. The humor signals a tone that pervades not only the *agōn* but the entire play, as if to acknowledge that, yes, making everyone (or even just the "just") rich might well be problematic if it were actually to happen, but it is so absurd to imagine that any sane person would ever *choose* to be poor that such a conversation is too emotionally depressing and philosophically arid to actually pursue, especially when one is in the theater to laugh. The plot certainly raises many topics that could be pondered seriously by an audience, but it also never really encourages them to do so – not, in any case, within the parameters of its own run-time.

Wealth at the Temple of Asclepius (633–770)

After the *agōn* and, as some manuscripts indicate, a choral entr'acte (although no actual text of this survives),[13] Chremyus and Cario prepare to take Wealth to the temple of Asclepius where his sight will be restored. The audience quickly understands that the actual visit to the temple took place off-site while the chorus performing, as Cario returns to the stage to congratulate them that they have now suddenly become rich. Chremlyus' wife appears to ask what all the fuss is about (641),

---

[12] The rest of this passage shows her to be a figure analogous to "Stronger Logos" in the *agōn* of *Clouds* (889–1153). Both Poverty and Stronger Logos claim to produce "better men," intellectually and physically. Poverty derides the men who have been brought up in wealth as "gout-ridden, potbellied, thick-legged, and disgustingly fat," while she produces men who are "thin, waspish, and painful to enemies" (559–561). Compare, e.g. Stronger Logos' remarks as *Clouds* 985–999.

[13] See Sommerstein's note (2001, p. 160) *ad loc.* on lines 321/22 for the indications in some manuscripts that choral dances would have appeared at certain junctures in performance.

and this gives Cario the opportunity to recount all the details of Wealth's temple cure. As has often been noted, Cario's narrative appears to parody a messenger speech from Greek tragedy, which is typically deployed to offer dramatic detail of scenes crucial to the plot but difficult to stage for either practical or aesthetic reasons.[14] Unlike a tragic messenger speech, however, Cario's account offers little information essential to the plot beyond the fact of Wealth's restored sight, and exists, as we shall see, mainly as a comic *tour de force*.

As an historical document, the passage is of great significance for the history of Greek medicine, providing as it does our earliest account of incubation at the temple of Asclepius, the process whereby afflicted patients sleep in the sanctuary with the expectation that the god will visit them in their dreams with specific instructions for a cure.[15] Despite the obvious comic purpose of Cario's narration, it is felt to offer a reasonably accurate account of the protocols and rituals of a visit to an Asclepieion. Cario describes a purification bath for Wealth "in the sea,"[16] offering sacrificial cakes on the altar, and lying down to sleep in the sanctuary (654–662). Even the increasingly silly description of what happens after the patients are supposed to be asleep probably reflects historical aspects of temple healing. Inscriptions describing cures of incubants at the temple of Asclepius at Epidaurus suggest that, despite the pretense that the cures were coming from the god himself, priests and their assistants, and even doctors, were on hand to carry out at least some of the god's prescriptions.[17] Cario also describes the application of cures but, doubtless for heightened dramatic effect, he claims he actually sees the god himself, along with his daughters Iaso and Panacea, physically appear to treat the incubating patients.

The entire episode at the temple, and particularly Cario's extended account of Wealth's actual cure, is a model of literary economy that deftly showcases Aristophanes' skill at simultaneously interweaving several of his hallmark comic conceits. After Wealth is put to bed in the sanctuary, which happens quickly at the beginning of the scene, Cario's account then sets the stage for an extended scene that combines farce, gratuitous (i.e. unmotivated by the plot) mockery, self-consciously lowbrow scatological and food jokes, political humor, and religious parody. Cario describes a lively, crowded sequence of events culminating in the description of Wealth's cure, but with cleverly crass sideshows along the way. Bookending Cario's account is the figure of Neocleides, a historical figure also mocked for his eye disease in *Eccleziasusae* (254–255),[18] who, like so many other contemporary figures making fleeting appearances in Aristophanes' plays, is brought into the scene for the sheer fun of ridiculing him and setting up an ironic joke. Both Neocleides and Wealth are brought to the temple because they are blind and are seeking a cure. Cario describes how the god himself applies medicine to their eyes, but in the case of Neocleides, instead of being cured, he gets punished for being a reprobate ("he's blind all right, but when it comes to stealing he's got sharper focus than the sighted!," 665–666). Instead of healing salves, the god applies a concoction of garlic, fig juice, and vinegar that stings his eyes and makes him jump and howl in pain. The god laughs at him, making it clear that he is being punished for his delaying tactics in the Athenian assembly (725).

This little vignette amounts to a kind of punch line to an extended joke about Neocleides' blindness, but between his first appearance at 565 and his perverted "cure" (714–725) Aristophanes has inserted another scene again for the sake of a derisive, and here, deliberately crass, punch line. Cario relates how he wanted to sneak away from his bed to get at a pot of porridge he saw nearby. The pot was sitting near the bed of an old woman, who tried to grab Cario while he was reaching for the pot. By hissing like one of Asclepius' sacred snakes, he frightens her, causing her – for the first

---

[14] On messenger scenes in Greek tragedy, see Bremer (1976) and Barrett (2002, esp. 14–22), with further bibliography.
[15] On Greek healing temples and their medical procedures, see Edelstein and Edelstein (1998), Parker (1996, pp. 175–187), Wickkiser (2008), Nutton (2013, pp. 104–115), Renberg 2017, (vol. 1) pp. 115–326.
[16] On this specific location in Athens, probably in the Piraeus, see Parker (1996, p. 185 n.102) and Renberg (2017, p. 185 n. 167).
[17] On the influence of doctors in Asclepieian healing practices, see Lloyd (1979, pp. 37–49) and Perilli (2006).
[18] On Neocleides, see Ussher (1973, p. 110 on line 254) and Sommerstein (2001, p. 181 on line 665).

punch line – to fart "more stinkily than a weasel" (693). A second punch line immediately follows ("I then did something really funny!" 697): because his stomach had become bloated from the porridge, he let out a huge fart himself (μέγα πάνυ ἀπέπαρδον, 698–699) just as the god approached him. Finally, the narrative interlude reaches its jocular climax – Cario is able to call the god a "shit-eater" (σκατοφάγον, 706). Whether or not some of the audience would have considered this a form of blasphemy is impossible to know, but there is no doubt that the joke relies on the assumption that someone *might* have thought it so.

The actual cure of Wealth occurs in a relatively short section of Cario's narrative, dispatched in a straightforward description at 727–739: the god and Panacea wrap Wealth's head in cloth, he summons his famous snakes, who lick at Wealth's eyelids under the wrappings, and – presto! – Wealth stands up and can see (738). The restoration of Wealth's sight is essential to move along the plot, but Aristophanes is curiously not especially interested in developing the drama of that event, preferring instead to stretch out the comic potential of non-essential, random characters such as Neocleides or the old woman under the blankets. Despite the familiar temptation to look for something deeper in such scenes of Aristophanic satire, we must remain firmly aporetic about whether Aristophanes has anything more in mind here than skillfully crafted and executed comedy. We are entitled to wonder, for example, if his ridicule of Neocleides amounted to a serious political statement, or if his portrayal of Asclepius and the rituals at his temple constituted religious parody or genuine skepticism about the efficacy of temple healing in the real world,[19] but aside from the obvious fact that we cannot access Aristophanes' thinking at the time of composition, in the case of comic literature it is virtually impossible to disentangle an author's goal of eliciting laughter from an audience from content that appears to be serious. This means that even in cases where an author may *appear* to deploy a joke in order to say something serious (e.g. "Neocleides really does *deserve* a public shaming for his behavior"), the primary goal of making even feigned serious content work as comedy will always complicate, if not entirely compromise, an audience's final reception of that joke.

The Cyclops Song (Parodos, 290–321)

Another set piece that raises interesting interpretive questions is the lyric section of the play's parodos (257–321), the scene where the chorus makes its first formal entrance. As noted earlier, the role of the chorus in *Wealth*, at least as a force in advancing the plot, is greatly diminished in comparison to the earlier plays,[20] and the parodos here is more a bantering exchange between the chorus and Cario than anything resembling an entrance processional. The chorus of *Wealth* is made up of "weak old men" (as they describe themselves, 258), poor farmers who make a perfect test case for the social good that a new system of wealth distribution could bring. They are called to the stage by Cario ostensibly to assist in the process of restoring Wealth's sight and they are a visual presence on stage throughout the play, but they have no significant speaking role after the brief parodos and only a handful of interjectory lines here and there outside of that scene (e.g. 486, the chorus leader introducing the *agōn*, or the final lines of the play where they announce their exit procession).

---

[19] It is worth remembering that the cult in Athens was relatively new at Athens at the time of the production of *Wealth*. Archeological evidence suggests that it was introduced to Athens as a private endeavor by an individual citizen named Telemachus in 420, and an Athenian location for his cult may have still been felt to be something of a novelty. See Beschi (1967/8), Clinton (1994, pp. 21–25), Parker (1996, pp. 177–180), and Renberg (2017, p. 187).

[20] On the diminishing importance of the chorus in late Aristophanes and fourth-century Attic comedy, see Sommerstein (2001, pp. 23–24). On the specific *lyric* contribution of the chorus, Parker's comment (1997, p. 555) is important: "The role of the chorus in reacting to events with the emotional heightening of lyric is reduced to a single short burst of joy in dochmiacs (637–640). Otherwise, the lyric element has dwindled to a single self-contained comic set piece (290–321), only tenuously connected with the plot."

If we trust the indications in the manuscripts that the chorus performed interludes between acts throughout the play,[21] we can assume that they were an important part of the whole spectacle, but their small role in the actual plot makes their appearance in the parodos all the more curious. After Cario reveals to the chorus that Chremylus has the god Wealth hidden in his house and he plans to make them all wealthy, the chorus leader responds in his elation by announcing a song and dance of joy (288–289). The song (290–315) is structured as two strophes with corresponding antistrophes plus a coda (316–321) in lyric iambic meters.[22] The theme of the song to which they dance, however, is so unmotivated by anything in the plot that one is not unjustified to wonder why it is even there.[23] At 290, Cario (note, not the chorus leader) chooses the theme of the song and says he will "lead them" in a performance in which he will play the role of Polyphemus, the Cyclops famous from Homer's *Odyssey* 9, and the chorus the role of Odysseus and his men as they plan to blind Polyphemus with a burning pole:

Cario:
Right, so I will want—dum-diddy-dum—to play the role (*mimoumenos*) of Cyclops
and lead you in a dance, leaping with both feet this way.... (290–291)

Chorus:
And we then will try, as we bleat— dum-diddy-dum—to catch hold of Cyclops
—that's you there!—while he's hungry... (296–297)

The second strophic grouping switches abruptly to another Homeric scene, with Cario impersonating Circe ("now I will be Circe, who mixes up potions," 302) and the chorus playing Odysseus ("And playing the role [*mimoumenoi*] of Laertes' son...we'll grab you...and hang you up by the balls," 309–312). Two aspects of this scene which we lack – the music and dance – would have presumably made it an entertaining spectacle in performance, but its high-spirited and irreverent lyrics also amalgamate a rich variety of specifically literary elements, emblematic of Aristophanic comic praxis more generally, to which we shall now turn.

The parody of Homer is, of course, obvious here, but according to a scholiastic comment, in the Cyclops strophe Aristophanes was also parodying a poem by Philoxenus of Cythera, a composer of dithyrambs from the late fifth to early fourth century, that is, roughly a contemporary of Aristophanes. Philoxenus' poem also concerned the Homeric Cyclops, Polyphemus, although his poem became celebrated for adding an unrequited love interest for Polyphemus, the nymph Galatea, which Aristophanes does not himself allude to. Philoxenus' *Cyclops* seems to have been performed between c. 406 and 388, when *Wealth* was performed, and Aristophanes' parody of it may have simply been motivated by the fact that it would have been a recent and memorable performance in the audience's minds.[24] Indeed, if the scholiast had not told us of the parody there might be little reason to assume it, especially since Philoxenus' text does not survive to which we could compare it.[25] But the mere fact that such a parody was operative in this episode opens a line of inquiry about what its purpose might have been in the larger context of the play as a whole. By this I do not mean to suggest that the parodos is somehow integral to the plot, or important for furthering a set of coherent, even serious, concerns. In fact, the reverse would seem to be true, and that in itself, as we shall see, has significant consequences for how we interpret other aspects of the play as well.

---

[21] See Sommerstein (2001, pp. 160–161 on lines 321–22), with further bibliography. Particularly helpful is Hamilton (1991), responding to Sommerstein (1984).
[22] For a full metrical analysis, see Parker (1997, pp. 554–561).
[23] As Parker notes (1997, p. 554), "The delight of the chorus at Carion's announcement that they are all to become rich provides the slender excuse for a piece of musical and terpsi-chorean buffoonery."
[24] On Philoxenus' poem, see Hordern (1999, 2004, p. 286), Rosen (2007, pp. 155–159), and Modini (2019, pp. 60–67); on Aristophanes' parody of Philoxenus in *Wealth*, see Kugelmeier (1996, pp. 255–262) and Sommerstein (2001, pp. 156–158). "The Aristophanic parody of the work may well point to a recent performance in Athens, perhaps the first, and it is hard to identify any more significant reason for mentioning the poem" (Hordern 1999, p. 445).
[25] As Sommerstein (2001, p. 158) (on 297) notes, since the details at 295–297 suggest a different narrative than we find in Homer's *Odyssey* 9, perhaps one would have to recall Philoxenus to understand the details.

The parodos in fact turns to play out in its few stanzas not only the specific literary ingredients that characterize Aristophanes' comedy but also what we might call the atmospherics of his comic agenda, including its performative tone and implicit assumptions about the role of laughter across an entire production. The parodos of *Wealth*, in fact, recalls the parodos of *Frogs*, produced 17 years earlier (405), which, while grander and more protracted than that of *Wealth*, also makes a point of calling attention to its comic methods and then enacting them in real time for all to see. The *Frogs* parodos even opens (354–371) with a warning from its chorus of Eleusinian initiates that those who do not understand what goes on in a comedy such as *Frogs* should stay away. The final example in their list of such persons is the public speaker who cannot endure being ridiculed in a comedy (*kōmōidētheis*) and wants to punish the poets by "gnawing away at" their stipends. With that proviso out of the way, and on the assumption that their audience will be sympathetic to their comic approach, the chorus begin their song and dance to honor Dionysus and Demeter, promoting aspects of the rituals associated with their worship, but especially comic mockery. Indeed, mockery, ridicule, and laughter become the main themes of the *Frogs* parodos, as they announce at 373: "the whole chorus can now advance bravely ....lampooning, jesting and insulting (*episkōptōn kai paizōn and khleuazōn*)." In the second antistrophe (389–393), addressing Demeter, the chorus prays that by saying "many funny things (*geloia*) as well as many serious things (*spoudaia*)," and by "jesting and lampooning" (*paisanta kai skōpsanta*) they will have success at her festival. There follows a series of iambic stanza (416–449) in which the chorus rouse themselves to begin mocking various contemporaries known to the audience, for no other apparent reason than that this is just what comic choruses typically "do" ("Hey, you want us to start ridiculing Archedemus?" 416; "...and I hear the son of Cleisthenes is plucking his asshole among the gravestones," 422–423; "and they say that Callias, son of Hippofuck, is doing a sea–battle with cunt, dressed in a lionskin," 428–430).

Returning to the parodos of *Wealth*, we find similar strategies and dynamics at work, where it becomes clear that the scene exists mostly as a vehicle for making rude comic jokes at the expense of various contemporaries. The homeric parodies never get off the ground as an actual enactment of anything homeric; instead, we see Cario (as Cyclops) accusing the chorus (imagined as the Cyclops' herd of goats) of the disreputable—but also funny—act of self-fellatio,[26] and then, claiming to be Circe, who immediately ridicules a contemporary Athenian named Philonides, infamous as a rich and unsavory character.[27] Cario announces he will become Circe the mixer of potions, but not so as to turn Odysseus' men into pigs as in Homer, but rather so as to become *Philonides'* followers. Like pigs, they will all "eat shit cakes" (*memagmenon skōr esthien*, 305) which Cario (as Circe) will make himself. By implication, Philonides too ends up a "shit-eater." Not to be outdone, the chorus responds in the antistrophe (308–315) saying that they will string up Cario by his testicles (dropping, of course, the pretense that they are dealing with a female character Circe!) and smear his nose with excrement. And that image allows them to take a jab at another Athenian, Aristyllus, who was evidently known for being a coprophage.[28]

The main focus of the parodos in *Wealth*, in short, is not only its raucous and derisive jokes against contemporary figures for their perceived transgressions but the joyful mood that the scene is crafted to create. The expression "out of sheer delight" (*hypo philēdias*) appears self-consciously twice in the parodos to characterize how the players in this parodic dance are imagined to be feeling as they engage in their scurrilous activities. In the second strophe, Cario playing Circe describes Philonides' shit-eating companions as grunting in their delight (*hypo philēdias*, 307), while in the antistrophe, the chorus, playing Odysseus and his men, describes their delight at the thought of stringing up Cario/Circe and smearing his face in shit with an echo of the same phrase (*hypo*

---

[26] 295: "...Follow me, with your foreskins pulled back; like goats you'll have breakfast." The scholia explains this as referring to the fact that goats lick their genitals after copulating (Sommerstein 2001, p. 187 *ad loc.*).

[27] Philonides also appears at *Wealth* 179, mentioned as an unattractive man whose wealth allowed keep a prostitute as his mistress.

[28] Aristyllus is also mentioned in Aristophanes *Ecclesiazusae* 647, on which see Sommerstein (1998, p. 195) *ad loc.*

philēdias, 311). The final flourish in which the chorus shifts the focus to the notorious deviant Aristyllus amplifies the atmospheric power of scatology and sexual humor.

There is in fact something rather disarming, almost – to put it in our own terminology – postmodern about the entire parodos, with its programmatic self-consciousness, its parodic pastiche, and its paradoxical claim that it is both enacting a specific scenario with its song and dance and, at the same time, *promising* to enact it at some future time. Note, for example, the future verbs used throughout: "I *will want* to play the Cyclops" (*boulēsomai*, 290), "we *will find* you starving" (*zētēsomai*, 296), "I *will play* the role of Circe" (*mimēsomai*, 306), and "I *will smear* your face with shit" (*minthōsomen*, 313). There may be a simple, practical explanation for the chorus' inability to act out their Homeric parodies. Cario had re-entered the stage at 253 already with the chorus in tow, and there is no break in the action between 287 (when Cario promises them that they will soon become rich) and 288 (when the chorus reacts by exclaiming that they want to dance for joy). Cario takes the cue by initiating the parodies in the lyric section to follow, but neither he nor the chorus has time to change their costumes or gather any props appropriate to the theme they propose. What is more, as if to call attention to the fact that their lyrical interlude was tossed in the play for its sheer entertainment value, after the two strophic sequences Cario calls an abrupt end to the whole parodic conceit in a short coda, 316–321:

> But hold on now, it's time to **abandon your jokes** (*skōmmatōn*)
> and **turn to some other style** (*eidos*).
> For my part, I'll want to evade
> my master and slink off
> to grab some bread and meat,
> and spend the rest of the day working hard at my chewing!

The word *eidos* ("style," "form") indicates Aristophanes' self-awareness of the generic play at work in the parodos, which it identifies as an exercise in a particular comic style marked by *aischrologia* and targeted mockery. Exactly what the instruction to "stop all the joking" and switch to a different "form" means is not entirely clear, and it may simply reflect Aristophanes' way of calling an end to targeted abuse and returning to the plot without further distraction from the unrelated hi-jinks of the parodos. Whatever we are supposed to think Cario has in mind with his dramaturgical intervention here, it highlights Aristophanes' awareness that his comedies rely on highly disparate, even disjointed, comic modes and styles.

Cario and Slavery

Enslaved characters appear in various roles across all of Aristophanes' comedies, with varying degrees of visibility.[29] The most celebrated Aristophanic enslaved character is undoubtedly Xanthias in *Frogs*, whose comic interplay with the god Dionysus is unusually well developed and integrated into the plot, and other prominent slave roles leave the impression that such characters were expected and admired by audiences in contemporary comedy.[30] Whether this is simply because comic playwrights of the period were interested in reflecting the realities of Athenian society – including its sizeable slave population – with some level of verisimilitude, or whether

---

[29] See Tordoff (2013, pp. 1–62) for a detailed overview of slavery in Greek comedy, which includes further bibliography. This essay forms the introduction to the excellent collection of essays on this topic in Akrigg and Tordoff (2013).

[30] Xanthias opens *Wasps* in a prolog (1–135) that offers a crucial, if comic, exposition of Aristophanic poetics. See Olson and Biles (2015, pp. 76–130) for commentary on these lines, with much discussion of the conversation in the prolog between the two slave characters, Xanthias and Sosias. For other conspicuous scenes involving enslaved characters, see Walin (2009) and Olson (2013).

they had more deliberate, intentional reasons for developing slave characters as they did, is impossible to tell.[31]

Recent scholarship on slave roles in Aristophanes has shown little uniformity in their presentation on the stage, although they tend to fall into several basic categories – "good" (honest, obedient, wise) and "bad" (disobedient, greedy, lazy, etc.), with most slave characters taking on qualities from both categories, depending on the comic needs of a given scene. Some plays seem to use the master–slave relationship as a heuristic to think through Athenian politics, as, for example, Olson (2013) has argued for *Knights*, where a notoriously "bad" slave (Paphlagonian, who allegorizes the demagogue Cleon) takes advantage of his weak master, the allegorical figure "Demos." Tordoff (2013, esp. 42, 51) has suggested more generally that Athenian audiences found depictions of slaves amusing because it allowed them to map on to them their own anxieties "about other relations of domination and subordination" – even free people, in other words, sometimes feel inferior to others with more social power, so identifying with the "clever slaves" offered the fantasy of at least a temporary superiority. There were doubtless many reasons why Athenian audiences enjoyed the various representations of master–slave interactions they saw on the comic stage, but one point is clear: there is no evidence that comic poets had any interest in offering an explicit critique of slavery as an institution. Comic slaves were allowed to be insubordinate, roguish, or even on occasion to "speak truth to power," but they never had the last word or the last laugh at the expense of established social hierarchies. Inept or buffoonish masters became great comic sport at the hands of their shrewd slaves, but the endpoint was a critique of masters who behaved this way, not of the ideology of slavery itself.[32]

While we may find little to consider socially radical in Aristophanes' depiction of slaves, however, he took great care in developing them for their full comic potential, especially since they were well positioned, as socially inferior, abject characters, to satirize the pretenses and cluelessness of their masters.[33] In *Wealth*, the slave Cario, as we have already begun to see in our earlier discussion, plays an unusually central role in the plot that anticipates comic slave characters in later Greek and comedy. As Sommerstein (2001, 24) succinctly notes, Cario is "the most prominent slave character in all of Aristophanic comedy, being present for well over half the length of the play [and] speaking about a quarter of its lines."[34] Hall (2020, p. 224) describes him as a "comic dramaturge, a sketch-writer, a comic actor, solo stand-up comedian, performance studies specialist, or a discourse analyst, [who] emerges as by far the most significant—because by far the funniest—character in the play." In so many ways, he embodies the qualities we come to expect in an Aristophanic *ponēros* – the roguish, mischievous character, who presents himself as a selfish creature of his appetites, intelligent and savvy but morally unpredictable.[35] The *ponēros* generates laughter from an audience precisely because he can embody all the hedonistic fantasies and excesses that they could never get away with in real life.[36]

---

[31] See Sommerstein (2009, pp. 136–154) takes up the question of whether or not the slave characters in Aristophanes functioned to validate the superiority of Athenian "free-adult-male-citizen" (138), arguing that "Aristophanic comedy rather consistently negates and subverts" the class distinctions between free-male and enslaved. Akrigg (2013) adds some necessary nuance to this debate.

[32] More generally, see Tordoff (2013, p. 61): "Antiquity, for all its achievements in other regards, did little to construct a critique of slavery sufficiently powerful to inspire political opposition to the institution on the analogy of the abolitionist movement in Enlightenment Europe." And, as Olson (1989, p. 198) observes for the slave Cario in *Wealth*, "...Cario is never liberated, despite his repeated laments earlier in the play about his servile condition (1–7; 147–148). This is not an ironic reflection on the new world, but a simple consequence of Old Comedy's exclusive orientation toward the concerns and fantasies of the male citizenry, and thus of the need to return this overbearing slave to his proper place."

[33] See Rosen (2007, pp. 243–248) on the abject posturing typical of the satirist, and here easily adopted by an enslaved character.

[34] On Cario, see also Dover (1972, p. 205) and Hall (2020).

[35] On Aristophanic *ponēria*, see Whitman (1964, pp. 21–58) and Rosen (2014, esp. 225–226). On the semantics and usages of *ponēria* more generally in fifth-century Athens, see Rosenbloom (2002), Rosen (2007, p. 244, n. 1), and Storey (2008, pp. 129–132).

[36] For more on Cario's orchestration of the play's laughter, see Hall (2020).

For all his prominence in *Wealth*, Cario's role as the energetic comic impresario of the play is ultimately traditional and unsurprising. As we have noted, there is no evidence that Aristophanes is particularly interested in confronting the social order with an actual critique of slavery. Nevertheless, if we attend closely to Cario's opening lines, one does suspect an allusion to at least some sort of contemporary discussion about the nature and morality of slavery:

> What a hard job it is—oh Zeus and the other gods—
> to be the slave of a master who's lost his mind!
> For if the servant happens to give the best advice,
> but his owner decides not to act on it,
> then the servant has to have a share in the bad things that result;
> For his fate doesn't allow him control over his own body,
> —that belongs to the one who bought him. (1–7)

Aristophanes seems to signal even in the first two lines that he is able to think himself into the mindset of a slave making a legitimate case for the moral badness of slavery. This opening sentence begins *almost* as if it will say just that – "it's *so hard* [*argaleon*] to be a *slave* [*doulos*]. . ." – but suddenly shifts at the end of line 2 to specify that the hardship is actually being the slave of a master who has "lost his mind" (*paraphronountos*). The *paraprosdokian* seems designed for the laugh, to emphasize just *how* bad it is to have to serve a mentally impaired master, when it is bad enough to be *any* kind of slave (as the opening lines start out by saying). While the tone of the passage is light, however, the language includes unusually explicit references to slaves as property (*kektēmenōi*, 4), to masters as buyers (*eōnēmenon*, 7), and to the jarring concept of one human with complete control over another human's *body* (*sōmatos*, 6). Aristophanes complicates Cario's status even more by having him reveal (147–148) that he was in fact formerly a free man (*etheutheros*) and was only forced into slavery because of a "little bit of money." His words here are an aside to the audience, affirming Chremylus' truism (146) that wealth ultimately drives everything in life, and offer no more explanation for how he fell into slavery, but the fact that Aristophanes went out of his way to imagine this slave figure as once having had a life of freedom, suggests some awareness – suppressed though it remains in the rest of the play – that the moral foundation of Athenian slavery may be less natural than was commonly supposed.[37]

Conclusion

It is always challenging to ponder what an Aristophanic play might have meant to its Athenian audience given our lack of direct and reliable information about how they experienced comic theater. There can be no question that *Wealth*, like all Aristophanic plays, frames its plot around a set of issues which, outside of comedy, at least, would be considered serious – the distribution of wealth across society, for example, the persistent injustice of bad people becoming rich and good people stuck in poverty, the fantasy of a "better world" when moral virtue would guarantee limitless wealth, and so on. These would surely have been familiar and much-discussed topics among Athenians, and it is tempting to conclude that Aristophanes considered his *Wealth* to be a substantive intervention in the debates of his day, that his fantasy of restoring the sight of a blind god Wealth reflected some kind of didactic, or at least some kind of serious purpose.[38] The simple truth,

---

[37] Akrigg (2013, p. 123): "At the same time as he personifies many of the tensions and contradictions in the institution of slavery, Karion is, in the end, a reassuring figure for an audience of slave owners. But his very presence reflects an anxiety about real slaves that would have been less prevalent in Athens at the height of the empire."

[38] Sommerstein's reading (1984) is emblematic of this approach, which views *Wealth* (along with *Ecclesiazusae*) as a "simultaneously moral and social comedy" (330), centered on the values of generosity and rectifying the unjust distribution of wealth. In a similar vein is McGlew (1997), who finds in *Wealth* a political intervention even amid all the comic mayhem: "*Wealth*. . .makes its political point despite its inability to propose constructive political solutions...[I]t combats the socially divisive tendencies of poverty by revealing as shared and common the hopes of each Athenian to escape it" (52–53). For a different approach that reads the play as a reflection on comic poetics, see Sfyroeras (1996).

of course, is that we cannot ever really know. But we can say that whatever glimmers of sober and coherent thinking about important issues of the day we might imagine emerge from the play, they existed in constant tension with – and likely always subordinate to – its comic strategies, which operated antithetically to the system and logic of the real world. As we have seen, *Wealth* revels in playing out these tensions for maximum laughter, sometimes with striking self-consciousness, and indeed one might even say that its pretenses of seriousness exist precisely *in order* for them to be subverted. The bricolage comic techniques so familiar from other Aristophanic plays – its eclectic jumble of literary parody, disjointed plotting, subversive slave characters, gratuitous, unmotivated mockery, and obscene jokes – are particularly pronounced in *Wealth*, suggesting that it may be time to abandon the traditional view that the play signals a fundamental shift in plotting and dramatic technique toward later forms of Greek comedy. It may also be time for us to abandon the traditional fixation on *Wealth*'s "lateness" as an explanation for its perceived inferiority in relation to Aristophanes' earlier plays, and indeed as a harbinger of "inferior" forms of comedy to come.

GUIDE TO FURTHER READING

For a translation of the text with extensive notes, see Sommerstein (2001). For interpretations of the play, particularly focusing on the question of an ironic reading, see Flashar (1967), McGlew (1997), and Konstan and Dillon (1981). On the portrayal of enslaved characters in *Wealth* and in comedy broadly, see the various essays in Akrigg and Tordoff (2013), Hall (2020), Olson (1989), and Walin (2009). On economic themes in the play, see Olson (1993), Sfyroeras (1996), and Sommerstein (1984). On Asclepius and religious medicine in Greece, see Clinton (1994), Nutton (2013), Parker (1996), Renberg (2017), and Wickkiser (2008).

REFERENCES

Akrigg, B. (2013). Aristophanes, slaves and history. In: *Slaves and Slavery in Ancient Greek Comic Drama* (ed. B. Akrigg and R. Tordoff), 111–123. Cambridge: Cambridge University Press.
Akrigg, B. and Tordoff, R. (ed.) (2013). *Slaves and Slavery in Ancient Greek Comic Drama*. Cambridge: Cambridge University Press.
Bakola, E. (2010). *Cratinus and the Art of Comedy*. Oxford: Oxford University Press.
Barrett, J. (2002). *Staged Narrative-Poetics and the Messenger in Greek Tragedy*. Berkeley, CA: University of California Press.
Beschi, L. (1967/8). Il monumento di Telemachos, fondatore dell'Asklepieion Ateniese. In: *Annuario della Scuola archeologica di Atene e delle Missioni italiane in Oriente*, 381–436. Athens.
Bianchi, F. (2017). *Kratinos. Einleitung und Testimonia. Fragmenta Comica, 3.1*. Heidelberg: Verlag Antike.
Bremer, J.M. (1976). Why messenger-speeches? In: *Miscellanea Tragica in Honorem J. C. Kamerbeek* (ed. S.L. Radt, J.M. Bremer, and C.J. Ruijgh), 29–48. Amsterdam: A. M. Hakkert.
Clinton, K. (1994). The Epidauria and the arrival of Asclepius in Athens. In: *Ancient Greek Cult Practice from the Epigraphical Evidence: Proceedings of the Second International Seminar on Ancient Greek Cult* (ed. R. Hägg), 17–34. Stockholm: Swedish Institute at Athens.
Dover, K.J. (1972). *Aristophanic Comedy*. London: B. T. Batsford.
Edelstein, E.J. and Edelstein, L. (1945). *Asclepius: Collection and Interpretation of the Testimonies*. Baltimore: Johns Hopkins University Press.
Flashar, H. (1967). Zur Eigenart des aristophanischen Spatwerkes. *Poetica* 1: 154–175. reprinted in H. Newiger (ed.) Aristophanes und die alte Komodie. Darmstadt (1975) 405–34, and translated as "The Originality of Aristophanes' Last Plays" in C. Segal (ed.) Oxford Readings in Aristophanes. Oxford, 314–28.
Gelzer, T. (1960). *Der epirrhematische Agon bei Aristophanes. Untersuchungen zur Struktur der attischen alten Komödie*. Munich: Beck.
Hall, E. (2020). In praise of Cario, the nonpareil comic slave of Aristophanes' *Wealth*. In: *Ancient Greek Comedy (Essays in Honour of Angus M. Bowie)* (ed. A. Fries and D. Kanellakis), 219–237. Berlin: de Gruyter.
Hamilton, R. (1991). Comic acts. *Classical Quarterly* 41: 346–355.

Henderson, J. (2007). *Aristophanes: Fragments*. (Loeb Classical Library). Cambridge, MA: Harvard University Press.
Hertel, O. (1969). *Die Allegorie von Reichtum und Armut*. Nuremberg: H. Carl.
Hordern, J.H. (1999). The Cyclops of Philoxenus. *Classical Quarterly, n.s.* 49: 445–455.
Hordern, J.H. (2004). Cyclopea: Philoxenus, Theocritus, Callimachus, Bion. *Classical Quarterly, n.s.* 54: 285–292.
Kaibel, G. (1899). Zur Attischen Komödie. *Hermes* 24: 35–66.
Konstan, D. and Dillon, M.J. (1981). The ideology of Aristophanes' *Wealth*. *American Journal of Philology* 102: 371–394. revised version in D. Konstan, Greek Comedy and Ideology. New York (1995), 75–90.
Kugelmeier, C. (1996). *Reflexe früher und zeitgenossischer Lyrik in der alten attischen Komödie*. Stuttgart: Teubner.
Lloyd, G.E.R. (1979). *Magic, Reason and Experience: Studies in the Origins and Development of Greek Science*. Cambridge: Cambridge University Press.
MacDowell, D.M. (1995). *Aristophanes and Athens: An Introduction to the Plays*. Oxford: Oxford University Press.
Marshall, C.W. (2014). Dramatic technique and Athenian comedy. In: *The Cambridge Companion to Greek Comedy* (ed. M. Revermann), 131–146. Cambridge: Cambridge University Press.
McGlew, J. (1997). After irony: Aristophanes' *Wealth* and its modern interpreters. *American Journal of Philology* 118: 35–53.
Miccolis, E. (2017). *Archippus: Kommentierung der Fragmente der griechischen Komödie*. Heidelberg: Verlag Antike.
Modini, F. (2019). The Cyclops' revenge Aelius Aristides on Plato, Philoxenus, and new music. *Greek and Roman Musical Studies* 7: 51–69.
Norwood, G. (1931). *Greek Comedy*. London: Methuen and Company Limited.
Nutton, V. (2013). *Ancient Medicine*, 2e. Oxford: Routledge.
Olson, S.D. (1989). Cario and the new world of Aristophanes' *Plutus*. *Transactions of the American Philological Association* 119: 193–199.
Olson, S.D. (1993). Economies and ideology in Aristophanes' *Wealth*. *Harvard Studies in Classical Studies* 93: 223–242.
Olson, S.D. (2007). *Broken Laughter: Select Fragments of Greek Comedy*. Oxford: Oxford University Press.
Olson, S.D. (2013). Slaves and politics in early Aristophanic comedy. In: *Slaves and Slavery in Ancient Greek Comic Drama* (ed. B. Akrigg and R. Tordoff), 63–75. Cambridge: Cambridge University Press.
Olson, S.D. and Biles, Z. (2015). *Aristophanes*. Oxford: Wasps.
Parker, R. (1996). *Athenian Religion*. Oxford: Oxford University Press.
Parker, L.P.E. (1997). *The Songs of Aristophanes*. Oxford: Oxford University Press.
Pellegrino, M. (2015). *Aristofane. Frammenti*. Lecce: Pensa Multimedia.
Perilli, L. (2006). 'Il dio ha evidentemente studiato medicina': Libri di medicina nelle biblioteche antiche: il caso dei santuari di Asclepio. In: *Stranieri e non cittadini nei santuari greci* (ed. A. Naso), 472–510. Florence: Le Monnier.
Renberg, G. (2017). *Where Dreams May Come: Incubation Sanctuaries in the Greco-Roman World*. Leiden: Brill.
Rosen, R.M. (2007). *Making Mockery: The Poetics of Ancient Satire*. New York and Oxford: Oxford University Press.
Rosen, R.M. (2014). The comic hero. In: *The Cambridge Companion to Greek Comedy* (ed. M. Revermann), 131–146. Cambridge: Cambridge University Press.
Rosenbloom, D. (2002). From *Ponêros* to pharmakos: theater, social drama, and revolution in Athens, 428–404 BCE. *Classical Antiquity* 21 (2): 283–346.
Sfyroeras, P. (1996). What wealth has to do with Dionysus: from economy to poetics in Aristophanes' *Plutus*. *Greek, Roman and Byzantione Studies* 36: 231.
Sommerstein, A.H. (1984). Aristophanes and the demon poverty. *Classical Quarterly* 34: 314–333.
Sommerstein, A.H. (1998). *Aristophanes: Ecclesiazusae*. Warminster: Aris & Phillips.
Sommerstein, A.H. (2001). *Aristophanes: Wealth*. Warminster: Aris & Phillips.
Sommerstein, A.H. (2009). *Talking about Laughter: And Other Studies in Greek Comedy*. Oxford: Oxford University Press.
Storey, I.C. and Allan, A. (2005). *A Guide to Ancient Greek Drama*. Malden, MA and Oxford: Blackwell Publishing.
Storey, I.C. (2008). Bad language in Aristophanes. In: *Kakos: Badness and Anti-Value in Classical Antiquity* (ed. I. Sluiter and R.M. Rosen), 119–141. Leiden: Brill.
Storey, I.C. (2011). *The Fragments of Old Comedy*, vol. 1. (Loeb Classical Library). Cambridge, MA: Harvard University Press.

Storey, I.C. (2012). Angling in Archippos: the Webster Lecture 2008-09. *Bulletin of the Institute of Classical Studies* 55: 1–19.

Tordoff, R. (2013). Introduction: slaves and slavery in ancient Greek comedy. In: *Slaves and Slavery in Ancient Greek Comic Drama* (ed. B. Akrigg and R. Tordoff), 1–62. Cambridge: Cambridge University Press.

Ussher, R.G. (1973). *Aristophanes: Ecclesiazusae*. Oxford: Oxford University Press.

Walin, D. (2009). An Aristophanic slave: *Peace* 819-1126. *Classical Quarterly* 59 (1): 30–45.

Whitman, C. (1964). *Aristophanes and the Comic Hero*. Cambridge, MA: Harvard University Press.

Wickkiser, B. (2008). *Asklepios Medicine and the Politics of Healing in Fifth-Century Greece: Between Craft and Cult*. Baltimore: Johns Hopkins University Press.

PART III

The Fragments of Greek Comedy

CHAPTER 18

Aristophanes' Lost Plays

Christian Orth

Introduction

Aristophanes is the only poet of Greek Comedy by whom complete plays have been preserved in medieval tradition. Nevertheless, the 11 extant plays are only about one-fourth of the production of Aristophanes still read (and quoted) by ancient scholars in the libraries of Alexandria and elsewhere. The central question of any study of Aristophanes' fragments is therefore how far the fragmentary plays add something to our knowledge of Aristophanes and modify the overall picture of his production – or, to put it the other way round, how representative the preserved plays are for Aristophanes' complete production.

There are various ways one can deal with this fragmentary material. One approach is to use each fragment exclusively as evidence for the reconstruction of the complete lost play. In this way, what we are really interested in is recovering a lost comedy using both the available evidence for a single play and more in general our knowledge of Aristophanes and Greek Comedy. To reconstruct what is lost from the evidence we have, is one of the central processes not only of the study of fragmentary material but also of all historical scholarship. Such an approach has the advantage to direct the attention away from the – often one-sided – preserved material to a more realistic picture of what may have been there. Even if there is no direct evidence, in order to have an even vague idea of a complete comedy of Aristophanes we are forced to ask questions like: Was there an agon and a parabasis? What was the role of the comic hero and the chorus in the play? How did the plot evolve? Such questions may give us a better idea of how much is lost, but they also may lead to the temptation to fill the gaps with arbitrary speculation.

Another – completely different – way is just to read the fragments as if they were little poems intended to be read in the state in which they are preserved. The concentration on what we actually have allows us to analyze the syntax, content, and allusions to realia and to explore the expressive potential of a fragment without entering into the more speculative questions of the function of the preserved vers(es) in the complete play. And it still allows to use the fragments as historical evidence for what is mentioned in the fragment. Unfortunately, such an approach is often hardly possible and may be even misleading. It is a fact that the fragments were not written as such, but as parts of a whole play, and to ignore this may lead to serious misunderstandings of the content of the fragment itself. And it is often impossible to analyze the incomplete syntax of a fragment without following up on its open ends and trying to get an idea of what may be missing.

A third way, somewhere in the middle between the two extremes mentioned above, seems to be more fruitful. To start not from the complete whole, but from the single pieces of evidence that we

---

A Companion to Aristophanes, First Edition. Edited by Matthew C. Farmer and Jeremy B. Lefkowitz.
© 2024 John Wiley & Sons, Inc. Published 2024 by John Wiley & Sons, Inc.

have, to analyze each of them as fully as possible, but with the awareness that these single pieces belonged to a lost complete play, and to follow up the hints that can be found in the fragments themselves in order to recover as much as possible of their lost context. If one studies the fragments of Aristophanes in such a way, it is, with varying degrees of probability, often possible to recover at least some elements of a lost play and at the same time to open up possibilities which may lead to a better understanding of the single fragments. The result of such a study of a fragmentary play by Aristophanes will be on the one hand a detailed discussion of each fragment with an open eye to the possibilities of its contextualization, and on the other hand a list of elements of the whole play that can still be recovered or plausibly guessed. This is, I believe, the best we can do in such a case.

When working with the fragments, we are constantly confronted with the paradox that we try to go beyond the preserved plays but are also dependent on them for understanding the fragments. It is nevertheless often possible to find in the fragments elements not attested in the complete plays or to show how an element that we know from the complete plays is treated in a different way in a lost one. And even if we fall from time to time into the trap of making the fragmentary plays look more similar to the preserved ones than they actually are, the damage is comparatively smaller than that of the opposite error. In general, it seems to be a good strategy to try to make every single fragment look as unremarkable as possible within the context of the production of Greek Comedy in general and Aristophanes in particular – and then to pay particular attention to the cases where this strategy does not really work well.

Preserved and Lost Plays

A look at the comedy titles alone suggests that the plays that have survived are by no means a representative selection from Aristophanes' complete works. A category that is missing in the preserved plays are, for example, the "mythical" titles such as Δαίδαλος, Δαναΐδες, Κώκαλος, and Πολύιδος (and see also Δράματα ἢ Κένταυρος and Δράματα ἢ Νίοβος). And while parody of Euripides also plays an important role in the extant plays, a direct reference to specific Euripidean tragedies is found only in the titles of lost plays (Αἰολοσίκων and Φοίνισσαι). Religion is another area that seems to be more prominent in the lost plays than in the surviving ones; cf. especially ἀμφιάραος, ἀνάγυρος, and the Ὧραι (perhaps also Λήμνιαι).

From a chronological point of view, too, the idea of Aristophanes' production that can be derived from the complete plays alone is quite fragmentary. The surviving plays are by no means evenly distributed over Aristophanes' career, and larger gaps exist between 421 (*Peace*) and 414 (*Birds*), between 411 (Lysistrata and *Thesmophoriazusae*) and 405 (*Frogs*), and especially between 405 (*Frogs*) and 392 or 391 (*Ecclesiazusae*). The latter gap is particularly regrettable insofar as interesting developments took place during this period, which – according to the conventional tripartite division of the genre – can be interpreted as the transition from Old to Middle Comedy. Also not preserved are the first two (*Daitales* and *Babylonians*) and the last two plays by Aristophanes (*Kokalos* and *Aiolosikon*), which would certainly be of particular interest for an understanding of the development of Aristophanes' style and its position in the history of Greek Comedy.

The Transmission of the Fragments

That we are still able to get at least an approximate idea of Aristophanes' lost plays is due to a highly complex and varied history of indirect transmission. In addition to the large number of individual sources of quotations, there is, on the diachronical axis, an often very complex history of the individual quotations in the indirect tradition. The author from whose work a fragment is known to us is almost never the same as the person who excerpted the fragment (often probably already in Hellenistic times) from a complete manuscript of the play in question. Here, the different (and only partially reconstructable) dependencies in the lexicographic tradition and the processes of progressive epitomization (which are also responsible for the many one-word fragments) must always be taken into account. A comparatively early stage of these processes is reached, for example, with authors such as Athenaeus, Pollux, Harpokration, Phrynichus, the Anti-Atticist, and Erotian, but also in the Scholia on Aristophanes and other authors, and the Lexicon of Photios contains much valuable material from earlier lexicographers such as Aelius Dionysius, Pausanias, Diogenian, and Phrynichus. But even here one is already a few steps away even from a late Alexandrian philologist like Didymus, who was active in the first century BCE, and whose extensive work represented an important transit point for many of the fragments that are still preserved today. One must always keep in mind the respective selection criteria of the sources of the fragments, which can easily lead to a one-sided picture. In Athenaeus, for example, culinary themes in the broadest sense are overrepresented, in Pollux the designations of individual objects, in Harpocration the legal and rhetorical terminology, in the scholia on Aristophanes the mockery of individual persons, in the paroemiographers (and also in the scholia on Plato) proverbs, in Hesychius rare words which were difficult to understand, in the Atticist lexicographers words whose Attic status could be questioned, in Erotian medical vocabulary, and in Hephaestion rare meters. The combination of different sources certainly mitigates the one-sidedness of the tradition – especially if one compares the situation with the fragments of the so-called Middle Comedy, knowledge of which is largely based on Athenaeus – but by no means completely invalidates it. A papyrus with randomly preserved parts of a lost play would certainly give a very different picture here.

It is also worth noting that not all fragmentary plays are equally well represented in the indirect tradition. Here is a ranking of the lost plays by the number of fragments (with translated titles from Henderson 2007): 1. Δαιταλῆς ("Banqueters", 51 frr.); 2. Ταγηνισταί ("Fry-Cooks", 39 frr.); 3. Γηρυτάδης ("Gerytades", 35 frr.); 4. Βαβυλώνιοι ("Babylonians", 34 frr.); 5. Ὁλκάδες ("Merchant Ships", 29 frr.); 6. Γῆρας ("Old Age", 28 frr.); 7. Θεσμοφοριάζουσαι β′ ("Thesmophoriazusae II", 28 frr.); 8. Γεωργοί ("Farmers", 27 frr.); 9. ἀνάγυρος ("Anagyrus", 26 frr.); 10. ἀμφιάραος ("Amphiaraus", 24 frr.); 11. Δαναΐδες ("Danaids", 21 frr.); 12. Ἥρωες ("Heroes", 21 frr.); 13. Λήμνιαι ("Lemnian Women", 20 frr.); 14. Σκηνὰς καταλαμβάνουσαι ("Women Claiming Tent-Sites", 17 frr.); 15. Αἰολοσίκων α′ β′ ("Aeolosicon I/II", 16 frr.); 16. Δαίδαλος ("Daedalus", 14 frr.); 17. Πελαργοί ("Storks", 14 frr.); 18. Τριφάλης ("Triphales", 14 frr.); 19. Νῆσοι ("Islands", 13 frr.; authorship doubted in antiquity); 20. Τελεμησσῆς ("Telemessians", 13 frr.); 21. Κώκαλος ("Cocalus", 13 frr.); 22. Ὧραι ("Seasons", 13 frr.); 23. Δράματα ἢ Κένταυρος ("Dramas or Centaur", 11–17 frr.; the uncertain number for the two Δράματα plays is due to the fact that there are six more fragments in PCG which may belong either to the first or the second Δράματα); 24. Δράματα ἢ Νίοβος ("Dramas or Niobus", 10–16 frr.; authorship doubted in antiquity); 25. Νεφέλαι α′ ("Clouds I", 10 frr.); 26. Προάγων ("Proagon", 10 frr.); 27. Πολύιδος ("Polyidus", 9 frr.); 28. Πλοῦτος α′ ("Wealth I", 8 frr.); 29. Φοίνισσαι ("Phoenician Women", 7 frr.); 30. Εἰρήνη β′ ("Peace II", 5 frr.); 31. Ποίησις ("Poetry", 2 frr.; authorship doubted in antiquity); and 32. Διόνυσος ναυαγός ("Dionysus Shipwrecked", 1 fr.; authorship doubted in antiquity). A general tendency can be observed that the late plays – especially those from the first decades of the fourth century – are cited less frequently than the early ones (the first two plays, *Banqueters* and *Babylonians*, are ranked first and fourth, the last two, *Aeolosicon* and *Cocalus*, fifteenth and nineteenth).

When working on the fragments of Aristophanes from indirect tradition, a close and detailed examination of the indirect tradition is important, not least in order to ultimately free oneself as far as possible from its clutches. A more accurate picture of the extent and the specific character of the falsifications caused by the indirect transmission can be obtained by examining the indirectly transmitted quotations from extant works. This has so far only been done to a limited extent for comedy (as well as for other genres). One can study either the quotations of a specific work, for example, a specific comedy by Aristophanes in different sources (see Dover 2000 on Aristophanes' *Frogs* and Orth forthcoming on Menander's *Dyskolos*), or the Aristophanic quotations from a specific author (see Olson 2015 on Athenaeus, and cf. on Menander in Stobaeus Millis 2020). The first approach has the advantage that it makes it easier to obtain comparative material that actually corresponds to the situation one is confronted with when working on a fragmentary comedy by Aristophanes; the latter allows more precise conclusions to be drawn about a single quoting author (which can then also be transferred to the same author's quotations from other genres). Just as a systematic recording of transmission errors in manuscripts can be used for the work of a textual critic, such an examination of the indirect transmission can also be used for the interpretation of lost works known only from quotations in indirect transmission.

Two Case Studies: *Babylonians* and *Anagyros*

The problems as well as the possibilities in the investigation of the fragmentary comedies of Aristophanes shall be illustrated here by two plays, *Babylonians* and *Anagyros*. I deliberately choose two plays that I myself have studied extensively elsewhere (Orth 2017), for – at least in my experience – a detailed examination of each piece of evidence is indispensable for any serious hypothesis on the content of a lost play. But they are also among the most interesting of Aristophanes' fragmentary plays, for various reasons: They (1) offer new insight into two important areas of Aristophanes' work which we find also in the preserved plays, Athenian politics at the times of the Peloponnesian War and parody of tragedy, especially Euripidean tragedy, they (2) are connected in interesting ways to specific preserved plays, and they (3) present a particularly wide range of different types of evidence, which results in a particularly rich and complex picture.

I will try to limit bibliographical references to a minimum (for more detailed discussion and bibliography cf. my commentary in Orth 2017). The translations of the fragments are taken from Henderson (2007) (with the exception of fr. 75 and 74, which are my own, and modifications in fr. 71, 78, 84, 59, 50, and 46).

The Babylonians

The *Babylonians* have always found much attention. The reason for this is a dispute between Aristophanes and Cleon, who seems to have accused Aristophanes of having spoken badly about the Athenian people in the presence of strangers. We know of this dispute mainly from Aristophanes' own words in the *Acharnians* and from the Scholia on the same play. These testimonia also provide some important clues to the content of the *Babylonians* themselves, which are difficult to assess, however, since Aristophanes' argumentative strategy must always be taken into account for the relevant passages in the *Acharnians*, and in the Scholia it is often difficult to distinguish between reliable information from now lost sources and autoschediastic speculation based on Aristophanes' own words. From *Acharnians* and the associated scholia, the following can be deduced for *Babylonians*: Aristophanes criticized Athenian officials, and perhaps also Cleon (Schol. Ar. Ach. 378), the play was interpreted by Cleon as a denigration of the *polis* and the *demos* (Ar. Ach. 377–82. 502–8), it treated the democracy in the allied cities or the rule of the Athenian people over them (Ar. Ach. 642), and envoys could also have appeared whose speeches were unmasked as insincere (Ar. Ach. 634–6).

While the testimonia here probably shed light on larger thematic complexes of the play but hardly reveal anything about their implementation in detail (and are also greatly overformed or even distorted by the interests of the sources from which they come), the literal fragments give much more precise but extremely selective information about individual moments, whose position in the play remains unclear in most cases. Nonetheless, any attempt to reconstruct *Babylonians* must rely mainly on these literal quotations.

Perhaps the most important is fr. 71 Σαμίων ὁ δῆμός ἐστιν; ὡς πολυγράμματος ("Is the demos the one of the Samians? How many-lettered!"), a verse that, according to the citation context in Phot. σ 150, is spoken by a character who sees "the Babylonians from the mill," while Photios explicitly states that the Babylonians were tattooed. From this, it can be deduced that the Babylonians in the play were tattooed mill slaves. A few other fragments can be assigned to the same thematic complex: Aristophanes called the tattooed forehead of the slaves "Istrian" (fr. 90), and also used the word στίγων for a tattooed slave; to the mill refer fr. 95 ζώντειον ("mill") and maybe also fr. 78 εἰς (or ἔχεις) ἄχυρα καὶ χνοῦν ("into (or: you have) bran and down") and fr. 96 θωμός (a word used, among other things, in the meaning of "heap of cereal grains"). When at Ar. Ach. 507–8 the metics are referred to as ἄχυρα ("husks") of the citizens and the citizens without the metics as περιεπτισμένοι ("with the husk stripped off"), Aristophanes seems deliberately to pick up the mill theme of the Babylonians (cf. Orth [2017] 353. 472).

Another interesting aspect of fr. 71 is that there is mentioned the "people (δῆμος) of the Samians." From this, scholars have repeatedly drawn the conclusion that the Babylonian mill slaves represented the Athenian allies (cf. Ar. Ach. 642). However, the wording of the verse must first be carefully examined before any far-reaching hypothesis is built on it. The association of the mill slaves with the Samian people here is probably no more than a spontaneous conjecture on the part of the speaker (comparable is Ar. Av. 284 Καλλίας ἄρ' οὗτος οὔρνις ἐστίν. ὡς πτερορρυεῖ) ("So this bird is Callias. What a lot of feathers he's lost!" [transl. A. Sommerstein]). Nevertheless, the verse does provide an important clue to such an identity, and it lies particularly in the definite article with δῆμος. For Σαμίων ὁ δῆμός ἐστιν can hardly mean simply "It is the δῆμος of the Samians|" (or, perhaps more likely, as a question: "Is it the δῆμος of the Samians?") but rather: "The δῆμος is that of the Samians" (or rather: "Is the δῆμος that of the Samians?"). The use of the article is more easily understood if the connection between the mill slaves and one or several δῆμοι is already presupposed, and the speaker just speculates about their exact identity. And the fact that he mentions the Samian people – perhaps with an allusion to the Samian alphabet, which had three more letters and, though officially introduced in Athens only in the year 403/2 BCE, was known (and used) there already from the middle of the fifth century on (cf. Threatte 1980, 26–45) – further supports the assumption that the δῆμοι he is thinking of are those of the Athenian allies from the islands.

If the Babylonian mill slaves stand for the Athenian allies, perhaps with a similar double identity as in the case of another famous Aristophanic slave, Paphlagon ~ Cleon in the *Knights*, three details of their portrayal in Aristophanes could be explained well: they are tattooed as fugitive slaves, because they were recaptured after an attempt to escape (the Mytilene revolt of 428–27 BCE). They work in a mill, perhaps alluding to the trade of one of the leading Athenian politicians of the time, Eucrates. And they are Babylonians, because according to Hdt. 3.150–160 the Babylonians attempted a revolt against the Persians, which was then punished as severely as that of Mytilene by the Athenians.

The mill would also be a suitable scenario for a picturesque and perhaps initially enigmatic prolog scene, in which – as often in Aristophanic prologs (see Arnott 1993) – the meaning of the situation was probably only gradually unfolded. In this case, fr. 81 (an iambic tetrameter) ἦ που κατὰ στοίχους κεκράξονταί τι βαρβαριστί ("I suppose by ranks they'll be screeching something in barbaric fashion") could derive from the *parodos* (as a comment by an observer as the chorus enters), but other interpretations are also possible.

Important additional information can be found in fr. 75, which shows that at one point in the play Dionysus reported how Athenian demagogues tried to blackmail him on the way to a trial. The definite article used in the paraphrase in Athenaeus (11494b–e) – ἐπὶ τὴν δίκην ἀπελθόντα ("having left for the trial") – indicates that this process may have played a role in the plot, and from ἀπελθόντα one can perhaps also conclude that, in one moment, Dionysus left the stage in order to take part in this process. One may compare how in *Knights* the sausage seller leaves the stage before the parabasis in order to go to the Council and confront Paphlagon, and after the parabasis returns and reports about his victory. If there was (as I suggested in my commentary) something similar in *Babylonians*, too, fr. 67 could come from such a report of Dionysus after he returned from the process. In any case, fr. 75 shows that Dionysus played a more important role in the action, and it is generally (and plausibly) assumed that he was the comic hero of the play (as he was later also in *Frogs*). The presence of Dionysus in a play in which Babylonian mill slaves appeared and presumably formed the chorus is reminiscent of the typical constellation of satyr plays, in which the satyrs have to do hard work (which is often inappropriate to their abilities and character) under different employers before they are freed in the course of the play and are able to return to their real master Dionysus.

Another element that can still be discerned from the fragments of the *Babylonians* is seafaring (cf. Starkey 2013), and this seems to involve in particular rowing ships, presumably triremes of the Athenian fleet. Attempts to assign the individual fragments to one specific scene of the play are problematic for reasons of both meter and content: Some are in iambic trimeters, others in anapaestic (or dactylic) meter, and some seem to directly comment on the arrival of a ship that is taking place at that moment, while others only speak of ships in general or even metaphorically: fr. 82 εὖ γ' ἐξεκολύμβησ' οὑπιβάτης ὡς ἐξοίσων ἐπίγυον ("the marine made a good dive to bring the stern-cable ashore") is an anapaestic tetrameter and may have come from a scene in which the arrival of a ship is observed, possibly in the *parodos* (this, however, would be inconsistent with a *parodos* in which the mill slaves come out of the mill). In fr. 86 ναῦς ὅταν ἐκ πιτύλων ῥοθιάζῃ σώφρονι κοσμῷ ("when a ship by sweep of oars dashes in sound order"), a hexameter or – if one adds at the beginning something like ⟨ἀλλ' ὥσπερ⟩ (cf. Menecrates fr. 1 ἀλλ' ὥσπερ παῖς ὅταν ἀστραγάλους ἐκκόψας ἀνταποπαίζῃ) – the end of an anapaestic tetrameter, a ship is only spoken of in a general subordinate clause with ὅταν and the subjunctive, and this could well be a political metaphor for an orderly state. fr. 80 ναυλόχιον ἐν τῷ μέσῳ ("anchorage in the middle"), apparently a description of a place where a ship can land, is probably the end of an iambic trimeter, and fr. 87 ἐς τὸν λιμένα (meter uncertain) is a proverb that can have occurred in various contexts. fr. 85 κατάγου ῥοθιάζων ("dash the ship onwards") could be accommodated both in an iambic trimeter and (more easily) at the end of an anapaestic tetrameter (and may then refer to the same arrival of a ship as fr. 82). It seems that ships (both metaphorical and non-metaphorical ones) somehow pervaded various parts of the play – which is hardly surprising in a comedy that explored Athens' relationship to its allies from the islands.

Many other fragments allow us to catch a glimpse of single moments of the play, which, however, can usually no longer be localized more precisely. In these cases, one should not too easily succumb to the temptation of creating links, and one should always pay particular attention to the elements of a fragment that stand in the way of such a link. So at first glance the temptation is great to combine fr. 68 (A.) δεῖ διακοσίων δραχμῶν./(B.) πόθεν οὖν γένοιτ' ἄν; (A.) τὸν κότυλον τοῦτον φέρε ("(A) Two hundred drachmas are needed./(B) So where will they come from?/(A.) Give this cup") directly with the blackmail of Dionysus by demagogues described in fr. 75; but an impartial reading of the fragment might point more to a situation in which two characters are contemplating how to get a needed sum of money, while the presence of a *kotylos* might point to a symposium. A symposium scene seems to be suggested also by fr. 69 πόσους ἔχει στρωτῆρας ἀνδρῶν οὑτοσί ("how many rafters does this banquet-hall have?"), and fr. 70 ὡς εὖ καλυμματίοις τὸν οἶκον ἤρεφεν ("how well he'd planked the roof of the house") is usually interpreted as a praising exclamation from a guest at a symposium who is admiring the beautiful ceiling (cf. Ar. Vesp. 1214–5). However, the imperfect ἤρεφεν ("used to cover with a roof") does not fit this assumption very well, and εὖ is anyway a conjecture of Bergk for the traditional (and not impossible) οὐ. In fr. 72, a group (of soldiers?) is asked to form three lines, and fr. 73 is an exclamation praising the appearance of a group of young men (perhaps soldiers again, or even the chorus after rejuvenation?). The man who in fr. 74 ἀνήρ τις ἡμῖν ἐστιν ἐγκινούμενος ("there is a man who is disturbing us") throws a group which includes the speaker into turmoil, could be a demagogue, and the fragment could then belong in an expository scene. fr. 76 μέσην ἔρειδε πρὸς τὸ σιμόν ("by the middle way push on toward the snub") is probably an order (again to soldiers?) to run up a hill, and in fr. 77 it is said that someone gives a sign to someone else to flee home. The proverb τὴν αὐτοῦ σκιὰν δέδοικεν ("he's afraid of his own shadow") in fr. 79 could refer to any fearful person (including a politician intimidated by demagogues). The anapaestic tetrameters fr. 83 ἢ βοιδαρίων τις ἀπέκτεινε ζεῦγος χολίκων ἐπιθυμῶν ("or someone wanting sausages killed a yoke of beeves") and fr. 84 ἢ δῶρ' αἰτῶν ἀρχὴν πολέμου μετὰ Πεισάνδρου πορίσειεν ("Or else, demanding gifts, should supply the beginning of a war") read like parts of a catalog of kinds of behavior that need to be prohibited or punished (cf. Ar. Ran. 147–51. 354–68 and Thesm. 335–48) and could originate from the anapaestic part of the *parabasis*. To assign both of them to the same catalog becomes, however, more difficult if one considers that in fr. 83 the indicative aorist (ἀπέκτεινε), and in fr. 84 the optative aorist (πορίσειεν) is used. And finally, there are interesting one-word fragments that may be connected with the reproach of favoring the side of the Spartans (fr. 97 λακεδαιμονιάζω "I Lacedaemonize" and fr. 100 ὠτοκάταξιν "broken-eared"), a motive that reappears in *Acharnians*.

The Anagyros

While *Babylonians* presents interesting elements of political satire and probably took some inspiration from satyr play, *Anagyros* seems to be concerned more with domestic life in the country and Euripidean parody. And while *Babylonians* is closely connected to *Acharnians*, *Anagyros* seems not only to be close in time but also to present some interesting similarities to the second version of *Clouds*.

The evidence here is even more diverse than for *Babylonians* and includes (besides the quotations from indirect tradition) a papyrus commentary that refers to the parabasis probably of this play, two versions of an Anagyros legend that help in understanding the title and also allow insights into the possible content of the play, and even a vase painting that may be directly related to this comedy. This evidence can be conveniently divided into elements that provide insight into the plot and those that relate to the parabasis or other similar extra-dramatic elements.

To the latter belong the two Eupolidean verses fr. 58 (ἐκ δὲ τῆς ἐμῆς χλανίδος τρεῖς ἀπληγίδας ποιῶν "from my cloak making three tunics") and fr. 59 (ἀλλὰ πάντας χρὴ παραλοῦσθαι καὶ τοὺς σπόγγους ἐᾶν "but everyone should bathe in the water of others and let the sponges be"). fr. 58 belongs (together with Ar. Nub. 553–4 and Eup. fr. 89) very probably to a debate between Aristophanes and Eupolis, in which the former accused the latter of having taken ideas from his plays (thus emphasizing his own originality). The χλανίς is probably *Knights*, the three ἀπληγίδες perhaps Eupolis' *Chrysoun genos*, *Marikas*, and *Poleis* (Orth 2017, 316–7, following a suggestion by Kyriakidi 2007, 178–84, who, however, identifies the χλανίς not with *Knights* but with Aristophanes' attack against Cleon in general). fr. 59 can be interpreted both as a political statement about rich and poor and as another comment on the lack of originality of Aristophanes' rivals. Both fragments would be placed in the main part of the parabasis on the basis of meter and content (Eupolideans are actually used in the parabasis of the extant second version of *Clouds* instead of the usual anapaestic tetrameters) were it not for important evidence from a papyrus published in 1968 which suggests that the main part of the parabasis of the *Anagyros* was, in all probability, in anapaestic tetrameters. This papyrus contains remains of a commentary on a comedy of Aristophanes and refers in its preserved section to a complete parabasis with the usual parts (main part in anapaestic tetrameters, ode, epirrhema in trochaic tetrameters, antode, antepirrhema in trochaic tetrameters). Due to an overlap of lines 33–5 τήν[ ]/βραγμένην· διαλελυμ[ένην]/εἶτα νεναγμένην πάλι[ν] with fr. 51 τήνδ' ἕωλον ἀναβεβρασμένην "this stale one having been brought to boil again" (ἀναβεβρασμένην and ἀναβεβραγμένην are little more than orthographic variants of the same word, see Orth 2017, 277) and other thematic similarities (cf. lines 6–10 with fr. 59 and lines 19–27 with fr. 62), this comedy can probably be identified with the *Anagyros*. fr. 58 and fr. 59 could then be from a second parabasis, for example, and perhaps the meter was determined not least by the debate with Eupolis (it is not clear why the verse was called Eupolidean – Eupolis certainly did not invent it, but possibly modified it, cf. Parker 1988, 117, and it is well possible that already Aristophanes associated it with Eupolis in particular, who is also one of the poets attacked in the parabasis of *Clouds*). The parabatic elements also provide the most important clues for dating the play to about 418 or 417 BCE (see in detail Orth 2017, 233–6), thus bringing the *Anagyros* into temporal proximity with the second *Clouds*.

Insights into the plot of *Anagyros*, on the other hand, emerge from some other fragments, most of them in the iambic trimeter: Thus, the speaker of fr. 41 is apparently looking (perhaps in vain) for some small coins, which he has hidden as a nest egg under his pillow. And fr. 42–44, which speak of horses (and cf. among the one- and two-word fragments also fr. 61, 64, and 66), suggest a similar passion of a young man for costly horses as in the *Clouds*. In fr. 46, there is talk of threatening weather (with clouds and thunder), and in fr. 48 of carrying small coins in the mouth, and the speaker of fr. 50 tells how someone fell into a ditch. However, the most important single element for interpreting the content of the play is the title ἀνάγυρος. The word designates both a stinking plant after which the Attic demos Anagyrous is named (its inhabitants are mentioned in fr. 54), and the eponymous hero of this demos, who according to a local legend preserved in two versions was responsible for the cruel punishment of an old farmer (we will soon return to this legend).

So far, however, the fragments (with the exception of fr. 54) do not obviously relate to the title, and the single pieces of evidence are not related in an obvious way to each other – but this situation changes when one takes a closer look at a group of thematically related fragments, which are all in anapaestic dimeters, frr. 53, 55, and 57 (and cf. also fr. 56). The female speaker of fr. 53 wishes to hunt (and eat) a cicada with a light stalk; fr. 55 is an order to set a mousetrap in case the person addressed catches nothing else; and fr. 57 speaks of a partridge that was lame yesterday (presumably playing on the word πέρδιξ "partridge" and the name of the lame tavern keeper Perdix, who is also mentioned in Ar. Av. 1292–3). All three fragments could belong to the same dialog – a dialog is indicated not only by the imperative in fr. 55 but also by καὶ μὴν . . . γ' in fr. 57 – in which the possibility of hunting various small animals is discussed, apparently, as fr. 53 shows, in order to eat them.

A key to understanding not only this scene but also *Anagyros* in general is provided by fr. 53 πρὸς θεῶν· ἔραμαι τέττιγα φαγεῖν/καὶ κερκώπην θηρευσαμένη/καλάμῳ λεπτῷ ("O gods, I long to eat cicada/and cricket, catching them myself/with a thin reed"). For this is a parody of some verses from the dialog, also in anapaestic dimeters, between Phaedra and her nurse in Euripides' *Hippolytus* (219–22 πρὸς θεῶν ἔραμαι κυσὶ θωΰξαι/καὶ παρὰ χαίταν ξανθὰν ῥῖψαι/Θεσσαλὸν ὅρπακ', ἐπίλογχον ἔχουσ'/ἐν χειρὶ βέλος "In heavens name, how I want to shout to the hounds and to let fly past my golden hair a javelin of Thessaly, holding in my hand the sharp-tipped lance!" [transl. D. Kovacs]). In the comic version, Phaedra's desire to go hunting, motivated by her love for Hippolytus, is deprived of much of its seriousness both by the choice of much smaller animals and by the fact that the speaker seems to be mainly concerned with eating them. If hunger should be her motive here, this stands in interesting contrast to the Euripidean Phaedra's attempt to starve herself to death.

What makes this parody of a passage of Euripides' *Hippolytus* particularly interesting is the fact that, on a larger scale, the already mentioned legend of the local hero Anagyros presents some striking parallels to the plot of Euripides' play. This legend is about an old peasant from the demos Anagyrous who cut down trees in the nearby grove of Anagyros and was punished for it by the fact that his concubine (παλλακή) fell in love with his son from a previous marriage and, when her advances were unsuccessful, slandered him before his father. As a result, the father mutilates the son and either walls him up or has him taken on a ship to a deserted island. Finally, the farmer and his concubine commit suicide (which in one version is explained by the bad rumors they are confronted with), the farmer hanging himself and the concubine falling into a well.

This reads almost like a variant of the Hippolytus myth transferred into the typical Attic rural everyday environment which is the setting of so many plays of Greek Comedy, and a poet like Aristophanes may have found it tempting to combine this local legend with direct allusions to and parody of Euripides' *Hippolytus*.

A good test for the plausibility of such a hypothesis is the question of whether it is compatible with other fragments of Aristophanes' play as well, or even helps to explain them more convincingly. And this seems to be actually the case here: First of all, the already mentioned fragments dealing with horses fit well into such a hypothesis, since the horses that Hippolytus uses in his chariot hunt, and that are also involved in the accident that leads to his death, are an important element of the plot of Euripides' play. fr. 43 ψῆχ' ἠρέμα/τὸν βουκέφαλον καὶ κοππατίαν ("gently curry/the ox-head and the koppa") can be associated especially with the scene in which Hippolytus returns from the hunt and orders his servants to prepare the meal and "rub down" the horses (Eur. Hipp. 108–112, especially 110–1 καὶ καταψήχειν χρεών/ἵππους), and the rare word ψήκτρα (fr. 66) is also attested in *Hippolytus* (1174 ψήκτραισιν ἵππων ἐκτενίζομεν τρίχας "we were scraping and combing the horses' coats" [transl. D. Kovacs]). fr. 50 (ἐκλιμάκισεν ὥστε εἰς μέσην ἔπεσε τὴν τάφρον "he dodged to the side, so that he fell into the middle of the ditch") could now be referred to an accident like that of Hippolytus, and one could speculate also about a connection of the thunder in fr. 46 (καὶ συννένοφε καὶ χειμέρια βροντᾷ μάλ' εὖ "it's cloudy and thundering in a quite wintry way") with the noise from the earth immediately before the accident, which is compared with thunder in *Hippolytus* (1201–2). And it is also conceivable that fr. 52 πλὴν ἀλεύρου καὶ ῥόας ("except wheat-gruel and pomegranate", a typical diet of a sick person) is related to the illness of

Phaedra – in which case the hunger of the woman in fr. 53 could be explained precisely by her scanty diet for the sick. Whether all these conjectures are correct, we cannot know; what can be said, however, is that these fragments all are well compatible with the assumption that *Hippolytus* was an important tragic model for Aristophanes' *Anagyros*, and that such an assumption offers attractive possibilities for their interpretation. At the same time, some of their details (like the mention of specific types of horses like βουκέφαλος and κοππατίας) still offer a glimpse of how these motives were presented in Aristophanes' play in a specifically comic mode.

But let us return for a moment to the parody of the dialog between Phaedra and the nurse – for here a quite different type of new evidence comes into play, which at the same time may allow us also interesting insights into the reception of *Anagyros*. A red-figure Lucan bell-crater made around or shortly before 400 BCE (Nicholson Museum, NM 2013.2) probably depicts a comic parody of this very Euripidean scene, and after what we have said so far it seems reasonable to assume that this image refers directly to *Anagyros* (for a detailed discussion of this vase, see Green 2014, who already thinks about Aristophanes, and Orth 2020, where I propose the attribution to *Anagyros*, and cf. already Orth 2017, 226). If this hypothesis is correct, then, for the first time, the previously known illustrations of Aristophanic comedies on South Italian vases, the "Würzburg Telephus" with a scene from *Thesmophoriazusae* and the "Berlin Heracles", probably referring to the prolog of *Frogs* (see Csapo 2010, 58–61), are joined by one from a play that has survived only in fragments – and it is perhaps no coincidence that in South Italy Aristophanes' "Euripidean" plays seem to have found particular interest.

One of the most interesting aspects of *Anagyros* that has not yet received full attention are some interesting parallels to the preserved second version of *Clouds* (whether or not some of them were already present in the lost first version of that play is impossible to say): Besides the already mentioned fragments about horses, both plays contain accusations against Eupolis for plagiarism, the speaker of fr. 41 seems to be in just as much need of money as Strepsiades in *Clouds*, and the same song by Terpander as in 595–7 seems to have been alluded to also in fr. 62 (for the complicated problems connected to this fragment cf. Orth 2017, 338–41). And one may even wonder how Aristophanes may have transformed the farmer of the Anagyros legend into a comic hero, and whether this comic hero was quite as unusual (and in the end unsuccessful) as Strepsiades in *Clouds*.

Conclusion

The two plays discussed here are among the best preserved of Aristophanes' fragmentary plays. Certainly, not all the other fragmentary plays offer the same possibilities of recovering at least some elements of their content. Each single case has to be considered in its own right, with an open mind to both the possibilities and limits of the extant evidence – and to the varying degrees of uncertainty that the results necessarily will have. And even if the interpretations presented here are correct – and most probably they are not, at least not in all details – there still remain large gaps that can no longer be filled. An indication of this is already provided by the many fragments, which still cannot be placed more precisely in a context, and even more by what we know about the content and structure of the completely preserved comedies by Aristophanes. A great mystery remains, for example, the agon of the *Babylonians* (if this play had a regular agon), and how in the play the elements concerning seafaring were integrated. And whether in the *Anagyros* the Euripides parody was indeed the central motif of the play must also remain open. It is at least conceivable that Aristophanes chose the Anagyros legend precisely because of its similarity to the plot of *Hippolytus*, and that this invention allowed him to combine the world of tragedy in an attractive (and potentially comic) way with the world of a rural Attic demos of his own time. In this respect, the play can perhaps also be seen as a precursor of a particular type of mythological comedies that was particularly popular from the end of the fifth to the middle of the fourth century BCE.

A plausible speculation is also still possible with regard to the direction of Aristophanes' criticism of the *Babylonians*. A comparison with statements in other comedies (see Orth 2017, 373–4 Anm. 65) makes it seem rather unlikely that Aristophanes simply took the side of the allied cities against the Athenians. It is more likely that he held the view that better treatment of the allies is in the interest of the Athenians themselves, and that individual demagogues like Cleon thus put Athens' success in the war with the Spartans at risk.

Let us now turn back for a moment to the question we asked at the beginning of our discussion: What do the fragmentary plays tell us beyond what we already know from the preserved ones? There may be different answers to this question, but four points seem to be particularly important: First of all, even in the examples chosen above – which are (or seem to be) both quite close in content to other, preserved, plays – we get a much clearer idea of how in Aristophanes' works similar ideas are being taken up several times, and how these ideas are constantly changed and fitted to new contexts. Second, we get further insight into the intergeneric play of comedy with genres like satyr play and tragedy (which seems to go a step beyond what we have in the preserved plays). Third, we may gain interesting comparative material which allows a better understanding of preserved plays like *Acharnians* and *Clouds*, and last but not least, we also come closer to the way a contemporary of Aristophanes may have looked at his production – long before more or less arbitrary processes of selection and canonization led to the corpus of 11 preserved plays that we still can read in their entirety.

GUIDE TO FURTHER READING

An overview of Aristophanes' fragmentary plays is provided by Gil (2010, 69–115) and Halliwell (2015, 235–254). The *Encyclopedia of Greek Comedy* edited by Alan Sommerstein (3 vols., 2019) includes entries on five fragmentary plays (*Daitales*, *Babylonians*, *Clouds I*, *Aiolosikon*, and *Cocalus*) as well as a chronological overview of Aristophanes' career including the fragmentary plays (in the entry on Aristophanes).

The standard (and by far the best) edition of Aristophanes' fragments is Kassel/Austin (1984). For an English translation of Aristophanes' fragments, see Henderson (2007), and for a commentary on all the fragmentary plays (with particular attention to the *realia*) Pellegrino 2015. On a larger scale, full commentaries on all the testimonia and fragments of Aristophanes are being prepared in the series *Fragmenta Comica* (2013–). Eight volumes on Aristophanes have appeared so far: *Aiolosikon – Babylonioi* (vol. 10.3, by Christian Orth, 2017), *Georgoi – Daidalos* (vol. 10.4, by Andreas Bagordo, 2022), *Eirene b' – Lemnia* (vol. 10.6, by Olimpia Imperio, 2023), *Nephelai a – Proagon* (vol. 10.7, by Maria Cristina Torchio, 2021), *Skenas katalambanousai – Horai* (vol. 10.8, by Andreas Bagordo, 2020), and three volumes of *fragmenta incertae fabulae* (vol. 10.9–10.11, by Andreas Bagordo, 2016, 2017, 2018).

There still remains much work to be done on the transmission of comic fragments and on the methodological issues of the interpretation and reconstruction of fragmentary comedy. Interesting reflections on how – and in what way – the preserved plays of Aristophanes may give a one-sided picture of the contemporary comic production may be found in Csapo (2000).

REFERENCES

Arnott, W.G. (1993). Comic openings. In: *Intertextualität in der griechisch-römischen Komödie* (Drama vol. 2) (ed. N.W. Slater and B. Zimmermann), 14–32. Stuttgart: Verlag für Wissenschaft und Forschung.

Bagordo, A. (2016). *Aristophanes fr. 590-674. Übersetzung und Kommentar (Fragmenta Comica 10.9)*. Heidelberg: Verlag Antike.

Bagordo, A. (2017). *Aristophanes fr. 675-820. Übersetzung und Kommentar (Fragmenta Comica 10.10)*. Heidelberg: Verlag Antike.

Bagordo, A. (2018). *Aristophanes fr. 821-976. Übersetzung und Kommentar (Fragmenta Comica 10.11)*. Göttingen: Vandenhoeck & Ruprecht.

Bagordo, A. (2020). *Aristophanes. Skenas katalambanousai – Horai (fr. 487-589). Übersetzung und Kommentar (Fragmenta Comica 10.8)*. Göttingen: Vandenhoeck & Ruprecht.

Bagordo, A. (2022). *Aristophanes. Georgoi - Daidalos (fr. 101–204). Übersetzung und Kommentar (Fragmenta Comica 10.4)*. Göttingen: Vandenhoeck & Ruprecht.

Csapo, E. (2000). From Aristophanes to Menander? Genre transformation in Greek comedy. In: *Matrices of Genre. Authors, Canons, and Society* (ed. M. Depew and D. Obbink), 115–133. Cambridge: Harvard University Press.

Csapo, E. (2010). *Actors and Icons of the Ancient Theater.* Chichester: Wiley.

Dover, K.J. (2000). Foreword: frogments. In: *The Rivals of Aristophanes. Studies in Athenian Old Comedy* (ed. D. Harvey and J. Wilkins), xvii–xx. London: Duckworth and The Classical Press of Wales.

Gil, L. (2010). *De Aristófanes a Menandro.* Madrid: Ediciones Clasicas.

Green, J.R. (2014). Two Phaedras: Euripides and Aristophanes? In: *Ancient Comedy and Reception. Essays in Honor of Jeffrey Henderson* (ed. S.D. Olson), 94–131. Berlin/Boston: Walter de Gruyter.

Halliwell, S. (2015). *Aristophanes. Clouds Women at the Thesmophoria Frogs.* A Verse Translation, with Introductions and Notes. Oxford.

Henderson, J. (2007). *Aristophanes. Fragments.* Edited and translated (Loeb Classical Library). Cambridge, MA and London: Harvard University Press.

Imperio, O. (2023). *Aristofane. Eirene II - Lemniai (fr. 305–391). Traduzione e commento (Fragmenta Comica 10.6).* Göttingen: Vandenhoeck & Ruprecht.

Kassel, R. and Austin, C. (1984). *Poetae Comici Graeci. Vol. III.2 Aristophanes. Testimonia et fragmenta.* Berolini et Novae Eboraci: Walter de Gruyter.

Kyriakidi, N. (2007). *Aristophanes und Eupolis. Zur Geschichte einer dichterischen Rivalität.* Berlin/New York: Walter de Gruyter.

Millis, B.W. (2020). *Fragments of Menander in Stobaeus* (ed. Lamari, Montanari, and Novokhatko), 647–661.

Olson, S.D. (2015). Athenaeus' Aristophanes and the problem of reconstructing lost comedies. In: *Fragmente einer Geschichte der griechischen Komödie – Fragmentary History of Greek Comedy* (ed. S. Chronopoulos and C. Orth), 35–65. Heidelberg: Verlag Antike.

Orth, C. (2017). *Aristophanes. Aiolosikon – Babylonioi (fr. 1-100). Übersetzung und Kommentar (Fragmenta Comica 10.3).* Heidelberg: Verlag Antike.

Orth, C. (2020). Fragmentary Comedy and the Evidence of Vase-Painting: Euripidean Parody in Aristophanes' Anagyros. In: *Fragmentation in Ancient Greek Drama* (eds. A. Lamari, F. Montanari, and A. Novokhatko), 481–500. Berlin/Boston: Walter de Gruyter.

Orth, C. (forthcoming). Die Zitate aus indirekter Überlieferung von Menanders Dyskolos. In: *Fragmente einer fragmentierten* (ed. F. Neuerburg, T. Tsiampokalos, and P. Wozniczka). Welt: Walter de Gruyter.

Parker, L.P.E. (1988). Eupolis the unruly. *PCPhS* 214: 115–122.

Pellegrino, M. (2015). *Aristofane. Frammenti.* Testo, traduzione e commento. Lecce-Brescia: Pensa Multimedia.

Sommerstein, A.H. (ed.) (2019). *The Encyclopedia of Greek Comedy, 3 vols.* Hoboken: Wiley-Blackwell.

Starkey, J. (2013). Soldiers and sailors in Aristophanes' *Babylonians. CQ* 63: 501–510.

Threatte, L. (1980). *The Grammar of Attic Inscriptions. I Phonology.* Berlin/New York: Walter de Gruyter.

Torchio, M.C. (2021). *Aristofane. Nephelai protai – Proagon (fr. 392-486). Traduzione e commento (Fragmenta Comica 10.7).* Göttingen: Vandenhoeck & Ruprecht.

CHAPTER 19

Aristophanes' Predecessors

Serena Perrone

Introduction

Aristophanes' 11 extant plays are only a tiny percentage of some 600 plays that were performed in the main Athenian dramatic festivals during the fifth century BCE and at the beginning of the fourth by at least some 50 comic poets (cf. Mensching 1964).

Many of these poets are hardly more than names for us, and we can try to recover a wider appreciation of what Old Comedy was only through *testimonia* and a multitude of fragments, rarely of more than one verse or even a single word (the point of reference is the monumental edition in eight volumes by Kassel and Austin 1983–2001).

The history of Athenian comedy before Aristophanes is particularly murky. We know very little about the inception of the comic genre and its first phases. Yet when Aristophanes officially started his career in 427 (leaving aside the possible previous "secret" period of apprenticeship, cf. Mastromarco 1979; Halliwell 1980; Rosen 2010, pp. 235–240), comedies had already been performed at the City Dionysia for about 60 years (on 486 BCE as the conventional date of the formal introduction of comedy in the city dramatic competitions, see *infra*), and for a dozen years at the Lenaea as well (whose official institution should have been sometime around 440). These first phases, albeit quite obscure, are undoubtedly important to fully understand what we can now read of Aristophanes's comedy. The previous comic production shaped the genre and the audience's expectations, and started settling the tradition within which Aristophanes's work must be placed, and against which he asserted its individuality, in terms of poetics, themes, and forms.

In recent decades, the study on comedy has definitely tried to overcome as far as possible the Aristophanocentric perspective and become more aware that the extant plays of Aristophanes are not necessarily representative of the whole genre, which indeed shows a great variety, particularly in its first phases. On the other hand, traits that we perceive as typically Aristophanean or innovative in his poetry may well have been not so. In any case, the poetical claims by Aristophanes himself about the novelty of his comedy can be understood only in the light of the comic tradition up to his time. As we will see, he makes implicit or explicit references to his predecessors at various points of his comedies, the most relevant example being in the *Knights*' parabasis.

The Obscure Prehistory of the Genre

The prehistory of the genre, before the formal introduction of comic performances at the City Dionysia in the early fifth century BCE, is really shadowy. Despite the lack of firm evidence on the ancestry of comedy, a multitude of candidates had been theorized (cf. Rusten 2006). Undoubtedly,

A Companion to Aristophanes, First Edition. Edited by Matthew C. Farmer and Jeremy B. Lefkowitz.
© 2024 John Wiley & Sons, Inc. Published 2024 by John Wiley & Sons, Inc.

many diverse performance traditions with comic elements did pre-exist and extended well outside Attica (cf. Csapo and Miller 2007), as we can see both from literary testimonies and archeological sources.

One of the main literary sources is Aristotle's *Poetics* (1448b29–1449b20), in which, however, ignorance is explicitly claimed about the early developments of comedy (who introduced the main innovations such as masks, prolog, number of actors, etc.), due to the fact that the official recognition of comedy was late, much later than tragedy and later than dithyramb (*Poet.* 1449a). Other information is in fact quite vague or inconsistent. Aristotle hints at an ideal derivation of the comic genre on one hand from Homeric poetry, and specifically the burlesque narrative of *Margites* (reputed to be by Homer), and on the other hand from the iambographic tradition of invective. Yet concerning the historical ancestry of comedy Aristotle could only report different opinions: comedy was developed by "those who lead phallic processions" (*phallika*) and from improvisation; a Doric origin of comedy is claimed (*Poet.* 1448a) both by mainland Dorians, in connection with the institution of a democratic regime in Megara, and from Sicilian Dorians, also on the basis of the disputed etymology of the very name of comedy from *kome*, Doric word for "village," rather than from *komos* "revel." As for a possible Sicilian ancestry, according to Aristotle the Syracusan Epicharmus was "much older than Chionides and Magnes" (see *infra*). Such an early chronology of the Sicilian comic poet is difficult to confirm from other evidence (the firmest dates point to the 470s), yet the beginnings of Epicharmus's long career could certainly predate the official comic performance at Athens. Aristotle also holds that the composition of plots (*mythoi*) originally came from Sicily. The actual influence of Epicharmus's comedy on the Athenian tradition has long been a debated issue, but an influence of this authoritative figure in fifth century. Athens is hardly deniable (cf. Cassio 1985; Rodríguez-Noriega Guillén 1996; Kerkhof 2001; Willi 2015).

We can thus summarize the main hypotheses emerging from Aristotle's *Poetics*:

(1) a literary development from (1a) Homeric or (1b) iambic tradition;
(2) an evolution from primitive choral performances attached to rituals, such as those of phallus-bearers or other reveling komasts (cf. the alternative etymology of comedy from *komos*);
(3) a Dorian origin (3a) from Sicilian comedy and specifically from Epicharmus or (3b) from Megarian farce.

Vase illustrations prompt some further evidence which could be in line with the possible evolution from primitive choral performances (2) and from a proto-comedy of the Peloponnesian area (3b). Some Corinthian vases dated late seventh/sixth century BCE depict groups of padded dancers: the reveling komasts have a grotesque costume with prominent belly and buttock and sometimes ithyphallic (2), recalling closely costumes of Old Comedy. Moreover, some 20 vases from sixth/early fifth century BCE display groups of men dressed up as animals (birds, horses mounted by armed men) or riding animals (dolphins), sometimes associated with a piper, an element that suggests a performative context. This iconographic evidence recalls suggestively plays like Aristophanes' *Birds* or *Knights* and has been associated with the theriomorphic choruses typical of many Old Comedy plays, like *Wasps*, *Frogs*, *Storks* by the same Aristophanes, or Crates's *Beasts*, Archippus's *Fishes*, and many others, cf. Sifakis (1971) and Rothwell (2007).

The possible origin of comedy in specific rituals, being Dionysiac processions or others, has been much discussed (at least since Cornford 1914). Worthy of note is that some of these alleged ancestors may also find an echo in Aristophanes's plays. As for rituals suffice to mention here the phallic procession in *Acharnians* 241–279, and the insults against individuals by the chorus of initiates in *Frogs* 416–430, which have been considered a dramatic adaptation of the insults from the bridge against the passers-by during the Eleusinian procession (*gephyrismos*), and thus led to the hypothesis of a possible ritual model for the personal verbal abuse (*onomastì komodein*) typical of Old Comedy and usually associated, rather, with the iambic tradition (Rosen 1988). As for a possible extra-Athenian origin, Aristophanes mentions the "Megarian laugh," criticizing it in the prologue of *Wasps* 54–66, and perhaps exemplifies it already in the scene of the Megarian and his daughters in *Acharnians* 729–835 (Konstantakos 2012; Ornaghi 2016, pp. 248–256). Yet in both cases, it could well be just the ethnic stereotypes of the Megarians as coarse and dull, more than a reference to a proper form of comedy.

Attached to a possible Megarian origin is also the first name that some ancient erudite tradition put forward for a putative father of comedy: SUSARION, the phantomatic figure of comedy inventor, who according to some sources was Megarian (test. 8, 10), according to others Ikarian (test. 1–2). The Parian Marble (264/263 BCE; FGrHist 239 A 39 = test. 1) provides the only chronological datum, mentioning Susarion as inventor when dealing with the institution of a comic chorus in Athens by the deme of Ikaria sometime between 582 and 561 BCE. Yet the lines are far from clear and, if this author did really exist, both the single known fragment (five iambic trimeters of a misogynistic invective) and other ancient sources (test. 11) may point to iambic poetry rather than comedy. On Susarion, see Rusten (2006), Bagordo (2014b), and Ornaghi (2016).

Any of these various primitive comic performances, literary models, or extra-Athenian antecedents could have provided some inspiration for the development of Athenian Comedy, but the sparseness of evidence does not allow any conclusion and each hypothesis of a diachronic evolution has in itself some inconsistencies. Basically, trying to find a single process seems quite pointless.

The First Generation of Comic Poets

The division of the fifth-century comic poets into generations cannot but be a conventional schematism. We rarely have firm chronological data, and the career of some playwrights of the "first generation" may have lasted quite long and overlapped with Aristophanes' generation (cf. following chapter), so that a clear-cut partition would not be viable, but out of convenience we would include under the label "first generation" those playwrights who were already active by the 440s of fifth century BCE.

As the prehistory, also the early history of the genre remains elusive. The substantial lack of documentation for the initial stages of comedy was a fact already in antiquity. Half at least of the production of Old Comedy did not reach the Alexandrian Library, and the loss was total for some of the first comic poets, even important ones like Magnes. Expectedly, the inherent problems of the textual transmission of performative texts, such as the Greek comedies, have been even more complex when dealing with early productions, before the emergence of a writing culture and the diffusion of book trade in Athens. That could have played a role in the obliteration of much of the earliest comic productions already by the Hellenistic age. This primary shortage of information often leads to confusion, incongruent chronology, autoschediastic reconstruction, and ultimately leads to unreliable testimonies.

We can gain at least partial perspective of this production, thanks to three main bodies of evidence:

(1) fragments of single authors, both from direct tradition (papyri) and, more often, from indirect tradition, that is, citations transmitted by later readers and scholars, whose specialized and idiosyncratic interests in the text may cause perspective distortions. The more frequent sources are Athenaeus' *The Learned Banqueters*, a treasure trove of quotations focused on food, drinking and dinner parties; ancient and Byzantine lexicographical or grammatical works, with a chiefly linguistic interest; and paremiographic or gnomologic collections, gathering proverbial expressions and moral sentences, respectively. On the textual transmission of the comic fragments, see Nesselrath (2010).
(2) testimonies provided by literary sources on the history of comedy, such as again Aristotle's *Poetics* chapter 5, as well as the anonymous treatises on Comedy preserved in some Aristophanes manuscripts, and other products of ancient scholarship like the biographical entries in the Byzantine encyclopedic lexicon Suda.
(3) substantial, albeit badly fragmentary, material from institutional records preserved in three series of Athenian inscriptions (third/second century BCE), providing didascalic information

about the City Dionysia and Lenaea festivals from the early fifth century BCE, that is, who competed in them and with which drama (Didascaliae IG II² 2319–2324), who won year-by-year at the City Dionysia (Fasti IG II² 2318), who were the winners and how many times in a list chronologically ordered by the first victory (Victors lists IG II² 2325). These epigraphic sources often play a key role in the reconstruction of the chronology and the production of the dramatic poets. The latest edition is that by Millis and Olson (2012).

Furthermore, as for the prehistory of the genre, the visual evidence from vase paintings has been used on occasion, particularly fourth-century BCE vases from South Italy, inasmuch they could have been inspired by the revival of specific plays and testify for the fortune of some comic motives, yet any identification inevitably rests on a precarious ground.

The nature of this evidence, distortive and often fragmentary, should always be borne in mind.

The canonical date 486 BCE for the official debut of comedy at the Dionysia rests on a dubious testimony of the *Suda* under the entry "CHIONIDES" (χ 318 = test. 1), according to which this Athenian poet was *protagonistes* of Old Comedy (assuming that the term here could be interpreted as "first competition winner") and produced eight years before the Persian Wars. This interpretation is not supported by the epigraphic evidence, and what we can get is only that Chionides was a "protagonist", one of the earliest and a first-rate representative of Old Comedy. Doubts regarding his chronology also arise from the fact that Aristotle (*Poet.* = test. 2) asserts that Epicharm was "much earlier" than him and Magnes. The same *Suda* lists three titles by him: *Heroes*, *Beggars*, and *Persians* or *Assyrians*. We only have eight fragments from *Heroes* and *Beggars*, half of which are cited by Athenaeus (frr. 4–7), three by lexicographical sources (frr. 1–3) and one, more surprisingly, by Vitruvius (fr. 8, but it is a mention rather than a proper fragment). The fragments are too scanty (and sometimes also of doubt authenticity) to get a sense of his comedy. Worthy of note are the variety of stylistic registers and possible metaliterary contents: a musical polemic against the virtually unknown poets Gnesippus and Kleomenes in fr. 4 and perhaps the title *Persians* might suggest a parody of the Aeschylean tragedy, cf. Bagordo (2014a).

Besides Chionides, the names emerging are many. Some of these recurs also in Aristophanes's comedies. In the parabasis of the *Knights*, Aristophanes justifies his hesitation to organize a chorus with the fickle tastes of the audiences and the ill-treatment suffered by his elder colleagues after honorable careers. He then recalls three poets of the old guard: Magnes, Cratinus, and Crates, in that order. The passage has been considered (improperly) a sort of history of comedy, yet the description Aristophanes made of the careers of his predecessors cannot be taken as a neutral informative review, since it is clearly part of a rhetorical construction of self-branding within an agonistic context. Aristophanes shapes his poetics in opposition to former comedy and present rivals. Albeit he asserts these three poets were trite and by then gone and forgotten, their fragments (at least in the cases of Cratinus and Crates, for whom we have more material) seem to tell a different story. In spite of their many limitations, from the fragments, we can have a sense of how much the comic tradition embodied in these authors was far from gone and had in fact a profound influence on Aristophanean production. In other words, fragmentary comedy makes it quite clear that Aristophanes was not a one-off genius, as he often represents himself, but rather a top practitioner within a lively and competitive field, which had for some decades established conventions and traditions.

Magnes

The verses of *Knights* 520–525 form much of the information on MAGNES (=test. 7).

> He knew what happened to Magnes, for one, as soon as the white hairs stole upon him: Magnes who had set up so many trophies of victory over his rivals' choruses, yet though he produced every kind of sound for you, twanging the lyre, flapping wings, speaking Lydian, buzzing like a fig wasp and dyeing himself frog green, he did not stay the course, but in the end, in his old age (never in his youth!), he was driven from the stage in his declining days because he ran short of jokes (transl. Sommerstein 1981 adapted).

According to Aristophanes's rhetorical construction, the late Magnes lost his humor (*skoptein*) after many successes and his production was various and full of sounds and animals (which brings to mind other well-known animal choruses). An ancient note on this passage (*scholia* ad *Knights* 522a) gives a list of titles by Magnes, arguably inferring some of them right away from Aristophanes's description: *Lyre Players* ("twanging the lyre"), *Birds* ("flapping wings"), *Lydians* ("speaking Lydian"), *Fig Wasps* ("buzzing like a gall-fly"), and *Frogs* ("dyeing himself frog-green"). Of these, only *Lydians* is attested independently with a couple of fragments (frr. 3–4). Other titles, known from different sources, are *Dionysus* (according to Athenaeus, in two different versions; frr. 1–2), *Weeding Woman* (fr. 5), and *Pytakides* (fr. 6), for a total of just eight fragments from four comedies.

We also have some epigraphic evidence (test. 4–5). The Victors List records as many as 11 victories at the Dionysia starting from 472 BCE for a poet whose name (short and ending in -s) falls mostly in lacuna (test. 4). "Magnes" is a likely integration here and is supported by an anonymous treatise on comedy (test. 3), which claims that he won precisely 11 times, a number worth the "so many trophies of victory" in Aristophanean verses (and an all-time record as far as we know). The same treatise says that nothing of his production survived anymore (arguably in the Library of Alexandria), and what was indirectly known as his work was under suspicion of inauthenticity. Athenaeus, too, when introducing quotations from Magnes (frr. 1–2), expresses doubts on the attribution.

Cratinus

Already in antiquity Cratinus was considered one of the most representative poets of Old Comedy, not by chance celebrated along with Aristophanes and Eupolis in the Horatian famous exameter *Eupolis atque Cratinus Aristophanesque poetae* (*Sat.* I 4, 1). He has been indeed much cited, and for us he is probably the best-known poet of Old Comedy after Aristophanes: we have 514 fragments from his plays and 29 titles.

With his long and successful career, he bridges the first and second generations of Athenian comic poets. He was active on the Athenian scene from 460/455 to 420 BCE roughly (for the chronology see now Bianchi 2017), gaining the first prize nine times, the first of which probably in 453 BCE and the last in 423 BCE. Thus, the latter Cratinus competed with the early Aristophanes. The rivalry between the two is well testified by mutual mockeries (Bianchi 2017, pp. 272–273; Sonnino 1998). Aristophanes teases his elder rival in *Acharnians*, describing him as shorn and stinky at ll. 848–853, and then imagining him accidentally hit with a fresh turd at ll. 1162–1173 (Cratin. test. 12–13).

In the *Knights*, Cratinus is explicitly cited already at l. 400 (= test. 14): "If I do not hate you (i.e. Paphlagon), may I become a blanket in Cratinus's bed," arguably implying a bed-wetting problem of the elderly rival. In the parabasis, after Magnes and before Crates, 11 lines are dedicated to Cratinus (ll. 526–536 = test. 9).

> Then, our poet remembered Cratinus, who once, gushing with your lavish applause, used to flow through the smooth plains, and uproot oak trees, plane trees, and rivals, sweep them from their places, and bear them downstream. At a party no song could be sung except "Goddess of Bribery, figwood-shod" and "Artificers of dextrous songs": so greatly did he flourish. And now you take no pity on him, though you see him driveling, with his pegs falling out, his tuning gone, and joints gaping; in his old age he wanders about, like Connas "wearing a garland old and sere, and all but dead with thirst," when in honor of his former victories he ought to be drinking in the Prytaneum, and instead of spouting drivel, should be setting sleek-faced in the audience by the side of Dionysus (transl. Sommerstein 1981 adapted).

His former comedy is depicted as vigorous, overwhelming, successful, and authoritative, a glorious past opposed in merciless comparison with a present of decay. No doubt, between the three predecessors evoked, Cratinus is the real target of the parabasis. He was in fact a rival of Aristophanes precisely in that competition, and by bundling him together with two past poets, surely dead or retired by 424, Aristophanes was mocking him as saying his heyday was over and he was clapped out. From the *argumenta* in Aristophanes' manuscripts (prefatory material to each play ultimately deriving information from the institutional records), we know that in 424 Aristophanes's *Knights* would have won over Cratinus's *Satyrs* (test. 7b), as the year before, when at the Lenaea Aristophanes's *Acharnians* won over Cratinus's *Storm-Tossed* (test. 7a), yet Cratinus would have taken his rematch at the Dionysia of the following year (423) winning the first prize with his *Wine-Flask* (*Pytine*) and thus defeating Aristophanes' original *Clouds*, placed only third (test. 7c). So, the two poets were in direct competition in three festivals at least.

Again, in *Peace* (700–703 = test. 10) Aristophanes jokes on the death of his predecessor, making Trigaeus reply to Peace that the sage Cratinus died during the Spartan invasion. This, rather than a reference to a real historic event (the last Spartan invasion before the staging of *Peace* was in 425, but Cratinus was still alive in 423), could be an allusion to the play *Spartans* by Cratinus himself (Mastromarco 2002), so that we have here not a biographical datum about Cratinus's physical death but rather a teasing insinuation about his professional death.

In 405 BCE, when Cratinus was dead and gone for sure, Aristophanes seems to celebrate his former rival in the parodos of the *Frogs*, mentioning him with an epithet of Dionysus in reference to a mystic initiation into the comic poetry: "the Bacchic mysteries of the tongue of the bull-eating Cratinus" (l. 357 = test. 11).

In this intertextual dialog between the two poets, we can have a glimpse also from Cratinus's side. According to our testimonia (an ancient note at *Knights* 400a = test. ii K.-A.), the victorious play *Wine-Flask* was Cratinus' reaction to Aristophanes's depiction of him as an old drunk in the *Knights*. The poet Cratinus himself was the main character of the play. His wife, Comedy, the embodied genre, sues him complaining about his inability to fulfill marital duties due to drunkenness (or Drunkenness embodied). The final was probably a reconciliation of the two. Likely this comedy is not only an isolated response to the caricature of him as an old drunk in the *Knights*, but reasserts elements of a recurrent self-representation of his poetic persona in the name of a genuine Dionysian inspiration, as opposed to new intellectualistic poetics and technicalities (Rosen 2000; Biles 2002; Bakola 2010), famous for the line "by drinking water you'll never produce anything good" (fr. *203, but the attribution to *Wine-Flask* is hypothetical and the fragment could be a paraphrasis rather than the *ipsissima verba* of Cratinus: cf. test. 45).

In an unidentified comedy (fr. 342, perhaps the same *Wine-Flask*?), Cratinus coined the verb *Euripidaristophanizein*, pointing out that Aristophanes, while parodying Euripides, actually imitates the tragic poet in subtleness and intellectualism. The same erudite source transmitting this fragment informs us that Aristophanes reacted in the play *Women Claiming Tent-sites* maintaining that he does use Euripidean "shapely" style, yet to express ideas far less vulgar than his ones (fr. 488).

The actual scope of the influence of Cratinus on Aristophanes is difficult to assess but is hardly questionable. Already the ancients noted cases of imitation, for example, suspecting forgery of Cratinus's scenes by Aristophanes in *Women at the Thesmophoria* (Cratin. fr. 90).

In particular, Cratinus has been traditionally considered the forerunner for Aristophanes in political comedy and harsh comic invective. The political dimension is undoubtedly a key element of his production. Yet we do not have enough evidence on contemporary productions to assert that Cratinus marked a turning point toward a "politicization" of Old Comedy in a sort of linear evolution (as Sifakis 2006, Henderson 2013, and Storey 2014, among many others). Political satire and personal attacks are not the unique ingredients in Cratinus's comedy and are often intertwined with mythological burlesque and metapoetry in "multiple plot strands" (Bakola 2010).

The relative abundance of material makes it possible to observe, better than for any other fragmentary comic poet, a great variety in Cratinus's production, both in terms of forms and themes. The fragments show multiple linguistic inventions and a wide assortment of meters. Already ancient sources remarked on his harsh and abusive style (test. 17, 19, 20, 25, 28, 33, 44), linking his poetry with that of Archilochus (test. 17). A close relationship with the poetical tradition, specifically Homeric epic and Aeschylus's tragedy, was probably part of Cratinus's poetic self-presentation (cf. Bakola 2010). The fragments do not allow for a real appreciation of the structural features, but according to some ancient testimonies, it was with Cratinus that the unorganized comedy of the earliest era became more structured, with the introduction of three actors and the development of coherent plots (test. 19, but cf. *infra* Crates test. 5). Fragments and titles display a broad range of subject matters. A good third of his titles has to do with mythological subjects, as many other plays from the period (cf. Bowie 2010). The best known is *Dionysalexander* (probably to be dated 429 BCE), for which we have not only a dozen verses from indirect tradition (frr. 39–51) but also a near-complete *argumentum*, thanks to a papyrus finding (P.Oxy. 663 = test. i):

> ... judgment, Hermes departs and these say some things to the spectators about (the adoptive sons?), and when Dionysus appears they mock and jeer at him. He, after the arrival of <the goddesses, and the offer> to him of unshakeable dominion by Hera, bravery in war by Athena, and becoming irresistibly attractive by Aphrodite, judges her the winner. After this he sails to Sparta, abducts Helen and returns to Ida. Shortly, he hears that the Achaeans are ravaging the countryside and [looking for] Alexandros. So he immediately hides Helen in a basket and transforms himself into a ram, and awaits developments. Alexandros arrives, and detects them both, and orders (the chorus) to take them to the ships so he can surrender them to the Achaeans. But since Helen is afraid, he takes pity on her and holds her back as his intended wife, but Dionysus he dispatches for surrender. The satyrs follow along, crying appeals and vowing not to give him up. In the play, Pericles is satirized very felicitously by innuendo as having brought the war upon the Athenians. (transl. Bakola 2010 adapted)

The play was a parody of a story of the Trojan saga, the Judgement of Paris (Alexander), with comic variations, such as the substitution of Dionysus for Paris. As the end of the summary explicitly reveals, the mythological burlesque incorporated political references, not to be intended as a consistent and systematic political allegory, but rather as indirect hints (*emphasis* is the technical term used in the *argumentum*) to contemporary situations, and specifically Pericles's responsibility for the war (the Archidamian War), and perhaps also the affair of the requested exemption of his son by Aspasia from his own citizenship law. The presence of the satyrs (as chorus probably) along with Dionysus speaks for a close relationship with satyr play, a non-isolated example of Cratinus's experimental engagement with other dramatic genres and other poetical traditions (see Bakola 2010).

Among the other mythological comedies are the *Odysseuses*, one of the many dramas inspired by the episode of the misadventure of Odysseus and his mate with the cyclops Polyphemus narrated in *Odyssey* IX, an epic model closely resembled in most of the 15 known fragments, even in lexical and metrical terms. The play possibly opened with a *parodos*, staging the hero and the chorus of his companions navigating the storm through the orchestra on board a spectacular stage boat (fr. 143). Another special theatrical effect, a giant stage egg, was in *Nemesis*, a comic adaptation of the myth of the union between Nemesis and Zeus in the form of a swan, and the subsequent birth of Helen from the egg hatched by Leda. In this mythological comedy too, as in the *Dionysalexander*, there were personal attacks on contemporary figures, and mockery of Pericles behind the figure of Zeus (fr. 118). The politics of Pericles is clearly a satirical target in *Cheirons* as well, and probably also in *Gods of Wealth* (429 BCE?), both criticizing the present decay in contrast with the good old days. *Gods of Wealth* deals with the theme of the fair wealth and envisages a utopic return to the golden age, after overthrowing the present tyranny of Zeus, back to the goodies of the time of Kronos (fr. 176) and the land of plenty (fr. 172).

Another key element of Cratinus's plays is indeed metapoetry. Besides the successful *Wine-Flask*, worth mentioning is *Archilochuses*, which stages (well before Aristophanes's *Frogs*) a poetic confrontation between two chief models of Cratinus, Homer (possibly associated with Hesiod) and Archilochus, with the respective supporters (two semi-choruses), awarding the final victory to the iambic poet. Here too, the fragments preserve references to contemporary personalities (frr. 1, 12, 14).

Men Who See Everything (*Panoptai*) seems to provide an example of "intellectual play," parodying contemporary philosophical trends and attacking the natural philosopher Hippon sometime before Aristophanes' *Clouds*, which apparently resumed a characterization from this play (fr. 167; cf. Carey 2000, pp. 426–427).

Crates

Crates' third position after Cratinus in the parabasis of the *Knights* is congruent with their relative chronology. They were nearly contemporary, but Crates seems to have started his career slightly after Cratinus (test. 2a). According to a marginal note in the manuscripts of the *Knights*, he was at first an actor for Cratinus, before becoming himself a comic poet (test. 3). His production probably spanned from the mid/late 450s to the early 420s of the fifth century BCE. By 424 (year of the staging of the *Knights*), he was no longer active or even dead, apparently, as Aristophanes speaks of him with verbs in the past tense, like for Magnes and unlike for Cratinus. This chronological priority of Cratinus over Crates finds support also in the Victors List (test. 9), where Crates' three victories at the Dionysia are recorded after those of Cratinus and those of the unknown Diopeithes (if the name restored is correct). His first victory should then have been in 451/450 BCE (cf. test. 7). Magnes, Cratinus, and Crates are cited in the same order also in other erudite sources (test. 2).

Aristophanes describes a career of ups and downs (many downs) and jokes on the recurrent imagery of the comic poet as a cook, depicting Crates's "cuisine" as both frugal and refined (537–540 = test. 6):

> And what rage and buffeting you made Crates endure, who used to send you home with a good lunch provided at small expense, kneading the most exquisite ideas from his so-refined lips! Indeed he alone held his own, sometimes failing, sometimes not. (transl. Sommerstein 1981 adapted)

Aristophanes' verses have been variously interpreted as praise of Crates's elegant comedy (e.g. Hartwig 2012, p. 202; Roux 1976; Neil 1901) or, on the contrary, as sarcastic mockery of his cheap comedy (Bonanno 1972, p. 44). Of course, these verses cannot be taken at face value but are a function of the rhetorical self-presentation of Aristophanes' poetics as the "haute cuisine" of comedy (Ruffell 2002; Biles 2002, 2011).

Crates has been traditionally considered one of the main exponents of a disengaged strand of Old Comedy, far away from the political engagement and satirical invective typical of mainstream comedy such as that of Cratinus, Aristophanes, and others (Bonanno 1972; Sidwell 2000; even the head of an alleged "school" for Norwood 1931). That view stemmed ultimately from a controversial interpretation of ancient testimonies about Crates, in particular Aristotle's *Poetics* (test. 5). According to Aristotle Crates was the first Athenian comic poet who, in the footsteps of the Sicilian comedy, discarded the iambic form and composed organically structured plots and dialogs. Crates is thus credited with a momentous development in the form of comedy, comparable with that of Aeschylus for tragedy. He is the beginner not of a new strand of comedy with generic contents and no invective, as someone interpreted it, but of the comedy itself as an achieved poetic form.

Another primacy held by Crates according to an ancient source (test. 2a) was that of introducing drunk characters on the Athenian comic stage (test. 2a, *Neighbours* test. i Storey).

In spite of the prime role attributed to Crates in antiquity, very few of his production survives: 11 titles (some dubious) and 60 fragments.

Political and social themes and topical issues may have been part of his comedy, as suggested by titles such as *Politicians, Metics, Samians*, and some fragments of controversial interpretation (e.g. fr. 37 naming the Persian general Megabyzos; cf. Perrone 2019, 2020). Several fragments display contents related to metapoetry (e.g. fr. 21 "three-cubits words"; fr. 28 contrasting comedy and tragedy), and unsurprisingly food, sex, and scatologic humor. The style seems to be characterized by linguistic inventiveness, with neologisms and several proverbial expressions, and diversified in stylistic registers, from highly poetic expressions (perhaps with paratragic intent) to prosaic and technical ones. In a couple of fragments, we can discern the use of non-Attic dialects (Ionic in fr. 1 concerning a lustful banquet of youths; Doric for the character of a doctor in fr. 46).

The more extensive fragments come from one of his latest plays, *Beasts*, and describe a utopic world where there is no need for slaves because the self-moving tools of the kitchen automatically prepare meals (fr. 16) and warm water spontaneously flows into the bathtub of everyone (fr. 17), perhaps as magic compensations promised to humans for renouncing to eat any animal meat (fr. 19). The play describes a vegetarian regime established by the chorus of Beasts, possibly with some elements of philosophical satire (fr. 19.2 echoes a Pythagorean dietary prescription as formulated in Empedocles fr. 31 B 141 D.-K.). Other comic fragments depicting utopic lands of plenty in the golden age are known from the same source, Athenaeus, who quotes them in chronological order from Cratinus's *Gods of Wealth*, Crates's *Beasts*, then Teleclides, Pherecrates, Nicophon, and Metagenes. For the government established by an animal chorus Crates's comedy could be confronted with Aristophanes' *Birds* and the motif of alive domestic utensils is then exploited also in Aristophanes's *Wasps* 936–966 and *Assemblywomen* 730–745.

Some of Crates's jokes earned enduring fame and are echoed by Aristophanes even after many years. The farting escape of the monster Lamia (fr. 20 from the homonymous play) is cited in *Wasps* 1177 by the gross Philocleon as an example of possible topic of conversation at dinner parties, and an allusion to Crates's Lamia is also in the *Assemblywomen* 77, as a marginal note in Aristophanes' manuscripts explains. Moreover, Crates's famous "ivory salt fish" (*tarichos elephantinon*) in the non-sense accumulation of fr. 32 from *Samians* was evoked by Aristophanes in parabatic verses of the second version of his *Women at the Thesmophoria* (fr. 347):

> what a great feeding comedy was when Crates considered brilliant *ivory salt fish*, effortlessly summoned, and of many other similar things he giggled

Here again with a culinary metaphor, Aristophanes rhetorically claims the complexity of his comedy (and of the tastes of his audience) in contrast with that of the time of Crates, who could easily get laughs with simple puns.

Other Predecessors

Besides the predecessors explicitly mentioned in the extant production of Aristophanes, there were of course several other contenders in the first decades of the comic competitions at the City Dionysia and in the early Lenaea. Some of them probably do not last long enough to compete with Aristophanes. Worth citing are at least:

ECPHANTIDES, who in the Victors list is right before Cratinus with four victories (test. 1), probably the first being in 454 BCE. Two title survives (*Peirai*, *Satyrs*) and only six fragments. Interestingly fr. 3 contains a metatheatrical reference to the Megarian comedy, and fr. 4 is a solemn invocation to Dionysus, cited in Cratinus fr. *361. Cratinus's rivalry against him emerges in other sources as well. Ecphantides was nicknamed "Smoky," possibly as a mockery of his obscure style (test. 5 K.-A. = Cratin. fr. 462), and Cratinus coined the compound *Choirilecphantides*, merging Ecphantides's name with that of the ancient tragic poet Choerilus (test. 7 = Cratin. fr. 502; cf. the aforementioned *Euripidaristophanizein* by the same Cratinus). On Ecphantides, see Bagordo (2014a, pp. 73–98).

CALLIAS, victorious at the City Dionysia in 446 BCE (Fasti = test. 3) and probably another time (Victors List = test. 5). Ancient sources cite him as a rival of Cratinus (test. 1–2). We know 8 titles down to the late 430s BC and 40 meager fragments, which offer a glimpse in a comedy with mythological parody (see titles *Atalantai*, *Cyclops*), animal choruses (the title *Frogs* again), and personal attacks against contemporary political and intellectual figures (persons of Pericles's entourage like Aspasia, the seer Lampon, Socrates, tragic poets including Euripides). Some of these mocked figures in the play *Men in Chains* leave open the hypothesis of a longer career since mid-410s (Storey 2011, p. I 146). On Callias, see Imperio (1998) and Bagordo (2014a, pp. 118–217).

Conclusion

Due to the sparse and flimsy evidence, an assessment of Attic comedy before Aristophanes is really difficult. What is clear is that we cannot simply apply the patterns working with Aristophanes's 11 plays when dealing with the production of his predecessors, and more generally with fragmentary plays. For example, we cannot assume that the formal structure of Aristophanes' extant plays was the one and only possible structure of Old Comedy, unchanging from the production of his predecessor (see Whittaker 1935, cf. e.g. Marsh 2020). Of course, poetic and dramatical features underwent many changes from the inception of the genre, yet not necessarily, nor even likely, in a singular, linear path of development over time.

The first phases of comedy seem to have been an intense experimentation period, with a production of various facets in terms of both forms and contents. An unbiased approach to the evidence clarifies that any clear-cut division of comedy in different strands makes little sense, as the traditional political versus evasion dichotomy, and even less the claim to assign each playwright to one or the other. Political and social issues, abusive attacks *ad personam*, trivial jokes, metaliterary contents, mythological burlesque, intellectual issues, and folk tales may coexist within the production of each author, and even within the single play indeed. Reconstruction of the storylines can only be highly speculative, yet even in this respect what seems to emerge is a variety of multi-layered plots.

We may find many comic elements that have long been received as hallmarks of Aristophanes already present in the fragments of his predecessors. Paratragedy and metapoetry are for sure extensively developed in Cratinus and probably in Crates, perhaps in Magnes too. Intellectual and philosophical plays are among the ones by Cratinus and Crates. Satire against demagogues and intellectuals, metaphors, utopic motifs, sex, and rituals are all ingredients well testified for in the first generation of comic poets, so that we cannot really affirm what is specifically typical or innovative of Aristophanes's genius. Aristophanes of course presents his comedy as new and better than ever (e.g. *Wasps* 1044–1056, *Clouds* 547–559), but these are bold self-promotional claims within the agonal dimension and we must not blindly trust in them.

In this respect, despite the huge gaps in our knowledge, testimonies and fragments of the first phases of Athenian comedy may provide new perspectives on Aristophanes, in his relationship with other authors and the comic tradition, and grant a more nuanced understanding of Old Comedy as a whole.

GUIDE TO FURTHER READING

For other synthetical overviews about the predecessors of Aristophanes, cf. Storey (2010) and Storey (2014). Studies on extra-Aristophanean Old Comedy have now become numerous, and I would suggest at least Heath (1990) and Harvey and Willis (2000). A helpful survey of the evidence on the history of comedy is in Rusten et al. (2011).

The reference edition for the fragments of Aristophanes's predecessors is that by Kassel and Austin (1983–2001). A rich selection of testimonies and fragments of Old Comedy with English translation in Storey (2011). A thematic anthology of comic fragments with comments and English translation is in Olson (2007). Much of the important bibliography is in languages other than English. In-depth commentary for each comic poet is provided within the ongoing multilingual project "Kommentierung der Fragmente der griechischen Komödie" (KomFrag) directed by Zimmermann (with new volumes appearing frequently from 2013). Magnes came out in the volume Fragmenta Comica 1.2 (Bagordo 2014b, in German). Four out of the six volumes on Cratinus are already available: general introduction and testimonies Fragmenta Comica 3.1 (Bianchi 2017, in Italian), Archilochoi – Empipramenoi Fragmenta Comica 3.2 (Bianchi 2016, in Italian), Seriphioi – Horai Fragmenta Comica 3.5 (Fiorentini 2022, in Italian), fragments *incertae fabulae* and *dubia* Fragmenta Comica 3.6 (Olson and Seaberg 2018, in English). Crates is treated in Fragmenta Comica 2 (Perrone 2019, in Italian). On Cratinus useful the thematic study by Bakola (2010).

REFERENCES

Bagordo, A. (2014a). *Alkimenes – Kantharos, Fragmenta Comica 1.1*. Heidelberg: Verlag Antike.
Bagordo, A. (2014b). *Leukon – Xenophilos, Fragmenta Comica 1.2*. Heidelberg: Verlag Antike.

Bakola, E. (2010). *Cratinus and the Art of Comedy*. Oxford and New York: Oxford University Press.
Bianchi, F.P. (2016). *Cratino. Archilochoi – Empipramenoi, Fragmenta Comica 3.2*. Heidelberg: Verlag Antike.
Bianchi, F.P. (2017). *Cratino: introduzione e testimonianze, Fragmenta Comica 3.1*. Heidelberg: Verlag Antike.
Biles, Z.P. (2002). Intertextual biography in the rivalry of Cratinus and Aristophanes. *American Journal of Philology* 123 (2): 169–204.
Biles, Z.P. (2011). *Aristophanes and the Poetics of Competition*. Cambridge: Cambridge University Press.
Bonanno, M.G. (1972). *Studi su Cratete Comico*. Padova: Editrice Antenore.
Bowie, A.M. (2010). Myth and ritual in comedy. In: *Brill's Companion to the Study of Greek Comedy* (ed. G.W. Dobrov), 143–176. Leiden & Boston: Brill.
Carey, C. (2000). Old comedy and the sophists. In: *The Rivals of Aristophanes: Studies in Athenian Old Comedy* (ed. D. Harvey and J. Wilkins), 419–436. London: Classical Press of Wale.
Cassio, A.C. (1985). Two studies on Epicharmus and his influence. *Harvard Studies in Classical Philology* 89: 37–51.
Cornford, F. (1914). *The Origin of Attic Comedy*. London: E. Arnold.
Csapo, E. and Miller, M.C. (ed.) (2007). *The Origins of Theater in Ancient Greece and Beyond. From Ritual to Drama*. Cambridge: Cambridge University Press.
Fiorentini, L. (2022). Cratino, Seriphioi – Horai (frr. 218–298): *traduzione e commento, Fragmenta Comica 3.5*, Göttingen: Verlag Antike.
Halliwell, S. (1980). Aristophanes' apprenticeship. *Classical Quarterly* 30: 33–45.
Hartwig, A. (2012). Comic rivalry and the number of comic poets at the Lenaia of 405 B.C. *Philologus* 156: 195–206.
Harvey, D. and Willis, J. (ed.) (2000). *The Rivals of Aristophanes. Studies in Athenian Old Comedy*. London: Classical Press of Wales.
Heath, M. (1990). Aristophanes and his rivals. *Greece & Rome* 37: 143–158.
Henderson, J. (2013). A brief history of Athenian political comedy (c. 440-c. 300). *TAPhA* 143: 249–262.
Imperio, O. (1998). Callia. In: *Tessere. Frammenti della commedia greca: studi e commenti*, 195–254. Bari: Adriatica ed.
Kassel, R. and Austin, C. (ed.) (1983–2001). *Poetae Comici Graeci*. vol. 8. Berlin: Walter de Gruyter.
Kerkhof, R. (2001). *Dorische Posse, Epicharm und Attische Komödie*. München: K. G. Saur.
Konstantakos, I. (2012). My kids for sale: the Megarian's scene in Aristophanes' Acharnians and Megarian comedy. *Logeion* 2: 121–166.
Marsh, L.D. (2020). The structure of mythological old comedy. *Philologus* 164 (1): 14–38.
Mastromarco, G. (1979). L'esordio segreto di Aristofane. *Quaderni di Storia* 10: 153–196.
Mastromarco, G. (2002). L'invasione dei Laconi e la morte di Cratino (Ar. *Pax*, 700–703). In: *Scritti in onore di Italo Gallo* (ed. L. Torraca), 395–403. Napoli: Edizioni scientifiche italiane.
Mensching, E. (1964). Zur Produktivität der alten Komödie. *Museum Helveticum* 21: 15–49.
Millis, B.W. and Olson, S.D. (2012). *Inscriptional Records for the Dramatic Festivals in Athens. IG II2 2318–2325 and Related Texts*. Leiden and Boston: Brill.
Neil, R.A. (1901). *The Knights of Aristophanes*. Cambridge: Cambridge University Press.
Nesselrath, H.G. (2010). Comic fragments transmission and textual criticism. In: *Brill's Companion to the Study of Greek Comedy* (ed. G.W. Dobrov), 423–453. Leiden-Boston: Brill.
Norwood, G. (1931). *Greek Comedy*. London: Methuen and Co.
Olson, S.D. (2007). *Broken Laughter: Select Fragments of Greek Comedy*. Oxford: Oxford University Press.
Olson, S.D. and Seaberg, R. (2018). *Kratinos frr. 299–514, Fragmenta Comica 3.6*. Göttingen: Vandenhoeck & Ruprecht.
Ornaghi, M. (2016). *Dare un padre alla commedia. Susarione e le tradizioni megaresi*. Alessandria: Edizioni dell'Orso.
Perrone, S. (2019). *Cratete: introduzione, traduzione e commento, Fragmenta Comica 2*. Göttingen: Verlag Antike.
Perrone, S. (2020). Crates and the polis. Reframing the case. In: *Fragmentation in Ancient Greek Drama* (ed. A.A. Lamari, A. Novokhatko, and F. Montanari), 353–368. Berlin and Boston: Walter de Gruyter.
Rodríguez-Noriega Guillén, L. (1996). *Epicarmo de Siracusa: testimonios y fragmentos*. Oviedo: Universidad de Oviedo, Servicio de Publicaciones.
Rosen, R.M. (1988). *Old Comedy and the Iambographic Tradition*. Atlanta: Scholars Press.

Rosen, R.M. (2000). Cratinus' *Pytine* and the construction of the comic self. In: *The Rivals of Aristophanes: Studies in Athenian Old Comedy* (ed. D. Harvey and J. Wilkins), 23–39. London: Duckworth and the Classical Press of Wale.

Rosen, R.M. (2010). Aristophanes. In: *Brill's Companion to the Study of Greek Comedy* (ed. G.W. Dobrov), 227–278. Leiden: Brill.

Rothwell, K.S. (2007). *Nature, Culture and the Origins of Greek Comedy. A Study of Animal Choruses.* Cambridge: Cambridge University Press.

Roux, G. (1976). Un maître disparu de l'ancienne comédie, le poète Cratès, jugé par Aristophane. *Revue de Philologie* 50: 256–265.

Ruffell, I.A. (2002). A total write-off. Aristophanes, Cratinus, and the rhetoric of comic competition. *Classical Quarterly* 52 (1): 138–163.

Rusten, J. (2006). Who 'invented' comedy? The ancient candidates for the origins of comedy and the visual evidence. *American Journal of Philology* 127: 37–66.

Rusten, J. et al. (2011). *The Birth of Comedy: Texts, Documents, and Art from Athenian Comic Competitions, 486–280.* Baltimore: Johns Hopkins University Press.

Sidwell, K. (2000). From old to middle to new? Aristotle's *Poetics* and the history of Athenian comedy. In: *The Rivals of Aristophanes: Studies in Athenian Old Comedy* (ed. D. Harvey and J. Wilkins), 247–258. London: Duckworth.

Sifakis, G.M. (1971). *Parabasis and Animal Choruses. A Contribution to the History of Attic Comedy.* London: Athlone Press.

Sifakis, G.M. (2006). From mythological parody to political satire: some stages in the evolution of old comedy. *Classica et Mediaevalia* 57: 19–48.

Sommerstein, A.H. (ed.) (1981). *The Comedies of Aristophanes*, Knights, vol. 2. Warminster: Aris & Phillips.

Sonnino, M. (1998). L'accusa di plagio nella commedia attica antica. In: *Furto e plagio nella letteratura del classicismo* (ed. R. Gigliucci), 19–51. Roma: Bulzoni Editore.

Storey, I.C. (2010). Origins and fifth-century comedy. In: *Brill's Companion to the Study of Greek Comedy* (ed. G. Dobrov), 179–225. Leiden: Brill.

Storey, I.C. (ed.) (2011). *Fragments of Old Comedy.* Cambridge, MA and London: Harvard University Press.

Storey, I.C. (2014). The first poets of old comedy. In: *The Oxford Handbook of Greek and Roman Comedy* (ed. M. Fontaine and A.C. Scafuro), 95–112. Oxford: Oxford University Press.

Whittaker, M. (1935). The comic fragments in their relation to the structure of old attic comedy. *Classical Quarterly* 29: 181–191.

Willi, A. (2015). Epicharmus, the Pseudepicharmeia, and the origins of attic drama. In: *Fragmente einer Geschichte der griechischen Komödie/Fragmentary History of Greek Comedy* (ed. S. Chronopoulos and C. Orth), 109–145. Heidelberg: Verlag Antike.

CHAPTER 20

Aristophanes' Contemporaries

Sarah N. Miles

Introduction: A Culture of Comedy

I was tempted to call this chapter: "Aristophanes' fragmentary companions" because this is a chapter about a shared knowledge and practice of comic drama among dramatists during the career of Aristophanes (420s–380s BCE). However, a *company* of Attic comedians is not merely one of companionship but also of *competition, rivalry, co-creativity,* and *self-promotion,* communicated through the medium of the ever-developing art form of live-performance comic drama (see, e.g. Biles 2011; Hughes 2012; Sells 2019). The element that links together all the dramatists explored here is that they are contemporary with the career of Aristophanes. The issue is that we have no complete plays for any of Aristophanes' contemporaries. The ancient audiences would recognize the distinct style of demagogue comedies of Eupolis, Platon, or Hermippus and be able to contrast these with the domestic comedies of Pherecrates, filled with *hetairai* (female companions) and household slaves; audiences would be familiar with Platon's penchant for reworking mythological stories in comedy and recognize these as distinct from the mythological comedies of Theopompus. Audiences could even appreciate the intricate Euripidean parodies by Strattis just as much as those of Aristophanes. However, in the twenty-first century, we are beholden to the 11 Aristophanic plays (25% of his total output) to give us an idea of what a complete comic drama looks like. Therefore, the extant comedies are all in the style of one man, Aristophanes, but there exists an array of remnants and fragments of the comic dramas of contemporary comic dramatists. This offers us a precarious but precious evidence set, and one that cannot be ignored in the study of Greek Comedy and Aristophanes.

I have started by drawing attention to the complexity of the relationship between comic dramatists, since this is something that will continue to emerge in the course of this chapter. It points to the key reasons why anyone exploring Greek drama, and indeed Aristophanes, must have recourse to the fragments of Aristophanes' contemporaries: (1) *fragments provide* **context** *for any discussion of comic drama and for the study of Aristophanes in particular;* (2) *only by placing Aristophanes in context can we begin to comprehend the* **culture** *of comedy that existed in 5th – 4th c.* BCE *Athens.* To put it another way: how can anyone claim to understand the comic drama of one individual if they do not place him alongside his contemporaries and competitors? How can we begin to determine the **esthetics**, the **values,** and the **impact** of Aristophanes' comedies if we do not situate these alongside the contemporary comic dramatists who were competing for the same prizes, the same *kudos*, the same laughs from the same receptive audiences? Equally, how can we lay claim to understanding a **culture of comedy** – for that is what existed from the fifth century BCE – if we look at it only through the eyes of Aristophanes?

The aim of this chapter is to open up these questions and to make it plain that Aristophanes should never be treated as the limit of fifth–fourth-century BCE comic drama, nor is analysis of

Aristophanes sufficient for anyone to use the label "Attic Greek Comedy" with conviction. To a member of the first audiences of comic drama Aristophanes was but one of a multitude of voices on the fifth-century BCE comic circuit of Athenian festivals (Lamari 2015; Csapo and Wilson 2020). Each and every year, a *host* of plays by a *variety* of comic dramatists was performed at a *number* of festivals across Athens. It is easy to lose sight of this when only viewing Greek comedy through an Aristophanic-shaped lens.

Live-performance comic drama offered a regularity, a familiarity, and a *rhythm* for audiences. But, instead of a ritual reperformance of identical stories every year, each comic dramatist could offer up a distinct comic drama, with the option of recycling and reworking their popular creations and those of each other (e.g. Ar. *Clouds* 553–9; discussed in Section 2). For all the developments in scholarship on Greek Comedy (Section 2), there continue to be publications in our field that talk of "Greek Comedy" when they really mean: "the extant plays of Aristophanes." This form of **synecdoche** has to stop. It limits our understanding of Greek comedy and distorts our knowledge of both Aristophanes and his comic contemporaries.

The focus of this chapter is on the **culture of comedy** in fifth–fourth-century BCE Athens. By exploring the contemporaries of Aristophanes, we gain a snapshot of the context and the culture of ancient comic drama of which Aristophanes was a part. To do this within the confines of a chapter, we can only touch the surface of this topic, using examples from the range of Aristophanes' contemporaries, and focusing on some of those who are best preserved through the remaining fragments of their work. They are listed here in order of their first recorded production or victory using *Testimonia* from *PCG*:

> Teleclides (445 BCE)
> Pherecrates (440s BCE)
> Eupolis (early 430s BCE)
> Hermippus (435 BCE – a victory)
> Phrynichus (430s BCE)
> Platon (410s BCE)
> Strattis (410s BCE)
> Archippus (late 5th/4th c. BCE)
> Theopompus (late 5th/4th c. BCE)

We can add Aristophanes to this picture by noting his first comedy, *Banqueters (Daitales)* appeared in 427 BCE, produced by Callistratus. The nine dramatists in the list also helpfully span the career of Aristophanes. This provides a means to contextualize all 11 extant Aristophanic comedies. The Attic comic dramatist Cratinus can be found in the earlier chapter: "Aristophanes' Predecessors" because Cratinus was influential on all the comic dramatists discussed in this chapter, and the end of Cratinus' career overlaps only with the start of Aristophanes'. Our time and space in this chapter are enough to demonstrate how important these contemporaries are both for understanding Aristophanes and equally for Greek Comedy in the fifth–fourth centuries BCE as a part of live-performance culture.

Survival and Scholarship: Always a Fragmentary Lens: From Aristophanes to Theopompus

The comic culture that I have outlined so far existed as a whole in fifth-century BCE Athens for its ancient audiences, but it reaches us in the twenty-first century in a far less wholesome form: all of the contemporaries of Aristophanes exist purely in the form of fragments, and incomplete plays. This fragmentation of Aristophanes' contemporaries and the imbalance of evidence compared to the 11 plays and nearly 1000 fragments of Aristophanes inevitably shapes the approach to our evidence and our interpretation of it. Therefore, as part of our foray into the fragments, it is important for anyone wishing to access the work of Aristophanes' contemporaries to be aware of the resources available as well as the methodological issues of working with fragments alongside the extant corpus of Aristophanes.

The most complete edited collection of comic fragments of Greek text is to be found in the multi-volumed work *PCG* by Kassel and Austin (1983–2001). In addition, commentaries on the Greek text of each comic dramatist are now emerging, thanks to Bernhard Zimmermann's *Kommentierung der Fragmente der griechischen Komödie (KomFrag)* with an ever-increasing number of publications by an array of scholars. The study of comic fragments still has a long way to go so that it is fully accessible to students and academics from other disciplines who rely on translation and English commentaries to interpret ancient sources. I look here, of course, to Alan Sommerstein's eye-watering achievement (Sommerstein 1980–2002) with Aris & Phillips to make all of Aristophanes' plays accessible with commentary, translation, and indexes. We currently lack, and certainly need, an equivalent for comic fragments, just as Cropp, Collard, and Lee began the work for tragic fragments (Collard et al. 1995–2004), with Matthew Wright recently providing summary guides (Wright 2016, 2019). Ian Storey's Loeb of *Fragments of Old Comedy* (Storey 2011) provides a starting point toward this work, but a comprehensive and accessible guide to comic fragments remains unpublished.

Each of the comic dramatists discussed in this chapter merits a monograph, although so far only Eupolis and Cratinus have been acknowledged in this way through the work of Ian Storey (2003) and Emmanuela Bakola (2010), respectively, alongside Olson (2007) which presents selected comic fragments by time period, by theme and with a translation. Alan Sommerstein's (2019) *The Encyclopedia of Greek Comedy* offers a highly accessible and vital resource, containing key summaries of individual comic dramatists, including all those discussed in this chapter. If you want a way into interpreting the fragments of Greek Comedy, these are the resources with which to begin, but there is much work still to be done.

Currently, Loeb editions are the friend of those investigating comic fragments without Greek (Storey 2011a,b,c), alongside Douglas Olson's (2006–2012) updated Loeb editions of Athenaeus' *The Learned Banqueters (Deipnosophistai)*, which is a major secondary source for citing from the works of Aristophanes' contemporaries as well as Aristophanes' 33 lost plays. For those new to working with fragments, a secondary source is one such as Athenaeus (second century CE) who incidentally provides us with quotations (i.e. fragments) from a lost comic play embedded within his overall work, *The Learned Banqueters*. This mode of transmission is by far the commonest way that fragments have reached us, outweighing the number of fragments that are found on papyri. This raises all forms of methodological issues about transmission, editing, and interpretation, because many fragments are embedded in an anachronistic context – Athenaeus was writing in the second century CE, for example, 650 years after the comic dramatists were creating and staging their comedies.

Each one of the comic dramatists discussed here is preserved across dozens of distinct secondary sources, such as Athenaeus, each with their own context of production and transmission, their own textual tradition, and their own interpretative issues. Therefore, the word "fragment" has an extra dimension: we are not just dealing with the broken pieces of a torn-up papyrus but with **a fragmented tradition of text,** that spans centuries, that crosses canonical boundaries, and that will always by definition remain "in pieces." It is very important for anyone approaching comic fragments and the related scholarship to be aware of the precarious nature of our evidence, and its interpretation, and of the full meaning that is bound up in the word: fragment.

When we compare the works of Aristophanes with the works of his contemporaries, the difference is that for fragments the holes are greater than the whole. We lack a complete play by any other comedian aside from Aristophanes. Therefore, his work holds the spotlight rightly on grounds of tracing narrative continuity within a play, but wrongly for thinking that we can extrapolate generalizations about comedy from the partially extant works of one man, Aristophanes. Indeed, only 25% of Aristophanes' output is extant, even if he is so much better preserved than his contemporaries. The imbalance of evidence rubs both ways. A methodology for working with fragments calls for a far greater care in making conjectures and hypotheses and using these as foundations for points. Scholarship has only recently turned full attention to this area in the edited volume of Anna Lamari,

Franco Montanari, and Anna Novokhatko (Lamari et al. 2020). With fragments, it is important that we as scholars hold up our hands and make it clear when we have moved into the world of conjecture. Otherwise, we risk constructing vast castles on sand.

To put Aristophanes into perspective: 61 is the number of comic dramatists whose careers cover the fifth and fifth—fourth centuries BCE, as listed in *PCG*. This number includes Aristophanes' predecessors and contemporaries. But the number of dramatists reduces to roughly 48, once those with only a name or play-title extant are discounted. Whole comic careers are lost to us. If we revisit the dramatists listed earlier (see Section 1), taking account of the surviving evidence, the full deficit of our evidence is laid bare. In the list below, I include in brackets the numbers of titles and fragments based on data from *PCG*, excluding *Dubia* (= fragments assigned without certainty to a dramatist), with the dramatists placed in order of number of fragments:

> Eupolis (15 titles, 489 fragments)
> Platon (28 titles, 292 fragments)
> Pherecrates (18 titles, 282 fragments)
> Theopompus (20 titles, 97 fragments)
> Hermippus (10 titles, 94 fragments)
> Strattis (19 titles, 90 fragments)
> Phrynichus (10 titles, 86 fragments)
> Teleclides (9 titles, 73 fragments)
> Archippus (6 titles; 61 fragments)

Out of all Aristophanes' predecessors and contemporaries, only **Cratinus, Eupolis, Pherecrates, and Platon** reach us with 200 (or more) fragments. Compare this to the nearly 1000 fragments of Aristophanes plus 11 extant plays, and the imbalance of evidence is brought into sharper focus. It is no coincidence that the best attested dramatists, Cratinus, Eupolis, Pherecrates, and Platon, are also the dramatists for whom we have the clearest sense of play contents, hints at plot and character, suggestions of thematic interests, of individual comic styles. The evidence is substantial enough for such analysis in these cases. For the 44 remaining comic dramatists, there are no fragments of more than 100 lines long. We need to acknowledge the deficit in evidence, and the huge power that Aristophanic comedy wields over how we interpret the comic fragments.

In light of this, it is then worth viewing with interest but added caution the passages in Aristophanic comedy where the other comic dramatists are caricatured. Aristophanes also acts as a secondary source in our understanding of the comic dramas of his contemporaries. An excellent example of this occurs in Aristophanes *Clouds* 553–9:

> First of all Eupolis hauled his *Marikas* on to the stage, serving a vile rehash of my *Knights* like the vile fellow he is, and adding on a drunken old woman for the sake of the kordax dance, the woman presented years ago by Phrynichos, the one the sea-monster tried to devour. Then Hermippos again wrote about Hyperbolos, and now all the others are piling into Hyperbolos, copying my similes about eels. (translation from Sommerstein 2000: 438)

This is part of Aristophanic rhetoric around his own exceptional and original talent, which leaves his competitors wanting. My focus here is on the Aristophanic snapshot that we receive of comic culture and that marks the variety and vibrancy of comedy in his contemporaries. We hear of Eupolis using female characters to dance drunkenly, and presumably obscenely, mocking old age and women; Phrynichus had introduced a character who was modeled on the mythical Andromeda (or perhaps who was Andromeda); Hermippus is seen to start a trend for attacking the demagogue Hyperbolus, and then everyone else is seen piling in, and repeating jokes using fish-based metaphors. The other element that shines out is that Aristophanes depicts a clear picture of comic dramatists building on and reworking each other's material. In the Aristophanic narrative, this becomes theft, which marks Aristophanes out as the superior comedian (i.e. worth stealing from), presented in a context where his competitors have no right to direct reply. The passage indicates the interconnectedness, the struggle, and the co-creativity of comic dramatists during this time.

When we look outside of the Aristophanic lens, we find fewer certainties, but intriguing possibilities. This can be seen from a brief examination of the parallels between Aristophanes, and his junior contemporary Theopompus. For example, we cannot tell if it is coincidence or careful calculation that led Theopompus to compose a *Peace,* calling for end to a war (fr. 8). We know that Aristophanes' *Peace* was mocked by Eupolis and Platon for using the statue of Peace as a character (Platon *Nikai* fr. 86; Eupolis *Autolycus* fr. 62), and so Theopompus would be assured attention by creating his own drama called *Peace.* It would also give Theopompus the opportunity to mock his elder predecessor, as Aristophanes had mocked Cratinus, or even to emulate him, as Aristophanes had emulated Magnes' *Frogs* with his own *Frogs.* Theopompus is doubly intriguing in this regard because he is the earliest comic dramatist to mock Plato (philosopher, not comedian), the follower of Socrates, who was the target of Aristophanes' *Clouds.* Here too Theopompus could be emulating Aristophanic comedy, and joining the public animosity between philosophers and comedians. Plato even refers to this in his *Apology* with a direct quotation from *Clouds.* There is not enough of Theopompus for us to reconstruct his relationship with Aristophanes fully, but there is more to be explored here. It is certainly the case that when Theopompus' career flourished, Aristophanes was the senior dramatist, open to the same mockery he had aimed at his older contemporaries, such as Cratinus.

Aristophanes and His Contemporaries: Individual Comedians with Common Characteristics

All of the facets, themes, and foibles that we find in Aristophanic comedy, and that are seen to characterize Aristophanes, are also found threaded through the fragments of his contemporaries. However, it is the weighting and balance that each dramatist brings to these that reflects the individual styles of each comic dramatist. Comedy in the late fifth–early fourth centuries BCE was based around humor and performance that was: plot-based, musical, choreographed, chorus-based, political, topical, personal (mocking named, real-life figures) and group-based, obscene, fantastical, mythical and parasitic on other performance modes, such as lyric, tragic, satyric, dithyrambic, epic, and with a ready ability to satirize, to parody, and to reperform them in a comically distorted fashion. It will be notable in this summary that I eschew the labels "Old," "Middle," and "New" for comedy, as being needlessly prescriptive for analyzing an already fragmentary corpus. Eric Csapo (2000) and Bernhard Zimmermann (2015) are among scholars to question the continued use of periodization of comedy.

This summary of comic drama tells us about the overall shared characteristics of comedy, but it does not help us to locate the individual styles of the dramatists. In this regard, the edited volume of Harvey and Wilkins (2000) was a game-changer for opening up discussion beyond Aristophanes, and demonstrating the benefits of so doing, while building on the earlier edited volume of Gregory Dobrov (1995). For example, in Harvey and Wilkins (2000), Jeffrey Henderson focused on the predominance of female characters in Pherecrates' comedies, who play a significant role in c. 33% of his extant plays, and many of these plays have a domestic setting and involve *hetairai* – female companions (Henderson 2000); Alan Sommerstein analyzed the demagogue comedies of Eupolis and Platon alongside Hermippus (Sommerstein 2000); Christopher Carey explored the roles of Socrates, sophists, and thinkers in comedies of Eupolis and Ameipsias, among others (Carey 2000). More recent scholarship takes account of fragments in varying degrees: Alan Hughes (2012) engaged with a selection of comic dramatists in his wide-reaching exploration of performing ancient comedy, while Donald Sells surveyed the evidence for slaves in the fragments of comedy, outlining trends in their characterization and function (Sells 2013, 92). This enables him to highlight the influential role of Pherecrates in this regard, due to the domestic setting of many of his comedies, a setting on which Menander a century later put his own stamp. Sarah Miles (2009) looked at the relationship between comedy and tragedy through the eyes of the comic dramatist Strattis, viewing the relationship as a form of ancient reception (Miles 2018). Matthew Farmer (2017) and

Donald Sells (2019) have provided a wider exploration of the relationship of Aristophanic comedy to other genres of poetry, particularly tragedy, incorporating fragments into their work.

Douglas Olson (2007, 2) notes that the comic fragments: "represent one of our most important sources of information about contemporary literary, political, and social life," building on the seminal work of Ehrenberg (1943) in this area. Furthermore, the comic fragments provide us with the best grasp of the culture of comedy, with comedy's variety, its self-image, its proclivities, and its cultural biases. Studying fragments encourages us to take a fresh look at Greek comedy and at Aristophanes from a different angle.

Snapshots of a Lost Culture of Comedy

I offer here a small cross-section through the layers of these comic fragments, which reveals to you the vibrancy, the richness, the complexity, and the culturally discriminatory aspects of ancient Athenian comedy that was alive in the work of all comic poets in the late fifth and early fourth centuries BCE, Aristophanes included. One need only look at the number of times that Aristophanes did not gain first prize to realize that there was a company of comedians capable of winning the approval of judges, as well as state, and/or citizen, and the wider audience beyond Athens. Paying attention to the fragments helps us to see that Aristophanes was one of many dramatists who gained public approval. But sadly, all that we have extant today is snapshots from this lost culture of comedy.

This was a male world of dramatists and performers but also a specifically *Athenian* male-only world of comic playwrights. As Michael Silk notes: "we know of no-one from outside Athens in the fifth century (or indeed the fourth) who composed comedies for performance there" (Silk 2020, 32). Certainly, the cultural biases of comic drama demand more attention in scholarship, in order to highlight the insular ideological nature of Attic comedy, and its defining cultural features, which include cultural norms around masculinity, sexuality and gender, roles of women, ethnicity, age (both youth and old age), non-Athenians, slaves, those living with illness, and disability. Aristophanic comedy provides one section of the picture here, but it is only alongside the fragments that the wider context falls into place.

As an example of this, I share one cross-section into the world that is co-created by Aristophanes and his contemporaries, and which highlights the cultural norms of this art form in relation to other performing arts. Comic dramatists constantly derided each other and other performance artists including tragic dramatists, actors, and dithyrambic composers for their perceived personal defects while also undermining their esthetic prowess. According to the internal co-created narrative of Attic comedy at this time, audiences received the following messages:

Aristophanes was "baldy," according to Eupolis (Eupolis *Baptai* (*Dippers*) fr. 89); Cratinus was a drunken "has been" and a bed-wetter in the eyes of Aristophanes (Ar. *Knights* 400, 526–36); Eupolis' *Maricas* had pinched Aristophanes' ideas from *Knights*, whereas Eupolis claims he collaborated with Aristophanes on that play (Ar. *Clouds* 553–4; Eupolis *Baptai* (*Dippers*) fr. 89); Platon and Eupolis found laughable Aristophanes' statue of Peace in 421 BCE (Platon *Nikai* fr. 86; Eupolis *Autolycus* fr. 62); Platon, like Aristophanes, says that he started his career writing material for other comic dramatists (Platon *Peisander* frr. 106–7); Aristophanes possibly credits Pherecrates for his move to female comic characters (*Lysistrata* 157–8; Henderson 2015, 156).

The picture is no less biting when we turn to the portrayal of tragedians: Acestor the tragedian was constantly nicknamed "Sacas," and his Athenian identity questioned in a racist slur, where "Sacas" is a non-Greek name (Cratinus *Cleoboulinai* fr. 92; Callias *Pedetai* fr. 17; Eupolis *Kolakes* fr. 172, Theopompus *Teisamenos* fr. 61, Metagenes *Philothutes* fr. 14, Aristophanes *Birds* 31, *Wasps* 1221); Sophocles receives little personal attention from comedians until his death, whereupon Phrynichus' *Muses* and Aristophanes' *Frogs* both refer to the tragedian but without the biting satire reserved for Euripides, who died in the same year as Sophocles; Euripides was the most popular tragedian for comedians to target and to (mis)quote during his lifetime and beyond (Miles 2009; Farmer 2017); Socrates was said to be a collaborator with Euripides in composing his tragedies (Callias *Pedetai* fr. 15; Teleclides frr. 41–2; Aristophanes *Clouds I* fr. 392; Aristophanes fr. 596); in the 420s BCE Socrates and Melanthius the tragedian were both influential and well known enough that multiple comic poets mocked each man at the same contest (Socrates in 423 BCE: Aristophanes' *Clouds*, Ameipsias *Konnos* fr. 9; Melanthius in 421 BCE: Eupolis *Kolakes* fr. 178, Aristophanes *Peace* 1009–14, and Leukon *Phrateres* fr. 3). In the case of Melanthius, at the end of the fifth century BCE Archippus' *Ichthues* (*Fishes*) could design a comedy in which this tragic dramatist was fed to the fishes in an apparent parody of Andromeda (cf. *Clouds* 553–9 discussed in Section 2 for Phrynichus' use of an Andromeda parody), possibly involving a tragic parody of Euripides' *Andromeda*.

Musicians, dithyrambic poets, and tragic actors escape no more lightly than tragedians: Cinesias was portrayed as a dire dithyrambic poet and a sickly human being (Platon fr. 200; Strattis' *Cinesias* and fr. 44 especially; Pherecrates, *Cheiron* fr. 155.8–13; Aristophanes *Birds* 1372–1409, *Frogs* 153, 1437, *Eccl.* 330; *Gerytades* fr. 156.9); according to Pherecrates' *Cheiron* fr. 155 a number of musicians were committing sexual violence against Music herself, as she tells us when she appears as a stage character, naming the perpetrators of her rape as the dithyrambists: Melanippides and Cinesias, the citharode Phrynis, and Timotheus who was both dithyrambist and citharode; Hegelochus was a tragic actor who bumbled his lines in Euripides' *Orestes* of 408 BCE and was never allowed to forget it (Strattis *Anthroporestes* frr. 1, 63; Ar. *Frogs* 303, Sannyrion fr. 8; cf. Platon fr. 235); meanwhile, the actor Callippides was the subject of a whole comedy in Strattis' *Callippides*, to which possibly Aristophanes makes reference (Braund 2000). This is particularly intriguing given the interest both authors share in tragedy and Euripides' *Phoenician Women* (Miles 2018 and see Section 6).

None of this co-created narrative, with its comic caricatures and public personas, needed to represent the reality of those individuals and their families, but they were all part of this publicly constructed narrative that was performed, inflated, and repeated by comic dramatists through the late fifth to early fifth centuries BCE. And this is the key point: year after year on the comic stage these caricatures were shaped, honed, and recreated on-stage by comic dramatist after comic dramatist. In this sense, they were real to the audience as they were part of the fabric of Attic comic culture at this time, all of which give a hint at the identity and status-based power struggles and insecurities at the heart of ancient Athenian culture that is too little spoken about. And it is this **comic culture** that we gain a view of by looking at all comic dramatists in fifth century BCE, and by viewing Aristophanes through the lens of fragments. Aristophanes was part of this culture but only a contributor to it.

Whether the comic targets were popular tragedians, dithyrambic poets, or political figures (the latter are discussed in Section 5), we can see that these were figures who had influence over the Athenian *demos*. More remarkably, we find annually a group of Athenian comic dramatists was given a designated place, time, and space to deride these popular influential figures, presumably at the behest of their opponents.

Comedy Snapshots 1: Eupolis, Biography, and Politics: Questioning Aristophanic Exceptionalism

According to the *Testimonia* for Eupolis (*PCG*; Storey 2003), we know how Eupolis died: he was either drowned in a shipwreck, or worse, thrown overboard by Alcibiades himself. As with all ancient biographical information, Aristophanes included, we should take the historicity of this with a pinch of salt while acknowledging its influence in the ancient reception of both dramatists (Lefkowitz 2012). In the case of Eupolis, these personal narratives developed from his *Dippers* (*Baptai*). We can see the parallels to Aristophanes' own relationship with Cleon that transcends the plays themselves. This points to a significant parallel between the works of Aristophanes and Eupolis: both poets were well-enough preserved after their initial performances that biographical traditions developed in relation to their work. Indeed, the ancient reception of Eupolis sees him form part of the triad of comedians, along with Cratinus and Aristophanes. In the case of these three comic dramatists, we have sizeable papyrus fragments, some recording c. 100 lines, as well as papyrus fragments of ancient commentaries on them.

Eupolis' *Demes* (*Demoi*) in particular stands out for its long-lived appearance in papyri (Telò 2007). Similarly, Eupolis and Aristophanes are the only two dramatists whose plays appear on the visual record of South Italian and Sicilian pottery (Csapo 2010). All of this should indicate the fame of Eupolis in his lifetime and in the centuries following his career, and this is a feature he shares in common with Aristophanes. At the same time, it is important to put Aristophanes and Eupolis in their place within the contexts of ancient reception of comedy. We can contrast the Hellenistic big three: Homer, Euripides, and Menander – who were the representatives of epic, tragedy, and comedy, as discussed in full by Sebastiana Nervegna (2013, 9–10).

We have already noted above accusations (comic or otherwise) that there was collaboration and plagiarism between Aristophanes and Eupolis (Section 3), and here we see two comedians taking the competition to each other, which points to the dual recognition that the one posed a threat to the other's success, at least within the narrative of the comic dramas themselves. Aristophanes used the same tactic in 405 BCE when Phrynichus' *Mousai* was competing against his *Frogs* (see Section 3). At the very start of *Frogs* (lines 12–15), Aristophanes mocks Phrynichus for his use of old-fashioned baggage scenes in comedy, before proceeding to engage in such a scene himself. Aristophanes would not have needed to employ such measures, unless Phrynichus was seen as a competent rival for first prize. Aristophanes repeatedly asserts the superiority of his own comedy, for example, *Knights* 507–46, *Clouds* 518–62, *Wasps* 54–63; 1046–7 *Peace* 736–43. In the case of Platon, curiously Aristophanes remains silent, as noted by Sommerstein (2000, 439), despite the latter's remarks about Aristophanes' *Peace* (see Section 3). But with only 25% of Aristophanes' plays extant, this silence is intriguing but not conclusive.

Certainly, a rivalry between individuals makes for a more exciting competition for audiences (Bakola 2008; Biles 2011). The shape of that rivalry is only partially visible to us, but whereas the biographical tradition pits Aristophanes against Cleon, Eupolis is portrayed as confronting Alcibiades. This might suggest a polarization of political standpoints and social backgrounds, but Eupolis also composed *Maricas,* in which he dedicated a full drama to satire of the demagogue Hyperbolus. By comparison, Aristophanes could mock Alcibiades' lisp in *Wasps* (44–6). We see here just as Cratinus, Hermippus, and Teleclides had taken on Pericles prior to Aristophanes (Cratinus' *Dionysalexandros* hypothesis; *Nemesis* fr. 118; *Thracian Women* fr. 73, *Cheirones* fr. 250, 258–9; Hermippus fr. 69; Teleclides *Hesiodoi* fr. 18, fr. 45), so the tradition continues with Aristophanes creating comedies centered around Cleon in the 420s. Subsequently, Hyperbolus becomes the target of Eupolis' *Maricas,* Hermippus' *Breadsellers* (*Artopolides*) and Platon's *Hyperbolus*. Later Platon composed a *Peisander* and *Cleophon* (Sommerstein 2000; Pirrotta 2009), which suggests a stylistic feature of Platon's comedies, that is later imitated in Archippus' *Rhinon*, and Theopompus composed a *Teisamenus,* which possibly refers to the political figure. Certainly, Aristophanes never composed a comedy using the name of his target as the title, and this marks an interesting distinction between the political satire of contemporaries Platon and Aristophanes.

Political targets are a feature and focus of many comic dramatist's works, but that is not the limit of their skills, anymore than Aristophanes being only associated with Cleon as a writer of demagogue comedies. Yet it is a risk that poets preserved in fragments become caricatured by the surviving lines of their work, plus being shaped by the Aristophanic lens (see Section 2). Eupolis certainly falls into this bracket, with scholarship focusing on his association with political subjects and with his rivalry with Aristophanes (Storey 2003; Bakola 2008), and not focusing on his repeated engagement with tragedy, to which our next section now turns.

Comedy Snapshots 2: Tragedy and Euripides in Eupolis and Strattis

Tragedy plays a big role in comedy. In the twentieth and early twenty-first centuries, scholars focused on cataloging and analyzing Aristophanes' engagement with tragedy (e.g. Rau 1967; Silk 1993; Foley 2008). This engagement was often termed "paratragedy," but it can involve a variety of modes, effects, and mimicry of tragedy transferred into a comic drama (Miles 2019). We see here another example of Aristophanic exceptionalism that has since been challenged, using the evidence from fragments to show how widespread engagement with tragedy is among all comic dramatists (Miles 2009; Farmer 2017). It is important to factor in the evidence that tragedians, and Euripides, in particular, were also a popular comic target. Euripides became an important reference point for comic dramatists during and after the tragedian's lifetime (Miles 2009; Hanink 2014; Farmer 2017).

Eupolis is usually overlooked for his engagement with tragedy, but his use of tragic quotation is striking, particularly in his ***Maricas, Demoi, Poleis,*** and ***Prospaltioi***. These are notable comedies that focused on contemporary politics and political figures. *Demoi* is particularly fascinating as it is the best preserved, thanks to papyrus finds (Storey 2003; Telò 2007). In *Demoi*, a comic protagonist sought out the help of deceased Athenian political figures: Aristides, Miltiades, Solon, and Pericles. *Demoi* contains comically adapted lines from a range of tragedies: Euripides' *Medea*, *Melanippe Desmotis*, and the opening phrase from his *Oineus*. This plot concept of seeking help from the dead pre-echoes Aristophanes' *Frogs*, and it is also found in Pherecrates' *Crapataloi* (date unknown) which is set in Hades and stars Aeschylus as a speaking character (fr. 100). Notably, Pherecrates *Miners (Metalles)* fr. 113 suggests another play with a setting in Hades, and Sells suggests the play contained a katabasis (Sells 2013, 106). We also find Aristophanes experimenting with Hades in his *Gerytades* where three ambassadors go to Hades: Sannyrion, Meletus, and Cinesias (representing composers of comedy, tragedy, and dithyramb, respectively). Therefore, *Demoi* is a comedy set in a recognizable mold that subsequent comedies continue to develop.

In Eupolis' *Demoi*, Miltiades is the speaker of a tragic line (*Demoi* fr. 106; Eur. *Med* 235), while Aristides employs tragic diction (e.g. *Demoi* fr. 99.35 and fr. 99.102). And so, in *Demoi*, Eupolis places tragic language in the mouths of characters from Athens' historical past. The key political figures of Athenian recent history are mythologized, or rather in the context of fifth-century BCE culture, they are turned into tragic protagonists. They speak and act in the manner of a tragic protagonist. Moreover, Eupolis is also the only other comedian who is known to use the word "trugedy," which is repeatedly found in Aristophanes (Ar. *Ach.* 499–500, 628; *Wa.* 1537; *Gerytades* fr. 156), and it occurs yet again in a passage of Eupolis' *Demoi* fr. 99.29, albeit in an excruciatingly fragmentary context. Its presence shows the variety of ways that comic poets could respond to tragedy, and it should guard further against Aristophanic exceptionalism.

A glance at Eupolis' wider use of tragic quotation in his other comedies indicates a characteristic feature of his work for re-quoting and misquoting tragic lines for comic ends: Eupolis' *Prospaltioi* fr. 260.23–6 replicates and adapts Sophocles' *Antigone* 712–5 indicating a substantial tragic parody. Eupolis' *Maricas* fr. 207 quotes Aeschylus' *Persians* 65, but the tragic line is amended in such a way as to aim a joke at Hyperbolus, who is the overall target of *Maricas*. Eupolis' *Poleis* fr. 231 uses the same word substitution technique, quoting Aeschylus' *Seven Against Thebes* 39, but replacing the name: "Eteocles" with the similar sounding: "Hierocles." Eupolis' *Helots* may have parodied suppliant tragedies (cf. Cratinus' Drapetides frr. 60–1). These points, taken together, alongside the sizeable evidence for *Demoi*, reveal the edges of a rich and tragically informed underbelly to Eupolis' comedies. Eupolis' manner of bringing historical political figures on-stage quoting tragic lines is a way to mythologize those characters, and it is not an Aristophanic method of employing tragedy in comedy. Here, we encounter an element of the Eupolidean style of comic drama.

Strattis comes after the careers of both Eupolis and Aristophanes were in full flow, and so we can see the later development of a comic dramatist engaging with tragedy. Strattis was second to none for paratragic material and his engagement with Euripidean tragedy. Strattis and Aristophanes both composed a ***Phoenician Women (Phoenissae)*** that directly engages with, and quotes from, Euripides' *Phoenician Women*. I and others have explored the relationship fully elsewhere (Miles 2009; Orth 2009; Fiorentini 2010; Farmer 2017; Miles 2018), and this is discussed in detail in the commentary by Christian Orth (Orth 2009). In brief, Strattis' *Phoenician Women* contains an on-stage Iocasta quoting her own Euripidean lines, but with a comic twist, indicating the closeness of Strattis to parts of his tragic model (Strattis *Phoenician Women* fr. 47 cf. fr. 48). There is also a fragment that contains an extended joke about Boeotian dialect (Strattis *Phoenician Women* fr. 49), which suits the Theban setting of the tragedy. Meanwhile, in fr. 46, we have preserved the entrance of Dionysus via the stage crane, quoting lines from Euripides' *Hypsipyle*. Perhaps Dionysus has entered the wrong play accidentally, since there is no Dionysus in Euripides' *Phoenician Women*. However, the most intriguing fragment from Strattis' *Phoenician Women* is in fr. 50, because it presents the earliest use of the verb παρατραγῳδέω = I paratragedize:

ἐγὼ γὰρ αὐτὸν παρατραγῳδῆσαί τι μοι
[[ε]]κε. [...] ι ọ
'For, I (say/ask/want) him to paratragedize for me'

This is the oldest recorded usage of the verb, and the only one in classical Greek, and so I have preserved the transliteration, because the precise meaning is not possible to reconstruct from the current context (Orth 2009 and Miles 2018 offer possible meanings). The concentration of Euripidean material in this single comedy, as well as the range of ways Strattis engages with it indicates that Aristophanes was certainly not alone in his Euripidean fanaticism (*pace* Jendza 2020). This is easier to see when taking account of the other fragments of Strattis, which include two jokes at the expense of Hegelochus the actor who messed up his lines for Euripides' *Orestes* in 408 BCE, and one of these jokes comes in his intriguingly named: *Anthroporestes* (*Man-Orestes*); there is also Strattis' *Medea*, where Strattis' play contains someone addressing Creon which suggests its link to Euripides' *Medea*. The evidence is tantalizing, all the more so because only 90 fragments of Strattis survive, often with mythological titles possibly tragic (Orth 2009 provides a comprehensive commentary). But this also warns of the limits of comparison with Aristophanes, for whom nearly 1000 fragments survive on top of 11 complete plays. When Strattis and Aristophanes are put alongside one another, it makes the extant paratragedy of Strattis all the more remarkable.

Comedy Snapshots 3: Pherecrates, Social Insects, Satire, and Myth

Sometimes the evidence is tantalizing but frustrating and yet still fruitful for understanding the culture of comedy in Athens in the late fifth to early fourth centuries BCE. Aristophanes' *Wasps* (422 BCE) involves a chorus of humanoid wasps, representing old men, who are Attic jurors and war veterans in a comic play that constantly blurs the line between animal, insect, and human in a visceral satire of Cleon. This can only whet one's appetite for the other comedies titled after social insects that we possess, given the poor state of their survival:

Magnes, Ψῆνες (*Fig-Wasps*)
Cantharus, Μύρμηκες (*Ants*)
Pherecrates, Μυρμηκάνθρωποι (*Antmen*)
Aristophanes' Σφῆκες (*Wasps*)
Platon, Μύρμηκες (*Ants*)
Diocles, Μέλιτται (Bees)

With the exception of Magnes, who pre-dates Aristophanes' career, all the comic dramatists listed above are contemporary with Aristophanes. The key point about social insects of the order hymenoptera, such as bees, ants, and wasps, is that they rely on cooperation and social interaction for survival, while different members of the collective carry out separate roles. We know Aristophanes was aware of this, from the jokes and metaphors he bases around drones, bees, bumble-bees, and bee larvae (Davies and Kathirithamby 1986; Miles 2018, 226–9), as well as the communal activity of the hive and swarms. Clearly, he would expect his audience to understand the jokes, and it gives us an insight into their level of knowledge, which is not surprising given the industry of bee-keeping (Wallace-Hare 2022) and the use of wasp similes in poetry such as

Homer (e.g. *Iliad* 12.167–70; 16.259–65). The parallels to group behavior extend to choral dancing, and that offers up possibilities for all the comedians listed above. Social insects were clearly successful material for comedies, offering a range of possibilities to the budding comic dramatist. Aristophanes, at the very end of *Wasps*, goes so far as to pit his comic wasp-juror chorus against four tragic dancing crabs, who represent the four sons of the general and tragedian Carcinus, whose name also means "crab." This takes *Wasps* to a vibrant, ludicrous high-energy inter-generic conclusion while maintaining the blurred lines between human, animal, and insect. It also warns that we should always recognize that we cannot reconstruct a lost comedy when only fragments survive.

Pherecrates' *Ant-men (Myrmekanthropoi)* is the best preserved of the comedies listed above, and it directly highlights the same insect–animal boundary as *Wasps*, but this time via its title. The title itself provides a new context within which to contemplate a pivotal line from Aristophanes *Wasps* 1090 where the chorus of juror wasps draws attention to their own dual identity:

μηδὲν Ἀττικοῦ καλεῖσθαι <u>σφηκὸς ἀνδρικώτερον</u>.
"nothing is more <u>manly</u> when compared to an Attic <u>wasp</u>!"

Notice, in particular, the juxtaposition in the Greek of "wasp" (σφηκὸς) and "more manly" (ἀνδρικώτερον), as if forming a hybrid term, that matches the make-up of the Pherecratean title: *Ant* (Μυρμηκ-) and *men* (-ἄνθρωποι). Barely 16 lines of Pherecrates' comedy survive, plus a few phrases of Greek, which should be the first point to note when approaching a fragmentary play. With that in mind, let us look at *Ant-men*, fr. 117:

[Character 1.]:
τί ληρεῖς; ἀλλὰ <u>φωνὴν</u> οὐκ ἔχειν
ἰχθύν γε φασι τὸ παράπαν.
[Character 2.]
                                νὴ τὼ θεώ,
κοὐκ ἔστιν ἰχθὺς ἄλλος οὐδεὶς ἢ <u>βόαξ</u>.

[Character 1. (male or female)]:
What are you babbling about!? *But, fish* don't have a <u>voice</u> –they definitely say that!
[Character 2. (female)]
That's right, by the two goddesses, and there's not one fish with a voice-box except for the <u>boax (shouting-fish)</u>!

The exchange between characters creates a joke that pivots on a pun around a type of fish, while also playing with the idea that fish can speak, which Character 1 sees as ridiculous. This punning on the noun: βοά (*boa*, "a shout") and the name of a fish: βόαξ (*boax*, "a shouting-fish") plays around with the human–animal boundary, all of which is recognizable from the copious amount of humor on the human–animal boundary in *Wasps* (Miles 2018, 226–9). We can also note the character dynamics, familiar from Aristophanic comedy, where one character expresses anger and outrage (setting up the joke), and the other character continues to escalate the anger with cheeky remarks (completing the joke). This is also seen in the characters sharing metrical lines, interrupting one another (cf. Philocleon and Bdelycleon in *Wasps*; *Lysistrata* and her interlocutors; Socrates and Strepsiades in *Clouds*). This demonstrates that both the **mechanics** of comedy (joke dynamics and character dynamics) and the **content** of comedy (animal puns and transgressing human–animal boundary) were common aspects of the comic culture of Aristophanes and his contemporaries. These are not Aristophanic techniques but rather comic techniques.

However, when it comes to the *plot* of *Ant-Men*, we move in a different direction from *Wasps*, as can be seen from *Ant-men*, fr. 125 where a character addresses the mythical figure Deucalion:

μηδέποτ' ἰχθύν, ὦ Δευκαλίων, μηδ' ἣν αἰτῶ παραθῇς μοι.
[Character 1. (male or female)]:
Never serve me fish, Deucalion! Not if I beg you!

This suggests that the mythical figure of Deucalion was a character in *Ant-men*, inviting the intriguing (but unanswerable) question around the plot of this comic drama. Deucalion and Pyrrha were already associated with the creation of people from stones after the flood sent by Zeus in Pindar *Olympian* 9.41ff (cf. Ovid *Met.* 1.381ff). Pherecrates' comedy now begins to look entirely distinct from Aristophanes' *Wasps* due to the involvement of mythical figures. However, it is worth remembering that Aristophanes' fragmentary comedies also could employ mythical figures, for example, Aristophanes' *Polyidus* (fr. 469 mentions Phaedra) and *Lemnian Women* (frr. 373–4 refers to Hypsipyle and the role of the women in killing their husbands). The proliferation of mythically based titles for comedies extends from Cratinus through Aristophanes and on through the fourth century BCE, with Platon, Strattis, and Theopompus among comedians with a large number of myth-based titles (Bowie 2010 provides an excellent overview of myth in comedy). And yet, a comic title alone is not sufficient to reconstruct the plot and contents of a comedy.

This example of social insect comedies indicates the creative range of possibilities confronting a comic dramatist, while starting from the common base of insect choruses. It also raises the warning, long ago signaled by scholars, concerning the over-interpretation of fragments: Kenneth Dover (2000) used a discussion of *Frogs* to draw attention to the issues of employing conjecture with partial evidence for Greek comedies. Douglas Olson (2015) similarly used the case study of Athenaeus to show how reconstructing lost comedies based on fragments creates an artificial and fictional image of a drama, just as Donald Mastronarde (2009) had done in the case of tragedy using Euripides' *Phoenician Women*.

Conclusion

There was a proliferation of comedy and of comic poets in the lifetime of Aristophanes. The fragments provide the context within which to situate Aristophanic comedy, and they hint at the lost culture of comedy that ancient audiences in the fifth–fourth centuries BCE experienced. We do a disservice to the evidence to ignore this material. If we want to understand the comedies of Aristophanes, his contemporaries, and the culture of comedy within which they operated, we need to include the extant work of his contemporaries. The purpose of this chapter in focusing on Aristophanes' contemporaries was to give these dramatists more attention in their own right and to demonstrate some of the benefits of the study of Aristophanes when we situate him more fully within the context of a culture of comedy. This was done using snapshots from some of Aristophanes' key contemporaries: from the parallels unspoken between Platon and Aristophanes to the borrowings and bickerings of Aristophanes and Eupolis, Pherecrates and Phrynichus, all the way down to Theopompus and Strattis as emulators and expanders of the comic dramas beyond the limits of Aristophanes and his generation.

The key change that I made in this chapter is methodological: I have spent our time focusing on the culture of comedy in order to explore **the dynamics between comic dramatists**, their overlaps and interactions their imitation and irritation with one another, and how this shapes the work and style of each dramatist. This approach is taken rather than viewing each dramatist in isolation. It enables us to move away from the commonly used tools of plot reconstruction or reconstituting the career of a dramatist, whose career is now (physically rather than figuratively) in tatters. Plot reconstruction tends toward layers of conjecture and reaches for questions that our evidence cannot always answer. Instead, the approach has been to change the lens: rather than viewing Greek Comedy through an Aristophanes-focused lens, I view Greek Comedy and Aristophanes through the fragmentary lens of his contemporaries. I have done so, not to champion my approach as superior, but because it provides a fresh and different lens through which to view Aristophanes, his contemporaries, and the culture of comedy in which they all operated. This means that the cracks, the holes, and the gaps in our evidence are more obvious, and the discomforts that go with it. This represents the reality of our evidence: no more "castles on the sand" without admitting that this is what we are all doing to a relative degree in classical scholarship.

This chapter has questioned Aristophanic exceptionalism by (re)introducing the key players of ancient performance comedy within the context of a culture of comedy that was marked by: *open competition, personal rivalry, co-creativity, self-promotion*, and a desire for success and celebrity. Aristophanes was one of many comic poets in the fifth–fourth century seeking prizes, esteem, societal backing, and the opportunity to compose ever more comedies, each of which reflected the individual style, esthetics, and values of the composer. At the same time, these comic dramas incorporated both collaboration and "theft" of comic material from one another, drawing on what had been successful with a particular audience. Comedy is a shared enterprise between actor, writer, and audience, and when something works with an audience, comedy repeats the joke, the joke structure, the comic character, the comic persona, the scene, and even plot structures. In this area, there is more that classical scholarship can do to engage with contemporary scholarship on comic performance.

The culture of comedy is at its heart a construct of the comic dramatists themselves. An ancient form of celebrity culture, if you will. It offers a creative space to play, in which we see emerging the rivalry, the fighting over jokes, and the endless put-downs that give us a hint of the struggles for dramatists to gain celebrity status. Exploring this culture of comedy encourages scholars to look at the cultural biases, discrimination, and deep-seated insecurities at the heart of Athenian society around gender, ethnicity, sexuality, age, and ablism, and there is much work for scholarship to do in this area for Greek Comedy. This work can only be achieved by embracing comic fragments alongside Aristophanic comedy. By viewing Aristophanes as part and a product of this culture of comedy, we have a means to contextualize Aristophanic work within its original setting, and to understand better the ancient audience experience. These audiences were used to seeing comedy after comedy, year upon year, by a wide selection of comic dramatists for a one-off unique performance. They did not live with the partial legacy of comedy, as we do now, but with **the live event and the lived experience of comic performance**.

Working with comic fragments is tricky, time-consuming, but rewarding for our understanding of the wider culture of comedy in fifth-century BCE Athens. With fragments, we need to acknowledge the gaps in our evidence and move beyond the well-trodden canonical authors and the canonical perspectives that persist around them. Comic fragments are now available in edited volumes, in translation, and in a growing number of commentaries. It is now to the next generation of scholars on Greek drama to embrace fully the complexity and the creativity of the fragments so that our understanding of drama, ancient, and contemporary continues to expand.

Greek comic fragments point up the precarity on which we place our interpretations of Aristophanes and of Greek drama more generally. Even when the evidence that remains is partial, interrupted, and fragmentary, for the ancient audiences of comic drama, there was a vibrant, lively continuous culture of comedy at Athens that extended from the fifth century BCE down to the time of Menander and beyond. Fragments are a legitimate source set that it should no longer be acceptable to ignore in any publication on Aristophanes, even if those fragments present a discomforting mirror to the delicacy of the work we do when we explore ancient Greek Comedy.

GUIDE TO FURTHER READING

The key edited volume of Greek comic fragments is *PCG* (*Poetae Comici Graeci*) by Kassel and Austin (1983–2001). Commentaries on the Greek text continue to emerge from Bernhard Zimmermann, *Kommentierung der Fragmente der griechischen Komödie* (*KomFrag*), with some volumes in English. For a Greek text with translation, there is Ian Storey's Loeb edition: *Fragments of Old Comedy* (2011), but a comprehensive and accessible guide to comic fragments in translation remains unpublished. Important monographs on individual comic dramatists are sparse: Ian Storey, *Eupolis Poet of Old Comedy* (2003); Mario Telò, *Eupolidis Demi* (2007); and Emmanuela Bakola, *Cratinus and the Art of Comedy* (2010). Douglas Olson's *Broken Laughter* (Olson 2007) provides a compilation of fragments arranged and discussed by theme, including translations. Alan Sommerstein's (2019) *The Encyclopedia of Greek Comedy* provides excellent summaries of each of Aristophanes' contemporaries. Key edited volumes include Gregory Dobrov, *Beyond Aristophanes: Transition and Diversity in Greek Comedy* (1995); David Harvey & John Wilkins, *The Rivals of Aristophanes: Studies in Athenian Old Comedy* (Harvey and Wilkins 2000), which remains the single-most influential work on my early encounters with comic fragments. Work to develop a sound and consistent methodology for working with comic fragments is still in its infancy: Anna Lamari, Franco Montanari, and Anna Novokhatko, *Fragmentation in Ancient Greek Drama* (Lamari et al. 2020).

REFERENCES

Bakola, E. (2008). The drunk, the reformer and the teacher: agonistic poetics and the construction of persona in the comic poets of the fifth century. *Cambridge Classical Journal* 54: 1–29.

Bakola, E. (2010). *Cratinus and the Art of Comedy*. Cambridge: Cambridge University Press.

Biles, Z.P. (2011). *Aristophanes and the Poetics of Competition*. Cambridge: Cambridge University Press.

Bowie, A. (2010). Myth and ritual in comedy. In: *Brill's Companion to the Study of Greek Comedy* (ed. G.W. Dobrov), 143–176. Leiden & Boston: Brill.

Braund, D.C. (2000). Strattis' Kallipides: the pompous actor from Scythia? In: *The Rivals of Aristophanes. Studies in Athenian Old Comedy* (ed. D. Harvey and J. Wilkins), 151–158. London: Duckworth and the Classical Press of Wales.

Carey, C. (2000). Old comedy and the sophists. In: *The Rivals of Aristophanes: Studies in Athenian Old Comedy* (ed. D. Harvey and J. Wilkins), 419–436. London: Duckworth and The Classical Press of Wales.

Collard, C., Cropp, M.J., and Lee, K.H. (1995–2004). *Selected Fragmentary Plays: Euripides*. Warminster: Aris & Phillips.

Csapo, E.G. (2000). From Aristophanes to Menander?: genre transformation in Greek comedy. In: *Matrices of Genre: Authors, Canons, and Society* (ed. M. Depew and D. Obbink), 115–133. Cambridge: Harvard University Press.

Csapo, E.G. (2010). *Actors and Icons of the Ancient Theater*. Malden, MA: Wiley Blackwell.

Csapo, E.G. and Wilson, P. (2020). *A Social and Economic History of the Theatre to 300 BC. Vol. II. Theatre Beyond Athens: Documents with Translation and Commentary*. Cambridge: Cambridge University Press.

Davies, M. and Kathirithamby, J. (1986). *Greek Insects*. New York: Oxford University Press.

Dobrov, G.W. (ed.) (1995). *Beyond Aristophanes: Transition and Diversity in Greek Comedy*. Atlanta, GA: Scholars Press.

Dover, K.J. (2000). Foreword: frogments. In: (ed. D. Harvey and J. Wilkins), xvii–xix. London: Duckworth and The Classical Press of Wales.

Ehrenberg, V. (1943). *The People of Aristophanes: A Sociology of Old Attic Comedy*. Oxford: Blackwell.

Farmer, M.C. (2017). *Tragedy on the Comic Stage*. New York: Oxford University Press.

Fiorentini, L. (2010). Elementi paratragici nelle Fenicie di Strattide. *Dionysus ex Machina* 1: 52–68.

Foley, H.P. (2008). Generic Boundaries in Late Fifth-Century Athens. In: *Performance, Iconography, Reception: Studies in Honour of Oliver Taplin* (ed. M. Revermann and P.J. Wilson), 15–36. Oxford: Oxford University Press.

Hanink, J. (2014). *Lycurgan Athens and the Making of Classical Tragedy*, 159–190. Cambridge: Cambridge University Press.

Harvey, D. and Wilkins, J. (ed.) (2000). *The Rivals of Aristophanes: Studies in Athenian Old Comedy*. Swansea, Wales: Duckworth and The Classical Press of Wales.

Henderson, J. (2000). Pherekrates and the women of Old Comedy. In: (ed. D. Harvey and J. Wilkins), 135–150. London: Duckworth and The Classical Press of Wales.

Henderson, J. (2015). Types and styles of comedy between 450 and 420. In: *Fragmente einer Geschichte der griechischen Komödie / Fragmentary History of Greek Comedy. Studia Comica, 5* (ed. S. Chronopoulos and C. Orth), 146–158. Heidelberg: Verlag Antike.

Hughes, A. (2012). *Performing Greek Comedy*. Cambridge: Cambridge University Press.

Jendza, C. (2020). *Paracomedy. Appropriations of Comedy in Greek Tragedy*. New York: Oxford University Press.

Kassel, R. and Austin, C. (1983–2001). *Poetae Comici Graeci*. Berlin & Boston: De Gruyter.

Lamari Anna, A. (ed.) (2015). *Reperformances of Drama in the Fifth and Fourth Centuries BC: Authors and Contexts, Trends in Classics 7.2*. Berlin & Boston: De Gruyter.

Lamari, A.A., Montanari, F., and Novokhatko, A. (ed.) (2020). *Fragmentation in Ancient Greek Drama, Trends in Classics 84.* Berlin & Boston: De Gruyter.
Lefkowitz, M.R. (2012). *The Lives of the Greek Poets.* Baltimore, MD: Johns Hopkins University Press.
Mastronarde, D.J. (2009). The lost Phoenissae: an experiment in reconstruction from fragments. In: *The Play of Texts and Fragments: Essays in Honour of Martin Cropp* (ed. J. Robert, C. Cousland, and J.R. Hume), 63–76. Leiden: Brill.
Miles, S. (2009). Strattis, Tragedy, and Comedy. PhD thesis, University of Nottingham.
Miles, S. (2018). Ancient Receptions of Euripides in Comedy: the Phoenissae of Euripides, Aristophanes and Strattis. *Frammenti sulla Scena. Studi sul dramma antico frammentario* 1: 175–200.
Miles, S. (2019). Paratragedy. In: *The Encyclopedia of Greek Comedy* (ed. A.H. Sommerstein), 660–662. Malden MA: Wiley-Blackwell.
Nervegna, S. (2013). *Menander in Antiquity: The Contexts of Reception.* Cambridge & New York: Cambridge University Press.
Olson, S.D. (2006–2012). *Athenaeus. The Learned Banqueters vol. I–VIII.* London & Cambridge, MA: Harvard University Press.
Olson, S.D. (2007). *Broken Laughter: Select Fragments of Greek Comedy.* Oxford: Oxford University Press.
Olson, S.D. (2015). 'Athenaeus' Aristophanes, and the problem of reconstructing lost comedies. In: *Fragmente einer Geschichte der griechischen Komödie / Fragmentary History of Greek Comedy. Studia Comica, 5* (ed. S. Chronopoulos and C. Orth), 35–65. Heidelberg: Verlag Antike.
Orth, C. (2009). *Strattis: Die Fragmente: Ein Kommentar.* Berlin: Verlag Antike.
Pirrotta, S. (2009). *Plato Comicus, Die fragmentarischen Komödien: Ein Kommentar.* Berlin: Verlag Antike.
Rau, P. (1967). *Paratragodia: Untersuchung einer komischen Form des Aristophanes.* Munich: Beck.
Sells, D. (2013). Slaves in the fragments of Old Comedy. In: *Slaves and Slavery in Ancient Greek Comic Drama* (ed. B. Akrigg and R. Tordoff), 91–110. Cambridge: Cambridge University Press.
Sells, D. (2019). *Parody, Politics, and the Populace in Greek Old Comedy.* London: Bloomsbury Academic.
Silk, M.S. (1993). Aristophanic paratragedy. In: *Tragedy, Comedy and the Polis* (ed. A.H. Sommerstein, S. Halliwell, J. Henderson, and B. Zimmermann), 477–504. Bari: Levante Editori.
Silk, M.S. (2020). Connotations of 'comedy' in classical Athens. In: *Ancient Greek Comedy: Genre - Texts – Reception* (ed. A. Fries and D. Kanellakis), 29–47. Berlin & Boston: De Gruyter.
Sommerstein, A.H. (1980–2002). *The Comedies of Aristophanes,* vol. 1–11. Warminster: Aris & Phillips.
Sommerstein, A.H. (2000). Platon, eupolis, and the 'Demagogue-Comedy. In: *The Rivals of Aristophanes: Studies in Athenian Old Comedy* (ed. D. Harvey and J. Wilkins), 439–452. London: Duckworth and The Classical Press of Wales.
Sommerstein, A. (ed.) (2019). *Encyclopedia of Greek Comedy.* Hoboken: Wiley Blackwell.
Storey, I.C. (2003). *Eupolis Poet of Old Comedy.* Oxford: Oxford University Press.
Storey, I.C. (2011). *Fragments of Old Comedy,* vol. I–III. Cambridge, MA: Harvard University Press.
Storey, I.C. (2011a). *Fragments of Old Comedy, Volume I: Alcaeus to Diocles. Loeb Classical Library, 513.* Cambridge, MA/London: Harvard University Press.
Storey, I.C. (2011b). *Fragments of Old Comedy, Volume II: Diopeithes to Pherecrates. Loeb Classical Library 514.* Cambridge, MA/London: Harvard University Press.
Storey, I.C. (2011c). *Fragments of Old Comedy. Volume III, Philonicus to Xenophon. Loeb Classical Library 515.* Cambridge, MA/London: Harvard University Press.
Telò, M. (2007). *Eupolidis Demi.* Florence: Felice Le Monnier.
Wallace-Hare, D. (2022). *New Approaches to the Archaeology of Beekeeping.* Oxford: Archaeopress Publishing Limited.
Wright, M. (2016). *The Lost Plays of Greek Tragedy,* vol. 1. London: Bloomsbury Academic.
Wright, M. (2019). *The Lost Plays of Greek Tragedy,* vol. 2. London: Bloomsbury Academic.
Zimmermann, B. (2015). Periodisierungszwänge als Problem und Herausforderung der Literaturgeschichtsschreibung. In: *Fragmente einer Geschichte der griechischen Komödie / Fragmentary History of Greek Comedy. Studia Comica, 5* (ed. S. Chronopoulos and C. Orth), 9–15. Heidelberg: Verlag Antike.

CHAPTER 21

Aristophanes' Successors

Anna Uhlig

Introduction

Before embarking on any examination of the comic "successors" of Aristophanes, it will be useful to consider just what is meant by "successor." Until relatively recently, this chapter would most likely have been given a title such as "New Comedy" or "Middle and New Comedy," adopting the conventional terminology that has been used to demarcate comic periodization since as early as the third century BCE (see Willi, Chapter 23). Ancient writers seem to have had no doubt that the categories of "Old" (*archaia*), "Middle" (*mese*), and "New" (*nea*) accurately described three distinct periods of comic drama. But since the late twentieth century, scholars have begun to seriously question the validity of this traditional taxonomy.

Many modern scholars have contributed to the reassessment of Ancient Greek comedy, but it is to Eric Csapo's masterful chapter "From Aristophanes to Menander: Genre Transformation in Greek Comedy" that the shift can most directly be attributed (Csapo 2000). There Csapo demonstrated the limitations of the traditional tripartite periodization with respect to both ancient and modern scholars. For the former, he observed, the schema served to support the author-based hierarchies favored by ancient literary criticism and was unlikely to reflect historical shifts in the genre as a whole.[1] In other words, the types of plot and humor that the ancients associated with distinct periods of Ancient Greek comedy were most probably part of the genre in some form from start to finish. For modern scholars, with our far more limited access to actual plays, Csapo notes that the focus on authors (rather than on the genre as a whole) is even more exaggerated, since we "tend to work not on comedy, but on Aristophanes or [his fourth-century successor] Menander around whom the traditional scheme is conveniently built" (Csapo (2000) 121). In other words, claims about the history and development of Ancient Greek comedy are, all too often, actually claims about the similarities and differences between the two practitioners to whom we have the greatest access: Aristophanes and Menander.

Csapo is undoubtedly correct in his diagnosis of the pitfalls of an "Aristophanes to Menander" narrative. Less clear is whether a convincing connected account of Ancient Greek comedy can be composed without recourse to the traditional tripartite periodization or narratives of generic

---

[1] "General opinion, trained by ancient habits, holds that great and significant changes took place in comedy at the end of the fifth century and again soon after the death of Alexander. The evidence, however, shows that what we normally think of as Old, Middle, and New Comedy designate synchronic, not period styles. This is not to say that there existed no qualitative difference between comedy in the fifth and comedy in the late fourth century, but rather that these differences are not characterizable by the broad categories of plot type of style of humor that we have inherited from ancient scholarship." Csapo 2000 121.

transformation. Rather than try to replace outdated models with a new and updated unified theory, this chapter offers an overview, necessarily brief and incomplete, of what we know about "Aristophanes' Successors" and, perhaps more importantly, how we know it. Each of the sections that follows introduces one important source of our current state of knowledge about post-Aristophanic comic drama. I begin with the indirect tradition: Athenaeus' *Scholars at Dinner*, Stobaeus' *Anthology*, and brief catalog of other ancient compilers and commentators. I then turn to material culture with particular emphasis on papyrological discoveries, both unidentified fragments and the large number of discoveries attributed to Menander. No attempt is made to synthesize these disparate fonts of evidence into a comprehensive narrative. However, the sections are all guided by the following methodological questions: What can we learn from the corpus if we choose *not* to view Aristophanes and Menander as broadly representative of a distinct style of comedy that held sway during the periods in which they were composed? How might our perception of Greek comic drama of the fourth and third centuries BCE look if we treat "succession" in purely chronological terms, without freighting it with the baggage of "inheritance" or "development?" Is it possible to emulate, or even to make a virtue of the fragmentariness of our evidence in the way that we think about ancient comedy?

Dramatis Personae

A cast of characters is always a good place to start when it comes to questions of theater. The sheer number of names of those we know to have been composing comic drama in Greek in the fourth and third centuries BCE provides a good counterweight to the "Aristophanes to Menander" narrative. We know of at least 186 Greek comic playwrights whose work enjoyed enough success in the years following Aristophanes' death in 386 BCE to be recorded in some form or another.[2] Their names or partial names, in alphabetical order with the century in which they worked in parentheses, are as follows:

Agathenor	(I)	Dionysius 2	(IV)	[?o]nesi[	(III)
Agathocles	(II)	Dionysius 3	(II)	Ophelio	(IV)
Alcenor	(IV)	[Dionysodo]rus	(IV)	Pandaetes	(III)
Alexander	(II-I)	Diosc[uride]s	(III)	Paramonus	(II)
Alexis	(IV-III)	Dioxippus	(IV)	Philemon	(IV-III)
Aminias	(IV-III)	Diphilus	(IV-III)	Philemon Junior	(III)
Amphichares	(II)	Dromon	(IV)	Philemon III	(II)
Amphis	(IV)	[Emm]enides	(II)	Philetaerus	(IV)
Anaxandrides	(IV)	Ephippus	(IV)	Philippides	(IV-III)
Anaxilas	(IV)	Epicrates 1	(IV)	Philippus	(IV)
Anaxippus	(IV-III)	Epi[crates] 2	(II)	Philiscus 1	(IV)
Antidotus	(IV)	Epigenes	(IV)	Philiscus 2	(III)
[Anti]genes	(II)	Epinicus	(III-II)	Philocles	(II)
Antiochus	(II)	Erato[	(III)	Philom[	(III)
Antiphanes 1	(IV)	Eriphus	(IV)	Philostephanus	(III-II)
Antiphanes 2	(III)	Eteagoras	(III)	[Philos]tratus	(III)
Antiphon	(II)	Euangelos	(III ?)	Philostratus	(II)
Anubion	(II)	Eubulides 1	(IV)	Phoenicides	(III)
Apollinaris	(IV)	Eubu[lides] 2	(III)	Po[	(II-I)
Apollodorus Carystius	(III)	Eubulus	(IV)	P[o]ly[	(III)
Apollodorus Geious	(IV-III)	Eudoxus	(III-II)	Polyclitus	(III)
Araros	(IV)	Eumedes	(III)	Poses	(I)

---

[2] This number, and the list of names that follows, is derived from the magisterial edition of Greek comic fragments *Poetae Comici Graeci* compiled and edited by Rudolph Kassel and Colin Austin.

Archedicus	(IV-III)	Euphanes	(IV)	Posidippus	(III)
Archi[	(III)	Euphron	(III)	[Posi]dipus	(II)
Archicles	(II)	Euthias	(IV)	Proclides	(IV)
Aristides	(III)	Eu<th>ycrates	(III)	Protarchus	(I)
Aristocl[es]	(II)	Germanicus	(I)	Pyr[ren]	(IV)
Aristocrates	(III-II)	Hegesippus	(III)	Pythod[	(III)
Ariston 1	(II)	Heniochus	(IV)	Satyron	(III)
Ariston 2	(I)	Heraclides	(IV)	Simylus	(III)
Ariston 3	(I)	Hipparchus	(III)	Soc[	(III)
Aristophon	(IV)	Iolaus	(II)	Sogenes	(II)
Aropus	(III)	Laines	(II)	Sophilus	(IV)
[Asclepiodo]rus	(IV)	Lampytus	(II)	Sosicrates	(III ?)
Athenio	(I ?)	Laon	(III)	So[sigenes	(II)
Athenocles	(IV)	Lynceus	(IV-III)	Sosipater	(III)
Augeas	(IV)	Machon	(III)	Sosippus	(IV-III)
Axionicus	(IV)	Menander	(IV)	Sotades	(IV)
Bato	(III)	Menestheneus	(III)	Stephanus	(IV-III)
Biottus	(II)	Metrodorus	(II)	Stratagus	(III)
[Bo]iscus	(I)	Mnasicles	(II)	Straton	(IV)
Callicrates	(IV)	[?m]nesi[	(III)	Theaetetus	(IV-III)
Callimachus	(III)	Mnesimachus	(IV)	Themis[	(III)
Chaerion	(II)	Musaeus	(III)	Theod[	(III)
Chariclides	(III)	Nausicrates	(IV)	[The]odorus	(III)
Chionnes	(I)	[N]eanthes	(III)	Theodor[us]	(III)
Chrysippus	(III)	[Ne]leus	(III)	Theognetus	(III)
Clearchus	(IV)	Nicarchus	(III-II)	Theo[n]	(?)
Cleo[	(II)	Nici[as]	(III)	Theophilus	(IV)
Cratinus Iunior	(IV)	Nicon	(IV-III)	Thymoteles	(II)
Crito 1	(II)	Nicodemus	(II)	Timocles	(IV)
Crito 2	(I)	Nicolaus	(II ?)	Timon	(IV)
Crobyllus	(IV)	Nicolaus Damascenus	(I)	Timostratus	(II)
Damoxenus	(III)	Nicomachus 1	(III)	Timotheus 1	(IV)
Demetrius	(III)	Nicomachus 2	(III-II)	Timotheus 2	(II)
Demonicus	(IV ?)	Nicostratus 1	(IV)	Timoxenus	(II)
Demophilus	(III-II ?)	Nicostratus 2	(IV-III)	Xenarchus	(IV)
Dexicrates	(III)	Nicostratus 3	(III-II)	Xeno	(III)
Dieuches	(I)	Novius	(II)		
Diodorus	(III)	O[	(II-I)		
Dionysius 1	(IV)	Oly[mp	(II)		

About many of these authors we know next to nothing apart from their names. Of others, we are far better informed (see Sommerstein 2019; for translations, see Rusten et al. 2017). None of them, not even Menander, has made it to the present day with anything like the clarity of Aristophanes and his 11 continuously transmitted scripts. Any attempt to comprehend the vibrant world of Greek comic drama that followed in the wake of Aristophanes is profoundly constrained by the vicissitudes of preservation. There is much that we may want to know, but often very little that can be said with certainty.

A Comic Feast

The most important source for our present knowledge about Ancient Greek comic drama, and especially about post-Aristophanic comedy, is a remarkable prose work entitled *Scholars at Dinner* written around 200 CE by a certain Athenaeus of Naucratis.[3] As the title suggests, Athenaeus' work

---

[3] Text and translation Olson 206–2013. For a general introduction to Athenaeus and his work, see Braund and Wilkins (2000); for the unreliability of Athenaeus as a source for understanding earlier poetry, see LeVen (2010).

is set at a fictional dinner party attended by a group of incredibly learned men.[4] As the almost impossibly long party progresses (in its current form, the work runs to 15 books; Rodriguez-Noriega Guillén 2000), the banqueters display their erudition by trading quotations from various works of poetry and prose. The topics range widely, but questions of food and drink – as befits the setting – are allotted the most attention.

Quotations from comic playwrights, particularly those dating to the fourth and third centuries BCE, comprise a significant proportion of the passages cited by Athenaeus' learned banqueters. The surviving text of *Scholars at Dinner* includes 2873 quotations attributed to comic authors.[5] This number dwarfs the 597 quotations from epic, the next most frequently cited poetic genre, and is more than double the 1280 passages from historical works (the second most popular genre overall). The name of the fourth-century comic playwright Alexis is the third most often spoken by the banqueters, behind only those of Homer and Aristotle. This generic bias is likely attributable to the comic tendency to celebrate food and wine, the subject most frequently discussed in *Scholars at Dinner*, in exuberant passages full of rich detail (Wilkins (2000a, b)), though we should keep in mind the possibility that we overestimate the prevalence of food-related themes in comedy due to the outsized influence of Athenaeus on the surviving record. Thus, for example, when Athenaeus' diners turn to the subject of the gray mullet, they offer up a medley from various comic poets:

> Anaxilas in *The Recluse* (fr. 20) accuses the sophist Maton of gluttony, saying:
> Maton grabbed the head of the gray mullet
> and gobbled it down; but I'm ruined.
> And the noble Archestratus[6] (fr. 43 Olson-Sens) says:
> Purchase a gray mullet from sea-girt Aegina
> and you will be counted among clever men.
> Diocles in *The Sea (fr. 6)*:
> A gray mullet leaps out of sheer joy.
> Archippus in *Heracles Getting Married* (fr. 12) says that *nêsteis* ("fasters") are a variety of gray mullet"
> fasting gray mullets
> Antiphanes in *Lampon* (fr. 136):
> You happen to have fasting gray mullets, but not
> fasting soldiers
> Alexis in *The Phrygian* (fr. 258):
> But I'm a fasting gray mullet running
> off home.
> Amipsias in *Cottbus-Players* (fr. 1):
> But I'm going to go to
> the marketplace and try to find a job. (B.) In that case you'd
> follow me around less like a fasting gray mullet.
> Euphro in *The Ugly Girl* (fr. 2):
> Midas is a gray mullet; he walks around
> fasting.
> Philemon in *Men Who Were Dying Together* (fr. 83):
> I bought a small roasted fasting gray mullet.
> Aristophanes in *Gerytades* (fr. 159)
> Is there a colony of gray mullet-men inside?
> Because it is known that they're fasting!

---

[4] Such dinner-party settings were popular amongst ancient prose authors. Modern scholars generally refer to them under the broad rubric of "sympotic literature."

[5] This and all other statistics related to Athenaeus included in this chapter have been compiled with the aid of Monica Berti's indispensable "Digital Athenaeus" platform (https://www.digitalathenaeus.org).

[6] Archestratus is the only author in this catalog who is not a comic playwright. His hexameter poem *Life of Luxury*, of which only fragments remain, is a guide to fine dining around the Mediterranean. For more, see Olson and Sens (2000).

Anaxandrides in *Odysseus* (fr. 35.8):
   A guy generally goes around without having had
   dinner; he's Fasting Mullet.
Eubulus in *Nausicaa* (fr. 68):
   who's been in the water for three days now,
   living the fasting life of a miserable gray mullet.
                                          (Athenaeus 7. 307c-f; trans. Olson)

We will return to the question of food and drink in the final section of this chapter. For now, we can set it alongside the many other topics, such as the names of famous courtesans, the behavior of chatterers and flatterers, or the entertainment value of riddles that prompt Athenaeus' diners to offer copious quotations from poetry. This last is a particularly interesting instance in which various forms of verse appear more or less on the same page, both literally and figuratively.

A brief section on punning and wordplay begins with the sixth-century lyric poet Lasus of Hermione:

One can also find many riddles [sc. in Lasus' song *Centaurs*]:
   I was born on Phanera, and saltwater enfolds my
   fatherland. But my mother is Number's child.
By Phanera he means Delos, which is surrounded by the sea, while the mother
   is Leto, who is the daughter of Coius; and the Macedonians use the word *koios* to mean "number."
                                          (Athenaeus 10. 455d; trans. Olson adapted)

Athenaeus then wends his way through fifth- and fourth-century comedy and undated, unidentified tragedy:

Antiphanes says in *The Man Who was in Love with Himself* (fr. 51):
   and linen-fleshed curdling. Do you understand? I'm referring to cheese.
Anaxandrides in *Aeschra* (fr. 6):
   He's just now finished the butchering, and the long-cut
   portions of flesh are being subdued in fire-formed bits of earth;
   thus Timotheus, at some point, gentlemen, referring, I believe, to a cookpot.
Timocles in *Heroes* (fr. 13):
                    And thus was carried away
   the nurse of life, enemy of starvation, guardian
   of friendship, healer of unbounded ravenousness –
   the table. (B.) Elaborately expressed, by heaven –
   when you could've just said "the table"!
Plato in his *Adonis* (fr. 3) reports that Cinyras received an oracle about his son Adonis, and says:
   Cinyras, king of the hairy-assed Cyprians,
   your son is the most amazingly beautiful person
   in the entire world. But two divinities will bring about his ruin,
   the goddess by being rowed with secret oars, the god by rowing.
He is referring to Aphrodite and Dionysus; because they were both in love with Adonis. Asclepiades in his *Stories Told in Tragedy* (FGrH 12 F 7a = AP 14.64) claims that the riddle of the Sphinx went as follows:
   There is a creature upon the earth that has two feet and four, a single voice,
   and three feet as well; of all that moves on land,
   and through the air, and in the sea, it alone alters its nature.
   But when it makes its way propped on the largest number of feet,
   then the swiftness in its limbs is weakest.
                                          (Athenaeus 10. 455d–456c; trans. Olson)

Athenaeus then pivots back to sixth-century lyric, this time that of the Cean poet Simonides:

The following passage composed by Simonides (fr. 69 Diehl) also has a riddling
character, according to Chamaeleon of Heracleia in his *On Simonides* (fr. 34 Wehrli):
   The father of a kid that grazes on anything and a miserable fish

> lean their heads close to one another. But when they take a child
> of night in with their eyes, they are unwilling to tend to
> the ox-slaying servant of King Dionysus.
> Some authorities claim that this text was inscribed on one of the ancient dedications in
> Chalchis, and that a billy-goat and a dolphin were depicted on this dedication and
> these lines describe them.
>
> (Athenaeus 10. 456c–d; trans. Olson)

The lack of differentiation between non-dramatic lyrics, tragedy, and comedy on display in this passage is a good illustration of how potentially misleading brief quotations can be. Absent crucial contextual information about the work as a whole, excerpts from wildly different genres can appear deceptively similar. (Likewise, connections or similarities between plays or authors may be entirely effaced.) Far from differentiating between the three ages of comic drama, Athenaeus is content to treat works from a range of poetic and prose genres as more or less interchangeable evidence in support of whatever particular point he is seeking to elucidate. What is more, as Douglas Olson has demonstrated, Athenaeus is quite willing to engage in "aggressive misreading" in the framing discussions of his source material when it serves his ends (Olson 2020). We do not know how Athenaeus accessed the thousands of lines that he quotes; it may be that he did not know much more about the plays that he quotes than what appears on the page. *Scholars at Dinner* makes mention of a number of ancient treatises on the subject of comedy, notably various catalogs of *komoidoumenoi* (lists of those mocked in comic drama). Modern scholars have suspected that earlier compendia like these, rather than the plays themselves, may have been the sources for the majority of Athenaeus' comic quotations (Nesselrath (2010) 426–7; Apostolakis 2020).

In addition to the names of comic playwrights, Athenaeus is generous in recording the titles of many of their works in the context of his quotations. Although it is rarely possible to divine much about the plot, even in outline, of a comic drama simply from knowledge of its title, there is still much that titles can tell us, particularly when we know so many of them. Take, for instance, the preponderance of titles associated with relatively low-status occupations; works such as the two plays entitled *Pimp* (*Pornoboskos*) by Eubulus and Posidippus, respectively (not to mention the *Antipimp* (*Antipornoboskos*) of Dioxippus, Menander's *Fishermen* (*Halieis*), Diphilus' *Merchant* (*Emporos*), Nicostratus' *Cook* (*Mageiros*), Anaxilas' *Cooks* (*Mageiroi*), Timocles' *Boxer* (*Puktos*), and Hermippus' *Baker* (*Artopolides*)) – to take a sampling at random.

Titles highlighting female-gendered occupations suggest important, often transgressive, roles for women within many of these dramas. Among those recorded by Athenaeus, we find *Wool Workers* (*Erithoi*), *Seamstress* (*Akestria*), *Female Harpist* (*Psaltria*), *Female Flute Player* (*Auletris*), *Nurse* (*Titthe*) or *Nurses* (*Titthai*), *Female Athletic Trainer* (*Aleiptria*), *Female Beggar* (*Ptoche*), and *Female Pythagorian* (*Pythagorizousa*). At times, these female-gendered titles are clearly sexualized, as with Menander's *Courtesan* (*Pallake*), or the many plays named after famous courtesans (e.g., Neaira, Nannion, and possibly the Lesbian poet Sappho[7]) or with the generic sobriquet for a hetaira, Chickee (*Neottis*). Other times they seem to focus on female vulnerability, as with Antiphanes' *Woman Fished* (*Halieuomene*), *Woman Abandoned* (*Apolipousa*), a title employed by both Diphilus and Crobylus, or Alexis' *Woman Poisoned by Mandrake* (*Mandragorizomene*).

Nor are women the only ones whose insecurity is foregrounded in the comic titles Athenaeus has collected for us. Comedies often take their titles from enslaved characters, as with Nicostratus' *Favored Slave* (*Habra*) or Menander's *Men Sold* (*Poloumenoi*). However, as the enslaved men who inspire the title of Menander's *Men at Trial* (*Epitrepontes*) remind us, there is a great deal of enslavement that is not explicitly legible in comic titles.

---

[7] However, see the cautious approach of Yatromanolakis (2007) 287–312 to the hyper-sexualization of Sappho in comedy.

Comic titles from Athenaeus can also help to dispel some misperceptions that tend to adhere to post-Aristophanic comedy. As Heinz-Günther Nesselrath had argued, comic titles reflect an important comic tradition of mythological parody that often goes unacknowledged (Nesselrath 1995). While Nesselrath highlights the preponderance of plots focused on the early childhoods of the gods in fourth-century comedy, also noteworthy is the popularity of divine marriage plays as well as heroic narratives, particularly those connected to Odysseus and Herakles. When it comes to representations closer to everyday life, titles such as Diphilus' *Lovers of Young Men* (*Paiderastai*) and Antiphanes' *Lover of Young Men* (*Paiderastes*) make clear that sexual relationships between men were hardly banished from the comic stage after the fifth century (Wright 2022a). Although the evidence is slightly less clear cut, the titles in Athenaeus also seem to reflect the continued importance of the chorus as an integral part of comic drama, at least in a handful of plays (on which see, most recently, Jackson 2020). It is certainly a mistake to assume that any plural agents in a dramatic title must constitute its chorus; the sheer number of plays entitled *Brothers*, *Sisters*, or *Twins* is a reminder of the degree to which post-Aristophanic comedy revels in doublets. Yet there are some titles – such as Posidippus' *Women in a Chorus* (*Choreuousai*), Euphron's *Muses* (*Mousai*), Anaxandrides' *Daughters of Nereus* (*Nereides*), or Timocles' *Icarian Satyrs* (*Ikarioi Satyroi*) – that are hard to envision without assuming a prominent role for an eponymous chorus.

So much for an impressionistic overview. What about cold, hard statistics? Like the fish that fill its pages, *Scholars at Dinner* offers sufficient comic quotations that one can happily prepare a variety of tasty dishes. It is possible, for example, to rank the comic playwrights mentioned by Athenaeus by frequency of citation. We find the top 20 in the following order (fifth-century authors in square brackets):

Author name:	# of quotations:
Alexis	335
Antiphanes	287
[Aristophanes	254]
[Epicharmus	163]
[Eupolis	161]
Eubulus	141
Menander	122
[Pherecrates	90]
[Cratinus	88]
Diphilus	80
Anaxandrides	67
[Plato	67]
Ephippus	58
Timocles	50
Amphis	40
Philemon	37
Anaxilas	35
Nicostratus	35
[Strattis	34]
[Theopompus	33][8]

---

[8] Macho of Sicyon (III) and Lyceus of Samos are excluded from this list since only a handful of the passages that Athenaeus includes from their work are from comic drama.

If, instead, we want to rank by number of plays (i.e., breadth of corpus represented), the top 20 author names look like this:

Author name:	# of named plays quoted:
Alexis	104
Antiphanes	96
Eubulus	46
Menander	46
[Aristophanes	43]
Diphilus	31
Timocles	24
Anaxandrides	23
[Plato	23]
Philemon	19
Nicostratus	18
[Pherecrates	18]
Amphis	16
Anaxilas	16
[Strattis	16]
[Theopompus	15]
Euhippus	13
[Eupolis	13]
Philetaerus	10
[Phrynichus	9][9]

This is a ranking by number of quotations not attributed to named plays (the actual number of plays represented by this ranking is, by definition, impossible to gauge):

Author name:	# of quotes w/out play:
Antiphanes	47
Alexis	39
Eubulus	20
[Aristophanes	17]
[Cratinus	17]
Alexandrides	10
Amphis	9
Diphilus	9
[Eupolis	8]
Euhippus	7
Philemon	7
Anaxilas	6

---

[9] Likely duplicates are not included here, but plays demarcated by "first" and "second" are counted twice.

Author name:	# of quotes w/out play:
[Pherecrates	6]
[Philyssius	6]
[Plato	6]
[Theopompus	6]
[Hermippus	5]
Menander	5
[Phrynichus	5]
Amipsias	4

By contrast, here are the ten most frequently quoted named plays:

Author name:	Play title:	# of quotes:
[Eupolis	*Flatterers*	122]
[Aristophanes	*Knights*	21]
[Aristophanes	*Gerytades*	19]
[Aristophanes	*Banqueters*	18]
[Archippus	*Fishes*	16]
Alexis	*Cauldron*	13
[Aristophanes	*Acharnians*	13]
[Aristophanes	*Broilers*	12]
[Aristophanes	*Birds*	11]
[Callias	*Cyclopes*	10]

The differences between these lists are striking. While the widest array of textual selections comes from post-Aristophanic comedy, nine of the ten most frequently quoted plays are from the fifth century, six from Aristophanes alone. In fact, it is only in the last list that anything like the primacy of Aristophanes can be detected. Elsewhere, it is Alexis and Antiphanes who stand above the fray. Less clear, however, is how much such rankings can tell us with significance beyond the text of Atheneaus. Some obvious points should give us pause. Of the six plays by Aristophanes in the final list, only three survive to the present day. Menander, who appears more or less middle of the pack in the first three lists is, in most other circumstances, unquestionably the most popular and well attested of post-Aristophanic comics. If Athenaeus necessarily serves as the Virgil guiding us among the underworld spirits of Ancient Greek comedy, we must recognize that the tour he leads may be an idiosyncratic one.

Words of Wisdom

In modern editions of comic fragments, the lines included by Athenaeus in his learned feast are often found alongside similarly presented excerpts recorded by the fifth-century CE prose author Stobaeus, a.k.a. Johannis of Stobi (the Roman provincial capital of Macedonia Salutaris). Though Stobaeus does resemble Athenaeus in some respects – a Greek-speaking author living under Roman rule who sought to preserve the memory of authors of poetry and prose from the past – the composite text that Stobaeus produced is of a quite different character than that of Athenaeus.

Stobaeus' *Anthology*, as the work is most often called, is a compendium of wise sayings ostensibly meant for the instruction of his son Septimius (a common framing device for ancient didactic literature). Stobaeus organizes his selections under headings such as "concerning virtue" or "concerning prudence," adducing lines from Greek authors of the past to illustrate the nature and challenges of each. There is nothing like Athenaeus' extreme preference for comedy in Stobaeus, and his selections from verse tend toward (what was then) the mainstream. In its current state, at least, the text offers a barebones catalog without any connecting prose beyond authors' names and, on occasion, the titles of the work being cited. Here, for instance, is a list of passages, comic and otherwise, under the heading "concerning intemperance":

> From Euripides' *Antiope*:[10]
>   Those who spend their lives concerned
>   with physical vitality are bad citizens,
>   if they mess up financially. Since a man habituated
>   to an intemperate stomach necessarily remains that way.
> From Philemon:
>   Tell me, what is free speech to you?
>   Do you babble amongst men, since you are one,
>   do you wander around the world, breathing the same
>   air as others? Do you, since you are such a man?
> From Cleanthes:[11]
>   Whoever wishes to refrain from a shameful deed
>   he will do so if he acts opportunely.
>   Where does the race of adulterers come from?
>   from a man who gave in to his lust.
> From Euphron:
>   There is no one evil greater than an adulterer.
>   he desires to live lasciviously amidst the misfortune of others.
> From Alexandrides:
>   Never make yourself a slave to pleasure.
>   For lust befits a woman, not a man.
> From Alexis:
>   Flee pleasure that will later cause harm
> From Menander's *Anger*:
>   No creature is worth more than an adulterer;
>   his price is death itself.
>
> (Stobaeus 3.6.1–3.6.8)

Many scholars suspect that Stobaeus, like Athenaeus before him, may be drawing his quotations from other compendia and learned works, often without any further knowledge of the works and authors that he quotes (Piccione 1994 and Reydams-Schils 2011). And, again like Athenaeus, he presents excerpts from various genres in such a way that their distinctive features are often occluded. But the scholarly tradition on which Stobaeus draws appears to be entirely separate from that of the treatises on comedy on which Athenaeus relied. As a result, the glimpse of comedy that he permits us is quite unlike that found in his predecessor. Where Athenaeus collected comic catalogs of fishes and names of famous courtesans, Stobaeus lists the many comic passages detailing the virtues of manly character and the manifold evils of marriage.

Perhaps the best way to appreciate the radically different perspectives represented by these superficially similar forms of execration is by examining a single play, as it looks from the vantage of each. Take, for example, the only two surviving fragments of the *Brothers* of Diphilus of Sinope, a playwright whom ancient critics counted as one of the top three "new comic" poets, alongside Menander and Philemon. Here are the lines excerpted by Athenaeus:[12]

>   What a rascally
>   little flagon, even if it belongs to men of means;
>   it is possible to secretly take it to the tasting area

---

[10] A fifth-century tragedy, much quoted by Stobaeus but otherwise almost entirely lost.
[11] A third second-century stoic philosopher.
[12] The section of the banquet in which it is quoted concerns names of vessels; specifically in this case the λάγυνος which I have translated here as "flagon."

and sell it until, just as at a potlatch, there is only
one vendor left who has been defrauded by a wine-merchant.

(Fr. 3 = Athenaeus 11.499.e)

Here are those quoted by Stobaeus:[13]

My good sir, you must know that as a mortal you will suffer misfortune
in order that you suffer only what you must
and not add to [your burdens] because of ignorance.

(Fr. 4 = Stobaeus 4.44.9)

The same experiment can be conducted on any number of authors and plays. Take these four surviving fragments from the *Rejuvenatrix* of Philippides. These two are from Athenaeus:

then, on top of it all, he arrived bringing a bunch
of testicles. The little ladies all pretended to be shocked,
but that man-killer Gnathaena laughed [...]
and said "They really are beautiful, these kidneys, by the good
Demeter" and she snatched up two and ate them off,
and they all fell on their backs from laughter.

(Fr. 5 = Athenaeus 9.384.e–f)

Always sponging food and insinuating himself

(Fr. 8 = Athenaeus 6.262.a)

And these two from Stobaeus:

I myself told you not to get married, but to live a pleasant life.
This is the Platonic good, Pheidylus:
do not take a wife nor hurl yourself into
the path of fortune in hopes of betterment

(Fr. 6 = Stobaeus 4.22.33)

[...] whenever you miss out on something, enjoy being bested;
for this is the greatest way to preserve one's good fortune

(Fr. 7 = Stobaeus 3.1.9)

Which of these compilers, if either, can be said to more accurately represent these plays? It is hard to say.

A Chorus of Ancient Scriveners

Athenaeus and Stobaeus may be the most fulsome compilers of Ancient Greek comic drama that have survived to the modern period, but they are certainly not the only ones. Our potpourri of comic fragments is further augmented by authors such as the second-century CE chronicler of philosophers' lives, Diogenes Laertius, who includes a variety of comic quotations that bear on his subjects or the twelfth-century CE scholar Eustatius, whose commentaries on the *Iliad* and *Odyssey* draw on the work of comic poets (alongside many other forms). Also important is the work of grammarians, such as the *Onomasticon* (a Greek-language thesaurus) of the second-century CE Roman subject Julius Pollux of Naucratis, the *Lexicon* the ninth-century CE Christian patriarch

---

[13] In a section entitled "That it is necessary to nobly endure misfortune and to live in accordance with virtue."

Photius of Constantinople, or the *Alphabetical Collection of All Words* compiled by the fifth-century CE lexicographer Hesychius. These ancient reference tools, and others like them, often illustrate words and their usages with lines from comic drama (as well as from a wealth of other genres). As with the works already discussed, these texts are invaluable sources of information about ancient comedy. Nonetheless, it is important to recall that they too are shaped in important ways by the compilers' particular interests and the resources to which they had access. As Nesselrath rightly observes: "it is clear that in these cases we are at the total mercy of the quoting author or work" (Nesselrath (2010) 437–8; see also Osborne 1987, Olson 2018).

Finally, we must grapple with the question of what and how we can learn about Ancient Greek comic drama through the far better-preserved plays of the Roman comic tradition. Beginning at some time in the third century BCE, Roman playwrights began to compose and perform plays that came to be known as *fabulae palliatae*, stories in Greek dress. These comic dramas were a conscious and overt adaptation for a Roman audience of characters and plots that enjoyed such success on the Greek comic stage. The era of *fabulae palliatae* is now known to us primarily through the surviving works of Plautus (c. 254–184 BCE) and Terence (c. 184?–160 BCE), in which we can see the Roman poets unabashedly, if somewhat facetiously, declare their reliance on Greek models. Terence begins his *Woman of Andros* (*Andria*) with an author's prolog stating:

> Menander wrote a "Woman of Andros" and a "Woman of Perinthos." If you know one, you know them both, since the plots are not very different, though they are written in a different language and style. Our author confesses that he has transferred anything suitable from the "Woman of Perinthos" to the "Woman of Andros" and made free use of it. (*Andria* 9–14, Barsby trans.)

Because the Roman playwrights so happily confessed their liberal borrowing from Greek models, scholars long presumed that the Roman plays were little more than copies of originals, now lost. With the recovery of a good deal of Menandrian drama (discussed below), it has been possible to appreciate the complex and artful ways in which the *fabulae palliatae* of Plautus and Terence are quite unlike Greek comedy (see, e.g., Goldberg 1986). Often, as with the Terence passage quoted above, multiple Greek comedies are combined to create a new composite drama. In certain instances, these Roman plays can provide important information with respect to plot; as in the case of Plautus' *Two Bacchises* (*Bacchides*) which helps to flesh out some details left unclear by the recently recovered fragments of Menander's *Twice Tricking* (*Dis Exapaton*). Even so, setting them side by side, we can see that Plautus' play is far from a direct translation of its Greek model. Far more commonly, however, the evidence of Roman adaptation leaves far more questions than answers. Such is the case with Plautus' *Little Ghost* (*Mostellaria*), which is generally agreed to have been based on a Greek original entitled *Ghost* (*Phasma*). The problem, however, is that we know of three Greek plays by that name – by Menander, Philemon, and Theognetus, respectively – and no one can satisfactorily determine which, if any, served as Plautus' model. It is sometimes thought that a barb aimed at Diphilus and Philemon in act five hints at the latter,[14] but such inferences hardly constitute a solid foundation on which to base further work.

Speaking Objects and Nameless Scripts

Up to this point, we have been exploring what remains to us of post-Aristophanic Greek comic drama by means of other texts that have, for one reason or another, remained part of an ongoing process of reading and preservation. In other words, these fragments have been preserved through a process of "secondary transmission" as a result of being excerpted for inclusion within the works of other authors. Aside from the 11 plays of Aristophanes, no work of Ancient Greek comedy is the beneficiary of continuous textual transmission (i.e., "primary transmission"). But that does not mean that all

---

[14] "If you're a friend of Diphilus or Philemon, tell them how your slave made fun of you: you'll give them first-rate stories of imposture for their comedies." (1149–51, de Melo trans.)

other comic works come to us as excerpts transmitted within the texts of others. In fact, there is a relatively large number of comic fragments, including the vast majority of what we now know of Menander, that come to us through another route: in the form of text written on papyrus.

Insofar as they are ancient artifacts preserved primarily through happenstance, papyri form part of the larger category of material culture which includes art and architecture, domestic and commercial tools and detritus, and just about any other physical objects that have survived from the ancient Mediterranean (on which see, e.g., Cooper 2020). As far as we know, none of the published comic papyri are "autographs" – that is, our written texts were not produced by the author of the play. Most often, we have little or no information about the scribes (or other artisans) who produced these objects (though two notable exceptions are discussed below). Like other ancient material artifacts, papyri have their own history and concomitant character. And while some papyrus fragments represent portions of what was once a complete text of a play (scripts for both reading and performance), others were already only partial excerpts before their physical fragmentation. Much as we have already found in our discussion of secondary transmission, this history should be recognized as a framing lens through which our understanding of each fragment is mediated.

Before turning to papyrological matters, however, we should note in passing two important forms of secondary transmission via material culture. On the one hand, inscriptional evidence provides important witness to the continued performance of Greek comic drama at festivals and competitions throughout the Mediterranean in the centuries following Aristophanes' death (see Csapo 2010, Le Guen 2014). On the other hand, the popularity of comedy as a subject for vase painting (Taplin 1993) and for other forms of architectural decor, most notably domestic mosaics, attests to the broad appeal of this form even beyond the confines of the theater (Nervegna 2013).

Like the indirect material evidence of inscriptions and visual art, papyrological finds offer us an eclectic and broad-ranging – albeit still highly mediated – record of the world of Ancient Greek Comedy. Rather than being collected for a distinct purpose, say moral instruction or lexical illustration, those comedies that have survived on papyrus have done so entirely as a result of happenstance. But the lack of editorial bias does not mean that papyri are necessarily representative of widespread trends. First, the number of papyri themselves, though substantial given our relative ignorance, hardly constitutes a meaningful proportion of the texts that circulated in the ancient Mediterranean. This numerical limitation might not be overly significant if the papyri represented a truly random sampling of this larger body of texts. But, as it happens, the papyri that have been preserved come almost exclusively from a single geographic area: the stretch of the Nile valley that is sometimes called "Middle Egypt." As such, they can offer astonishing insight into this particular location (see, e.g., Bagnall 1995; Hickey 2011). Less clear, however, is how much they can tell us about the Greek-speaking Mediterranean more broadly (*pace* Netz 2020).

Approximately, half of the more than 300 papyri containing text identifiable as comic drama can be further attributed to a known author, and sometimes even a specific play (Perrone (2009) 204–5). Following the circular reasoning outlined at the beginning of this chapter, this group is dominated by the two best-known comic poets: Aristophanes and Menander. Otherwise, identification is most often made through overlap with known fragments preserved through the indirect manuscript tradition. So, for example, a Roman-era school exercise now housed in Cairo (P. Cairo 56226) contains the first line of a Philemon fragment ("Why did Prometheus, who they say molded us. . .") that is preserved, along with ten additional lines, in Stobaeus (in the section "Concerning vice"):

> Why did Prometheus, who they say molded us
> and all the other living things, to the beasts
> give one nature to each of the races?
> All lions are brave
> But all rabbits are cowardly.
> There isn't one fox who is tricksy,
> and one who is forthright; but if you bring together
> thirty thousand foxes, you'll see they all have

one nature and one character.
But when it comes to us, you'll see as many different
characters as there are different kinds of bodies. (Fr. 93)

The roughly 150 remaining comic papyri are so-called *adespota*, fragments that cannot be confidently attributed to a known author. As Serena Perrone rightly notes, the anonymous status of these fragments cannot be disentangled from the distinctive nature and history of the papyri themselves. Fragments that fall under the label *adespota* are, by definition, those "that have not survived via the Byzantine tradition, [and are not] attributable to a specific author on the basis of their formal characteristics or context. The author might very well be one of the 'major' or 'minor' playwrights, or possibly someone completely unknown to us" (Perrone (2009) 204; see also the discussion of Nesselrath 2011) As a result, multiple claims can be made about the same lines; as happened, for instance, with a remarkably well-preserved 44 line dramatic fragment preserved on a second-century BCE papyrus now housed at the Musée du Louvre (P. Louvre 7172, for more on this papyrus, see Thompson (1988) 259–61). This exciting fragment finds its speaker in the midst of a dilemma "Oh father, you ought to have said what I say! But now we must consider whether it is better for you or for me to speak when it is required." It was first attributed to Euripides by Nauck in 1889 and then to Menander by Koerte in 1910 (on the porous boundaries between dramatic genres, see Hanink 2014). The passage is now generally agreed to come from a comedy, but its authorship is considered uncertain and it goes by the name Com. Adesp. 1000 Kassel-Austin.

Longer fragments, such as Com. Adesp. 1000, give us a better sense of the range of comedy beyond the circumscribed interests of literary compilers. But they can also, in certain circumstances, tell us about the ways that comedy featured in the everyday lives of those living in Greco-Roman Egypt. One particularly rich fragment in this regard is the 28 lines that go under the label Com. Adesp. 1064 Kassel-Austin. The text, in which a father makes plans for a wedding, is transmitted on a papyrus dated to the late third-century BCE which was collected at Tebtunis in 1899 (hence its papyrological moniker P. Tebt. 693) and is now housed at the University of California, Berkeley. Alongside the comic fragment, this papyrus contains two draft letters written by a flax farmer petitioning for early release from prison.[15] As Silvia Barbantani demonstrates, it seems probable that both petitions were written around the same time as the comic fragment, likely all from the man's prison cell (Barbantani n.d.). The papyrus is thus a poignant witness to the role that comedy played at a significant moment in the life of an individual. Could it be, as Barbantani suggests, that the comic fragment's "allusions to good food and happiness [. . .] provided him a brief moment of escapism"? (Barbantani n.d.). Even if we can never know for certain why this particular prisoner opted to copy out this particular comic passage, the object nonetheless invites us to reflect on the many non-traditional ways that Ancient Greek Comedy was part of the quotidian experience of the ancient Mediterranean.

The Underground Comedian

There is no comic poet, and perhaps no other Ancient Greek poet full stop, whose corpus of extant works has been expanded by papyrus finds to the extent that Menander's has. In 1897, Jules Nicole published text from a papyrus comprising 87 continuous lines from a play identifiable as Menander's *Farmer* (*Georgos*) (Nicole 1897–8). Ten years later, the publication of a significantly lengthier papyrus, the so-called Cairo Codex of Menander, by Gustave Lefebvre revealed extended sections of four Menandrian plays: *Woman from Samia* (*Samia*), *Woman with Shorn Hair* (*Perikeiromene*), *Men at Trial* (*Epitrepontes*), and *Hero* (*Heros*) (Lefebvre 1907; For a history of the papyrus and discussion of its ancient owner, Dioscorus of Aphroditopolis, see Gagos and van Minnen 1995). The century that followed added more lines to all of these plays and introduced substantial portions

---

[15] The first draft, which is on the front side of the papyrus, goes under the title P. Tebt. 769.

of *Shield* (*Aspis*), *Hated Man* (*Misoumenos*), *Sikyonians* (*Sikyonioi*), and a nearly complete text of *Dyscolos* (*Grouchy Man*), as well as shorter fragments from a handful of other plays.

This startling transformation of Menander from a playwright known only through indirect transmission into one of the Ancient Greek playwrights best represented in modern libraries has yet to be fully reflected in the work of literary scholars. Nor has the field of classics adequately grappled with the deeply troubling, often straightforwardly illegal means by which many of these papyri were "recovered" for academic study (but see Nongbri 2018). It is not within the purview of this chapter to attempt to remedy either of these shortcomings, but I hope some of its readers may be moved to do so in future.

With respect to our understanding of post-Aristophanic comedy, access to a number of relatively lengthy passages from Menander provides a wealth of insight. First and foremost, the ability to situate fragments from the indirect tradition within the broader context of dramatic plot and characterization shines a spotlight on the extreme limits of the information conveyed by brief excerpts, particularly the one- or two-line quotations typical of ancient compilations. So, as Eric Handley details, a passage which in the indirect tradition was taken as earnest praise of those who offer the simplest sacrifices as expressing the greatest piety takes on a distinctly different tenor when placed in the mouth of the Grouchy Man (at line 447–53 of the play of the same name) complaining about the noise made by those sacrificing near his house (Handley (2011) 143; see also the methodological reflections of Olson (2020) 139–44). Indeed, as Matthew Wright has recently argued, this type of ironizing embedding of gnomic wisdom and maxims seems to have been a regular means of generating humor in Greek comedy (Wright 2022b). In Menander and elsewhere, it is crucial to remember that the views expressed in comic fragments are always voiced by characters within a play. Without an idea of who the speaker of a passage might be, or what work a given utterance is doing with regard to their particular aims, the knowledge that we can hope to gain from fragments is necessarily circumscribed in a number of consequential ways.

Conversely, our ability to examine dramatic arcs in Menander permits an appreciation of certain stock characters and motifs that tend to appear in the works of a variety of playwrights. We already noted the prominence of courtesans and other professional identities among the titles collected by Athenaeus. Menandrian dramas like *Dyscolos* and *Samia* allow us to see certain roles, like that of the foreign courtesan or the hired cook, deployed within a specific narrative frame. In light of the regularity with which cooks are brought onto Menander's stage and permitted to hold forth on the topic of their trade, we might better appreciate how Athenaeus was able to fill his fifteen books of dinner talk. It is not so much that comedy was "about" food as that the cook's speech – like the car chase in a contemporary action movie – was a kind of set piece within the genre, on which a poet-wright could put a new spin if he was so inclined (Lämmle 2013 explores a related poetics of repetition in satyr drama). Thanks in large part to Athenaeus, we can appreciate just how wide a range of expression this stock figure enjoyed: from the chef-protagonists (e.g., Peisetaerus in *Birds*, Trygaeus in *Peace*, on which see Wilkins (2000a, b) 371–9) to the poetically inspired cooks of Antiphanes who describe their culinary creations in elaborately elegant language (Dobrov 2002), to the commercially savvy hired hands of Menander, such as Sikon, who plays a critical role in the action of *Grumpy Man* and boasts of his ability to acquire all manner of equipment he needs through shameless flattery (489–97). Indeed, it would seem that the figure of the cook provided yet another opportunity for the kind of joyous intra-generic commonplace that Matthew Farmer has so aptly identified in the pervasive insulting of tragedians on the comic stage (Farmer (2017) 34–65).

Alongside these comically rendered cooks, the now-ample remains of Menander also permit us to see the casual violence and commodification of human life that is a central feature of Ancient Greek comic drama in context. In *Shield* (*Aspis*), the "comic" action hinges on whether the greedy old Smikrines will be able to take possession of Kleostratus' young sister – given neither name nor speaking lines in our extant fragments – together with the equally nameless and silent crowd of slaves (*aichmatón ochlos* 36–7) that are paraded on stage at the beginning of the play. In *Samia*, as the rape of a young citizen woman and the ejection of a foreign woman from her home are resolved by the marriage of the former to her rapist and the reconciliation of the latter to the man who had condemned her to the life of a two-bit prostitute, the comedy's "happy" ending is inaugurated by a violent physical attack on the enslaved Parmenon, who brings news of the resolution to his initially incredulous owner (676–82). The scapegoating of the enslaved in the service of tranquility across gender lines echoes the conclusion of Aristophanes' *Lysistrata*. Perhaps this is one facet of comedy on which, however widely they might otherwise diverge, ancient Greek comic playwrights could agree.

All Difficulties Are Resolved by a Happy Ending

This, broadly speaking, is what we know about post-Aristophanic comedy in 2022. There is a rich trove of evidence, and much of it remains to be explored. Yet it is undeniable that our ability to speak about the vibrant world of Greek comic drama in the centuries that followed the death of Aristophanes in 386 BCE is and will remain extremely limited. Why is it that scores of names have fallen by the wayside? How did it come to pass that a playwright as universally beloved as Menander did not see his works preserved alongside those of Homer and Euripides (the only two Greek poets who could claim greater popularity in the Roman period)? Here, too, we must face up to the cold comfort of unyielding ignorance. However much narratives of canon formation give credence to claims for the inherent value of those works that have survived and are thus familiar and beloved to contemporary scholars, we simply cannot construct a satisfactory account of why Aristophanes "made it" and no other comic poet did. The picture that we have is just that; a snapshot that is in focus in some places and blurred in others, whose boundaries cut off far more than they include. We can be grateful that the image has survived at all, but we cannot pretend that it affords us a true window into the past.

GUIDE TO FURTHER READING

The best source for translations of the fragments of post-Aristophanic comedy is Rusten et al. (2017). For the development of fourth-century comedy, see Csapo (2000), Le Guen (2014), Nesselrath (1995), and Hunter (1985). For the challenges of reading comic fragments, see Olson (2020) and Wright (2022a). For Menander, see Lape (2003), Traill (2008), Handley (2011), Nesselrath (2011), and Nervegna (2013). For comic fragments in literary papyri, see Bagnall (1995), Barbantani (n.d.), and Perrone (2009). For Athenaeus' preservation of comic fragments, see Apostolakis (2020), Braund and Wilkins (2000), Nesselrath (2010), and Olson (2018). For Stobaeus as a source of comic fragments, see Piccione (1994), Reydams-Schils (2011), Mills (2020). For maxims in comedy, see Wright (2022b).

REFERENCES

Apostolakis, K. (2020). Increasing comic fragmentation: some aspects of text re-uses in Athenaeus. In: *Fragmentation in Ancient Greek Drama* (ed. A. Lamari, F. Montanari, and A. Novokhatko), 603–616. Berlin: De Gruyter.

Bagnall, R. (1995). *Reading Papyri, Writing Ancient History*. Oxford: Routledge.

Barbantani, S. (n.d.). The Provenance of the Literary Papyri P. Tebt. III 691, 693: An Overview of Cartonnage Papyri from Mummy 104. Paper delivered at the American Society of Papyrologists Summer Seminar at the University of Berkeley in 2004.

Braund, D. and Wilkins, J. (ed.) (2000). *Athenaeus and his World: Reading Greek Culture in the Roman Empire*. Liverpool: Liverpool University Press.

Cooper, C. (ed.) (2020). *New Approaches to Ancient Material Culture in the Greek and Roman World*. Leiden: Brill.

Csapo, E. (2000). From Aristophanes to Menander: genre transformation in Greek comedy. In: *Matrices of Genre Authors, Canons, and Society* (ed. M. Depew and D. Obbink), 115–133. Cambridge: Harvard University Press.

Csapo, E. (2010). *Actors and Icons of the Ancient Theater*. Chichester: Wiley-Blackwell.

Dobrov, G.W. (2002). Mageiros poietes: language and character in Antiphanes. In: *The Language of Greek Comedy* (ed. A. Willi), 169–190. Oxford: Oxford University Press.

Farmer, M. (2017). *Tragedy on the Comic Stage*. Oxford: Oxford University Press.

Gagos, T. and van Minnen, P. (1995). *Settling a Dispute: Toward a Legal Anthropology of Late Antique Egypt*. Ann Arbor: University of Michigan Press.

Goldberg, S. (1986). *Understanding Terence*. Princeton, NJ: Princeton University Press.

Le Guen, B. (2014). The diffusion of comedy from the age of Alexander to the beginning of the Roman Empire. In: *The Oxford Handbook to Greek and Roman Comedy* (ed. M. Fontaine and A. Scafuro), 359–377. Oxford: Oxford University Press.

Handley, E. (2011). The Rediscovery of Menander. In: *Culture in Pieces* (ed. D. Obbink and R. Rutherford), 138–159. Oxford: Oxford University Press.

Hanink, J. (2014). Crossing Genres: Comedy, Tragedy, and Satyr Play. In: *The Oxford Handbook to Greek and Roman Comedy* (ed. M. Fontaine and A. Scafuro). Oxford: Oxford University Press.

Hickey, T. (2011). Writing histories from the papyri. In: *The Oxford Handbook to Papyrology* (ed. R. Bagnall), 495–520. Oxford: Oxford University Press.

Hunter, R. (1985). *The New Comedy of Greece and Rome*. Cambridge University Press.

Jackson, L. (2020). *The Chorus of Drama in the Fourth Century BCE*. Oxford: Oxford University Press.

Lämmle, R. (2013). *Poetik des Satyrspiels*. Heidelberg: Winter Verlag.

Lape, S. (2003). *Reproducing Athens: Menander's Comedy, Democratic Culture, and the Hellenistic City*. Princeton University Press.

Lefebvre, G. (1907). *Fragments d'un manuscrit de Ménandre*. Cairo: L'Institut français d'archéologie orientale.

LeVen, P. (2010). New music and its myths: Athenaeus' reading of the aulos revolution. *Journal of Hellenic Studies* 130: 35–47.

Mills, B.W. (2020). Fragments of Menander in Stobaeus. In: *Fragmentation in Ancient Greek Drama* (ed. A. Lamari, F. Montanari, and A. Novokhatko), 647–662.

Nervegna, S. (2013). *Menander in Antiquity: Contexts of Reception*. Cambridge: Cambridge University Press.

Nesselrath, H.-G. (1995). Myth, Parody and Comic Plots: The Birth of the Gods and Middle Comedy. In: *Beyond Aristophanes: Transition and Diversity in Greek Comedy* (ed. G. Dobrov), 1–28. Atlanta, GA: Scholars Press.

Nesselrath, H.-G. (2010). Comic fragments: transmission and textual criticism. In: *Brill's Companion to the Study of Greek Comedy* (ed. G. Dobrov), 423–453. Leiden: Brill.

Nesselrath, H.-G. (2011). Menander and his Rivals: New Light from the Comic Adespota? In: *Culture in Pieces* (ed. D. Obbink and R. Rutherford), 119–137. Oxford: Oxford University Press.

Netz, R. (2020). *Scale, Space and Canon in Ancient Literary Culture*. Cambridge: Cambridge University Press.

Nicole, J. (1897–8). *Le Laboureur de Ménandre: fragments inédits sur papyrus d'Égypte*. Oxford: Oxford University Press.

Nongbri, B. (2018). *God's Library: The Archaeology of the Earliest Christian Manuscripts*. New Haven: Yale University Press.

Olson, S.D. (2006–2013). *Athenaeus: The Learned Banqueters*. Cambridge: Loeb Classical Library, 8 vols.

Olson, D. (2018). Athenaeus 'Fragments' of prose authors. *AJP* 139 (3): 423–450.

Olson, D. (2020). Fragments of Aristophanes' Gerytades: methodological considerations. In: *Fragmentation in Ancient Greek Drama* (ed. A. Lamari, F. Montanari, and A. Novokhatko), 129–144.

Olson, S.D. and Sens, A. (2000). *Archestratos of Gela: Greek culture and cuisine in the fourth century BCE*. Oxford: Oxford University Press.

Osborne, C. (1987). *Rethinking Early Greek Philosophy: Hippolytus of Rome and the Presocratics*. London: Duckworth.

Perrone, S. (2009). Lost in Tradition: Papyrus commentaries on comedies and tragedies of unknown authorship. *Trends in Classics* 1 (2): 203–240.

Piccione, R.M. (1994). Sulle fonti e le metodologie compilative di Stobeo. *Eikasmós* 5: 281–317.

Reydams-Schils, G. (ed.) (2011). *Thinking Through Excerpts. Studies on Stobaeus*. Turnhuout.

Rodriguez-Noriega Guillén, L. (2000). Are the fifteen books of the Deipnosophistae an Excerpt? In: *Athenaeus and his World: Reading Greek Culture in the Roman Empire* (ed. D. Braund and J. Wilkins), 244–255. Exeter: University of Exeter Press.

Rusten, J. et al. (ed.) (2017). *The Birth of Comedy: Texts, Documents, and Art from Athenian Comic Competitions*, 486–280. Baltimore: Johns Hopkins University Press.

Sommerstein, A. (ed.) (2019). *The Encyclopedia of Greek Comedy*. Hoboken, NJ: Wiley-Blackwell.

Taplin, O. (1993). *Comic Angels and Other Approaches to Greek Drama through Vase-paintings*. Oxford: Clarendon Press.

Thompson, D. (1988). *Memphis Under the Ptolemies*. Princeton, NJ: Princeton University Press.

Traill, A. (2008). *Women and the Comic Plot in Menander*. Cambridge University Press.

Wilkins, J. (2000a). *The Boastful Chef*. Oxford: Oxford University Press.

Wilkins, J. (2000b). Dialogue and comedy: the structure of the Deipnosophistae. In: *Athenaeus and his World: Reading Greek Culture in the Roman Empire* (ed. D. Braund and J. Wilkins), 23–38. Exeter: University of Exeter Press.

Wright, M. (2022a). Comic sex and 'fragmentary thinking': Damoxenus, Fr. 3 PCG. *The Classical Quarterly* 72 (1): 191–201.

Wright, M. (2022b). Wisdom in inverted commas: Greek comedy and the quotable maxim. *Cambridge Classical Journal* 68: 244–267.

Yatromanolakis, D. (2007). *Sappho in the Making: The Early Reception*. Washington, DC: Center for Hellenic Studies, Trustees for Harvard University.

PART IV

Aristophanes and His Readers

CHAPTER 22

Aristophanes Between Plato and Aristotle

Pierre Destrée

Introduction

The reception of Aristophanes among ancient philosophers has been rather contrasted, ranging from sheer condemnation to boundless admiration. In line with a fairly widespread judgment among ancient critics,[1] Cicero enthusiastically praised Old Comedy for its "refined, urbane, clever, witty kind of jokes" (iocandi genus . . . elegans, urbanum, ingeniosum, facetum, *De officiis* 1.104), and especially Aristophanes, whom he takes to be the "wittiest poet of Old Comedy" ("facetissumus poeta veteris comoediae," *De legibus* 2.37). On the other side of the spectrum, Plutarch has launched a definitive condemnation against Aristophanes, without any hope of parole. True, in the *Parallel Lives*, he quite often mentions passages from Aristophanes' plays, and he never hesitates to quote a verse or two. So Plutarch knew very well his Aristophanes: whenever writing down the life of one of his fifth-century BCE Athenian heroes, he uses Aristophanes' plays as a reservoir for (allegedly) historical details. But when it comes to literary appreciation, Plutarch's judgment is the most negative one can imagine:

> "Old Comedy, he writes in *Table-Talk*, is unsuitable for drinkers because of its unevenness. The seriousness and outspokenness of what are called the "parabases" are too unrelieved and intense, while the tendency to jests and buffoonery is altogether excessive and unrestrained, and improper expressions and indecent words abound. Moreover, just as at princely dinners every guest has his own wine waiter, so every reader needs his own grammarian to explain all the details . . . so that the party becomes a class-room, or else the jokes go by ineffectively and without significance" (*Quaestiones Convivales* 7. 8. 4; tr. Russell).

What is condemned is first of all indecency: in the context of a symposium (where passages from comedies were read aloud), indecent jokes are quite simply not what suit educated citizens. And even the decent, not obscene jokes, Plutarch adds, need explanation, which of course spoils the amusement. In the summary that we have of *A comparison between Aristophanes and Menander*, Plutarch is even harsher: "Coarseness (*to phortikon*), vulgarity (*to thumelikon*), and triviality (*to banauson*) of language are to be found in Aristophanes, but not in Menander. Aristophanes' style captivates the ordinary, uneducated reader for whom he writes, but disgusts the educated. This is due to its antitheses, rhymes, and puns. Menander thinks such tricks need careful handling, and employs them sparingly and with due thought. Aristophanes has them often, with no regard to occasion, and with a frigid effect" (1. 853b; tr. Russell). What Plutarch seems to condemn is not only the violence and

---

[1] See Quadlbauer 1960 for the main texts; and Dobrov 2010 and Slater 2016 for recent surveys.

obscenity of Aristophanes' language, it is even the way the comedic poet uses all the rhetorical figures that we commonly associate with jokes: antitheses, rhymes, and puns. And he cites numerous examples from Aristophanes' plays, which we modern readers usually admire for their cleverness such as the famous verses where Dikaiopolis mocks Lamachos (*Ach.* 1124–1125). Also, Plutarch is well aware that Aristophanes himself condemned "coarseness" and easy jokes and praised sophisticated jokes which he hopes he succeeds to convey – something Plutarch himself fully takes over as how one should tell jokes in social gatherings of well-educated citizens. But he dismisses Aristophanes' own characterization out of hand: "Where his reputed ingenuity lies, in speeches or characters, I have no notion." And he concludes his essay: "Whatever he imitates he makes worse; smartness becomes malice instead of urbanity, rusticity becomes silliness instead of simplicity, humor is not amusing but absurd, love not joyous but indecent. He seems not to have written his poetry for respectable people at all; the impropriety and indecency appear to be intended for the licentious, the invective and bitterness for the spiteful and malicious" (4. 854C,D; tr. Russell).[2]

Such a condemnation can be seen as the radicalization of Plutarch's two main sources of inspiration: Plato, who most of all condemns the violence of the derision against people, and Aristotle, who rejects the idea that obscene speech and jokes are what makes a good comedy. And yet, for all their critiques and condemnation, Plato and Aristotle also (implicitly or explicitly) recognized their admiration for Aristophanes. Aristophanes never hesitated to pepper his plays with obscenities and aggressive jokes. But he was also a great master of humor. In his youth, Plato (presumably) attended some of his plays in the theater, and he surely read them extensively. He must have recognized how powerful laughter can be, and it is no wonder that when writing his *Dialogs*, he was happy to use its power for his own, philosophical, purposes. Scholars often speak of Plato's wish to replace Homer and the poets with his own writings; one might add that in the comic vein, he emulated Aristophanes in his philosophical uses of humor. Considering philosophy and poetry to be two domains that must obey different agendas and rules, Aristotle did not have such an ambition (even though he also uses humor in his work). In writing the second book of his *Poetics* on comedy, he was only focusing on the way spectators should be appreciative of the humor that took place in the theater; and since Aristophanes was viewed as a great master of comedy, it would have been odd if Aristotle had not considered him as such too.

Let me review in turn how these two major philosophical figures dealt with the "wittiest poet of Old Comedy" as Cicero called Aristophanes.

Plato and the Emulation of Aristophanes

"Although you condemn comedy, you yourself satirize (*komôdein*) Hippias, Prodicus, Protagoras, Gorgias, Euthydemus, Dionysodorus, Agathon, Cinesias, and everyone on earth. Satirizing these may not really matter, but when it comes to Aristophanes himself – well, who is this who is satirizing him? Someone who himself has a rich vein of comedy (*komôdia*) in him, one might well say." (*Orations* 614, tr. M. Trapp mod.)

This very lively passage comes from Aelius Aristides (a second-century CE rhetor belonging to the so-called second sophistic). It very well captures the problem all scholars, from antiquity on, have had with Plato and his ambiguous relationship with comedy, Aristophanes, in particular.[3] Remember the passages that Aelian alludes to:

- *Condemnation of comedy*: "No writer of comedy, or of any iambic or lyric song, shall be permitted to make fun of any of the citizens in any way at all – neither verbally nor by mimicry, whether in anger or not; if anyone disobeys, those running the games are to impose an outright ban,

---

[2] On Plutarch and this treatise, see Hunter (2009), pp. 78–89.
[3] Aelius' passage takes place in a long tradition. See also the judgment that is reported by Athenaeus, which Gorgias made about the eponymous dialog where Plato mocks him: "Plato very well knows to satirize (*iambizein*)" (505D,E).

there and then, on his being in the country, or else fine him 3 minas (to be dedicated to the god whose games these are)" (*Laws* 11.935e–36a; tr. Griffith).
- *Satirizing sophists, tragedians, and other poets*: see Plato's *Hippias, Protagoras, Gorgias, Euthydemus*, where these sophists are repeatedly mocked. In the *Symposium*, the tragedian Agathon gets refuted by a rather mocking Socrates; and the dithyramb poet Cinesias and his father Meles are harshly dismissed in the *Gorgias* (501e–502a).
- Satirizing Aristophanes: see esp. *Symposium* where Aristophanes is overwhelmed with hiccuping.

Thus, while he explicitly and most strongly condemns one of the most distinctive traits of Old Comedy, the vituperative attack against a certain person (*to onomasti komôdein*), Plato has Socrates no less harshly mock his own contemporaries (Protagoras or Hippias were perhaps not citizens of Athens, but Agathon and Aristophanes were). And that's because, Aelius suggests, perhaps sarcastically, he has "a rich vein of comedy (*komôdia*) in him," or more literally, "he has plenty of mockery to spare." In other words, Plato's stance on comedy seems to be deeply puzzling, if not incoherent: while he condemns comedy in the strongest terms, he regularly mocks and satirizes people, including Aristophanes himself, in a similar way Aristophanes did.

Many scholars have tried to solve this puzzle by mitigating the negative aspects of Plato's attacks and mockeries. When Plato mocks sophists or poets, he admittedly does so without recurring direct insults and obvious obscenities as Aristophanes often does; and in the *Symposium*, the relationships between Socrates and all other symposiasts, including Aristophanes, show no trace of enmity. But this is how a symposium should take place: having (in 416 BCE, the date when the *Symposium* is supposed to have taken place) a Socrates harshly counter-attacking Aristophanes (whose *Clouds* was staged a few years before, in 423 BCE) would have entirely spoiled the venue and jeopardized Plato's philosophical commitments. And yet, such an amicable ambiance does not prevent Plato from insulting Aristophanes, if indirectly, in the famous scene of the hiccup. Caused by "too much eating or whatever such cause" (185c), hiccupping is a bodily phenomenon that is of the same sort as farting, which Aristophanes himself condemns as being vulgar and obscene (see esp. *Frogs* 1–11): is not it a rather cruel way to turning the table against Aristophanes? Also, this episode of hiccup, which is described in a very detailed manner, is probably nothing less than a kind of literary show of being overwhelmed by laughter, which Plato strongly condemns elsewhere (*Rep.* 3, 388e): is not it a way to present Aristophanes as incapable to dominate his bodily affects, he who even needs a doctor to help him cure his hiccup? (Note that Eryximachos' name means "the fighter of the belch," something Plato hints at 185d where the name is repeated no less than three times in three lines).

As to Aristophanes' speech, it is arguably the most brilliant of the speeches in honor of Erôs which precede Diotima's speech. It is also a very witty speech, which the real Aristophanes could have written, with many funny details that seem to echo passages from Aristophanes' own plays: see, for example, the description of the people cut into two like a platyfish – a reminder of *Lys.* 115–16: "And I'd be willing to cut myself in half/And serve myself as a sacrificial flat-fish!" (tr. Halliwell). On the philosophical level, Aristophanes introduces a few topics that have not been put forward in the previous speeches, such as the centrality of happiness (*eudaimonia*), and the "power" (*dunamis*) of love (189c,d) – two topics that will prove of central importance in Diotima's speech. Thus, did not Plato consider Aristophanes to be a serious partner in this philosophical symposium on the importance of love?

This is, I suggest, a trap which Plato himself warns his readers not to fall into. As scholars have ever since acknowledged, Aristophanes' speech is the only one that is explicitly mentioned by Diotima who rejects it straightaway: "There is a theory [and actually a speech: logos] that says that those who are looking for their second half are in love. But my theory [and my speech] says that there is no such thing as the love for one's half or whole unless it happens to be good one way or another [. . .]For, there is nothing but the good that human beings desire" (205e). And the fact that alone among the other symposiasts "who praise" Socrates for his/Diotima's speech, Aristophanes wants to speak, that is, retort to (or criticize) that speech which "had mentioned him and his speech" before he is interrupted by Alcibiades' entrance (212c) shows that this is a crucial point of contention. And, most importantly, one should note that this is already alluded to in the middle of Aristophanes' speech itself. When he presents the true love that should lead to happiness, Aristophanes has Hephaistos speak to all lovers: "Is this your desire, to be always together, as close as possible, and never parted from each other day or night? If this is what you want, I am ready to join you together and fuse (*sumphusênai*) you until, instead of two, you become one. For your whole lives long the two of you will live together as one, and when you die you will die together and even in the Underworld you will be one rather than two. Tell me if this is what you long for and if it will satisfy you to achieve this" (192d,e).

Many modern readers have taken this as if Plato were serious.[4] But ancient readers would have immediately recognized this as a rewriting of the famous scene in the *Odyssey*, where Aphrodite and Ares are caught up in a metal net made by Aphrodite's own husband, Hephaistos (*Od.* 8.267–328). In the *Odyssey*, the scene is meant to be extremely funny: when seeing the naked lovers trapped by the cuckooed husband, all the gods burst into an "unquenchable laughter at such a clever trap Hephaestus set" (321–322), that is, presumably, at the incongruous scene of the two naked lovers trying to move out from that devilish "finely woven spider web" (280). Similarly here, we Plato's readers are meant to laugh at such an odd, incongruous proposal, as if being reunited with your second half should make you happy forever (note also that the mention of the Underworld can be interpreted as a parodic anticipation of the theme of immortality that plays an important role in Diotima's speech). Admittedly, Aristophanes fully recognizes that "sexual intercourse (*aphrodisión sunousia*)" is not what brings true happiness, which will prove to be of central importance in Diotima's own praise of love (notably in her advocating "right pederasty," 211b). But true love or intercourse is not to be seen as the fusion (*sumphusênai*) of two persons as Aristophanes proposes, but as "living with the form of beauty" – where the verb *suneinai* also means "having intercourse" (212a) – which only could lead to happiness everyone desires.

Plato has written an extraordinarily sophisticated speech on behalf of Aristophanes, and he goes as far as presenting Aristophanes rightly guessing the importance of a few crucial topics. But it all should be read as a parody, and we readers are meant to be amused, and laugh at the speech holder. True, to Eryximachos who warns to watch him out in case he would say something ridiculous, Aristophanes replies: "Don't watch over my speech as what I fear is not to say funny jokes – after all, this would be a bonus and typical of my Muse – but things that would make people laugh at me" (189b). But of course it is Plato who has his character Aristophanes say that, and one should then read this as a kind of rather sarcastic way of warning his reader to see for herself whether or not this will prove true.

Another key passage where Aristophanes is taken to task is the beginning of the *Apology of Socrates*. There, in his first speech before the court, Socrates blames at length Aristophanes by name for being his oldest and actually his most dangerous accuser (18a–19d). Many scholars tend to view this as a kind of rhetorical figure that should not be taken at face value.[5] And indeed, Aristophanes had also repeatedly mocked Cleon, especially in the *Knights*; but far from being hurt (let alone condemned to death as Socrates will soon be) Cleon was elected general in the year after that play was performed. Also, as several ancient sources claim, Socrates seems to have attended the performance of *Clouds* without being upset or hurt in any significant way.[6] But the testimonies about Socrates' reactions are very late and can hardly be taken as historically reliable (see, for example, the case of Seneca who presents a proto-stoic Socrates impassible in front of Aristophanes' mockeries).[7] And one should always remind ourselves that it is Plato, not Socrates, who wrote the *Apology*. So the question is not whether Socrates actually said this in the court, or if Aristophanes really was at the beginning of the accusation that Socrates now faces. The question is why Plato wanted to emphasize the importance of the humorous vilification that is at the center of *Clouds* (note that

---

[4] Saxonhouse (1985) offers a committed defense of such a tendency; but see Hooper (2013) for a devastating critique.
[5] A good example of such a reading is Platter. See Bouvier for a vigorous critique.
[6] For all references, see Bouvier (2000).
[7] On this, see Bouvier for all testimonies.

Xenophon does not mention it in his *Apology*). Also, one could not but relate this importance of *Clouds* in Socrates' trial to the no less emphatic notion of the "ancient quarrel between poetry and philosophy" that concludes Plato's second critique of poetry in *Republic* 10. For, by this "quarrel," Plato alludes more specifically to the attacks that comedic poets launched against philosophers for being "great in the empty eloquence of fools," "a mob of overly wise critics," and "subtle hair splitters who are beggars all" (607b–c). If we cannot say who wrote these invectives, they all sound very similar to how Aristophanes spoke of Socrates. (As one scholar suggested, they might even come from the first version of *Clouds*.)[8]

In both passages, Plato seems to take Aristophanes' attacks against Socrates very seriously. In vilifying Socrates, Aristophanes actually attacks the very possibility of philosophy as Plato understands it. But then how are we to solve our puzzle? If Plato really meant to counter-attack and harshly mock Aristophanes in his turn, how could he also have no less strongly condemned comedy for its attacks against citizens?

The first question we need to face is this: why does Plato so strongly condemn the satire of citizens? As Plato clearly states in the quoted passage from the *Laws*, such violent satires only awake our *thumos*, that is, your spirited emotional reactions (which include anger and indignation), especially when people are still young. Spirit (*thumos*, corresponding to the *thumoeidés* part of the soul) is not a bad thing per se. In the *Republic*, Plato proposes that a right education consists in making one's spirit the ally of reason; with a good, well-nurtured spirit (notably by listening to the right kind of music), reason is to grow robust enough to fight against one's epithumetic (i.e., bodily, irrational) desires. This is probably the main bone of contention between Plato and Aristophanes (and the other poets): contrary to what they may claim, poets do not have any knowledge, and more than that, they are not guided by reason whatsoever. This is the main claim Plato makes in both the *Ion* and the famous critique of poetry in *Rep.* 10. Contrary to what they claim (or to what people claim about them), poets are no *sophoi*, they do not obey or promote reason, and hence the pleasure they seek is never for the sake of the good, which only reason can determine. One might say that comedic poets nurture our spirit with the wrong objects. As Plato says of the comedic poet, "It is a fool who finds anything ridiculous except what is bad, or tries to raise a laugh at the sight of anything except what is stupid or bad, or – putting it the other way around – who takes seriously any standard of what is beautiful other than what is good" (*Rep.* 5, 452d–e; tr. Reeve). The problem with comedians, and Aristophanes, in particular, who is the target in *Rep.* 5, is that they laugh at the wrong objects: not knowing what is right and wrong, they actually take the good things to be ridiculous and they laugh at them. All of which Plato summarizes in making himself a good joke while quoting Pindar: "As to the man who laughs at the sight of naked women, when their athletic training is for the best, he is 'plucking the unripe fruit of the wisdom' . . . of laughter – he knows nothing, it seems, about what he is laughing at or what he is doing" (457b, tr. Reeve mod.). With this bon mot (*Fr. 209* Bergk), Pindar apparently mocked some presocratic philosopher for his claims he believed were off the mark (the adjective *atelés* here means "unripe," but literally it means "not reaching its goal"). In adding the unexpected, incongruous, coda ". . .of laughter," Plato adds his own bon mot and mocks Aristophanes who makes his audience laugh at things he mistakenly thinks are ridiculous.

Thus, what Plato condemns is not laughter as such, nor even satire or mockery, but the wrong, irrational way comedians use them. Aristophanes often claims that he has a certain *sophia* that would allow him to teach a few serious councils or lessons to his audience. Whether Aristophanes himself meant it seriously, or as a kind of second-order joke, Plato takes him at his word, except that he thinks his targets are totally ill chosen.[9]

On the other hand, and this is crucial to solve our puzzle, Plato fully understood that laughter can be a powerful tool to transmit or transform certain views – which is why he could not be but admirative of Aristophanes' techniques. Read the *Apology* passage again: what Plato has Socrates

---

[8] For a detailed analysis of these quotations, see Most (2011) (the suggestion by D. Obbink is reported by Most 2011, p. 12).

[9] On this, see esp. Nightingale.

say is that his judges saw *Clouds* when there were still young – indeed more than 20 years ago – and they thus have been imbued by the views of a Socrates as an idle, atheist, and morally dangerous sophist. Historically speaking, one may doubt that *Clouds* exercised any such strong influence, and one may even argue that Aristophanes choose to stage the quite idiosyncratic person of Socrates (who was ugly and went barefoot like a beggar and yet had a huge charism on his young pupils) just for the sake of fun. But for Plato, the fact that Socrates' indictment sounded similar to how Aristophanes depicted Socrates was a kind of proof that comic plays exercise an important influence, and more generally that laughter works as a very powerful tool in persuading people of such and such. At least in the eyes of Plato, through his jokes, Aristophanes managed to persuade his theater audiences that Socrates was a potentially dangerous sophist who went so far as to deny the existence of Zeus. Everyone must have remembered the last scene of *Clouds* where Strepsiades put the "thinkery" on fire. Surely (and contrary to what many scholars have claimed), Socrates and his disciples do not die on the pyre: as the last verse alludes to, they all go all around the "thinkery" in flames – indicating how the staging took place with all characters running all around in a kind of great carnivalesque dance. But one may well imagine that Plato took it seriously, making the parallel between this last scene where the place that symbolizes philosophy goes destroyed, and Socrates' death.

Plato may have (purposefully) exaggerated the importance of that "ancient quarrel" that comic poets made with the philosophers, as well as that of *Clouds* in the condemnation of Socrates. But he fully recognized the power that laughter can have. Laughter is both an automatic and a very pleasurable reaction that no one can resist. He thus must have realized that using such a tool could be extremely useful when it comes to persuade people to the importance of philosophy, which he took to be the necessary condition of a happy, truly human life. According to the late neo-platonic philosopher Olympiodorus (sixth century CE), Plato "liked Aristophanes and Sophron so much that, it is said, when he died, their works were found in his bed" (which modern scholars usually render as "under his pillow") as if he had to read a little bit of Aristophanes every night to get some inspiration for the next day of his writing the *Dialogs*. And as if he wanted to confirm that saying, Olympiodorus adds an epigram that, he says, "Plato himself wrote": "The Graces sought a sacred enclosure that would never fall: they found the soul of Aristophanes" (*Vita Platonis*, 74). Without much doubt, both the story and the authorship of the epigram have no historical basis. But both attest of the importance of Aristophanes as a master of humor in Plato's own writings.

Aristophanes' proximate aim was to get his audience laugh, with the final goal of winning a competition. As Aristotle says about making jokes, "If poets do not do this well, their public failure is keenest; if they do it well, they are popular" (*Rhet*. 3.11. 1413a10–11). To be sure, Plato did not want to win a competition in the theater. But it was a higher competition as it were that he wanted to win. As he clearly says in concluding his critique of poetry in *Rep.* 10: "It is a great struggle (*agôn*), my dear Glaucon, greater than people think, to become good rather than bad. So we must not be tempted by honor, money, or any sort of office whatever – not even by poetry! – into neglecting justice and the rest of virtue" (608b; tr. Reeve). Since Plato always carefully chooses his words, it is probably not by chance that in the final sentence of his long critique of poetry, Plato uses the word *agôn* which also commonly means a theater performance, or competition. So the real competition, Plato means to say, is not to win in the theater, but in the real life. Poetry can be a temptation that should be avoided when its only aim is emotional pleasure that is not guided by reason. But – to paraphrase the famous challenge Plato just made a little earlier in the same text – if jokes and laughter can prove that they be "both pleasurable and beneficial" (*Rep.* 10. 607d), one would welcome them in our philosophical practice. In the eyes of Plato, Aristophanes' humorous invectives were powerful enough to prepare the ground for the rejection of philosophy, and eventually the condemnation of Socrates. Using the same, powerful humorous devices should help philosophy to prepare the ground for rational persuasion. A joke is not a rational argument of course. But it may very well help the laugher who enjoys it wonder about such and such, and eventually better see and understand such and such a point that proves crucial in the whole process of argumentation. That is how Plato meant to both rebuke and emulate Aristophanes.

As we have seen from Olympiodorus' report, the ancient readers of Plato fully recognized the importance of the comedic aspects in Plato's art of writing. And it has been noticed by several commentators that Plato took over several techniques that are proper to Aristophanes (or at least, that we find prominently in Aristophanes): the unexpected use of colloquial language or trivial matters in the middle of a serious exchange; parodic use of serious features; invention of, and puns on, proper names; the coinage of words, especially oddly long words; animalistic imagery; slapstick scenes; and sexual jokes.

Let me give a very few sample of these humorous devices:[10]

Unexpected use of colloquial language or trivial matters in the middle of a serious exchange. One typical example of this comes from the beginning of *Frogs* when Dionysios while he was reading Euripides' Andromeda Dionysius is suddenly overwhelmed by a "most intense desire," yes "a terrible longing that's piercing [him] through and through." When summoned by Heracles to explain himself, Dionysius insists that his desire is really difficult to explain and that he will have to "speak through enigmas": "Have you ever been struck, he asks Heracles, by a sudden desire for – soup?" (Such a thick soup made with peas or beans was the most simple and cheap meal of poor people). And as if the contrast between the desire that consumes Dionysius which seems to be so difficult to explain and the clarifying example were not immediately evident (perhaps for the less sophisticated members of his audience), Aristophanes has him add a quotation of Euripides himself: "Am I making my point quite clear? Do you need more hints?" (51–65; tr. Halliwell).

In Plato, the most emblematic example of such a humorous device comes from the *Hippias Major*. When asked what he takes to be beautiful, Hippias gives Socrates lots of examples such as a young girl, a horse, and a lyra, all of which everyone would readily agree to consider beautiful. And then all of a sudden, (through the anonymous voice) Socrates asks Hippias: "Then, my best friend, what about a beautiful pot? Isn't it something beautiful?" An unexpected example of something beautiful that must have made Plato's readers chuckle (as Hippias himself makes it clear: "What a boor he is to dare in an august proceeding to speak such vulgar speech that way!"). And the example comes again further down, when Hippias suggests to define beauty through appropriateness; there Socrates comes with a wooden spoon that is much more appropriate, and hence beautiful, than a golden one when it comes to handle soup in a pot: it gives the soup a better taste, Socrates explains, and it will not break the pot! These two trivial examples are particularly funny because Hippias is presented to be a "beautifully dressed and beautifully shod" (291a). And they are meant to help us better see how empty and actually not fine/beautiful Hippias' suggestions are.

Parodic use of serious features. One very serious framework that seems to have been much admired, yes revered, in Athens was the institution of being fed at the Prytaneum which was the greatest possible honor that particularly successful athletes and other people were gratified with. It comes as no surprise then that it also gave rise to parody, and Aristophanes refers to it a few times, notably in *Knights*, for example, where Paphlagon (i.e., Cleon who was granted such an honor) says: "I pray to our Lady Athena, sovereign of the City, that if I have been the worthiest of all servants of the Athenian people [. . .] I may dine in the Prytaneum for having done. . . nothing" (763–66). We find a very similar parodic use of this venerable institution in the *Apology*, when Socrates notoriously proposes to be fed at the Prytaneum for all he has done for Athens (37a). For the jury, this is the last outrage that one could have thought of. But it is a good joke for us readers, which is meant to accompany our commitment to the very fact that (contrary to how Aristophanes sees Cleon) indeed Socrates was the perfect and true "hero," and that he therefore should be fed there if one takes seriously into account his commitments to help his Athenian fellow citizens toward virtue and true happiness; and by the same token, it also highlights the profound mistake and real outrage of Socrates' condemnation.

Puns on proper names. These are very common in all of Aristophanes' plays, and they are numerous in Plato too (Gorgias: *Symp.* 198c; Meletus: *Ap.* 25c; Bias: *Hp. Mai.* 281d; Demos: *Grg.* 481d, 513b; Ariston: *Rep.* 580b; Stesichorus: *Phdr.* 244a; and Agathon: *Symp.* 174b. Note that

---

[10] Many of them have been conveniently put together in the path-breaking article by Roger Brock (Brock 1990). For a more recent review, see Trivigno (forthcoming).

Aristophanes too made a pun on Agathon, calling him the *agathos poiêtês*: *Frogs* 83–84). An interesting, often unnoticed, instance comes at the end of *Symposium*, when Alcibiades enters the house of Agathon and shouts as loudly as he can: "Where on earth is Agathon/Mister Goodness, where is he then? I order you to lead (*agein*) me to Agathon/the Good – now!" (212d; my admittedly over-translation takes into account the way the verbs are emphatically used in the present tense). With the repetition of the name/adjective *agathon*, this is a genuine way to start staging the funny scene of a very drunk man who impatiently wants to meet with the honorand of the day. That repetition, as well as the emphatic verb *agein* which was used earlier by Diotima at 210c8 in the case of the guidance to the Form of the Good (210c8; 211c2; see also *paidagôgein*: 210e2), point also to the fact that Socrates' most talented pupil and lover really wanted to aim at a good life when he was young, but because of his overwhelming desire of glory, completely failed and eventually became a traitor of his city. And indeed, the good life, or more precisely the Form of the Good that one must "see" in order to become truly virtuous and happy (212a), is something that is no easy reach; hence, Plato's insistence on Diotima's toponym, *mantinikê* (201d), "from Mantinea," which can easily be heard as meaning "who has the art of divination" (taking *mantinikê* as derived from *manteia*, "divination"), which (perhaps for the readers who would not have noticed it) Plato has Socrates explicitly alludes to a little later: "I would need divination (*manteia*) to get what you are saying, I don't understand you" – with a further pun with *manthanein*, "understand" (206b).

Coinage of words. When in the *Poetics* Aristotle review the various classes of words, the example he gives for words made of different parts (most probably) comes from a comedy (*Poet.* 21, 1457a36–b1). And indeed, such words are quite common in Aristophanes where we even find the longest word that any Greek writer has ever written: (*Assembly Women* 1169–1175). Contrary to how the passage seems to be usually read by scholars, it must be the case that the longest word in Plato's corpus (*enneakaieikosikaieptakosioplasiakis*: "729 times") has to be read as a joke, which is meant to make us wonder ("What an extraordinary account!" says Glaucon) and ponder on how huge the difference is between the amount of pleasure that a king enjoys and that a tyrant does. Other instances are much shorter but no less funny. If Aristophanes famously coined the word *trugôdia*, literally: "the tragedy for drunks" (from *trugos*, "vine") as a kind of humorous nickname for comedy, Plato's *theatrocracy* (*Laws* 701a) no less became a catchword.

Diminutives. These seem to have been another specialty of Old Comedy, Aristophanes in particular of whom Aristotle cites a few examples from his *Babylonians* (*Rhet.* 3.2. 1405b29–33). In Plato (Rep. 475e), one such diminutive, *technudrion* (a little *technê*), may not sound terribly funny to our ears. But it is a hapax (and perhaps Plato's coinage), which accompanies other words that Plato has arguably coined as well: *philotheamones* (the "philotheater people") and *philêkooi* (the "philomusic people"). Like the numerous philo-words that peper the beginning of *Wasps*, where Philocleon's illness is finally revealed as being a *philêliastês*, a philo-court person, these two words that describe the people who are the opposite of the 'philosophers,' were certainly meant to be funny, which this description corroborates: 'just as if their ears were under contract to listen to every chorus, they run around to all the Dionysiac festivals'. Thus, when adding that they are 'craving to learn all about all possible techni. . . calities', Plato wants to make sure his readers laugh at them, before he introduces the philosophers who are the worthy "philotheater" people, eager to learn all what is needed in order to finally "see" the Good.

Animalistic imagery. When Plato has Socrates compare himself to a gadfly (*Ap.Soc.* 30e) and to a stingray (*Meno* 80a), this is certainly meant to be amusing; but of course, we readers are also invited to take the metaphor in all seriousness: Socrates is indeed the one who will endlessly annoy you until you take the path of virtue, and his replies are meant to put you in a state of *aporia*, and thus wake you up to philosophical questions. Or again when Philebus (apparently an invented name, meaning "the man who is found of young men") decides to stay silent and is thus dubbed a "jellyfish," Plato wanted us to chuckle but also to reflect on how a life made only of physical pleasures is not very different from the life of such a mindless animal which of course no one would live (*Phil.* 21c). And finally, what about the most notorious image, that of the half-human, half-animal Silenus, which Alcibiades presents as the most genuine image of Socrates (*Symp.* 216d–e)? Scholars have endlessly wondered where this image might come from and how to read it. As Andrea Capra has forcefully suggested, it might very well owe its origin in one of Aristophanes' lost plays. But here, in contrast to the gadfly and stingray images that were probably invented by Plato (or Socrates) himself, this image was meant by Aristophanes to be utterly ridiculous: hence, the detailed explanation of Alcibiades who makes everything he can to justify why such a comparison proves to be actually right.[11]

Slapstick scenes. In Plato, the most obvious example of such a scene is at beginning of *Charmides*: the beautiful Charmides' "coming caused a lot of laughter, because every one of us who was already seated began pushing hard at his neighbor so as to make a place for him to sit down. The upshot of it was that we made the man sitting at one end get up, and the man at the other end was toppled off sideways" (155b–c). Presumably, Plato is parodying a boy game similar to our musical chairs, which is played by these male adults, who are all sexually aroused at the sight of the beautiful young Charmides. Such a parody must have been funny in itself, but at the beginning of a *Dialog* dedicated to the virtue of moderation (*sophrōsunê*), what amused readers are meant to understand is arguably the very fact that these men are not at all a good example of that virtue – including Socrates who then gets a glimpse into Charmides' cloak and could not help but be sexually aroused in his turn (155d).

Stylistic parody. Parody of tragedy plays an important role in Aristophanes who never tires of having characters speaking in an elevated style in a comic atmosphere – something that the coined *trugódia* is meant to capture very well. In Plato, several *Dialogs* contain large portions of sheer parody, from the entire *Menexenus*, a parody of funeral oration, up to the main part of the *Cratylus* which mocks the etymological explanations that the Sophists were found of. Also, in the *Symposium*, Pausanias' speech recalls the typically long, alliterative, sentences of his master Gorgias, which ends with the formidable coda "When Pausanias finally took a pause" (185c).

Sexual jokes. As to sexual jokes, Plato admittedly avoids the most graphic insults such as the recurrent (in)famous *euryprōktos* ("having his arsehole widely open"). But perhaps surprisingly (at least for modern readers) we do find some explicit sexual jokes in the *Dialogs* which are no less obscene than Aristophanes'. The most obscene joke is probably to be found in the *Gorgias* (494c–e). Trying to refute Callicles' position that "happiness consists in the capacity of fulfilling all of our desires" (considered as lacks), Socrates asks him whether he would then consider the person who has an itch and scratches it "abundantly" and "all his life long" could also be considered happy. "Nonsense" is Callicles' first answer. But he must admit that for such a man, scratching is pleasurable, and hence (since he had admitted that pleasure makes happiness) this must make him happy. This refutation does not seem enough to persuade Callicles, though, and Socrates asks further: "What if he scratches only his head – or what am I to ask you further? [. . .] And isn't the climax of this sort of thing, the life of a catamite [i.e. a passive male sexual slave], a frightfully shameful and miserable one? Or will you have the nerve to say that they are happy as long as they get everything they want in abundance?" The usually shameless Callicles is now shocked for good ("Aren't you ashamed, Socrates, to bring our discussion to such matters"), which shows that the last question is an utterly obscene joke amounting to something like: "the more semen they are filled with, the merrier!" Why such a joke here? Quite obviously, because despite his own contradictions, Callicles has obstinately remained unconvinced so far; thus making him indignant at such a shameful thought should help him recognize the truth of Socrates' argument – and it should help us laughing readers to better appreciate the oddity of Callicles' hedonistic stance.

A very similar joke comes up in the *Symposium*, when Socrates mocks Agathon who wants Socrates to sit next to him and get his knowledge through his contact: "It would be splendid, Agathon, if knowledge was the sort of thing that could flow from the fuller to the emptier of us when we tough one another, like water that flows through a piece of wool from a fuller cup to an emptier one. If wisdom is really like that, I regard it as a great privilege to share your couch: I expect to be filled up from your rich supply of fine wisdom" – a clear allusion to anal penetration here too. It is a symposium where all guests are expecting such jokes, and they indeed must be imagined to

---

[11] See Capra (2018).

have great fun which might be at its peak when Agathon replies with a good sense of humor: "You are a mocker (*hybristés*), Socrates," where *hybristés* can also mean "sexual offender" (175d–e). But the joke is also supposed to convey the most possible serious message: philosophical knowledge cannot be transmitted from one person to another but must be sought through a long quest. That quest will eventually be described by Diotima. But perhaps Diotima's speech might have sounded a little bit too serious and abstract for these symposiasts, and Plato felt compelled to add a kind of "satyric drama" (as he has Socrates characterize it, 222d) to Diotima's "elevated," that is, characteristic of tragedy, speech. When Alcibiades tells his hilarious story of his attempts to seduce Socrates, all symposiasts are enjoying themselves a lot, especially when they hear Alcibiades addressing them as if they were the "judges" (with the typical address, "ô judges," that people use in a court) of how Socrates "had abused him by despising his beauty" (219c; which is of course a reminder of Agathon's joke at the beginning)! This very funny speech is meaningful at different levels: it exonerates Socrates from being the teacher of Alcibiades; it repeats the point made in the first sexual joke, that philosophy is not to be conceived as a transmission from one person to another; and since Alcibiades is depicted as in deep love with Socrates, it ultimately makes Aristophanes' speech off the mark: loving a person may be important at the beginning of the so-called ladder of love, but true love is love of the Form of the Beautiful, or the Good.

Besides these humorous devices, and their philosophical uses, there are two main targets against which Plato seems to be particularly eager to emulate Aristophanes.

The first target of Plato's humorous attacks is Aristophanes himself. As we have already seen, the hiccup scene in the *Symposium* should be taken as a derisive depiction of Aristophanes. Also, one should bear in mind that Aristophanes is trying to cope with his hiccup all along doctor Eryximachos makes his own praise to Erôs, which is to be viewed as a powerful way to make readers laugh not only at Aristophanes but also at Eryximachos and his grand theory of universal love.[12] Another joke that Plato makes against Aristophanes is a pun on his very name, when at 189a7–8, he writes: "And then Eryximachus: my good, he said, Aristophanes, mind what you are doing!" This literal translation sounds weird, but it just captures the very odd word order of the address Ὠγαθέ, φάναι, Ἀριστόφανες. I suggest that careful ancient Greek ears must have noticed the double pun, one semantic (Ὠγαθέ – Ἀριστό = good – best), and one purely phonetic (φάναι – φανες), which is to make us readers understand (and have fun at) the fact that Aristophanes is indeed the one who only seems (*phanes* as a suffix from the verb *phainomai*, to appear) to be the best, but is not.[13]

A second target are the Sophists. Of course for Aristophanes, the paradigmatic sophist is Socrates. Hence, the insistence is made by Plato in most of his *Dialogs* to differentiate his master from the Sophists. One recurrent theme is money: the poor Socrates never got paid for his meetings with young people while the sophists earned fortunes from their teaching. But as if this (perhaps historical) argument would not be sufficient, Plato never misses an opportunity to make fun of the Sophists by using the same sort of humorous devices that Aristophanes used when mocking Socrates. The clearest example of this is the hilarious beginning of *Protagoras*. Scholars have long noted the similarity of this beginning with the (now lost) play of Eupolis, the *Parasites* (which Plato himself seems to be alluding to, notably in describing the way the sophists are moving around like a chorus: 315a–b). The very few fragments that we have from that play do not allow us to say much more. But some features are clearly reminiscent of those that we find in Aristophanes. After a long discussion along their way about what makes a sophist, Socrates arrives with his young friend Hippocrates at the house of Callias who is hosting the renowned sophist. In a similar way, Strepsiades must fight against the slave porter who does not want to let him in the "Thinkery," Socrates is first rebuked by Callias' porter slave who opens the door and screams: "Oh boy! Here are some of these sophists – well, he has no time for you!" – and he slams the door on them with full force. And it is only when repeating that they are no sophists but want to meet Protagoras that they are finally let in. This joke is only the first in a long series, where all the prominent sophists of the time are

---

[12] Here too quite a few interpreters have tried to "save" Eryximachos from being the butt of Plato, but see Trivigno (2017) for a forceful defense of the parodic aspects of it.
[13] For a detailed defense of this reading, see Destrée (2015).

satirized. In the *Clouds*, Socrates is taken to be (and perhaps actually was, at that time) known for his research on astronomy; hence, the jokes on his being near his research object: "I'm air-walking and spinning my thoughts around the sun" (an image that Plato refers to in the *Apology*: 19c). Similarly, Plato takes one typical feature of each sophist and makes a parody of it. Especially funny and meaningful, the satire of the polymath Hippias "he was sitting on a chair, delivering sentences all the while he was responding to all their questions" about the physical and astronomical worlds (315c), as if he were a judge who can decide and state about everything in the world!

Aristotle, or the Appreciation of Sophisticated Jokes à la Aristophanes

The case of Aristotle is hard to assess as we do not have the second book of the *Poetics* that was dedicated to comedy, where he seems to have dealt with the "various kinds of jokes" as one passage from his *Rhetorics* alludes to (1419b6-7). But in the *Nicomachean Ethics*, in the chapter on "the good sense of humor" (*eutrapelia*), he clearly rejects obscene speech (*aischrologia*) from the jokes that well-educated people are supposed to make and hear: "there are some things that it is appropriate for such a person to say and to listen to by way of amusement, and the amusement of a gentleman differs from that of a slavish person, and that of an educated person from that of an uneducated. One can also see this from old and new comedies: to the earlier writers, bad language was what was funny, while, to the later, it was innuendo (*hyponoia*), which makes a great difference when it comes to refinement" (1128a19-22). True, comedy is mentioned as an analogy to humor in a social framework such as a symposium. But it seems quite evident that this condemnation of obscenity must have been valid in the case of comedy too. A good joke, Aristotle seems to be saying, is a joke where innuendo is used, not sheer obscenity. Scholars usually explain this difference as if Aristotle was primarily concerned with ethical standards. But innuendo (*hyponoia*) refers to the use of intelligence.[14] "Innuendo" thus points to the fact that a good joke is a sophisticated joke, which needs some sort of search on the part of the hearer and invention on the part of the joker. In other words, an obscene joke is what we call an "easy joke," not sophisticated or demanding enough for well-educated people.

This normative theory of humor is actually not at all new. It is Aristophanes himself who condemns obscene and graphic jokes for being "easy jokes," which could only please the mob; sophisticated people want to hear innovative, unexpected jokes that only clever (*dexios*) poets can offer. (Also note that in that chapter, Aristotle uses the word *epidexios* as a synonym for *eutrapelos*.) Thus, Aristotle may have owed this theory of humor to Aristophanes. Or at least, since he certainly read Aristophanes' plays (which he quotes a few times), it is difficult not to be struck by the similarity of their respective demands.

True, Aristotle never hints at such an origin, and as I recalled, he clearly says that "in old comedies, what makes laugh is obscene speech." And of course, he must have noticed that, despite his own precepts, Aristophanes himself never hesitates making an obscene joke whenever he can. But there is no reason to take that comparison to be more than a comparison that helps see or understand something: the difference between obscene speech and innuendo is best seen in the difference that is obvious between the old comedies and the newest ones; this does not imply though that Old comedy is nothing but obscene speech or that the Old comedic poets considered obscene speech to be what should count as the best jokes. And as to the obscene jokes in Aristophanes, Aristotle must also have noticed that all these jokes are almost always uttered by not educated characters (and should probably be heard in a kind of mockery made against these) – thus hardly as something that would go against Aristophanes' own ideal. And he must also have noticed that

---

[14] Note that in Plato, the word means "allegorical meaning" (*Rep.* 378d). In his commentary on that passage of the *Nic. Ethics*, Aspasius speaks of "divination" (125.33–34). For a more detailed defense of this reading, see Destrée (2020).

besides those obscene jokes, very sophisticated jokes abound, even in the case of sexual jokes. This is not pure speculation. Actually, it is what Aristotle seems to have been clearly aware of in the third book of his *Rhetoric*. There, when dealing with bons mots and witticisms (*asteia*) (literally "urbane" bons mots, not "rough" or vulgar ones), he quotes quite a few verses from comedies. I will only mention two of them which Aristotle gives as his apparently preferred example of how one should conceive of how a joke should work.

Let us call the first one the "Thracian joke." It is an example of a witticism that is based on the unexpected change of one or two letters, that is, what we call a pun. In the play from which the joke comes, apparently one character named Nicon, a cithara player from Thrace, is readying himself to play. But instead of saying "you going to playing the cithara" (θράττεις σύ/*thratteis su*), as the audience would have expected, his protagonist on stage unexpectedly says "you are a Thracian girl" (Θρᾷττ' εἶ σύ/*Thratt' ei su*; *Rhet.* 3.11.1412a33–b1) – a adapted translation would read: instead of saying, "Now, are you going to play something on your trumpet?" that protagonists says: "Now, are you going to play the ... stumpet?" Probably no one nowadays would find this joke particularly clever and witty, since it is based on homophobia, misogyny, and racism taken together, as the poor Nicon is called a female slave prostitute from Thrace (a region Athenians commonly despised and from which many slaves came). But it would be a mistake to think that this joke was not a good example of a witty innuendo in the eyes of Aristotle (and his contemporaries). For Nicon is a cithara player who actually comes from Thrace, as Aristotle emphasizes: "if the audience did not take Nicon to be Thracian, it would not seem witty." And, if Thracian people were usually despised by Athenians, it also remains true that cithara playing was intimately linked to Thrace; according to Pindar, the paradigmatic player of the cithara (and "the father of song," *Pythian Odes* 4.4.315), Orpheus, was Thracian by origin (fr.128c), and it was therefore common to speak of a Thracian cithara too. If one takes this into consideration, which of course educated minds in Athens did, the joke sounds much more like a clever innuendo. Aristotle does not tell who wrote that witticism. But he reports it from the fifth-century BCE rhetorician Theodorus of Byzantium; it is thus a joke that must come from an Old Comedy play, perhaps even from Aristophanes.

Let us call our second example the "Sandal joke," which Aristotle reports as another example of a good pun. In a verse, such a pun can be especially effective when the humorous word has exactly the same accentuation and length as the word that was normally expected: "'There he was walking around with ... blisters (*chímethla*) on his feet,' where the hearer thought he would have said 'slippers' (*pédila*)" (Rhet. 3.11.1412a31–32). The funniness of the verse comes of course from the pun but not only. For an educated audience, the amusement comes also from the awareness that this is a parody of Homeric verses, where the description "walking with fine sandals" normally applies to gods or goddesses. Especially if you think of the verse where the sandals are described as being "in gold" (*Od.* 1.96; *Il.*24.340), the incongruity is blatant.

That funny verse may come from a Middle comedy play. But we do have a very similar joke in Aristophanes already. Bdelycleon wants Philoclean to put so-called Laconian sandals, to which the latter replies: "What? O my (*tlaiên*)! Are you seriously expecting me to put on/undergo [the verb *hypoduein* can mean undergo a danger, or put on shoes] our enemies' hostile ... footwear (*echthrón ... dusmenê kattumata*)?" The second verse is most certainly the parody of a tragic verse (announced by the typically tragic "O my") such as Euripides' *Heraclidae* 1006: "the hostile offspring of an enemy lion (*echthrou ... dusmenês blastêmata*)." So, here the sophisticated members of the theater audience must have appreciated the double meaning of the verb *hypoduein*, the (possible) pun on *kattumata*, and the parodic flavor of the whole passage.

GUIDE TO FURTHER READING

For the reception of Aristophanes in Plato, see Bouvier (2000), Brock (1990), Dobrov (2010), and Quadlbauer (1960); in Aristotle, see Destrée (2020) and Janko (2002). For the portrait of Aristophanes in Plato's *Symposium*, see Capra (2018), Dover (1966), Hooper (2013) and Hooper (2022).

REFERENCES

Bouvier, D. (2000). Platon et les poètes comiques: peut-on rire de la mort de Socrate? In: *Le rire des Grecs. Anthropologie du rire en Grèce ancienne* (ed. M.L. Desclos), 425–440. Grenoble: J. Millon.

Brock, R. (1990). Plato and Comedy. In: *'Owls to Athens': Essays on Classical Subjects Presented to sir Kenneth Dover* (ed. E.M. Craik), 39–49. Oxford: Clarendon Press.

Capra, A. (2018). Aristophanes' iconic socrates. In: *Socrates and the Socratic Dialogue* (ed. A. Stavru and C. Moore) 64–83. Leiden/Boston: Brill.

Destrée, P. (2015). The allegedly best speaker: a note on Plato on Aristophanes (*Symp.* 189a7). *Classical Philology* 110 (4): 360–366.

Destrée, P. (2020). Aristotle on aristophanic humour. In: *Aristophanic Humour: Theory and Practice* (ed. E. Hall and P. Swallow), 101–116. London: Bloomsbury.

Dobrov, G. (2010). Comedy and her critics. In: *The Brill's Companion to the Study of Greek Comedy*, 3–34. Brill.

Dover, K. (1966). Aristophanes' Speech in Plato's Symposium. *The Journal of Hellenic Studies* 86: 41–50.

Hooper, A. (2013). The greatest hope of all: Aristophanes on human nature in Plato's symposium. *Classical Quarterly* 63: 567–579.

Hooper, A. (2022). Aristophanes' Hiccups and Pausanias' Sophistry in Plato's Symposium. *Arethusa* 55: 101–119.

Hunter (2009). *Critical Moments in Classical Literature*. Cambridge.

Janko, R. (2002). *Aristotle on Comedy: Towards a Reconstruction of Poetics II*. Bloomsbury.

Most, G. (2011). What Ancient Quarrel between Philosophy and Poetry? In: *Plato and the Poets* (ed. P. Destrée and F.G. Herrmann), 1–20. Leiden/Boston: Brill.

Quadlbauer, F. (1960). Die Dichter der griechischen Komödie im literarischen Urteil der Antike. *Wiener Studien* 73: 40–82.

Saxonhouse, A.W. (1985). The net of Hephaestus: Aristophanes' speech in Plato's symposium. *Interpretation* 13: 15–32.

Trivigno, F. (2017). A Doctor's folly: diagnosing the speech of Eryximachus in Plato's. In: *Plato's 'Symposium': A Critical Guide. Cambridge critical guides* (ed. P. Destrée and Z. Giannopoulou). Cambridge, New York: Cambridge University Press.

CHAPTER 23

Ancient Scholarship on Aristophanes

Andreas Willi

Introduction

Scholarship on Greek comedy started when the genre was still flourishing, in the fourth century BCE. Besides the cursory remarks **Aristotle** has to offer on the subject in his (extant) *Poetics*, and possibly a more in-depth treatment by the same author and/or subsequent Peripatetic studies feeding into later sources such as the so-called *Tractatus Coislinianus* and the late-antique *Prolegomena de comoedia* (cf. "Scope and Themes" section), one may think here in particular of Aristotle's compilation of the Athenian dramatic *Didaskaliai*.[1] By making available in book form the official records that listed for each year and for each dramatic festival the names of the competing tragic, dithyrambic, and comic poets, together with the titles of their respective plays, this was to become a crucial reference work for subsequent literary historians. Referring to it, the Alexandrian scholar **Callimachus** was able to draw up a *Catalogue and List of Dramatists in Chronological Order from the Beginnings*, supplementing his general catalog (*pinax*) of the holdings in the newly established library at Alexandria (cf. Callim. frr. 454–456 Pfeiffer); and later on in the third century BCE the great Aristophanes of Byzantium equally used the didascalies when prefacing each of the comic plays he edited with a brief *hypothesis* including key data such as the date of production and the ranking achieved in the comic agon alongside a plot summary.[2] Given their aims, it is natural if none of these works paid more attention to Aristophanes than to other comic poets of the classical period. It is important to bear this in mind when looking at "ancient scholarship on Aristophanes." Much of the latter simply forms part of a much wider field of ancient scholarship on comedy. If we are better informed about scholarship on Aristophanes than on, say, Cratinus or Eupolis, this is mainly a consequence of selection and canonization processes that were at best indirectly related to scholarly endeavors in the field – nor can we really tell what it was that led to Aristophanes still being read in late antiquity when the texts of other comic authors had more or less disappeared from the scene.[3] The availability of accessible commentaries (cf. below) may well have played a role

---

[1] For the inscriptional remains of the *Didaskaliai*, see Millis and Olson (2012). The fragments of ancient treatises on drama are collected in Bagordo (1998); cf. also the survey in Rusten (2011, pp. 737–741). On the *Tractatus Coislinianus* and its possible relationship to Aristotle's *Poetics* and/or the Peripatetic tradition, see Janko (1984) and Nesselrath (1990, pp. 102–149).

[2] But the metrical *hypotheseis*, which are explicitly ascribed to Aristophanes of Byzantium in the manuscripts, are generally considered spurious; cf. Achelis (1913–1916), Radermacher (1954, pp. 79–83), Pfeiffer (1968, pp. 192–196), and Montanari (1970–1972).

[3] Cf. Trojahn (2002, pp. 144–149), with statistics.

in this, but if the interest in Cratinus and Eupolis had not begun to ebb, equally useful commentaries would have continued to be produced on these authors as well. That Aristophanes' status was a special one even within the triad of the great three representatives of Old Comedy, who are often named together (e.g. Hor. *sat.* 1.4.1, Pers. 1.123, Quint. *inst.* 10.1.65–66, [Dion. Hal.] *art. rhet.* 8.11), is, however, confirmed by him not only being singled out already in Aristotle (*Poet.* 1448a25–27), or later Cicero (Cic. *leg.* 2.37; cf. Gell. 13.25.7) and some writers on style and rhetoric (Demetr. *eloc.* 128, [Longin.] *subl.* 40.2; cf. the assessment in *Proleg. de com.* III.36–37 Koster), but also by Aristophanes being chosen as the negatively judged counterpart to elegant Menander in Plutarch's half-stylistic, half-ethical *Comparison* of the two poets (Plut. *Comp. Ar. Men.* = *Mor.* 56, 853a–854d).

On the whole, though, ancient rhetoric and literary criticism tend to turn a blind eye to comedy, and it is not here that we find much evidence for scholarly engagement with Aristophanes. Nor should we make too much of the interest shown for Aristophanes' work among the lexicographers in the Roman imperial period. Especially during the second and third centuries CE, an ideological war was raging between the so-called "**Atticists**," who advocated various degrees of linguistic purism and a general revival of "classical" Greek as used in the fifth and fourth centuries BCE, and their opponents who denounced this as a silly exercise in anachronism, which was moreover often based on questionable evidence.[4] In this debate, Aristophanic comedy served as a treasure trove for the Atticists, who could discover in it many everyday lexemes that had long been forgotten, but potentially also as an ammunition depot for the other side whenever they happened to find in one of the plays a word or expression the Atticists were frowning on without noticing that *even* Aristophanes had already used it. None of this deserves the label of *Aristophanic* scholarship as the objectives of either camp were not to elucidate, explain, or critically assess Aristophanes' oeuvre in its own right.

The Sources

By and large, therefore, we have just two main sources of evidence to concentrate on when enquiring into Aristophanic scholarship as such. The first, and less substantial one, is fragments of ancient papyrus scrolls and papyrus or parchment codices containing either editions of Aristophanic plays with accompanying marginal annotations of variable extent or self-standing commentaries (*hypomnēmata*) that were meant to be consulted alongside a separate text of a given play. In none of these cases are we able to assign a specific scholar's name to such a partially preserved commentary or set of annotations. The relevant papyri that are currently known range from the first century CE to the sixth century CE, with one-quarter of the two dozen items collected in the Aristophanes volume of *Commentaria et lexica Graeca in papyris reperta* (*CLGP*) belonging to the *hypomnēma* type and the rest to an annotated edition (Esposito and Montana 2012). Apart from the plays that are also known through the medieval manuscript tradition, we occasionally come across other comedies as well here: one of the earliest pieces containing marginal comments belongs to the lost *Heroes* (*CLGP* 11), and one of the earliest *hypomnēmata* deals with a play possibly to be identified with the *Anagyrus* (*CLGP* Ar. 27). However, from the fourth century onward, such evidence supplementing the medieval canon disappears. We may therefore infer that plays other than the 11 comedies still known to us in their entirety stopped being read and studied at around that time.[5]

The second, and more informative, source consists of marginal (or more rarely interlinear) annotations in some of the medieval manuscripts of Aristophanes, the so-called *scholia* (Koster

---

[4] On these debates, see, e.g. Swain (1996), Schmitz (1997), and Kim (2010), on the individual scholars involved Dickey (2007), pp. 94–99). Galen compiled a five-volume treatise on *Ordinary Words in Aristophanes* (alongside similar works on Cratinus and Eupolis): cf. Galen. *De libris propriis* p. 19.48 Kühn.

[5] See Esposito and Montana (2012, pp. 3–12); Trojahn (2002, pp. 153–199) proposes a broad categorization into (1) scientific *hypomnēmata*, (2) extensive/succinct commentaries, and (3) reading aids.

et al. 1960–2007).⁶ What differentiates these from the ancient annotations just mentioned is not so much their content as the fact that they are less fragmented and that their initial compilation (cf. below) ostensibly aimed for comprehensiveness. Although not all the extant plays are equally well served by scholia, for those with extensive coverage – including not only the three plays most commonly read in Byzantine times, *Plutus*, *Clouds*, and *Frogs*, but also other highlights such as *Birds*, *Wasps*, *Knights*, and *Peace* – the material is abundant. Its exploration, however, is rendered difficult by the process that led to the final product we now have, namely different selections of notes, which sometimes but not always overlap across witnesses, in manuscripts each of whose copyists may have had their own ideas on what was or was not worth including, and which amalgamate the results of the activity of commentators over a period of more than a millennium. One may therefore compare the scholiastic corpus to a stretch of sedimentary rock grown over a very long time, but with the added complication that someone has broken up the rock into countless pieces, mixed them up more or less randomly, and glued them together again. Now to reassign each of the fragments to its original layer is impossible, and even where there are lucky hints in the structure of a given item – or even a rare "label" (the name of a commentator) assigning it to a specific stratum – we always have to reckon with the possibility that it nevertheless contains extraneous elements as well or that the layering we think we can infer is in fact erroneous.

That readers of Aristophanes never stopped commenting on what they read is in any case illustrated by the comparatively straightforward separation of "old" and "recent" scholia. The former of these are by and large the scholia preserved in manuscripts that predate the work of Byzantine scholars such as John Tzetzes (in the twelfth century) or Thomas Magister and Demetrius Triclinius (in the fourteenth century);⁷ or else, where this is not the case, scholia in later copies that show significant similarities in content and wording with those in the earlier manuscripts. Yet, the fact that there is a clearly discernible corpus of "recent" scholia at all – alongside a full-scale commentary on several of the comedies by Tzetzes himself – brings home the fundamental continuity that connects the ancient *hypomnēmata* with the modern Aristophanic commentaries of our times.

In view of the overlaps between the scholia in different manuscripts, coupled with the surprisingly common phenomenon that even a single manuscript may contain several annotations with similar content on a single word or line, it seems clear that the bulk of the scholiastic corpus derives from some large-scale master version that brought together the exegetical efforts of previous scholarship. This could have taken the form of a luxury edition of Aristophanic comedy with very ample margins into which the information presented in various earlier annotated texts and/or separate *hypomnēmata* were copied. There has been much debate over the date at which such a scholiastic archetype could have been written.⁸ The latest plausible point in time would be the ninth century, not just because this is when the introduction of the Byzantine minuscule script might have acted as an incentive to produce a new full edition but also because the step must in any case have been taken before the Byzantine lexicon **Suda** was compiled, a great many of whose entries are in fact explanatory notes on Aristophanic words and passages (i.e. to be treated like a further manuscript alongside the "normal" transmission of the scholia) (Adler 1928–1938, 1931). On the other side, though, it has also been pointed out that we have some limited evidence for text editions with marginal comments on a large scale already in the sixth century.

For our purposes, however, this is less important than the fact that the scholiastic archetype itself gathered together information from more than one scholarly source. It is the date and character of these sources that are of real relevance for a proper understanding of the evolution of ancient Aristophanic scholarship. Luckily, at the end of the scholia on some of the plays, an end note

---

⁶ For an overview of the main manuscripts of Aristophanes, see Sommerstein (2010, pp. 412–420). For the older scholia, R[avennas 429], V[enetus Marcianus 474], E[stensis gr. 127], and Γ (Laurentianus XXXI 15 + Vossianus gr. F 52) are particularly important.
⁷ On these scholars, see Wilson (1996, pp. 190–196, 247–256).
⁸ Cf. Montana (2011), who assesses the opposite views of Zuntz (1975) and Maehler (1994) on the one hand (late) and Wilson (1967) and McNamee (1995, 1998) on the other (early).

(*subscriptio*) gives a pertinent reference. For *Clouds* and *Peace*, we thus learn that "[*hypomnēmata*] by Phaeinus and Symmachus" were mainly used, alongside a metrical analysis by the first-century metrician **Heliodorus**,[9] for *Birds* the work of Symmachus "and other scholia." In the scholia on the other plays, no such end notes are found, but we may confidently assume that **Symmachus** in particular must have been of crucial significance there too. Unlike **Phaeinus**, who is otherwise cited by name only in a small handful of banal or questionable notes on *Knights* and of whose work or date we know nothing else, Symmachus – a scholar whose activity is datable to the second century CE – is referred to quite frequently also in individual annotations on nearly all the comedies (with the exception of *Lysistrata* and *Ecclesiazusae*, but the scholia on all three "women's plays" are meager anyway, no doubt because they were the least read of all the extant works of Aristophanes).[10] Although we have to allow for a limited amount of further accretion of (largely insignificant) material after the second century, we can thus conclude that Symmachus' commentary represented the last important stage of real scholarship on Aristophanes in antiquity – the last substantial sedimentary layer, so to speak – and that, in all likelihood, it was through Symmachus' work that most of what the scholia still tell us about earlier scholars' opinions was mediated and handed down (cf. already Schneider 1838). If this is correct, Phaeinus might perhaps have produced a shorter, digested version of what Symmachus had offered, with personal additions here or there, but without many insights from independent research. In any case, it is noteworthy that the grammarians Herodian and Phrynichus and the rhetorician Athenaeus, all of whom were active during the reign of Marcus Aurelius in the second half of the second century CE, are among the latest writers referred to by name in the scholia; and since Symmachus may have been a contemporary of theirs – rather than living slightly earlier, as is often assumed because Herodian once cites him – it is even conceivable that virtually *no* such scholarly reference is post-Symmachean (with one likely exception being sch. Ar. Plut. 725h, where the late-antique [fourth/fifth century?] grammarian Salustius is quoted). Moreover, it has been observed that there are noticeable coincidences in wording and substance between the fragmentary remnants of a few fourth- and fifth-century *hypomnēmata* (*CLGP* Ar. 1, 15, 17) with the medieval scholia, whereas there are no such coincidences between the scholia and marginal annotations or *hypomnēmata* fragments before the fourth century. For what it is worth, this too suggests that by around 300 CE at the latest, there should have been one generally acknowledged scholarly reference point for readers of Aristophanes – and it then stands to reason to identify this with Symmachus' commentary.

A Historical Sketch

The preceding remarks have already hinted at the many unknowns we are facing when trying to untangle the evolution of ancient Aristophanic scholarship. Much of the information in the following historical sketch has to be read against this background of fundamental uncertainty.[11] Even apart from the many question marks regarding the identities and biographies of several figures in this history, the general impression we gain from our sources about their individual interests, achievements, and shortcomings could well be flawed because of the selective and haphazard character of the primary data. On the positive side, though, the very fact that our sources are so piecemeal also has one advantage. *If* certain patterns do emerge across a body of evidence that is as fragmentary as ours, the danger that these patterns reflect nothing but a selectivity bias is reduced.

---

[9] Heliodorus and his metrical scholia are discussed in detail by White (1912, pp. 384–421); cf. also Boudreaux (1919, pp. 138–143).
[10] On Symmachus see further the "A Historical Sketch" section, Schauenburg (1881), Boudreaux (1919, pp. 144–160), Gudeman (1931), and Montana (2003); on Phaeinus Boudreaux (1919, pp. 161–164), Strout and French (1938), and Montana (2015).
[11] For a fuller treatment, see Boudreaux (1919); cf. also Schneider (1838, esp. 86–96), Rutherford (1905, pp. 417–434) (assembling the pertinent scholia), Trojahn (2002, pp. 117–142).

If, for example, a scholar X is repeatedly associated with a simple type of lexical explanation but hardly ever cited for some piece of factual information, it seems legitimate to assume that this is due to the nature and focus of his scholarship, no matter how little else we know about it. Were this not so, little more than a mere list of ancient scholars' names could be given.

In order for research on Aristophanic comedy to become possible, the plays first had to be collected into one corpus. A Byzantine source, which is certainly drawing on ancient information, tells us that it was **Lycophron of Chalcis** who was encharged with assembling the texts of Greek comedy soon after the establishment of the Alexandrian library in the early third century BCE (*Proleg. de com.* [Tzetzes] XIa.I.1–8, XIa.II.1–3/22–24).[12] In addition, the same Lycophron wrote a treatise *On Comedy* whose title resembles that of similar writings by members of the Peripatos and Academy schools in Athens. However, whereas the latter may have been mainly interested in social–historical and/or dramaturgical aspects of comedy, the references to Lycophron in the Aristophanic scholia suggest that his focus was primarily lexical. Since we usually learn only that "Lycophron explained word X as meaning Y" (e.g. sch. Ar. Pax 702a, "Lycophron [said] that *hōrakiān* [= 'faint'] is used for *ōkhriān* [= 'become pale']"), the method by which he arrived at his conclusions is hard to establish. Most likely at this early stage of lexicographical research the meanings of unfamiliar words were inferred from the immediate context, perhaps with some recourse to etymological considerations, but without reference to other occurrences of the word outside comedy.

It did not take long to realize that the results thus achieved could be questionable. In several cases where the scholia cite Lycophron, his opinion on the meaning of a word is juxtaposed with a correction by **Eratosthenes of Cyrene** (c. 275–195 BCE), one of the greatest scholars of the Hellenistic period who is most famous for his work on astronomy, geography, and chronology but who also wrote a large-scale treatise *On Ancient Comedy* in at least 12 books.[13] That Eratosthenes' corrections to Lycophron (e.g. sch. Ar. Pax 702a [cont.], "but Eratosthenes said [*hōrakiān*] refers to suffering from vertigo as a result of fainting, a consequence of which may perhaps be to become pale") were to be found in this work is at least plausible, and the same goes for one or two notes that cite him for an opinion on a detail of text constitution. More importantly, however, the treatise also discussed matters of wider literary-historical significance. Thus, in opposition to Callimachus who, in writing his *Catalogue*, had diagnosed an error in Aristotle's *Didaskaliai* as they dated Aristophanes' *Clouds* to 424/3 BCE although the parabasis mentions Eupolis' *Marikas* dated to 422/1 BCE, Eratosthenes inferred that the text of *Clouds* we read (and he read) must be a partially revised version (cf. sch. Ar. Nub. 553); and by means of a similar reasoning he also tentatively inferred that there may have been two versions of *Peace*, only one of which was preserved in the library at Alexandria (argum. A2 in Ar. Pac.).

Messy transmission situations like the one of *Clouds*, where the originally staged version got lost, underline the importance of being able to read and critically assess a properly edited text. It is uncertain whether Lycophron had already tried not just to collect manuscripts of the Aristophanic comedies for the library but also to collate them and establish on this basis a true *diorthōsis* or vulgate version. Even if he did, the result must have been only preliminary since the task of coming up with a truly reliable edition of the plays was left to **Aristophanes of Byzantium** (c. 257–180 BCE).[14] Best known for his editorial work on Homer, in which he pioneered the use of critical and exegetical signs, he appears to have made use of these in his Aristophanes edition too. According to a scholion on *Frogs*, he put a *sigma* and *antisigma* against Ran. 152 and 153, to signal either that these two lines were mutually exclusive alternatives or that the originality of Ran. 152 was doubtful (sch.

---

[12] On Lycophron, who was also a poet but whose authorship of the extant iambic poem *Alexandra* remains disputed, see Strecker (1884), Ziegler (1927), Pfeiffer (1968, pp. 106, 119–120), Bagordo (1998, 35–36, 150), Meliadò (2019), and Pellettieri (2020).
[13] On Eratosthenes, see Strecker (1884), Knaack (1907), Pfeiffer (1968, pp. 152–170), Bagordo (1998, pp. 37–40, 127–136), Geus (2002), and Montana (2020, pp. 185–190).
[14] On Aristophanes of Byzantium, see Cohn (1895b), Boudreaux (1919, pp. 25–47), Pfeiffer (1968, pp. 171–209), Slater (1986), and Montana (2020, pp. 191–200).

Ar. Ran. 152). Furthermore, since he is credited with the invention of lyric colometry, it is also likely that he was the first to set apart cola in lyric passages of comedy as well, rather than writing them out as continuous text; and his idea of prefacing each play with a *hypothesis* (cf. "Introduction" section) was again to find many followers in later centuries.

It is unprovable, but not implausible, that such a careful establishment of the Aristophanic text not only preceded but inspired the compilation of a running commentary. For all we know, this novel format may have been tried out here for the very first time – even before *hypomnēmata* on Homer began to be written by Aristarchus and others – by a regrettably shadowy scholar called **Euphronius**.[15] One source explicitly speaks of a *hypomnēma* of his on Aristophanes' *Plutus* (Orus in *Lexicon Messanense*, ed. Rabe 1892, p. 411), and Euphronius' name also appears with reasonable frequency in the scholia on other plays (*Clouds*, *Wasps*, *Birds*, *Frogs*). His date, however, is most uncertain. On the one hand, we are told by the Byzantine scholar Choeroboscus that one Euphronius was counted by "some" as a member of the Alexandrian Pleiad, a group of poets associated with Ptolemy II Philadelphus (r. 283–246 BCE); this would make him a rough contemporary of Eratosthenes. On the other hand, the same Choeroboscus speaks of Euphronius as a teacher of Aristarchus, thereby placing him in the same generation as Aristophanes of Byzantium (Choerob. *Heph.* 9.3 and 16.2 Consbruch). Obviously, only the latter chronology would allow us to assume that his activity as a commentator postdates the editorial activity of Aristophanes. One consideration that speaks in favor of this view is that according to one notice he commented on the accentuation of the word for "owl," *glaux* (sch. Ar. Vesp. 1086a). This presupposes a text with written accents, and that is yet another innovation with which Aristophanes of Byzantium is generally credited. On the whole, Euphronius' notes seem to have been fairly cursory and superficial, as one may expect of such a pioneer work. However, they already went beyond the mere explanation of lexical details and also discussed, at least, the identity of individuals mocked in the plays (*kōmōidoumenoi*) – though sometimes basing hasty conclusions on a one-dimensional reading of the comic text. Thus, Euphronius' inference from Av. 997 that the geometer Meton came from the Attic deme of Kolonos is unwarranted and was subsequently corrected by another, better-informed, scholar (sch. Ar. Av. 997a).

When Euphronius is referred to in the scholia, his name is often paired with that of **Callistratus**, a commentator who is known to have worked also on epic, lyric, and tragic poetry and who must have belonged to the circle of Aristophanes of Byzantium's students.[16] Many of Callistratus' notes were, again, concerned with points of detail, regarding the comic lexicon including phraseology (cf. *CLGP* Ar. 28, frr. C+D+E, col. I.12–16) but also prosody, grammar, and textual criticism. It is clear that he was at times responding to Euphronius, as when he sought to clarify the association of Meton with the Kolonos according to the scholion just cited. In his discussion of other *kōmōidoumenoi* too, Callistratus may have drawn more strongly than his predecessor on sources external to comedy itself. For instance, his identification of the Dracontides mentioned at Vesp. 157 with Dracontides of Aphidna, one of the Thirty Tyrants of 404/3 BCE, was certainly not based on anything in the text (sch. Ar. Vesp. 157a; cf. Montana 1996, pp. 191–198); whether it was correct is a different matter. In this context, it is worth remembering that specialist treatises on *kōmōidoumenoi* were not yet available to commentators at the time. Such repertories were subsequently written, still in the second century BCE, by Aristarchus' pupil and successor Ammonius (cf. sch. Ar. Vesp. 1238a) as well as Herodicus of Babylon, who belonged to the Pergamene school of Crates of Mallus (cf. Athen. 13.586a).[17]

---

[15] On Euphronius see Strecker (1884), Cohn (1907), Boudreaux (1919, pp. 50–51), Pfeiffer (1968, pp. 160–161), Montana (2020, pp. 200–201), and Novembri (2020).
[16] On Callistratus see Schmidt (1848), Boudreaux (1919, pp. 48–51), Gudeman (1919), and Montana (2008a, 2020, pp. 201–203).
[17] On Ammonius and Herodicus, see Blau (1883, pp. 5–13), Cohn (1894), Steinhausen (1910, pp. 6–49), Gudeman (1912), Düring (1941), Bagordo (1998, pp. 50–51, 74–77, 142–143), Montana (2006a), Pagani (2009b), and Montana (2020, pp. 231–232).

That Callistratus' relationship with **Aristarchus of Samothrace** (c. 215–144 BCE), the most illustrious student of Aristophanes of Byzantium, was fraught is sometimes assumed, mainly because he is said to have criticized Aristarchus for not dressing well enough (Athen. 1.21c; cf. Montana 2008b).[18] Be that as it may, for all the evident sensibility of Aristarchus' famous philological principle of "explaining Homer out of Homer," that is, treating epic poetry as a closed (literary) universe (cf. Nünlist 2015; Schironi 2018, pp. 735–742), the confidence with which he dissected the epic text was not appreciated by everyone; and, more crucially for our purposes, a similar isolatory approach was far less appropriate when dealing with the rather different genre of comedy. In commenting on (at least some) of the comedies of Aristophanes, Aristarchus was no doubt aware of this, but it remains striking that the one scholion which refers to a view of his not on a literary or philological point but on a historical matter, shows him go wrong. Unlike Callistratus, who rightly saw that Ran. 1422 must be read against the background of Alcibiades' voluntary absence from Athens in 407 BCE, Aristarchus thought that Alcibiades' exile of 415 BCE was at issue (sch. Ar. Ran. 1422c/d). Moreover, Aristarchus' literary judgment on comedy does not always seem impeccable either. That, for example, the verses Ran. 1437–1441, where Euripides proposed to turn Cleocritus and Cinesais into an airship and to squirt vinegar into the eyes of the enemy, are "coarse and cheap" may be true, but *that* is hardly a reason to athetize them with Aristarchus (sch. Ar. Ran. 1437–1441a); Aristarchus' idea that the chorus of initiates in *Frogs* must have been divided into two half-choruses at Ran. 354 is not really compelling (cf. sch. Ar. Ran. 440a, taking issue with Aristarchus' view as recorded in sch. Ar. Ran. 354a, 372c); and his (mis)understanding of the joke at Ran. 308–309, where Xanthias comments on Dionysus who has shat himself, is hardly redeemed by the willingness instead to attribute to Aristophanes a rather complex piece of wordplay involving an exchange of the words for "red" and "yellow" (sch. Ar. Ran. 308a). However, too negative an assessment of Aristarchus' work on Aristophanes would be equally unfair since elsewhere we also see him engage in careful textual scholarship (e.g. sch. Ar. Ran. 191c, where Aristarchus defended the reading "the battle about the flesh" instead of "…about the corpses" based on some proper lexicographical research) or check and assess intertextual connections proposed by previous scholars (sch. Ar. Ran. 1206a/b/c, on an alleged borrowing from Euripides' *Archelaus*). To what extent the concentration of Aristarchean references in the scholia on *Frogs* is a coincidence, that is, merely due to the fact that the transmission and selection history was different for the scholia of each play, is difficult to tell; but given the intrinsic interest *Frogs* held for any literary scholar, it is not impossible that Aristarchus' notes on other plays, though securely attested by occasional citations here or there, were less rich.

Like all inspirational scholarship, Aristarchus' work also provoked dissent. With regard to Aristophanic comedy, we witness this most clearly with **Demetrius of Adramyttium**, who was nicknamed Ixion – after a mythical king who killed his father-in-law – precisely because he criticized his former teacher Aristarchus in the most vitriolic terms.[19] Although Demetrius' polemical attitude was no doubt most prominent in Homeric matters, the Aristophanic scholia also reflect some of it in one or two cases, as when he attacked Aristarchus' take on a controversial word play at Ran. 970. Puzzled by the politician Theramenes being called there "not a Chian, but a Keian," Aristarchus apparently preferred to read "…Koan" since the worst and best throws of a dice were called the "Chian" and the "Koan" throws, respectively; but Demetrius found this "completely ignorant" since it overlooked the *para prosdokian* joke Aristophanes created precisely by substituting "Keian" for the expected "Koan" (sch. Ar. Ran. 970b). However, Demetrius' counter-claim that Theramenes was a native of Keos itself looks like a misinference from the passage, and similarly his defense of the "battle about the corpses" reading at Ran. 191 (cf. above) is so strained that it seems to result primarily from a desire to oppose Aristarchus (sch. Ar. Ran. 191e, attributable to Demetrius thanks to Phot. κ 1069).

---

[18] The bibliography on Aristarchus is vast but mainly focused on his Homeric studies: see e.g. Cohn (1895a), Pfeiffer (1968, pp. 210–233), Schironi (2018), and Montana (2020, pp. 204–217). On Aristarchus in the Aristophanes scholia, see especially Gerhard (1850), Boudreaux (1919, pp. 52–74), and Muzzolon (2005).

[19] On Demetrius Ixion, see Staesche (1883), Blau (1883, pp. 19–20), Cohn (1901), Boudreaux (1919, pp. 84–85), Ascheri (2009), and Montana (2020, pp. 230–231).

A very different attitude toward Aristarchus is inferable for a critic who is generally cited as **Apollonius** in the scholia. Since Apollonius is about as distinctive a name as English *John* would be, a secure identification of this person is impossible. However, a scholion on *Wasps* once mentions more specifically an Apollonius son of Chaeris (sch. Ar. Vesp. 1238b), and it is reasonable to think this is the same man as the Apollonius of the other scholia. If so, this would make Apollonius slightly later than Demetrius, toward the end of the second century BCE, because his father Chaeris is himself considered a pupil of Aristarchus'.[20] Even so, Apollonius would still be among the "heirs" of Aristarchus, and it therefore makes sense if the two are mentioned in one breath (sch. Ar. Ran. 1124) or if we learn, for example, that Apollonius concurred with Aristarchus' athetesis of Ran. 1437–1441 (cf. above); significantly, though, he managed to improve the strength of the case by observing, not without reason, that the lines "have no bearing on the overall argument of the passage" (sch. Ar. Ran. 1437–1441b). The clearest testimony to the conscientiousness and quality of Apollonius' scholarship, meanwhile, comes from another scholion on *Frogs*, commenting on a line where Dionysus says to Xanthias that the latter will "look like the flogging-slave from Melite" once he has put on Heracles' attire (Ran. 501). Here, Apollonius adopted an earlier line of interpretation which suspected a prosopographical allusion, perhaps to Callias the son of Hipponicus, behind the "flogging-slave from Melite"; but what makes his contribution really interesting is the circumspect way in which he both addressed potential criticism (e.g. relating to the fact that no actual name occurs in the passage) and dissected the alternative view according to which the line contains a *para prosdokian* joke for "*Heracles* from Melite," that is, a reference to a particular shrine and cult image of the hero (sch. Ar. Ran. 501c). Even if Apollonius' chronological and linguistic objections are not completely watertight, they here show an argumentative stringency that is closer to modern scholarship than what we usually see attested in the scholia.

All the Aristophanic scholars who have been discussed so far were either active in, or at least closely associated with, Ptolemaic Alexandria as *the* hub of learning in the early Hellenistic period. From the middle of the second century onward, however, Pergamum in Asia Minor began to compete with the Egyptian capital as the Attalid kings fostered their own cultural ambitions – it is hardly a coincidence if the quarrelsome Demetrius Ixion eventually came to work here. The question thus arises to what extent Aristophanic comedy was also studied by others in Pergamum. The leading Pergamene scholar, **Crates of Mallus**, is mentioned very rarely in the scholia, although it is noteworthy that he seems to have had access to a second Aristophanic play called, or version of, *Peace*, as is shown by a remark to this effect in a hypothesis of the transmitted comedy (argum. A2 in Ar. Pac.). Beyond that, the scholiastic references to Crates are of a lexicographical nature and could be based, not on *hypomnēmata* or specialist treatises on comedy, but on a work *On the Attic Dialect* (cf. Broggiato 2001, p. xlvi).[21]

More in-depth engagement with Aristophanes at Pergamum might be indicated if the **Asclepiades** whom the scholia mention repeatedly were to be identified as Asclepiades of Myrlea, a scholar commonly associated with the Pergamene tradition. However, one scholion in the early modern Aldine edition of *Clouds* speaks of an Asclepiades of Alexandria (sch.^Ald. Ar. Nub. 37), and while this man is generally believed to have been a different person, who also wrote an exegetical treatise on the archaic laws of Solon (cf. e.g. Plut. Sol. 1), it is impossible to tell whether that entails that the Asclepiades mentioned in other Aristophanic scholia is equally to be kept apart from Asclepiades of Myrlea, or even yet another figure.[22] In any case, there is nothing in those scholia to point to a

---

[20] On Apollonius son of Chaeris and Apollonius the Aristophanic commentator, see Schrader (1866), Blau (1883, pp. 50–56), Cohn (1895c, 1895d), Berndt (1902, pp. 50–52), Boudreaux (1919, pp. 77–78), and Montana (2002).
[21] On Crates of Mallus, see Boudreaux (1919, pp. 79–83), Kroll (1922), Pfeiffer (1968, pp. 234–243), Broggiato (2001), Pagani (2009a), and Montana (2020, pp. 222–227). The attribution is further complicated by the slight possibility that the author of the dialect treatise was not Crates of Mallus, but his namesake Crates of Athens, a third-century academic scholar who also wrote about comedy (*FGrH* 362; cf. Bagordo 1998, pp. 61, 216–218).
[22] On Asclepiades of Myrlea, Asclepiades of Alexandria, and Asclepiades the Aristophanic commentator, see Wentzel (1896a, 1896b, 1896c), Boudreaux (1919, pp. 86–88), Pfeiffer (1968, p. 273), Pagani (2007) and Pagani (2009c) (on Asclepiades of Myrlea), Pagani (2009d) (on Asclepiades of Alexandria), Pagani (2009e) (on the Aristophanic scholar), Montana (2020, pp. 236–237).

fundamentally different attitude from what we find among all the Alexandrian scholars, and certainly nothing that is reminiscent of the allegorical exegesis that characterized Asclepiades of Myrlea's treatise *On Nestor's Cup*. One common concern of the earlier commentators had long been to pin down the intertextual models of parodistic lines and quotations in Aristophanes (cf. e.g. sch. Ar. Nub. 1264 for Euphronius). Once the most uncontroversial cases had been set out, less obvious connections could then also be suggested (just as they are in modern commentaries); and Asclepiades may have been a little bolder in this respect than his predecessors. If, for example, Aristarchus and Apollonius had been unable to find an intertextual source for Ran. 1269/70, a line with which the stage Euripides of *Frogs* clearly intends to parody Aeschylus in one way or another, and if Asclepiades then "assigned" that line to Aeschylus' *Iphigeneia* (sch. Ar. Ran. 1269b), it is unlikely that an incontrovertible model verse had simply been overlooked until then. Probably, Asclepiades merely found in Aeschylus' play a less immediate similarity, just as he ostensibly did in the case of Ran. 1331–1333: these latter verses he presented as an imitative allusion to Eur. *Hec.* 68–69 although the resemblance is a very general one, not one involving any specific verbal echo (sch. Ar. Ran. 1331b). Inevitably, there is a danger of going too far in establishing such connections, and at least twice Asclepiades even fell into the trap of suspecting a reminiscence that must be excluded on chronological grounds (by arguing that Av. 348 and Av. 422–424 hark back to Euripides' *Andromeda* and *Phoenician Women*, respectively, although *Birds* was staged earlier than either of these plays) (cf. sch. Ar. Av. 348a/b). However, we should also positively acknowledge that, by going beyond the obvious, suggestions like those of Asclepiades fostered less mechanical ways of reading Aristophanes.

Besides Alexandria and Pergamum, the island of Rhodes developed into a further center of learning during the second and first centuries BCE. When Ptolemy VIII expelled many intellectuals from Alexandria in 145 BCE, it was in Rhodes, for example, that the great grammarian Dionysius Thrax found refuge. As far as Aristophanic scholarship is concerned, we find it represented on the island by a certain **Timachidas**, who wrote a commentary on *Frogs* (in addition to working on Euripides and Menander), and who may have been the same man as the Timachidas who was in charge of drafting the Lindian temple chronicle in 99 BCE.[23] Unfortunately, the occasional references to Timachidas in the scholia on *Frogs* are not very informative, nor do his contributions seem to have been particularly valuable. For instance, the suggestion that the vinegar-flask joke in Ran. 1440 (and Ran. 1453) was inspired by Euripides' mother allegedly being a greengrocer is far-fetched, though still of some interest because it shows that Timachidas cannot have accepted Aristarchus' (and Apollonius') athetesis of Ran. 1437–1441 (cf. above; sch. Ar. Ran. 1453).

Having reached the first century BCE, we return to Alexandria where the activity of **Didymus of Alexandria** (c. 80–10 BCE?) constitutes a caesura in the history of Aristophanic scholarship. Nicknamed "Bronze-Guts" (*Khalkenteros*) because of his incredible learning and scholarly output, which encompassed works on grammar, lexicography, and mythology alongside literary exegesis (also of epic, lyric, and tragic poetry as well as oratory), Didymus made more than one major contribution to the study of comedy.[24] On the one hand, he compiled a large-scale *Comic Lexicon*, which was based on his own and other people's research on the vocabulary of comedy and which (indirectly) constitutes a major source for the comic lemmata in the late-antique dictionary of Hesychius (cf. Hsch. *epist. in Eulog.* 3–8 L.-C.); this will have quickly eclipsed the only slightly earlier, but no doubt less ambitious, collection of comic words by Artemidorus of Tarsus (for which cf. e.g. sch. Ar. Vesp. 1169b, 1238).[25] On the other hand, Didymus wrote a series of *hypomnēmata*,

---

[23] On Timachidas, see Boudreaux (1919, pp. 88–89), Ziegler (1936), Montana (2006b), Montana (2020, pp. 238–239), and Matijašić (2014, 2021).

[24] On Didymus, see Schmidt (1854), Cohn (1903), Roemer (1908, pp. 366–410), Boudreaux (1919, pp. 91–137), Pfeiffer (1968, pp. 274–279), Braswell (2013, pp. 27–103), Montana (2020, pp. 246–253), Benuzzi (2020), and Benuzzi (2023).

[25] On Artemidorus and his work, see Wentzel (1895) and Bagordo (1998, pp. 63, 98–100). *P.Oxy.* 1801 (with *CLGP* Ar. 3, 7, 12, 24, 26, 30, 31) might contain, or be based on, Artemidorus' collection, but the *Lexicon* of Artemidorus' son Theon or indeed that of Didymus are other possibilities: see Esposito and Montana (2012, p. 41 n. 1).

among other things on (probably all) comedies of Aristophanes. In preparation for these *hypomnēmata*, he extensively excerpted the commentaries and treatises of previous researchers, and it is assumed that whenever the scholia tell us that a pre-Didymean scholar X or Y said this or that about an Aristophanic passage, we owe the preservation of this information to Didymus' reports. However, Didymus' research was not merely derivative. Not only did he often disagree with what others had said, and typically sought to support his own views with substantial and sometimes out-of-the-way references to parallel passages (cf. e.g. sch. Ar. Av. 1283a, with a quotation from some Doric comedy [?]); he also extended the scope of the commentaries by bringing in sources that had not been consulted by previous commentators at all, notably with regard to factual and historical information (cf. e.g. sch. Ar. Lys. 313a, which suggests that Didymus used the Hellenistic historian Craterus' *Collection of [Athenian] Decrees*). It is in this respect, rather than the philological establishment and discussion of the text (as a basis of which he probably still used the edition of Aristophanes of Byzantium) that Didymus' legacy was greatest. In particular, his familiarity with the widest possible range of comic *and* non-comic literature had the potential to act as a corrective to the old habit of drawing problematic conclusions (e.g. in prosopographical matters) from oblique or allusive statements in the plays themselves (though see sch. Ar. Thesm. 31 for an instance of Didymus making the same mistake), or also to enrich a reader's understanding where matters of daily life were concerned (such as the Athenian festival calendar or the ingredients of an Athenian dried-fish wrap: see sch. Ar. Ach. 1076a and sch. Ar. Ach. 1101a, respectively). The downside, meanwhile, is that Didymus sometimes worked too hastily, or was carried away by excessive learning. The latter we see in a case like sch. Ar. Av. 13a, according to which Didymus saw in Peisetaerus' straightforward remark "The guy from the bird-market (*houk tōn orneōn*) really gave us a terrible deal" a complicated allusion to the Peloponnesian town of Orneai (cf. Av. 399) and through this to the battle of Mantineia that had taken place a few years before the production of *Birds*. As for the former, one may think of Didymus' rejection of Aristophanes of Byzantium's sensible reading of the poet Alcaeus' name in Thesm. 162, preferring a reference to the more recent tragedian Achaeus (sch. Ar. Thesm. 162a); when, following a rethink, Didymus did realize that "Alcaeus" was in fact the better option, he still did not have the grace to retract entirely, but insisted that another Alcaeus, a citharode from Sicily, must be meant. However, the most serious error that has been imputed on Didymus – on the basis of circumstantial and doubtful evidence, it has to be said[26] – is that he was the commentator who believed, when dealing with the *Plutus*, that the play he had in front of him was not the late composition of 388 BCE, but rather a homonymous comedy that had been staged some 20 years earlier (cf. esp. sch. Ar. Plut. 972i). This did create serious chronological problems, but they were brushed aside by means of somewhat specious assumptions (cf. sch. Ar. Plut. 173b, 179a, 1146d).

Once Didymus' comprehensive commentaries were available, readers of Aristophanes who wanted to get up-to-date information on specific points of interest would naturally turn to them, rather than go back to older works; and similarly, anyone wanting to put together a shorter, more eclectic, *hypomnēma* would also take them as the starting point (cf. e.g. *CLGP* Ar. 27, 28). There is in any case little evidence for substantial further developments in the main areas of Aristophanic scholarship for roughly 200 years. As already mentioned ("The Sources" section), it is only in the second century CE that **Symmachus** felt the need to overhaul Didymus' work.[27] What prompted him to do so we do not know. It can hardly have been a conviction that scholarship had made so much progress in the intervening time that a "new Didymus" had to be produced; for not only was the one major contribution of the first century CE, the metrical analysis by Heliodorus ("The Sources" section), not integrated into Symmachus' *hypomnēmata* (as it is still cited separately in the *subscriptio* of *Peace*), but it is also not the case that the scholia preserve many other references to scholars belonging to the

---

[26] His name is not given in the relevant scholia, but the "Didymean" appearance of some of their information induced Boudreaux (1919, pp. 133–137) to attribute the mistake to him. In his discussion of the complex issue Sommerstein (2001, pp. 28–33) wisely just speaks of "one of the ancient commentators"; cf. now also Willi (2023).

[27] For literature on Symmachus, see above, fn. 10.

period between Didymus and Symmachus. Heliodorus' student Irenaeus (Pacatus) is mentioned a few times, for grammatical minutiae (e.g. sch. Ar. Vesp. 900b), and so are Seleucus, a grammarian of the Tiberian age (e.g. sch. Ar. Thesm. 840) and the slightly later lexicographer Epaphroditus (sch. Ar. Eq. 1150a), but none of them should be supposed to have worked specifically on Aristophanes. It is therefore likely that Symmachus simply disapproved of Didymus' ideas often enough to make him wish for a modernized alternative. This is not to say that we never see the two scholars agree when both of their names are mentioned on a single matter, with Symmachus at best refining Didymus' points (cf. e.g. sch. Ar. Av. 1273a/b, sch. Ar. Av. 1705a); and we also have to take into account that where only Symmachus is cited, this might be due to incomplete referencing in the scholia as much as to Symmachus really having been the first to come up with a given explanation. However, there are in fact also a number of instances where Symmachus diverges from his most important predecessor. Looking at Av. 1121, for example, Symmachus thought that the description of the panting messenger as "breathing Alpheius-style" (*Alpheion pneōn*) must imply that the messenger "is running as hard as a runner in the Olympic foot-race [sc. by the Alpheius river]," whereas Didymus had more boldly suggested an intertextual reference to a Pindaric line that spoke of the "venerable breath/resting-place (*ampneuma*) of the Alpheius" (sch. Ar. Av. 1121a); and on Av. 439–442, where we obscurely hear of a "knife-maker monkey who made a pact with his wife not to pull his testicles," Symmachus preferred to assume that this is no more than a hint at some popular fable, rather than a prosopographical jibe at a certain monkey-like cook's son called Panaetius, as Didymus had suspected (cf. sch. Ar. Av. 440). From this and other examples, including one where Symmachus openly confesses his inability to make sense of a line as transmitted (sch. Ar. Av. 1681b), we can infer a healthily sober attitude, which no doubt helped his work to supersede that of Didymus. Even so, his was not always the last word either, for any later reader could of course still come to different conclusions and reject what he had offered (e.g. sch. Ar. Thesm. 393a, 710b). In that sense, and as noted before ("The Sources" section), ancient Aristophanic scholarship must not be thought to have come to a complete halt with him. All we can state with some confidence is that Symmachus' *hypomnēmata* – the precise extent of which we ignore: they almost certainly included a commentary also on at least one play now lost, the *Merchantmen* (cf. sch. Ar. Av. 1283a), but did he still cover *all* the Aristophanic plays? – represent the last *major* stop on the road that eventually led to the medieval scholiastic corpus (cf. "The Sources" section).

Scope and Themes

If we look at the scholia in their entirety, and together with the much more limited papyrus evidence, we see that many of the things that modern commentaries deal with are already present. The most numerous notes are quite elementary as they offer lexical and grammatical – including at times "rhetorical" – elucidation, often by glossing or paraphrasing words and expressions but sometimes also by highlighting differences between classical Attic and later (i.e. for the commentators/readers: contemporary) usage (cf. e.g. sch. Ar. Thesm. 572 on *homou genesthai ~ eggus genesthai* "get together," sch. Ar. Nub. 439b on a morphological difference, which is misclassified in the scholion). Recording textual variants (including conjectures) belongs to this basic layer as well, although the scale of this is much more limited than in a modern critical apparatus and real text-critical discussions are rare (e.g. sch. Ar. Av. 66a; often a variant is just added with abbreviated *gr.* = *graphetai* "one [sc. alternatively] writes"). That the attribution of lines, or parts of lines, to speakers is not always clear triggers many pertinent annotations, and the commentators may also express views on other matters of performance (entries/exits, movements on stage, vocal expression), not least because stage directions were only exceptionally written within the text itself (*parepigraphai*: cf. e.g. sch. Ar. Thesm. ante 277 on the text between Thesm. 276 and 277). As mentioned before, meter was originally dealt with separately, but commentators were of course aware of the metrical exigencies of comic verse: they do on occasion, and again not always correctly, comment on scansion (cf. e.g. sch. Ar. Nub. 818 and sch. Ar. Av. 1283a, with two doubtful scansional claims by Symmachus). Beyond that, there is much information about historical people and realia, the quality of which is variable. Unfortunately, we are ourselves often dependent on what the scholia tell us and hence unable to decide how much trust we should place in them in such matters. To give just one example, there has been considerable debate in modern scholarship about the historicity (and/or scope) of a decree proposed by a certain Syracosius forbidding the act of "lampooning by name" (*onomasti kōmōidein*); the only positive evidence we have for this is a scholion on a passage of *Birds* where Syracosius is compared to a garrulous jay (sch. Ar. Av. 1297a; cf. e.g. Halliwell 1991, pp. 58–63; Sommerstein 2004, pp. 208–211). It is telling that the scholion introduces the relevant claim by a hedge ("he *seems* [*dokei*] to have brought in a decree"), which may imply that this was merely an inference from a comic passage cited in support (Phrynichus fr. 27 K.-A.); but since we know that at least one of Aristophanes' commentators was conscientious enough to consult, where appropriate, a published *Collection of Decrees* (cf. the "A Historical Sketch" section on Didymus), how sure can we be that there was not really some form of speech injunction in decree form with which Syracosius was associated? Similar questions arise with regard to many of the intertextual sources of Aristophanic parody identified in the scholia. When we no longer possess the original texts as such, we frequently cannot decide whether the dependency relationship between a given expression/verse and a proposed model was obvious and indisputable or more or less plausible speculation (as with some of the examples from Asclepiades cited in the "A Historical Sketch" section).

Compared to all this, what one might call the really *literary* exploration of the text is marginal in the scholia, more so than in modern commentaries. Partly this may be ascribed to the format because line-by-line or word-by-word annotation does not lend itself so easily to the exploration of wider interpretive matters (though cf. e.g. sch. Ar. Pax 619, 1204 containing a critical assessment of the build-up of entire passages of *Peace*). But even where the format need not have acted as a deterrent, we notice a certain lack of engagement. Although the ancient commentators were not blind to the mechanisms of Aristophanic humor and regularly highlighted speaking names (e.g. sch. Ar. Pax 190 on Trygaeus, sch. Ar. Lys. 838a on Cinesias), puns (e.g. sch. Ar. Nub. 710a, 730b; also, without reticence, obscene ones: e.g. sch. Ar. Ach. 801 on *erebinthos* = "chickpea"/"penis"), or the many *para prosdokian* jokes (for which the term *par' hyponoian* is normally used: e.g. sch. Ar. Plut. 27a/c with rudimentary analysis), they were much less attuned to other aspects of comic verbal art. For example, comic compounds may be dissected into their component parts (e.g. sch. Ar. Vesp. 220b/c), but nothing is said about their stylistic impact; the user of the commentary is rarely told with sufficient clarity whether an unusual lexeme is a comic coinage or simply a word of the classical language that has lost currency; and where parody is purely stylistic, without echoing a specific model, the chances of it being picked up are much reduced (though tragic and dithyrambic style fare slightly better than the rest: cf. e.g. sch. Ar. Ach. 1190b *paratragōidei*, Ar. Vesp. 1484 *paratragikeuetai*; para-dithyrambic: sch. Ar. Av. 930b, 1379b [Symmachus]).

Finally, there is the question of macroscopic interpretation. In modern commentaries, this is typically presented in introductory sections. These do not exist as such in the scholia. There are the *hypotheseis*, which became increasingly substantial and, while still containing the basic facts as at the time of Aristophanes of Byzantium (cf. "Introduction" section), sometimes outline the plot in considerable detail. However, even in such longer hypotheses, the readers are seldom told much about how to read a given play. At best, a general judgment is formulated and the presumed central message extracted. Thus, *Acharnians* is "one of those plays that are particularly well-made, and it advocates peace in every way" (argum. 1 in Ar. Ach.); *Knights* "is composed against Cleon, the Athenian demagogue" (argum. A1 in Ar. Eq.); *Clouds* "is written against Socrates the philosopher, arguing that he intentionally teaches the young people in Athens bad things, because the comedians are in opposition to the philosophers; not, however, as some say, prompted by Archelaus the king of the Macedonians because he thought better of him [Socrates] than of Aristophanes" (argum. A1 in Ar. Nub.); *Wasps* "criticizes the Athenians as fond of lawsuits and encourages the people to be reasonable and abandon them" (argum. II in Ar. Vesp.), and so on. As these illustrations show, the proposed readings tend to assume a straightforward social-corrective and moral function of the plays, often in response to some specified historical situation. The roots of this approach must be sought in Peripatetic scholarship on comedy, and it perfectly matches what Platonius, a perhaps late-antique (?) critic, wrote in his treatise *On the Difference between [Types of] Comedies*, an abbreviated version of which has come down to us among the *Prolegomena de comoedia*, general essays on comedy that were collected by Byzantine scholars and prefaced to a number of Aristophanes manuscripts (cf. Perusino 1989). According to Platonius, in the period of Old Comedy "the poets were free to ridicule generals, judges who passed bad judgment, and some of the citizens who were greedy for money or lived licentious lives" since "we know how naturally opposed ordinary people (*dēmos*) are to the rich, so as to enjoy when they fare badly" (*Proleg. de com.* I.6–11 Koster). This does not exclude that "the Athenians" as a community may on occasion be thought of as being censured too (cf. e.g. sch. Ar. Eq.219a, sch. Ar. Plut. 98, 338), but it leaves little room for additional (e.g. kathartic or ritualistic) dimensions to be made out in the genre.

Conclusion

When we look at the extant remains of ancient scholarship on Aristophanes, there is a constant danger of paying more attention to its shortcomings than to its achievements. It is therefore important to remember how much easier scholarly research has become since antiquity and not to expect from the academic work of our remote predecessors that it complies with our own standards of quality. Moreover, it is precisely these standards that should prevent us from neglecting the scholia and other evidence discussed in this chapter when we ourselves read Aristophanes. First, as already hinted at ("Scope and Themes" Section), by consulting them we quickly realize how dependent our own learning is on the wealth of information that has been assembled in antiquity: to brush the latter aside without further ado would often mean to saw off the branch on which we are sitting. Second, all this material may also serve as a reminder that our own ways of understanding Aristophanes are, in many ways, no less subjective, selective, or biased: perhaps we should even ask ourselves from time to time what an Aristarchus or a Didymus would have thought if they had been able to read a modern monograph on Aristophanes' art. And third, however one-sided we may find the evidence that has come down to us, and however much we may therefore be tempted to contrast it with the sophisticated *literary* response to Aristophanes someone like Lucian manages to create (cf. Rosen 2016), we must also acknowledge that there is enough in it to disprove the notion of Aristophanes having been read throughout antiquity *only* because of the plays' historical or linguistic appeal. That scholars are good at taking the fun out of funny texts is as true today as it was back then, but that is simply the price their students have to pay for being enabled to appreciate to the full what it is that makes those texts worth reading.

GUIDE TO FURTHER READING

The Aristophanic scholia, both old and recent and including the commentaries of Tzetzes as well as the hypotheses, are now accessibly edited in Koster et al. (1960–2007); the first volume of this series contains the *Prolegomena de comoedia*. None of the material assembled there is translated; a translation of many of the scholia on *Frogs* and *Plutus* into French can be found in Chantry (2009), and for all the plays some assistance with understanding the often difficult scholiastic comments is given in the annotated edition of the scholia in the important Ravenna manuscript (R) by Rutherford (1896). The third volume of Rutherford's work (Rutherford 1905) offers a meticulous, if rather dismissive, overview of much of the content of the scholia arranged by ancient instructional categories.

The papyrus evidence is collected in fasc. I.1.4 of *Commentaria et Lexica Graeca in papyris reperta* (*CLGP*), which contains Italian translations (Esposito and Montana 2012; cf. also Trojahn 2002). Montana (2011) surveys the many controversial issues regarding the formation of medieval scholiastic corpora from such ancient annotations and *hypomnēmata*.

For a very readable history of scholarship in antiquity, see still Pfeiffer (1968); but there are now also the detailed and up-to-date chapters by A. Novokhatko (Pre-Hellenistic period), F. Montana (Hellenistic period), S. Matthaios (Roman period), and F. Pontani (Byzantine period) in Montanari (2020). Specifically for

Aristophanes, Dunbar (1995, pp. 31–49) is an ideal starting point, while White (1914, pp. ix–lxxxv) and Boudreaux (1919) remain essential. Dickey (2007) is an incredibly useful bibliographical and practical guide to all kinds of ancient scholarly texts, including sample passages and a pertinent glossary. Though focused on Homer, the discussion by Nünlist (2009) of the literary-critical concepts present in ancient scholia is also important for an exploration of the Aristophanic material.

REFERENCES

Achelis, T.O.H. (1913–1916). De Aristophanis Byzantii argumentis fabularum. *Philologus* 72: 414–441, 518–545; 73: 122–153.
Adler, A. (1928–1938). *Suidae Lexicon* (4 vols.). Leipzig: Teubner.
Adler, A. (1931). Suidas 1. *RE* ser. 2, 4/1, 675–717.
Ascheri, Paola (2009). 'Demetrius [14] Ixion'. *LGGA*. https://doi.org/10.1163/2451-9278_Demetrius_14_Ixion.
Bagordo, A. (1998). *Die antiken Traktate über das Drama. Mit einer Sammlung der Fragmente.* Stuttgart/Leipzig: Teubner.
Benuzzi, F. (2020). Didymus on comedy. In: *Didymus and Graeco-Roman Learning* (= *BICS* 63/2) (ed. T.R.P. Coward and E.E. Prodi), 51–61. London: Institute of Classical Studies.
Benuzzi, F. (2023). *Supplementum Grammaticum Graecum, 8: Didymus Alexandrinus. The Fragments of the Commentaries on Comedy*. Leiden/Boston: Brill.
Berndt, R. (1902). *De Charete Chaeride Alexione grammaticis eorumque reliquiis, i. Charetis Chaeridisque fragmenta, quae supersunt.* Diss. Königsberg.
Blau, A. (1883). *De Aristarchi discipulis*. Diss. Jena.
Boudreaux, P. (1919). *Le Texte d'Aristophane et ses commentateurs*. Paris: de Boccard.
Braswell, B.K. (2013). *Didymos of Alexandria: Commentary on Pindar Edited and Translated with Introduction, Explanatory Notes and a Critical Catalogue of Didymos' Works*. Basel: Schwabe.
Broggiato, M. (2001). *Cratete di Mallo: I frammenti* (ed. with introduction and notes). La Spezia: Agorà.
Chantry, M. (2009). *Scholies anciennes aux* Grenouilles *et au* Ploutos *d'Aristophane* (with introduction, translation, and commentary). Paris: Les Belles Lettres.
Cohn, L. (1894). Ammonios 16. *RE* 1/2, 1865–1866.
Cohn, L. (1895a). Aristarchos 22. *RE* 2/1, 862–873.
Cohn, L. (1895b). Aristophanes 14. *RE* 2/1, 994–1005.
Cohn, L. (1895c). Apollonios 77. *RE* 2/1, 135.
Cohn, L. (1895d). Apollonios 78. *RE* 2/1, 135.
Cohn, L. (1901). Demetrios 101. *RE* 4/2, 2845–2847.
Cohn, L. (1903). Didymos 8. *RE* 5/1, 445–472.
Cohn, L. (1907). Euphronios 7. *RE* 6/1, 1220–1221.
Dickey, E. (2007). *Ancient Greek Scholarship. A Guide to Finding, Reading, and Understanding Scholia, Commentaries, Lexica, and Grammatical Treatises, from Their Beginnings to the Byzantine Period*. Oxford/New York: Oxford University Press.
Dunbar, N. (1995). *Aristophanes: Birds* (ed. with introduction and commentary). Oxford: Clarendon Press.
Düring, I. (1941). *Herodicus the Cratetean: A Study in Anti-Platonic Tradition*. Stockholm: Wahlström & Widstrand.
Esposito, E. and Montana, F. (2012). Aristophanes. In: *Commentaria et Lexica Graeca in papyris reperta (CLGP), pars I: Commentaria et lexica in auctores*, vol 1: Aeschines–Bacchylides, fasc. 4: Aristophanes–Bacchylides, 2nd edn. (ed. G. Bastianini et al.), 3–241. Berlin/Boston: De Gruyter.
Gerhard, O. (1850). *De Aristarcho Aristophanis interprete*. Diss. Bonn.
Geus, K. (2002). *Eratosthenes von Kyrene. Studien zur hellenistischen Kultur- und Wissenschaftsgeschichte*. München: Beck.
Gudeman, A. (1912). Herodikos 1. *RE* 8/1, 973–978.
Gudeman, A. (1919). Kallistratos 38. *RE* 10/2, 1738–1748.
Gudeman, A. (1931). Symmachus 10. *RE* ser. 2, 4/1, 1136–1140.
Halliwell, S. (1991). Comic satire and freedom of speech in Classical Athens. *The Journal of Hellenic Studies* 111: 48–70.
Janko, R. (1984). *Aristotle on Comedy. Towards a Reconstruction of Poetics II*. London: Duckworth.
Kim, L. (2010). The literary heritage as language: Atticism and the second sophistic. In: *A Companion to the Ancient Greek Language* (ed. E.J. Bakker), 468–482. Chichester: Wiley-Blackwell.

Knaack, G. (1907). Eratosthenes 4. *RE* 6/1, 358–388.
Koster, W.J.W. et al. (1960–2007). *Scholia in Aristophanem* (18 vols.). Groningen/Amsterdam: Bouma/Forsten.
Kroll, W. (1922). Krates 16. *RE* 11/2, 1634–1641.
LGGA = Montanari Franco, Montana Fausto, and Pagani Lara (eds.) (2015), *Lexicon of Greek Grammarians of Antiquity*.
Maehler, H. (1994). Die Scholien der Papyri in ihrem Verhältnis zu den Scholiencorpora der Handschriften. In: *La Philologie grecque à l'époque hellénistique et romaine* (ed. F. Montanari), 95–141. Vandoeuvres/Genève: Fondation Hardt.
Matijašić, I. (2014). Timachidas di Rodi. Introduzione, edizione dei frammenti, traduzione e commento. *Annali della Scuola Normale Superiore di Pisa, Classe di Lettere e Filosofia*, ser. 5, 6: 113–185.
Matijašić, I. (2021). *Supplementum Grammaticum Graecum, 4: Timachidas Rhodius*. Leiden/Boston: Brill.
McNamee, K. (1995). Missing links in the development of scholia. *Greek, Roman, and Byzantine Studies* 36: 399–414.
McNamee, K. (1998). Another chapter in the history of scholia. *The Classical Quarterly* 48: 269–288.
Meliadò, C. (2019). Lycophron. *LGGA*. https://doi.org/10.1163/2451-9278_Lycophron.
Millis, B.W. and Olson, S.D. (2012). *Inscriptional Records for the Dramatic Festivals in Athens. IG II² 2318–2325 and Related Texts* (edited with introductions and commentary). Leiden/Boston: Brill.
Montana, F. (1996). *L'Athenaion politeia di Aristotele negli scholia vetera ad Aristofane*. Pisa/Roma: Istituti Editoriali e Poligrafici Internazionali.
Montana, F. (2002). Apollonius [8] Chaeridis filius. *LGGA*. https://doi.org/10.1163/2451-9278_Apollonius_8_Chaeridis_filius.
Montana, F. (2003). Symmachus [1]. *LGGA*. https://doi.org/10.1163/2451-9278_Symmachus_1.
Montana, F. (2006a). Ammonius [2] Alexandrinus. *LGGA*. https://doi.org/10.1163/2451-9278_Ammonius_2_Alexandrinus.
Montana, F. (2006b). Timachidas. *LGGA*. https://doi.org/10.1163/2451-9278_Timachidas.
Montana, F. (2008a). Callistratus. *LGGA*. https://doi.org/10.1163/2451-9278_Callistratus.
Montana, F. (2008b). Il grammatico Callistrato nella *diadoche* alessandrina. *Museum Helveticum* 65: 77–98.
Montana, F. (2011). The making of Greek scholiastic *corpora*. In: *From Scholars to Scholia. Chapters in the History of Ancient Greek Scholarship* (ed. F. Montanari and L. Pagani), 105–161. Berlin/New York: De Gruyter.
Montana, F. (2015). Phainus. *LGGA*. https://doi.org/10.1163/2451-9278_Phainus.
Montana, F. (2020). Hellenistic scholarship. In: *History of Ancient Greek Scholarship. From the Beginnings to the End of the Byzantine Age* (ed. F. Montanari), 132–259. Leiden/Boston: Brill.
Montanari, O. (1970–1972). Note agli *Argumenta metrica* delle commedie di Aristofane. *Museum Criticum* 5–7: 128–145.
Montanari, F. (ed.) (2020). *History of Ancient Greek Scholarship. From the Beginnings to the End of the Byzantine Age*. Leiden/Boston: Brill.
Muzzolon, M.L. (2005). Aristarco negli scolii ad Aristofane. In: *Interpretazioni antiche di Aristofane* (ed. F. Montana), 55–109. Sarzana: Edizioni di Storia e Letteratura.
Nesselrath, H.-G. (1990). *Die attische Mittlere Komödie. Ihre Stellung in der antiken Literaturkritik und Literaturgeschichte*. Berlin/New York: de Gruyter.
Novembri, V. (2020). Euphronius. *LGGA*. https://doi.org/10.1163/2451-9278_Euphronius.
Nünlist, R. (2009). *The Ancient Critic at Work. Terms and Concepts of Literary Criticism in Greek Scholia*. Cambridge: Cambridge University Press.
Nünlist, R. (2015). What does Ὅμηρον ἐξ Ὁμήρου σαφηνίζειν actually mean? *Hermes* 143: 385–403.
Pagani, L. (2007). *Asclepiade di Mirlea: I frammenti degli scritti omerici*. Roma: Edizioni di Storia e Letteratura.
Pagani, L. (2009a). Crates [1]. *LGGA*. https://doi.org/10.1163/2451-9278_Crates_1.
Pagani, L. (2009b). Herodicus Crateteus. *LGGA*. https://doi.org/10.1163/2451-9278_Herodicus_Crateteus.
Pagani, L. (2009c). Asclepiades [2]. *LGGA*. https://doi.org/10.1163/2451-9278_Asclepiades_2.
Pagani, L. (2009d). Asclepiades [3]. *LGGA*. https://doi.org/10.1163/2451-9278_Asclepiades_3.
Pagani, L. (2009e). Asclepiades [5]. *LGGA*. https://doi.org/10.1163/2451-9278_Asclepiades_5.
Pellettieri, A. (2020). Lycophron Chalcidensis. In: *Supplementum Grammaticum Graecum, 3: Glossographi, Lycophron Chalcidensis* (eds. E. Dettori and A. Pellettieri). Leiden/Boston: Brill.
Perusino, F. (1989). *Platonio: La commedia greca*. Urbino: Quattroventi.
Pfeiffer, R. (1968). *History of Classical Scholarship from the Beginnings to the End of the Hellenistic Age*. Oxford: Clarendon Press.

Rabe, H. (1892). Lexicon Messanense de iota ascripto. *Rheinisches Museum für Philologie* 47: 404–413.
Radermacher, L. (1954). *Aristophanes' 'Frösche'. Einleitung, Text und Kommentar*, (2nd edn., ed. W. Kranz). Vienna: Rohrer.
Roemer, A. (1908). Philologie und Afterphilologie im griechischen Altertum. I: Die Parodien und die Lehren der Alexandriner über dieselben; II: Didymus als Erklärer des Aristophanes. *Philologus* 67: 238–278 and 366–410.
Rosen, R. (2016). Lucian's Aristophanes: on understanding Old Comedy in the Roman Imperial period. In: *Athenian Comedy in the Roman Empire* (ed. C.W. Marshall and T. Hawkins), 141–162. London/New York: Bloomsbury Academic.
Rusten, J. (2011). *The Birth of Comedy: Texts, Documents, and Art from Athenian Comic Competitions, 486–280*. Baltimore: Johns Hopkins University Press.
Rutherford, W.G. (1896). *Scholia Aristophanica Being Such Comments Adscript to the Text of Aristophanes as Have Been Preserved in the Codex Ravennas* (2 vols.). London/New York: Macmillan.
Rutherford, W.G. (1905). *A Chapter in the History of Annotation Being Scholia Aristophanica vol. III*. London/New York: Macmillan.
Schauenburg, A. (1881). *De Symmachi in Aristophanis interpretatione subsidiis*. Diss. Halle-Wittenberg.
Schironi, F. (2018). *The Best of the Grammarians: Aristarchus of Samothrace on the Iliad*. Ann Arbor, MI: University of Michigan Press.
Schmidt, R. (1848). Commentatio de Callistrato Aristophaneo. In: *Aristophanis Byzantii grammatici Alexandrini fragmenta* (ed. A. Nauck), 307–338. Halle: Lippert et Schmidt.
Schmidt, M. (1854). *Didymi Chalcenteri grammatici Alexandrini fragmenta quae supersunt omnia*. Leipzig: Teubner.
Schmitz, T. (1997). *Bildung und Macht. Zur sozialen und politischen Funktion der zweiten Sophistik in der griechischen Welt der Kaiserzeit*. Munich: C.H. Beck.
Schneider, O. (1838). *De veterum in Aristophanis scholiorum fontibus*. Stralsund: C. Loeffler.
Schrader, H. (1866). Der Aristarcheer Apollonios. *Jahrbücher für classische Philologie* 12: 227–241.
Slater, W.J. (1986). *Aristophanis Byzantii Fragmenta*. Berlin/New York: de Gruyter.
Sommerstein, A.H. (2001). *The Comedies of Aristophanes, Wealth* (ed. with introduction and commentary), vol. 11. Warminster: Aris and Phillips.
Sommerstein, A.H. (2004). Comedy and the unspeakable. In: *Law, Rhetoric, and Comedy in Classical Athens: Essays in Honour of Douglas M. MacDowell* (ed. D.L. Cairns and R.A. Knox), 205–222. Swansea: Classical Press of Wales.
Sommerstein, A.H. (2010). The history of the text of Aristophanes. In: *Brill's Companion to the Study of Greek Comedy* (ed. G.W. Dobrov), 399–422. Leiden/Boston: Brill.
Staesche, T. (1883). *De Demetrio Ixione*. Diss. Halle-Wittenberg.
Steinhausen, J. (1910). *Kōmōidoumenoi. De grammaticorum veterum studiis ad homines in comoedia Attica irrisos pertinentibus*. Diss. Bonn.
Strecker, K. (1884). *De Lycophrone, Euphronio, Eratosthene comicorum interpretibus*. Diss. Greifswald.
Strout, D. and French, R. (1938). Phaeinos 2. *RE* 19/2, 1505–1506.
Swain, S. (1996). *Hellenism and Empire. Language, Classicism and Power in the Greek World, AD 50–250*. Oxford: Clarendon Press.
Trojahn, S. (2002). *Die auf Papyri erhaltenen Kommentare zur Alten Komödie. Ein Beitrag zur Geschichte der antiken Philologie*. Leipzig: Saur.
Wentzel, G. (1895). Artemidoros 31. *RE* 2/1, 1331–1332.
Wentzel, G. (1896a). Asklepiades 28. *RE* 2/2, 1628–1631.
Wentzel, G. (1896b). Asklepiades 29. *RE* 2/2, 1631.
Wentzel, G. (1896c). Asklepiades 30. *RE* 2/2, 1631.
White, J.W. (1912). *The Verse of Greek Comedy*. London: MacMillan and Co.
White, J.W. (1914). *The Scholia on the Aves of Aristophanes with an Introduction on the Origin, Development, Transmission, and Extant Sources of the Old Greek Commentary on his Comedies*. Boston/London: Ginn.
Willi, A. (2023). Didymus Chalcenterus and Aristophanes' two *Plutus* plays. *The Journal of Hellenic Studies* 143: 167–188.
Wilson, N.G. (1967). A chapter in the history of Scholia. *The Classical Quarterly* 17: 244–256.
Wilson, N.G. (1996). *Scholars of Byzantium*, 2nd edn. London: Duckworth.
Ziegler, K. (1927). Lykophron 8. *RE* 13/2, 2316–2381.
Ziegler, K. (1936). Timachidas. *RE* ser. 2, 6/1, 1052–1060.
Zuntz, G. (1975). *Die Aristophanes-Scholien der Papyri*. Berlin: Seitz.

CHAPTER 24

Aristophanes in Roman Literature

Jennifer L. Ferriss-Hill

Introduction

That Aristophanes and Old Comedy more generally were known to ancient Roman readers in the first and second centuries BCE and CE is not in doubt. The form or forms in which the Greek dramatic genre was known, however, have been the subject of considerable and continued debate. Were plays of Old Comedy ever performed in Rome and, if so, in what periods, and was this done with any regularity? Alternatively, were the plays known only as texts? If texts, were they read in their entireties by educated speakers of Latin, or was the primary or only form in which they were available that of florilegia, collections of pithy or humorous excerpts? Was, in short, the Romans' interaction with Aristophanes of a rather fossilized, limited nature, or could organic and productive literary conversations by means of allusions, borrowings, and reworkings take place? These questions lie at the heart of any assessment of Aristophanes in Roman Literature, even as Roman literature is itself the source for various answers that have been teased out from it. This survey seeks to address the questions posed above and to provide an overview and insight into what Roman writers were doing, or trying to do, from the second century BCE through the second century CE, in Latin prose and verse alike, when they named and looked to Aristophanes and other poets of Old Comedy.

Greek Comedy in Rome

The beginning of Roman literature is traditionally, if artificially, pinpointed as the performance at a festival in 240 BCE of a comedy and a tragedy written by Livius Andronicus.[1] Livius found his models for comedy in New Comedy rather than Old, however, and this preference for Menander, Diphilus, and Philemon over Aristophanes, Eupolis, and Cratinus persisted through the careers of Plautus and Terence. If New Comedy provided the model, the earliest Roman writers may still have found inspiration in Old Comedy, however, and work surely remains to be done on traces of Old Comedy in earlier Latin literature, especially theater. Beta (2014), for example, rightly notes that even if Old Comic plays were not freely translated and adapted for the Roman stage as plays by Menander were, they nevertheless exerted their influence on at least one playwright, Naevius, and likely such influence can be found in other early playwrights as well. While comedy and tragedy, as

---

[1] Conte (1994, pp. 1–42) remains useful on the origins of literature at Rome.

A Companion to Aristophanes, First Edition. Edited by Matthew C. Farmer and Jeremy B. Lefkowitz.
© 2024 John Wiley & Sons, Inc. Published 2024 by John Wiley & Sons, Inc.

well as epic, lyric, iambic, pastoral, and more, would find themselves given Latin form over the next century, the Romans would have to wait until the creation of Roman verse Satire beginning in the late second century BCE for any semblance of Old Comedy rendered Roman.

A more sustained engagement with Aristophanes first comes in the waning decades of the Roman Republic in the works of Cicero who, perhaps to our surprise, possesses not merely what appears to be a fairly extensive knowledge of Old Comic plays but also a particular fondness for Aristophanes. Studying the quotations from Greek and Roman plays in Cicero and the references to playwrights and actors by name in his 1931 study, *Cicero and the Theater*, F. Warren Wright says that "no other Roman Writer has given us such a picture of the theatre" and concludes that the quotations found in Cicero's letters suggest "perhaps mistakenly, considerable familiarity ... with the Greek drama" (79–80). Wright's cautiously offered impression bears up under scrutiny as not mistaken at all. While some of the references in Cicero are incidental, even accidental, others are richer. Alongside comments on a type of anapest termed Aristophanean (*Orat.* 190),[2] two instances in which Cicero quotes part or all of *Wasps* 1431 (*Att.* 5.10.3 in Greek and *Tusc.* 1.41 in Latin), or a request to Atticus to emend the name Eupolis to that of Aristophanes in his copy of *Orator* (*Att.* 12.6.3),[3] for example, are found others in which Aristophanes is used as a yardstick of sorts. Cicero refers to Aristophanes's apparent preference for longer iambic poems by Archilochus as an analog for his own desire for longer letters from Atticus (16.11.2).[4] He describes another letter as "both delightful and serious very much in the Aristophanic way" (*Aristophaneo modo valde mehercule et suavem et gravem, Q Fr.* 3.1.19).[5] At *De Finibus* 5.50, Cicero invokes Aristophanes, alongside Archimedes, Pythagoras, and Plato, among others, as an exemplum of "zeal for learning" (*ardorem studii*), marveling again at the enthusiasm with which he devoted his life to writing (*quo studio Aristophanem putamus aetatem in litteris duxisse*).[6] Similar is *De Oratore* 3.132, where Aristophanes and Callimachus, along with the musicians Damon and Aristoxenus, the mathematicians Euclid and Archimedes, and the physician Hippocrates are invoked to make the point that holistic, humanistic study is preferable to over-specialization and the compartmentalization of disciplines. Beyond such instances, Cicero also gives at least one synopsis of a play no longer extant – *Horae* at *Leg.* 2.37.11 – that is substantial enough to indicate that it was generated from a more-or-less complete text of this play, no longer available to us (though admittedly there may be some uncertainty as to whether Cicero generated this synopsis himself or copied it from another source).

What is evident consistently in Cicero's references is admiration toward Aristophanes,[7] whom he praises as "the wittiest poet of Old Comedy" (*facetissumus poeta veteris comoediae, Leg.* 2.37), and it is hard to envision the degree of admiration expressed without also envisioning a thorough familiarity on Cicero's part with Aristophanes's works. Moreover, Cicero expects the evaluative judgments he expresses to be understandable to his readership; that is, the considerable familiarity and facility with Aristophanes evinced would not have been Cicero's alone. Comparable is the opening of Horace's address to Maecenas in *Epistles* 1.19, which presupposes that the patron knew Cratinus's

---

[2] This meter is discussed in other ancient sources as well, for example, Servius (repeatedly in *De Centum Metris*).

[3] On this passage and Cicero's error and the request to correct it, see Mesturini (1983). On the discussion of humor in *De Oratore* 2, where Cicero contrasts Roman with Greek Comedy, see Graf (1997).

[4] Curiously, in probably the late second century CE, Terentianus Maurus (*De Litt., De Syll., De Metr.* 2243) would also compare Aristophanes favorably with Archilochus, saying that the former's "enormous cleverness sparkles" (*ingens micat sollertia*) and that "often with his multi-form new meters" he rivaled Archilochus (*saepe metris multiformibus novis*). This raises the possibility that a comparison of the two poets was in some way standard, despite their having written in different periods and genres, that is, that this is a fossilized rather than a living or originally generated comparison.

[5] Some editions emend Aristophanes to Aristotle, but the combination of seriousness and playfulness alludes compellingly to the *spoudogeloion* so characteristic of Old Comedy.

[6] As at some other moments, there is room for uncertainty here as to whether Cicero has the Old Comic poet in mind or Aristophanes of Byzantium, the Hellenistic grammarian. In this instance, the company Aristophanes keeps weighs in favor of Cicero having the Old Comic poet in mind.

[7] Cicero's fondness for Aristophanes has been noted also by Cooper (1922, pp. 39, 91–92, 102) and Wright (1931, pp. 81–82).

Pytine, or at the very least its premise, also familiar from fragment 120W of Archilochus, that "no poems can be pleasing nor live long if they are written by water-drinkers" (*nulla placere diu nec vivere carmina possunt/quae scribuntur aquae potoribus*, 2–3). The references to Aristophanes throughout Cicero's works, then, suggest knowledge of Aristophanes as a sort of literary-cultural currency among his correspondents and close intellectual friends (as well as perhaps the posterity whom he also had in mind when he gathered and published his letters). This need not imply one-upmanship or showing off; rather, as Cucchiarelli says of Horace, Cicero likewise seems to have been "working within a well-established cultural practice," whereby Old Comedy and especially the plays of Aristophanes were not only known fairly extensively but were known as texts, and ones "to be appreciated above all for their literariness" (2009, p. 15).

References such as the one in *Epistulae ad Atticum* 12.6.3 or at *Orator* 29, where Cicero paraphrases Aristophanes's description at *Acharnians* 530–531 of Pericles "lightening and thundering and mixing up Greece" (*fulgere tonare permiscere Graeciam*) in a section on rhetorical style, might indicate a familiarity merely with excerpts and one liners (indeed, Quintilian would later refer also to Aristophanes's comparison of Pericles to lightning, *Inst.* 12.10.65). And such allusions that have about them a proverbial flavor might indicate that they were taken from previously compiled collections rather than being selected by Cicero himself from the text of a whole play. The same might be said of the types of fragments preserved in, for example, Pliny the Younger in the first century CE,[8] who once quotes Eupolis describing Pericles's oratorical skill (*Ep.* 1.20), a passage that Sherwin-White (1966, p. 134) notes was "much quoted in antiquity" and that Storey (2003, p. 35) likewise sees as having "become a 'quotation', cited often by the ancients, sometimes with proper attribution, more often not" since these seven lines had "entered the realm of popular knowledge."[9] Aulus Gellius in the second century might be evidence of much the same when he quotes what were evidently well-known passages from *Frogs* describing Aeschylus's style in humorous terms (*NA* 1.15.19, 13.25.7). Other moments, however, in Cicero as well as in other Latin writers, speak to knowledge of entire works of Old Comedy as late as the second century CE. The six-line quotation from *Frogs* in the preface to *Noctes Atticae* (20–21) or the four-line quotation from *Thesmophoriazusae* at *NA* 15.20.7 illustrating hatred of women go on at sufficient length to suggest that Aulus Gellius was copying it from a fuller text than a florilegium. Gellius seems, in fact, to describe himself doing this very thing when he states his intention to "borrow a few anapaests from a chorus of Aristophanes" (*mutuabor ex Aristophanae choro anapaesta pauca*) to introduce his work, or when he has a character who is explaining the term νάνοι, "dwarves," recall, "if my memory does not fail me, this was written in a comedy of Aristophanes, one called *Olcades*" (*si memoria . . . mihi non labat, scriptum hoc est in comoedia Aristophanis, cui nomen est Ὁλκάδες*, *NA* 19.13.3). The four-line quotation from *Thesmophoriazusae*, moreover, is followed by another multi-line quotation from Alexander Aetolus (of whose works only some titles and fragments remain today), suggesting that Gellius had both texts open in front of him and was able to copy from each whatever portions he wished. (Notably, Aulus Gellius seems to share Cicero's admiration for Aristophanes, calling him "that liveliest man" [*ille homo festivissimus*, pr. 20] and "the wittiest poet" [*facetissimus poeta*, 1.15.19]. We may be justified in wondering, however, whether comments such as these are evidence of Gellius's own reading and opinions or whether they are indicative of a certain prestige or caché associated with sharing Cicero's esthetic discernment.) Finally, a range of writers, and well into late antiquity, give the impression that they were working from an array of texts spread out before them when they cite numerous works in support of one point or another: Aristophanes "not in (just) one book" (*non uno libro*) describes old-fashioned musical education

---

[8] This Pliny's uncle, Pliny the Elder, had in turn known Aristophanes's plays well enough to mine them for information on plants, as at *NH* 21.29.3 and 22.80.5; unless, of course, he was already relying on information culled from these sources by a previous writer, though the monumental and originary nature of his *Natural History* perhaps speaks against such a conclusion.

[9] Similar is Alfonsi's (1970) study of the appearance of a proverbial expression in overall sense rather than exact wording from Aristophanes's *Clouds* through Plautus, Cato, and Cicero.

(Quint. *Inst.* 1.10.18); Crates, Chionides, Aristophanes, and Alexis are referenced together for what they say regarding children's obligations to their parents (Vitr. *De arch.* 6.pr.3); and Orpheus, Aristophanes, and Ephorus are noted for the information they give about Achelous (Serv. *In Vergilii Georgicon Libros* 1.8.36). It seems clear enough that while it might well be "very probable that in Hellenistic and Roman times the vast majority of the plays were known even to highly educated readers – to the extent they were known at all – only at second hand through anthologies, commentaries, lexica, specialist essays, and the like" (Olson 2007, p. 32), some Roman readers, among them practicing poets (let us not forget Cicero's *carmina*), had access to and knew well entire plays of Old Comedy into at least the second century CE, and that among these were plays we no longer possess today.

The evidence for Old Comic performances/performances of full Old Comedies in Rome is considerably more limited but no less intriguing. In the course of a discussion of public shows, Suetonius records that Augustus "took great pleasure in old comedy" (*delectabatur etiam comoedia veteri*) and that he even had this put on "often" at games (*saepe eam exhibuit spectaculis publicis, Aug.* 89). Although this passage is the only extant mention in a Roman author of *comoedia vetus* being performed in Greek at Rome,[10] and although such a reading is not widely accepted, it seems at least possible (if far short of certain), given that *vetus/prisca comoedia* consistently has the marked sense of Old Comedy, that Augustus and his contemporaries (among them Horace) could have watched Old Comic plays revived.[11]

An anecdote from Pliny the Younger offers up a different possibility. Noting that he is "one of those who admires the ancients" (*ex iis qui mirer antiquos*), Pliny recalls that he had recently heard a person, Vergilius Romanus, performing a recitation of a play "written on the model of Old Comedy" (*ad exemplar veteris comoediae scriptam*) for "a small audience" (*paucis, Ep.* 6.21.1–2). Here, too, there has been skepticism: Sherwin-White, for example, says that "pure Aristophanic comedy can hardly have been possible, even under Trajan" and suggests that the play Pliny describes was not a genuine Old Comedy but rather a satire of contemporary society. Hunter (2009, p. 97) likewise takes Vergilius's work to be a "satirical" one, although Cucchiarelli (2009–2010, p. 251) says that "it is very difficult to imagine that he attacked the *primores populi*." If satire of prominent contemporary figures seems unthinkable, why could the play not have been a free translation or an adaptation of an Old Comedy, as Cucchiarelli (2009, pp. 1–2) also suggests, or a play set in fifth-century BCE Athens and written in Greek? Whatever the nature of Vergilius's play, which is surely unrecoverable, certain details of Pliny's description point to a deeper knowledge of Old Comedy, on the parts of both Vergilius and himself, than could be gleaned simply from the excerpts preserved in florilegia or in plot synopses. Other details speak strongly in favor of *vetus comoedia* as the marked term for Old Comedy:[12] that Pliny has in mind "ancients" (*antiquos*) and not "talents of our own times" (*temporum nostrorum ingenia*); that Vergilius's imitation was so excellent as to be indistinguishable from an original (*tam bene ut esse quandoque possit exemplar*); that the description of his Old Comic (*vetere comoedia*, 6.21.4) composition comes on the heels of Vergilius's skill in writing in mimiambs and comedies on the models of Menander, Plautus, and Terence (i.e. that *veteris comoediae* is something distinct from the writings of these latter three named authors); and that Vergilius's play was characterized by "vigor" (*vis*), "greatness" (*granditas*), "subtlety" (*subtilitas*), "bitterness"

---

[10] That it was performed in Greek seems reasonable given Suetonius's emphasis at *Aug.* 89 that Augustus was also familiar with Greek poetry (cf. Cucchiarelli 2009, p. 16 n. 29).
[11] Whereas Fraenkel (1957, p. 396 n. 1) says that the term "can only refer to the *fabula palliata*," Cucchiarelli (2001, pp. 53–55, 2009, pp. 15–16, 2009–2010, pp. 247–248) more reasonably says that "Old Comedy" is at least possible. The evidence for performances of other genres of Greek comedy at Rome in this period is not much clearer. Horace is widely assumed to be very familiar with New Comedy, but as Fantham (1984, pp. 303, 309) says, the evidence for Roman audiences ever having seen an entire play of Menander staged in Greek is "uncomfortably vague." See also Yardley (1972). Wiseman (1988, p. 12) argues for satyr plays at Rome, but only of a generically contaminated variety, written by Roman authors such as Sulla (although this would, it seems, suggest extensive knowledge of the original).
[12] So, too, Cucchiarelli (2009, p. 1) who sees any "lexical ambiguity" of the phrase *veteris comoediae* as "resolved by the subsequent description."

(*amaritudo*), "sweetness" (*dulcedo*), and "elegance" (*lepos*) – all standard attributes of Old Comedy,[13] along with "elevating virtues and hunting vices" (*ornavit virtutes, insectatus est vitia*, 6.21.5) through appropriate references to individuals under both their real names and pseudonyms (*fictis nominibus decenter, veris usus est apte*), as Pliny also praises Vergilius for having done.

The argument that Roman readers had access to and in fact read entire plays of Old Comedy does not seem to have been made seriously until the efforts of Ian Storey in 2003 and Andrea Cucchiarelli in his 2001 monograph and his 2009 and 2009–2010 articles. Storey reviews the evidence for knowledge of Eupolis in the opening section, "Who knows Eupolis?" (34–40), of his introductory chapter, "Eupolis in Antiquity." Eupolis, of course, unlike Aristophanes for whom 11 plays are extant, did cease to be known in the form of complete plays at some point, though we have reason to believe that plays of Eupolis, like those of Cratinus, were read in their entirety in Egypt in the third and second centuries BCE.[14] Storey worries that if the *Demoi*, "Eupolis' best-known and most-cited comedy," was known to Roman writers such as Pliny in the form of quotations, however, this "does not augur well for the rest of his plays" and he notes that "by far the majority of the fragments are cited for some technical or scholarly reason" such as "another occurrence of an Aristophanic *kōmōdoumenos*, an unusual word or term, or linguistic usage." Nevertheless, at moments such as Juvenal 2.91–92, Storey sees "a reading knowledge of the plays": Juvenal writes, *talia secreta coluerunt orgia taeda/Cecropiam soliti Baptae lassare Cotyto* ("they performed such rites with a secret torch, the Baptae accustomed to tire out Cecropian Cotyto"), where the "very rare term *Baptae*" repeats the title of a play by Eupolis, and Juvenal goes on to give a more extended description of the likely contents of that play. Storey sees evidence of much the same in Aelius Aristides, writing in Greek during the Second Sophistic, in Galen, and in Lucian. Regarding Eupolis, Storey is willing to conclude that "someone in the third or fourth century AD was copying and presumably reading Eupolis' *Demoi*" but nevertheless believes that it is "much more doubtful" that he was "read at length or for pleasure." Storey is certainly right to distinguish between how different types of readers were reading Eupolis at different times, and looking further back he finds it unlikely that when "Quintilian (10. 1. 65) names the troika of Old Comedians with approving remarks about their 'pure grace of Attic speech'," such a comment would have been the result of "autopsy."

Aristophanes in Roman Literature

I now shift focus from appearances of Aristophanes and Old Comedy in Latin writings in somewhat microscopic fashion, to Aristophanes in Roman *literature*. To the extent that there is sustained and pervasive *literary* engagement with Old Comedy in Roman literature, it is across the genre of Roman verse Satire, whose poets saw the Greek genre as both a source and foil for their own poetry. Originating with Lucilius's 30 books of *saturae* in the late second century BCE (he seems to have lived from perhaps 180 to around 102/1 BCE), the genre went on to be taken up by Horace in his two books of *Sermones*, published probably in 35 and 30 BCE. Persius, living 34–62 CE, would follow with a 6-poem collection prefaced by a short prologue, before the genre culminated with Juvenal, who produced a 16-poem collection, arranged into 5 books, under several emperors in the late first and early second centuries CE. As I have argued elsewhere (2015), Roman Satire may fruitfully be read as Old Comedy reinvented for Rome. Old Comedy's lengthy plays, performed for the public on cyclic, civic occasions, become smaller poems, performed for a select group or read privately by an elite readership on any day of the year. A moral concern of a type almost entirely absent from Old Comedy runs through Roman Satire, and what was outward-looking and revivifying has become introverted and at times markedly sneering and cynical. Nevertheless, the genres find

---

[13] Compare Quintilian's description of Old Comedy at *Inst.* 10.1.65 as "almost alone preserving the authentic grace of Attic speech" (*sinceram illam sermonis Attici gratiam prope sola retinet*), as "exemplary in hunting out vices" (*in insectandis vitiis praecipua*), and as being "lofty and elegant and charming" (*grandis et elegans et venusta*).
[14] *Enciclopedia Oraziana* s.v. *Cratino*.

themselves united in their poet, who is decidedly urban and who purports to be consistently under-appreciated and misunderstood. The type of poetry that these poets produce appears easy to write but is in fact the result of great effort, yet despite this professed abjection, the poet is a figure of strength, and the ways that he is underestimated and maligned are, if paradoxically, a source of this strength.[15] Above all, the poets of Old Comedy and Roman Satire, as personae in their verses, devote a remarkable amount of lines and energy to discussing their own poetic programs and, in particular, to policing its bounds and to teasing out what counts and what does not count as their particular type of poetry. Allied to this, both genres also promote a mythology of transgression, which exists to underscore the potential usefulness of their verses to society: in his quest to remediate misbehavior, the poet of Old Comedy and Roman Satire is in perpetual danger of overstepping the boundary of free speech into criminal speech, that is, slander. Aristophanes (via Dicaeopolis) mentions in *Acharnians* (425 BCE) that the demagogue Cleon had supposedly attempted to bring charges against him for "slandering the city in the presence of strangers" (ξένων παρόντων τὴν πόλιν κακῶς λέγω, 502–503; cf. 377–381) in an earlier play (*Babylonians*, 427 BCE), while Horace worries in the opening of his second book of *Satires* that while some have found his satire too mild, others have found him "too fierce" (*nimis acer*) and as "stretching" his satire "beyond the law" (*ultra/legem tendere opus, Sat.* 2.1.1–4). The later tradition held that a law (of dubious historicity, but conveniently dated to around the shift from Old to Middle Comedy in 404 BCE) was responsible for the demise of the genre of Old Comedy itself. This law banned slander and (therefore) silenced the Old Comic chorus – a narrative perpetuated, among others, by Horace at *Ars Poetica* 281–284, who claims that a parallel law also silenced the Italian Fescennine verse form (*Epist.* 2.1.145–154) associated with satire.

The poets of both genres also present themselves as being in competition with one another and frame their poetry as forged in this crucible – plausible in the case of Old Comedy where the poets actually competed for first prize at the annual dramatic festivals, but striking in the case of Roman Satire where no poet could have met any other, given their non-overlapping life spans. Yet this lack of contemporaneity does not hinder Horace from continually presenting his poetry as existing in relation to that of Lucilius, their genre's "discoverer" (*inventor, Sat.* 1.10.48): where Lucilius was "muddy" (*lutulentus*) and overgrown in his poetic flow, and prolix and careless in his compositional process (*Sat.* 1.4.6–13, 1.10.1, 1.10.50–51, 1.10.64–71), Horace is slender and careful after the model of Callimachus[16] even as he writes "what Lucilius once wrote" (*olim quae scripsit Lucilius, Sat.* 1.4.57). Accordingly, *Satires* 1.9 may be read as the uneasy, anxious dance between a literary successor and his predecessor.[17] Nor does the lack of contemporaneity any less prevent Persius from recalling with admiration how "Lucilius sliced up the city" (*secuit Lucilius urbem*) and how Horace worms his way into people's affections to humorously critique their vices (1.114–118). Nor does it deter Juvenal from framing his poetic program as an explanation of "why he likes to perform maneuvers in this field through which the great scion of Aurunca," that is, Lucilius, "steered his horses" (*cur tamen hoc potius libeat decurrere campo, /per quem magnus equos Auruncae flexit alumnus*, 1.19–20) or from referring to certain material as worthy of Horatian scrutiny (1.51). Thus, in writing *sermo* the Roman Satirists engage in a sustained conversation (*sermo*) with one another, albeit selectively (Juvenal, for example, ignores Persius altogether). The Old Comic theme of competition is simultaneously fronted in other ways throughout Roman Satire, too, as in the head-butting conversations among various imagined speakers or in such agon-like scenes as the famous debate between the Country Mouse and the City Mouse in Horace's *Satires* 2.6, which has strong resonances of the agon between Right Argument and Wrong Argument in Aristophanes's *Clouds*. It is the combination of agon and parabasis, of competition and self-exposition (even around the theme of competition), that marks each of Roman Satire and Old Comedy and binds them to each other.

---

[15] See especially Rosen (2000, p. 35) on this idea.
[16] See especially Thomas (1979, 1983, 1993), Scodel (1987), and Hunter (2006) (whose study goes considerably beyond Horace).
[17] Ferriss-Hill (2011).

In the "swirling mixture of the effluent" (Gowers 1995, p. 32) from the various literary genres and other art forms, high and low, that make up Roman Satire, Old Comedy thus looms among the larger. In *Satires* 2.3.11–12, Horace's interlocutor Damasippus wonders about the books the poet has stuffed into his luggage to take to the country with him, perhaps implying that Horace will not spend much time actually reading during his holiday: "What was the point of cramming in Plato with Menander, Eupolis with Archilochus, and taking away with you such great companions?" (*quorsum pertinuit stipare Platona Menandro?/Eupolin, Archilochum, comites educere tantos?*). The list allows Horace to enumerate Roman Satire's most fertile sources: New/Roman Comedy (Menander), Old Comedy (Eupolis), Iambus (Archilochus), and philosophy and the dialogic form (Plato), with a second allusion to Old Comedy thrown in, too, since the reference to Plato admits of also being construed as a reference to Plato Comicus, and Horace is the type of thinker and poet who would both anticipate such an ambiguity and use it to his own poetic advantage. Horatian satire, according to this recipe, is a stuffed (*stipare*) mixture made up of one measure each of New Comedy and iambus, half a measure of philosophy, and one and a half of Old Comedy – proportions that give prominence to the plays of Cratinus, Eupolis, and Aristophanes in Horace's satirical program. This sense is further amplified by *tantos*, indicating both the literal size of these volumes, presumably entire plays, and their importance to Horace's satire.[18] Above all, Horace conceives of all of these authors as texts to be read, as he does also in *Satires* 1.10.16–19 when he disparages "fancy Hermogenes" and "that ape, clever at nothing but parroting Calvus and Catullus" specifically for never having read the writers of Old Comedy (*illi scripta quibus comoedia prisca viris est/... quos neque pulcher/ Hermogenes umquam legit neque simius iste/nil praeter Calvum et doctus cantare Catullum*).[19]

The prominence accorded implicitly to Old Comedy in *Satires* 2.3 is articulated explicitly in the opening to *Satires* 1.4, one of the two programmatic, framing, anchoring poems of Horace's first book, alongside 1.10:

Eupolis atque Cratinus Aristophanesque poetae
atque alii quorum comoedia prisca virorum est,
si quis erat dignus describi, quod malus ac fur,
quod moechus foret aut sicarius aut alioqui
famosus, multa cum libertate notabant.
hinc omnis pendet Lucilius, hosce secutus
mutatis tantum pedibus numerisque.

(*Sat.* 1.4.1–7)

The poets Eupolis and Cratinus and Aristophanes and the other men to whom Old Comedy belongs, if anyone was worthy of being noted down on the grounds that he was villainous and a thief, an adulterer or a murderer or infamous in some way, they would brand him with great freedom. From here Lucilius hangs entirely, having followed these men with only feet and rhythm altered.

In these words, his first "as a theorist" (Freudenburg 1993, p. 96) and in the manner of an Alexandrian scholar ("un filologo alessandrino," Cucchiarelli 2001, p. 33), Horace claims that Lucilius descends from the by-now-canonical triad of Old Comic poets. The nature of this filiation has been and continues to be discussed extensively. Whereas the prevailing view had been, as Freudenburg (53) summarizes, that "Horace quickly abandons any real pretensions to the role of the Old Comic poet and ... champions Aristotle's theory of the liberal jest against the traditions of Old Comedy and the iambic idea," more recently scholars have started from the premise that Horace ought to be taken seriously: "perché dunque non prendere sul serio Orazio?" (Cucchiarelli 2001, p. 34). What, in short, are the Old Comic poets for Horace and his satirical program?

---

[18] Ruffell (2003) suggests that Horace omits reference to the various Roman models for his satire (Plautus, Terence, Atellan farce, Fescennine verse, and more) out of a desire to elevate satire by associating it only with more reputable Greek genres and "segregating" it especially from popular Latin verse forms.
[19] Cf. Cucchiarelli (2009, p. 14): Horace "advocates actually reading" Old Comic works.

Since the passage is both simple and evocative, absolute and open-ended, scholars have naturally proposed a range of explanations for what Horace had in mind when he confidently waved a hand and proclaimed Lucilian satire as hanging "entirely" (*omnis*) from Old Comedy with "only" (*tantum*) the meter changed.[20] Even as both genres are united by a shared "freedom of speech" (*libertas*), Lucilius was manifestly not a social policeman in the manner that the Old Comic poets could be thought of; yet, they similarly do not fulfill the role that Horace ascribes to them: "how often, an uncooperative reader might ask, does Aristophanes name and/or disgrace murderers in his extant plays? How many adulteries does he expose on stage?" (Freudenburg 2001, p. 18). Perhaps, others have suggested, Horace is nodding to Varro, who may have been the first to posit a connection between Old Comedy and Roman Satire, and while the presence of Varro specifically is debatable (he is often conjured up to explain gappy references), it seems reasonable enough to see Horace both alluding to and parodying scholarly traditions, among them the desire to claim a Greek origin.[21] The elephant in the room, of course, remains Horace's own place in the lineage: it is all well and good for him to say that his predecessor and the founder of the genre of Roman Satire descended wholesale from Old Comedy, but where does that leave Horace himself?

One thing the opening of *Satires* 1.4 does accomplish, as I have argued (2015, pp. 5–7), is to Romanize the trio of Old Comic poets. The motley procession of criminals in lines 3–5 culminates in the verb *notabant*, the technical term for what Roman censors did when they "made a note" of a citizen's crimes. The resulting image is jarringly comic: a toga-clad Eupolis, Cratinus, and Aristophanes hold the highest elected office of the *cursus honorum*, and administer the citizen role and carry out the census from their offices in the Tabularium on Rome's Capitoline Hill.[22] The image also affords Horace himself a place in the tradition: the censors oversaw the public *scribae*, among them the *scriba quaestorius*, an office that Horace had held (*Sat.* 2.6.36), rendering the three Old Comic poets his direct supervisors. Horace thus humorously does to Old Comedy what he boasts elsewhere of doing for two other Greek genres: he was "the first to show Parian iambs to Rome" (*Parios ego primus iambos ostendi Latio, Epist.* 1.19.23–24) and "the first to have brought the Aeolian song," that is, lyric, "to Italian measures" (*princeps Aeolium carmen ad Italos/deduxisse modos, Carm.* 3.30.13–14). The verb *notare* also paternalizes the Old Comic poets in their relation to Horace, since he uses the same verb a little later in *Satires* 1.4 to describe how his own father, a stereotypical stern Terentian parent as Leach (1971) has shown, taught him "how to avoid certain sins by pointing out examples of each" (*ut fugerem exemplis vitiorum quaeque notando*, 106). Finally, the opening of *Satires* 1.4 takes a step toward setting up the artistic dichotomy that Horace insists on between himself and Lucilius, even as his use of the canonical triad elides the fact that these three poets were qualitatively quite distinct from one another. Horace will consistently align Lucilius with the stylistic pole occupied by Cratinus, Aeschylus, and Pindar as verbose, roaring, and insufficiently honed; he himself, on the other hand, aligns with Euripides, Callimachus, and Aristophanes, for whom he can thus claim to be the Latin equivalent.[23]

Horace's implied statement at the opening of the programmatic *Satires* 1.4 that he did for Old Comedy what he would also do for iambic and lyric bears fruit throughout his books and sets a precedent for Persius and Juvenal as well. Wasting no time, Horace offers in *Satires* 1.5 what Cucchiarelli (2001, 2009, 2009–2010) discerned is a reimagining of Aristophanes's *Frogs*.[24] Lucilius's *Iter Siculum* was long held to be the model for *Satires* 1.5, and while it inarguably provides the framework of pit stops at a series of Italian towns, the parallels among the three works may be

---

[20] It might be noted that Lucilius's earlier books of satires (26–29) are indeed written in the senarius and septenarius, the Latin counterparts to the Old Comic iambic trimeter and trochaic tetrameter.
[21] See Freudenburg (2013) on Roman theorizing about satire's origins, and Hose (2013) for the argument that Horace, not Varro, invented this Old Comic Lucilius.
[22] Brill's Neue Pauly *s.v. censores* and *scriba*.
[23] On the dominant stylistic dichotomy of the *genus grande* (grand form) and *genus tenue* (slender form) from the Greek Classical period through the Hellenistic and into the Latin Augustan poets, O'Sullivan (1992) remains foundational. On Aristophanes as successor to Cratinus and Horace as successor to Lucilius, see Müller (1992).
[24] Horace also reworks *Frogs* 1030–1036 at *Ars Poetica* 391–407, likewise indicating extensive familiarity with the whole play.

more abiding than has been generally recognized if Sommerstein (2011) is correct that Lucilius's poem itself also drew on *Frogs*.²⁵ Sommerstein (2011, pp. 30–34), summarizing Cucchiarelli and adding his own observations, outlines the following as essential points of contact among Aristophanes's *Frogs*, Lucilius's *Iter Siculum*, and Horace, *Satires* 1.5: "mud and heavy roads" (*Ran.* 145, 273; Lucil. fr. 109M; Hor. *Sat.* 1.5.94–97); "upset digestion" (*Ran.* 237–238, 308, 479–490; Lucil. fr. 136; Hor. *Sat.* 1.5.7–8); "a boat trip" (*Ran.* 180–270; Lucil. fr. 125–127; Hor. *Sat.* 1.5.11–24); "plebeian transport animals" (*Ran.* 21–32; Lucil. fr. 1207; Hor. *Sat.* 1.5.13, 18, 22, 47); "contests or conflicts with a strong verbal element" (*Ran.* 209–268, 605–673, 830–1478; Lucil. fr. 117–122; Hor. *Sat.* 1.5.11–13, 14–17, 51–70); "an inn with simple food" (*Ran.* 549–578; Lucil. fr. 128, 132–135; Hor. *Sat.* 1.5.71–72); "an engagement with tragedy" (*Ran. passim*; Hor. *Sat.* 1.5.63–64); and "solitary orgasm, induced, or spontaneous" (*Ran.* 542–545, 752–753; Lucil. fr. 1248; Hor. *Sat.* 1.5.82–85). The correspondences are striking in both quantity and quality, but one in particular goes to the heart of Old Comedy and Roman Satire: the theme of competition.

At *Frogs* 180–270, incompetently and with much complaining, Dionysus helps to row Charon's boat across to the Underworld. He does so to the accompaniment of and in competition with a chorus of frog swans (βάτραχοι κύκνοι): the frog swans provide Dionysus with a beat to assist with his rowing tempo, yet as the chorus sings the praises of Dionysus, whom they worship, they end up in a shouting match, each insisting that they will beat the other. Next, Dionysus and his slave, Xanthias, engage in a contest in which Aeacus, the judge of the Underworld, attempts to discern which of them is the god and which is the mortal (605–673). Finally, the culminating contest of the play and its formal *agon* is of course that between Aeschylus and Euripides, as they compete for the title of best tragic poet (830–1478). In *Satires* 1.5, sailors and slaves shout at one another (11–13) and a drunken sailor sings "in competition" (*certatim*) with a traveler about his girlfriend while "awful gnats and marsh frogs" (*mali culices ranaeque palustres*) prevent everyone from sleeping (*avertunt somnos*, 14–17). These singing contests prefigure the central one between Sarmentus and Cicirrus, which seems to have an analog in Lucilius (fr. 117–122) and also to draw on the Italian dramatic genre of Atellan farce. If *Satires* 1.4 gave us an Old Comic parabasis in Latin in its opening lines, right on its heels *Satires* 1.5 gives us an agon, and a threefold one on the model of *Frogs* at that, and Cucchiarelli (2009, p. 7) is certain that "the poem's first readers ... must have been able to hear in the lines of *Sat.* 1, 5 the ancient echo of Aristophanes' *Frogs*." Looking beyond these correspondences, we would do well to ask what the point of them is, and Sommerstein is convincing when he connects the "political aim" of *Frogs* (namely, "nothing less than to save Athens from the threat of destruction") with the political "failure" of *Satires* 1.5: Horace is famously silent on the "important business" of "reconciling friends who have fallen out" that is supposedly the purpose of this journey to Brundisium (*missi magnis de rebus uterque/legati, aversos soliti conponere amicos*, 1.5.28–29). The poem winks at the treaties of 40, 38, and 37 BCE but its details do not quite fit any of these and as Gowers (1993a, p. 49) has seen, "the poem seems designed to annoy us" by hinting that it will offer a glimpse into an important historical moment and then focusing instead on "the discomforts of traveling, the little picaresque adventures" (Sommerstein 2011, p. 30). In this, too, however, Horace is Aristophanic: both genres are a mixture of the high and the low, the serious and the trivial, "saying both many amusing things and many earnest ones" (καὶ πολλὰ μὲν γέλοιά μ' εἰ-/πεῖν, πολλὰ δὲ σπουδαῖα, *Ran.* 389–390) and allowing that "the laughing man can speak the truth" (*ridentem dicere verum*, Hor. *Sat.* 1.10.24).

At the close of his first, and also programmatic, hexameter poem, Persius invites a very specific reader to his satire:

> audaci quicumque adflate Cratino
> iratum Eupolidem praegrandi cum sene palles,
> aspice et haec, si forte aliquid decoctius audis.
> inde vaporata lector mihi ferveat aure.
>
> (1.123–126)

---

²⁵ Zimmermann (2001) also looks for Old Comic references in the fragments of Lucilius more generally.

Whoever you are, you who, inspired by bold Cratinus, grow pale at angry Eupolis along with the great old man, look also to these writings, to see if you perhaps hear something even more boiled down. Let my reader, with his ear steamed clean from there, be on the boil for me.

Although the words have been read as evidence that by Persius's time, "the relation of Latin satire to Old Comedy" had become "purely traditional and theoretical" (Van Rooy 1965, pp. 149–150), and as late as 2009 Cucchiarelli was able to say that "the fact that Persius refers to the poets of Old Comedy as relevant to his satiric project has, until recently, been treated as a matter of no particular significance" since he was "seen as indulging in a tired literary-critical convention that had already been authorised by Horace" (10), it seems clear that Persius should be doing much more at this key juncture than merely regurgitating a Horatian trope. Relihan (1989, p. 155) suggests that Persius's request for a *reader* of Aristophanes is "a call for an antiquary and a pedant, for only these read Old Comedy at this time" and, amusingly enough, if we think of *Satires* 1.10.16–19 and 2.3.11–12, Horace would have been just such a pedant. The passage affirms, however, that for both satirists, Old Comedy had a textual existence. For Persius, the affinity is not a matter of the poet's own generic descent (*hinc omnis pendet*) but rather of his *reader's* qualifications: this reader should come to Persius's verses fresh from his Cratinus, Eupolis, and "great old man" Aristophanes and with his "ear steamed clean" by these Old Comic poets. *Decoctius* unambiguously describes something that is more concentrated, but scholars have wondered how, exactly, Old Comedy undergoes densification in Persius's hands, becoming a "concentrated essence" of itself. The various explanations ventured can coexist productively: Persius's six satires are Horace's two books compressed into one-third of the length (Gowers 1993b, pp. 140, 180), the genre becoming reduced even as it is supposed to be stuffed (*satura*; Gowers 1994, pp. 131, 133); *decoctius* is Persius's allusion "explicitly to the value of brevity" of a Horatian, Callimachean sort (Cucchiarelli 2012, p. 177); and, since "to decoct was ... a well-known procedure for transforming the alimentary into the medicinal," Persius's satire is presented as "Lucretius' wormwood without the honeyed cup" and, as such, anti-Horatian (Bartsch 2015, p. 72).

What does Persius go on to do with Old Comedy and with Aristophanes after this provocative opening? Where Horace had followed his parabatic *Satires* 1.4 with the agonistic 1.5, Cucchiarelli (2009, pp. 11–12) sees Persius's words instead recasting earlier portions of his first satire in Aristophanic terms. The recitation scene that is Persius's scathing commentary on the state of literature and literary criticism at Rome, which Freudenburg (2001, pp. 151–172) has aptly dubbed "Faking it in Nero's Orgasmatron," compellingly renders into Latin satire *Thesmophoriazusae* 130–133. In place of Aristophanes's poet Agatho who, dressed in women's garb, causes his listener, Mnesilochus, to experience "a tickling in his very backside" (ὑπὸ τὴν ἕδραν αὐτὴν ὑπῆλθε γάργαλος) with his "effeminate and wantonly-kissed and shocking" song (καὶ θηλυδριῶδες καὶ κατεγλωττισμένον/καὶ μανδαλωτόν), in Persius a bejeweled reciter makes his audience of "burly Tituses tremble in a manner not morally upright and moan with possessed voice, when the poems enter their loins and the itch in their most intimate of places is scratched" (*tunc neque more probo videas nec voce serena/ingentis trepidare Titos, cum carmina lumbum/intrant et tremulo scalpuntur ubi intima versu*, 19–21). Beyond continuing Horace's (and probably Lucilius's) Old Comic poetics of self-reflection and competition, Persius's words at 1.123–126 also encourage us to read other, non-programmatic poems in Old Comic terms as well. As I have suggested (2015, pp. 246–249), Persius's generally overlooked fourth satire, a dialog between Socrates and Alcibiades, evokes Aristophanes's *Clouds* and also his *Thesmophoriazusae* and *Frogs*, as well as Old Comedy more generally via Horace. Much like Horace, then, Persius has rendered Old Comedy Roman and, more specifically, Neronian. In place of kindly, Socratic irony and the festal license of the comic festivals[26] is found a harsher, less redemptive humor as Persius experiments

---

[26] On this idea, which originates in Mikhail Bakhtin's *Rabelais and His World*, in Roman Satire see especially Miller (1998, 2012), D'Alessandro Behr (2009), and Sharland (2010).

with Platonic dialogue to produce a typically compressed, crammed poem full of familiar yet dislocated language and motifs.

Juvenal's dramatic allegiances lie not with comedy but rather tragedy, as he declares at the close of his sixth poem his intention to "take up the high boot of tragedy" (*altum satura sumente coturnum*, 6.634–637) and to "go out beyond the boundary and law of our predecessors" (*finem egressi legemque priorum*) and "rage some great song with a Sophoclean gaping mouth, one unknown to the Rutulian mountains and the Latin sky" (*grande Sophocleo carmen bacchamur hiatu, /montibus ignotum Rutulis caeloque Latino?*). Although this "tragic" satirist never mentions *vetus/prisca comoedia* or any of its poets by name, Juvenal, too, seems to have read entire plays of Old Comedy, and Freudenburg (2013, p. 306) goes so far as to say that "Juvenal seems to have modeled much of his second satire ... on the *Baptae* of Eupolis," the play that Storey (2003) also discerned echoes of in the poem. Braund (2005, p. 390) has said that "to view satire as a kind of drama is perhaps the most illuminating approach available" and this certainly goes some way toward explaining the pervasive references to comedy, Old and New, Greek and Roman, throughout Roman Satire. Juvenal can be seen as having "expand[ed] satire's theatrical identity" (Keane 2006, pp. 13–41), but even within this he, too, makes Old Comic references to "black frogs in the Stygian whirlpool" (*Stygio ranas in gurgite nigras*, 2.150). It could also be said that as "conversation," *sermo*, the other of the two genre terms for satire alongside *satura*, Roman Satire is predisposed to be dialogic in the manner of drama. Within the dialogic form, moreover, there is considerable room for a wide range of agonistic, competitive, back-and-forth activities.

Conclusion

In addition to the authors and works surveyed here, I suspect that much can still be done on Aristophanes in Roman literature, not least through more fully explicating already-noticed correspondences. Mallan (2016) argues that Aristophanes, *Plutus* 292–295 helps to make sense of a joke about Tiberius purportedly licking genitals in goat-like fashion, and this observation could be further contextualized within what Suetonius's knowledge of Old Comedy may have been. More extensive is the study by Chiarini (2019) of how the Latin phrase *nihil dicere*, found exclusively in Plautus, Terence, and Cicero, may go back to Aristophanes; again, however, this raises the question of how else Plautus and Terence might have made use of Aristophanic phrases and of Old Comic motifs and themes more generally. In broad strokes, however, and beyond the circuitous ways in which certain phrases trickled down from Old Comedy into Latin texts, the presence of Old Comedy in Roman literature may be characterized in the following twofold way. On the one hand, Old Comedy is present because the stylistic dichotomy that happens to be codified in Aristophanes's *Frogs* persisted as the dominant stylistic dichotomy through the Hellenistic and into the Augustan period of artistic output.[27] *Frogs* was, and remains, inescapable as the earliest place in which the notion of the *genus grande* versus the *genus tenue* was articulated explicitly – a self-consciousness permitted within the confines of Old Comedy – and even without an author having *Frogs* in mind, their style can be understood in the terms outlined there. On the other hand, Old Comedy erupts into Roman literature at various points – Lucilius, Cicero, Horace, Persius, Pliny, Juvenal, and Aulus Gellius – because Latin writers found that it allowed them to participate in a shared vernacular with contemporaries or predecessors or to say something particular, even about the role of comedy (and satire) in society.

---

[27] O'Sullivan (1992) is clear that Aristophanes was not himself responsible for inventing the stylistic dichotomy or its associated terminology; rather, he was recording (and parodying) something in the contemporary cultural consciousness. Porter (2006) writes about *Frogs* as classicizing: the presentation of both Aeschylus and Euripides in the agon scene is not merely "retrospective, tinged with nostalgia, venerating, canonizing, and so on," but also "goes beyond a musealizing admiration" to involve "a sense of vividness and presence in the face of what is definitively past."

GUIDE TO FURTHER READING

Ralph Rosen's *Old Comedy and the Iambographic Tradition* (Scholars Press, 1988) and *Making Mockery: The Poetics of Ancient Satire* (Oxford University Press, 2007) are foundational on the ancient tradition of poetry that critiques and ridicules, from ancient iambic through Old Comedy to Roman Satire. Following him, Freudenburg (1993, 2001, *Satires of Rome: Threatening Poses from Lucilius to Juvenal*, Cambridge: Cambridge University Press) and Ferriss-Hill (2015) have continued the study into the affinities between Old Comedy and Roman Satire, specifically, while scholars such as Sommerstein (2011) and Cucchiarelli (as above; see also his 2006 article, "La commedia greca antica a Roma," *Atene e Roma: rassegna trimestrale dell'Associazione Italiana di Cultura classica* 51.4 [2006, pp. 157–177]) have focused their investigations on individual poems. In the work of Kenneth Reckford, *Aristophanes' Old-and-New Comedy, Volume 1: Six Essays in Perspective* (Chapel Hill: The University of North Carolina Press, 1987) and *Recognizing Persius* (Princeton: Princeton University Press, 2009), the topic of Aristophanes in Roman literature is also addressed.

REFERENCES

Alfonsi, L. (1970). Il proverbio di Aristoph. Nub. 1417 e la sua diffusione nel mondo latino. *Dioniso: Rivista Trimestrale di Studi sul Teatro Antico* 44: 7–9.

Bartsch, S. (2015). *Persius: A Study in Food, Philosophy, and the Figural*. Chicago, IL: The University of Chicago Press.

Beta, S. (2014). *Libera lingua loquemur ludis Liberalibus*: Gnaeus Naevius as a Latin Aristophanes? In: *Ancient Comedy and Reception: Essays in Honor of Jeffrey Henderson* (ed. S.D. Olson), 203–222. Berlin; Boston: De Gruyter.

Braund, S.M. (2005). The masks of satire. In: *Latin Verse Satire: An Anthology and Reader* (ed. P.A. Miller), 390–397. London: Bristol Classical Press.

Chiarini, S. (2019). Οὐδὲν λέγειν/*nihil dicere*: a lexical and semantic survey. *Mnemosyne* 72: 114–149.

Conte, G.B. Trans. Joseph B. Solodow (1994). *Latin Literature: A History*. Baltimore, MD: The Johns Hopkins University Press.

Cooper, L. (1922). *An Aristotelian Theory of Comedy*. New York: Harcourt, Brace and Company.

Cucchiarelli, A. (2001). *La satira e il poeta: Orazio tra Epodi e Sermones*. Pisa: Giardini.

Cucchiarelli, A. (2009). Old frog songs: four points on the Roman Aristophanes. *mediAzioni* 6: 1–22.

Cucchiarelli, A. (2009–2010). Frogs songs: literary reception of old Greek comedy in Rome. *Ordia Prima* 8–9: 235–255.

Cucchiarelli, A. (2012). *Venusina lucerna*: Horace, Callimachus, and imperial satire. In: *A Companion to Persius and Juvenal* (ed. S. Braund and J. Osgood), 165–189. Hoboken, NJ: Wiley-Blackwell.

D'Alessandro Behr, F. (2009). Open bodies and closed minds? Persius' *Saturae* in the light of Bakhtin and Voloshinov. In: *Persius and Juvenal* (ed. M. Plaza), 222–254. Oxford; New York: Oxford University Press.

Fantham, E. (1984). Roman experience of Menander in the late republic and early empire. *Transactions of the American Philological Association* 114: 299–309.

Ferriss-Hill, J.L. (2011). A stroll with Lucilius: Horace, Satires 1.9 reconsidered. *American Journal of Philology* 132 (3): 429–455.

Ferriss-Hill, J. (2015). *Roman Satire and the Old Comic Tradition*. Cambridge: Cambridge University Press.

Fraenkel, E. (1957). *Horace*. Oxford: The Clarendon Press.

Freudenburg, K. (1993). *The Walking Muse: Horace on the Theory of Satire*. Princeton, NJ: Princeton University Press.

Freudenburg, K. (2001). *Satires of Rome: Threatening Poses from Lucilius to Juvenal*. Cambridge: Cambridge University Press.

Freudenburg, K. (2013). The afterlife of Varro in Horace's *Sermones*: generic issues in Roman satire. In: *Generic Interfaces in Latin Literature: Encounters, Interactions, and Transformations* (ed. T.D. Papanghelis, S.J. Harrison, and S. Frangoulidis), 297–336. Berlin: De Gruyter.

Gowers, E. (1993a). Horace, Satires 1.5: an inconsequential journey. *Proceedings of the Cambridge Philological Society* 39: 48–66.

Gowers, E. (1993b). *The Loaded Table: Representations of Food in Roman Literature*. Oxford: The Clarendon Press.

Gowers, E. (1994). Persius and the decoction of Nero. In: *Reflections of Nero: Culture, History, and Representation* (ed. J. Elsner and J. Masters), 131–150. Chapel Hill, NC: University of North Carolina Press.

Gowers, E. (1995). The anatomy of Rome from capitol to cloaca. *The Journal of Roman Studies* 85: 23–32.

Graf, F. (1997). Cicero, Plautus and Roman laughter. In: *A Cultural History of Humour: From Antiquity to the Present Day* (ed. J.N. Bremmer), 29–39. Cambridge: Polity Press.

Hose, M. (2013). Wie Horaz und ein Philologe die Satire erfanden. In: *Epos, Lyrik, Drama. Genese und Ausformung von literarischen Gattungen. Festschrift für E.-R. Schwinge zum 75. Geburtstag* (ed. B. Dunsch, A. Schmitt, and Th. A. Schmitz), 301–314. Heidelberg: Winter.

Hunter, R. (2006). *The Shadow of Callimachus: Studies in the Reception of Hellenistic Poetry at Rome (Roman Literature and Its Contexts)*. Cambridge: Cambridge University Press.

Hunter, R. (2009). *Critical Moments in Classical Literature: Studies in the Ancient View of Literature and Its Uses*. Cambridge: Cambridge University Press.

Keane, C. (2006). *Figuring Genre in Roman Satire*. New York: Oxford University Press.

Leach, E.W. (1971). Horace's *Pater Optimus* and Terence's Demea: autobiographical fiction and comedy in *Sermo* 1.4. *American Journal of Philology* 92 (4): 616–632.

Mallan, C. (2016). Tiberius the goat: an addition to Champlin's Mallonia. *Histos* 10: 15–16.

Mesturini, A.M. (1983). Aristofane-Eupoli e Diodoro. A proposito di una citazione ciceroniana. *Maia: Rivista di Letterature Classiche* 35: 195–204.

Miller, P.A. (1998). The bodily grotesque in Roman satire: images of sterility. In: *Vile Bodies: Roman Satire and Corporeal Discourse (Arethusa 31.3)* (ed. S.M. Braund and B.K. Gold), 257–283. Baltimore, MD: The Johns Hopkins University Press.

Miller, P.A. (2012). Imperial satire as saturnalia. In: *A Companion to Persius and Juvenal* (ed. S. Braund and J. Osgood), 312–333. Hoboken, NJ: Wiley-Blackwell.

Müller, C.W. (1992). Aristophanes und Horaz: Zu einem Verlaufsschema von Selbstbehauptung und Selbstgewißheit zweier Klassiker. *Hermes* 120 (2): 129–141.

Olson, S.D. (ed.) (2007). *Broken laughter: select fragments of Greek comedy*. Oxford, New York: Oxford University Press.

O'Sullivan, N. (1992). *Alcidamas, Aristophanes and the Beginnings of Stylistic Theory*. Stuttgart: Franz Steiner Verlag.

Porter, J.I. (2006). Feeling classical: classicism and ancient literary criticism. In: *Classical Pasts: The Classical Traditions of Greece and Rome* (ed. J.I. Porter), 301–352. Princeton, NJ: Princeton University Press.

Relihan, J.C. (1989). The confessions of Persius. *Illinois Classical Studies* 14: 145–167.

Rosen, R. (2000). Cratinus' *Pytine* and the construction of the comic self. In: *The Rivals of Aristophanes: Studies in Athenian Old Comedy* (ed. D. Harvey and J. Wilkins), 23–39. London: Duckworth and the Classical Press of Wales.

Ruffell, I.A. (2003). Beyond satire: Horace, popular invective and the segregation of literature. *The Journal of Roman Studies* 93: 35–65.

Scodel, R. (1987). Horace, Lucilius, and Callimachean polemic. *Harvard Studies in Classical Philology* 91: 199–215.

Sharland, S. (2010). *Horace in Dialogue: Bakhtinian Readings in the Satires*. Oxford: Peter Lang.

Sherwin-White, A.N. (1966). *The Letters of Pliny: A Historical and Social Commentary*. Oxford: The Clarendon Press.

Sommerstein, A.H. (2011). *Hinc omnis pendet?*: old comedy and Roman satire. *Classical World* 105 (1): 25–38.

Storey, I. (2003). *Eupolis: Poet of Old Comedy*. Oxford: Oxford University Press.

Thomas, R.F. (1979). New comedy, Callimachus, and Roman poetry. *Harvard Studies in Classical Philology* 83: 179–206.

Thomas, R.F. (1983). Callimachus, the Victoria Berenices, and Roman poetry. *The Classical Quarterly* 33 (1): 92–113.

Thomas, R.F. (1993). Callimachus back in Rome. In: *Callimachus* (ed. M.A. Harder, R.F. Regtuit, and G.C. Wakker), 197–215. Groningen: Forsten.

Van Rooy, C.A. (1965). *Studies in Classical Satire and Related Literary Theory*. Leiden: Brill.

Wiseman, T.P. (1988). Satyrs in Rome? The background to Horace's Ars Poetica. *The Journal of Roman Studies* 78: 1–13.

Wright, F.W. (1931). *Cicero and the Theater*. Menasha, WI: The Collegiate Press.

Yardley, J.C. (1972). Comic influences in Propertius. *Phoenix* 26 (2): 134–139.

Zimmermann, B. (2001). Lucilius und Aristophanes. In: *Der Satiriker Lucilius und seine Zeit* (ed. G. Manuwald), 188–195. Munich: Beck.

CHAPTER 25

Aristophanes and the Second Sophistic

Inger N.I. Kuin

Introduction

A man travels to the heavens, using an eagle's right wing and a vulture's left wing to get there, with the purpose of learning the truth about the gods and the universe. He tried studying with the philosophers first but found them to be vain and quarrelsome idle talkers. On the way up, he observes the laughable depravity of humans. Once in heaven he meets with the gods and finds them weak, indecisive, and nervous, but they have him delivered back to earth unscathed.

This, in a nutshell, is the plot of Lucian's comic dialogue *Icaromenippus*, written sometime in the second century CE. The piece is a mishmash of Aristophanic motifs and ideas: the protagonist's stint with the philosophers reminds us of the Thinkery in *Clouds*, his creative mode of ascent alludes to *Peace* and *Birds*, while the comic portrayal of the gods bears traces of those two plays, and of *Wealth* and *Frogs*. The bird's eye view of human shortcomings sounds a lot like the revelation in *Clouds* – among other Aristophanic moments – that the entire audience consists of tainted, disgusting individuals, even if in Lucian the details of the accusation are less crass.

In the Greek-speaking Roman East of the early imperial period Aristophanes continued to be read widely. Authors from this period show in their own works that they had direct access to complete texts of Aristophanes's plays, and papyrological and (in one instance) even epigraphic evidence supports this (Matijašić 2017); in late antiquity, there is a slight increase in the number of Aristophanic papyri, suggesting that his plays became more popular during the heyday of the Second Sophistic movement (Wilson 2014).

We have no certainty as to whether or not Lucian and his contemporaries would still have been able to see Aristophanes's plays performed in the theater. Two Greek inscriptions from the imperial period attest to performances of "old comedy" specifically, pointing either to revivals of works by Aristophanes and his peers or to new compositions mimicking their style, and there is plentiful epigraphic evidence for performances of comedy as such (Jones 1993, 43–48; Graf 2016; Slater 2016, 20; Peterson 2019, 73–75). Additionally, one of the orations of Aelius Aristides (see Section "Critics: Plutarch & Aristides") corroborates the ongoing presence of Old Comedy in one form or another on the theatrical stage.

The label "Second Sophistic" is here used to denote the literary production in Greek of the first and second centuries CE. Others have used it in a narrower sense to refer only to the traveling rhetorical performers and teachers of Philostratus's *Lives of the Sophists* but also in a broader sense to include the third and fourth centuries CE or to incorporate Latin authors like Aulus Gellius and Apuleius (Whitmarsh 2005, 4–10; Johnson and Richter 2017a, 3–6). When it comes to Aristophanes, his presence is felt most strongly in the Greek literature of the early imperial period. Authors used

---

A Companion to Aristophanes, First Edition. Edited by Matthew C. Farmer and Jeremy B. Lefkowitz.
© 2024 John Wiley & Sons, Inc. Published 2024 by John Wiley & Sons, Inc.

him to define what it meant to write "good" Greek, a highly contentious issue at the time (Section "The Atticists' Aristophanes"). He also stood at the center of a collective investigation into the ethical implications of comic mockery: Plutarch and Aelius Aristides both formulate a moral critique of Old Comedy through Aristophanes (Section "Critics: Plutarch & Aristides"), while Dio Chrysostom performs an intricate dance with the playwright, alternating between rejection and appropriation (Section "Dio Chrysostom"). Lucian, in turn, took great interest in both of these debates and successfully inserted Aristophanes's imaginative, utopian spirit into his own comic performances (Section "Lucian of Samosata").

The Atticists' Aristophanes

With his vulgarities, virtuosic neologisms, and tongue-twisting nonsense words (see Chapter 5), Aristophanes seems an unlikely model for traditionalist linguistic purism. And yet, this is exactly what he became for Second Sophistic authors. By the imperial period, "Atticizing" means reproducing the orthography, morphology, vocabulary, and syntax of the Attic dialect spoken in the fifth century BCE, which differed significantly from the *koine* Greek used in the Roman East at the time. This linguistic Atticism developed out of the earlier stylistic Atticism, which had focused on emulating classical, not just Attic authors, and continued to hold sway as well (Kim 2017, 41–53). Relying on the work of Hellenistic scholars (see Chapter 24), Atticizing lexicographers crowned Aristophanes a source of correct Attic usage and vocabulary. What this meant was that you could point to a precedent in Aristophanes in order to rebuff someone questioning your *bona fides* as an Atticist.

Julius Pollux assembled an Attic vocabulary containing hundreds of references to Aristophanes in the second century CE. Around the same time, Phrynichus wrote his *Selection of Attic Verbs and Nouns*, which has been transmitted only in a fragmentary state. But Photius, patriarch of Constantinople in the Byzantine period, writes that Phrynichus counted Aristophanes among "the best standards, norms, and models of undiluted and pure Attic speech" (*Library* 158). The so-called Anti-Atticist, an anonymous author also from the second century CE, argued by means of his own lexicon that many words rejected by contemporary Atticists in fact had been used by Attic writers from the classical period. In this work, Aristophanes looms large as well, which shows that linguistic Atticism was far from an exact science, and Aristophanes a major pawn in these language wars (Willi 2010, 473–477; Peterson 2019, 7–9).

Along with the anonymous Anti-Atticist, some well-known authors also pushed back against the combativeness of their Atticizing contemporaries. Lucian plays a complicated role in this regard. His prose generally adheres to the standards of Atticism, but he will deviate from them to avoid obscurity, occasionally adopting *koine* syntax and vocabulary, and non-Attic morphology instead (Bompaire 1994, 65–70). In his works, Lucian engages with Atticism directly, frequently ridiculing its proponents but sometimes also those who fail to live up to its requirements (Swain 1996, 298–329; 2007, 18–23).

In Lucian's *Lexiphanes*, a hyper-Atticizing character by that name recites his own *Symposium*, which is presented as an attempt to emulate Plato, another approved model for Atticizers. Immediately, however, we enter the world of comedy: Lexiphanes's *Symposium* contains an excruciatingly long list of foodstuffs, described in ornate and outlandish language. Lexiphanes's antagonist Lycinus anticipated this by saying the reading would be "a feast." The piece culminates in Lexiphanes vomiting up, with Lycinus's help, his Atticisms – like noxious bile.

Talk of food evokes comedy as such, but *Lexiphanes* also gestures at Aristophanes specifically. Just as Lycinus does for the new *Symposium*, Dionysus in *Frogs* compares tragic poetry to soup to help Heracles understand his longing for Aeschylus and succeeds. The Attic-word-purging scene has been compared to *Acharnians*, where Cleon is instead made to vomit up coins (Sidwell 2000, 138; Storey 2016, 175–176; Martin 2018, 512). In satirizing the Atticist movement, Lucian purposely makes fun of their reliance on the vocabulary of Old Comedy: Lexiphanes has gorged himself on Aristophanic language to sound sophisticated but is instead forced to spit it out again, like the butt of a joke from Aristophanes's real work.

Galen, Lucian's contemporary and a medical writer, was an even more outspoken critic of Atticism. In his own works, he generally, though not entirely, avoids Atticizing archaism. In *The Order of My Own Books*, he writes that Attic vocabulary "is not in itself worth fussing about" and mocks those who "use words badly" and "establish new meanings for Greek words" (5.6), presumably the kind of Atticizing sophists of whom Lucian's character Lexiphanes is a caricature. At the same time, Galen took a keen interest both in Attic vocabulary and in Old Comedy. He wrote a work titled *On False Attic Usage*, a large Attic dictionary, and a treatise on the vocabulary of Aristophanes, none of which survive. In *On Medical Names*, which has been transmitted only in Arabic, he argues that doctors should follow Aristophanes's usage of words because the language of the comic theater is intelligible to the general population (Coker 2019).

Galen is having his cake and eating it too. He distances himself from fussy Atticizers: unlike their vain pursuits, his study of language is for the sake of clarity of expression alone. Yet, in doing so, he takes every opportunity to show his mastery of Aristophanes's Attic vocabulary, the Atticists' own mascot. If he had known, Aristophanes, the man who composed a choral ode out of croaking frogs repeating "*brekkekex koax koax*," would likely have been rather surprised to be called on as an ally in a debate over language purism, more than five-hundred years after his death.

Critics: Plutarch and Aristides

When it comes to content instead of language, New Comedy (Menander in particular) rivaled and perhaps surpassed Aristophanes in popularity in the Second Sophistic. There are some obvious reasons why this might have been so: New Comedy was much less embedded in Athenian society and culture than Old Comedy, and with its focus on family life it was more readily transferable to later settings, as the indebtedness of Plautus and Terence to Greek New Comedy for their plots amply shows. But the fifth-century Athenian-ness of Aristophanes would also have appealed to Second Sophistic authors, who looked backward to the culture and history of classical Athens broadly (Bowie 1970; Whitmarsh 2001, 41–89).

Plutarch's first-century CE work *The Comparison of Aristophanes and Menander* is a key text for assessing Second Sophistic attitudes to Aristophanes as a comic author, but unfortunately it has been transmitted only in summary form. In what remains, Plutarch compares the two authors in terms of what moral value audiences might derive from them, and his approach is somewhat circular: educated, good people enjoy good, wholesome comedy, and vice versa. Menander comes out on top: "Coarseness in words, aggression, and vulgarity are present in Aristophanes, but not at all in Menander. This is to be expected, since the uneducated, ordinary person is captivated by what that man Aristophanes says, but the educated man will loathe it" (*Moralia* 853B). Conversely, for the educated man, Menander "is a rest from their concentrated and intense studies, receiving the mind like a flowery, shady meadow full of breezes" (*Moralia* 854C).

Plutarch disapproves of Aristophanes's verbal humor: too much and too blunt. He praises Menander's realistic characterization through language, while in Aristophanes you can never tell who is speaking. Old woman or hero, god or country bumpkin, they all sound the same. While Menander's wit is "like the salt of the sea from which Aphrodite was born," Aristophanic humor is "bitter and harsh, containing a wounding, biting fierceness" (*Moralia* 854C). Finally, Aristophanes renders worse whatever he takes from real life for the stage: "roguishness is not urbane but malicious, anything rustic is silly rather than innocent, anything funny is ridiculous instead of playful, and love not joyous but licentious" (*Moralia* 854D). Plutarch's piece betrays the influence of Plato and Aristotle throughout (on their views on Aristophanes, see Chapter 23), but in particular the last comment recalls Aristotle's often cited claim from *Poetics*, that comedy shows people worse than they are, while tragedy makes them look better (1448a).

Plutarch equivocates on the appeal of Aristophanic comedy in his *Comparison*. He started out saying that "common" people like it, but later on he says that they find it too haughty and that the only reason to go to the theater is to see Menander's plays performed. Taken together with Menander's greater prevalence in the papyri from the period, this seems to bolster his edging out

Aristophanes in popularity. But just because Plutarch thinks nobody ought to like Aristophanes does not make it so: the fierceness of his attack rather suggests that his contemporaries needed to be dissuaded from enjoying Aristophanes's plays (Peterson 2019, 28, 38).

What remains of the *Comparison* largely aligns with what Plutarch says about Aristophanes in his other essays: it is too dangerous, too free, and too obscene (Bréchet 2005, 13–18; Hunter 2009, 78–89). The frankness of, in particular, the *parabasis* risks offending fellow citizens and might destabilize the community, and the obscenities are inappropriate for an educated audience. As moral education Aristophanes is useless because there are no realistic characters (protreptic or apotreptic) whose behavior the audience might learn from. Finally, Old Comedy has become so obscure, that if one were to read it at a party, teachers would have to stand by to explain the details and references (*Moralia* 711F–712A).

Given Plutarch's dislike of Aristophanes, it is remarkable that he still refers to him around sixty times. (He mentions Menander only slightly more often.) Plutarch features all of Aristophanes's comedies except for *Women at the Thesmophoria* and quotes from most of the plays as well (Bréchet 2005, 12–13). Ironically, Plutarch sometimes uses details from Aristophanes's plays for his biographies of the leading men of classical Athens in his *Parallel Lives* – those obscure references are suddenly helpful source material (Peterson 2019, 40–50)! Just as Galen could not afford to be ignorant of Atticism and the vocabulary of Old Comedy, Plutarch, both as literary critic and as biographer, had no choice but to engage with Aristophanes.

Aelius Aristides lived and worked roughly a century after Plutarch. He was from Mysia in Asia Minor and is best known for his extensive and sophisticated account of his experiences at the sanctuary of Asclepius in Pergamon, *Sacred Tales*. Aristides also wrote speeches and encomia on various topics and numerous prose hymns for individual gods. Like his contemporaries, Aristides knew Aristophanes well, and quotes or alludes to him on occasion (Bowie 2007, 34, 44–49). But like his predecessor Plutarch, he too had strong misgivings about Old Comedy as a suitable genre for entertainment.

Aristides's oration *Concerning the Prohibition of Comedy (Oration* 29*)* is addressed to the inhabitants of Smyrna. He argues that they should no longer include performances of Old Comedy in their celebration of the Dionysia. The speech corroborates the presence of new compositions in the style of Old Comedy on the imperial stage: he criticizes them for the slanderous humor characteristic of Old Comedy and complains that unlike fifth-century Old Comedy they do not include a *parabasis* offering "warnings and education" (*Oration* 29.28; Peterson 2019, 72–73). In his condemnation of new Old Comedy, Aristides presents two arguments: slanderous, obscene jokes are unsuitable to the context of a religious festival, and the alleged utility of such jokes for moral education is a fiction.

Aristides's assumption that scurrility is at odds with worshipping the gods because it would be hateful to them stems from his fundamentally Platonic understanding of the divine as purely good. But laughter and obscenity had a long, ongoing legacy within Greek and Roman religious life (Halliwell 2008, 160–191). With his wholesale rejection of ridicule from the religious sphere, Aristides goes further than Plato, Aristotle, or Dio Chrysostom (see Section "Dio Chrysostom"), who all accepted mockery as a viable component of divine worship (Kuin 2023, 70–74).

The failure of Old Comedy as moral corrective has some practical reasons. Only the innocent will get slandered because unlike the guilty they will not pay bribes to prevent it, and, says Aristides, the masses are unfit to learn anyway. Yet, Aristides already on principle views humor as an inappropriate vehicle for education: being exposed to shameful language does audiences more harm than good, no matter what the context or purpose is.

Aristides does not mention Aristophanes, or any of the canonized writers of Old Comedy by name in his speech. But for fellow connoisseurs of classical literature, the comments on new Old Comedy lacking a *parabasis* would strongly evoke the *parabasis* from Aristophanes's *Frogs*. Aristides calls the new plays "counterfeit" and adds that while it would be all right to "suffer from a worthy piece of wood" – meaning, presumably, being reproached by a good, old-fashioned *parabasis* – the new plays contain only wickedness. Both of these phrases are taken from Aristophanes (*Frogs* 721, 736).

Aristides chose to take these phrases specifically from the *parabasis* of *Frogs*, which stands out in Aristophanes's corpus for referring in detail to contemporary political events. Hellenistic scholars believed that the Athenians were so grateful for it that they crowned Aristophanes with an olive branch and arranged for the play to be re-performed (Halliwell 2015, 153–154, 168–170). By inserting phrases from the *parabasis* of *Frogs* into his discussion of the lack of a *parabasis* in new Old Comedy, Aristides signals his knowledge of Aristophanes and the scholarly traditions about him. Taking into account the religious motivation of Aristides's rejection of Old Comedy as a genre, *Frogs* is also a remarkable choice: it contains the most shameful depiction of a god in Aristophanes, Dionysus himself no less.

Aristides has built up an intricate argument a fortiori against the Old Comedy style plays of his contemporaries: even Aristophanes's most "useful" play from a civic point of view is still inappropriate, the new plays which all lack a *parabasis* are that much worse. In the course of doing so, he flaunts his knowledge of Aristophanes, but only those who are as well educated as he is will notice. This is for the best since Old Comedy is far too dangerous for everyone else.

Plutarch and Aristides were both anxious about Aristophanes's comedy, and did not think that it deserved to be read or re-performed. The intensity of their pleas supports the ongoing popularity of Aristophanes's plays among their contemporaries, as does their eagerness to show themselves well-versed in his plays even as they discredit them. At the core of the critique was a rejection of Old Comedy's use of obscenity and of (personal) invective. The remainder of this chapter will be concerned with authors defending and adopting the Aristophanic "spirit," who, in spite of their much more positive attitude toward Old Comedy, also generally shy away from its explicit obscenities and aggressive name-calling. What caused this reluctance? Was the "ethos" of the Second Sophistic morally more conservative, and was there less freedom for comedy because of political and legal restrictions?

Such questions about the Second Sophistic's rejection of key ingredients of Old Comedy can and were asked about earlier periods as well. Ancient scholars of Greek comedy sought to explain the disappearance of harsh, personal invective from the stage after Aristophanes's lifetime. A popular hypothesis, often taken over by modern scholars, was that toward the end of the classical period legal restrictions were placed on the use of defamatory speech in comedy, and that this is why Middle and New Comedy differ from Old Comedy in this regard. The evidence for such restrictions, however, is weak, and the fact that the decrease in the use of personal invective was "a gradual change in style and tone, not a sudden and enforced exclusion" argues against this hypothesis; rather, comedy's freedom and its styles of humor arose out of "the inventiveness of playwrights and the changing taste of mass audiences" (Halliwell 1991, 64, 70).

In the imperial period, the juxtaposition of fifth-century BCE Athens as a haven of comic freedom with the restrictive environment of one's own time was a popular framework (Fields 2020, 13). With respect to legal restrictions on speech in drama and other literature, there is no evidence of systematic censorship or libel laws in Rome (Fantham 1977; Howley 2017). Nonetheless, there were "conventions . . . that made poets largely avoid direct criticism of contemporary public individuals and of concrete political actions" on the stage (Manuwald 2015, 108).

From the Principate onward, incidental punitive repercussions for criticism inside or outside literature fostered a sufficiently threatening atmosphere such that authors negotiated, sometimes openly, what they should and should not say, with some emperors giving more license than others (Free 2015, 179–254; Strunk 2017, 133–166). Even if in legal terms the difference between what Aristophanes or, for instance, Aristides could say was less stark than we might expect, it clearly matters a great deal that authors of the Second Sophistic felt that they lived under tighter restrictions.

The issue of obscenity in part falls under the same rubric as criticism and invective: authors would have self-censored themselves if they felt they were at risk of getting into trouble by using certain vocabulary. At the same time, just as with the transition from Old to Middle and New Comedy in Greece, taste will have been an important factor. Critics like Plutarch and Aristides represent and reinforce the view that "bad" language is inappropriate for self-respecting readers and listeners. Other authors like Dio and Lucian are still prepared and even eager to describe sex acts or unseemly bodily affects in the service of invective or other contexts, but they – often coyly and self-consciously – use modest language to do so, for fear of alienating their audience otherwise.

Dio Chrysostom

Dio Chrysostom's *First Tarsian* (*Oration* 33) is devoted entirely to condemning a certain type of inappropriate bodily activity, but at no point does the speaker disclose what the activity is exactly. Dio says that he cannot describe the Tarsians' behavior clearly, because decent language falls short (33.32–33). Several solutions to this puzzle have been suggested, from snorting to nasal singing, speaking in an undesirable accent, and even farting. But Dio's elusiveness most likely was intentional: "the indefinition itself engendered suspicions of something much more scandalous, more repulsive, more depraved" (Kim 2013, 49). The speech is, in a way, a perfect illustration of Dio's attempts to adopt the harsh, abusive voice of Old Comedy without taking on the stain of improper language, and it shows that such attempts can be rather effective.

In *First Tarsian*, Dio himself offers a brief history of Old Comedy. The Athenians on the advice of the god Dionysus went "to the theater in order to be abused" and watched insulting plays by Aristophanes, Cratinus, and Plato (the playwright) without punishing them, while they were unable to endure Socrates's unadorned criticism; over time, Old Comedy degenerated, and the playwrights started to flatter the people, "biting softly and with a laugh . . . filling the city with arrogance, rude jokes, and buffoonery" (33.9–10). For this reason, Dio brings in the iambic poet Archilochus as the true model for rebuking citizens and launches into his lengthy attack on the Tarsians' morals (33.11–18) – a ploy which in itself may derive from a lost play by Cratinus, called *Archilochoi* (Hawkins 2014, 203–205).

It is uncertain whether or not Dio actually delivered this speech to the Tarsians, but if he did it would have been a bold, body-focused, and rather Aristophanic attack on the audience in front of him. Toward the end of the speech Dio appears to acknowledge a return to the model of Old Comedy. He says that not even Archilochus would be able to address such depravity as the Tarsians have fallen victim to (33.61), and in his closing remarks he connects the mysterious behavior to men's shaving more and more of their bodies, for which "the comic poet" said they should be burned "upon a heap of sixteen fig-wood phalluses." This is an otherwise unknown fragment, but it is likely Aristophanic (Di Florio 2001, 69). The very last word of the speech, addressed to the audience, is "androgynes," clearly intended as an insult.

Dio builds up a speaking persona to distance himself from Old Comedy: by refusing to name the behavior, he is more innocent, yet by avoiding flattery he is more stern. By the end of the work, though, this posturing has evaporated. The audience has been given its fair share of buffoonery, some of it lifted directly from Aristophanes and Cratinus. Dio held out the promise of a prim diatribe, but instead – probably to the relief of the audience – delivered something much more colorful. This dynamic in itself is reminiscent of the opening exchange in *Frogs*, where through *praeteritio* and meta-jokes Aristophanes exploits the same comic register that Dionysus purports to reject.

In sharp contrast to Aristides, in *First Tarsian* Dio sanctions the comic as divine: Dionysus instituted the performance of Old Comedy at his festival, while Apollo sanctioned Archilochus's blame poetry (33.12). In the *Alexandrian Oration* (*Oration* 32), which critiques the people of that city for their vulgar tastes in entertainment, Dio again uses the Athenians of Aristophanes's day as a positive example, because they allowed themselves to be slandered at the religious festival (Hunter 2014, 384–386). His own mockery, too, is salutary, and Dio takes up his role as critic driven, just like Plato's Socrates, by the gods: "I feel that I have chosen this not of my own volition but by the will of some deity" (32.12).

Within his *Alexandrian*, Dio cites Aristophanes's *Knights*, and an unknown Eupolis fragment (32.6). Toward the end, he includes an insult that strongly alludes to the giant beetle's diet of dung cakes in Aristophanes's *Peace*: "though you have often listened to so-and-so and can well recall his jokes, and also the songs of what's-his-name, I am not sure that you have ever heard Theophilus; just as someone has said of the beetles in Attica, that, though Attica has the purest honey, the beetles never taste of it, not even if it is poured out for them, but only of the other food" (32.98). With the help of Aristophanes, Dio says that the Alexandrians, as they ignore wise men and consume bad art instead, behave like dung-eating beetles (Jazdzewska 2015, 259).

In the *Alexandrian* and *First Tarsian*, Dio specifically engages with Old Comedy as a model for humorous rebuke that he, as an orator, can adopt or (pretend to) reject. By itself this approach appears to offer only a limited view of Aristophanic comedy, reducing it to a vehicle for criticizing the citizens as a group or individually. But Dio does not only talk about Old Comedy he also does Old Comedy, when he borrows vivid imagery and comic techniques from Aristophanes. His *On Aeschylus, Sophocles, and Euripides on the Bow of Philoctetes* (*Oration* 52) is in its entirety a witty reworking of Aristophanes's *Frogs*, even if it contains little obscenity or mockery (Hunter 2009, 39–48).

Dio compares the Big Three of tragedy by putting their *Philoctetes* plays side by side. In his introduction, he remarks how lucky he is to be able to have them compete with each other: the Athenians might have been able to see Aeschylus and Sophocles at the same festival and also Sophocles and Euripides, but never all three because of chronological constraints (52.3). In *Frogs*, Aristophanes has Aeschylus and Euripides compete, but he can only do so by setting their *agon* in the underworld. Dio one-ups Aristophanes by adding Sophocles as well, who is notoriously absent in *Frogs*. That ultimately Sophocles is handed the palm in the speech as the perfect mean between Euripides and Aeschylus, puts further emphasis on Dio's "emendation" of Aristophanes. And, in case any audience member still failed to notice, he closes the speech quoting Aristophanes (from an unknown play), to say that Euripides enriched his plays by "licking the honey-covered lips of Sophocles" (52.17).

One final technique that Dio borrows from Aristophanes is that of comic dialogue. Several of Dio's epideictic speeches take the form of dialogues, either narrated or mimetic, but they are modeled primarily on Plato's dialogues (Trapp 2000, 230) and are not very humorous. An important exception to this is the *Achilles* (*Oration* 58). It is a narrated dialogue between a young Achilles and Cheiron. The boy petulantly complains about Cheiron's archery and riding lessons, on the grounds that such skills are for cowards, while he wants to learn hand-to-hand combat. Achilles makes fun of Cheiron for being a centaur and for fleeing from danger rather than standing his ground (58.4). Cheiron, exasperated, calls Achilles the "bad, arrogant spawn of a briny mother" and says he will never be a brave warrior (58.5). This is the end of the piece; Achilles is denied a comeback. Homer's *Iliad*, of course, is the main intertext of this short work in terms of contents, but the prickly repartee between the two heroic characters is closely related to Aristophanic dialogue. As such it points ahead to the works of the self-appointed inventor of comic dialogues for epideictic performance: Lucian of Samosata.

Lucian of Samosata

Lucian's piece *Icaromenippus*, as discussed in the Section "Introduction," contains many Aristophanic elements. It is a mimetic dialogue, in which the protagonist Menippus tells the story of his ascent to the heavens to an anonymous friend. The character Menippus is an allusion to the third-century BCE Cynic philosopher Menippus of Gadara. He is featured in several of Lucian's pieces, but as a character he is not stable. As he does with most of his recurring characters, Lucian adapts Menippus to the context of each individual piece. In *Icaromenippus*, Menippus fulfills the role of the Aristophanic hero: he has a radical, bold vision, and obtains his goal against all odds. Menippus wants to see for himself what the gods are like. His plan for doing so seems patently absurd – fly up on stolen bird wings and just knock on heaven's door – and yet, just like Trygaeus in *Peace* and Pisthetaerus in *Birds*, he succeeds.

Among Second Sophistic writers, Lucian is by far the most indebted to Aristophanes of the authors whose works are extant. Conversely, if one takes a *longue durée* view of literature, Lucian is the most important torchbearer of Aristophanic comedy after Aristophanes. The presence of Aristophanes and, more broadly, Old Comedy as a genre in Lucian's works has many different layers, ranging from simple direct quotation to complex and allusive debates over the function, status, and remit of Lucian's performed comic dialogue (an invention claimed by the author in *Double Indictment* and *You are a Prometheus with words*) through the prism of Old Comedy. Lucian's refashioning of the Aristophanic comic hero and his liberal borrowing of plot motifs in *Icaromenippus* exist in between these two poles: nowhere in that dialogue is Aristophanes named or cited directly, but Lucian's reliance on Aristophanic comedy in the piece is obvious nonetheless.

Generations of scholars have by now cataloged and studied Lucian's quotations from Aristophanes and the narrative motifs he has borrowed (Kock 1888; Ledergerber 1905; Householder 1941, 4–5; Bompaire 1958, 627–642; Bowie 2007, 44–49; Storey 2016; Anderson 2019, 149–159). His programmatic engagement with Old Comedy and with Aristophanes in particular is most prominent in the pieces *Double Accusation* and *Fisherman* (Sidwell 2014; Rosen 2016). In her monograph *Laughter on the Fringes: The Reception of Old Comedy in the Imperial Greek World*, Anna Peterson has shown how in these works and in his introductory pieces (*prolaliae*) Lucian uses Aristophanes to craft his own comic persona and to define and defend his literary project, either adopting a parabatic voice or staging satiric personae in plots borrowed from Old Comedy (Peterson 2019, 82–142).

In what follows one particular play, Aristophanes's *Birds* (see Chapter 12) will serve as a framework for illustrating the relation of Lucian's works to Aristophanic comedy. Not because it is the most prominent Aristophanes play in Lucian's corpus – that prize goes to *Clouds* – but rather because it offers an especially rich picture of the different ways in which Lucian harkens back to his comic predecessor.

Lucian's *True Histories* famously starts out announcing that the reader will be deceived from beginning to end: the narrator says that the work will contain nothing but lies, other than this prefatory admission, that is (*VH* 1.4). While this passage strongly evokes the (already well-known) Cretan liar paradox, the fantastical narrative of the work itself leaves no doubt that it is indeed fantasy. Toward the end of the first book, after visits to the moon, the morning star, and a town inhabited by lamps, the narrator and his companions catch sight of the city Cloudcuckootown. They admire it, but cannot visit because of unfavorable wind. The narrator adds: "It made me think of Aristophanes the poet, a wise and truthful man whose writings are disbelieved without reason" (*VH* 1.29).

The sighting of Cloudcuckootown is an explicit reference to the name that Pisthetaerus decides to give to his new bird *polis* in the sky in *Birds* (819), and Lucian's narrator immediately follows this up with a mention of Aristophanes himself. *Birds* is arguably Aristophanes's most fantastic writing, so it is highly ironic for the narrator to praise him for his truthfulness at precisely this moment (Ní Mheallaigh 2010, 88). The narrator is here pointing back to his opening discussion of truth and lies, but there is also an echo of the first parabasis of *Birds* and its claims of truth for a theogony in which birds came into being before the gods (685–736).

Throughout his works, Lucian appropriates the (attempted) anonymity of Aristophanes's parabatic voice through personae and masks like the Syrian and Parrhesiades. In *True Histories*, he takes this game to its extreme: the narrator withholds his name for most of the work only to reveal toward the end that it is actually "Lucian" (*VH* 2.29)! By pretending that the narrator's experiences equal the author's in a context where this is obviously impossible, Lucian pokes fun at the elusive parabatic voices in his own works and in Aristophanes.

The delayed disclosure of the narrator's name once again points back to the opening of *True Histories*. There the narrator says that by lying he will follow "not uncomically" in the footsteps of poets, historians, and philosophers of old whom he will not mention "by name," though he immediately proceeds to call out Ctesias and Homer (*VH* 1.2–3). The pretend reluctance to name names alludes to the speculation, mentioned in the Section "Critics: Plutarch & Aristides," by ancient readers about the legality of personal invective in Old Comedy (Sidwell 2000, 139–140), while Aristophanes's name – just like the narrator's – is pointedly withheld. At the same time, such implicit gesturing at the dangers of mocking individuals openly is a trope of satirical literature which goes back to Aristophanes himself, most notably his so-called feud with Cleon (Rosen 2014).

When Aristophanes's name finally is mentioned, the narrator also purports to name the ruler of Cloudcuckootown, but instead of Pisthetaerus, he calls him Crow the Son of Blackbird (*VH* 2.29), two species that both feature in *Birds* repeatedly. The narrator continues Aristophanes's game of naming and not naming, hiding, and revealing. *Birds'* Pisthetaerus, seemingly an amalgam of any number of quarrelsome and opportunistic Athenians, has no known real-life referent, but the play is still bursting with names, both of birds and contemporary politicians (e.g., 1280–1308). The narrator of *True Histories* mocks by name the many heroes of Greek *paideia* in the underworld narrative of the second book, even as he so coyly continues to hide his own identity.

In *Birds*, Pisthetaerus joins the birds to build a new society and a new city, because he wants to escape the stress of Athens. Cloudcuckootown is planned out as a paradise of abundance and freedom for the birds and their hybrid leader. In *True Histories*, Lucian uses an account of life on the Island of the Blessed likewise as a canvas for sketching a utopian society of unlimited resources and pleasure. But the utopian scenarios of both authors quickly turn sour. Cloudcuckootown dissolves into painfully familiar strife, bureaucracy, and oppression – as it turns out, much of what Pisthetaerus wanted to escape is actually contained within himself. On the Island of the Blessed the shades fight wars, and quarrel with each other over status and women: even under the most blessed of circumstances humans manage to be profoundly unhappy (Kuin 2021, 261–268).

In *True Histories*, but also in the impossible egalitarian utopia of *Dialogues of the Dead*, Lucian takes up the imaginative utopianism of (inter alia) Aristophanes's *Birds*. Yet in doing so, Lucian simultaneously shows himself attuned to the pessimism that is baked into Aristophanes's fantasy. Even during the span of the performance, the utopia of *Birds* is shown to be an *ou-topia* ("no place") rather than an *eu-topia* ("good place"). Dreaming of a better, different world is fun and perhaps even wholesome, but the dreams can never come true. The fact that in *True Histories* the narrator and his friends are unable to actually go to Cloudcuckootown gestures at the impossibility of its existence. Furthermore, in his own utopian fantasies, Lucian, just like Aristophanes, emphasizes the fundamental inescapability of our human flaws.

In *Birds*, Aristophanes depicts the gods both as sexual predators (556–560) and as gluttons desperate for food (1230–1233, 1575–1692). The latter is caused by the wall that the birds have built at Pisthetaerus's insistence: sacrifices can no longer get through from earth to the gods in heaven. Lucian appropriates the motif of a sacrificial strike in two of his pieces. Both in *Icaromenippus* and in *Tragic Zeus* the gods contemplate what would happen if humans stopped sacrificing to them under the influence of philosophical critiques of divine providence. This scenario fills them with great dread, as they anticipate exactly the situation that Aristophanes depicts in *Birds* (and in *Wealth* as well): they would be miserably famished.

A sacrificial strike, actual or anticipated, reduces the supposedly powerful gods to weakness and want through humorously exaggerated anthropomorphism. At the same time, this narrative motif functions as a comic exploration of the meaning of alimentary sacrifice to the gods – why feed them unless you expect them to go hungry without? (Kuin 2023, 88–114). Similarly, showing the gods susceptible to erotic desire is both a natural component of the gods' anthropomorphism and a reflection of the threat of sexual violence perpetrated by (primarily) male gods against (primarily) female human victims in myth. In *Birds*, preventing the male gods from going down to earth to rape women is presented as a secondary motivation for building the wall. In Lucian's *Dialogues of the Gods*, the many shades of sexual desire among the gods, ranging from sweet and seductive to terrifying predation, is a dominant theme.

For Lucian, the humorous representation of the gods is more important as a tool than it is for Aristophanes, the gods feature as comic characters in the majority of his works, and there are important differences between the two authors in how they use this tool. As is to be expected, the jokes about the lust of Zeus and Dionysus in Aristophanes are more explicit than Lucian's handling of this theme. Furthermore, Lucian's depiction of the gods is informed by the history of thought and religion that happened in between: his Zeus is afraid of Epicureans and fails hard at Stoicism in pieces like *Tragic Zeus*, and his comic arsenal also includes jokes about Mithras and imperial cult. Nonetheless, it is hard to imagine Lucian having as much riotous fun with the gods as he does without the example of Aristophanes's cowardly yet lascivious Dionysus in *Frogs* or his desperate Poseidon and Heracles from *Birds*.

GUIDE TO FURTHER READING

Peterson's 2019 monograph (discussed in the Section "Lucian of Samosata") *Laughter on the Fringes* is an outstanding overview of the engagement with Old Comedy as a genre by Greek imperial authors, including chapters on Plutarch, Aristides, Lucian, and Libanius in which Aristophanes looms large. The volume *Athenian Comedy in the Roman Empire* (Marshall and Hawkins 2016) covers Aristophanic reception in these same authors and has excellent treatments of Dio Chrysostom and Aelian as well. *Ancient Comedy and Reception* (Olson 2014) also offers several chapters on Second Sophistic authors; of special note is the discussion of Old Comedy in the ancient novel (Smith 2014) and a chapter on Old Comedy in Latin rhetoric and satire (Ruffell 2014). Two chapter-length introductions to the topic of Aristophanes in the Second Sophistic are Bowie (2007, which includes a helpful chart of citations) and Hunter (2014). For Aristophanes in Athenaeus, see Sidwell (2000), for Apuleius see May (2009, 198–201). In the imperial period, much Cynic literature (Oenomaus of Gadara, the pseudo-epigraphic *Cynic Letters* and Diogenes Laërtius's *Life of Diogenes of Sinope*) was written in Greek; for Aristophanes and Old Comedy in the Cynic tradition, see Bosman (2006).

REFERENCES

Anderson, G. (2019). *Fantasy in Greek and Roman Literature*. London: Routledge.

Bompaire, J. (1958). *Lucien écrivain: Imitation et Création*. Paris: Belles Lettres.

Bompaire, J. (1994). L'atticisme de Lucien. In: *Lucien de Samosate. Actes du colloque international de Lyon organisé au Centre d'études romaines et gallo-romaines, les 30 septembre-1er octobre 1993* (ed. A. Billault), 65–75. Lyon: De Boccard.

Bosman, P. (2006). Selling Cynicism: the pragmatics of Diogenes' Cynic performances. *CQ* 56 (1): 93–104.

Bowie, E. (1970). Greeks and their past in the Second Sophistic. *P&P* 46: 3–41.

Bowie, E. (2007). The ups and downs of Aristophanic travel. In: *Aristophanes in Performance, 421 BC-AD 2007: Peace, Birds and Frogs* (ed. E. Hall and A. Wrigley), 32–51. London: Legenda.

Bréchet, C. (2005). Aristophane chez Plutarque. *Pallas* 67: 11–23.

Coker, A. (2019). Galen and the language of old comedy: glimpses of a lost treatise at *Ind.* 23b-28. In: *Galen's Treatise Περὶ Ἀλυπίας (De Indolentia) in Context* (ed. C. Petit), 63–90. Leiden: Brill.

Di Florio, M. (2001). Tra Aristofane e Menandro: per un'estetica del comico in Dione di Prusa. In: *Ricerche su Dione di Prusa* (ed. P. Volpe and F. Ferrari), 65–84. Napels: Luciano.

Fantham, E. (1977). Censorship, Roman style. *EMC* 21: 41–53.

Fields, D. (2020). *Frankness, Greek Culture, and the Roman Empire*. London: Routledge.

Free, A. (2015). *Geschichtsschreibung als Paideia: Lukians Schrift 'Wie man Geschichte schreiben soll'*. Munich: Beck.

Graf, F. (2016). Comedies and comic actors in the Greek East: an epigraphical perspective (ed. Marshall and Hawkins), 117–130. Bloomsbury.

Halliwell, S. (1991). Comic satire and freedom of speech in classical Athens. *JHS* 111: 48–70.

Halliwell, S. (2008). *Greek Laughter: A Study of Cultural Psychology from Homer to Early Christianity*. Cambridge and New York: Cambridge University Press.

Halliwell, S. (transl.) (2015). *Aristophanes: Birds and Other Plays*. Oxford: Oxford University Press.

Hawkins, T. (2014). *Iambic Poetics in the Roman Empire*. Cambridge: Cambridge University Press.

Householder, F.W. (1941). *Literary Quotation and Allusion in Lucian*. New York.

Howley, J. (2017). Book-burning and the uses of writing in ancient Rome: destructive practice between literature and document. *JRS* 107: 213–236.

Hunter, R. (2009). *Critical Moments in Classical Literature: Studies in the Ancient View of Literature and Its Uses*. Cambridge: Cambridge University Press.

Hunter, R. (2014). Attic comedy in the rhetorical and moralising traditions. In: *The Cambridge Companion to Greek Comedy* (ed. M. Revermann), 373–386. Cambridge: Cambridge University Press.

Jazdzewska, K. (2015). Do not follow the Athenians! The example of Athens in Dio Chrysostom's orations. *CP* 110 (3): 252–268.

Johnson, W.A. and Richter, D.S. (2017a). Periodicity and scope (ed. Johnson and Richter), 3–10. Oxford University Press.

Johnson, W.A. and Richter, D.S. (ed.) (2017b). *The Oxford Handbook of the Second Sophistic*. Oxford: Oxford University Press.

Jones, C.P. (1993). Greek drama in the Roman Empire. In: *Theater and Society in the Classical World* (ed. R. Scodel), 39–52. Ann Arbor: University of Michigan Press.

Kim, L. (2013). Figures of Silence in Dio Chrysostom's *First Tarsian Oration* (*Or.* 33): *Aposiopesis, Paraleipsis*, and *Huposiópésis*. *Greece & Rome* 60: 32–49.

Kim, L. (2017). Atticism and Asianism (ed. Johnson and Richter), 41–66. Oxford University Press.

Kock, T. (1888). Lucian und die Komödie. *Rheinisches Museum* 34: 29–59.

Kuin, I.N.I. (2021). Laughter in Lucian's utopia of the dead. In: *Ancient Utopias* (ed. P. Destrée, J. Opsomer, and G. Roskam), 255–276. Berlin: De Gruyter.

Kuin, I.N.I. (2023). *Lucian's Laughing Gods: Religion, Philosophy, and Popular Culture in the Roman East*. Ann Arbor: University of Michigan Press.

Ledergerber, P.I. (1905). *Lukian und die altattische Komödie*. Einsiedeln: University of Fribourg Press.

Manuwald, G. (2015). Censorship for the Roman stage? In: *The Art of Veiled Speech: Self-Censorship from Aristophanes to Hobbes* (ed. H. Baltussen and P.J. Davis), 94–115. Philadelphia: University of Pennsylvania Press.

Marshall, C.W. and Hawkins, T. (ed.) (2016). *Athenian Comedy in the Roman Empire*. London: Bloomsbury.

Martin, P. (2018). Cleansing the palate: vomit and satire in Lucian's Lexiphanes. *ICS* 43 (2): 507–520. https://doi.org/10.5406/illiclasstud.43.2.0507.

Matijašić, I. (2017). Base di statua da Rodi con citazione di Aristofane. *Axone* 1 (2): 215–223. https://doi.org/10.14277/2532-6848/Axon-1-2-17-16.

May, R. (2009). *Apuleius and Drama: The Ass on Stage*. Oxford: Oxford University Press.

Ní Mheallaigh, K. (2010). The game of the name: Onymity and the contract of reading in Lucian. In: *Lucian of Samosata. Greek Writer and Roman Citizen* (ed. F. Mestre and P. Gómez Cardó), 121–132. Barcelona: University of Barcelona Press.

Olson, S.D. (ed.) (2014). *Ancient Comedy and Reception: Essays in Honor of Jeffrey Henderson*. Berlin: De Gruyter.

Peterson, A. (2019). *Laughter on the Fringes: The Reception of Old Comedy in the Imperial Greek World*. Oxford: Oxford University Press.

Rosen, R.M. (2014). Comic parrhesia and the paradoxes of repression (ed. Olson), 13–28. De Gruyter.

Rosen, R.M. (2016). *Lucian's Aristophanes: On Understanding Old Comedy in the Roman Imperial Period* (ed. Marshall and Hawkins), 141–162. Bloomsbury.

Ruffell, I. (2014). Old Comedy at Rome: rhetorical model and satirical problem (ed. Olson), 275–308. De Gruyter.

Sidwell, K. (2000). Athenaeus, Lucian and fifth-century comedy. In: *Athenaeus and his World: Reading Greek Culture in the Roman Empire* (ed. D. Braund and J. Wilkins), 136–152. Exeter: University of Exeter Press.

Sidwell, K. (2014). "Letting it all hang out": Lucian, Old Comedy and the origins of Roman satire (ed. Olson), 259–274. De Gruyter.

Slater, N.W. (2016). Aristophanes in antiquity: reputation and reception. In: *Brill's Companion to the Reception of Aristophanes* (ed. P. Walsh), 1–21. Leiden: Brill.

Smith, S.D. (2014). From drama to narrative: the reception of comedy in the ancient novel (ed. Olson), 322–345. De Gruyter.

Storey, I. (2016). Exposing frauds: Lucian and Old Comedy (ed. Marshall and Hawkins), 163–180. Bloomsbury.

Strunk, T. (2017). *History After Liberty: Tacitus on Tyrants, Sycophants, and Republicans*. Ann Arbor: University of Michigan Press.

Swain, S. (1996). *Hellenism and Empire. Language, Classicism, and Power in the Greek World, AD, 50–250*. Oxford: Oxford University Press.

Swain, S. (2007). The three faces of Lucian. In: *Lucian of Samosata Vivus et Redivivus* (ed. C. Ligota and L. Panizza), 17–44. London and Turin: The Warburg Institute.

Trapp, M. (2000). Plato in Dio. In: *Dio Chrysostom: Politics, Letters, and Philosophy* (ed. S. Swain), 213–239. Oxford: Oxford University Press.

Whitmarsh, T. (2001). *Greek Literature and the Roman Empire: The Politics of Imitation*. Oxford: Oxford University Press.

Whitmarsh, T. (2005). *The Second Sophistic*. Oxford: Oxford University Press.
Willi, A. (2010). The language of Old Comedy. In: *Brill's Companion to the Study of Greek Comedy* (ed. G. Dobrov), 471–510. Leiden: Brill.
Wilson, N. (2014). The transmission of Aristophanes. In: *The Oxford Handbook of Greek and Roman Comedy* (ed. M. Fontaine and A. Scafuro), 655–666. Oxford: Oxford University Press.

CHAPTER 26

Renaissance and Early Modern Reception of Aristophanes

Malika Bastin-Hammou

Introduction

The rediscovery of Aristophanes in the Latin West happened quite early. While manuscripts circulated in fourteenth-century Italy, the *editio princeps* was printed in Venice by Alde Manuce in 1498 (Musurus 1498). From then on, Aristophanes' comedies have been re-edited, translated, imitated, adapted, and performed continuously.

In the *editio princeps*, *Wealth* was printed first, in keeping with the history of the transmission of Aristophanes. *Plutus* is the best transmitted of Aristophanes comedies, and it was, with *Clouds* and *Frogs*, the first of the three plays forming the "byzantine triad." This preeminence lasted during the Renaissance and Early Modern era. On the other side, *Lysistrata* and *Thesmophoriazusae* were missing in the 1498 edition, before they were first printed in 1516 Florence by the Giunti. They were never printed separately during this same period nor imitated or performed, while Lysistrata is nowadays the most popular of Aristophanes' comedies.

This can be related to the fact that Aristophanes, during the Renaissance and Early Modern era, was mainly used to learn Greek. Very often printed and translated into Latin, his comedies were less often imitated and adapted by dramatists, who overwhelmingly chose Latin comedy as a model, and rarely performed. There were, though, interesting exceptions. Aristophanes was imitated and sometimes performed, but these experiences were often related, again, to the world of scholars and professors.

In this chapter, we will examine the trends in editing, translating, adapting, and performing Aristophanes before the important turn that occurred at the end of the eighteenth century, with the rediscovery and systematic use of the *Ravennas* manuscript, which coincides with the disparition of Latin translations in favor of the vernacular, and the upsurge of modern performances of Aristophanes. Even though the line between editing, translating, imitating, adapting, and performing is sometimes difficult to draw, and an evolving one, as the definition of those concepts changed during this period, for the sake of clarity, this chapter will be divided into three sections, which sometimes overlap.

Our point in this chapter is to show that this Early Modern reception of Aristophanes shaped the interpretations of the comic poet for a long time. While religious and moral issues were at the heart of the mere possibility of reading Aristophanes in Early Modern Europe, they do not really matter any more today. But satirical attack, and especially the role of Aristophanes' *Clouds* in the death of Socrates, was also a problem that Early Modern readers faced: while some condemned the comic poet, others highlighted the positive political role played by his comedies in fifth-century Athens, and these two interpretations still coexist today. As for obscenities, they did not seem to be a problem, except when related to homosexuality. While this understudied period of reception undoubtedly had its specificities, it also shaped the ways the comic poet has been and to some extent still is read today.

Editing

Sixteenth-Century Editions: Giving Access to the Text of the 11 Comedies

The first editions of Aristophanes were printed in Italy, until the study of Greek developed in Germany and the low countries, in the second decade of the sixteenth century, and in France, in the third decade. By the middle of the sixteenth century, European hellenists could have easily access to complete editions of the comic poet.

Aristophanes was one of the first Greek authors printed by Alde Manuce. The famous venitian printer published his *editio princeps* in 1498 (Musurus 1498), before that of Sophocles (1502), Euripides (1503), and Aeschylus (1518). In his Latin preface to this edition, Alde underlined the virtues of Aristophanes for learners of the Greek language: the purity of his attic Greek and his eloquence make him very suitable and he must be read as often as Terence.

After the printing of nine comedies by Alde Manuce, the Giunti press printed 1516 *Lysistrata* and *Thesmophoriazusae*, but these two comedies were absent from the 1525 juntine: the first complete edition is not an Italian but a German one.

During the second and third decades of the sixteenth century, the study and printing of Greek increased outside Italy, especially in Germany and in the low countries. There were first several separated editions of *Wealth*: in 1517, Petrus Mosellanus edited *Wealth* and had it printed by Thomas Anshelm (Mosellanus 1517); in 1518, Thierry Martens printed the same comedy in Antwerp (Martens 1518). Then, in the third decade, came editions of other comedies: in 1521, Melanchthon edited *Clouds* (Melanchthon 1521) and in 1524, Froben edited *Frogs* (Froben 1524).

In the paratexts of their editions, all explicitly made for students of Greek, those editors justified their choice of editing the comic poet. Following Alde, they described Aristophanes as the best of the Greek poets regarding the purity of the language, prayed for his freedom of speech when used to criticize vices, and considered his comedies as useful to learn eloquence. When editing separate plays, they also took good care to justify their choice of such or such comedy. These humanist paratexts shaped the modern reception of those comedies for a long time. Mosellanus and Martens considered *Wealth* as both the best composed ("argumenti commoditate," "foecunditatem argumenti") and the most decent ("morum correctione") of Aristophanes plays. Interestingly, Melanchthon justified his choice to publish Aristophanes *Clouds* by the idea that young people – meaning students – should know how much the Ancients despised philosophy and philosophers. Froben, prefacing *Frogs*, praised Aristophanes' poetry and especially the songs of frogs, comparing them to nightingales.

The first complete edition of the comic poet came from the same German circle. It was printed in Basel in 1532 by Andreas Cratander and edited by Simon Grynaeus, professor of Greek in Basel (Grynaeus 1532). In his longue preface, Grynaeus explained how professors should avoid corrupting their students when teaching Aristophanes. The comic poet, he wrote, should be used to show them vices in order to teach them the true Christian virtues. This defying attitude toward Aristophanes lasted for a long time.

At about the same time, Aristophanes started to be printed and taught in France, where Greek studies had developed too. In 1528, Gilles de Gourmont printed the same nine comedies contained in the aldine *princeps*, edited by Jean Chéradame. Like Grynaeus, Chéradame was mainly concerned with the difficulty to make Aristophanes compatible with Christian virtues, at a time when being a hellenist in Paris could be dangerous. But with the founding of the Collège des lecteurs royaux by

François the First in 1530, the study of Greek suddenly increased in France and by 1540 two other editions of Aristophanes were printed in Paris and the comic poet was taught at the Collège by one of the first Lecteurs royaux de grec, Jacques Toussain. We have annotated exemplars of students of Toussain that give us a glimpse at what it meant to teach Aristophanes in sixteenth-century Paris. It seems that the lectures consisted mainly in commenting upon the vocabulary used by the comic poet.

The second half of the century did not see any major new edition and focused on translating Aristophanes into Latin.

Seventeenth- and Eighteenth-Century Editions: From Editing the Text to Adding Fragments and New Tools

During the seventeenth century, as the Greek text had been printed several times and made accessible through Europe, scholars offered new editions of the comic poet which provided Latin translations, commentaries, index, and, later on, fragments. In 1607 was printed in Geneva the first complete edition containing the text of the 11 comedies and their translation into Latin, by different translators, but also ancient and new scholia written in Greek by Édouard Biset de Charlais (Portet 1607). These were presented on the title page as the most important part of this new edition. Samely, in 1625, was printed by Johannes Maire in Leyde a new complete edition claiming on the title page that it contained an index of sentences (Cum *indice Paroemiarum selectiorum*), new emendations by different scholars among which the famous hellenist Scaliger and unedited fragments (Scaliger 1625). In the second half of the century, a new edition printed in Amsterdam by Johannes Ravestein (Ravestein 1670) also claimed the edition of fragments and of a new translation of *Assemblywomen* by Tanneguy Le Fèvre, to which we will return (Section "XVIth c. Editions: Giving Access to the Text of the 11 Comedies"). These seventeenth-century editions do not differ from the sixteenth-century ones regarding their attitude toward Aristophanes: the comic poet is useful to learners of the Greek language because he is pleasant to read and his language is pure attic Greek.

In the continuity of the expansion of the Dutch press in the seventeenth century, the two major editions of the seventeenth century were published in Amsterdam and Leiden. Ludolf Kuster (1670–1716) published a new complete edition with a Latin translation in Amsterdam with Thomas Fritsch in 1710 (Kuster 1710). The work marked important philological progress and will serve as a reference edition during the whole century, until the publication of Brunck's edition in 1783 (Brunck 1783). Starting from the text of the Geneva edition of 1607, corrected thanks to the collation not only of editions but also of numerous manuscripts listed in the Preface, the edition opens with a series of texts about Aristophanes and his works and closes with four indexes.

Pierre Burman's edition marked an intermediate stage between the two major editions of Kuster and Brunck, at both ends of the century, and differed from them in its intended audience. Indeed, it excluded the Greek scholia and proposed to give shorter notes and literal translations. The Greek text is that of Kuster, sometimes corrected with the help of earlier editions and scholia. The main interest of the brief notes lies in their attention to what will later be called "paratragedy" by Rau, which is systematically pointed out and explained here for the first time (Burman and Bergler 1760).

At the end of the eighteenth century, the edition of Richard François Philippe Brunck was printed in Strasbourg (Brunck 1783). This edition is at the crossroads of two eras and two traditions in the understanding of the comic poet.

Brunck belongs to the period which goes from the Renaissance to the Revolution, which he closes, because he is the last one not to use the *Ravennas* 429, which was first used in 1516 and then forgotten; but by the philological method he adopts, he belongs already to the nineteenth century. The *Ravennas* is a manuscript from the beginning of the tenth century that Giovanni Aurispa brought back from Greece with 227 other manuscripts purchased at the request of Niccolo Niccoli in 1423. It is the only manuscript that contains the 11 comedies of the poet that we have, and it is also the oldest. It had certainly been used by Euphrosinus Boninus who, thanks to it, had been able to publish *Lysistrata* and the *Thesmophoria* at the presses of Bernardo Giunta as early as 1516

(Boninus 1516), but it had then been forgotten until a Roman lawyer, Filippo Invernizzi, found it. Invernizzi used it in his edition of Aristophanes published in 1794 in Leipzig, and since then its value has been widely recognized (Invernizzi 1794–1834). This marks the end of the Early Modern editions of Aristophanes and the beginning of a new era.

Translating

Even if the *editio princeps* of the comic poet was printed at the end of the fifteenth century, attempts at translating his comedies occurred earlier (Lockwood 1909). These first translations were in Latin, and of a very different kind, varying from *ad verbum* to loose paraphrases of the Greek text. Later on came vernacular translations, which did not replace Latin translations before the end of the eighteenth century: both coexisted through the Early modern era; they just aimed at different readers. Just as *Wealth* was, at the beginning of the period, the most edited comedy, it was also the most translated one, until came, progressively, complete translations. By the end of the period, the 11 comedies had been translated into Latin, Italian, and French, and the most popular ones in English, German, and Spanish (Giannopoulou 2007; Hall and Wrigley 2007). The translators were mainly scholars and professors of Greek but sometimes also students, poets, and dramatists.

The Latin Aristophanes

During the fifteenth century in Italy, several scholars attempted at translating *Wealth* into Latin, whose manuscripts have gained recent interest from scholars. Leonardo Bruni, who theorized the practice of translation in his *De interpretatione recta* (c.1420), translated c.1440 the first 269 lines of *Wealth* (Cecchini and Cecchini 1965; De Cesare 2006) and so did by the same time Pietro da Montagnana (Gamba 2016; De Cesare 2006). Some 20 years later, Alessandro d'Otranto gave an *ad verbum* translation of the whole play (Chirico 1991) and so did Ludovicus de Puppio in the last quarter of the fifteenth century (Muttini 2023). While Montagnana, Otranto, and Puppio translated *ad verbum*, Bruni transposed the beginning of *Plutus* by using the codes of Latin comedy, omitting some words, adding others, and sometimes even rewriting the text to make it more understandable, but also morally acceptable to sixteenth-century Italian readers. A joke involving male homosexuality, for instance, was erased and remodeled with reference to female prostitutes instead of male.

The first printed translation of *Wealth*, by Franciscus Passius, appeared at the turn of the sixteenth century in Venice (Passius 1501). It belongs to the tradition illustrated by Bruni, as Passius translated the comedy in verse and sometimes digressed from the text. Furthermore, Passius added a new prolog, in the manner of the prologus of Latin comedy, which is completely absent from the Greek original (Beta 2017). The same approach is to be found in Alciatus translation of *Frogs*, c.1517. Alciatus also translated the play into Latin verse and added a prolog in the manner of Latin comedy at the beginning of the play. But he did not add or omit lines or changed the content to make it more acceptable to a modern audience (Penguilly 2019; Bastin-Hammou 2023a; Bastin-Hammou et al. 2023). In this respect, he was announcing a new way of translating the comic poet which flourished in the third decade of the century among northern scholars, such as Thomas Venatorius or Adrianus Chilius, who both translated *Wealth* not *ad verbum* but *ad versum* (Venatorius 1531; Van Kerchove 1974). On the first page of Venatorius translation, one can read a short poem explaining that translating a Greek comedy in Latin verse is as difficult as writing a brand-new comedy. In a way, those translators presented themselves as poets and put forward the creativity as well as the philological accuracy of their work.

Completely different is the approach of Andreas Divus, an Istrian scholar who, in 1538, had printed in Venice by Pocatela the first complete translation of the 11 comedies into Latin (Divus 1538; Quaglia 2006; Beta 2012). Divus translated *ad verbum* and in prose. He was clearly not aiming at competing with the original he translated, or with contemporary poets; his translation was made for students of Greek, and it is sometimes barely understandable without the Greek text. However, this translation was widely reprinted in different formats and places. Andreas Cratander reprinted it in Basel in 1539 and again in 1542. It seems that it opened the path to the translation of other comedies that Wealth. While this comedy was still frequently retranslated, other comedies – mainly *Clouds*, *Knights*, and *Frogs* – were also retranslated in separate or uncomplete editions. In 1556, Coriolanus Martiranus translated *Wealth* and *Clouds* (Martiranus 1556), and this same year Lambertus Hortensius translated *Wealth*, a year later *Clouds* and in 1561 *Knights* and *Frogs* (Hortensius 1556, Hortensius 1557, Hortensius 1561). In 1586, another German scholar, Nicodemus Frischlinus, translated the same four comedies, to which he added *Acharnians* (Frischlinus 1586; Hadley 2015).

Finally, some neglected comedies were also retranslated. Nicasius Ellebodius, c.1575, translated and annotated *Thesmophoriazusae* and *Lysistrata*, unpublished at the time of his death in 1577 and in 1589 Florent Chrestien translated and commented upon *Peace* (Chrestien 1589; Bastin-Hammou 2015) and, without having them printed though, upon *Wasps* and *Lysistrata*. Just as Passius and Alciatus at the other end of the century, Chrestien composed new prologs for *Peace* and *Wasps* which were meant to articulate those comedies to the political and religious situation in France, which was then torn apart by the "guerres de religions" – religious wars (Bastin-Hammou 2024; Bastin-Hammou et al. 2024).

Latin translations of the sixteenth century thus fall roughly into two categories. While many of them, generally *ad verbum* and in prose, are meant to help the learners of Greek to understand the Greek original, others, translated *ad versum* and, though not adaptations, aim at being understandable to a modern audience. To achieve this goal, they relate to different codes of Latin comedy, for instance, by composing a liminar prolog addressed to the audience and exposing the plot of the play.

During the seventeenth and eighteenth centuries, this poetic approach tends to disappear and translations into Latin become mainly pedagogical tools, while Aristophanes is increasingly associated with and condemned for his role in the death of Socrates and, more generally, his satirical content. Those who still dare to translate Aristophanes seem to do it not in spite of this negative reputation, but because of it, as if it made the comic poet all the more so attractive. This is the case of the singular scholar Taneguy Le Fèvre, who in 1665 had printed in his correspondence a long letter in which he translated and commented upon *Ecclesiazusae* (Le Fèvre 1665). This comedy had not been translated into Latin since Divus's translation in 1538. Le Fèvre translated it in Latin prose, though not *ad verbum*. But the most interesting – and transgressive – features of his work do not lie so much in the translation itself as in the notes that come with it. These notes are both pedagogical, of high erudition and completely free – as when Le Fèvre digresses at length on the practice of cunnilingus. But this is an exception. The seventeenth- and eighteenth-century Latin translations are mostly pedagogical and scholarly tools. What characterizes them is the disparition of humanist and classical, meaning sixteenth century, translation features, as translating *ad versum*, defining acts and scenes and, more broadly, using the codes of Latin comedy.

The complete translation printed in 1760 with the new edition of Stephan Berglerus and Peter Burman is entirely in prose. Three translations had already been printed, and the other eight are new. Translated by Peter Burman, they are not only in prose but very literal. Indeed, Berglerus and Burman theorized this practice. The same Berglerus composed the new translations and the commentaries. Instead of compiling different translations and *addenda*, the edition stands for a coherent school book, Berglerus being the distant teacher, thus emerges the idea that Aristophanes works are to be translated and understood as a whole, that his comedies are inter-related, and so should be their translations and interpretations. This comes with the assertion of the role of the translator as an interpret.

In 1781, Richard Brunck has his *Comoediae in latinum sermonem conversae* printed in Strasbourg (Brunck 1781). This translation is, in fact, not a new one. Brunck merely revised Berglerus' translation, because his printer, Godfried Bauer, asked him to join a translation to his new edition. But for Brunck, Aristophanes should not be translated: if one wants to know the comic poet, one should not read a Latin translation... but learn ancient Greek.

Latin translations lasted all through the Early Modern period and coexisted for some time with vernacular translations. But by the end of the eighteenth century, even scholars considered they were of no use. From then on, to read Aristophanes, one would have the choice between learning Greek or read translations in the vernacular.

Aristophanes Speaks Vernacular

Vernacular translations had somehow an independent life from Latin ones, and this life depends heavily on the language considered. While Italian and, to a lesser extent, French attempts started as early as the sixteenth century, translations into English and German came later on. With the exception of Italian, most translators focused on *Wealth* and *Clouds*. Among those translations, some gained much attention, circulated widely, and were themselves translated into other vernacular, as it is the case for Pierre Brumoy French versions printed in the third volume of his *Théâtre des Grecs* (Brumoy 1730). It seems that some of those vernacular translations aimed at giving an Aristophanes understandable to a large audience, including dramatists, on whom they had an important influence. Some adaptations were probably prompted by this larger access to the comic poet.

Aristophanes in Italian

As for editions and Latin translations, Italy started first when the Rositini gave, as early as 1545, less than 50 years after the *editio princeps*, the first complete translation of Aristophanes in vernacular (Rositini and Rositini 1545; Beta 2013). The Rositini brothers were not scholars but physicians, and their translation was widely criticized. They were basically accused to have translated not the Greek text but the Latin translation of Andreas Divus, printed a few years earlier. This has been contested (Beta 2023). This shows, however, that translations have a life of their own, not necessarily depending on the original text they pretend to translate, and can have a tremendous influence on later reception of such or such author. This is definitely the case of Divus' translation. The Rositini's complete translation, though, did not seem to have a wide afterlife, as translating into Latin remained the mainstream way to translate Aristophanes. One has to wait until the middle of the eighteenth century to be able to read the comic poet in new Italian translations but limited to *Wealth* and *Clouds* (Beta 2024). After the Rositini, nobody cared to give a new complete translation of the comic poet in Italian before the nineteenth century.

Untranslatable Aristophanes? The French Aristophanes

The picture is slightly different in France, where the first complete printed translation of Aristophanes in French appeared in 1784 three years after Brunck's last complete Latin translation (Brunck 1781). It was preceded, though, by many attempts which should be related to the strong will to give major, that is, classical, authors in the French language which humanists wanted to "defend and illustrate" ("défence et illustration de la langue française"). Aristophanes benefited to some extent from this will; but to some extent only, as he was also perceived by some as uncompatible with the French language and thus untranslatable into French (Bastin-Hammou 2013).

As early as 1550, Ronsard translated into French the beginning of *Wealth*. At that time, it was a common exercise for student of Greek to translate this play but into Latin. Ronsard, who belonged to the Pleiad's circle ("cercle de la Pléiade"), which was eager to develop the French language, chose French, probably prompted by his Professor of Greek Jean Dorat (Céard et al. 1993, Bastin-Hammou 2015). But this bit of translation was not published, and one had to wait until 1684 to be able to read for the first time Aristophanes in French. This year, Anne Le Fèvre, daughter of Tanneguy Le Fèvre, had her French translation of *Wealth* and *Clouds* printed in Paris (Le Fèvre 1684, Bastin-Hammou 2010). This was quite an audacious move from this brilliant hellenist. The woman who would become best known for her role in the Querelle d'Homère, a revival of the Querelle des Anciens et des Modernes, was no longer a beginner. When she turned to Aristophanes, she had already successfully edited several volumes of the collection *ad usum Delphini*, Callimachus, Sappho, and Anacreon. Then she became interested in theater and translated three comedies by Plautus. An excellent philologist, trained by her own father, who had himself edited and translated into Latin the sulfurous *Assemblywomen*, she was then the partner of André Dacier, also a philologist and theater enthusiast.

Her choice to translate Aristophanes into French appears to have been well thought out. In addition to her personal taste for the author, it corresponded to a turning point in her career. It was indeed a daring choice, for Aristophanes did not have good reputation at the time. But the audacity was controlled: theater was then fashionable and, far from tackling, like her father, a scandalous comedy like the *Assemblywomen*, she prudently chose to translate the two best-known comedies, "the only ones that can be well put into our language," as she wrote in her Preface.

Her translations came with long "Remarques," where she explained what she sometimes considered impossible to translate. This concerned not only the language but also the very conception of the comic genre.

Even though Le Fèvre claimed, with great modernity, her will to "Lose sight of this century" to understand Aristophanes, she still tried to show that the poet respected the unity of time in *Wealth*, and of place in *Clouds*. She also tried to make the comedies undergo a division into acts and scenes, in accordance with the use which one applied to the Latin comedies since the Renaissance. This influence of the reception of the Latin comedy on that of the Greek comedy affected, in particular, *Clouds*' parabasis, which she moved to the beginning of the play, turning it into a prolog. The process allowed her especially to make the play conform to the rules of her century, that is to say, to avoid any rupture of the dramatic illusion, as she explained in the Preface. This translation was hugely appreciated and followed by numerous reprints, in and outside France, up to 1762.

Le Fèvre's attention to the context of the comedies and their alterity was to be found again, but amplified, in 1729 translation of *Birds* by Boivin and even more in Pierre Brumoy's *Théâtre des Grecs*.

The Jesuit proposed, with this sum of 1500 pages in three volumes, to give access, in French, to the entire Greek theater. This was intended to be as complete as possible: it was not only a question of translating the texts but of "making them heard." In the line of Boivin, but in a much more systematic and developed way, Brumoy endeavored to provide the reader with the elements of context necessary to the comprehension of the Greek theater, and to fight the prejudices which prevailed against it. He linked these prejudices to an attitude that consisted of judging this theater by the criterion of modern theater. In this perspective, his translations are framed by a whole pedagogical material aiming at facilitating their access. All of them are preceded by an introduction, accompanied by notes and followed by historical comments but also by large extracts, or even the entirety of Latin, French, and foreign plays proposed for comparison. Brumoy thus hopes to disseminate to a public that does not read Greek but is interested in theater, a body of work to which it does not have access, and which, in a context still marked by the Querelle, seems to him to be unjustly disparaged. The enterprise is thus both pedagogical and polemical. The third volume of the Théâtre des Grecs was entirely dedicated to Aristophanes. To give access to the comic poet, far from translating everything, he decided *not* to translate the complete comedies. When he considered that the text was too obscure, or that the long choral songs could bore the readers, he summarized them in a few words: The jokes which required a knowledge of the historical context were left aside. The "licentious words" were neglected, because they were considered "unworthy of the curiosity of honest people, & deserve to remain eternally in the obscurity which is appropriate to them." The comedies themselves did not seem to him worthy of interest from an aesthetic point of view. Indeed, if Brumoy devoted a whole volume to Aristophanes, it was not because of a literary or even dramaturgical interest in ancient comedy, certainly not because of its licenses but, in addition to the concern of exhaustiveness which animated him, the exceptional contribution which Aristophanes constituted regarding historical knowledge of the classical Athens. Thus, instead of translating, he used an alternative method made of presentations that are as many "exact analyses" of the four domains of his interest: the history of the comic genre, the history of the people of Athens, and the attitude of Aristophanes toward the tragic authors and toward the gods. The presentation of the comedies, which did not exclude the translation of certain passages, was thus oriented toward the analysis of these questions. Strange as it is, with its translations that are not translations and its enormous pedagogical apparatus, the *Theatre of the Greeks* had the immense merit of making Aristophanes exist in a way that was different from what Plutarch said about him and that had been repeated ever since. It thus played a major role in the history of the reception of Aristophanes, not so much for the snippets of translations it offers as for its immense diffusion and the curiosity it aroused in the public. Limited in his translations, Brumoy produced a text which, by its very ellipses, made people want to know more about the comic poet.

This curiosity, however, had to wait for more than 50 years before it was satisfied, with the publication of the first complete translation in French of Aristophanes by de Sivry (1784).

In the meantime, the practice of translation evolved and, as regards Greek theater, the so-called irreducibility of the Greek poets progressively disappeared. Translators henceforth dared to approach them head-on and freed them from the important pedagogical apparatus which seemed until then necessary to their understanding. The work of Louis Poinsinet de Sivry is, however, less revolutionary than it seems. A specialist in antiquity, author like Anne Dacier of a translation of Anacreon, he was a member of the Academies of Nancy, Dijon, and Rome. In addition to translation, he practiced poetry, theater, and journalism, without much success. Brother-in-law of Palissot, the author of the comedy "Les Philosophes," which caused a scandal in 1760 because of the mistreatment of philosophers, Poinsinet was also a fervent defender of Aristophanes. But unlike Dacier or Brumoy, Poinsinet de Sivry did present himself as a scholar, but as a translator. He prefaced the comedies with a "translator's foreword," something new in the history of Aristophanes' translations, and perhaps a proof of the emergence of the profession as such. This foreword, which would suggest a reflection on the work to which he has devoted himself, is however invaded by the quarrel of *Clouds*. The play opens the volume, flouting the chronological order that had been re-established by Brumoy. Rather than defending Aristophanes, as his predecessors had done, Poinsinet attacked Socrates in a very virulent way.

His translations are very elegant, but Poinsinet refused to translate what could shock and, contrary to his predecessors, did not take the trouble to explain and to justify by notes his choices. The scatological and obscene passages are the first to suffer from this elegant paraphrase.

This excessive modesty, which will be the distinctive mark of the nineteenth-century translations of Aristophanes, should however not hide the innovation that Poinsinet showed in terms of metric. His translation of Aristophanes is indeed "part verse, part prose" and he rejected the alexandrin.

To Le Fèvre's concern for philological accuracy, to Boivin's and especially to Brumoy's concern for historical precision, is added, at the end of the eighteenth century, the concern for the elegance of the translation and that of the metric. The question is no longer whether it is possible to translate Aristophanes but how to translate him *well*, that is, as a poet, and the solution now lies, it is thought, in the hands of the translators.

It appears that the path that leads from the first translations to complete translations of Aristophanes is far from being linear. The oldest translations are not the least faithful, and, paradoxically, it even appears that the more time passes, and the more plays are translated, the more translators deviated from the original text – and the less they justified these deviations.

The Long Emergence of English and German Aristophanes

Translations into English and German really gained momentum in the nineteenth century and emerged later than translation into Italian and French. Translations into English started in the middle of the seventeenth century and into German in the eighteenth century. They focused, unsurprisingly, on *Wealth* and *Clouds*, with the notable exception of the 1783 German translation of *Frogs*, *Die Frösche. Ein Lustspiel aus dem Griechischen des Aristophanes*, by Johann Georg Schlosser, brother-in-law of Goethe. Some of those translations come with stage directions, such as the 1784 *Die Wolken. Eine Komödie des Aristophanes*. Indeed, the emergence of vernacular translations is often to be related to a will not only to read but to stage the comic poet.

Imitating, Adapting, and Performing Aristophanes

Imitating and Adapting Aristophanes

At the same time when Aristophanes was edited and translated, his comedies were also adapted, imitated, and even staged, but rarely in the same circles (Stefani 1986).

As early as 1415, Rinuccio da Castiglione wrote a short and moralizing play called *Fabula Penia* which is a loose adaptation of Aristophanes' *Plutus* paraphrasing the scene featuring Πενία (l. 400–426) (Ludwig 1975, Radif 2011). While the adaptation of the Penia scene was quite loose, some lines seemed to be translated (403–409, 413–414, 489–610), though with omissions. Rinucci probably had the Greek text, which he sometimes translated, but also rewrote. This attitude toward the original, oscillating between translating it and completely rewriting it, is to be found again in many adaptations of Aristophanes.

As can be expected, those adaptations rarely came with the Greek text they adapt, as they were not meant for learners of the Greek language. Some did not pay any tribute to Aristophanes – Rinucci never mentioned his name – while others used the name of the comic poet to underline the paradoxical newness of their work: writing and Old Comedy, in the sixteenth century and even the seventeenth century, was presented as a way to renew the genre of Comedy, traditionally inspired by Latin Comedy.

In this respect, the features of Attic Old Comedy were exhibited. The satirical tone of the genre was a real asset for dramatists willing to attack their contemporaries, as Aristophanes legitimated their assaults. Machiavel, for example, is said to have written in 1504 a play overtly based on *Clouds* in which he attacked fiercely some contemporary figures (Giannopoulou 2007). Alciatus, who had translated *Clouds* c.1517, wrote in turn a Neo-Latin Old Comedy called *Philargyrus* c.1523 in which he used what he considered to be the main features of the Greek comedy genre, among which, again, satirical attacks (Nogara 2016). In the prolog of the play, Alciatus underlined comedy's ethical and political virtues, a *topos* of the interpretation of Aristophanes. But he also used a chorus, and the names of his characters have a meaning, just like Aristophanes'. Besides, in keeping with Aristophanes satirical content, he attacked his fellow citizens, especially friars and jurists and their obscure language (Bastin-Hammou 2023a).

Wealth was the most often adapted comedy in Early Modern Europe, whether it be in Germany with Hans Sachs' 1531 *Pluto dem Gott der Reichtumb* (Holzberg and Brunner 2020, 75–78) or in England with 1651 London *Ploutophtalmia ploutogamia: A pleasant comedie, entituled Hey for honesty, down with knavery*, an adaptation by Thomas Randolph (Steggle 2007; Miola 2014). But *Clouds* came close behind, because of its satirical content. In 1607, the professor of philosophy Cesare Cremonini wrote *Le Nubi* in which he attacked his colleague Ragusea, accusing him of corrupting his students (Giannopoulou 2007); in 1760, Charles Palissot de Montenoy composed a comedy called *Les philosophes* in which he ridiculed contemporary philosophers as Diderot (de Montenoy 1760; Ferret 2002). A few years later, in 1776, Jakob Michael Reinhold Lenz also wrote a play based on *Clouds* in which he attacked Christoph Martin Wieland.

However, beyond *Wealth* and *Clouds*, other comedies were also adapted. *Birds* was very loosely adapted, for example, in 1579 Pierre Le Loyer' *Néphélococcygie*, where two Toulousains, and not Athenians, flee the city of Toulouse not because they have debts but because they are "cuckolds," both birds and deceived husbands (Doe and Cameron 2004, Bastin-Hammou 2015). And in 1668, the young and not yet famous Jean Racine wrote his only comedy, *Les Plaideurs*, inspired by *Wasps* from which he took mainly the scene of the trial.

Performing Aristophanes Before the Nineteenth Century

Though some of these adaptations were clearly meant to be staged, and sometimes were, Aristophanes comedies were rarely performed before the nineteenth century. In 1512, Eufrosino Bonini wrote the *Comedia di giustizia*, an adaptation of the first 800 lines of *Wealth*, which was performed at the Medici palace (Giannopoulou 2007) and, at the other end of the period, in 1780 a German adaptation of *Birds*, *Die Vögel*, by Johann Wolfgang von Goethe, was performed in Weimar.

But performances of translations or adaptations of Aristophanes were mostly, before the nineteenth century, pedagogical stagings linked to the teaching of Greek, which explains the predominance of stagings of *Wealth*, though an interest in Ancient comedy satirical content, and thus for *Clouds*, was also present.

In this pedagogical context, many of these performances were conducted in ancient Greek, with varying devices to help the audience understand what was going on on stage. In 1521, George Agricola directed in Zwickau performances of *Wealth*, in both Latin and Greek, acted by his students (Giannopoulou 2007; Boas 1914, 16). Ten years later, in 1531, the same *Wealth* was performed again in Greek at Zürich in the circle of Zwingli, who, according to Boas, composed the music for the choruses (Boas 1914, 16; Giannopoulou 2007).

This desire to stage Greek comedies in Greek is also to be linked to an interest in and intense debates about the pronunciation of the language, especially in a British context. In 1536, *Wealth*, again, was performed in Greek by students at Saint John's College in Cambridge during Christmas, with the new pronunciation promoted by John Cheke (Boas, 17).

But at the same time some tried to perform Aristophanes' comedies in a language that could be understood by a larger audience: that is, in Latin, but also in the vernacular. This is the case of the first translation of *Wealth* in French attributed to Pierre de Ronsard, which is limited to the beginning of the play and is said to have been staged at the Collège de Coqueret in either 1549 or 1550 (Bastin-Hammou 2015), and of the 1613 Strasbourg Performance of *Clouds*. This performance was in ancient Greek, but Isaac Fröreisen published a German translation, *Nubes*, especially for the audience. Thus, performances, even when they were conducted in Ancient Greek, seem to have stimulated the development of translations in the vernacular.

Conclusion

The Renaissance and Early Modern Aristophanes was a multi-faceted one. The comic poet, in keeping with his late antique and byzantine transmission, was mostly used to teach and learn Greek. This explains his early and numerous editions but also his abundant and continuous translations into Latin. But, at a time were vernacular and national theaters were developing, his comedies, though not being used as models, as Latin comedies, sometimes interested those who wanted to renew the genre. His satirical content, especially, attracted authors of adaptations who, under the protection of the name of this Ancient and famous predecessor, wanted to disparage their contemporaries. This satirical reception, as often decried as used, lasted after the Early Modern period, opening a new era where neglected comedies such as *Lysistrata* and *Assembly Women* gained more and more interest, in keeping with the nineteenth-century craze for the staging of Ancient Drama.

GUIDE TO FURTHER READING

Sommerstein's (2019) *The Encyclopedia of Greek Comedy* has many entries on Renaissance and Early Modern Reception of Aristophanes. Lord's (1963) monograph *Aristophanes, his plays and his influence* is an old but still useful overview of the reception of Aristophanes from Antiquity to the twentieth century. For the French reception, see Bastin-Hammou (2015) on Florent Chrestien's Latin translation of Aristophanes' *Peace*, Dudouyt (2016) on two French adaptations of Aristophanes, Le Loyer's *Néphélococcugie* (1588) and Racine's *Les Plaideurs* (1679). Hadley's *Athens in Rome, Rome in Germany: Nicodemus Frischlin and the rehabilitation of Aristophanes in the sixteenth century* (2015) is a thorough study of Aristophanes in sixteenth-century Germany. For England, Miola "Aristophanes in England, 1500-1660" (Miola 2014) and Steggle "Aristophanes in Early Modern England" (Steggle 2007) are good introductions. A very useful list of translations, including Early Modern translations, in all languages, is given by Giannopoulou (2007). The volume

Translating Greek Drama in Early Modern Europe (Bastin-Hammou et al. 2023) has three chapters dedicated to the reception of Aristophanes in the Renaissance. Muttini concentrates on a fifteenth-century Latin translation of *Plutus*, Beta's on the first vernacular translation of Aristophanes' *Knights* by the brothers Rositini in 1545; Bastin-Hammou compares two of Alciatus' works on Aristophanes, his Latin translation of *Clouds* and his *Philargyrus*, an attempts to write an aristophanic comedy in Latin. The school and scholarly reception of Aristophanes in the sixteenth and seventeenth centuries is analyzed in Bastin-Hammou (2019), "Teaching Greek with Aristophanes in the French Renaissance," and Bastin-Hammou (2020), "Aemilius Portus, Greek Scholar and Latin Humanist. Some Reflexions on Aemilius Portus's Edition of Aristophanes (1607)." Many of these Early Modern editions, translations, and adaptations have been digitized and can be read on Google Books.

REFERENCES

Bastin-Hammou, M. (2010). Anne Dacier et les premières traductions françaises d'Aristophane: l'invention du métier de femme philologue. *Littératures classiques* 72: 85–99.

Bastin-Hammou, M. (2013). Traduire ou ne pas traduire: 1684-1784, de Madame Dacier à Poinsinet de Sivry, un siècle de 'traductions' des comédies d'Aristophane en français. In: *Traduire en français à l'âge classique: Génie national et génie des langues* (ed. Y.-M. Tran-Gervat), 117–135. Paris: Presses Sorbonne Nouvelle.

Bastin-Hammou, M. (2015). Les 'Traductions' d'Aristophane en français au XVIe siècle. In: *Histoire des Traductions en Langue Française – XVe – XVIe siècle* (ed. V. Duché), 1209–1216. Paris: Editions Verdier.

Bastin-Hammou, M. (2019). Teaching Greek with Aristophanes in the French renaissance. In: *Receptions of Hellenism in Early Modern Europe – 15th-17th Centuries* (ed. N. Constantinidou and H. Lamers), 72–93. Leiden/Boston: Brill.

Bastin-Hammou, M. (2020). Aemilius Portus, Greek scholar and Latin humanist. Some reflexions on Aemilius Portus's edition of Aristophanes (1607). In: *Post-Byzantine Latinitas. Latin in Post-Byzantine Scholarship (1453–1821)* (ed. V. Vaiopoulos, I. Deligiannis, and V. Pappas), 77–90. Turnhout.

Bastin-Hammou, M. (2023a). From Translating Aristophanes to Composing a Greek Comedy in XVIth c. Europe: The Case of Alciato. In: *Translating Ancient Greek Drama in Early Modern Europe: Theory and Practice (15th–16th Centuries)* (ed. Bastin-Hammou, D. Di Martino, and Jackson), 37–52. Berlin, Boston: De Gruyter.

Bastin-Hammou, M. (2024). *Le prologue de Florent Chrestien à sa traduction latine des Guêpes d'Aristophane: un texte polémique à la destinée contrariée* (ed. D. Bastin-Hammou and Hermand). Geneva: Librairie Droz.

Bastin-Hammou, M., Dedieu, A., and Hermand, L. (ed.) (2024). *Florent Chrestien, un poète, traducteur et polémiste en son temps*. Geneva: Presses Sorbonne Nouvelle.

Bastin-Hammou, M., Di Martino, G., Dudouyt, C., and Jackson, L. (ed.) (2023). *Translating Greek Drama in Early Modern Europe*. Berlin/Boston: Brill.

Beta, S. (2012). La prima traduzione latina della *Lisistrata*. Luci e ombre della versione di Andrea Divo. *Quaderni Urbinati di Cultura Classica* 129: 95–114.

Beta, S. (2013a). *Aristophanes Venetus*: i fratelli Rositini e la prima traduzione italiana del poeta comico greco (1545). *Cahiers d'études italiennes* 17: 57–70.

Beta, S. (2017). Francesco Passi Versipellis. Fra Aristofane e Plauto. In: *A Maurizio Bettini. Pagine stravaganti per une filologo stravagante* (ed. A. Romaldo), 47–50. Milano: Mimesis.

Beta, S. (2023). *The Sausage-Seller Suddenly Speaks Vernacular. The Rositini Brothers and the First Italian Translation of Aristophanes' Knights* (ed. Bastin-Hammou, D. Di Martino, and Jackson), 53–67. Berlin/Boston: De Gruyter.

Beta, S. (2024). Mulier quidem sum, mens inest tamen mihi. Florent Chrestien et sa traduction latine de la Lysistrata d'Aristophane. In: *Florent Chrestien, un poète, traducteur et polémiste en son temps* (ed. M. Bastin-Hammou, A. Dedieu, and L. Hermand). Geneva: Librairie Droz.

Boas, F.S. (1914). *University Drama in the Tudor Age*. Oxford: Oxford University Press.

Boninus, E. (1516). In hoc parvo libro haec insunt. In: *Aristophanes. Cereris sacra celebrantes ejusdem Lysistrate*. Florence: Filippo Giunta.

Brumoy, Pierre (1730), *Le Théâtre des Grecs*, par le R. P. Brumoy, de la Compagnie de Jésus, à Paris, Rollin Père, Jean-Baptiste Coignard et Rollin fils.

Brunck, R.F.P. (1781). *Aristophanis Comoediae in Latinum Sermonem Conversae*. Strasbourg: Bauer & Treuttel.

Brunck, R.F.P. (1783). *Aristophanis Comoediae ex Optimis Exemplaribus Emendatae Studio Rich. Franc. Phil. Brunck.* Strasbourg: Bauer & Treuttel.

Burman, P. and Bergler, S. (1760). *Aristophanis comoediae undecim, grace & latine, ad fidem optimorum codicum Mss. emendatae etc.* (ed. S. Leiden and J. Luchtmans). Leiden: S. and J. Luchtmans.

Céard, J., Ménager, D., and Simonin, M. (ed.) (1993). *Pierre de Ronsard, Œuvres Complètes.* Paris: Gallimard.

Cecchini, M. and Cecchini, E. (1965). *Leonardo Bruni, Versione del Pluto di Aristofane, (introduzione e testo critico di).* Firenze: Sansoni Editore.

de Cesare, Z. (2006). *Le traduzioni latine del Pluto di Aristofane nel XV secolo: Rinuccio di Arezzo, Leonardo Bruni et Pietro da Montagnana.* Tesi di Dottorato in Filologia Latina, Università degli studi di Parma.

Chirico, M.L. (1991). *Aristofane in terra d'Otranto.* Napoli: Press of the University of Naples Federico II.

Chrestien, F. (1589). *Q. Septimii Florentis Christiani in Irenam vel Pacem Commentaria Glossemata: Vbi aliquot ueterum Grammaticorum aliorumque auctorum loci aut correcti aut animaduersi.* In: *Cum Latina Graeci Dramatis Interpretatione Latinorum Comicorum Stylum Imitata.* Paris: Fédéric Morel.

Divus, A. (1538). *Aristophanis, comicorum principis, Comoediae undecim, è Graeco in Latinum, ad verbum translatae, Andrea Divo Iustinopolitano interprete.* Venice: Jacopo Pocatela.

Doe, M. and Cameron, K. (ed.) (2004). *Pierre Le Loyer. La Néphélococugie ou la Nuée des Cocus.* Paris: Librairie Droz.

Dudouyt, C. (2016). Aristophanes in early-modern fragments: Le Loyer's *La Néphélococugie* (1579) and Racine's *les Plaideurs* (1688). In: *Brill's Companion to the Reception of Aristophanes* (ed. P. Walsh), 173–194. Leyden/Boston: Brill.

Ferret, O. (ed.) (2002). *Palissot. La comédie des Philosophes et autres textes.* Saint-Étienne: Publications de l'Université de Saint-étienne.

Frischlinus, N. (1586). *Nicodemi Frischlini Aristophanes, veteris comoediae princeps: poeta longe facetissimus et eloquentissimus: repurgatus a mendis, et imitatione Plauti atque Terentii interpretatus etc.* Frankfurt am Main: Johannes Spies.

Froben, I. (1524). *Aristophanes Inter Comicos Summi, Ranae.* Basel: Ioannes Froben.

Gamba, E. (2016). Pietro da Montagnana: la vita, gli studi, la biblioteca di un homo trilinguis. In: *Tesi di Dottorato in Filologia Latina.* Parma: Università degli studi di.

Giannopoulou, V. (2007). *Aristophanes in Translation Before 1920* (ed. Hall and Wrigley), 309–342. London: Legenda.

Grynaeus, S. (1532). ΑΡΙΣΤΟΦΑΝΟΥΣ ΕΥΤΡΑΠΕΛΩΤΑΤΟΥ κωμωιδίαι ἕνδεκα *ARISTOPHANIS FACETISSIMI comoediae undecim.* Basel: Andreas Cratander et Ioannis Bebelius.

Hadley, P. (2015). *Athens in Rome Rome in Germany: Nicodemus Frischlin and the Rehabilitation of Aristophanes in the 16th Century.* Tübingen: Narr Francke Attempto Verlag.

Hall, E. and Wrigley, A. (ed.) (2007). *Aristophanes in Performance 421 BC-AD 2007. Peace, Birds, and Frogs.* London: Legenda.

Holzberg, N. and Brunner, H. (ed.) (2020). *Hans Sachs. Ein Handbuch.* Berlin/Boston: De Gruyter.

Hortensius, L. (1556). *Aristophanis clarissimi comici, Plutus, interprete Lamberto Hortensio Montfortio.* Utrecht: Hermannus Borculous.

Hortensius, L. (1557). *Aristophanis comici clarissimi nebulae Lamberto Hortensio Montfortio interprete.* Utrecht: Hermannus Borculous.

Hortensius, L. (1561). *Aristophanis comici clarissimi equites Lamberto Hortensio Montfortio interprete.* Utrecht: Hermannus Borculous.

Invernizzi, F. (1794–1834). *Aristophanis Comoediae auctoritate libri praeclarissimi saeculi decimi emendatae a Philippo Invernizio.* Leipzig: Weidmann.

Kuster, L. (1710). *Aristophanis comoediae undecim, graece et latine, ex codd. Mss. emendatae etc.* Amsterdam: Thomas Fritsch.

Le Fèvre, T. (1665). *Tanaquilli Fabri Epistolae pars altera. Additae sunt Aristophanis concionatrices, cum interpretatione nova, notis et emendationibus.* Saumur: Daniel de Lerpinière et Jean Lesnie.

Le Fèvre, A. (1684). *Le Plutus et les Nuées d'Aristophane. Comédies grecques traduites en françois. Avec des Remarques & un Examen de chaque Piece selon les regles du Theatre. Par Mademoiselle Le Fèvre.* Paris: Denis Thierry et Claude Barbin.

Lockwood, D.P. (1909). Aristophanes in the fifteenth century. *TAPA* 40: lvi–lvii.

Lord, L.E. (1963). *Aristophanes, his Plays and his Influence.* New York: Cooper Square.

Ludwig, W. (1975). *Die Fabula Penia des Rinucius Aretinus; herausgegeben, eingeleitet und kommentiert von Walther Ludwig.* München: Fink.

Martens, T. (1518). *ΑΡΙΣΤΟΦΑΝΟΥΣ ΠΛΟΥΤΟΣ ARISTOPHANIS PLUTUS, Alost.* Thierry Martens.

Martiranus, C. (1556). *Coriolani Martirani Cosentini Episcopi Sancti Marci. Tragoediae. VIII. Medea. Phoenissae. Electra. Cyclops. Hippolytus. Prometheus. Bacchae. Christus. Comoediae. II Plutus. Nubes. Odysseae Lib. XII. Batrachomyomachia. Argonautica.* Naples: Giovanni Maria Simonetta.

Melanchthon, P. (1521). *Aristophanis Poetae Comici Nubes.* Wittenberg: Melchior Lother Iunior.

Miola, R. (2014). Aristophanes in England, 1500-1660. In: *Ancient Comedy and Reception. Essays in Honor of Jeffrey Henderson* (ed. S. Douglas Olson), 479–502. Leiden/Boston: Brill.

de Montenoy, C.P. (1760). *Les Philosophes. Comédie en trois actes, en vers.* Paris: Duschene.

Mosellanus, P. (1517). *Aristophanis Comici Facetissimi Plutus.* Haguenau: Thomas Anshelm.

Musurus, M. (1498). *Aristophanis Comoediae Novem.* Venice: Aldus Manutius.

Muttini, M. (2023). *Aristophanes Renaissance Readers and Translators in XVth c. Italy. The Latin Plutus of MS 4697 in the National Library of Spain* (ed. Bastin-Hammou, D. Di Martino, and Jackson). 19–36. De Gruyter.

Nogara, A. (2016), 'Gli otia di un giurista filologo: il Philargyrus di Andrea Alciato, *Laboratoire italien* 17, online.

Passius, F. (1501). *Plutus antiqua comoedia ex Aristophane quae nuper in linguam latinam translata est.* Parma: Angelo Ugoleto.

Penguilly, T. (2019). *Huiusmodi, hercle, Aristophanes si cerneret. . .* La première traduction latine des *Nuées* d'Aristophane par André Alciat. In: *Rire et sourire dans la littérature latine au Moyen Âge et à la Renaissance* (ed. B. Gauvin and C. Jacquemard), 183–199. Dijon: Press of the University of Dijon.

Portet, É. (1607). *Aristophanis Comoediae Vndecim, Cum Scholis Antiquis, Quae Tudio & Opera Nobilis Viri Odoardi Biseti Carlaei Sunt Quamplurimis Locis Acurate Emendata, & Perpetuus Novis Scholiis Illustrata. Adque Etiam Accesserunt Ejusdem in Duas Posteriores Novi Commentarii: Opera Tamen & Studio Doctissimi Viri D. Aemylii Franscisci Porti Cretensis Filii ex Biseti Autographo Excripti & in Ordinem Digesti. Quae Ad Hanc Editionem Accesserunt Praeterea Pagina 36. Demonstrat.* Geneva: Société caldorienne.

Quaglia, R. (2006). Su alcune traduzioni italiane di Aristofane: azzeccagarbugliando tra i secc. XVI e XIX. *Maia* 57: 349–357.

Radif, L. (ed.) (2011). *Rinuccio Aretino.* Florence: Penia.

Radif, L. (2014). Aristofane mascherato: un secolo (1415-1504) di fortuna e « sfortuna ». In: *Ancient Comedy and Reception: Essays in Honor of Jeffrey Henderson* (ed. S.D. Olson), 397–409. Berlin, Boston (MA): De Gruyter.

Ravestein, J. (1670). *Aristophanis comoediae undecim, grace & latine, ut et fragmenta earum quae amissae sunt cum emendationibus virorum doctorum etc.* Amsterdam: Jean Ravestein.

Rositini, P. and Rositini, B. (1545). *Le comedie del facetissimo Aristofane, tradutte di Greco in lingua commune d'Italia, per Bartolomio & Pietro Rositini de Prat' Alboino, con privilegio de lo Illustrissimo Senato Veneto per anni diece.* Venice: Vincent Vaugris.

Scaliger, J.J. (1625). *Aristophanis comoediae undecim, grace & latine, cum indice paroemiarum selectiorum & emendationibus virorum doctorum etc.* Leiden: Ioannes Maire.

de Sivry, L.P. (1784). *Théâtre d'Aristophane traduit en français, partie en vers, partie en prose avec les fragmens de Ménandre et de Philémon par M. Poinsinet de Sivry.* Paris: Didot jeune.

Sommerstein, A. (2019). *The Encyclopedia of Greek Comedy.* Hoboken: Wiley Blackwell.

Stefani, L. (ed.) (1986). *Tre commedie fiorentine del primo 500; edizione critica e introduzione di Luigina Stefani.* Ferrara: Legare Street Press.

Steggle, M. (2007). *Aristophanes in Early Modern England* (ed. Hall and Wrigley), 52–65.

Van Kerchove, D. (1974). The Latin translation of Aristophanes' *Plutus* by Hadrianus Chilius, 1533. *Humanistica Lovaniensia* 23.

Venatorius, T. (1531). *Aristophanis facetissimi comici plutus. [. . .].* Nuremberg: J. Petrius.

PART V

Aristophanes Today

CHAPTER 27

Performing Aristophanes

Philip Walsh

Introduction

Published in March 2000, Gonda Van Steen's *Venom in Verse: Aristophanes in Modern Greece* introduced a new scholarly paradigm to the fields of performance history and classical reception studies.[1] The book explored significant productions of Aristophanic comedy in modern Greece and clearly demonstrated how the plays were utilized in debates about politics, culture, and national identity. Over the last 20 years, Van Steen's nimble research methodologies and perceptive conclusions have proven influential as others have delivered fresh insights into the global receptions of Aristophanes. At the same time, scholars and practitioners, in the process of documenting diverse performances and representing the enduring potential of Aristophanic comedy, have also begun to question its relevance for the twenty-first century. In an era marked by economic disruptions, technological innovations, environmental uncertainties, political upheavals, a catastrophic pandemic, and gradual encroachments of the liberal world order, "Why Aristophanes?" becomes a crucial question with no easy or universal answers.

To her credit, Van Steen posed this question in the prolog of *Venom in Verse*, but perhaps she was anticipating different concerns – for instance, the book's relevance to mainstream ancient Greek studies.[2] As this chapter will suggest, though, *Venom in Verse* was immediately successful in expanding the universe of classical studies. It broadened scholarly horizons with respect to Aristophanic comedy, and it deepened our appreciation for its seemingly ubiquitous presence in modern Greek culture. In subsequent years, Van Steen has continued to research and publish on performance history and reception, and her book has been read and digested by a new generation of students and scholars who have applied its cross-disciplinary methods in different cultural contexts.[3]

Today, performance history and classical reception studies are mature fields, and while Van Steen cannot take full credit for their rise in prominence, she was a persistent and enthusiastic pioneer who

---

[1] I would like to thank Gonda Van Steen, whom I interviewed in June 2021, and who read an early version of this essay. I would also like to thank Matthew Farmer, who spoke with my students about ancient Greek comedy in October 2021, and whose support, with Jeremy Lefkowitz, helped to bring this essay together.

[2] Responding to Green's positive review in the *TLS* (28 April 2000), Greenwood remarks, "While I endorse Green's praise, I am less convinced about the relevance of this study for students of the ancient Greek world. To my mind, *Venom in Verse* is a work that poses greater relevance for students of modern Greek culture and those interested in reception theory and the history of performance. While Classicists who do not fall into these categories will definitely enjoy this work and learn from it, they may bridle at Van Steen's conscious decision not to discuss Aristophanes in the context of Ancient Greece" (Greenwood 2001).

[3] For instance, see Van Steen (2002, 2007a, b, 2014a, b, 2016a, b, 2019).

parried skepticism, promoted new work, encouraged the exchange of ideas, and elevated scholarly consciousness. With all of this in mind, and given the profound shifts in society, politics, and education since *Venom in Verse* appeared, the time is right for reflection, and this chapter will revisit the book by taking up Porter's idea of "reception of reception." It will elucidate significant methods and conclusions, assess subsequent scholarship, and identify trends and novel avenues of study. No critical survey can claim comprehensiveness, but charting representative research will "bring the focus of reception studies up to the present or near-present – always an uncomfortable thing, but essential just the same" (Porter 2008, 477). Finally, this chapter will conclude with a case study of performance: *7 Wilde Clouds*, an integrated arts project completed at St. Andrew's School (Middletown, DE) during a physically distanced era of COVID-19. This study is important not just because of the many practical challenges that were surmounted but also because of the unusual creative and intellectual circumstances under which the project came about. The significance of Aristophanic comedy was a central consideration from the start, and it became amplified as we moved away from in-person instruction to virtual learning. The key deliverable proved to be the creative process itself – a surprising and incremental journey of collaboration, uncertainty, and joy. Ultimately, the process became paramount, and I believe it yielded a new answer to that relevant question, "Why Aristophanes?"

Remembering *Venom in Verse*: Innovative Methods and Conclusions

To argue that only in Greece did the regular reception history of a classic become, once again, a practice of engaged public performance, I have used sources and techniques that rarely figure in conventional treatments of Aristophanes, let alone in studies of Greek civilization and politics, whether ancient or contemporary. My conclusions cross boundaries between classical philology, actual performance, and critical theory, and they subvert a record of Attic comedy characterized by denial or distortion. The claim that an ancient author provides insight into a modern society and vice versa might strike classicists and historians as bold, whereas Neohellenists might perceive the argument for Aristophanes' broad presence in nineteenth- and twentieth-century Greece as exaggerated. Nonetheless, comic revivals in contemporary Greece have been as ubiquitous and politically motivated as were the original performances in antiquity. At once classical (because of the long philological tradition) and popular (because of his humor's immediacy), the poet's work has been a choice battleground in the interplay between old and new (Van Steen 2000, 5).

Van Steen opens *Venom in Verse* with a clear agenda, and this quotation, found in the prolog, introduces a theoretically informed approach to document the myriad presences of Aristophanes in the post-classical Greek world.[4] One of the most striking characteristics of Van Steen's book is how adeptly she uses primary source material – for example, theater programs, cartoons, scripts, newspaper clippings, oral testimonies, and personal memorabilia – alongside traditional scholarship to track socio-political, historical, literary, and cultural changes over time. As she suggests, much of this evidence, despite its rich and revealing qualities, was ignored, unappreciated, or undiscovered, and part of her project was to demonstrate how these "texts" matter – that is, to substantiate how various artistic, intellectual, and political figures unlocked the authority of Aristophanic satire in order to engage with a public receptive to biting humor and big ideas. This approach allows Van Steen to introduce an open-minded, "democratic" framework to performance history and reception studies that eschews arid or elitist interpretations; moreover, the treasure trove of source materials that she presents suggests that appreciation for Aristophanes in modern Greece was much deeper than anyone had previously understood. For instance, she devotes a whole chapter to Karolos Koun's important production of *Birds* (1959), and in her discussion of the controversies surrounding its opening night (29 August 1959), she reproduces a satirical cartoon of the politician Konstantinos Tsatsos, who would later serve as president of Greece. Tsatsos had banned the remaining three performances of *Birds* on esthetic and religious grounds, which really served as

---

[4] She cites, among others, the work of Jauss, Foucault, Bakhtin, Dolan, Edmunds, Martindale, and Dracoulides.

cover for concerns about the "antigovernment and anti-American" politics of Koun's translator, Vasiles Rotas (Van Steen 2000, 127). In the image, which was originally published in the newspaper *Anexartetos Typos* (September 2, 1959), a tiny Tsatsos is holding a chicken (he was ridiculed as "the Chicken" for banning *Birds*) and quakes at the sight of a giant Aristophanes, who holds a copy of the play (ΟΡΝΙΘΕΣ) under his arm.[5] Despite any feelings of anger or disappointment, the media attention and public debates on Koun's *Birds* raised its profile both in Greece and internationally. As Van Steen describes, "The condemned *Birds* proved to be Koun's largest failure and his greatest success. . . [becoming] perhaps the biggest landmark in the modern Greek reception history of Aristophanes" (Van Steen 2000, 134–5, 135).

In demonstrating the breadth and depth of modern Greece's reception of Aristophanes, Van Steen traces the gradual evolution of performances of Aristophanic comedy, beginning in the middle of the eighteenth century, and continuing, in fits and starts, through the end of the twentieth century. Important to her methodology is the concentrated, geographical focus on modern Greece, which had received little to no serious attention in Anglophone scholarship. Such intentionality helped to expand the vistas of classical receptions: not only did it put Aristophanes and ancient Greek comedy back "on the map" but it also created a space for Greece itself to reclaim its position alongside other cultural centers around the world (see Holtermann 2004; Piana 2005; Walsh 2008).[6] In addition, her methodology can be likened to a meticulous archeological excavation, contextualizing people and performances in historical and cultural moments, sifting through the social and political terrains into which the plays by Aristophanes were introduced, and compiling the data to tell a nuanced and compelling story of performance reception. Her critical approach is evident in the documentation of two nineteenth-century amateur productions: *Plutus* (January 1868), a success because of "its conscious intent to entertain a larger urban audience of lower- and middle-class theatergoers"; and *Clouds* (May 1868), "a didactic academic exercise [in strict Kathareuousa] that resuscitated, in all its minute detail, the form but not the humor of Aristophanic comedy" (Van Steen 2000, 73, 71).

The conclusions that Van Steen draws in *Venom in Verse* are equally as significant as her methods and questions. One point that becomes eminently clear is how the plays of Aristophanes were utilized across the socio-political spectrum in modern Greece. From militant leftists to antifeminists, satirical journalists, and anticommunists, "the Aristophanic experience is plural, transient, and above all open-ended" (Van Steen 2000, 224). This is evident when evaluating Aristophanes' political views, one of the most essential interpretative functions when studying Old Attic Comedy. Van Steen cites the historian Gomme, who dismissed the importance of knowing Aristophanes' political opinions, but takes a more "radical" position than his, suggesting "the impossibility of reading singular intention, of determining final meaning (even of assuming that we can equate the author's intentionality and the meaning of his or her text), given the multiple and contradictory deductions made by modern Greek translators and theater practitioners" (Van Steen 2000, 186). This observation productively complicates an earlier claim: namely, that a modern Greek "*re*performance" of Aristophanes (like Koun's *Birds*, which was often revived post-1960) could follow or adapt a modern playscript different from the ancient original. In Van Steen's view, "any new interpretation chooses to interact with or to displace a modern legacy's authority. It ultimately re-members Aristophanes in its own way" (Van Steen 2000, 149).[7] Her conclusion here is grounded in "middle course" interpretations of Aristophanes' political views that reject clear binaries, and

---

[5] See the work of Mitchell (2016), who assembles over 40 posters advertising performances of *Lysistrata* in the United States, the United Kingdom, Australia, Canada, and France. His "archeological perspective" allows him to read posters as signs, symbols, and visual synecdoches for the themes of the play and particular performances. These ephemera are of a piece with Van Steen's interest in playbills, photographs, and other visual media.

[6] Michelakis describes *Venom in Verse* as providing "the first systematic and detailed account of performances of Aristophanes in modern times. In this respect it sets a precedent for the study of the reception of Greek and Roman comedy elsewhere in Europe and America. . . [the book] explores a largely unmapped territory, and it is to V.'s credit that it does so with clarity and elegance" (Michelakis (2002) 200).

[7] Kotzamani also notices the significance of this argument: "A particularly interesting feature of Aristophanic reception in Greece has been the existence of strong theatrical traditions that have established discourses focused on performance, rather than on the original texts. Thus, Karolos Koun's 1959 landmark production of *The Birds* acquired primacy over the Aristophanic text in validating and influencing later interpretations" (Kotzamani (2000) 453).

although she does not explicitly engage with those scholarly debates, her thinking reflects post-modern readings of Aristophanes that prefer multi-dimensionality to definitiveness (see Walsh 2009, 69–70; Rosen 2020; Osborne 2020; Cartledge 2020).[8]

Building on the notion of interpretive diversity, Van Steen articulates another important insight: that since the mid-1970s the reception of Aristophanes in modern Greece has been characterized by "the realization of the 'marketplace' of Aristophanes, both through the expansion of literary and theater criticism and through the institutionalization or 'framing' of the comic revival stage." She describes not only how Aristophanes was assimilated into routine public discourse in newspapers and periodicals but also how institutions like universities, playhouses, lecture halls, and museums "were essential in shaping the history of production and consumption of Aristophanes in public life" (Van Steen 2000, 190, 193). She compels the reader to understand the receptions of Aristophanes wholistically and inclusively – that is, to document and appreciate modern productions of Aristophanic comedy, whether they run during important national festivals or in local coffee shops. In addition, she democratizes the study of Aristophanes' reception by recognizing and honoring his emerging presence in "television, film, and video; institutions of higher education and other public bodies; and children's and comic books" (Van Steen 2000, 210). Although *Venom in Verse* did not explore all these sites of mass media reception, it suggested that these might yield any number of new and useful insights.

In the Shadow of *Venom in Verse*: A Scholarly Survey

Today, the methods, questions, and conclusions of *Venom in Verse* may seem familiar, but it is important to remember that in the 1990s, when Van Steen was researching and writing the book, the fields of performance history and classical reception studies were undertheorized, understudied, and relegated to the fringes of the discipline. Van Steen, however, is a confident storyteller, and she ends the book by inviting others to learn from her "map" and to chart new ground. Several scholars have taken up the charge, advancing our understanding of the performance history of Aristophanic comedy in modern Greece. For instance, Kiritsi (2016) describes the significance of Dimitris Potamitis' *The Stories of Grandfather Aristophanes* (1979) and Karmen Rouggeri's *Ecclesiazusae Like a Fairy Tale* (1997–8), both produced in an educational context for school-age children. Her essay offers a brief historical survey of Aristophanes in the Greek classroom and shows how Potamitis and Rouggeri creatively adapted Aristophanic plots so that they could be digested and understood by young minds. In the twenty-first century, Aristophanes remains popular with modern Greek and Cyprian artists, whose productions often respond to and reflect contemporary economic austerity and political crises. Zira tracks several "melancholic" productions of Aristophanes (including her own *Frogs*, staged in Cyprus in 2012), contending that "The artists involved wanted to bring into relief the dichotomy between dramatic poetry on the one hand and social disintegration on the other" (Zira 2020, 203).[9]

As Van Steen noted in *Venom in Verse*, educational institutions are places where the plays of Aristophanes are often mounted. Gamel's account of *The Julie Thesmo Show*, an adaptation of *Thesmophoriazusae* performed at the University of California, Santa Cruz (May 2000), and Case Western Reserve University in Cleveland, Ohio (February 2001), is riveting in the details and sets a standard for more rigorous theoretical analysis. Reflecting on the ephemerality of performance and the diversity of audience response, she concludes that "Awareness of such multiplicity and instability should temper sweeping assertions that seek to fix a single meaning on a script—whether

---

[8] Given the importance of these debates, perhaps Greenwood (2001) has a point: "Van Steen's refusal to attempt to understand 'Aristophanes per se' (p.10) means that many of the perspectives and insights of classicists who have written about Aristophanes remain unacknowledged or unexploited."
[9] See also Simpson (2008), who situates Mikis Theodorakis' "operatic" *Lysistrata* (Athens, 2002) in the contemporary context of the US invasion of Iraq and conflicts between Israel and Palestine.

that meaning is the intention behind the text or its effect on the audience" (Gamel 2002, 495–6).[10] While Anglophone case studies continue to be popular, one scholarly trend over the past 20 years is to look beyond established cultural centers (like educational institutions in Europe and North America) in order to chart Aristophanes' global receptions. In *Aristophanes in Performance*, Hall and Wrigley spotlight *Peace*, *Birds*, and *Frogs*, which were not necessarily Aristophanes' most popular comedies, but which "were known to have enjoyed longer and certainly more *varied* afterlives in performance since the Renaissance than Aristophanes' other plays" (Hall 2007, 3). In addition to tracking performances in North America and Britain, the book commits to a historical and cross-cultural focus. Case studies investigate and analyze performances in modern Greece, East Germany, South Africa, France, and Italy.

Edited collections with international foci have become more prominent, and two recent books, Olson's *Ancient Comedy and Reception* and van Zyl Smit's *A Handbook to the Reception of Greek Drama*, have contributed much to our understanding of the global Aristophanes. Interestingly, both volumes chart performances outside of the live theater and include radio adaptations, television, and cinema. In Olson's book, Wrigley describes mid-twentieth-century BBC Radio and Television performances of Aristophanes. She rightly notes that radio could reach a huge number of people compared to other media, but she stresses the cultural symbiosis between radio, the stage, and television, as well as print publications and higher education. Aristophanic comedy was a known quantity in Britain, and while the BBC productions were popular, they elicited a wide range of responses: "Listeners and viewers were interested, bored, enraged, and felt themselves to have been educated by these productions, a rich spectrum of engagement which testifies to the significance of mass media within the reception of Aristophanes" (Wrigley 2014, 870; see also Wrigley 2011, 2015).[11] However, his broad appeal – so evident in twentieth-century Britain and in Greece – did not necessarily translate to other countries and cultures. In van Zyl Smit's *Handbook*, Treu reports that due to fears of censorship or retribution Aristophanes was not popular in Fascist Italy (1922–43), and during the 1950s Aristophanes "was still an unwelcome guest in Syracuse and at other official festivals" (Treu 2016, 227). It was only in the 1990s that interest in performing Aristophanes gained momentum, under the influence of Italian playwright, director, and teacher, Marco Martinelli (see Treu 2007, 262–5). Sommerstein's *Encyclopedia of Greek Comedy*, though not an edited collection of essays, is a collaborative project with extensive entries on Aristophanes' ancient and modern performance and reception. The *Encyclopedia* presents surveys of modern productions divided by individual country (e.g., Israel), and linguistic groups (e.g., German-speaking counties), as well as by region, like Eastern Europe, where Aristophanic comedy was adapted as early as 1825 (*Knights* in Russia), but where (as in Belarus) it is still banned under censorship laws (Śmiechowicz 2019, 753–4).

Scholars and artists have long noted the challenges of translating and performing Aristophanic comedy. Perceptions of aggressive language, unrelenting ribaldry, and sexual antics have stymied interest in Aristophanes at different moments and in different cultures around the world. These tensions are especially felt in the Middle East and North Africa, where "it remains an open question to what extent Arab theater can accommodate Aristophanic comedy and recast it to so that it can be effective in modern Arab culture and can confront contemporary issues" (Almohanna 2019, 768). Nonetheless, limited appreciation for Aristophanic comedy emerged in the first half of twentieth century, and scholars have recently considered the work of Tawfiq Al-Hakim, an Egyptian playwright educated in Paris whose adaptation of *Ecclesiazusae*, *Braksa aw Muskilat al-Hukm* (*Praxa or The Problem of Ruling*), was performed at Damascus in 1960 (see Almohanna 2016;

---

[10] In a different study, Gamel considers the authenticity in the performance reception of ancient Greek drama and the challenges of Aristophanes' topical humor: "Aristophanes' plays challenge later producers because of their profusion of Athenian topical allusions. Substituting allusions to those a modern audience can understand... is the only way to create inductive authenticity" (Gamel (2010) 160). For more recent case studies of performance in an educational context, see Given and Rosen (2016) and Bullen (2020).

[11] Summarizing Aristophanes' importance in modern Greece, see Van Steen (2016b) 216: "Aristophanes, however, remained the one who consistently reached broader audiences than did any Classical tragedian, especially among the popular strata of Greek society."

Pormann 2014). In a stimulating evaluation of Al-Hakim and Aristophanes, Nooter sees two authors with "an abiding interest in confronting and reflecting the history of the genres to which they are contributing" (Nooter 2013, 141).[12] Al-Hakim, it seems, not only found inspiration in the plays of Aristophanes but also an identity – for himself and for a developing dramatic tradition in the Arab world.

With the advent of the internet and the explosion of digital media outlets, performances of Aristophanes can be experienced live and in person, but also documented, recorded, uploaded, commented on, and archived for posterity. Early insight into the performance history of Aristophanes was offered by the Archive of Performances of Greek and Roman Drama (APGRD), whose online presence includes a searchable productions database (see Marshall 2019, 74; Macintosh 2012). One entry, for example, details a performance of *The Acharnians* (2009) by Stanford Classics in Theater (SCIT), which has produced adaptations of Greek and Roman Comedy since its founding in 2008. SCIT maintains its own website, and for the performance of *Acharnians*, it has conveniently archived the translation used, the program, an advertising poster, and videos of selected scenes.[13] Describing itself as "part of a growing movement toward adapting and performing ancient theater for pedagogical, research, and entertainment purposes," the SCIT website, like the APGRD, represents a way to combat the ephemerality of the live theater (SCIT n.d.; see also SCIT 2015). Although watching a recording of a performance is certainly not the same as the magic of a live, in-person show, digital media preserves, catalogs, and allows access to the cultural frameworks, political contexts, and artistic inspirations of individuals actively engaged in interpreting Aristophanes at a specific time and place.

In March 2020, the COVID-19 pandemic and the ensuing global lockdowns prohibited communities from coming together for months on end, but this disruption created opportunities for innovative and (sometimes) international collaboration that would not have otherwise existed. The appropriately named Out of Chaos Theatre (UK), in partnership with Harvard University's Center for Hellenic Studies (CHS) and the Kosmos Society, conceived *Reading Greek Tragedy Online*, a project that hoped "to foster dialogues between actors and academics, and to create an educational resource for a wide range of students. . . to explore how we can make theatre online and in different spaces, and to build an international ensemble of performers" (Reading Greek Tragedy Online Project Background (n.d.); see also Barnes 2020). Tragedy, of course, was the main focus, but three plays of Aristophanes, *Clouds* (20 July 2020), *Assemblywomen* (27 October 2020), and *Frogs* (23 December 2020), were performed in the first season. Hosted by Professor Joel Christensen (Brandeis University), performances were held live online and later posted to the CHS's YouTube channel. For each episode, Christensen was joined by a guest expert, and after the readings participants would engage in thoughtful conversation about the play and its themes. For instance, at the end of *Frogs*, actor Tony Jayawardena, who played Dionysus (and previously Socrates in *Clouds*), reflected on the unique experience of performing on Zoom: "What is lovely is. . . working with people you've never met before, which is absolutely brilliant. What I absolutely love is how mixed we are as a group: men, women of all different ages, colors, sizes etc.. . . and it's been an absolute lifesaver for me in terms of lockdown." Credit goes to artistic director Paul O'Mahony, whom Christensen praised for intentional cross-casting "against age and typical expectations. It's been a powerful thing, and I think in the future when students look at these performances, it's going to rewrite some of our expectations" (*The Frogs, Aristophanes* (2021)). While it may be too soon to

---

[12] This idea substantiates her earlier claim for "reflective studies," not reception studies: ". . . to indicate the proposition that reception studies might be used to reflect more assertively our understanding of the classical texts themselves, even in their 'original' contexts, and to help us hear them better. I suggest that reception studies might be rethought as reflecting instead of receiving, and be constituted by explorations of how other peoples compose, produce and approach the theatre in ways that are analogous to how fifth-century Athenians engaged in these activities" (Nooter (2013) 139).

[13] SCIT has done the same for other adaptations of Aristophanes: *Clouds* (2010), *Wasps* (2011), *Women on Top* [*Ecclesiazusae*] (2012), *Nerds* [*Birds*] (2015), *The Republican Party in Pieces: A Comedy in Fragments* [includes Aristophanes' *Banqueters*] (2016), and *Men's Rites: An Alt-Comedy* [*Thesmophoriazusae*] (2017).

measure the ultimate significance of *Reading Greek Tragedy Online*, its organizers took the initiative to build an inclusive, human community in response to a shared experience of loneliness and disconnection. At the same time, their performances were critical interventions, challenging traditional notions of Aristophanic comedy and empowering actors who could bring new perspectives and identities to their roles.

One lesson from studying the modern reception of Aristophanes is that many societies turn to the Aristophanic corpus during crisis, revolution, and catastrophe, but since the end of the nineteenth century, *Lysistrata* has dominated the popular imagination. For some, the play is fascinating because it is a satirical time capsule of the city of Athens during the Peloponnesian War. For others, its dual plots are outrageous and funny; its heroine, memorable, resolute, and charismatic. Its reputation as a raucous peace play or as a proto-feminist play attracts eager audiences; its potential for "productive misreadings" allows for malleability in performance (Revermann 2010, 71). Foremost in the effort to document and explain the modern performance history of *Lysistrata* has been Marina Kotzamani, who has written about the play in several different contexts. She describes a 1923 Soviet production for Moscow Art Theatre's Musical Studio, as "Perhaps the most remarkable political interpretation of *Lysistrata* in the twentieth century. . . an exemplary model of the new revolutionary theatre. . . the official representative of state policy on culture at the time" (Kotzamani 2005, 79).[14] This modernist adaptation was well received when it came to New York City in 1925, and it served as a model for Gilbert Seldes' Broadway production of *Lysistrata* directed by Norman Bel Geddes (1930). Kotzamani notes that the political climates out of which these two adaptations emerged were very different, distinguishing the Seldes *Lysistrata* as "distinctly American in its capitalist ideological orientation." While the Soviet adaptation de-emphasizes Lysistrata's independence, the American version "magnifies and idealizes" Lysistrata as a powerful leader (Kotzamani 2014, 812, 811).[15]

Like Koun's *Birds*, Seldes' *Lysistrata* maintained its popularity in the years after its debut. In 1946, it re-ran on Broadway with an all-black cast (including the young actor Sidney Poitier) but closed after four performances. Ten years earlier, in Seattle, Washington, the Negro Repertory Company (NRC), also an all-black company, held one performance of *Lysistrata of Aristophanes: An African Version* before it was shut down over concerns about the show's "themes of activist resistance and political overthrow," not to mention "entrenched white anxieties about black sexuality and power" (Klein 2014, 43, 44; see also Hill 2015). According to Wetmore, *Lysistrata* is the only Aristophanic comedy to be adapted in an African-American context and suggests that interest derives from the play's concern with "sexual power, [and] the ability of the disenfranchised (women in ancient Athens, women of color in contemporary America) to use what power they have to affect the political process" (Wetmore 2014, 788).

While American adaptations of *Lysistrata* tend to highlight the potential of an individual (woman) enacting political change, contemporary Arabic responses to the play present a bleak, circumscribed vision. Kotzamani, after interviewing several theater practitioners from Egypt, Palestine, and Morocco about how they would stage the play, explains that their proposals "focus on exploring, in sophisticated ways, the power dynamics preventing the underprivileged to express themselves freely and to have political influence." For artists like the Egyptian Lenin El-Ramly, whose adaptation of *Lysistrata*, *Salam El-Nisaa (Peace of Women)* was performed in Cairo in December 2004, Aristophanes becomes "a political author of postcolonial or alternative views, that is, as an author going against the mainstream, or the Western mainstream" (Kotzamani 2006, 18; see also Hardwick 2010; Robson 2016). In wondering what it means to stage *Lysistrata* for Arabic

---

[14] See also Given (2015) 305–7, who describes the influence of Constructivism on set design and the synthetic theater on the play's psychological realism.
[15] Klein concludes her chapter on Seldes' *Lysistrata* by situating the play in the context of American politics: "While he did not take up the new and emerging concerns of the Depression in his adaptation, he did bring innovation to the Great White Way. Representing the intersections of bodies at war and bodily desire on a mainstream stage was part of Seldes' grand effort to democratize American culture. By helping to parse questions about gender roles and the cost of war still lingering from the last decade, he readied the cultural scene for a more aggressively political theatrical climate that would dominate the 1930s" (Klein (2014) 42).

audiences, Kotzamani was responding to the well-known Lysistrata Project (2003), which originated in the United States to protest the Iraq War, but which reached 59 countries and hundreds of thousands of people. In evaluating the nature of the Project, Dutsch highlights the "reterritorialization" of the play, which "turned away from the play's topical ancient Greek implications. . . recasting the *Lysistrata* in terms of modern ideologies" (Dutsch 2015, 576).

Rosa Andújar is certainly aware of the diverse readings/misreadings of *Lysistrata* over the past century. In her evaluation of Francisco Arriví's *Club de Solteros* (*Bachelor's Club*, 1951–3), she cites Revermann's notion of a "productive misreading," as well as Morales' contention that "*Lysistrata* has become the go-to trope for any women's activism involving the withdrawal of sex" (Morales 2013, 284). Andújar identifies "the modern Lysistrata paradigm" as "Wholly focused on the aggressive actions of the protesting women. . . [and] fundamentally uninterested in any nuanced dynamics between men and women, unlike the ancient play which crucially features a chorus divided by gender while performing various versions of both masculinity and femininity." Arriví's adaptation, which is relatively unknown even in his native Puerto Rico, inverts the paradigm by staging a sex strike organized by men. This was an interesting choice because Arriví "refocuses the absurdity and the misogyny of the ancient, features that are often lost or de-emphasized in modern adaptations" (Andújar 2020, 137–8). At the same time, the play, which was written and performed at a time when Puerto Rico was again struggling with its identity as the US commonwealth, reflects modern tensions and volatile emotions.

Andújar ends her essay on *Club de Solteros* by considering "whether Aristophanic comedies can continue to address fraught political situations in modernity" (Andújar 2020, 143).[16] For many countries and cultures, even those with a modest tradition of performing Aristophanic comedy, the answer is yes, because performances make tangible abstract ideas about democracy, war, peace, and gender relations. However, as this survey has suggested, the question of "Why Aristophanes?" remains, with any "answer" revealing deep-seated cultural assumptions about what is funny, what is beautiful, what is wise, what is acceptable, what is political, what is canonical, and what is true. As for new avenues of research, the global pandemic has accelerated social, political, and educational trends, and scholars should pay careful attention to what roles and applications that technology can and will have in performances of Aristophanic comedy. Physical spaces that support live performance will remain vital, but what of virtual spaces? What of social media? What of the emerging metaverse? Will *Lysistrata* continue to dominate stages? Or will another play emerge as global circumstances change? These are just some of the questions that will animate thinking about performance and reception of Aristophanes in the years to come.

Process, Not Perfection: An Integrated Arts Performance in the Era of COVID-19

When I first envisioned bringing Aristophanic comedy to St. Andrew's School, an all-boarding high school in Middletown, DE, I imagined an integrated art project that would be performed in front of a live audience.[17] In late 2019, I began brainstorming with faculty colleagues in the arts, and

---

[16] See also Ford, who studies Franklin Domínguez's *Lisístrata odia la política* (*Lysistrata Hates Politics*, 1981), a prize-winning adaptation from the Dominican Republic: "With *Lisístrata odia la política*, Domínguez challenges the ideas of who is included within the Western canon and forces the reader-spectator to rethink definitions of identity. Ironically, like the source text, he does this within the parameters of these definitions, which is precisely why he is effective" (Ford (2020) 145–6).

[17] I would like to thank my faculty colleagues, Avi Gold, Fred Geiersbach, Navanjali Kelsey, Erin Ferguson, Ashley Hyde, and Ann Taylor, who contributed in large ways and small to the success of *7 Wilde Clouds*. I am also grateful to the high school students who were involved in this project as musicians, readers, dancers, and artists: Zadoc B., Piper J., Leila W., Adelaide D., Pearl M., Elizabeth R., Will D., Javier I., Jake K., Kyle S., Daniel K., and Julian P.

although we realized that a full-scale production of an Aristophanic play was too big a project to take on, we were committed to engaging with "fragments" of Aristophanes: a few staged readings, with students working from significant English translations; a choreographed, theatrical dance routine, with accompanying music and scene design; and interpretative media like a playbill and a promotional poster that would reflect the themes of our project. Our pedagogical objectives were straightforward: (1) to introduce Aristophanic comedy to students of ancient Greek and Latin, as well as the broader school community; (2) to engage participating students in creative, collaborative, interdisciplinary work; and (3) to include students in the research process by having them assist with interviews, read relevant scholarship, and interact with subject matter experts.

In February 2020, my first sustained conversation was with Avi Gold, Director of Dance at St. Andrew's, and given our mutual appreciation for Oscar Wilde, we decided to anchor the dance portion of the project around Wilde's "Chorus of Cloud Maidens" (1874–5), a verse translation of *Clouds* 275–90 and 298–313. Published in *Dublin University Magazine* (November 1875), Wilde's translation indicates (in Greek) that the lines come from Aristophanes' *Clouds*, but he detaches the strophe and antistrophe from the original context of the play. His translation, therefore, is a fragment of a pagan past, a poem that celebrates physical beauty, the natural world, and the magnificent city of Athens.[18] In order to showcase the talents of our ancient Greek students, we planned to record them reading Aristophanes' Greek and Wilde's translation. We also hoped to collaborate

---

[18] See Walsh (2016a) 227–8. Wilde's translation is below:

"Chorus of Cloud Maidens"
Στρόφη
  Cloud-maidens that float on forever,
  Dew-sprinkled, fleet bodies, and fair,
  Let us rise from our Sire's loud river,
  Great Ocean, and soar through the air
To the peaks of the pine-covered mountains where the
  pines hang as tresses of hair!
  Let us seek the watch-towers undaunted,
    Where the well-watered cornfields abound,
And thro murmurs of rivers nymph-haunted
    The songs of the sea-waves resound;
  And the sun in the sky never wearies of spreading his
  radiance around!
  Let us cut off the haze
    Of the mists from our band,
  Till with far-seeing gaze
    We may look on the land!
Ἀντιστροφη
  Cloud-maidens that bring the rain-shower,
    To the Pallas-loved land let us wing,
  To the land of stout heroes and Power,
    Where Kekrops was hero and king,
  Where honour and silence is given
    To the mysteries that none may declare,
  Where the gifts to the high gods in heaven
    When the house of the gods is laid bare,
  Where are lofty-rooft temples and statues well-carven and fair;
    Where are feasts to the happy immortals
  When the sacred procession draws near,
    Where garlands make bright the bright portals
  At all seasons and months of the year;
    And when Spring days are here,
  Then we tread to the wine-god a measure
    In Bacchanal dance and in pleasure,
  'Mid the contests of sweet-singing choirs,
    And the crash of loud lyres!

with students and faculty proficient in other languages by having them recite translations of *Clouds* in order to demonstrate Aristophanes' varied reception history through time and space. Those recordings, paired with original music, would serve as a backdrop to the student dancers, and we had ideas for elaborate costuming, stage designs, and lighting effects. We were very excited to get started, with the goal of weekend performances in May 2020, but that initial meeting was the last time that I would see Avi in person for several months. The COVID-19 pandemic and ensuing lockdown sent our students home and disrupted our plans. Realizing that we would not be able to utilize an indoor theater for the foreseeable future and unsure about our school schedule, I began thinking about how we could create a physically distanced and asynchronous arts project that would tell a meaningful story about Aristophanic comedy.

Inspired by the Center for Hellenic Studies' *Reading Greek Tragedy Online* (see above), Avi and I decided to pivot to digital media as a way to assemble and integrate the fragments of dance, drama, music, and visual art. Instead of rehearsing for a live performance in a theater space, we would instead focus on an incremental creative process that would take place over the entire academic year. We were confident about delivering an arts-rich and student-centered learning experience, but questions remained: How could we thoughtfully introduce Aristophanes' *Clouds* while students were at home or physically distanced on campus? Given the harsh realities of the pandemic, would we be able to accomplish what we intended? What would be lost, but more importantly, what insights could be gained? Finally, we thought about a question that perhaps Aristophanes himself considered: What is the power of art in a time of crisis and catastrophe?

We were fortunate that St. Andrew's was able to reconvene in-person classes in the fall of 2020. Immediately, Avi and I connected with Fred Geiersbach, our school's Director of Instrumental Music. That fall, Fred was teaching a semester-long introductory music theory course with four talented students, and he relished the opportunity to learn about Aristophanic comedy and to reexamine the ancient Greek modes. He built the arts project directly into his course: in December 2020, as a final assessment, his students read Wilde's "Chorus of Cloud Maidens," and then composed music based on their understanding of the translation. They also engaged in a question-and-answer session with my ancient Greek students who listened and responded to each piece. One of the student musicians, Javier I., inventively picked up on the idea of the "Chorus," created several guitar tracks, and digitally placed them and the sound of rippling water on top of one another. What results is a slow play of reverberation, euphony, and dissonance; moody, peaceful, mysterious, and replete with sound, the piece captures the stylized beauty of Aristophanes' original song.[19]

While the music theory students were working on their compositions, students in my ancient Greek classes learned about Old Comedy and carefully examined the entrance hymn of the Clouds. We talked about elements of meter, diction, and dramatic setting, and students read and reread the lines aloud in ancient Greek. To provide context to our work, students watched and then wrote responses to the CHS production of *Clouds*; in addition, they connected virtually with Professor Matthew Farmer (Haverford College), who presented a slide deck on Old Comedy, focusing on the festival context of the Athenian theater, and utilizing vase paintings to suggest the boisterous physicality of Aristophanic comedy. Responding to Prof. Farmer's lecture and the CHS *Clouds*, one of my Greek students, Elizabeth R., decided to draw a charcoal of Socrates (Figure 27.1). Initially, we thought that we would use her artwork to advertise our project, but once we committed to digital media, we decided to incorporate her drawing at the open and close of the video. With the help of visual arts teacher, Navanjali Kelsey, Elizabeth meticulously sketched her Socrates based on a sculpture bust of the ancient philosopher. She worked for several weeks, and the final product, with its haunting contrast of light and shadow, reminds the viewer of Socrates' prominent role in Aristophanes' play. In the digital video, Avi added two effects that represent important themes of the project: floating stone fragments that seem to break off the image of Socrates; and colorful clouds that pass through, in, and around the ancient philosopher.

---

[19] See the following link to hear this track (featured at the beginning through 2:35) and to watch *7 Wilde Clouds*: https://youtu.be/-vsqJmqF6Eg. The video includes all four student compositions, as well as a fifth by another St. Andrew's student, who heard about our project, independently composed a piece, and submitted it for use.

Figure 27.1 Elizabeth Rainey, *Socrates*. Print. Source: From Matt Troutman.

As for the name of our project, we decided on *7 Wilde Clouds*, with the number 7 representing the different languages that we hoped to spotlight: the ancient Greek original (c. 420 BCE), as well as translations into Latin (Nicodemus Frischlin, c. 1586), French (Anne Dacier, 1684), German (Johann Gustav Droysen, 1835), English (Oscar Wilde, 1874–5), modern Greek (Georgios Souris, 1910), and Russian (Adrian Ivanovich Piotrovsky, 1970). We successfully recruited students and faculty to record themselves reading in all of these different languages, with the exception of French, but we kept the number 7 by including both Wilde's English strophe and antistrophe.[20] With the music, charcoal drawing, and voice recordings completed, we turned to choreograph a dancing sequence, film it, and produce the video, but because of scheduling challenges and indoor physical distancing protocols, we waited until May of 2021 ("when Spring days are here," as Wilde writes) to record outside. For a dancing space, we utilized St. Andrew's labyrinth, a verdant, circular area nestled in a quiet spot on campus. It seemed to invoke something of the ancient Greek *orchestra* and captured the majestic beauty of Wilde's translation. We featured two dancers, Leila W. and Zadoc B., and they performed two routines that we interspersed in the editing process. The first was improvisational: a dance with smoke torches, highlighting flow and movement in a three-dimensional space. In the video, we manipulated time, speed, and color, and we experimented with augmented reality by adding an ancient temple in the background. The effects achieve a sense of timelessness; at 6:22, for instance, images of Leila are blended so that she moves forward and backward at the same time ("Cloud-maidens that float on forever"). The second routine, independently choreographed by Zadoc, was linear, two-dimensional, and playful in its poses. When filming, we used a 360-degree camera to manipulate the world, creating an Aristophanic, "topsy turvy" effect while the dancers performed in the labyrinth.

In sum, we believe that *7 Wilde Clouds* was a successful experiment in performance pedagogy – not in a traditional or linear sense but in a way that honored the creative process and confirmed the

---

[20] The final version of the integrated arts project includes versions of the strophe in English, ancient Greek, and Latin, and versions of the antistrophe in English, German, Russian, and modern Greek.

importance of cross-disciplinary collaboration. Our initial pedagogical objectives were met, and we gained insight into how highly visual and esthetically beautiful Aristophanic comedy can be. The students involved in this project demonstrated passion, curiosity, initiative, content knowledge, and resilience. They did not have the chance to perform in front of a live audience, but they took great personal satisfaction from what they learned and created. It was, after all, the journey that mattered, a journey that connects them to all who revive Aristophanic comedy. In the epilog of *Venom in Verse*, Van Steen concludes that "Aristophanes has been essential to Greek survival, knowledge, and self-knowledge" (Van Steen 2000, 224). During the global pandemic, the plays of Aristophanes have played a similar role for students at St. Andrew's School; for the actors, organizers, and audiences of *Reading Greek Tragedy Online*; and for other individuals and communities who have chosen to make Aristophanic comedy new. Our answer to the question "Why Aristophanes?" was simple: the rituals of art brought communities together, threading past and present, and providing hopeful visions of the future.

GUIDE TO FURTHER READING

The work of Van Steen (2000) remains an invaluable starting place for modern performance and reception studies of Aristophanes. Davis (2008) and Schechner (2020) offer helpful overviews of the field of performance studies and its interdisciplinary methodologies. The edited collections of Hall and Wrigley (2007); Stuttard (2010), Olson (2014), Bosher et al. (2015), Walsh (2016b), van Zyl Smit (2016), and Andújar and Nikoloutsos (2020) include many interesting case studies of performance, translation, and adaptation. The information gathered by Sommerstein (2019) is a roadmap for future work on Aristophanes' global reception.

REFERENCES

Almohanna, M. (2016). Greek drama in the Arab world. In: *A Handbook to the Reception of Greek Drama* (ed. B. van Zyl Smit), 364–381. Malden, MA, Oxford, Chichester: Wiley–Blackwell.

Almohanna, M. (2019). Productions, modern (Middle East and North Africa). In: *The Encyclopedia of Greek Comedy* (ed. Sommerstein), 768. Wiley.

Andújar, R. (2020). Distorting the *Lysistrata* Paradigm in Puerto Rico: Francisco's Arriví's *Club de Solteros*. In: *Greeks and Romans on the Latin American Stage* (ed. Andújar and Nikoloutsos), 131–143. Bloomsbury Academic.

Andújar, R. and Nikoloutsos, K.P. (ed.) (2020). *Greeks and Romans on the Latin American Stage*. London: Bloomsbury Academic.

Barnes, C. (2020), "Reading Greek tragedy online: a podcast with Paul O'Mahony, Joel Christensen, and Lanah Koelle," APGRD Podcast 5. <http://www.apgrd.ox.ac.uk/sites/default/files/podcast-transcript-episode-5.pdf>

Bosher, K., Macintosh, F., McConnell, J., and Rankine, P. (ed.) (2015). *The Oxford Handbook of Greek Drama in the Americas*. Oxford: Oxford University Press.

Bullen, D. (2020). Saving classics with the clouds: a case study in adapting Aristophanes. In: *Aristophanic Humour: Theory and Practice* (ed. P. Swallow and E. Hall), 205–214. Bloomsbury Academic.

Cartledge, P. (2020). Afterword: the Boy from Cydathenaeum some concluding reflections. In: *Aristophanes and Politics: New Studies* (ed. R. Rosen and H.P. Foley), 273–278. Brill.

Davis, T.C. (ed.) (2008). *The Cambridge Companion to Performance Studies*. Cambridge, UK: Cambridge University Press.

Dutsch, D. (2015). Democratic appropriations: *Lysistrata* and political activism. In: *The Oxford Handbook of Greek Drama in the Americas* (ed. K. Bosher, F. Macintosh, J. McConnell, and P. Rankine), 575–594. Oxford: Oxford University Press.

Ford, K. (2020). Challenging the Canon in the Dominican Republic: Lisístrata odia la política by Franklin Domínguez. In: *Greeks and Romans on the Latin American Stage* (ed. Andújar and Nikoloutsos), 145–156. Bloomsbury Academic.

Gamel, M.K. (2002). From *Thesmophoriazousai* to 'The Julie Thesmo Show': adaptation, performance, reception. *American Journal of Philology* 123: 465–499.

Gamel, M.K. (2010). Revising 'Authenticity' in staging ancient Mediterranean Drama. In: *Theorising Performance: Greek Drama, Cultural History, and Critical Practice* (ed. E. Hall and S. Harrop), 153–170. London, UK: Duckworth.

Given, J. (2015). Aristophanic comedy in American Musical Theater, 1925–1969. In: *The Oxford Handbook of Greek Drama in the Americas* (ed. K. Bosher, F. Macintosh, J. McConnell, and P. Rankine), 301–332. Oxford Univeristy Press.

Given, J. and Rosen, R.M. (2016). Teaching Aristophanes in the American college classroom. In: *Brill's Companion to the Reception of Aristophanes* (ed. Walsh), 88–108. Brill.

Greenwood, E.J.M. (2001). Venom in Verse: Aristophanes in Modern Greece. *Bryn Mawr Classical Review* <https://bmcr.brynmawr.edu/2001/2001.08.05/>

Hall, E. (2007). Introduction: Aristophanic laughter across the centuries. In: (ed. E. Hall and A. Wrigley), 1–29. London: Legenda.

Hall, E. and Wrigley, A. (ed.) (2007). *Aristophanes in Performance, 421 BC-AD 2007.* London: Legenda.

Hardwick, L. (2010), *Lysistrata*s on the modern stage, In: *Looking at Lysistrata: Eight Essays and a New Version of Aristophanes' Provocative Comedy* (ed. D. Stuttard), 80–90. Bloomsbury Academic.

Hill, L.M. (2015). A new stage of laughter for Zora Neale Hurston and Theodore Browne: *Lysistrata* and the negro units of the federal theatre project. In: *The Oxford Handbook of Green Drama in the Americas* (ed. K. Bosher, F. Macintosh, J. McConnell, and P. Rankine), 286–300. New York: Oxford University Press.

Holtermann, M. (2004). *Der deutsche Aristophanes: die Rezeption eines politischen Dichters im 19. Jahrhundert.* Hypomnemata 155, Göttingen.

Kiritsi, S. (2016). Aristophanes, education, and performance in modern Greece. In: *Brill's Companion to the Reception of Aristophanes* (ed. Walsh), 67–87. Brill.

Klein, E. (2014). *Sex and War on the American Stage: Lysistrata in Performance 1930-2012.* New York.

Kotzamani, M. (2000). Venom in Verse (review). *Journal of Modern Greek Studies* 18 (2): 453–455.

Kotzamani, M. (2005). Lysistrata joins the soviet revolution: Aristophanes as engaged theatre. In: *Rebel Women: Staging Ancient Greek Drama Today* (ed. J. Dillon and S.E. Wilmer), 78–111. London, UK.

Kotzamani, M. (2006). Lysistrata on the arabic stage. *PAJ: A Journal of Performance and Art* 28: 13–41.

Kotzamani, M. (2014). Lysistrata on broadway. In: *Ancient comedy and reception: essays in honor of Jeffrey Henderson* (ed. S.D. Olson), 807–824. Berlin, Boston (MA): De Gruyter.

Macintosh, F. (2012). Museums, archives and collecting. In: *The Cambridge Companion to Theatre History* (ed. D. Wiles and C. Dymkowski), 267–280. UK: Cambridge.

Marshall, C.W. (2019). Archive of performances of Greek and roman drama. In: (ed. Sommerstein), 74.

Michelakis, P. (2002). G.A.H. Van Steen: Venom in Verse: Aristophanes in Modern Greece. *The Classical Review* 52 (1): 199–200.

Mitchell, A. (2016). Classical reception in posters of *Lysistrata*: the visual debate between traditional and feminist imagery. In: (ed. Walsh), 331–368.

Morales, H. (2013). Aristophanes' *Lysistrata*, the Liberian 'Sex Strike', and the Politics of Reception. *Greece & Rome* 60: 281–295.

Nooter, S. (2013). Reception studies and questions of identity in Aristophanes and Tawfiq Al Hakim. *Ramus, Special Issue: New Approaches to Greek Drama* 42 (1–2): 138–161.

Olson, S.D. (ed.) (2014). *Ancient Comedy and Reception: Essays in Honor of Jeffrey Henderson.* Boston.

Osborne, R. (2020). Politics and laughter: the case of Aristophanes' Knights. In: *Aristophanes and Politics: New Studies* (ed. Rosen and Foley), 24–44. Brill.

Piana, R. (2005). La réception d'Aristophane en France de Palissot à Vitez, 1760–1962. Diss. Université Paris VIII.

Pormann, P.E. (2014). Arabs and Aristophanes, Menander among the Muslims: Greek humour in the Medieval and Modern Middle East. *International Journal of the Classical Tradition* 21 (1): 1–29.

Porter, J.I. (2008). Reception studies: future prospects. In: *A Companion to Classical Receptions* (ed. L. Hardwick and C. Stray), 469–481. UK: Oxford.

Reading Greek Tragedy Online Project Background (n.d.). Website. <https://chs.harvard.edu/programs/reading-greek-tragedy-online/#background%22>

Revermann, M. (2010). On misunderstanding the *Lysistrata*, productively. In: *Looking at Lysistrata: Eight Essays and a New Version of Aristophanes' Provocative Comedy* (ed. Stuttard), 70–79. Bloomsbury Academic.

Robson, J. (2016). Aristophanes, gender, and sexuality. In: *Brill's Companion to the Reception of Aristophanes* (ed. Walsh), 44–66. Brill.

Rosen, R.M. (2020). Prolegomena: accessing and understanding Aristophanic politics. In: *Brill's Companion to the Reception of Aristophanes* (ed. Rosen and Foley), 9–23. Brill.

Schechner, R. (2020). *Performance Studies: An Introduction*, 4e. New York: Routledge.
SCIT (2015). Adapting Aristophanes in Silicon Valley. *Eidolon* December 28.
SCIT, (n.d.), Archive Website. Accessed 12 August 2021. https://scit.stanford.edu/archive.html.
Simpson, A.E. (2008). Against Whatever War: Mikis Theodorakis' Operatic *Lysistrata*. *Syllecta Classica* 19: 203–219.
Śmiechowicz, O. (2019). Productions, modern (Eastern Europe). In: *The Encyclopedia of Greek Comedy* (ed. Sommerstein), 753–755. Wiley.
Sommerstein, A.H. (ed.) (2019). *The Encyclopedia of Greek Comedy*. Medford.
Stuttard, D. (ed.) (2010). *Looking at Lysistrata: Eight Essays and a New Version of Aristophanes' Provocative Comedy*. London: Bloomsbury.
The Acharnians (2009), Website. Accessed 15 August 2021. http://www.apgrd.ox.ac.uk/productions/production/10919
The Frogs, Aristophanes (2021, 23 December), Tony Jayawardena and Joel Christensen in conversation [1,10:10-1:11:29]. YouTube. <https://www.youtube.com/watch?v=LHh4G2NeEjA>
Treu, M. (2007). Poetry and politics, advice and abuse: the Aristophanic chorus on the Italian stage. In: *Aristophanes in Performance, 421 BC–AD 2007* (ed. Hall and Wrigley), 255–266. London: Legenda.
Treu, M. (2016). The history of ancient Drama in modern Italy. In: *A Handbook to the Reception of Greek Drama* (ed. van Zyl Smit), 221–237. Wiley.
Van Steen, G.A.H. (2000). *Venom in Verse: Aristophanes in Modern Greece*. Princeton.
Van Steen, G.A.H. (2002). Trying (on) gender: modern Greek productions of Aristophanes'. Thesmophoriazusae. *American Journal of Philology* 123: 407–427.
Van Steen, G.A.H. (2007a). Politics and Aristophanes: watchword 'Caution!'. In: *The Cambridge Companion to Greek and Roman Theatre* (ed. M. McDonald and J.M. Walton), 108–123. Cambridge, UK: Cambridge University Press.
Van Steen, G.A.H. (2007b). From scandal to success story: Aristophanes' birds as staged by Karolos Koun. In: *Aristophanes in Performance, 421 BC–AD 2007* (ed. Hall and Wrigley), 155–178. Legenda.
Van Steen, G.A.H. (2014a). Snapshots of Aristophanes and Menander: from spontaneous reception to belated reception study. In: *The Cambridge Companion to Greek Comedy* (ed. M. Revermann), 433–450. Cambridge, UK: Cambridge University Press.
Van Steen, G.A.H. (2014b). Close encounters of the comic kind: Aristophanes' *Frogs* and *Lysistrata* in Athenian Mythological Burlesques of the 1880s. In: *Ancient Comedy and Reception: Essays in Honor of Jeffrey Henderson* (ed. Olson), 747–761. De Gruyter.
Van Steen, G.A.H. (2016a). Comedy and Tragedy in Agon(y): The 1902 Comedy *Panathenaia* of Andreas Nikolaras. In: *Brill's Companion to the Reception of Aristophanes* (ed. Walsh), 240–262. Brill.
Van Steen, G.A.H. (2016b). Greece: a history of turns, traditions, and transformations. In: *A Handbook to the Reception of Greek Drama* (ed. van Zyl Smit), 201–220. Wiley.
Van Steen, G.A.H. (2019). Production, modern (Greece and Cyprus). In: *The Encyclopedia of Greek Comedy* (ed. Sommerstein), 762–764. Wiley.
Walsh, P. (2008), "Comedy and Conflict: The Modern Reception of Aristophanes," Diss. Brown University.
Walsh, P. (2009). A study in reception: the British debates over Aristophanes' politics and influence. *Classical Receptions Journal* 1: 55–72.
Walsh, P. (2016a). The verbal and the visual: Aristophanes' nineteenth-century English translators. In: *Brill's Companion to the Reception of Aristophanes* (ed. Walsh), 217–239. Brill.
Walsh, P. (ed.) (2016b). *Brill's Companion to the Reception of Aristophanes*. Leiden/Boston: Brill.
Wetmore, K. (2014). She (Don't) Gotta Have It: African-American Reception of *Lysistrata*. In: *Ancient Comedy and Reception: Essays in Honor of Jeffrey Henderson* (ed. Olson), 786–796. De Gruyter.
Wrigley, A. (2011). *Performing Greek Drama in Oxford and on Tour with the Balliol Players*. Exeter.
Wrigley, A. (2014). Aristophanes at the BBC, 1940s–1960s. In: *Ancient Comedy and Reception: Essays in Honor of Jeffrey Henderson* (ed. Olson), 849–870. De Gruyter.
Wrigley, A. (2015). *Greece on Air: Engagements with Ancient Greece on BBC Radio, 1920s–1960s*. Oxford.
Zira, M. (2020). *Melancholia* and Laughter: Modern Greek productions of aristophanes in the twenty-first century. In: *Aristophanic Humour: Theory and Practice* (ed. Swallow and Hall), 193–204. Bloomsbury Academic.
van Zyl Smit, B. (ed.) (2016). *A Handbook to the Reception of Greek Drama*. Malden: Wiley Blackwell.

CHAPTER 28

Teaching Aristophanes

Elizabeth Scharffenberger

Comedy Tonight![1]

Let me acknowledge straightaway the provisional nature of the ideas about teaching shared in this essay. As Plato's Socrates points out (*Phaedrus* 275d–276a), a piece of writing cannot replicate a face-to-face conversation, which would let us get acquainted and give me the chance to offer individually tailored suggestions. There are so many contexts in which you could be teaching and so many variables we might want to consider: the type of course you are teaching ("Gen Ed" Humanities? literature survey? drama? myth? gender and sexuality? ancient history? comedy?), its format (discussion? lecture? performance workshop?), and the level of your students (high school? college? graduate?). We might even want to talk about your school and its culture, and also your region and its culture and politics. These factors are trickier to reckon with, because we cannot read them off like a course title, such as "Survey of Greek Literature 101" or "Ancient Athenian Democracy" or "Drama Through the Ages." But they can matter, since conditions in your instructional environment as well as your local community's standards may influence how you teach Aristophanes.

Also worth noting is the fact that Aristophanes can play different roles in different types of courses. Indeed, the wonderful thing about his comedies is that they lend themselves to being enjoyed in many contexts and also to exploring many phenomena, topics, and questions. If you want to focus on the special features and appeal of comic imagination and fantasy, the various items in the toolbox of comedy and humor (e.g., exaggeration, distortion, fantasy, caricature, parody, irony, distancing, wordplay, sight gags, slapstick), or the social and psychological effects of humor and laughter, what better case study is there than a play by Aristophanes? Students of playwrighting and creative writing can learn a lot by unpacking how Aristophanes manipulates features of plot, theme, characterization, song, dance, visual spectacle, and verbal echoing. Alternatively, your focus could be historically oriented, and your aim could be to gain insight into the distribution of political, social, and economic privileges in classical Athens/Attica[2]; or constructions of identity according to gender, age, legal status, social standing, area of residence, occupation, and nationality; or the expression of social anxieties and prejudices; or practices relating to labor, property, and enslavement; or the conventions of prominent forms of public discourse ranging from political

---

[1] The opening number of Stephen Sondheim's *A Funny Thing Happened on the Way to the Forum* (1962).
[2] Whereas local communities ("demes") in the peninsula of Attica had some political independence, Athens was the urban center of the city-state (*polis*). Hence, the city-state comprising the Attic peninsula is generally referred to as "Athens," which gives rise to phrases such as "Athenian democracy." The adjectives "Athenian" and Attic," however, are often used interchangeably to describe drama, vase painting, religious festivals, and the calendar.

A Companion to Aristophanes, First Edition. Edited by Matthew C. Farmer and Jeremy B. Lefkowitz.
© 2024 John Wiley & Sons, Inc. Published 2024 by John Wiley & Sons, Inc.

speech to poetry. You might be interested as well in the reception and reconfiguration of traditional myths and legends in the fifth century BCE, or even aspects of practice and participation in the many religious festivals and rituals of the Athenian city-state (*polis*). In that case, Aristophanic comedies will be welcome additions to your syllabus, because they offer perspectives that add nuance to the information we derive from other sources handed down from antiquity.

To keep this essay's project manageable, I am adopting the following parameters for imagining the circumstances that prompt you to seek out someone else's thoughts about teaching Aristophanes. You are teaching Aristophanes in translation at the college level to students who do not know how to read Greek. Your course is "generalist": a survey of literature or drama or comedy, or a course on myth, history, politics, or gender. You need to keep moving through the syllabus and therefore do not have a lot of time to devote to any one play or to Aristophanes in general. You are also interested in encouraging discussion among your students and finding other ways of engaging them. You probably do not read Greek. Even if you do, you are not a specialist in Attic drama of the classical period.

Since presenting meaningful pedagogical suggestions about multiple dramas is not feasible in a short essay, I focus on *Lysistrata*, which is the most commonly taught comedy.[3] My hope is that, even though my suggestions for preparatory assignments, discussion questions, in-class exercises, essay topics, and creative projects are oriented toward this one comedy, you will be able to adapt them to work for others. And I hope that, even if you find yourself in disagreement with me about one thing (or many!), you will find something useful in my suggestions.

In the Background (General)

You will want to be aware of the basics concerning the performance conditions of dramas during the classical period in the Theater of Dionysus on the southern slope of the Athenian Acropolis. In addition to the essays on "Aristophanes the Poet" in the first section of this volume, Csapo/Slater (1994) is a comprehensive scholarly resource for what we know – and do not know – concerning the annual religious festivals in Athens (the "Great Dionysia," which is sometimes referred to as the "City Dionysia," and the "Lenaea") that honored the god Dionysus and at which dramas were performed. Csapo/Slater also surveys information about the physical footprint(s) of the Theater of Dionysus, the processes by which dramas were selected for the "awarding of choruses" and paid for by well-to-do citizens obliged to serve as *choregoi* ("producers"), actors and choruses, costuming and staging conventions, judging and the awarding of prizes, the transmission of the texts from antiquity, and much else. There are many other sources of information to which you might turn, such as the Wikipedia pages on "Theatre of Ancient Greece" (https://en.wikipedia.org/wiki/Theatre_of_ancient_Greece) and "Theater of Dionysus" (https://en.wikipedia.org/wiki/Theatre_of_Dionysus). Not all Wikipedia pages are consistent and reliable, but these two are well composed, with up-to-date references and helpful links to other sites. Departments of Classics, Theater, and other disciplines at many colleges and universities also have publicly accessible webpages devoted to Attic drama, such as Reed College's https://www.reed.edu/humanities/110Tech/Theater.html.

Vase paintings supply near-contemporary evidence for comic costuming (masks, padding, and *phalloi*). Taplin (1993), Compton-Engle (2015), and Piqueux (2022) present plates and illustrations of many vase images that you can also find online and make available to your students. Because of its easily readable depiction of what a comedy may have looked like in performance, my favorite vase painting to show in class is on the Choregoi Vase, a South Italian red-figure bell krater (i.e., a vessel for mixing wine and water) that dates to 400–380 BCE.[4] The Choregoi Vase is

---

[3] Chirico/Younger 2020: 9.
[4] Naples, Museo Archeologico Nazionale, 248778 (formerly Getty 96.AE.29), discussed most recently by Piqueux 2022: 32–4, 97–8, 306 (with bibliography). Theater-related scenes are rare on Attic vases dating to the fifth century (Taplin 1993: 6–11, Piqueux 2022: 15–19). But many vases manufactured in Southern Italy during the fourth century BCE feature images of comic performance, and it is widely accepted today that these images capture key elements of the staging and costuming used in performances of Attic comedies during the fifth and fourth centuries. Taplin 1993: 1–20 offers an account of how Attic drama was "exported" to non-Athenian Greeks.

particularly useful because the scene it depicts (from a comedy about theatrical productions?[5]) gives a sense of how comic costumes and masks differed from those used in tragedy. I also like to show the image on the Würzburg Telephus, another South Italian bell krater dating to the same period, which depicts the parody of Euripides' *Telephus* in Aristophanes' *Thesmophoriazusae*.[6] It is a great asset if you are teaching a comedy that features female characters (*Lysistrata, Thesmophoriazusae, Ecclesiazusae*) or a tragic parody (*Acharnians, Peace, Birds, Thesmophoriazusae, Frogs*).[7]

Aside from the basics concerning costuming, role-sharing (necessitated by the limited number of actors who could take on speaking roles), and other aspects of production, three oft-discussed points about the performance contexts of Aristophanes' comedies that I emphasize (though not necessarily via introductory lectures) are:

- the competitive nature of the productions of comedies and tragedies at the Athenian festivals (and also dithyrambic poems at the Great Dionysia). There were many other comedians active in Athens before, during, and after Aristophanes' time. These guys – and the *choregoi* who financed their productions – were competing for prizes, and they wanted to win!
- the spare physical resources in the Theater of Dionysus for the outdoor staging of plays on festival days in all kinds of weather. This means no to elaborate sets, but yes to some painted scenery, yes to lots of props and other movables items, and yes to the crane (*mēkhanē*) that suspended performers, often when playing gods, above the stage, and to the trolley (*ekkyklema*) that was used to bring into view the interior of the stage building, which likely featured more one entrance.[8]
- the importance of the choruses, which means the importance of choral songs, and the general importance of music and song in all ancient drama, which was "musical theater" in the truest sense. The confrontation of the two half-choruses in 614–705 illustrates one type of deployment of choral lyric in *Lysistrata*.[9] In the two pairs of matching stanzas, a *strophe* sung by the male half-chorus (616–25, 658–71) is countered by an *antistrophe* sung by the female half-chorus (636–47, 682–95).

Although less widely discussed, the fourth point I touch on is that Aristophanes' spectators, who *qua* spectators were participants in religious festivals with profound civic significance, would not have been self-selecting.[10] This constitutes one way in which the experience of Aristophanic comedies in ancient Athens could have differed significantly from the experiences of most audiences today, who typically exercise choice over what they watch or read. It is important to keep in mind especially if you and your students compare "comedy past and present." It also might influence how we approach interpreting the comedies, since – unlike today's comic performers and writers – Aristophanes could not assume that his spectators were in agreement with each other on any topic, even something as momentous as the Peloponnesian War.[11]

---

[5] This interpretation, advanced by Taplin 1993: 55–66, is accepted by Piqueux 2022: 32–4 and challenged by Gilula 1995.

[6] Würzburg, Martin-von-Wagner Museum der Universität, H5697, discussed most recently by Piqueux 2022: 34–6, 271–2, 310 (with bibliography).

[7] Piqueux 2022: 137–89.

[8] Revermann 2006 details the "busy-ness" of the comic stage.

[9] Since different translations of *Lysistrata* can use different line numbers (if any at all), I cite the standard line numbers of the Greek text in Henderson 1987.

[10] Though concerned primarily with the performances of tragedy at the Great Dionysia, Goldhill 1990 provides a helpful discussion of the festival's civic and political importance. Since it was such a significant event in the communal life of Athens, we might wonder whether the festival's participants (and hence Aristophanes' spectators) included women, children, and other residents of Attica otherwise excluded from political franchise, such as non-citizen residents ("metics") and slaves. Reviewing the ancient evidence, Csapo/Slater 1994: 286–7 concludes that women, minor children, and non-citizens including slaves were permitted to attend the Lenaea as well as the Great Dionysia and to witness their dramatic competitions. Henderson 1991 also makes the case for the presence of women at dramatic festivals.

[11] Henderson 1990 and Olson 2012: 76 offer counterpoints to my view, arguing (as Olson puts it) that comedians aimed to express "what average citizens were thinking and feeling about the state via the fantasies [they] presented on stage," and that their goal was "to capture the common mood."

The episodic structure of Aristophanes' comedies resembles the episodic structure of tragedies by Aeschylus, Sophocles, and Euripides. The basic pattern consists of a prologue, a choral entrance song ("parodos"), a series of episodes followed by choral songs, and a concluding finale. Many (though not all) comedies have two additional elements not found in tragedies: (1) a formal contest scene or *agón* (pl. *agónes*) that typically features a debate between two characters with opposing viewpoints, and (2) a *parabasis* (pl. *parabases*) in which the chorus "steps aside" and addresses spectators directly. *Lysistrata* nicely illustrates the flexibility Aristophanes enjoyed in handling these formal elements. It features a formal *agón* (476–607), but the scene is just "a kind of rowdy news conference" in which the male magistrate who challenges Lysistrata, instead of debating, becomes the women's "captive audience."[12] Moreover, there is no *parabasis*; instead, the half-choruses confront one another in 614–705.

Please be confident that you are the best judge of how to share background information with your students and of how much they need to know and when. It is perfectly OK to let the comedies themselves raise questions about composition and performance, and then let these questions raise other questions in turn. To take just one of many examples: you do not have to tell your students in advance that the female speaking and choral roles in *Lysistrata* and every drama performed in Athens in the classical period were always played by mask-wearing male actors in exaggeratedly padded "woman-suits,"[13] and that everyone involved in dramatic productions was male. You can let them discover this fact on their own or introduce it once your discussion is underway, and then let them explore whether (or how) this fact affects their interpretation of *Lysistrata*'s action.

In the Background (*Lysistrata*)

The original performance of *Lysistrata* in the Theater of Dionysus dates to the latter half of the year in the Athenian lunar calendar that corresponds to July 412 BCE–June 411 BCE in the modern calendar.[14] Ancient sources preserve no information about whether it was staged at the Lenaea (in the winter month Gamelion, so February of 411) or at the Great Dionysia (in the month Elaphebolion, during which the spring equinox of 411 occurred).[15] Dominating the play's background is the Peloponnesian War, first referred to as "the war" in *Lys.* 112, that the Athenians and Lacedaemonians (i.e., Spartans) along with their respective allies and partners had been waging since 431, but for a few truces, on several fronts. The Lacedaemonians' recent defeat of Athenian forces on Sicily in 413 is a more specific context for *Lysistrata*'s action. Conspicuously, the unnamed magistrate who confronts Lysistrata and her partners in *Lys.* 387–610 is identified as a *proboulos*, that is, a member of the board of senior officials with broad supervisory mandates that was specially created in late 413 to stabilize the city-state's finances after the great loss of life and resources (particularly ships) in Sicily.[16] This loss, along with the recent Lacedaemonian occupation of Decelea in Attica, caused considerable tension in Athens and Attica, to the point that its democratic institutions were suspended during a short-lived coup d'état that began in the spring of 411, thanks to the machinations of pro-oligarchical agitators. *Lysistrata* makes no direct reference to this domestic political crisis. Nonetheless, one might agree with Olson (2012: 77–8; cf. 72–3) that the action

---

[12] Henderson 1987: 128.
[13] Scholars debate whether mute, nude female figures who appear in the finales of several comedies, like "Reconciliation" in *Lysistrata* 1106–88, were played by "male actors wearing female masks and tights with breasts and pubic hair" (Henderson 1987: 195–6) or by naked female performers of non-citizen status, perhaps slaves or freeborn sex-workers (*hetairai*), as argued for by Marshall 2001.
[14] The comedy is dated to the year of the "archonship of Callias" in its first *hypothesis*. *Hypotheses* are ancient prefaces based on scholarship from the third century BCE that are included in the medieval manuscripts of Aristophanes' comedies.
[15] Parke 1977: 104–106 and 125–36; also Goldhill 1990. Sommerstein 1977, Henderson 1987: xv–xxv, and Olson 2012 survey the tumultuous events of 412/411. All three argue that Lysistrata was performed at the Lenaea.
[16] Thucydides 8.3–4.

effected and recommended by Lysistrata, insofar as it can be viewed as "a 'well-intentioned' overthrow of the democracy and a 'hygienic' purge of the citizen body" (Olson 78), anticipates the actual events of the coup, although perhaps in an entirely coincidental manner unintended by Aristophanes and therefore indicative of neither awareness nor approval of the agitators' plans.[17]

There is no evidence for a "women's suffrage movement" in classical Attica, and the scenario imagined in *Lysistrata* – of women striving to shape public policy – would have seemed fantastical to Aristophanes' audience.[18] But women did play crucial roles in other aspects of civic life, especially in religion.[19] The similarity of the character's name "Lysistrata" to "Lysimache," the name of the current priestess of Athena Polias ("Guardian of the City"), may also gesture toward these important roles, although, to quote Henderson, "[w]e should probably not conclude that Lysistrata was modelled on Lysimache."[20]

Lysistrata: Starting the Conversation

Given that Lysistrata seeks to unite the women of Greece[21] in a sex strike designed to force male combatants on both sides to negotiate a lasting resolution to the Peloponnesian War (*Lys.* 119–24), the usual focal points for scholarly discussions concerning *Lysistrata* are war, women, gender roles, and gender stereotypes.[22] If your students look to online resources to help them understand the comedy, they will likely find a raft of essays (free and for sale), blogs, and postings that center on these topics. I encourage you to embrace this likelihood, because these are practical focuses for your conversations about *Lysistrata*. That said, my preferred approach to teaching *Lysistrata* is to ease into discussions of war, women, and gender via an indirect route, by encouraging my students to think first about the logic of the protagonist's plan and of the plot's construction, and hence about the interplay of plot, theme, and setting. I then aim to use the ideas and questions generated by this conversation as springboards for investigations of the comedy's representations of the agency, capability, and desire of females, and also of the perspectives it offers on the Peloponnesian War and on war in general. This indirect approach is effective for other comedies as well. Its virtue is that it directs attention away from preoccupations with immediately and definitively identifying the "messages" or "lessons" of the comedy in question, and it opens up paths to appreciating the richness of Aristophanes' playful humor and to exploring the diverse ways in which the comedies might be meaningful as well as entertaining.

As a way of getting the class conversation started, I like to present questions such as the following about the "pretzel logic" of *Lysistrata*'s plot. You can ask your students these questions at the beginning of class, but they also can be incorporated into an informal, pre-class discussion written assignment.

- Twist #1: According to Lysistrata's plan, women will go home and refuse to have sex with their husbands, who will be compelled by frustration to capitulate to their wives' demands and make peace (149–54). But the problem with the war is that it takes men away from home (99–107). So, if the men are not present at home, vulnerable to their wives' teasing, how is the strike supposed to work?
- Twist #2: Like the women from other Greek city-states, the women of Attica are supposed to disperse to their homes, where they will frustrate their husbands into negotiating a peace treaty.

---

[17] See also Henderson 1987: 132.
[18] Henderson 1987: xxxiv–xxxv.
[19] As Olson 2012: 75 notes, *Lys.* 640–7 highlights the roles that girls and women from elite Athenian families played in the cults of Artemis (at Brauron) and Athena (on the Acropolis).
[20] Henderson 1987: xxxix. "Lysistrata" literally means "she who releases/dissolves armies," and "Lysimache" means "she who releases/dissolves battle(s)." In 554, Lysistrata uses the name Lysimache in the plural to refer to the women who have joined her cause.
[21] I.e., the legally recognized spouses of the male citizens in the city-states participating in the war.
[22] See Giluhly 2024 in this volume.

But the Athenians do not go home; instead, they take over the temple complex on the Acropolis, and the setting of most of *Lysistrata*'s action is at the entryway to this complex. Again, how is the strike described in 149–54 supposed to work?
- Twist #3: Lysistrata's plan and the comedy in general pretend that Greek males had sexual relations only with the women they legally married. This was manifestly not the case!
- More questions: Are these twists (illogicalities, inconsistencies, contradictions – whatever!) obstacles to your enjoyment of the comedy? If so, how in particular? If not, what elements in the comedy help you look past them?

Goals

Despite – or maybe because of – the unpredictability of your students' responses, especially concerning their enjoyment, I find these sorts of questions useful for stimulating conversation about the following topics:

- Although the execution of Lysistrata's plan does not follow through on the originally proposed strategy, the comedy's plot finds some coherence in (paradoxically) the Athenian wives' occupation of the Acropolis, which is initially conceptualized as a means for older women (i.e., the women's half-chorus) to take over temple's treasury and thus prevent further expenditures on the war (175–9). However, when they take refuge on the Acropolis, Lysistrata and her partners effect a fantastic "domestication" of the civic space of the temple precinct, essentially turning it into the home environment that women habitually occupy.[23] This domestication culminates in the scene in which Myrrhine faithfully executes Lysistrata's original plan, as she makes the space in front of the Acropolis' entrance function as a bedroom for her sexually frustrated husband Cinesias (831–952).[24]
- The abrupt shift in setting at 254, the freedom with which the women take over important public spaces and resources, and Myrrhine's surprising fulfillment of Lysistrata's plan are great examples of the "comic freeness" that is enjoyed by Aristophanes (*qua* playwright) and his characters (*qua* agents). The contrast between uninhibited "comic freeness" and restrictive "tragic necessity" is something I emphasize when teaching every Aristophanic comedy: Aristophanes and his characters can get away with *almost* anything, and that is part of the basic fun of comedy! But there are limits to this freeness, and you and your students might also spend a bit of time exploring what "*almost* anything" means in *Lysistrata* or any other comedy. That which is off limits to a comically uninhibited treatment is just as important as whatever is treated as fair game.

A few additional examples of "comic freeness" in *Lysistrata* that you might want to discuss are the vulgar language and frank descriptions of sexual activity; the ease with which women from many Greek city-states are able to travel to Athens; Lysistrata's confrontational treatment of the magistrate, who first has women's accoutrements thrust upon him (532–8) and is then "dressed" for burial (599–607)[25]; Aristophanes' elision of the real-life opportunities that men had for sexual gratification outside of marriage; the sudden introduction of sexy Reconciliation in the finale.

Women, War, Etc.: Approaches, Assignments, and Topics

Discussions of the actions of *Lysistrata*'s female characters, particularly their domestication of civic space, are excellent points of departure for exploring the comedy's representations of women. Your explorations can encompass a variety of specific topics that include (but are not limited to!): the characterization(s) of the goals of the women's sex strike; the comedy's perspective(s) on the roles, influence, and contributions of women in domestic and civic spheres; the reliance on stereotyping

---

[23] Hulton 1972, Vaio 1973, and Foley 1982 discuss the comedy's plot manipulations and its play with domestic and civic space.
[24] As Henderson 1987: xli observes, the common Athenian names "Cinesias" (also transliterated "Kinesias") and "Myrrhine" take on sexual double-entendres in *Lysistrata*.
[25] Compton-Engle 2015: 52–3 offers an illuminating discussion of this confrontation.

humor about women's penchant for "transgression" and their lack of self-restraint regarding physical satisfaction; the objectification of the female body, most obviously in the finale with Reconciliation; the seemingly casual acceptance of domestic violence (160–6, 520). The big question your class might end up debating is whether the perspectives on women and gender roles in *Lysistrata* are "feminist," "sexist," "misogynistic," "progressive," "conservative," or maybe something else, something in between, or all of the above. You might also consider the implications of Olson's thought-provoking suggestion that gender, far from being a main focus in *Lysistrata*, is "a comic red herring" that can be "removed from the equation" by interpreters (2012: 74).

Since the Peloponnesian War is what brings *Lysistrata*'s female characters to the stage, your discussion about the comedy's treatment of women and gender will naturally raise questions about the perspectives it offers on this war in particular and possibly on war in general. When performed or adapted today, *Lysistrata* is often characterized as an expression of opposition to war and violence in general.[26] A basic question that you might explore with your students is whether the comedy should be called "anti-war," "anti-violence," and/or "pacifist."

Your class discussion can compartmentalize considerations of gender and war, or weave back and forth between the two topics. Following are suggestions for facilitating these considerations that can be used singly or in combinations. The shared goals of these questions, assignments, and projects are to foster close attention to details of text and performance and to encourage reflections on the significance of these details.

Staged Reading for Exploring the Representations of Females (Preplanned In-class Group Project)

Recruit volunteers to perform a segment of a scene (maybe 50–100 lines) as a staged reading (i.e., with texts in hand, but maybe with some gestures and movement, depending on the layout of your classroom and your students' comfort with performing). Perhaps another set of volunteers can lead post-performance reflections. The idea is to choose a scene that in your (individual or collective) estimation exemplifies how females are "impersonated" in *Lysistrata* and how the desires and abilities of women are represented. Virtually every scene can work for this project, but, in some classroom settings, you may want to avoid asking performers to enact a scene that features language or action that is too sexually explicit, such as the oath sworn in the prologue (181–239), Myrrhine's teasing of Cinesias (870–953), or the negotiations over the "map" provided by Reconciliation's body (1112–85). If sensitivity is a concern, a workable option might be the last hundred or so verses of the confrontation between Lysistrata and the magistrate (505–610). You might also consider following the excellent template for staging a performance of the "dueling" half-choruses outlined by Mills (2020). To expand the scope of a staged-reading exercise, you can ask your students about their alternate choice for a scene to read/perform in class. You do not have to actually read or perform it, but exploring the reasons why a certain scene is their alternate choice will almost certainly add depth to your discussions of the scene they choose for performance.

Goals
This project gives students the chance to explore how performance choices inflect interpretation of the text. One choice that Aristophanes could *not* make is to cast female actors to impersonate his speaking female characters. If possible, you might try replicating this limitation in your class's performance by experimenting with non-traditional casting.[27] A question this experiment might raise is: What are the effects of having "women" represented on stage not by actors who identify as female, but by actors who do not? Other details to bring into the mix are (1) male comic actors

---

[26] As in the many performances and productions associated with 2003's *Lysistrata Project* (http://lysistrataprojectarchive.com/lys/) and Spike Lee's 2015 film adaptation *Chi-raq*.
[27] Credit for this suggestion is owed to Anna Andes, Joshua Streeter, and other attendees at the October 2021 meeting of the Comparative Drama Conference at Rollins College, Orlando FL.

playing female roles would have been outfitted with masks and exaggerated padding that, while recognizably "feminine," did not aim at realism, and (2) every single female figure in *Lysistrata* and every other Athenian drama is the product of a male playwright's imagination and, with the possible exception of mute female figures like Reconciliation, was impersonated by a male performer.[28]

If a staged reading is not feasible, consider showing your students a video clip from a production of *Lysistrata* as a basis for exploring staging and performance. Videos of several productions (usually filmed in front of live audiences) are available on YouTube and Vimeo, such as the 2004 production at Loyola University New Orleans (https://www.youtube.com/watch?v=4Qp5DP6a-2c) or the 2013 performance by Human-Kind Productions (https://vimeo.com/55719340). Other options that may pique your students' interest are adaptations such as Spike Lee's *Chi-raq* (2015).

Performance choices were/are by no means limited to those concerning the representation of gender. For example, Conner (2001): 22–3 notes the strategies that English-language translators employ to replicate the "stage Doric" dialect spoken by Aristophanes' Lacedaemonian characters (Lampito in 81–253, the herald and ambassador in 980–1321), and a staged reading can help focus attention on the choices that Aristophanes (and his translators) make to underscore cultural differences between Athenians and their main opponents in the Peloponnesian War. As Conner observes (2001: 23–4), attention to language will necessarily pertain to the choices of the translator rather than the comedian. But other types of choices, including (if you care to go there) the Lacedaemonian ambassador's fixation with anal intercourse (1148–74), are Aristophanes'.[29]

Comparing Translations (A Preparatory Exercise, or Spontaneously Introduced in Class)

Conner (2001) details how she and her students improvised a productive conversation about the choices made by translators of *Lysistrata* when, unbeknownst to her, students came to class having read different translations in different editions of a drama anthology. You can intentionally replicate her improvised experiment. If it is impractical for your students to read multiple translations cover to cover, compose a handout or powerpoint with different translations of one or two passages.

Goals

Conner acknowledges, "Aristophanes got lost in translation that day." Yet, she continues, great gains were achieved by the "illuminating moment . . . engendered by the chance appearance of both texts in the room, since their dual presence made it impossible for any one translation to be received as having an authoritative, transparent relationship to *Lysistrata*." The exercise afforded "a perfect pedagogical opportunity to compare/critique/deconstruct the role of translation" (2001: 23).

Since the manuscripts preserving the texts of Aristophanes' comedies offer no extra-textual stage directions, all stage directions in translations are inferred and are sometimes products of interpretation. Questioning the rationales for stage directions in translations can be a productive component of this comparative exercise.

Wish Lists (Study Questions, or a Preparatory Written Exercise, or Spontaneously Introduced in Class)

Ask your students to come up with two "wish lists," one for the female figures and one for the male figures. What do the female figures in the comedy want, and why do they want it? What do the male figures want, and why?

---

[28] Case 1985. See note 13 above for questions about the gender of the performers of figures like Reconciliation.
[29] Henderson 1987: 202. Compton-Engle 2015: 49–52 also draws attention to the "man-handling" of non-Athenian females in 78–92.

Goals

This exercise is designed to encourage students to explore the insights the comedy yields into the motivating factors behind (1) Lysistrata's objective – soon adopted by the other female figures – to bring an end to the Peloponnesian War and (2) the resistance to ending the war exhibited by male characters.

Like the staged reading project, this exploration affords opportunities for considering how females and "what women want" are represented in *Lysistrata* and, more generally, for discussing whether *Lysistrata* should be considered "feminist." I'll leave the judgment on "feminist or not" to you and your students. That said, it is worth noting that the ultimate aim of Lysistrata and her partners is to find a way back to the life that was once enjoyed at home with their husbands (99–106, 1182–7). The problems she focuses on are the war's disruption of everyday existence (557–64) and its thwarting of young girls' prospects for marriage (588–97). A return to conventional domesticity, and not permanent franchise for women, is the strike's objective.[30] The orientation of the female characters to the household – women's traditional sphere of influence – is apparent even and especially when they seem most transgressive. They seize control of the public treasury, but transform the Acropolis into domestic space; as they rudely send off the magistrate/*proboulos* outfitted as a corpse (599–607), they enact the traditional female labor of preparing the dead for burial.

Exploring what the comedy intimates about its male characters' commitment to continuing their fight with the Lacedaemonians is just as interesting! As Lysistrata predicts (154), sexual frustration eventually jumpstarts the peace process. Yet, even as the male ambassadors ogle the most intimate areas of Reconciliation's body, the rival claims they persist in staking to the territories mapped onto her body almost cause a breakdown of negotiations (1162–72). A question to consider is: Does this scene – and the comedy as a whole – cast the eagerness of its male characters to keep fighting as the consequence of a kind of erotic fixation?

This exercise provides opportunities for discussing other dimensions of Aristophanes' representations of "what women really want" – i.e., their libidinousness and bibulousness (e.g., 124–34, 194–7, 387–419, 708–80). Jokes about women's lack of self-restraint, especially regarding sex, food, and wine, abounded in the comic drama of Aristophanes' day, and Aristophanes freely exploits humor that stereotypes women as sex-crazed boozers and objectifies the female body. Your students might want to spend some time thinking about *how* this humor is contextualized and perhaps complicated by, for example, Myrrhine's display of self-discipline in her encounter with Cinesias (845–951).

Moreover, this exercise furnishes a useful point of entry for discussing the words and actions of the two half-choruses of older women and men. Both half-choruses express a willingness to inflict violence on their "opponents" (e.g., 269–70, 358–9).[31] Do your students think that the "desire to hurt" belongs on the wish lists they compose? Why or why not?

An intriguing supplement to (or substitute for) this exercise is to treat gender as a "red herring," as Olson suggests (2012: 74 [above, p. 429]), and (re-)frame the wish lists without reference to gender. Are there shifts in your students' impressions of what each side wants, and of the legitimacy of their goals, when gender is "removed from the equation"?

The Wool-working Analogy in Lys. 574–86 – Option #1 (For Study Questions, or Pre-discussion Written Exercise, or Spontaneously Introduced in Class)

To what extent can details of the analogy be correlated to practical policies that could inform a strategy for governing a political community? Does an identifiable political ideology – or an identifiable set of political goals – seem to sit behind this analogy? What is the analogy's relevance to the problems of the Peloponnesian War as Lysistrata identifies them?

---

[30] Fletcher 1999, 2011: 220–40, and Culpepper-Stroup 2004 detail how Lysistrata and her partners at first stray from the norm of "respectable" married women and, in the case of their oath (181–239), coopt privileges reserved for men.
[31] Henderson 1987: 99.

The Wool-working Analogy in Lys. 564–86 – Option #2 (Preplanned In-class Group Project)[32]

You will probably not be able to bring in a fleece that needs to be cleaned and carded, spun into thread, and woven into a piece of cloth. But how about engaging your students, divided into small groups (maybe two or three apiece), in a less ambitious fiber-oriented project like untangling a knotty wad of string or yarn? (The thicker the better, since you want your students to work on something big enough for everyone in the group to put their hands on.) Allot just a little time if you like, and do not worry if the detangling does not get finished.

Goals

The exercises described above are actually designed to be a bit, well, frustrating! This is because (1) the details of the fleece-cleaning/wool-working analogy can admit quite different interpretations, and (2) it takes a good deal of effort to engage in an activity that mimics just a fragment of the intensive labor involved in transforming fleece into a garment.[33]

The element of Lysistrata's metaphor that most generates interpretational dilemmas is the description in 575–8 of "washing the dung out of the city-state," "flogging out the rascals and plucking out the burrs," "carding out those who form coalitions and pack themselves into public offices and plucking off their heads." Henderson (1987): 143 and Olson (2012): 72–3 emphasize the violence of Lysistrata's description, but differ in their interpretations of who exactly her targets are in the context of the strained political circumstances of the comedy's premiere. Are the people to be removed from the "fleece-of-state" only the members and supporters of the established "deliberately deaf and domineering pseudo-democratic order" that led Athens to disaster in Sicily (Olson 2012: 78), or does the description take aim at pro-oligarchic agitators as well as those who profited from the status quo of Athenian democracy (Henderson 1987: 143)? And/or is the metaphor developed so as to have a generic, all-purpose appeal ("Throw the bums out – whoever they are!") that would resonate differently with different spectators? You and your students may not be able to settle these questions to your satisfaction. But a set of questions you can profitably consider is: How do the description in 575–8 and the subsequent components of the metaphor (579–86), which describe less aggressive activities of blending, spinning, and weaving, mutually inform one another? Does the violence in 575–8 overshadow the second part, or does the creative activity described in 579–86 soften the initial impression of violence? And should we construe Lysistrata's vision as somehow reflecting something Aristophanes personally wanted to occur? Why or why not?[34]

A hands-on detangling project can help underscore the ways the analogy models the task of policy-making/governing as a collaborative effort, since all the activities Lysistrata describes would not have been performed by one person working alone, but through collective labor.[35] If spending time in class unknotting yarn is unfeasible, you might look into a more manageable hands-on project, such as assembling small jigsaw puzzles. Alternatively or additionally, consider showing your students the image on the *lekythos* (oil flask) attributed to the Amasis Painter (c. 550–530 BCE) that depicts women weighing wool, weaving cloth on an upright loom, and folding the finished product.[36] The painting illuminates what might be the most basic (perhaps reassuringly anodyne) point of the analogy: it takes a village.

---

[32] Credit for this inventive classroom exercise is owed to Kelly Younger.
[33] See Orenstein 2023.
[34] Henderson 1987: 141 states that in the metaphor Aristophanes "express[es] *his* programme" (my emphasis). A general counterpoint is offered by Rosen 2010, who outlines the difficulties of discerning specific "programs" in Aristophanic comedies.
[35] Working with tangled yarn can also afford opportunities for thinking about the manipulation of props on stage. In the description, Lysistrata probably is not demonstrating the tasks she describes with props, but there are plenty of physical items manipulated by performers throughout this scene and the entire comedy.
[36] Metropolitan Museum of Art, New York, NY, 253348 (https://www.metmuseum.org/art/collection/search/253348).

Casting Call (Pre- or Post-discussion Written Exercise, or Spontaneously Introduced in Class)

Ask your students to imagine that they will be able to recruit a well-known contemporary performer for the role of the magistrate/*proboulos* in their production of *Lysistrata*. Whom would they cast, and why? What features of this character do they think this performer is suited to capture?

Goals
This is a roundabout way to coax your students into interpreting aspects of the behavior of the *proboulos*, although keeping the focus on the Aristophanic character rather than the more familiar contemporary performer can sometimes be a challenge! The "casting call" can be used as a vehicle for analyzing any/every character, including the choruses. What the focus on the *proboulos* provides is an opportunity for analyzing his role as the "blocking figure" that is a standard component of so many comedies through the ages. Showing some clips of blocking figures in popular films could be a helpful way of sparking discussion of how the friction provided by the Proboulos' resistance generates an important inflection point in *Lysistrata*'s plot.

Point/Counterpoint (Pre- or Post-discussion Written Exercise, or Spontaneously Introduced in Class)

Ask your students to evaluate the relative merits of opposing perspectives on *Lysistrata*, as exemplified by these quotations (all recently gleaned from online sources) or by others of your choosing. Ask them not only to identify the opinions they favor, but also to explain why specific passages in the comedy dispose them to favor one view over another.

POINT[37]: "The theme, or central message conveyed by the author, is feminism; however, there are also other themes to consider. It is clear that the play has a feminine heroine, Lysistrata. She is a strong-willed woman who directs the action of the play . . . Perhaps the most obvious view of feminism is the fact that while men are seen as violent, women are seen as peacemakers . . . Another way in which feminism is present is in the portrayal of women's sexuality. The women are in complete control of their sexuality and have the power to decide when and if they'll have sex with their partners, which leads to the theme of sex itself."

COUNTERPOINT[38]: "*Lysistrata* could never have been considered feminist due to the nature of Old Comedy, which made fun of the status of ancient Athenian women. Those who hail Lysistrata as a feminist icon simply have no context in which to understand that she was never intended to be anything more than a joke. This comic female protagonist possessed no qualities of ancient Athenian women. Lysistrata was a female turned masculine to keep the other women, controlled by their insatiable vices, in order . . . In fact, the play is rampantly anti-feminist when its context is understood. Although some modern artists and audiences may see this play as a beacon of feminism, it is clear that Lysistrata was simply created to make fun of women and to make men laugh, nothing more."

POINT + COUNTERPOINT, COMBINED[39]: "Modern adaptations of *Lysistrata* are often feminist and/or pacifist in their aim . . . The original play was neither feminist nor unreservedly pacifist. Even when they seemed to demonstrate empathy with the female condition, dramatic poets in classical Athens still reinforced sexual stereotyping of women as irrational creatures in need of protection from themselves and from others . . . In fact the play might not even be a plea for an end to the war so much as an imaginative vision of an honorable end to the war at a time when no such ending was

---

[37] From "*Lysistrata*: Feminism and Other Themes," https://study.com/academy/lesson/lysistrata-feminism-other-themes.html. Found via online search for "What is the main message of *Lysistrata*?"
[38] From "Lysistrata: Modern Day Feminist, Ancient Joke," https://digitalcommons.kean.edu/cgi/viewcontent.cgi?article=1021&context=keanquest. Found via online search for "Is *Lysistrata* a Feminist Play?"
[39] From https://en.wikipedia.org/wiki/Lysistrata.

possible ... According to Sarah Ruden, *Lysistrata* (Hackett Classics, 2003), the play 'nowhere suggests that warfare in itself is intolerable, let alone immoral' (87)."

Goals

Staging a "point/counterpoint" debate featuring different perspectives/assessments is one of the best techniques I know for encouraging students to sift through interpretative options and develop considered opinions they can defend about which option makes the most sense to them. While not asking students to do the difficult work of developing from scratch a point of view that they then must support, it encourages them to look carefully at and interpret specific passages in the text so that they can explain why they favor View X over View Y, or vice versa, or why both views have merit, but each omits something important. Agonistic confrontations between opposing viewpoints are at the heart of every comedy by Aristophanes, including *Lysistrata*, and this assignment thus incorporates in a playfully self-conscious fashion a feature of the comedy your students are studying.[40] Very Aristophanic!

Beyond *Lysistrata*: More Approaches, Assignments, and Projects

Big-Picture Point/Counterpoint

Exercises and assignments that confront opposing interpretative options can be used to explore all types of claims, general as well as specific. Here are two of many possibilities.

(1) A widely repeated claim about Aristophanes that your students will surely encounter, especially in discussions of *Clouds, Frogs, Wasps, Knights,* and *Lysistrata*, is that the comedian is a "conversative" whose comedies consistently promote the "good old ways" by advocating a return to the values of standards of previous generations and modeling the rejection of "radical new influences" in Athenian society promulgated by the likes of Socrates, Euripides, and the political leader Cleon.[41]

This judgment can be scrutinized and tested from any number of perspectives.[42] A couple of questions your students can reflect on are: Because characters in Aristophanic comedies denigrate Socrates (or Euripides or Agathon or Cleon), should we assume that their views reflect personal opinions that Aristophanes cared to impress on his audiences? Does Dionysus' selection of Aeschylus in *Frogs*, or Strepsiades' violent attack on Socrates in the finale of *Clouds*, convey what the comedian would do if he could? Which specific passages might support affirmative answers, and which might incline one to respond differently? More basically: what are the meanings of labels like "conservative" (or "progressive")? Can modern understandings of "conservatism" be accurately mapped onto conceptions of "conservatism" that Aristophanes and his contemporaries could have grasped?

(2) Eco (1984): 7 defines comedy, or "the comic," as an expression of "authorized transgression" that promises "liberation," but is ultimately "only an instrument of social control" and "can never be a form of social criticism." Eco distinguishes comedy from "humor," which "does not act in order to make us accept [a] system of values," even though "it obliges us to acknowledge its existence." He continues: "Very seldom does the business of entertainment display real humor ... When a real piece of humor appears, entertainment becomes avantgarde: a supreme philosophical game. We smile because we feel sad for having discovered, only for a moment, the truth" (Eco, 8).

Using Eco's definitions, ask your students: Does Aristophanes present "comedy" or "humor"?

---

[40] Credit for this observation is owed to Jeremy Leftkowitz.
[41] Here is a short list of sites that feature articulations of this view: https://en.wikipedia.org/wiki/Aristophanes; https://en.wikipedia.org/wiki/The_Frogs; https://aristophanes-clouds.gr; https://www3.dbu.edu/mitchell/aristoph.htm; https://www.sparknotes.com/drama/theclouds/themes/; https://www.ipl.org/essay/Analysis-Of-The-Clouds-By-Aristophanes-PKK93C4NFJE86.
[42] Rosen 2010: 241–5, 262–77.

Jump Right In! – Another Way To Break The Ice

With some comedies, I do the opposite of "easing in" to discussions of the big interpretative issues. For example, since the Hellenistic period, *Clouds* has been construed as an attack on Socrates; the comedy's first ancient *hypothesis* states that it "has been written against Socrates."[43] When teaching *Clouds*, I quote this statement and ask, "Is this a fair assessment?" The process of responding to this question leads to considerations of not only the scope, but also the limits, of *Clouds*' interest in Socrates, and it opens the door to taking stock of aspects of *Clouds* that have nothing to do with Socrates, such as the protagonist Strepsiades' "debt-crisis" and his dysfunctional relationship with profligate son Pheidippides. Further questions I aim to explore with my students when using this approach are: What is the substance of the "new learning" offered in Socrates' "Thinkery" (*phrontisterion*), and what exactly do Strepsiades and Pheidippides learn? Are the two "corrupted" by what they learn? How should we interpret Strespsiades' stated desire to cheat his creditors (116–7) and Pheidippides' disrespect for his father (119–25) in the prologue?

Creative (Re)writings

According to the sixth ancient hypothesis of *Clouds*, the burning of the Thinkery in the final scene (1484–1511) was not depicted in the comedy when it premiered in 423 BCE, and perhaps the entire episode after Strepsiades and Pheidippides' *agon* (1452–1511) belongs to the revised script that is now the only text of the comedy.

Since the ending preserved in the manuscripts is Aristophanes' alternative ending, ask your students to "ghost-write" their own alternative endings for Aristophanes. How would they finish off the action of *Clouds*, and why would they make these choices?

Or, ask your students to imagine what might happen if *Clouds* continued after the burning of the Thinkery[44] . . . or if *Lysistrata* continued after the party on the Acropolis broke up and the wives went home with their husbands. . . or if *Frogs* continued after Dionysus and Aeschylus returned to Athens from Hades. Again, what guides their choices about how to script the next "act" of the comedy?

Or, ask your students to re-imagine the *agón* between the Arguments in *Clouds*, or between Aeschylus and Euripides in *Frogs*, as a contemporary debate.[45] Yet again, what prompts their updated interpretations of the terms of debate between "old" and "new"?

Are You Choosing Your Own Comedy?

Fantastic! Please consider choosing *Knights* (424 BCE). Yes, it is off the beaten path, full of topical references, and jam-packed with obscenity and nastiness. But experience teaches me that today's students, raised in the era of 24-hour news cycles and rampant political scandals, are primed to "get" this comedy, even if what they are "getting" is its very cynical vision of how politicians gain and lose power – a vision that may (or may not) be tempered by a finale that is "all's well that ends well" or "too good to be true," depending on how one interprets its details. Excellent guides for the rough yet rewarding ride that is *Knights* are Scholtz (2004), Rosen (2010), and Ruffell (2011).

---

[43] *Apology* 19a8-d7 shows that, in Plato's view, *Clouds* damaged Socrates' reputation, but does not suggest that Plato considered the harm intentionally inflicted.
[44] As in *The State v. Versa*, a collectively written performance piece created and directed by Liz Peterson in July 2021 (https://lizpeterson.org/clouds).
[45] Burt Shevelove and Stephen Sondheim's adaptation of *Frogs*, whose *agón* substitutes William Shakespeare for Aeschylus and G. B. Shaw for Euripides, is a high-profile example of such reimagining.

GUIDE TO FURTHER READING

For further reading beyond the materials cited in the notes, I recommend collections of essays by multiple contributors (such as this one!) because the plurality of perspectives makes them supremely useful. Recent collections of English-language essays generally focused on Aristophanes and ancient Greek comedy include Kozak/Rich (2006), Dobrov (2010), Marshall/Kovacs (2012), Olson (2014), and Rosen/Foley (2020). Swallow/Hall (2020) has a narrower focus on the "theory and practice" of Aristophanes' humor, which is also the subject of Ruffell (2011). A seminal collection on Athenian drama is Winkler/Zeitlin (1990), whereas Stott (2014) is a helpful general study of comedy. Chirico/Younger (2020) is an inspirational volume with concrete classroom exercises for dramas of every era. It is worth taking a look at their wealth of pedagogical suggestions to see what can be adapted for your classroom.

Recent English (North American and UK) translations of all 11 extant Aristophanic comedies are published in paperback by Penguin Books and the University of Pennsylvania Press. Harvard University Press's Loeb Classical Library features the plays and fragments in a five-volume set, with facing Greek text and English translation. Hackett Publishing offers translations of several commonly studied comedies, including *Lysistrata* and *Clouds*, as does Oxford's World's Classics. Most translations feature introductions (usually by the translator) and notes. These introductions and notes bear careful reading, because your students will absorb from them information that may need to be taken with grains of salt. Because of the brief shelf-life of comic translations, recent translations are generally preferable; I also find it easier to work with a translation that uses line numbers. Nonetheless, despite its age and lack of line numbers, I still use Douglass Parker's 1964 translation of *Lysistrata*, now reissued as an inexpensive mass-market paperback by Signet. Though dated in some regards, Parker's translations exude real verve, and Judith Fletcher's introduction is excellent.

When using free translations accessible online, be aware that many of them are available only because their copyrights have expired, and they therefore may be too outdated for your purposes. The exceptions to this caveat are the very fine, recent translations in (North American) English available on the websites of Ian Johnston (http://johnstoniatexts.x10host.com) and George Theodoridis (https://bacchicstage.word press.com/aristophanes/). Johnston offers free downloadable versions of his translations of seven Aristophanic comedies, including *Lysistrata*, *Clouds*, *Frogs*, and *Knights*; Theodoridis' site has free links to his translations of all 11 extant plays. Many heartfelt thanks are due to both translators for sharing the fruits of their labors *gratis* with the public.

REFERENCES

Case, S.-E. (1985). Classic drag: the Greek creation of female parts. *Theatre Journal* 37: 317–327.

Chirico, M. and Younger, K. (ed.) (2020). *How To Teach A Play: Essential Exercises for Popular Plays*. London and New York: Methuen Drama.

Compton-Engle, G. (2015). *Costume in the Comedies of Aristophanes*. Cambridge University Press.

Conner, L. (2001). Gained in translation: classroom conversations on *Lysistrata*. *Metamorphoses* 9: 16–25.

Csapo, E. and Slater, W.J. (1994). *The Context of Ancient Drama*. Ann Arbor: University of Michigan Press.

Culpepper-Stroup, S. (2004). Designing women: Aristophanes' *Lysistrata* and the 'hetairization' of the Greek wife. *Arethusa* 37 (1): 37–73.

Dobrov, G. (ed.) (2010). *Brill's Companion to the Study of Greek Comedy*. Leiden and Boston MA: Brill.

Eco, U. (1984). The 'frames' of comic freedom. In: *Carnival!* (ed. U. Eco, V.V. Ivanov, M. Rector, and T.A. Sebeok), 1–9. Berlin and New York: Mouton Publishers.

Fletcher, J. (1999). Sacrificial bodies and the body of the text in Aristophanes' *Lysistrata*. *Ramus* 28 (2): 108–125.

Fletcher, J. (2011). *Performing Oaths in Classical Greek Drama*. Cambridge University Press.

Foley, H. (1982). The 'Female Intruder' reconsidered: women in Aristophanes' *Lysistrata* and *Ecclesiazusae*. *Classical Philology* 77: 1–21.

Giluhly, Kate. 2024. "*Lysistrata*: sexuality." In this volume.

Gilula, D. (1995). The Choregoi vase: comic yes, but angels? *Zeitschrift für Papyrologie und Epigraphik* 109: 5–10.

Goldhill, S. (1990). The great Dionysia and civic ideology. In: *Nothing To Do With Dionysus?: Athenian Drama in Its Social Context* (ed. J.J. Winkler and F.I. Zeitlin), 97–129. Princeton NJ: Princeton University Press.

Henderson, J. (ed.) (1987). *Aristophanes: Lysistrata.* Oxford: Oxford University Press.

Henderson, J. (1990). The *demos* and the comic competition. In: *Nothing To Do With Dionysus?: Athenian Drama in Its Social Context* (ed. J.J. Winkler and F. Zeitlin), 271–313. Princeton NJ: Princeton University Press.

Henderson, J. (1991). Women and the Athenian dramatic festivals. *Transactions of the American Philological Association* 121: 133–147.

Hulton, A.O. (1972). The women on the Acropolis: a note on the structure of the *Lysistrata. Greece and Rome* 19: 32–36.

Kozak, L. and Rich, J. (ed.) (2006). *Playing Around Aristophanes: Essays in Honour of Alan Sommerstein.* Oxford: Oxbow Books.

Lee, S.(2015). *Chi-raq.* Amazon Studios; 40 Acres and a Mule Filmworks.

Marshall, C.W. (2001). Female performers on stage? (*PhV* 96 [RVP 2/33]). *Text and Presentation* 21: 13–25.

Marshall, C.W. and Kovacs, G. (ed.) (2012). *No Laughing Matter: Studies in Athenian Comedy.* London: Bristol Classical Press.

Mills, J. (2020). *Lysistrata* by Aristophanes. In: *How To Teach A Play: Essential Exercises for Popular Plays* (ed. M. Chirico and K. Younger), 37–39. London and New York: Methuen Drama.

Olson, S.D. (2012). Lysistrata's conspiracy and the politics of 412 BC. In: *No Laughing Matter: Studies in Athenian Comedy* (ed. C.W. Marshall and G. Kovacs), 69–81. London: Bristol Classical Press.

Olson, S.D. (ed.) (2014). *Ancient Comedy and Reception: Essays in Honor of Jeffrey Henderson.* Berlin and Boston: De Gruyter.

Orenstein, P. (2023). *Unraveling: What I Learned About Life While Shearing Sheep, Dyeing Wool, and Making the World's Ugliest Sweater.* Harper.

Parke, H.W. (1977). *Festivals of the Athenians.* Ithaca NY: Cornell University Press.

Piqueux, A. (2022). *The Comic Body in Ancient Greek Theatre and Art, 440–320 BCE.* Oxford: Oxford University Press.

Revermann, M. (2006). *Comic Business: Theatricality, Dramatic Technique, and Performance Contexts of Aristophanic Comedy.* Oxford: Oxford University Press.

Rosen, Ralph M. 2010. Aristophanes. In: *Brill's Companion to the Study of Greek Comedy* (ed. G. Dobrov), 227–78. Leiden: Brill.

Rosen, R.M. and Foley, H.P. (ed.) (2020). *Aristophanes and Politics: New Studies.* Leiden and Boston: Brill.

Ruffell, I.A. (2011). *Politics and Anti-Realism in Athenian Old Comedy.* Oxford: Oxford University Press.

Scholtz, A. (2004). Friends, lovers, and flatterers: demophilic courtship in Aristophanes' *Knights. Transactions of the American Philological Association* 134: 263–293.

Sommerstein, A. (1977). Aristophanes and the events of 411. *Journal of Hellenic Studies* 97: 112–126.

Stott, A. (2014). *Comedy,* second ed. New York and London: Routledge.

Swallow, P. and Hall, E. (ed.) (2020). *Aristophanic Humour: Theory and Practice.* London and New York: Bloomsbury Publishing.

Taplin, O. (1993). *Comic Angels and Other Approaches to Greek Drama Through Vase-Painting.* Oxford: Oxford University Press.

Vaio, J. (1973). The manipulation of theme and action in Aristophanes' *Lysistrata. Greek, Roman, and Byzantine Studies* 14: 369–380. Open access at https://grbs.library.duke.edu/index.php/grbs/article/view/9051/.

Winkler, J.J. and Zeitlin, F.I. (ed.) (1990). *Nothing To Do With Dionysus?: Athenian Drama in Its Social Context.* Princeton NJ: Princeton University Press.

Index

Note: *Italic* page numbers refer to figures and page numbers followed by 'n' refer to notes. Titles of Greek texts are listed by their most commonly used English title, followed by alternate titles in parentheses.

absurdity 100, 151, 155, 233, 242, 416
abuse 44, 66, 109, 121, 149, 154, 219, 273
acropolis 79, 82, 84, 196, 197, 201, 202, 204, 222, 223, 266, 428, 431
actors 21, 22, 24–26, 35, 65, 66, 298, 299, 414, 415, 424, 425, 429
Aeschylus 26, 39, 43, 44, 46, 52, 63, 64, 81, 91, 93–94, 98, 100–101, 139, 143, 170, 219, 224, 228, 231, 233, 235–239, 241–242, 267, 299, 312, 360, 375–376, 382, 387, 394, 426, 434–435
   Eumenides 171
   Libation Bearers 39
   Prometheus 170
affordances 27–32
allegory 79–80, 108, 111, 228–246, 298
Amipsias 130, 145, 322, 327
   Connus 127, 130, 135, 145
ancient scholarship 127, 294, 319, 352–365
animal choruses 61, 235, 296, 300
antistrophe 35, 36, 38, 40–44, 133, 271, 272, 417, 419
Apollonius (*schol.*) 359–360
Aristarchus of Samothrace 358–360, 364
Aristophanes, plays of,
   Acharnians (Akharnians) 8, 12–14, 26–28, 37–39, 41, 47, 48, 60, 66, 71, 73, 91–106, 107–108, 116, 119, 132, 161, 167, 170, 172, 173, 216, 219, 220, 284

Anagyros 284, 287–289
Assemblywomen (Ecclesiazusae, Ekklesiazusai) 8, 16–18, 35, 37–39, 47, 81–83, 190, 191, 199, 213, 223, 247–26, 300, 399, 414
Babylonians 8, 73, 91, 108, 115, 159, 161, 282–287, 289
Banqueters 91, 94, 128
Birds 8–11, 35, 38, 39, 41, 44, 58, 77–78, 92, 93, 119, 135, 136, 138, 171, 175, 177, 183–195, 220, 254, 293, 300, 309, 310, 327, 388–389
Clouds 10, 26, 37, 39, 43, 47, 58, 75, 91, 94, 95, 109, 127–148, 149, 158, 162, 172, 287, 289, 298, 307–310, 344, 381, 393, 394, 397–399, 401, 402, 414, 417, 418, 435
Clouds II 128, 142
Frogs 14–15, 23, 35, 39, 43, 44, 52, 63–68, 80–81, 94, 95, 98, 117–119, 167, 219, 224, 225, 228–246,, 308, 360, 376, 378, 381, 384, 385, 414
Knights (Cavalrymen) 8–9, 39, 43, 44, 47, 51, 53, 72–75, 77, 91, 92, 107–127, 149, 159–161, 166, 172, 174, 292, 295–297, 299, 435
Lysistrata 8, 11–13, 16, 35, 37–39, 72, 79, 84, 95, 119, 120, 175, 176, 196–211,, 213, 222–223, 247, 250, 257, 393, 415, 416, 426–429, 431, 433
Peace 8, 23, 40–42, 76–77, 79, 92, 97–98, 119, 165–182, 220, 308, 381

A Companion to Aristophanes, First Edition. Edited by Matthew C. Farmer and Jeremy B. Lefkowitz.
© 2024 John Wiley & Sons, Inc. Published 2024 by John Wiley & Sons, Inc.

Peace II 173
Wasps 26, 39, 44, 75–76, 91, 108, 115, 128, 149–165, 166, 167, 172, 313, 314
Wealth (Ploutos, Plutus) 8, 17–18, 35, 37–39, 83, 98, 171, 190–194, 262–277, 381, 393, 396, 398, 401–402
Women at the Thesmophoria (Thesmophoriazusae) 27–31, 38–39, 62–64, 72, 75, 79–80, 84, 93, 94, 98, 100 117, 119, 212–227, 247, 370, 393, 394, 425
Aristophon 321
Plato 136
Aristophanes of Byzantium 353, 356–358, 361, 363
Aristotle 339–350
Poetics 22, 93, 352
Politics 138
Asclepiades (*schol.*) 359–360, 363
Asclepius 264, 265, 268, 269, 384
astronomy 129, 130, 132, 139, 349, 356
Athenaeus 39, 62, 98, 158, 204, 283, 285, 294, 295, 296, 300, 306, 315, 320–329, 333–334, 340, 355, 390
Deipnosophistai (Learned Banqueters, Scholars at Dinner) 39, 62, 204, 283–285, 294–296, 300, 306, 315, 320, 321–329, 333, 355
Athenian audiences 9, 27, 96, 103, 191, 274, 275
Athenian citizens 70, 73, 76, 92, 95, 118, 151, 205
Athenian democracy 12, 74, 83, 92, 97, 157, 247, 432
Athenian society 7, 75, 99, 128, 191, 247, 253, 256, 265, 273, 316
Athenian women 12, 199, 221, 255, 257
atticists 283, 353, 382–383

Callias 300
The Letter Play 39
Callimachus 369, 375, 399,
Callimachus (*schol.*) 352, 356
Callistratus (*schol*) 357–358
chorus leader 15, 38, 40, 41, 144, 189, 240, 267, 271
City Dionysia 77, 79, 92, 97, 101, 166, 172, 222, 292, 295, 300
Cloud–cuckoo–land 77, 186, 192, 195, 220
competition 24, 92, 108–113, 219, 220, 311, 344, 373, 376, 377
corruption 9, 109, 114, 116, 118, 151, 153, 155, 166, 174,
Crates 299–300
Crates of Mallus (*schol.*) 357, 359
Cratinus 49–54, 71, 94, 115–117, 121, 128, 130–131, 136, 141, 149, 216, 224, 254, 263–264, 295–299, 301, 305–312, 315, 353, 369–374, 386
Damianus 127

Dionysalexander (Dionysalexandros) 115, 298, 311
Seasons 136
Trophonius 141
Wine-Flask (Pytine) 51, 149, 297, 369–70
cult 142, 171, 172, 177, 193, 194, 203, 220, 233

Demetrius of Adramyttium 358–359
democracy 11–17, 70, 80, 81, 83, 84, 99, 152, 155, 249
demos/the *dēmos* 9, 11, 12, 16, 47, 70, 71, 75, 79–80, 107–116, 118, 153, 155, 174, 175 284
Demosthenes (*orat.*) 116, 151, 153
On the False Embassy 116
Didymus of Alexandria 360–364
Dio Chrysostom 382, 386–387
dystopia 184–186

Ecphantides 300
education 91, 111, 115, 118, 149, 158, 267, 384, 410, 412, 413
embodiment 29, 145, 229, 233, 241, 242
Eratosthenes of Cyrene 356–357
Euphronius 357, 360
Eupolis 49–50, 53–54, 58, 67–68, 71, 117, 119, 121, 129–131, 136, 171, 287–289, 296, 304–305, 307–312, 348, 353, 368–378
Demes (Demoi) 311, 372
Taxiarchoi 57–58, 67
Euripides 93–95, 103
Aeolus 143
Bacchae (Bacchai) 16, 168, 248, 250, 253
Bellerophon 40, 168, 171
Helen 30–31, 213–219, 221–222
Hippolytus 289
Orestes 52–53, 310, 313
Palamedes 30, 216
Telephus 62, 93–98, 100–104, 215, 216, 221 268

Galen 353, 372, 383, 384
On False Attic Usage 383
On Medical Names 383
Ordinary Words in Aristophanes 353
The Order of My Own Books 383
gender 28, 29, 197, 198, 207, 225, 247–249, 251, 252, 257, 423, 429, 431
roles 112, 120, 255, 427, 429

Heliodorus (*met.*) 355, 361, 362
Hesiod 205, 298, 194
Theogony 109
Works and Days 194

Homer 91–93, 98–99, 135, 142, 188, 231, 271, 272, 293, 298, 311, 314, 322, 334, 340, 357, 358, 365, 388
   Iliad 77, 99, 100, 179, 188, 329
   Odyssey 74, 150, 217, 271, 298, 329, 342
humor 82, 83, 149, 200, 201, 242, 319, 340, 345, 348, 349, 384, 385, 423, 431, 434

incongruity 48, 50, 242, 257, 350
intellectuals 13, 16, 128–130, 134, 136, 138, 142, 301, 360

The Julie Thesmo Show 412
jurors and jury service 75–76, 149—161

language 46–55, 208, 224, 229, 243, 257, 339, 340, 383–385, 399, 402, 419
Latin translations 393, 395–398
Lucian 141, 213, 364, 381–283, 385, 387–389
   Dialogues of the Courtesans 213
Lycophron of Calcis 356

Magnes 295–296
manuscripts 262, 268, 271, 284, 354, 356, 393, 395, 396, 430, 435
masculinity 118, 197, 214, 215, 248, 249, 251, 309, 416
Menander 46, 48–49, 156, 175, 283, 308, 311, 316, 319–320, 325–327, 330–334, 339, 353 360, 368, 371, 374, 383–384
   Men at Court (Epitrepontes) 324, 332
metaphors 51–53, 109, 110, 205, 229, 230, 235, 237, 238, 241–243, 432
meter 35–44
   anapaestic tetrameters 286, 287
   dactylic meter 36
   dactylo–epitrite meter 43
   dialog meters 36–39
   iambic trimeters 35–37, 40, 41, 286, 287, 294
   ionic meter 39
   lyric meters 39–44
   trochaic tetrameters 37, 40
modern Greece 409–413
mythological comedies 289, 298, 304

New Comedy 3, 49, 82, 191, 258, 319, 368, 383, 385

obscenity 46–55, 121, 339–341, 384, 385, 387
old women 18, 65, 192, 215, 218, 221, 256–258, 265–267, 269, 307
oligarchs and oligarchy 12, 14, 15, 79, 80, 81, 118, 155, 240, 251
opsis 22
oracles 39, 41, 92, 94, 107, 113, 177, 191, 196, 323

panathenaic procession 82, 256
papyri 283, 287, 294, 306, 311, 312, 331–333, 353, 383
parabasis 35, 38, 40, 102, 139, 143, 150, 161, 166, 172, 215, 221, 285, 287, 296, 384, 385, 426
   speech 36, 38, 40
paratragedy 50, 215, 216, 218, 222, 224, 301, 311, 395
parodos 37, 38, 134, 138, 221, 224, 271–273, 285, 286, 297, 298
Peisandros 12
personification 9, 75, 77, 79, 140, 173, 241, 242
persuasion 143, 160, 237, 251, 257
Phaeinus 355
philosophy 129–144
Philostratus 381
   Lives of the Sophists 381
Phrontisterion 130–137, 139, 140, 142, 144, 145
Plato 339–350
   Apology 94, 132, 145, 152, 199, 308, 342, 343, 345, 349
   Laws 121
   Phaedrus 132
   Republic 77, 81, 97, 190, 254, 343
   Symposium 10, 119, 135, 156, 208, 286, 339, 341, 346–349, 382
   Theaetetus 132, 137
Plutarch 47–50, 121, 339–340, 353, 382, 383–385 400
   Table-Talk 339
   The Comparison of Aristophanes and Menander 383
political satire 107, 108, 113–116, 119, 122, 128, 287, 297
   in Aristophanic Comedy 114–120
politicians 53, 107–109, 112–117, 119, 120, 149, 155, 160
politics 91–93
   and Athenian Justice System 151–156
   comedy and 70–84
poverty 18, 79, 81, 83, 191, 193, 263, 265, 267, 268, 275
prostitutes 160, 201–203, 206, 208, 209, 256

reception 3, 21, 27, 173, 224, 394, 398, 399, 409, 412, 413
   early modern 393–402
renaissance 393–402, 413
rhetoric 129–144
Roman Literature 368–378
   Aristophanes in 372–378
   Greek comedy in 368–372
Roman Satire 372–376, 378

sacrifice 11, 18, 23, 41, 60, 77, 81, 82, 100, 112, 139, 143, 175, 177, 204–205, 208–209, 213, 216, 220, 224, 266, 389
7 Wilde Clouds 410, 416n17, 419
sex and sexuality 17, 18, 84, 196–209, 198, 201, 203–205, 207, 209, 223, 254, 256, 433
slavery and slaves 37. 41, 66, 81, 83, 107, 11, 117, 118, 150, 158, 188, 240, 253 273–275
sophistry 129–144
Sophocles 26, 46, 50, 64, 168, 232, 309, 312, 387, 394, 426
  Antigone 37, 39, 312
  Oedipus Tyrannos 97
  Philoctetes 168
spectators 23–25, 142, 143, 145, 167, 233, 235, 236, 249, 425, 426
The Stories of Grandfather Aristophanes 412
Strepsiades 75
style 46–55, 58, 273, 315, 378, 381, 385
Symmachus 355, 361–363

teachers and teaching 1–3, 129, 136, 139, 144, 145, 186, 348, 357, 381, 384, 413, 418, 423–435
theatrical audience 23–25, 29 249–251
Thesmophoria Festival 27, 28, 30, 32

Timachidas 360
tragedy 24–26, 28, 35–37, 39, 91, 93, 98, 103, 216 219, 224, 236, 237, 241, 311 312
tragic poets 27, 28, 44, 224, 297, 300
translations and translators 2, 3, 194, 330, 371, 394–401, 417–419, 430, 436

utopia 2, 83, 183–195, 220, 223, 253–256, 258–259, 389

vases, Greek,
  Apulian red–figure bell krater 62
  attic black–figure amphora 61
  New York Goose Vase 65, 66
  West Greek 61–63
Venom in Verse: Aristophanes in Modern Greece 409–416
violence 121, 158, 176, 194, 208, 339, 340, 429, 432

war 165–180
women 12, 27, 79, 119, 196, 199–208, 212–216, 219, 220, 222, 223, 248–251, 253, 259, 332, 427, 428
  chorus of 212, 218, 222, 225